# Leith's Cookery Bible

# Leith's Cookery Bible

PRUE LEITH
AND CAROLINE WALDEGRAVE

First edition published in 1991
This edition published in 1996
Bloomsbury Publishing Plc, 2 Soho Square, London W1V 6HB

A CIP catalogue record for this book is available from the British Library

ISBN 0 7475 2799 7

10 9 8 7 6 5 4 3 2 1

Photographs by Andrea Heselton
Assisted by: Sarah Mac, Nesa Mladjenovic
Stylist: Roisin Nield
Home economists: Polly Tyrer, Fiona Traill Stevenson, Jackie Brewer
Assisted by: Louise Bacon

Line drawings by: Kate Simunek

Typeset by Hewer Text Composition Services, Edinburgh
Printed in Great Britain by The Bath Press, Bath

# CONTENTS

# ACKNOWLEDGEMENTS

This book is officially by Prue Leith and me. In fact this is not really true. The book is the result of 21 years in the life of Leith's School of Food and Wine. Teachers, students and friends alike have all contributed. Recipes have been unashamedly adapted from magazines, newspaper articles and other cookery books, including *Leith's Fish Bible, Leith's Contemporary Cooking, Leith's Easy Dinner Parties, Leith's Complete Christmas* and *Leith's Guide to Wine*.

We see or hear of a recipe that we like the idea of and then test it and adapt it as we see fit. It then undergoes a more rigorous testing as it is cooked by 96 students, all of whom follow it to the letter, and we certainly know if we've got it wrong! It then gets rewritten and becomes part of the *Bible*.

We have acknowledged other people's recipes when we can – but sometimes, I'm afraid, we no longer know where they first came from, and hope their creators will forgive us. Prue and I are not trying to take the credit for these recipes. We have simply tried to build up the collection which we now rather grandly call our Bible.

Past and present staff have contributed enormously to this end and I would particularly like to acknowledge the work of the following people: Sally Procter, Fiona Burrell, Caroline Yates, Barbara Stevenson, Charlotte Lyon, Sarah Staughton, Alison Cavaliero, Lesley Waters, Richard Harvey, CJ Jackson, Puff Fairclough, Be Kassapian, Emma Crowhurst, Maxine Clarke, Sue Spaull, Eithne Swan, Janey Orr, Roz Denny and Karen Sorensen.

We would also like to thank Judy van der Sande, Annie Simmonds and Maureen Flynn for all their very hard work typing the often illegible manuscript. This book could not have been produced without the editorial brilliance and the extreme patience of Helen Dore.

Finally, we would like to thank all those people who helped so much with the production of this book. Polly Tyrer, Fiona Traill Stevenson and Jackie Brewer all cooked the food for the photographs that were taken by Andrea Heselton. They were a joy to work with, as was Kate Simunek, who drew the pictures. The mushrooms in the colour photograph of wild mushrooms were identified by Antonio Carlucci of the Neal Street Restaurant.

CAROLINE WALDEGRAVE

# FOREWORD

There are not many cookbooks whose recipes have been tested over and over again by 100 students and 15 teachers. However, this book has been 10 years in the making and can probably claim to include the most tried, tested and true set of instructions ever offered to the keen cook, greedy gourmet or addicted recipe reader.

What we have tried to do in this book is to reproduce the style of cooking taught at Leith's School. Frankly, we threw out recipes, however classic and time-honoured, if the teachers and students did not like the results. This has meant the demise of rock buns, nut cutlets and many an uninspiring stew. It has also meant the inclusion of dozens of 'new classics' – the fresh, imaginative cooking that has been such an inspiration to today's chefs. It has meant that Oriental, Indian and South American vegetarian dishes have come into their own. It has meant due regard for healthy eating, alongside the *haute cuisine* of rich butter sauces and high-cholesterol puddings and the hearty, homely cooking of the modern brasserie.

What we have guarded determinedly against is gimmickiness or pretentiousness. Thus, we have included a fruit coulis only when it improves the flavour as well as the appearance of a dessert. We have kept garnishes, decorations and trimmings to the edible and relevant minimum.

The whole point of cooking, it seems to us, is to lift food from the merely nutritive to the positively pleasurable. There was never a good cook with a Calvinist heart. By which I don't mean that good cooks are profligate, extravagant or wasteful. Waste is as painful to a true cook as second-rate ingredients are.

Another thread running through the recipes, however simple or grand, is the love of doing things well. For there really is great satisfaction for the cook (more, perhaps, even than for the diner) in a perfectly balanced and executed meal. There is no buzz quite like that of surveying a buffet, every dish of which you have got exactly right, before the marauding guests descend. That feeling of pride and pleasure is worth all the hard work.

But of course this book is more a practical manual than a paean to the joy of creativity. It is essentially the tool by which such pleasures (and profit) are reached. It will be, we hope, the mentor and guide of newly fledged cooks, and will become the trusted old friend and helpmeet of experienced chefs. Caroline Waldegrave and her team of teachers have put into it everything we think a professional might turn to for reference, and enough to turn the amateur into a professional.

Above all, I hope that this book will spread the gospel: good cooking is enjoyable and rewarding for everyone – not least the cook.

PRUE LEITH

# CONVERSION TABLES

The tables below are approximate, and do not conform in all respects to the conventional conversions, but we have found them convenient for cooking. Use either metric or imperial measurements. But do not mix the two.

## Weight

| Imperial | Metric | Imperial | Metric |
|---|---|---|---|
| ¼oz | 7–8g | ½oz | 15g |
| ¾oz | 20g | 1oz | 30g |
| 2oz | 55g | 3oz | 85g |
| 4oz (¼lb) | 110g | 5oz | 140g |
| 6oz | 170g | 7oz | 200g |
| 8oz (½lb) | 225g | 9oz | 255g |
| 10oz | 285g | 11oz | 310g |
| 12oz (¾lb) | 340g | 13oz | 370g |
| 14oz | 400g | 15oz | 425g |
| 16oz (1lb) | 450g | 1¼lb | 560g |
| 1½lb | 675g | 2lb | 900g |
| 3lb | 1.35kg | 4lb | 1.8kg |
| 5lb | 2.3kg | 6lb | 2.7kg |
| 7lb | 3.2kg | 8lb | 3.6kg |
| 9lb | 4.0kg | 10lb | 4.5kg |

## Australian cup measures

| | Metric | Imperial |
|---|---|---|
| 1 cup flour | 140g | 5oz |
| 1 cup sugar (crystal or caster) | 225g | 8oz |
| 1 cup brown sugar, firmly packed | 170g | 6oz |
| 1 cup icing sugar, sifted | 170g | 6oz |
| 1 cup butter | 225g | 8oz |
| 1 cup honey, golden syrup, treacle | 370g | 12oz |
| 1 cup fresh breadcrumbs | 55g | 2oz |
| 1 cup packaged dry breadcrumbs | 140g | 5oz |
| 1 cup crushed biscuit crumbs | 110g | 4oz |
| 1 cup rice, uncooked | 200g | 7oz |
| 1 cup mixed fruit or individual fruit, such as sultanas | 170g | 6oz |
| 1 cup nuts, chopped | 110g | 4oz |
| 1 cup coconut, desiccated | 85g | 3oz |

## Approximate American/European conversions

| | USA | Metric | Imperial |
|---|---|---|---|
| Flour | 1 cup | 140g | 5oz |
| Caster and granulated sugar | 1 cup | 225g | 8oz |
| Caster and granulated sugar | 2 level tablespoons | 30g | 1oz |
| Brown sugar | 1 cup | 170g | 6oz |
| Butter/margarine/lard | 1 cup | 225g | 8oz |
| Sultanas/raisins | 1 cup | 200g | 7oz |
| Currants | 1 cup | 140g | 5oz |
| Ground almonds | 1 cup | 110g | 4oz |
| Golden syrup | 1 cup | 340g | 12oz |
| Uncooked rice | 1 cup | 200g | 7oz |
| Grated cheese | 1 cup | 110g | 4oz |
| Butter | 1 stick | 110g | 4oz |

## Liquid measures

| Imperial | ml | fl oz |
|---|---|---|
| 1 teaspoon | 5 | |
| 2 scant tablespoons | 28 | |
| 4 scant tablespoons | 56 | |
| ¼ pint (1 gill) | 150 | 5 |
| ⅓ pint | 190 | 6.6 |
| ½ pint | 290 | 10 |
| ¾ pint | 425 | 15 |
| 1 pint | 570 | 20 |
| 1¾ pints | 1000 (1 litre) | 35 |

## Australian

| 250ml | 1 cup |
|---|---|
| 20ml | 1 tablespoon |
| 5ml | 1 teaspoon |

## Approximate American/European conversions

| American | European |
|---|---|
| 1 teaspoon | 1 teaspoon/5ml |
| ½fl oz | 1 tablespoon/½fl oz/15ml |
| ¼ cup | 4 tablespoons/2fl oz/55ml |
| ½ cup plus 2 tablespoons | ¼ pint/5fl oz/150ml |
| 1¼ cups | ½ pint/10fl oz/290ml |
| 1 pint/16fl oz | 1 pint/20fl oz/570ml |
| 2½ pints (5 cups) | 1.1 litres/2 pints |
| 10 pints | 4.5 litres/8 pints |

## Useful measurements

| Measurement | Metric | Imperial |
|---|---|---|
| 1 American cup | 225ml | 8fl oz |
| 1 egg, size 3 | 56ml | 2fl oz |
| 1 egg white | 28ml | 1fl oz |
| 1 rounded tablespoon flour | 30g | 1oz |
| 1 rounded tablespoon cornflour | 30g | 1oz |
| 1 rounded tablespoon caster sugar | 30g | 1oz |
| 2 rounded tablespoons fresh breadcrumbs | 30g | 1oz |
| 2 level teaspoons gelatine | 8g | ¼oz |

30g/1oz granular (packet) aspic sets 570ml/1 pint liquid.

15g/½oz powdered gelatine, or 3 leaves, will set 570ml/1 pint liquid. (However, in hot weather, or if the liquid is very acid, like lemon juice, or if the jelly contains solid pieces of fruit and is to be turned out of the dish or mould, 20g/¾oz should be used.)

## Wine quantities

| Imperial | ml | fl oz |
|---|---|---|
| Average wine bottle | 750 | 25 |
| 1 glass wine | 100 | 3 |
| 1 glass port or sherry | 70 | 2 |
| 1 glass liqueur | 45 | 1 |

## Lengths

| Imperial | Metric |
|---|---|
| ½in | 1cm |
| 1in | 2.5cm |
| 2in | 5cm |
| 6in | 15cm |
| 12in | 30cm |

## Oven temperatures

| °C | °F | Gas mark | AMERICAN | AUSTRALIAN |
|---|---|---|---|---|
| 70 | 150 | ¼ | COOL | VERY SLOW |
| 80 | 175 | ¼ | COOL | VERY SLOW |
| 100 | 200 | ½ | COOL | VERY SLOW |
| 110 | 225 | ½ | COOL | VERY SLOW |
| 130 | 250 | 1 | VERY SLOW | VERY SLOW |
| 140 | 275 | 1 | VERY SLOW | SLOW |
| 150 | 300 | 2 | SLOW | SLOW |
| 170 | 325 | 3 | MODERATE | MODERATELY SLOW |
| 180 | 350 | 4 | MODERATE | MODERATELY SLOW |
| 190 | 375 | 5 | MODERATELY HOT | MODERATE |
| 200 | 400 | 6 | FAIRLY HOT | MODERATE |
| 220 | 425 | 7 | HOT | MODERATELY HOT |
| 230 | 450 | 8 | VERY HOT | MODERATELY HOT |
| 240 | 475 | 8 | VERY HOT | HOT |
| 250 | 500 | 9 | EXTREMELY HOT | HOT |
| 270 | 525 | 9 | EXTREMELY HOT | VERY HOT |
| 290 | 550 | 9 | EXTREMELY HOT | VERY HOT |

# CATERING QUANTITIES

Few people accurately weigh or measure quantities as a control-conscious chef must do, but when catering for large numbers it is useful to know how much food to allow per person. As a general rule, the more people you are catering for the less food per head you need to provide, e.g. 225g/8oz stewing beef per head is essential for 4 people, but 170g/6oz per head would feed 60 people.

## SOUP
Allow 290ml/½ pint soup per head, depending on the size of the bowl.

## POULTRY
**Chicken and Turkey** Allow 450g/1lb per person, weighed when plucked and drawn. An average chicken serves 4 people on the bone and 6 people off the bone.
**Duck** A 2.7kg/6lb bird will feed 3–4 people; a 1.8kg/4lb bird will feed 2 people. 1 duck makes enough pâté for 6 people.
**Goose** Allow 3.6kg/8lb for 4 people; 6.9kg/15lb for 7 people.

## GAME
**Pheasant** Allow 1 bird for 2 people (roast); 1 bird for 3 people (casseroled).
**Pigeon** Allow 1 bird per person.
**Grouse** Allow 1 young grouse per person (roast); 2 birds for 3 people (casseroled).
**Quail** Allow 2 small birds per person or 1 large boned stuffed bird served on a croûton.
**Partridge** Allow 1 bird per person.
**Venison** Allow 170g/6oz lean meat per person; 1.8kg/4lb cut of haunch weighed on the bone for 8–9 people.
**Steaks** Allow 170g/6oz per person.

## MEAT
### LAMB OR MUTTON
**Casseroled** 285g/10oz per person (boneless, with fat trimmed away).
**Roast leg** 1.35kg/3lb for 3–4 people; 1.8kg/4lb for 4–5 people; 2.7kg/6lb for 7–8 people.
**Roast shoulder** 1.8kg/4lb shoulder for 5–6 people; 2.7kg/6lb shoulder for 7–9 people.
**Grilled best end cutlets** 3–4 per person.
**Grilled loin chops** 2 per person.

### BEEF
**Stewed** 225g/8oz boneless trimmed meat per person.
**Roast (off the bone)** If serving men only, 225g/8oz per person; if serving men and women, 200g/7oz per person.
**Roast (on the bone)** 340g/12oz per person.
**Roast whole fillet** 1.8kg/4lb piece for 10 people.
**Grilled steaks** 200–225g/7–8oz per person depending on appetite.

### PORK
**Casseroled** 170g/6oz per person.
**Roast leg or loin (off the bone)** 200g/7oz per person.
**Roast leg or loin (on the bone)** 340g/12oz per person.
**2 average fillets** will feed 3–4 people.
**Grilled** 1×170g/6oz chop or cutlet per person.

### VEAL
**Stews or pies** 225g/8oz pie veal per person.
**Fried** 1×170g/6oz escalope per person.

### MINCED MEAT
170g/6oz per person for shepherd's pie, hamburgers, etc.
110g/4oz per person for steak tartare.

85g/3oz per person for lasagne, cannelloni, etc.
110g/4oz per person for moussaka.
55g/2oz per person for spaghetti.

## FISH

**Whole large fish** (e.g. sea bass, salmon, whole haddock), weighed uncleaned, with head on: 340–450g/12oz–1lb per person.
**Cutlets and steaks** 170g/6oz per person.
**Fillets** (e.g. sole, lemon sole, plaice): 3 small fillets per person (total weight about 170g/6oz).
**Whole small fish** (e.g. trout, slip soles, small plaice, small mackerel, herring) 225–340g/8–12oz weighed with heads for main course; 170g/6oz for first course.
**Fish off the bone** (in fish pie, with sauce, etc) 170g/6oz per person.

## SHELLFISH

**Prawns** 55–85g/2–3oz per person as a first course; 140g/5oz per person as a main course.
**Mixed shellfish** 55–85g/2–3oz per person as a first course; 140g/5oz per person as a main course.

## VEGETABLES

Weighed before preparation and cooking, and assuming 3 vegetables, including potatoes, served with a main course: 110g/4oz per person, except (per person):
**French beans** 85g/3oz.
**Peas** 85g/3oz.
**Spinach** 340g/12oz.
**Potatoes** 3 small (roast); 170g/6oz (mashed); 10–15 (Parisienne); 5 (château); 1 large or 2 small (baked); 110g/4oz (new).

## RICE

**Plain, boiled or fried** 55g/2oz (weighed before cooking) or 1 breakfast cup (measured after cooking).
**In risotto or pilaf** 30g/1oz per person (weighed before cooking) for first course; 55g/2oz per person for main course.

NOTE: As a general rule men eat more potatoes and less 'greens' than women!

## SALADS

Obviously, the more salads served, the less guests will eat of any one salad. Allow 1 large portion of salad, in total, per head – e.g. if only one salad is served make sure there is enough for 1 helping each. Conversely if 100 guests are to choose from 5 different salads, allow a total of 150 portions – i.e. 30 portions of each salad.
**Tomato salad** 450g/1lb tomatoes (average 6 tomatoes), sliced, serves 4 people.
**Coleslaw** 1 small cabbage, finely shredded, serves 10–12 people.
**Grated carrot salad** 450g/1lb carrots, grated, serves 6 people.
**Potato salad** 450g/1lb potatoes (weighed before cooking) serves 5 people.
**Green salad** Allow a loose handful of leaves for each person (i.e. a large Cos lettuce will serve 8, a large Webb's will serve 10, a Dutch hothouse 'butterhead' will serve 4).

## SANDWICHES

2 slices of bread make 1 round of sandwiches.
**Cucumber** 1 cucumber makes 15 rounds.
**Egg** 1 hardboiled egg makes 1 round.
**Ham** Allow 20g/¾oz for each round.
**Mustard and cress** For egg and cress sandwiches, 1 punnet makes 20 rounds.
**Tomatoes** 450g/1lb makes 9 rounds.
**Smoked salmon** Allow 20g/¾oz for each round.

## COCKTAIL PARTIES

Allow 10 cocktail canapés per head.
Allow 14 cocktail canapés per head if served at lunchtime when guests are unlikely to go on to a meal.
Allow 4–5 canapés with pre-lunch or pre-dinner drinks.
Allow 8 cocktail canapés, plus 4 miniature sweet cakes or pastries per head for a wedding reception.

## PUDDINGS

**Cooking apples** Allow 225g/8oz per head for puddings.
**Fruit salad** Allow 8 oranges, 2 apples, 2 bananas and 450g/1lb grapes for 8 people.
**Mousses** Allow 290ml/½pint double cream inside and 290ml/½ pint to decorate a mousse for 8 people.
**Strawberries** Allow 110g/4oz per head.

## MISCELLANEOUS

**Brown bread and butter** 1½ slices (3 triangular pieces) per person.

**French bread** 1 large loaf for 10 people; 1 small loaf for 6 people.

**Cheese** After a meal, if serving one blue-veined, one hard and one soft cheese: 85g/3oz per person for up to 8 people; 55g/2oz per person for up to 20 people; 30g/1oz per person for over 20 people.

At a wine and cheese party: 110g/4oz per person for up to 8 people; 85g/3oz per person for up to 20 people; 55g/2oz per person for over 20 people. Inevitably, if catering for small numbers, there will be cheese left over but this is unavoidable if the host is not to look mean.

**Biscuits** 3 each for up to 10 people; 2 each for up to 30 people; 1 each for over 30 people.

**Butter** 30g/1oz per person if bread is served with the meal; 45g/1½oz per person if cheese is served as well.

**Cream** 1 tablespoon per person for coffee; 3 tablespoons per person for pudding or dessert.

**Milk** 570ml/1 pint for 18–20 cups of tea.

**Sliced bread** A large loaf, thinly sliced, generally makes 18–20 slices.

**Butter** 30g/1oz soft butter will cover 8 large bread slices.

**Sausages** 450g/1lb is the equivalent of 32 cocktail sausages; 16 chipolata sausages; 8 pork sausages.

**Bouchées** 675g/1½lb packet of puff pastry makes 60 bouchées.

**Chicken livers** 450g/1lb chicken livers will be enough for 60 bacon and chicken liver rolls.

**Dates** 50 fresh dates weigh about 450g/1lb.

**Prunes** A prune (with stone) weighs about 10g/⅓oz.

**Mushrooms** A button mushroom weighs about 7g/¼oz.

**Bacon** A good sized rasher weighs about 30g/1oz.

**Button onions** A button onion weighs about 15g/½oz.

**Choux pastry** 6-egg choux paste makes 150 baby éclairs. They will need 570ml/1 pint cream for filling and 225g/8oz chocolate for coating.

**Short pastry** 900g/2lb pastry will line 150 tartlets.

# PLANNING A LARGE PARTY

Cooking for a party can be daunting, but if you are well prepared it can also be terrific fun and it is deeply satisfying to look at perfectly presented food and realize that the occasion is going to be a success.

## FORWARD PLANNING

**1.** Decide where you are going to have the party, decide on a convenient date and book the venue.
**2.** Decide on the type of party – cocktail party, buffet, sit-down dinner, dancing or disco.
**3.** Work out how many people can come to the party. Allow 3 square metres/10 square feet per person for a sit-down party and 2 square metres/ 6 square feet for a drinks party.
**4.** If chairs have to be removed to allow space for dancing, make sure that you hire stackable chairs.
**5.** Is the kitchen area big enough? Are there good reheating facilities or should you hire extra ovens?
**6.** Are there adequate toilet facilities or will you need to hire a portacabin?
**7.** Think about the colour scheme, particularly if you are having a marquee that has to be ordered well in advance.
**8.** Get invitations printed – and expect one-third refusals.
**9.** If the party is a commercial event, organize a licence and extend your employer's liability insurance.
**10.** If the party is for charity, set up a committee to organize the tombola, programme advertising, and most importantly the sale of tickets.

## MEDIUM-TERM PLANNING

**1.** Plan the menu (see page 17).
**2.** Work out the hire list. Once you know the menu it is simple to work out how many knives, forks, plates, coffee cups and glasses you will

need and how many chairs and tables to hire, but don't forget any of the following:

*4 or 5 extra place settings*
*serving dishes and cloths*
*butter dishes*
*serving trays for food and glasses*
*serving spoons and forks*
*1½ glasses per head for a cocktail party*
*menu holders (if required)*
*cake stand (for a wedding)*
*coffee urns for a big party*
*table mats*
*knife and board for lemons*
*ice buckets*
*water jugs*
*corkscrews*
*coffee pots, milk jugs, sugar bowls, teaspoons*
*punch bowl and ladle*
*tablecloth and napkins*
*cocktail shakers*
*ashtrays, plenty, all the same size*
*dustbins in which to chill wine*
*salt and pepper pots (check that they are full)*
*bread baskets*
*plate stackers (for piling up plates of ready plated food)*
*fruit baskets*
*coat rail and hangers*
*candlesticks*
*drugget (cloth for the floor behind the bar)*
*stand for the seating plan*
*extra ovens or hot cupboards*

Establish that the hired linen is returned dirty and agree a delivery time.

**3.** Hire a van to deliver food if necessary – start saving boxes to deliver food in.

**4.** Plan the wine to go with the menu (see pages 86–9). Allow a bottle per head and hope to have some left over. Order on sale or return and only chill wine as you need it so that the labels don't drop off. Many wine firms will supply ready-chilled wine and glasses.

**5.** Book a master of ceremonies if necessary.

**6.** Book staff if necessary. The general rule is that for silver service, one waitress can cope with 6 people, and for butler service one waitress can look after 10 people. At a buffet, one waitress can look after 25 people. One barman can cope with 30 people if it is a full bar and with 50 people for a simple bar. Decide whether you need to hire kitchen staff, kitchen porters, cloakroom ladies, security staff or any other help. Decide on the kind of staff you want.

**7.** Think about parking arrangements. Do you need to give car registration numbers to security? Find out from what time you can have access and from what time you can lay the tables. Check what time you need to leave the building and the latest time you can have the hired equipment collected in the morning. Check how the equipment can be delivered to the right place – is there a goods lift, etc?

**8.** Hire and order flower arrangements and table decorations as necessary.

**9.** Order the band, discotheque, casino, etc. Discuss electrical requirements.

**10.** Go to the party venue and make a plan of action so that you can establish if there are any gaps in your forward-planning scheme.

## A WEEK BEFORE THE PARTY

**1.** Order the food (see catering quantities pages 11–13) to arrive 2 days before the party. Don't forget to order sandwiches for the staff.

**2.** Order the ice. Champagne is generally served colder than other wine. Make sure that the containers for ice are delivered before the ice arrives.

**3.** Order other drinks, such as orange juice, mineral water and whisky.

**4.** Talk over the plan of the party with a friend to make sure there are no gaps.

## A DAY BEFORE THE PARTY

**1.** Prepare as much of the food as you can. Separate into small batches to cool as quickly as possible and chill well. The easiest way to cook in large quantities is to do one process at a time. If making sandwiches make all the fillings, soften all the butter, butter all the bread and then put the sandwiches together.

**2.** Get all the equipment you need to take, such as:

*matches*
*loo paper, cloakroom soap and towels, flowers for loos*
*clingfilm*
*absorbent kitchen paper*
*kitchen foil*
*dustbin liners (lots)*
*knives, whisks, fish slices, etc.*
*carving knife and fork*
*electric carving knife*
*oven gloves*
*tea towels*
*washing-up liquid*
*mop and bucket*
*broom and dustpan and brush*
*J-cloths*
*plenty of boxes for taking home dirty equipment*
*first-aid box*
*pins*
*screwdriver*
*needles and cotton*
*rubber gloves*
*chopping boards*
*scissors*
*lemons*
*petty cash (for tipping people)*
*tea bags, milk, sugar for staff*
*cold drinks for staff*

## ON THE DAY OF THE PARTY

**1.** Get someone to the venue reasonably early to check off the deliveries, sign slips, persuade people to take equipment to the right place and generally organize the setting-up and laying of tables, the seating plan, the flowers, the microphone, the lighting, the table decorations, tidying the cloakroom and warding off potential problems.

**2.** Meanwhile, finish off all the cooking, pack up the food, undecorated, and deliver it with all the equipment and garnishes.

**3.** Set up an efficient working kitchen, work tidily and stick to a time plan.

**4.** Serve the food by the agreed method and enjoy the party.

## PLANNING A BUFFET PARTY

If you are going to be cooking for a buffet party, here are a few hints that may be helpful when planning your menu and arranging your food.

• The larger the choice of dishes, the more generous you have to be, and therefore if you are cooking for a small number the increased costs can be significant.

• Think about ease of both serving and eating – if there are not many places for guests to sit down it should be a fork buffet.

• Think about what the food will look like once people have started to fill their plates. We decorate the underplates with fresh flowers or bunches of herbs and leave the dishes themselves very simply garnished. Do not put too many flowers on the table – let the food speak for itself.

• Have more than one service point with only about 16 sets of knives, forks and plates in any one pile – the crockery must not dominate the table. If you are cooking for 100 people, you will need at least 4 service points. Think carefully about the appearance of the food – it should be a good mixture of colours.

• Try to make the table look attractive by using height. Place the food on cake stands and put boxes under the tablecloths.

• Don't decorate the front of the tablecloth with garlands of flowers – they'll get crushed and look untidy.

• Always think about what the buffet will look like at the end of the meal.

• If possible change the tablecloth in between courses – if not, then certainly after coffee.

• Use linen napkins to hide spills.

• Never underestimate the number of helpers you'll need – people helping themselves often have eyes bigger than their stomachs. For 100 people you will need 4 people serving the food.

• Make sure that there is easy access to all service points and that there is a choice of all the dishes beside each pile of plates.

• It is possible to buy (from disposable products suppliers) little plastic holders so that the wine glasses can be attached to plates.

• Don't use linen napkins – they are too cumbersome at a buffet.

• Precut and slice most of the food but for the sake of appearance leave some whole.

• Never put out all the food – keep some back so that the last shall be first. Always hide the vegetarian dishes – you could run out and genuine vegetarians would not be able to have any.

• Try to avoid individual dishes as they dictate how many people can have how much of a certain dish – you may well calculate tastes incorrectly.

• If people have to queue you'll find that only about two-thirds of the guests will come back for puddings, and only about half will come back again for coffee. Obviously you have to cater for full take-up but don't be over-generous.

# MENU PLANNING

Once a menu is planned, cooking becomes much easier. It is making the decisions that can be so daunting. Here are a few hints that may help. One of the most important things is to make the menu relevant to the people for whom you are cooking; giving a rugger XV grilled aubergines with pesto would be as absurd as giving a ladies' lunch party carbonnade of beef with savoury crumble. The menu should stay in style throughout. The figurative leap from the South of France, with aubergine flan, to the Nursery, with steak and kidney pudding, apart from being badly balanced, would also give your guests an uncomfortable culture shock. One of the many skills of cooking is to think of the people for whom you are cooking and choose a menu that you know they will like. Here are a set of guidelines that can help:

• Never repeat the same basic ingredients in a menu – for example, do not have pastry in two courses or serve smoked salmon in the first and main courses. However, it is perfectly acceptable to have a fish first course, such as a seafood salad, followed by a fish main course.
• Try to devise a menu that is full of colour. This is particularly important when planning a buffet party. For a conventional lunch or dinner party, always think about the appearance of the main course plate.
• Think about the balance of the menu. Do not be so inclined to generosity that you daunt your guests. If there is to be a great number of courses then serve a sorbet halfway through to refresh the palate. If you decide to serve a very rich pudding, always offer a light alternative.
• The texture of a meal is important – it should vary.
• Try not to have too many exciting and exotic tastes in one menu. If you get carried away, sometimes the basic flavour of a delicious ingredient can be drowned. If the menu is to include a highly seasoned dish, don't follow it with a subtle dish – your guests simply won't be able to appreciate it.

• Most people love sauces, so if you serve a sauce be generous.
• We would always recommend serving a salad with any rich meal.

At Leith's there is always much discussion about the order of a meal. In England we conventionally serve the pudding followed by the cheese. In France it is more usual to serve the cheese before the pudding – the theory being that the red wine is finished with the cheese and then the pudding is served with a sweet white wine. We rather like the French approach for both its wine appreciation factor and also for its practicality in that it means that the host or hostess can nip off to the kitchen and do any last-minute cooking necessary for the pudding.

Finally, we would say don't overtax yourself. A dinner party is meant to be fun. Don't try to cook three hot courses and sit down to each successive course feeling slightly more flushed. Prepare as much as you can in advance – work out a timetable of how you are going to cope, and enjoy the meal with your guests.

# CREATIVE LEFTOVERS AND INSTANT COOKING

When not cooking for a special occasion most of us spend some time foraging in the refrigerator or store cupboard looking for inspiration. Some types of dishes are particularly suitable for leftover cooking such as:

**Soups:** leftover vegetables
**Soufflés:** cheeses
**Flans:** vegetables
**Pies:** cooked meats
**Stir-fries:** cooked meats
**Warm salads:** cooked chicken, turkey, etc.
**Gougères:** cooked game, chicken, fish
**Stuffed pancakes:** fish, meat, vegetables
**Risottos:** fish, meat, vegetables
**Pilaffs:** fish, meat, vegetables
**Rice, noodle and pasta salads:** fish, meat, chicken
**Pasties:** cooked meat
**Ice creams:** 'tired' fruit

The important thing when cooking with leftovers is not to try to be too clever – don't be tempted to use too many different ingredients in one recipe. There are a number of store cupboard ingredients that can make leftover cooking more exciting and instant cooking easier:

*Good-quality oils such as walnut, hazelnut, extra virgin olive*
*Fresh herbs (these keep well, stalks down, in the refrigerator)*
*Soy sauce*
*Stem ginger*
*Pinenuts*
*Chinese noodles*
*Sesame seeds*

*Pasta, different types*
*Cheeses, including Parmesan*
*Chestnut purée, sweetened and unsweetened*
*Fruit cordials such as elderflower, etc.*
*Rice, all types – basmati, organic, etc.*
*Dried milk*
*Boxed juices*
*Worcestershire sauce*
*Sundried tomatoes*
*Olives*
*Capers*
*Hoisin sauce*
*Vinegar, including balsamic*
*Canned tomatoes*
*Passata (sieved tomatoes)*
*Canned beans*
*Dried mushrooms*
*Dried beans and lentils*
*Good-quality canned fruits, such as figs*

Sometimes it is not necessary to be particularly creative. If you have some delicious cold meat all you need do is to cheer up the dinner with an instant chutney made from chopped fruit, chopped mint, stem ginger, balsamic vinegar and olive oil. If you have some pasta but no time to make a sauce, use passata mixed with a little stem ginger syrup to make a tomato and ginger sauce. A fruit salad can be made more sophisticated by adding alcohol or a cordial such as elderflower.

# DICTIONARY OF COOKING TERMS AND KITCHEN FRENCH

**Abats** French for offal (hearts, livers, brains, tripe, etc.). Americans call them 'variety meats'.

**Bake blind** To bake a flan case while empty. In order to prevent the sides falling in or the base bubbling up, the pastry is usually lined with paper and filled with 'blind beans'. See below.

**Bain-marie** A roasting tin half-filled with hot water in which terrines, custards, etc. stand while cooking. The food is protected from direct fierce heat and cooks in a gentle, steamy atmosphere. Also a large container that will hold a number of pans standing in hot water, used to keep soups, sauces, etc. hot without further cooking.

**Bard** To tie bacon or pork fat over a joint of meat, game bird or poultry, to be roasted. This helps to prevent the flesh from drying out.

**Baste** To spoon over liquid (sometimes stock, sometimes fat) during cooking to prevent drying out and to promote flavour.

**Bavarois** Creamy pudding made with eggs and cream and set with gelatine.

**Beignets** Fritters.

**Beurre manié** Butter and flour in equal quantities worked together to a soft paste, and used as a liaison or thickening for liquids. Small pieces are whisked into boiling liquid. As the butter melts it disperses the flour evenly through the liquid, thereby thickening it without causing lumps.

**Beurre noisette** Browned butter; *see* Noisette.

**Bisque** Shellfish soup, smooth and thickened.

**Blanch** Originally, to whiten by boiling, e.g. to boil sweetbreads or brains briefly to remove traces of blood, or to boil almonds to make the brown skin easy to remove, leaving the nuts white. Now commonly used to mean parboiling, as in blanching vegetables when they are parboiled prior to freezing, or precooked so that they have only to be reheated before serving.

**Blanquette** A stew made without prior frying of the meat. Usually used for lamb, chicken or veal.

The sauce is often thickened with an egg and cream liaison.

**Blind beans** Dried beans, peas, rice and pasta used to fill pastry cases temporarily during baking.

**Bouchées** Small puff pastry cases like miniature vol-au-vents.

**Bouillon** Broth or uncleared stock.

**Bouquet garni** Parsley stalks, small bay leaf, fresh thyme, celery stalk, sometimes with a blade of mace, tied together with string and used to flavour stews, etc. Removed before serving.

**Braise** To bake or stew slowly on a bed of vegetables in a covered pan.

**Brunoise** Vegetables cut into very small dice.

**Canapé** A small bread or biscuit base, sometimes fried, spread or covered with savoury paste, egg, etc., used for cocktail titbits or as an accompaniment to meat dishes. Sometimes used to denote the base only, as in champignons sur canapé.

**Caramel** Sugar cooked to a toffee.

**Chapelux** Browned breadcrumbs.

**Châteaubriand** Roast filled steak from the thick end for 2 people or more.

**Chine** To remove the backbone from a rack of ribs. Carving is almost impossible if the butcher has not 'chined' the meat.

**Clarified butter** Butter that has been separated from milk particles and other impurities which cause it to look cloudy when melted, and to burn easily when heated.

**Collops** Small slices of meat, taken from a tender cut such as neck of lamb.

**Concasser** To chop roughly.

**Consommé** Clear soup.

**Coulis** Essentially a thick sauce, such as coulis de tomates, thick tomato sauce; raspberry coulis, raspberry sauce.

**Court bouillon** Liquid used for cooking fish.

**Cream** To beat ingredients together, such as butter and fat when making a sponge cake.

**Crêpes** Thin French pancakes.

**Crépin** Pig's caul.

**Croquettes** Pâté (stiff purée) of mashed potato and possibly poultry, fish or meat, formed into small balls or patties, coated in egg and breadcrumbs and deep-fried.

**Croustade** Bread case dipped in butter and baked until crisp. Used to contain hot savoury mixtures for a canapé, savoury or as a garnish.

**Croûte** Literally crust. Sometimes a pastry case, as in fillet of beef en croûte, sometimes toasted or fried bread, as in Scotch woodcock or scrambled eggs on toast.

**Croûtons** Small evenly sized cubes of fried bread used as a soup garnish and occasionally in other dishes.

**Dariole** Small castle-shaped mould used for moulding rice salads and sometimes for cooking cake mixtures.

**Déglacer** To loosen and liquefy fat, sediment and browned juices stuck at the bottom of a frying pan or saucepan by adding liquid (usually stock, water or wine) and stirring while boiling.

**Deglaze** See Déglacer.

**Dégorger** To extract the juices from meat, fish or vegetables, generally by salting then soaking or washing. Usually done to remove indigestible or strong-tasting juices.

**Dépouiller** To skim off the scum from a sauce or stock: a splash of cold stock is added to the boiling liquid. This helps to bring scum and fat to the surface, which can then be skimmed more easily.

**Dropping consistency** The consistency where a mixture will drop reluctantly from a spoon, neither pouring off nor obstinately adhering.

**Duxelles** Finely chopped raw mushrooms, sometimes with chopped shallots or chopped ham, often used as a stuffing.

**Egg wash** Beaten raw egg, sometimes with salt, used for glazing pastry to give it a shine when baked.

**Emulsion** A stable suspension of fat and other liquid, e.g. mayonnaise, hollandaise.

**Entrecôte** Sirloin steak.

**Entrée** Traditionally a dish served before the main course, but usually served as a main course today.

**Entremet** Dessert or sweet course, excluding pastry sweets.

Escalop A thin slice of meat, sometimes beaten out flat to make it thinner and larger.

**Farce** Stuffing.

**Fecule** Farinaceous thickening, usually arrowroot or cornflour.

**Flamber** To set alcohol alight. Usually to burn off the alcohol, but frequently simply for dramatic effect. (Past tense flambé or flambée; English: to flame).

**Flame** See Flamber.

**Fleurons** Crescents of puff pastry, generally used to garnish fish or poultry.

**Fold** To mix with a gentle lifting motion, rather than to stir vigorously. The aim is to avoid beating out air while mixing.

**Frappé** Iced, or set in a bed of crushed ice.

**Fricassé** White stew made with cooked or raw poultry, meat or rabbit and a velouté sauce, sometimes thickened with cream and egg yolks.

**Fumet** Strong-flavoured liquor used for flavouring sauces. Usually the liquid in which fish has been poached, or the liquid that has run from fish during baking. Sometimes used of meat or truffle-flavoured liquors.

**Glace de viande** Reduced brown stock, very strong in flavour, used for adding body and colour to sauces.

**Glaze** To cover with a thin layer of shiny jellied meat juices (for roast turkey), melted jam (for fruit flans) or syrup (for rum baba).

**Gratiner** To brown under a grill after the surface of the dish has been sprinkled with breadcrumbs and butter and, sometimes, cheese. Dishes finished like this are sometimes called gratinée or au gratin.

**Hors d'oeuvre** Usually simply means the first course. Sometimes used to denote a variety or selection of many savoury titbits served with drinks, or a mixed first course (hors d'oeuvres variés).

**Infuse** To steep or heat gently to extract flavour, as when infusing milk with onion slices.

**Julienne** Vegetables or citrus rind cut in thin matchstick shapes or very fine shreds.

**Jus or jus de viande** God's gravy, i.e. juices that occur naturally in cooking, not a made-up sauce. Also juice.

**Jus lié** Thickened gravy.

**Knock down or knock back** To punch or knead out the air in risen dough so that it resumes its pre-risen bulk.

**Knock up** To separate slightly the layers of raw puff pastry with the blade of a knife to facilitate rising during cooking.

**Lard** To thread strips of bacon fat (or sometimes anchovy) through meat to give it flavour, and, in the case of fat, to make up any deficiency in very lean meat.

**Lardons** Small strips or cubes of pork fat or bacon generally used as a garnish.

**Liaison** Ingredients for binding together and thickening sauce, soup or other liquid, e.g. roux, beurre manié, egg yolk and cream, blood.

**Macédoine** Small diced mixed vegetables, usually containing some root vegetables. Sometimes used of fruit meaning a fruit salad.

**Macerate** To soak food in a syrup or liquid to allow flavours to mix.

**Mandolin** Frame of metal or wood with adjustable blades set in it for thinly slicing cucumbers, potatoes, etc.

**Marinade** The liquid described below. Usually contains oil, onion, bay leaf and vinegar or wine.

**Marinate** To soak meat, fish or vegetables before cooking in acidulated liquid containing flavourings and herbs. This gives flavour and tenderizes the meat.

**Marmite** French word for a covered earthenware soup container in which the soup is both cooked and served.

**Medallions** Small rounds of meat, evenly cut. Also small round biscuits. Occasionally used of vegetables if cut in flat round discs.

**Mirepoix** The bed of braising vegetables described under Braise.

**Mortifier** To hang meat, poultry or game.

**Moulè-à-manqué** French cake tin with sloping sides. The resulting cake has a wider base than top, and is about 2.5cm/1in high.

**Napper** To coat, mask or cover, e.g. éclairs nappés with hot chocolate sauce.

**Needleshreds** Fine, evenly cut shreds of citrus zest (French julienne) generally used as a garnish.

**Noisette** Literally 'nut'. Usually means nut-brown, as in beurre noisette, i.e. butter browned over heat to a nut colour. Also hazelnut. Also boneless rack of lamb rolled and tied, cut into neat rounds.

**Nouvelle cuisine** Style of cooking that promotes light and delicate dishes often using unusual combinations of very fresh ingredients, attractively arranged.

**Oyster** Small piece of meat found on either side of the backbone of a chicken. Said to be the best-flavoured flesh. Also a bivalve mollusc!

**Panade or panada** Very thick mixture used as a base for soufflés or fish cakes, etc., usually made from milk, butter and flour.

**Paner** To egg and crumb ingredients before frying.

**Papillote** A wrapping of paper in which fish or meat is cooked to contain the aroma and flavour. The dish is brought to the table still wrapped up. Foil is sometimes used, but as it does not puff up dramatically, it is less satisfactory.

**Parboil** To half-boil or partially soften by boiling.

**Parisienne** Potato (sometimes with other ingredients) scooped into small balls with a melon baller and usually fried.

**Pass** To strain or push through a sieve.

**Pâte** The basic mixture or paste, often used of uncooked pastry, dough, uncooked meringue, etc.

**Pâté** A savoury paste of liver, pork, game, etc.

**Pâtisserie** Sweet cakes and pastries. Also a cake shop.

**Paupiette** Beef (or pork or veal) olive, i.e. a thin layer of meat, spread with a soft farce, rolled up, tied with string and cooked slowly.

**Piquer** To insert in meats or poultry a large julienne of fat, bacon, ham, truffle, etc.

**Poussin** Baby chicken.

**Praline** Almonds cooked in sugar until the mixture caramelizes, cooled and crushed to a powder. Used for flavouring desserts and ice cream.

**Prove** To put dough or yeasted mixture to rise before baking.

**Purée** Liquidized, sieved or finely mashed fruit or vegetables.

**Quenelles** A fine minced fish or meat mixture formed into small portions and poached. Served in a sauce, or as a garnish to other dishes.

**Ragoût** A stew.

**Réchauffée** A reheated dish made with previously cooked food.

**Reduce** To reduce the amount of liquid by rapid boiling, causing evaporation and a consequent strengthening of flavour in the remaining liquid.

**Refresh** To hold boiled green vegetables under cold running water, or to immerse them immediately in cold water to prevent their cooking further in their own steam, and set the colour.

**Relax or rest** Of pastry: to set aside in a cool place to allow the gluten (which will have expanded during rolling) to contract. This lessens the danger of shrinking in the oven. Of batters: to set aside to allow the starch cells to swell, giving a lighter result when cooked.

**Render** To melt solid fat (e.g. beef, pork) slowly in the oven.

**Repere** Flour mixed with water or white of egg used to seal pans when cooking a dish slowly, such as lamb ragoût.

**Revenir** To fry meat or vegetables quickly in hot fat in order to warm them through.

**Roux** A basic liaison or thickening for a sauce or soup. Melted butter to which flour has been added.

**Rouille** Garlic and oil emulsion used as flavouring.

**Salamander** A hot oven or grill used for browning or glazing the tops of cooked dishes, or a hot iron or poker for branding the top with lines or a criss-cross pattern.

**Salmis** A game stew sometimes made with cooked game, or partially roasted game.

**Sauter** Method of frying in a deep-frying pan or sautoir. The food is continually tossed or shaken so that it browns quickly and evenly.

**Sautoir** Deep-frying pan with a lid used for recipes that require fast frying and then slower cooking (with the lid on).

**Scald** Of milk: to heat until on the point of boiling, when some movement can be seen at the edges of the pan but there is no overall bubbling. Of muslin, cloths, etc.: to immerse in clean boiling water, generally to sterilize.

**Seal or seize** To brown meat rapidly usually in fat, for flavour and colour.

**Season** Of food: to flavour, generally with salt and pepper. Of iron frying pans, griddles, etc.: to prepare new equipment for use by placing over high heat, generally coated with oil and sprinkled with salt. This prevents subsequent rusting and sticking.

**Slake** To mix flour, arrowroot, cornflour or custard powder to a thin paste with a small quantity of cold water.

**Soft ball** The term used to describe sugar syrup reduced by boiling to sufficient thickness to form soft balls when dropped into cold water and rubbed between finger and thumb.

**Supreme** Choice piece of poultry (usually from the breast).

**Sweat** To cook gently, usually in butter or oil, but sometimes in the food's own juices, without frying or browning.

**Tammy** A fine muslin cloth through which sauces are sometimes forced. After this treatment they look beautifully smooth and shiny. Tammy cloths have generally been replaced by blenders or liquidizers, which give much the same effect.

**Tammy strainer** A fine mesh strainer, conical in shape, used to produce the effect described under Tammy.

**Terrine** Pâté or minced mixture baked or steamed in a loaf tin or earthenware container.

**To the thread** Of sugar boiling. Term used to denote degree of thickness achieved when reducing syrup, i.e. the syrup will form threads if tested between a wet finger and thumb. Short thread: about 1cm/½in; long thread: 5cm/2in or more.

**Timbale** A dish that has been cooked in a castle-shaped mould, or a dish served piled high.

**Tomalley** Greenish lobster liver. Creamy and delicious.

**Tournedos** Fillet steak. Usually refers to a one-portion piece of grilled fillet.

**To turn vegetables** To shape carrots or turnips to a small barrel shape. To cut mushrooms into a decorative spiral pattern.

**To turn olives** To remove the olive stone with a spiral cutting movement.

**Velouté** See under Sauces, p. 249.

**Vol-au-vent** A large pastry case made from puff pastry with high raised sides and a deep hollow centre into which chicken, fish, etc. is put.

**Well** A hollow or dip made in a pile or bowlful of flour, exposing the tabletop or the bottom of the bowl, into which other ingredients are placed prior to mixing.

**Zest** The skin of an orange or lemon, used to give flavour. It is very thinly pared without any of the bitter white pith.

## CLASSIC GARNISHES

**Américane** For fish. Slices of lobster tail and slices of truffles.

**Anglaise** Braised vegetables such as carrots, turnips and quartered celery hearts (used to garnish boiled salted beef).

**Aurore** A flame-coloured sauce obtained by adding fresh tomato purée to a béchamel sauce: used for eggs, vegetables and fish.

**Bolognese** A rich sauce made from chicken livers and/or minced beef flavoured with mushrooms and tomatoes. Usually served with pasta.

**Bonne femme** To cook in a simple way. Usually, of chicken, sautéed and served with white wine gravy, bacon cubes, button onions and garnished with croquette potatoes. Of soup, a simple purée of vegetables with stock. Of fish, white wine sauce, usually with mushrooms; and served with buttered mashed potatoes.

**Boulangère** Potatoes and onions sliced and cooked in the oven in stock. Often served with mutton.

**Bouquetière** Groups of very small carrots, turnips, French beans, cauliflower florets, button onions, asparagus tips, etc. Sometimes served with a thin demi-glace or gravy. Usually accompanies beef or lamb entrées.

**Bourgeoise** Fried diced bacon, glazed carrots and button onions. Sometimes red wine is used in the sauce. Used for beef and liver dishes.

**Bourguignonne** Button mushroom and small onions in a sauce made with red wine (Burgundy). Used for beef and egg dishes.

**Bretonne** Haricot beans whole or in a purée. Sometimes a purée of root vegetables. Usually served with a gigot (leg) of lamb.

**Chasseur** Sautéed mushrooms added to a sauté of chicken or veal.

**Chiffonnade** Chopped lettuce or sorrel cooked in butter to garnish soup.

**Choron** Hollandaise sauce with prawns and tomato.

**Clamart** Garnish of artichoke hearts filled with buttered petits pois. Sometimes a purée of peas, or simply buttered peas.

**Doria** A garnish of cucumber, usually fried in butter.

**DuBarry** Denotes the use of cauliflower; potage DuBarry is cauliflower soup. Also, cooked cauliflower florets masked with mornay sauce and browned under grill, used for meat entrées.

**Flamande** Red cabbage and glazed small onions used with pork and beef.

**Florentine** Spinach purée, or leaf spinach. Also a 16th-century name for a pie.

**Hongroise** Normally implies the addition of paprika.

**Indienne** Flavoured with curry powder.

**Jardinière** Garnished with fresh vegetables.

**Joinville** Slices of truffle, crayfish tails and mushrooms with a lobster sauce, used for fish dishes.

**Lyonnaise** Denotes the use of onions as garnish – the onions are frequently sliced and fried.

**Meunière** Of fish, lightly dusted with flour, then fried and served with beurre noisette and lemon juice; also frequently (but not classically) chopped fresh parsley.

**Milanese** With a tomato sauce, sometimes including shredded ham, tongue and mushrooms. Frequently served with pasta.

**Minute** Food quickly cooked, either fried or grilled. Usually applied to a thin entrecôte steak.

**Mornay** With a cheese sauce.

**Nantua** With a lobster sauce.

**Napolitana** Tomato sauce and Parmesan cheese (for pasta). May also mean a three-coloured ice cream.

**Nicoise** Name given to many dishes consisting of ingredients common in the South of France, such as tomatoes, olives, garlic, fish, olive oil.

**Normande** Garnish of mussels, shrimps, oysters and mushrooms. Or creamy sauce containing cider or Calvados, and sometimes apples.

**Parmentier** Denotes the use of potato as a base or garnish.

**Paysanne** Literally, peasant. Usually denotes the use of carrots and turnips sliced across in rounds.

**Portuguaise** Denotes the use of tomatoes or tomato purée.

**Princesse** Denotes the use of asparagus (usually on breast of chicken).

**Printanière** Early spring vegetables cooked and used as a garnish, usually in separate groups.

**Provençal** Denotes the use of garlic, and sometimes tomatoes and/or olives.

**Rossini** With collops of foie gras and truffles tossed in butter, served with a rich meat glaze.

**St Germain** Denotes the use of peas, sometimes with pommes Parisienne.

**Soubise** Onion purée, frequently mixed with a béchamel sauce.

**Vichy** Garnish of small glazed carrots.

# METHODS OF COOKING

## WAYS OF COOKING MEAT

The tougher the meat, or the larger its volume, the more slowly it must be cooked. The quick methods of cooking – frying, deep-fat frying and grilling – are suitable for small pieces of tender meat, whereas the slower methods – braising, stewing, etc. – are best for the tougher cuts.

Three factors determine the toughness of a particular cut of meat: the age of the animal (the older it is the tougher it will be); the activity of the particular joint (the neck, shoulders, chest and legs are used far more than the back of a quadruped and are therefore tougher); and finally the texture of the fibres.

Muscle tissue is made up of long thin cells or muscle fibres bound together by sheets of connective tissue. Individual fibres can be as long as the whole muscle. Bundles of fibres are organized in groups to form an individual muscle. The lengthways structure of muscles is known as the grain of the meat. It is easier to carve and also to chew in the direction of the grain, which is why meat is cut across the grain. The connective tissue is the harness of the muscle and is visible as gristle, tendons, etc. Connective tissue is made up of three main proteins: collagen, which can be converted by long, slow cooking into gelatine; elastin, which is elastic and not changed by heat; and reticulen, which is fibrous and not changed by heat.

Tender cuts of meat such as sirloin steak have relatively few connective tissues and as they cook the meat fibres shrink and lose moisture. If overcooked, the juices finally dry up and a once tender piece of meat becomes tough and dry. However, a tough cut of meat such as oxtail, which has a lot of connective tissue, can become very moist during cooking. The collagen is converted into gelatine and the meat becomes almost sticky in its succulence.

As meat should be tender and juicy rather than dry and tough, it is important to cook it in such a way as to minimize fluid loss and to maximize the conversion of the tough collagen in the connective tissue into water-soluble gelatine.

It is possible to tenderize meat before cooking it. This can be done by cutting, pounding and grinding to break down the structure of the muscle bundles. It can also be done by marinating. The acid in citrus fruit or wine produces protein-digesting enzymes that can break down muscle and connective tissue.

### POT-ROASTING

Pot-roasting is not really roasting but rather baking food enclosed in a pot, either in the oven or over a low heat. It is an ancient, economical method of cooking that was much used in the days before domestic ovens. Roasting proper is a much faster, 'dry' method used for cooking choicer, more tender cuts of meat and poultry by exposing them to direct heat. (Full instructions for roasting meat are given on page 367.) Pot-roasting involves cooking meat in its own juices and might better be called a simpler, quicker version of braising. It is ideal for cooking joints with plenty of connective tissue. On the other hand, a tender joint will toughen when pot-roasted or braised.

Traditionally there is very little liquid in a pot-roast, other than the fat needed for browning, as moisture from the meat provides most of the liquid during cooking.

A casserole with a tightly fitting lid creates a small oven. Steam is formed inside the pot from the moisture given off by the added liquid or by the food itself, and this tenderizes and cooks the meat. If the lid does not fit tightly, the steam can escape. Similarly, if the casserole or pan is too big, the liquid spreads over too large an area and is more likely to boil away. To make sure a lid fits tightly, cover the top of the casserole or pan with a piece of greaseproof paper and place the lid on top, jamming it down firmly.

If you have a flameproof casserole, you can brown meat on the hob and pot-roast in the oven in one vessel. Otherwise, brown the meat in a frying pan and transfer it with all the pan juices to a casserole for pot-roasting.

A traditional tip when pot-roasting is to cook the browned meat on a piece of pork rind. This adds flavour, and prevents the meat from scorching. Coarsely cut root vegetables are sometimes placed under the meat for the same reason. They can be either raw or browned in the same fat as the meat, though the meat should be removed from the pan while browning the vegetables. Once cooked, they can be served with the meat.

One way to ensure tender meat is to marinate it before cooking. A mixture of oil, wine and other flavourings penetrates the outer layer of the meat when it is left to marinate overnight in the refrigerator. The acid in the marinade also helps to break down tough fibres, and the oil prevents moisture evaporation and adds richness. Save some of the marinade to use as the cooking liquid.

Another way to make sure that a large piece of pot-roasted meat is succulent is to lard it. This is especially important with some lean joints such as the beef 'leg of mutton' cut. Cut thin strips of pork back fat longer than the joint and thread them all the way through the meat about 1cm/½in apart. This is easily done with a larding needle which, when removed, leaves the strips of fat in place. As the meat cooks, the fat partially melts, making the meat juicy and adding flavour and richness to the sauce. As long as the meat cooks slowly, the liquid in the pan is not likely to boil, or, more importantly, to evaporate. This liquid becomes a richly flavoured sauce for the meat after cooking. Any vegetables cooked with the meat will help to thicken it.

Transfer the pot-roasted joint to a warmed serving dish or board to carve and remove any strings or skewers. If there is too much liquid left in the pan, simply reduce it by boiling or thicken it with beurre manié (see page 241). Serve separately.

## GRILLING

Intense heat is the secret of successful grilling. Although this method requires active attention from the cook, its advantages are that the food cooks quickly and the charred surface gives great flavour.

To produce succulent, perfectly grilled meat with a crisp brown outside and pink juicy inside, it is absolutely essential to preheat the grill to its highest setting. This may take 10 or even 20 minutes for the grill on a good domestic cooker. Under a cooler grill, the meat's surface will not brown quickly, leaving the meat tasteless and unattractive by the time it is cooked through. If the grill cannot be adequately preheated to brown meat and fish quickly, fry the steaks instead.

When grilling over an open charcoal fire, it may take 2 hours before the embers are flameless yet burn with the necessary intensity. But their fierce heat will cook a small lamb cutlet perfectly in 2 minutes and the charcoal will give it a wonderfully smoky flavour. Charcoal, when ready, glows bright red in the dark and has an ashy grey look in daylight.

Unlike braising, grilling will not tenderize meat, so only tender, choice cuts should be grilled. They should not be so much thicker than 5cm/2in because of the high temperatures involved. Any thicker and the meat will remain cold and raw when the outside is black. Even so, unless the cut of meat is fairly thin, once it browns it must be moved further away from the heat source so that the interior can cook before the surface burns. Basting with the delicious pan juices or with olive oil or butter adds flavour and shine. Turning is necessary for even cooking, and should be done halfway through the estimated cooking time, when the first surface is attractively brown.

When grilling over, rather than under, heat, use a fine grill rack or wire mesh grill to support delicate cuts of fish and grease the grill rack or mesh well. Fish cuts can be wrapped in greased foil and cooked over heat, but they then cook in their own steam rather than grill in the true sense.

The following points should be remembered when grilling:

**1.** Take food out of the refrigerator or freezer in plenty of time to bring it to room temperature before grilling. An almost frozen steak will still be cold inside when the outside is brown and sizzling. This is particularly important if the steak is to be served very rare (blue, see below).

**2.** Do not salt food much in advance. The salt draws moisture from the food. Salt after, during or immediately before grilling.

**3.** Brush the food with butter, oil or a mixture of the two to keep it moist and to speed the browning process. This is also essential to prevent delicate foods such as fish from sticking.

**4.** The more well done meat or fish is, the tougher it will be to the touch and the palate.

**5.** To avoid piercing the meat and allowing the juices to escape, turn the grilling food with tongs or spoons, not a sharp instrument.

**6.** Serve immediately. Grilled food, even if well sealed, inevitably loses moisture, dries up and toughens if kept hot for any length of time.

## GRILLING STEAKS

All grilled meats should be well browned on the surface, but the varying degrees of 'doneness' are defined as follows:

BLUE The inside is almost raw (but hot).
RARE Red inside with plenty of red juices running freely.
MEDIUM RARE As rare, but with fewer free-flowing juices and a paler centre.
MEDIUM Pink in the centre with juices set.
WELL DONE The centre is beige but the flesh is still juicy.

The best way to tell if meat is done is by its texture. Feel the meat by pressing firmly with a finger. Rare steak feels soft, almost raw; medium steak is firmer with some resilience to it; well-done steak feels very firm. With practice there will soon be no need to cut-and-peep.

COOKING TIME FOR STEAKS varies with the heat of the grill, the distance of the food from the heat, the thickness of the cut and its fat content. The density of the meat also affects the cooking time. Open-textured steak such as sirloin will cook faster than the same thickness and weight of closer-textured rump.

## GRILLING FISH

Lay fish steaks and fillets on greased foil on the grill rack, and set close under the preheated grill. This prevents the delicate flesh from sticking to the rack and breaking up when turned.

## FRYING AND SAUTÉING

Frying, sometimes referred to as 'shallow frying', and sautéing are both quick cooking methods which are suitable for small, not-too-thick, tender pieces of meat and other foods. The difference between the two methods is the amount of fat used in cooking. For sautéing, an almost dry pan with no more than 1 tablespoon of fat is used; for frying, food is cooked up in 5mm/¼in of fat.

The processes are similar to grilling but when grilling small pieces of meat some fat is lost in the pan juices which may or may not be eaten with the meat. When fried, the meat cooks in fat, at least some of which is eaten with the meat. For this reason the fat used for frying is an important consideration as its distinctive flavour – or the lack of it – will affect the taste of the dish. Olive oil, butter, bacon dripping, lard and beef dripping will each give distinctive flavour to fried foods, while corn, safflower, peanut and most other vegetable oils have little or no flavour. Potatoes fried in goose fat may taste delicious, but not when they are served with fish.

When choosing a fat, remember that some can be heated to much higher temperatures than others before they break down and start to burn. For example, clarified butter – butter with all its milk solids removed (see page 686) – can be heated to a higher temperature than untreated butter; pure bacon dripping, lard, beef dripping and solid frying fat can generally withstand more heat than margarine, butter or vegetable oil. Fats tend to lose their molecular structure ('break down') if heated for too long, and this causes them to smoke (and smell) unpleasantly at a lower temperature than when fresh. Eventually they will give an unappetizing flavour to any food fried in them. However, even solid fresh fats (if they contain an emulsifier) will smoke and burn at cooler temperatures than pure fats without additives.

## FRYING

Techniques vary depending on the texture and size of the food and the effect the cook wishes to achieve. For instance, when frying steaks or chops remember to:

**1.** Fry in an uncovered wide pan. A lid traps the steam and the food stews or steams rather than frying crisply.

**2.** Preheat the fat. If the fat is cool when the food is put into it, the food will not brown. It will then lack flavour, look unattractive and may even absorb some of the cool fat and become too greasy.

**3.** Fry a little at a time. Adding too much food at one time to hot fat lowers the temperature and, again, hinders the browning.

**4.** Fry fast until the meat is completely browned on all sides. Then turn down to medium heat to cook the inside through.

Fried food should be served as soon as possible after cooking. Juices gradually seep out and meat toughens on standing; potatoes lose their crispness, become leathery and tough-skinned; fritters deflate, and everything loses its newly fried shine.

Fish is cooked à la meunière by dusting it with flour and shallow-frying in butter until it is brown on both sides. The slight coating of flour helps to prevent sticking and adds crispness to the skin. The fish is then put on a warmed platter. Chopped fresh parsley, lemon juice, salt and pepper are added to the butter in the pan and, once sizzling, this is poured over the fish.

STIFFENING Some recipes require gentle frying without a coating of flour. When this method is used, the fat, though hot, is not fearsomely so, and the food can be gently fried to a very pale brown, or cooked without browning. This is particularly useful with kidneys and liver, which tend to burst and become grainy if fried too fast; with shellfish, which toughens if subjected to fierce heat; and with thin slices of fish (such as salmon to be served in a sorrel sauce), where the taste of butter-frying is required without a browned surface.

ENGLISH BREAKFAST FRYING Eggs should be fried in clean fat. Frying them in a pan in which bacon or sausages have been cooking leads to sticking and possible breaking of the yolks. If eggs are to be fried in the same pan as other items, fry the bacon, ham, sausages, potatoes, mushrooms and bread first as this will all keep in a warm oven for a few minutes. Tip the fat into a cup. Rinse the pan, removing any stuck sediment, dry it, then pour the fat back into the pan. Using enough sizzling fat to spoon over eggs speeds up the process and prevents the edges of the whites from overcooking before the thicker parts are set.

Sausages generally have skins which, as the stuffing expands in the hot pan, can burst or split open. Avoid this by pricking them carefully all over with a thin needle (large holes like those made by the prongs of a fork provide weak points where the skin will split), and/or by cooking slowly. Shake the pan with rapid but careful side-to-side or forward-and-backward movements; this will dislodge any pieces that are stuck with less damage than a prodding utensil. Fry the sausages slowly until evenly browned all over and firm to the touch.

Bacon rashers can be fried in an almost dry pan as they readily produce their own fat. However, they cook faster and more evenly in shallow fat.

GLAZING VEGETABLES Vegetables are sometimes given a final shiny, slightly sweet glaze by frying them in a mixture of butter and sugar. The sugar melts and caramelizes to a pale toffee and the vegetables brown in the butter and caramel mixture. Constant shaking of the pan is necessary to prevent burning and sticking. This method is particularly successful with shallots, baby onions, mushrooms and root vegetables.

SAUTÉING is used on its own to cook foods such as chicken pieces, mushrooms or apple rings, but is most frequently used in conjunction with other forms of cooking. For example, whole small onions may be sautéed to brown them before they are added to liquid in a stew or a sauce. Sautéing is also employed after boiling to give cooked or partially cooked foods, such as potatoes, a lightly browned and buttered exterior.

Browning gives a sautéed dish its essential character. After browning, some meats, such as liver or veal escalopes, are often removed and then served with a relatively small amount of well-flavoured sauce which has been made in the same pan. Meats such as pork chops or chicken pieces may be given an initial browning and then cooked with added ingredients that will eventually form the sauce. The range of such sauces is almost endless – as various as the liquids and other flavourings that can be used in making them. Stages in sautéing are as follows:

**1.** Fry the main ingredients together with any others, browning them in minimal fat. Remove them from the pan and keep them hot.
**2.** Deglaze (see page 20) the pan with a liquid such as stock, cream or wine.
**3.** Add the flavourings for the sauce.
**4.** If the initial browning has cooked the main ingredients sufficiently, reduce the sauce by rapid boiling and pour it over the dish. Garnish and serve immediately.
**5.** If the main ingredients need further cooking, simmer them in the sauce until they are tender, then proceed as above.

## DEEP-FRYING

Deep-frying is one of the fastest possible methods of cooking small, tender cuts of meat and fish. It is also suitable for many vegetables, and for dough mixtures such as fritters and doughnuts.

Because of the very high temperatures the fat reaches, most foods are given a protective coating before frying. This seals in their juices and prevents overcooking as well as too much spluttering of the hot fat, caused by moisture rapidly vaporizing on the surface of uncoated wet food.

Some foods, such as potato crisps, are in and out of the hot fat so quickly that they do not need any coating. Chips are given a first frying at a low temperature to cook them through, then a second frying at a higher temperature to brown them.

Most other foods need a coating, either of flour or crumbs or a flour-and-liquid batter. While the coating fries to a crisp brown, the food stays moist and tender. One of the pleasures of deep-fried food is the contrast between interior and exterior. For the driest and crispest coating, drain off all excess fat on absorbent kitchen paper after cooking and serve as soon as possible.

If the coating covers the food completely, as it should, the flavour of the fried food will not

contaminate the fat, which may then be used again. Filter the fat clean of any food particles after frying. As soon as it shows signs of breaking down, by becoming dark, odorous or cloudy, it should be replaced. Such fat smokes and burns at a lower temperature than fresh fat, smells stale and gives an unpleasant flavour to anything cooked in it.

BATTER Batter is a farinaceous mixture of a thick liquid consistency. It is used to give a crisp protective coating to food that might otherwise burn or splatter when deep- or shallow-fried.

### USING A DEEP-FRYER

**1.** If the deep-fryer is not thermostatically controlled, use a thermometer to test the temperature of the fat by dropping a crumb or cube of bread into it. If the bread browns in 60 seconds, the fat is about 182°C/360°F and suitable for gentle frying; if it browns in 40 seconds, the oil is moderately hot, about 190°C/375°F; if it browns in 20 seconds, the fat is very hot, about 195°C/385°F. If the bread browns in 10 seconds, the fat is dangerously hot and should be cooled down. Turn off the heat and fry several slices of bread in it to speed up the cooling.
**2.** Cook food in small amounts. Adding too many pieces at one time lowers the temperature of the fat so that the coating will not form a crisp crust. The food then absorbs fat and loses its juices in the cooking fat. This is particularly important if you are frying food that is still frozen, such as fish fingers, commercially prepared chips or Chinese spring rolls, which will of course cool the fat greatly. However, do not attempt to remedy this problem by frying in very hot fat. Comparatively cool fat is needed (about 180°C/350°F) to allow the inside to thaw and cook before the coating browns.
**3.** Drain the cooked fat well on absorbent paper.
**4.** If the food is not served right away, spread it out in a single layer on a hot baking sheet or tray and keep it uncovered in a warm oven with the door ajar to allow the free circulation of air. Covering or enclosing the food will make the crust soggy. Try not to fry far ahead of serving.
**5.** Add salt, or a sprinkling of caster sugar if the food is sweet, after frying. This accentuates the

flavour and the dry, crisp texture.

**6.** After use, cool the fat and strain it through muslin or a coffee filter paper. This removes food particles which, if left in the fat, will become black and burned with repeated fryings. As soon as the fat becomes at all dark, it should be changed, as it is beginning to break down, will smoke readily and give a rancid flavour to fried food.

### STIR-FRYING

Choose a carbon iron wok with a round base and one long wooden handle. The best size is about 35cm/14in. The advantage of stir-frying is that there is a large surface area all at the same temperature, so the food cooks fast and retains all its flavour, colour and texture. The trick is to stir with a Chinese ladle, strainer or spoon with one hand while shaking and jerking the wok with the other. When stir-frying vegetables add the firmest vegetables first, and the more tender ones a few minutes later.

## BRAISING

Braising, in the true sense of the word, is a method of slowly cooking meat on a mirepoix, a thick bed of finely diced mixed vegetables with the addition of strong stock. In practice, the term braising is often confused with pot-roasting, as in both methods food is cooked slowly in a pan with a tightly-fitting lid to give deliciously tender results. The main difference is that pot-roasted food is cooked with little, if any, liquid other than the fat used for browning the ingredients, and braising involves some liquid and at least some cut-up vegetables to add moisture to the pan, even if a true mirepoix is not used. A pot-roast should taste 'roasted' and be decidedly fattier than a braise, which is closer to a stew and depends more on juices and stocks than on fat for flavour.

Braising can also mean 'sweating'. This is a method of gently cooking vegetables, frequently onions and shallots, in butter or oil in a covered pan, which is shaken frequently to prevent burning and sticking. Once cooked through, softened and exuding their juices but not coloured, the vegetables are usually added to stews, sauces or soups, to which they give a subtle flavouring but no colouring. For example, to braise red cabbage, a finely chopped onion is sweated in butter until tender, then shredded cabbage, a little vinegar, sugar, apple and seasoning are added. These are left over a low heat, covered tightly, to sweat for 2–3 hours. The result is braised red cabbage, even though neither meat nor mirepoix has been included.

Occasionally the term braising is used to mean baking in a covered pan with only a little liquid. Braised celery hearts, for example, consists of quarters of celery head cooked in a little stock in a covered pan in the oven. Braised fennel is cooked with lemon juice, butter and stock.

Beef fillet and sirloin or lamb best end should be roasted or grilled, but otherwise whole joints or smaller pieces of meat can be braised with advantage. The meat should be fairly lean and any fat that melts into the stock should be skimmed off before serving. Poultry may be braised unless it is old and tough, when stewing or poaching are more suitable cooking methods as all the flesh, which will tend to be stringy and dry, is submerged in liquid.

The vegetables for the mirepoix should be browned quickly in hot fat and stirred constantly to ensure even colouring, then transferred to a heavy casserole or pan. The meat can be browned in the same fat before it is placed on top of the vegetables and stock is added. As the vegetables cook they will disintegrate, helping to thicken the stock.

Making a strong, reduced, well-flavoured stock is time-consuming, but it is one of the key factors in good braising. The best stock is one made from chopped-up beef shin bones that have been browned all over and then simmered and skimmed frequently for hours (see page 243).

As with pot-roasting, meat may be marinated overnight in the refrigerator and large pieces of exceptionally lean meat may be larded to ensure that they remain moist. Dry the meat well before browning it.

The exacting and by no means easy steps for braising red meat to ideal tenderness and almost sticky juiciness are as follows:

**1.** Fry the mirepoix of vegetables and a few tablespoons of diced salt pork or bacon slowly in oil and butter, shaking the pan and stirring until they are evenly browned all over.
**2.** Brown the meat on all sides and place it on top of the vegetable bed in a heavy casserole.

**3.** Add stock, made from gelatinous meats such as knuckle of veal or beef shin bones, to cover the meat. If the stock is not rich and solidly set when cold, the braise will not have the correct 'melting' stickiness. Then stew, without basting, until half-cooked.

**4.** Lift out the meat, strain the stock, and discard the mirepoix, which will by now have imparted all its flavour.

**5.** Return the meat to the casserole and reduce the stock by rapid boiling until it is thick and syrupy, then pour it over the meat.

**6.** There will no longer be enough stock to cover the meat and there is a danger, even in a covered pan, of the exposed top drying out, so turn the meat every 15 minutes and baste it with the stock.

By the end of the cooking time, when the meat is tender, the stock should be so reduced as to provide a shiny coating that will not run off the meat. It will penetrate the flesh, moistening it and giving it the slightly glutinous texture of perfectly braised meat.

## STEWING

The term stew is so widely used that it can mean almost anything. A stew is essentially food that has been slowly and gently cooked in plenty of liquid. Most cooks envisage meat cut into smallish pieces before cooking, but the term is sometimes used for sliced, sautéed meat or poultry served in a sauce, or for a whole joint or bird poached in liquid. Many stews require preliminary frying of the meat, and sometimes of onions, shallots, carrots or mushrooms too. This gives a richer flavour to the ingredients and adds colour and flavour to the sauce, which will be made using the browned sediment and dried-on juices sticking to the pan after frying. These are called brown stews. White stews are made without preliminary browning and are less rich, less fatty, altogether gentler and more easily digestible than brown ones.

Both brown and white stews are served in their cooking liquid, which is usually thickened to a syrupy sauce.

The principles of shallow-frying (see page 27) apply to the preliminary frying for a brown stew. If the sauce is not to taste insipid, or be pale in colour, you must start with a good even colour on both sides of each slice or all sides of each cube of meat. Good stews are made or lost in the early stages – so take care to fry only a few pieces at a time, to keep the temperature hot enough to sizzle and to take the time to get an even colour. Deglaze the pan as often as necessary. Deglazing serves three essential purposes: it prevents the stuck sediment in the pan from burning; it allows the flavour of that sediment to be captured and incorporated into the sauce; and it cleans the pan ready for the next batch of meat.

Beef stew with suet crust is a traditional stew, classically made. But the same principles can be used to make a lamb navarin, for example. Follow the same procedure, using lean cubes of lamb instead of the beef and omitting the suet crust. Young spring vegetables such as broad beans, French beans, tiny whole carrots, peas or sprigs of cauliflower, can be added to the stew for the last 10 minutes of stewing time to give a navarin d'agneau printanier.

## BOILING AND POACHING

BOILING is a blanket term for cooking food submerged in liquid by one of several techniques: from fast, agitated bubbling – a rolling boil – to a gentle simmer, when bubbles will appear in one part of the pan only, or to the barest tremble of the liquid, which is poaching. The techniques suit different foods and achieve different effects.

Cooking green vegetables quickly in rapidly boiling water in an open pan tenderizes them, yet ensures they retain their crispness and bright colour. The water should be well salted (1 tablespoon for every 1.75 litres/3 pints), as it then boils at a higher temperature, cooking the vegetables even more quickly.

Rapid boiling in an open pan protects the vivid colours of some vegetables, such as runner beans, while enhancing the colours of others, such as artichokes. When covered, discoloration can be caused by enzymes from the vegetables, which collect in the condensation on the lid and fall back into the water. The best method is to bring the water to the boil without the vegetables, add the vegetables and cover with a lid to bring them back to the boil as fast as possible, then remove the lid to allow the escape of steam.

Vegetables that would be damaged by vigorous boiling are cooked by the more gentle simmering methods. Vegetables unlikely to discolour, like potatoes, carrots, parsnips, beetroot and other root vegetables, are traditionally cooked in a covered pan to preserve heat and contain fuel costs. Hence the adage: 'If it grows in the light, cook it in the open; if it grows in the dark, keep it covered.'

REFRESHING Once cooked, refresh the vegetables by rinsing them briefly under cold running water, then put them into a warmed serving dish. Refreshing prevents further cooking by the heat retained in the vegetables, and thus sets the colour. Vegetables that hold their colour well, such as carrots, or small quantities of vegetables, such as French beans for 4 people, do not need refreshing, but for large quantities it is vital, especially if there is to be any delay before serving. They can be reheated briefly before serving by any of the following methods: by being dipped in boiling water; by rapid steaming; by being given 30 – 60 seconds in a microwave oven; by being tossed quickly in butter over high heat. Slow reheating in the oven will discolour most green vegetables, frozen peas being the exception, although even these will eventually lose their brilliant hue.

BLANCHING Some foods, especially vegetables and fruit, are immersed in boiling water without being fully cooked. This is called blanching and has various uses:

1. To remove strong flavours, e.g. from liver or kidneys before frying.
2. To facilitate the removal of skin, e.g. from tomatoes or peaches.
3. To lessen the salt content, e.g. from ham before cooking.
4. To destroy enzymes in vegetables destined for the freezer and to prevent discoloration.
5. To shorten the roasting time of vegetables such as potatoes, onions and parsnips by parboiling first.
6. Simply to semi-cook or soften food, e.g. fennel in salad.

FAST BOILING Rice and pasta cook well at a good rolling boil. The boiling water expands the starch granules and makes them tender, while the rapid agitation prevents the pieces of pasta or rice grains from sticking together or to the pan. Adding 1 tablespoon oil to the water also helps to prevent sticking. Long-grain rice boiled in a large pan of heavily salted water takes 10 – 11 minutes to cook. The grains should then mash to a paste when pressed between the thumb and index finger, though a little 'bite' is preferable to an all-over soft texture.

Similarly, pasta should always be cooked *al dente*, i.e. firm to the bite. Remember that fresh or homemade pasta, which already contains moisture, cooks 4 times faster than the dried commercial equivalents. The cooking time also depends on the thickness. Dried vermicelli cooks in 2 – 3 minutes, while dried lasagne takes 15 – 16.

Sometimes rapid boiling is used to drive off moisture and reduce liquids to a thicker consistency. With sugar mixtures, the essential high temperatures are most rapidly achieved by a galloping boil.

EGGS are often boiled, yet there is considerable confusion about the correct method of doing this. The easiest and most foolproof is as follows:

1. Prick the rounded end of the egg with an egg-pricker or a needle to allow air to escape.
2. Bring a pan of water to the boil. Have the eggs at room temperature. (If chilled, add 30 seconds to cooking time.)
3. Carefully lower the eggs into the water on a perforated spoon.
4. Time the cooking from the moment of immersion, keeping the water simmering or gently boiling, and not boiling too vigorously, which tends to crack the shells and toughen the whites.

Three minutes will cook a medium-sized egg until the white is barely set; indeed, the white closest to the yolk will still be slightly jelly-like. Four minutes give a runny yolk and a just-set white. Six minutes give a well-set white and moist but runny yolk (set on the rim and thick but wet inside). Eight minutes give a nicely hardboiled egg. Ten minutes will give a yolk sufficiently cooked to be dry and crumbly when mashed. Fifteen minutes will give a yellow-green rim to the dry yolk and make the white tough and unpalatable. For hardboiling eggs, see page 112.
SIMMERING Dried pulses are also cooked by boiling.

As there is no colour loss to worry about, and the process is a long one, they may be simmered rather than fast-boiled. Rapidly boiling water evaporates very fast, risking boiling dry and burning. They may even, with advantage, be slowly stewed – cooked in a covered pan in liquid that only partially covers them – either on top of the stove or in the oven. If the proportion of liquid to pulses is right, they absorb all the liquid during cooking. There is nothing to throw away and little loss of flavour and nutrients. The amount of water needed obviously depends on the age, and therefore dryness, of the pulses and the speed of boiling, but twice the volume of water to pulses is a good guide.

It is often recommended that pulses be soaked in water before cooking, but this is not always necessary, especially if the pulses are last season's crop. Dried beans that are known to be 2 – 3 years old can be cooked without any prior soaking, but they will absorb more water, take longer to become tender, and will not taste as good as fresher pulses. As a general rule, soaking is a good idea, especially for the larger beans.

Pressure-cooking works well for pulses and eliminates the need for soaking. Pressure cookers vary and it is obviously sensible to consult the manufacturer's instructions. As a general rule, 450g/1lb dried peas or beans, unsoaked, will need 1 litre/2 pints water and will cook in 30 minutes at 7kg/15lb pressure.

Like pulses, some vegetables can be slowly stewed until all the liquid is either absorbed or has evaporated. For example, even-sized pieces of carrot can be put into very lightly salted water with a lump of butter. The carrots are cooked slowly so that when all the water has evaporated they are just tender, and coated in the butter. They are then called Vichy carrots.

POACHING is another long, slow, gentle cooking method, but the food is generally completely submerged in liquid that is barely trembling, either on the hob or in the oven. It is an excellent method for delicate items, such as eggs, fish or soft fruit, which would break up if subjected to vigorous agitation. For poaching an egg, see page 666.

Tough meat becomes more tender and succulent the more slowly it is cooked. A cut such as oxtail takes at least 3 hours of simmering on the hob until it is acceptably tender. Poached in

the oven at 150°C/300F/gas mark 2 for 5 hours, it would be even more tender, falling from the bone and gelatinous.

A ham or large piece of bacon is cooked when the meat has shrunk back from the bone or, if boneless, when it has visibly shrunk in size by about one-fifth. The rind or skin will then peel off easily and a skewer will penetrate the meat unimpeded. But until you are experienced and confident, it is wise to stick to the cooking times given in recipes.

## STEAMING

Steaming is the cooking of food in hot vapours over boiling liquid (usually water) rather than in liquid. It occurs to some extent in braising and pot-roasting, because of the closed pans and the relatively small amounts of liquid used. In true steaming, however, the food never touches the liquid, so the loss of many vitamins is significantly reduced. Furthermore, steamed food is not browned first, so it can be cooked without fat. This makes the food more easily digestible and particularly suitable for invalids and those on low-fat diets. The method has regained great favour with the new-wave nouvelle cuisine chefs because of its simplicity and purity. But excellent ingredients are essential for steaming – there is no browning, so the food must taste good without such assistance.

A variety of equipment for steaming food is available. Most common are oval or round steamers, which are like double saucepans, except that the top has holes in its base. Steam from boiling water in the lower pan rises through the holes to cook the food, while the lid on the upper pan keeps in the steam.

Another popular steaming device is a stainless steel or aluminium basket that opens and folds shut and is used with an ordinary lidded saucepan. The basket stands on its own short legs to keep it clear of the boiling water. It fits inside most saucepans and is particularly suitable for foods that do not need long cooking time as otherwise the water underneath the short legs would have to be replaced too frequently. The saucepan must have a tightly fitting lid.

VEGETABLES are the food most commonly steamed as they cook quickly and retain more of their colour and texture this way. Careful timing is essential as steamed food can be tasteless if even slightly overcooked. Today steaming times for vegetables are short, giving bright-coloured, *al dente*, palpably fresh results. Some vegetables can be steamed in their own juices. Spinach, for example, may be trimmed and put wet from washing into a covered saucepan over medium heat, and shaken occasionally until limp and cooked, but still very green. This takes about 5 minutes.

Floury potatoes that tend to break up when boiled before they are cooked are best steamed; choose potatoes that are about the same size, so that they cook at the same time. If they are very large or different sizes, cut them into bite-sized pieces before steaming. For most other root vegetables, such as turnips, parsnips and swedes, cut them into 1cm/½in dice and steam them until tender before seasoning and adding butter to serve.

FISH AND POULTRY Steaming fish is simple and quick and always produces a delicate result if the fish is not allowed to overcook. Put the fish on to a piece of muslin or cheesecloth to prevent it from sticking to the steamer bottom. Oval steamers and folding baskets are suitable for small quantities of fish, but for larger fish or cooking a number of small fish, shellfish, fish steaks or fillets, a fish kettle (usually used for poaching whole fish) may be used. Made of metal, these come in sizes to take whole fish on a perforated rack inside the kettle. Ramekins can be placed under the rack to keep it well above the boiling liquid. Whole fish can be stuffed and cooked over liquid in a covered kettle on top of the stove. Allow about 8 minutes per 450g/1lb of fish.

Delicate poultry such as chicken breasts or whole small quail may be steamed similarly.

Plate steaming is an excellent method of cooking small quantities of fish in their own juices. Put the fish fillets or steaks on a lightly buttered plate, season well and cover with another upturned buttered plate or buttered kitchen foil. Set the covered plate on top of a pan of gently boiling water or on a trivet inside a large frying pan of bubbling water and cook for 8–10 minutes, depending on the thickness of the fish.

STEAMED PUDDINGS Traditional English sweet and savoury puddings (particularly suet crust puddings) are also cooked by steaming, but here the food is cooked in a container heated by steam. This gives the suet mixture its distinctive soft, open texture. The easiest way to cook the pudding is to put its container in a saucepan with hot water that comes halfway up the sides of the container. The pan is covered and the pudding cooked over low heat to steam gently for a long time, and water is added to the pan as necessary. Take care to cover the pudding with a double thickness of kitchen foil, pleated to allow for expansion of the crust, and put a band of folded foil under the basin with ends projecting up the sides to act as handles.

CHINESE COOKING traditionally involves a good deal of steaming. Fish, shellfish and tender cuts of meat, often wrapped in pastry or vegetable leaves, are quickly steamed. Food in one or more stacked rattan or metal baskets with a lid is placed over steaming liquid in a pan or wok for quick cooking.

MICROWAVING In conventional oven cooking the air is heated and the heat is passed slowly into the centre of the food by conduction. In microwaving the microwaves cause the moisture molecules in the food to vibrate, causing friction which results in heat. The heat that is generated in the food begins to cook it from the inside. Microwaves only penetrate about 5cm/2in into the food. The centre of large pieces of food is cooked by the conduction of the heat produced near the food's surface. The microwaves are reflected off the metal cavity of the oven and form criss-cross patterns. The food absorbs waves from all directions. The waves pass through china, glass, paper, etc., all of which make suitable microwave containers. Metal must not be used for microwaving as the waves are reflected and bounce off.

Microwave ovens can cook all foods but with varying results. They are very useful for cooking vegetables that would normally be boiled, such as peas and asparagus, saving on washing up and preserving vitamins and minerals, but not so good for those that would naturally be baked – a microwave-'baked' jacket potato tastes boiled.

A microwave is excellent for reheating, melting butter and defrosting food in small quantities. However, it is less suitable for defrosting large joints of meat or poultry: as the food begins to thaw, the microwaves are attracted to the defrosted water molecules and keep causing vibration/friction in the same place, while other parts remain frozen. The joint or bird should be removed from the oven and left to stand every so often so that the heat can be conducted to the centre. The speed at which a microwave cooks means that food benefiting from long cooking, such as roast beef, simply does not have the depth of flavour that a conventionally cooked piece has. On the other hand, it is good for cooking fish, which it will steam or poach beautifully.

There is no need to preheat a microwave oven but the colder the food is the longer it will take to cook. There is only a set amount of energy coming into the oven so when more than one item of food is put in, the energy is divided between them. Thus five potatoes will take considerably longer to cook than one. The shape of the food should also be taken into account – the more even the shape the more evenly it will cook. Thinner areas of food can be covered with smooth-edged tin foil to prevent further cooking. Very dense foods, such as shepherd's pie, are more difficult to reheat than those with a light, open texture, such as a sponge pudding.

Do not cover food to be microwaved with tin foil, which reflects the waves; instead use clingfilm, which should be pierced to prevent it from bursting. As a general rule moist food should be pricked.

At Leith's we have decided that a microwave is most useful for:

• Melting butter
• Softening butter for cake making (be careful not to oversoften and melt)
• Cooking vegetables in a minimum of water
• Cooking small pieces of fish
• Cooking chestnuts (pierce the tops and place on absorbent kitchen paper, cook on High for 2 minutes and peel while warm)
• Reheating plated meals and cups of coffee
• Making caramel (make it in a dish. See note on page 495 for making caramel for Crème Caramel in a microwave)

Do not use the following utensils in the microwave:

• Metal containers, which reflect the waves
• Dishes with gold or silver decoration, which cause arcing (blue flashes)
• Packets with a gold line, which will get so hot that the paper will burst into flames
• Anything containing glue
• Pottery, which often has a metallic glaze
• Melamine or similar, which will absorb the waves
• Crystal glass, which contains lead
• Thin-stemmed glasses, which may break
• Jagged pieces of tin foil, which may cause arcing. If foil is used to prevent cooking, make sure it has smooth edges.

HOME-SMOKING Smoking food can be a fairly messy business, therefore attempting it at home requires a certain degree of determination.

A selection of domestic smokers is available, varying in price and sophistication. All home-smokers are for hot-smoking, where the food cooks and smokes at the same time.

The home-smoker is a simple affair, easily assembled. We use a tall metal cylinder with a trivet which sits on the bottom and an assortment of baskets that fit inside the cylinder or hang from the lid. The wood shavings are sprinkled on the bottom; the trivet, containing a little water or other liquid, sits on top, and then the food is arranged over the trivet and the smoking takes place.

The smoke is created by the use of wood shavings. Oak, beech or fruit wood shavings are best as they give a subtle flavour and burn easily. Resinous woods such as pine should never be used. Other flavourings can be mixed with the shavings to give an extra dimension. Whole spices such as dried chilli peppers, cumin, caraway, coriander, cinnamon sticks and star anise are excellent. Tea leaves also give an interesting flavour.

The shavings and flavourings are sprinkled, dry, on to the base of the smoker. The food can be either very lightly smoked, giving a very subtle flavour, or heavily smoked for a pronounced flavour, according to the amount of wood shavings used. The small amount of liquid in the trivet is essential during the smoking, as the steam created helps to keep the food moist. Water can be infused with herbs and spices, or wine or a marinade can be used.

The food is then arranged in the baskets. It is important that they do not touch: the smoker must not be overcrowded with food. The smoker is set over a low heat and the food is cooked for 30 – 45 minutes, depending on size. Avoid lifting the smoker lid too much during cooking or smoke will escape. The end-result is delicious and well worth the effort.

It is perfectly possible to smoke food at home without the use of a special smoker. Instead, a large roasting tin can be effectively used, with a cake tin or small metal dish acting as the trivet, and a wire cake rack placed over the tin can hold the food. When the shavings, liquid and food are in place, the whole thing can be covered in kitchen foil and the smoking process begun.

## FOOD PRESENTATION

If food looks delicious, people are predisposed to find that it tastes delicious. If you have spent a long time cooking, it is a shame just to dump the food on a plate. At Leith's School we have gradually developed a set of rules which can be used as guidelines when presenting food. Fashion may dictate the method – be it stylish nouvelle cuisine or chunky real food – but the guidelines are the same.

### 1. Keep it simple
Over-decorated food often looks messed about – no longer appetizing, but like an uncertain work of art. The more cluttered the plate, the less attractive it inevitably becomes.

### 2. Keep it fresh
Nothing looks more off-putting than tired food. Sprigs of herbs used for garnish should always be absolutely fresh. Pot herbs now widely available in supermarkets make this easy to ensure. Salad wilts when dressed in advance; sautéed potatoes become dull and dry when kept warm for hours, and whipped cream goes buttery in a warm room, so don't risk it.

### 3. Keep it relevant
A sprig of fresh watercress complements lamb cutlets nicely. The texture, taste and colour all do something for the lamb. But scratchy sprigs of parsley, though they might provide the colour, are

unpleasant to eat. Gherkins cut into fans do nothing for salads, tomato slices do not improve the look of a platter of sandwiches – they rather serve to confuse and distract the eye. It is better by far to dish up a plate of chicken mayonnaise with a couple of suitable salads to provide the colour and contrast needed, than to decorate it with undressed tomato waterlilies or inedible baskets made out of lemon skins and filled with frozen sweetcorn.

### 4. Centre height
Dishes served on platters, such as chicken sauté, meringues, profiteroles or even a bean salad, are best given 'centre height' – arranged so the mound of food is higher in the middle with sides sloping down. Coat carefully and evenly with the sauce, if any. Do not overload serving platters with food, which makes dishing up difficult. Once breached, an over-large pile of food looks unattractive.

### 5. Contrasting rows
Biscuits, petits fours, little cakes and cocktail canapés all look good if arranged in rows, each row consisting of one variety, rather than dotted about. Pay attention to contrasting colour, taking care, say, not to put 2 rows of chocolate biscuits side by side, or 2 rows of white sandwiches.

### 6. Diagonal lines
Diamond shapes and diagonal lines are easier to achieve than straight ones. The eye is more conscious of unevenness in verticals, horizontals and rectangles.

### 7. Not too many colours
As with any design, it is easier to get a pleasing effect if the colours are controlled – say, just green and white, or just pink and green, or chocolate and coffee colours or even 2 shades of one colour. Coffee icing and hazelnuts give a cake an elegant look. Adding multi-coloured icings to a cake, or every available garnish to a salad, tends to look garish. There are exceptions of course: a colourful salad Niçoise can be as pleasing to the eye as a dish of candy-coated chocolate drops.

### 8. Contrasting the simple and the elaborate
If the dish or bowl is elaborately decorated, contrasting simple food tends to show it off better. A Victorian fruit epergne with ornate stem and silver carving will look stunning filled with fresh strawberries. Conversely, a plain white plate sets off pretty food design to perfection.

### 9. Uneven numbers
As a rule, uneven numbers of, say, rosettes of

cream on a cake, baked apples in a long dish, or portions of meat on a platter look better than even numbers. This is especially true of small numbers. Five and three invariably look better than four, but there is little difference in effect between 11 and 12.

### 10. A generous look

Tiny piped cream stars, or sparsely dotted nuts, or mean-looking chocolate curls on a cake look amateurish and stingy.

### 11. Avoid clumsiness

On the other hand, the temptation to cram the last spoonful of rice into the bowl, or squeeze the last slice of pâté on to the dish leads to a clumsy look, and can be daunting to the diner.

### 12. Overlapping

Chops, steaks, sliced meats, even rashers of bacon, look best evenly overlapping. This way, more of them can be fitted comfortably on the serving dish than if placed side by side.

### 13. Best side uppermost

Usually the side of a steak or a cutlet that is grilled or fried first looks the best, and should be placed uppermost. Bones are generally unsightly and, if they cannot be clipped off or removed, they should be tucked out of the way.

### 14. Individual plating

Until the advent of nouvelle cuisine in the 1970s it was considered a caterer's short-cut trick to plate dishes individually. Suddenly it became the only way to present food. When plating individually the same rules apply to presentation. Keep it simple and keep it relevant. We add two extra caveats. First, think of the rim of the plate as a picture frame: do not put any food on the 'frame'. Second, stick to your original idea. If a dish has been plated up and then changed, it will inevitably look messy.

## SERVING STYLE

How much formal convention is followed at an informal family table or at a simple supper with friends, depends of course on the character and personal style of the host or hosts. But it is useful to know how things ought to be done, so that, at an elegant dinner party or if cooking for someone else, the cook at least won't make any blunders.

### LAYING THE TABLE

As a rule, cutlery is laid so that the diner works from the outside in – his first-course knife will be furthest from the plate, and on the right, because he is to pick it up with his right hand. His first-course fork will be on his left, and furthest from his plate. Similarly, if the first course is soup, the soup spoon will be on the right (because most people are right-handed), at the extreme outside of the cutlery collection.

If a knife-and-fork first course is followed by soup, the soup spoon will be in second place, and so on, working inwards to dessert spoon and fork, or cheese knife. Dessert or pudding cutlery is sometimes put across the top of the diner's place, the spoon above or beyond the fork and the handles pointing towards the hand that will pick them up – i.e. spoon handle towards the right hand, fork handle towards left hand.

Logic prevails in the same way with glasses, which are set out just beyond the knife tip, in a diagonal row, first one (say for a white wine to go with the first course) a little further away, and the dessert wine glass at the end of the row. The bread plate is placed on the diner's left, to the left of the cutlery. Napkins either go on this plate, or in the middle of the diner's place if the first course is not yet on the table. Individual ashtrays, fingerbowls, salt cellars are placed within comfortable reach.

The commonest mistakes made in laying tables are to fail to leave enough space between the banks of cutlery for the dinner plate to fit comfortably (leaving the guest foraging under his plate for a knife or fork), to line up the tips of the cutlery instead of the bases, which gives an untidy unprofessional look, and to arrange flowers or candles in such a way that diners cannot see each other across the table. Low flowers are best, and candles should be checked to make sure they do not confuse sight lines. Nothing is so irritating as having to peer round an obstruction to carry on a conversation.

### THE ETIQUETTE OF SERVING

At a formal dinner convention holds that women are served before men, starting with the most important female guest and ending with the hostess. Usually the top female guest will be seated on the right of the host. The men are then served, the most important male guest (who will be seated at the right of the hostess) being served first, then the others and, lastly, the host. Once everyone is served the hostess starts to eat which is a signal for everyone else to begin.

## HOW MUCH TO SERVE

A daunting plateful tends to take away the appetite, so do not over-help guests to food. Take trouble to arrange things neatly and attractively on the plate. Place the first spoonful (say the meat) to one side, not in the middle, then work round with vegetables and garnishes, keeping them separate. Slops and drips look bad, so take time when spooning a sauce to let any excess run off the spoon before moving away from the main dish, and make sure the serving dish and diner's plate are as close together as possible.

If waiting formally, by the diner's side, hold the platter with one hand almost over his plate and use a spoon and fork in the other hand to serve him. This is called 'silver service'. If the diner is helping himself, hold the platter very low close to the table and close to his plate, to the side of it, so he can manage the awkward business of turning and wielding spoon and fork. This is called 'butler service'. With silver service the server serves food to the diners' left. With butler service diners are offered food to their right. Plates are always cleared from the diners' right. But in awkward or crowded corners it is better to forget convention and do whatever is least likely to disturb conversation.

## SERVING WINE

The wine should be served at the same time as the food, or even before, but not too long afterwards – waiting is a strain and drinking is permitted straight away even if eating is not. The host tastes the wine – if he has not already done so – then everyone is served, ladies then men.

Good waiters, or hosts, do not constantly top up glasses, but do so positively when they are down to about a third. Glasses should not be filled more than two thirds full – the idea is to leave room for the drinker to be able to get his nose into the glass to smell it without getting the tip wet! It also means he can swill the wine about, which encourages the release of its bouquet.

## CLEARING THE TABLE

This should happen as unobtrusively as possible. Nothing should be touched until everyone has finished his food and indicated the fact by putting knife and fork firmly together. Then the plates are removed, but not stacked one on top of other or scraped within sight of the diners. Such unattractive operations should be performed out of sight. When the plates are cleared, everything connected with the just-removed course is cleared too – salt and pepper, mustard, sauces, salad dishes and, if the savoury courses are now over, bread plates and bread and butter. Nothing connected with the pudding should go on the table before everything pertaining to the previous course is off it. The same goes for coffee – it should not appear, nor should the bitter mints or petits fours, until the pudding has vanished, with its sauce jugs, cream, etc.

# HEALTHY EATING

## by Caroline Waldegrave

Healthy recipes form an integral part of this book, in that you will find
some that are low in saturated fat, sugar and salt. It is not a health
book as it is designed to cover all aspects of cooking that most of us
need to know about. However, I am very keen on bringing up my
children as healthily as possible and many of our ex-students are asked
to cook carefully for overweight, over-stressed businessmen.

Nutritionists seem to have changed their advice dramatically over the past few years and this can be very confusing. But in fact they are responding to the considerable advance in knowledge made recently as well as to changing social conditioning. Earlier this century, the national diet was high in inexpensive carbohydrate foods like bread and potatoes and often dangerously low in the more costly protein foods like meat. The more affluent post-war years have seen a great change in the way the nation eats, however, and now the danger is seen to be not so much in an excess of protein as in too much saturated fat in the diet. Saturated fat comes from high-protein foods like meat and cheese as well as from more obvious sources like butter and cream. Moreover, we no longer eat enough carbohydrate to provide adequate dietary fibre.

We are told now to reduce our intake of saturated fat, but we are also sometimes told that a small increase in polyunsaturated fat may be a good thing. What is the difference between these two types of fat? It is a matter of the chemical structure of the fatty acids that make them up. Fatty acids are long chains of carbon atoms joined by a chemical bond, which may be either double or single. A fatty acid with no double bonds is called saturated; where there is only one double bond: it is known as monounsaturated, and where there are two or more, polyunsaturated. Most fats are made up of a mixture of many fatty acids. For example, the fat in butter is 63 per cent saturated, 3 per cent polyunsaturated and 34 per cent monounsaturated fatty acids. So when you hear that butter is a saturated fat, this really means that it is higher in saturated fat than in any other kind. Unsaturated bonds can be converted back into single (saturated) bonds by a process called hydrogenation; a food that undergoes this process, therefore, will become higher in saturated fats. Hydrogenation is used in some food-refining processes to make liquid fats solidify.

Why are saturated fats now considered to be bad for us? Medical research suggests that a high level of saturated fat in the blood blocks and damages the arteries and impedes blood circulation. This increases the risk of cardiovascular disease, which is one of the major killers in this country. Polyunsaturated fat makes the blood less 'sticky' and so prevents it from attaching itself to arterial walls and causing blockages. Thus it has a beneficial effect on health, unless you eat so much of it that your weights starts to become a health problem. Monounsaturated fat has no effect on the blood.

Saturated fat is also thought to be a factor in the level of cholesterol in the blood. Cholesterol is a common source of confusion. It is a substance associated with fat and can originate in two ways.

Blood (serum) cholesterol is manufactured by the human liver and is an essential part of all healthy cells. The liver makes enough cholesterol for our needs, and in some people a high level of saturated fat in the diet makes the liver produce more cholesterol than is needed by the body.

Dietary cholesterol is cholesterol found in foods. Animal foods that are high in saturated fat are also high in cholesterol; some low-fat foods contain high levels as well. You should be concerned about eating too much fat overall, but not about eating prawns, brains, liver and kidney which, although high in cholesterol, are low in other fats. The important point is still to reduce the proportion of saturated fats in your diet.

All fat is fattening, that is, high in calories: 1 gram of fat releases about 9 calories, while 1 gram of carbohydrate releases only about 4. Calories are a unit of heat energy, but if the food you eat releases more calories than you need, your body will store the extra energy as body fat. If you are trying to lose weight, cutting fats out of your diet is therefore the best way. You would find it hard, and it would be foolish, to cut them out entirely, however, as some intake of fat is essential to several metabolic processes.

It is now recommended that no more than 30–35 per cent of daily calories should come from fats of any sort, even if you are not trying to lose weight. Fat in the diet comes from many sources, from the obvious fatty foods such as butter, cream and cheese to hidden sources such as many ready-prepared and processed foods. Meat products, such as sausages, pork pies and so on, are generally high in fat, and especially high in saturates. Some cuts of meat are very fatty and, again, the fat is mostly saturated. The leanest meats are chicken – especially when skinned – turkey, rabbit, game, liver and kidney. Many fish, such as tuna, salmon, herrings and mackerel, are oily, but the fat is mainly monounsaturated and polyunsaturated. If you buy fish canned in oil, however, drain away the oil as it may be high in saturated fat unless, for example, soya oil is used. White fish and shellfish are low in fat.

Nutritionists also advise us to reduce the amount of sugar we eat. Too much sugar has no direct link with heart disease, but sugar is quite fattening and obesity is a major cause of heart disease. Sugar is also bad for your teeth. The calories released by sugar are 'empty', that is, they provide no nutritional advantages.

I am always amazed when I go into health food shops. They are often stuffed full of jars of honey (another form of sugar), 'healthy bars' (often full of more sugar) and mueslis (often far

from free of sugar). Also in health food shops you sometimes see cheesy pies (full of saturated fat) and carob cakes (full of another form of sugar). Sometimes they also have spring rolls and samosas (often deep-fried and actually tasting greasy).

The basic message is to cut down on fat – saturated fat in particular – sugar, salt and processed foods. And to increase your intake of fresh fruit, vegetables and cereals. Obviously one must not go 'over the top' by sprinkling bran on everything. Apart from making food fairly unpalatable, this can cause diarrhoea and bowel obstructions. Eating no salt at all would be harmful and everything would taste deadly dull.

At home, I avoid saturated fats in my cooking. This means I do not use butter, lard, cream, dripping, coconut oil, blended cooking fat, mixed blended vegetable oil, solid vegetable fat, or margarines unless they are labelled 'high in polyunsaturated fat'. For general cooking purposes I use sunflower or grapeseed oil as they are both high in polyunsaturated fat. Corn oil is also a good choice but it has a strong flavour, and safflower is high in polyunsaturated fat but very expensive. For special occasions, I buy walnut oil, as it is fairly high in polyunsaturated fat and tastes delicious, as does hazelnut oil, which is high in monounsaturated fatty acids. I also like to use extra virgin olive oil, which is high in monounsaturated fatty acids. Use a polyunsaturated margarine instead of butter, but most low-fat spreads are not suitable for cooking, because they tend to separate on contact with heat.

When cooking conventionally, cream is often an important part of a recipe. Cream is high in saturated fat, so I use low-fat natural yoghurt, buttermilk, low-fat soft cheese (quark), tofu, fromage frais and cottage cheese in place of cream.

Greek yoghurt is higher in fat than ordinary natural yoghurt but makes a very good cream substitute for special occasions when you would normally serve cream as an accompaniment.

Unfortunately none of these substitutes is capable of remaining stable if boiled, so they must be added at the last minute. Cottage cheese must be whizzed or sieved before use and the others should be slaked. Greek yoghurt can be momentarily boiled.

Skimmed or semi-skimmed milk can easily be

substituted for full-fat milk and after a couple of weeks you will not notice the difference. Nuts are a high-fat food although their fat is mainly monounsaturated and polyunsaturated. There are two exceptions: coconut contains saturated fat and chestnuts are very low in fat.

Of all the foods high in saturated fats, cheese is the one I find hardest to give up. On the whole I try to eat low-fat cheese such as quark or cottage cheese, but for a treat I have Brie and, for a real treat, farmhouse Cheddar. Looking at labels on cheese can be confusing, as in other parts of Europe the fat content is measured at a different stage in the manufacturing process. They measure the amount of fat in the 'dry matter', that is, the fat content of the cheese minus water. Many French cheeses, like Brie, have a high water content. Here in Britain the amount of fat given per 100g is the amount of fat you actually eat. When you see a Brie labelled in the French way as containing 45 per cent fat, it is only about 23 per cent fat by British standards: that is, the same as the rather bland Edam that dieters have always been told to eat.

A change to healthy eating can involve imitating conventional recipes in a healthier way, making shepherd's pie with more vegetables and less mince, for example. But there are some dishes that you cannot imitate. What is the point of a yoghurt-based crème brûlée? Or a carob, polyunsaturated oil, wholemeal flour and raw sugar chocolate cake? Either you allow yourself the occasional treat, or you try to find equally sophisticated puddings that are low in fat. You want, after all, to keep to your new way of eating. Although after 10 years of healthy eating my tastebuds have learned to appreciate slightly different tastes, it has taken time and patience: much better to go slowly and stick to it than be too dramatic and too restrictive and then give it up. Begin by allowing yourself occasional treats: after 6 months you will not want them any more! The gentle and almost subversive route to health is a smooth path.

# FAT CONTENTS OF VARIOUS FOODS

| Bacon | Fat (g/100g) |
|---|---|
| Collar joint, boiled, lean and fat | 27.0 |
| Collar joint, boiled, lean only | 9.7 |
| Gammon, boiled or grilled, lean and fat | 18.9 |
| Gammon, boiled or grilled, lean only | 5.5 |
| Rashers, grilled, lean only | 18.9 |
| Rashers, back, lean and fat | 33.8 |
| Rashers, streaky, lean and fat | 36.0 |
| Rashers, middle, lean and fat | 35.1 |

| Beef | |
|---|---|
| Brisket, boiled, lean and fat | 23.9 |
| Forerib, roast, lean and fat | 28.8 |
| Forerib, roast, lean only | 12.6 |
| Rump steak, grilled, lean and fat | 12.1 |
| Rump steak, grilled, lean only | ;6.0 |
| Stewing steak, lean and fat | 11.0 |
| Topside, roast, lean and fat | 12.0 |
| Topside, roast, lean only | 4.4 |

| Lamb | | |
|---|---|---|
| Breast, roast, lean and fat | | 37.1 |
| Breast, roast, lean only | | 16.6 |
| Chops, grilled, lean and fat | without | 29.0 |
| Chops, grilled, lean only | bone | 12.3 |
| Leg, roast, lean and fat | | 17.9 |
| Leg, roast, lean only | | 8.1 |
| Scrag and neck, stewed, lean and fat | | 21.1 |
| Scrag and neck, stewed, lean only | | 15.7 |

| Pork | | |
|---|---|---|
| Chops, grilled, lean and fat | without | 24.2 |
| Chops, grilled, lean only | bone | 10.7 |
| Leg, roast, lean and fat | | 19.8 |
| Leg, roast, lean only | | 6.9 |

## Veal

| | |
|---|---|
| Cutlets, grilled | 5.0 |
| Fillet, roast | 11.5 |

## Chicken

| | |
|---|---|
| Roast, meat and skin | 14.0 |
| Roast, meat only | 5.5 |

## Grouse

| | |
|---|---|
| Roast | 3–5 |

## Partridge

| | |
|---|---|
| Roast | 4–7 |

## Pheasant

| | |
|---|---|
| Roast | 5–10 |

## Pigeon

| | |
|---|---|
| Roast | 5–13 |

## Turkey

| | |
|---|---|
| Roast, meat and skin | 6.5 |
| Roast, meat only | 2.7 |

## Rabbit

| | |
|---|---|
| Stewed | 3–7 |

## Hare

| | |
|---|---|
| Stewed | 3–7 |

## Offal

| | |
|---|---|
| Hearts, stewed | 3–6 |
| Kidneys | 5–7 |
| Liver, grilled, etc. | 5 |

| Cooking Fat | Total fat content (g/100g) |
|---|---|
| Butter | 82.0 |
| Margarine | 82.0 |
| Gold | 40.7 |
| Outline | 40.7 |
| Cream, single | 21.2 |
| Cream, soured | 21.2 |
| Cream, whipping | 35.0 |
| Cream, double | 48.2 |

## Cheese

| | |
|---|---|
| Camembert, Brie, etc. | 23.2 |
| Cheddar, Cheshire, Gruyère, Emmental, etc. | 33.5 |
| Danish Blue, Roquefort, etc. | 29.2 |
| Edam, Gouda, St. Paulin, etc. | 22.9 |
| Parmesan | 29.7 |
| Stilton | 40.0 |
| Cream cheese | 47.4 |
| Low-fat cottage cheese (see carton) | 0–4 |
| Medium-fat curd cheese | 25 |
| Medium-fat Mozzarella, etc. | 25 |

## Fish

| | |
|---|---|
| Eel, stewed | 13.2 |
| Herring, grilled | 13.0 |
| Bloater, grilled | 12.9 |
| Kipper, baked | 6.2 |
| Mackerel, grilled | 6.2 |
| Salmon, steamed | 13.0 |
| Sardines, canned (drained) | 13.0 |
| Sprats, grilled (estimated value) | 13.0 |
| Trout, steamed | 3.0 |
| Tuna, canned (includes oil) | 22.0 |
| Tuna, canned (drained, estimated value) | 13.0 |

# NUTRITION

## by Karen Sorensen
### Director of Nutrition and Dietetics, Guy's and St Thomas' Hospital Trust

Food plays a vital role in all our lives. At its most basic, it provides the nutrients essential to existence and general health. A regular intake of food is required by the body to work, grow and repair itself.

Food also influences physical and mental well-being, and plays an important part in social activities. It is used to celebrate and commiserate, to reward and to give pleasure, and as a sign of affection and caring.

A balanced variety of foods needs to be eaten for the body to function most efficiently, as well as fulfilling these wider functions. All foods are made up of the same main constituents: protein, fat, carbohydrate, vitamins and minerals, in differing amounts. All these elements, known as nutrients, must be included in the diet, although specific requirements for each nutrient vary according to individual needs, circumstances and activity.

## ENERGY REQUIREMENTS
### NORMAL REQUIREMENTS
Energy provides fuel for the body, and is often referred to by one of its measurements – calories.

The energy requirement for each individual is the amount of energy ingested from food that balances the amount of energy used by the body to maintain its normal processes. This amount differs from person to person, and is affected by a variety of factors, such as age, gender and level of physical activity. Almost three-quarters of the energy utilized by the body is used in basic involuntary activities such as breathing, keeping the heart beating and maintaining body temperature. This is often known as the Basal Metabolic rate or BMR. Additional energy is used during processes such as digestion of food and physical activity. It is the latter which can affect weight loss or weight gain.

Periods of intense growth, such as childhood, adolescence and pregnancy, significantly increase energy needs. As an example, a one-year-old child needs about 1200 calories per day, an adolescent boy about 2700 calories per day, and an adult male about 2500 calories per day. Women have slightly lower requirements on average than men.

### FAT AND CARBOHYDRATE AS ENERGY SOURCES
The main energy sources in the diet are fat and carbohydrate. Protein can be used as an energy source, but this is a complex process, and protein is needed first by the body for its growth and repair functions.

Carbohydrate foods such as bread, potatoes, rice, pasta and cereals provide the majority of energy in the British diet, along with spreading fats and fat in food. A healthy diet contains a higher proportion of energy from starchy carbohydrate foods, especially those high in fibre. Weight for weight, fat has more than twice the calories of carbohydrate or protein. This makes it an excellent energy source where requirements are particularly high, but it needs to be taken in moderation in a normal diet.

## PROTEIN
### STRUCTURE AND FUNCTION
Protein foods are made up of amino acids, which are small organic compounds. When food containing protein is digested, it is broken down into its constituent amino acids. Amino acids are usually classified into those which the body can synthesize or make itself and are therefore non essential, and those which have to be obtained from the diet and are known as essential amino acids. There are nine essential amino acids.

The body requires a variety of protein foods to supply its needs. Some of these foods (generally from animal sources) contain all the essential amino acids, and are known as high biological value (HBV) protein. Foods which have small amounts of some essential amino acids are known as low biological value protein (LBV), and these are usually proteins from vegetable sources.

However, a combination of plant protein foods, such as beans and bread, can provide a meal which in total has a high biological value. This principle is essential in planning a well-balanced vegetarian or vegan diet.

Protein is essential to life. The body needs protein to provide for repair and growth of tissues, and to provide vital supplies of nitrogen and other chemicals.

### NORMAL REQUIREMENTS

Individual requirements for protein vary from person to person, although requirements are usually expressed as figures for population groups.[1] Protein in the body is constantly being broken down and resynthesized, especially during periods of growth, such as childhood, adolescence and pregnancy.

Unlike fat and carbohydrate, protein in excess of immediate requirements cannot be stored by the body. Any protein foods not used as a protein source will be converted to provide a further energy source for the body. Protein foods need to be eaten daily to fulfil the body's requirements for protein.

The current Dietary Reference Values for Protein[2] suggest protein intakes of 45g (women) and 55.5g (men) of protein per day for an adult between 19 and 50. Older adults and pregnant and lactating women have slightly higher requirements. There are separate figures for children, who have proportionally higher needs, because of their increased rate of growth.

The average protein intake in the UK is significantly higher than this. A person consuming a modest 570ml/1 pint of milk, 55g/2oz of cheese at lunch, and 110g/4oz (uncooked weight) of meat or fish at dinner is already consuming 56g of protein, before the substantial contribution from bread and cereals is taken into account.

### SOURCES OF PROTEIN IN FOODS

Meat, fish, poultry, offal, eggs, cheese, milk, yoghurt
Beans, peas, lentils, nuts and seeds
Bread, flour, cereals, pasta, rice

## CARBOHYDRATE

### STRUCTURE AND FUNCTION

Dietary carbohydrate is made up of sugars and starches. Carbohydrates contribute to the taste and texture of food, and provide essential supplies of dietary fibre.

Sugars and starches are made up of chemical units called saccharides. Sugars are either made up of one unit (monosaccharides or simple sugars, such as glucose, fructose) or of two units (disaccharides, such as sucrose, lactose). Starches contain many saccharide units (polysaccharides). Some foods contain non-starch polysaccharides which cannot be digested, and it is these which constitute dietary fibre.

The main role of carbohydrate in the diet is as an energy source. Carbohydrates are digested by the body and broken down to form glucose, which is absorbed into the bloodstream. It is this glucose which acts as the fuel for the body, in the same way that petrol is the fuel for a car.

### SUGARS

Sugar in the diet provides an easily and quickly absorbed form of energy. Much has been made of the adverse though well-documented effects of sugar, such as dental caries. It is more useful to look at sugars as part of the overall diet. Sugars can be divided into those which are naturally present in food as part of cells (intrinsic sugars), such as the sugar in fruit, and those which are not (extrinsic sugars). Milk, which contains an extrinsic sugar (lactose), is an exception to this rule. Knowing this allows us to look at the overall quality of a diet. Naturally occurring sugars (intrinsic and milk sugars) should form a higher proportion of the sugar in the diet than non-milk extrinsic sugars, such as sucrose (table sugar). A diet high in added sugar is likely to be poor in other nutrients, and the small volume in which it is consumed and its attractive sweetness make it easy to eat too much sugar, which may lead to obesity.

Sugars have important properties in cooking, keeping gluten soft in cakes, providing a medium for yeast in baking, and strengthening the structure of egg white.

Starch is the main carbohydrate present in all foods, and forms a major part of our diet. In cooking, starch swells, and the starch cells burst and gelatinize, improving digestibility, palatability and texture. Starch is composed of complex links of glucose units, and these are broken down to provide energy.

NON-STARCH POLYSACCHARIDES

Non-starch polysaccharides are more commonly (and less accurately) known as dietary fibre. They are a form of carbohydrate which cannot be digested by the body. From this characteristic comes the beneficial effects of fibre in improving bowel function, reducing constipation and the risk of bowel diseases. Some foods, particularly oats and pulses, contain soluble forms of fibre, such as pectin, and these have been shown to be effective in controlling glucose and cholesterol levels in the blood.

Foods high in fibre are filling and add bulk to the diet, which is particularly helpful for those trying to cut down on fat, or to lose weight.

NORMAL REQUIREMENTS

Starch (complex carbohydrates) should provide the main source of energy in the diet. Individual requirements vary, depending on levels of activity, for example. However, general health recommendations suggest that an overall increase in carbohydrate intake, particularly from cereals, fruit and vegetables, is beneficial. At least half the energy from food should come from starchy foods. Meals should contain plenty of potatoes, rice, pasta, bread or cereals.

To give an example: an average woman who requires 2000 calories per day, obtaining half her energy intake from carbohydrate, would be eating 5 tablespoons breakfast cereal, 4 slices of bread, a large portion of spaghetti, 3 portions of fresh fruit, 2 portions of vegetables (one beans or peas), 290ml/ 1/2 pint semi-skimmed milk, as well as other foods to make up a normal diet.

SOURCES OF CARBOHYDRATE IN FOOD

Bread, breakfast cereals, rice, pasta, potatoes (wholegrain varieties are best sources of fibre)
Fruit, vegetables, milk
Sugar, confectionery, cakes and biscuits, preserves

# FATS

STRUCTURE AND FUNCTION

Fat acts as an energy source, and forms the major part of adipose tissue, the fatty layer beneath the skin which protects body tissue and organs and helps to maintain body temperature. Fat in the diet consists of triglycerides (which are composed of fatty acids), cholesterol and phospholipids.

Some fatty acids are essential to the body, and fat also acts as a carrier for fat-soluble vitamins.

Triglycerides form the largest component of dietary fat, and are made up of three (hence tri-) fatty acids and glycerol. It is the different types of fatty acid, and their chemical make-up, which determine their nutritional properties, as well as whether they are liquid or solid at room temperature. The essential fatty acids (linoleic and linolenic acids) are those which the body cannot make itself. All fatty acids are used in the body for a variety of important processes, such as immune function.

Fatty acids are distinguished chemically into saturated, monounsaturated and polyunsaturated fatty acids.

Fats containing saturated fatty acids are mainly solid at room temperature, and are usually found in foods from animal sources.

Unsaturated fatty acids are generally found in foods of vegetable origin, and are liquid at room temperature.

Monounsaturated fatty acids are found primarily in olive oil.

Cholesterol is a complex steroid compound which is not only essential, but is synthesized by the body itself. Plasma (blood) cholesterol is not affected by cholesterol in the diet, but by the total fat in the diet.

Fat in food provides flavour, smooth texture and fullness.

NORMAL REQUIREMENTS

Some fat is necessary in the diet, to provide the essential fatty acids, but this can easily be obtained from foods which contain fat naturally, such as milk, meat and oily fish. It is not necessary to add fat to foods for spreading and cooking, but fat does make food more palatable, and small amounts of it can be used in a healthy diet. Too much fat in the diet, especially fat with a high proportion of saturated fatty acids, is linked to a high incidence of coronary heart disease.

Choosing more foods from vegetable sources, and replacing some red meat with chicken and fish will reduce the overall fat intake. Further information about changes which can usefully be made in the normal diet is available in the chapter on Healthy Eating.

SOURCES OF FAT IN FOOD
Butter, margarine, oil, lard, fat on meat
Nuts, seeds, milk, cheese, cream, eggs, oily fish
Pastry, cakes, biscuits, crisps, fried foods

## VITAMINS

Vitamins are a group of organic compounds, so called because they are vital to life, essential in the body in small amounts. They perform specific roles in the metabolic process: energy metabolism, blood clotting, absorption of other nutrients.

Vitamins are divided into two groups; those which are fat-soluble, and are found in association with fat, and those which are water-soluble. Special care must be taken in preparation and cooking to preserve the water-soluble vitamins.

Vitamin requirements for groups of the population are defined in tables.[3] Vitamins are found in a wide range of food sources, and a well-balanced diet based on a wide variety of foods includes plenty of fresh fruit and vegetables, should provide adequate vitamin intakes for most people. Supplementary vitamins are only necessary in exceptional cases.

The growing role of antioxidant vitamins, particularly those in fresh fruit and vegetables, has led to the 'Take Five' initiative internationally – encouraging intake of at least 5 portions of fruit and vegetables per day.

A number of vitamins have now been recognized as having strong antioxidant properties. These are Vitamin C, Vitamin E and beta carotene. Antioxidants neutralize the effect in the body of free radicals, substances produced during the body's normal processes, but potentially harmful to the body if not mopped up. Free radicals are believed to play a role in cardiovascular disease, ageing and cancer.

## WATER-SOLUBLE VITAMINS

| Vitamin | Functions | Sources in food |
|---|---|---|
| Vitamin C | Maintains connective tissue, e.g. skin, gums. Important role in wound healing. Antioxidant. | Potatoes, green vegetables, fruits, especially citrus. |
| Vitamin B1 (Thiamine) | Release of energy from carbohydrate. | Milk, wholemeal bread, fortified bread and cereals, meat, especially offal. |
| Vitamin B2 (Riboflavin) | Utilization of energy from food. | Milk, dairy produce, meat, especially liver, yeast extracts. |
| Vitamin B3 (Niacin) | Utilization of energy from food. | Meat, especially liver, fish, wholemeal cereals |
| Vitamin B6 (Pyridoxine) | Metabolism of amino acids and formation of haemoglobin | Occurs widely in foods, especially meats and fish, eggs, wholegrain cereals. |
| Vitamin B12 | Growth and metabolism. Red blood cells. | Occurs only in animal products. Offal, fish, eggs, milk and dairy foods. |
| Folic acid | Many functions in body. Important for reduction of risk of neural | Offal, green leafy vegetables, fortified bread and cereals. |

# FAT-SOLUBLE VITAMINS

| Vitamin | Functions | Sources in food |
|---|---|---|
| Vitamin A (Retinol) Only in animal products, but body can convert beta-carotene in fruit and vegetables into Retinol. | Essential for healthy skin and tissues. Resistance to disease, light perception. | Fish liver oils, offal, eggs, carrots, green and yellow vegetables, margarine (fortified by law). |
| Vitamin D Produced by action of sunlight on skin, in addition to dietary sources. | Controls and maintains absorption of calcium, essential for healthy bones and teeth. | Margarine (fortified by law), fatty fish, eggs, fortified cereals, butter. |
| Vitamin E | Antioxidant, protects cell membranes. | Plant sources, especially wheatgerm and green vegetables. |
| Vitamin K | Blood clotting. | Green vegetables, egg yolk, liver. |

## MINERALS AND TRACE ELEMENTS

Minerals are naturally occurring chemicals essential in small quantities for the body to function normally. Trace elements are needed in even smaller quantities, and usually act in enzyme systems.

Like vitamins, minerals and trace elements occur in a wide variety of foods, and normal requirements should be obtained from a balanced, varied diet which provides adequate energy.

| Mineral | Functions | Sources in food |
|---|---|---|
| Iron | Formation of haemoglobin which transports oxygen around the body. Deficiency can lead to anaemia. | Meat, especially offal. Cereal products, egg yolk and green leafy vegetables. Absorption improved in combination with foods containing Vitamin C. |
| Calcium | Gives strength to teeth and bones, in combination with phosphorus. Required for muscle contraction, nerve activity, normal blood clotting. | Milk and dairy produce, green leafy vegetables, fish with edible bones, flour, bread. |
| Sodium | Essential for muscle and nerve activity. High intakes related to increased blood pressure. | Table salt, bread, cereals, meat products, e.g. bacon, ham. Processed foods. |

| Potassium | Complements sodium in function of cells, and fluid balance. | Fruit, fruit juices, vegetables, meat and milk. |
|---|---|---|
| Magnesium | Enzyme function and energy utilization. | Wide range of foods, especially those of vegetable origin. |
| Zinc | Wound healing. Component of many enzymes. | Meat, dairy produce, eggs and oysters. |

## WATER

Water is an essential component of all the cells and tissues in the body. An adult body consists of about 60 per cent water. Water is the main constituent of body fluids, such as blood and urine, and acts as a solvent for minerals and vitamins. Lack of fluid, especially in the elderly, can be a major cause of constipation. Fluid is therefore an essential part of any diet. Intake can be in the form of plain water, or as drinks, sauces, etc. Normal fluid intake should be not less than 1.5 litres/2½ pints per day, which is about 6–8 cups.

## SPECIAL DIETS

All special diets require modification of one or more components of the diet. It is essential that professional help and advice are sought when preparing special diets for medical conditions. Changes in the diet need expert supervision to ensure that all nutrients continue to be provided.

A few of the most common diets are outlined below. Local hospital Dietetic Departments can give further advice on the cooking modifications needed for these and other therapeutic diets.

### WEIGHT-REDUCING, DIABETIC AND LIPID-LOWERING DIETS

All medical conditions which need these diets require a change to a healthy lifestyle, which includes a diet based on fresh foods and high in fibre and low in fat. The emphasis should be on wholegrain bread and cereals, fresh fruit and vegetables, with moderate portions of lean meat and fish. These dietary modifications are all based on healthy eating principles, and as such can easily be followed by partners and the rest of the family. Drastic changes should be avoided, as this generally means the diet is difficult to keep to. The appropriate changes made to diet and lifestyle can be incorporated into the normal diet permanently.

### GLUTEN-FREE DIET

This diet is specifically for the treatment of coeliac disease. It requires complete avoidance of gluten, a protein found in wheat, rye, barley and oats. All foods containing these, even in small amounts, must be avoided. Gluten-free flour, bread, pasta and biscuits are available on prescription and from chemists: the flour can be used to make gluten-free versions of many foods. Rice, soya, corn and potato flour are naturally gluten-free, and can also be used. Gluten is the component of flour which gives it stretchiness and air-holding qualities, and it takes time to adapt to gluten-free flours.

Many manufactured products contain gluten, and labels must be carefully checked. If in doubt, omit it.

## DIETARY CHANGE ON RELIGIOUS AND MORAL GROUNDS

Many people choose to follow a specific set of dietary rules for ethnic, cultural, moral and religious reasons. These may be dictated by religious texts, such as the Koran for Muslims. They may also involve special methods of preparation and/or slaughter of animals, or the avoidance of certain foods together at the same meal. It is very important when cooking for other people to find out if they have any such dietary restrictions, and to adhere strictly to them.

The information given below outlines the generally accepted guidelines for the most widely used of these diets. There are also a number of religious festivals, which may provide the opportunity for special foods, or fasting for periods of time.

### HINDU

Orthodox or strict Hindus are vegetarian. Many, particularly women, do not eat eggs, and will only eat vegetarian cheese, which does not contain animal rennet. Hindus never eat beef, as the cow is considered a sacred animal. Some non-Orthodox

Hindus may eat chicken, mutton and occasionally fish. Milk, yoghurt and butter are permitted.

## MUSLIM

Muslims can only eat meat which is halal and has been killed according to Islamic law. This can be obtained from a halal butcher. Pork is strictly forbidden, as are all of its products. Care must be taken with cooking fats, which must be of vegetable origin, or from halal sources.

Fish, eggs, milk and dairy products are allowed. Alcohol is strictly avoided by most Muslims, and should not be used in cooking.

At certain times of the Islamic calendar, such as Ramadan, Muslims will fast during the hours of daylight, and eat late at night and early in the morning. There are a number of important festivals, which are celebrated by special food customs.

## JEWISH

Jews can only eat meat from animals which have been ritually slaughtered and prepared to render them kosher. Pork is forbidden, but kosher lamb, beef and goat are acceptable.

Fish which have fins and scales are allowed, but shellfish are not. Chicken, turkey, duck, goose, partridge and pheasant are allowed, but other game birds are not.

The other important aspect of the Jewish diet is that meat and dairy foods must be kept apart in cooking, and must not be eaten at the same meal.

## VEGETARIAN

Some people choose not to eat meat, poultry or fish in their diet. Within this group, there are a number of variations. Protein foods need to be combined in vegetarian meals, to provide all the essential amino acids.

**Demi-vegetarians**, while not strictly vegetarian, will eat fish, but not meat.

**Lacto-vegetarians** will eat milk, cheese and dairy products. Cheese should not be made with animal rennet. Seemingly vegetarian foods, such as vegetable soups made with meat stock, are not acceptable.

**Lacto-ovo-vegetarians** eat eggs in addition to the above foods.

## VEGAN

A vegan diet avoids animal foods of any sort, including dairy foods, and relies entirely on plant foods. Protein is obtained from foods such as soya beans and nuts. A vegan diet is deficient in Vitamin B12, which is only present in animal products, or in synthetic form. A number of yeast extracts fortified with Vitamin B12 are available, which can be used in a variety of ways to fortify the diet.

## FOOD ADDITIVES

Many people express concern about additives in food. Certainly, a diet based mainly on a variety of fresh ingredients, well prepared and freshly cooked, is ideal. However, many food products rely on some form of additives, such as preservatives, to ensure that they are safe to eat. The range of foods available would be severely restricted if these were not used in moderation. Similarly, many foods would look unpalatable after processing if some colouring were not added to them.

The legislation governing additives in the UK is extensive, and all foods containing additives are labelled as such. 'E' numbers show that an additive is accepted as safe throughout the European Community. Many of these are derivatives of natural products, like red colouring derived from beetroot (E162).

The key is to base the diet on fresh foods, using processed foods in moderation.

Excellent information on additives and food labelling is available from The Ministry of Agriculture, Fisheries and Food.[4]

## CONCLUSION

For all its life-giving and therapeutic properties, food is to be enjoyed. If a variety of food is eaten, chosen from a range of food groups, in appropriate portions, anyone's diet can provide for both the body's fundamental physical requirements and the important psychological aspects of the enjoyment of food. The recipes in this book are designed to provide a happy balance of these two interlinked roles of food in our lives.

REFERENCES
**1.** Dietary Reference Values for Food Energy and Nutrients for the United Kingdom; Department of Health. 1991.
**2.** Ibid.
**3.** Ibid.
**4.** Ministry of Agriculture, Fisheries and Food: information on food matters available from Food Sense, London SE99 7TT.

# FOOD SAFETY

Food safety and hygiene are essential in the kitchen as many foods may contain harmful organisms. The cook must be aware of these bacteria and of how to prevent them multiplying to dangerous levels in food which would cause food poisoning.

Salmonella is one of the commonest causes of food poisoning and is most often brought into the kitchen on poultry and meat. Campylobacter (the symptoms of which may not appear for 10 days) usually enters on raw poultry. Clostridium perfringens is often present on raw meats, or unwashed vegetables. The origin of Staphylococcus aureus is usually a food handler with an inadequately covered skin infection. The latter two organisms can produce illness within a few hours of eating. Listeria is commonly found in many foods but listeriosis is very rare as most people's immune system copes well. Special dietary advice regarding listeriosis applies only to vulnerable groups who are particularly at risk. These are pregnant women and those with underlying illness which results in impaired resistance to infection. These special groups are advised to avoid pâtés and soft ripened cheeses of the Brie, Camembert and blue vein types, and to reheat cooked chilled meals and ready-to-eat poultry until piping hot rather than eat them cold.

## PREVENTING THE GROWTH OF BACTERIA

Bacteria will grow to toxic levels if given the chance. What they need to do their evil work is warmth, time and moisture – ideal conditions, from the bugs' point of view, would be lukewarm food left out in a hot kitchen for several hours. A tiny (and therefore harmless) colony of bacteria could multiply rapidly to such an extent that anyone eating that food could become very ill and require hospitalization. If the victim was a baby (with an immune system not fully developed) or an elderly person or invalid (whose immunity might be impaired), death could result.

Fortunately, some simple precautions can be taken to prevent food poisoning. You can wash off bacteria (such as listeria from salad vegetables, etc.); you can kill the organisms with heat; you can arrest their growth by refrigeration; and you can prevent cross-contamination by practising good hygiene in the kitchen.

## THE GOLDEN RULES ARE:

BUYING Buy only very fresh food from suppliers you can trust.

WASHING Wash all food if it is to be eaten raw. It is good practice to wash all fruits and vegetables, even if they are to be peeled, as they could contaminate other foods. Wash free-range eggs just before cooking – salmonella is more likely to be present on the egg shell than in the egg.

REFRIGERATION Refrigerate all meat, fish and chicken, all dairy products and eggs. Until the discovery of salmonella in eggs, refrigeration of eggs was not thought to be necessary. The danger is still small, but why take any unnecessary risks? Besides, eggs lose their freshness and become stale much more quickly when they are not stored in a refrigerator.

Keep food refrigerated as much as you can. Never leave it on the side in the kitchen waiting to be used, and never leave cold, cooked food at room temperature for more than an hour or so.

Although the original cooking will have destroyed any bacteria, food can be re-infected and, if left in a warm atmosphere, can become harmful.

Do not put hot food in the refrigerator. It will warm up the atmosphere inside and encourage the growth of any bacteria present in other foods in the cabinet.

As far as possible, always keep raw and cooked food separated until serving. Bacteria can enter the kitchen on raw food, and can then be transferred to cooked food where they might easily be left to multiply in peace if the food is not to be re-cooked.

COOKING Cook food sufficiently to kill any bacteria that may be present. In particular chicken, chopped meats, rolled joints, burgers and re-formed steaks must be cooked thoroughly as food-poisoning bacteria may be present in the centres of these. If cooking for the very young, the very old or the infirm, egg yolks should be cooked hard. (Soft-cooked eggs may not have reached a sufficiently high temperature to kill salmonella.)

RAW MEAT AND FISH Consumption of raw meat and fish carries a risk of food poisoning. Meat and fish that are traditionally served raw, such as sushi and steak tartare, must be of the freshest, best quality, and should be prepared and eaten on the day they are purchased. Some traditional dishes, such as gravad lax, smoked salmon, or Parma ham, although they are raw, can be kept safely under refrigeration because they have been cured either with salt or smoke, or both.

REHEATING If reheating food, make sure that you serve it really hot, i.e. near boiling point, even right in the middle.

Do not pour hot sauces on to cold food unless you are going to reheat it right through at once. Don't add warm food to cold food. Don't mix yesterday's soup with today's without reboiling. Always reheat any mixture immediately if adding two things of different temperatures together. Remember that the cool one might contain a few bacteria, and the hot one will provide enough heat to start them multiplying, but not enough to kill them.

Reboil stocks, soups and sauces frequently in hot weather. Even in winter, reboil them every three days. In theory, you can keep the same stockpot on the go for ever if you reboil it every time you add anything to it. And remember that the stronger the stock, the firmer the jelly it will set to, and the better it will keep in the refrigerator. If reheating aspic, bring to the boil, then let it cool enough to use.

KEEPING FOOD WARM If food must be kept warm, first make sure that it is heated through

sufficiently to kill all bacteria; then keep it really hot, not lukewarm. Do not pour a warm sauce over, say, cold poached eggs and keep them warm in a hot cupboard or warming drawer.

FREEZING Do not refreeze completely thawed food without cooking it first. Although the freezing and thawing do not harm, it is easy to forget just how many periods at room temperature the food has had, and it is therefore impossible to guess how large the concentration of bacteria may be. Never refreeze chicken that has been frozen and thawed.

COOKING FROM FROZEN Do not cook large items (such as whole chickens) when frozen. When the bird looks cooked, the inside (where salmonella is most likely to be present on the surface of the cavity) may still be lukewarm and raw. For the same reason, it is unwise to stuff large birds. The stuffing may prevent the heat from penetrating the cavity and killing any bacteria present.

THAWING Thaw food slowly in the refrigerator or in a leakproof plastic bag under cold water. Do not try to thaw things fast by putting them in a warming drawer or under hot water. The outer layer will stay at incubating temperature too long. However, microwaving to thaw is safe because it is so fast that the bacteria do not have time to breed. But cook the food as soon as it is thawed, just in case your microwave has warmed it up too much.

COOLING Cool large quantities of food fast. If a stew is left to cool in a heavy pan, the centre of it will provide perfect bacteria breeding conditions: warmth, moisture and time. And a stir with a non-sterile wooden spoon could easily provide the parent bacteria to start the colony. Commercial caterers cool food in a blast chiller, but small kitchens do not have this luxury. So either tip the stew into shallow flat containers to cool, or cool the pot fast by standing it in a bowl in the sink, and continuously running the cold tap into the bowl, to keep the waterjacket round the pan cool. Give it an occasional stir to speed things up.

Nor should you leave hot food covered with a heavy lid. Open food cools quicker. If you want to avoid the food drying out or forming a skin, place some wet greaseproof paper (which is thin enough not to hinder cooling) flat on the surface of the food.

WRAPPING Take care when wrapping hot food in clingfilm – if there are any air spaces between the food and the film, greenhouse-like incubating conditions will be produced. Instead, wrap the food loosely in kitchen foil, and refrigerate as soon as it is cold.

UTENSILS Don't use the same knife or board for raw and cooked food without washing it between jobs. If you have just jointed a raw chicken and then slice cooked beef with the same knife, you could transfer bacteria from the chicken to the beef. The micro-organisms in the chicken will get cooked to death, but they could grow with impunity in the beef. Caterers have separate refrigerators and boards for storing and preparing hot and cold food, and large-production kitchens very often have separate kitchen areas and separate cooks. The home cook, however, who is dealing with small quantities of food that are cooked, eaten or refrigerated fast, need not go to such lengths but should practise good food hygiene and take sensible precautions, always washing utensils thoroughly after use.

Keep the kitchen area clean. This means frequently washing tools in near-boiling water, scrubbing boards and surfaces with detergent, washing out the refrigerator weekly with weak bleach, and making sure that tea-towels and cloths are changed as soon as they are dirty or damp. A damp cloth left over a warm cooker, or a crack in the wooden handle of a much-used knife, provides the perfect incubating conditions for germs.

'OFF' FOODS Don't ever serve food that smells or looks at all peculiar. Although salmonella is completely tasteless and has no discernible odour, unpleasant odours or appearance are an indication of age and poor condition, and food-poisoning organisms are likely to be present along with the ones causing the obvious deterioration. Always err

on the safe side and throw out any food that looks or smells dubious – don't take risks.

SALMONELLA IN EGGS Consumption of raw eggs or uncooked dishes made from them, such as home-made mayonnaise, mousse and ice cream, carries the risk of food poisoning. However, if you do use raw eggs to make these dishes, make sure you use only the freshest, that the dishes are eaten as soon as possible after making and that they are never left for more than 1 hour at room temperature.

For healthy people there is little risk from eating cooked eggs, however they have been prepared – boiled, fried, scrambled or poached. Vulnerable people such as the elderly, the sick, babies, toddlers and pregnant women should only eat eggs that have been thoroughly cooked until the white and yolk are solid. These vulnerable people should avoid egg recipes which require light cooking, such as meringues and hollandaise sauce.

Lightly cooked egg dishes should be eaten as soon as possible after cooking and if the dishes are not for immediate use they should be stored in the refrigerator after cooling. Pasteurized egg, which is free from harmful bacteria, is often used by caterers in these dishes and is available as a useful alternative in the home.

POISONOUS FOODS Some foods are naturally poisonous and must be treated with care. For example, red kidney beans must be boiled for 10 minutes to destroy an enzyme which is potentially fatal. Cooking the beans until soft at a very low temperature is not sufficient to do this, so, if using a 'slow cooker', give the beans a good boil before putting them into the pot.

Green potato skins, rhubarb leaves and many wild mushrooms are mildly poisonous and can cause gastric upsets in some people. Indeed, a few wild mushrooms are lethal. Do not cook mushrooms unless purchased from a reputable supplier and you are certain they are safe. Do not gather and cook wild mushrooms unless you have the knowledge to distinguish between the safe and poisonous varieties.

# CHOOSING AND STORING PRODUCE

This chapter has been written to offer a few guidelines on how to recognize good-quality food and how best to store it. For freezability please see the chapter on freezing (see page 64). When shopping we would always suggest buying organic ingredients as their taste is naturally better. Organic foods are more highly priced than non-organic ingredients so the purse inevitably dictates your final decision.

## MEAT

When choosing meat, the general principle is to look for signs that it has come from a young animal. It should not be too fatty, the joints should be reasonably small, it should be of a firm texture and not have too much gristle, although obviously there are different expectations about the quantity of acceptable fat and gristle depending on the particular cut of meat. Meat should never be slimy; it should be moist but not gelatinous and it should not smell. Any exposed bones should be pinkish-blue in colour and the paler the fat the better.

### STORAGE

Always allow meat to breathe, so if it comes tightly wrapped up, pierce the clingfilm and refrigerate for not more than 2 – 3 days. Raw meat should always be stored at the bottom of the refrigerator so that no raw blood can drop on to cooked food – this can be a cause of food poisoning.

### BEEF

Generally you should look for a deep, dull red piece of meat rather than a bright, orange-red joint. This is difficult in a supermarket because managers assume that their customers want 'bright' meat so there is much use of clever lighting as well as the widespread use of adding anti-oxidants. The fat on beef should be a pale creamy yellow colour. When choosing beef, ask for meat from a traditional beef herd.

### VEAL

The flesh should be pale pink, soft but not flabby, and finely grained. There should be a very little creamy white fat. Do not worry if there is a lot of gelatinous tissue around the meat as this is a natural characteristic of a very immature animal.

### LAMB

The colour of the meat varies with the breed of lamb. The fat should be creamy white (if it is yellow it indicates old age) and it should not be oily. All joints should be plump and compact rather than long and thin. The skin should be pliable; not hard and wrinkled. Welsh or English lamb is considered to be superior to New Zealand lamb.

### PORK

The meat should be pale pink, close-grained and firm to the touch. It should not have enlarged glands or abscesses (pigs kept too close together, reasonably enough, bite each other). The fat should be firm and white, not oily, and without a greyish tinge. There should be an even covering of fat. Try to find free-range pork; it has an excellent flavour.

### OFFAL

Offal has often been called 'awful offal' in the past, but at last it is gaining the recognition it deserves as a delicacy. It tends to be low in fat and high in iron and is very healthy. All offal must be eaten very fresh.

LIVER

It should not have a strong smell; it should be shiny and a little bloody.

CALVES' LIVER It should be a pale milky brown colour with a fine even texture. Dutch liver is considered better than English.

LAMBS' LIVER This is darker in colour than calves'.

PIGS' LIVER This is dark and close-textured. It is used in pâtés and terrines.

OX LIVER This is dark bluish-brown with a very strong flavour. Used occasionally in stews and pies but it is very inferior to other sorts of liver and is best avoided.

KIDNEY

Kidneys are sold loose or still in their suet. To store kidneys, remove them from the suet and refrigerate for a maximum of 24 hours. Make sure that they are not tightly wrapped in clingfilm – they must be allowed to breathe.

VEAL KIDNEYS These are delicious. They should be a pale milky brown with a creamy white suet. They look rather like a bunch of grapes.

LAMBS' KIDNEYS These are medium brown, faintly bluish, firm-textured and egg-shaped.

PIGS' KIDNEYS These are pale brown with a rather strong flavour, similar in shape to lambs' kidneys.

OX KIDNEYS These look like huge veal kidneys but are much darker in colour. They are only suitable for pies and puddings.

SWEETBREADS As with all offal, the calves' sweetbreads are the best, then the lambs' and then the ox breads. Pigs' sweetbreads are not sold.

HEADS AND BRAINS

CALVES' HEADS These are sometimes available if ordered specially. They are used mainly for boiling and serving hot. Salted, they are used for brawn.

CALVES' BRAINS The most delicate and expensive they are soaked and blanched to remove all traces of blood before cooking, and skinned of membrane and sinew after blanching. They are excellent fried plain or in a crumb coating and have an almost creamy texture when cooked.

PIGS' HEADS These are made into brawn, fresh or salted, and can be used for sausages. The cheeks of certain long-faced breeds of pig are lightly salted and sold as Bath Chaps. They are rather fatty, but have a good flavour, and are usually eaten crumbed and fried, or cold like ham. A pig's head is sometimes used on banqueting tables as a stand-in for the now unavailable boar's head. Pigs' brains are sold in the heads.

SHEEP'S HEADS These can be boiled or stewed for use in broths and pie fillings, but are seldom available, and involve a lot of labour for very little meat.

SHEEP'S BRAINS These are less fine and delicate than calves', but more readily available. They are treated in exactly the same way.

OX CHEEK This is sold for brawns and stews.

HEART

Heart is highly nutritious, but needs slow cooking to tenderize it. It is also very lean, and requires a sauce or plenty of basting to keep it moist. Hearts must be cleaned of all sinew and the tubes removed before cooking.

OX HEART This is large, very tough, strongly flavoured, coarse and muscular and bluish-red. It is generally used chopped or minced with other ingredients – perhaps for a pie.

LAMBS' HEARTS The smallest and most tender of the hearts, but stuffing to add flavour, slow cooking and careful basting are still necessary to moisten and tenderize the naturally lean and tough flesh.

PLUCK

The pluck is the name given to the lights (lungs), liver, pancreas and spleen. Today, lights are sold generally for pet food. The liver is sold separately. Sheep's pluck is sometimes minced for haggis.

FEET AND TROTTERS

CALVES' FEET These are seldom sold to the public. They are good for stock and calf's foot jelly due to the high concentration of gelatine present in the feet. Pigs' trotters are high in gelatine, and good for setting stocks, and for brawn. They can be boned, stuffed, braised, served hot with mustard sauce, or hot or cold with vinaigrette. Sheep's trotters and ox feet are not sold. Cow heel is treated before sale, and looks and tastes similar to tripe. It consists of the whole foot and heel of the animal.

### TRIPE

Tripe can come from all cud-chewing animals, being the first and second stomachs, but in practice only ox tripe is sold. The first stomach (blanket tripe) is smooth, the second honeycombed.

Tripe is sold parboiled, but needs further long boiling to tenderize it. It is wise to ask the butcher how much more boiling it will need. Grey, slimy, flabby, strong-smelling tripe should be avoided. It should be thick, firm and very white. Tripe can be stewed, boiled or deep-fried. A specialist taste, it's either loved or loathed!

### OXTAIL

Oxtail is sold skinned and usually jointed. Choose large fat tails, with plenty of meat on them. Cow tails, which are skinny and rather tasteless, are sometimes passed off as oxtail. The meat should be dark and lean, and the fat creamy white and firm. Oxtail is high in gelatine content, so it cooks to a tender, almost sticky, stew. It is good for soups and very rich in flavour.

### MARROW BONES

Marrow bones are from the thigh and shoulder bones of beef. They are sawn across in short cylinders by the butcher. They are boiled whole and served in a napkin, the diner extracting the soft rich marrow and eating it on toast. Marrow is also used as a flavouring in other dishes, such as entrecôte à la Bordelaise, where it moistens and flavours the steak.

## TONGUE

To get a pig's tongue you must buy the whole head, while calves' tongues are very rarely available. Ox and lambs' tongues can be bought, however.
OX TONGUE It should feel soft to the touch, though it may have a rough, pigmented skin.

LAMBS' TONGUES They are very small and are generally sold by the kilo. They should be pale pink: the roughish skin may be light or dark grey.

### BLOOD

Pigs' blood is used in the making of black pudding. It is mixed with fat, and stuffed into intestines like a sausage.

NOTE: Brains, oxtail and marrow-bones are currently not eaten because of the BSE controversy. Doubtless they will come back into fashion: we have included recipes for them.

## GAME

If you want to roast your game, try to buy young tender birds or animals. You can recognize a young bird by its smooth legs and pliable feet and beaks. If it has already been plucked, feel it for pliability in the backbone. See the end of this section (page 55) for a seasonal table of game.

### STORAGE

If it has not been hung already, you should hang game, undrawn (except for rabbits, which are paunched, or gutted, as soon as they are killed), in a cool, dry place. Birds are hung by the neck and animals by the feet. The hanging time varies according to the animal and the weather, but a rough guide is given below with a brief description of each bird or animal. The less well hung it is, the easier it is to pluck and draw. If the game is already prepared, store it loosely wrapped in the bottom of the refrigerator.

### GROUSE

Hanging time: anything from 2–10 days.
After 2 days it does not have a strong flavour but after 10 it will be very gamey. Red or Scottish grouse is best. Allow one grouse per head.

### PARTRIDGE

**Hanging time: 3 – 4 days.**
We think that a partridge, particularly the grey British as opposed to the French red leg, is the nicest of all game birds. Plucked birds should have a pale skin and plump breast. Allow one partridge per head (some people can eat 2).

PHEASANT

**Hanging time: 3 – 8 days.**

As with most game birds the hen pheasant is juicier than the cock. Pheasant is fairly mild in terms of 'gameyness'. Allow one pheasant to 2–3 people.

PIGEON AND SQUAB

These are in season all the year round. Squab are fledgling pigeons. The pigeon breast should be moist, glistening dark red meat. It is difficult to judge the age of a pigeon by its appearance so you have to trust the game dealer. Allow one pigeon per head or 3 breasts each.

QUAIL

Eat quail fresh – preferably 24 hours after being killed. Most of today's quails are farmed and should look plump for their size. They have a slightly gamey flavour. Allow 2 quails per person.

SNIPE

**Hanging time: 4 days.**

This is a small bird with a long bill which is sometimes served pushed into the body of the bird, like a skewer, drawing the head through the legs before roasting. It is traditionally roasted ungutted and served on a croûte. Snipe are very hard to find unless you shoot them yourself.

WILD DUCK, TEAL AND WIDGEON

Wild duck varies in size from the large mallard to the tiny teal. All wild ducks should be eaten fresh. It tends to be rather dry and can have a fishy flavour. This can be overcome by stuffing the cavity with an orange, by marinating or by parboiling the plucked bird.

WOODCOCK

Like the snipe, it is also roasted undrawn. It is very rarely available to buy: you have to be given woodcock as a present by a rather good shot.

VENISON

**Hanging time: 3 – 10 days.**

Venison should be a good deep red colour with a firm texture and should not be slimy. It should be moist but not gelatinous with very little fat, and it therefore needs to be cooked carefully. Venison that has been hung for 3 days tastes like rather delicious beef. However, once it has been hung for 10 days it has a very gamey flavour.

# SEASONAL TABLE FOR GAME

| Grouse | 12 August – 10 December |
|---|---|
| Partridge | 1 September – 1 February |
| Pheasant | 1 October – 1 February |
| Pigeon and squab | In season all year round |
| Quail | Available all year round |
| Snipe | August – January |
| Wild duck, teal and widgeon | Various, starting in August and finishing in March |
| Woodcock | October – January |
| Venison | Seasons are complicated; however, frozen venison is often available all year round |
| Rabbit | Wild or farmed available all year |
| Hare | September – March |

# STATUTORY CLOSE SEASONS FOR DEER

| Species | Sex | England and Wales | Scotland |
|---|---|---|---|
| Red | Stags | 1 May – 31 July | 21 October – 30 June |
| | Hinds | 1 March – 31 October | 16 February – 20 October |
| Fallow | Bucks | 1 May – 31 July | 1 May – 31 July |
| | Does | 1 March – 31 October | 16 February – 20 October |
| Roe | Bucks | 1 November – 31 March | 21 October – 31 March |
| | Does | 1 March – 31 October | 1 April – 20 October |
| Sika | Stags | 1 May – 31 July | 21 October – 30 June |
| | Hinds | 1 March – 31 October | 16 February – 20 October |
| Red/Sika | Stags | | 21 October – 30 June |
| Hybrids | Hinds | | 16 February – 20 October |

In addition The British Deer Society recommends the following close seasons for which there is no statutory provision at present

| | | | |
|---|---|---|---|
| Muntjac | Bucks | 1 March – 31 October | |
| | Does | 1 March – 31 October | |
| Chinese Water | Bucks | 1 March – 31 October | |
| Deer | Does | 1 March – 31 October | |

RABBIT

**Hanging time: 24 hours.**

Wild or farmed rabbit is available all the year round. Rabbits are paunched (gutted) as soon as they are killed. Wild rabbit is gamier and less tender than farmed, whose pale flesh is rather like chicken. If the rabbit has not been skinned, look for smooth, sharp claws and delicate soft ears.

HARE

**Hanging time: 5 – 6 days, unpaunched.**

If the hare has not been skinned, look for smooth sharp claws and delicate soft ears. A leveret (young hare) has a hardly noticeable hare lip – this becomes deeper and more pronounced in an older animal. If the hare has been skinned, look for deep claret flesh. Only young tender joints of hare are suitable for roasting, and even they need much basting. Older hares and the tougher joints are traditionally jugged.

## POULTRY

STORAGE OF ALL POULTRY

If the bird has been sold with giblets remove them as soon as you get home, and unwrap the bird so that it can breathe. Store at the bottom of the refrigerator for not more than 2–3 days.

CHICKENS

The more you spend on a chicken, the better it will probably taste. A frozen supermarket bird, battery-raised and fed on fishmeal until the moment of slaughter, has little chance of tasting good, however well cooked. Try to buy free-range birds. They may look scrawnier than the plump-breasted oven-ready bird but the flavour is far superior.

POUSSINS These are 4–6 weeks old. They serve one person and look appetizing but have very little flavour.

DOUBLE POUSSINS These are 6–10 weeks old. They serve 2 people and have quite a good flavour.

SPRING CHICKENS These are 10–12 weeks old. They serve 3 people and have a similar flavour to that of double poussins.

ROASTERS These are usually over 3 months old and can have an excellent flavour as long as they have been reasonably raised. They normally serve 4 people.

CORN-FED CHICKENS These are normally free-range chickens fed on corn. They are yellow in colour and have a very good flavour. The French corn-fed chickens generally seem to have a better flavour than the English ones.

POULET NOIR This is a French black-legged chicken. It is more like a guinea fowl than a chicken in both shape and texture. The poulet noir is more expensive than a conventional chicken but is really worth the occasional burst of extravagance.

CAPONS These were castrated cockerels who, having lost their interest in sex, ate voraciously and became very plump and tender. They have been banned by the EC.

BOILING FOWLS These are very rare today. They require long, slow cooking and have an excellent flavour.

DUCK
Most ducks sold today are ducklings of 7–9 weeks. A 1.8kg/4lb duck feeds only 2–3 people. Young duck is delicious, but do not buy frozen duck as you will not be able to judge the pliability of the backbone, which is the tell-tale sign of age. The skin of a fresh duck should be dry, soft and smooth. It should not be slimy and should not smell strongly. The Aylesbury duck is a very superior bird.

GOOSE
This is at its best when it weighs 4.6kg/10lb, i.e. when it is 6–9 months old. A goose can be utterly delicious but make sure that you choose a young bird as old geese can be very tough. Fresh goose

has a clean white skin, which is soft and dry to the touch.

TURKEY
Try to buy fresh rather than frozen turkeys as they tend to have a better flavour. The flesh should be snow-white and firm, and the skin dry and soft. A turkey can often smell a little high. Remove all the giblets as soon as possible because they deteriorate quickly, and wipe the bird inside and out before storing.

GUINEA FOWL
This is normally a little smaller than the average-sized chicken and looks rather scrawny. The taste is that of a very delicious, slightly gamey chicken. Be warned: it needs careful cooking as it should have very little fat.

## DAIRY PRODUCTS
EGGS
CHICKEN EGGS There is no nutritional difference between a battery and a free-range egg, but somehow the idea of a battery egg is depressing. If the box says 'farm eggs' it simply means battery-farmed eggs. You cannot judge the freshness of an egg from its outward appearance so buy eggs from somewhere with a rapid turnover. You can test for freshness by breaking an egg into a saucer: the yolk should be well domed and there should be 2 distinct layers of egg white, the inner circle being rather gelatinous and the outer circle a little thinner. When an egg is stale, the yolk is flatter and the 2 layers of white intermingle. Store eggs pointed end downwards so that the air pocket in the rounded end is uppermost. They should keep for a minimum of 2 weeks in the refrigerator. If the eggs have been separated, the whites can be frozen and the yolks kept refrigerated for 2–3 days. Cover them with a little cold water to prevent a hard crust from forming, then cover with clingfilm.

Eggs can be tainted easily so keep them well separated from other foods. The easiest thing is to keep them in the egg box in which they have been bought.

GOOSE, DUCK, PLOVER, GULLS, TURKEY AND QUAIL EGGS All eggs should be stored in the same way as chicken eggs. The following eggs are now available fresh from farms, from specialist shops and from the occasional supermarket.

TURKEY, GOOSE AND DUCK EGGS These have too strong a flavour to be eaten in the normal way as eggs but are useful for cooking. Goose eggs make particularly good sponge cakes.

QUAIL, GUINEA FOWL AND GULLS EGGS These make very good first courses served with celery salt, paprika, brown bread and butter. Quail eggs take 3 minutes to boil, guinea fowl eggs take 5, and gull eggs are always sold ready cooked and are only in season in May and June.

MILK, CREAM AND YOGHURT
Always refrigerate milk as quickly as possible and keep it covered as it can easily be tainted by other foods in the refrigerator. An open bottle or carton of milk will go off more quickly than an unopened one. Milk keeps for about 3 days. Milk is standardized by its fat content. Most milk has been pasteurized to kill off harmful bacteria.

SKIMMED MILK A thin, slightly grey-coloured milk from which virtually all the fat has been removed. It goes off a little more quickly than 'fattier' milks.

SEMI-SKIMMED MILK As skimmed milk but with a little more fat.

'REGULAR' MILK This is the standard milk with about 3.8 per cent fat.

'RAW' MILK This unpasteurized milk is very rarely available.

HOMOGENIZED MILK This has been pasteurized and then homogenized to distribute the cream evenly throughout the milk. It has a particularly unpleasant flavour.

LONG-LIFE MILK This is milk that has been sterilized or heat-treated to give it a long shelf life unrefrigerated. It is a useful emergency stopgap but has a rather nasty flavour. Once opened, treat as fresh.

BUTTER
This is either salted or unsalted, and either pasteurized or ripened. Most English and New Zealand butter is pasteurized. Whether you buy salted or unsalted depends on your personal taste, but unsalted butter is better (although more expensive) for cooking as it contains less sediment and is consequently less likely to burn. It should be used for all butter sauces.

Unsalted butter will keep for only 2 weeks whereas salted butter can be kept for up to 4 weeks. It must always be refrigerated and should be kept tightly wrapped to prevent it drying out or becoming tainted by other foods in the refrigerator.

CHEESE
CHOOSING CHEESE Many shops proudly sell unpasteurized cheese. However, I have married into a farmhouse cheesemaking family where this foodie fad is met with scorn and derision. If the milk is not pasteurized it is probably not filtered either as the filter is an integral part of the pasteurizing machine. It might have been filtered into the milk lorry but there will be lots of twigs, hairs and worse still left in the milk. Pasteurization does not change the consistency or the taste of the milk; it only heats it up to 74°C/160°F (boiling is 100°C/212°F) and it simply kills any bugs. No responsible parent would give their children unpasteurized milk, nor should they give them unpasteurized cheese. A certain cynicism exists in my in-laws' minds – they suggest that not all cheese labelled 'unpasteurized' is in fact so. There is a logical problem in keeping the milk fresh long enough to make the cheese.

It is difficult to choose cheese in a supermarket if it has been tightly wrapped in clingfilm and is deceptively coloured by supermarket lighting.

HARD CHEESE (E.G. CHEDDAR, DOUBLE GLOUCESTER) Try to find a mature cheese that has a rind. It should have a good strong smell but should not smell of whey (i.e. sour milk) and nor should it smell of ammonia. If there is no odour at all, it is probably too bland. It should feel hard rather than soft and should not be sweaty, or have any mould or be cracked.

SOFT FRESH CHEESES (E.G. COTTAGE CHEESE, CURD CHEESE) They should look and smell fresh and the packaging should be undamaged.

SOFT MATURED CHEESES (E.G. BRIE, CAMEMBERT)
There are a huge number of soft matured cheeses available but many of them are rather dull. We think that the best are Brie and Camembert, but fear that the imitation Somerset Brie bears little resemblance to the real thing. Buy a soft runny cheese that does not have a chalky white rind. If it has a strong smell of ammonia do not buy it as it will have an unpleasant flavour.

FIRM MATURED CHEESES (E.G. PONT L'EVEQUE, REBLOCHON) These cheeses can vary from the rather tasteless (Port Salut) to the utterly delicious and very strong Pont l'Eveque. Firm matured cheeses should be pale, creamy and fairly firm in texture.

BLUE CHEESES (E.G. STILTON, ROQUEFORT) These cheeses can be soft or firm, and should have strong blue veins with no brown blotches.

STORING CHEESE
Ideally cheese should be kept in a larder, but as few houses have one, the next best thing is to wrap it tightly in clingfilm and keep it in the refrigerator. Remove at least 1 hour before serving. If left in the warmth of a centrally heated house it will sweat.

YOGHURT
CHOOSING YOGHURT There are many different types of yoghurt now widely available. Take no notice of the labels that proudly say 'live' – all yoghurt is live unless specified as having been pasteurized, in which case it cannot be used as a starter for making your own yoghurt. Most yoghurt is labelled 'low fat' as it is made from skimmed milk. Greek yoghurt, which is now widely available in supermarkets as well as delicatessens, is a little higher in fat than most yoghurts but the taste is utterly delicious.

STORAGE
Store in the refrigerator for 3–4 days. Note that Greek yoghurts tends to go off more quickly than other yoghurts.

## FISH
For fish classifications and methods of preparation see the chapter on fish (page 265).

Fish must be purchased and eaten when it is still very fresh. Some fish is frozen on board trawlers, so do not be put off buying a frozen fish as it may well be significantly fresher than a 'fresh' fish. It is easy to tell if fish is fresh, firstly by its smell – if it has a strong fishy smell it is probably quite stale. Scaly fish should have plenty of scales and all fish should have bright eyes, red gills and firm flesh. If you press your finger into a fish and the flesh does not spring back into place immediately, it is probably not fresh.

Shellfish are often sold live in order to guarantee freshness – if buying raw shellfish, I would opt for frozen rather than for dead raw shellfish. Chinese supermarkets are often the best place to buy good-quality raw frozen shellfish. If you want to buy cooked shellfish it must be very fresh. Some fishmongers will buy and cook lobsters and crayfish to order. Cooked 'shell-on' prawns are delicious but they must be bought from a reputable source and eaten on the day of purchase. If you just need a few cooked prawns for a recipe, I would recommend that you buy frozen ones and defrost them slowly sprinkled with a little lemon juice and freshly ground black pepper.

STORING FISH
Store fish, gutted, for as short a time as possible. Refrigerate it, lightly covered with clingfilm, and eat on the day of purchase. Smoked fish will keep for a couple of days and vacuum-packed smoked fish will stay fresh for much longer (check the sell-by date), but as with all 'long-life' products it must be treated as fresh once opened. To store live shellfish, such as crabs, lobsters, mussels and oysters, put them curved side down to prevent them losing their juices on a tray in the bottom of the refrigerator and cover with a damp cloth. They can be kept overnight.

## VEGETABLES AND HERBS
See the vegetable chapter (page 215) for detailed descriptions and uses for vegetables and herbs.

CHOOSING
The most important thing about choosing vegetables is that they should be young and fresh. Old-fashioned gardeners and many producers take pride in their enormous turnips and giant

parsnips but, in fact, nothing can be nicer than a tiny roasted parsnip or a minute braised turnip. The only vegetables that I like reasonably old (but not stale) are carrots. Young carrots can be rather flavourless compared to large, deep orange ones. Very old carrots, however, are horrid as they have woody cores.

TO CHOOSE GOOD-QUALITY VEGETABLES It is obvious from a carrot's wrinkled skin that it is old, or from a lettuce's limp leaves that it has wilted. As a general rule of thumb, the vegetables you choose should be small (of their type), brightly coloured, unwrinkled, unblemished and should look 'alert' – for example, pea pods should snap open. Fruit vegetables, such as tomatoes, avocado pears and aubergines, can be large but they should still look and feel ripe. They should also feel heavy for their size.

STORING
Unwrap any vegetables that have been sold tightly wrapped in clingfilm. Store them in the warmest part of the refrigerator (i.e. the salad compartment) or in a larder. The air in a refrigerator is very dry and, to prevent dehydration, you should store root vegetables (which like to be in the dark) in brown paper bags, and above-ground vegetables in polythene bags. Make sure that the vegetables are not squeezed into too small a space. If there is no room in the refrigerator and the vegetables have to be kept in a warm room do not put them in polythene bags as they will sweat and rot. Small packets of fresh herbs will keep in their cartons for a day or two. Large bunches can be kept in polythene bags or, like flowers, in jugs of water. Watercress is best kept leaves downwards in a jug of water.

# CHOOSING FRUIT
It is fairly easy to choose good-quality fresh fruit – it should look bright-skinned and, usually, should be heavy for its size. It should also have a fairly strong scent without being overpowering. Some fruits, such as pears, are very rarely perfect in the shops as they are only perfectly ripe for one day and should therefore be purchased in advance and ripened at home.

STORING FRUIT
SOFT FRUIT Do not store for more than 2 days in the refrigerator. Do not prepare until ready for use – an unhulled strawberry will keep longer than a hulled one. If the fruit cannot be used in time, freeze and use for dishes such as ice creams, purées and pies.

CITRUS FRUITS AND HARD FRUITS Ideally these should be kept refrigerated in polythene bags. If there is no room in the refrigerator, do not leave them in polythene bags as they will rot. To store these fruits for more than a week: wrap each piece of fruit individually in newspaper and place in a box in a cool place. Some fruits (especially if under-ripe), such as quinces, apples and pears, will keep well like this for 2–3 months. Citrus fruits can be kept for 2–3 weeks. Seville oranges will only keep for 1 week but may be frozen. (Freezing will not spoil the marmalade.)

BANANAS AND AVOCADO PEARS Do not refrigerate but leave in a cool place. To ripen firm avocado pears, place in a paper bag and keep in a warm place.

STONE FRUITS (E.G. APRICOTS, PLUMS, GRAPES, ETC.) Store in a cool place, preferably the refrigerator.

NOTE: Strong-smelling fruit, such as cut pineapple or melon, must be well wrapped if kept in the refrigerator as their fragrance will taint cheese, butter and milk.

# LARDER INGREDIENTS

We have called this section larder ingredients, not that many people have larders any more, but the word conjures up a pleasing image of a cool room filled with stone storage jars. This section describes our store room at Leith's School – i.e. the basic dry ingredients that are useful to have to hand, and where necessary we have made a few notes.

MUSTARD

Buy in small pots – once opened, mustard deteriorates quite rapidly. We have smooth Dijon mustard. Dry English mustard is also useful for cheese sauces, mayonnaise and some spicy recipes.

VINEGAR

We keep Dufrais white wine vinegar as a basic ingredient although balsamic and flavoured ones, e.g. herb vinegars, are a welcome additional ingredient. Malt vinegar is very useful for cleaning and the occasional recipe.

FLOURS

We have 100 per cent wholemeal (once opened it goes off quite quickly so keep in a sealed container), 85 per cent wholemeal, strong flour (including '00' grade for making pasta), plain flour, granary flour, self-raising flour, cornflour, arrowroot and rice flour.

OILS

Sunflower is good for general cooking use; extra virgin olive oil for special salads; and sesame oil for Chinese dishes. We usually have some hazelnut, walnut and sometimes pinenut oil in the refrigerator. The expensive oils tend to deteriorate quite quickly and so should be bought in small jars.

PASTA

Dried pasta keeps well in sealed containers and we always have a selection of different shapes. The versatility and reliability of dried pasta makes it a useful standby ingredient.

DRIED HERBS AND SPICES

Ideally, all herbs and spices should be fresh, but in practice this is not possible. Store them out of the sunlight and buy in small jars from a supermarket with a quick turnover as they go stale quite quickly. At Leith's we have the following dried herbs and spices:

| Herbs | Spices |
|---|---|
| Bay leaves | Whole and ground nutmeg |
| Herbes de | Whole and ground cinnamon |
| Provence | Whole and ground mace |
| Rosemary | Whole and ground cardamom |
| Tarragon | Vanilla pods |
| Oregano | Juniper berries |
| | Allspice |
| | Cloves |
| | Coriander |
| | Cumin |
| | Turmeric |
| | Mixed spice |
| | Saffron |
| | Chilli |
| | Paprika |
| | Cayenne |

BOTTLES

Soy sauce, Worcestershire sauce, Heinz tomato ketchup, vanilla extract, rosewater, orange blossom water, passata (sieved tomatoes), stem ginger in syrup.

CANS

Plum tomatoes, flageolet beans, kidney beans, chick peas, tuna fish, sardines, anchovies, smoked oysters, red peppers, green peppercorns, petits pois, water chestnuts, palm hearts and sweetcorn kernels.

GRAINS

Basmati rice (brown and white), long-grain rice, risotto rice, pudding rice, brown rice, couscous, cracked wheat (burghul), semolina and polenta.

NUTS

Almonds, grounded, nibbed, flaked and whole; walnuts, halved; hazelnuts, whole; pinenuts, whole.

SEEDS

Sesame, poppy, mustard, pumpkin.

JAMS

Apricot, redcurrant jelly – for glazing. Honey.

SUGAR

Granulated, caster, icing, preserving, demerara, lump and muscovado.

CHOCOLATE

Chocolate Menier is an excellent all-purpose cooking chocolate. Chocolate couverture is an especially high-quality chocolate with a high proportion of cocoa solids.

DRIED FRUIT

Raisins, currants, sultanas, apples, apricots and prunes. Try to find those that have not been treated with sulphur dioxide.

COFFEE AND TEA

Earl Grey, camomile and PG Tips, Melitta filter coffee, Gold Blend instant and Café Hag decaffeinated.

GELATINE

Gelatine, available powdered and in leaves, is obtained from the bone and connective tissue of certain animals. Connective tissue is the physical harness of muscles, it is made up of three basic proteins – collagen, elastin and reticulin. Collagen is converted by long slow cooking into gelatine.

Acids weaken the setting power of gelatine so when following a recipe such as lemon soufflé an increased amount of gelatine is called for.

*How to use powdered gelatine*

1. Pour a small amount of liquid into a saucepan.
2. Slowly sprinkle on the required amount of gelatine.
3. Leave the gelatine to 'sponge' i.e. swell, for 3–5 minutes.
4. Melt the gelatine over a very low heat. Do not allow to boil. Do not stir. It should become clear and warm.
5. Pour into the mousse/soufflé base. Stir briskly: if the base is too cold the gelatine can set quickly in streaks. Gelatine is generally poured from a height to help cool it down.
6. When the mousse has reached setting-point other light ingredients such as cream or whisked egg whites can be added. If the cream or egg whites are added too early the base mix will not support their weight and the soufflé will separate into layers. If the cream or whites are added too late the mixture has to be beaten hard to incorporate the additions and the result is heavy.

Setting-point is when the base mixture will support its own weight and when a spoon is drawn through the mixture the bottom of the mixing bowl will remain visible for 2–3 seconds.

*How to use leaf gelatine*

1. Soak the leaves in a small amount of cold water for 5 minutes.
2. Dissolve over a gentle heat until liquid.
3. Use as powdered gelatine.

## Gelatine Conversion table

| 1 level teaspoon | 5–7g | ¼oz | 1½ leaves |
| 3 level teaspoons | 15g | ½oz | 3 leaves |
| 6 level teaspoons | 30g | 1oz | 6 leaves |

AGAR AGAR

Agar agar, a seaweed, is cooked, pressed, freeze-dried and then flaked or powdered for use as a setting agent in vegetarian cooking.
1 teaspoon powder has the setting power of 1 tablespoon flakes. Agar agar's setting qualities are affected by the nature of the food to which it is added, and so required quantities will vary, but

as a general rule 1 teaspoon powder or 1 tablespoon flakes will set 570ml/1 pint, and twice the quantity should be used to set a firm jelly.

*How to use agar agar*
1. Soak the agar agar in the full liquid measurement specified in the recipe, in a saucepan; leave powder for 5 minutes, flakes for 10–15 minutes.
2. Dissolve the agar agar in the pan over a medium heat, stirring continuously. Turn up the heat and boil for 2–3 minutes, continuing to stir to prevent sticking. Use as required. (Agar agar may be re-boiled without impairing its setting ability.)
3. If properly prepared, agar agar sets quickly on contact with anything much cooler than itself. Therefore, the ingredients to which it is added must be no colder than room temperature. To test whether it is ready for use, spoon a small quantity on to a cold plate: a skin should form very quickly, and wrinkle if a finger is pulled over the surface.

# FREEZING

Freezing is a method of preserving food – not indefinitely, but for some weeks or months. Bacterial action, which causes spoilage, is prevented by keeping the food at extremely low temperatures. Note that some deterioration in the taste, texture and colour of food will take place if it is kept frozen for longer than the recommended times. Providing that the following simple instructions for freezing are followed religiously, many foods can be stored successfully without any loss of nutritional value or quality.

## RAPID FREEZING

The quicker the freezing process, the smaller will be the ice crystals formed in the food. Large ice crystals, resulting from slow freezing, damage the cell walls of the food itself, and consequently, when it is thawed, liquid will be lost, including some soluble nutrients. Meat, in particular, will lose moisture on thawing if frozen too slowly, and will be dry when cooked.

### PACKING THE FREEZER

In order to facilitate rapid freezing, only small amounts of unfrozen food should be put into the freezer at one time (for different types of freezer, see page 69). Large quantities of food at room temperature would raise the temperature in the freezer and, inevitably, the freezing process would be slower. For the same reason, food should not be packed in large parcels, and the items should be separated in the freezing compartment, allowing the air to circulate around them. Once they are frozen, however, they can be – and indeed should be for economy's sake – packed tightly together with as little space between them as possible. A full freezer costs less to run than a half-empty one. Many freezers contain a fast-freeze compartment for the actual freezing process, and larger compartments for storage.

### WRAPPING THE FOOD

Because the cold atmosphere of a freezer is very drying, and direct contact with the icy air causes 'freezer burn' (dry discoloured patches) on some foods, most foods need careful wrapping before freezing. Heavyweight polythene bags are the cheapest and best wrappers, because it is possible to see through them, and they take various shapes of food without creating too much air spaces. However, an airtight container will suffice. Foil is sometimes used, as are rigid plastic containers, old yoghurt cartons, bowls with lids, etc.

Whatever container you use, it must be robust enough to withstand some rough handling in the freezer, and it must be possible to label it clearly. Freezer labels, or polythene bags with white labels on which it is possible to write with a freezer pen, are best. Once the food is packed into the container, as closely wrapped as possible, it should be labelled with the contents and the date, and frozen immediately. Liquids can be poured into a polythene bag set in square containers and frozen. Once solid, the bag is lifted out of the outer container and thus stored. This means fewer kitchen containers are out of use in the freezer, and liquids can be stored in space-saving rectangular shapes. Liquids in plastic tubs or containers should be frozen with a 2.5cm/1in gap between bowl and lid to allow for expansion. Food should be used up in the right order – for example, peas frozen the previous week should not be eaten before the batch that was frozen 2 months ago. To facilitate this, a record or inventory of what is in the freezer can be kept on it, in it or near it, with additions and subtractions made each time food is put in or taken out.

## OPEN FREEZING

If frozen in a mass, fruit and vegetables will emerge from the freezer in a solid block. This can be inconvenient for thawing in a hurry, or if only a small quantity of the food is needed, and the fruit and vegetables may also lose their individual shape and texture. For this reason, many foods are frozen on open trays so that each raspberry, pea, broad bean or sprig of cauliflower is individually frozen before packing into bags. The frozen produce will then be free-flowing and separate. Use this method for sausages, beefburgers, breadcrumbs, bread rolls, etc. as well as for fruit and vegetables. Decorated cakes and puddings can be open-frozen, then packed when the decoration is hard enough to withstand the tight wrapping around it.

## MASS FREEZING

If the food to be frozen is not suitable for open freezing, make sure that the block is not too thick. This will make cooking and thawing easier and quicker. For example, meatballs in tomato sauce should be laid one deep in a plastic box, not piled one on top of each other; spinach should be in a flattish pack so that it can be cooked from frozen (a thick block would mean overcooked outside leaves while the middle was still frozen). Air should be excluded as far as possible. This is especially important with casseroles, where the chicken or meat should be coated or covered completely by the sauce. Otherwise, the meat may become dry and fall apart on reheating.

## THAWING

Thawing should be as slow as possible. Rapid thawing leads to loss of moisture and subsequent dryness or tastelessness of the food. However, it is sometimes imperative to thaw food in a hurry. To do this, put it into an airtight polythene bag and immerse it in cold, not hot, water. Hot water tends to cook the outside of the food and encourages bacterial activity which would cause the food to go bad if not completely cooked immediately. Meat should be thawed completely, and should be at room temperature before it is cooked.

## RE-FREEZING FROZEN FOOD

Freezing does not kill bacteria present in food; it simply inhibits growth. So when food is removed from the freezer the bacteria in it will multiply normally. When put back, the now considerably increased population of bacteria will cease breeding, to start afresh when the food is brought back into the warmth. For this reason, frozen food manufacturers caution purchasers not to refreeze the product once it has been thawed. They are justly nervous that if the food is taken in and out of the freezer, it could contain germs in dangerous concentrations. However, the cook may still regard the product as being perfectly fresh because it has just emerged from the freezer. The foods most likely to cause illness are commercial ice cream and seafood, as both deteriorate rapidly. But this is not to say that no food should ever be refrozen. It is merely a matter of common sense.

## FOODS THAT CANNOT BE FROZEN SUCCESSFULLY

Although most food will be prevented from going bad if kept at freezing point, some foods cannot be frozen successfully as their texture is ruined by freezing. This is particularly true of foods with a high water content. However, some of these may be frozen if wanted for soups or purées, in which case they should normally be frozen in purée form. Examples are bananas, cucumbers, lettuce and watercress.

**Emulsions** such as mayonnaise or hollandaise sauce do not freeze successfully as they separate when thawed.

**Yoghurt, milk and cream** can be frozen but will not be totally smooth when thawed. Double cream freezes better if whipped first. Storage time: 4 months.

**Eggs** cannot be frozen in the shell, but both whites and yolks freeze well, either lightly beaten together or separated. Storage time: 9 months

**Jelly**, both savoury and sweet, loses its texture if frozen, and would have to be reboiled and allowed to set again after thawing if required jellied.

**Mousses and soufflés** set with gelatine tend to go rubbery.

**Strawberries** keep their colour and flavour well, but become soft on thawing.

**Melon** is too watery to remain crisp when thawed. It is best frozen in balls in syrup, but even this is not totally satisfactory.

**Tomatoes** emerge mushy when thawed, but are

good for soups and sauces. One bonus of freezing tomatoes whole is that they can be easily peeled if placed, still frozen, under running hot water. They can, of course, be frozen as purée or juice.

**Fats**, or foods with a high fat content, freeze less successfully as a rule than less fatty foods. They have a tendency to develop a slightly rancid flavour if stored for more than 3 months.

## FOODS THAT FREEZE SUCCESSFULLY

Most foods freeze well if some care is taken with wrapping, etc. But some foods freeze so well that no one would ever know that they had been frozen. Baked or raw pastries, breads, bread or biscuit doughs, cakes and sandwiches containing not-too-wet fillings, are good examples. As a general rule, raw food keeps better and longer than cooked. But cooked food, especially if well covered in a sauce, or under a potato or pastry crust, keeps well.

**Vegetables** freeze well if they are to be eaten cooked. They cannot be frozen if intended to be eaten raw. In order to prevent enzyme activity, green vegetables are boiled briefly, then cooled rapidly, before freezing. They may be frozen without this 'blanching' but their storage time would be reduced, and it is foolish to lose food through lazy freezing. Only the best vegetables, very fresh, should be used. They should be washed, or picked over, or otherwise prepared as if for immediate cooking. A large saucepan of water is brought to a rapid boil, and the vegetables (not more than 450g/1lb or so at a time) lowered into it. Accurate timing of the blanching process is important: the minutes are counted from the time the water reboils. As soon as the time is up, the vegetables are lifted out, and immediately cooled in a sink full of cold water, if possible. Once stone-cold, the vegetables are lifted out, drained well, patted dry if necessary, and frozen. The same blanching water can be used for several batches of vegetables. Some vegetables (onions, mushrooms, potatoes) may be cooked completely in butter or blanched in oil instead of water. They are allowed to cool normally before freezing.

**Fruits** (storage time: 9 months) Only freeze fruit that is in prime condition. Unripe, over-ripe or blemished fruit gives poor results. Three methods, as follows, are generally used to freeze raw fruit. (Cooked fruit may also be frozen whole or puréed.)

### OPEN FREEZING

Suitable for most soft fruit such as raspberries and currants. Spread the fruit out on a baking sheet or tray and place in the freezer uncovered. When hard, pack into polythene bags or a rigid container, with or without adding sugar.

### DRY SUGAR PACK

Suitable for most fruit to be used in cooked puddings. Prepare the fruit, toss it in sugar and freeze, with any juices that may have run from it during preparation. Care should be taken to exclude air, which may cause discoloration of the fruit.

### PURÉE

Suitable for any fruits. Stew the fruit and mash, liquidize or sieve. Allow the purée to cool. Pack into containers, leaving head space, cover, label and freeze. Raw purées freeze well, too.

### HERBS

(Storage time: 3 months) Herbs should be frozen dry in small polythene bags or packets, or chopped finely, put into ice trays and just covered with water. The frozen cubes can be transferred to labelled bags.

### MEAT AND FISH

(Storage time: raw meat, 9 months; cooked meat, 4 months; raw fish, 5 months; cooked fish, 3 months) Special care should be taken in wrapping to prevent freezer burn.

### CAKES AND BREAD

(Storage time: 12 months) Both raw and cooked doughs and pastries freeze well.

### STOCKS

Reduce stocks by boiling rapidly until very concentrated. Freeze in ice trays and when thawed use as stock cubes.

# VEGETABLES

Where a choice of times is given, the shorter time is for smaller vegetables,
the longer for larger ones.

| Vegetable | Preparation | Blanching time in minutes | Storage time in months |
|---|---|---|---|
| **Asparagus** | Do not tie in bunches | 3–4 | 12 |
| **Artichoke (globe)** | Remove stalks and outer tough leaves | 7 | 6 |
| **Artichoke (Jerusalem)** | Freeze once cooked into a purée | – | 6 |
| **Beans, broad** | Sort by size | 3 | 12 |
| **Beans, French** | Trim ends | 2–3 | 12 |
| **Beans, runner** | Slice thickly | $1^1/_2$–2 | 6 |
| **Beetroot** | Freeze completely cooked and skinned. Slice if large | – | 6 |
| **Broccoli** | Trim stalks | $2^1/_2$–4 | 12 |
| **Brussels sprouts** | Choose small, firm sprouts. Remove outer leaves | 4–6 | 12 |
| **Carrots** | Choose small young ones with good colour. Scrape. Freeze whole | 5–6 | 12 |
| **Cauliflower** | Break heads into florets | 3–4 | 6 |
| **Celery** | Will be soft when thawed, but good for soups and stews | 3 | 12 |
| **Corn on the cob** | Remove husks and silks | 6–10 | 9 |
| **Courgettes** | Use only very small ones. Do not peel | 1 | 12 |
| **Kale** | Remove stalks | 1 | 6 |
| **Leeks** | Slice thinly; chop in chunks or leave whole | 1–3 | 12 |
| **Mushrooms** | Do not peel. Freeze unblanched for up to 1 month. For longer storage, cook in butter | – | 4 |
| **Onions** | Store unblanched onions, sliced or chopped, for up to 3 months. Sliced or chopped onions can be blanched in water or oil. Button onions can be blanched whole | 1–3 | 5 |
| **Peas** | Choose young, very fresh peas | 1–2 | 12 |
| **Potatoes** | Chips: blanch in oil. Boiled or mashed: freeze cooked and cold | 4 | 6 |
| **Root vegetables** | Cut into chunks; blanch, or cook completely | 3 | 12 |
| **Spinach** | Move about in water to separate leaves | 1 | 12 |
| **Tomatoes** | Do not blanch. Freeze whole, in slices or as juice or purée, cooked or raw | | |

# EQUIPMENT AND UTENSILS

When buying kitchen equipment, the basic rule for standard items is to buy the best that you can possibly afford. Good kitchen equipment will probably last for 15 years and is worth the investment. When buying small or specialist equipment that may be used once only, be as economical or extravagant as your purse dictates.

The following is not intended to be a complete list of the kitchen equipment available, but includes all the utensils that the home cook could possibly want, while excluding certain specialist items like preserving and cake-decorating equipment, barbecues, smokers and storage equipment.

## UTENSILS
The following items of equipment are essential for any cook (further details on individual items are given on pages 70–76):
1 cook's knife with 18cm/7in blade
1 cook's knife with 7.5cm/3in blade
1 filleting knife with 14cm/5in blade
1 fruit knife
1 carbon-steel knife
1 palette knife
1 large saucepan 21cm/8in diameter with lid
1 medium saucepan 19cm/7in diameter with lid
1 small saucepan 12cm/5in diameter
1 frying pan with 20cm/8in diameter base
1 colander
2 wooden spoons
1 fish slice
1 rubber spatula
1 sieve (bowl strainer)
1 potato peeler
1 set of scales
1 measuring jug
1 pair poultry shears
3 gradated pudding basins
1 cheese grater
1 wooden board
1 roasting tin
1 salad bowl
1 whisk

## OTHER KITCHEN EQUIPMENT
The home cook will also find the following items useful, and often time- or labour-saving:

**Bottle opener**
**Bottle stopper**
**Breadboard and knife**
**Can opener** Wall-mounted ones are easiest to use and cannot be mislaid.
**Casserole dishes** Buy several sizes as food must be cooked in the right-sized pot or it will dry out during the long slow cooking. Make sure that the lids fit tightly. We recommend dishes made of enamelled cast iron (or other heavy duty metal) as they can be used on the hob and in the oven. Earthenware and heat-resistant glass must not be put on to the hob.
**Chicken brick** This is a clay container for cooking chicken in its own juices and makes for very succulent birds. Never wash it with detergent, which will be absorbed into the brick and taint the food.
**Clock** This is essential for accurate timing and to avoid guesswork.
**Coffee maker** There are a huge variety of coffee machines available on the market, but one of the nicest and simplest ways to make coffee is to pour boiling water into a large earthenware jug. Add 4 heaped tablespoons of medium ground coffee per

570ml/1 pint water, stir once or twice with a large spoon and leave to stand and infuse in a warm place for 5 minutes. The coffee will sink to the bottom of the jug. Pour, through a small strainer, into prewarmed cups.

**Cafétière** This is a glass jug with a central plunger. The coffee is made by infusion (as in the jug method) but the plunger isolates the ground coffee and acts as a filter.

**Filter** Filter systems range from the simple drip filter with jug to sophisticated electric machines. Use fine ground coffee. Experts recommend that you choose a machine that doesn't use filter paper, which gives the coffee a poor flavour. The ultimate in coffee-filter machines is the one that grinds and filters in one process – and does not use filter paper.

**Percolator** This does not make very good coffee. If you have one, used medium ground beans.

**Corkscrew** Choose one with a very thin sharp coil that disturbs the wine as little as possible.

**Electric kettle**

**Freezer** Chest freezers are cheaper than upright freezers, but are less convenient to use and lose more energy when they are opened. Upright freezers take up less floor space than chest freezers.

**Microwave oven** This can be very useful for defrosting food (like loaves of bread and packets of butter), reheating precooked vegetables and melting butter, chocolate and jam (see Microwaving, pages 33–4). But we would not recommend them for cooking unless you are in a rush.

**Oven** Choose the largest (think of the Christmas turkey!) and best oven that you can afford. You are not likely to replace it often. If you can, buy a double oven so that food can be cooked at different temperatures. Gadgets can often be a snare – as they often go wrong. So choose an oven with only the gadgets that you are sure you will find useful. Make sure that it is easy to clean with no dirt traps. Ideally, buy a self-cleaning oven. Check that it has a good grill.

**Fan-circulated ovens** The efficient fan-assisted ovens and convection ovens (rather than radiant ovens) heat up very quickly. Fan ovens can be run at up to 20 per cent lower temperatures than conventional ovens.

**Oven cloth/gloves**

**Refrigerator** Choose the largest refrigerator that will fit into your kitchen; you can never have enough fridge space. Make sure that it is easy to clean and sturdy. The ice tray should be made of strong, flexible rubber.

**Salad spinner** Almost a 'spin-dryer' for salad leaves, this is operated by a handle. It is a cheap and very useful piece of kitchen equipment.

**Salt and pepper mills** Choose wooden ones with matt screw-tops rather than handles.

**Tea towels** You can never have enough.

**Timer** Buy the type that you hang around your neck – that way it goes with you when you leave the kitchen.

**Toaster** This uses less energy than a grill.

**Vegetable brush** A shaving brush is useful as it can be stood upright.

## MEASURING AND WEIGHING

It is essential to have accurate weighing and measuring equipment for successful cooking. Useful charts can be found on pages 8–10. The following measuring equipment is necessary for accuracy and good results.

**American cup measures** American recipes call for cups or parts of a cup. A cup is 225ml/8fl oz. A set of cup measures is available from specialist kitchen shops in multiples of one cup.

**Measuring jug** Buy a large jug, so that you can measure both large and small quantities, with both imperial and metric gradations.

**Scales** Balance scales last a lifetime and are more accurate than other types. They are used with expensive, but very accurate, metal weights, which can be imperial or metric.

**Thermometers** The thermometers on the market fall into the following broad categories:

**Freezer thermometer** To check that the freezer is running at the required temperature.

**Meat thermometer** This is particularly useful when roasting a large joint. It helps to indicate the degree of 'closeness'.

**Oven thermometer** For the accurate measurement of oven temperature.

**Sugar or deep-fat thermometer** This gauges when fat is ready for deep-frying and indicates the degree of 'crack' of boiling sugar. It is normally made of glass, so it should be warmed before use.

# TYPES OF FUEL: ADVANTAGES AND DISADVANTAGES

| | Gas | Electricity | Solid fuel |
|---|---|---|---|
| Expense | Cheaper than electricity | | Cheaper than gas or electricity |
| Hobs | Quick to heat | Needs preheating | Provides a constant source of heat. |
| | Any pans can be used | Some ceramic hobs need flat-based saucepans | Needs very flat, very heavy saucepans |
| Ovens | Drier heat than electricity therefore better for roasts, cakes and meringues. | | Excellent for long, slow cooking |
| | Uneven heat; top of oven hotter than bottom, though this can be very useful | Even heat throughout oven | Temperature of oven can be guaranteed, but normally there are only three settings from which to choose |
| | The flame can go out at low-temperature settings | Good for low simmering | Good for low simmering, but the hotplate is not always hot enough for fast frying |
| | | | **Room heating:** can make the kitchen too hot in the summer, but is an excellent radiator in the winter |

## POTS, PANS AND OTHER VESSELS

Always buy as heavy a pan as you can afford. The very best ones are made of copper with tin lining, or heavy aluminium or steel. Heavy pans conduct heat better and more evenly than light ones. A cheap pan might last two years, but it will dent and burn. A good, heavy pan could last 50 years and will not burn easily. Buy pans that are stable when empty, the right size for your burners or hot plates and have lids that fit well. If you have an Aga or range, you will need heavy pans with flat bases that conduct the heat evenly across the surface. You can buy these from specialist dealers and cookware shops. Non-stick pans are particularly useful for low-fat cookery and can be relined at specialist shops.

**Colander** Choose a large standing colander; the legs keep the contents clear of draining liquid and it frees hands to empty heavy pans.

**Double saucepan** This is for making delicate sauces and melting chocolate. The bottom saucepan is very useful for boiling eggs if your other saucepans are made of heavy aluminium, in which eggs tend to discolour. The handles of both pans are angled towards each other to facilitate picking them up as one unit.

**Fish kettle** Buy a fish kettle with a steaming platform. The kettle is made to accommodate the shape of a large fish, and should be big enough to hold at least one 50cm/20in long. The matching platform should fit well and have handles that stand proud of the liquid.

**Frying pan** For general use, choose a heavy-duty pan with a 20cm/8in diameter base.

**Crêpe pan** This is a small, round-edged frying pan used only for making French pancakes. The ideal size has a 15cm/6in diameter base.

**Deep-fat frying pan** This is thicker and deeper than an ordinary frying pan. Make sure that it is big enough for all your needs (including frying pieces of fish, etc.), has good handles and a fine mesh to keep the fat free of food particles.

**Omelette pan** A small carbon-steel frying pan with edges curving into the base, making the folding and serving of omelettes easier. Keep it just for omelettes.

**Girdle** This is a heavy aluminium, iron or steel plate for girdle (pronounced 'griddle') scones and crumpets. Make sure that the base is thick and quite flat. The handle should drop down for easy storage.

**Head diffuser** This is made of a circular piece of metal with a wooden handle to reduce heat under glass and earthenware vessels on top of the stove, and for controlled simmering.

**Paella pan** This broad, shallow, flat-bottomed, two-handled pan gets its name from the traditional Spanish rice dish. (The paella is cooked and served in the pan.) Pans are usually made of cast iron.

**Pan rest** A wooden triangle that prevents hot pans from marking work surfaces.

**Pizza plate** A round, metal baking sheet with a slightly raised lip to support the edges of the pizza crust. Buy two. The most common size is 25cm/10in diameter.

**Pressure cooker** This is extremely useful for speeding up cooking processes and wonderful for making preserves.

**Roasting pans and racks** Get several sizes, but make sure that the large one fits into your oven; a small roast in a large pan allows the juices to spread too thinly and burn. Choose pans made of heavy stainless steel with rolled edges and high sides. Many new ovens are supplied with roasting pans. Buy roasting racks to fit.

**Saucepans** Buy 3 or 4 saucepans ranging in capacity from 900ml/1½ pints to 6–7.2 litres/10–12 pints. They should be deep and straight-sided to hold the heat well and minimize evaporation. A sloping-sided saucepan (without a lid) is invaluable for making sauces.

**Sauté pan** This is like a frying pan with deeper, straighter sides which allow for vigorous shaking of food. It is used for sauté dishes such as chicken casseroles. Buy one with a 30cm/12in diameter base, and one with a 20cm/8in diameter base.

**Splash guard** A fine wire mesh with a long handle which covers pans but allows steam to escape. It is very useful when frying.

**Steamers** You can buy steamers in the form of a saucepan with a second, perforated pan that fits on top. This is rather more expensive than the readily available perforated steamer top, with lid, with gradated bottom that fits on to any saucepan.

**Chinese rice steamer** A perforated aluminium, hinged, spherical container that is attached to the side of a saucepan for steaming rice.

**Folding steaming platform** This perforated platform stands on legs with adjustable, folding side panels and is particularly useful for steaming small quantities of vegetables. It fits into any size of saucepan.

**Steaming basket for wok** A small bamboo cage that fits neatly into the wok, leaving about a 5cm/2in gap between it and the wok's base.

**Stock pot** A deep and straight-sided pot for long slow cooking with minimal evaporation. It can be made of light aluminium as it will be used essentially for boiling. Choose one that holds at least 8.5 litres/15 pints. Some pots have small taps near the bottom to draw off fat-free stock.

**Wok** Buy a wok set complete with a lid, stand and scoop. Choose one made of carbon iron, with a round bottom, wooden handles and domed lid. The best size is 35cm/14in.

## KNIVES AND CUTTING IMPLEMENTS

The basic principle when buying a knife is to choose one that feels comfortable in your hand: heavy and well balanced. Pivot the handle/blade junction on the edge of your open hand – the handle should fall back gently into the palm.

The part of the blade that extends into the handle of the knife is called the tang. Those knives that have a full tang running the whole length of the handle give the best overall balance; blades that are not riveted in place in this way inevitably come loose. The heads of the rivets should be flush with the surface of the handle as this makes for easy cleaning.

Carbon-steel knives are easy to sharpen and stay sharp for a long time. However, they rust easily and must be wiped clean and dried immediately after use. They also discolour, especially from onions and highly acidic food. Stainless steel knives are strong, do not rust and can be used on onions and highly acidic food. Unfortunately, they are difficult to sharpen and blunt readily. High-carbon stainless steel knives have all the advantages of carbon-steel and stainless steel knives, and none of the disadvantages, but they are very expensive.

Knives must be looked after carefully. Always wipe clean and dry them immediately after use. Sharpen them regularly with a steel suitable for the type of knife. Do not store them in a drawer – they will damage each other's blades and may cut your hands. Use a wooden knife block. When carbon-steel knives get very stained, clean them with half a lemon sprinkled with salt. If that does not work, use a scouring pad, but only occasionally. To remove rust, rub the blade with a burnt cork.

**Apple corer** Choose one with a sharp, strong and rigid stainless steel blade to withstand the force of twisting when coring.

**Boning knife** The thin, very rigid blade must be at least 10cm/4in long, and particularly sharp, especially at the tip, which does most of the work.

**Canelle knife** A stainless steel blade with sharpened notch for cutting decorative grooves.

**Carbon steel** The bigger the better. Choose one that has a good guard at the hilt and a handle with a good grip. Steels do wear out eventually, after several years.

**Carving knife and fork** The knife should have a broad and rigid blade at least 20cm/8in long. The fork should be about 25cm/10in long. If the prongs are curved, they can be useful for roasts – for larger roasts; longer, straighter prongs are necessary. The guard, which is essential, protects you against the knife slipping.

**Cheese wire** The simplest is a stainless steel wire with 2 wooden handles. Cheese wires are useful only for slicing large pieces of cheese.

**Cherry stoner** Choose a sturdy stainless steel stoner – very useful for stoning both cherries and olives.

**Chinese cleaver** This is similar to a meat cleaver but with a finer, sharper edge for precise slicing and chopping.

**Chip cutter** This is only for people who eat a lot of chips. After the potatoes are peeled, the chip cutter is pushed down on top of each potato. Perfect chips emerge.

**Citrus zester** A wooden-handled implement with stainless steel blade which has a row of holes with sharpened edges to remove the zest-filled top layer of citrus fruits, leaving the bitter pith behind. Various sizes are available.

**Clam knife** This is similar to an oyster knife, but with a longer, more blunted blade and rounded tip.

**Cook's knife** A cook's knife has a gentle curve from the blade to the tip giving a neatly pointed end for fine work. Using the tip as a pivot, the blade gives an efficient chopping action. On a large cook's knife, the broad, heavy flat of the blade makes a useful mallet. Cook's knives come in a wide variety of sizes from a 25cm/10in blade to a 7.5cm/3in blade. The small one is particularly useful for boning small birds and fine work like dicing shallots.

**Double-handed herb chopper or 'mezzaluna'** A double-handled knife with a wide curved stainless steel blade. Use for chopping herbs. It can come with up to 4 blades in parallel for chopping herbs in bulk.

**Egg pricker** This has a steel pin for pricking eggs to prevent cracking during boiling. It is invaluable.

**Egg slicer** A stainless steel wire cutter that will slice an egg without crumbling the yolk.

**Filleting knife** Choose a pointed straight-edged filleting knife with a fine, flexible blade that is about 14cm/5in long.

**Food mill** A hand-operated mill for puréeing. Choose one with several discs of different gauges.

**Freezer knife** This has a rigid blade at least 30cm/12in long, serrated deeply on both sides and used like a saw. It has a hooked tip for prising and lifting.

**Fruit knife** This has a stainless steel blade with a serrated edge to cut through skins and 'saw' slices without squashing delicate fruit and a sharp tip for piercing skins prior to peeling.

**Grapefruit knife** This has a stainless steel, slightly flexible blade, serrated and curved to fit the shape of the fruit.

**Graters** Hand-held graters come in a variety of shapes and sizes. We recommend a stainless box-shaped grater for general purposes, a tiny conical grater for nutmeg and a hand-operated rotary grater for cheese. Use a pastry brush rather than a knife to clean the faces of the graters.

**Lobster crackers** These are for cracking lobsters' legs. They look rather like pliers and can also be used to remove small bones from smoked salmon.

**Lobster pick** A steel prong for getting meat out of lobsters' legs and claws.

**Mandoline** A mandoline grater is useful both for slicing and grating. It has adjustable steel blades – 1 rippled and 1 straight – and is mounted on a wooden or plastic base. Food processors have, to a certain degree, replaced mandolines but they are still useful for small quantities.

**Meat cleaver** Buy one that is as heavy as you can handle with ease. For storage, hang by the hole in the blade.

**Melon baller** A small stainless steel metal scoop with a wooden handle used for making balls from potatoes and melons.

**Mincers** Choose one with a clamp rather than a suction base. Sharpen or replace the blades regularly. Ensure that they come apart easily for cleaning.

**Oyster knife** For opening oysters. Short, rigid, pointed blade with a good grip and a guard to save hands if the knife slips.

**Palette knife** The blade should be sturdy and evenly flexible along its full length and have a blunt edge for easing under cakes and breads. It is also useful for smoothing iced surfaces. Buy a large one.

**Paring knife** A small stainless steel blade (7.5cm/3in) for peeling soft fruit or vegetables.

**Potato peeler** There are 2 types of potato peeler: the swivel type has a blade that pivots freely to adapt to the shape of the item being peeled. One with a double cutting edge means that you can peel in both directions. The fixed-blade type is used like a knife. Left-handed people must choose a left-handed peeler. This type can also be used for extracting bones from salmon. Both have pointed ends for clipping out potato eyes, but neither type can be sharpened well.

**Poultry shears** These can be used both as scissors and shears. They should be made of stainless steel because they are often immersed in water and you don't want them to rust. They should be at least 25cm/10in long to cope with all varieties and sizes of birds. The notch cracks bones; the spring keeps the blade open between cuts, and one blade is usually serrated for cutting cartilage.

**Saw** A lightweight saw can be very useful for sawing large thigh bones or frozen meat. Get the kind with a replaceable blade.

**Scissors** Choose kitchen scissors that can be unscrewed for easy cleaning and sharpening. Make sure that the blades meet smoothly along their full length.

**Smoked salmon/ham knife** The blade should be at least 25cm/10in long, and only slightly flexible. The blade often has indentations to reduce friction and keep thin slices intact.

## BAKEWARE AND MOULDS

There is a large variety of moulds available on the market, many of which have been designed with a specific use in mind, but inevitably, they are not always used for that purpose. For instance, how many people own both a ring mould and a savarin mould? Moulds that are intended for baking, like terrines and cake tins, are made of a fairly heavy-duty material, whereas moulds that are intended for chilling are usually made of thinner more malleable metal.

The following list does not cover all the moulds available, but only those that it would be fun or useful to own. It also includes many of the different cake tins, baking sheets and flan rings that you can purchase.

**Angel cake tin** The central funnel allows for better conduction of heat. Choose a non-stick tin as angel cakes tend to stick.

**Baking sheets** You will need several. Make sure that they fit into your oven. Heavy steel sheets with one lip are suitable for most uses: you can slide reluctant flans off them and the lip makes for easier handling. A lipped baking sheet is useful when there is the likelihood of an overflow.

**Blind beans** Ceramic baking beans are for baking blind and can be re-used continually. Uncooked rice is a perfectly good substitute.

**Bombe mould** For moulding ice cream and making ice-cream bombes. The best ones have a vacuum-release top; otherwise the bombe is very difficult to dislodge.

**Brioche tins** Fluted, tinned metal moulds for making brioches. They come in a variety of sizes and some have funnelled centres to aid the conduction of heat.

**Cake moulds** These are made of steel and come in a variety of sizes and shapes – chickens, rabbits, etc. They are held together by clips.

**Cake racks** They are either rectangular (for all types of baked food) or circular (specifically for cakes). They are used for cooling cakes and biscuits without sweating. Buy one that is large and stands fairly high off the work surface.

**Charlotte mould** A classic shaped mould for charlotte pudding. It can be used hot for apple charlotte, say, or cold for charlotte russe.

**Confectionery mould** A rubber mould with 50 or more holes in several different shapes for sweet mixtures. Its flexibility makes for easy unmoulding.

**Copper bowl** An expensive and non-essential piece of kitchenware equipment. It is unlined and used solely for holding egg whites while they are being whisked. Some people say that there is a chemical reaction between the egg whites and copper that aids beating.

**Coeur à la crème mould** A porcelain heart-shaped mould with a perforated base to drain the whey produced when making coeurs à la crème.

**Dariole moulds** These small, deep sloping-sided tins are used for individual hot mousses and timbales. Many people use ramekins instead, but these metal dariole moulds are better because the heat is conducted quickly throughout.

**Deep cake tin** Buy 2 of these – 1 square, 1 round – for fruit cakes. Make sure that they are heavy-duty for long, slow baking. Select ones with loose bottoms.

**Easter egg moulds** Stainless steel, glass or plastic moulds, either plain or patterned.

**Fish mousse mould** A metal or porcelain fish-shaped mould for fish mousses set with gelatine.

**Flan rings** Buy several metal flan rings, plain and fluted, of different sizes. They are preferable to porcelain flan dishes for pastry as they conduct heat well, thereby preventing soggy pastry.

**Flour dredger or sifter** Buy one with a handle. Better still, buy 2 – a big one and a small-holed one – for heavy and light dredging.

**Folding pâté tin** Metal with folding sides for pies and pâté en croûte.

**Jelly moulds** There is a large variety of metal decorative jelly moulds, often made of copper with a tin lining. However, they are rarely ovenproof.

**Loaf tin** This can also be used for terrines.

**Madeleine sheet** This is similar to a patty tin, but shaped for making madeleines.

**Marble slab** An ideal surface on which to make pastry, as it stays cool.

**Mixing bowls** Get several different sizes of white china pudding basins and one larger ceramic mixing bowl.

**Moulè-á-manqué** For French génoise cake. The sloping sides ease unmoulding and decoration.

**Pastry brush** Buy a good-quality small paint brush with thick, tightly packed bristles that will not shed. A shaving brush also makes a good pastry brush as it is very soft and will stand upright when you are not using it.

**Pastry cutters** Buy an assortment of metal cutters, round, fluted, plain, animal shapes, ornamental shapes, etc. The top edge is rolled to safeguard fingers and to keep the shape rigid. The cutting edge must be sharp.

**Pastry moulds** Buy a variety of different shaped metal moulds for tarts, tartlets, boat-shaped moulds, petits fours moulds, etc.

**Patty tin** The larger the better – not all the moulds need be filled.

**Pie dishes** Get a large and a small pie dish – usually deep, glazed ceramic dishes. They must be deep so that the filling can cook before the crust burns.

**Piping bag and nozzle** Nylon bags with sewn seams last longer than plastic bags. Buy both a small and a large bag and a selection of metal nozzles.

**Raised pie mould** A wooden block to shape hot watercrust pastry and make a traditional raised pie.

**Raised pie tin** This is not for traditionally raised pies, but for pies that are to be decorated and made to look like a raised pie. The sides unclip and detach from the base. The advantage of these tins is that you can use a pâte à pâté pastry for making a raised pie; this rich pastry would not hold its shape if baked as a self-supporting raised pie.

**Ramekin dishes** These small soufflé dishes are for individual servings.

**Ring mould** This jelly mould has a hole in the centre which can be filled with a suitable accompaniment.

**Rolling pin** Buy a wooden pin without handles that gives even pressure, covers the maximum surface area and is easy to wipe clean. Buy a fairly long one.

**Sandwich tins** Buy 2 × 20cm/8in diameter tins for Victoria sandwich cake. Tins with levers ease unmoulding.

**Savarin mould or ring mould for jellies** The ring mould shape gives maximum surface for good heat conduction.

**Soufflé dishes** Get 2 or 3 soufflé dishes ranging from 0.5 litre/¾ pint to 1 litre/1¾ pints. They must have straight sides, be good and deep for high rising and made of very fine porcelain to aid conduction of heat.

**Sponge finger sheet** This is similar to a madeleine sheet, but shaped for making sponge fingers.

**Spring form tin** Use when unmoulding is difficult. The sides unclip.

**Spring form tube tin** For kugelhopf; the funnel helps to get heat to the centre of the tin and the clips ease unmoulding.

**Swiss roll tin** Make sure that the sides are at least 2.5cm/1in high. The tin should be 35 × 25cm/14 × 10 in.

**Terrine** Make sure that the lid has a steam hole. A terrine can also be used as a pie dish.

**Wooden board** Choose a large, thick one made of maple or another hard wood. Make sure that it is reinforced. Ideally, the grain of the main part should run in the opposite direction to that on the reinforced ends.

## FOOD PROCESSING MACHINES
The following machines should be considered.

**Deep-fryer** Buy an electric thermostatically controlled deep-fryer with a charcoal filter lid, which prevents smells in the kitchen. Make sure that it is easy to clean.

**Food mixer** Although food mixers have been superseded by food processors, they are remarkably versatile and have a huge variety of attachments, the most useful of which are: mincer, liquidizer, coffee grinder, electric sieve (which gives perfect mashed potatoes), can opener, sausage maker, dough hook and juice extractor. Buy a heavy-duty model with rotating whisks that reach to the bottom of the bowl and are capable of whisking very small quantities.

**Hand-held whisk** An electric hand-held whisk is a very useful piece of kitchen equipment. Buy one with a heavy-duty motor. It is ideal for making whisked sponge cakes and mayonnaise.

**Ice-cream machines** Electric ice-cream machines make wonderful ice-creams and sorbets and are very easy to use. However, they are expensive and take up a lot of space.

**Liquidizer** This often comes as an attachment to a food mixer but can be bought as a separate machine. Liquidizers are better for blending soups than food processors, but other than that they have become outdated. Choose a large liquidizer made

of clear roughened glass or heavyweight plastic.

**Pasta machine** Buy a hand-operated machine for kneading, rolling and cutting pasta dough. It should be made of rust-resistant metal and be able to be clamped securely to a work surface. Choose one with rollers that adjust to several positions to alter the thickness of the dough and with rotary cutters that give a range of different widths of cut strips. Electric machines are available but are very expensive.

**Processor and julienne attachment** This is not an essential piece of equipment, but once you have used one you cannot live without it! It chops, slices, grates, minces, shreds and beats. It does not whisk egg whites successfully, though. Choose the most compact model that you can find with as quiet a motor as possible. It should have a circuit breaker to prevent over-heating or burning out. Choose one that will not operate unless the cover is in position.

## HAND TOOLS AND SIEVES
**Basting spoon** Choose a large one with a pierced or hooked handle if you want to hang it up. It should be heavy-duty, deep and long-handled.

**Bowl strainer (sieve)** Choose a stainless steel sieve as carbon steel discolours some purées, and nylon sieves break easily, sometimes melt and look old relatively quickly. Double-mesh strainers are used for very fine puréeing. Make sure that the sieve will sit securely.

**Bulb baster** A syringe-type baster in plastic with a rubber bulb. It is also useful for skimming off fat or for extracting fat-free stock from under a layer of fat. Wash and dry carefully.

**Conical strainer (Chinois or tammy strainer)** There are 2 types of conical strainer: a firm metal one for heavy purées and a wire mesh one for straining large quantities of liquid into a single stream.

**Drum sieve** This is good for sifting but not easy to clean, so it is not suitable for making purées.

**Fish slice** Make sure that it has a pierced or hooked handle if you want to hang it up. Choose one that is broad enough to lift and turn large objects.

**Fruit juice press** Very useful for squeezing quantities of citrus fruits.

**Funnel** Get one that is heat-resistant, with a wide flared top and a tube that fits narrow bottles.

**Garlic press** This is best with thick handles and a pivoted pressing foot. Some have cherry or olive stoners integrated in the handle. Garlic presses are invaluable in the kitchen as the smell of garlic is difficult to remove from wooden boards or a pestle and mortar.

**Ice-cream scoop** Spring action, moulds ice cream or firm vegetable purées into a ball shape.

**Ladle** Make sure that it has a pierced or hooked handle if you want to hang it up. Choose one with a large bowl and long handle.

**Larding needle** Lengths of lard are gripped by the teeth at the end of the needle. The lard is then threaded through the meat.

**Lemon squeezer** There are 2 types of lemon squeezer. One is made of glass or toughened plastic for squeezing citrus fruits, but the plastic ones with a container underneath are the most useful. The other is a wooden gadget used to push into fruit halves for extracting a few drops.

**Meat-tenderizing mallet** A spiked wooden mallet for flattening and tenderizing meat by breaking down the meat fibres.

**Metal tongs** For lifting and turning food. These are particularly useful when grilling. Make sure that the ends meet.

**Pasta wheel** Useful for cutting pasta.

**Pastry blender** A wooden handle with circular-shaped wires for easy blending.

**Perforated jam skimmer** A flat perforated spoon for removing fat from liquids and scum from jams and stocks.

**Perforated spoon** Choose a large one with a pierced or hooked handle if you want to hang it up. It is excellent for lifting poached food out of the poaching liquid.

**Pestle and mortar** A pestle crushes herbs and spices in a mortar bowl. Stone is more effective than glass or wood, as wooden mortars tend to absorb flavours. Stone has the advantage of being heavy and has an excellent rough texture for fine grinding. The pestle and mortar must be made of the same material, or one will grind away the other.

**Potato masher** Although we recommend making potato purées by pushing the cooked potato through a bowl strainer, a potato masher can be very useful when you are in a hurry.

**Scraper** The best are steel with a metal handle for scraping pastry boards clean. Scrapers are also invaluable for scraping up vegetables after chopping.

**Skewers** Metal butchers' skewers are used to hold meat in place. Metal kebab skewers are used for grilling and should be about 40cm/16in long.

**Spaghetti rake** This looks like a giant wooden hairbrush. The spaghetti does not slip off the wooden prongs.

**Spatulas** These come in rubber or wood. The rubber variety is more effective than the wooden type. Choose one with a long wooden handle, making it ideal for getting the last bits of food out of jars and for scraping bowls. A wooden spatula is particularly useful for use on non-stick saucepans.

**Steak bat** This is flat and made of metal or wood.

**Trussing needle** A large metal needle with a large eye for sewing up stuffed meat and poultry.

**Waffle iron** An aluminium or cast-iron toaster or waffle iron for use on an open-flame burner. Check that the 2 halves fit smoothly and that the handles are long and insulated.

**Whisk** A device for beating air in and lumps out of a mixture. But you need the right type for the job in hand.

**Balloon whisk** A simply designed whisk of several loops of wire. The large heavy-duty ones with a wooden handle are the best for whisking in plenty of air.

**Flat whisk** A neat efficient whisk which is ideal for shallow whisking.

**Sauce whisk** A tiny flat whisk which is invaluable for whisking out lumps from sauces and mounting sauces with butter.

**Wire 'spider' or ladle** Used for lifting solids from liquids.

**Wooden spoons** Get a good assortment of sizes – the ones with long handles are sturdier and better beaters than are short-handled ones.

**Wooden spoon with hole** This allows liquid to pass through and prevents spillage during stirring.

**Wooden spoons with square corner** This is particularly useful for getting into the corners of saucepans.

# WINE

### by Richard Harvey M.W.

In Britain we are fortunate in having the widest selection of wines from the most varied outlets in the world. Being only a minor producer of wine, we are less prone to the natural chauvinism that exists in most wine-growing regions and countries. The assiduous research of the buyers for British importers has resulted in an enormous range of wines now being available not only in specialist wine shops but also in most supermarkets and off-licences. So where should you go to buy wine, whether it's for everyday consumption or a special occasion?

## WHERE TO BUY

### SUPERMARKETS

These account for most of the retail wine sales in the UK. They have been responsible for bringing wine to many new consumers, with the result that, today, no matter where you live, there is a wide range of wines available. By virtue of their size, the major supermarket groups have great buying power with the result that they can offer the customer very competitive prices. However, their size is also a disadvantage in that normally they are required to buy from the larger producers, and therefore cannot realistically offer the often more characterful wines made by smaller growers.

The second, and more important, disadvantage to buying in a supermarket is the lack of any personal advice. Many stores have overcome this to a small extent by the use of information slips on the shelves, or on back labels of the bottles, but this is rarely sufficient for the really interested consumer. The supermarkets, therefore, are the place to buy everyday drinking wines at affordable prices at the lower end of the price scale as well as their own-label champagnes and fortified wines. (The best supermarket groups for wine at the moment are Sainsbury's, Tesco and Waitrose.)

### RETAIL CHAINS

These groups have suffered most from the development and rapid growth of wine sales through the supermarkets over the last 20 years. Although having similar buying power to the supermarkets, they have tended to become simply outlets for the major brands of their parent companies (for example, Victoria Wine is owned by Allied Domecq). Although these stores can offer personal advice, it is all too rarely knowledgeable. The notable exceptions are Oddbins, the idiosyncratic chain which, although owned by Seagrams, is allowed to follow its own successful path, and Thresher's and their Wine Rack stores, both of which offer a wide and interesting range of wines, with knowledgeable and enthusiastic staff on hand to advise the customer.

### SPECIALISTS

The specialist wine merchants, with perhaps only one or two outlets, or even working from home, have proliferated over the last 20 years, since the major brewery groups bought up most of the existing wine-merchant businesses in the 1960s. Some of these specialists offer the most comprehensive range of wines available, such as Lay and Wheeler of Colchester, or perhaps specialize in the wines of a particular country or region, such as Yapp's of Mere which sells wines mainly from the Rhône and Loire Valleys of France. What these specialists can offer is expert advice, since often, especially in the case of one-man bands, you will be buying from the person who has actually visited the vineyard and selected the wine. Whilst these specialists often cannot compete in price with the supermarkets at the lower end of the scale, what they can offer is wines, often only available in small quantities, that have a really individual character. These are certainly the places to buy once you have exhausted the supermarkets' more basic ranges.

## MAIL ORDER

This area was for a long time the domain principally of the Wine Society, founded in 1874. It remains the largest operator in this field, but has been joined by many of the specialist merchants mentioned above. This is a good way to buy wine if you do not live near a good wine shop, and many of the wine lists sent out by firms who offer this service are extremely informative. However, the consumer has to bear the cost of delivery, either directly or indirectly, and this can add to the cost significantly for small orders of the less expensive wines. Also, the minimum quantity that you can order is a dozen bottles, although usually these can be mixed.

## AUCTIONS

Wine auctions have also developed considerably during the last 20 years, although they have existed since the nineteenth century. The majority of wine sold at auction, mostly through Christie's and Sotheby's, is fine claret and vintage port, but other smaller auctions around the country also offer a range of everyday wine. It is important to check on the wine and ensure that it has been well stored, and is not simply stock that a wine merchant has been unable to sell. The other disadvantage is that normally lot sizes are in the order of 2 to 5 dozen cases. However, for individual purchasers, or groups of purchasers, who know specifically which fine wine they want to buy, the major London auction houses can be cheaper than a traditional merchant.

## ABROAD

Since January 1993, there have been no limits on personal imports from the European Union. This has opened up a new market for people to bring back as much wine as they wish, either direct from the vineyard, or purchased from shop or supermarket; the mail-order option has been stifled by H.M. Customs & Excise! The result has been a burgeoning of British-owned wine shops in the French Channel ports, which offer a vastly superior selection and service to most French wine shops or supermarkets.

## WHAT TO BUY

Having decided where to buy, the next question is what to buy. Normally, the first criterion in the mind of the consumer is the price. So it is worth examining how the cost of a bottle of wine is determined. In the United Kingdom, we have high rates of excise duty based on the alcoholic strength of the product (and a higher rate for sparkling wines). Because this tax is not related to the cost of the wine, a significantly high percentage of the selling price of less expensive wines is made up by the fixed costs, as the table below shows.

# HOW THE RETAIL PRICE IS MADE UP

| Retail price | £3.00 | £5.00 | £8.00 |
|---|---|---|---|
| Duty and VAT | 50% | 35% | 30% |
| Shipping, distribution and retailing | 30% | 25% | 20% |
| Wine | 20% | 40% | 50% |

It is apparent therefore that the less expensive wines offer the lowest value in terms of wine for money.

## READING THE LABEL

In the absence of any personal advice from an expert, the consumer's buying choice must be based on the information given on the label. This can sometimes be very informative, although only a minimum of information has to be given by law: the country of origin of the wine, the quantity in the bottle (a standard bottle is now 75 centilitres), the alcoholic strength, the name and address of the bottler responsible, and, for wines produced within the EC, the quality of the wine. This latter designation is important as it distin- guishes quality wines produced from a specified

# WINE LABELS

| Country | Description of table wine | Description of regional wine | Description of quality wine | Description of top-quality wine |
|---------|---------------------------|------------------------------|----------------------------|---------------------------------|
| **France** | Vin de Table | Vin de Pays | VDQS (Vin Délimité de Qualité Supérieure) | AOC (Appellation d'Origine Contrôlée) |
| **Italy** | Vino da Tavola | IGT Indicazione Geographica Tipica | DOC (Denominazione di Origine Controllata) | DOCG (Denominazione di Origine Controllata e Garantita) |
| **Germany** | Deutscher Tafelwein | Landwein | QbA (Qualitätswein bestimmter Anbaugebiete) | QmP (Qualitätswein mit Prädikat) |
| **Spain** | Vino de Mesa | Vino de la Tierra | DO (Denominación de Origen) | DOC (Denominación de Origen Calificada) |
| **Portugal** | Vinho de Mesa | Vinho Regional | Indicacaode Proveniencia Regulamentada | Denominacao de Origen |

region from table wines that have no specific geographical designation.

The name and address of the bottler is also a good guide to the quality of the wine within the bottle, and it is worth looking for wines labelled as being bottled by the grower, or at the domaine, estate or château. Apart from giving greater assurance of authenticity, such wines will normally have more individual character than blends put together by large merchant houses or co-operatives. Most French, Italian, German and Spanish wines are named after the region, or village, in which they are produced. The grape variety is sometimes indicated, especially if it is not the norm for the area or, as in Germany, if the same named wine can be produced from different varieties. The quality-wine laws of France and Italy specify the permissible varieties for any particular quality wine.

By contrast, the wines produced in what is called the New World (United States, Australia, New Zealand, South Africa and South America) are usually named after the grape variety, as a producer may make several wines in the same region from a number of different grape varieties, and the concept of the *terroir,* vineyard, is considered of less importance.

## WHAT IS WINE?

Wine is the alcoholic drink resulting from the fermentation of the sugars in the grape by natural yeasts. The alcoholic content of most wines is between 8 per cent and 15 per cent alcohol by volume. The wine may be white, pink (rosé) or red. It may be the produce of only one year (a vintage wine) or a blend of wines produced in different years (a non-vintage wine).

The style of any particular wine is influenced by the following factors: the climatic conditions in which the grapes are grown; soil in which the vine's roots develop; the particular grape variety grown; the methods used to cultivate the vine; the techniques used to make the wine; and any particular variations that occur from year to year. Climatic conditions mean that grapes which receive higher levels of sunshine will have higher degrees of sugar, and thus the resulting wines will be higher in alcohol (generally described as fuller wines).

Conversely, wines produced from grapes grown in cooler climates will be lower in alcohol, higher in acidity, and normally described as being lighter. Cooler climates are generally better suited to the production of white wines, which require a balance of acidity to give them a fresh, crisp style.

White wine is produced only from the juice of the grape, which is usually colourless, so that either white or black grapes can be used. Red wine achieves its colour from the skins remaining in contact with the juice for a period of time. In addition to colour, the skins also give tannin to the wine – a natural acid, which diminishes in time but can often make young red wines appear quite tough and dry. Rosé wines are produced from a very brief contact with the red grape skins.

Sweetness in wines is achieved either by not fully fermenting the grape sugars into alcohol, thereby leaving residual sugar in the wine, or by adding a concentration of unfermented grape juice to the wine prior to bottling, which is the usual practice for German and English wines. Almost all red wines are dry, but white and rosé wines can be dry, medium or sweet. Sparkling wines are produced by inducing a second fermentation in the wine and retaining the carbon dioxide gas that is produced naturally. Champagne, the best-known sparkling wine, can only be produced in the delimited Champagne region of north-eastern France by secondary fermentation in the bottle. Wines made by this method elsewhere will usually show the term *méthode traditionelle* on the label.

Fortified wines are made by the addition of grape spirit either during or after fermentation. This spirit is normally brandy, the distillate of wine. These wines are normally between 15 and 20 per cent alcohol by volume and include: sherry, which can be dry, medium or sweet; port, which is normally sweet (although a little dry white port is made); Madeira; Marsala; and the sweet Muscat wines from the South of France.

# SOME USEFUL TERMS

## France

**Sec** – dry
**Demi-sec** – medium-sweet
**Doux** – sweet
**Moelleux** – sweet
**Brut** – very dry (sparkling wine)
**Blanc de Blancs** – white wine produced only from white grapes
**Supérieur** – normally 0.5° or 1.0° higher in alcohol

## Italy

**Secco** – dry
**Amarone** – dry (literally bitter)
**Abboccato** – medium-sweet
**Amabile** – medium-sweet
**Dolce** – sweet
**Recioto** – wine made from selected (i.e. riper) bunches of grapes
**Riserva** – wine that has undergone a longer period of ageing
**Classico** – wines that come from the best part of the denomination

## Germany

**Kabinett** – grower's selection
**Spätlese** – late-picked grapes with more sugar
**Auslese** – selected bunches of very ripe grapes
**Beerenauslese** – selected berries
**Trockenbeerenauslese** – selected berries with the greatest concentration of sugar
**Trocken** – dry
**Halbtrocken** – medium-dry (most German wines are medium to sweet)

## Spain

**Crianza** – wine that has not been aged in cask
**Riserva** – wine aged in cask
**Gran Riserva** – wine aged in cask for a longer period

## MAJOR WINE-PRODUCING AREAS

### WHITE WINES

FRANCE produces many of the greatest white wines of the world, both dry and sweet. The Loire Valley produces mostly crisp, dry white wines, such as Muscadet and the Sauvignon-based Sancerre and Pouilly-Fumé, with their fresh, almost tart, gooseberry flavour. Burgundy is the home of the classic white wines produced from the Chardonnay grape – from Chablis in the north to Mâcon and Pouilly-Fuissé in the south, with the finest, most concentrated and richest wines coming from Meursault and Puligny-Montrachet in the middle, just south of the town of Beaune. Alsace produces fine, fruity wines, which, because they come mostly from German grape varieties, are often confused with German wines. They are mostly dry with a wonderful, intense, spicy flavour. Bordeaux, although producing some good dry white wine in Entre-Deux-Mers and Graves, is best known for the lusciously sweet dessert wines made in Sauternes and Barsac, from grapes that have achieved a super-rich concentration of sugars.

GERMANY is best known for its slightly sweet, delicate and fruity white wines, the best of which are made from the Riesling grape. They also produce drier styles, called trocken or halbtrocken, but these can appear rather hard and acidic to British tastes.

ITALY produces a vast range of white wines, mostly inexpensive and easy to drink, like Soave, Frascati and Orvieto. More interesting wines can be found in the north of the country, often from French grape varieties.

SPAIN has turned its production mostly from heavy, oaked, alcoholic white wines to fresher, crisper styles.

PORTUGAL is best known for Vinho Verde, traditionally a light, slightly acidic wine, which is usually white and sweetened for the British market.

EASTERN EUROPE Austria and Hungary in particular are making good-quality, inexpensive white wines.

AUSTRALIA makes very good, ripe, buttery wines from Chardonnay grapes, and lighter, more lemony-tasting wines from Semillon.

NEW ZEALAND produces very fine examples of Chardonnay and particularly good Sauvignon, the equal of Sancerre or Pouilly-Fumé.

CALIFORNIA also makes Chardonnay- and Sauvignon-based wines which are generally fuller and fatter than those of New Zealand, due to the hotter climate

CHILE makes very good Sauvignon Blanc and Chardonnay.

SOUTH AFRICA is producing increasing quantities of good-quality Chardonnay, Sauvignon Blanc and Chenia Blanc.

### RED WINES

FRANCE, traditionally recognized as producing the finest red wines in the world, be they Bordeaux or Burgundy, now faces competition from around the world. Claret, the English term for red wines from Bordeaux, is made predominantly from the Cabernet-Sauvignon grape in the Médoc and Graves, and the Merlot grape in St-Emilion and Pomerol. The wines are, at their best, deeply coloured, tannic when young, with the characteristic blackcurrant flavour of the Cabernet. Bordeaux is an enormous wine-producing region which also offers a vast variety of good-value red wines, often under a château label Burgundy, in contrast, produces only a fraction of the quantity of red wines made in Bordeaux, and is generally expensive. The finest wines, from the Pinot Noir grape, produced in well-known villages such as Nuits-St-Georges, Gevrey-Chambertin or Beaune, are softer and generally lighter than those of Bordeaux, with a raspberry fruitiness which matures quicker than the more tannic Cabernet. Beaujolais, France's best-known red wine, has been devalued by the excessive production of wine sold as Nouveau, but true Beaujolais is an easily drinkable, fruity wine from the Gamay grape. The Rhône Valley makes deeply coloured, rich spicy reds from the Syrah grape, such as Hermitage, and, further south, wines like Châteauneuf-du-Pape have a full, peppery alcoholic flavour derived from the Grenache grape. The South of France, in the past the source of vast quantities of unexciting table wines, is now producing many interesting wines, such as Corbières and Minervois and Vin de Pays.

ITALY generally makes better red wines than white, whether traditional ones such as Chianti, Barolo or Barbaresco or new wines made outside the DOC laws and labelled simply as Vino da Tavola. The traditional wines were made to accompany the local cuisine, and can often appear somewhat tannic and astringent to the unaccustomed palate, without the balance of a cuisine based predominantly on olive oil.

SPAIN is best known for Rioja. This, like most Spanish reds, is a full, soft wine, with the pronounced oaky flavour that comes from being aged in oak barrels.

PORTUGAL produces many interesting red wines from local grape varieties.

BULGARIA has become a leader in inexpensive red wines, particularly Cabernet Sauvignon. The better ones have a geographical designation.

AUSTRALIA'S best red wines come from the Cabernet Sauvignon and Shiraz (Syrah) grapes. They are rich, very concentrated wines with masses of ripe fruit flavours.

CALIFORNIA has also produced some very fine wines from the Cabernet Sauvignon, which, with the warmer temperatures, tend to be softer and riper than those from Bordeaux, with less tannin.

SOUTH AFRICA is making fine red wines from Cabernet and Merlot. Those made from Cinsault and Pinotage are usually less interesting.

SOUTH AMERICA, notably Chile and Argentina, is making increasingly good red wines from Cabernet Sauvignon and Merlot.

ROSÉ WINES
Rosé wines are little appreciated in Britain – the most common being slightly sweet. There are, however, some fine dry rosé wines produced in France – the best, such as Tavel, coming from the southern Rhône. Other very good examples are made in the Languedoc, but the wines of the Côtes de Provence are usually priced in relation to their quality.

SPARKLING WINES
Whilst few people would dispute the supremacy of the best producers of champagne, there are also some very good sparkling wines made by secondary fermentation in the bottle (*méthode traditionelle*), which are available at a third of the price of champagne. Saumur and Vouvray in the Loire make fine examples from the local Chenin and Cabernet grapes. Spain produces good wines in the Penedes region south of Barcelona, labelled as Cava. There are also some very good sparkling wines made in Italy, Australia and California, both inexpensive and top-quality.

FORTIFIED WINES
SHERRY denotes a wine that can only come from a delimited area around the town of Jerez in Andalucía, in Spain. Although similar-style wines are made in Cyprus and South Africa, for example, they do not have the classic flavours associated with true sherry. The drier styles, fino, manzanilla and amontillado, make excellent aperitifs, whereas the full, sweeter oloroso-based wines are better after a meal.

PORT is the traditional after-dinner drink. The most common styles, ruby and tawny (relating to their colour), are being overtaken in favour by higher-quality Vintage Character (an older ruby-style), 10-, 20- and 30-year-old tawnies, and vintage and late-bottled vintage ports. This last style is wine from a single year which does not need decanting, an essential requirement for a vintage or crushed port, which has matured for years in the bottle.

MADEIRA AND MARSALA are fortified wines which today are somewhat out of favour as drinks, although appreciated in the kitchen. The sweet, fortified Muscat wines from the South of France, such as Beaumes-de-Venise, are popular as dessert wines in the United Kingdom, although in France they are drunk as aperitifs (as with many sweet wines, and even port).

## STORING WINE

Any wines which are going to be kept for longer than a few weeks must be stored correctly. There is no greater disappointment than holding high expectations of a bottle of wine which has been maturing for years, only to find it virtually undrinkable. Today very few houses have traditional underground cellars, and purpose-built ones are extremely expensive. However, it is not too difficult to replicate ideal conditions in some part of most homes. The following are the most important factors to bear in mind.

TEMPERATURE The ideal temperature for storing wine for any length of time is around 12°C. Equally important, though, is to maintain a constant temperature; far better to keep the wine at a steady 10°C or 14°C than to fluctuate between 8°C and 16°C, ending up at an average 12°C, which is what can happen if the wine is stored in a centrally heated room, where the temperature rises and falls during each twenty-four-hour period. As a general rule, wine stored at a higher temperature will mature sooner than if stored at cooler temperature.

HUMIDITY The ideal humidity for storing wine is 100 per cent; unfortunately this quickly damages the cartons and labels. The best compromise is a relative humidity of around 75–80 per cent at 12°C.

LIGHT Ultra-violet damages wine, therefore it should always be stored in a dark area.

SMELL Wine can become tainted by smell, through the cork, so a clean atmosphere is important.

VIBRATION The maturation of wine can be upset by vibration, so any movement must be avoided if possible.

STORING POSITION Finally, and most importantly, it must be remembered that all wine bottles must be stored on their sides, if they are to be kept for any length of time. This ensures that the wine keeps the cork moist which would otherwise start to dry and contract and allow air into the bottle. The wine would oxidize very quickly, and become undrinkable.

## TASTING WINE

Tasting wine must be viewed as an objective exercise, whereas drinking wine is much more subjective, a question of personal like or dislike. The reason for tasting, rather than just drinking, a wine is to assess its qualities. The taster's aim should be to provide someone who has not tasted a particular wine with as accurate a description as possible. Personal prejudices have to be put aside. Learning to taste is easy; all that is required is a little concentration and an idea of the elements to look for. Tasting wine involves the senses of sight and smell as well as taste.

### THE APPEARANCE OF A WINE
CLARITY

Wine should look clear and bright. If it is cloudy, there is either an intrinsic fault with the wine or it has been badly handled, causing sediment in the bottle to have become mixed with the wine.

Some wines will contain small bubbles of carbon dioxide gas; *pétillance*, as this is known, is encouraged deliberately by some producers, particularly of white wines, to enhance freshness. It is achieved by not allowing all the carbon dioxide produced during fermentation to escape. The best-known example is Muscadet de Sèvre et Maine; if it is labelled 'Sur Lie', it means that the wine has not been racked off the yeast sediment following the alcoholic fermentation, but has been filtered and bottled early, directly from the vat, while some carbon dioxide is still being created.

Sugar-like crystals, often found on the cork or in the bottom of a bottle, are simply tartrates which have been precipitated by cold; they are entirely harmless.

### COLOUR

Colour can give a good indication of the style of wine to be tasted. White wines will vary from pale, watery white to deep, golden yellow, covering all shades in between. The palest-coloured wines usually come from cooler wine-producing regions, such as the Moselle or Loire valleys. Chablis will usually have a pronounced greenish tinge. Many Australian and Californian Chardonnays will be straw-yellow in colour, as a result of the hotter climate in which they are produced. Sweet wines produced from over-ripe, or 'botrytized', grapes will often be a beautiful golden yellow. However, it would be wrong to assume that all sweet wines will be this colour; many sweet German wines, for example, are quite pale. A golden-yellow colour can also be an indication of age; white wines become more yellow as they mature, finally turning brown, which could indicate that they have become oxidized (i.e. they are too old), or, in extreme cases, maderized (i.e. they have taken on the burnt caramel colour of Madeira).

Red wines, when young, will usually be purplish in colour. Light reds, particularly some Italian wines such as Valpolicella and Bardolino, often have a cherry-red colour. Normally, ruby-red is more typical, the deeper-coloured wines again usually indicating warmer climates. As red wines age they take on a more brick-red hue, finally turning tawny and brown. Unlike white wines, these tawny-coloured reds may not be completely oxidized; long ageing in cask prior to bottling is traditional for many Italian wines, and the Pinot Noir grape of Burgundy produces wines which take on an orangey-brown colour much sooner than, for instance, Cabernet Sauvignon-based wines.

### THE BOUQUET OR SMELL OF A WINE

It is possible to obtain a reasonably good indication of a wine's style from its smell. Any faults not apparent on sight will also be noticeable in the smell. The most common fault, other than an oxidized wine, will be one that is corked. This is the result of a rotten cork, which may have been infected with cork weevil, as a result of a failure in the sterilization process which all wine corks undergo. The wine will smell musty and woody, although there may be no visual indication on the cork itself. A fault which is becoming less and less common, thankfully, is the smell of sulphur, caused by excessive use of sulphur dioxide as an anti-oxidant and anti-yeast agent during the wine-making process.

To gain the most from a wine's bouquet, it is essential to swirl the wine around the glass, which will help release the aromas. Many of the primary elements of the wine – fruit flavours, sweetness, acidity and alcohol – may be noticed. Certain grape varieties have very distinctive aromas – Cabernet Sauvignon of blackcurrants, Sauvignon Blanc of gooseberries or elderflowers. Sweetness on the nose may not necessarily indicate residual sugar in the wine, as it is not a volatile element. Acidity and alcohol can often be apparent.

### TERMS DESCRIBING THE BOUQUET OF A WINE

**Fruity** Attractive fruit quality, as in blackcurrants (Cabernet Sauvignon) or gooseberries (Sauvignon Blanc)

**Grapey** Often produced by wines with some residual sugar

**Floral** Flowery aromas such as elderflower (Sauvignon Blanc) or roses (Gewürztraminer)

**Grassy** Sappy, green smell

**Stalky** Green, woody (Cabernet Franc)

**Vegetal** Mature Pinot Noir

**Dumb** or **closed** Little smell, often from a young or undeveloped wine

**Corked** See above

**Oxidized** See above

**Acetic** Vinegar smell from excess volatile acidity

**Sulphury** See above

### THE TASTE OF WINE

Taste should be a confirmation and development of sight and smell. When tasting wine it is important to swirl it well around the mouth. The human tongue picks up sweetness at the tip and acidity at the back. It also helps to draw in air through the teeth to aerate the wine and thereby appreciate its development.

### THE PRIMARY ELEMENTS OF TASTE

**Sweetness** Often detected first

**Acidity** Can carry right through

**Alcohol** Constitutes part of the body of a wine: a light wine may still be high in alcohol, although a full-bodied wine is rarely low in alcohol

**Fruit** This can be carried through from the nose but may be more or less intense on the palate

**Tannin** Tannic acid is found in young red wines, as a result of the skin maceration required to obtain colour. It will leave a dry, slightly bitter taste in the mouth, although the same effect can be the result of wine which has been allowed to age too long, and has lost its fruit and started to dry out.

A wine in which all these elements are in balance will appear complete, although it must be remembered that a young red wine may have noticeably high levels of tannin until it reaches maturity.

TERMS DESCRIBING THE TASTE OF A WINE

SWEETNESS

**Dry** Wine with all its grape sugars fermented out

**Sweet** Wine containing residual grape sugars

ACIDITY

**Fresh, crisp, green, sharp, tart** Noticeable or excessive acidity

**Flat, flabby** Lack of acidity

ALCOHOL

**Body** A light, medium or full-bodied wine is determined by the amount of alcohol and extract

**Extract** The soluble solids in a wine

**Thin** Wine with little extract or body

**Big** Wine with plenty of extract and alcohol

**Heavy** Wine with too much extract and alcohol

FRUIT

**Ripe** Wine made from mature grapes

**Rich** Wine full of fruit, alcohol and extract

**Nutty** Often the taste of full, dry white wines

**Spicy** Often found in wines from the Syrah grape

**Peppery** Often found in wines from the Grenache grape

**Neutral** Bland, little fruit flavour

**Mouldy, musty, woody** 'Off' flavours – perhaps corked wine

TANNIN

**Hard, tough** Excess of tannin

**Round, smooth, soft, supple** Little tannin

Finally, it is important to appreciate the length of time the taste remains after swallowing or spitting out the wine. This is known as the after-taste or finish and its length is a good indicator of quality – a wine can be described as having good length. When little taste remains after swallowing, a wine is described as short.

## SERVING WINE

The enjoyment of wine is greatly enhanced if it is served correctly. This requires a little forethought, particularly as far as serving temperature is concerned.

TEMPERATURE

White and rosé wines are best served around 7°C. The best way to chill wine is to put the bottle into a refrigerator for a couple of hours. If the wine is going to be drunk sooner, then 15 minutes in a bucket of ice and water, or in a freezer, will achieve the same result. However, it is important to remember that too cold a temperature will deaden the bouquet and flavour of a wine.

Sparkling wines should be served well chilled, 5–7°C; the low temperature helps to reduce the pressure of carbon dioxide gas in the bottle.

Light fortified wines, such as pale dry, fino or manzanilla sherry should also be served well chilled. It is also not uncommon to serve light tawny port chilled; otherwise, fortified wines are best served at ambient room temperature.

Red wines are traditionally served at what is called 'room' temperature. This term originated before central heating, and nowadays there is a tendency to serve red wine too warm. But there is also a fashion for serving some light red wines, particularly those from the Loire Valley, chilled. Certainly, lighter styles such as these, or Beaujolais, or Valpolicella and Bardolino from Italy, are best served cool, around 12°C. Fuller-bodied red wines are best served warmer, around 16°C. It is dangerous to try to raise a red wine's temperature quickly; if the wine is 'cooked' or 'boiled' it will be completely spoilt. If a red wine cannot be allowed to rise to ambient room temperature naturally and slowly, it can be put in a bucket of warm, not hot water, but it should never be put under boiling water, in an oven or on a radiator.

OPENING

Many red wines benefit from being opened some time before serving. As a general rule, the younger and more full-bodied the wine, the longer it will need to breathe. Old wines should only be opened up to an hour before drinking, as they can deteriorate very quickly once they have come in contact with air. Otherwise a couple of hours is generally sufficient.

CORKSCREWS

The best corkscrew for opening bottles of wine will have a broad wide spiral which ensures good purchase on the cork, whereas a thick screw can pull out a hole through the middle of a cork.

DECANTING

Red wines which have been made to mature in the bottle will begin to throw a sediment after a number of years. It is therefore always safer to decant a wine more than 10 years old, in order to separate the wine from the deposit in the bottle. Decanting also helps to aerate a wine as it is being poured, and so also serves to soften full-bodied, young red wines.

GLASSES

The enjoyment of any wine is enhanced by serving it in good glasses. The best glasses for wine are the simplest, made of clear, thin glass, narrower at the lip than in the bowl to concentrate the bouquet, and with a stem long enough to keep the hand away from the bowl. Glasses, especially for red wine, should be generous in size; they should be no more than two-thirds filled to allow space for the bouquet to develop as the wine is swirled around the glass. Finally, it is important to ensure that glasses are clean and not carrying any smell of detergent.

KEEPING OPENED WINE

Once a wine has been opened the exposure to the air means that it will start to oxidize and deteriorate. The length of time any opened wine can be kept depends not only on the wine itself, but also on the amount left in the bottle in proportion to the air. A bottle with only one glassful taken from it will last for 3 or 4 days, whereas a bottle with one glassful remaining in it may not be drinkable the following day. White wines which have been opened should always be kept in the refrigerator, and red wines keep better in a cool place. Wines made from certain grape varieties, notably Pinot Noir and Gamay, do not really keep at all well, whereas others, such as Nebbiolo, can actually improve the day after being opened.

Various products claim to maintain freshness in an opened bottle of wine; the best system is an inert gas spray which, being heavier than air, forms a blanket on top of the wine.

# WINE AND FOOD

Most wines taste different when tasted on their own or drunk with food. Different elements in each react with each other. Traditionally, matching wine and food had little to do with anything other than geographical association. For centuries, the purpose of wine production was simply to provide wine for meals. While different areas discovered that certain grape varieties and styles were better suited to their climate and soil than others, wines were primarily being made to suit the local foods.

The increasing consumption of wine without food has contributed to the popularity of New World wines with their ripe, sweet fruit flavours and soft tannins. A lot of these wines have a variety of flavours which often conflict with the different flavours in many dishes; they are at their best accompanying simple roast or grilled foods. Many Italian red wines, on the other hand, can taste rather dry and astringent on their own, but soften dramatically when drunk with food, especially a cuisine based on olive oil. German wines, generally light in body and slightly sweet, are best drunk on their own.

There are two specific criteria for matching wine with food. First, the two must complement each other: a strong-tasting food will kill a light wine, just as a rich, full-bodied wine will overwhelm light food. Muscadet and Chablis are perfect with shellfish but would be killed by game. Equally important is contrast. A wine with good acidity and dryness can be a perfect match for oily food – Sancerre, or New Zealand Sauvignon Blanc, with smoked salmon, for example – white claret, with its dry tannins, is the perfect complement for the fattiness of lamb.

Certain combinations which have developed over the years can seem strange. The most striking is drinking Sauternes with foie gras; one of the richest foods accompanied by rich, strong, sweet white wine. An equally good match would be a strong, dry, spicy white from Alsace.

When selecting wine to match a specific dish, it is important to remember that it is not just a question of choosing the wine to match the particular type of meat or fish; the sauce in which they are cooked can have greater effect on the wine. Cream- or butter-based sauces demand wines with acidity rather than alcohol to help cut the richness; Sauvignon grape-based wines, Bourgogne Aligote or Muscadet for white wines; cool-climate red wines, such as those from the Loire Valley, Beaujolais, or even light Burgundy. Dishes rich in oil need dry, full-bodied wines, such as whites or rosés from southern France, or Bordeaux or Piedmontese red wines. Hot, spicy foods will kill just about any wine, and are best accompanied by water or beer.

One of the hardest ingredients with which to match wine is vinegar, its natural antithesis. Any dish with a dressing containing vinegar will be detrimental to wine. The best solution for salad dishes is to serve a full-bodied, dry white wine with low acidity. Chocolate is also difficult, but not impossible – a fortified Muscat, such as Beaumes de Venise with its orangey sweetness, can make a good match, as can rich Australian Liqueur Muscat, or Malaga from Spain.

Strong, dry cheeses are usually best eaten with red wine, but this is not the ideal accompaniment to all cheese. Creamy blue cheeses can often be delicious with sweet white wine. Port may be fine for Stilton, but only if it is drunk with it, not poured into it.

If you are serving different wines during a meal, and especially if they are its focal point, it is important to serve them in the right order:

Dry before sweet
Light before full-bodied
Young before old

| FOOD | STYLE OF WINE | SUGGESTION |
| --- | --- | --- |
| **FISH DISHES** | | |
| Terrine | Light dry wine | Chablis |
| Soups | | Sancerre/Pouilly |
| Mayonnaise | Crisp dry white | Fumé |
| Buttery sauce | | Burgundy |
| Smoked | | |
| Chinese-style | Spicy white | Alsace |
| Barbecued | | Tokay/Riesling |
| **CHICKEN DISHES** | | |
| Mayonnaise | Clean, dry white | Soave |
| Buttery sauce | | |
| Chinese-style | Full white | Mâcon |
| Roast | Light, fruity red | Beaujolais |
| Casseroled | | |
| Barbecued/Indian/ Tandoori | Fuller red | Côtes du Rhône |
| **VEAL** | | |
| Buttery sauce | Light, fruity red | Valpolicella |
| Roast | | |
| Casserole | Fuller red | Chianti Classico |
| **PORK** | | |
| Buttery sauce | | Beaujolais |
| Spicy/ | Light red | Villages |
| Chinese style | | |
| Stewed/Cassoulet | Full red | Corbières |

| | | |
|---|---|---|
| Roast<br>Barbecued | Medium red | Burgundy |

**LAMB**

| | | |
|---|---|---|
| With Hollandaise | Light to medium red | Chinon/Bourgueil |
| Stewed<br>Roast | Fuller red | Claret/Rioja |
| Spiced/curried/<br>barbecued | Spicy red | Crozes-Hermitage |

**BEEF**

| | | |
|---|---|---|
| With Hollandaise | Medium red | Burgundy |
| Casserole<br>Roast | Fuller red | Rhône/Châteauneuf du Pape |
| Spiced/<br>barbecued | Full, spicy red | Australian Shiraz<br>Australian/CalifornianCabernet |

**VENISON**

| | | |
|---|---|---|
| | Rich red | Australian Shiraz |

**DUCK**

| | | |
|---|---|---|
| | Medium red | Burgundy |

**GAME BIRDS**

| | | |
|---|---|---|
| | Full red | Claret |

**COLD COLLATIONS/ SALMIS**

| | | |
|---|---|---|
| | Rosé or light red | Tavel Rosé<br>Valpolicella |

**PATÉS/TERRINES**

| | | |
|---|---|---|
| | Spicy red | Côtes du Rhône |

**FOIE GRAS**

| | | |
|---|---|---|
| | Sweet wine | Sauternes |

**SOUPS**

| | | |
|---|---|---|
| Light | Fortified | Dry sherry/Madeira |
| Creamy | Dry white | Burgundy |

**VEGETABLE DISHES**

| | | |
|---|---|---|
| | Light dry wine | Soave |

**CHEESE**

| | | |
|---|---|---|
| Soufflé | | Alsace Tokay |
| Soft, creamy<br>Blue | Light, sweet wine | Loire (Coteaux du Layon) |
| Hard | Medium red | Burgundy |

**PUDDINGS**

| | | |
|---|---|---|
| Plain fruit | Slightly sweet wine | German Spätlese/Auslese |
| Light fruit puddings | Sweet white | Coteaux du Layon |
| Ice creams/sorbets | | Italian Moscato |
| Rich creamy puddings | Rich, sweet, white | Sauternes |
| | | Champagne |
| Hot soufflés | Sweet | |
| Chocolate puddings | Fortified | Muscat de Beaumes de Venise |
| | | Australian Liqueur |
| | | Muscat |

| WINE STYLE | STYLE OF FOOD |
|---|---|
| Very dry white (Muscadet, Sauvignon grape wines, Chablis) | Shellfish, salmon, oily fish |
| Dry white (Soave, Frascati, Chardonnay wines, Burgundy) | White fish |
| Spicy dry white (Alsace, some dry German and English wines) | Smoked fish |
| Medium dry white (Moselle, Vouvray, VinhoVerde) | Chicken |
| Medium sweet white (German Spätlese/Auslese, Italian Moscato) | Soft, creamy cheese<br>Fruit and fruit puddings |
| Sweet white (Sauternes, Barsac, Muscat de Beaumes de Venise) | Foie gras<br>Rich puddings<br>Chocolate puddings |
| Rosé (Tavel, Provence) | Bouillabaisse<br>Cold meats |
| Light red (Beaujolais, Valpolicella) | Chicken, veal<br>Pork |
| Soft red (Burgundy) | Pork, duck |
| Medium red (Claret, Côtes du Rhône, Chianti, Rioja) | Lamb<br>Game birds |
| Full red (Châteauneuf du Pape, Cabernet-Sauvignon wines) | Beef |
| Very full red (Crozes-Hermitage, Barolo, Australian Shiraz) | Rich stews<br>Venison |

# A DICTIONARY OF TASTING TERMS

## APPEARANCE

**Bright** All wines in sound condition should be bright.

**Colour** White wines can be:

**Pale** Usually indicating they come from a cool climate.

**Straw-yellow** A deeper colour from a hot climate.

**Green** Usually indicates a young wine.

**Purple** The colour of young red wine, turning **ruby or cherry red** before becoming **brick red or tawny** with age.

**Deep-coloured** Wines that usually come from hot climates.

## SMELL

**Bouquet** The particular smell of a wine.

**Fruity** Attractive fruit quality, not necessarily:

**Grapey** Aroma produced by certain grape varieties.

**Grassy** Green, woody smell often found in young wine.

**Dumb** or **Closed** Little smell, usually from a young or undeveloped wine.

**Corked** Distinct smell of cork – the result of a diseased cork leading to a wine becoming:

**Oxidized** . . . or worse.

**Maderized** White wine turned brown in colour.

**Acetic/vinegary** Excess volatile acidity.

**Sulphury** Excess of sulphur used in the wine's production.

## TASTE

**Acidity** Natural component of wine. High-acid wines are described as **crisp, green, sharp, tart.** Low-acid wines taste **flat** or **flabby** and lack **freshness.**

**Alcohol** Indicated by the weight of a wine. Low-alcohol wines tend to be **light.**

**Extract** The soluble solids in a wine. Wines with plenty of extract and alcohol are described as having plenty of **body**, or as being **big** or **full-bodied** wines. These tend to come from hot climates and will usually have more alcohol and extract than those from cool climates.

**Heavy** Wine with too much alcohol and extract.

**Thin** Wine with little extract or flavour.

**Flavour** The particular taste of a wine. Useful terms in this area are:

**Fruity** Not necessarily grape tastes.

**Nutty** Found in full, dry white wines.

**Peppery** Raw taste often found in young red wine, but also from certain grape varieties.

**Spicy** Rich taste found in certain grape varieties.

**Ripe** Wine made from mature grapes – or a wine ready to drink.

**Rich** Full fruit flavour with alcohol and extract, not necessarily sweet.

**Round** No rough edges.

**Smooth** No rough edges.

**Soft** No rough edges.

**Supple** No rough edges.

**Neutral** Bland flavour.

**Oxidized** Flat, stale taste – the result of the wine's exposure to air.

**Mouldy** Off flavour.

**Musty** Off flavour.

**Woody** Off flavour.

**Dry** Wine with all grape sugars fermented out.

**Sweet** Wine with high sugar content.

**Tannin** Tannic acid derived from grape skins during fermentation therefore found only in young red wines. Leaves dry taste in mouth and around teeth. Wine with an excess of tannin is described as **hard or tough.**

**Finish** The end-taste of a wine. The time it lasts is described as **length.**

# TRADITIONAL
# FIRST COURSES

# CAVIAR

*30g/1oz per person*

Leave the caviar in its pot. Chill, and stand on a napkin. Serve 1 teaspoon on each individual plate, and offer, from another platter, wedges of lemon, chopped hardboiled egg white and sieved yolk (in separate piles), chopped fresh parsley and very finely chopped raw onions. Serve with hot toast.

# BROWN SHRIMPS

*150ml/¼ pint per person*

Serve the shrimps in piles, unpeeled, on individual plates with hot bread, good butter, lemon wedges and salt and freshly ground pepper. The guests peel their own shrimps. Provide finger bowls.

# POTTED SHRIMPS

*1 small pot per person*

Warm the pots gently in a low oven, and when the butter is just melted, or at least soft, turn out on to individual plates. Offer toast (no butter) and lemon wedges separately, and a knife and fork to eat them with. This is the traditional way of serving shrimps, but today they are sometimes turned out cold and eaten, like pâté, on rather than with the toast. They are better just warm, however. Do not rechill them once melted.

# GULL'S EGGS

*2 per person*

Gull's eggs are normally sold ready-cooked. Serve in a basket lined with lettuce leaves or a napkin, and offer sea or rock salt, celery salt or oriental salt, freshly ground black pepper and cayenne pepper separately. Serve brown bread and butter. The guests peel the eggs and eat them with their fingers.

NOTE: Plover's and quail's eggs may be served in the same way. Plover's eggs (4 per person): boil for 6 minutes. Quail's eggs (6 per person): boil for 2 minutes.

# OYSTERS

*9 or 12 per person*

Serve 6 each if there is a big meal to come, but oyster lovers like a lot! Order the oysters and ask for them to be opened only when you collect them, or as late as possible. Keep refrigerated until serving. If the fishmonger has not loosened the oysters from the bottom shell, do so with a sharp knife. Check that there are no bits of shell or grit on the saucer-shaped bottom shells, but leave any sea water or juices with them. Discard the top shells. Put the oysters on to oyster plates, or failing them, on to dinner plates covered by a napkin to keep them from tipping or rolling. Hand Tabasco sauce, or chilli pepper, freshly ground black pepper, white pepper, wedges of lemon and vinegar separately, and serve with brown bread and butter. The diner eats the oysters with a fork, and drinks the juice from the shell as from a cup.

# OURSINS (SEA URCHINS)

*3 per person*

Serve exactly as oysters, with the same accompaniments, but with a teaspoon for the guest to extract the flesh. The fishmonger cuts off the top of the shell, like the top of a boiled egg.

# SMOKED SALMON

*85g/3oz per person*

Arrange slices in a single layer on dinner plates. Hand lemon wedges or halves and brown bread and butter separately. To slice smoked salmon: use a salmon or ham knife. Put the fish skin-side down on a board. Slice the top thin layer of smoked skin-like flesh off, then feel for the row of lateral bones whose tips will be sticking like pins straight up in a row between the 2 fillets of flesh, in a line running the length of the fish. Pull them out, one by one, with tweezers or pliers. Then slice the flesh horizontally in paper-thin pieces. Keep covered or painted with salad oil to prevent drying out.

# SMOKED TROUT

*1 fish per person*

Use kitchen scissors to cut the smoked skin carefully round the neck and tail before loosening it with the fingers and peeling it off, leaving head and tail intact. Serve on individual plates with lemon wedges, handing brown bread and butter and horseradish sauce separately.

# SMOKED MACKEREL

*½ fish per person*

Peel the fish and carefully lift the fillets off the backbone. There will be 4 of them. Arrange 2 per person on individual plates with lemon wedges and hand mustard, mayonnaise or horseradish sauce separately. Serve with brown bread and butter.

# ASPARAGUS

*6 fat or 12 thin spears per person*

Cut off the woody ends. Peel the fibrous stalks. Wash well. Tie in bundles. Boil in an asparagus cooker (the stalks stand in the water, the tips cook in the steam), or simmer lying down in salted water in a frying pan, until the stalk is tender halfway down. Drain well. Serve from a platter lined with a napkin to absorb the moisture. Hand melted clarified butter, hollandaise or beurre blanc separately if hot; vinaigrette if cold.

# GLOBE ARTICHOKES

*1 per person*

Twist and pull the stalk off the artichoke very close to the base so that it will stand without rolling. Trim the tips of the bottom few rows of leaves off straight if they are hard or cracked and if the tip spines are prickly. Leave the smaller higher leaves. Boil for 45 minutes in salted water with a cut-up lemon and 1 tablespoon oil. When an inner leaf will pull out easily, drain the artichokes upside down. When cool enough to handle, prise open the middle leaves and lift out the central cluster of tiny leaves. Using a teaspoon, scrape out the fibrous choke and discard it. Serve the artichokes on individual plates on a folded napkin. Give each guest a small pot of clarified melted butter if the artichokes are hot, or vinaigrette dressing if cold. The guest pulls the leaves off the flowerhead, dips the flesh end into the butter or sauce, eats the softer part with his fingers and discards the leaves.

# SOUPS

# GAZPACHO I

This recipe assumes that the cook has a blender.

SERVES 6
*900g/2lb fresh, very ripe tomatoes, peeled*
*1 large mild Spanish onion*
*2 red peppers*
*1 small cucumber*
*1 thick slice of white bread, crust removed*
*1 egg yolk*
*2 large cloves of garlic*
*6 tablespoons olive oil*
*1 tablespoon tarragon vinegar*
*450g/1lb canned tomatoes*
*1 tablespoon tomato purée*
*freshly ground black pepper*
*plenty of salt (preferably sea salt)*

To serve
*a large bowl of croûtons (see page 686)*

**1.** Chop or dice finely a small amount of the fresh tomato, onion, red pepper and cucumber and put into separate small bowls for garnish. Roughly chop the remaining vegetables to prepare them for the blender.
**2.** Put the bread, egg yolk and garlic into the blender. Turn it on and add the oil in a thin steady stream while the motor is running. You should end up with a thick, mayonnaise-like emulsion.
**3.** Add the vinegar and then gradually add all the soup ingredients in batches and blend until smooth.
**4.** Sieve the soup to remove the tomato seeds and check for seasoning.

NOTES: Gazpacho should be served icy cold with the small bowls of chopped vegetables and fried croûtons handed separately. Sometimes crushed ice is added to the soup at the last minute.

If you prefer a thinner soup, dilute it with iced water or tomato juice.

 *CRISP DRY WHITE*

# GAZPACHO II

This recipe by Christopher Buey is from *The Taste of Health* and is lower in fat than the previous recipe.

SERVES 4
*ice cubes*
*285g/10oz tomatoes*
*½ cucumber*
*½ green pepper*
*½ red pepper*
*1 medium onion*
*570ml/1 pint canned or fresh tomato juice*
*1 clove of garlic*
*2 tablespoons tarragon vinegar*
*salt and freshly ground black pepper*
*2 tablespoons olive oil*

To garnish
*1 tablespoon chopped fresh herbs, such as parsley, chervil, tarragon, chives*

**1.** Cut all the vegetables into chunks. Set aside a little of each for the garnish.
**2.** Place half the tomato juice in a food processor or blender with the vegetables and garlic, and liquidize for 2–3 minutes. Gradually add the remaining tomato juice, the vinegar, salt and pepper and finish with the olive oil.
**3.** Add the ice cubes to the soup and refrigerate for 10 minutes.
**4.** Remove the ice cubes and serve the soup garnished with the reserved chopped raw vegetables and herbs.

 *CALIFORNIAN CHARDONNAY*

# CUCUMBER AND MELON GAZPACHO

SERVES 6
*2 large cucumbers, peeled and deseeded*
*1 medium Galia melon, peeled and deseeded*
*1 bunch of rocket*
*3 sprigs of fresh dill*
*3 sprigs of fresh mint*

2 tablespoons tarragon vinegar
1 small clove of garlic, peeled
1 small green chilli, deseeded
290ml/½ pint carrot juice or mixed vegetable juice
150ml/¼ pint Greek yoghurt
6 tablespoons olive oil
salt and freshly ground black pepper

To garnish
ice, crushed sprigs of fresh dill

**1.** Finely dice half 1 cucumber and 1 slice of melon and reserve.
**2.** Chop the remaining cucumber and melon roughly and put into a blender with the rocket, dill, mint, vinegar, garlic, chilli and half the carrot or mixed vegetable juice. Liquidize to a smooth paste and gradually blend in the remaining juice, yoghurt and oil. Season to taste with salt and pepper. Refrigerate until cold.
**3.** To serve: pour into 6 individual soup bowls and garnish with the reserved cucumber and melon, crushed ice cubes and sprigs of dill.

 *FINO SHERRY*

# LEBANESE CUCUMBER AND YOGHURT SOUP

SERVES 4
1 large cucumber, peeled
290ml/½ pint single cream
140g/5fl oz plain yoghurt
2 tablespoons tarragon vinegar
1 tablespoon chopped fresh mint
salt and freshly ground white pepper

**1.** Grate the cucumber coarsely.
**2.** Stir in the remaining ingredients and season to taste with salt and pepper.
**3.** Chill in the refrigerator for 2 hours before serving.

NOTE: This soup may be garnished with cold croûtons; chopped fresh chives; a spoonful of soured cream added just before serving; chopped gherkins; a few pink shrimps. It is also good flavoured with garlic.

 *WHITE BURGUNDY*

# CHILLED CREAM CHEESE SOUP

SERVES 4
1 × 340g/12oz can of jellied consommé
170g/6oz mild cream cheese
1 teaspoon curry powder
1 squeeze of lemon juice

**1.** Reserve 1 cupful of consommé for the top.
**2.** In a food processor or blender, liquidize the remaining consommé with the cheese, curry powder and lemon juice. Pour into cocotte dishes.
**3.** Chill in the refrigerator until set.
**4.** Spoon over the remaining consommé (which should be cool, on the point of setting) and chill again until ready to serve.

NOTE: Some canned consommé will not set. Test it by chilling for 1 hour. If the soup is still liquid, melt 1 teaspoon powdered gelatine in the consommé and allow to cool. Consommé with 'serve hot' on the label is generally non-setting.

 *WHITE BURGUNDY*

# ICED VICHYSSOISE SOUP

SERVES 4
55g/2oz butter
1 medium onion, finely chopped
the white part of 3 large or 5 small leeks, chopped
110g/4oz potatoes, peeled and sliced
salt and freshly ground white pepper
290ml/½ pint white stock (see page 213)
290ml/½ pint creamy milk
2 tablespoons single cream
chopped fresh chives

**1.** Melt the butter in a heavy saucepan and add the onion and leek.
**2.** Sweat the vegetables for 15 minutes or so. They must soften without crisping or browning.
**3.** Add the potatoes, salt and pepper and the stock. Simmer until the potatoes are soft.
**4.** Liquidize the soup in a food processor or blender and push it through a sieve.

5. Add the milk and cream. (Check the consistency before adding all the milk.)
6. Check the seasoning. Chill in the refrigerator.
7. Add the chives just before serving, and perhaps an extra swirl of cream.

NOTE: The soup is good hot, too. Reheat without boiling.

 *WHITE BURGUNDY*

# COLD CUCUMBER SOUP

SERVES 4
*2 cucumbers, peeled and sliced*
*290ml/½ pint water*
*salt and freshly ground white pepper*
*30g/1oz plain flour*
*570ml/1 pint white stock (see page 243)*
*1 bay leaf*
*2 cloves*
*150ml/¼ pint soured cream*
*1 tablespoon chopped fresh dill*
*finely grated zest of 1 lemon*

1. Cook the cucumber in the water until tender. Liquidize in a blender or food processor or push through a sieve and add salt and pepper to taste.
2. Mix the flour with 4 tablespoons of the stock. Heat the remaining stock.
3. Add a little of the hot stock to the flour and stock mixture and return this to the pan. Stir until the liquid boils and thickens.
4. Add the cucumber purée, bay leaf and cloves. Bring slowly to the boil, then simmer for 2 minutes. Strain into a bowl.
5. Allow to cool. Stir in the soured cream, dill and lemon zest. Chill in the refrigerator before serving.

 *MUSCADET/SAUVIGNON*

# SIMPLE VEGETABLE SOUP

SERVES 8
*45g/1½oz butter*
*225g/8oz onions, chopped*
*450g/1lb carrots, chopped*
*110g/4oz celery, chopped*
*225g/8oz potatoes, chopped*
*860ml/1½ pints water*
*salt and freshly ground black pepper*
*425ml/¾ pint milk*

1. Melt the butter in a large heavy pan with 2 tablespoons water. Add the onions, carrots and celery, stir and cover with a lid. Cook over a slow heat until soft but not coloured, stirring occasionally (about 45 minutes).
2. Add the potatoes and water. Season with salt and pepper and simmer, without a lid, for 15 minutes.
3. Liquidize the soup in a food processor or blender, with the milk, and pass through a sieve.
4. Pour into the rinsed-out pan. Season to taste and add water if the soup is too thick. Reheat carefully.

 *DRY WHITE/LIGHT RED*

# CREAMY VEGETABLE SOUP

SERVES 4
*30g/1oz butter*
*225g/8oz onions, very thinly sliced*
*225g/8oz leeks, thinly sliced*
*1 small head of celery, finely sliced*
*1 large potato, peeled and thinly sliced*
*570ml/1 pint white stock (see page 243)*
*salt and freshly ground white pepper*
*nutmeg, freshly grated*
*290ml/½ pint creamy milk*
*1 tablespoon single cream*
*1 tablespoon port (optional, but very good)*

1. Melt the butter in a very large, heavy saucepan. Add the onions, leeks and celery and sweat with the lid on, stirring occasionally, until the whole

mass is soft and cooked (about 45 minutes).

**2.** Add the potatoes and stock, bring to the boil, stirring, and boil for 1 minute. Add the salt, pepper and nutmeg to taste and simmer gently for 20 minutes.

**3.** Liquidize the soup in a blender or food processor and pass through a sieve.

**4.** Add the milk, reheat, and add the cream and port. Use white port if you would prefer the soup not to go faintly pink.

NOTE: Do not add all the milk if the soup looks too thin.

 *WHITE LOIRE/SAUVIGNON*

# ARTICHOKE SOUP

SERVES 4
*55g/2oz butter*
*1 medium onion, sliced*
*675g/1½lb Jerusalem artichokes*
*570ml/1 pint milk, scalded*
*570ml/1 pint water*
*salt and freshly ground white pepper*

**1.** Melt the butter in a saucepan and gently cook the onion in it until soft but not coloured.

**2.** Peel the artichokes and leave in a bowl of cold acidulated water (water with lemon juice or vinegar added) to prevent discoloration.

**3.** Slice the artichokes and add to the pan. Continue cooking, covered, for about 10 minutes, giving an occasional stir.

**4.** Add the milk and water, season well with salt and pepper and simmer for a further 20 minutes. Do not allow it to boil, or it will curdle.

**5.** Liquidize in a food processor or blender and push through a sieve. Check for seasoning – this soup needs plenty of salt and pepper.

 *LIGHT WHITE ALSACE*

# CHESTNUT SOUP

SERVES 4
*1 onion, finely chopped*
*1 carrot, finely chopped*
*30g/1oz butter*
*675g/1½lb fresh chestnuts, peeled*
*1 bouquet garni (see page 19)*
*860ml–1 litre/1½ pints white stock (see page 243)*
*150ml/¼ pint single cream*
*salt and freshly ground black pepper*

To garnish
*1 Cox's apple, diced*
*15g/½oz butter*
*1 teaspoon caster sugar*
*finely chopped fresh parsley*

**1.** Sweat the onion and carrot in the butter until tender. Add the chestnuts and sweat for a further 5 minutes.

**2.** Add the bouquet garni and stock. Bring up to the boil, then simmer for 20–30 minutes or until the chestnuts are tender.

**3.** Liquidize the soup and strain into a clean saucepan. Add the cream, bring up to scalding point (just below the boil) and season to taste with salt and pepper.

**4.** Meanwhile, prepare the garnish: fry the apple in the butter, add the sugar and let the apple caramelize. Add the parsley.

**5.** Tip the soup into a warmed soup tureen and scatter with the apple garnish.

NOTE: If fresh chestnuts are not available use 1 large can whole, peeled chestnuts.

 *WHITE ALSACE OR LIGHT RED*

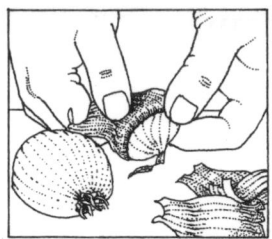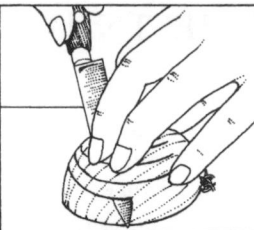

*Peel onion from pointed end. Cut horizontal slices*

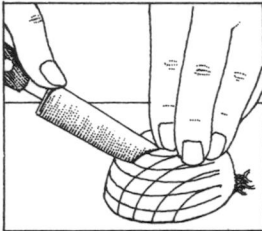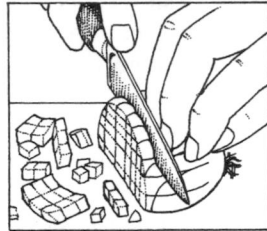

*Cut vertical slices, leaving root intact*

# PEA SOUP

SERVES 4

*15g/½oz butter*
*1 onion, finely chopped (see above)*
*1 potato, peeled and diced*
*340g/12oz frozen peas*
*1 litre/2 pints ham stock (see page 243) or water*
*salt and freshly ground black pepper*
*4 tablespoons single cream*

**1.** Put the butter into a large, heavy saucepan, melt over a low heat and add the onion and potato. Cover with a piece of greased greaseproof paper and leave to sweat for 10 minutes.
**2.** Add the peas, stock or water, salt and pepper. Bring to the boil, then simmer slowly for 15 minutes.
**3.** Remove the soup from the heat, liquidize it very well in a food processor or blender, then pass it through a sieve into a clean saucepan.
**4.** Reheat for 1–2 minutes, add the cream and check the seasoning.

 *ROSÉ/LIGHT RED*

# LETTUCE AND DILL SOUP

SERVES 4–6

*3 lettuces, washed*
*30g/1oz butter*
*225g/8oz onion, very thinly sliced*
*400g/14oz potatoes, peeled and thinly sliced*
*1 litre/2 pints white stock (see page 243)*
*salt, freshly ground white pepper and freshly grated nutmeg*
*1 bunch of fresh dill, roughly chopped*
*2 tablespoons single cream*

**1.** Shred the lettuces finely. Melt the butter in a large, heavy saucepan and add the onion and potato. Cover and sweat for 10 minutes.
**2.** Add the stock, bring to the boil, season with salt, pepper and nutmeg and simmer gently for 5 minutes.
**3.** Add the lettuce, and simmer for 10 minutes.
**4.** Add the dill, and simmer for 1 minute.
**5.** Liquidize the soup in a food processor or blender and push through a sieve into rinsed-out pan.
**6.** Bring back to the boil, add the cream and tip into a warmed soup tureen.

 *LIGHT DRY WHITE*

# STILTON SOUP

SERVES 4

*1 medium onion, finely chopped*
*2 sticks of celery, finely chopped*
*55g/2oz butter*
*45g/1½oz plain flour*
*5 tablespoons dry white wine*
*1 litre/1¾ pints white stock (see page 243)*
*290ml/½ pint milk*
*225g/8oz Stilton cheese, grated or crumbled*
*2 tablespoons single cream*
*salt and freshly ground black pepper*

**1.** Soften the onion and celery in the butter over a low heat. Add the flour and cook for 1 minute.
**2.** Remove from the heat and stir in the wine and stock. Return to the heat and bring slowly to the

boil, stirring continuously until the soup thickens, then simmer for 25 minutes.

**3.** Add the milk and simmer for 2 minutes. Remove from the heat and whisk in the Stilton. Liquidize in a food processor or blender and push through a sieve.

**4.** Add the cream and salt and pepper. Reheat the soup, taking care not to let it boil, or it will curdle.

NOTES: White port, well chilled, is delicious with this soup.

The soup can be served chilled. In this event streak the cream into the soup just before serving, giving it an attractive marbled appearance.

 *BEAUJOLAIS*

# MUSHROOM SOUP

SERVES 4
*55g/2oz butter*
*340g/12oz flat mushrooms, chopped*
*3 tablespoons chopped fresh parsley*
*½ clove of garlic, crushed*
*2 large slices of bread, crusts removed, crumbled*
*860ml/1½ pints white stock (see page 243)*
*a pinch of freshly grated nutmeg or ground mace*
*salt and freshly ground black pepper*
*150ml/¼ pint single cream*

**1.** Melt the butter in a very large, heavy saucepan.
**2.** Add the mushrooms and most of the parsley. Cook over a low heat, stirring, until soft. Add the garlic and the bread. Stir until the bread and mushrooms are well mixed, then add the stock, nutmeg or mace and salt and plenty of pepper to taste. Bring to simmering point, then cook slowly for 10 minutes.
**3.** Liquidize the soup in a food processor or blender or put it through a vegetable mill. If the soup is to be served cold, allow to cool, sprinkle on the parsley and swirl in the cream. Alternatively, add the parsley and cream and reheat.

 *ALSACE GEWÜRZTRAMINER*

# CHINESE MUSHROOM BROTH

SERVES 4
*85g/3oz dried Chinese black mushrooms*
*860ml/1½ pints white stock (see page 243)*
*2 tablespoons soy sauce*

To garnish
*1 spring onion, thinly sliced*
*sesame oil*

**1.** Soak the mushrooms, caps up, in a bowl of warm water until they are soft (about 30 minutes). Squeeze to remove excess water. Remove the stems and cut each cap into 5mm/¼in slices.
**2.** Put the stock, soy sauce and mushrooms into a small saucepan and bring to the boil, then simmer for 15 minutes.
**3.** Sprinkle on the spring onion and about 4 drops of sesame oil. Serve.

 *DRY SHERRY*

# CHILLED BEETROOT SOUP WITH SOURED CREAM

SERVES 4
*675g/1½lb raw beetroots, washed*
*salt and freshly ground black pepper*
*570–860ml/1–1½ pints white stock (see page 243)*
*1–2 teaspoons ground cumin or caraway seeds*
*caster sugar*
*salt and freshly ground black pepper*
*290ml/½ pint soured cream*

To garnish
*chopped fresh herbs*

**1.** Place the whole raw beetroots in a large saucepan of cold water, and season with salt and pepper. Bring to the boil and cook until *al dente* (about 1 hour, depending on the size of the beetroots).
**2.** Drain and leave to cool.

3. Peel the beetroots, cut roughly into small pieces and liquidize in a food processor or blender.

4. Push the purée through a fine sieve, then add the stock to give a thick consistency which will still easily run from a spoon.

5. Season the soup to taste with cumin or caraway, sugar, salt and pepper. Chill in the refrigerator.

6. Ladle the beetroot soup into three-quarters of an ice-cold soup plate, holding the plate at an angle. Then ladle the soured cream into the remaining (uppermost) quarter of the plate, gently lowering the plate as you do so.

7. Feather the cream into the beetroot soup at the 'join', using a cocktail stick or thin skewer. Sprinkle with herbs. Serve cold.

 *ALSACE TOKAY*

# CLEAR BORSCHT

SERVES 6
*900g/2lb raw beetroots*
*1.7 litres/3 pints white stock (see page 243)*
*6 black peppercorns*
*8 coriander seeds*
*½ teaspoon fennel seeds*
*1 parsley stalk, bruised*
*1 onion, chopped*
*1 carrot, peeled and chopped*
*1 clove of garlic, unpeeled*
*salt and freshly ground black pepper*
*4 teaspoons malt vinegar*
*1 tablespoon caster sugar*

1. Wash and peel the beetroots and cut each one into quarters.

2. Put the beetroot into a large clean saucepan with the stock.

3. Put the peppercorns, coriander and fennel seeds into a small piece of muslin and tie up. Add to the pan with the parsley stalk. Bring to the boil, then simmer for 1 hour.

4. Add the onion, carrot, garlic, salt and pepper and cook very slowly for a further 20 minutes. Add the vinegar and sugar. Check the seasoning.

5. Strain the soup through a muslin-lined sieve into a clean saucepan. Reheat and pour into individual soup bowls.

 *LIGHT ALSACE WHITE*

# LENTIL SOUP

SERVES 4
*340g/12oz orange lentils*
*1 litre/2 pints water*
*1 small bacon bone*
*1 bay leaf*
*55g/2oz onion, sliced*
*1 parsley stalk*
*3–4 tablespoons single cream*

To garnish
*chopped fresh mint*

1. Wash the lentils and drain them. Put them into a saucepan with the water, bacon bone, bay leaf, onion and parsley stalk, and boil for about 30 minutes.

2. When the lentils are soft, remove the bone and flavourings. Liquidize in a food processor or blender, then sieve the soup.

3. Return the soup to the rinsed-out pan with the cream and heat through. Serve sprinkled with a little mint.

 *LIGHT RED*

# CORN CHOWDER

SERVES 4
*110/4oz rindless streaky bacon, chopped*
*30g/1oz butter*
*3 sticks of celery, chopped*
*1 large onion, chopped*
*1 large yellow pepper, cored, deseeded and finely*
*    chopped*
*1 bay leaf*
*1 large potato, peeled and diced*
*30g/1oz plain flour*
*570ml/1 pint milk*
*4 cobs of sweetcorn*
*salt and freshly ground black pepper*

To garnish
*chopped fresh parsley*

1. Fry the bacon in the butter. When brown but not crisp add the celery, onion, yellow pepper and

bay leaf. Reduce the heat and cook slowly until the onion looks soft and transparent. Add the potato after 5 minutes.

**2.** Remove the pan from the heat; mix in the flour, cook for 1 minute and then add the milk.

**3.** Return the pan to the heat; stir until boiling.

**4.** Scrape the kernels from the cobs and add them to the soup. Scrape the cobs with a sharp knife to extract all the juice and add this too. Season to taste with salt and pepper. Simmer for 5 minutes or until the vegetables are soft but not broken.

**5.** Serve sprinkled with parsley.

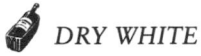 *DRY WHITE*

# PRAWN BISQUE

SERVES 4
*900g/2lb shell-on cooked prawns*
*2 tablespoons oil*
*110g/4oz butter*
*2 shallots, chopped*
*juice of ½ lemon*
*3 tablespoons brandy*
*1 litre/1¾ pints well-flavoured fish or shellfish*
  *stock (see page 245)*
*1 bay leaf*
*1 parsley stalk*
*1 blade of mace*
*45g/1½oz plain flour*
*salt and freshly ground white pepper*
*Tabasco sauce*
*3 tablespoons single cream*

**1.** Peel all but 4 of the prawns, and reserve the shells. Wash the prawns, remove the dark veins and reserve any roe.

**2.** In a large, heavy saucepan heat the oil, add 30g/1oz of the butter and fry the prawn shells for 2 minutes. Add the shallots, lemon juice and brandy and continue to cook for a further 2 minutes. Add the stock, bay leaf, parsley stalk and blade of mace and cook for 30 minutes (this will help to give the bisque flavour and colour).

**3.** Meanwhile, blend or pound together all the peeled prawns with about 45g/1½oz butter and any reserved roe.

**4.** Melt the remaining butter in a saucepan. Add the flour and cook for 30 seconds. Strain in the

stock and bring slowly to the boil, stirring constantly. Simmer for 2 minutes, strain in the pan juices, and whisk in the prawn butter.

**5.** Season with salt, pepper and Tabasco. Add the cream and the reserved prawns.

NOTE: If there is no roe to be found, whisk 1 tablespoon tomato purée into the bisque to give it a better colour.

 *CHABLIS*

# LOBSTER BISQUE

SERVES 4
*1 × 675g/1½lb live lobster*
*2 tablespoons oil*
*110g/4oz butter*
*2 shallots, chopped*
*juice of ½ lemon*
*3 tablespoons brandy*
*1 bay leaf*
*1 parsley stalk*
*1 blade of mace*
*1 litre/1¾ pints fish, shellfish or vegetable stock*
  *(see page 245)*
*45g/1½oz plain flour*
*3 tablespoons single cream*
*salt and freshly ground white pepper*
*a pinch of cayenne pepper*

**1.** Preheat the oven to 180°C/350°F/gas mark 4.

**2.** Kill the lobster by pushing a sharp knife through its nerve centre (marked by a well defined cross on the back of the head).

**3.** Lay the lobster flat on a board and split it in half lengthways. Remove and discard the little stomach sac from the head and the thread-like intestine. Remove the coral (if any) and reserve.

**4.** In a large flameproof casserole, heat the oil with 30g/1oz of the butter. Sauté the lobster, flesh side down, for 5 minutes. Add the shallot, lemon juice and brandy. Cover and place in the preheated oven for 15 minutes.

**5.** Remove all the meat from the lobster, adding the greenish creamy paste from the head.

**6.** Break up the shells in the pan, add the bay leaf, parsley stalk, mace and stock, and simmer for 30 minutes. Set aside. (This will help to give the bisque flavour and colour.)

**7.** Meanwhile, blend or pound together all but a small chunk of the lobster meat with about 45g/1½oz butter and the coral. Cut the reserved meat into neat dice and set aside for garnish.

**8.** Strain the stock. Melt the remaining butter, add the flour and cook for 30 seconds. Add the stock and bring slowly to the boil, stirring all the time. Simmer for 2 minutes, add the pan juices and whisk in the lobster butter.

**9.** Add the cream and finally the lobster pieces. Check the seasoning. Serve sprinkled with a pinch of cayenne pepper.

 *CHABLIS*

# BOUILLABAISSE

Recipes for this Mediterranean stew are many and varied according to the availability of fish and

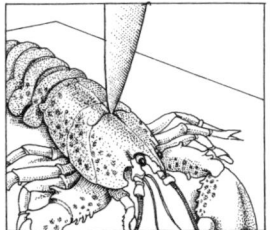 

*Push a sharp knife through the lobster's nerve centre*

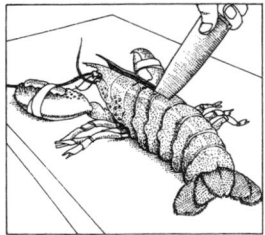 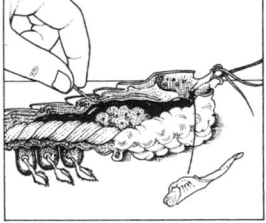

*Split the lobster in half and remove the stomach sac*

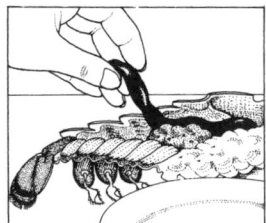 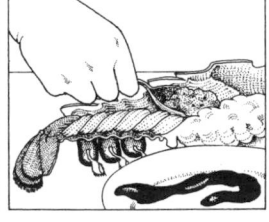

*Remove the thread-like intestine and the greeny black roe*

vegetables. The sad truth is that it is only possible to make a real bouillabaisse on or near the Mediterranean coast. Imitations made at home never have quite the freshness and authenticity of the original.

This recipe is an adaptation of many recipes but we have relied mostly on Jane Grigson's in *Fish Cookery*.

Use a selection of the following fish: rascasse, bay scallops, mussels, monkfish, conger eel, John Dory, gurnard, crayfish, lobster, Dublin Bay prawns, scampi.

Traditionally the fish are cooked and served unfilleted but they can be skinned and filleted if preferred. The cooking time would need to be reduced accordingly.

SERVES 10
*150ml/¼ pint good-quality olive oil*
*2 onions, chopped*
*2 cloves of garlic, crushed*
*white part of 2 leeks, chopped*
*1 small bulb of Florence fennel, sliced*
*1 small green chilli, deseeded and chopped*
*2 very large tomatoes, peeled and chopped*
*7 filaments of saffron, dissolved in 4 tablespoons*
*    hot water*
*cayenne pepper*
*salt*
*3 litres/5 pints fish stock (see page 245)*
*1 small bunch of fresh parsley*
*2.7kg/6lb fresh fish, cleaned*

To serve
*10 slices of French bread, toasted lightly in the*
*    oven, fried in olive oil and rubbed with garlic*
*a bowl of rouille (see page 259)*
*a bowl of aïoli (garlic mayonnaise – see page 250)*

**1.** Put the oil into a large, heavy saucepan. Add the onions, garlic, leeks, fennel and chilli. Sweat for 5 minutes.

**2.** Add the tomatoes, saffron liquid, cayenne pepper, salt, stock and parsley. Bring to the boil and boil well to enable the oil and water to emulsify. Reduce to a simmer.

**3.** Gradually add the fish. Conger eel will take about 20 minutes to cook; crayfish about 15 minutes; unfilleted white fish about 10 minutes, and most shellfish 5 minutes.

**4.** Remove the fish to a warmed serving dish, split the crayfish head in two and slice the tail. Leave the shellfish unshelled. Check the seasoning of the soup.

5. Bring the soup to the boil and boil hard for a few moments to emulsify the liquid, then strain into a warmed soup tureen. Serve immediately with the fish, hot bread, rouille and aïoli.

 *ROSÉ DE PROVENCE OR WHITE RHÔNE*

# COCK-A-LEEKIE SOUP

This is an unthickened chicken broth, and it should have plenty of chicken and leeks in it. At the end of the cooking process there should be about 1 litre/1¾ pints of soup.

SERVES 6
*6 prunes*
*1.35kg/3lb chicken*
*2 teaspoons salt*
*freshly ground black pepper*
*1 bay leaf*
*a few parsley stalks*
*6 leeks, cut into matchstick lengths*

To garnish
*chopped fresh parsley*

1. Soak the prunes in cold water for 6 hours. Remove the stones.
2. Joint the chicken and place the pieces in a pan with enough water to cover them generously. Reserve the giblets. Add salt and pepper, the bay leaf, giblets (except the liver) and parsley. Bring to the boil and skim. Cover and simmer for about 45 minutes.
3. Skim the fat from the soup, add the leeks and prunes and simmer for a further 45 minutes.
4. Remove the chicken, giblets, bay leaf and parsley stalks. Skin the chicken and cut the flesh into small, neat dice. Add the diced chicken to the soup.
5. Check the seasoning and serve hot with a little parsley sprinkled over at the last minute.

NOTES: You may prefer to reserve the chicken breast and use it for another dish, rather than adding it to the soup. Chicken portions (thighs and drumsticks) can be bought more cheaply than whole chickens, but this means no giblets. Best of all, use a boiling fowl, but remember this will need a total of 3 hours simmering, with the water being topped up as necessary.

If there is no time to soak the prunes they may be cooked whole in the soup and the stones removed afterwards.

# FRENCH ONION SOUP

SERVES 4–6
*55g/2oz butter*
*450g/1lb onions, sliced*
*½ clove of garlic, crushed*
*1 teaspoon plain flour*
*1.1 litres/2 pints good stock, preferably brown (see page 243)*
*salt and freshly ground black pepper*
*55g/2oz Gruyère cheese, grated*
*1 teaspoon dry English mustard*
*4 slices of French bread*

1. Melt the butter in a large, heavy saucepan and slowly brown the onions: this should take at least 1 hour and the onions should become meltingly soft and greatly reduced in quantity. They must also be evenly golden-brown all over and transparent. Add the garlic after 45 minutes.
2. Stir in the flour and cook for 1 minute.
3. Add the stock and stir until boiling. Season with salt and pepper and simmer for 20–30 minutes.
4. Preheat the oven to 200°C/400°F/gas mark 6.
5. Mix the Gruyère cheese with the mustard and pepper. Spread this on the bread slices and put them on the bottom of an earthenware tureen. Pour over the soup. The bread will rise to the top. Put the soup (uncovered) in the oven until well browned and bubbling.

 *BEAUJOLAIS*

# BEEF CONSOMMÉ

SERVES 6
*1.75 litres/3 pints very well-flavoured brown stock (see page 243)*
*225g/8oz lean shin of beef, minced*
*salt and freshly ground black pepper*
*3 egg whites and shells*
*5 tablespoons medium sherry or Madeira*

1. Place the bouillon, beef and sherry in a large clean metal saucepan. Season very well with salt and pepper.

**2.** Put the crushed egg shells and the whites into the bouillon. Place over the heat and whisk steadily with a balloon whisk until the mixture boils. Stop whisking immediately and remove the pan from the heat. Allow the mixture to subside. Take care not to break the crust formed by the egg white.

**3.** Bring the consommé just up to the boil again and then again allow to subside. Repeat this once more. (The egg white will trap the sediment in the stock and clear the soup.) Allow to cool for 2 minutes.

**4.** Fix a double layer of fine muslin over a clean basin and carefully strain the soup through it, taking care to hold the egg white crust back. When all the liquid is through (or almost all of it) allow the egg white to slip into the muslin. Then strain the soup again, this time through both egg-white crust and cloth. Do not try to hurry the process by squeezing the cloth as this will produce murky soup: it must be allowed to drip through at its own pace. The consommé is now ready for serving.

NOTES: All equipment for clarifying the consommé should be scalded before use.

To serve the consommé en gelée (jellied), pour the liquid into a shallow pan or tray to cool and refrigerate until set. Chop roughly with a knife and spoon into ice-cold soup cups. Serve with a wedge of lemon and toast.

 *DRY SHERRY*

# GARNISHES FOR CONSOMMÉ

### AUX POINTES DES ASPERGES
Place cooked asparagus tips at the bottom of a warmed tureen and pour the soup over.

### À LA JULIENNE
Add mixed carrot, turnip, leek and celery cut into julienne strips to the consommé and cook until tender. Chopped fresh chervil or parsley is sometimes added at the last minute.

### LADY CURZON
Chill the consommé in ovenproof cups. Flavour 2 tablespoons double cream with curry powder, salt and pepper and pour over each consommé. Place under a hot grill to brown the top. Put into a warm oven to heat the soup.

### AUX PROFITEROLES
Season choux pastry with Parmesan, mustard and cayenne, pipe in pea-size pieces and bake until crisp. Place in the bottom of a hot tureen, pour the soup over and serve immediately before the profiteroles can become soggy.

### AUX QUENELLES
Poach small chicken quenelles in stock. Float these in the consommé and sprinkle with chopped fresh chervil or parsley.

### AUX VERMICELLI
Cook vermicelli in stock until tender. Rinse well, place in a warmed tureen and pour the soup over. (Other small-size pastas are also used.)

# CONSOMMÉ ROYALE

SERVES 6
*1 egg white*
*4 tablespoons double cream*
*salt and freshly ground white pepper*
*beef consommé (page 105)*

**1.** Mix the egg white with a fork and beat in the cream, salt and pepper.
**2.** Place in a heatproof dish and stand in a pan of gently simmering water until set.
**3.** Cool, cut into neat strips and add to the consommé just before serving.

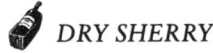 *DRY SHERRY*

# SPICY TOMATO SOUP

SERVES 4
*15g/¹/₂oz butter*
*¹/₂ onion, finely chopped*
*15g/¹/₂oz plain flour*
*1 × 200g/7oz can of tomatoes*
*425ml/³/₄ pint white stock (see page 243)*
*1 bay leaf*
*a pinch of freshly grated nutmeg*
*salt and freshly ground black pepper*
*¹/₂ teaspoon paprika*
*1 clove*
*¹/₂ teaspoon caster sugar*
*a squeeze of lemon juice*
*1–2 tablespoons port*
*110g/4oz fresh tomatoes, peeled, deseeded and*
  *slivered*

**1.** Melt the butter in a saucepan. Add the onion and cook gently until pale yellow and transparent.
**2.** Stir in the flour, cook for 1 minute, then add the canned tomatoes and the stock. Stir until the mixture boils.
**3.** Add the bay leaf, nutmeg, a pinch each of salt and pepper, the paprika, clove, sugar and lemon juice.
**4.** Simmer, stirring occasionally, for 30 minutes.
**5.** Push the soup through a sieve and return it to the saucepan.
**6.** Add the port and the fresh tomatoes. Reheat and check the seasoning.

 *AUSTRALIAN CHARDONNAY*

# LEITH'S RESTAURANT'S TOMATO AND BASIL SOUP

SERVES 6
*2.3kg/5lb tomatoes*
*24 large fresh basil leaves*
*170g/6oz salted butter*
*salt and freshly ground black pepper*
*85g/3oz fromage blanc*

**1.** Make a small slit in the skin of each tomato and blanch in boiling water for 5–7 seconds. They are ready to peel when the skin starts to lift away from the knife slits. Skin, then halve the tomatoes, scooping the seeds and juice into a sieve set over a bowl. Sieve the juice and reserve, then cut the tomato flesh into small strips.

**2.** Roughly chop all but 6 of the basil leaves. Put the tomato strips, reserved juice and chopped basil into a large deep frying pan. Add 55g/2oz of the butter and place over a medium heat, shaking the pan and stirring.
**3.** When the tomato strips start to break up, turn up the heat and briskly stir in the remaining butter. When all the butter has been added, the tomatoes should be only half cooked. Season to taste with salt and pepper.
**4.** Fill individual soup bowls with the tomato soup, then spoon fromage blanc into the middle of each bowl. Garnish each soup bowl with a fresh basil leaf and serve immediately.

 *SOAVE*

# WATERCRESS AND POTATO SOUP

SERVES 4
*30g/1oz butter*
*1 medium onion, chopped*
*225g/8oz potatoes, diced*
*570ml/1 pint white stock (see page 243)*
*2 bunches of watercress, chopped*
*290ml/¹/₂ pint creamy milk, scalded*
*salt and freshly ground black pepper*
*a pinch of freshly grated nutmeg*

To garnish
*chopped fresh chives*

**1.** Melt the butter, add the onion and cook over a low heat until soft but not coloured. Add the potatoes and stock and simmer for 10 minutes or until the potatoes are tender.
**2.** Liquidize the soup with the watercress in a food processor or blender and push it through a sieve. Pour into the rinsed-out pan.
**3.** Add enough of the milk to get the required consistency and season to taste with salt, pepper and nutmeg. Reheat until the soup is just below boiling point.
**4.** Serve in a warmed soup tureen, garnished with chives.

 *WHITE LOIRE*

# CARROT AND CORIANDER SOUP WITH PUFF PASTRY TOPS

SERVES 4

675g/1½lb carrots, peeled and sliced
1 onion, finely chopped
15g/½oz butter
1 bay leaf
860ml/1½ pints white stock (see page 243) or water
salt and freshly ground black pepper
1 tablespoon chopped fresh parsley
1 tablespoon chopped fresh coriander
4 tablespoons double cream
225g/8oz flour quantity puff pastry (see page 464)
beaten egg, to glaze

1. Put the carrots and onion into a large, heavy saucepan with the butter. Sweat for 10 minutes or until beginning to soften. Add the bay leaf, stock, salt and pepper. Bring to the boil, then simmer as slowly as possible for 25 minutes. Remove the bay leaf.
2. Liquidize the soup with the parsley and coriander in a food processor or blender and push through a sieve into a clean saucepan. Check the consistency. If a little thin, reduce by rapid boiling, if a little thick, add extra water.
3. Add the cream and season to taste with salt and pepper. Leave to get completely cold.
4. Preheat the oven to 220°C/425°F/gas mark 7.
5. Put 200ml/7fl oz of the cold soup into 4 large ovenproof soup bowls.
6. Roll out the pastry very thinly and cut out 4 circles a little larger than the rim of the bowl (allowing about 1cm/½in extra). Brush a little of the beaten egg around the edge of each circle and use this to attach the pastry to the bowl, pressing firmly to make a good seal. Trim off any uneven edges. Brush the pastry with remaining egg glaze. Chill well in the refrigerator.
7. Place the soup bowls on a baking sheet and bake near the top of the preheated oven for 20 minutes until well risen and golden-brown.

 *AUSTRALIAN/NEW ZEALAND SAUVIGNON BLANC*

# MINESTRONE

SERVES 6

85g/3oz dried haricot beans
1 tablespoon oil
3 rashers of rindless streaky bacon, diced
2 cloves of garlic, crushed
1 large onion, sliced
2 carrots, diced
1 stick of celery, chopped
2 medium potatoes, peeled and diced
1.1 litres/2 pints ham stock (see page 243)
1 bouquet garni (3 leaves fresh basil, 2 parsley stalks, bay leaf, tied together with string)
1 tablespoon tomato purée
110g/4oz white cabbage
3 large tomatoes, peeled and chopped
55g/2oz broken spaghetti or other small pasta
salt and freshly ground black pepper
freshly grated Parmesan cheese

1. Soak the beans in cold water for 3–4 hours.
2. Heat the oil in a heavy saucepan, add the bacon and garlic, onion, carrot and celery and cook for 2 minutes, stirring. Add the potato and cook until the oil has been absorbed and the vegetables are soft.
3. Add the stock, bring to the boil, add the bouquet garni, tomato purée and drained beans. Simmer for 45 minutes.
4. Add the cabbage, tomato and spaghetti and continue to simmer for a further 15 minutes, or until the beans are soft and the spaghetti is tender.
5. Just before serving remove the herbs and check the seasoning. Serve sprinkled with Parmesan cheese.

 *LIGHT CHIANTI OR VALPOLICELLA*

# NEW ENGLAND CLAM CHOWDER

SERVES 6

3 rashers of rindless streaky bacon, chopped
55g/2oz butter
1 large or 2 medium onions, chopped
1 stick of celery, chopped
1 leek, chopped
48 clams (soft- or hard-shelled)
425ml/¾ pint water
3 medium potatoes, peeled and finely diced

*425ml/³/4 pint creamy milk*
*a pinch of dried thyme*
*a small piece of bay leaf*
*salt and freshly ground black pepper*
*30g/1oz plain flour*
*4 tablespoons double cream*

**1.** Put the bacon into a heavy saucepan and fry in its own fat until crisp and slightly brown.
**2.** Add half the butter and the onion, celery and leek. Cook slowly until the vegetables are softened but not coloured.
**3.** While the vegetables are cooking, scrub the clams well, using a brush to remove any sand. Put the clean clams into a second saucepan and pour on the water. Cook slowly until the shells have opened wide (about 10 minutes).
**4.** Lift out the clams and reserve their liquid. Remove the clams from their shells and chop the flesh. Strain the cooking liquid through a fine cloth to remove any sand.
**5.** Add the potato, milk, thyme and bay leaf to the onion mixture and season with salt and pepper. If the potatoes are not covered by the liquid, top up with a little water. Cover the pan and simmer gently until the potatoes are almost tender (about 12 minutes).
**6.** Meanwhile, melt the remaining butter and stir in the flour. Cook gently for 30 seconds, then remove the pan from the heat and stir in the strained liquid reserved from poaching the clams. Stir steadily until the mixture boils. Simmer for 2 minutes. Add the clams.
**7.** Stir the thickened clam liquid into the chowder. Check the seasoning. Stir in the cream and serve immediately.

NOTE: Canned clams can be used as a substitute for fresh. They should be added once the soup has cooked, and simmered for 3–4 minutes before serving. If using canned clams, substitute good fish stock for water.

 *CALIFORNIAN SAUVIGNON*

# SOUPE AU PISTOU

This is a Mediterranean peasant soup which calls for fresh basil and very fresh garlic.

SERVES 6
*450g/1lb dried haricot beans, soaked overnight*
*2 tablespoons oil (preferably olive)*
*225g/8oz potatoes, peeled and diced*
*2 leeks, thinly sliced*
*2 carrots, thinly sliced*
*110g/4oz green beans, sliced or chopped*
*1.7 litres/3 pints white stock (see page 243)*
*¹/2 teaspoon coarsely ground black pepper*
*2 tablespoons vermicelli or other small pasta*
*4 ripe tomatoes, peeled and chopped*
*1 teaspoon salt*

For the pistou
*4 cloves of garlic, crushed*
*4 tablespoons chopped fresh basil*
*3 tablespoons olive oil*

To serve
*grated Gruyère cheese*

**1.** Cook the beans in boiling water for about 1 hour, until half tender.
**2.** Heat the oil and add the potatoes, leeks and carrots. Cover and cook over a low heat until the vegetables are soft.
**3.** Add the half-cooked dried beans, the green beans, stock and pepper. Simmer until the haricot beans are soft (about 1½ hours). Add the pasta and tomatoes, season with salt and cook for a further 10 minutes, or until the pasta is tender. Allow to cool a little before adding the pistou.
**4.** Make the pistou: put the garlic and the basil in a mortar or blender and pound to a paste. Add the oil, drop by drop (as when making mayonnaise), mixing all the time, to form an emulsion. Just before serving, stir the pistou into the soup. Hand the cheese separately.

NOTE: Recipes for this soup vary along the Mediterranean according to local tradition and season. Courgettes, cabbage and onions sometimes make their appearance. The Italian version of pesto (page 255), from which pistou is derived, is sometimes added to the soup, which is itself a version of Italian minestrone.

 *RED OR ROSÉ DE PROVENCE*

# EGG FIRST
# COURSES

# EGG MAYONNAISE

SERVES 4
*290ml/½ pint mayonnaise (see page 250)*
*water*
*6 hardboiled eggs (see below), shelled*

To garnish
*strips of cucumber skin or chopped fresh parsley*
*paprika pepper*

**1.** Thin the mayonnaise slightly by adding a little water, to achieve a reluctant dropping consistency.
**2.** Cut the eggs in half lengthways and arrange, cut side down, on a plate. Carefully coat each egg with mayonnaise.
**3.** Garnish half the eggs with a small diamond shape cut from cucumber skin or a neat sprinkling of chopped parsley. Garnish the remaining eggs with paprika pepper.

NOTE: Other suitable garnishes for egg mayonnaise include thin strips of anchovy fillet in a criss-cross pattern, pitted black olives, rings of radish or watercress leaves.

 *GERMAN RIESLING*

# HARDBOILED EGGS

There are two tried and tested methods for hardboiling an egg:

**1.** If you are cooking a lot of eggs, lower them carefully into a saucepan of boiling water and simmer for 12 minutes.
**2.** If you are just boiling one or two eggs put them into a saucepan of cold water, bring the water up to the boil and then simmer for 10 minutes.
   Once the eggs are cooked, drain and put to cool in a bowl of cold water.

NOTES: If you have an egg pricker, prick the rounded end of the raw egg to allow the air under the shell to escape. This will prevent cracking when boiling.
   Fresh eggs take longer to cook than stale eggs. Add 30 seconds if the eggs are new-laid and 30 seconds if they are straight from the refrigerator.

# CODDLED EGGS

SERVES 4
*15g/½ oz butter*
*4 medium eggs at room temperature*
*salt and freshly ground black pepper*

**1.** Preheat the oven to 180°C/350°F gas mark 4.
**2.** Butter 4 egg coddlers or ramekins and stand them in a roasting pan or ovenproof dish half-filled with hot water (a bain-marie).
**3.** Break an egg carefully into each dish and season with salt and pepper.
**4.** Cover with the coddler lid or a piece of greased greaseproof paper and cook in the centre of the oven for 12–15 minutes until the whites are set and the yolks still runny.

 *MUSCADET*

# SCRAMBLED EGGS ON ANCHOVY TOAST

SERVES 1
*2 eggs*
*1 tablespoon cream or creamy milk*
*salt and freshly ground black pepper*
*1 slice of crustless buttered toast, spread with anchovy paste*
*15g/½ oz butter*

**1.** In a bowl mix together the eggs, cream or milk, salt and pepper.
**2.** Get the toast ready. Place on a heated plate and keep warm.
**3.** Melt the butter in a saucepan. Tip in the egg mixture and using a wooden spoon keep it constantly moving until thickened and creamy.
**4.** Pile on to the prepared toast and serve immediately.

 *DRY GERMAN WHITE*

# SMOKED SALMON AND SCRAMBLED EGGS

Most recipes for smoked salmon and scrambled eggs suggest chopping up the smoked salmon and adding it to the eggs just before they are ready to serve. We serve the salmon cold as we feel warm smoked salmon can taste a little like smoked ham.

SERVES 4
*110g/4oz Scotch smoked salmon*
*salt and freshly ground black pepper*
*8 eggs*
*4 tablespoons double cream*
*30g/1oz butter*

**1.** Divide the smoked salmon into 4 and arrange on one half of 4 side plates. Grind over a little pepper.
**2.** Mix together the eggs, cream, salt and pepper. Beat well.
**3.** Melt the butter in a small saucepan. Tip in the egg mixture and using a wooden spoon stir constantly until thickened and creamy, but still moist.
**4.** Pile on to the plates and serve immediately.

 *ALSACE WHITE*

# PLAIN FRENCH OMELETTE

SERVES 1
*3 eggs*
*salt and freshly ground black pepper*
*a pinch of freshly grated Parmesan cheese*
   *(optional)*
*1 tablespoon cold water*
*15g/½oz butter*

**1.** Break the eggs into a bowl and with a fork mix in the seasoning, Parmesan cheese and water.
**2.** Melt the butter in a heavy 15cm/6in omelette pan and swirl it around so that the bottom and sides are coated. When foaming, pour in the egg mixture.
**3.** Hold the pan handle in your left hand and move it gently back and forth over the heat. At the same time, move the mixture slowly, scraping

up large creamy flakes of egg mixture. As you do this some of the liquid egg from the middle of the omelette will run to the sides of the pan. Tilt the pan to help this process. Leave over the heat until the bottom has set and the top is creamy. Remove from the heat.
**4.** With a fork or palette knife fold the nearside edge of the omelette over to the centre and then flick the whole omelette over on to a warmed plate with the folded edges on the underside. Alternatively, fold the omelette in two and slide it on to the plate.

NOTE: Grated cheese, fresh chopped herbs, fried mushrooms or other flavourings can be added to the basic omelette mixture.

 *LIGHT RED*

# OMELETTE ARNOLD BENNETT

SERVES 4
*1 slice of onion*
*1–2 slices of carrot*
*1 bay leaf*
*4 black peppercorns*
*150ml/¼ pint milk*
*110g/4oz smoked haddock*
*45g/1½oz butter*
*15g/½ oz plain flour*
*3 eggs, separated*
*3 tablespoons single cream*
*fresh ground black pepper*
*1 tablespoon freshly grated Parmesan cheese*

**1.** Put the onion, carrot, bay leaf, peppercorns and milk into a saucepan and heat slowly.
**2.** When the milk is well infused, add the haddock and poach gently for 10 minutes, or until the fish is just cooked.
**3.** Take out the fish and skin, bone and flake it. Strain and reserve the cooking liquor.
**4.** Melt 15g/½oz of the butter in a small saucepan, add the flour and stir over the heat for 1 minute.
**5.** Add 150ml/¼ pint of the strained cooking liquor. Stir until boiling.
**6.** Beat the egg yolks with 2 tablespoons of the cream. Season with pepper only (do not add salt as the haddock is salty). Stir into the sauce. Add the haddock and half the cheese. Check the seasoning.

**7.** Whisk the egg whites to medium peaks and fold into the sauce.

**8.** Preheat the grill to its highest setting.

**9.** Melt the remaining butter in an omelette pan over a medium-high heat, tipping the pan so that the bottom and sides are coated. When the foaming begins to subside quickly pour in the egg mixture.

**10.** When the omelette is beginning to set, sprinkle on the remaining cheese, pour over the remaining tablespoon of cream and brown quickly under the hot grill.

**11.** Slide the omelette on to a warmed dish.

 *ALSACE WHITE*

# HERB OMELETTE SALAD

SERVES 2–4

For the omelette
*5 eggs*
*3 tablespoons olive oil*
*1 tablespoon chopped fresh parsley*
*salt and freshly ground black pepper*

For the salad
*2 red peppers, quartered and deseeded*
*2 large tomatoes, peeled and cut into strips*
*1 cucumber, peeled, deseeded and cut into strips*
*1 head of lettuce*
*1 bunch of fresh chives, roughly chopped*
*12 fresh basil leaves, chopped*

For the dressing
*1 clove of garlic, crushed*
*2 anchovy fillets, mashed*
*1 teaspoon Dijon mustard*
*2 tablespoons wine vinegar*
*8 tablespoons olive oil*
*salt and freshly ground black pepper*

To garnish
*10 small black olives, pitted*

**1.** Make the omelette: in a bowl, mix together the eggs, 2 tablespoons of the oil, the parsley, salt and pepper.

**2.** Use the remaining oil to fry the omelette. Lightly grease the base of an omelette pan. When hot, add enough of the omelette mixture to cover the base of the pan. The omelette mixture should be the thickness of a pancake. Cook the omelette for about 1 minute. Slide on to a plate and leave

to cool. Continue to cook the remaining omelette mixture in the same way.

**3.** When cool, cut the omelettes into thin strips.

**4.** Meanwhile, prepare the salad: place the peppers under a hot grill. When charred, hold under cold running water and scrape off the skin, then cut the flesh into 1cm/½in strips.

**5.** Prepare the dressing: mix together all the ingredients, and whizz in a blender. Season with salt and pepper.

**6.** Mix together all the salad ingredients, the omelette strips and the herbs. Add the dressing and toss well.

**7.** Pile on to a serving dish and scatter over the olives.

 *LIGHT TO MEDIUM RED*

# TORTILLA

SERVES 4
*oil for frying*
*450g/1lb floury potatoes, peeled and thinly sliced*
*1 small onion, thinly sliced*
*salt and freshly ground black pepper*
*4 eggs, beaten*

**1.** Heat about 1cm/½in of oil in a frying pan, add the potatoes and onion, season with salt and pepper and fry slowly until soft but not coloured (up to 20 minutes).

**2.** Tip all the oil, but for a thin film, out of the pan and into the egg mixture. Beat, then pour the egg mixture into the pan.

**3.** Cook the omelette over a medium heat until it is set, then slip on to a plate. Turn it over and put it back into the frying pan with the uncooked side down.

**4.** Cook for 1 further minute, then turn out on to a serving plate. Serve warm or cold, cut into wedges.

NOTE: Frying the potatoes from raw is the usual Spanish method. But if the potatoes are small and waxy it is better to boil them first, then slice and fry. Boiled potatoes give a light, soft omelette.

 *RED RIOJA*

# FRITTATA (ITALIAN OMELETTE)

SERVES 2

*225g/8oz red or white onions, very thinly sliced*
*3 tablespoons olive oil*
*3 eggs*
*30g/1oz Parmesan cheese, freshly grated*
*salt and freshly ground black pepper*
*20g/³/4oz butter*

**1.** Cook the onions slowly in the oil until reduced in quantity, soft, and a rich golden-brown. Tip the onions into a sieve over a bowl. Leave to cool.
**2.** Beat the eggs until lightly mixed. Mix all but 3 tablespoons of the egg with the onions, cheese, salt and pepper. Mix well.
**3.** Melt the butter in an 18cm/6in frying pan over a medium heat. When foaming, add the egg and onion mixture. Reduce the heat to very low.
**4.** Cook very slowly for 15 minutes. The eggs should be set and the surface runny. Pour over the reserved egg. Place under a hot grill until set but not brown. Loosen with a spatula and slide on to a round dish. Serve cut into wedges.

 *LIGHT CHIANTI*

# BAKED EGGS

SERVES 4

*4 medium eggs at room temperature*
*salt and freshly round black pepper*
*4 teaspoons single cream*
*15g/¹/2oz butter*

**1.** Preheat the oven to 180°C/350°F/gas mark 4.
**2.** Brush 4 cocotte dishes with butter and stand them in a roasting pan half-filled with hot water (a bain-marie).
**0.** Break an egg carefully into each dish and season with salt and pepper. Spoon over a little cream and place a knob of butter on top.
**4.** Bake uncovered in the centre of the preheated oven for about 10 minutes, until the whites are set and the yolks runny.

NOTES: The eggs will continue cooking for a short time after removing from the oven, so be very careful not to overcook.

Tarragon eggs can be made by adding 2 fresh tarragon leaves to each egg before spooning over the cream.

 *LIGHT RED*

# BAKED EGGS WITH MUSHROOMS

SERVES 4

*45g/1¹/2oz butter*
*1 shallot, finely chopped*
*110g/4oz mushrooms, finely chopped*
*2 teaspoons chopped fresh parsley*
*salt and freshly ground white pepper*
*4 eggs*
*4 tablespoons single cream or creamy milk*

**1.** Preheat the oven to 180°C/350°F/gas mark 4. Lightly butter 4 ramekin or cocotte dishes.
**2.** Melt half the remaining butter, add the shallot and cook until very soft but not coloured.
**3.** Add the remaining butter with the mushrooms. Cook slowly over a low heat until the mushrooms are soft. Add the parsley and season to taste with salt and pepper.
**4.** Divide this mixture between the 4 dishes, make a dip in each cocotte and break an egg into each. Spoon 1 tablespoon cream on to each egg and season with salt and pepper.
**5.** Stand the dishes in a roasting pan half-filled with hot water (a bain-marie) and bake in the preheated oven for 10–12 minutes, until the whites are just set and the yolks still runny.

 *LIGHT RED*

# OEUFS FLORENTINE

Eggs for poaching must be very fresh; if not, a little vinegar can be added to the water to help the white coagulate but this will have an adverse effect on the taste.

SERVES 4

*450g/1lb fresh spinach, cooked and chopped*
*15g/¹/2oz butter, melted*
*salt and freshly ground black pepper*
*a good pinch of freshly grated nutmeg*
*4 eggs, chilled*
*290ml/¹/2 pint mornay sauce (see page 247)*
*a little grated cheese*
*browned breadcrumbs*

**1.** Turn the spinach in the melted butter. Season with salt, pepper and nutmeg. Place in the bottom of an ovenproof dish.

**2.** Preheat the oven to 150°C/300°F/gas mark 2. Preheat the grill.

**3.** Poach the eggs: three-quarters fill a large shallow pan with water. Bring to the boil, then lower the temperature to a simmer. Break an egg into a cup and slip it into the water. Immediately raise the temperature slightly so that the bubbles help to draw the white round the yolk. Poach for about 3 minutes, then lift out with a slotted spoon.

**4.** Trim the whites neatly with a pair of scissors or a stainless steel knife and drain thoroughly by shaking the slotted spoon.

**5.** Arrange the eggs on top of the spinach and coat with the cheese sauce. Sprinkle over the cheese and crumbs.

**6.** Brown the top under the hot grill.

 *LIGHT RED*

# SCOTCH EGGS

SERVES 4

*340g/12oz good-quality sausagemeat*
*salt and freshly ground black pepper*
*4 hardboiled eggs, shelled (see page 112)*
*seasoned plain flour*
*oil for frying*
*beaten egg*
*2 tablespoons dried white breadcrumbs*

**1.** Season the sausagemeat with salt and pepper. Divide it into 4 equal pieces.

**2.** Roll the eggs in seasoned flour. Dip your hands in a little water and mould the sausagemeat around each egg, making sure they are completely and evenly covered.

**3.** Place at least 3.5cm/1½in of oil in a deep-fryer and begin to heat it up slowly.

**4.** Dip the eggs in seasoned flour, brush with beaten egg and coat with breadcrumbs.

**5.** Place the prepared eggs in the deep-fryer basket and when the oil is hot enough to sizzle gently when a breadcrumb is added, put in the eggs and fry for about 12 minutes. Drain well on absorbent kitchen paper.

 *MEDIUM RED*

# QUAIL'S EGGS EN CROUSTADE

SERVES 4

*8 quail's eggs*
*4 thin slices of bread*
*unsalted butter*
*1 shallot, finely chopped*
*1 rasher of rindless streaky bacon, finely chopped*
*85g/3oz flat mushrooms, finely chopped*
*chopped fresh parsley*
*salt and freshly ground black pepper*
*beurre blanc (see page 253)*

**1.** Preheat the oven to 170°C/325°F/gas mark 3.

**2.** Cut the bread into circles with a large fluted pastry cutter and press very firmly into large patty tins. Brush with melted unsalted butter. Bake in the preheated oven for 15 minutes. Remove from the tins, turn upside down and bake for a further 10 minutes or until crisp and lightly browned.

**3.** Meanwhile, prepare the duxelles: cook the shallot and bacon in butter. Add the mushrooms and cook for a further 2 minutes. Boil away the liquid. Add the parsley and season to taste with salt and pepper. The mixture should be very dry.

**4.** Bring a saucepan of water to simmering point. Break 2 quail's eggs at a time on to a saucer, then tip carefully into the saucepan and poach for about 2 minutes. Repeat with the remaining eggs.

**5.** Divide the duxelles mixture between the croustades. Place 2 eggs on top of each and coat with the beurre blanc.

 *LIGHT RED*

# OEUFS EN MEURETTE

SERVES 4

This recipe has been adapted from a recipe by Anne Willan.

*½ × 75cl bottle of red Burgundy*
*250ml/8 floz white stock, made with veal bones*
*    (see page 243)*
*4 fresh free range eggs*

For the sauce
20g/³⁄₄oz unsalted butter
½ onion, thinly sliced
½ carrot, thinly sliced
½ stick of celery, thinly sliced
½ clove of garlic, crushed
1 bouquet garni (see page 19)
4 black peppercorns
15g/½oz plain flour

To garnish
15g/½oz unsalted butter
55g/2oz pancetta, blanched and cut into 1cm/½in
    lardons
12 button onions, peeled
45g/1½oz button mushrooms
4 fried bread croûtes, 6cm/2½in in diameter
salt and freshly ground black pepper

1. Poach the eggs: put the wine and stock into a frying pan or shallow sauté pan and bring to the boil, then reduce to a simmer.
2. Break an egg into a cup and slip carefully into the simmering liquid. Immediately raise the heat slightly so that the bubbles help to draw the white around the yolk. Poach for about 3 minutes, then lift the egg out with a perforated spoon.
3. Trim the white neatly with a pair of kitchen scissors and put the poached egg into a bowl of cold water until ready for use. Repeat the process for the remaining 3 eggs.
4. Strain the poaching liquid and set aside.
5. Make the sauce: melt 7g/¼oz of the butter in a small heavy saucepan, add the onion, carrot and celery and cook until soft but not brown. Add the garlic and cook for 2 minutes.
6. Add the strained poaching liquid, bouquet garni and peppercorns. Bring to the boil, then reduce the heat and simmer for 20–25 minutes, until the liquid has reduced by half its original quantity.
7. Meanwhile, prepare the garnish: put half the butter into a large heavy saucepan and slowly brown the pancetta in it. Remove and reserve.
8. Add the onions, shaking the pan to brown them evenly all over.
9. Add the mushrooms, fry fast for a further 2 minutes, then lift out with the onions and keep warm.
10. Finish the sauce: when the liquid has reduced, strain it into a small saucepan.
11. Mix the remaining butter and the flour together to a smooth paste. Whisk this gradually into the hot liquor, and whisk steadily until the sauce is smooth. Bring to the boil, then simmer for 2 minutes.
12. Meanwhile, reheat the eggs by slipping them into hot water for 1 minute. Lift out with a slotted spoon and drain thoroughly.
13. To serve: put the eggs on to the croûtes, divide the garnish on top of each and coat with the sauce.

 *LIGHT RED BURGUNDY*

# VEGETABLE
# AND SALAD
# FIRST COURSES

## STUFFED CREAM CHEESE TOMATOES

SERVES 2

*4 tomatoes, peeled*
*110g/4oz good cream cheese or sieved cottage*
*    cheese*
*1 tablespoon chopped fresh mint*
*a squeeze of lemon juice*
*¼ small clove of garlic, crushed*
*salt and freshly ground black pepper*
*1 tablespoon chopped fresh parsley*
*French dressing (see page 254)*
*sprigs of watercress*

To serve
*brown bread and butter*

1. Slice a quarter of each tomato off at the rounded end. Scoop out the flesh and seeds. Discard the seeds and coarsely chop the flesh. Leave the tomatoes to drain while making the filling.
2. Mix a little of the tomato flesh with the cream cheese, mint, lemon, garlic and the salt and pepper.
3. Fill the hollow tomatoes with this mixture and stick the tops back at a jaunty angle. Arrange on a plate.
4. Add the parsley to the dressing and shake or mix well. Spoon this over the tomatoes, and garnish with the watercress.
5. Serve with brown bread and butter.

 *LIGHT RED*

## STUFFED MUSHROOMS

SERVES 4

*4 large flat mushrooms about 7.5cm/3in in*
*    diameter*
*salt and freshly ground black pepper*
*70g/2½oz pancetta or streaky bacon, diced*
*2 shallots, finely chopped*
*½ clove of garlic, crushed*
*55g/2oz fresh white breadcrumbs*
*1 tablespoon chopped fresh parsley*
*1 tablespoon Sercial Madeira or dry sherry*
*1 tablespoon freshly grated Parmesan cheese*

1. Preheat the oven to 180°C/350°F/gas mark 4.
2. Wipe the mushrooms and peel them if necessary. Cut off the stems, dice and set aside.
3. Put the mushrooms in a single layer into a shallow ovenproof dish. Season with salt and pepper.
4. Sauté the pancetta or bacon for 1 minute over a medium-high heat, then reduce the heat to medium and add the shallots. Cook for a further 4 minutes, stirring frequently.
5. Add the diced mushroom stalks and continue to cook until the pancetta is lightly browned and the onions are golden (about 2 minutes).
6. Add the garlic and cook for 1 further minute. Remove from the heat.
7. Stir in the breadcrumbs, parsley and Madeira or sherry. Season to taste with salt and pepper.
8. Heap the stuffing mixture into the mushroom caps, pressing down lightly. Sprinkle with the Parmesan cheese.
9. Bake in the preheated oven for 20–25 minutes, or until the mushrooms are tender when pierced with a skewer and the stuffing is golden-brown.

## STUFFED VINE LEAVES (DOLMADES)

SERVES 8

*about 30 small young vine leaves*
*1 onion, finely chopped*
*2 tablespoons olive oil*
*225g/8oz cooked rice*
*a pinch of ground allspice*
*½ teaspoon chopped fresh mint*
*salt and freshly ground black pepper*
*white stock (see page 243)*
*1 tablespoon lemon juice*
*plain yoghurt or tomato sauce II (see page 258)*

1. Plunge the vine leaves into a saucepan of boiling salted water for 10 seconds. Rinse under cold running water and drain well. Lay the leaves, smooth side up, side by side on a worktop or board.
2. Fry the onion in the oil until soft but not coloured. Mix the onion (with its oil) together with the rice, allspice and mint. Season to taste with salt and pepper.

**3.** Lay a teaspoon of rice mixture on each vine leaf and roll up the leaf, tucking in the ends to make a small parcel. Squeeze the rolls in the palm of your hand – this will ensure that the dolmades hold their shape and will not need tying up. Pack all the dolmades into a wide saucepan and add enough stock to half-cover them. Sprinkle over the lemon juice. Cover tightly, preferably with a small plate that fits inside the pan (this will prevent the dolmades moving during cooking) and a lid. Simmer for 1 hour.

**4.** Lift out the dolmades with a slotted spoon and arrange on a serving dish. Chill. Coat with yoghurt or tomato sauce.

NOTE: Dolmades may be served hot, with the yoghurt or sauce handed separately.

 *CHIANTI*

# AVOCADOS STUFFED WITH CRAB

SERVES 4
*2 ripe avocados*
*French dressing (see page 254)*
*170g/6oz white crabmeat*
*1 stick of celery, finely chopped*
*3 tablespoons mayonnaise (page 250)*
*1 tablespoon single cream*
*1 teaspoon finely grated lemon zest*
*salt and freshly ground black pepper*

**1.** Cut the avocados in half lengthways, remove the stones and immediately brush the cut surface with French dressing to prevent discoloration.
**2.** Pick over the crabmeat and remove any pieces of inedible cartilage.
**3.** Mix the crabmeat and celery with the mayonnaise lightened by the addition of the cream and lemon zest. Season to taste with salt and pepper and pile into the avocado halves.

 *WHITE LOIRE*

# AVOCADOS WITH STRAWBERRY VINAIGRETTE

SERVES 4
*6 tablespoons oil*
*2 tablespoons lemon juice*
*4 strawberries*
*salt and freshly ground black pepper*
*a pinch of caster sugar*
*2 avocados*

**1.** Make the strawberry vinaigrette: liquidize the oil, lemon juice, strawberries, salt, pepper and sugar in a food processor or blender. The mixture should become fairly thick. Taste and add more sugar or salt as required.
**2.** Cut the avocados in half lengthways. Remove the stones and skin. Lay rounded side up and slice fairly thinly or cut into fans.
**3.** Spoon the strawberry vinaigrette on to 4 side plates, making sure that the base of each plate is completely covered. Arrange overlapping slices of avocado on top of the strawberry vinaigrette.

# TZATZIKI

Recipes for this are legion: some include mint; some do not call for garlic.

SERVES 6
*1 medium cucumber, grated*
*570ml/1 pint low-fat plain yoghurt*
*1 clove of garlic, crushed*
*freshly ground black pepper*

**1.** Place the cucumber in a sieve, sprinkle lightly with salt and leave to degorge for 30 minutes. Drain and pat dry.
**2.** Mix the cucumber with the yoghurt, garlic and plenty of pepper.

NOTE: The yoghurt can be thickened by draining it in a muslin-lined sieve; this will make for a creamier finish.

 *WHITE ALSACE*

# AUBERGINE LOAF

340g/12oz aubergines, peeled and diced
2 cloves of garlic, crushed and fried in ½
    tablespoon olive oil
2 eggs
225ml/8fl oz Greek yoghurt
a pinch of ground cumin
30g/1oz creamed coconut
salt and freshly ground black pepper

To serve
tomato sauce II (see page 258)

1. Preheat the oven to 150°C/300°F/gas mark 2. Oil
a 450g/1lb loaf tin and line with greaseproof paper.
2. Steam the aubergines for about 10 minutes or
until softened.
3. Mix together the garlic, eggs, yoghurt, cumin,
coconut, salt and pepper. Add the aubergines.
4. Pour into the prepared loaf tin and cover with
kitchen foil. Place in a roasting pan half-filled
with hot water (a bain-marie) and cook in the
preheated oven for 40 minutes or until firm.
5. Remove from the oven and allow to cool. Turn
out and serve cut in slices with the tomato sauce.

 *MEDIUM RED*

# TOMATO CHARTREUSE (JELLIED TOMATO RING)

SERVES 4
560g/1¼lb canned tomatoes
2 teaspoons tomato purée
salt and freshly ground white pepper
1 teaspoon caster sugar
1 clove of garlic
1 bay leaf
2 parsley stalks
about 6 fresh basil leaves
6 black peppercorns
tomato juice
2 tablespoons water
15g/½oz powdered gelatine
a squeeze of lemon juice

To serve
French dressing (see page 254)
about 30 fresh mint leaves

To garnish
watercress

1. Put the tomatoes, tomato purée, salt, pepper
and sugar into a heavy saucepan. Add the garlic,
bay leaf, parsley stalks, basil and peppercorns.
Simmer gently for 15 minutes.
2. Strain the mixture into a measuring jug. Make
up to 425ml/¾ pint with tomato juice. Taste and
season well with salt and pepper. Allow to cool.
3. Put the water into a small heavy saucepan and
sprinkle over the gelatine. Set aside for 5 minutes
to become spongy.
4. Wet a ring mould, jelly mould or savarin tin.
5. Dissolve the gelatine over a gentle heat until
liquid and clear. Stir into the tomato mixture, add
the lemon juice, and pour into the wetted mould.
Leave in the refrigerator to set for at least 2 hours.
6. Liquidize the French dressing with all but 10 of
the mint leaves in a food processor or blender.
7. Turn out the jelly on to a round plate: dip the
bottom of the mould briefly into hot water, put the
plate over the jelly, and turn plate and jelly over
together so that the jelly slips out on to the plate.
8. Garnish the jelly with the remaining mint and
watercress leaves. Hand the French dressing
separately.

 *CALIFORNIAN SAUVIGNON*

# TOMATO, AVOCADO AND MOZZARELLA SALAD

55g/2oz tomatoes per person, peeled and sliced
¼ avocado per person, sliced
55g/2oz mozzarella cheese per person, sliced
shredded fresh basil
French dressing (see page 254)
black olives
salt and freshly ground black pepper

1. Arrange the tomato, avocado and cheese in
overlapping slices on a serving dish.
2. Add the basil to the dressing. Pour over the
salad and sprinkle with a few olives. Season well
with salt and plenty of pepper.

 *SOAVE/FRASCATI*

# MUSHROOM AND PRAWN SALAD

SERVES 4
*170g/6oz frozen peeled, cooked prawns*
*lemon juice*
*freshly ground black pepper*
*170g/6oz button mushrooms, sliced*

For the French dressing
*3 tablespoons olive oil*
*1 tablespoon lemon juice*
*½ clove of garlic, crushed*
*salt and freshly ground black pepper*
*2 teaspoons chopped fresh mint*

To garnish
*1 teaspoon chopped fresh parsley*

**1.** Sprinkle the frozen prawns liberally with lemon juice and black pepper and leave to defrost.
**2.** Mix together the ingredients for the French dressing and add the mushrooms. Leave to marinate for 6 hours.
**3.** Add the prawns, mix well and put into a clean serving dish. Garnish with the parsley.

 *CHABLIS*

# THREE-PEA SALAD

SERVES 8
*110g/4oz brown lentils*
*110g/4oz chickpeas, soaked for 3 hours*
*110g/4oz split green peas*
*150ml/¼ pint French dressing (see page 254)*
*1 teaspoon chopped fresh mint*
*1 tablespoon chopped fresh parsley*
*1 teaspoon French mustard*
*salt*

**1.** Cook the lentils, chickpeas and split green peas in separate saucepans of boiling water. The lentils and split peas will take anything from 30 to 75 minutes, and the chickpeas up to 2 hours. Rinse them all under cold running water and drain well.
**2.** Shake the dressing in a jar until well emulsified.

Add the herbs and mustard and shake again. Mix with the lentils, chickpeas and peas and pile into a serving dish.

NOTE: Other pulses, such as soya beans, red kidney beans and haricot beans, are good treated similarly.

 *ALSACE WHITE*

# SHELL SALAD

This recipe has been adapted from *Cooking with Michael Smith*.

SERVES 4
*8 cooked king prawns*
*1 avocado, sliced*
*2 oranges, cut into segments*
*110g/4oz cooked mangetout*
*110g/4oz cooked cauliflower florets*
*French dressing (see page 254)*
*chopped fresh chives*
*chopped fresh parsley*
*salt and freshly ground black pepper*

**1.** Mix all the ingredients together, season and serve, well chilled, on individual plates.

 *WHITE LOIRE*

# PEASANT SALAD

SERVES 4
*1 curly endive lettuce*
*110g/4oz piece of rindless bacon*
*2 slices of thick white bread*
*oil*
*French dressing made with plenty of garlic (see page 254)*

**1.** Wash and trim the lettuce. Spin dry.
**2.** Cut the bacon and bread into 2cm/¾in cubes.
**3.** Fry the bacon in oil in a frying pan until it begins to brown. Remove and keep warm. Add the bread to the pan and fry until brown and crisp.
**4.** Toss together and serve immediately.

 *ALSACE WHITE/LIGHT RED*

# MELON, CUCUMBER AND TOMATO SALAD

*6 tomatoes, peeled, deseeded and cut into slivers*
*1 cucumber, cubed*
*1 medium ripe melon, deseeded and cut into chunks*
*French dressing (see page 254)*
*1 tablespoon chopped fresh mint*

**1.** Mix all the ingredients together with the French dressing and mint. Serve well chilled.

# FOIE GRAS AND ARTICHOKE HEART SALAD

SERVES 6
*2 handfuls of bitter salad leaves*
*French dressing (see page 254)*
*4 warm artichoke hearts*
*110g/4oz pâté de foie gras*

**1.** Wash, pick over and pull to smallish pieces the bitter salad leaves. Dry well. Toss in some of the French dressing and arrange on 6 side plates.
**2.** Slice the still warm artichoke hearts and toss in the remaining French dressing. Pile them on top of the salad leaves.
**3.** Slice the foie gras very thinly and arrange the slices on top of the artichoke hearts. Serve immediately.

 *MOSELLE*

# BACON AND QUAIL'S EGG SALAD

SERVES 6
*2 handfuls of very young spinach or beet leaves*
*1 handful of young dandelion leaves, or*
*    watercress if not available*
*French dressing (see page 254)*
*12 raw quail's eggs*
*3 rashers of rindless streaky smoked bacon*
*2 tablespoons oil for frying*
*1 slice of bread*

**1.** Wash and pick over the spinach and dandelion leaves and pull them into small pieces, discarding any stalks or thick ribs. Dry well. Toss in the dressing and arrange on 6 individual plates.
**2.** Break the quail's eggs carefully on to a plate. Get a frying pan or shallow sauté pan of water bubbling on the heat. Slide the eggs into it. Reduce the heat and poach for 1 minute. Remove from the pan and slip into a bowl of warm water until ready for use.
**3.** Cut the bacon across into thin strips. Brown them rapidly in the oil. Remove them. Cut the bread into small dice and fry in the hot fat until evenly browned. Remove with a perforated spoon and drain on absorbent kitchen paper.
**4.** Arrange 2 well-drained eggs per person on the salads. Add a sprinkling of bacon, then the fried croûtons, still warm, and serve immediately.

 *DRY WHITE*

# PINENUT AND DUCK BREAST SALAD

SERVES 4
*2 handfuls of bitter salad leaves, such as mâche,*
*    watercress, chicory, radicchio*
*2 tablespoons French dressing, made with walnut oil*
*15g/¹/₂oz unsalted butter*
*1 duck breast, skinned and halved horizontally*
*55g/2oz pinenuts*

**1.** Wash and pick over the bitter salad leaves and pull them into small pieces. Dry well. Toss in the French dressing and arrange on 4 individual plates.
**2.** Heat the butter in a frying pan until it has ceased to foam. Add the duck breast pieces and fry fairly fast to brown on both sides – about 3 minutes in all. They are done when they feel firm when pressed and are pink, not blue, when cut. Lift out on to a board.
**3.** Put the pinenuts into the frying pan and shake over the heat until pale brown and crisp.
**4.** Cut the duck diagonally into thin slices and scatter over the salad with the pinenuts. Serve immediately.

 *LIGHT/SOFT RED*

# GRILLED PEPPER SALAD

SERVES 4
*2 large red peppers*
*2 large green peppers*
*2 large yellow peppers*
*3 hardboiled eggs*
*6 anchovy fillets*
*2 tablespoons extra virgin olive oil*
*freshly ground black pepper*

**1.** Cut the peppers into quarters and remove the stalks, inner membranes and seeds. Preheat the grill to its highest setting.
**2.** Grill the peppers, skin side uppermost, until the skin is black and blistered. Using a small knife, scrape off all the skin.
**3.** Cut the flesh into shapes like petals, and arrange them like a flower on a flat round dish, garnishing with the hardboiled eggs, cut into quarters, and the anchovy fillets. Pour over the olive oil and sprinkle with a little pepper.

 *ALSACE WHITE*

# DUCK LIVER AND MANGETOUT SALAD

SERVES 6
*450g/1lb mangetout, topped and tailed*
*225g/8oz duck livers*
*crisp salad leaves, such as radicchio or middle leaves of cos*
*3 spring onions, finely chopped*
*French dressing (see page 254)*
*15g/¹/₂oz butter*

**1.** Blanch the mangetout in rapidly boiling salted water for 3–4 minutes. Rinse under cold running water and drain very well.
**2.** Pick over the duck livers.
**3.** Toss the salad leaves, spring onions and mangetout in the French dressing. Drain off any excess dressing and arrange on 6 individual plates.
**4.** Just before serving, slice the livers and sauté them in a little butter for 1 minute – they should

become just firm but not cooked. Lift them out of the pan with a slotted spoon and scatter on top of the salad.

 *CLARET*

# MANGO AND LOBSTER SALAD

SERVES 4
*4 handfuls of bitter salad leaves, such as endive, lamb's lettuce and radicchio*
*French dressing (see page 254)*
*2 ripe mangoes*
*2 × 450g/1lb cooked lobsters*

**1.** Wash and dry the salad leaves. Toss in some of the French dressing and arrange on 4 individual plates.
**2.** Cut a thick slice from each side of the mangoes, keeping as close to the stone as possible.
**3.** Carefully peel off the skin and slice the flesh horizontally.
**4.** Cut the heads and claws off the lobsters and remove the shell, rather like peeling a large prawn. Cut the body flesh into neat slices or collops. Crack the claws but leave whole.
**5.** Arrange alternate slices of lobster and mango on each diner's plate. Pour over the remaining French dressing and garnish with a claw.

 *WHITE BURGUNDY*

# SCALLOP AND ROCKET SALAD

SERVES 4
*12 scallops*
*seasoned plain flour*
*hazelnut oil*
*balsamic vinegar*
*fresh chives*
*a large handful of rocket, washed*

**1.** Clean the scallops (*see page 128*). Remove the muscular white frill found opposite the roe. Rinse off any black matter. Slice them in half horizontally, trying to keep the roe attached to the scallop.

**2.** Dip the scallops into seasoned flour. Heat some oil in a frying pan and fry the scallops quickly on both sides until lightly browned and just cooked. Sprinkle over some vinegar.

**3.** Tip the scallops on to the rocket leaves. Turn lightly and place on 4 individual plates.

 *DRY WHITE*

# SALADE TIÈDE

SERVES 4
*1 tablespoon olive oil*
*110g/4oz piece of rindless bacon, diced*
*150ml/¼ pint olive oil*
*4 slices of white bread, cut into 1cm/½ inch cubes*
*salt*
*225g/8oz chicken livers, cleaned*
*5 spring onions, sliced on the diagonal*
*1 tablespoon tarragon vinegar*
*1 small frisée lettuce*
*1 bunch of watercress*
*1 small radicchio*
*French dressing (see page 254)*
To garnish
*1 bunch of chervil, roughly chopped*

**1.** Heat 1 tablespoon of the oil in a frying pan and cook the bacon until it is evenly browned all over. Lift it out with a slotted spoon and keep it warm in a low oven.

**2.** Heat 150ml/¼ pint oil in another frying pan and cook the bread until golden-brown. Drain well and sprinkle with a little salt. Keep the croûtons warm in the oven.

**3.** Tip most of the oil out of the frying pan and gently cook the livers until slightly stiffened and fairly firm but not hard to the touch. They should be light brown on the outside and pink in the middle. Add the spring onions and fry for 30 seconds.

**4.** Add the tarragon vinegar to the pan and shake the livers and spring onions in the vinegar for 10 seconds.

**5.** Toss the salad leaves in the well-seasoned

French dressing and divide it between 4 dinner plates.

**6.** Scatter the croûtons, the bacon, the spring onions and livers over the salad. Sprinkle the salad with the chervil and serve immediately.

 *SPICY DRY WHITE*

# ITALIAN BREAD SALAD

SERVES 6
*225g/8oz Italian bread (see page 614)*
*1 large red onion, roughly chopped*
*3 sticks of celery, roughly chopped*
*½ cucumber, peeled, sliced and deseeded*
*10 fresh basil leaves, roughly chopped*
*2 tablespoons capers, drained and rinsed*
*450g/1lb beef tomatoes, peeled and finely chopped*
*salt and freshly ground black pepper*
*110ml/4fl oz good-quality olive oil*
*1–2 tablespoons red wine vinegar*

To garnish
*5 fresh basil leaves*
*radicchio*

**1.** Soak the bread in cold water for 30 minutes. Squeeze out the water and put the bread on a large flat dish.

**2.** Lay the onion on top of the bread followed by the celery, cucumber, basil leaves, capers and tomato.

**3.** Cover and refrigerate for at least 2 hours.

**4.** Transfer to a large bowl. Add salt and pepper to taste, then the oil and vinegar. Toss very well, sprinkle over the remaining basil leaves, then garnish with a few radicchio leaves.

 *DRY WHITE*

# WARM MEDITERRANEAN SALAD WITH POLENTA

SERVES 10 (AS A FIRST COURSE)
*1 litre/1³/4 pints white stock (see page243)*
*200g/7oz freshly polenta (coarse cornmeal)*
*140g/5oz Parmesan cheese, grated*
*salt and freshly ground black pepper*
*85ml/3fl oz olive oil, infused with a sliced clove of garlic*
*2 medium aubergines*
*2 large courgettes*
*1¹/2 tablespoons chopped fresh oregano*
*140g/5oz prosciutto, thinly sliced*
*¹/2 head of radicchio, washed*
*140g/5oz mesclun, washed*
*2 teaspoons balsamic vinegar*
*30g/1oz fresh Parmesan cheese*

**1.** Heat the stock in a large saucepan until simmering. Slowly pour in the polenta, stirring all the time until thick. Reduce the heat to as low as possible, cover the pan and cook, stirring frequently, for 30–40 minutes. Add 125g/4¹/2oz of the Parmesan cheese and season with pepper. Cover and set aside to cool slightly.

**2.** Pour the polenta on to a damp baking sheet and smooth the surface with a wet spatula. The polenta should be about 1cm/¹/2in thick.

**3.** Preheat the grill.

**4.** When the polenta is cool, cut into diamond shapes, place on a lightly greased baking sheet, brush with the flavoured oil and grill under the hot grill. When brown and crisp turn the shapes over, brush with more oil and grill on the other side. Dust with the remaining grated Parmesan cheese.

**5.** Cut the aubergines into long strips 1cm/¹/2in wide and salt them lightly. Leave for 30 minutes, then rinse and dry. Brush with the flavoured oil and grill until soft.

**6.** Slice the courgettes on the diagonal into 5mm/¹/4in pieces. Brush with the flavoured oil and grill on both sides until just cooked and lightly browned. Toss with the oregano.

**7.** Heat some of the remaining flavoured oil in a frying pan, add the prosciutto and fry briskly until crisp and brown.

**8.** Arrange the radicchio and mesclun on 10 individual serving plates. Distribute the aubergine, courgettes and prosciutto between the plates. Mix 2 tablespoons of the flavoured oil with the vinegar and sprinkle over the salads. Scatter with shavings of Parmesan cheese. Put 2 warm polenta shapes on each plate.

 *CHILLED LIGHT RED*

# SMOKED CHICKEN SALAD

SERVES 4
*1 small smoked chicken*
*85g/3oz butter*
*1 teaspoon chopped fresh parsley*
*salt and freshly ground black pepper*
*radicchio and lamb's lettuce*
*1 teaspoon dry English mustard*
*French dressing (see page 254)*

**1.** Separate the legs from the body of the chicken.

**2.** Mince or pound the leg flesh (without the skin) in a food processor with the butter and parsley. Season to taste with salt and pepper.

**3.** Shape this pâté into a cylinder and roll up in a piece of kitchen foil. Chill, then unwrap and cut into slices.

**4.** Carve the chicken breast into thin slices and divide them between 4 individual plates, overlapping the slices attractively.

**5.** Add a slice or two of the pâté to each plate with a few crisp salad leaves.

**6.** Add the mustard to the French dressing and whisk until smooth. Spoon a little dressing over each salad before serving.

 *SPICY/MEDIUM DRY WHITE*

# ROCKET AND BUTTERNUT SQUASH SALAD

SERVES 4
*1 large butternut squash*
*oil*
*2 large handfuls of rocket leaves*
*1 tablespoon roughly chopped fresh basil*
*1 quantity French dressing (see page 254)*

**1.** Peel the squash as best you can. Remove any seeds and cut the flesh into 5mm/¼in thick slices.
**2.** Heat the oil in a frying pan with a ridged base, add the squash and fry until lightly coloured and just tender. Drain lightly.
**3.** Put the rocket into a salad bowl, add the squash and basil and toss together with the French dressing. Serve as soon as possible.

# SCALLOP AND ASPARAGUS SALAD

SERVES 4
*225g/8oz young asparagus, trimmed*
*salt and freshly ground black pepper*
*12 scallops*
*endive*
*radicchio*
*lamb's lettuce*
*French dressing (see page 254)*
*unsalted butter*
*lemon juice*

**1.** Cook the asparagus in boiling salted water until just tender. Drain well.
**2.** Clean the scallops, removing the muscular white frill found opposite the roe. Rinse off any black matter. Separate the roes from the body and slice both in half horizontally.

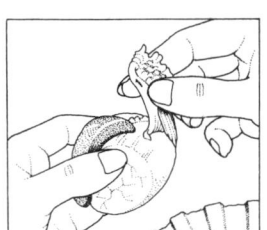

*Remove the muscular white frill found opposite the scallop roe*

**3.** Toss the well-washed salad leaves in French dressing and divide between 4 individual plates.
**4.** Arrange the still warm asparagus on top of the salad leaves.
**5.** Fry the scallops quickly in a little butter. Cool slightly, and add the lemon juice, salt and pepper.
**6.** Divide the scallops, with their pan juices, between the 4 plates.

 *WHITE LOIRE*

# VEGETABLE RIBBON SALAD

SERVES 4
*4 carrots*
*4 medium courgettes*
*French dressing (see page 254)*

To garnish
*1 tablespoon finely chopped fresh chives*
*1 tablespoon toasted poppy seeds*

**1.** Peel the carrots, then continuing to use the vegetable peeler, shred them into long thin ribbons.
**2.** Top and tail the courgettes, then proceed as for the carrots, and shred the courgettes into long thin ribbons.
**3.** Toss the carrots and courgettes in the French dressing at least 2 hours before serving so that the vegetables begin to curl.
**4.** Arrange on individual plates and garnish with the chives and poppy seeds.

Above: Provençal Fish Soup.

Above: Herb Omelette Salad. Right: Aubergine Loaf.

Left: Mango and Lobster Salad. Above: Marinated Italian Aubergines and Courgettes.

Above: Aubergine Charlotte. Right: Red Pepper Bavarois with Red Pepper Salad.

Left: Terrine de Ratatouille Niçoise. Above: Leith's Restaurant's Artichoke and Green Olive Pie.

Above: Jams Californian Vegetables. Right: Potato Cakes with Smoked Salmon.

Left: Ceviche. Above: Squid Salad with Cucumber and Cumin.

Above: Arbroath Smokies Pots. Right: Easy Fish Quenelles

**Above: Wild Mushrooms.** 1. St George. 2. Velvet shank. 3. Blackening Russula. 4. Cep. 5. Wood blewit. 6. Shiitake. 7. Oyster (pink). 8. Oyster (yellow). 9. Chanterelle. 10. Oyster (wild). 11. Morel. 12. Fairy Ring Champignon.

# TABOULEH

Recipes for this are legion. The important thing is that the salad should be green and have a good lemon flavour.

SERVES 4
*110g/4oz burghul (cracked wheat)*
*1 tomato, peeled, deseeded and chopped*
*1/2 cucumber, deseeded and chopped*
*10 fresh mint leaves, finely chopped*
*a good handful of fresh parsley, finely chopped*
*1 shallot, finely chopped*
*3 tablespoons olive oil*
*salt and freshly ground black pepper*
*lemon juice*

**1.** Soak the wheat in cold water for 15 minutes – it will expand greatly. Drain and wrap in a clean tea towel. Squeeze out the moisture. Spread the wheat on a tray to dry further.
**2.** Mix all the ingredients together, adding salt, pepper and plenty of lemon juice to taste.

 *MUSCADET*

# CRUDITÉS

A selection of:
*celery*
*red pepper*
*cauliflower*
*radishes*
*spring onions*
*carrots*
*young asparagus*
*tiny mangetout*
*baby sweetcorn*
*celeriac*

For the dressing
*1 clove of garlic, crushed (optional)*
*150ml/1/4 pint mayonnaise (see page 250)*

**1.** Prepare the vegetables, making sure they are perfectly clean, and as far as possible evenly sized.
Celery: wash and cut into sticks.
Pepper: wipe and cut into strips, discarding the inner membrane and seeds.

Cauliflower: wash and break into florets. Peel the stalks if tough, blanch and refresh if required.
Radishes: wash and trim off the root and long leaves, but leave a little of the green stalk.
Spring onions: wash. Cut off most of the green part, and the beard (roots). Leave whole, or cut in half lengthways if large.
Carrots: peel and cut into sticks the same shape and size as the celery.
Asparagus: peel the tough outer stalk and trim away the hard root ends.
Celeriac: peel and cut into strips. Blanch and refresh if required.
**2.** Mix the garlic, if using, with the mayonnaise. Spoon it into a small serving bowl.
**3.** Arrange the raw prepared vegetables in neat clumps on a tray or flat platter with the bowl of mayonnaise dip in the centre.

 *ROSÉ DE PROVENCE*

# CUCUMBER WITH SOURED CREAM

*1 medium cucumber*

For the dressing
*3 tablespoons oil*
*1 tablespoon white wine vinegar*
*salt and freshly ground white pepper*
*a pinch of caster sugar*
*1 tablespoon chopped fresh mint*

For the topping
*55g/2oz soft cream cheese*
*2 tablespoons soured cream*
*1 small clove of garlic, crushed*
*juice of 1/2 lemon*

**1.** Slice the cucumber thinly. Sprinkle the slices lightly with salt and leave for 20 minutes.
**2.** Put the dressing ingredients into a screw-top jar and shake until well emulsified.
**3.** Beat the cream cheese until soft, then gradually stir in the soured cream. Add the garlic, and season with salt, pepper and lemon juice to taste.
**4.** Rinse, drain and dry the cucumber thoroughly. Toss the slices in the French dressing and put

them into a serving dish, or on to individual plates. Spoon the cream cheese mixture on top.

NOTE: This makes a good salad, with others, for a party, or can be served with hot bread and butter as a light first course.

 *MEDIUM DRY WHITE*

# MARINATED ITALIAN AUBERGINES AND COURGETTES

This recipe has been adapted from a similar recipe by Sophie Grigson.

SERVES 8
*450g/1lb small courgettes (yellow or green)*
*450g/1lb small aubergines*
*salt and freshly ground black pepper*
*olive oil*
*1 large onion, roughly chopped*
*1 carrot, diced*
*5 fresh sage leaves, roughly torn*
*juice of 1 lemon*
*4 tablespoons dry white wine*
*225ml/8fl oz white wine vinegar*
*3 juniper berries*
*1 bay leaf*
*2 sprigs of fresh parsley*

1. Trim the ends off the courgettes and aubergines and cut into quarters lengthways.
2. Place in a colander, sprinkle with salt and leave to degorge for 30 minutes.
3. Rinse and dry the vegetables and fry in oil until lightly browned and just tender. The aubergines will take considerably longer to cook than the courgettes. Transfer, skin side up, to a heatproof dish.
4. Meanwhile, put the remaining ingredients into a large saucepan. Bring them to the boil and simmer for 2 minutes.
5. When all the courgettes and aubergines are cooked, reheat the vinegar marinade and pour it over the vegetables. Leave to cool. Cover and refrigerate for 2 days.

6. Remove and discard any bedraggled herbs and vegetables. Bring back to room temperature before serving.

# AUBERGINES ROBERT

SERVES 4
*2 aubergines*
*150ml/¹/4 pint French dressing (see page 254)*
*1 teaspoon chopped fresh chives*

1. Slice the aubergines and soak them in the dressing for 2 hours.
2. Preheat the grill.
3. Grill the aubergines on both sides until pale brown. Sprinkle well with chives and more dressing and grill again for 1 minute or until golden-brown. Turn the slices over, sprinkle again with dressing and chives, and grill until a good brown.
4. Allow to cool. Chill well before serving.

 *ROSÉ*

# GRILLED AUBERGINES WITH PESTO

SERVES 4
*2 medium aubergines, sliced*
*salt*
*150ml/¹/4 pint French dressing (see page 254)*
*2 teaspoons French mustard*
*parsley pesto sauce (see page 255)*

1. Sprinkle the aubergine slices liberally with salt and leave to degorge for 30 minutes.
2. Make the French dressing and season with the mustard.
3. Rinse the aubergines, drain and dry well. Soak them in the French dressing for 2 hours. Drain well.
4. Preheat the grill.
5. Grill the aubergines for about 10 minutes on each side, or until soft and pale brown.
6. Spread one side of the aubergine with the parsley pesto sauce and return to the grill for 1 minute.
7. Arrange on a round plate.

 *LIGHT RED/ROSÉ*

# CELERIAC RÉMOULADE

SERVES 4

*3 tablespoons mayonnaise (see page 250)*
*½ teaspoon Dijon mustard*
*2 teaspoons finely chopped gherkin*
*2 teaspoons finely chopped fresh tarragon or*
*  chervil*
*2 teaspoons finely chopped capers*
*1 anchovy fillet, finely chopped*
*450g/1lb celeriac*

**1.** Mix together all the ingredients except the celeriac.
**2.** Peel the celeriac and cut into very fine matchstick lengths. Blanch briefly in boiling acidulated water, refresh and drain well. Mix with the sauce, before it has time to discolour.
**3.** Turn into a clean dish.

NOTE: Rémoulade sauce is a mayonnaise with a predominantly mustard flavour. The other ingredients, though good, are not always present.

 *SPICY DRY WHITE*

# MUSHROOMS À LA GRECQUE

SERVES 4

*425ml/¾ pint water*
*1 tablespoon tomato purée*
*2 tablespoons olive oil*
*2 tablespoons dry white wine*
*2 shallots, finely chopped*
*1 clove of garlic, crushed*
*6 coriander seeds, well crushed*
*1 teaspoon chopped fresh fennel*
*freshly ground black pepper*
*a small pinch of salt*
*a pinch of caster sugar*
*a good squeeze of lemon juice*
*450g/1lb button mushrooms, wiped and trimmed*
*2 teaspoons chopped fresh parsley*

**1.** Place all the ingredients except the mushrooms and parsley in a saucepan and simmer gently for 15–20 minutes.

**2.** Add the mushrooms and simmer for 10 minutes, then remove.
**3.** Unless it tastes very strong, reduce the liquid by boiling to about 190ml/⅓ pint. Put the mushrooms back and allow to cool.
**4.** Check the seasoning and tip into a shallow bowl or dish. Sprinkle with the parsley.

 *BEAUJOLAIS*

# MUSHROOM ROULADE

SERVES 4–6

*450g/1lb mature flat mushrooms, roughly*
*  chopped*
*30g/1oz butter*
*30g/1oz plain flour*
*1 teaspoon tomato purée*
*1 teaspoon mushroom ketchup (optional)*
*a pinch of freshly grated nutmeg*
*salt and freshly ground black pepper*
*4 eggs, separated*

For the filling
*225g/8oz cream cheese*
*4 tablespoons fromage frais or plain yoghurt*
*4 medium spring onions, thinly sliced*
*1 tablespoon chopped fresh mixed herbs, such as*
*  parsley, thyme, sage, chervil*
*salt and freshly ground black pepper*

**1.** Preheat the oven to 200°C/400°F/gas mark 6. Place the mushrooms in a food processor with 1 tablespoon water. Process until very finely chopped.
**2.** Melt the butter in a large saucepan, add the flour and cook together for 30 seconds.
**3.** Add the mushrooms and stir well. Heat steadily and cook, stirring occasionally, until the mushrooms are fairly dry. (They will, at first, exude a lot of liquid which needs to be evaporated. This may take up to 20 minutes.) Meanwhile, line a large roasting pan with a double sheet of lightly greased greaseproof paper or non-stick baking parchment, allowing the edges to stick up above the sides of the pan.
**4.** Remove the mushrooms from the heat and add the tomato purée, mushroom ketchup, nutmeg,

and salt and pepper to taste. Stir in the egg yolks and turn into a large bowl.

**5.** In another large bowl whisk the egg whites with a balloon whisk until they will hold their shape. Take a spoonful of egg white and add to the mushroom mixture, stirring it in to loosen the mixture.

**6.** Fold the remaining egg whites into the mixture and carefully spread the mixture into the prepared roasting pan, taking care not to lose any air.

**7.** Cook in the preheated oven for about 12 minutes, or until the roulade is firm to the touch.

**8.** Meanwhile, prepare the filling. Using a wooden spoon, combine the cream cheese carefully with the fromage frais, stirring well to ensure no lumps are left. Add the spring onions, herbs, salt and pepper.

**9.** When the roulade is cooked, turn it on to a piece of greaseproof paper, trim the edges, spread over the filling and roll it up carefully, letting it rest on the seam. Wrap tightly with the greaseproof paper and place in the refrigerator for about 30 minutes, or until cold.

 *LIGHT RED*

**2.** Prepare the filling: melt the butter in a saucepan and gently cook the mushrooms in it. Remove the pan from the heat, add the flour and mix well. Return the pan to the heat and cook for 30 seconds. Add the milk and bring to the boil, stirring continuously until you have a very thick creamy sauce. Add the cream and parsley and season to taste with salt and pepper.

**3.** Preheat the oven to 190°C/375°F/gas mark 5.

**4.** Make the roulade: gradually beat the egg yolks and butter into the spinach and season with salt, pepper and nutmeg. Whisk the egg whites until stiff but not dry and fold them into the spinach. Pour the mixture into the prepared roasting pan and spread it flat. Bake in the preheated oven for 10–12 minutes, or until it feels dry to the touch.

**5.** Put a piece of greaseproof paper on top of a tea towel. Turn the roulade out on to the paper and remove the original piece of paper. Spread the filling on to the roulade and roll it up as you would a Swiss roll, removing the paper as you go. Serve whole on a warmed dish. Slice to serve

 *SOFT RED*

# SPINACH ROULADE

SERVES 4
*4 eggs, separated*
*15g/¹/₂oz butter*
*450g/1lb fresh spinach, or 170g/6oz frozen leaf*
*spinach, cooked and puréed*
*salt and freshly ground black pepper*
*a pinch of freshly grated nutmeg*

For the filling
*15g/¹/₂oz butter*
*170g/6oz mushrooms, chopped*
*15g/¹/₂oz plain flour*
*150/¹/₄ pint milk*
*4 tablespoons double cream*
*1 tablespoon chopped fresh parsley*
*salt and freshly ground black pepper*

**1.** Line a roasting pan with a double sheet of lightly greased greaseproof paper or non-stick baking parchment. Allow the edges to stick above the sides of the tin.

# SPINACH ROULADE WITH SMOKED SALMON AND CRÈME FRAÎCHE

SERVES 4
*15g/¹/₂oz butter*
*4 eggs, separated*
*450g/1lb fresh spinach, or 170g/6oz frozen leaf*
*spinach, cooked and puréed*
*salt and freshly ground black pepper*
*a pinch of freshly grated nutmeg*

For the filling
*290ml/¹/₂ pint crème fraîche*
*110g/4oz smoked salmon, chopped*
*2 teaspoons chopped fresh dill*

**1.** Preheat the oven to 190°C/375°F/gas mark 5. Line a large roasting pan with a double sheet of lightly greased greaseproof paper or non-stick baking parchment, allowing the edges to stick up above the sides of the pan.

**2.** Make the roulade: beat the butter and egg yolks into the spinach and season with salt, pepper and nutmeg. Whisk the egg whites until stiff but not dry and fold them into the spinach. Pour the mixture into the prepared roasting pan and spread it flat. Bake in the preheated oven for 10–12 minutes, or until it feels dry to the touch.
**3.** Mix together the filling ingredients.
**4.** Turn the roulade out on to a piece of greaseproof paper. Spread the filling on to the roulade and roll it up as you would a Swiss roll, removing the paper as you go. Serve on a warmed dish.

NOTE: Extra soured cream can be served separately with this dish.

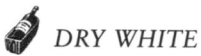 *DRY WHITE*

## SPINACH AND RICOTTA STRUDELS

These strudels can be made easily with bought filo pastry.

SERVES 6
*450g/1lb fresh spinach, cooked and finely chopped*
*170g/6oz ricotta cheese*
*1 egg, lightly beaten*
*salt and freshly ground black pepper*
*freshly grated nutmeg*
*340g/12oz flour quantity filo or strudel pastry (see page 466)*
*melted butter*

**1.** Preheat the oven to 200°C/400°F/gas mark 6.
**2.** Mix the spinach with the ricotta cheese, egg, salt, pepper, and nutmeg to taste.
**3.** Cut the strudel sheets into 13cm/5in squares. Brush each square immediately with melted butter. Lay 2 or 3 squares on top of each other.
**4.** Put a spoonful of the spinach mixture on each piece of pastry. Fold the sides of the pastry over slightly to prevent the filling escaping during cooking, then roll the strudels up rather like a Swiss roll.

**5.** Brush with more melted butter, place on a greased baking sheet and bake in the preheated oven for 15 minutes.

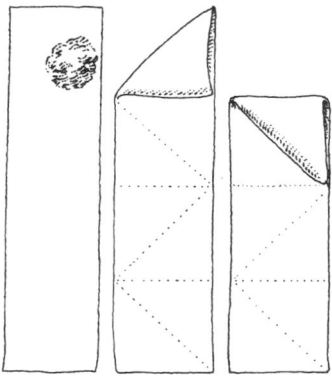

*Put a spoonful of filling in the top right-hand corner and fold the pastry into successive triangles*

NOTE: Alternatively, the strudel pastry can be cut into long strips, a spoonful of the filling placed in the top right-hand corner and the pastry folded into successive triangles as illustrated.

 *SPICY DRY WHITE/LIGHT RED RED*

## SPINACH MOULDS

SERVES 6
*30g/1oz butter*
*675g/1½lb spinach leaves, destalked and washed*
*225g/8oz ricotta cheese*
*30g/1oz Gruyère cheese, grated*
*30g/1oz fresh Parmesan cheese, grated*
*2 eggs*
*4 tablespoons single cream*
*freshly grated nutmeg*
*salt and freshly ground black pepper*

**1.** Lightly butter 6 ramekins.
**2.** Blanch 10 spinach leaves, refresh, drain and dry well.

3. Arrange the leaves inside the ramekin dishes, overlapping the edges.

4. Cook the remaining spinach leaves for 2 minutes, then drain very well by pressing between 2 plates. Chop finely. Preheat the oven to 200°C/400°F/gas mark 6.

5. Mix together the cheese, eggs, cream, nutmeg, salt and pepper.

6. Fill the ramekins with alternate layers of the cheese mixture and the chopped spinach. Fold the spinach leaves over the top to cover.

7. Dot butter on each ramekin. Set in a roasting pan half-filled with hot water (a bain-marie) and bake in the preheated oven for 25–30 minutes until set. Remove from the oven and allow to rest for 2 minutes before unmoulding.

## SPINACH TIMBALE

SERVES 4–6
*675g/1½lb fresh spinach*
*30g/1oz butter*
*85g/3oz fresh white breadcrumbs, sieved*
*2 eggs, beaten*
*1 egg yolk*
*a pinch of freshly grated nutmeg*
*salt and freshly ground black pepper*
*340ml/12fl oz milk*

To serve
*tomato dressing (see page 254)*

1. Wash the spinach well and remove the tough stalks. Blanch, refresh and drain 15 of the biggest and best leaves. Put the remaining still wet spinach into a saucepan with a lid and, holding the pan in one hand and the lid on with the other, shake and toss the spinach over heat until it is tender and reduced in quantity.

2. Squeeze all the water from the spinach, pressing it between 2 plates. Tip on to a board and chop very finely. Butter a 15cm/6in cake tin or soufflé dish and line it with the whole spinach leaves.

3. In a saucepan melt the butter, add the spinach and stir until very dry looking. Remove from the heat and add the breadcrumbs, eggs, egg yolk, nutmeg, salt and pepper.

4. Heat the milk and stir it into the mixture.

5. Spoon the spinach mixture into the lined cake tin or soufflé dish and cover with buttered kitchen foil or greaseproof paper.

6. Preheat the oven to 180°C/350°F/gas mark 4. Stand the tin or dish in a roasting pan half-filled with hot water (a bain-marie). Remove from the oven and allow to rest in the preheated oven for 45 minutes, or until the mixture is firm.

7. Turn out on to a warmed serving dish.

NOTE: Individual spinach timbales can be made in ramekin dishes. They will take 20–30 minutes to cook. The finer the china, the more quickly the mixture will cook.

## CARROT AND SPINACH TIMBALES

SERVES 6
*450g/1lb carrots, peeled and sliced*
*2 eggs, beaten*
*290ml/½ pint double cream*
*a pinch of ground cumin*
*salt and freshly ground black pepper*
*450g/1lb spinach, tough stalks removed*
*a pinch of freshly grated nutmeg*

1. Cook the carrots in boiling salted water until very tender. Drain well, whizz in a food processor and push through a sieve. Cool.

2. Stir in half the beaten egg and half the cream, and season well with cumin, salt and pepper.

3. Cook the spinach in a very little boiling water until tender. Drain very well, cool slightly and whizz in a food processor with the remaining beaten egg and cream. Season well with nutmeg, salt and pepper.

4. Line the bottom of 6 timbale moulds or ramekins with circles of greased greaseproof paper. Spoon in the carrot then carefully pile on the spinach purée.

5. Preheat the oven to 180°C/350°F/gas mark 4. Cook the timbales in a roasting pan half-filled with hot water (a bain-marie) for about 40 minutes or until set. Turn out on to warmed individual plates to serve.

NOTE: If spinach is not available, broccoli can be used instead.

 *MEDIUM DRY WHITE*

# CARROT AND GRUYÈRE TIMBALES

SERVES 4
*170g/6oz carrots, grated*
*85g/3oz Gruyère cheese, grated*
*1 egg, beaten*
*salt and freshly ground black pepper*
*1/2 teaspoon dry English mustard*
*2 tablespoons double cream*
*butter*

To serve
*tomato sauce I (see page 258)*

**1.** Preheat the oven to 190°C/375°F/gas mark 5.
**2.** Blanch the carrot in boiling water for 30 seconds. Refresh under cold running water and drain well on absorbent kitchen paper. Mix together the carrot, cheese, egg, salt, pepper, mustard and cream. Beat well.
**3.** Butter 4 dariole moulds and pour in the carrot and cheese mixture. Cover with lids or kitchen foil and put the moulds into a roasting pan half filled with hot water.
**4.** Bake in the preheated oven for 20 minutes. Carefully turn the moulds out on to a warmed serving dish or individual plates. Hand the tomato sauce separately.

 *LIGHT RED*

# COURGETTE TIMBALES

SERVES 6
*450g/1lb courgettes*
*salt and freshly ground black pepper*
*2 eggs*
*1 egg yolk*
*55g/2oz fresh white breadcrumbs, sieved*
*290ml/1/2 pint milk*
*1 tablespoon chopped fresh thyme*

To serve
*tomato sauce II (see page 258)*

**1.** Preheat the oven to 170°C/325°F/gas mark 3.

**2.** Oil and line 6 ramekins with circles of greased greaseproof paper.
**3.** Top, tail and grate the courgettes. Sprinkle sparingly with salt. Leave to degorge in a sieve for 30 minutes. Rinse and dry well on absorbent kitchen paper.
**4.** Lightly beat the eggs and egg yolk together. Add the breadcrumbs, milk, thyme and courgettes. Season well with salt and pepper.
**5.** Pour the mixture into the prepared ramekins. Cover with greased greaseproof paper and place in a roasting pan half-filled with hot water (a bain-marie). Bake in the centre of the preheated oven for 40 minutes, or until the timbales are set.
**6.** Turn out on to warmed individual serving plates and serve warm, with the tomato sauce handed separately.

 *DRY WHITE*

# COURGETTE AND CARROT ROULADE

SERVES 6
*110g/4oz carrots*
*110g/4oz courgettes*
*4 eggs, separated*

For the filling
*110g/4oz cream cheese*
*2 tablespoons plain yoghurt*
*4 spring onions, thinly sliced*
*1 tablespoon finely chopped fresh mixed herbs,*
*    such as parsley, thyme*
*grated zest of 1/2 lemon*
*salt and freshly ground black pepper*

**1.** Line a large roasting pan with a double sheet of greased greaseproof paper or non-stick baking parchment, making sure the edges stick up above the sides of the pan. Preheat the oven to 190°C/375°F/gas mark 5.
**2.** Grate the carrots and courgettes. Place in a colander and sprinkle lightly with salt. Leave for 10 minutes, then pat dry. Mix together with the egg yolks and season well with salt and pepper. Whisk the egg whites to medium peaks and fold them carefully into the carrots and courgettes.

**3.** Pour the mixture into the prepared roasting pan and spread it flat. Bake in the preheated oven for 10–12 minutes, or until it feels dry to the touch.

**4.** Meanwhile, mix together the ingredients for the filling. Season to taste.

**5.** When the roulade is cooked, turn it out on to a clean sheet of greaseproof paper. Trim the edges, spread with the filling and roll up carefully. Serve cold.

 *DRY WHITE*

# VEGETABLE TERRINE

SERVES 8

*10 large fresh spinach leaves, blanched and refreshed*
*550g/1lb 2oz large carrots, peeled and sliced*
*salt and freshly ground black pepper*
*grated zest and juice of 1/2 lemon*
*3 tablespoons water*
*20g/3/4oz powdered gelatine*
*1 large ripe avocado*

**1.** Line a loaf tin first with clingfilm, then with the spinach leaves, overlapping them neatly without any gaps.

**2.** Cook the carrots in a minimum quantity of water until tender, then drain and whizz them in a food processor until they are absolutely smooth. Season the carrots and add the lemon zest.

**3.** Put the water into a small saucepan, sprinkle on the gelatine and set aside for 5 minutes to become spongy.

**4.** Dissolve the gelatine over a gentle heat until it is liquid and clear, then stir into the carrot purée.

**5.** Spoon half the carrot purée into the prepared loaf tin, smooth it down, cover the tin and leave the terrine to set in the refrigerator.

**6.** Peel and slice the avocado, sprinkle it with lemon juice and arrange on top of the carrot purée. Cover it with the remaining carrot purée, smooth the top down and fold over the spinach leaves carefully to seal the terrine. Cover with clingfilm and refrigerate the terrine again until set.

**7.** To serve: place a large serving plate over the loaf tin. Turn the tin and plate over together. Give a sharp shake, and remove the tin. Slice the terrine with a serrated knife.

 *MEDIUM DRY WHITE*

# LEEK TERRINE WITH STILTON DRESSING AND GRIDDLED SCALLOPS

SERVES 8

*27 tiny leeks, cleaned and boiled in salted water*
*    until tender*
*4 tablespoons olive oil*
*1 tablespoon wine vinegar*
*1 teaspoon made English mustard*
*55g/2oz Stilton cheese, crumbled*
*salt and freshly ground black pepper*
*radicchio leaves*

To serve
*8 scallops, cleaned (see page 128)*
*unsalted butter*

**1.** Cut the leeks in half lengthways. Lay them lengthways in a 450g/1lb loaf tin, making sure they lie head-to-tail, half of them one way, half the other.

**2.** Put another loaf tin on top to press them down, turn both tins upside-down so the water can drain out, turn over again, and put a 900g/2lb weight on top to press the leeks. Leave for 4 hours.

**3.** Meanwhile, prepare the dressing: mix together the oil, vinegar, mustard and Stilton cheese and season with salt and pepper.

**4.** Cut the scallops in half horizontally. Season with pepper.

**5.** Unmould the terrine and carefully cut into slices. Lay a slice on each of 8 individual serving plates. Quickly fry or griddle the scallops in butter and arrange beside the terrine. Surround with the radicchio leaves and serve with the dressing.

 *DRY WHITE*

# VEGETABLES EN GELÉE

SERVES 8

This is a complicated recipe but a very pretty dish that justifies the effort. Other vegetables can obviously be substituted depending on availability of ingredients.

*2 small artichokes, washed, with stems removed*
*225g/8oz carrots, peeled, sliced and boiled*
*225g/8oz courgettes, peeled, sliced and boiled*
*225g/8oz turnips, peeled, sliced and boiled*
*110g/4oz French beans, topped, tailed and boiled*
*225g/8oz asparagus, scraped and cooked until*
   *tender*
*725ml/1¼ pints well-flavoured aspic (see page*
   *244)*

For the sweet pepper sauce
*1 onion, sliced*
*1 tablespoon sunflower oil*
*2 tomatoes, peeled, deseeded and cut into eighths*
*1 red pepper, peeled (by singeing over a flame),*
   *deseeded and cut into strips*
*1 clove of garlic, crushed*
*1 bouquet garni (see page 19)*

**1.** Cook the artichokes in boiling salted water for about 45 minutes, or until tender. Leave to drain.
**2.** Meanwhile, make the sauce: cook the onion in the oil until just beginning to soften. Add the tomatoes, red pepper, garlic and bouquet garni. Add 4 tablespoons water and season lightly. Cover and cook slowly for 20 minutes. Liquidize until smooth in a blender or food processor, then push through a sieve. Chill.
**3.** Remove the leaves from the artichokes and slice the hearts. Drain all the vegetables very well, keeping them separate.
**4.** Melt the aspic very gently. Pour about 5mm/¼in into the base of a well-chilled 900g/2lb loaf tin. Refrigerate until set.
**5.** Pour 4 tablespoons of aspic into a deep dish or soup plate and dip the asparagus spears in it until they are thoroughly soaked. Arrange on top of the aspic in the tin. Pour in a little more aspic and refrigerate until set.
**6.** Gradually layer up all the vegetables and aspic in the loaf tin, finishing with a smooth layer of aspic. Refrigerate until completely set.

**7.** To serve: dip the tin briefly in hot water. Invert a serving dish over the tin and turn both over together. Give a sharp shake and remove the tin. Hand the chilled sauce separately.

NOTES: An alternative method is to make 4 individual vegetables in aspic in small soup bowls. The pepper sauce can be spread on the base of 4 side plates and an individual vegetable in aspic unmoulded on top.

   Cook the vegetables in minimal amounts of water so that they need little or no draining. This will prevent too much leaching out of vitamins.

 DRY WHITE

# MOUSSES
# AND SOUFFLÉS

---

# TUNA FISH MOUSSE

SERVES 4
2 teaspoons powdered gelatine
285g/10oz canned tuna fish
150ml/¼pint mayonnaise (see page 250)
salt and freshly ground black pepper
lemon juice
1 tablespoon chopped fresh parsley
150ml/¼ pint Greek yoghurt
oil for greasing

To garnish
thin slices of cucumber
pitted black olives

1. Put 2 tablespoons cold water into a small saucepan, sprinkle on the gelatine and set aside for 5 minutes to become spongy.
2. Oil a mould and leave upside down to drain.
3. Pour off the oil from the tuna fish and flake the fish with a fork. Mash to a pulp. Stir in the mayonnaise, salt, pepper, lemon juice and parsley.
4. Place the gelatine over a gentle heat; when it is liquid and clear, stir into the tuna mixture.
5. Fold in the yoghurt. Pour into the mould. Refrigerate until set.
6. To turn out, invert a serving dish over the mould and then turn both the dish and the mould over together. Give both a sharp shake, and remove the mould.
7. Garnish with cucumber slices and olives.

NOTE: If the mousse is to stand for more than 1 hour after garnishing, the cucumber slices should first be degorged, i.e. salted, allowed to stand for 30 minutes, rinsed well and patted dry. If this is not done the cucumber will weep when left on the sides of the mousse.

 SPICY DRY WHITE

# EGG MOUSSE

SERVES 4
2 teaspoons powdered gelatine
6 hardboiled eggs
6 tablespoons mayonnaise (see page 250)
2 teaspoons anchovy essence

3 tablespoons double cream, lightly whipped
salt and freshly ground white pepper
cayenne pepper

To garnish
thin slices of cucumber

1. Put 1 tablespoon cold water into a small saucepan and sprinkle over the gelatine. Set aside for 5 minutes to become spongy.
2. Oil a soufflé dish or mould and leave it upside down to drain.
3. Chop the eggs and mix them with the mayonnaise, anchovy essence and cream, and season with salt, pepper and cayenne.
4. Place the gelatine over a gentle heat and when liquid and clear, stir it into the mixture.
5. Pour into the mould or dish. Refrigerate until set.
6. Loosen the mousse round the edge, using fingers or thumb, and turn out on to a serving plate. Garnish with cucumber slices.

NOTE: If the mousse is to stand for more than 1 hour after garnishing, the cucumber slices should first be degorged, i.e. salted, allowed to stand for 30 minutes, rinsed well and patted dry. If this is not done the cucumber will weep when left on the sides of the mousse.

 PROVENCE ROSÉ

# HADDOCK MOUSSE

SERVES 6
225g/8oz haddock
150ml/¼ pint milk
2 slices of onion
1 bay leaf
6 white peppercorns
15g/½oz butter
15g/½oz plain flour
8g/¼oz powdered gelatine
2 hardboiled eggs
150ml/¼ pint double cream, lightly whipped
3 tablespoons mayonnaise (see page 250)
salt and freshly ground white pepper
1 teaspoon anchovy essence

To garnish
*thin slices of cucumber*

**1.** Preheat the oven to 180°C/350°F/gas mark 4. Oil a 10cm/4in soufflé dish and leave it upside down to drain.
**2.** Place the haddock in an ovenproof dish. Pour over the milk and add the onion, bay leaf and peppercorns. Cover and poach in the preheated oven for 20–30 minutes, or until the haddock is cooked.
**3.** Skin the haddock and strain the milk into a bowl. Taste to check for saltiness.
**4.** Melt the butter in a saucepan and add the flour. Stir over a gentle heat for 1 minute. Remove from the heat and add the milk the fish was cooked in. Return to the heat and bring gently to the boil, stirring continuously. You should now have a very thick white sauce. Remove from the heat and set aside to cool.
**5.** Put 3 tablespoons cold water into a small saucepan and sprinkle over the gelatine. Set aside for 5 minutes to become spongy.
**6.** Meanwhile, chop the hardboiled eggs. Flake the fish carefully, removing any bones.
**7.** Mix the cream and mayonnaise with the cooled sauce, the eggs and the fish. Season to taste with salt, pepper and anchovy essence.
**8.** Place the gelatine over a gentle heat until liquid and clear. Using a large metal spoon, stir the gelatine thoroughly into the fish mixture. Add the cream. Pour into the prepared soufflé dish. Cover and refrigerate until set, preferably overnight.
**9.** To turn the mousse out, invert a wetted plate over the top of the dish. Turn dish and plate over together and give a sharp shake. The mousse should come out immediately. (Wetting the plate makes it easier to shift the mousse, should it not turn out in the centre.) Garnish with cucumber slices.

NOTE: If the mousse is to stand for more than 1 hour after garnishing, the cucumber slices should first be degorged, i.e. salted, allowed to stand for 30 minutes, rinsed well and patted dry. If this is not done the cucumber will weep when left on the sides of the mousse.

*MUSCADET*

# CUCUMBER MOUSSE

SERVES 4
*1 large cucumber, peeled if preferred*
*110g/4oz cream cheese*
*150ml/¼ pint double cream, whipped, or plain*
    *yoghurt or soured cream*
*salt and freshly ground white pepper*
*a pinch of freshly grated nutmeg*
*juice of 1 lemon*
*150ml/¼ pint white or vegetable stock (see pages*
    *243, 246)*
*15g/½oz powdered gelatine*

**1.** Grate the cucumber, reserving about 2.5cm/1in to slice for decoration. Put the grated cucumber into a sieve. Leave to drain for 15 minutes.
**2.** Oil a soufflé dish or mould, and leave upside down to drain.
**3.** Beat together the cream cheese and whipped cream, yoghurt or soured cream. Mix in the grated cucumber and season well with salt, pepper and nutmeg. Add the lemon juice.
**4.** Put the stock into a small saucepan, sprinkle over the gelatine and set aside for 5 minutes until spongy. Then place over a gentle heat until the gelatine is liquid and add to the cucumber mixture, mixing gently but thoroughly.
**5.** Pour into the prepared mould and refrigerate.
**6.** To turn the mousse out, invert a wetted plate over the mould and turn plate and mould over together. Give a sharp shape to dislodge the mousse. Garnish with cucumber slices.

NOTES: If a velvety texture is required, blend the cucumber with the yoghurt or cream in a blender.
    This mousse does not keep well. Eat within 24 hours.

 *DRY WHITE*

# HAM MOUSSE

SERVES 4

200ml/7fl oz aspic (see page 244)
300g/11oz cooked lean ham
200ml/7fl oz chicken velouté sauce (see page 249)
salt and freshly ground white pepper
6 leaves of gelatine (see page 62)
6 tablespoons hot brown stock (see page 243)
230ml/8fl oz double cream, lightly whipped

1. Coat 6 × 110ml/4fl oz moulds with a little aspic and leave to set.
2. Cut up the ham and mince it. Purée in a food processor or blender with the velouté. Push through a sieve and season carefully, taking care with the salt.
3. Soften the gelatine leaves in water and squeeze out. Drop the gelatine into the hot stock and allow to dissolve, then add to the ham purée.
4. Chill the mixture in the refrigerator to setting point, then fold in the lightly whipped cream.
5. Fill the moulds with the ham mousse, smooth the tops and refrigerate until set. Once set, cover with a thin layer of aspic and refrigerate again until set.
6. To serve: dip the moulds quickly into boiling water and invert on to a serving plate.

 *ALSACE WHITE OR LIGHT RED*

# RED PEPPER BAVAROIS WITH RED PEPPER SALAD

SERVES 8

3 red peppers, quartered and deseeded
3 small cloves of garlic, finely chopped
1 onion, thinly sliced
1 tablespoon olive oil
salt and freshly ground black pepper
4 large egg yolks
290ml/1/2pint milk
20g/3/4oz powdered gelatine
150ml/1/4 pint double cream
150ml/1/4 pint low-fat plain yoghurt
1 teaspoon chilli sauce

To serve
red pepper salad (see page 237)

1. Preheat the grill to its highest setting. Grill the peppers, skin side up, until they are blistered and blackened all over. Place under cold running water and remove the skins. Cut the pepper flesh into strips.
2. Cook the peppers, garlic and onion gently in the olive oil until soft but not brown. Allow to cool, then purée in a food processor and push through a sieve. Season with salt and pepper.
3. Beat the egg yolks. Put the milk into a saucepan and heat until scalding. Pour on to the egg yolks, stirring all the time. Return the mixture to the saucepan and heat gently until it coats the back of a wooden spoon. Do not allow to boil. Strain into the red pepper purée.
4. Put 3 tablespoons cold water into a small saucepan, sprinkle over the gelatine and leave for 5 minutes until spongy. Lightly oil a charlotte mould or 20cm/9in cake tin. Place the gelatine over a gentle heat until liquid and clear. Add it to the purée. Allow to cool and thicken.
5. Whip the cream lightly and mix it with the yoghurt and the chilli sauce.
6. Fold the cream mixture into the red pepper custard and pour into the prepared mould. Refrigerate until set.
7. Dip the mould quickly into very hot water and turn out on to a serving plate. Serve with the red pepper salad.

 *MEDIUM DRY WHITE*

# AVOCADO MOUSSE WITH PRAWNS

SERVES 4

15g/1/2oz powdered gelatine
2 ripe avocados
lemon juice
salt and freshly ground black pepper
290ml/1/2 pint Greek yoghurt
85g/3oz peeled, cooked prawns
French dressing (see page 254)

To serve
brown bread and butter

1. Lightly oil a ring mould.
2. Put 3 tablespoons cold water into a small saucepan, sprinkle over the gelatine and set aside for 5 minutes until spongy.

**3.** Meanwhile, peel the avocados and mash or purée until smooth. Add the lemon juice, salt and pepper.
**4.** Place the gelatine over a gentle heat until liquid and clear, then stir into the avocado mixture. Fold in the yoghurt, using a large metal spoon.
**5.** Pour into the prepared mould and refrigerate until set. Dip the mould quickly into very hot water and turn out on to a round serving plate. Mix the prawns with the French dressing and pile into the centre of the mousse. Serve with brown bread and butter.

 *SPICY DRY WHITE*

# SMOKED TROUT MOUSSE

SERVES 4
*2 large smoked trout*
*150ml/¹/4 pint double cream, lightly whipped*
*a squeeze of lemon juice*
*¹/2 teaspoon horseradish cream (see page 246)*
*freshly ground black pepper*
*4 slices of smoked salmon*

To serve
*brown bread and butter*

**1.** Cut the heads and tails off the trout. Skin the fish and remove the bones. Mince or pound the flesh and mix with the cream, lemon juice, horseradish and pepper to taste.
**2.** Shape the mixture into a shallow mound on a serving plate. Cover neatly with the slices of smoked salmon.
**3.** Serve with brown bread and butter.

NOTE: Individual mousses can be made by covering small mounds of mousse with a slice of smoked salmon.

 *SPICY DRY WHITE*

# CHEESE SOUFFLÉ

SERVES 2
*40g/1¹/4oz butter*
*dried white breadcrumbs*
*30g/1oz plain flour*
*¹/2 teaspoon dry English mustard*

*a pinch of cayenne pepper*
*290ml/¹/2 pint milk*
*85g/3oz strong Cheddar or Gruyère cheese, grated*
*4 eggs, separated*
*salt and freshly ground black pepper*

**1.** Preheat the oven to 200°C/400°F/gas mark 6. Melt a knob of the butter and brush a 15cm/6in soufflé dish with it. Dust lightly with the breadcrumbs.
**2.** Melt the remaining butter in a saucepan and stir in the flour, mustard and cayenne pepper. Cook for 45 seconds. Add the milk and cook, stirring vigorously, for 2 minutes. The mixture will get very thick and leave the sides of the pan. Remove from the heat.
**3.** Stir in the cheese, egg yolks, salt and pepper. Taste; the mixture should be very well seasoned.
**4.** Whisk the egg whites until stiff but not dry, and mix a spoonful into the cheese mixture. Then fold in the remainder and pour into the soufflé dish, which should be about two-thirds full. Run your finger around the top of the soufflé mixture. This gives a 'top hat' appearance to the cooked soufflé.
**5.** Bake in the preheated oven for 25–30 minutes and serve immediately. (Do not test to see if the soufflé is done for at least 20 minutes. Then open the oven just wide enough to get your hand in and give the soufflé a slight shove. If it wobbles alarmingly, cook for a further 5 minutes.)

 *SPICY DRY WHITE*

# COURGETTE SOUFFLÉ

SERVES 4
*melted butter, for greasing*
*625g/1lb 6oz small dark green courgettes*
*salt and freshly ground black pepper*
*55g/2oz unsalted butter*
*45g/1¹/2oz plain flour*
*150ml/¹/4 pint milk, infused with 1 slice of onion*
*30g/1oz fresh Parmesan cheese, grated*
*30g/1oz Cheddar cheese, grated*
*2 egg yolks*
*4 egg whites*

To serve
*tomato sauce I (see page 258)*

1. Preheat the oven to 180°C/350°F/gas mark 4. Brush 6 ramekins with melted butter.
2. Trim the courgettes. Slice 450g/1lb of them very thinly. Place in a colander or sieve and sprinkle with a little salt. Mix in well and allow to drain for at least 1 hour.
3. Cut the remaining courgettes into 5mm/¼in dice. Salt lightly then leave to drain.
4. Rinse the sliced courgettes and put in a pan with 150ml/¼ pint water. Bring to the boil, then simmer for 5 minutes. Liquidize in a blender or food processor until smooth.
5. Melt 45g/1½oz of the butter in a medium saucepan, add the flour and cook over a gentle heat for about 1 minute, stirring occasionally. Remove from the heat and allow to cool slightly.
6. Gradually add the flavoured milk and courgette purée to the flour and butter. Bring to the boil, then cook over a gentle heat for about 15 minutes, stirring occasionally. Add more water to the sauce if it gets too thick. Remove from the heat.
7. Add the grated cheeses, stir well, allow to cool slightly and then beat in the egg yolks.
8. Melt the remaining butter in a small pan and cook the rinsed, drained and diced courgettes until slightly brown and crisp.
9. Season the sauce well with salt and pepper. Whisk the egg whites until medium peaks are formed. Fold carefully into the courgette sauce.
10. Half fill each prepared ramekin with the soufflé mixture. Divide the diced courgettes between the ramekins and cover with the remaining mixture.
11. Place the ramekins in a roasting pan half-filled with hot water (a bain-marie) and bake at the top of the preheated oven for 25–30 minutes, or until well risen and brown on the top. Serve immediately with the tomato sauce.

# TWICE-BAKED CHEESE SOUFFLÉS

These little soufflés are wonderfully rich. They can be cooked a few hours before serving and then re-baked at the last minute.

SERVES 6
*290ml/½ pint milk*
*1 slice of onion*
*a pinch of freshly grated nutmeg*
*45g/1½oz butter*
*40g/1¼oz plain flour*
*a pinch of dry English mustard*
*a pinch of cayenne*
*110g/4oz strong Cheddar cheese, grated*
*3 eggs, separated*
*salt and freshly ground black pepper*
*200ml/7fl oz single cream*

1. Generously butter 6 ovenproof teacups or ramekins.
2. Preheat the oven to 180°C/350°F/gas mark 4. Heat the milk slowly with the onion and nutmeg. Remove the onion.
3. Melt the remaining butter in a saucepan and stir in the flour, mustard and cayenne. Gradually add the milk, off the heat, stirring until smooth.
4. Return to the heat and stir until the sauce boils and thickens. Remove from the heat and add three-quarters of the cheese and finally the egg yolks. Season with salt and pepper.
5. Whisk the egg whites until stiff but not dry, and fold into the cheese mixture. Spoon into the cups to fill two-thirds full. Stand the cups in a roasting pan of boiling water half-filled with hot water (a bain-marie) and bake for 15 minutes, or until set. Allow to sink and cool.
6. Run a knife round the soufflés to loosen them. Turn them out on to your hand, giving the cups a sharp shake. Put them, upside down, on to an overproof serving dish.
7. Twenty minutes before serving, sprinkle the remaining cheese on top of the soufflés. Season the cream with salt and pepper and pour all over the soufflés, coating them completely. Put the dish into a hot oven, 220°C/425°F/gas mark 7, for 10 minutes or until the soufflé tops are pale gold. Serve immediately before they sink.

 *SPICY DRY WHITE*

# CAULIFLOWER AND STILTON PUDDING

SERVES 4
1 medium cauliflower
150ml/¼ pint milk
30g/1oz butter
30g/1oz plain flour
salt and freshly ground black pepper
freshly grated nutmeg
55g/2oz Stilton cheese, crumbled
4 eggs, separated
1 tablespoon grated Cheddar cheese
1 teaspoon dried breadcrumbs

1. Cut the cauliflower into florets and steam them until very tender. Drain very well and liquidize in a blender, or sieve to a pulp, with the milk.
2. Melt the butter in a saucepan, stir in the flour and cook, stirring, for 1 minute. Pour in the cauliflower purée. Stir until the sauce is boiling and has thickened. Remove from the heat and season very well with salt, pepper and nutmeg.
3. Preheat the oven to 180°C/350°F/gas mark 4. Butter a 15cm/6in soufflé dish.
4. Stir the Stilton into the cauliflower mixture, returning the pan to the heat only if the cheese does not melt, but being careful not to boil the mixture. Allow to cool slightly. Check the seasoning.
5. Beat the egg yolks into the cauliflower mixture.
6. Whisk the whites until stiff but not dry and fold into the mixture. Pour into the soufflé dish.
7. Sprinkle the top sparingly with cheese and crumbs. Bake in a roasting pan half-filled with hot water (a bain-marie) in the preheated oven) for 20–25 minutes, or until well risen, brown on top and fairly steady when given a slight shake. If the soufflé wobbles alarmingly, cook for a further 5 minutes.

 *MEDIUM DRY WHITE*

# SMOKED HADDOCK AND SPINACH SOUFFLÉ

This is more of a 'pudding' than a soufflé.

SERVES 4
melted butter for greasing
2 tablespoons fresh white breadcrumbs
170g/6oz smoked haddock fillet
290ml/½ pint milk
1 bay leaf
½ small onion
6 black peppercorns
450g/1lb fresh spinach
30g/1oz butter
30g/1oz plain flour
salt and freshly ground black pepper
a pinch of dry English mustard
4 large eggs, separated

1. Preheat the oven to 200°C/400°F/gas mark 6 and place a baking tray on the middle shelf. Brush a 1.2 litre/2 pint soufflé dish with the melted butter and coat with the breadcrumbs.
2. Lay the smoked haddock in a shallow ovenproof dish and pour on half the milk. Add the bay leaf, onion and peppercorns, cover lightly with a lid or foil and bake in the preheated oven for 20–30 minutes, or until the fish is cooked.
3. Strain the milk through a sieve and reserve. Mash the haddock finely with the back of a fork, then set it aside.
4. Rinse and shake excess water from the spinach and put it into a large non-aluminium saucepan. Set it over a low heat and cook gently for 3–4 minutes or until tender. Drain very well, cool a little, then chop finely
5. Melt the butter in a saucepan, stir in the flour and cook for 30 seconds. Remove the pan from the heat and gradually add the reserved and the remaining milk. Return the pan to the heat and bring the sauce to the boil. Simmer for 1 minute, then remove from the heat, season with salt and pepper and add the mustard powder.
6. Allow the sauce to cool slightly, then beat in the egg yolks. Stir in the mashed haddock and spinach.
7. Whisk the egg whites until stiff. Fold 2 large spoonfuls into the sauce to slacken it, then gently

fold in the remaining egg whites. Spoon the mixture into the prepared soufflé dish, place on the heated baking tray and bake in the preheated oven for 25 minutes, or until well risen and rich brown in colour. Serve immediately.

 *VERY DRY WHITE*

# GRUYÈRE SPOONBREAD WITH VEGETABLES AND BUTTER SAUCE

This recipe has been adapted from a recipe cooked at the school by a Mouton Cadet competition entrant.

Spoonbread is a cornmeal-based dish similar to a soufflé but with a denser texture; it is less fragile and temperamental than a soufflé. It is an old American dish based on native American Indian cooking. Other green vegetables can be substituted if broccoli and courgettes are not to hand.

SERVES 6
For the Gruyère spoonbread
*570ml/1 pint milk*
*150ml/¼ pint double cream*
*125g/4½oz fine white or yellow cornmeal*
*70g/2½oz butter*
*1 teaspoon salt*
*½ teaspoon freshly grated nutmeg*
*1 teaspoon paprika pepper*
*170g/6oz Gruyère cheese, grated*
*4 eggs, separated*

For coating
*melted butter*
*dried white breadcrumbs*

For the vegetables
*110g/4oz dried flageolet beans*
*450g/1lb broccoli*
*70g/2½oz walnuts, chopped*
*butter for sautéing*
*3 small courgettes, cut into batons*
*½ small head of radicchio*

For the butter sauce
*70g/2½oz shallots, finely chopped*
*150ml/¼ pint wine vinegar or white wine*
*285g/10oz butter*
*salt and freshly ground black pepper*

1 . Boil the flageolets for 10 minutes, then simmer for 1 hour or until tender. Drain and set aside. Boil the broccoli until *al dente*. Cut into bite-sized pieces.

2 . Make the spoonbread: bring the milk and cream to the boil and reduce the heat. Gradually add the cornmeal, stirring constantly until thick (3–5 minutes).

3 . Remove from the heat and stir in the butter, salt, nutmeg, paprika, cheese and egg yolks. The batter can be prepared in advance up to this point, and stored in the refrigerator until 45 minutes before serving.

4 . Generously butter a 1.5 litre/3 pint ring mould and coat with breadcrumbs. Preheat the oven to 180°C/350°F/gas mark 4.

5 . Whisk the egg whites until stiff but not dry, and fold them into the cornmeal mixture. Pour gently into the prepared mould, and bake in the preheated oven for 30–40 minutes, until the top is crusty and the centre soft.

6 . Sauté the walnuts in butter for 2 minutes over a medium heat. Add the courgettes and sauté for 1 further minute. Pull off about half the leaves of the radicchio and tear into smaller pieces. Add to the sauté pan, along with the broccoli and flageolet beans, and sauté until the radicchio leaves turn dark and lose their bitterness (about 5 minutes).

7 . Make the butter sauce: cook the shallots and vinegar over a high heat until reduced by about half. Reduce the heat and add the butter slowly, in little pieces, whisking constantly until creamy (about 10 minutes). Season with salt and pepper.

8 . Unmould the spoonbread on to a platter as soon as it comes out of the oven, and gently heap the vegetables into the centre and around the edges of the platter. Pour the butter sauce over the vegetables.

 *DRY WHITE*

# PÂTÉS AND TERRINES

# SARDINE AND LEMON PÂTÉ

SERVES 6–8
*110g/4oz butter*
*225g/8oz canned sardines*
*110g/4oz cream cheese*
*½ teaspoon French mustard*
*juice of ½ lemon*
*salt and freshly ground black pepper*

To garnish
*6 black olives, pitted*

To serve
*hot toast*

**1.** Beat the butter until soft and creamy.
**2.** Add the sardines with their oil and beat.
**3.** Add the cream cheese, mustard, lemon, salt and plenty of pepper and mix well. (Alternatively all the above ingredients can be combined in a blender.)
**4.** Pile on to a dish and garnish with olives. Serve with hot toast.

 *MUSCADET*

# SMOKED TROUT PÂTÉ

This recipe is a low-fat version of smoked trout mousse (page 143). It is also delicious made with smoked salmon.

SERVES 4
*2 smoked trout*
*170g/6oz low-fat cottage cheese, very well drained*
*1 teaspoon grated horseradish*
*freshly ground black pepper*
*lemon juice*

**1.** Skin and bone the trout.
**2.** Blend all the ingredients together in a food processor. Alternatively, mince the trout or chop very finely. Sieve the cottage cheese and beat in the trout. Add the horseradish, pepper and lemon juice to taste.
**3.** Pile into a dish and refrigerate for 3 hours.

 *SPICY DRY WHITE*

# KIPPER PÂTÉ

SERVES 4
*340g/12oz kipper fillets*
*85g/3oz unsalted butter, softened*
*85g/3oz cream cheese*
*freshly ground black pepper*
*horseradish cream (see page 246)*
*lemon juice*

To garnish
*4 black olives*

**1.** Skin and mince the kipper fillets.
**2.** Beat the butter until very creamy (but do not melt it) and beat in the cream cheese. Add the kippers and beat well.
**3.** Beat until completely incorporated.
**4.** Season well with pepper, horseradish and lemon juice.
**5.** Pile into a dish and garnish with olive slivers.

 *SPICY DRY WHITE*

# POTTED TURKEY

SERVES 4
*225g/8oz smoked turkey*
*110g/4oz butter, clarified (see page 686) and cooled*
*freshly ground black pepper*

**1.** Mince the turkey and pound it with three-quarters of the butter. Season with pepper.
**2.** Press the mixture tightly into small pots, making sure that there are no air pockets.
**3.** Melt the remaining butter, allow to cool until on the point of setting, and pour over the pots. Leave to set. Store in a cool place. It will keep for 2 weeks or more in a refrigerator.

 *ROSÉ/LIGHT RED*

# CHICKEN LIVER PÂTÉ

SERVES 6
*225g/8oz butter*
*1 large onion, very finely chopped*
*1 large clove of garlic, crushed*
*450g/1lb chicken livers, or 225g/8oz duck livers
    and 225g/8oz chicken livers*
*1 tablespoon brandy*
*salt and freshly ground black pepper*
*85g/3oz clarified butter (see page 686), if the pâté
    is to be stored*

**1.** Melt half the butter in a large, heavy frying pan and gently fry the onion until soft and transparent.
**2.** Add the garlic and continue cooking for 1 further minute.
**3.** Discard any discoloured pieces of liver as they will be bitter. Rinse under water.
**4.** Add the livers to the pan and fry, turning to brown them lightly on all sides, until cooked. Flame the brandy and add to the livers.
**5.** When the flames subside, add salt and plenty of pepper.
**6.** Mince the mixture or liquidize in a blender or food processor with the remaining butter. Put it into an earthenware dish or pot.
**7.** If the pâté is to be kept for more than 3 days, cover the top with a layer of clarified butter.

NOTE: If making large quantities of chicken liver pâté simply bake all the ingredients together under foil or a lid in the oven preheated to 190°C/375°F/gas mark 5 for 40 minutes. Cool for 15 minutes, then proceed from step 6.

 CLARET

# SMOOTH DUCK PÂTÉ

SERVES 6
*1 × 2.3kg/5lb ovenready duck*
*1 bay leaf*
*1 carrot, sliced*
*1 onion, peeled and sliced*
*1 blade of mace*
*10 black peppercorns*
*1 stick of celery, sliced*

*1 tablespoon chopped fresh sage*
*salt and freshly ground black pepper*
*60–85g/2½–3oz butter, softened*
*grated zest and juice of 1 orange*
*85g/3oz clarified butter (see page 686)*

**1.** Put the duck into a saucepan with the bay leaf, carrot, onion, mace, peppercorns and celery and cover with water. Bring to the boil, then poach for 1½–2 hours until the duck is tender, when the legs will feel loose and wobbly. Remove from the heat and allow to cool.
**2.** Remove the duck from the stock. Strain the stock and reserve. Remove the flesh from the duck, discarding the fat, skin and bones. Cut up the flesh and place in a food processor with the sage, salt and pepper. Whizz until smooth. Add the butter, orange zest and juice and 5 tablespoons of the reserved stock. Check the seasoning.
**3.** Spread the pâté flat in a serving dish, cover and leave to cool. When completely cold, melt the clarified butter and pour it over the top of the pâté.

 RED BURGUNDY

# TARAMASALATA

SERVES 6
*1 slice of white bread, crusts removed*
*225g/8oz fresh smoked soft roe, skinned*
*1 large clove of garlic, crushed*
*about 150ml/¼ pint each sunflower oil and olive
    oil*
*freshly ground black pepper*
*juice of ½ lemon*

**1.** Hold the bread slice under the tap to wet it. Squeeze dry and put it into a bowl with the cod roe and the garlic. Using a wooden spoon or electric whisk, beat very well.
**2.** Now add the oils very slowly, almost drop by drop (as with mayonnaise), beating all the time. The idea is to form a smooth emulsion, and adding the oil too fast will result in a rather oily, curdled mixture.
**3.** The amount of oil added is a matter of personal taste: the more you add, the paler and

creamier the mixture becomes and the more delicate the flavour. Stop when you think the right balance is achieved.

**4.** Add pepper and lemon juice to taste. If the mixture seems too thick or bitter add a little hot water.

NOTE: Taramasalata can be served as a spread for cocktail snacks, or with toast or fresh rolls, but it is best served as a first course with hot Greek bread (pitta).

If it begins to separate, add a little boiling water.

 *RETSINA OR DRY WHITE*

# HUMMUS

This is a spicy hummus and has been adapted from a recipe by one of Leith's most popular guest lecturers, Claudia Roden.

SERVES 4
*225g/8oz chickpeas*
*salt and freshly ground black pepper*
*2 teaspoons ground cumin*
*2 cloves of garlic, crushed*
*juice of 1 lemon*
*4 tablespoons olive oil*
*a pinch of cayenne pepper*

To garnish
*flat-leaf parsley*

To serve
*pitta bread*

**1.** Soak the chickpeas overnight in cold water.
**2.** Drain the chickpeas and cook slowly in fresh water for 1–1½ hours. Add the salt towards the end of cooking. Drain and reserve the cooking liquor.
**3.** Cool for a few minutes, then tip into a food processor. Whizz and add the remaining ingredients. Add enough of the cooking liquor to produce a soft cream.
**4.** Serve on a flat plate garnished with the parsley. Hand hot pitta bread separately.

 *RETSINA OR DRY WHITE*

# TUNA FISH PÂTÉ

SERVES 8
*225g/8oz boned tuna fish*
*170g/6oz butter, softened*
*1 teaspoon anchovy essence*
*a little lemon juice*
*salt and freshly ground black pepper*

To garnish
*nasturtium leaves or thin slices of cucumber*

**1.** Mash the tuna fish. Add the butter, mixing very well. Season with anchovy, lemon juice, salt and pepper.
**2.** Pile into a soufflé dish, spread it flat and garnish with nasturtium leaves or cucumber.

NOTE: Young nasturtium leaves look very pretty as a garnish and are delicious to eat, with a peppery flavour. This pâté is good served with hot buttered toast.

 *MUSCADET*

# GUACAMOLE

This authentic Mexican recipe calls for 3 chillies. We found this too hot and think one is enough, but use according to taste.

SERVES 4
*1–3 fresh green chillies*
*1 large clove of garlic, crushed*
*1 teaspoon salt*
*3 tablespoons fresh coriander leaves*
*juice of 1 lime*
*2 ripe avocados*
*1 large tomato, quartered and deseeded*
*1–2 spring onions, thinly sliced on the diagonal*
  *(optional)*

To serve
*crudités or tortilla chips*

**1.** Wearing rubber gloves, quarter the chillies, remove the seeds and roughly chop the flesh. Place in a food processor or blender with the garlic, salt and coriander and process to a fine pulp. Scrape down the sides of the bowl or goblet with a spatula as often as necessary. Use a little lime juice to help the mixture move, if necessary.

**2.** Peel and stone the avocados; reserve the stones. Place the avocado flesh in a mixing bowl and mash to a rough-textured purée with a fork. Spoon in the chilli mixture to taste and combine well. Add lime juice to taste.

**3.** Cut each tomato quarter into 4 thin slivers. Stir into the avocado mixture with the spring onions, if using.

**4.** Serve with crudités or tortilla chips.

NOTE: Guacamole cannot be made too far in advance or it will discolour. To help prevent discoloration keep the reserved stones in the mixture until it is served.

 *FULL-BODIED RED*

# AUBERGINE CAVIAR

SERVES 8
*4 medium aubergines*
*4 tablespoons good-quality olive oil*
*4 cloves of garlic*
*2 tablespoons chopped fresh parsley*
*salt and freshly ground black pepper*
*lemon juice to taste*

**1.** Preheat the oven to 190°C/375°F/gas mark 5.
**2.** Brush the aubergines with a little oil and bake them in the preheated oven for 40–60 minutes, until soft. After 20 minutes add the whole cloves of garlic.
**3.** Allow the aubergines and garlic to cool. Peel.
**4.** Put the garlic into a food processor with the aubergine flesh, parsley, salt and pepper. Whizz to a smooth purée.
**5.** Gradually beat in the remaining oil and when the mixture is stiff stir in the lemon juice and season to taste with salt and pepper.
**6.** Refrigerate for 2 hours before serving.

# HARLEQUIN OMELETTE

This recipe has been adapted from Roger Vergé's *Cuisine of the Sun*.

SERVES 4–6
*5 tablespoons olive oil*
*400g/14oz very ripe tomatoes, peeled, deseeded and diced*
*a pinch of thyme flowers*
*salt and freshly ground black pepper*
*500g/1lb 2oz fresh spinach, well washed*
*2 cloves of garlic, peeled*
*9 eggs*
*8 tablespoons whipping cream*
*freshly grated nutmeg*
*75g/2½oz Gruyère cheese, grated*

**1.** Preheat the oven to 180°C/350°F/gas mark 4.
**2.** Heat 2 tablespoons of the olive oil in a medium saucepan. Add the tomato together with the thyme and a pinch of salt and allow to cook until the moisture from the tomato has evaporated completely.
**3.** Put the remaining oil into a larger saucepan and add the spinach, garlic and a pinch of salt. Stir with a wooden spoon and cook until the moisture has completely evaporated.
**4.** When the tomatoes and spinach are cooked put them on 2 separate plates. Remove the garlic, chop the spinach finely and allow to cool.
**5.** Break 3 eggs into each of 3 bowls. Add the spinach, 3 tablespoons of the cream, a grating of nutmeg and salt and pepper to the eggs in the first bowl and whisk everything together. Add the tomatoes, 2 tablespoons of the cream and salt and pepper to the eggs in the second bowl and whisk. Add the Gruyère cheese, remaining cream and salt and pepper to the eggs in the third bowl and whisk.
**6.** Lightly oil the inside of a terrine, and pour in the tomato mixture. Stand the dish in a roasting pan half-filled with hot water (a bain-marie) and cook in the preheated oven for 30 minutes.
**7.** Pour the cheese mixture very gently into the terrine and return to the oven for a further 10 minutes. Finally pour in the spinach mixture and cook for a further 20 minutes.

8. When the omelette is cooked, let it rest for 10–15 minutes in a warm place before turning it out on to a serving dish. Serve warm, cut into slices.

NOTES: This omelette can also be served cold, as a first course, with a little extra virgin olive oil sprinkled on each slice.

Cooking times for each omelette can vary, so check that the tomato is just set before adding the cheese and that the cheese is just set before adding the spinach.

 *DRY WHITE*

# TERRINE DE RATATOUILLE NIÇOISE

SERVES 10–12
*20 large spinach leaves, blanched and refreshed*
*salt and freshly ground black pepper*
*2 red peppers*
*2 yellow peppers*
*2 green peppers*
*2 aubergines*
*1 bulb of Florence fennel*
*3 medium courgettes*
*olive oil*

For the mousse
*olive oil*
*½ onion, roughly chopped*
*2 cloves of new season garlic, crushed*
*3 red peppers, chopped*
*2 tomatoes, chopped*
*2 tablespoons tomato purée*
*12 fresh basil leaves*
*1 sprig of fresh thyme*
*1 tablespoon caster sugar*
*150ml/¼ pint dry white wine*
*290ml/½ pint water*
*10 leaves of gelatine, soaked in cold water (see*
*  page 62)*

For the basil sauce
*25 fresh basil leaves*
*150ml/¼ pint mayonnaise (see page 250)*
*150ml/¼ pint single cream*
*lemon juice to taste*
*salt and freshly ground black pepper*

1. Line a 900g/2lb terrine first with clingfilm, then with the spinach leaves, overlapping them neatly without any gaps. Season lightly with salt and pepper.
2. Prepare the vegetables as follows. Cook the peppers in olive oil in the oven preheated to 220°C/425°F/gas mark 7 for 20–25 minutes. Cool, then remove the skins and seeds. Cut the aubergines into quarters lengthways. Cook in olive oil in the oven for 20 minutes. Peel the fennel, separate the layers and blanch in boiling water for 5–8 minutes. Refresh in iced water and pat dry. Cut the courgettes into quarters lengthways and shape neatly into pencil thickness. Blanch and refresh, then dry.
3. Prepare the mousse: heat a little oil in a large saucepan, and add the onion, garlic, peppers, tomatoes and tomato purée. Add the herbs and sugar, and cook for 4–5 minutes.
4. Add the wine and cook until reduced by half. Add the water and cook gently on the edge of the stove until the vegetables are well cooked (about 15–20 minutes).
5. When cooked, add the soaked gelatine, remove the pan from the heat and allow to cool.
6. Purée the mixture in a blender, then pass the purée through a fine sieve. Allow to cool completely and check the seasoning.
7. Prepare the terrine: pour 2 tablespoons of the mousse into the bottom of the spinach-lined terrine. Cut the yellow peppers to fit and cover the terrine from end to end. Season with salt and pepper as you go.
8. Pour another 2 tablespoons of the mousse on top, then add the aubergine, skin side down first to make a good colour contrast, then another 2 tablespoons of mousse followed by the courgettes. Repeat the process, alternating layers of mousse and vegetable in the following sequence: red pepper, fennel, green pepper, aubergine, yellow pepper. Finish with a layer of mousse.
9 Fold over the spinach leaves carefully to seal the terrine, then cover with clingfilm. Press the terrine

with a weight and leave for 8–24 hours in the refrigerator.

**10.** Prepare the basil sauce: place all the ingredients in a blender and liquidize. Check the seasoning and consistency.

**11.** Pour a little sauce on to a plate, cut a slice of terrine and place it on the sauce. Serve chilled.

 *ROSÉ/DRY WHITE*

# CHICKEN AND SPINACH TERRINE

SERVES 4
*2 chicken breasts, skinned and boned*
*900g/2lb fresh spinach, cooked and chopped*
*1 bunch of fresh tarragon, chopped*
*white stock (see page 243)*

**1.** Preheat the oven to 180°C/350°F/gas mark 4.

**2.** Slice the chicken breasts horizontally.

**3.** Layer up the spinach, tarragon and chicken in a small non-stick loaf tin. Pour in a little chicken stock.

**4.** Place the loaf tin in a roasting pan half-filled with hot water (a bain-marie), cover with damp greaseproof paper and bake in the preheated oven for 1 hour. Allow to cool for 30 minutes. Drain very well.

**5.** To turn out: invert a serving dish over the loaf tin and then turn both the dish and the tin over together. Give both a sharp shake and remove the tin.

 *LIGHT RED*

# PORK AND LIVER TERRINE

Make this terrine the day before serving.

SERVES 6
*110g/4oz pig's liver, minced*
*225g/8oz rindless belly of pork, minced*
*225g/8oz lean veal, minced*
*2 shallots, finely chopped*

*1 clove of garlic, crushed*
*2 teaspoons brandy*
*a pinch of ground allspice*
*salt and freshly ground black pepper*
*225g/8oz thin rashers of rindless streaky bacon*
*110g/4oz chicken livers, cleaned*

**1.** Preheat the oven to 10°C/325°F/gas mark 3.

**2.** Mix together the pig's liver, belly pork, veal, shallots, garlic, brandy and allspice. Season with salt and pepper.

**3.** Line a medium terrine or loaf tin with the bacon.

**4.** Tip in half the prepared mixture and spread it flat.

**5.** Trim any discoloured parts from the chicken livers, then place in an even layer over the mixture and top up with the other half of the mixture. Lay the bay leaves on the surface.

**6.** Cover with a piece of greased greaseproof paper. Stand the terrine in a roasting pan half-filled with hot water (a bain-marie) and bake in the preheated oven for 1¼ hours. The mixture should feel fairly firm to the touch.

**7.** Remove from the roasting pan, place a weight on the terrine (a can of fruit in a second terrine will do) and leave overnight to cool and harden. Then refrigerate until needed, and turn out on to a plate to serve.

NOTE: Kitchen foil may be used to cover the terrine during baking, but it must be well greased, or lined with a butter wrapper or other paper. If this is not done the foil will corrode into small holes while baking, and the top of the terrine will be covered in metallic spots.

 *CLARET*

# PROVENÇAL LAMB TERRINE

SERVES 8

12 *large spinach leaves*
400g/14oz *lamb fillet*
*salt and freshly ground black pepper*
1 *tablespoon chopped fresh rosemary*
1 *tablespoon chopped fresh thyme*
7 *tablespoons olive oil*
1 *large aubergine*
2 *teaspoons salt*
1 *large red pepper*
1 *large yellow pepper*
6 *medium courgettes*
1 *large bulb of Florence fennel*
30g/1oz *butter*
1 *onion, finely chopped*
4 *cloves of garlic, crushed*
1 *bay leaf*
1 × 800g/28oz *can of plum tomatoes, liquidized*
    *and sieved*
1 *teaspoon tomato purée*
8 *fresh basil leaves, torn*
85ml/3fl oz *water*
30g/1oz *powdered gelatine*
6 *artichoke hearts, cut in half*
3 *ripe tomatoes peeled, seeded and quartered*
1 *tablespoon extra chopped mixed fresh herbs*

To serve
450g/1lb *cherry tomatoes*
45g/1½oz *pinenuts, toasted*
*fresh basil leaves*
*fresh thyme leaves*
*French dressing (see page 254)*

1. Wash the spinach and blanch in boiling water for a few seconds. Refresh with cold water and pat dry. Remove the tough stalks.
2. Trim any fat off the lamb and cut into 1cm/1/2in strips. Season with salt, pepper, rosemary and thyme.
3. Heat 1 tablespoon of the oil in a frying pan and quickly fry the lamb until the strips are brown on the outside but pink in the middle (about 2 minutes).
4. Cut the aubergine in half lengthways and cut each half again lengthways into 4–5 equal pieces. Salt lightly and leave to degorge for 30 minutes.

5. Heat the remaining oil in a frying pan. Rinse and dry the aubergine and cook each piece until golden-brown and soft. Drain on absorbent kitchen paper.
6. Cut the peppers in half. Remove the seeds and membrane and cut into quarters. Place under a hot grill until the skins are blackened and scorched. Remove the skins.
7. Trim the courgettes and cut in half lengthways. Pull the fennel bulb apart. Blanch both in boiling water and then refresh under cold running water.
8. Melt the butter in a saucepan and sweat the onion over a low heat until soft. Add the garlic, bay leaf, tomatoes and tomato purée. Simmer for 10 minutes, then add the basil. Remove the bay leaf.
9. Meanwhile, put the water into a small saucepan, sprinkle over the gelatine and set aside for 5 minutes to become spongy. Then place over a gentle heat until the gelatine is liquid and clear. Add to the tomato sauce.
10. Line a 2 litre/3½ pint terrine or loaf tin with the spinach leaves, leaving some overhanging the edge. Spread a layer of tomato sauce over the spinach and layer the vegetables and lamb in the following order, coating each layer with a film of sauce to bind: aubergine, yellow pepper, red pepper, courgettes, fennel, artichokes, lamb fillets and tomatoes. Season carefully between the layers with salt, pepper and herbs.
11. Fold the spinach leaves over the top and tap firmly to settle the layers. Weight the top and refrigerate overnight to set.
12. Turn the terrine out on to a serving dish and serve at room temperature, garnished with the cherry tomatoes, pinenuts and herbs tossed in the dressing.

 *CÔTES DU RHÔNE*

# ALEX FLOYD'S FOIE GRAS TERRINE

To make this terrine the duck liver must be soft.

*2 fattened duck livers (foie gras), total weight about 1kg/2¼lb*
*20g/¾oz coarse sea salt (you need 20g salt for every kilo of foie gras)*
*freshly ground white pepper*
*1 glass of white port*
*1 glass of Cognac or Armagnac*

**1.** When the duck liver is soft and pliable, remove as many veins as you can without breaking up the lobes.
**2.** Preheat the oven to 80°C/176°F/gas mark ¼.
**3.** Put the livers into a roasting pan. Sprinkle with the salt and pepper. Pour over the port and Armagnac. Turn the livers so that they are evenly seasoned.
**4.** Place in the oven for 8 minutes or until blood temperature. If the foie gras gets too hot it is ruined. If it does not reach the correct temperature it is of course not cooked.
**5.** Remove from the oven. Lay the lobes on a clean kitchen cloth. Reserve the pan juices.
**6.** Put the lobes into a terrine and refrigerate for 24 hours. Serve as required.

NOTES: Tip all the pan juices into a bowl and leave in the refrigerator to set. Remove from the refrigerator and lift off the fat. Discard the pan juices (they will be bitter, salty and alcoholic). Let the fat reach to room temperature. This fat can then be whizzed with room-temperature unsalted butter and used in a variety of different sauces.

Literally translated foie gras means fattened liver. There is a general misconception that foie gras inevitably means goose liver (this may simply be because foie is French for goose). In fact both duck and goose liver can be used. At Leith's Restaurant we generally use duck liver, finding the flavour more subtle.

When preparing foie gras for cooking, try to disturb the lobes as little as possible: remove any tubes but try to keep the liver intact. The easiest way to do this is to make sure the liver is at room temperature before you prepare it.

When cooking foie gras it is essential that the recipe is followed very accurately. If overcooked the liver oozes fat and becomes unpalatable. If undercooked it will, not surprisingly, be raw. A thermometer to guarantee temperature control is useful.

 *SPICY DRY WHITE*

# VENISON TERRINE AND CUMBERLAND SAUCE

SERVES 8
*225g/8oz back pork fat*
*225g/8oz lean pork*
*225g/8oz lean venison*
*1 onion, finely chopped*
*1 clove of garlic, crushed*
*8 juniper berries, crushed*
*½ teaspoon ground mace*
*½ teaspoon ground allspice*
*4 tablespoons red wine*
*2 tablespoons brandy*
*salt and freshly ground black pepper*
*2 eggs*
*285g/10oz rashers of streaky bacon, cut very thin and stretched with a knife*

To serve
*Cumberland sauce (see page 260)*

**1.** Cut half the pork fat into small cubes. Mince the pork, remaining fat and venison and mix with the onion, garlic, diced fat, juniper berries, spices, wine, brandy, salt, pepper and eggs. Beat very well and check for seasoning.
**2.** Line a 1 litre/1¾ pint terrine with bacon and fill with the mixture. Cover with the remaining bacon rashers.
**3.** Refrigerate for at least 3 hours for the flavour to develop – the longer the better.
**4.** Preheat the oven to 170°C/325°F/gas mark 3.
**5.** Put the terrine into a roasting pan half-filled with hot water (a bain-marie). Cook in the preheated oven for 1½–2 hours. It is cooked when the terrine shrinks away from the side of the dish and no pink juices come out when it is pierced with a skewer.
**6.** Keep the terrine in the refrigerator for a couple of days to mature the flavour.
**7.** Serve the terrine with Cumberland sauce.

 *FULL RED*

# WILD BOAR TERRINE

This recipe is from Time Life's *Terrines, Pâtés and Galantines.*

SERVES 10
*900g/2lb boned loin of wild boar, fat removed*
*1 small onion, chopped*
*1 clove of garlic, crushed*
*salt and freshly ground black pepper*
*1 teaspoon ground allspice*
*5 juniper berries*
*a good pinch of ground cloves*
*1 teaspoon green peppercorns*
*1 teaspoon chopped fresh thyme*
*1 bay leaf*
*55g/2oz fresh white breadcrumbs*
*150ml/¼ pint strong red wine, preferably Rioja*
*560g/1¼lb pork fat*
*1 egg, beaten*
*30g/1oz black truffles, finely chopped*
*55g/2oz shelled pistachios, skinned and roughly*
*    chopped*
*400g/14oz pork fat, thinly sliced*

To garnish
*1 fresh bay leaf*
*1 sprig of fresh thyme*

1. Trim the wild boar of fat and sinew and cut into strips. Place in a bowl with the onion, garlic, 2 teaspoons salt, the spices, herbs, breadcrumbs and wine. Leave to marinate for 24 hours.
2. Discard the wine, then put the wild boar and all the marinade ingredients through the finest blade of the mincer or whizz in small batches in a food processor until very finely chopped but not puréed. Chill thoroughly in the refrigerator.
3. Preheat the oven to 160°C/325°F/gas mark 3.
4. Cut two-thirds of the pork fat into strips with which to line the terrine and dice the remainder. Work the egg, truffles, pistachios and diced pork fat into the wild boar mixture. Season with plenty of salt and pepper.
5. Line the terrine with the fat strips and fill with the stuffing. Fold over the excess fat and cover with the slice pork fat. Garnish with the bay leaf and thyme. Cover with a double layer of oiled greaseproof paper and seal the edges.
6. Cook in a bain-marie (a roasting pan half-filled

with hot water) in the bottom of the preheated oven for about 1 hour. The terrine is ready when a skewer inserted into the centre of the terrine for a few seconds comes out hot.
7. When the terrine is cooked, remove from the bain-marie. Weight the top down and leave to cool. Refrigerate for several hours before serving.

NOTES: Wild boar are considered a delicacy up to the age of 18 months when they became very tough and strong-flavoured. They can live up to 30 years but only the head of old boar is ever cooked.

A marcassin (young boar up to the age of 6 months) is highly esteemed for its flesh. A bête rousse is a boar from 6–12 months old.

All wild boar must be marinated for 24 hours before cooking.

 *SPICY ALSACE WHITE*

# PÂTÉ EN CROÛTE

SERVES 10
For the filling
*1 shallot, very finely chopped*
*15g/½oz butter*
*4oz/110g chicken livers, membranes and blood*
*    vessels removed*
*2 tablespoons brandy*
*6oz/170g lean veal, minced*
*6oz/170g lean pork, minced*
*6oz/170g pork fat, minced*
*1 egg*
*1oz/30g fresh white breadcrumbs*
*1 teaspoon dried mixed herbs*
*1½ teaspoons ground allspice*
*salt and freshly ground black pepper*
*1 pig's caul, about 45cm/18in square*
*290ml/½ pint aspic (see page 244), seasoned with*
*    Madeira or tarragon vinegar*

To garnish
*110g/4oz lean ham*
*110g/4oz lean veal*
*2 tablespoons brandy*
*1 tablespoon chopped fresh thyme*

For the pastry
*450g/1lb plain flour*
*1 teaspoon salt*
*225g/8oz butter, cubed*
*1 egg*
*2–3 tablespoons very cold water*
*beaten egg, to glaze*

**1.** Make the filling: sweat the shallot in the butter until soft but not coloured. Add the chicken livers and sauté gently.

**2.** Warm the brandy in a ladle, set alight with a match and then pour over the chicken livers and allow to flambé until the flames subside.

**3.** Whizz the mixture in a food processor until smooth, then set aside to cool.

**4.** Mix all the meats together with the pork fat, egg, breadcrumbs, herbs, allspice and seasoning. Mix in the liver purée. Leave to marinate overnight.

**5.** Meanwhile, prepare the garnish: cut the ham and veal into strips 1cm/½in thick and marinate in the brandy with the thyme overnight.

**6.** Make the pastry: sift the flour with the salt into a bowl. Rub in the fat until the mixture resembles coarse breadcrumbs.

**7.** Beat the egg with 2–3 tablespoons of water. Stir into the flour with a knife and bring together to form a stiff but not dry dough, adding more water if necessary.

**8.** Roll out a large rectangle no thinner than a £1 coin. Chill in the refrigerator for 20 minutes.

**9.** Assemble the pâté: cut a long strip 10cm/4in wide off the edge of the pastry and reserve for the top. Place the remaining rectangle of pastry on a baking sheet.

**10.** Lay the piece of pig's caul over the pastry, to cover it entirely.

**11.** Take one-third of the meat filling and lay it in a neat rectangle about 20 × 7.5cm/8 × 3in on the pastry. Arrange half the garnish strips of ham and veal on top and season with salt and pepper. Repeat with another layer of meat. Arrange the remaining garnish on top and cover with the remaining meat.

**12.** Cut the corners out of the pastry, wet the edges and lift the pastry up to the sides of the meat, forming a terrine shape. Seal at the corners and crimp. Cut the reserved strip of pastry down to the exact size and lay over the top. Decorate the edges by crimping. Make 4 steam holes in the pastry on top at the sides.

**13.** Meanwhile, preheat the oven to 425°C/210°C gas mark 7.

**14.** Glaze the pastry all over with beaten egg. Garnish with pastry trimmings cut into decoration shapes. Chill in the refrigerator for 30 minutes.

**15.** Glaze the pastry again with beaten egg. Bake in the top of the preheated oven for 15 minutes, then turn down the oven temperature to 170°C/325°F/gas mark 3, transfer the pâté en croûte to the bottom of the oven and bake for a further 1–1½ hours. It is cooked when a skewer inserted into the centre of the terrine comes out clean. Remove from the oven and place on a cooling rack until completely cold.

**16.** Using a plastic baster, pour the aspic into the steam holes to fill up any air pockets inside the pastry. If there are any holes, block them with softened butter.

**17.** Chill the pâté en croûte again for 1 hour before serving.

 *AUSTRALIAN/CALIFORNIAN CHARDONNAY*

# FRUIT FIRST
# COURSES

---

# PEARS WITH STILTON AND POPPY SEED DRESSING

SERVES 4
*85g/3oz Stilton cheese*
*85g/3oz cream cheese*
*4 ripe dessert pears, washed but not peeled*

To garnish
*1 small bunch of watercress*

For the dressing
*3 tablespoons oil*
*1 tablespoon lemon juice*
*2 teaspoons poppy seeds, toasted*
*salt and freshly ground black pepper*

1. Put all the dressing ingredients together in a screw-top jar and shake until well emulsified. Check the seasoning.
2. Beat together the Stilton and cream cheese until soft. Spoon into a piping bag fitted with a large plain nozzle.
3. Using an apple corer, remove the centre of the pears. Pipe in the cheese mixture. Refrigerate until ready to serve (at least 2 hours).
4. Slice each pear across into thin round slices. Spoon over the poppy seed dressing and garnish with watercress.

NOTE: To toast the poppy seeds, place in a heavy saucepan over a medium heat for a couple of minutes.

 *SPICY DRY WHITE*

# PINEAPPLE WITH TARRAGON SABAYON

SERVES 4
*1 fresh pineapple*
*caster sugar*

For the tarragon sabayon dressing
*1 egg*
*3 tablespoons tarragon vinegar*
*2 tablespoons caster sugar*
*a pinch of salt*
*2 tablespoons cream, lightly whipped*

1. Slice the pineapple in half lengthways, cutting through the fruit and the leaves. Using a grapefruit knife, cut out the flesh in one piece from each pineapple half. Remove and discard the woody core. Slice the flesh and return it rounded side up to the pineapple shell. Sprinkle with sugar and leave to stand while preparing the dressing.
2. Put the egg into a heatproof bowl with the vinegar, sugar and salt. Stand the bowl over a pan of simmering water and stir slowly until lightly thickened, then whisk continuously until thick and creamy. Allow to cool.
3. Stir in the cream and spoon the dressing over the pineapple.

 *VOUVRAY*

# GRAPE AND GRAPEFRUIT COCKTAIL

SERVES 4
*2 grapefruit*
*110g/4oz white grapes*
*1 teaspoon sugar*
*1 tablespoon sunflower oil*
*1 tablespoon chopped fresh mint*
*salt and freshly ground black pepper*

To garnish
*30g/1oz flaked almonds, toasted*

To serve
*brown bread and butter*

1. Halve the grapefruit and, using a grapefruit knife, remove all the segments, leaving the membranes attached to the shell. Put the segments, with the juice, into a bowl. Reserve the grapefruit shells.
2. Dip the grapes into boiling water for 4 seconds, then peel them. Cut them in half lengthways and discard any pips. Add the grapes to the grapefruit with the sugar, oil, mint, salt and pepper. Leave for at least 30 minutes.
3. Pull the membrane from the grapefruit shells and fill the shells with the grapes and grapefruit mixture.
4. Scatter the almonds on top. Serve with brown bread and butter.

NOTE: If the grapes are soft-skinned and nice looking do not bother to peel them.

# MELON AND PRAWN COCKTAIL

SERVES 6
*1 small honeydew melon*
*150ml/¼ pint thick mayonnaise (see page 250)*
*2 tablespoons double cream*
*1 tablespoon tomato ketchup*
*1 drop of Tabasco sauce, or a pinch of cayenne*
    *pepper*
*1 teaspoon lemon juice*
*a few fresh tarragon leaves, finely chopped*
*450g/1lb peeled, cooked prawns*
*salt and freshly ground black pepper*

To garnish
*6 shell-on prawns*
*chopped fresh chervil*

1. Cut the melon into 6. Remove the skin and cut the flesh so that it can be attractively arranged on 6 small plates.
2. Mix together the mayonnaise, cream, ketchup, Tabasco, lemon juice and tarragon. Add the peeled prawns.
3. Taste, and add salt and pepper if necessary.
4. Arrange the prawn mayonnaise beside the melon.
5. Remove the legs and roe (if any) from the whole prawns, and arrange on top of the prawn mayonnaise. Sprinkle with the chervil.

 *MUSCADET*

161

# FLANS, TARTS AND YEAST-BASED FIRST COURSES

---

# QUICHE LORRAINE

SERVES 2

*110g/4oz flour quantity rich shortcrust pastry (see page 461)*

For the filling
*½ small onion, finely chopped*
*55g/2oz rindless bacon, diced*
*7.5g/¼oz butter*
*5 tablespoons milk*
*5 tablespoons single cream*
*1 egg*
*1 egg yolk*
*30g/1oz strong Cheddar or Gruyère cheese, grated*
*salt and freshly ground black pepper*

**1.** Roll out the pastry and use to line a 15cm/6in flan ring. Refrigerate for about 45 minutes to relax – this prevents shrinkage during baking.
**2.** Preheat the oven to 200°C/400°F/gas mark 6. Bake the pastry case blind (see page 459) and remove from the oven.
**3.** Fry the onion and bacon gently in the butter. When cooked but not coloured, drain well.
**4.** Mix together the milk, cream and eggs. Add the onion, bacon and cheese. Season with salt and pepper (the bacon and cheese are both salty, so be careful not to overseason).
**5.** Reduce the oven temperature to 150°C/300°F/ gas mark 2.
**6.** Pour the mixture into the prepared flan case. Bake the flan in the centre of the preheated oven for about 40 minutes.
**7.** Remove the flan ring and bake for a further 5 minutes to allow the pastry to brown. The top of the quiche should be pale and set.
**8.** Serve hot or cold.

 *WHITE ALSACE*

# SPINACH FLAN

SERVES 2

*110g/4oz flour quantity rich shortcrust pastry (see page 461)*
For the filling
*½ onion, finely chopped*
*15g/½oz butter*
*5 tablespoons milk*
*5 tablespoons single cream*
*1 egg*
*1 egg yolk*
*340g/12oz spinach, cooked, drained and chopped*
*30g/1oz cheese strong Cheddar or Gruyère cheese, grated*
*salt and freshly ground black pepper*
*freshly grated nutmeg*

**1.** Roll out the pastry and use to line a 15cm/6in flan ring. Refrigerate for about 45 minutes to relax – this prevents shrinkage during baking.
**2.** Preheat the oven to 200°C/400°F/gas mark 6.
**3.** Bake the pastry case blind (see page 459) and remove from the oven.
**4.** Reduce the oven temperature to 150°C/300°F/ gas mark 2.
**5.** Sweat the onion slowly in the butter. When thoroughly cooked but not coloured, drain well.
**6.** Mix together the milk, cream and eggs. Add the onion, spinach and cheese. Season carefully with salt, pepper and nutmeg (the cheese is salty, so be careful not to overseason).
**7.** Pour the mixture into the prepared flan case. Bake the flan in the centre of the preheated oven for 30–40 minutes.
**8.** Serve hot or cold.

 *LIGHT RED*

# AUBERGINE FLAN

SERVES 6
*340g/12oz flour quantity lemon pastry (see
    page 469)*

For the filling
*1 medium aubergine, sliced*
*6 tablespoons olive oil*
*2 medium onions, thinly sliced*
*3 cloves of garlic, crushed*
*6 large tomatoes, peeled and chopped*
*a pinch of chopped fresh thyme*
*a pinch of chopped fresh rosemary*
*a pinch of cayenne pepper*
*salt and freshly ground black pepper*
*4 eggs*
*150ml/¼ pint single cream*
*85g/3oz Cheddar cheese, grated*
*30g/1oz Parmesan cheese, freshly grated*
*12 black olives, pitted*

**1.** Sprinkle the aubergine slices lightly with salt
and leave in a colander for 30 minutes to extract
any bitter juices.
**2.** Roll out the pastry and use to line a loose-
bottomed flan ring about 26.5cm/11in in
diameter. Chill in the refrigerator for about 45
minutes to allow the pastry to relax and prevent
shrinkage during baking.
**3.** Preheat the oven to 200°C/400°F/gas mark 6.
**4.** Bake the pastry case blind (see page 459).
Remove from the oven and turn the temperature
down to 180°C/350°F/gas mark 4.
**5.** Rinse the aubergines well and pat dry. Fry them
in about 2 tablespoons of the oil until golden-
brown. Drain on absorbent kitchen paper.
**6.** Heat the remaining oil, add the onions and fry
until lightly browned. Add the garlic and fry for a
further 30 seconds. Add the tomatoes, thyme,
rosemary, cayenne, salt and pepper. Cook for 5–6
minutes or until a rich pulp.
**7.** Beat the eggs, and stir in the cream and cheeses.
Mix with the tomato mixture. Season to taste
with salt and pepper.
**8.** Spoon half the mixture into the baked flan
case, cover with the fried aubergines and then
spoon in the remaining tomato mixture with the
olives. Bake in the oven for 40 minutes, or until
set and slightly risen.

 *LIGHT RED/ROSÉ*

# ONION TART

SERVES 4
*170g/6oz flour quantity rich shortcrust pastry (see
    page 461)*
*55g/2oz butter*
*1 tablespoon olive oil*
*675g/1½lb onions, sliced*
*2 eggs*
*2 egg yolks*
*150ml/¼ pint single cream*
*salt and freshly ground black pepper*
*freshly grated nutmeg*

**1.** Preheat the oven to 200°C/400°F/gas mark 6.
**2.** Roll out the pastry and use to line a 20cm/8in
flan ring. Refrigerate for 20 minutes to relax –
this prevents shrinkage during baking.
**3.** Melt the butter in a large frying pan, add the
oil and onions and cook very slowly until soft but
not coloured (up to 30 minutes). Remove from
the heat and leave to cool.
**4.** Bake the pastry case blind (see page 459), then
reduce the oven temperature to 180°C/350°F/gas
mark 4.
**5.** Mix together the eggs, cream and onions.
Season to taste with salt and pepper. Pour into the
prepared flan case and sprinkle with nutmeg.
Bake until golden and just set (about 20 minutes).

 *BEAUJOLAIS/ALSACE WHITE*

# LEEK AND BACON FLAN
# WITH MUSTARD

SERVES 4
*170g/6oz flour quantity rich shortcrust pastry (see
    page 461)*

For the filling
*15g/½oz butter*
*white part of 5 small or 3 large leeks, washed and
    finely chopped*
*55g/2oz rindless bacon, chopped*
*2 egg yolks*
*150ml/¼ pint double cream*
*salt and freshly ground black pepper*
*good-quality coarse-grain mustard*
*Parmesan cheese, freshly grated*

1. Roll out the pastry and use to line a 20cm/8in flan ring. Refrigerate for 30 minutes to relax – this prevents shrinkage during baking.

2. Preheat the oven to 190°C/375°F/gas mark 5.

3. Bake the pastry case blind (see page 459). Remove from the oven and reduce the temperature to 170°C/325°F/gas mark 3.

4. Melt the butter in a frying pan and cook the leeks until fairly soft. In a second pan fry the bacon, in its own fat, until it begins to brown. Drain well.

5. Mix together the egg yolks and cream. Add the leeks and bacon. Season carefully with salt and pepper.

6. Spread a fairly thick layer of mustard on the base of the flan and then pour in the filling. Sprinkle evenly with Parmesan cheese. Bake in the oven for 30 minutes or until the filling is set.

 *VERY DRY WHITE*

# LEEKS EN CROÛTE WITH RED PEPPER SAUCE

SERVES 4
*30g/1oz butter*
*900g/2lb leeks, trimmed and thinly sliced*
*3 tablespoons double cream*
*salt and freshly ground black pepper*
*450g/1lb flour quantity puff pastry (see page 464)*
*4 fresh basil leaves*
*1 egg yolk*

To serve
*red pepper sauce (see page 258)*

1. Melt the butter in a sauté pan and add the leeks. Cook over a low heat for about 15 minutes, or until the leeks have softened. Add the cream and cook until the juices have evaporated. Season with salt and pepper and allow to cool completely.

2. Flour a work surface lightly. Roll the pastry out to the thickness of a £1 coin. Using a 10cm/4in and a 13cm/5in cutter, cut out 4 rounds of each size. If you need to re-roll the pastry, lay the scraps on top of each other and re-roll.

3. Take the 4 smaller circles and divide the leeks

between them, leaving a 1cm/½in border clear. Top each mound of leeks with a basil leaf. Dampen the edges lightly with water.

4. Take the larger circles of pastry and carefully place over the filling, ensuring no air is trapped inside. Press the edges lightly together, knock up and scallop the edges.

5. Brush with the egg yolk, then, using the back of a sharp knife, mark a criss-cross pattern on the top.

6. Put the leeks en croûte on a baking sheet and chill in the refrigerator for 30 minutes.

7. Meanwhile, preheat the oven to 200°C/400°F/ gas mark 6.

8. Bake the leeks en croûte in the oven for 15–20 minutes, or until they are risen and brown.

9. To serve: put a leeks en croûte on each diner's plate and spoon a little sauce around the edge.

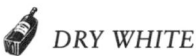 *DRY WHITE*

# CREAMY FISH FLAN WITH BURNT HOLLANDAISE

SERVES 4
*170g/6oz flour quantity shortcrust pastry (see*
*    page 461)*
*1 small onion, finely chopped*
*30g/1oz butter*
*30g/1oz plain flour*
*1 bay leaf*
*290ml/½ pint milk*
*salt and freshly ground black pepper*
*1 egg*
*225g/8oz white fish, cooked and flaked*
*1 tablespoon chopped fresh parsley*
*a squeeze of lemon juice*
*55g/2oz butter quantity hollandaise sauce (see*
*    page 251)*

1. Preheat the oven to 190°C/375°F/gas mark 5. Roll out the pastry and use to line a 20cm/8in flan ring. Refrigerate for 20 minutes to relax – this prevents shrinkage during baking.

2. Bake blind (see page 459), then remove from the oven.

3. Reduce the oven temperature to 180°C/350°F/ gas mark 4.

**4.** Cook the onion in the butter in a saucepan until soft but not coloured. Add the flour and bay leaf. Cook, stirring, for 1 minute. Remove from the heat, stir in the milk, and bring slowly to the boil, stirring continuously. Taste and season as necessary with salt and pepper. Simmer for 2 minutes, remove the bay leaf and allow to cool for 5 minutes.

**5.** Separate the egg and beat the yolk into the sauce. Stir in the fish, parsley and lemon juice to taste. Whisk the egg white until stiff but not dry and fold into the mixture. Pour into the pastry case. Bake in the centre of the preheated oven for about 25 minutes.

**6.** Preheat the grill 10 minutes before the flan is cooked.

**7.** Prepare the hollandaise sauce and spoon over the flan. Put the flan under the hot grill until the top is nicely browned. Serve immediately.

NOTE: If the fish has been poached in milk, reserve the cooking liquor for the white sauce.

 *CHABLIS*

# SPINACH AND OLIVE TART

This recipe has been adapted from Roger Vergé's *Entertaining in the French Style*.

SERVES 6
*285g/10oz flour quantity thyme rich shortcrust*
*    pastry (see page 461)*
*2 tablespoons virgin olive oil*
*2 onions, finely chopped*
*450g/1lb fresh spinach, cooked and chopped*
*3 cloves of garlic, crushed*
*3 eggs*
*3 tablespoons double cream*
*salt and freshly ground black pepper*
*340g/12oz small black Niçoise olives in oil, pitted*
*1 teaspoon fresh thyme leaves*

**1.** Preheat the oven to 200°C/400°F/gas mark 6.
**2.** Heat the oil in a large frying pan, add the onions, and cook over a low heat for about 15 minutes until beginning to soften and brown. Add the

spinach and garlic and continue to cook over low heat until all the liquid has evaporated (about 8 minutes). Remove from the heat and leave to cool.

**3.** Beat the eggs with the cream. Add the onion and spinach mixture. Mix well and season lightly to taste.

**4.** Roll out the pastry and use to line the base of a 30cm/12in loose-bottomed flan ring. Refrigerate for 20 minutes to relax.

**5.** Bake the pastry case blind (see page 459) in the centre of the preheated oven.

**6.** Reduce the oven temperature to 180°C/350°F/gas mark 4.

**7.** Pour the spinach and onion mixture into the flan case and spread it evenly over the base. Bake in the centre of the oven for 10 minutes. Remove the flan ring to allow the sides of the pastry to cook and sprinkle the olives evenly over the tart. Dust with the fresh thyme leaves and bake for a further 5 minutes.

**8.** Serve hot or cold.

 *PROVENCE ROSÉ*

# MUSHROOM AND RICOTTA TART

SERVES 6
*225g/8oz flour quantity herb wholemeal pastry*
*    (see page 463)*
*225g/8oz medium mushrooms, stalks removed*
*30g/1oz butter*
*juice of ½ lemon*
*900g/2lb ricotta cheese*
*2 teaspoons canned green peppercorns, rinsed and*
*    crushed*
*1 clove of garlic, crushed*
*3 eggs*
*4 tablespoons double cream*
*4 tablespoons chopped fresh mixed herbs, such as*
*    chives, parsley, dill, sage*
*salt and freshly ground black pepper*

**1.** Preheat the oven to 400°F/200°C/gas mark 6.
**2.** Roll out the pastry and use to line a 28cm/11in flan ring. Refrigerate for 20 minutes to relax.
**3.** Bake the pastry case blind (see page 459), then

remove from the oven and turn the temperature down to 150°C/300°F/gas mark 3.

**4.** Cook the mushrooms in half the butter and the lemon juice for about 5 minutes. Remove from the heat and leave to cool.

**5.** Beat together the ricotta cheese, peppercorns, garlic, eggs, cream and herbs. Season to taste with salt and pepper.

**6.** Carefully spoon the mixture into the flan case and smooth it flat.

**7.** Place the mushrooms, stalk side down, on top of the filling. Brush with the remaining butter, melted, and bake in the centre of the oven for 30 minutes. Serve hot.

 *LIGHT RED*

# LEITH'S RESTAURANT'S ARTICHOKE AND GREEN OLIVE PIE

SERVES 6–8
*10 fresh globe artichokes*
*30g/1oz butter*
*10 shallots, finely diced*
*2 small cloves of garlic, crushed*
*chopped fresh thyme*
*chopped fresh sage*
*4 tablespoons dry white vermouth or white wine*
*150ml/¼ pint double cream*
*170g/6oz green olives, pitted and chopped*
*salt and freshly ground black pepper*
*225g/8oz flour quantity puff pastry (see page 464)*
*1 egg, beaten, to glaze*

**1.** Peel the artichokes to the core and put them immediately into acidulated water, to prevent discoloration.

**2.** Preheat the oven to 190°C/375°F/gas mark 5.

**3.** Cut the artichokes into 5mm/¼in cubes and cook very slowly in the butter, with the shallots, garlic, thyme and sage, until soft.

**4.** Add the vermouth or wine. Add the cream and reduce, by boiling, to a coating consistency. Stir the sauce every so often to prevent it from catching on the bottom of the saucepan.

**5.** Add the olives and season carefully to taste with salt and pepper. Leave to cool.

**6.** Roll out the pastry and use half to line a 20cm/8in flan ring. Pile in the artichoke and olive mixture and cover the pie with the remaining pastry.

**7.** Brush with beaten egg and bake in the centre of the preheated oven for 15–20 minutes or until golden brown.

NOTE: If fresh artichokes are not available, canned artichoke bottoms may be used.

 *DRY WHITE*

# BRIOCHE STUFFED WITH WILD MUSHROOMS

SERVES 4
*225g/8oz flour quantity brioche dough (1) (see page 620), sugar omitted*

For the filling
*340g/12oz wild mushrooms, sliced*
*20g/¾oz butter*
*1 tablespoon chopped fresh parsley*
*a squeeze of lemon juice*
*salt and freshly ground black pepper*
*4 tablespoons double cream*
*a little beaten egg to glaze*

**1.** Grease a large brioche mould. Roll three-quarters of the dough into a ball and put it into the mould. Make a dip in the centre. Roll the remaining dough into a ball and press into the prepared dip. Press a wooden spoon handle through the smaller of the 2 balls into the brioche base to anchor the top in place during baking.

**2.** Cover with greased clingfilm and leave in a warm place until risen to the top of the mould (about 30 minutes).

**3.** Preheat the oven to 220°C/425°F/gas mark 7.

**4.** Meanwhile, make the filling: fry the mushrooms in the butter over a low heat for 1 minute. Add the parsley, lemon juice, salt, pepper and cream. Taste and set aside.

**5.** Brush the brioche with beaten egg and bake in

the preheated oven for 25 minutes. Remove the 'top knot' and some of the inside brioche dough.

**6.** Heat up the mushroom mixture and spoon it into the brioche cavity. It does not matter if it does not all fit in as the final dish looks very attractive served with some of the filling on the side of the plate. Replace the top and serve immediately.

 *WHITE ALSACE*

# BLINIS

MAKES 15
*225g/8oz wholemeal flour*
*225g/8oz plain flour*
*salt*
*3 eggs*
*45g/1½oz fresh yeast*
*10ml/2 teaspoons sugar*
*720ml/1¼ pints warm milk*
*1 tablespoon melted butter*
*lard for frying*

**1.** Sift the flours into a bowl, add the salt and any bran left in the sieve.
**2.** Make a well in the centre and drop in 2 whole eggs and 1 egg yolk, reserving 1 egg white.
**3.** Cream the yeast with the sugar and add the milk. Mix well.
**4.** Pour the yeasty milk gradually into the flours and mix to a smooth batter. Add the melted butter.
**5.** Cover with a sheet of greased clingfilm or a cloth and leave in a warm place for 1 hour.
**6.** Just before cooking, whisk the remaining egg white and fold it into the mixture.
**7.** Grease a heavy frying pan lightly with oil. Heat it gently over steady heat. When the frying pan is hot, pour enough of the batter on to the surface to make a blini the size of a saucer. When bubbles rise, turn it over and cook the other side to a light brown.
**8.** Keep the blinis warm in a cool oven between sheets of greaseproof paper.

To serve
CAVIAR: Butter the hot blini, place a spoonful of caviar (or Danish lumpfish roe) on top and surround with soured cream. Serve immediately.
SMOKED SALMON: Butter the hot blini, spread liberally with soured cream and place a roll of smoked salmon on top. Serve immediately.
PICKLED HERRING: Mix herring fillets with soured cream. Butter the blini and top with the herring and soured cream mixture. Serve immediately.

NOTES: If using dried yeast use half the amount called for, mix it with 3 tablespoons of the liquid (warmed to blood temperature) and 1 teaspoon sugar. Leave until frothy (about 15 minutes), then proceed. (If the yeast does not froth it is dead and unusable.)

Blinis are very good made with buckwheat flour in place of some or all of the wholemeal flour. They can also be made with all white flour.

 *VERY DRY OR SPICY WHITE*

# FISH FIRST
# COURSES

# MARINATED KIPPER FILLETS

SERVES 4
*8 kipper fillets*
*1 small onion, sliced*
*2 bay leaves*
*freshly ground black pepper*
*1 teaspoon dry English mustard*
*150ml/¼ pint olive oil*
*1 teaspoon soft light brown sugar*
*1–2 tablespoons lemon juice*

To serve
*lemon wedges*
*brown bread and butter*

**1.** Skin the kipper fillets and cut into wide strips on the diagonal.
**2.** In a small dish layer the fillets with the onion and bay leaves, grinding black pepper between the layers.
**3.** Place the mustard, oil, sugar and lemon juice in a jar with a lid and shake vigorously. Pour over the fillets.
**4.** Cover the dish well with a lid or clingfilm and refrigerate for at least 2 days, preferably a week.
**5.** Drain off most of the oil and discard the onion and bay leaves.
**6.** Serve with lemon wedges. Hand brown bread and butter separately.

 *VERY DRY WHITE*

# GRAVAD LAX

This Scandinavian pickled salmon is best made with a whole fish. The recipe is for a 2.25kg/5lb salmon which would serve 15–20 people, but it can be made with a pound or two of salmon fillet. The fillet should come from a large fish – the larger the fish the oilier and better flavoured. Frozen salmon gives good results.

SERVES 20
*1 salmon, filleted into 2 sides and pin-boned (see page 268) but not skinned*

*olive oil*
*about 3 tablespoons granulated sugar*
*1½ tablespoons coarse sea salt*
*1 tablespoon brandy*
*1 tablespoon chopped fresh dill*
*crushed white peppercorns*

To serve
*mustard sauce (see page 256)*
*brown bread and butter*

**1.** Smear the sides of salmon all over with oil. Put one of them skin side down on a board.
**2.** Mix together the sugar and salt and pack this mixture in a layer on the flesh side of the fillet. Sprinkle with brandy to moisten and cover the top with dill – there should be enough dill to cover the sugar/salt completely. Sprinkle generously with the peppercorns.
**3.** Put the second side on top of the first, skin side up, so that you have a salmon sandwich with a thick sugar and dill filling.
**4.** Wrap the whole thing up very tightly in 2–3 layers of kitchen foil and put it in a tray or dish with a good lip. Put another tray on top and weight it down with something heavy such as a couple of large cans of fruit. Leave for 4 hours at room temperature.
**5.** Unwrap the parcel, taking care not to lose any of the juice, turn the whole sandwich over and rewrap. Weight down again for a further 4 hours and then refrigerate.
**6.** The gravad lax will be ready when it has been marinating for at least 12 hours. Slice the salmon thinly and serve with the juices that have run from the fish. Hand mustard sauce and brown bread and butter separately.

 *SANCERRE/SAUVIGNON*

# POTATO CAKES WITH SMOKED SALMON

MAKES 8
*450g/1lb floury potatoes, peeled and halved*
*55g/2oz butter, melted*
*1 egg yolk*

salt and freshly ground black pepper
plain flour
1 tablespoon creamed horseradish
2 tablespoons mayonnaise (see page 250)
2 tablespoons soured cream
grated zest of ½ lemon
225g/8oz smoked salmon, cut into strips

To garnish
55g/2oz salmon roe
1 small bunch of fresh chives, snipped

**1.** Preheat the oven to 180°C/350°F/gas mark 4.
**2.** Cook the potatoes until just tender. Drain and cool.
**3.** Mash the potatoes, add the butter and egg yolk and stir until well mixed. Season with salt and pepper.
**4.** Divide the mixture into 8 equal pieces and with floured hands shape into flattish circles about 9cm/4½in in diameter.
**5.** Place on a lightly oiled baking sheet and bake in the preheated oven for 20 minutes, then turn over and bake for a further 20 minutes.
**6.** Meanwhile, prepare the filling: mix together the horseradish, mayonnaise, soured cream and lemon zest, and season to taste with salt and pepper.
**7.** Sandwich the potato cakes together with the filling and the smoked salmon. Garnish each one with salmon roe and chives.

 *VERY DRY WHITE*

# MOULES MARINIÈRE

SERVES 4
2kg/4lb or 2 litres/4 pints mussels
2 medium onions, very finely chopped
2 shallots, chopped
2 cloves of garlic, chopped
1 tablespoon chopped fresh parsley
150ml/¼ pint water
150ml/¼ pint dry white wine
45g/1½oz butter
salt and freshly ground black pepper

To garnish
extra chopped fresh parsley

**1.** Clean the mussels by scrubbing them well under a running tap. Pull away the 'beards' (seaweed-like threads). Throw away any mussels that are cracked or that remain open when tapped.
**2.** Simmer the onion, shallot, garlic, parsley, water and wine together in a large saucepan for 5–10 minutes. Add the mussels, put on the lid and leave to steam over a low heat until the shells open, shaking the pan occasionally (about 5 minutes). Tip the mussels into a colander set over a bowl.
**3.** Throw away any mussels that have not opened. Pour the mussel liquid from the bowl into a saucepan. Boil and reduce well. Lower the heat and whisk in the butter, then season to taste with salt and pepper.
**4.** Transfer the mussels to a warmed soup tureen or wide bowl, pour over the sauce and sprinkle with parsley.

NOTES: Moules marinière recipes vary from port to port in France. In Normandy cream is sometimes added to the sauce instead of, or as well as, butter. Sometimes the juice is thickened by the addition of beurre manié. Herbs other than parsley are frequently used in sophisticated restaurants. Sometimes one mussel shell from each mussel is removed and discarded after cooking, as is the 'rubber band' found round the mussel. The mussels are served in the remaining shells, neatly piled on a dish.

Extra soup plates or bowls should be provided to take the pile of discarded shells.

 *MUSCADET*

# BAKED MUSSELS PROVENÇALE

SERVES 4
2kg/4lb or 2 litres/4 pints mussels
290ml/½ pint water
1 onion, chopped
a few sprigs of fresh parsley
1 bay leaf
170g/6oz butter
2 small cloves of garlic, crushed

*1 shallot, finely chopped*
*3 tablespoons finely chopped fresh parsley*
*2 tablespoons grated Gruyère cheese*
*2 tablespoons dried wholemeal breadcrumbs*

**1.** Scrub the mussels well, discarding any that are cracked or will not close when tapped.
**2.** Heat the water, onion, parsley and bay leaf in a large saucepan. When simmering add the mussels and cover. Shake the pan occasionally until the mussels have opened (about 2 minutes).
**3.** Strain through a colander, discarding any mussels which have not opened.
**4.** Completely open the mussel shells, throwing away the top halves. Remove the 'rubber band' around each mussel.
**5.** Preheat the oven to 200°C/400°F/gas mark 6.
**6.** Cream the butter and stir in the garlic, shallot and parsley. Spread each mussel with the garlic butter and place on a flat ovenproof serving dish. Mix the cheese with the breadcrumbs and sprinkle the mixture over each shell.
**7.** Bake in the preheated oven until hot and browned (about 10 minutes).

NOTE: The water in which the mussels were stewed will make an excellent base for a fish sauce or soup.

 *VERY DRY WHITE*

# GRILLED OYSTERS

SERVES 4
*24 oysters*
*150ml/¼ pint single cream*
*freshly grated Parmesan cheese*
*cayenne pepper*
*melted butter*
*dried white breadcrumbs*

**1.** Open the oysters: wrap a tea-towel around your left hand. Place an oyster on your palm with the flat side upwards. Slip a short, wide-bladed kitchen or oyster shucking knife under the hinge and push it into the oyster. Press the middle fingers of your left hand on to the shell and with your right hand jerk up the knife and prise the two shells apart. Free the oyster from its base.

**2.** Preheat the grill.
**3.** Rinse and dry the bottom oyster shells, spoon a little cream into each and replace the oysters. Sprinkle with Parmesan cheese, a very little cayenne, melted butter and breadcrumbs. Grill for 3–4 minutes or until hot and lightly browned.

 *CHAMPAGNE OR CHABLIS*

# STEAMED CLAMS

*4–6 soft-shelled clams per person, depending on size*

**1.** Clean the clams thoroughly with a brush under cold running water.
**2.** Place the clams on a flat heatproof dish.
**3.** Put the dish in a steamer and allow to steam for 7–8 minutes or until the shells open.

 *DRY WHITE*

# GOUJONS WITH TARTARE SAUCE

*110g/4oz white fish fillets, skinned, per person*
*oil for deep-frying*
*seasoned plain flour*
*beaten egg*
*dried white breadcrumbs*
*salt*

To serve
*tartare sauce (see page 251)*
*lemon wedges*

**1.** Cut the fish, across the grain or on the diagonal if possible, into finger-like strips.
**2.** Heat the oil in a deep-fryer until a crumb will sizzle in it.
**3.** Dip the fish into the seasoned flour, then into the beaten egg, and toss to coat the breadcrumbs.
**4.** Fry a few goujons at a time until crisp and golden-brown. Drain well on absorbent kitchen paper and sprinkle with salt. Serve with tartare sauce and lemon wedges.

 *LOIRE WHITE*

# CEVICHE

SERVES 4

*450g/1lb fillet of monkfish, halibut or salmon,*
*    skinned and cut into thin slices or small strips*
*1 onion, sliced*
*juice of 2 lemons or 4 limes*
*1 tablespoon good-quality olive oil*
*a pinch of cayenne pepper*
*1 fresh chilli pepper, deseeded and cut into strips*
*    (optional)*
*1 tablespoon chopped fresh dill or chives*
*1 avocado, peeled and sliced*
*1 tomato, peeled and cut into fine strips*
*½ yellow pepper, cut into fine strips*
*salt and freshly ground black pepper*

**1.** Put the fish, onion, lemon juice, oil, cayenne pepper, chilli, if using, and half the dill or chives into a dish and leave in a cool place for 6 hours, giving an occasional stir. (If the fish is really thinly sliced, as little as 30 minutes will do; it is ready as soon as it looks 'cooked' – opaque white rather than glassy.)

**2.** Remove the onion from the marinade.

**3.** Season with salt and pepper. Arrange on a serving dish with the avocado, tomato and pepper, and sprinkle liberally with the remaining dill or chives.

 *CHABLIS*

# BRANDADE

SERVES 4–6

*150g/1lb salt cod*
*lemon juice*
*6 black peppercorns*
*2 thick slices of white bread, crusts removed*
*4–5 tablespoons olive oil*
*2 cloves of garlic, crushed*
*juice of 1 lemon*
*salt and freshly ground black pepper*
*4–5 tablespoons mayonnaise (see page 250)*

To garnish
*1 tablespoon capers, rinsed and drained*

**1.** Soak the salt cod in cold water for 24 hours. Change the water twice to ensure that as much salt as possible is extracted.

**2.** Drain the salt cod on absorbent kitchen paper and poach the fish in fresh water with the lemon juice and peppercorns. Leave it to cool in its own juice.

**3.** Drain the cod. Remove the skin and bones.

**4.** Soak the bread in a little water with 1 tablespoon of the olive oil. Squeeze dry.

**5.** Put the salt cod, bread and garlic into a food processor, then gradually add the remaining oil, whizzing until thoroughly incorporated.

**6.** Add the lemon juice and salt and pepper to taste.

**7.** Stir in the mayonnaise and season with more salt and pepper if required.

**8.** Pile into a serving dish and garnish with the capers.

 *CALIFORNIAN PINOT NOIR*

# TUNA FISH AND PASTA SALAD

SERVES 8

*85g/3oz pasta shells*
*salt and freshly ground black pepper*
*oil and lemon for cooking*
*150ml/¼ pint French dressing (see page 254)*
*1 × 200g/7oz can of flageolet beans, rinsed and*
*    drained*
*1 × 200g/7oz can of borlotti beans, rinsed and*
*    drained*
*1 × 200g/7oz can of red kidney beans, rinsed and*
*    drained*
*1 bunch of spring onions, chopped diagonally*
*1 box of mustard and cress*
*1 tablespoon chopped fresh chives*
*1 tablespoon finely chopped fresh parsley*
*a squeeze of lemon juice*
*1 × 200g/7oz can of tuna fish, drained*
*15 small black Niçoise olives, pitted*

**1.** Cook the pasta shells in plenty of boiling salted water, with 1 tablespoon oil and 1 slice of lemon, until just tender (about 10 minutes.)

**2.** Drain and rinse the pasta well.

**3.** Soak the pasta in the French dressing for 30 minutes, seasoning well with salt and pepper.

**4.** Mix the pasta with the beans, spring onions, half the mustard and cress, half the chives and parsley and the lemon juice.

**5.** Add the tuna fish and gently mix so as not to break it up.

**6.** Pile into a serving dish and scatter over the remaining herbs and mustard and cress and the olives.

 *VERY DRY WHITE*

## FISH NIÇOISE

SERVES 4
*4 fillets of pink trout*
*grapeseed oil*
*freshly ground black pepper*
*110g/4oz French beans, topped, tailed and*
*blanched*
*1 small cauliflower, broken into florets and*
*blanched*
*4 tomatoes, peeled, deseeded and cut into slivers*
*8 black olives, pitted*

To serve
*French dressing (see page 254), made with*
*hazelnut oil*

**1.** Preheat the grill to its highest setting.

**2.** Brush the trout fillets with a little oil, season with pepper and grill until tender (2–3 minutes on each side). Heat a meat skewer until red-hot and use it to score a lattice pattern on each fillet. Leave to cool.

**3.** Arrange the fish, beans, cauliflower, tomatoes and olives on a serving plate. Pour over the dressing.

 *DRY WHITE*

## SMOKED SALMON AND PASTA SALAD

SERVES 4
*170g/6oz fresh green and white tagliatelle*
*sunflower oil for cooking*
*170g/6oz good-quality smoked salmon, cut into*
*thin strips*
*French dressing (see page 254)*

To garnish
*4 sprigs of fresh dill*

**1.** Cook the pasta in plenty of rapidly boiling water with 2 tablespoons oil. When cooked, drain and refresh by pouring boiling water over it. Leave to cool.

**2.** Mix together the pasta, smoked salmon and French dressing. Arrange on 4 individual serving plates and garnish each with a sprig of fresh dill.

 *WHITE LOIRE*

## MARINATED SALMON AND MELON SALAD

A simple, light and refreshing first course.

SERVES 6
*225g/8oz piece fresh salmon, skinned*
*juice of 1 lime*
*2 teaspoons canned green peppercorns, well rinsed*
*2 handfuls of bitter salad leaves*
*1 small melon*
*French dressing (see page 254)*
*salt and freshly ground black pepper*

**1.** Slice the salmon finely and marinate overnight in the lime juice and green peppercorns. Turn occasionally.

**2.** Wash and spin-dry the salad leaves.

**3.** Cut the melon in half. Scoop out the seeds. Cut into quarters, cut off the skin and slice thinly. Toss the salad leaves in the French dressing, arrange on 6 small serving plates and cover with salmon and melon. Season well with salt and pepper.

# SAUMON MARINÉ ET FROMAGE BLANC AU POIVRE

SERVES 4

*1 small bunch of fresh dill*
*225g/8oz filleted fresh salmon, skinned*
*2 teaspoons canned green peppercorns, well*
   *rinsed and drained*
*1 shallot, very finely chopped*
*1 tablespoon coarse sea salt*
*4 tablespoons olive oil*
*4 tablespoons fromage blanc*
*1 tablespoon whipped cream*
*1 tablespoon chopped fresh mixed herbs, such as*
   *chives, chervil, tarragon*
*salt*
*juice of 1 lemon*

To serve
*hot toast*

**1.** Blanch the dill, reserving 1 sprig for decoration.
**2.** Slice the salmon thinly and marinate with the
dill, half the peppercorns, the shallot, sea salt and
olive oil for 30 minutes.
**3.** Remove the salmon from the marinade and
scrape down, making sure all the salt is removed.
**4.** Divide the salmon between 4 individual serving
plates and refrigerate.
**5.** Drain the fromage blanc, add the cream, mixed
herbs, the remaining peppercorns and salt to
taste. Form this mixture into quenelle shapes
using 2 wet dessertspoons and place 1 quenelle on
each plate.
**6.** Just before serving, brush the salmon with the
lemon juice and garnish with the reserved dill.
Serve immediately with hot toast.

 *LIGHT WHITE*

# ITALIAN SEAFOOD SALAD

SERVES 6
*450g/1lb fresh squid*
*a few slices of onion*
*a few parsley stalks*

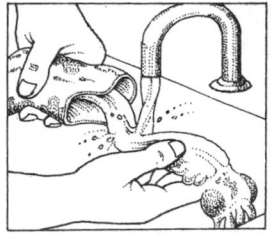
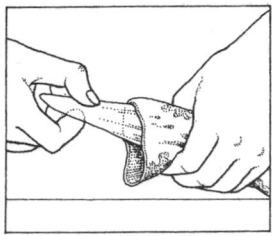

*Remove the squid entrails and cartilage*

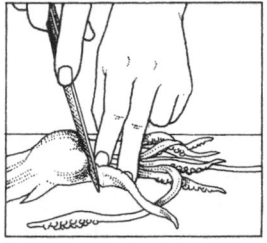
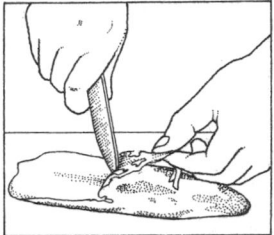

*Cut off the head and scrape away the membrane*

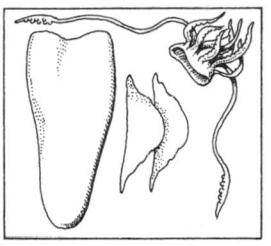

*Body, fins and tentacles*

*1 bay leaf*
*2 slices of lemon*
*salt*
*1 medium leek*
*1 medium carrot*
*55g/2oz peeled, cooked prawns*
*55g/2oz cooked cockles*
*55g/2oz white button mushrooms, thinly sliced*

For the dressing
*1 tablespoon good-quality olive oil*
*2 tablespoons mild salad oil*
*1 teaspoon wine vinegar*
*1 teaspoon lemon juice*
*salt and freshly ground black pepper*
*1 small clove of garlic, crushed*
*1 tablespoon finely chopped fresh parsley*

**1.** Ask the fishmonger to clean and skin the squid.
Alternatively tackle it yourself – it is rather messy,

but quite easy: see diagram on page 177. Remove the blood (ink) and the entrails under cold running water – they will come out easily. Remove the clear plastic-like piece of cartilage (the quill) that runs the length of the body on the inside. Cut off and throw away the head (it is the round middle bit with two large eyes). Scrape off the pinkish-purple outside skin – a fine membrane – from the body and the tentacles. Don't worry if you cannot get all the tentacles completely clear of it. Wash the body and tentacles to remove all traces of ink: you should now have a perfectly clean, white, empty squid.

**2.** Cut it into thin strips. Put them into a saucepan and just cover with water. Add the onion, parsley stalks, bay leaf, lemon slices and a pinch of salt. Simmer gently until the squid is tender. This will probably take 2–3 minutes but can take up to 1 hour for strips cut from a large squid. Drain well.

**3.** Wash the leek and discard the tough outside leaves and the dark green part. Shred the remainder finely and plunge it into boiling salted water for 1 minute until just tender but still bright green. Rinse under cold running water to set the bright colour. Drain well.

**4.** Peel the carrot. Using a potato peeler, shred it into long thin ribbons.

**5.** Combine the ingredients for the dressing in a screw-top jar and shake well.

**6.** When the squid is cool, drain it (but keep the stock for some future use, such as a soup or sauce – it is delicious), discard the onion, bay leaf, lemon slices and parsley stalks and put the squid into a bowl. Add the prawns, cockles, mushrooms, carrot strips, leek and dressing. Toss. Chill well in the refrigerator before serving.

NOTE: Other seafood can be used too.

FRESH COCKLES: Leave for 1 hour in salty water and turn often to rid them of sand before cooking as for mussels.

MUSSELS: Scrub well under running water. Pull away the 'beards' and discard any that are broken or which will not close when tapped. Put into a heavy pan with a little white wine, cover, and shake over heat for 5 minutes until the shells have opened. Discard any that remain closed. Remove the mussels from the shells and discard the 'rubber bands'.

FROZEN COOKED PRAWNS: Thaw slowly, season

with lemon juice, salt and freshly ground black pepper.

FROZEN RAW 'SCAMPI': Simmer in a court bouillon for 3–4 minutes.

RAW WHOLE PRAWNS: Simmer in a court bouillon for 4 minutes. (The shells will be bright red when they are cooked.) Shell carefully. If using any whole for garnish, remove the legs and any roe after cooking.

 *SOAVE/FRASCATI*

# SQUID SALAD WITH CUCUMBER AND CUMIN

SERVES 4
*450g/1lb squid*
*150ml/¼ pint water*
*150ml/¼ pint dry white wine*
*1 onion, chopped*
*1 bay leaf*

For the salad
*1 cucumber*
*6 spring onions, thinly sliced*

For the dressing
*1 teaspoon Dijon mustard*
*2 tablespoons crème fraiche, or Greek yoghurt*
*2 tablespoons olive oil*
*½ teaspoon ground cumin*
*salt and freshly ground black pepper*
*grated zest and juice of 1 lime*
*1 tablespoon chopped fresh mint and chives*

**1.** Clean the squid (see page 177). Chop the tentacles into 2.5cm/1in lengths and cut the body into rings.

**2.** Place the water, wine, onion and bay leaf into a saucepan and bring to the boil, then simmer for 10 minutes. Strain and bring back to the boil, then add the squid and remove from the heat. Leave to stand for 5 minutes, or until the squid is tender and opaque, then lift out and allow to cool.

**3.** Peel the cucumber and cut into quarters lengthways. Using an apple corer, remove the seeds and then slice the cucumber into rings about the same size as the squid rings.

**4.** Make the dressing by mixing all the ingredients together. Check the seasoning.

**5.** Toss the squid, cucumber, and spring onion in the dressing.

 *DRY WHITE*

# GRILLED CHILLI SQUID WITH LIME

SERVES 4
*16 small squid, prepared (see page 177)*
*salt*
*1 tablespoon chilli oil*
*Tabasco sauce*

For the dressing
*1 red chilli, deseeded and chopped*
*grated zest and juice of 1 lime*
*3 tablespoons grapeseed oil*
*1 tablespoon chopped fresh coriander*
*1 tablespoon chopped fresh parsley*
*½ teaspoon Sichuan peppercorns*
*1 teaspoon sugar*
*salt and freshly ground black pepper*

To serve
*225g/8oz bulghur (cracked wheat)*
*salt and freshly ground black pepper*

**1.** Preheat the grill to its highest setting.

**2.** Season the squid bodies and tentacles with salt. Brush with the chilli oil and add a splash of Tabasco sauce. Set aside.

**3.** Make the dressing: put all the ingredients into a blender and whizz until well mixed. Season to taste with salt and pepper.

**4.** Put the bulghur wheat into a bowl, cover with boiling water and leave to soak for 15 minutes. Drain, first in a sieve and then on absorbent kitchen paper. Season well with salt and pepper.

**5.** Grill the squid bodies and tentacles for 2–3 minutes or until the bodies have puffed up and turned opaque.

**6.** To serve: divide the bulghur wheat between 4 individual plates, arrange 4 squid on each and spoon over the dressing. Serve warm.

NOTE: Any grain, such as quinoa or couscous, may be used instead of bulghur wheat.

 *DRY MUSCAT*

# ARBROATH SMOKIES POTS

This recipe has been taken from *La Potinière and Friends* by David and Hilary Brown.

SERVES 6
*3 large Arbroath smokies*
*3 eggs*
*285g/10oz fromage frais*
*juice of ½ lemon*
*salt and freshly ground black pepper*
*melted butter*

To serve
*tomato, basil and olive oil sauce (see page 257)*
*sprigs of fresh dill*

**1.** Preheat the oven to 160°C/325°F/gas mark 3.

**2.** Place the smokies in an ovenproof dish and cook in the oven for 10 minutes.

**3.** Remove from the oven and carefully remove the skin and bones.

**4.** Place the flesh in a food processor and process until smooth. Add the eggs one at a time and continue to blend. Gradually add the fromage frais, lemon juice and seasonings to taste. Be careful with the salt.

**5.** Brush 6 ramekins with melted butter and line the bases with circles of greased greaseproof paper.

**6.** Divide the fish mixture between the dishes and place them in a roasting pan half filled with hot water (a bain marie).

**7.** Bake in the centre of the oven for 35–40 minutes, or until set.

**8.** Meanwhile, make the sauce.

**9.** Remove the mousses from the oven and allow to rest for 2 minutes. Run a knife around the edges of the ramekins and turn the mousses out on to warmed individual serving plates.

**10.** Spoon a tablespoon of the warm sauce over each mousse and garnish with a sprig of dill.

 *SPICY DRY WHITE*

# FISH QUENELLES

SERVES 4

675g/1½lb fish fillet, such as sole, salmon or pike
2 egg whites
salt and freshly ground black pepper
cayenne pepper
290ml/½ pint double cream
290ml/½ pint court bouillon or fish stock (see
    page 245)
fish beurre blanc (see page 253)

To garnish
slivers of peeled tomatoes
whole fresh chervil leaves

**1.** Process the fish well in a food processor, adding
a little egg white if necessary. Season with the
pepper only.
**2.** Remove from the processor. Season with salt.
Place in a large bowl set in a roasting pan of ice.
Beat well and gradually add first the egg white
and then the cream, making sure that the mixture
remains fairly firm. Taste and season with
cayenne – it should be well seasoned.
**3.** Heat the court bouillon or stock.
**4.** Using 2 wet dessertspoons, mould the mixture
into 12 egg shapes and drop them into the hot
court bouillon or stock. Poach for 3–5 minutes,
or until the quenelles feel firm to the touch.
**5.** Flood the base of 4 individual serving plates
with the beurre blanc and arrange 3 quenelles on
each plate. Garnish with the tomatoes and chervil
leaves.

NOTE: In this recipe much of the beating is done
over ice. This is to prevent the mixture from
separating, which it may do in a food processor,
especially if you are working with large quantities
in hot weather.

 *WHITE LOIRE*

# PAIN DE POISSON

SERVES 4

285g/10oz sole, salmon or pike
1 egg white
230ml/8fl oz double cream
salt and freshly ground white and black pepper
cayenne pepper
1 egg
55g/2oz fresh white breadcrumbs
2 tablespoons chopped fresh parsley
1 tablespoon mixed chopped fresh tarragon and
    chives

To serve
hollandaise sauce (see page 251)

**1.** Preheat the oven to 150°C/300°F/gas mark 2.
**2.** Skin the fish and remove any bones. Cut into
pieces and pound in a food processor. Add 1 egg
white and process well. Remove to a bowl and
gradually beat in approximately two-thirds of the
cream. Everything should be very cold. If not,
place the bowl over iced water as the cream is
added. Season well with salt, white pepper and
cayenne. Place in the refrigerator.
**3.** Whisk the egg and add the remaining cream.
Add the breadcrumbs and herbs. Season with salt
and black pepper.
**4.** Oil a 450g/1lb loaf tin and line the base with a
piece of greaseproof paper cut to size and also
lightly oiled.
**5.** Spread the fish mixture round the base and
sides of the tin to about 1cm/½in thickness.
**6.** Place the herb mixture in the middle and cover
with the remaining fish.
**7.** Cover with a double sheet of damp greaseproof
paper. Place in a roasting pan half-filled with hot
water (a bain-marie) and bake in the preheated
oven for 1–1¼ hours.
**8.** Allow to cool in the tin slightly, then turn out
and serve with hollandaise sauce.

 *WHITE BURGUNDY*

# FISH TERRINE WITH CHIVE AND LEMON DRESSING

This recipe is very quick to make in a food processor.

SERVES 6
*2 teaspoons canned green peppercorns, rinsed and*
 *drained*
*1 large carrot, peeled and cut into batons*
*45g/1½oz French beans, topped and tailed*
*680g/1½lb sole fillets, skinned*
*3 egg whites, lightly beaten*
*salt and freshly ground black pepper*
*290ml/½ pint double cream*
*15g/½oz butter*

For the dressing
*1 large bunch of fresh chives*
*150ml/¼ pint soured cream*
*290ml/½ pint mayonnaise (see page 250)*
*salt and freshly ground black pepper*
*juice of ½ lemon*

To garnish
*sprigs of watercress*

**1.** Rinse the green peppercorns under cold running water for 2–3 minutes. Drain well. Steam the carrots and beans over boiling water until very tender. Rinse under cold running water and drain on absorbent kitchen paper.
**2.** Preheat the oven to 180°C/350°F/gas mark 4. Pound the sole fillets in a food processor with a little egg white. Season with salt. Place in a large bowl set in a roasting pan of ice. Beat well and gradually add first the remaining egg whites and then the cream, making sure that the mixture remains fairly firm. Beat in the pepper. Taste: the mixture should be well seasoned.
**3.** Lightly butter a medium loaf tin or terrine, line the base with greaseproof paper and spoon in a quarter of the fish mixture. Spread it flat with a spatula. Arrange 4 parallel lines of green beans down the length of the tin. Cover with a second quarter of the fish mixture. Spread flat. Arrange 4 parallel lines of carrot batons immediately above

the beans. Cover with a third quarter of the fish mixture. Spread flat. Arrange 4 parallel lines of green peppercorns immediately above the carrots. Cover with the remaining fish mixture and smooth over with a spatula. Cover with a piece of damp greaseproof paper.
**4.** Stand the terrine in a roasting pan half-filled with hot water (a bain-marie). Bake in the preheated oven for 35 minutes. Remove from the oven, leave to cool and refrigerate overnight.
**5.** Make the sauce: put the chives and soured cream into a blender and whizz until pale green. Remove from the blender, mix with the mayonnaise and season to taste with salt, pepper and lemon juice.
**6.** To serve: invert a plate or wooden board over the terrine and turn the whole thing over. Give a gentle shake and remove the tin. Cut into even slices. Serve with the chive dressing and garnish with watercress.

NOTE: If you do not have a food processor the fish should be pushed through a sieve before adding the egg whites (quite a task!).

 *MUSCADET*

# PÂTÉ OF FISH TRICOLOUR

If whiting is not available, any other white fish can be used

SERVES 4
For the fish mousse
*675g/1½lb whiting fillets, skinned*
*2 egg whites*
*1 teaspoon salt*
*½ teaspoon freshly ground white pepper*
*425ml/¾ pint double cream*

For the fish
*170g/6oz salmon fillet*
*4 large sole fillets (about 140g/5oz each), skinned*
 *and lightly pounded*

For the herb mousse

*4–5 shallots, roughly chopped*
*225ml/8fl oz dry white wine*
*a pinch of freshly ground white pepper*
*½ teaspoon salt*
*110g/4oz spinach leaves*
*1 small bunch of watercress leaves, chopped*
*2 teaspoons chopped fresh tarragon, or chives*
*2 tablespoons chopped fresh parsley*

For the sauce

*1 large tomato, peeled, deseeded and roughly*
*   chopped*
*½ teaspoon good paprika pepper*
*a pinch of cayenne pepper*
*1 teaspoon salt*
*a pinch of freshly ground white pepper*
*1 tablespoon good red wine vinegar*
*1 egg yolk*
*225ml/8fl oz virgin olive oil*

TO PREPARE THE FISH MOUSSE:

**1.** Preheat the oven to 140°C/275°F/gas mark 1.
**2.** Place the whiting in a food processor and process for 1 minute with the egg whites, salt and pepper, slowly pouring in half the cream with the motor still running.
**3.** Fold the remaining cream into the fish mixture.

TO PREPARE THE HERB MOUSSE:

**4.** Put the shallots, wine, pepper and salt into a saucepan and bring to the boil, then reduce by boiling rapidly to 3 tablespoons. Add the spinach and cook until the liquid is reduced to 1 tablespoon.
**5.** Put into a clean food processor with the watercress, tarragon or chives and the parsley. Process until smooth, then mix with 3 tablespoons of the whiting mousse.

TO ASSEMBLE THE TERRINE:

**6.** Grease a 1.7 litre/3 pint mould or 2 × 450g/1lb loaf tins with butter and line the bottom with greaseproof paper. Line the bottom and sides of the mould with 1cm/½in of the fish mousse.
**7.** Cut the salmon fillet into 1cm/½in slices and line the fish mousse with a layer of the salmon slices.
**8.** Sprinkle with salt and pepper and spread a thin layer of fish mousse on top.

**9.** Place half the pounded sole fillets over the fish mousse.
**10.** Place the herb mousse in the centre.
**11.** Cover with the remaining sole fillets, spread with some more fish mousse and slices of salmon.
**12.** Thinly cover the last layer of salmon with the remaining fish mousse, smooth the top and cover with non-stick baking parchment. Place damp greaseproof paper over the top.
**13.** Place the mould or loaf tins in a roasting pan three-quarters filled with hot water (a bain-marie). Bake in the preheated oven for 1½ hours. Remove from the oven and allow to cool.

MEANWHILE, PREPARE THE SAUCE:

**14.** Combine all the sauce ingredients, except the oil, in a food processor and blend until smooth. Add the oil slowly with the machine running as for mayonnaise. Check the seasoning. If the sauce is too thick, thin down to a creamy consistency with a little lukewarm water.

TO SERVE:

**15.** Unmould the cooled terrine and cut into 5mm/¼in slices. Spread about 2 tablespoons of the sauce on to the base of each of 4 individual serving plates. Arrange a slice of the terrine on top of the sauce.

*The finished layers of the terrine*

NOTE: This terrine is quite difficult to slice – if you have an electric carving knife it makes life much easier.

 *CHABLIS*

# THAI DEEP-FRIED NOODLE BALLS

MAKES 22
*200g/7oz egg noodles or fine spaghetti*
*salt and freshly ground black pepper*
*400g/14oz crabmeat*
*4 large eggs*
*4 tablespoons chopped fresh coriander leaves*
*55g/2oz Parmesan cheese, freshly grated*
*70g/2½oz plain flour*
*1 onion, finely chopped*
*3 cloves of garlic, crushed*
*oil for deep-frying*

For the sauce
*125ml/4½fl oz Thai sweet chilli sauce*
*½ cucumber, peeled, deseeded and finely diced*
*55ml/2fl oz rice vinegar*

**1.** Cook the egg noodles in plenty of salted boiling water until just cooked. Drain well, then cut into small lengths. Place in a large bowl.
**2.** Add all the remaining ingredients except the oil to the bowl and mix to a firm, slightly sticky mixture.
**3.** Mould the mixture into balls about the size of golf balls. Chill well in the refrigerator.
**4.** Preheat the oil in a deep-fryer to 160°C/300°F. Fry about 4 balls at a time until golden-brown, being careful not to overload the fryer as this will reduce the temperature of the oil. Drain well on absorbent kitchen paper.
**5.** Meanwhile, make the sauce by mixing the ingredients together in a small bowl.
**6.** To serve: arrange 3 Thai noodle balls on individual serving plates with a small dish of sauce. Offer the remaining balls separately.

 *FULL DRY WHITE*

# SCALLOP MOUSSE WITH CRAYFISH SAUCE

This recipe has been adopted from Michel Guérard's *Cuisine Gourmande*.

SERVES 4
*450g/1lb scallops*
*salt and freshly ground white pepper*
*1 egg*
*340ml/12fl oz double cream*
*30g/1oz butter, melted*

For the sauce
*2 tablespoons olive oil*
*3 tablespoons groundnut oil*
*20 freshwater crayfish*
*2 small carrots, peeled and diced*
*½ onion, chopped*
*1 shallot, chopped*
*1 unpeeled clove of garlic, crushed*
*1 bouquet garni (see page 19)*
*2 tablespoons Armagnac*
*2 tablespoons port*
*200ml/7fl oz dry white wine*
*2 tomatoes, peeled, quartered, deseeded and diced*
*1 tablespoon tomato purée*
*salt and freshly ground black pepper*
*290ml/½ pint double cream*
*1 teaspoon chopped fresh tarragon*

To garnish
*a few sprigs of lamb's lettuce*

**1.** Remove the tough muscle (found opposite the roe) from the scallops (*see page 128*). Process the scallops briefly in a food processor with salt and pepper. When smooth, add the egg and process for 1 minute. Refrigerate until fairly firm (about 30 minutes).
**2.** Now process in the cream. The mousse should be fairly thick. Check the seasoning.
**3.** Preheat the oven to 170°C/325°F/gas mark 3. Brush 4 ramekins with melted butter and fill with the scallop mousse. Place in a roasting pan half-filled with hot water (a bain-marie) and bake in the preheated oven for 30 minutes. Remove from the oven and keep warm in the bain-marie.
**4.** Make the sauce: heat the oils in a very large

sauté pan, add the crayfish and cook, covered with a lid, for 10–12 minutes, or until red and cooked. Remove from the heat and take the crayfish out of the sauté pan. Shell them and remove the black vein but do not throw away the shells.

**5.** Pound the shells in a mortar (or grind in a food processor). Add to the sauté pan with the vegetables, garlic and bouquet garni. Cook slowly without browning. Add the Armagnac and port and simmer until reduced by half.

**6.** Add the wine, tomatoes and tomato purée. Season with salt and pepper and reduce by one-third by rapid boiling.

**7.** Add the cream and tarragon and simmer slowly for 10 minutes. Stir every so often to prevent the sauce from catching.

**8.** Push the sauce through a fine sieve, pressing well to extract all the flavour.

**9.** Arrange 5 shelled crayfish on each individual serving plate. Turn out the warm mousses beside them.

**10.** Just before serving, coat each mousse with the hot sauce and garnish with a sprig of lamb's lettuce.

 *WHITE BURGUNDY*

# ARRANGED SEAFOOD SALAD WITH BASIL AÏOLI

This first course is quite extravagant, but ideal for an easy dinner party. For a main course dish, simply increase the amount of seafood.

SERVES 8
For the basil aïoli
*2 cloves of garlic, crushed*
*2 egg yolks*
*a generous handful of basil leaves*
*salt and freshly ground white pepper*
*290ml/½ pint grapeseed oil*
*2 tablespoons lemon juice*

*a selection of seafood, such as:*
*16 small oysters, shucked*
*16 tiger prawns, cooked, peeled and deveined*

*225g/8oz smoked salmon*
*225g/8oz smoked halibut*
*225g/8oz smoked mussels*
*225g/8oz slender asparagus spears*
*Tabasco sauce*
*juice of 1 lemon*
*freshly ground black pepper*

To garnish
*sprigs of basil*

**1.** Make the basil aïoli: put the garlic, egg yolks and basil into a liquidizer or food processor. Season with a little salt and pepper. Whizz until well puréed. With the motor running, pour the oil in a thin stream on to the egg yolks. When a thick emulsion has formed, add the lemon juice and season to taste with salt and pepper. Pour into a small dish and set aside.

**2.** Prepare the seafood: remove the top shell of the oysters and cut the smoked salmon and halibut into long strips. Arrange the fish and asparagus in an attractive pattern on a large platter.

**3.** Season the oysters with a dash of Tabasco. Season the smoked fish with a little lemon juice and pepper.

**4.** Garnish with sprigs of basil and hand the basil aïoli separately.

 *SANCERRE*

# MEAT FIRST
# COURSES

# MINTED PIGEON BALLS

SERVES 6
*3 pigeons*
*85g/3oz unsalted butter, well chilled*
*2 small shallots, finely chopped*
*fresh mint leaves*
*170g/6oz piece of rindless streaky bacon*
*sprigs of fresh thyme and a few fresh rosemary*
  *leaves*
*a little brandy*
*salt and freshly ground black pepper*

1. Skin the pigeons and remove the flesh from the bones. Keep the carcases for stock or soup.
2. Cut 75g/2½oz of the butter into cubes the size of a hazelnut and put them into the freezer or a very cold refrigerator.
3. Cook the shallots in the remaining butter until soft.
4. Blanch the mint leaves in boiling water, refresh and drain well.
5. Put the pigeon flesh, bacon, shallots, thyme, rosemary and brandy into a food processor and process until smooth.
6. Remove the butter from the freezer or refrigerator. Moisten your fingers with water and shape pigeon mixture around each butter cube. Place a mint leaf firmly on each ball.
7. Put the balls on a steamer rack over boiling water and steam, covered, for 8 minutes. Serve immediately.

 *MEDIUM DRY WHITE*

# SNAILS WITH GARLIC BUTTER

SERVES 4
*170g/6oz butter*
*juice of ½ lemon*
*2 tablespoons chopped fresh parsley*
*6 cloves of garlic*
*salt*
*24 shelled snails and 24 shells*

To serve
*French bread*

1. Soften the butter and beat in the lemon juice and parsley. Crush the garlic with salt and beat this into the butter. Leave in a cool place.
2. Using a teaspoon handle, push a snail, tail first, into each shell. Fill the remaining cavity of the shell with the garlic butter, scraping off the top neatly. Keep in the refrigerator until needed.
3. Preheat the oven to 200°C/400°F/gas mark 6. Place a snail, butter upwards, in each indentation of 4 snail dishes and cook in the preheated oven for 8 minutes or until the butter has completely melted and starts to sizzle, but no longer. (Overcooking snails toughens them.)
4. Serve immediately with fresh French bread.

NOTE: Because preparing fresh snails is a specialized and lengthy process, ready-to-use snails are bought in cans, even by top French restaurants. Shells are bought separately and can be reused.

 *LIGHT WHITE*

# CHINESE CHICKEN BALLS

SERVES 4–6
*450g/1lb boneless, skinned chicken meat, finely*
  *minced*
*4 large spring onions, chopped*
*2.5cm/1in piece of fresh root ginger, peeled and*
  *finely chopped*
*1 clove of garlic, crushed*
*1 small green chilli, deseeded and finely chopped*
*2 tablespoons soy sauce*
*1 tablespoon wine vinegar*
*½ teaspoon ground, roasted Sichuan peppercorns*
*1 egg, lightly beaten*
*570ml/1 pint white stock, made with chicken*
  *bones (see page 243)*

To serve
*150ml/¼ pint low-fat plain yoghurt*
*1 teaspoon sesame oil*
*a dash of Tabasco sauce*

To garnish
*1 small bunch of watercress*

1. Mix together the chicken, spring onion, ginger, garlic, chilli, soy sauce, vinegar and peppercorns. Check the seasoning. Add the egg and beat well.

2. With wet hands shape the mixture into balls the size of ping-pong balls and place in the top half of a steamer, on a plate if the holes are large. Put the stock into the bottom half of the steamer. Bring to the boil and steam the balls for 20 minutes.

3. Meanwhile, make the sauce: mix together the yoghurt, oil and Tabasco and pour into a small dish.

4. Serve the balls on a warmed serving plate, garnished with sprigs of watercress.

# CHICKEN PARFAIT WITH CHICKEN LIVERS AND MUSHROOMS

SERVES 6–8
*butter for greasing*
*300g/11oz white chicken meat, finely minced*
*salt and freshly ground white pepper*
*a generous pinch of ground ginger*
*a generous pinch of ground cardamon*
*1 egg white, lightly beaten*
*55g/2oz flour quantity panada, sieved (see next recipe)*
*350ml/12fl oz double cream, lightly whipped*
*150g/5oz chicken livers*
*1–2 tablespoons oil*
*150g/5oz mushrooms, washed and diced*
*570ml/1 pint aspic (see page 244), flavoured with 3 tablespoons Madeira*
*3 tablespoons chopped fresh parsley*

1. Grease a 1 litre/1¾pint mould or loaf tin and line the base with a piece of greased greaseproof paper.

2. Cut the chicken into strips and sprinkle with salt, pepper and the spices. Chill in the refrigerator for at least 2 hours.

3. Preheat the oven to 150°C/300°F, gas mark 2.

4. Put the chicken into a bowl. Set in a bowl of ice, beat in the egg white and then add the panada.

5. Push the mixture through a drum sieve and then beat in the lightly whipped cream, a spoonful at a time, over ice.

6. Remove all the membrane and blood vessels from the chicken livers and cut into small pieces. Fry quickly in a little oil, season with salt and pepper and allow to cool.

7. Fry the mushrooms in a little more oil and season with salt and pepper. Drain and allow to cool. Mix together the mushrooms and chicken livers.

8. Put half the chicken mixture into the prepared mould and spread flat. Cover with the chicken liver and mushroom mixture. Add the remaining chicken mixture and spread flat. Cover the mould with greased greaseproof paper or foil and place in a roasting pan half filled with very hot water (a bain-marie). Bake in the centre of the preheated oven for about 40 minutes.

9. Allow the parfait to cool, then turn out carefully on to a plate and remove the lining paper. Coat carefully with one third of the Madeira-flavoured aspic and sprinkle with parsley. Allow to set and coat with a second layer of Madeira aspic.

10. Chill the remaining Madeira aspic until firm, then dice. Serve the parfait on a bed of the diced aspic.

 *SPICY WHITE ALSACE OR BEAUJOLAIS*

# PANADA

*100ml/3½fl oz milk*
*20g/¾oz butter*
*salt and freshly ground white pepper*
*freshly grated nutmeg*
*55g/2oz plain flour, sifted*
*1 egg*

1. Bring the milk, butter and seasoning up to the boil in a small saucepan. Add all the flour at once and mix well over the heat. Beat well until it comes away from the sides of the pan.

2. Allow the panada to cool slightly, then beat in the egg. Transfer to a bowl and leave to cool completely.

3. Push the cold panada through a sieve. Use as required.

# WONTON AND PANCAKE FIRST COURSES

# CHICKEN AND SPRING ONION WONTONS

MAKES 12
For the stuffing
*140g/5oz boneless, skinned chicken meat*
*5 spring onions, thinly sliced*
*2 teaspoons soy sauce*
*a few drops of sesame oil*
*salt and freshly ground black pepper*
*110g/4oz packet wonton skins*
*peanut oil*
*oil for frying*

To garnish
*2 tablespoons peanut oil*
*2 tablespoons sesame seeds*
*1 teaspoon peeled and grated fresh ginger root*
*10 spring onions, thinly sliced*

1. Make the stuffing: finely chop or process the chicken flesh. Place in a bowl and add the spring onions, soy sauce, sesame oil, salt and pepper. Mix well.
2. Place a teaspoon of the stuffing mixture in the centre of a wonton skin. Brush the edges of the skin with water and place a second skin on top, then press the edges together to seal. Repeat until all the filling and wonton skins are used.
3. Cook the stuffed wonton skins in boiling salted water for 2 minutes. Drain, then refresh under cold running water. When cold, drain well and toss in a little peanut oil.
4. When ready to serve, fry the wontons. Heat 3 tablespoons oil in a frying pan and cook the wontons until golden-brown on both sides. You may well need to add extra oil for each batch of wontons.
5. Prepare the garnish: heat the oil in a frying pan, add the sesame seeds and cook, stirring, until just turning brown. Add the ginger and spring onions and cook for a further minute.
6. Arrange the stuffed wonton skins on a serving dish and scatter the garnish over the top.

 *WHITE ALSACE*

# PORK AND CHINESE LEAF WONTON STUFFING

This is an alternative filling for the chicken and spring onion wontons (in the previous recipe).

MAKES 12
*225g/8oz Chinese leaves*
*1 teaspoon salt*
*freshly ground black pepper*
*110g/4oz pork, finely chopped*
*3 spring onions, finely chopped*
*1 tablespoon sesame oil*
*1 tablespoon corn oil*
*1 teaspoon Shaoxing wine or medium-dry sherry*

1. Chop the Chinese leaves very finely, discarding any tough stalks, and put into a bowl. Cover with water and add half the salt. Leave for 30 minutes.
2. Mix together the remaining salt, the pepper, pork, spring onions, sesame and corn oil and wine. Beat well.
3. Drain the Chinese leaves, squeeze dry and add to the pork mixture. Mix thoroughly.
4. Follow the recipe above to stuff and cook the wontons.

 *WHITE ALSACE*

# PEKING PANCAKES WITH DUCK, PORK AND PRAWN FILLINGS

SERVES 6
For the Peking pancakes
*450/1lb plain flour*
*290ml/½ pint very hot water*
*2 tablespoons sesame oil*

For the prawn filling
*1 tablespoon finely chopped spring onions*
*5cm/2in piece of fresh root ginger, peeled and finely chopped*
*1 tablespoon dry sherry*
*1 teaspoon soy sauce*

*1 tablespoon white stock (see page 243)*
*225g/8oz peeled cooked prawns*

*For the Peking duck*
*1 oven-ready duckling*
*1 lemon*
*1 litre/1³/₄ pints water*
*3 tablespoons clear honey*
*3 tablespoons soy sauce*
*150ml/¹/₄ pint dry sherry*

*For the pork and cashew filling*
*1 tablespoon oil*
*¹/₂ red chilli pepper*
*340g/12oz minced pork*
*55g/2oz cashew nuts*
*2 tablespoons soy sauce*
*1 tablespoon dry sherry*
*1 teaspoon caster sugar*
*salt and freshly ground black pepper*

*To serve*
*hoisin sauce*
*2 bunches of spring onions, cleaned and cut into*
*thin strips*
*¹/₂ cucumber, cut into thin sticks*

**1.** Prepare the duck the day before cooking. Wash and dry it well with absorbent kitchen paper. Slice the lemon thickly and put it into a saucepan with the water, honey, soy sauce and sherry. Bring to the boil, then simmer for about 30 minutes.

**2.** Ladle the honey and lemon syrup over the duck several times, until it is completely coated with the mixture. Hang the duck in a cool, well-ventilated place and leave to dry overnight. Place a roasting pan underneath it to catch any drips.

**3.** The following day, prepare the pancakes: sift the flour into a large bowl. Gradually add enough of the hot water to form a soft but not sticky dough. Knead the dough for 10 minutes until it is soft and smooth, cover it with a damp cloth and leave for 30 minutes.

**4.** After the dough has rested, knead it again for 5 minutes. Shape it into 2 sausages, each about 30cm/12in long, and cut each roll into 2cm/1in pieces. Shape each piece into a ball.

**5.** Take 2 balls at a time and dip one side of one ball in the sesame oil, put the oiled side on top of the other ball and roll the 2 together into a 15cm/6in circle.

**6.** Heat a heavy frying pan or griddle and cook the pancake until it has dried on one side, then cook the other side. Remove from the pan and peel the 2 sides apart. Continue to roll and cook the pancakes. Cover tightly in clingfilm until you are ready to use them.

**7.** To finish the duck: preheat the oven to 250°C/500°F/gas mark 9. Place the duck breast-side up on a wire rack. Stand the rack over a roasting pan containing 150ml/¹/₄ pint water. Cook the duck in the preheated oven for 15 minutes, then reduce the oven temperature to 180°C/350°F/gas mark 4 and cook for 1 further hour, or until the juices from the cavity are no longer pink. Allow the duck to stand for 10 minutes, then remove the meat from the bone and cut both meat and skin into neat slices. Keep warm.

**8.** Make the prawn filling: put the spring onions, ginger, sherry, soy sauce and stock into a frying pan or wok. Bring to the boil, then simmer for 2 minutes. Add the prawns and cook for a further 2 minutes. Turn into a warmed serving dish and keep warm in a low oven.

**9.** Make the pork and cashew filling: heat the oil in a wok or frying pan, add the chilli and fry until it turns dark, then remove from the pan. Stir-fry the pork in the oil, breaking up any lumps of meat. Remove the pork from the pan and drain off all but 1 tablespoon of the fat. When the fat is very hot, add the cashew nuts and stir-fry for 1 minute. Return the pork to the pan and add the soy sauce, sherry and sugar, and season with salt and pepper. Continue to stir-fry for 5 minutes or until the meat is cooked. Turn into a warmed serving dish and keep warm.

**10.** To serve the pancakes: give each guest a tiny dish of hoisin sauce. Dry the spring onion and cucumber well and put into serving dishes. Steam the pancakes to reheat them and serve immediately with the various hot fillings. The guests help themselves to duck, spring onions and cucumber (dipped into hoisin sauce if they like) or to the other fillings, wrap them in the pancakes and eat with chopsticks or fingers.

 *SPICY DRY WHITE*

# SPECIAL SPRING ROLLS

MAKES 16
*16 spring roll wrappers*

For the filling
*55g/2oz beansprouts*
*55g/2oz French beans*
*55g/2oz carrots, peeled and cut into julienne strips*
*1 stick of celery, trimmed and cut into julienne strips*
*1 courgette, cut into julienne strips*
*110g/4oz lean veal or pork, cut into fine julienne strips*
*1 tablespoon oil*
*1 × 1cm/½in piece of fresh root ginger, peeled and sliced*
*1 clove of garlic, peeled and sliced*
*1 tablespoon soy sauce*
*salt and freshly ground black pepper*

To cook
*lightly beaten egg white*
*oil for deep-frying*

1. First make the filling: blanch the beansprouts in boiling water for 15 seconds. Drain and refresh under cold running water. Top and tail the French beans and cut them in half lengthways. Mix the sprouts and beans with the carrots, celery and courgette.
2. Mix in the veal or pork.
3. Heat the oil in a wok or frying pan, add the ginger and garlic and cook over a low heat for 2 minutes. Remove the ginger and garlic – the oil should by now be well infused with their flavour.
4. Turn up the heat and quickly stir-fry the meat and vegetables. Season with the soy sauce, salt and pepper. Remove from the heat and leave to cool.
5. Divide the filling between the spring roll wrappers. Put the filling in the centre of each wrapper and fold 2 opposite corners on top of it. Then roll up from one of the exposed corners to the other to form rolls.

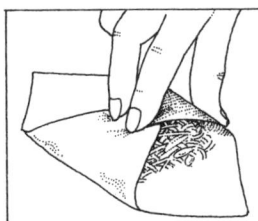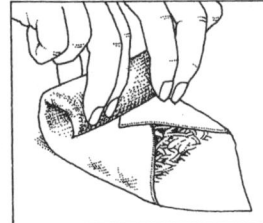

*Put the filling in the centre and fold and roll up*

6. Brush the rolls with the beaten egg white.
7. Heat oil in a deep-fryer until a crumb will sizzle vigorously in it and add the spring rolls. Fry until golden-brown, then drain well on absorbent kitchen paper. Sprinkle with salt, and serve.

 WHITE ALSACE

# SPRING PANCAKE ROLLS WITH CHINESE VEGETABLES

This has been adapted from a recipe by Paul Gayler in *Take Six More Cooks*.

MAKES 20
*2 medium-large heads of celeriac*
*a squeeze of lemon juice*
*30g/1oz mouli (Chinese radish)*
*¼ red pepper*
*¼ green pepper*
*¼ yellow pepper*
*2 carrots*
*30g/1oz beansprouts*
*3 spring onions*
*30g/1oz mangetout*
*30g/1oz butter*
*a little sesame oil*
*¼ teaspoon crushed garlic*
*a small piece of fresh root ginger, peeled and finely chopped*
*2 egg yolks*
*4 tablespoons arrowroot*
*4 tablespoons clarified butter (see page 686) for frying*

For the tomato coriander sauce
*55g/2oz butter*
*2 shallots, finely chopped*
*2 cloves of garlic, crushed*
*4 tomatoes, roughly chopped*
*1 tablespoon tomato purée*
*5 tablespoons sherry vinegar*
*150ml/¼ pint white wine*
*290ml/½ pint water*
*2 tablespoons soy sauce*
*10 fresh coriander leaves, finely shredded*

To garnish
*fresh coriander leaves*

**1.** Peel the celeriac and slice into very thin circles, preferably on a mandolin. Blanch the celeriac in boiling water with a squeeze of lemon juice for 10 seconds, then plunge into iced water to refresh. Remove, drain and dry on a clean cloth.

**2.** Make the filling: finely shred all the other vegetables. Heat the butter and the sesame oil in a wok or frying pan. Add the garlic, then the shredded vegetables and the ginger. Cook for 2–3 minutes, keeping the vegetables crisp. Remove the ingredients from the pan and allow to cool.

**3.** Make the celeriac pancake rolls: place 2 celeriac circles overlapping on a clean surface. If using smaller celeriac, you may need several circles. Bind the egg yolks and arrowroot together to form a paste and brush this mixture lightly around the edge of the celeriac circles.

**4.** Place a portion of Chinese vegetables in the centre of each celeriac circle and roll up to form a pancake roll. Leave in the refrigerator for 30 minutes to set.

**5.** Make the sauce: put the butter, shallots, and garlic into a saucepan and cook without allowing to colour. Add the tomatoes and the tomato purée, and cook for a further 5 minutes.

**6.** Add the vinegar and wine and cook until reduced by half. Pour in the water, cover with a lid and cook gently for 20 minutes.

**7.** Pass the sauce through a fine sieve. Finish by adding the soy sauce and the coriander.

**8.** Fry the celeriac pancake rolls in the clarified butter until golden. Arrange 2 on each individual serving plate and pour a little of the coriander and tomato sauce alongside.

**9.** Garnish with fresh coriander leaves and serve immediately.

NOTES: Smaller versions of these rolls make excellent hot canapés.

If celeriac is not available, filo pastry, spring roll wrappers or wonton skins can be used instead.

 *WHITE ALSACE*

# SAVOURY STUFFED PANCAKES

SERVES 4
*12 French pancakes (see page 471)*
*450g/1lb smoked haddock*
*290ml/½ pint milk*
*1 bay leaf*
*1 slice of onion*
*3–4 black peppercorns*
*1 parsley stalk*
*salt and freshly ground black pepper*
*15g/½oz butter*
*15g/½oz plain flour*
*a pinch of dry English mustard*
*a pinch of cayenne pepper*
*55g/2oz Cheddar cheese, grated*
*1 teaspoon chopped fresh tarragon*
*30g/1oz melted butter*
*dried white breadcrumbs*
*1 tablespoon freshly grated Parmesan cheese*

**1.** Preheat the oven to 190°C/375°F/gas mark 5.

**2.** Place the smoked haddock skin side up in an ovenproof dish with the milk, bay leaf, onion, peppercorns and parsley stalk.

**3.** Cover the dish and cook in the preheated oven for 15 minutes, or until the fish will flake easily with a fork.

**4.** Strain off and reserve the liquor and flake the fish, taking care to remove any bones and skin. Taste the liquor and if it is too salty, dilute with a little water.

**5.** Melt the butter in a saucepan, add the flour, mustard and cayenne and cook for 1 minute. Remove the pan from the heat, pour on the reserved liquor and bring to the boil, stirring continuously.

**6.** Remove the sauce from the heat, stir in half the Cheddar cheese and season with salt, pepper and tarragon. Stir in the fish. Preheat the grill.

**7.** Place a good spoonful of the fish mixture on each pancake and roll up. Lay the pancakes side by side in a buttered ovenproof dish. Brush with melted butter. Sprinkle with the remaining Cheddar cheese, the breadcrumbs and the Parmesan cheese.

**8.** Place under the hot grill until well browned.

 *BEAUJOLAIS*

# OTHER FIRST
# COURSES

# TOASTED GOAT'S CHEESE WITH SESAME SEEDS

SERVES 6

6 small or 3 medium goat's cheeses (crottins)
85g/3oz sesame seeds, lightly toasted
6 slices of wholemeal toast, cut into circles just
    larger than the cheeses
2 heads of radicchio, washed and dried

For the dressing
2 tablespoons olive oil
2 tablespoons white wine vinegar
1 clove of garlic, crushed
2 tablespoons chopped fresh chives
salt and freshly ground black pepper

**1.** Preheat the oven to 200°C/400°F/gas mark 6.
**2.** If you are using 3 medium goat's cheeses, cut
them in half horizontally. Roll the cheeses in the
sesame seeds until completely coated.
**3.** Place the circles of toast on a baking sheet and
place the cheeses on top. Bake in the preheated
oven for 5–10 minutes, until the cheese is soft and
on the point of melting.
**4.** Meanwhile, combine all the ingredients for the
dressing and mix well. Separate the radicchio into
leaves and toss in the dressing. Arrange on 6
individual serving plates and place the hot toast
and cheese on each leaf. Serve immediately.

 *SAUVIGNON BLANC*

# GOAT'S CHEESE WITH SESAME SEEDS IN FILO

SERVES 6

6 small or 3 medium goat's cheeses (crottins)
85g/3oz sesame seeds, lightly toasted
3 sheets of filo pastry (see page 466)
30g/1oz butter, melted
2 heads of radicchio

For the dressing
2 tablespoons olive oil
2 tablespoons white wine vinegar
1 clove of garlic, crushed

2 tablespoons chopped fresh chives
salt and freshly ground black pepper

**1.** Preheat the oven to 200°C/400°F/gas mark 6. If
you are using 3 medium goat's cheeses, cut them
in half horizontally. Roll the cheese in the sesame
seeds until completely coated.
**2.** Spread out the filo pastry, brush with melted
butter and cut into 12 × 15cm/6in squares. Layer
one square on top of another. Place a whole or half
goat's cheese in the centre of each square. Draw up
the pastry to form a pouch. Lightly dot the outside
of the pastry with melted butter, place on a baking
sheet and bake in the preheated oven for 5 minutes.
**3.** Meanwhile, combine all the ingredients for the
dressing and mix well. Separate the radicchio into
leaves and toss in the dressing. Arrange on 6
individual serving plates and place the filo parcels
on top.

 *WHITE LOIRE*

# FRIED POLENTA

Polenta is a classical dish of Northern Italy. It can be
eaten as soon as it is cooked, served with roasts,
grills, casseroles or poultry. Or it can be left to cool,
sliced and then grilled or fried. Fried polenta is
particularly good served with fried wild mushrooms.

SERVES 4–6

2 litres/3½ pints white stock (see page 243)
teaspoon salt
285g/10oz polenta  (coarse cornmeal)
oil for frying

**1.** Put the stock and salt into a large saucepan and
bring to the boil.
**2.** Remove from the heat and sprinkle on the
polenta, whisking quickly to prevent lumps from
forming. Reduce the heat.
**3.** Return the pan to the heat and cover it as the
mixture will bubble and spatter.
**4.** Continue cooking until the polenta is very thick
(about 35–40 minutes), stirring often to prevent
sticking and burning.
**5.** The polenta can be served at this stage piled
high on a plate, or it can be fried as below.

**6.** Lightly oil a shallow tin 28 × 18cm/11 × 7in. Spread the mixture out evenly, allow to cool, and refrigerate for about 1 hour.

**7.** Turn the polenta out of the tin, and cut into 4cm/1½in slices.

**8.** Fill a large deep frying pan with enough oil to come 2cm/¾in up the sides of the pan. Heat until very hot.

**9.** Add the polenta slices, being careful not to overcrowd the pan as this will make turning difficult, reduce the heat and fry gently until golden-brown on both sides. Remove with a fish slice, taking care to drain off excess oil.

 *YOUNG RED*

# SPINACH GNOCCHI

SERVES 6
*170g/6oz fresh spinach, cooked and chopped*
*225g/8oz ricotta cheese*
*85g/3oz Parmesan cheese, freshly grated*
*1 egg*
*salt and freshly ground black pepper*
*freshly grated nutmeg*
*plain flour*
*45g/1½oz butter, melted*

**1.** Combine the spinach, ricotta and half the Parmesan cheese in a bowl with the egg, salt, pepper and plenty of nutmeg. Mix thoroughly.

**2.** Bring a large saucepan of salted water to simmering point.

**3.** Meanwhile, shape the spinach mixture into egg shapes, using a tablespoon and the palm of your hand. Roll the gnocchi lightly in flour. Place them in the simmering water a few at a time and poach gently until they rise to the surface (about 2–3 minutes).

**4.** Preheat the grill. Remove the gnocchi from the pan with a slotted spoon, allowing excess liquid to drain off. Arrange in an ovenproof dish.

**5.** Pour over the melted butter, and sprinkle with the remaining Parmesan cheese. Place under the hot grill for a few minutes until the cheese is bubbly and golden-brown. Serve immediately.

 *SOAVE*

# FRIED GNOCCHI

SERVES 6
*570ml/1 pint milk*
*1 onion, sliced*
*1 clove*
*1 bay leaf*
*6 parsley stalks*
*110g/4oz semolina*
*200g/7oz strong Cheddar cheese*
*2 tablespoons freshly grated Parmesan cheese*
*1 tablespoon chopped fresh parsley*
*salt and freshly ground black pepper*
*a pinch of dry English mustard*
*a pinch of cayenne pepper*
*oil for deep-frying*
*beaten egg*
*dried white breadcrumbs*

**1.** Infuse the milk in a saucepan with the onion, clove, bay leaf and parsley stalks over a very gentle heat for 7 minutes. Bring up to boiling point, then strain.

**2.** Sprinkle in the semolina, stirring continuously, and cook, still stirring, until the mixture is thick (about 1 minute). Remove the pan from the heat and add the cheeses, parsley, salt, pepper, mustard and cayenne. Taste: the mixture should be well seasoned. Spread this mixture into a neat round on a wet plate and refrigerate for 30 minutes.

**3.** Cut the gnocchi paste into 8 equal wedges. Refrigerate again.

**4.** Heat oil in a deep-fryer until a crumb will sizzle vigorously in it. Dip the gnocchi into beaten egg and coat with breadcrumbs.

**5.** Deep-fry in hot oil until golden-brown (about 2 minutes). Drain well on absorbent kitchen paper. Sprinkle with salt and serve.

NOTES: A thin tomato sauce (see page 258) is good with fried gnocchi.

If you do not like the idea of deep-frying, bake the gnocchi in the oven preheated to 190°C/375°F/gas mark 5 for 20 minutes, then grill until well-browned on both sides.

 *LIGHT RED ITALIAN*

# GNOCCHI ALLA ROMANA

SERVES 4–6
1 litre/1¾ pints milk
1½ teaspoons salt
freshly grated nutmeg
225g/8oz coarse-ground semolina
3 egg yolks
85g/3oz Parmesan cheese, freshly grated
85g/3oz butter

1. Lightly oil a baking tray.
2. In a large saucepan, bring the milk, salt and plenty of nutmeg to the boil, then remove from the heat and sprinkle over the semolina, stirring continuously with a wooden spoon.
3. Reduce the heat and return the pat to the heat. Continue to cook, uncovered, for 10–15 minutes, stirring occasionally to prevent burning and sticking, until the spoon is able to stand upright, unsupported, in the mixture. Remove from the heat and allow to cool slightly.
4. Beat in the egg yolks, 30g/1oz of the cheese and 30g/1oz of the butter. Check the seasoning.
5. Pile into the prepared tray and smooth over with a wet spatula to about 5mm/¼in thick. Refrigerate for about 1–1½ hours until firm.
6. Preheat the oven to 230°C/450°F/gas mark 8. Melt the butter and lightly brush a shallow ovenproof dish with a little of it.
7. Cut the semolina into circles, using a 4cm/1½in plain pastry cutter. Arrange the circles slightly overlapping in the prepared dish.
8. Pour over the remaining butter and sprinkle with the remaining cheese. Bake in the preheated oven for 15–20 minutes, or until crisp and golden-brown.

 *LIGHT RED ITALIAN*

# TEMPURA

SERVES 4
1 small aubergine
salt
oil for deep-frying
1 medium courgette, cut into batons
110g/4oz baby sweetcorn, halved lengthways
225g/8oz scampi, seasoned with lemon juice and
    freshly ground black pepper

For the batter
225g/8oz plain flour
2 small egg yolks
340ml/12fl oz water
a pinch of salt

For the sauce
2 teaspoons sesame oil
2 tablespoons red wine vinegar
2 tablespoons soy sauce
3 tablespoons ginger syrup (from a jar of
    preserved ginger)
2 tablespoons clear honey
1 small bunch of spring onions, shredded

1. Slice the aubergine thinly, score the flesh lightly and place in a colander, sprinkling each layer with salt. Leave to degorge for 30 minutes.
2. Mix together all the ingredients for the sauce, except for the spring onions.
3. Heat oil in a deep-fryer until a crumb will sizzle vigorously in it.
4. Wash the aubergines well and pat dry on absorbent kitchen paper.
5. When the oil is hot, mix the batter ingredients together – it should not be smooth.
6. Dip the prepared aubergine, courgette, sweetcorn and scampi into the batter and deep-fry in small batches. Drain well on kitchen paper and sprinkle lightly with salt. Arrange on a large warmed serving dish.
7. Scatter the shredded spring onions on top of the sauce and hand separately.

 *SPICY DRY WHITE*

# FARINACEOUS

---

# FARINACEOUS

Farinaceous staples – rice, pasta, and potatoes – are fundamental to the diet worldwide. Details on making pasta are to be found on page 470. Here we give information and cooking instructions for rice and potatoes.

## RICE

### by Roz Denny

It is said that around two-thirds of the world's population are nourished daily with rice. Unlike any other major food, rice is central to the cultures, and in some cases the religion, of many countries, particularly in Asia. The cultivation of rice requires great skills of irrigation which in turn has demanded levels of social organization unknown in the West. Rice farmers had to co-operate amicably if their paddy fields were to receive sufficient water for the two or more crops a year needed to sustain their families and fellow villagers. Small wonder, then, that the rice-growing nations of the world hold rice in great esteem and consider it central to their exciting and sophisticated cuisines. Unfortunately, we in the West have barely exploited the potential of rice in the kitchen, relegating it frequently to a small side accompaniment on a plate and requiring only that it should not stick!

In fact, the beauty of rice is that it has very many qualities, and it is well worth learning to discriminate between different types and brands. Texture and flavour play an important part in assessing the culinary worth of rice. This depends on the variety and growing conditions. Good rice can be compared to fine wine in that it can take on the characteristics of the soil and climate where it is grown. Unfortunately, there is no equivalent of an *appellation contrôlée* for rice sold in the West and therefore little way of knowing which is the best quality. Even higher prices are no guide. Whilst cheaper supermarket own-brand rices may well be of poorer quality than well-known brands, a well-advertised brand may lack finesse of flavour and simply be milled to a consistent, bland, non-stick standard. You are merely paying more for marketing and advertising costs.

The best guide to buying quality rices is to seek out brands bought by rice-eating people – Indians, Chinese, Thais, Arabs, and so on. Another assurance of quality is to look for the country of origin on the pack. Rice sold without a country of origin may well be a blend of grains milled to a basic standard with little to commend it to the cook.

### TYPES OF RICE

Estimates on the varieties of rice grown vary, but there are believed to be approximately 7,000, all with their own individual styles of taste, texture, colour and cooking quality. Rice is categorized botanically into either long-grain (*Oryza indica*) or short-grain (*Oryza japonica*). Indica rices (e.g. basmati) are higher in amylose starch, which keeps the grains more separate after cooking, whilst Japonica rices (e.g. sushi or risotto) are higher in amylopectin, which makes them appear more starchy. And some grains fall in between the two categories. Long-grain rices are generally more slender and longer. Short-grain rices have plumper grains and cook to a more starchy consistency, either more creamy or more sticky.

LONG-GRAIN RICES

Originally called Patna, after the popular rice grown in India, but little rice is now sold as such. Generally it will be classified simply as long-grain. One of the biggest exporters of long-grain rice is the USA. American long-grain rice is a high-quality grain giving excellent results, sometimes said to have a natural 'popcorn' flavour. The best American long-grain is grown in Arkansas, on the delta of the Mississippi, but production is also prolific in California and Texas. Long-grain rice may also come from Spain, India, Surinam, Thailand and Australia.

When rice is sold with the bran layer intact it is known as wholegrain or brown rice.
USES: General accompaniment for casseroles and curries. Good for chilli con carne, Caribbean dishes, salads and pilafs.

Basmati

The Prince of Rices! An elegant long-grain rice with a legendary flavour. The name basmati means 'the fragrant one' in Hindi, and good basmati will smell deliciously aromatic even in its uncooked state. The smell of basmati cooking is even better. There are very many varieties and qualities of basmati, which is grown in Iran, Pakistan and Northern India. The best comes from the state of Haryana in the foothills of the Himalayas and is sold under a brand name for export to the Middle East, Europe and the USA. Good basmati will lengthen to three times its dried length once cooked and retain a white, delicate, separate fluffiness.

Basmati is also available as wholegrain or brown basmati.
USES: For curries, pilafs and kedgerees as well as salads, casseroles, koulibiacs, to serve with sauces and even as rice puddings.

Thai rice

Thailand, known as the rice bowl of Asia, is the world's greatest exporter of rice. (The great rice-eating nations of China, Japan and India produce most of their own rice to support their billion-plus populations and export relatively little.) Many rices are produced in Thailand but rice

known specifically as Thai rice is lightly sticky or glutinous, displaying some characteristics of short-grain rices, yet retaining a good bite to the grain. This is the rice Chinese cooks like to serve at home and it is becoming increasingly popular in the West. High-quality Thai rices have a silky sheen and a wonderful natural fragrance, like a milky, sweet nuttiness, often likened to the smell of jasmine flowers. It can be sold as Thai Fragrant or specifically Thai Jasmine.
USES: An ideal accompaniment to all Thai and Indonesian dishes as well as Indian food, Chinese and other Oriental dishes. It is excellent, too, as a stir-fry rice as the light stickiness separates out during re-frying. It also makes excellent rice puddings and rice cakes, and is good as a sushi rice.

SHORT-GRAIN RICES

Japonica varieties include risotto and pudding rices (both from Italy) and sticky rices from China and Japan.

Risotto rices

As with basmati, there are different qualities of risotto rices, and choosing the right one can make or break a dish. Risotto rices are grouped into superfini and semifini qualities. The most highly rated risotto rices are Carnaroli and Arborio, which are superfini quality, although the semifino Vialone Nano grain is highly prized by risotto connoisseurs because of its smaller, firmer grain. A good risotto grain should absorb up to five times its volume in stock and impart a creaminess to the dish while still retaining a good *al dente* bite. When risotto is left to cool it becomes solid and can be shaped into rissoles or savoury cakes. The arborio grain is particularly suitable for this use. Risottos are made differently from pilafs in that hot stock is stirred gradually into the rice, allowing each addition to be absorbed, thus encouraging the starch in the grain to give a natural creaminess to the dish. Risottos, like soufflés, should always be served immediately.
USES: Real Italian risottos, paella, puddings, rissoles/fritters, cakes.

Paella rice

The Moors brought rice-growing into Spain and from there it was introduced into the lush valleys of the Po river in Italy during medieval times. Paella rice is similar to risotto rice in that it is a medium-short grain rice with a creamy texture. A classic paella is shaken, not stirred, in the pan, so the right grain should be not quite as creamy as a risotto rice. However, true paella rices, such as Valencia and Bomba, are not easy to buy in the UK and USA and an arborio grain is fine as a substitute.

## Pudding rice

Most of this short-grain rice comes from Italy, although at one stage the Carolinas in North America were abundant producers, hence the one-time term Carolina rice, which is not now used in the industry. Pudding rice imparts a lot of creaminess to a dish, but the grain breaks down completely on cooking and so has little else to offer the cook in the way of flavour or texture. Increasingly, chefs and cooks are experimenting with using other more flavoursome grains such as risotto, Thai or basmati rices in desserts.
USES: Puddings either baked in a slow oven or stirred in a saucepan, to be served hot or cold.

## OTHER RICES
### Wild rice

Botanically not a true rice at all, but an aquatic grass that is native to Canada and the USA, producing dark brown grains with a delicious nutty flavour and texture. During cooking, good wild rice imparts a wonderful smell like that of new-mown grass. This is a grain that helped sustain the early settlers of North America and consequently is particularly popular in the USA around Thanksgiving and Christmas, served with turkey and game as a 'dressing' or stuffing. The best-quality wild rice has long, unbroken, dark brown, glossy grains and is grown organically around lakes in Canada where it is still hand-harvested by native Americans in canoes. Again, look for good branded wild rice rather than grains sold loose or as own-label. 'Wild' rice is also cultivated and these grains are smaller and paler in colour. Cultivated grains can be passed through a system of rollers that scratches the outside of the grain (known as scarified rice), enabling water to enter the grain quicker during cooking and so shorten the otherwise long cooking time. This grain is increasingly sold blended with basmati or white long-grain rice.
USES: As a dressing/stuffing for turkey, also good

with fish, mixed with white rice as an accompaniment, and for salads.

## Red Camargue rice

A hybrid rice discovered as a happy accident by a member of the Griotto family of rice farmers in the traditional rice-growing region of the Camargue, southern France. It has a reddish-brown colour and a rather pleasant flavour slightly reminiscent of buckwheat. The texture is nutty but breaks down somewhat in cooking. It is good as an accompaniment and should be treated as a cross between wild rice and brown rice.
USES: Similar to wild rice, for stuffings, as an accompaniment and in salads.

## Glutinous black rice

This rice from South East Asia is used primarily as a pudding rice, cooked with sugar, coconut milk and lemon grass. It has a nice nutty texture and a delicious, sweet, milky taste.
USES: As a dessert served with sliced mango, star fruits, etc.

## Wehani rice

A reddish-brown, nutty-style rice from the USA, developed by the Lundburg family in California. It should be treated as brown rice and is good as an accompaniment or for stuffings and puddings.

## EASY-COOK RICES

The rice-milling process called par-boiling is actually based on an ancient Persian technique of treating rice grains so that they could be stored for longer. In Europe we call these rices 'easy-cook'; in the USA the term used is 'par-boiled'. After the removal of the outer bran layer, rice grains are subjected to short bursts of intense steam which hardens the outside of the grain, causing the gelatinization of the starch. The process also has the benefit of driving the vitamins on the outside of the grain into the centre, thus making it marginally more nutritious. Manufacturers claim this makes the rice non-stick, but par-boiling deprives the grain of a lot of its natural flavour, and some would say makes the rice seem quite chewy. Easy-cook rice takes longer to cook than some varieties and the par-boiling makes the grains look yellowish, although the rice is more resistant to careless cooking. An easy-cook basmati rice seems to survive the process quite well, and much of the original flavour continues to shine through.

## COOKING METHODS

*Allow 55g/2oz uncooked rice per person*
Choosing the right grain for a dish is the secret of successful rice cooking. It is hard to make a pilaf with a risotto rice, or a risotto with an easy-cook rice. Also, many grains need differing amounts of water and cooking times: most brown rice, for example, needs considerably longer cooking than white. The best guide is to follow instructions on the pack. There are four main methods (see below) of cooking rice, apart from risotto and pudding rices: The first method, the open-pan, is quick and easy and so ideal for inexperienced cooks. For specific rice recipes, see pages 204–6. Note that all rice benefits from a standing time of about 5 minutes after cooking and draining so that excess water is absorbed back into the grain. Allow for this before serving. In addition, basmati rice benefits from rinsing and sometimes a little pre-soaking. This is not essential but does give a lighter, more traditional result (see box below).

### 1. OPEN-PAN/FAST BOILING

Suitable for basmati, easy-cook basmati, brown basmati and other brown rices, long-grain, wild rices and wild rice blends.

Allow 1.2 litres/2 pints water and 1 teaspoon salt for each 110g/4oz rice.

Bring a saucepan of water to a rolling boil. Add salt, then stir in the rice. Return to a medium boil and cook for the following times.
- Basmati and Thai rices: 10 minutes
- American long-grain: 12 minutes
- Easy-cook basmati and easy-cook long-grain: 15 minutes
- Brown basmati and wild rice with white rice blends: 20–25 minutes
- Brown long-grain rices: 25–30 minutes
- Wild rice: 40–50 minutes

Drain in a large sieve and rinse in hot water. Allow to stand in the sieve for 5 minutes before forking through with melted butter or oil.

### 2. COVERED PAN/ABSORPTION METHOD

Suitable for Thai rice, sushi rice, basmati (rinsed), brown basmati, brown rice, wild rice, wild rice with white rice blends, easy-cook rices. A measured amount of water is absorbed during cooking, so there is no need to drain. Follow the instructions below according to the rice variety.

- Put rice, water and salt to taste into a saucepan. Bring to the boil, stir once, then cover and lower the heat to a gentle simmer. Do not lift the lid.
- After the calculated cooking time (see below) remove from the heat, still uncovered, and allow to stand 5 minutes before forking through with butter or oil.

For each (225ml/8fl oz) cup of rice allow:
*Thai and Sushi rice*: 1¼ cups water. Cook for 10–12 minutes.
*Basmati rice*: 1½ cups water. Cook for 10–12 minutes.
*Brown basmati, wild rice with white rice blends, easy-cook rices*: 2 cups water. Cook for 20–25 minutes.
*Wild rice and brown long grain rice*: 2½–3 cups water. Cook for 40–50 minutes.

### 3. STEAMING/MICROWAVE

Suitable for basmati, long-grain and Thai rices.

- Rinse first if using basmati. Par-boil in plenty of boiling salted water for 5 minutes. Drain in a sieve and rinse under cold running water for a good minute or two. Drain again.
- Place in a non-metallic heatproof bowl. Cover with clingfilm and vent the side very slightly.
- Microwave on full power (100%) for 5 minutes (Thai and basmati), 7 minutes for long-grain rice.
- Allow to stand (still covered) for 5 minutes before forking through with butter or oil.

### 4. PILAF

Suitable for basmati, easy-cook basmati and long-grain rices. Rinse first if using basmati.

- Fry 1 chopped onion and 2 crushed cloves of garlic in 3 tablespoons sunflower or olive oil for 5 minutes.
- Stir in 250g/9oz rice and cook gently for 1–2 minutes, stirring occasionally.

- Pour in 450ml/¾ pint stock or water for basmati, 600ml/1 pint for other rices.
- Add salt and pepper to taste. Bring to the boil, then cover and simmer gently for 10 minutes for basmati, 12–14 minutes for long-grain rices and 20 minutes for easy-cook basmati.
- Allow to stand, still covered, for 5 minutes, then fork through with butter or oil.

---

*RINSING AND SOAKING BASMATI*

For a traditional, light and fluffy grain.

- Place the rice in a deep bowl. Cover with cold water and stir well with your hand. Tip out the water (the grains sink to the bottom, so there is no need for a sieve)
- Fill with more cold water, and repeat the process three more times until the water becomes clearer.
- Fill again with cold water and leave to stand for 10–15 minutes. This also helps shorten the cooking time slightly. Drain well before cooking.

---

## RICE AND YOUR HEALTH

Rice is an excellent food for a well-balanced, healthy diet. For a start, it is a complex carbohydrate starchy food, and as such one of the foods nutritionists and doctors tell us we must eat more of. In fact, half our daily calorie intake should come from starchy foods such as rice. A good 50g/2oz portion (uncooked weight) which swells to 150g/5oz cooked weight provides approximately 170 calories, with useful amounts of B group vitamins, a small amount of easy-to-digest protein, the minerals iron and zinc and useful amounts of fibre. The starchy carbohydrate in rice does not give the body immediate energy. Rather, the energy is released slowly into the bloodstream. In other words, it is better-value energy and keeps us going longer. Rice is therefore an invaluable food for athletes and sportsmen and women.

ROZ DENNY

# BOILED RICE

*55g/2oz long-grain white rice per person, rinsed*

1. Fill a large saucepan with salted water (1 cup of rice will need at least 6 cups of water, but the exact quantities do not matter as long as there is plenty of water). Bring to the boil.
2. Tip in the rice and stir until the water returns to the boil.
3. Boil for 10 minutes and then test: the rice should be neither hard nor mushy, but firm to the bite: *al dente*.
4. Drain the rice in a colander or sieve. Allow to stand for 10 minutes.

# BOILED BROWN RICE

Brown rices vary enormously, and though this method is suitable for the majority of them, some may require longer, slower cooking.

*55g/2oz brown rice per person*
*salt*

1. Cook the rice in a large amount of boiling salted water for 20 minutes. Drain well. Allow to stand for 5 minutes.

# BASMATI RICE I

Allow 55g/2oz rice per head. Rinse and soak the rice (see above). Put it into a saucepan and add enough cold water to cover, a pinch of salt, a cinnamon stick, 1 teaspoon lightly fried mustard seeds, and the crushed seeds from 2–3 cardamom pods. Bring to the boil, cover and simmer until the rice is cooked and the water absorbed (about 10 minutes). Remove the cinnamon stick.

# BASMATI RICE II

Allow 55g/2oz rice per head. Rinse and soak the rice (see above). Put into a saucepan with a pinch of salt. Add enough cold water to just cover the rice. Bring to the boil, then simmer for 4–5 minutes, cover and remove from the heat. After about 10 minutes the rice should be perfectly cooked and all the water absorbed.

# STEAMED RICE

This recipe has been taken from *The Wok Cook Book* by Yan-Kit So.

*2 cups or about 375g/13oz long-grain white rice*
*2 cups or 450ml/³/4 pint water*
*1 tablespoon vegetable oil*

**1.** Wash the rice in several changes of water until the water is no longer milky. Drain well.
**2.** Put the rice into a cake tin or a Pyrex pie dish. Add the water and oil. Put the tin or dish on a steaming stand in a wok.
**3.** Steam, covered, over a high heat for about 25 minutes in a cake tin or 35 minutes in a Pyrex dish. The rice should be firm but cooked through. Fluff up and serve.

# FRIED RICE

SERVES 4
*8 tablespoons long-grain rice*
*55g/2oz pinenuts (optional, browned)*
*4 tablespoons oil*
*2 spring onions, finely chopped*
*salt and freshly ground black pepper*

**1.** Bring a large saucepan of salted water to the boil and tip in the rice. Stir, bring back to the boil, and cook for 10 minutes or until the rice is just tender.
**2.** Fry the pinenuts in 1 tablespoon of the oil until lightly browned all over.
**3.** Rinse plenty of hot water through the rice to remove the excess starch and drain well. While it is draining, turn it over occasionally with a spoon to allow trapped steam to escape.
**4.** Pour the remaining oil into the frying pan with the spring onions. Put in the rice, which should now be quite dry. Fry, turning all the time to brown evenly. Season to taste with salt and pepper.
**5.** Stir in the pinenuts.

NOTE: 'Easy-cook' or polished rice is much easier to fry evenly.

# CHINESE FRIED RICE

This recipe is adapted from Yan-Kit So's Mixed Fried Rice. As Yan-Kit says, this recipe can be changed to use up leftovers in the refrigerator as long as the essential ingredients – rice, spring onions and egg – are included.

SERVES 4–6
*3 tablespoons sunflower oil*
*1 × 110g/4oz can of bamboo shoots, drained*
*½ cucumber, diced*
*110g/4oz petits pois, cooked*
*6 spring onions, cut into small rounds, white and*
   *green parts separated*
*2 eggs, lightly beaten with ¼ teaspoon salt*
*steamed rice (see above)*
*½ teaspoon salt*
*225g/8oz lean bacon, grilled and diced*
*225g/8oz cooked chicken, diced*
*1 tablespoon light soy sauce, plus extra to taste*

**1.** Heat a wok, add 1 tablespoon of the oil and when hot add the bamboo shoots and cucumber. Stir-fry for 30 seconds, then remove and mix with the petits pois. Wipe the wok clean.
**2.** Heat the remaining oil, add the white spring onions and stir-fry for 30 seconds. Add the eggs and allow to set very slightly. Add the rice. Stir-fry vigorously, mixing the eggs thoroughly into the rice. When the mixture is hot add the salt, bacon and chicken.
**3.** Add the bamboo shoots, cucumber and peas and stir again until very hot. Add the soy sauce and green spring onions. Stir and add extra soy sauce to taste.

 *DRY WHITE*

# BROWN RICE PILAF WITH SESAME SEEDS

SERVES 4–6
*225g/8oz brown rice*
*1 small onion, finely chopped*
*30g/1oz butter*
*720ml/1¼ pints white or vegetable stock (see*
*    pages 243, 246)*
*salt and freshly ground black pepper*
*3 tablespoons sesame seeds, toasted*
*1 tablespoon chopped fresh mixed herbs*
*paprika pepper*

**1.** Soak the rice in cold water for 30 minutes.
**2.** Cook the onion in the butter in a saucepan until soft but not coloured.
**3.** Add the rice and fry, stirring, until it is slightly transparent (about 1 minute).
**4.** Add the stock, salt and pepper. Bring to the boil, then cover and cook very slowly for 45 minutes, by which time the liquid should be completely absorbed and the rice tender. Add the seeds and herbs.
**5.** Serve sprinkled with a little paprika.

# POTATOES

In Britain potatoes are often classified according to when they are harvested:
First earlies (new): end May–July
Second earlies (new): August–March
Main crop: September–May

The growing season for early potatoes is short. They are harvested when the tubers are immature; the skin is not 'set' and can be rubbed off easily, and they should be eaten soon after purchase as they do not keep well.

Main crop varieties are lifted when fully mature and will keep through to next year's harvest if correctly stored.

The three most popular varieties of main crop potatoes grown in Britain are, in descending order, Maris Piper, Record and Cara.

## BUYING AND STORING

Look for potatoes that are well-shaped, firm and free from blemishes. Avoid those with green patches as these indicate exposure to light and the production of toxins (non-deadly poisons) under the skin. Buy new potatoes in small quantities as they do not keep well.

Always remove potatoes from the plastic bag in which they have been sold.

Main crop potatoes will keep well if they are stored, unwashed, in a dark, cool, frost-free, airy place away from smells. Light turns potatoes green, and warmth and dampness can cause them to sprout, shrivel and rot.

# SELECTION OF POTATO VARIETIES

| NAME | CROP | USES | COMMENTS |
|---|---|---|---|
| ARRAN PILOT | First early. | Salads, chipped, baked. | White skin and flesh; waxy texture when cooked. |
| ASPERGE LA RATTE/ CORNICHON | Second early. | Salads, steamed. | Yellow skin; creamy flesh; waxy texture when cooked. |
| CARA | Main. | All rounder. | Large; round; white skin; pink eyes; creamy flesh; creamy texture when cooked. |
| CHARLOTTE | Second early. | Salads, steamed, boiled. | Pale yellow skin and flesh; good flavour waxy texture when cooked. |
| DESIRÉE | Main. | All rounder. | Red skin; pale yellow flesh; waxy texture when cooked. |
| ESTIMA | Second early. | Baked, chipped, boiled. | Pale yellow skin and flesh; waxy texture when cooked. |
| GOLDEN WONDER | Main. | Salads, baked, mashed. | Brown skin; pale yellow flesh; floury texture when cooked. |
| KING EDWARD | Main. | All rounder. | Large; pale skin with pink patches; creamy flesh; floury texture when cooked. |
| MARIS BARD | First early. | Salads, boiled, baked when mature. | White skin and flesh; waxy texture when cooked. |
| MARIS PIPER | Main. | All rounder. | Thin white skin; cream coloured flesh; floury texture when cooked. |
| PENTLAND DELL | Main. | All rounder. | Long oval shape; white flesh and skin; firm texture when cooked. |
| PENTLAND JAVELIN | First early. | Salads, boiled, steamed. | Smooth white skin; white flesh; waxy texture when cooked. |

| NAME | CROP | USES | COMMENTS |
|------|------|------|----------|
| PENTLAND SQUIRE | Main. | Baked, roasted, chipped, mashed. | White skin (russeted); white flesh; floury texture when cooked. |
| PINK FIR APPLE | Main. | Salads, boiled. | Pink skin; pinky-yellow flesh; new potato characteristics; waxy texture when cooked. |
| ROMANO | Main. | Baked, boiled, roasted, chipped. | Red skin; creamy flesh; waxy texture when cooked. |
| RECORD | Main. | Grown mainly for processing, such as | Short oval; yellow skin; pigments on exposure to light; crisps, waffles etc. yellow flesh; firm; slightly waxy texture. |
| ULSTER SCEPTRE | First early. | Salads, boiled. | Elongated oval shape; white skin and flesh; very waxy; firm texture when cooked. |
| WILJA | Second early. | Boiled, baked, chipped. | Rough yellow skin; pale yellow firm flesh; slightly dry but firm texture when cooked. |

# MOST SUITABLE COOKING METHODS

| BOILING | MASHING | BAKING |
|---------|---------|--------|
| Cara | Golden Wonder | Arran Pilot |
| Charlotte | King Edward | Cara |
| Desirée | Maris Piper | Estima |
| Estima | Pentland Dell | Golden Wonder |
| King Edward | Pentland Squire | King Edward |
| Maris Piper | Romano | Maris Piper |
| Maris Bard | Wilja | Pentland Dell |
| Pentland Javelin | Desirée | Romano |
| Pentland Squire | | Wilja |
| Pink Fir Apple | | Desirée |
| Romano | | |
| Ulster Sceptre | | |
| Wilja | | |

| CHIPPING | ROASTING | SALADS |
|---|---|---|
| Arran Pilot | King Edward | Asperge |
| King Edward | Maris Piper | Desirée |
| Maris Piper | Pentland Dell | Golden Wonder |
| Maris Bard | Romano | Maris Bard |
| Pentland Dell | Wilja | Pentland Javelin |
| Romano | Desirée | Pentland Squire |
| Desirée | | Wilja |
| | | Charlotte |
| | | Pink Fir Apple |
| | | Ulster Sceptre |

| STEAMING | PROCESSING |
|---|---|
| Asperge | Record |
| Pentland Javelin | |
| Ulster Sceptre | |
| Wilja | |

# POTATOES IN COCONUT MILK

This recipe has been adapted from *Curries and Oriental Cookery* by Josceline Dimbleby.

SERVES 4
*55g/2oz unsweetened desiccated coconut*
*290ml/½ pint milk*
*675g/1½lb potatoes, peeled and cut into chunks*
*salt*
*1 small green chilli*
*2–3 small bay leaves*
*3 × 2.5cm/1in cinnamon sticks*

1. Put the coconut into a bowl. Bring the milk to the boil and pour on to the coconut, stir and set aside.
2. Boil the potatoes in salted water for 7–10 minutes, until just cooked but not breaking up, then drain.
3. Cut open the chilli under cold running water, discard the seeds and stem and chop the flesh finely.
4. Return the drained potatoes to the rinsed-out saucepan and strain the coconut milk over them through a fine sieve, pressing to extract all the liquid. Add the bay leaves, the chilli, a little salt and the cinnamon sticks. Bring to the boil, then simmer for 8–10 minutes. Transfer to a warmed serving dish.

# FONDANT POTATOES

SERVES 4
*900g/2lb potatoes*
*55g/2oz butter*
*2 bay leaves*
*200ml/7fl oz white stock (see page 243)*
*salt and freshly ground black pepper*

1. Wash and peel the potatoes and trim into 8-sided barrel shapes.
2. Melt the butter in a sauté pan, add the potatoes and brown lightly on all sides.
3. Add the bay leaves, stock, salt and pepper and cover with damp greaseproof paper. Cook over a low heat for about 40 minutes, or until the stock is absorbed and the potatoes tender.
4. Carefully lift the potatoes out of the pan and place in a warmed serving dish. Pour over any remaining butter and juices from the sauté pan.

# ROAST POTATOES

SERVES 4
*900g/2lb potatoes*
*salt*
*4 tablespoons dripping or oil*

**1.** Preheat the oven to 200°C/400°F/gas mark 6.
**2.** Wash and peel the potatoes and, if they are large, cut them into 5cm/2in pieces.
**3.** Bring them to the boil in salted water. Simmer for 5 minutes. Drain well, return to the pan and shake the potatoes.
**4.** Melt the dripping or oil in a roasting pan and when hot add the potatoes, turning them so that they are coated all over. Season with salt and pepper.
**5.** Roast, basting occasionally, and turning the potatoes over halfway through cooking. See note below.

NOTES: Potatoes can be roasted at almost any temperature, usually taking 1 hour in a hot oven, or 1½ hours in a moderate one. They should be basted and turned over once or twice during cooking, and they are done when a skewer glides easily into them. Potatoes roasted in the same pan as meat have the best flavour, but this is not always possible if the joint or bird is very large, or if liquid has been added to the pan.

The water in which the potatoes were parboiled can be saved and used for making gravy if no stock is available.

# CHÂTEAU POTATOES

SERVES 4
*900g/2lb small, even-sized potatoes*
*oil or beef dripping*
*salt and freshly ground black pepper*

**1.** Wash and peel the potatoes. Trim each one into a barrel shape.
**2.** Preheat the oven to 190°C/375°F/gas mark 5.
**3.** Heat a few spoons of oil or dripping in a sauté pan. Add the potatoes and brown gently on all sides, shaking the pan constantly, until they are just brown. Season with salt and pepper.
**4.** Cover the pan and cook in the preheated oven for about 30 minutes or until the potatoes are tender. (Alternatively, they can be cooked on the hob, but care must be taken that they do not burn: shake the pan frequently. Do not remove the lid as this allows the steam to escape, and the potatoes will fry rather than cook gently.)

# BAKED POTATOES WITH CHIVES AND SOURED CREAM

SERVES 1
*1 medium potato, well scrubbed*
*2 tablespoons soured cream*
*1 teaspoon chopped fresh chives*
*salt and freshly ground black pepper*

**1.** Preheat the oven to 200°C/400°F/gas mark 6.
**2.** Prick the potatoes with a fork to prevent them from bursting in the oven.
**3.** Bake in the preheated oven for 1 hour, or until a skewer glides easily through the largest potato.
**4.** Mix together the soured cream and chives and season with salt and pepper.
**5.** Split the potatoes without cutting them quite in half and fill with some of the soured cream mixture.
**6.** Serve immediately, with the remaining soured cream and chives handed separately.

NOTE: There is some controversy about preparing potatoes for baking: oiling and wrapping them in foil gives a soft shiny skin, wetting them with water and sprinkling them with salt gives a dull but very crisp skin.

# BAKED NEW POTATOES EN PAPILLOTE

These scented potatoes with their slightly crinkly skin must be baked in greaseproof paper, not kitchen foil in which they tend to steam.

SERVES 4
675g/1½lb new potatoes
1 tablespoon sunflower oil
salt and freshly ground black pepper
1 sprig of fresh rosemary
1 clove of garlic, unpeeled

1. Preheat the oven to 200°C/400°F/gas mark 6.
2. Put the potatoes on a large piece of greaseproof paper. Turn them lightly in the oil and season with salt and pepper.
3. Add the rosemary and garlic and wrap the potatoes up in the greaseproof paper, sealing the parcel tightly so that the steam does not escape.
4. Bake in the preheated oven for about 50 minutes, or until tender.

# BOULANGÈRE POTATOES

SERVES 4
45g/1oz butter
675g/1½lb floury potatoes, very thinly sliced
1 small onion, very thinly sliced
salt and freshly ground black pepper
200ml/7fl oz white stock (see page 243)

1. Preheat the oven to 170°CC/325°F/gas mark 3.
2. Butter a pie dish and arrange the potatoes in layers with the onion, adding a little salt and pepper as you go.
3. Arrange the top layer of potatoes in over lapping slices.
4. Dot with the remaining butter and pour in the stock. Press the potatoes down firmly – they should be completely submerged in the stock.
5. Bake in the preheated oven for about 2 hours, or until the potatoes are tender and the top browned.

# LEITH'S GOOD FOOD'S DAUPHINOISE POTATOES

1 onion, thinly sliced
1 clove of garlic, crushed (optional)
15g/½oz butter
900g/2lb old floury potatoes, peeled and thinly sliced
425ml/¾ pint mixed single and double cream
150ml/¼ pint soured cream, thinned down to double cream consistency with milk
salt and freshly ground black pepper

1. Preheat the oven to 170°C/325°F/gas mark 3.
2. Cook the onions and garlic in the butter until soft but not brown.
3. Layer up the potatoes and creams with the onions and seasoning in a lightly buttered dish, and bake in the preheated oven for 1½ hours, or until tender.

# POMMES ANNA

SERVES 4
675g/1½lb potatoes, peeled and thinly sliced
55g/2oz butter, clarified (see page 686)
salt and freshly ground black pepper
freshly grated nutmeg

1. Preheat the oven to 200°C/400°F/gas mark 6. Brush a heavy ovenproof pan with the clarified butter.
2. Arrange a neat layer of overlapping potato slices on the bottom of the pan. Brush the potatoes with butter and season well with salt, pepper and nutmeg.
3. Continue to layer the potatoes, butter and seasoning until all the potatoes have been used. Finish with butter and seasoning.
4. Set the pan over direct medium heat for 2 minutes to brown the bottom layer of potatoes.
5. Remove from the heat and cover with greased paper and a lid or kitchen foil. Bake in the preheated oven for about 45 minutes or until the potatoes are tender.
6. Invert a serving plate over the pan and turn the potatoes out so that the neat first layer is on top.

# INDIVIDUAL POMMES ANNA

*450g/1lb small potatoes, peeled and thinly sliced*
*45g/1½oz unsalted butter, melted*
*salt and freshly ground black pepper*
*freshly grated nutmeg*

**1.** Preheat the oven to 200°C/400°F/gas mark 6.
Brush 12 individual patty tins with the melted butter.
**2.** Arrange one slice of potato on the bottom of
each patty tin and then neatly overlap the slices
with more melted butter and seasoning. You need
8 layers of potatoes.
**3.** Bake at the top of the preheated oven for 30
minutes, or until golden-brown and tender.
**4.** Remove the potatoes from the patty tins and
serve immediately.

# MASHED POTATOES

SERVES 4
*675g/1½lb potatoes, peeled*
*salt and freshly ground black pepper*
*about 100ml/3½fl oz milk*
*55g/2 oz butter*
*a little freshly grated nutmeg*

**1.** Boil the potatoes in salted water until tender.
Drain thoroughly.
**2.** Push the potatoes through a sieve or mouli.
Return them to the dry saucepan. Heat carefully,
stirring to allow the potato to steam-dry.
**3.** Push the potato to one side of the pan. Set the
exposed part of the pan over direct heat and pour
in the milk. Add the butter, salt, pepper and
nutmeg. Tilt the pan to allow the milk to boil and
the butter to melt.
**4.** When the milk is boiling, or near it, beat it into
the potato. Check the seasoning.

NOTE: This recipe is for soft mashed potatoes. If
you want a stiffer consistency, add less milk.

# SAUTÉ POTATOES

SERVES 4
*675g/1½lb floury potatoes*
*salt and freshly ground black pepper*
*2 tablespoons oil*
*45g/1½oz butter*
*1 tablespoon chopped fresh parsley or rosemary*

**1.** Cook the potatoes until tender in boiling salted
water. Drain and allow to dry. Cut into 2.5cm/1in
irregular chunks.
**2.** Heat the oil in a large sauté or frying pan, add
the butter and wait until the foam subsides. Add
all the potatoes at once.
**3.** Season with salt and pepper and shake the
potatoes gently over the heat while they fry
slowly until pale brown. Turn them only
occasionally or they will break up too much.
They should in any case be fairly dry and
crumbly. This should take up to 40 minutes.
**4.** When delicately brown and crisp add the parsley
or rosemary and tip into a warmed serving dish.

# POMMES PARISIENNE

SERVES 4
*6 large potatoes, peeled*
*2 tablespoons oil*
*a knob of butter*
*salt*

**1.** Scoop the potatoes into small balls, using a
melon baller. As you prepare the balls, drop them
into a bowl of cold water to prevent
discoloration. Float a plate on top to keep them
submerged.
**2.** Heat the oil in a sauté pan and add the butter.
Dry the potato balls well and toss them in the pan
until completely coated with fat. Fry very slowly
until they are browned and tender, shaking the
pan frequently to prevent them from sticking.
**3.** Drain well, sprinkle with salt and serve
immediately.

NOTE: Allow 15 Parisienne potatoes per head.
The larger the potatoes, the easier it is to scoop
them into balls.

# CHIPS

SERVES 4
*657g/1½lb potatoes*
*oil for deep-frying*
*salt*

1. Cut the potatoes into 5 × 1cm/2 × ½in sticks. Keep them in a bowl of cold water until ready for cooking. This will prevent any discoloration and remove excess starch, which tends to stick the chips together.
2. Heat oil in a deep-fryer to a medium temperature – when a crumb of bread is dropped in it should sizzle gently.
3. Dry the potatoes carefully and place a few at a time in the chip basket – too many will stick together.
4. Fry for 7–8 minutes until soft. Remove from the oil.
5. Heat the oil again, until a crumb of bread will sizzle and brown in just 30 seconds.
6. Repeat the frying process in the hotter oil until the chips are well browned and crisp.
7. Drain the chips on absorbent kitchen paper. Sprinkle with salt.
8. Serve immediately. Do not cover the chips or they will lose their crispness.

NOTE: Chips are cooked in two stages because if the fat is hot enough to crisp and brown them, the middle of the potato will not be cooked. On the other hand, if the oil is cooler, although the chip will cook through, it will be soggy. The second frying, to create the crisp brown outside, should be done just before serving.

# GAME CHIPS

SERVES 4
*450g/1lb large potatoes*
*oil for deep-frying*
*salt*

1. Wash and peel the potatoes. If you want even-sized chips trim each potato into a cylinder shape.
2. Slice them very thinly across the cylinder, preferably on a mandolin. Soak in cold water for

30 minutes to remove the excess starch – this will prevent them from discolouring or sticking together.
3. Heat oil in a deep-fryer until a crumb will sizzle vigorously in it.
4. Dry the chips very thoroughly on a tea towel.
5. Lower a basket of chips into the hot oil. They are cooked when they rise to the surface and are golden-brown.
6. Drain on absorbent kitchen paper, sprinkle with salt and serve immediately.

NOTE: Commercial plain potato crisps will do very well as game chips. Simply heat them, uncovered, in a moderate oven.

# MATCHSTICK POTATOES (POMMES ALLUMETTES)

SERVES 4
*450g/1lb potatoes*
*oil for deep-frying*
*salt*

1. Wash and peel the potatoes. Cut them into tiny even matchsticks and soak in cold water for 15 minutes. This is to remove the excess starch and will prevent the potatoes from sticking together. Dry them very thoroughly on a tea towel.
2. Heat oil in a deep-fryer until a crumb will sizzle vigorously in it. Fry the chips in a chip basket for 2–3 minutes, until golden brown and crisp. Drain on absorbent kitchen paper. Sprinkle with salt and serve immediately.

# GAME CHIP BASKETS FILLED WITH CHESTNUTS

SERVES 4
*675g/1½lb potatoes*
*oil for deep-frying*
*45g/1½ butter*
*30g/1oz pinenuts*
*1 × 400g/14oz can of whole unsweetened*
  *chestnuts*
*a handful of raisins*
*1 small bunch of white grapes, halved and any*
  *pips removed*

1. Peel the potatoes. Slice thinly, using a mandolin or a patterned cutter so that the finished basket will look like woven straw.

2. Dip a small wire strainer or sieve into the oil to get it well greased. Heat oil in a deep-fryer until a crumb will sizzle vigorously in it.

3. Line the strainer with potato slices overlapping each other. Using a small ladle to prevent the chips floating away from the strainer as you cook them, deep-fry the 'basket' until golden and crisp.

4. Drain well on absorbent kitchen paper.

5. Melt the butter and add the pinenuts. Brown them lightly, then add the chestnuts, raisins and grapes. Fry until hot.

6. Fill the baskets with this mixture just before serving.

NOTE: A gadget for making the baskets is available in shops selling to the catering trade, but the sieve and ladle method works perfectly well.

## RÖSTI POTATOES

SERVES 4

*1 Spanish onion, finely chopped*
*55g/2oz rindless streaky bacon, finely chopped*
*oil*
*675g/1½lb large waxy potatoes, peeled*
*salt and freshly ground black pepper*
*butter*

1. Cook the onion and bacon in 1 tablespoon oil in a 23cm/9in frying pan over a low heat until the onion is transparent and soft but not coloured. Remove from the heat.

2. Grate the potatoes coarsely. Place in a bowl and season with salt. Leave to stand for 20 minutes, then squeeze dry. Season with pepper. Fork in the onion and bacon.

3. Heat 1 tablespoon mixed butter and oil in the frying pan. Add the potato mixture. Pat it lightly into a flat cake with straight sides.

4. Fry over a low heat until the underside is crusty and golden-brown (about 15 minutes). Shake the pan from time to time to ensure that the cake does not stick.

5. Place a plate larger than the frying pan over the pan, turn both plate and pan over and tip the rösti out on to the plate. Slip it immediately back into

the pan for 5 minutes to cook the other side. Place in a warm oven for 15 minutes, if necessary. Serve on a large flat dish, cut into wedges like a cake.

NOTES: Finely grated raw carrots are sometimes added to the mixture. The potato cake can be baked in the oven preheated to 190°C/375°F/gas mark 5 for about 30 minutes rather than fried.

## INDIVIDUAL RÖSTI POTATOES

SERVES 4–6

*1 Spanish onion, finely chopped*
*2 tablespoons oil*
*2 slices of smoked ham*
*675g/1½lb large waxy potatoes, peeled*
*salt and freshly ground black pepper*
*30g/1oz butter, melted*

1. Cook the onion in half the oil until soft but not coloured.

2. Preheat the oven to 200°C/400°F/gas mark 6.

3. Cut the ham into short thin strips. Grate the potatoes coarsely. Season with salt and leave to stand for 20 minutes. Season with pepper and mix with the onion and ham.

4. Divide the mixture into 12 and place in patty tins. Spoon over the melted butter and bake in the preheated oven for about 15 minutes, or until golden-brown.

# VEGETABLES

# VEGETABLES

Vegetables in Britain are usually served as an accompaniment to a main meat course. It is worth considering them, however, as first courses on their own, or as main courses if served in sufficient variety or with a sauce. For a salad or first course they may be served raw or cooked, warm or cold, and with a dressing.

## TO PREPARE VEGETABLES

Always wash vegetables before preparing them. Vegetables are an excellent source of vitamins and minerals but these can easily be leached if the vegetables are cut up too far in advance of cooking, if they are left to soak in cold water (vitamin C particularly is lost in this way), if they are cut up with a blunt knife, which damages the cells, or if they are cooked with bicarbonate of soda in an attempt to preserve colour.

## FRESH GREEN VEGETABLES

BLANCHING AND REFRESHING. This method of cooking vegetables is commonly used in restaurants where some advance preparation is vital. It is worth doing when coping with a large selection of vegetables.

BOILING. Boil the vegetables separately: bring the water to a good boil and drop in the vegetables. Use enough water to barely cover them and add 1 teaspoon salt for each 570ml/1 pint water. Boil as rapidly as you dare (delicate vegetables like broccoli can break up if too rapidly boiled.) As soon as they are tender, drain them and serve or rinse under cold running water to prevent further cooking and to set the colour. This is called refreshing. Just before serving, toss the vegetables separately in melted butter over a good heat.

NOTE: As the cooking liquid contains most of the vitamins and minerals it should, if possible, be preserved and used for soups or sauces.

SWEATING. Put the prepared vegetables into a heavy saucepan with 1 tablespoon butter or oil. Cover tightly with a lid. Cook over a very low heat. Shake the pan frequently until the vegetables are tender. Season with salt and dish up.

STEAMING. Steaming in a proper steamer is an excellent method of cooking root vegetables, but is less successful with green ones as their bright colour is sometimes lost. It is nutritionally superior to boiling – although vegetables take longer to cook, there is no leaching of vitamins or minerals into the water.

STIR-FRYING. This cooking method, much beloved of Chinese cooks, is excellent for green vegetables. It preserves vitamins and minerals, and the vegetables remain bright in colour. The disadvantage is that you must stand over the vegetables while they cook, but cooking time is short.

Slice the vegetables as thinly as you can, then put into a large deep-sided frying pan (a Chinese wok is perfect) with a splash of oil. Toss the vegetables in the hot oil over a fierce heat. Shake the pan, and stir and turn the vegetables continually until they are just tender. Sprinkle with salt and serve.

## FRESH NON-GREEN VEGETABLES

BOILING. Put the vegetables into cold salted water and bring slowly to the boil. Cook, covered, until completely tender. With the exception of carrots (which are good with a bit of bite to them), root vegetables should be cooked until tender. Drain and brush with melted butter if required. New potatoes are usually put into boiling salted water.

REFRESHING. It is sometimes advisable to rinse carrots briefly in cold water after cooking, as this sets the bright colour, but it is not necessary.

SWEATING OR HALF-STEAMING. Slice the vegetables fairly thickly. Cook them slowly in butter or oil in a covered saucepan. They will absorb more fat than green vegetables. This is a very good method for mushrooms.

STEAMING. This is excellent for all root vegetables, particularly for large potatoes, which might otherwise break up while boiling.

## DRIED PULSES

Dried peas and beans (lentils, split peas, chickpeas, green peas, black-eyed peas, haricot beans, lima beans, butter beans, brown beans, red kidney beans, etc.) are generally cheaper than their fresh or canned equivalents, are easy to cook and are very nutritious. They should be bought from grocers with a good turnover, and as a rule small butter beans are better than large ones.

Most pulses need soaking until softened and swollen before cooking. Soaking can take as much as 12 hours (butter beans) or as little as 20 minutes (lentils). Do not soak for more than 12 hours in case the beans start germinating or fermenting. If there is no time for preliminary soaking, unsoaked pulses may be cooked either in a pressure cooker or very slowly in a saucepan; but remember that enough water must be used to allow the beans first to swell and then to cook. Preliminary soaking is less hazardous.

To cook the pulses, cover them with fresh cold water, bring to the boil and then simmer for 5 minutes. Change the water and cook until tender. Boiling times vary according to the age and size of the pulses: new season's pulses will cook faster. Small lentils may take as little as 15 minutes and large haricot beans or chickpeas can take as long as 2 hours.

NOTE: Red kidney beans must be boiled fast for at least 15 minutes to destroy dangerous toxins.

# CABBAGE WITH CARAWAY

SERVES 4
*30g/1oz butter*
*2 onions, sliced*
*450g/1lb white cabbage, finely shredded*
*1 teaspoon caraway seeds*
*1 teaspoon vinegar or lemon juice*
*salt and freshly ground black pepper*

**1.** Melt the butter in a frying pan and add the sliced onions. Cook over a low heat until soft but not coloured.
**2.** Put the cabbage into a saucepan of boiling salted water. Simmer for about 5 minutes until tender, then drain well.
**3.** Add the caraway seeds and vinegar to the onion and cook gently for 1 further minute.
**4.** Stir this into the drained cabbage and season well with salt and pepper.

# SPRING CABBAGE WITH CREAM AND NUTMEG

SERVES 4–6
*675g/1½lb spring cabbage*
*salt and freshly ground black pepper*
*a pinch of freshly grated nutmeg*
*15g/¼oz butter*
*2 tablespoons soured cream*

**1.** Shred the cabbage finely and rinse it under cold running water. Place in boiling salted water and return to the boil. Boil rapidly for 3–5 minutes until slightly soft but crunchy.
**2.** Drain the cabbage well, then return it to the heat to evaporate excess moisture, shaking the pan and tossing the cabbage so that it dries but does not burn.
**3.** Sprinkle with pepper and nutmeg. Toss in the butter. Remove from the heat and stir in the soured cream.

# BRUSSELS SPROUTS AND CHESTNUTS

SERVES 4
*450g/1lb very small Brussels sprouts*
*225g/8oz fresh chestnuts*
*30g/1oz butter*
*salt and freshly ground black pepper*
*freshly grated nutmeg*

**1.** Wash and trim the sprouts, paring the stalks and removing the outside leaves if necessary.
**2.** Make a slit in the skin of each chestnut and put them into a saucepan of cold water. Bring to the boil, then simmer for 15 minutes and remove from the heat. Remove 1–2 nuts at a time and peel. The skins come off easily if the chestnuts are hot but not too well cooked.
**3.** Melt the butter in a frying pan, and slowly fry the chestnuts, which will break up a little, until brown.
**4.** Bring a large saucepan of salted water to the boil, and tip in the sprouts. Boil fairly fast until they are cooked, but not soggy: their flavour changes disastrously if they are boiled too long. Drain them well.
**5.** Mix the sprouts and chestnuts together gently, adding the butter from the frying pan. Season with salt, pepper and nutmeg.

# VICHY CARROTS

SERVES 4
*560g/1¼lb carrots*
*2 teaspoons butter*
*½ teaspoon salt*
*1 teaspoon caster sugar*
*freshly ground black pepper*
*2 teaspoons mixed chopped fresh mint and*
  *parsley*

**1.** Peel the carrots and cut them into sticks or even-sized barrel shapes; or if they are very young leave them whole.
**2.** Put all the remaining ingredients except the pepper and herbs into a saucepan, half-cover them with water and boil until the water has almost evaporated and the carrots are tender.

Then turn down the heat and allow the carrots to brown slightly in the remaining butter and sugar, watching to make sure they do not burn.
**3.** Season with pepper and mix in the herbs.

NOTE: It is important not to oversalt the water. When the water has evaporated the entire quantity of salt will remain with the carrots.

# MUSHROOMS WITH LEMON AND PARSLEY

SERVES 4
*675g/1½lb button mushrooms, halved*
*juice of ½ lemon*
*150ml/¼ pint white stock (see page 243)*
*1 tablespoon chopped fresh parsley*

**1.** Cook the mushrooms in a covered saucepan with the lemon juice and stock for about 3 minutes, until tender.
**2.** Lift the mushrooms, using a perforated spoon, into a warmed serving dish. Reduce the cooking liquor by boiling rapidly to 3–4 tablespoons. Add the parsley and pour over the mushrooms.

# GLAZED VEGETABLES

SERVES 6–8
*450g/1lb large potatoes*
*450g/1lb carrots*
*450g/1lb turnips*
*12 button onions*
*1 tablespoon bacon or pork dripping*
*½ teaspoon caster sugar*
*salt and freshly ground black pepper*
*55g/2oz butter*
*110g/4oz button mushrooms*
*juice of ½ lemon*
*1 tablespoon chopped fresh parsley*

**1.** Wash and peel the potatoes, carrots and turnips. Using a melon baller, scoop the flesh of the potato into balls. Dry them in a clean cloth. Trim the carrots and turnips into small barrel shapes.

**2.** Peel the onions. (Dipping them into boiling water for 10 seconds makes this easier.)

**3.** Preheat the oven to 200°C/400°F/gas mark 6.

**4.** Put the prepared vegetables in a roasting pan and baste with the dripping. Roast, shaking the pan occasionally and turning the vegetables over, for 45 minutes.

**5.** When the vegetables are tender, put the roasting pan over direct heat, add the sugar and shake the pan until the vegetables are browned to a good even colour. Season with salt and pepper. Keep warm.

**6.** Melt the butter over a good heat and toss the mushrooms in it. Shake the pan to make sure that every mushroom is coated with butter. When they are beginning to brown, add the lemon juice and allow this to sizzle and evaporate a little. Add salt, pepper and the parsley.

**7.** Serve the vegetables mixed together on a heated dish.

NOTES: If these vegetables are to accompany roast meat, the root vegetables can be cooked in the meat roasting pan. Add them about 30 minutes before the meat is due to come out.

The root vegetables can be 'pot roasted' instead of cooked in the oven. This is a good idea if nothing else is being baked or roasted at the time, when it would be wasteful to heat the oven just for this dish. Toss the vegetables in the fat in a heavy casserole or saucepan. Cover with a lid, and turn the heat down low. Cook for 20 minutes or until the vegetables are tender, giving the casserole or pan a shake every now and then to prevent sticking. When the vegetables are cooked, brown them with the sugar, and fry the mushrooms as described above.

# PROVENÇAL TOMATOES

SERVES 4
*4 medium tomatoes*
*30g/1oz butter*
*1 onion, finely chopped*
*½ clove of garlic, crushed*
*4 tablespoons stale white breadcrumbs*
*salt and freshly ground black pepper*
*a pinch of freshly grated nutmeg*

*2 teaspoons chopped fresh parsley*
*1 teaspoon chopped fresh tarragon*

To garnish
*chopped fresh parsley*

**1.** Preheat the oven to 200°C/400°F/gas mark 6.

**2.** Cut the tomatoes in half horizontally. Spoon out and strain the tomato pulp.

**3.** Melt the butter in a frying pan and cook the onion in it over a low heat until soft. Add the garlic and cook for 1 further minute.

**4.** Mix the breadcrumbs, salt, pepper, nutmeg, herbs, and the onion mixture together with a fork. Add enough strained tomato to make a moist but not soggy stuffing.

**5.** Pile the mixture into the tomatoes.

**6.** Put the tomatoes into an ovenproof dish and bake in the preheated oven for about 20 minutes, or until the breadcrumbs are golden.

**7.** Sprinkle with the parsley.

# BAKED TOMATOES

SERVES 4
*4 tomatoes*
*butter*
*salt and freshly ground black pepper*

**1.** Preheat the oven to 190°C/375°F/gas mark 5.

**2.** Remove the stalks from the tomatoes. Using a sharp knife cut a shallow cross in the rounded end of each tomato.

**3.** Brush with a little melted butter and season with salt and pepper.

**4.** Put the tomatoes into a roasting dish and bake for about 10 minutes, until soft but not out of shape.

# BASHED NEEPS

SERVES 4
*675g/1½lb swedes*
*30–55g/1–2oz butter*
*salt and freshly ground black pepper*
*freshly grated nutmeg*
*caster sugar (optional)*

1. Peel the swedes and cut them into chunks.
2. Boil the swedes in salted water until tender.
3. Drain very well.
4. Mash with a potato masher. Beat in the butter and salt, pepper and nutmeg, and a little sugar if necessary.

NOTE: The Scots call a swede a neep (or turnip). Very confusing.

## CELERIAC PURÉE

SERVES 4
*2 medium potatoes*
*225g/8oz celeriac*
*150ml/¼ pint milk*
*55g/2oz butter*
*salt and freshly ground white pepper*

1. Wash and peel the potatoes and place them in a saucepan of cold salted water. Bring to the boil, cover and simmer for about 25 minutes until tender.
2. Meanwhile, wash the celeriac, peel it and cut into chunks. Simmer slowly in the milk for about 20–30 minutes, or until tender.
3. Mash the celeriac with its milk, which should by now be much reduced.
4. Drain the potatoes and mash or sieve them. Place the potatoes and celeriac together in a clean heavy saucepan. Beat over a low heat, adding the butter as you mix. Season to taste with salt and pepper.
5. Pile into a serving dish and serve immediately.

## PEA PURÉE

SERVES 4
*1 medium onion*
*45g/1½oz butter*
*150ml/¼ pint white stock (see page 243)*
*450g/1lb frozen or podded fresh peas*
*salt and freshly ground black pepper*
*225g/8oz mashed potatoes (see page 212)*

1. Chop the onion finely and put it with the butter, stock and peas into a saucepan. Add a

little salt and pepper. Cover the saucepan and simmer until the peas are tender. If the peas are fresh, or frozen in a solid block, it may be necessary to add a splash more stock during cooking as the cooking time will be longer.
2. Liquidize the peas with any remaining juice in a blender or food processor, or push through a sieve. Turn into a bowl.
3. Gradually beat the potato into the peas. The purée should be soft but hold its shape. Check the seasoning and turn into a warmed dish.

## CARROT AND CHERVIL PURÉE

SERVES 4
*450g/1lb carrots*
*570ml/1 pint white or vegetable stock (see pages 243, 246)*
*2 cardamom pods, crushed*
*1 bay leaf*
*2 tablespoons crème fraîche*
*1 tablespoon chopped fresh chervil*
*salt and freshly ground black pepper*

1. Peel and slice the carrots. Cook in the stock with the cardamom and bay leaf for 20 minutes, or until very soft.
2. Remove from the heat and allow to cool slightly, then remove the cardamom pod and bay leaf. Drain well but reserve a little of the liquor.
3. Whizz the carrots with the crème fraîche in a blender or food processor to make a firm but soft purée. If too firm, add a little of the reserved cooking liquor. Add the chervil and season to taste with salt and pepper.

# JAMS CALIFORNIAN VEGETABLES

This recipe was inspired by Jams Restaurant, New York, where they serve a similar beautifully colourful selection of attractively prepared vegetables.

SERVES 4

12 small new potatoes, washed but not peeled
12 baby carrots, or 3 carrots peeled and sliced on the diagonal
1/4 red pepper, deseeded and cut into 4 strips
1/4 yellow pepper, deseeded and cut into 4 strips
4 baby sweetcorn
4 button turnips
16 French beans, topped and tailed
4 broccoli florets
2 courgettes, each cut into 6 diagonal slices
12 radishes
12 strips of cucumber, deseeded
30g/1oz butter
freshly ground black pepper

1. Cook the potatoes and carrots in boiling salted water until just tender. Drain.
2. Blanch all the remaining vegetables except the cucumber in boiling salted water for 2 minutes. Drain.
3. Melt the butter in a sauté pan, add the cucumber and toss all the vegetables in it until lightly glazed. Pile on to a warmed serving dish or divide between 4 individual serving plates and serve immediately.

# STIR-FRIED VEGETABLES

This recipe can be adapted according to what you have in your refrigerator but most people would expect it to include mangetout and baby sweetcorn.

SERVES 4–6

2 tablespoons sunflower oil
1 × 2.5cm/1in piece of fresh root ginger, peeled and cut into slivers
1 clove of garlic, peeled and cut into slivers
110g/4oz baby sweetcorn, cut in half lengthways
110g/4oz mangetout, topped and tailed
3 sticks of celery, cut into julienne strips
2 carrots, peeled and cut into julienne strips
1 red pepper, peeled (after singeing over a flame), deseeded and cut into strips
3 spring onions, sliced on the diagonal
85g/3oz Chinese leaves, finely shredded
2 tablespoons soy sauce
2 teaspoons sesame oil

1. Heat the oil in a heavy wok. Add the ginger and garlic and fry gently for 1–2 minutes.
2. Add the baby sweetcorn, mangetout, celery and carrots. Stir-fry for 1–2 minutes.
3. Add the red pepper, spring onions and Chinese leaves. Stir-fry until the Chinese leaves begin to wilt. Add the soy sauce and sesame oil and serve immediately.

# PETITS POIS À LA FRANÇAISE

SERVES 4

225g/8oz peas, shelled (use frozen peas if fresh are not available)
1 large mild onion, very thinly sliced
1 small lettuce, shredded
150ml/1/4 pint water
30g/1oz butter
a handful each of fresh mint and parsley
1/2 clove of garlic crushed (optional)
salt and freshly ground black pepper
1 teaspoon caster sugar

1. Mix the peas, onion and lettuce together in a flameproof casserole. Add the water, butter, mint, parsley, garlic (if using), salt, pepper and sugar.
2. Cover tightly. Put a double seal of greaseproof paper over the casserole before pressing down the lid to make a good seal.
3. Cook for about 30 minutes over a very low heat until the peas are almost mushy or, better still, bake in the oven preheated to 170°C/325°F/ gas mark 3 for 1–2 hours.

NOTE: The liquid may be thickened by the addition of beurre manié (see page 241) if preferred, but care should be taken not to mash the peas while stirring.

# VEGETABLE STEW

SERVES 6
110g/4oz haricot beans
55g/2oz butter
3 small whole onions, peeled
2 leeks, washed and cut up
2 courgettes, cut into chunks
2 medium carrots, peeled and cut into chunks
2 sticks of celery, cut into chunks
3 small tomatoes, peeled and quartered
290ml/½ pint vegetable stock (see page 246)
3 new potatoes, cut into chunks
salt and freshly ground black pepper
¼ cauliflower, broken into florets
2 teaspoons plain flour
2 teaspoons chopped fresh parsley
2 teaspoons fresh chopped mint

To serve
brown rice (see page 204)

1. Soak the haricot beans for 3 hours. Cook them in fresh boiling water until tender (1–2 hours). Drain well.
2. Melt half the butter, add the onions and cook them over a low heat for 1 minute, then add the leeks, courgettes, carrots, celery and tomatoes. Pour on the stock and bring to the boil. Add the potatoes, season with salt and pepper and simmer for about 30 minutes. Add the cauliflower and beans and continue to simmer for about 15 minutes until all the vegetables are tender.
3. Mix the remaining butter and the flour to a smooth paste (beurre manié). Slip a little at a time down the side of the pan and into the mixture, stirring gently. When all the beurre manié has been added you should have a smooth, slightly thickened sauce for the vegetables. Simmer the stew for 3 minutes to cook the flour. Add the parsley and mint. Check the seasoning. Serve with brown rice.

# BRAISED CELERY

SERVES 4
15g/½oz butter
1 small onion, finely chopped
1 carrot, finely chopped
1 head of celery, cut into batons
290ml/½ pint white stock (see page 243)
1 bay leaf
salt and freshly ground black pepper
15g/½oz butter
15g/½oz plain flour

1. Preheat the oven to 180°C/350°F/gas mark 4.
2. Melt the butter in a heavy roasting pan and cook the onions and carrots in it until soft but not coloured.
3. Add the celery, stock, bay leaf, salt and pepper and bring to the boil.
4. Cover with a lid or kitchen foil and bake in the preheated oven for about 30 minutes until tender.
5. Mix the butter and the flour to a smooth paste (beurre manié).
6. When the celery is tender, place the roasting pan over direct heat. When the liquid boils, stir in a little of the beurre manié to thicken the sauce. Do not add too much at a time. Stir until boiling.
7. Simmer for 2 minutes to cook the flour. Check the seasoning.
8. Remove the bay leaf. Transfer the celery and liquid to a warmed serving dish.

# BAKED FENNEL WITH SUN-DRIED TOMATOES AND GOAT'S CHEESE

SERVES 4
4 even-sized bulbs of fennel
30g/1oz butter
1½ teaspoons chopped fresh parsley
juice of 1 lemon
1 tablespoon olive oil
4 tablespoons water
1 onion, finely diced
6 whole sun-dried tomatoes, soaked in boiling water for 10 minutes
30g/1oz pinenuts
140g/5oz goat's cheese log, such as Roubillac
salt and freshly ground black pepper

1. Preheat the oven to 180°C/350°F/gas mark 4.
2. Discard any damaged outside leaves from the fennel and cut the bulbs neatly in half. Carefully remove some of the dense core.
3. Put the fennel halves into an ovenproof dish, cut side uppermost. Melt the butter in a saucepan and add the parsley and lemon juice. Pour over the fennel, add the water and cover tightly with a lid or kitchen foil. Bake in the preheated oven for about 1 hour or until cooked.
4. Heat the oil in a small saucepan, add the onion and cook over a low heat until soft and transparent. Slice the sun-dried tomatoes finely and mix with the pinenuts, diced goat's cheese and onion.
5. Increase the oven temperature to 200°C/400°F/gas mark 6.
6. Remove the fennel from the oven, take off the foil and pile the cheese mixture on top. Return to the oven for 15–20 minutes.
7. Serve immediately.

NOTE: There is no need to soak sun-dried tomatoes that have been packed in oil.

 *FULL-BODIED WHITE*

# RATATOUILLE

SERVES 4
*2 small aubergines*
*2 courgettes*
*olive oil*
*1 large onion, sliced*
*1 clove of garlic, crushed*
*1 medium green pepper, cored, deseeded and sliced*
*1 small red pepper, cored, deseeded and sliced*
*6 tomatoes, peeled, quartered and deseeded*
*salt and freshly ground black pepper*
*a pinch of ground coriander*
*1 tablespoon chopped fresh basil (optional)*

1. Wipe the aubergines and courgettes and cut into bite-sized chunks. Degorge (sprinkle with salt and leave to drain for about 30 minutes). Rinse away the salt and dry the vegetables well.
2. Melt a little oil in a large heavy saucepan and add the onions and garlic. When soft but not brown, add the aubergine and fry until pale

brown, adding more oil if necessary. Add the peppers and courgettes, cover and cook over a low heat for 25 minutes.
3. Add the tomatoes, salt if necessary, pepper and coriander. Cook, covered, for about 20 minutes.
4. Dish up and sprinkle with basil, if using. Serve hot or well chilled.

NOTE: If you are making large quantities of ratatouille try this catering trick. Deep-fry the aubergines, peppers and courgettes in oil. Drain them and put into the saucepan with the onions, which you have gently fried in olive oil, and the tomatoes. Cook, covered, for 10 minutes with the flavourings. Deep-frying saves a lot of time, but the oil must be clean.

# RED RATATOUILLE

SERVES 4
*1 medium aubergine*
*olive oil*
*2 red onions, sliced*
*1 clove of garlic, crushed*
*1 large red pepper, cored, deseeded and sliced*
*400g/14oz can of tomatoes*
*a pinch of caster sugar*
*salt and freshly ground black pepper*
*a pinch of ground coriander*
*1 tablespoon chopped fresh purple basil (optional)*

1. Wipe the aubergine, cut into bite-sized chunks and degorge (sprinkle with salt and leave to drain for about 30 minutes). Rinse away the salt and dry the aubergine well.
2. Heat a little oil in a large heavy saucepan, add the onions and garlic and fry until soft but not brown. Add the aubergine and fry until pale brown. Add the red pepper and fry over a low heat for another couple of minutes until the pepper softens a little.
3. Add the tomatoes, sugar, salt, pepper and coriander. Cover with a lid and simmer gently for about 20 minutes until the vegetables have softened but not broken up. (If the ratatouille is too wet, remove the lid and reduce the juices.)
4. Check the seasoning and serve sprinkled with purple basil, if using.

# RED CABBAGE

SERVES 6
*1 small red cabbage*
*1 onion, sliced*
*30g/1oz butter*
*1 small cooking apple, peeled and sliced*
*1 small dessert apple, peeled and sliced*
*2 teaspoons soft light brown sugar*
*2 teaspoons wine vinegar*
*a pinch of ground cloves*
*salt and freshly ground black pepper*

1. Shred the cabbage and discard the hard stalks. Rinse well.
2. In a large heavy saucepan, fry the onion in the butter until it begins to soften.
3. Add the drained but still wet cabbage, the apples, sugar, vinegar and cloves, and season with salt and pepper.
4. Cover tightly and cook over a very low heat, mixing well and stirring every 15 minutes or so. Cook for 2 hours, or until the whole mass is soft and reduced in bulk. (During the cooking it may be necessary to add a little water.)
5. Taste and add more salt, pepper or sugar if necessary.

# ROAST PARSNIPS

SERVES 4
*675g/1½lb parsnips*
*salt*
*oil*
*salt and freshly ground black pepper*

1. Preheat the oven to 200°C/400°F/gas mark 6.
2. Wash and peel the parsnips. Cut them in half lengthways.
3. Boil in salted water for 5 minutes. Drain well.
4. Heat 1cm/½in of oil in a roasting pan in the preheated oven. When the oil is hot, add the parsnips. Season with salt and pepper.
5. Roast the parsnips, basting and turning during cooking, until they are crisp and golden brown (about 30 minutes).

# CAULIFLOWER CHEESE

SERVES 4–6
*1 large or 2 small cauliflowers*
*salt*
*290ml/½ pint mornay sauce (see page 247)*
*1 teaspoon dried white breadcrumbs*
*1 tablespoon grated Cheddar cheese*

1. Break the cauliflower into florets and cook in boiling salted water until just tender. Drain well.
2. Preheat the grill.
3. Reheat the mornay sauce. Put the cauliflower into an ovenproof dish and coat with the sauce.
4. Sprinkle with the breadcrumbs and cheese and place under the hot grill until brown.

# VEGETABLE MORNAY

SERVES 6
*1 small cauliflower*
*salt*
*225g/8oz shelled fresh or frozen peas*
*450g/1lb carrots, peeled and cut into batons*
*3 tomatoes, peeled and halved*
*570ml/1 pint mornay sauce (see page 247)*

To finish
*dried white breadcrumbs*
*grated cheese*

1. Break the cauliflower into florets and cook them in boiling salted water until just tender but not soft.
2. Boil the peas. Boil the carrots in salted water until just tender. Preheat the oven to 200°C/400°F/gas mark 6.
3. Put all the vegetables into an ovenproof dish.
4. Heat the mornay sauce and pour it over the vegetables. Sprinkle with the breadcrumbs and cheese.
5. Bake in the preheated oven until bubbling and brown on top. If necessary, the finished dish can be placed briefly under a hot grill.

# SALSIFY (OR SCORZONERA) IN MORNAY SAUCE

Salsify and scorzonera are classified as different vegetables but they taste very alike and are treated similarly, the only practical difference being that salsify is peeled before cooking and scorzonera afterwards. In fact both may be peeled before cooking, but the flavour of scorzonera boiled in its skin is considered to be superior.

SERVES 4
*12 roots of salsify or scorzonera*
*salt*
*lemon juice (for salsify only)*
*290ml/½ pint mornay sauce (see page 247)*
*grated cheese*
*dried white breadcrumbs*

**1.** For salsify, wash, peel and cut each root into 3–4 pieces.
**2.** Place in a pan with a cupful of salted water with a little lemon juice and simmer, with a tightly closed lid, for 12–20 minutes, or until tender, topping up with water if necessary.
**3.** Drain well and arrange in a serving dish.
**4.** Coat with the hot mornay sauce, sprinkle with the breadcrumbs and cheese and brown under a hot grill.

**1.** For scorzonera, wash and cut each root into 3–4 pieces.
**2.** Place unpeeled in a pan of boiling salted water and simmer until tender (15–20 minutes).
**3.** Drain well and peel off the skin.
**4.** Proceed as for salsify.

# HOT RAW BEETROOT

SERVES 4
*450g/1lb raw beetroot*
*55g/2oz butter*
*salt and freshly ground black pepper*
*a squeeze of lemon juice*

**1.** Peel the beetroot and put it through the julienne blade of a food processor or grate it on a coarse cheese grater or mandolin.
**2.** Melt the butter. Toss the beetroot in it for 2 minutes until hot but by no means cooked. Season with salt, pepper and lemon juice.

NOTE: Raw beetroot in a mustardy vinaigrette is also very good.

# COOKED CUCUMBER WITH DILL

SERVES 4
*2 cucumbers*
*salt and freshly ground white pepper*
*30g/1oz butter*
*a squeeze of lemon juice*
*2 teaspoons chopped fresh dill*

**1.** Peel the cucumbers and cut them into 1cm/½in cubes.
**2.** Drop them into boiling salted water and cook for 30 seconds.
**3.** Rinse under cold running water and drain well.
**4.** Melt the butter in a frying pan and when foaming add the cucumber.
**5.** When the cucumber is beginning to turn a delicate brown, reduce the heat, season with pepper and lemon juice and shake briefly to glaze. Add the dill.

NOTE: If cucumbers are cheap and plentiful it is worth shaping them into balls with a melon baller – wasteful but very pretty.

# SPINACH BHAJEE

SERVES 4

900g/2lb fresh spinach, cooked and roughly
  chopped
3 tablespoons oil
1 medium onion, finely chopped
1 green chilli pepper, deseeded and chopped
1 clove of garlic, crushed
2.5cm/1in piece of fresh root ginger, peeled and
  grated
2 teaspoons ground coriander
1 teaspoon ground cumin
6 cardamom pods
1 tomato, deseeded and sliced
salt and freshly ground black pepper

1. Heat the oil in a saucepan and fry the onion
until golden. Add the chilli, garlic, ginger and
spices and cook together very slowly and carefully
for 1 minute.
2. Add the tomato and stir over a low heat for
about 2 minutes. Add the spinach and cook for a
further 4 minutes. Season with salt and pepper. If
necessary, boil away any extra liquid.

# CAULIFLOWER FRITTERS

SERVES 4

1 large cauliflower
lemon juice
salt and freshly ground black pepper
oil for deep-frying
150ml/¼ pint fritter batter (see page 472)

To serve
290ml/½ pint tomato sauce I (see page 258)

1. Cut the cauliflower into florets. Boil them in
salted water for 3 minutes.
2. Drain the florets well. When dry, sprinkle
liberally with lemon juice and season with pepper.
3. Heat oil in a deep-fryer until a crumb will
sizzle in it.
4. Dip each piece of cauliflower into the seasoned
fritter batter and drop carefully into the hot oil.
5. The batter will puff up and the cauliflower is
ready when golden-brown. Drain well and serve
immediately with tomato sauce.

NOTE: Although this dish makes a good
vegetable accompaniment to plain meat dishes, it
is delicious on its own as a lunchtime dish.

# FRENCH BEANS WITH ALMONDS

SERVES 4

450g/1lb whole French beans, topped and tailed
salt and freshly ground black pepper
20g/¾oz butter
30g/1oz flaked almonds
a squeeze of lemon juice

1. Cook the beans in a saucepan of boiling salted
water until just tender.
2. Meanwhile, melt the butter and, when foaming,
add the almonds. Fry until golden-brown, cool for
30 seconds, then add the lemon juice.
3. Drain the beans well and mix with the buttery
almonds. Sprinkle with pepper.

# BROAD BEANS AND BACON

SERVES 4

3 rashers of rindless streaky bacon
450g/1lb shelled broad beans
7g/¼oz butter, melted
salt and freshly ground black pepper
1 tablespoon chopped fresh savory or thyme

1. Dice the bacon and fry in its own fat until crisp
and brown but not brittle.
2. Boil the beans in salted water for 8 minutes.
3. Drain well and toss in the melted butter. Season
with salt and pepper, then stir in the diced bacon,
any bacon fat, and the savory or thyme.

NOTE: Large, tough broad beans are delicious if
the inner skins are removed after boiling. Boil the
beans as usual, then leave under cold running
water until cool enough to handle. Slip off the
skins and put the bright green beans into a frying
pan with the butter, bacon and savory or thyme.
Toss carefully to reheat – they are inclined to
break up.

# PIEDMONT BEANS

SERVES 4
*900g/2lb French beans, topped and tailed*
*salt and freshly ground black pepper*
*30g/1oz butter*
*1 clove of garlic, crushed*
*1 egg*
*55g/2oz Edam or Gruyère cheese, grated*

To finish
*freshly grated Parmesan cheese*
*dried white breadcrumbs*

**1.** Preheat the oven to 180°C/350°F/gas mark 4.
Butter an ovenproof serving dish.
**2.** Cook the beans in a saucepan of boiling salted
water until just tender. Drain well and mince or
push through a vegetable mill, or chop finely.
**3.** Melt the butter and, when foaming, add the
beans and garlic. Shake over direct heat for 1
minute. Tip into a mixing bowl.
**4.** Separate the egg and beat the yolk and Edam
or Gruyère cheese into the bean mixture. Taste
and season with salt and pepper. Be careful not to
overseason as cheese is salty.
**5.** Whisk the egg white until stiff but not dry, then
using a large metal spoon, fold into the beans.
**6.** Turn the mixture into the prepared dish and
sprinkle with the Parmesan cheese and
breadcrumbs. Bake in the preheated oven for 40
minutes.

# MJADARA

SERVES 4
*225g/8oz brown lentils, soaked for 2 hours*
*1 litre/1³⁄₄ pints salted water*
*55g/2oz long-grain rice*
*2 tablespoons olive or vegetable oil*
*1 large onion, thinly sliced*
*salt and freshly ground black pepper*

To garnish
*1 raw red onion, thinly sliced*
*1 raw tomato, thinly sliced*

**1.** Drain the lentils and cook in salted water in a
large saucepan for about 1 hour, or until just
tender but not broken.
**2.** Add the rice and stir, making sure that there is
enough water to cook it. Cook for about 20
minutes, or until the rice is tender. At the end of
the cooking time the water should be absorbed by
the rice and lentils. If it is not, boil the mixture
rapidly until the liquid is reduced to leave the
cereals moist but not swimming.
**3.** Meanwhile, heat the oil in a frying pan and
cook the onion over a very low heat until soft and
just brown. Pour this into the rice and lentil dish,
stir well and season with salt and pepper.
**4.** Transfer to a warmed flat dish. Garnish with
the onion and tomato.

NOTE: This is a Middle Eastern peasant dish. It
is good served with a salad of finely shredded
cabbage dressed with yoghurt, lemon and garlic.

# VEGETABLE COUSCOUS

Couscous is made from wheat. It is similar to
semolina, but coarser.

SERVES 4
*110g/4oz chickpeas*
*salt and freshly ground black pepper*
*110g/4oz couscous*
*425ml/³⁄₄ pint vegetable stock (see page 246)*
*4 button onions, peeled*
*2 leeks, roughly chopped*
*1 carrot, peeled and roughly chopped*
*1 stick of celery, roughly chopped*
*2 courgettes, roughly chopped*
*1 tomatoes, peeled and quartered*
*1 teaspoon chopped fresh mint*
*2 teaspoons chopped fresh parsley*
*a pinch of dried oregano*
*a pinch of saffron or a few shreds soaked in 1*
    *tablespoon water*

For the sauce
*2 tablespoons hot vegetable stock*
*1 teaspoon ground cumin*
*1 teaspoon ground coriander*
*¹⁄₂ teaspoon chilli powder*
*2 tablespoons tomato purée*

1. Soak the chickpeas for 3 hours. Drain them, then simmer for 1–2 hours in fresh water until tender. Drain well.

2. Cover the couscous with 230ml/8fl oz cold water and leave to absorb the liquid for 20 minutes.

3. Put the stock, salt, pepper and onions into a large saucepan. Bring slowly to the boil and add the leeks, carrots and celery.

4. Set the couscous to steam in a muslin-lined sieve or couscoussière above the cooking vegetables. Cover the sieve with kitchen foil or a cloth to prevent too much steam escaping, and simmer for 30 minutes.

5. Add the courgettes to the vegetables. Fork through the couscous to remove any lumps and return the lid. Cook for 2 minutes.

6. Add the tomatoes, mint, parsley and oregano to the vegetable mixture and again cover and cook for 2 minutes. Pour the couscous into a dish and keep warm.

7. Add the chickpeas and the saffron, with its water if soaked, to the vegetables, and heat for 2 minutes. Drain off some of the stock.

8. For the sauce, mix the hot stock with the cumin, coriander, chilli powder and tomato purée.

9. Spread the couscous over a flat serving dish and pile the vegetables, with a cupful or so of stock, on top. Serve the spiced sauce separately.

# ZUCCHINI FRITTERS

This is one of Italy's most popular courgette recipes, hence the use of the Italian word for courgettes (also used in the USA).

SERVES 4
*450g/1lb courgettes (zucchini)*
*salt and freshly ground black pepper*
*plain flour*
*oil for deep-frying*
*2 egg whites*

1. Cut the courgettes into thin chip-like strips. Sprinkle with salt and leave to degorge for 30 minutes. Rinse, drain and pat dry.

2. Season the flour well with salt and pepper.

3. Heat the oil in a deep-fryer until a crumb will sizzle vigorously in it.

4. Whisk the egg whites until stiff but not dry.

5. Put the courgettes into a sieve. Add the seasoned flour and toss them in it. Then turn them in the egg white.

6. Fry a few at a time in the hot oil until brown. Drain on absorbent kitchen paper. Season with salt and pepper. Serve immediately.

# SEAWEED

This recipe has been adapted from Yan-Kit So's excellent *Classic Chinese* cookbook. She says: 'This Northern dish uses a special kind of seaweed which is not available elsewhere. However, the adapted ingredients used below do produce the desired delicious result.'

SERVES 4
*450g/1lb spring greens*
*oil for deep-frying*
*¼ teaspoon salt*
*2 teaspoons caster sugar*

1. Remove and discard the tough stalks from the spring greens. Wash, then lay them out on a large tray to dry thoroughly.

2. Fold 6–7 leaves, or however many you can handle at a time, into a neat roll and, using a sharp knife, slice very finely into shreds. Lay out on the tray again to dry. The drier the better.

3. Heat oil in a deep-fryer until a cube of stale bread will brown in 40 seconds. Add half the spring greens and fry for 30 seconds or until bright green and crisp. Remove with a large strainer and deep-fry the remaining spring greens.

4. Sprinkle with salt and sugar and mix thoroughly.

# SALADS

# EVERYTHING GREEN SALAD

*1 lettuce (any kind)*
*French dressing (see page 254)*
*Choice of the following:*
*cucumber*
*fennel*
*celery*
*chicory*
*spring onions*
*watercress*
*green beans*
*peas*
*1 teaspoon chopped fresh mint, parsley or chives*

**1.** Prepare the salad ingredients.
Lettuce: Wash, drain and shake to allow to drip dry. Do not twist or wring the leaves together, which bruises them, but tear each lettuce leaf individually and place in a salad bowl.
Cucumber: Peel or not, as desired. Slice thinly.
Fennel: Wash and shave into thin slices.
Celery: Wash and chop together with a few young leaves.
Chicory: Wipe with a damp cloth. Remove the tough core with a sharp knife and cut each head on the diagonal into 3–4 pieces.
Spring onions: Wash and peel. Chop half the green stalks finely. Keep the white part with the rest of the salad.
Watercress: Wash and pick over, discarding the thick stalks and any yellow leaves.
Beans and peas: Cook in boiling salted water until just tender and cool under cold running water. Drain well and pat dry in a tea towel.
**2.** Add the herbs and the spring onion tops to the dressing.
**3.** Mix the salad ingredients together and just before serving toss them in French dressing.

# FRILLY BITTER SALAD

*slightly bitter leaves: watercress; young kale; curly endive; young spinach; chicory; lamb's lettuce; radicchio; rocket; frisée*

*For the dressing*
*3 tablespoons salad oil*
*1 tablespoon olive oil*
*1 tablespoon red wine vinegar*
*1 teaspoon French mustard*
*salt and freshly ground black pepper*

**1.** Put the dressing ingredients into a screw-top jar and shake well.
**2.** Wash and dry the salad leaves, discarding any tough stalks.
**3.** Toss the salad in the dressing and tip into a clean bowl.

# CAESAR SALAD

SERVES 4
*2 large cloves of garlic, slivered*
*150ml/¼ pint olive oil*
*2 tablespoons lemon juice*
*dry English mustard*
*freshly ground black pepper*
*1 egg, boiled for 1 minute*
*2 anchovy fillets, finely chopped*
*2 slices of bread, crusts removed, cubed*
*1 cos lettuce*
*2 tablespoons freshly grated Parmesan cheese*

**1.** Mix the garlic with the oil. Leave to stand for 10 minutes. Strain off 3 tablespoons of the oil to make the dressing.
**2.** Add it to the lemon juice, mustard, pepper and egg. Whisk well. Add the anchovies.
**3.** Pour the remaining oil and the garlic into a frying pan. There should be at least 1cm/½in oil. Heat slowly. When the garlic shreds begin to sizzle, remove, add the bread cubes and fry, turning frequently with a fish slice or spoon, until the croûtons are crisp and brown. Using a perforated spoon, lift out the croûtons and drain and allow to cool on absorbent kitchen paper.
**4.** Toss the lettuce in the dressing. Sprinkle over the croûtons and cheese.

# TOMATO AND BASIL SALAD

SERVES 4
*6 tomatoes, peeled and sliced*
*8–10 fresh basil leaves, roughly chopped*
*French dressing (see page 254)*

**1.** Arrange the tomato slices on a plate.
**2.** Mix the dressing and basil together and spoon over the tomatoes.

# CARROT AND MINT SALAD

SERVES 4
*½ teaspoon caster sugar*
*a large pinch of ground cumin*
*French dressing (see page 254)*
*8 large carrots*
*2 tablespoons chopped fresh mint*
*salt and freshly ground black pepper*

**1.** Mix the sugar and cumin with the dressing.
**2.** Peel the carrots and grate coarsely into the French dressing.
**3.** Add the mint and toss the salad well. Check the seasoning.

# FENNEL AND WALNUT SALAD

SERVES 6
*2 large or 3 small bulbs of Florence fennel*
*110g/4oz fresh shelled walnuts, roughly chopped*
*1 tablespoon chopped fresh marjoram*
*French dressing made with walnut oil (see page 254)*

**1.** Remove the feathery green tops of the fennel and set aside. Wash, then finely slice the fennel heads, discarding any tough outer leaves or discoloured bits.
**2.** Blanch the fennel in boiling water for 1 minute to soften slightly. Refresh under cold running

water until cool. Drain well on absorbent kitchen paper, or dry in a tea towel.
**3.** Mix together the fennel, nuts and marjoram and moisten with a little French dressing. Pile into a salad bowl.
**4.** Chop the green fennel leaves and scatter them over the salad.

# FENNEL, RED ONION AND RED PEPPER SALAD

SERVES 4–6
*1 large or 2 small heads of fennel*
*1 red pepper*
*½ medium red onion, sliced*

For the dressing
*1 tablespoon wine vinegar*
*3 tablespoons salad oil*
*a pinch of dry English mustard*
*salt and freshly ground black pepper*

**1.** Remove the feathery green tops of the fennel and set aside. Thinly slice the fennel heads, discarding any tough outer leaves. Blanch in boiling salted water for 1 minute. Refresh under cold running water. Drain well.
**2.** Remove and discard the seeds and membrane from the pepper. Cut the flesh into quarters. Place, skin side up, under a very hot grill. Grill until very black. Cool, skin and cut the flesh into strips.
**3.** Mix all the dressing ingredients together in a jar, shaking well to form an emulsion.
**4.** Toss everything in the dressing and tip into a clean salad bowl. Chop the green fennel leaves and scatter over the salad

# CARROT AND POPPY SEED SALAD

SERVES 4
4 large carrots
French dressing made with hazelnut oil (see
    page 254)
2 spring onions, chopped
2 teaspoons poppy seeds

1. Peel the carrots into ribbons. Toss in the French dressing with the onions.
2. Put the poppy seeds into a heavy saucepan and place over a medium heat. Cover and dry-roast for 2 minutes. Leave to cool, then sprinkle over the salad.

# JAPANESE-STYLE CUCUMBER AND CARROT SALAD

This recipe is by Madhur Jaffrey from *The Taste of Health*.

SERVES 4–6
1 large cucumber
1 small carrot
1 tablespoon unhulled sesame seeds
2 tablespoons soy sauce
2 dessertspoons distilled white vinegar

1. Peel the cucumber and cut it diagonally into wafer-thin, long, oval shapes. Put them into a bowl.
2. Peel the carrot and cut this similarly. Put into the bowl with the cucumber.
3. Put the sesame seeds into a small cast-iron frying pan and place over a low heat. Cook, shaking the pan, until the sesame seeds begin to brown evenly (just a few minutes). When the seeds start popping, they are ready. You can also spread the sesame seeds out on a tray and roast them under a hot grill. They should turn just a shade darker.
4. Pour the soy sauce and vinegar over the salad, and mix thoroughly. Sprinkle on the sesame seeds and mix again. Serve immediately.

# CHINESE CABBAGE AND APPLE SALAD

SERVES 4
450g/1lb Chinese cabbage (Chinese leaves)
2 dessert apples
chopped fresh parsley

For the dressing
3 tablespoons oil
1 tablespoon wine vinegar
3 tablespoons chopped fresh mint
2 tablespoons soured cream
salt and freshly ground black pepper

1. Mix all the dressing ingredients together in a screw-top jar and shake until well emulsified. Season well with salt and pepper.
2. Shred the cabbage finely. Slice the apples but do not peel them.
3. Toss the cabbage and apple in the dressing.
4. Tip into a wooden salad bowl and sprinkle with plenty of parsley.

# MUSHROOM AND CORIANDER SEED SALAD

SERVES 4
225g/8oz button mushrooms
French dressing (see page 254)
2 teaspoons coriander seeds, lightly toasted
1 onion, sliced
sunflower oil
freshly ground black pepper

1. Wipe the mushrooms, slice fairly thinly and leave to marinate in the French dressing.
2. Crush the coriander seeds very well in a pestle and mortar and add to the mushrooms. Leave for 2 hours.
3. Cook the onion until soft but not brown in a minimum amount of oil in a non-stick frying pan. Remove from the heat and cool, then add to the mushrooms and season well.

# SPINACH SALAD WITH BACON AND YOGHURT

SERVES 4
*450g/1lb fresh young spinach*
*6 rashers of rindless streaky bacon*

For the dressing
*2–3 tablespoons plain yoghurt*
*2 tablespoons oil*
*2 teaspoons wine vinegar*
*1 teaspoon French mustard*
*½ clove of garlic, crushed*
*salt and freshly ground black pepper*
*caster sugar to taste*

**1.** Preheat the grill.
**2.** Wash the spinach and remove the stalks. Drain well and shred finely.
**3.** Grill the bacon for about 2 minutes on each side until brown and crispy. Cool, then chop.
**4.** Mix all the dressing ingredients together.
**5.** Toss the spinach and bacon in the dressing just before serving.

# SALADE NIÇOISE

SERVES 3–6
*3 tomatoes, peeled and quartered*
*225g/8oz cooked French beans*
*1 × 200g/7oz can of tuna fish*
*½ red onion, thinly sliced*
*1 red pepper, cored, deseeded and sliced*
*1 lettuce heart*
*6 anchovy fillets, split lengthways*
*2 hardboiled eggs, quartered lengthways*
*8 black olives*

For the dressing
*1 tablespoon wine vinegar*
*3 tablespoons olive oil*
*salt and freshly ground black pepper*
*½ clove of garlic, crushed*
*1 tablespoon finely chopped fresh mixed herbs*

**1.** Put all the dressing ingredients into a large bowl and whisk well.

**2.** Reserving a few colourful ingredients for the top, put all the remaining salad ingredients into the bowl. Turn them gently in the dressing. Do not over-mix.
**3.** Tip carefully into a clean salad bowl and put the reserved ingredients on the top.

# BEAN AND BEAN SALAD

SERVES 4
*450g/1lb fresh French beans, topped and tailed*
*450g/1lb cooked or canned haricot beans or butter beans*
*2 tablespoons chopped fresh basil or spring onion tops*
*1 tablespoon lemon juice*
*salt and freshly ground black pepper*
*1 small clove of garlic, crushed*
*3 tablespoons salad oil*

**1.** Boil the French beans in salted water until just tender. Drain and refresh under cold running water to prevent further cooking and preserve their colour. Drain well.
**2.** Drain the haricot or butter beans if they are canned and rinse away any starchy water. When they are dry mix them with the cooked French beans and put into a dish.
**3.** Place the basil or spring onions in a jar, add the lemon juice, seasoning, garlic and oil and shake vigorously. Pour over the salad.

NOTE: All types of beans are good – fresh broad beans (especially if the inner skins are removed after cooking), dried lima beans, canned flageolets, etc.

# WATERCRESS SALAD WITH CROÛTONS

SERVES 4–5
*oil for deep-frying*
*4 slices of white bread, crusts removed, cubed*
*2 bunches of watercress, trimmed*

For the dressing
*3 tablespoons oil*
*1 tablespoon wine vinegar*
*salt and freshly ground black pepper*
*½ clove of garlic, crushed*
*1 teaspoon chopped fresh parsley*
*a pinch of sugar (optional)*

**1.** Combine all the dressing ingredients in a screw-top jar and shake well.
**2.** Make the croûtons: heat oil in a deep-fryer until a crumb will sizzle vigorously in it. Fry the bread cubes until golden-brown and crisp. Drain well on absorbent kitchen paper. Sprinkle lightly with salt.
**3.** Just before serving toss the watercress in the French dressing, tip into a clean salad bowl and sprinkle the warm croûtons on top.

# SALAD OF ROAST TOMATOES AND SPRING ONIONS

SERVES 4
*10 medium ripe tomatoes*
*olive oil*
*salt and freshly ground black pepper*
*caster sugar to taste*
*sprigs of fresh thyme*
*30g/1oz butter*
*½ bunch of spring onions, trimmed and cleaned,*
    *sliced on the diagonal*

For the dressing
*1 teaspoon Dijon mustard*
*2 teaspoons tarragon vinegar*
*2 teaspoons white wine vinegar*
*2 tablespoons olive oil*

To garnish
*3 tablespoons vegetable oil*
*½ bunch of flat-leaf parsley, chopped*

**1.** Preheat the oven to 200°C/400°F/gas mark 6. Cut the tomatoes in half vertically and scoop out the seeds. Drain the tomatoes thoroughly on absorbent kitchen paper.
**2.** Brush a baking sheet with oil. Arrange the tomatoes cut side up on the sheet. Season with salt, pepper and sugar. Scatter with sprigs of thyme and drizzle over more oil.
**3.** Roast in the preheated oven for 10–15 minutes until the tomato flesh just gives when touched.
**4.** Arrange 5 tomato halves, cut side down, on each individual serving plate.
**5.** Melt the butter in a frying pan and sauté the spring onions for about 2 minutes. Scatter around the roasted tomatoes.
**6.** Whisk the dressing ingredients together, check the seasoning, and drizzle over the tomatoes. Sprinkle with parsley.

NOTE: This dish is ideally made with plum tomatoes.

# PASTA AND RED PEPPER SALAD

SERVES 4
*225g/8oz pasta, preferably spirals*
*salt*
*1 tablespoon oil*
*2 red peppers*
*110g/4oz broccoli*
*French dressing (see page 254)*
*chopped fresh sage*

**1.** Cook the pasta in plenty of boiling salted water with oil. Drain well and leave to cool.
**2.** Cut the peppers into quarters and remove the stalk, inner membrane and seeds. Preheat the grill to its highest setting.
**3.** Grill the peppers, skin side uppermost, until the skin is black and blistered. Using a small knife, remove all the skin. Cut the flesh into strips.
**4.** Cook the broccoli in boiling salted water. Refresh under cold running water. Drain well and leave to cool.
**5.** Toss the pasta, pepper, broccoli, French dressing and sage together.

# RICE SALAD

Almost any vegetables can be added to cold cooked rice to make a salad, but it is important to have approximately equal quantities of rice and vegetables, or the result may be lifeless and stodgy. The dressing should moisten, not soak, the dish.

SERVES 8
*225g/8oz long-grain rice*
*110g/4oz frozen peas*
*1/2 green pepper, cored, deseeded and chopped*
*1/2 red pepper, cored, deseeded and chopped*
*1 small stick of celery, chopped*
*1/4 cucumber, peeled and chopped*
*2 tomatoes, peeled and cut into strips*
*a few black olives, pitted*
*finely chopped fresh parsley, mint, chives or dill*

For the dressing
*3 tablespoons salad oil*
*1 tablespoon vinegar*
*1/2 small onion, very finely chopped*
*salt and freshly ground black pepper*

1. Boil the rice in plenty of water until just tender (about 10 minutes). Rinse in boiling water and leave to drain well.
2. Cook the peas.
3. Put all the dressing ingredients into a screw-top jar and shake well.
4. Mix everything together and add salt and pepper if necessary.

NOTE: Rice salad looks pretty when turned out of a ring mould, a jelly mould, or even a mixing bowl. Push it down firmly in the oiled mould, then invert it on to a dish. If simply served in a bowl or on a dish, keep back a few olives and tomato pieces for the top.

# POTATO SALAD

SERVES 4
*675g/1 1/2lb new potatoes*
*salt*
*1 sprig of fresh mint*
*4 tablespoons French dressing (see page 254)*
*150ml/1/4 pint soured cream*
*1 tablespoon mayonnaise (page 250)*
*2 tablespoons chopped fresh chives*

1. Boil the potatoes with the mint in a saucepan of salted water until just tender. Do not peel small new potatoes. Peel larger potatoes after boiling. Drain well. Cut up if large.
2. Toss the potatoes in the French dressing while still hot. Leave to cool.
3. Mix the soured cream with the mayonnaise. Add half the chives.
4. Turn the potatoes in this creamy dressing and tip into a salad bowl.
5. Sprinkle liberally with the remaining chives.

# BARLEY AND BEETROOT SALAD

SERVES 4
*30g/1oz barley*
*salt*
*1 large beetroot, cooked and chopped*
*1/2 small onion, very finely chopped*
*1/2 green dessert apple, chopped*
*French dressing (see page 254)*

1. Boil the barley in plenty of salted water for about 1 hour, until tender. Drain well.
2. Toss the barley with the beetroot, onion and apple in the French dressing.

# NEW POTATOES VINAIGRETTE

SERVES 4
*675g/1½lb small new potatoes*
*salt*
*1 small bunch of fresh mint*
*French dressing (see page 254)*
*1 tablespoon chopped fresh chives*
*1 shallot, finely chopped*

**1.** Wash the potatoes and scrape them, but do not peel. Cook in boiling salted water with a sprig of mint until tender. Chop 8–10 mint leaves finely.
**2.** Mix the French dressing with the chopped mint, chives and shallot.
**3.** Drain the potatoes well and toss immediately in the French dressing. Leave to cool and toss again just before serving. Decorate with fresh mint leaves.

NOTE: There is always controversy about peeling new potatoes. The best, very new, pale ones need little more than washing. Most need scraping, and some – usually large, dark and patently not very new – need peeling after cooking.

# COLESLAW WITH RAISINS AND WALNUTS

SERVES 4
*225g/8oz firm white cabbage, very finely shredded*
*3 small carrots, coarsely grated*
*3 tablespoons mayonnaise (see page 250)*
*1 teaspoon French mustard*
*1 teaspoon sugar*
*salt and freshly ground black pepper*
*1 tablespoon raisins*
*1 tablespoon chopped walnuts*

**1.** Toss the cabbage and carrots together in a bowl.
**2.** Mix the mayonnaise with all the remaining ingredients and combine it with the cabbage and carrots.

NOTE: Mayonnaise for coleslaw is delicious made with cider vinegar.

# ORANGE AND WATERCRESS SALAD

SERVES 4
*6 oranges*
*1 large bunch of watercress, trimmed*

**1.** Peel the oranges with a knife as you would an apple, making sure that all the pith is removed. Reserve the juice.
**2.** Cut the oranges into slices horizontally, removing all the pips, or cut into segments.
**3.** Arrange the oranges and watercress attractively on a plate and spoon over the reserved orange juice.

# ORANGE AND FRISÉE SALAD

SERVES 4
*2 oranges, peeled with pith removed*
*1 small frisée lettuce*

For the dressing
*3 tablespoons hazelnut oil*
*1 tablespoon raspberry vinegar*
*salt and freshly ground black pepper*

**1.** Segment the oranges and keep the juice.
**2.** Combine the dressing ingredients and add the reserved orange juice.
**3.** Toss the frisée and oranges in the dressing.

# AVOCADO, APPLE AND LETTUCE SALAD

SERVES 4
*1 dessert apple*
*French dressing (see page 254)*
*1 ripe avocado*
*1 small cos or round lettuce*

**1.** Cut the unpeeled apple into chunks, and put straight into the French dressing.
**2.** Peel and cut the avocado into cubes and turn carefully with the apple in the French dressing until completed coated.
**3.** Toss the lettuce with the avocado and apple.

# RED PEPPER SALAD

SERVES 4
*4 red peppers*
*1 clove of garlic*
*½ teaspoon salt*
*3 tablespoons extra virgin olive oil*
*4 anchovy fillets*
*1 teaspoon chopped fresh oregano*
*3 tablespoons pitted black olives*

**1.** Preheat the grill to its highest setting. Cut the peppers into quarters and remove the membrane and seeds. Grill the skin side of the peppers until they are blistered and blackened all over. Place under running cold water and remove the skins. Cut the flesh into strips.
**2.** Crush the garlic with the salt and add the oil and anchovies. Mash well together. Add the oregano and toss in the red pepper strips. Mix with the olives.

# GRILLED RADICCHIO SALAD

SERVES 4
*2 large heads of radicchio, each cut into 8 wedges*

For the dressing
*3 tablespoons hazelnut or walnut oil*
*1 tablespoon balsamic, sherry or raspberry vinegar*
*chopped fresh chives*

**1.** Preheat the grill.
**2.** Mix the oil with the vinegar. Toss the radicchio in this dressing.
**3.** Grill half the radicchio wedges until brown around the edges but pink in the middle.
**4.** Toss the grilled radicchio with the ungrilled radicchio and add the chives. Serve immediately.

# QUINOA AND LIME SALAD

SERVES 8
*225g/9oz quinoa*
*720ml/1¼ pints water*
*salt*

For the dressing
*juice of 6 limes*
*125ml/4fl oz groundnut oil*
*salt and freshly ground black pepper*
*1 tablespoon caster sugar*
*1 tablespoon dry-roasted Sichuan peppercorns, ground*
*4 small cloves of garlic, crushed*
*1 tablespoon each chopped fresh flat-leaf parsley, basil and coriander*

To serve
*10 Kalamata olives, pitted and slivered*
*140g/5oz cooked kidney beans*
*1 head of radicchio*
*1 small bunch of fresh basil or coriander*

**1.** Rinse and drain the quinoa well before use to remove bitterness. It can then be lightly toasted in oil to enhance the flavour, if you wish.
**2.** Put the quinoa into a saucepan with the water and salt. Bring to the boil, then reduce the heat, cover and cook for 15–20 minutes or until the liquid has been absorbed and the quinoa looks transparent. If not all the liquid has been absorbed, drain well.
**3.** Remove from the heat and fluff up with a fork. Allow to cool.
**4.** Make the dressing: put the ingredients into a blender and process until smooth, then season well to make a strong-flavoured dressing.
**5.** Mix the dressing with the quinoa and mix in most of the olives and the kidney beans, reserving a few for garnish.
**6.** Line a serving bowl with the radicchio leaves, spoon in the quinoa, scatter over the reserved olives and kidney beans and garnish with basil or coriander leaves.

NOTES: Quinoa is a grain similar to tapioca. It is available in large supermarkets and health food shops.

The dressing is also very good with hot or cold pasta. It should be made on the day that it is eaten. It loses some of its brilliant green if kept overnight.

# STOCKS AND
# SAVOURY
# SAUCES

---

# STOCKS AND SAVOURY SAUCES

Behind every great soup and behind many a sauce stands a good strong stock. Stock is flavoured liquid, and the basic flavour can be fish, poultry, meat or vegetable. Stock cubes and bouillon mixes are usually over-salty and lack the intense flavour of properly made stock, making food taste the same. As an emergency measure, or to strengthen a rather weak stock, they are useful. But a good cook should be able to make a perfect stock.

## MAKING A STOCK

The secret of stocks is slow, gentle simmering. If the liquid is the slightest bit greasy, vigorous boiling will produce a murky, fatty stock. Skimming, especially for meat stocks, is vital: as fat and scum rise to the surface they should be lifted off with a perforated spoon, perhaps every 10–15 minutes.

Rich, brown stocks are made by first frying or baking the bones, vegetables and scraps of meat until a good, dark, even brown. Only then does the cook proceed with the gentle simmering. Care must be taken not to burn the bones or vegetables: one burned carrot can ruin a gallon of stock. Brown stocks are usually made from red meats or veal, and sometimes only from vegetables for vegetarian dishes. Brown fish stock can be very useful.

White stocks are more delicate and are made by simmering only. They are usually based on white poultry or vegetables.

The longer meat stocks are simmered the better flavoured they will be. A stockpot will simmer all day in a restaurant, being skimmed or topped up with water as the chef passes it, and only strained before closing time. However, it is important not to just keep adding bits and pieces to the stockpot and to keep it going on the back burner for days, because the pot will become cluttered with cooked-out bones and vegetables that have long since given up any flavour. At least 3, and up to 8 hours over the gentlest flame, or in the bottom

oven of an Aga, is ample cooking time.

In the Aga, skimming is unnecessary – as the liquid hardly moves there is no danger of fat being bubbled into the stock, and it can be lifted off the top when cold.

Fish stocks should never be simmered for more than 30 minutes. After this the bones begin to impart a bitter flavour to the liquid. For a stronger flavour the stock can be strained, skimmed of any scum or fat, and then boiled down to reduce and concentrate it.

Similarly, vegetables stocks do not need long cooking. As they contain very little fat, even if the vegetables have been browned in butter before simmering, they are easily skimmed, and can then be boiled rapidly to concentrate the flavour. An hour's simmering or 30 minutes' rapid boiling is generally enough.

THE BONES. Most households rarely have anything other than the cooked bones from a roast available for stocks. These will made good stock, but it will be weaker than that made with raw bones. Raw bones are very often free from the butcher, or can be had very cheaply. Get them chopped into manageable small pieces in the shop. A little raw meat, the bloodier the better, gives a rich, very clear liquid.

WATER. The water must be cold, as if it is hot the fat in the bones will melt immediately and when the stock begins to boil much of the fat will be bubbled into the stock. The stock will then be murky, have an unattractive smell and a nasty flavour. Cold water encourages the fat to rise to the surface; it can then be skimmed.

JELLIED STOCK. Veal bones produce a particularly good stock that will set to a jelly. A pig's trotter added to any stock will have the same jellifying effect. Jellied stock will keep longer than liquid stock, but in any event stocks should be reboiled every 2 or 3 days if kept refrigerated, or every day if kept in a larder, to prevent them going bad.

SALT. Do not add salt to stock. It may be used later for something that is already salty, or boiled down to a concentrated glaze (glace de viande), in which case the glaze would be over-salted if the stock contained salt. (Salt does not boil off with the water, but remains in the pan.)

STORAGE. A good way of storing a large batch of stock is to boil it down to double strength, and to add water only when using. Or stock can be boiled down to a thick, syrupy glaze, which can be used like stock cubes. Many cooks freeze the glaze in ice cube trays, then turn the frozen cubes into a plastic box in the freezer. They will keep for at least a year if fat-free.

## SAUCES

Larousse defines a sauce as a 'liquid seasoning for food', and this covers anything from juices in a frying pan to complicated and sophisticated emulsions.

FLOUR-THICKENED SAUCES. The commonest English sauces are those thickened with flour, and these are undoubtedly the most practical for the home cook. The secret is not to make them too thick (by not adding too much flour), to beat them well and to give them a good boil after they have thickened to make them shine. They will also look professionally shiny if they are finished by whizzing in a blender, or if they are 'mounted' with a little extra butter, gradually incorporated in dice, at the end.

The butter and flour base of a sauce is called a roux. In a white roux, the butter and flour are mixed over a gentle heat without browning; in a blond roux, they are allowed to cook to a biscuit colour; and in a brown roux, they are cooked until distinctly brown.

Another way of thickening a sauce with flour is to make a beurre manié. Equal quantities of butter and flour are kneaded to a smooth paste and whisked into a boiling liquid. As the butter melts the flour is evenly distributed throughout the sauce, thickening the liquid without allowing lumps to form. Cornflour and arrowroot are also useful thickeners. They are 'slaked' (mixed to a paste with cold water, stock or milk), added to a hot liquid and allowed to boil to thicken it for a couple of minutes.

EMULSIONS AND LIAISONS. Emulsions are liquids that contain tiny droplets of oil or fat evenly distributed in suspension. Like liaisons, they may be unstable.

STABLE EMULSIONS. Mayonnaise is the best known of the cold and stable emulsion sauces, in which oil is beaten into egg yolks and held in suspension. If the oil is added too fast the sauce will curdle.

WARM EMULSIONS. The most stable warm emulsions, like cold emulsions, are based on egg yolks and butter. The best known is hollandaise. Great care has to be taken not to allow the sauce to curdle.

EGGLESS EMULSIONS. These have become the more fashionable butter sauces. The classic is beurre blanc. Eggless emulsions curdle very easily, so great care should be taken to follow the recipe precisely.

UNSTABLE EMULSIONS. French dressing will emulsify if whizzed or whisked together, but will separate back to its component parts after about 15 minutes.

SABAYONS. Egg yolks are whisked over heat and the flavouring ingredient is gradually whisked in. The suspension is temporary and most sabayons collapse after 30–40 minutes.

LIAISONS. Egg yolk can be mixed with cream to form a liaison. It is then used to thicken and enrich sauces. The yolks must not boil or the sauce will curdle.

# SAUCE TABLE

| Flour-thickened | | Emulsions | | Combinations and other |
|---|---|---|---|---|
| Mother | Daughter | Mother | Daughter | |
| White sauce | Anchovy | Mayonnaise | Aïoli | Apple sauce |
| | Béchamel | | Rémoulade | Tomato sauce |
| | Cardinale | | Tartare | Mint sauce |
| | Crème | | Andalouse | |
| | Egg | | Elizabeth | **Savoury butters** |
| | Cheese | | | Almond, Anchovy, |
| | Onion | Hollandaise | Béarnaise | Garlic, Green, |
| | Parsley | | Choron | Maître d'hotel, |
| | Green | | Moutarde | Mint and Mustard |
| | | | Mousseline | |
| Blond (velouté) | Aurore | | | Cumberland sauce |
| | Poulette | Beurre blanc | Chicken | Yoghurt sauce, Cranberry |
| | Suprême | | Fish | sauce |
| | Mushroom | | Orange | Bread sauce, Horseradish |
| | | | Saffron | cream |
| | | | | Soured cream, Onion sauce, |
| | | | | Mint sauce |
| | | | | Tomato and cream sauce |
| Brown | Chasseur | | | Red pepper sauce, Black bean |
| | Robert | | | sauce |
| | Madeira | French dressing | | Ginger and tomato sauce |
| | Bordelaise | | | Uncooked pasta sauce |
| | Poivrade | | | Exotic sauce |
| | Diane | | | Tomato and whisky sauce |
| | Reforme | | | Salsa Pizzaiola, Salsa |
| | Périgueux | | | Romesco |
| | | | | |
| | | | | **Sabayons** |
| | | | | Leek and watercress |
| | | | | |
| | | | | **Liaisons** |
| | | | | As in Blanquette de Veau |
| | | | | |
| | | | | **Reduction and Pan sauces** |
| | | | | Wild mushroom sauce |

# BROWN STOCK

*900g/2lb beef and veal bones*
*1 onion, peeled and chopped, skin reserved*
*1 carrot, roughly chopped*
*1 stick of celery, chopped*
*green part of 2 leeks, chopped (if available)*
*parsley stalks*
*a few mushroom peelings (if available)*
*2 bay leaves*
*6 black peppercorns*

**1.** Preheat the oven to 220°C/425°F/gas mark 7.
**2.** Put the beef bones into a roasting pan and brown in the oven (up to 1 hour).
**3.** Brown the onion, carrot, celery, and leeks, if using, in the oil in a large stock-pot. It is essential that they do not burn.
**4.** When the bones are well browned add them to the vegetables with the onion skins, parsley stalks, mushroom peelings, if using, bay leaves and peppercorns. Cover with cold water and bring very slowly to the boil, skimming off any scum as it rises to the surface.
**5.** When clear of scum, simmer gently for 6–8 hours, or even longer, skimming off the fat as necessary and topping up with water if the level gets very low. The longer it simmers, and the more liquid reduces by evaporation, the stronger the stock will be.
**6.** Strain, cool and lift off any remaining fat.

NOTE: Lamb stock can be made in the same way with lamb bones but is only suitable for lamb dishes.

# GLACE DE VIANDE

*570ml/1 pint brown stock (see above), absolutely*
*free of fat*

**1.** In a heavy saucepan reduce the brown stock by boiling over a steady heat until thick, clear and syrupy.
**2.** Pour into small pots. When cold cover with clingfilm or jam covers and secure with rubber bands.
**3.** Keep in the refrigerator until ready for use.

NOTE: Glace de viande keeps for several weeks and is very useful for enriching sauces.

# WHITE STOCK

*onion, sliced*
*celery, sliced*
*carrot, sliced*
*chicken or veal bones*
*parsley*
*thyme*
*bay leaf*
*black peppercorns*

**1.** Put all the ingredients into a saucepan. Cover generously with water and bring to the boil slowly. Skim off any fat, and/or scum.
**2.** Simmer for 3–4 hours, skimming frequently and topping up the water level if necessary. The liquid should reduce to half the original quantity.
**3.** Strain, cool and lift off all the fat.

# HAM STOCK

The best-flavoured ham stock is generally the well-skimmed liquor from boiling a ham or gammon (see page 413), but this recipe works well with a cooked ham bone.

*1 cooked ham bone*
*1 onion, chopped*
*1 carrot, chopped*
*1 bay leaf*
*fresh parsley stalks*
*black peppercorns*

**1.** Place all the ingredients together in a large saucepan. Cover with cold water and bring gradually to the boil. Skim off any fat and/or scum. Simmer for 2–3 hours, skimming frequently and topping up the water level if necessary.
**2.** Strain and use as required.

NOTE: Ham stock is usually salty and should not be reduced.

# TURKEY STOCK (1)

Ideally all stocks are made from raw bones. However, no one is likely to have raw turkey bones. If you are making stock before Christmas you will have to make it from the giblets. This recipe can be used for making goose, pheasant and chicken stock as well. Never add liver to a stock pot; it will make the stock taste bitter.

*the neck of the turkey*
*giblets, well washed, without the liver*
*1 onion, sliced*
*1 stick of celery, sliced*
*1 carrot, sliced*
*1 parsley stalk, bruised*
*1 sprig of fresh thyme*
*2 bay leaves*
*10 black peppercorns*

**1.** Put all the ingredients into a large saucepan. Cover generously with cold water and bring slowly up to the boil. Skim off any fat.
**2.** Simmer slowly for 2–3 hours, skimming frequently and topping up the water level if necessary. The liquid should reduce to half the original quantity.
**3.** Strain and cool.

# TURKEY STOCK (2)

This recipe for making stock uses the cooked turkey bones. It is important that the water is very cold; if it is hot, the fat in the turkey skin will melt immediately and, when the stock begins to boil, much of the fat will bubble into the stock. This stock can be used in any of the recipes that call for chicken stock.

*cooked turkey bones*
*1 onion, sliced*
*a stick of celery, sliced*
*1 carrot, sliced*
*1 parsley stalk, bruised*
*1 sprig of fresh thyme*
*2 bay leaves*
*10 black peppercorns*

**1.** Put all the ingredients into a large saucepan. Cover generously with cold water and bring slowly to the boil. Skim off any fat and/or scum.
**2.** Simmer slowly for 2–3 hours, skimming frequently and topping up the water level if necessary. The liquid should reduce to half the original quantity.
**3.** Strain and cool.

# ASPIC

*1 litre/1³/4 pints well-flavoured white stock (see above)*
*15–30g/¹/2–1oz powdered gelatine, as necessary*
*2 egg shells, crushed*
*2 egg whites*

**1.** Lift or skim any fat from the stock.
**2.** Put the stock into a large saucepan and sprinkle on the gelatine, if using. If the stock is liquid when chilled, use 30g/1oz gelatine; if the stock is set when chilled, gelatine will not be necessary. Dissolve over a low heat, then allow to cool.
**3.** Put the shells and egg whites into the stock. Place over the heat and whisk steadily with a balloon whisk until the mixture begins to boil. Stop whisking immediately and remove the pan from the heat. Allow the mixture to subside. Take care not to break the crust formed by the egg white.
**4.** Bring the aspic just to the boil again, and again allow to subside. Repeat this once more (the egg white will trap the sediment in the stock and clear the aspic). Allow to cool for 2 minutes.
**5.** Fix a double layer of fine muslin over a clean basin and carefully strain the aspic through it, taking care to hold the egg-white crust back. When all the liquid is through (or almost all of it) allow the egg white to slip into the muslin. Then strain the aspic again – this time through both egg white crust and cloth. Do not try to hurry the process by squeezing the cloth, or murky aspic will result.

NOTE: When clearing, the saucepan, sieve and whisk should be scalded before use.

# COURT BOUILLON

*1.1 litre/2 pints water*
*150ml/¼ pint wine vinegar*
*1 carrot, sliced*
*1 onion, sliced*
*1 stick of celery*
*12 black peppercorns*
*2 bay leaves*
*salt*

**1.** Bring all the ingredients to the boil in a large saucepan and simmer for 20 minutes. Allow to cool, then strain.
**2.** Use as required.

# WHITE FISH STOCK

*onion, sliced*
*carrot, sliced*
*celery, sliced*
*fishbones, skins, fins, heads or tails of white fish*
*parsley stalks*
*bay leaf*
*a pinch of chopped fresh thyme*
*6 black peppercorns*

**1.** Put all the ingredients together into a saucepan, with water to cover, and bring to the boil. Turn down to simmer and skim off any scum.
**2.** Simmer for 20 minutes if the fish bones are small, 30 minutes if large. Strain.

NOTE: The flavour of fish stock is impaired if the bones are cooked for too long. Once strained, however, it may be strengthened by further boiling and reducing.

# BROWN FISH STOCK

This is not a classic stock but can be used when a stronger flavour is required. It is a good alternative to chicken stock.

*2 shallots*
*½ bulb of Florence fennel*
*½ carrot*
*1 stick of celery*

*2 tablespoons oil*
*2 teaspoons plain flour*
*1 litre/1¾ pints water*
*fish bones, skins, fins, etc. and crustacean and mollusc shells*
*1 bouquet garni (see page 19)*
*1 clove of garlic*
*½ teaspoon tomato purée*

**1.** Cut the vegetables into large even dice.
**2.** Heat the oil in a large saucepan and add the vegetables. Cook over a very low heat until the vegetables are soft but not coloured.
**3.** Add the flour to the pan and continue to cook until the flour and the vegetables are a good russet-brown. Do not allow the vegetables to burn.
**4.** Remove the pan from the heat and add the water, fish bones, trimmings and shells, the bouquet garni, garlic and tomato purée.
**5.** Bring up to the boil, then reduce the heat and cook for 30 minutes. Skim regularly.
**6.** Strain and use as required.

# SHELLFISH STOCK

*1 onion, sliced*
*1 carrot, sliced*
*1 stick of celery, sliced*
*a selection of crustacean and mollusc shells, such as prawn shells, mussel shells, lobster or crab cases*
*1 bouquet garni (see page 19)*
*6 black peppercorns*

**1.** Put all the ingredients into a saucepan. Cover with water and bring to the boil, then reduce the heat and simmer for 30 minutes. Skim regularly. Strain and reduce to two-thirds of the original quantity by boiling rapidly. Use as required.

# FISH GLAZE

Fish glaze (glace de poisson) is simply very well-reduced, very well-strained fish stock, which is used to flavour and enhance fish sauces. It can be kept refrigerated for about 3 days or frozen in ice cube trays and used as required.

# VEGETABLE STOCK

MAKES 290–425ML/½–¾ PINT
*4 tablespoons oil*
*1 onion, roughly chopped*
*1 leek, roughly chopped*
*1 large carrot, roughly chopped*
*2 sticks celery, roughly chopped*
*a few cabbage leaves, roughly shredded*
*a few mushroom stalks*
*2 cloves of garlic, crushed*
*a few parsley stalks*
*6 black peppercorns*
*sea salt*
*1 large bay leaf*
*6 tablespoons dry white wine*
*570ml/1 pint water*

**1.** Heat the oil in a large saucepan. Add the vegetables, cover and cook gently for 5 minutes or until softening.
**2.** Add the garlic, parsley stalks, peppercorns, salt, bay leaf, wine and water and bring to the boil. Reduce the heat and simmer for 30 minutes or until the liquid is reduced by half.
**3.** Strain the stock through a sieve, pressing hard to remove as much of the liquid as possible. Discard the vegetable pulp. Allow to cool and skim off any fat.
**4.** Use as required.

NOTE: The stock can be kept, covered, in the refrigerator for up to 1 week. It can also be frozen.

# HORSERADISH CREAM

*150ml/¼ pint double cream*
*1–2 tablespoons grated fresh horseradish*
*2 teaspoons white wine vinegar*
*½ teaspoon made English mustard*
*salt and freshly ground white pepper*
*sugar to taste*

**1.** Put all the ingredients into a bowl and whisk to the required consistency.

# UNCOOKED PASTA SAUCE

This sauce should be served on the day after it has been made in order to allow the flavours to develop. It can be served with hot or cold pasta.

*6 large tomatoes, peeled and finely chopped*
*1 red onion, finely chopped*
*2 cloves of garlic, finely chopped*
*4 tablespoons chopped fresh basil*
*1 tablespoon chopped fresh parsley*
*6 tablespoons extra virgin olive oil*
*juice of ½ lemon*
*salt and freshly ground black pepper*

**1.** Put the tomatoes into a sieve and drain them for 30 minutes.
**2.** Mix the tomatoes with the onion, garlic and herbs. Add the oil and lemon juice. Season to taste with salt and pepper.

# GINGER AND TOMATO SAUCE

This is a very simple sauce that can be used to accompany fish, chicken, pasta and vegetable dishes. This quantity fills 2 sauceboats.

*1 × 400g/14oz can of tomatoes*
*3 spring onions*
*2 teaspoons very finely peeled and chopped fresh root ginger*
*1 large clove of garlic*
*2 tablespoons fresh lime juice*
*2 teaspoons caster sugar*
*1 fresh chilli, deseeded (under cold running water) and chopped*
*2 tablespoons roughly chopped fresh coriander*
*salt and freshly ground black pepper*

**1.** Simply process or liquidize together all the ingredients

# TOMATO AND CREAM SAUCE

3 large tomatoes, peeled, deseeded and finely
    diced
3 tablespoons double cream
1 teaspoon wine vinegar
1 teaspoon strong Dijon mustard
1 teaspoon Cognac
salt
cayenne pepper or Tabasco sauce
10 fresh leaves tarragon, finely chopped
1 tablespoon finely chopped fresh parsley
1 teaspoon finely chopped fresh chervil

**1.** Put the tomatoes into a sieve and leave to
drain.
**2.** Pour the cream into a bowl and add the
vinegar, mustard, Cognac, salt and cayenne
pepper or Tabasco. Whisk until the cream just
thickens, but do not let it separate.
**3.** Add the tomatoes, tarragon, parsley and
chervil. Add more salt if necessary. Keep in a cold
place and serve in a sauceboat.

# WHITE SAUCE

This is a quick and easy basic white sauce.

20g/³/4oz butter
20g/³/4oz plain flour
a pinch of dry English mustard
290ml/¹/2 pint creamy milk
salt and freshly ground white pepper

**1.** Melt the butter in a heavy saucepan.
**2.** Add the flour and the mustard and stir over the
heat for 1 minute. Remove the pan from the heat,
pour in the milk and mix well.
**3.** Return the sauce to the heat and stir
continuously until boiling.
**4.** Simmer for 2–3 minutes and season with salt
and pepper.

# BÉCHAMEL SAUCE

290ml/¹/2 pint creamy milk
1 slice of onion
1 blade of mace
a few fresh parsley stalks
4 white peppercorns
1 bay leaf
30g/1oz butter
20g/³/4oz plain flour
salt and freshly ground white pepper

**1.** Place the milk with the onion, mace, parsley,
peppercorns and bay leaf in a saucepan and
slowly bring to simmering point.
**2.** Remove from heat and leave for the flavour to
infuse for 8–10 minutes.
**3.** Melt 20g/³/4oz of the butter in a heavy saucepan,
stir in the flour and stir over heat for 1 minute.
**4.** Remove from the heat. Strain in the infused
milk and mix well.
**5.** Return the sauce to the heat and stir or whisk
continuously until boiling. Add the remaining
butter and beat very well (this will help to make
the sauce shiny).
**6.** Simmer, stirring well, for 3 minutes.
**7.** Season to taste with salt and pepper.

NOTE: To make a professionally shiny béchamel
sauce, pass through a tammy strainer before use
or whizz in a blender.

# MORNAY SAUCE (CHEESE SAUCE)

20g/³/4oz butter
20g/³/4oz plain flour
a pinch of dry English mustard
a pinch of cayenne pepper
290ml/¹/2 pint milk
55g/2oz Gruyère or strong Cheddar cheese, grated
15g/¹/2oz Parmesan cheese, freshly grated (optional)
salt and freshly ground black pepper

**1.** Melt the butter in a heavy saucepan and stir in
the flour, mustard and cayenne pepper. Cook,
stirring, for 1 minute. Remove the pan from the
heat. Pour in the milk and mix well.

**2.** Return the pan to the heat and stir until boiling. Simmer, stirring well, for 2 minutes.
**3.** Add all the cheese, and mix well, but do not reboil.
**4.** Season to taste with salt and pepper.

# PARSLEY SAUCE

290ml/<sup></sup>*1/2 pint creamy milk*
*1 slice of onion*
*a good handful of fresh parsley*
*4 black peppercorns*
*a bay leaf*
*20g/³/4oz butter*
*20g/³/4oz plain flour*
*salt and freshly ground black pepper*

**1.** Put the milk, onion, parsley stalks (but not leaves), peppercorns and bay leaf into a saucepan and slowly bring to simmering point.
**2.** Remove from heat and leave for the flavour to infuse for about 10 minutes.
**3.** Melt the butter in a heavy saucepan, stir in the flour and cook, stirring, for 1 minutes.
**4.** Remove from the heat. Strain in the infused milk and mix well.
**5.** Return the sauce to the heat and stir continuously until boiling, then simmer for 2–3 minutes. Season to taste with salt and pepper.
**6.** Chop the parsley leaves very finely and stir into the hot sauce. Serve immediately.

# SOUBISE SAUCE

For the soubise
*30g/1oz butter*
*225g/8oz onions, very finely chopped*
*4 tablespoons double cream*

For the béchamel sauce
*20g/³/4oz butter*
*1 bay leaf*
*20g/³/4oz plain flour*
*290ml/¹/2 pint milk*

**1.** Make the soubise: melt the butter in a heavy saucepan. Add the onions and cook over a very

low heat, preferably covered with a lid to create a steamy atmosphere. The onions should become very soft and transparent, but on no account brown. Add the cream.
**2.** Now prepare the béchamel: melt the butter in a saucepan, add the bay leaf and flour and cook, stirring, for 1 minute. Remove from the heat and stir in the milk. Return to the heat and bring slowly to the boil, stirring continuously. Simmer for 2 minutes. Remove the bay leaf and mix with the soubise.

NOTE: This sauce can be liquidized in a blender or pushed through a sieve if a smooth texture is desired.

# GREEN SAUCE

*30g/1oz butter*
*30g/1oz plain flour*
*290ml/¹/2 pint milk*
*salt and freshly ground black pepper*
*2 bunches of watercress, trimmed and chopped*

**1.** Melt the butter in a heavy saucepan and stir in the flour. Cook, stirring for 1 minute.
**2.** Remove from the heat and pour in the milk. Mix well. Return to the heat and stir continuously until boiling. Simmer for 2 minutes.
**3.** Add the watercress to the sauce. Cook for 1 minute. Season to taste.
**4.** Liquidize the sauce thoroughly. Do not keep it warm for too long or the colour will dull.

# ENGLISH EGG SAUCE

*3 hardboiled eggs, peeled*
*45g/1¹/2oz butter*
*45g/1¹/2oz plain flour*
*570ml/1 pint fish or white stock (see pages 245, 243)*
*3 tablespoons cream*
*4 tablespoons chopped fresh parsley*
*salt and freshly ground white pepper*

**1.** Using a stainless steel knife, chop the eggs roughly.
**2.** Melt the butter in a heavy saucepan. Stir in the flour and cook for 1 minute. Remove from the heat, add the stock and mix well.

**3.** Return the sauce to the heat and stir continuously until boiling, then simmer for 2–3 minutes, stirring occasionally.

**4.** Just before serving, add the remaining ingredients and season to taste. This sauce does not keep warm well.

NOTE: The liquid in which fish or chicken is cooked is suitable as stock. Chicken stock will do for veal, fish or chicken dishes, but fish stock is of course only good for fish dishes.

## VELOUTÉ SAUCE

20g/³⁄₄oz butter
20g/³⁄₄oz plain flour
290ml/¹⁄₂ pint white stock, strained and well
    skimmed (see page 243)
2 tablespoons double cream
salt and freshly ground white pepper
a few drops of lemon juice

**1.** Melt the butter in a heavy saucepan, add the flour and cook, stirring, over a low heat until straw coloured. Remove from the heat. Add the stock and mix well.

**2.** Return to the heat. Bring to the boil, stirring, and simmer until slightly syrupy and opaque. Stir in the cream. Season to taste with salt, pepper and lemon juice.

## CHICKEN VELOUTÉ SAUCE

20g/³⁄₄oz butter
20g/³⁄₄oz plain flour
100ml/3¹⁄₂fl oz milk, infused with bay leaf, celery,
    onion and peppercorns
100ml/3¹⁄₂fl oz white stock, made with chicken
    bones (see page 243)

**1.** Melt the butter in a small saucepan and add the flour. Cook over a low heat for 1 minute. Add the milk and stock and bring up to the boil stirring all the time. Simmer for 2 minutes and use as required.

## SAUCE ESPAGNOLE

4 tablespoons oil
1 small carrot, diced
1 small onion, diced
1 stick of celery, diced
2 teaspoons plain flour, browned
570ml/1 pint brown stock (see page 243)
¹⁄₂ teaspoon tomato purée
a few mushroom stalks
1 bouquet garni (2 parsley stalks, bay leaves,
    blade of mace, tied together with string)

**1.** Heat the oil in a heavy saucepan, add the vegetables and fry until they begin to soften.

**2.** Stir in the flour and continue to cook slowly, stirring occasionally, scraping the bottom of the pan to loosen the sediment. Cook to a good russet-brown.

**3.** Remove from the heat, add three-quarters of the stock, the tomato purée, mushroom stalks and bouquet garni.

**4.** Return to the heat and bring to the boil, then simmer for 30 minutes.

**5.** Skim twice to remove scum: add a splash of cold stock to the boiling liquid to help bring the scum and fat to the surface. Tilting the pan slightly, skim the surface with a large metal spoon. Strain.

NOTE: The flour can be browned in the oven (200°C/400°F/gas mark 6). This gives the sauce a good colour.

## DEMI-GLACE SAUCE

Demi-glace sauce is a refined sauce espagnole. Simmer together equal quantities of sauce espagnole and brown stock. Reduce by boiling to half original quantity. Skim off impurities as they rise to the surface. Pass through a fine chinois (conical strainer), reboil and check seasoning.

# MADEIRA SAUCE

3 tablespoons Madeira
1 teaspoon glace de viande (see page 243)
290ml/½ pint sauce espagnole (see page 249)
a nut of butter

1. Place the Madeira and glace de viande together in a small heavy saucepan. Boil until reduced by half.
2. Add the sauce espagnole and heat up.
3. Beat in the nut of butter.

# SAUCE ROBERT

1 tablespoon chopped onion
a little butter
150ml/¼ pint wine vinegar
290ml/½ pint demi-glace sauce (see page 249)
3 gherkins, chopped
1 teaspoon Dijon mustard
1 teaspoon chopped fresh parsley

1. Soften the onion in the butter in a heavy saucepan over a low heat. Add the vinegar and boil until the liquid has reduced to 1 tablespoon. Pour in the demi-glace sauce, stir, and simmer for 15 minutes.
2. Immediately before serving, add the gherkin, mustard and parsley.

# AÏOLI

This is a speciality of Provence.

6 cloves of garlic, peeled and crushed
3 egg yolks
3 tablespoons fresh white breadcrumbs
salt and freshly ground white pepper
4 tablespoons white wine vinegar
290ml/½ pint good-quality olive oil
1 tablespoon boiling water

1. Put the garlic, egg yolks, breadcrumbs, salt, pepper and vinegar into a food processor. Whizz to a paste.
2. With the motor running, add the oil slowly to make a thick, emulsified sauce. Add the boiling water. Season to taste and use as required.

# MAYONNAISE

2 egg yolks
salt and freshly ground white pepper
1 teaspoon dry English mustard
290ml/½ pint olive oil, or 150ml/¼ pint each olive and salad oil
a squeeze of lemon juice
1 tablespoon white wine vinegar

1. Put the yolks into a bowl with a pinch of salt and the mustard and beat well with a wooden spoon.
2. Add the oil, literally drop by drop, beating all the time. The mixture should be very thick by the time half the oil is added.
3. Beat in the lemon juice.
4. Resume pouring in the oil, going more quickly now, but alternating the dribbles of oil with small quantities of vinegar.
5. Season to taste with salt and pepper.

NOTE: If the mixture curdles, another egg yolk should be beaten in a separate bowl, and the curdled mixture beaten into it drop by drop.

# ELIZABETH SAUCE

This sauce was invented by the staff at the Cordon Bleu School for the Coronation of Queen Elizabeth II in 1953 and has become a classic.

1 small onion, chopped
2 teaspoons oil
2 teaspoons curry powder (see page 688)
½ teaspoon tomato purée
3 tablespoons water
1 small bay leaf
4 tablespoons red wine
salt and freshly ground black pepper
2 teaspoons apricot jam
1 slice of lemon
1 teaspoon lemon juice
290ml/½ pint mayonnaise (see above)
2 tablespoons double cream

1. Cook the onion gently in the oil for 10 minutes.
2. Add the curry powder and fry gently for 1 minute.

**3.** Add the tomato purée, water, bay leaf, wine, salt, pepper, jam, lemon slice and juice and simmer for 8 minutes.

**4.** Strain the mixture, pushing as much as possible through the sieve. Leave to cool.

**5.** When cold, use this sauce to flavour the mayonnaise to the desired strength.

**6.** Half-whip the cream and stir into the sauce.

NOTE: This sauce is also delicious made with Greek yoghurt instead of mayonnaise.

# GREEN MAYONNAISE

*1 bunch of watercress*
*290ml/¹/2 pint mayonnaise (see page 250)*
*salt and freshly ground black pepper*

**1.** Pick over the watercress to remove the stalks and any yellowed leaves. Blanch and refresh. Dry thoroughly and chop very finely.

**2.** Add to the mayonnaise and season to taste with salt and pepper.

NOTE: Cooked and very well-drained spinach can be used instead of watercress.

# TARTARE SAUCE

*150ml/¹/4 pint mayonnaise (see page 250)*
*1 tablespoon chopped capers, rinsed*
*1 tablespoon chopped gherkins, rinsed*
*1 tablespoon chopped fresh parsley*
*1 shallot, finely chopped*
*a squeeze of lemon juice*
*salt and freshly ground black pepper*

**1.** Mix all the ingredients together. Check the seasoning.

NOTE: Chopped hardboiled eggs make a delicious addition.

# RÉMOULADE SAUCE

*150ml/¹/4 pint mayonnaise (see page 250)*
*1 teaspoon Dijon mustard*
*¹/2 tablespoon finely chopped capers*
*¹/2 tablespoon finely chopped gherkin*
*¹/2 tablespoon finely chopped fresh tarragon or chervil*
*1 anchovy fillet, finely chopped*

**1.** Mix all the ingredients together.

NOTE: Rémoulade sauce is a mayonnaise with a predominantly mustard flavour. The other ingredients, though good, are not always present.

# HOLLANDAISE SAUCE

*3 tablespoons wine vinegar*
*6 black peppercorns*
*1 bay leaf*
*1 blade of mace*
*2 egg yolks*
*salt*
*110g/4oz unsalted butter, softened*
*lemon juice*

**1.** Place the vinegar, peppercorns, bay leaf and mace in a small heavy saucepan and reduce by simmering to 1 tablespoon.

**2.** Cream the egg yolks with a pinch of salt and a nut of the butter in a small heatproof bowl. Set over, not in, a saucepan of gently simmering water. Using a wooden spoon, beat the mixture until slightly thickened, taking care that the water immediately around the bowl does not boil. Mix well.

**3.** Strain on the reduced vinegar. Mix well. Stir over the heat until slightly thickened. Beat in the softened butter bit by bit, increasing the temperature as the sauce thickens and you add more butter, but take care that the water does not boil.

**4.** When the sauce has become light and thick remove from the heat and beat or whisk for 1 minute. Check the seasoning and add lemon juice, and salt if necessary. Keep warm by standing the bowl in hot water. Serve warm.

NOTE: Hollandaise sauce will set too firmly if allowed to get cold and it will curdle if overheated. It can be made in larger quantities in either a blender or a food processor: simply put the eggs and salt into the blender and blend lightly. Add the hot reduction and allow to thicken slightly. Set aside. When ready to serve, pour in warm melted butter, slowly allowing the sauce to thicken as you pour.

# BÉARNAISE SAUCE

*3 tablespoons white wine vinegar*
*6 black peppercorns*
*1 bay leaf*
*1 small shallot, chopped*
*1 sprig of fresh tarragon*
*1 sprig of fresh chervil*
*2 egg yolks*
*salt and freshly ground black pepper*
*110g/4oz unsalted butter, softened*
*1 teaspoon chopped fresh tarragon*
*1 teaspoon chopped fresh chervil*
*a nut of glace de viande (see page 243)*

**1.** Place the vinegar, peppercorns, bay leaf, shallot, tarragon and chervil in a heavy saucepan and reduce over a medium heat to 1 tablespoon.
**2.** In a small heatproof bowl cream the egg yolks with a pinch of salt and a nut of butter. Set the bowl over, not in, a saucepan of gently simmering water using a wooden spoon, beat the mixture until slightly thickened.
**3.** Strain on the reduced vinegar. Mix well and beat until thickened. Beat in the remaining butter bit by bit, increasing the temperature as the sauce thickens and you add more butter, but take care that the water does not boil immediately round the bowl.
**4.** When all the butter is added, stir in the tarragon, chervil and glace de viande. Check for seasoning.

NOTE: See the note at the end of hollandaise sauce (page 251) for cooking in larger quantities.

# HERBY HOLLANDAISE SAUCE

*1 shallot, finely chopped*
*fresh tarragon*
*fresh chervil or parsley*
*4 tablespoons white wine vinegar*
*6 white peppercorns*
*1 bay leaf*
*2 egg yolks*
*110g/4oz unsalted butter*
*a pinch of salt*
*a pinch of cayenne pepper*
*lemon juice*

**1.** Put the shallot, tarragon and chervil or parsley stalks, the wine vinegar, peppercorns and bay leaf into a small saucepan and simmer until the liquid is reduced to about 1 tablespoon. Cool slightly and strain into a small heatproof bowl. Add the egg yolks and mix well. Chop the herbs finely, to give 2 tablespoons of each
**2.** Fit the bowl over a saucepan of water, making sure that the water does not touch the bottom of the bowl. (Alternatively set the bowl in one end of a roasting pan full of water. Place the empty end of the pan over enough heat to make the water bubble only in that area, leaving the water immediately around the bowl hot but not bubbling.) Bring the water under and around the bowl to simmering point, stirring the egg yolk mixture with a wooden spoon all the time. Allow to thicken slightly and then gradually add the butter, a teaspoon at a time. The trick is to add the next small blob of butter only when the last one is safely absorbed without curdling. The mixture must stay warm enough for the egg yolk to thicken slightly but must never boil or it will curdle. When all the butter is absorbed you should have a sauce the consistency of soft mayonnaise. Add salt, cayenne and a very little lemon juice to taste. Stir in the chopped herbs. Serve in a warmed sauceboat.

NOTE: See the note at the end of hollandaise sauce (see page 251) for cooking in larger quantities.

# HERB AND CREAM HOLLANDAISE SAUCE

The addition of cream to the hollandaise sauce means that it is stabilized and can be gently reheated, though it will curdle if allowed to boil. This recipe has glace de poisson in it, so is only suitable for fish dishes.

*2 egg quantity hollandaise sauce (see page 251)*
*1 teaspoon fish glaze (see page 245)*
*85ml/3fl oz double cream*
*1 tablespoon chopped fresh mixed herbs, such as*
*    chives, chervil, tarragon, fennel*

**1.** Make the hollandaise sauce and stir in the fish glaze, double cream and herbs.
**2.** Reheat over a very low heat as and when required.

# BEURRE BLANC

*225g/8oz unsalted butter, chilled*
*1 tablespoon chopped shallot*
*3 tablespoon white wine vinegar*
*3 tablespoons water*
*salt and freshly ground white pepper*
*a squeeze of lemon juice*

**1.** Cut the butter in 3 lengthways, then across into thin slices. Keep cold.
**2.** Put the shallot, vinegar and water into a heavy sauté pan or small shallow saucepan. Boil until reduced to about 2 tablespoons. Strain and return to the saucepan.
**3.** Lower the heat under the pan. Using a wire whisk and plenty of vigorous continuous whisking, gradually add the butter, piece by piece. The process should take about 5 minutes and the sauce should become thick, creamy and pale – rather like a thin hollandaise. Season to taste with salt, pepper and lemon juice.

# FISH BEURRE BLANC

*225g/8oz unsalted butter, chilled*
*1 shallot, finely chopped*
*5 tablespoons very strong fish stock (see*
*    page 245)*
*1 tablespoon white wine vinegar*
*salt and freshly ground white pepper*
*a squeeze of lemon*

**1.** Cut the butter in 3 lengthways, then across into thin slices. Keep cold.
**2.** Put the shallot, stock and vinegar into a small heavy saucepan and boil until reduced to 2 tablespoons. Strain and return to the pan.
**3.** Keep the stock hot, not boiling. Using a wire whisk and plenty of continuous whisking, gradually add the butter, piece by piece. The process should take about 5 minutes and the sauce should become thick, creamy and pale, rather like a thin hollandaise. Season to taste with salt, pepper and lemon juice.

# CHICKEN BEURRE BLANC

*225g/8oz unsalted butter, chilled*
*1 shallot, finely chopped*
*5 tablespoons very strong white stock, made with*
*    chicken bones (see page 243)*
*1 tablespoon white wine vinegar*
*salt and freshly ground white pepper*
*a squeeze of lemon juice*

**1.** Cut the butter in 3 lengthways, then across into thin slices. Keep cold.
**2.** Put the shallot, stock and vinegar into a small heavy saucepan and boil until reduced to 2 tablespoons. Strain and return to the pan.
**3.** Keep the stock hot but not boiling. Using a wire whisk and plenty of continuous whisking, gradually add the butter, piece by piece. The process should take about 5 minutes and the sauce should become thick, creamy and pale, rather like a thin hollandaise. Season to taste with salt, pepper and lemon juice.

# LIME BEURRE BLANC

*225g/8oz unsalted butter, chilled*
*75ml/3fl oz white wine*
*juice of 2 limes*
*finely grated zest of 1 lime*
*1 tablespoon chopped fresh parsley*
*100ml/3½fl oz double cream*
*salt and freshly ground white pepper*

1. Cut the butter into small, even pieces. Keep cold.
2. Put the wine, lime juice and zest into a small saucepan, bring to the boil and reduce to 3 tablespoons.
3. Lower the heat under the pan. Using a wire whisk and plenty of vigorous continuous whisking, gradually add the butter piece by piece. This process should take about 5 minutes, and the sauce should become thick and creamy.
4. Add the parsley and cream and season to taste with salt and pepper.

# FRENCH DRESSING (VINAIGRETTE)

*3 tablespoons salad oil*
*1 tablespoon wine vinegar*
*salt and freshly ground black pepper*

1. Put all the ingredients into a screw-top jar. Before using, shake until well emulsified.

NOTES: This dressing can be flavoured with crushed garlic, mustard, a pinch of sugar, chopped fresh herbs, etc., as desired.

If kept refrigerated, the dressing will more easily form an emulsion when whisked or shaken, and has a slightly thicker consistency.

# TOMATO DRESSING

*1 tomato*
*4 tablespoons oil*
*1 tablespoon water*
*1 tablespoon tarragon vinegar*
*a small pinch of dry English mustard*
*a small pinch of caster sugar*

1. Chop the tomato and whizz in a blender with the remaining ingredients.
2. When well emulsified push through a sieve. If the dressing looks as though it might separate add a little very cold water.

# SOY, GARLIC AND OLIVE DRESSING

This dressing is delicious with cold meats and particularly good with cold butterfly leg of lamb (see page 411). Scatter the olives and rosemary over the meat and hand the sauce separately.

*1 small clove of garlic, unpeeled*
*2 teaspoons olive oil*
*290ml/½ pint plain yoghurt*
*1 tablespoon light soy sauce*
*2 teaspoons sesame oil*
*salt and freshly ground black pepper*

To serve
*55g/2oz black olives, pitted*
*1 tablespoon roughly chopped fresh rosemary*

1. Preheat the oven to 200°C/400°F/gas mark 6.
2. Brush the clove of garlic with a little of the olive oil, place on a baking sheet and bake in the preheated oven for 15 minutes. Peel the garlic and mash well.
3. Mix together the mashed garlic, yoghurt, soy sauce, sesame oil and remaining olive oil. Season to taste with salt and pepper. Serve with the olives and rosemary as required.

## TAPENADE

*110g/4oz black olives, pitted*
*2 tablespoons capers, rinsed*
*1 medium clove of garlic, chopped*
*75ml/3fl oz olive oil*
*freshly ground black pepper*

1. Put the olives, capers and garlic into a food processor and process until smooth. While the motor is still running, pour in the oil. Season with pepper.

## PESTO SAUCE

*2 cloves of garlic*
*2 large cups of fresh basil leaves*
*55g/2oz pinenuts*
*55g/2oz Parmesan cheese, freshly grated*
*150ml/¹/4 pint olive oil*
*salt*

1. In a blender or mortar, grind the garlic and basil together to a paste. Add the nuts, cheese, oil and plenty of salt. Keep in a covered jar in a cool place.

NOTE: Pesto is sometimes made with walnuts instead of pinenuts, and the nuts may be pounded with the other ingredients to give a smooth paste.

## PARSLEY PESTO

*2 cloves of garlic*
*a large handful of freshly picked parsley, roughly*
  *chopped*
*30g/1oz blanched almonds*
*150ml/¹/4 pint olive oil*
*55g/2oz Cheddar cheese, finely grated*
*salt and freshly ground black pepper*

1. Process or liquidize the garlic and parsley together to a paste.
2. Whizz in the nuts, then add the olive oil slowly with the motor still running. Whizz in the cheese quickly. Season to taste with salt and pepper.
3. Keep in a covered jar in a cool place.

## DILL PESTO

*a large handful of fresh dill*
*55g/2oz blanched almonds*
*2 cloves of garlic*
*30g/1oz Parmesan cheese, freshly grated*
*150ml/¹/4 pint extra virgin olive oil*
*salt and freshly ground black pepper*

1. Put the dill, almonds and garlic into a food processor and whizz to a paste. Add the cheese and continue to blend until well mixed.
2. With the motor running, gradually pour the oil into the herb mixture in a steady stream. It should be well emulsified. Season to taste with salt and pepper.
3. Keep in a covered jar in a cool place.

## ROCKET PESTO

*55g/2oz rocket*
*55g/2oz blanched almonds*
*85ml/3fl oz olive oil*
*55g/2oz Parmesan cheese, freshly grated*
*salt and freshly ground black pepper*

1. Put all the ingredients into a blender and process until smooth. Season to taste with salt and pepper. If the paste begins to look oily and too thick, add 1 tablespoon water.

## RED PESTO

*2 cloves of garlic*
*1 small bunch of fresh basil*
*55g/2oz pinenuts*
*55g/2oz sundried tomatoes, chopped*
*150ml/¹/4 pint olive oil*
*55g/2oz Pecorino cheese, finely grated*
*salt and freshly ground black pepper*

1. In a food processor or blender, whizz the garlic and basil together to a paste.
2. Add the nuts and sundried tomatoes and whizz again, then add the oil slowly with the motor still running. Add the cheese and whizz quickly.
3. Season to taste with salt and pepper. Keep in a covered jar in a cool place.

# MUSTARD SAUCE

1 tablespoon Dijon mustard
6 tablespoons oil
2 tablespoons wine vinegar
1 tablespoon chopped fresh dill
salt and freshly ground black pepper

1. Put the mustard into a small bowl and gradually whisk in the oil, then the vinegar. Mix in the dill and season to taste with salt and pepper.
2. Put all the ingredients into a screw-top jar.

# WILD MUSHROOM SAUCE

30g/1oz butter
2 shallots, chopped
110g/4oz wild mushrooms, such as horn of
    plenty, chanterelles, etc.
55g/2oz flat mushrooms, sliced
425ml/$^3$/4 pint brown stock (see page 243)
100ml/3$^1$/2fl oz dry white wine
170g/6oz unsalted butter, chilled and cut into
    small pieces

1. Melt the butter in a sauté pan, add the shallots and cook until soft. Increase the heat and cook until golden-brown.
2. Add the mushrooms and cook for 1–2 minutes.
3. Add the stock and wine. Remove the mushrooms with perforated spoon and reserve. Boil the stock and wine until reduced to about 150ml/1/4 pint. Lower the heat under the pan.
4. Using a small wire whisk and plenty of vigorous continuous whisking, gradually add the butter, piece by piece. This process should take about 5 minutes and the sauce should become thick and creamy. Check the seasoning.
5. Return the mushrooms to the sauce and serve.

# MUSHROOM SAUCE

2 handfuls of mixed fresh herbs, such as tarragon,
    parsley, chervil
150ml/$^1$/4 pint white stock (see page 243)
220ml/8fl oz double cream
30g/1oz butter

110g/4oz button mushrooms
110g/4oz oyster mushrooms
salt and freshly ground black pepper

1. Drop the herbs into a saucepan of boiling salted water. Bring back to the boil, then strain through a sieve. Pour cold water on to the herbs and squeeze out any excess moisture. Put into a blender.
2. Put the stock and cream into a saucepan, bring up to the boil and simmer until a coating consistency is achieved. Pour into the blender and liquidize with the herbs until smooth and green.
3. Melt the butter in a sauté pan and cook the mushrooms until soft and any liquid has evaporated. Add the herb sauce to the pan and reheat. Season to taste with salt and pepper.

# SALSA PIZZAIOLA

This recipe has been taken from *A Taste of Venice* by Jeanette Nance Nordio.

1 onion, chopped
2 tablespoons olive oil
3–4 cloves of garlic, chopped
1kg/2$^1$/4lb canned plum tomatoes
2 tablespoons tomato purée
2 teaspoons dried oregano
1 teaspoon dried basil
1 bay leaf
2 teaspoons sugar
salt and freshly ground black pepper

1. In a saucepan, sweat the onion in the oil until transparent.
2. Add the garlic and cook for 1 further minute, then stir in the tomatoes with their liquid, the tomato purée, oregano, basil, bay leaf, and sugar. Season to taste with salt and pepper. Bring to the boil, then cook very gently for about 1 hour.
3. Remove the bay leaf and check the seasoning. This sauce should be quite thick and rough but you may purée it if you wish.

# TOMATO, BASIL AND OLIVE OIL SAUCE

*55ml/2fl oz olive oil*
*1 clove of garlic, flattened but not crushed*
*2 medium tomatoes, peeled, deseeded and finely*
*    chopped*
*4 large fresh basil leaves*
*salt and freshly ground black pepper*

**1.** Place the oil and the garlic in a small saucepan and set over a low heat to infuse for a few minutes.
**2.** Remove the garlic and add the tomatoes and basil. Season to taste with salt and pepper.
**3.** Serve warm.

# TOMATO AND MINT SALSA

*1 shallot, finely diced*
*1 tablespoon wine vinegar*
*3 tablespoons extra-virgin olive oil*
*4 tomatoes, peeled, deseeded and finely chopped*
*1 clove of garlic, crushed*
*1 tablespoon chopped fresh mint*
*salt and freshly ground black pepper*

**1.** Mix together the shallot, vinegar and oil and allow to stand for 10 minutes. Add the tomatoes, garlic and mint and season to taste with salt and pepper.

# WARM RED SALSA

SERVES 10
*2 red peppers*
*2 large tomatoes, peeled, deseeded and finely*
*    diced*
*1 tablespoon chopped fresh basil*
*1 tablespoon olive oil*
*juice of ½ lemon*
*juice of ½ orange*
*salt and freshly ground black pepper*

**1.** Preheat the oven to 180°C/350°F/gas mark 4.
**2.** Place the peppers on a baking sheet and roast in the preheated oven for about 30 minutes, or until the peppers are soft and the skins will come off easily.
**3.** Leave the peppers until cold, then cut them in half and remove and discard the seeds, membrane and skin. Dice the flesh finely and mix with the remaining ingredients. Season to taste with salt and pepper.
**4.** Just before serving, heat through very gently until just warm.

# THICK ONION AND MINT SAUCE

*1 large Spanish onion*
*55g/2oz butter*
*2 tablespoons chopped fresh mint*
*salt and freshly ground black pepper*
*a pinch of caster sugar (optional)*

**1.** Chop the onion very finely. Cook slowly in the butter until very soft but not coloured. Push through a sieve, or liquidize in a blender.
**2.** Mix in the mint and season to taste with salt and pepper, and sugar if necessary.

# EXOTIC SAUCE

This sauce has been adapted from a recipe by Josceline Dimbleby. It is a very useful accompaniment to fish, chicken or veal.

*2 large green chillies, finely chopped*
*450g/1lb tomatoes, peeled and chopped*
*2–3 cloves of garlic, crushed*
*1 teaspoon ground cardamom*
*2 teaspoons caster sugar*
*1 tablespoon tomato purée*
*juice of ½ lemon*
*1 tablespoon chopped fresh coriander*
*110g/4oz button mushrooms, thinly sliced*
*salt and freshly ground black pepper*

1. Put the chilli peppers, tomatoes, garlic, cardamom, sugar, tomato purée and lemon juice into a saucepan. Bring to the boil, then simmer for 10 minutes.

2. Add the coriander and mushrooms. Season to taste with salt and pepper.

NOTE: If this sauce is too thick it can be thinned to the required consistency with water.

# TOMATO SAUCE I

*1 large onion, finely chopped*
*3 tablespoons oil*
*10 tomatoes, roughly chopped*
*salt and freshly ground black pepper*
*a pinch of caster sugar*
*150g/¼ pint white stock (see page 243)*
*1 teaspoon fresh thyme leaves*

1. Sweat the onion in the oil in a saucepan. Add the tomatoes, salt, pepper and sugar, and cook for a further 25 minutes. Add the stock and cook for 5 minutes.

2. Liquidize the sauce and push through a sieve. If it is too thin, reduce, by boiling rapidly, to the desired consistency. Take care: it will spit and has a tendency to catch.

3. Add the thyme. Check the seasoning.

# TOMATO SAUCE II

*1 × 400g/14oz can of tomatoes*
*1 small onion, chopped*
*1 small carrot, chopped*
*1 stick of celery, chopped*
*½ clove of garlic, crushed*
*1 bay leaf*
*parsley stalks*
*salt and freshly ground black pepper*
*juice of ½ lemon*
*a dash of Worcestershire sauce*
*1 teaspoon caster sugar*
*1 teaspoon chopped fresh basil or thyme*

1. Put all the ingredients together in a heavy

saucepan, cover and simmer over a medium heat for 30 minutes.

2. Liquidize and sieve the sauce and return it to the pan.

3. If it is too thin, reduce by boiling rapidly. Check the seasoning, adding more salt or sugar if necessary.

# BARBECUE SAUCE

This sauce is particularly suitable for fried, barbecued, grilled or roasted pork. Brush some of the sauce on the meat and heat the remainder and use as a sauce.

*55g/2oz unsalted butter*
*4 spring onions, white part only, thinly sliced*
*1 teaspoon finely grated lime zest*
*1 teaspoon peeled and finely grated fresh root ginger*
*juice of 2 oranges, strained*
*75ml/2½fl oz soy sauce*
*30g/2oz soft light brown sugar*
*75ml/2½fl oz water*
*2 teaspoons cornflour*

1. Melt the butter in a saucepan and add the spring onions. Sweat for 3 minutes or until soft.

2. Add the lime zest, ginger, orange juice, soy sauce and sugar and simmer for 5 minutes.

3. Mix the water with the cornflour and add to the glaze mixture; mix well. Return to the heat and bring to the boil stirring continuously, then simmer gently for 4 minutes. Use as required.

# RED PEPPER SAUCE

*1 onion, finely chopped*
*1 tablespoon sunflower oil*
*2 tomatoes, chopped*
*1 red pepper, peeled (by singeing over a flame), cored, deseeded and cut into strips*
*1 clove of garlic, crushed*
*1 bouquet garni (see page 19)*
*6 tablespoons water*
*salt and freshly ground black pepper*

1. Cook the onion in the oil in a saucepan until just beginning to soften. Add the tomatoes, red pepper, garlic and bouquet garni. Add the water and season lightly with salt and pepper. Cover and cook over a low heat for 20 minutes.
2. Liquidize until smooth, then push through a sieve. Chill.

# BLACK BEAN SAUCE

3 tablespoons fermented black beans
1 tablespoon sunflower oil
2 spring onions, chopped
1 clove of garlic, sliced
2.5cm/1in piece of fresh root ginger, peeled and
    sliced
2 tablespoons soy sauce
2 tablespoons sherry
1 teaspoon sugar
290ml/1/2 pint water
2 teaspoons sesame oil

1. Wash the beans several times.
2. Heat the oil in a saucepan, add the spring onions, garlic and ginger and cook for 1 minute.
3. Add the soy sauce, sherry, beans, sugar and water. Bring slowly to the boil, then simmer for 15 minutes to allow the flavour to infuse.
4. Stir in the sesame oil. Use as required.

# PEANUT AND CORIANDER SAUCE

This sauce is delicious served hot with deep-fried aubergines or stir-fried vegetables. It is also good as a cold dressing for dark salad leaves, such as oakleaf or lollo rosso, where the colours are not affected by the darkness of the sauce.

55ml/2fl oz light soy sauce
55ml/2fl oz red wine vinegar
55g/2oz fresh root ginger, peeled and chopped
2 teaspoons red chilli sauce
3 tablespoons crunchy peanut butter
3 tablespoons black bean sauce (see above)
1 tablespoon caster sugar

5 tablespoons chopped fresh coriander
85ml/3fl oz groundnut oil
2 tablespoons sesame oil

1. Beat all the ingredients in a bowl, or mix in a food processor or blender, until well emulsified.

# ROUILLE

The traditional accompaniment to Bouillabaisse (see page 104).

3 cloves of garlic, crushed
1 red chilli pepper, deseeded and chopped
1 green pepper, halved, deseeded and blanched
1 red pepper, halved, deseeded, grilled and peeled
6 tablespoons olive oil
2 tablespoons fresh white breadcrumbs
salt and freshly ground pepper
Tabasco sauce

1. Blend the garlic, chilli and green and red peppers in a liquidizer until smooth. With the motor still running, very slowly pour the oil on to the purée. Add the breadcrumbs to bind the sauce.
2. Season to taste with with salt, pepper and Tabasco.

# APPLE SAUCE

450g/1lb cooking apples
finely grated zest of 1/4 lemon
3 tablespoons water
2 teaspoons sugar
15g/1/2oz butter

1. Peel, quarter, core and chop the apples.
2. Place in a heavy saucepan with the lemon zest, water and sugar. Cover with a lid and cook very slowly until the apples are soft.
3. Beat in the butter, cool slightly and add extra sugar if required. Serve hot or cold.

# MINT SAUCE

*a large handful of fresh mint*
*2 tablespoons caster sugar*
*2 tablespoons hot water*
*2 tablespoons wine vinegar*

**1.** Wash the mint and shake it dry. Remove the stalks and chop the leaves finely. Place in a bowl with the sugar.
**2.** Pour on the hot water and leave for 5 minutes to dissolve the sugar. Add the vinegar and leave to soak for 1–2 hours.

# BREAD SAUCE

This is a very rich sauce. The quantity of butter may be reduced, and the cream is optional.

*1 large onion, peeled*
*6 cloves*
*290ml/1/2 pint milk*
*1 bay leaf*
*10 white peppercorns, or a pinch of freshly*
    *ground white pepper*
*a pinch of freshly grated nutmeg*
*salt*
*55g/2oz fresh white breadcrumbs*
*55g/2oz butter*
*2 tablespoons single cream (optional)*

**1.** Cut the onion in half. Stick the cloves into the onion pieces and put with the milk and bay leaf into a saucepan.
**2.** Add the peppercorns, nutmeg, and a good pinch of salt. Bring to the boil very slowly, then remove from the heat and leave to infuse for 30 minutes. Strain.
**3.** Reheat the milk and add the breadcrumbs, butter and the cream, if using. Mix and return to the saucepan.
**4.** Reheat the sauce carefully without boiling. If it has become too thick, beat in more hot milk. It should be creamy. Check the seasoning.

# CUMBERLAND SAUCE

*2 oranges*
*1 lemon*
*225g/8oz redcurrant jelly*
*1 shallot, chopped*
*150ml/1/4 pint port*
*1/2 teaspoon Dijon mustard*
*a pinch of cayenne pepper*
*a pinch of ground ginger*

**1.** Peel 1 orange and the lemon, removing only the outer skin. Cut the zest into fine shreds.
**2.** Squeeze the fruit juice and strain into a pan. Then add the remaining ingredients with the needleshreds. Simmer for 10 minutes and cool.

# DIPS AND SAVOURY BUTTERS

# DIPS AND SAVOURY BUTTERS

Soft pâtés, dips and spreads are useful for serving with raw vegetables (crudités), biscuits or toast, or on cocktail canapés. Tartare dip is good with fried fish or chicken, and cream cheese dip is delicious on iced consommé. Quantities in these recipes would fill 2 good-sized cups. Flavoured butters are good served with grilled or fried fish or shellfish, or with plainly grilled chicken or meat dishes. They are also excellent with hot toast or bread. After preparation the butter should be shaped into a cylinder, rolled up in foil or damp greaseproof paper and chilled in the refrigerator. It can then be sliced and used as required. If it is to be kept for more than 2 days it should be frozen.

## AVOCADO DIP

*2 avocados, mashed*
*1 clove of garlic, crushed*
*1 tablespoon chopped fresh chives*
*juice of ½ lemon*
*salt and freshly ground black pepper*

**1.** Combine all the ingredients, beat well, and season to taste with salt and pepper.

## TARTARE DIP

*2 tablespoons chopped gherkins*
*2 tablespoons chopped capers, rinsed*
*1 tablespoon chopped fresh parsley*
*½small onion, finely chopped*
*½ pint mayonnaise (see page 250)*
*salt and freshly ground black pepper*
*a squeeze of lemon juice*

**1.** Mix the gherkins, capers, parsley and onion with the mayonnaise. Season to taste with salt, pepper and lemon juice.

## CREAM CHEESE DIP

*225g/8oz cream cheese*
*1 tablespoon soured cream*
*2 tablespoons chopped fresh chives*
*salt and freshly ground black pepper*
*a little milk*

**1.** Mix the cream cheese with the soured cream and chives, season with salt and pepper and add enough milk to bring the dip to the required consistency.

## BLUE CHEESE DIP

*225g/8oz blue cheese*
*1 shallot, very finely chopped*
*1 teaspoon white wine vinegar*
*4 tablespoons soured cream*
*salt and freshly ground black pepper*

**1.** Beat the cheese with a wooden spoon and mix in the shallot and vinegar. Beat in the soured cream and season to taste with salt and pepper.

# MUSTARD DIP

*150ml/¼ pint mayonnaise (see page 250)*
*150ml/¼ pint soured cream*
*2 tablespoons moutarde de Meaux or other*
  *coarse-grain mustard*

**1.** Combine all the ingredients.

# ALMOND BUTTER

*55g/2oz butter*
*30g/1oz ground almonds*
*a squeeze of lemon juice*
*salt and freshly ground white pepper*

**1.** Beat the butter to a light cream. Mix the almonds with the lemon juice and beat this paste into the softened butter. Season to taste with salt and pepper. Chill.

# ANCHOVY BUTTER

*2 anchovy fillets*
*½ clove of garlic*
*55g/2oz butter*
*freshly ground black pepper*
*anchovy essence*

**1.** Pound the anchovies and garlic and mix well with the butter. Season with pepper and anchovy essence. Chill.

# GARLIC BUTTER

*55g/2oz butter*
*1 large clove of garlic, crushed with salt*
*2 tablespoons lemon juice*
*salt and freshly ground black pepper*

**1.** Beat all the ingredients together. Chill.

# GREEN BUTTER

*2 springs of watercress*
*1 small bunch of fresh tarragon*
*1 sprig of fresh parsley*
*55g/2oz butter*
*1 shallot, minced*
*salt and freshly ground black pepper*

**1.** Blanch the watercress, tarragon and parsley for 30 seconds in boiling salted water. Refresh under cold running water. Drain well and pat dry. Chop very finely.
**2.** Cream the butter and beat in the shallot, watercress and herbs. Season to taste with salt and pepper. Chill.

# MAÎTRE D'HÔTEL BUTTER

*55g/2oz butter*
*2 teaspoons lemon juice*
*1 teaspoon finely chopped fresh parsley*
*salt and freshly ground black pepper*

**1.** Cream the butter, stir in the lemon juice and parsley and season to taste with salt and pepper. Mix well and chill.

# MINT AND MUSTARD BUTTER

*110g/4oz butter*
*1 teaspoon Dijon mustard*
*1 tablespoon finely chopped fresh mint*
*salt and freshly ground black pepper*

**1.** Cream the butter until very soft and beat in the mustard and mint
**2.** Season with salt and pepper. Chill.

# FISH AND SHELLFISH

# FISH AND SHELLFISH

Freshwater fish are divided into coarse fish, fished mainly for sport and generally thrown back live into the rivers, and game fish, which are caught both for sport and commercially. Much freshwater fish in fact comes from fish farms. Many freshwater fish, such as bass, sturgeon, sea trout and salmon spend most of their adult lives in the sea, swimming back up the rivers to spawn, but they are still classified as freshwater fish despite the fact that most of them are caught by trawl in the sea. Coarse river fish, such as roach, gudgeon and tench, are not sold commercially and are seldom eaten except by anglers' families.

Most of our fish comes from the sea. It is increasingly difficult today to get locally caught fish. Fish is frozen or deep-chilled on trawlers and immediately exported. For the cook this is sad. Fish is a valuable source of protein, vitamin D (in oily fish), calcium and phosphorus (found especially in the edible bones of whitebait, sardines, etc.), iodine, fluorine and some of the B vitamins. Fish contains very little fat, and even oily fish seldom has more than 20 per cent fat content. The fat in fish is polyunsaturated and contains essential fatty acids that cannot be obtained elsewhere.

Like meat, fish is composed of muscle fibres that vary in length and thickness according to type. For example, lobster has long and coarse fibres and herring very fine fibres.

The fibres are generally shorter than in meat and are packed in flakes with very little connective tissue between them. The fat is dispersed among the fibres. The connective tissue is very thin and is quickly converted to gelatine when cooked. Because of its structure, fish is naturally more tender than meat, and over-vigorous or overlong cooking will cause dryness and disintegration as the connective tissue dissolves and the flakes fall apart. The protein in the fibres coagulates, the fish begins to shrink and the juices are extracted – in dry heat there is a more rapid loss of juices. In moist heat soluble nutrients and flavouring minerals are lost into the liquid, making an overcooked fish dry, tough and tasteless.

Fish should be cooked quickly by grilling or frying, or slowly by poaching. If frying or grilling, the fish should be protected from the fierce heat by a coating of seasoned flour, beaten egg, breadcrumbs or a batter. If poaching, use a well-seasoned court bouillon and then use this liquid to make the sauce so that none of the flavour is lost. Do drain fish well after it has been poached, and do not keep it warm as it will dry out and become tough and tasteless. Fish does not keep well and should be eaten as fresh as possible. A plausible theory explaining this is that as fish live in cold water, they are cold-blooded and their enzymes work at very low temperatures. Thus they continue, unlike meat, to deteriorate in the refrigerator.

## PREPARATION FOR COOKING

REMOVING THE SCALES. Large fish have dry scales which should be removed before cooking. To do this, scrape a large knife the wrong way along the fish (from tail to head). This can be a messy business as the scales tend to fly about; it can be cleanly done in a plastic carrier bag to prevent this. However, unless you are buying fish from a wholesale market, the fishmonger will do it for you.

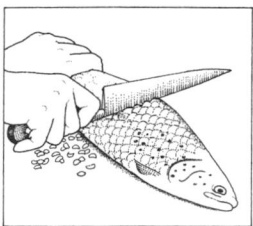

*Remove the scales with the back of a knife*

GUTTING AND CLEANING. The fishmonger will probably clean the fish, but if you are to do it yourself you will need a very sharp knife. Fish skin blunts knives faster than anything else. If the fish is to be stuffed or filleted it does not matter how big a slit you make to remove the entrails. If it is to be left whole, the shorter the slit the better. Start just below the head and slit through the soft belly skin. After pulling out the innards, wash the fish under cold water. If it is large, and of the round type, make sure all the dark blood along the spinal column is removed. Now carefully cut away the gills. Take care not to cut off the head if you want to serve the fish whole. If you do not, cut off head and tail now. To remove the fins, cut the skin round them, take a good grip (if you salt your fingers well it will stop them slipping) and yank sharply towards the head. This will pull the fin bones out with the fin.

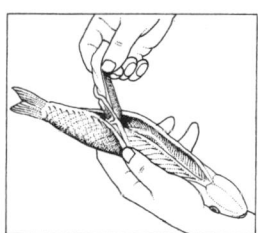

*Remove the innards and wash thoroughly*

SKINNING AND FILLETING FLAT FISH. Fish skin is easier to remove after cooking. But sometimes the fish must be skinned beforehand. Most whole fish are not skinned or filleted before grilling, but sole (and lemon sole, witch and plaice) are skinned on at least the dark side, and sometimes on both sides. To do this, make a crossways slit through the skin at the tail, and push a finger in. You will now be able to run the finger round the edge of the fish loosening the skin. When you have done this on both edges, salt your fingers to prevent slipping, take a firm grip of the skin at the tail

end with one hand, and with the other hold the fish down. Give a quick strong yank, peeling the skin back towards the head. If necessary, do the same to the other side.

Flat fish are generally filleted into four half-fillets. To do this, lay the fish on a board with the tail towards you. Cut through the flesh to the backbone along the length of the fish. Then, with a sharp pliable knife, cut the left-hand fillet away from the bone, keeping the blade almost flat against the bones of the fish. Then swivel the fish round so the head is towards you and cut away the second fillet in the same way. Turn the fish over and repeat the process on the other side. (If you are left-handed, tackle the right-hand fillet first.)

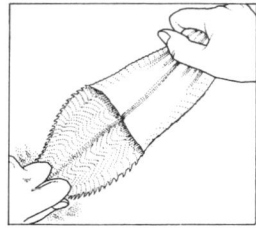

*Remove the skin from a flat fish in one piece*

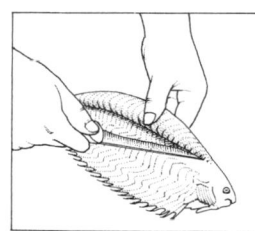

*To fillet a flat fish, stroke the flesh away from the bones*

FILLETING AND SKINNING ROUND FISH. Round fish are filleted before skinning. If they are to be cooked whole, they are cooked with the skin, but this may be carefully peeled off after cooking, as in the case of a whole poached salmon. To fillet a round fish, lay it on a board and cut through the flesh down to the backbone from the head to the tail. Insert a sharp pliable knife between the flesh and the bones, and slice the fillet away from the bones, working with short strokes from the backbone and from the head end. Remember to keep the knife as flat as possible, and to keep it against the bones. When the fillet is almost off the fish you will need to cut through the belly skin to detach it completely. Very large round fish can be filleted in four, following the flat fish method, or the whole side can be lifted as described here, and then split in two once off the fish.

TO SKIN A FISH FILLET. Put it skin side down on a board. Hold the tip down firmly, using a good pinch of salt to help get a firm grip. With a sharp, heavy, straight knife, cut through the flesh, close to the tip, taking care not to go right through the skin. Hold the knife at right angles to the fish fillet, with the blade almost upright. With a gently sawing motion, work the flesh from the skin, pushing the fillet off rather than cutting it. The reason for keeping the knife almost upright is to lessen the danger of cutting through the skin, but with practice it is possible to flatten the knife slightly, so that the sharp edge is foremost, and simply slide it forward, without the sawing motion.

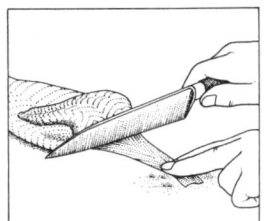

*To skin a fillet, grip the tail with one hand and push the flesh off the fillet with a knife*

TO BONE SMALL FISH. Split the fish open completely, clean thoroughly and lay, skin side up, on a board. With the heel of your hand, press down firmly on the backbone of the fish. This will loosen it. Turn it over, cut through the backbone near the head, and pull it out with all the side bones, or nearly all the side bones, attached to it.

PINBONING FISH. This is done to remove all the small irritating bones that run along the flanks of the fish, and which are the reason why some people do not enjoy eating fish.

Any cut of fish should be pinboned before cooking. Run the tips of the fingers of one hand over the surface of the flesh to locate the ends of the small bones. Pull the bones out with tweezers or pliers. The fish is now ready for cooking.

SKINNING EEL. Cut through the skin round the neck and slit the skin down the length of the

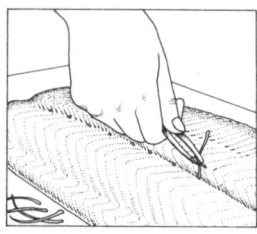

*Remove the bones with tweezers or pliers*

body. Hang the eel up by its head – a stout hook through the eyes is best. Using a cloth to get a good grip, pull hard to peel off the skin from neck to tail.

STUFFING FISH. Round fish are more suitable for stuffing whole than flat fish, as there is more space in the body cavity after gutting. Stuffings usually contain breadcrumbs, which swell during cooking, so care should be taken not to overfill the fish. Fish fillets can be sandwiched with stuffing, or rolled up round the mixture. Well-flavoured expensive fish is less often stuffed than the more tasteless varieties, which need the additional flavour of an aromatic filling.

SLICING SMOKED SALMON. Place the side of salmon, skin side down, on a board. Run the tips of the fingers of one hand over the surface of the flesh to locate the ends of the small bones. Pinbone (see above). Now slice the flesh in horizontal paper-thin slices, using a long, sharp ham knife. The slices should be long and wide. It is customary to remove the central narrow stripe of brownish flesh, but this is not strictly necessary – it tastes excellent. If the whole side is not to be sliced, place a piece of clingfilm on the cut surface of the remaining salmon to prevent drying out.

# SEASONAL TABLE OF COMMERCIAL FISH AVAILABLE IN THE U.K.

| FISH FAMILY | SEASON | CATEGORY | TYPE |
|---|---|---|---|
| **SALMONIDAE** Salmon – farmed | all year | OILY/FRESH AND SEAWATER | MAINLY PELAGIC |
| Salmon – wild | May–Sept | | |
| Trout – farmed | all year | ROUND | |
| Trout – wild | various | | |
| Others include: Char Pacific salmon   species | | | |
| **GADIDAE** Cod | June–Feb | WHITE/SEAFISH | MAINLY DEMERSAL |
| Haddock | May–June | ROUND | |
| Coley | August–Feb | | |
| Pollack | May–Sept | | |
| Ling | June–Feb | | |
| Whiting | June–Feb | | |
| Hake | June–March | | |
| **SCOMBRIDAE** | | OILY/SEAFISH | PELAGIC SHOALING |
| Mackerel | All year | | |
| Tuna | All year | ROUND | |
| **CLUPEIDAE** Herring | May–Dec | OILY/SEAFISH | PELGAIC SHOALING |
| Anchovy | June–Dec | ROUND | |
| Sardine | Jan/Feb/April/ Nov/Dec | | |
| Sprat | Oct–March | | |
| **BOTHIDAE** Turbot | April–Feb | WHITE/SEAFISH | DEMERSAL |
| Brill | June–Feb | FLAT | |
| **PLEURONECT** Plaice | May–Feb | WHITE/SEAFISH | DEMERSAL |
| Halibut | June–March | FLAT | |
| Lemon sole | May–March | | |
| **SOLIDAE** Dover/Slip soles | May–Feb | WHITE/SEAFISH FLAT | DEMERSAL |
| **RAJIDAE** Skate | May–Feb | WHITE/SEAFISH FLAT | DEMERSAL |
| **LOPHIIDAE** Monkfish | All year | WHITE/SEAFISH ROUND | DEMERSAL |
| **ZEIDAE** John Dory | All year | WHITE/SEAFISH ROUND | PELAGIC |
| **TRIGLIDAE** Gurnard | July–Feb | WHITE/SEAFISH ROUND | DEMERSAL |

| FISH FAMILY | SEASON | CATEGORY | TYPE |
|---|---|---|---|
| **MULLIDAE**<br>Red mullet | May–Nov | WHITE/SEAFISH<br>ROUND (Highest oil<br>content of all white fish) | DEMERSAL |
| **MUGLIDAE**<br>Grey mullet | Sept–Feb | WHITE/SEAFISH<br>ROUND | DEMERSAL<br>AND<br>PELAGIC |
| **MORONIDAE**<br>Seabass | August–March | WHITE/SEAFISH<br>ROUND | PELAGIC/<br>SHOALING |
| Others include:<br>Wrasse<br>Ocean perch<br>Rockfish | | ROUND | |
| **IMPORTED<br>SPECIES INC.**<br>Mahi mahi<br>Red snapper<br>Croakers<br>Orange roughy<br>Barracudas<br>Grouper<br>Sea bream<br>Pomfrets<br>etc . . . | All year<br><br><br><br><br><br><br>(previously<br>frozen) | ROUND | |
| **DEEPSEA<br>DWELLERS**<br>Marlin<br>Swordfish<br>Shark family<br>Includes:<br>Porbeagle<br>Tope<br>Mako<br><br>also<br>Huss | All year<br><br><br><br><br><br>(previously<br>frozen) | VARIOUS<br><br>ROUND<br><br>(mainly white) | VARIOUS |
| **SHELLFISH** | | | |
| CRUSTACEA<br>Crabs<br>Brown Edible<br>Spider<br>Many other<br>species | <br><br>April–Dec<br>April–Oct | | |
| Lobster<br>Rock/Spiny | April–Nov | | |
| Prawns<br>Various<br>species | All<br>year<br>worldwide | | |
| Others include:<br>Crayfish<br>Dublin Bay prawn (scampi) | | | |

# FISH AND SHELLFISH

| FISH FAMILY | SEASON | CATEGORY | TYPE |
|---|---|---|---|
| MOLLUSCS BIVALVE | | | |
| | | | |
| Mussel | Sept–March | | |
| Oyster | All year | | |
| Scallop | Sept–March | | |
| Clam | All year | | |
| Cockle | May–Dec | | |
| | | | |
| GASTROPODS Univalve | | | |
| Whelk | Feb–August | | |
| Winkle | Sept–April | | |
| | | | |
| CEPHALAPODS Octopus | May–Dec | | |
| Squid | May–Oct | | |
| Cuttlefish | May–Dec | | |
| | | | |
| SMOKED Hot Some herrings including: Kippers Trout Eel | | | |
| | | | |
| Cold Salmon Haddock Some trout Halibut Salt cod | | | |

## DEFINITIONS OF TERMS

Demersal: fish that live and feed on the seabed
Pelagic: fish that live and feed on the surface of the water
Crustacea: shellfish that are multijointed, legs and pincers

Molluscs subdivided into three categories:-
Bivalve: hinged/double shell (mussel/oyster)
Gastropod: (univalve) single shell (whelk/winkle)
Cephalopod: shellfish with modified internal shell (octopus/squid)

## SHELLFISH

Edible shellfish can be divided into two main categories:

**Crustaceans:** lobsters, crabs, crawfish, langoustines, prawns and shrimps, which have 5 pairs of legs and live encased in a jointed, multi-hinged shell.

**Molluscs:** *Gastropods* (univalves) or single-shelled creatures, including whelks and winkles, and *bivalves* or double-hinged shelled creatures, such as mussels, oysters and scallops. These are also known as filter-feeders.

*Cephalods,* creatures with tentacles and a modified internal shell – octopus, squid and cuttlefish.

The shellfish industry is a multi-million-pound business and is growing. In the UK molluscan shellfish can only be marketed and sold commercially in the EU if harvested from an area that has met with government approval and has been designated as safe by scientific research. It is unwise to gather these species yourself from any area you are not completely confident about. This is particularly important where bivalves or filter-feeders are concerned as they filter a considerable amount of water through their systems each day and in doing so they can pick up any toxins and bacteria in the water. This does not affect the shellfish but, if the water is polluted, could have an adverse effect on the consumer.

Freshness is of paramount importance in shellfish, so always buy from a reputable supplier. For instructions on preparation, see individual recipes on pages 104, 128, 177 and 301.

# GRILLED FISH CUTLETS

This recipe is suitable for brill, cod, halibut, haddock, turbot or salmon cutlets. The pieces of fish should, if possible, be cut to a uniform thickness.

SERVES 4
*4 × 170g/6oz fish cutlets*
*melted butter*
*freshly ground black pepper*
*juice of ½ lemon*

To garnish
*sprigs of fresh parsley or watercress*
*lemon wedges*

**1.** Preheat the grill. Brush the cutlets and the bottom of the grill pan with melted butter. Season the cutlets with pepper and lemon juice. Lay them in the grill tray (not on the wire tray where they might stick).

**2.** Grill them until pale brown. Turn over and brush with more melted butter. Season again with pepper and lemon juice and grill for a further 3 minutes or until cooked. They will feel firm to the touch, and the flesh will flake easily.

**3.** Serve on a warmed dish with the pan juices poured over, garnished with parsley or watercress and lemon wedges.

 *CRISP DRY WHITE*

# FISH IN BATTER

SERVES 4
*4 cutlets or steaks of any white fish*
*oil for deep-frying*
*2 teaspoons oil*
*55g/2oz plain flour*
*a pinch of salt*
*1 egg yolk*
*3 tablespoons warm water*

To serve
*lemon wedges*

**1.** Heat the oil in a deep-fryer until a crumb will sizzle gently in it.

**2.** Mix the 2 teaspoons oil with the flour in a shallow bowl and add the salt, egg yolk and water.

**3.** Dip the fish into this batter, hold it with tongs and lower it into the hot oil. Increase the temperature of the oil.

**4.** Fry for 4–10 minutes depending on the thickness of the fish pieces.

**5.** Drain well on absorbent kitchen paper and sprinkle lightly with salt. Serve with lemon wedges.

 *WHITE LOIRE*

# POACHED FISH, HOT OR COLD

Use salmon, haddock, etc., either whole or in a large piece. If the fish weighs over 1.35kg/3lb, double the court bouillon quantities.

For the fish
*see above*

For the court bouillon
*about 1.1 litres/2 pints water*
*1 teaspoon salt*
*150ml/¼ pint white wine vinegar*
*1 medium onion, sliced*
*1 bunch of fresh parsley*
*1 sprig of fresh thyme*
*1 bay leaf*
*6 black peppercorns*

For cold fish
*watercress, trimmed*
*cucumber slices, blanched*
*mayonnaise (see page 250)*

For hot fish
*lemon wedges*
*boiled potatoes*
*melted butter*

1. Simmer together all the court bouillon ingredients for 1 hour. Strain and cool.
2. Put the fish into the cold court bouillon and heat gently, bringing up to poaching temperature. Do not allow the water to simmer or boil – it should barely move. Poach for 4 minutes.
3. If the fish is to be served cold, turn the heat off now and leave the fish to cool. It will finish cooking as it does so. Check the fish every 10 minutes or so, and when cooked, remove it carefully from the court bouillon and leave to get cold. When cold, skin the fish, garnish it with watercress and cucumber and hand the mayonnaise separately.
4. If the fish is to be served hot, poach it for 4 minutes per 450g/1lb, then carefully lift it out. Skin it if necessary, garnish with lemon wedges, surround with hot potatoes and pass the melted butter separately.

NOTE: Starting with a cooled court bouillon is considered to produce moister flesh, but it is not always practicable. If the fish has to be put into a hot court bouillon allow 6 minutes per 450g/1lb and remove immediately from the pan.

 *DRY WHITE*

# SPICY FISH CURRY

Any firm white fish will do for this curry. Be very careful not to overcook the fish or it will begin to fall apart and look unattractive. This is a fairly mild curry but can be made hotter by using an extra green chilli pepper. Remove the seeds of the green chilli under cold running water.

*675g/1½lb monkfish, filleted and skinned*
*1 large onion, chopped*
*1 green pepper, cored, deseeded and sliced*
*1 green chilli, deseeded and chopped*
*sunflower oil*
*1 × 1cm/½ in piece of fresh root ginger, peeled*
  *and cut into slivers*
*1 clove of garlic, crushed*
*1 teaspoon ground cumin*
*1 teaspoon ground coriander*
*1 teaspoon ground cinnamon*
*1 teaspoon ground turmeric*
*450ml/¾ pint water*
*salt and freshly ground black pepper*
*110g/4oz Greek yoghurt*

To garnish
*roughly chopped fresh mint*

1. Cut the monkfish into 2.5cm/1in cubes.
2. Fry the onion, pepper and chilli in a little oil in a frying pan and allow to soften without browning for 2–3 minutes. Add the ginger, garlic and dry spices and cook for a further 2 minutes. Stir regularly and add a little extra oil if the mixture is getting too dry.
3. Remove the pan off the heat. Add the water and bring to the boil. Season well with salt and pepper. Add the fish and simmer for 10 minutes. Remove the fish with a slotted spoon. Reduce the sauce, by boiling rapidly, to a syrupy consistency.
4. Beat the yoghurt with a little water, add some of the hot fish juices, mix well and return to the

pan. Bring to the boil but do not allow to get too hot. Return the fish to the pan.

5. Pile into a warmed serving dish and serve garnished with the mint.

 *SPICY DRY WHITE*

# FISH PIE

SERVES 6

*900g/2lb haddock, whiting or cod fillet or a
    mixture of any of them*
*425ml/³/4 pint milk*
*½ onion, sliced*
*6 black peppercorns*
*1 bay leaf*
*salt and freshly ground black pepper*
*5 hardboiled eggs, quartered*
*1 tablespoon chopped fresh parsley*
*30g/1oz butter*
*30g/1oz plain flour*
*2 tablespoons double cream*
*675g/1½lb mashed potatoes (see page 212)*

1. Preheat the oven to 180°C/350°F/gas mark 4.
2. Lay the fish fillets in a roasting pan.
3. Heat the milk with the onion, peppercorns, bay leaf and a pinch of salt.
4. Pour over the fish and cook in the preheated oven for about 15 minutes, until the fish is firm and creamy-looking.
5. Strain off the milk and reserve it for the sauce. Flake the fish into a pie dish and add the eggs. Sprinkle over the parsley.
6. Melt the butter in a saucepan, stir in the flour and cook for 1 minute. Remove from the heat and gradually add the reserved milk.
7. Return to the heat and stir, bringing slowly to the boil. Season to taste with salt and pepper. Stir in the cream and pour over the fish, mixing the sauce in carefully with a palette knife or spoon.
8. Spread a layer of mashed potatoes on the top and mark with a fork in a criss-cross pattern. Or pipe the potatoes on top of the pie. Dot with butter. Place on a baking sheet and brown in the oven for about 10 minutes, or longer if the pie has been made in advance.

 *DRY WHITE*

# EEL PIE

SERVES 6

*340g/12oz flour quantity puff pastry (see page 464)*
*900g/2lb fresh spinach, cooked and chopped*
*freshly grated nutmeg*
*freshly ground black pepper*
*900g/2lb smoked eel, skinned and boned*

For the sauce
*55g/2oz unsalted butter*
*15g/½oz plain flour*
*150ml/¼ pint milk*
*2 egg yolks*
*beaten egg to glaze*

1. Preheat the oven to 200°C/400°F/gas mark 6.
2. Take one-third of the pastry and roll it out to a 15 × 20cm/6 × 8 in rectangle. Place on a wet baking sheet and prick all over with a fork. Bake in the preheated oven for about 20 minutes until golden-brown. Transfer the pastry to a wire rack to cool but do not turn the oven off.
3. Season the spinach with nutmeg and pepper.
4. Make the sauce: melt 15g/½oz of the butter, add the flour and cook for 30 seconds. Remove from the heat and stir in the milk. Return to the heat and stir until boiling.
5. Cool slightly, then beat in the remaining butter and the egg yolks. Season with pepper.
6. Arrange half the spinach on the cooked pastry base and cover with the eel. Spread the béchamel sauce over the eel and cover with the remaining spinach.
7. Roll the remaining pastry on a floured board into a 'blanket' large enough to overlap the edges of the pie. Lay it gently over the spinach. Using a sharp knife, cut off the corners to the size of the pie. Reserve the pastry trimmings.
8. Lift one side of the overlapping pastry and brush the underside with a little beaten egg. Tuck the 'blanket' neatly underneath the cooked base. Repeat with the other three sides.
9. Shape the trimmings into leaves. Brush the whole pie with beaten egg. Arrange the pastry on top and brush again.
10. Bake in the oven for 40–45 minutes. Serve hot or cold.

NOTE: To counteract the saltiness of the smoked eel, salt is not added to the sauce or to the spinach.

# TURBOT WITH SPRING ONIONS AND GINGER SAUCE

Any firm white fish such as halibut, haddock, monkfish or turbot can be used for this recipe – the firmer the fish, the easier it is to cook.

SERVES 2–3
*450g/1lb turbot fillet*
*sesame oil for frying*
*2 cloves of garlic, cut into slivers*
*1cm/½in piece of fresh root ginger, peeled and cut into slivers*
*8–10 spring onions, shredded*

For the marinade
*1 tablespoon soy sauce mixed with 1 tablespoon dry sherry*

For the sauce
*½ teaspoon ground ginger*
*½ teaspoon caster sugar*
*1 tablespoon soy sauce*
*1 tablespoon dry sherry*

**1.** Cut the fish fillets into strips the size of your little finger.
**2.** Add the fish to the marinade and leave it to stand for 30 minutes.
**3.** Mix all the ingredients for the sauce together and set aside.
**4.** Heat a sauté pan (preferably non-stick), add a little oil, and when hot add the garlic and ginger. Cook quickly until the garlic is lightly browned. Lower the heat and add the fish, in its marinade, and fry briefly. Pour in the sauce, stir and add the spring onions. Serve immediately.

 *SPICY DRY WHITE*

# TURBOT SAUSAGES WITH WATERCRESS SAUCE

SERVES 4
*340g/12oz turbot fillet, skinned*
*110g/4oz whiting or haddock fillet, skinned*
*2 egg whites*
*290ml/½ pint double cream*
*salt and freshly ground black pepper*
*cayenne pepper*
*beaten egg*
*fine dried white breadcrumbs*
*oil and butter for frying*

For the sauce
*30g/1oz butter*
*30g/1oz plain flour*
*290ml/½ pint fish stock (see page 245)*
*150ml/¼ pint double cream*
*1 bunch of watercress, trimmed, blanched and refreshed*
*salt and freshly ground black pepper*

To garnish
*watercress leaves*

**1.** Keeping everything as cool as possible, process the fish with a little egg white in a food processor until smooth and season with salt. Place in a large bowl and set in a roasting pan of ice. Beat well, and gradually add the remaining egg whites, then the cream, salt, pepper and cayenne.
**2.** Roll the mixture up in clingfilm in the shape of sausages.
**3.** Poach for 10–15 minutes in simmering water. Remove the clingfilm. Allow to cool, then brush with egg and roll in breadcrumbs.
**4.** Make the sauce: melt the butter in a saucepan and add the flour. Cook for 30 seconds. Remove from the heat. Add the stock and cream. Return to the heat and bring to the boil, then simmer for 4 minutes. Add the watercress and whizz briefly. Season to taste with salt and pepper.
**5.** Fry the turbot sausages in oil and butter. Garnish with watercress leaves and serve with the sauce.

 *WHITE BURGUNDY*

# HADDOCK FILLING FOR GOUGÈRE

SERVES 4
*45g/1oz butter*
*30g/1oz plain flour*
*290ml/½ pint milk*
*freshly ground black pepper*
*2 tablespoons chopped fresh parsley*
*4 tablespoons double cream*
*1 gougère case (see page 321)*
*340g/12oz smoked haddock fillet, cooked and flaked*
*4 tomatoes, peeled, deseeded and cut into slivers*

**1.** Melt the butter in a saucepan. Add the flour, stir well and draw off the heat.
**2.** Add the milk, pepper, parsley and cream. Return to the heat and stir until boiling. Simmer for 1–2 minutes.
**3.** Stir in the haddock and tomatoes. Use to fill a gougère case (see page 321).

# HADDOCK WITH ENGLISH EGG SAUCE

SERVES 4
*675/1½ lb haddock fillets*
*570ml/1 pint milk*
*1 onion, sliced*
*1 bouquet garni (see page 19)*
*salt and freshly ground black pepper*

To serve
*570ml/1 pint English egg sauce, (see page 248) made with the reserved cooking liquor*

**1.** Preheat the oven to 170°C/325°F/gas mark 3.
**2.** Wash the fish, scrape off any scales and lay skin side up in a roasting pan.
**3.** Pour in the milk and add the onion, bouquet garni, salt and pepper.
**4.** Cover the dish with greased paper or a lid and bake in the oven for 30 minutes, or until the fish is tender to the touch of a skewer.
**5.** Remove the fish, skin, drain and remove any bones. Reserve the fish liquor for the sauce. Arrange the fish on a flat ovenproof dish.

**6.** Cover again with the paper and keep warm while you make the sauce.
**7.** Pour the sauce over the fish and serve.

NOTE: Cooking times for baking fillets of fish depend on the size of the fillets, the type of roasting pan and the heat of the milk as well as the oven temperature.

 *DRY WHITE*

# HADDOCK WITH TOMATOES AND CHIVES

SERVES 4
*4 × 170g/6oz haddock fillets*
*salt and freshly ground black pepper*
*290ml/½ pint fish stock (see page 245)*
*150ml/¼ pint dry white wine*
*30g/1oz butter*
*30g/1oz plain flour*
*150ml/¼ pint double cream*
*2 large tomatoes, peeled, deseeded and cut into slivers*
*1 tablespoon chopped fresh parsley*
*1 tablespoon chopped fresh chives*

**1.** Preheat the oven to 180°C/350°F/gas mark 4. Wash the haddock fillets and season with salt and pepper.
**2.** Lay the fish skin side up in an ovenproof dish. Pour over the strained stock and the wine. Cover with buttered greaseproof paper or foil and bake in the preheated oven for 15–20 minutes.
**3.** Lift out the fish. Strain the cooking liquor into a small heavy saucepan and boil rapidly until reduced to 290ml/½ pint.
**4.** Melt the butter in another saucepan, add the flour and stir for 1 minute. Remove from the heat and strain in the reduced fish liquor. Return to the heat, bring slowly to the boil, and simmer for 2 minutes. Remove from the heat. Season to taste with salt and pepper and add the cream, tomatoes, parsley and chives.
**5.** Skin the fish and lay it in a serving dish. Pour over the sauce.

 *MUSCADET*

# ROAST COD WITH GARLIC

This recipe is best made with narrow rather than wide fillets of fish.

SERVES 4
*4 × 170g/6oz cod fillets, unskinned*
*salt and freshly ground black pepper*
*seasoned flour*
*150ml/5fl oz good-quality olive oil*
*4 cloves of garlic, unpeeled*

To serve
*lemon wedges*

**1.** Preheat the oven to 200°C/400°F/gas mark 6.
**2.** Pinbone the cod fillets if necessary (see page 268). Season with salt and pepper and dip them, skin side down, into the seasoned flour. Shake off excess.
**3.** Heat the oil in a roasting tin. Add the garlic and bake in the oven for 15 minutes. Remove the tin from the oven and increase the oven temperature to its highest setting.
**4.** Set the oil in the tin over direct heat and add the cod, skin side down. Let it sizzle for 2 minutes.
**5.** Turn the cod skin side uppermost, and roast in the oven for 3 minutes or until cooked (it should be opaque and firm).
**6.** To serve: place the cod, skin side uppermost, on a serving dish with the baked garlic and lemon wedges.

 *CALIFORNIAN PINOT NOIR*

# SALT COD RAGOÛT

SERVES 4
*450g/1lb salt cod*
*150ml/¼ pint olive oil*
*2 onions, thinly sliced*
*5 cloves of garlic, crushed*
*2 yellow peppers, grilled, deseeded and peeled*
*2 red peppers, grilled, deseeded and peeled*
*6 tomatoes, peeled, deseeded and chopped*

*1 tablespoon chopped fresh thyme*
*450g/1lb potatoes, peeled and sliced thickly*
*290ml/½ pint fish stock (see page 245)*

To garnish
*12 olives, pitted and halved*
*1 tablespoon capers, rinsed*

**1.** Soak the salt cod in cold water for 24 hours. Change the water several times to extract as much salt as possible.
**2.** Drain the salt cod on absorbent kitchen paper. Remove the skin and bones and break the flesh into large flakes. Lay on a flat serving dish and pour over the oil. Cover and refrigerate for 2 hours.
**3.** Preheat the oven to 180°C/350°F/gas mark 4.
**4.** Heat 2 tablespoons of the cod soaking oil in a saucepan. Add the onions and cook over a very low heat until soft. Add the garlic and cook for 2 further minutes.
**5.** Cut the peppers into strips and add to the onions and garlic with the tomatoes and thyme.
**6.** Arrange the potato slices in the bottom of a large casserole and pour over the stock.
**7.** Lift the salt cod from the oil, mix with the tomato and pepper mixture and spoon on to the potatoes. Cover and cook in the oven for 50 minutes, or until the cod and potatoes are tender.
**8.** Sprinkle over the olives and capers and serve hot.

 *DRY ROSÉ BORDEAUX*

# HALIBUT AU GRATIN

SERVES 4

*4 × 170g/6oz halibut steaks*

For the court bouillon
*570ml/1 pint water*
*2 tablespoons white wine vinegar*
*1 carrot, sliced*
*1 onion, sliced*
*4 cloves*
*salt*
*6 black peppercorns*
*parsley stalk*
*1 sprig of fresh thyme*
*1 bay leaf*

For the sauce
*30g/1oz butter*
*20g/³⁄4oz plain flour*
*150ml/¹⁄4 pint milk*

For the topping
*dried breadcrumbs*
*30g/1oz Gruyère or strong Cheddar cheese, grated*

**1.** Make up the court bouillon: combine all the ingredients, bring to the boil, simmer for 10 minutes, then allow to cool.
**2.** Preheat the oven to 180°C/350°F/gas mark 4. Place the halibut steaks in a buttered dish. Strain on the court bouillon and cover with a piece of greased paper, foil or a lid. Poach in the oven or over a gentle heat for 10–15 minutes. Reduce the oven temperature to 70°C/150°F/gas mark 1.
**3.** Lift out the fish. Strain the fish liquor into a saucepan and reduce it by rapid boiling to 150ml/¹⁄4 pint.
**4.** Skin the halibut and remove the bones. Drain well. Place the fish steaks on an ovenproof serving dish, cover, and return to the oven.
**5.** Preheat the grill.
**6.** Make the sauce: melt the butter in a small saucepan and stir in the flour. Cook for 1 minute, then remove from the heat. Pour in the reduced fish liquor and milk. Return to the heat and bring slowly to the boil, stirring until you have a smooth creamy sauce. Simmer for 2 minutes. Season to taste with salt and pepper.
**7.** Spoon the sauce over the fish. Sprinkle with breadcrumbs and grated cheese.
**8.** Grill until well browned.

 *WHITE BURGUNDY*

# MACKEREL WITH GOOSEBERRY SAUCE

SERVES 4

*4 × 225g/8oz mackerel*

For the gooseberry sauce
*340g/12oz young gooseberries*
*30g/1oz caster sugar*
*30g/1oz butter*
*a pinch of ground ginger*

To garnish
*lemon wedges*

**1.** Preheat the grill.
**2.** Clean the mackerel, cut off the fins and make 2 or 3 diagonal slashes into the flesh through the skin.
**3.** Prepare the gooseberry sauce: top and tail the berries and place them in saucepan with a little water and the sugar. Simmer until tender.
**4.** Push the gooseberries through a sieve. Beat in the butter and ginger and taste for sweetness.
**5.** Grill the mackerel for about 5 minutes on each side, depending on size, or until cooked.
**6.** Arrange the mackerel on a warmed serving dish. Garnish with lemon wedges. Hand the sauce separately.

 *ALSACE WHITE*

# MONKFISH WITH HERBY HOLLANDAISE

SERVES 4

*900g/2lb monkfish, skinned and filleted*

For the court bouillon
*1.1 litres/2 pints water*
*5 tablespoons white wine vinegar*
*1 carrot, sliced*
*1 onion, sliced*
*1 bunch of fresh parsley*
*1 bay leaf*
*1 stock of celery*
*6 black peppercorns*
*¹⁄4 teaspoon salt*

To finish
*herby hollandaise sauce (see page 252)*
*sprigs of fresh chervil*

**1.** Combine all the court bouillon ingredients into a saucepan and bring to the boil. Simmer for 30 minutes. Strain and cool the liquid.
**2.** Put the fish into a saucepan and pour over the court bouillon. Cover and bring slowly to simmering point, then reduce the heat until it barely moves; it must not boil. Poach the fish for 10 minutes.
**3.** Lift out the fish. Remove any remaining skin or bones.
**4.** Slice the fish and arrange on a warmed serving dish. Coat with the herby hollandaise and garnish with the chervil.

 *MUSCADET*

# MONKFISH SALAD WITH EXOTIC SAUCE

This recipe has been adapted from *The Josceline Dimbleby Collection* published for Sainsbury's. It is one of our most popular recipes and is ideal for a cold buffet.

SERVES 10
*1.25kg/2½lb monkfish, skinned and cubed*
*4 tablespoons olive oil*
*2 large green chillies, deseeded and chopped*
*2–3 cloves of garlic, crushed*
*450g/1lb tomatoes, peeled and chopped*
*1 teaspoon ground cardamom*
*1 teaspoon caster sugar*
*1 tablespoon tomato purée*
*juice of ½ lemon*
*salt*
*1 good bunch of fresh coriander*
*110g/4oz button mushrooms, thinly sliced*

**1.** Heat the oil in a large frying pan and cook the fish over a medium heat for 5–7 minutes, turning gently. Turn off the heat, remove the fish with a slotted spoon and set aside in a bowl. Leave the fish juices in the pan.

**2.** Pour any juices that have drained from the fish into the bowl back into the pan. Bring the juices to the boil and add the chillies, garlic, tomatoes, cardamom, sugar, tomato purée and lemon juice. Stir and allow to simmer over a low heat for 7–10 minutes until the tomato is soft. Season to taste with salt and turn off the heat.
**3.** Chop about three-quarters of the coriander and stir into the hot sauce. Pour the sauce over the fish in the bowl and gently mix in. Stir the mushrooms into the mixture. Leave until cold.
**4.** When the salad has cooled, pile it into a clean serving dish. Pull the whole leaves off the remaining sprigs of coriander and scatter them over the fish.

NOTE: The sauce can be made separately and used with chicken or veal dishes.

 *AUSTRALIAN/CALIFORNIAN CHARDONNAY*

# GIRARDET'S RED MULLET WITH ROSEMARY SAUCE

This recipe was published by Robert Carrier in the *Sunday Express.*

SERVES 4
*4 × 140–200g/5–7oz red mullet*
*55g/2oz butter*
*2 medium shallots, finely chopped*
*1 sprig of fresh rosemary, cut into 4*
*100ml/3½fl oz dry white wine*
*290ml/½ pint double cream*
*juice of ½ lemon*
*salt and freshly ground black pepper*
*2 tablespoons olive oil*

To garnish
*sprigs of fresh rosemary*

**1.** Prepare the mullet. Cut off the head and tail. Using a sharp kitchen knife, cut down either side of the backbone. Lift off the 2 fillets and remove the scales and remove the pin-sized bones along the centre of the fillets. Finely chop the fish livers. Chop the heads, bones and trimmings.

**2.** Make the stock: melt half the butter in a heavy saucepan, add the fish trimmings, and simmer for 2–3 minutes, pressing them into the butter with the back of a wooden spoon to extract all the juices.

**3.** Add the shallot and continue to simmer for a further 2 minutes, stirring constantly. Add the rosemary, wine and an equal quantity of water and simmer for a further 7 minutes. Remove the rosemary and discard.

**4.** Pass the stock through a fine sieve into a clean saucepan, pressing down with a wooden spoon to extract all the juices. Set the pan over a high heat and reduce the stock by boiling rapidly to half its original quantity.

**5.** Pour the reduced stock on to the cream in a bowl. Return to the pan and continue to reduce until the sauce is thick enough to coat the back of a wooden spoon, stirring frequently to prevent the sauce from catching.

**6.** Remove the pan from the heat and gradually beat in the remaining butter, a little at a time. Add the chopped fish livers and lemon juice and season to taste with salt and pepper. Keep warm.

**7.** Cook the fish fillets: heat 2 heavy frying pans. Pour half the oil into each pan and arrange 4 fillets, skin side up, in each pan. Season generously with salt and pepper. Cook gently for 2 minutes.

**8.** To serve: cover 4 warmed dinner plates with the sauce; place 2 fillets on each plate, skin uppermost, and garnish with the rosemary.

 *WHITE ALSACE*

For the sauce
*2 shallots, diced*
*100ml/3⅓fl oz red wine*
*100ml/3⅓fl oz white fish stock (see page 245)*
*55ml/2fl oz brown fish stock (see page 245)*
*55g/2oz butter, chilled and cut into cubes*

**1.** Remove any scales and pinbones from the mullet fillets (see pages 267 and 268). Season with salt and pepper.

**2.** Peel the new potatoes and cut them into cork shapes. Slice thinly. Arrange the sliced potatoes on the skinned side of the mullet to resemble scales.

**3.** Meanwhile, make the sauce: put the shallots into a saucepan with the wine and reduce by boiling rapidly until syrupy. Add the white and brown fish stock. Reduce by boiling rapidly to half the original quantity. Strain into a clean pan.

**4.** Reduce the heat under the pan. Using a wire whisk and a continuous vigorous whisking action, gradually add the butter, piece by piece. The process should take about 2 minutes and the sauce should become thick, creamy and pale.

**5.** Heat the clarified butter in a large, heavy frying pan. Pan-fry the mullet fillets, potato side down, until the potatoes are golden-brown. Turn over and cook for 2 further minutes or until the fish is just cooked (it should be opaque and firm).

**6.** To serve: place the mullet fillets on a serving plate, potato side up, and spoon around the sauce.

 *RULLY ROUGE BURGUNDY*

# RED MULLET WITH POTATO SCALES

We saw this dish demonstrated by the Cordon Bleu School at the BBC Good Food Show at Olympia.

SERVES 6 AS A FIRST COURSE
*3 × 225g/8oz red mullet, filleted (see page 267)*
*salt and freshly ground black pepper*
*22g/8oz new potatoes*
*55g/2oz butter, clarified (see page 686)*

# RED MULLET WITH FENNEL AND CHIVES

This is a very low-fat dish.

SERVES 4
*4 × 250g/8oz red mullet, filleted (see page 267)*
*the fish trimmings*
*1 litre/1³/4 pints water*
*1 stick of celery, sliced*
*1 onion, sliced*
*1 bay leaf*
*3 slices of lemon*
*6 black peppercorns*
*100ml/3¹/2fl oz dry white wine*
*1 small bulb of Florence fennel, chopped, leaves reserved*
*1 bunch of fresh chives, chopped*

**1.** Remove any scales and pinbones from the mullet fillets (see pages 267 and 268).
**2.** Clean the fish trimmings and put into a large saucepan with the water, celery, onion, bay leaf, lemon slices and peppercorns. Bring gradually up to the boil, then reduce the heat and simmer very gently for 20 minutes.
**3.** Strain, pushing the trimmings well into the bottom of the sieve to extract as much flavour as possible, into a large flat saucepan.
**4.** Put the mullet fillets into the saucepan, skin side uppermost, with the white wine and fennel, and simmer very slowly for 2 minutes.
**5.** Remove the fish with a fish slice and keep warm on a serving dish. Boil the stock rapidly until reduced to 150ml/¹/4 pint.
**6.** To serve: add the chives and pour over the fillets. Garnish with a few of the fennel leaves.

 *WHITE RHÔNE OR PROVENCE*

# GRILLED TUNA FISH STEAKS WITH GREEN CHILLI PESTO

Tuna is wonderful if carefully cooked. If overdone it becomes very dry and rather cardboard-like in texture.

SERVES 4
*4 × 170g/6oz tuna steaks, skinned (see page 267)*

For the marinade
*6 tablespoons olive oil*
*2 tablespoons balsamic vinegar*
*freshly ground black pepper*

For the chilli pesto
*2 green chillies*
*1 bunch of fresh coriander*
*55g/2oz pinenuts*
*2 cloves of garlic, crushed*
*55g/2oz Parmesan cheese, freshly grated*
*6 tablespoons olive oil*
*salt and freshly ground black pepper*

To garnish
*sprigs of fresh coriander*

**1.** Pinbone the tuna steaks (see page 268), place in a flat dish and pour over the marinade ingredients. Cover and refrigerate for 2 hours.
**2.** Preheat the grill to its highest setting.
**3.** Make the chilli pesto: slit the chillies carefully and remove the seeds. Put the chillies, coriander, pinenuts and garlic into a blender. Blend well, add the Parmesan cheese, and with the motor still running pour on the oil in a thin stream until well emulsified. Season to taste with salt and pepper.
**4.** Lift the tuna steaks from the marinade, place on the grill rack and grill for about 3 minutes on each side, until cooked (they should be opaque, lightly browned and firm but still moist).
**5.** To serve: place the tuna steaks on a serving dish, spoon the chilli pesto on top and garnish with coriander.

NOTE: Take care when handling chillies: the volatile oil contained in the juice can burn sensitive skin badly. It is a good idea to wear rubber gloves when chopping chillies.

 *CALIFORNIAN CHARDONNAY*

# ORIENTAL RED SNAPPER SALAD

SERVES 4

1.35kg/3lb whole red snapper, filleted and
   skinned
2 tablespoonfuls olive oil

For the marinade
1 teaspoon salt
2 teaspoons sugar
1 teaspoon peeled and grated fresh root ginger
1 teaspoon dry English mustard
½ teaspoon ground turmeric
1 teaspoon curry powder (see page 688)
freshly ground black pepper

For the salad
110g/4oz beanshoots
1 red pepper, deseeded and cut into strips
225g/8oz mangetout, blanched
225g/8oz baby sweetcorn, blanched
110g/4oz broccoli spears, blanched

1. Pinbone the red snapper fillets if necessary (see page 268). Cut into 5cm/2in chunks.
2. Mix all the marinade ingredients together. Coat the snapper with the marinade and leave, covered, in the refrigerator for at least 2 hours, preferably overnight.
3. Heat the oil in a wok or large frying pan and fry the marinated snapper fillets for 2–3 minutes or until just cooked through.
4. Toss the salad ingredients together with the fish and serve immediately.

NOTE: This can also be served with a hot salad. Just toss the prepared vegetables into the wok after frying the fish and heat through well. Sprinkle with a little sesame seed oil and light soy sauce.

 *NEW WORLD DRY WHITE*

# SALMON WITH FISH MOUSSELINE AND TOMATO SAUCE

SERVES 4

4 × 170g/6oz tail-end slices of fresh salmon
110g/4oz fresh salmon trimmings
2 egg yolks
150ml/¼ pint double cream
1 tablespoon Pernod
1 tablespoon very finely chopped fresh chives
salt and freshly ground white pepper
freshly grated nutmeg

For the sauce
1 shallot, very finely chopped
225ml/8fl oz dry white wine
2 large tomatoes, peeled and deseeded
tomato purée
15g/½oz butter

To garnish
1 small bunch of fresh chervil

1. Prepare the salmon slices: cut them in half horizontally and remove any grey flesh. Place each one between two pieces of clingfilm and batter them slightly so that they increase their size by about a quarter.
2. You should now have 8 thin pieces of salmon shaped like flattened triangles.
3. Now prepare the mousse filling. Put the salmon trimmings into a food processor with the egg yolks. Process quickly, then add half the cream and process again. Season with the Pernod, chives, salt, pepper and nutmeg. Chill in the refrigerator for 20 minutes.
4. Preheat the oven to 180°C/350°F/gas mark 4.
5. Divide the filling between the 8 pieces of salmon and roll them up.
6. Put the salmon cones into a lightly greased baking dish. Sprinkle with the shallot, pour over the wine, cover and bake for 10 minutes.
7. Meanwhile, cut the tomatoes into julienne strips and leave to drain in a sieve.
8. Remove the salmon fillets to a warm place while you make the sauce.
9. Reduce the cooking liquor by boiling rapidly, then add a little tomato purée and the remaining cream. The sauce should be fairly thin.

**10.** Melt the butter in a frying pan and heat the tomatoes through very quickly.

**11.** Partially flood the base of 4 dinner plates with the sauce. Slice the salmon and arrange on the plates. Garnish with the warm tomatoes and the chervil leaves.

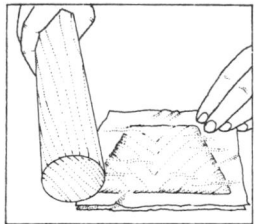

*The pieces of salmon should be shaped like flattened triangles*

SANCERRE/POUILLY-FUME

## SALMON IN FILO PASTRY WITH WATERCRESS

This recipe is similar to a Moroccan Bstilla dish.

SERVES 6
*110g/4oz watercress, trimmed*
*8 eggs*
*55ml/2fl oz single cream*
*100ml/3½fl oz fish stock (see page 245)*
*salt and freshly ground black pepper*
*olive oil*
*400g/14oz filo pastry*
*1 tablespoon cumin seeds, dry-dried*
*900g/2lb salmon fillets, skinned*
*1 tablespoon lemon juice*

**1.** Place the watercress in a sieve and immerse in boiling water to blanch it. Remove after 2 seconds and refresh under cold running water. Drain well.

**2.** Place the watercress, eggs, cream, fish stock, salt and pepper in a blender and liquidize until smooth and pale green. Pour into a small saucepan and stir over a low heat until the mixture is creamy and nearly set. It will be very slightly scrambled.

**3.** Preheat the oven to 400°F/200°C/gas mark 6.

**4.** Brush an ovenproof dish large enough to take the salmon in one layer with oil. Line the dish with a sheet of filo pastry (there will be a lot of overlap). Brush the pastry with oil. Cover with a further 5 sheets of oiled filo. Bake in the preheated oven for 5 minutes.

**5.** Sprinkle with the cumin seeds and spoon over half the watercress mousseline.

**6.** Lay the salmon on top of the watercress in a single layer. Sprinkle with pepper and lemon juice. Spoon over the remaining watercress mousseline. Smooth the surface.

**7.** Arrange 4 sheets of filo pastry on top of the watercress cream, brushing with oil as you go. Fold over the overlapping piece of pastry, trim to get a good fit, brush with more oil and cover with the last sheet of filo. Brush with oil. Score the surface of the pastry into diamond shapes.

**8.** Bake in the preheated oven for 35–40 minutes until golden brown. Serve hot or cold.

CRISP DRY WHITE

## NOISETTES OF SALMON WITH SAFFRON SAUCE AND DILL PESTO

SERVES 4
*4 × 170g/6oz salmon cutlets, cut 3.5cm/1½in*
  *thick*
*1 tablespoon oil*
*salt and freshly ground black pepper*
*1 quantity dill pesto (see page 255)*

For the saffron sauce
*100ml/3½fl oz dry white wine*
*1 shallot, finely chopped*
*½ teaspoon saffron filaments*
*150ml/¼ pint double cream*
*salt and freshly ground black pepper*

To garnish
*sprigs of fresh dill*

**1.** Prepare the salmon noisettes: carefully remove the bones from the cutlets. Using a sharp knife, slice the skin away from the flesh halfway round the cutlet. Fold the skinned piece of fish into the centre and wrap the rest of the cutlet round the outside. Tie with string. Press the noisettes between 2 plates and chill in the refrigerator for at least 1 hour.

**2.** Preheat the grill to its highest setting.

**3.** Make the saffron sauce: put the wine, shallot and saffron into a saucepan. Bring to the boil, then lower the heat and simmer until the wine is reduced to half its original quantity. Add the cream and reduce until syrupy by boiling rapidly. Season to taste with salt and pepper.

**4.** Brush the salmon noisettes on both sides with oil and season with salt and pepper. Grill the salmon noisettes for about 4 minutes on each side or until cooked (they should be opaque and firm).

**5.** To serve: remove the string and skin and arrange the salmon noisettes on 4 dinner plates. Spoon a little of the saffron sauce around one side and a little pesto around the other. Garnish each salmon noisette with a sprig of dill.

 *CHILEAN SAUVIGNON BLANC*

# SALMON STEAKS WITH TOMATO AND BASIL

SERVES 4
*4 × 170g/6oz salmon steaks*
*sunflower oil*
*10 tomatoes, roughly chopped*
*1 onion, chopped*
*2 tablespoons water*
*2 tablespoons chopped fresh basil*
*55g/2oz pinenuts*
*5 spring onions, chopped*

**1.** Wipe the salmon steaks. Cut 4 circles of kitchen foil, each large enough to wrap a salmon steak. Brush with oil. Put a salmon steak on top of each circle of foil. Preheat the oven to 180°C/350°F/gas mark 4.

**2.** Put the tomatoes into a large saucepan with the onion and water. Cook over a very low heat until quite a lot of liquid seeps out of the tomatoes. Increase the heat and simmer for 15 minutes. Liquidize in a blender, then push through a sieve into a clean saucepan. Reduce, by rapid boiling,

to a thick consistency, Remove from the heat and allow to cool slightly, then add the basil.

**3.** Divide the tomato mixture between the salmon steaks, wrap up in the foil and bake in the preheated oven for 15–20 minutes.

**4.** Meanwhile, cook the pinenuts in a little oil, being careful not to let them burn.

**5.** Just before serving, open the parcels slightly and sprinkle each one first with pinenuts and then with the spring onions.

 *FULL DRY WHITE*

# SUMMER SALMON EN PAPILLOTE WITH LIME AND CHIVES

SERVES 4
*8 × 85g/3oz thin slices of salmon fillet*
*oil*
*8 tomatoes, peeled and thinly sliced*
*salt and freshly ground black pepper*
*2 limes*
*1 small bunch of fresh chives, very finely chopped*
*55g/2oz butter, melted*
*2 tablespoons dry white wine*
*lime beurre blanc (see page 254)*

To garnish
*4 small sprigs of watercress*

**1.** Preheat the oven to 220°C/425°F/gas mark 7. Cut out 8 × 20cm/8in circles of kitchen foil. Brush with oil.

**2.** Sandwich the fillets of salmon with the tomato slices. Season well with salt and pepper.

**3.** Place each salmon sandwich on one half of a circle of foil.

**4.** Slice one of the limes into eighths and squeeze the juice from the second lime.

**5.** Put 2 slices of lime and a sprinkling of chives on each salmon sandwich and sprinkle with the lime juice, melted butter and wine.

**6.** Fold over the foil to make a parcel rather like an apple turnover. There must be space inside for circulation of air. Twist and press hard to make a good seal.

**7.** Lightly brush a baking sheet with oil and put it into the preheated oven for 5 minutes to heat. Then carefully put the papillotes on the baking sheet, taking care that they do not touch each other. Bake in the oven for 12 minutes.

**8.** Unwrap the salmon sandwiches and place on warmed dinner plates. Garnish with small sprigs of watercress. Hand the sauce separately.

 *CALIFORNIAN SAUVIGNON BLANC*

# SALMON MAYONNAISE

The recipe is for boned salmon mayonnaise. It is an excellent idea to bone the salmon for a large party as it makes it easy to serve.

*1 whole salmon, cleaned*

For the court bouillon
*150ml/¼ pint white wine vinegar*
*3 bay leaves*
*1 onion, sliced*
*1 large bunch of fresh parsley*
*1 carrot, peeled and sliced*
*12 black peppercorns*
*1 teaspoon salt*

To garnish
*cucumber slices, blanched*
*lemon wedges*
*1 bunch of watercress, trimmed*
*290ml/½ pint mayonnaise (see page 250)*

**1.** Half fill a fish kettle with water and add the remaining court bouillon ingredients. Simmer together for 20 minutes. Strain and cool.

**2.** Put the salmon into the cold court bouillon and bring slowly to the boil. Poach gently for 5 minutes.

**3.** Remove from the heat and leave the fish to cook and cool in the cooking liquid. Check it every 10 minutes or so and when the salmon is cooked, remove it carefully and leave to get cold. The salmon is cooked when the eyes are cloudy, the skin lifts easily and the flesh is opaque.

**4.** Tidy up the salmon and remove the fins. Skin the top half of the salmon, leaving the head and

eyes intact. Lift off the 2 top fish fillets and turn them over on to a serving plate so that they are skinned side down. Remove any remaining little bones.

**5.** Cut the backbone out from the 2 bottom fillets and remove any remaining little bones. Lift the bottom fillets and turn them over on to the top fillets to reassemble the fish. Skin the 2 top fillets.

**6.** Now garnish the salmon as you wish, using cucumber slices, lemon wedges and watercress. Hand the mayonnaise separately.

NOTE: Starting with a cooled court bouillon is considered to produce moister flesh, but it is not always practicable. If the fish has to be put into a hot court bouillon allow about 6 minutes for every 450g/1lb and remove as soon as it is cooked.

 *SANCERRE/POUILLY-FUMÉ*

# SALMON EN CROÛTE

SERVES 10
*1 × 2.3 kg/5lb salmon*
*450g/1lb flour quantity puff pastry (see page 464)*
*a few tablespoons fine semolina*
*butter*
*lemon juice*
*tarragon leaves*
*freshly ground white pepper and salt*
*beaten egg, to glaze*

For the stock
*bones, skin and head from the salmon*
*2 slices of onion*
*1 bay leaf*
*1 small bunch of fresh parsley*
*6 black peppercorns*
*salt*
*water*

For the sauce
*55g/2oz butter*
*20g/¾oz plain flour*
*290ml/½ pint fish stock (see page 245)*
*55ml/2fl oz dry white wine*
*1 teaspoon chopped fresh tarragon or parsley*
*2 tablespoons double cream*
*salt and freshly ground white pepper*

1. Fillet the salmon, keeping the 4 fillets as intact as possible. Skin the fillets.

2. Use the bones and other trimmings for the stock. Put all the ingredients for the stock into a saucepan and simmer for 30 minutes. Strain, measure, and reduce, by boiling to 290ml/½ pint.

3. Preheat the oven to 230°C/450°F/gas mark 8.

4. Roll out a third of the pastry into a long, narrow rectangle, about the thickness of a £1 coin. Cut it to roughly the size and shape of the original salmon.

5. Place on a damp baking sheet, and prick all over with a fork. Leave to relax in a cool place for 15 minutes. Bake it in the preheated oven until the pastry is brown and crisp. If, when you turn it over, it is soggy underneath, put it back in the oven, soggy side up, for a few minutes. Allow to cool.

6. Sprinkle the cooked pastry evenly with semolina to prevent the fish juices making the pastry soggy.

7. Reassemble the salmon fillets on the cooked pastry, dotting them with plenty of butter and sprinkling with lemon juice, tarragon, salt and pepper as you go.

8. Roll out the remaining pastry into a large sheet, slightly thinner than the base, and lay it over the salmon. Cut round the fish, leaving a good 2.5cm/1in border beyond the edge of the bottom layer of pastry. Carefully tuck the top sheet under the cooked pastry, shaping the head and tail of the fish carefully.

9. Brush with beaten egg. Using the back of a knife, mark the pastry in a criss-cross pattern to represent fish scales, or mark scales with the rounded end of a teaspoon. Cut some pastry trimmings into fine strips and use them to emphasize the tail fins and gills, and use a circle of pastry for the eye. Brush again with beaten egg.

10. Bake in the oven for 15 minutes to brown and puff up the pastry, then turn down the oven temperature to 150°C/300°F/gas mark 2 for a further 30 minutes to cook the fish. Cover the crust with damp greaseproof paper if the pastry looks in danger of over-browning. To test if the fish is cooked, push a fine skewer through the pastry and fish from the side: it should glide in easily.

11. Make the sauce, melt half the butter in a saucepan, add the flour and cook, stirring, for 1 minute or until the butter and flour are pale biscuit-coloured and foaming. Remove from the heat, then add the stock and wine. Return to the heat and stir until boiling and smooth. Boil rapidly until you have a sauce of coating consistency.

12. Add the tarragon or parsley and the cream. Season to taste with salt and pepper. Beat in the remaining butter, piece by piece. Pour into a warmed sauceboat.

13. Slide the salmon en croûte on to a board or salmon dish.

14. Hand the sauce separately.

 *WHITE BURGUNDY*

# SALMON KOULIBIAC

This is a simple version of a classic dish normally made with brioche dough.

SERVES 4
*110g/4oz long-grain rice*
*170g/6oz flour quantity rough puff pastry (see page 463)*
*55g/2oz butter*
*1 onion, finely diced*
*30g/1oz mushrooms, chopped*
*1 tablespoon chopped fresh parsley*
*juice of ½ lemon*
*285/10oz cooked salmon, flaked*
*2 hardboiled eggs, roughly chopped*
*salt and freshly ground black pepper*
*1 egg, beaten with a pinch of salt, to glaze*

1. Preheat the oven to 200°C/400°F/gas mark 6.

2. Cook the rice in a large saucepan of boiling water for 10–12 minutes. Drain in a colander or sieve and swish plenty of hot water through it. Stand the colander on the draining board. With the handle of a wooden spoon, make a few draining holes through the pile of rice to help the water and steam escape. Leave for 30 minutes.

3. Roll a third of the pastry into a rectangle as thick as a £1 coin. Leave to relax in the refrigerator for 10 minutes.

4. Place the pastry on a damp baking sheet. Prick lightly all over with a fork and bake in the preheated oven for about 15 minutes, until

golden-brown. Transfer to a wire rack and leave to cool but do not turn the oven off. Rinse the baking sheet under cold running water until cool.

**5.** Melt the butter over a medium heat and add the onion. When nearly cooked add the mushrooms and cook gently for 1 minute.

**6.** Put the cooked rice into a bowl and fork in the onion, mushrooms, parsley, lemon juice, salmon, eggs and plenty of salt and pepper.

**7.** Place the cooled pastry base on the damp baking sheet and pile on the rice mixture. Shape it with your hands into a neat mound, making sure that it covers the base completely.

**8.** Roll the remaining pastry into a blanket large enough to cover the mixture with an overlap of 2.5cm/1in. Using a sharp knife, cut the corners off the blanket at right angles to the cooked base. Working carefully with a palette knife, lift the base and tuck the pastry blanket underneath it. Brush with beaten egg to seal. Repeat with the other 3 sides. Refrigerate for 10 minutes.

**9.** Meanwhile, shape the discarded pastry corners into leaves, marking the veins and stem with the back of a knife.

**10.** Brush the koulibiac with more beaten egg, decorate with the pastry leaves and brush again with egg. Bake in the oven for 30 minutes, until the pastry is golden-brown. Serve hot or cold.

NOTES: If a sauce is required, serve plain soured cream, seasoned with salt and pepper.

This is also delicious made with cooked chicken instead of salmon.

 *WHITE BURGUNDY*

# FLAT SALMON PIE

SERVES 4
*450g/16oz flour quantity pâte à pâte (see page 467)*
*55g/2oz Gruyère or Cheddar cheese, grated*
*30g/1oz Parmesan cheese, grated*
*85g/3oz unsalted butter, melted*
*55g/2oz fresh white breadcrumbs*
*225g/8oz smoked salmon, chopped*
*2 tablespoons chopped fresh dill*
*1 large clove of garlic, crushed*

*150ml/¼ pint soured cream*
*freshly ground black pepper*
*lemon juice*
*beaten egg to glaze*

**1.** Roll out the pâte à pâte into 2 rectangles, one to fit a Swiss roll tin, the other slightly larger.

**2.** Preheat the oven to 200°C/400°F/gas mark 6.

**3.** Lightly grease and flour the back of a Swiss roll tin or baking sheet. Put the smaller rectangle of pastry on it and prick all over with a fork. Bake in the preheated oven for 15 minutes until half-cooked. Loosen it on the baking sheet so that it does not stick and leave to cool.

**4.** Mix together the Gruyère or Cheddar cheese, the Parmesan, the melted butter and the breadcrumbs. Sprinkle half of this mixture all over the half-cooked pastry, leaving 1cm/½in clear round the edge.

**5.** Scatter the smoked salmon on top of the cheese mixture. Then scatter over the dill.

**6.** Mix the garlic with the soured cream and spread all over the salmon. Season well with pepper but not salt.

**7.** Sprinkle evenly with lemon juice and top with the remaining cheese mixture. Wet the edge of the bottom piece of pastry lightly with beaten egg and put the top sheet of pastry in place, pressing the edges to seal it well.

**8.** Use any pastry trimmings to decorate the pie and brush all over with beaten egg.

**9.** Bake until the pastry is crisp and pale brown. Serve hot or cold.

NOTE: Off-cuts and trimmings of smoked salmon can be bought more cheaply than slices, and do well for this dish.

 *ALSACE RIESLING*

# SALMON FISH CAKES

SERVES 4

*450g/1lb cooked salmon, flaked*
*340g/12oz mashed potatoes (see page 212)*
*salt and freshly ground black pepper*
*30g/1oz butter, melted*
*1 tablespoon chopped fresh parsley*
*2 eggs, beaten*
*dried white breadcrumbs*
*6 tablespoons oil for frying*
*290ml/1/2 pint parsley sauce (see page 248)*

To serve
*lemon wedges*

1. Mix the salmon and potato together. Season well with salt and pepper.
2. Add the melted butter, parsley and enough beaten egg to bind the mixture until soft but not sloppy. Allow to cool.
3. Flour your hands and shape the mixture into 8 flat cakes 2.5cm/1in thick. Brush with beaten egg and coat with breadcrumbs.
4. Heat the oil in a frying pan and fry until the fish cakes are brown on both sides.
5. Serve with parsley sauce and lemon wedges.

 *DRY WHITE*

# GRILLED GRAVAD LAX WITH SAFFRON NOODLES

SERVES 6

*900g/2lb salmon fillets*
*170g/6oz sea salt*
*170g/6oz caster sugar*
*15g/1/2oz white peppercorns, freshly ground*
*1 bunch of fresh dill, chopped*

To serve
*saffron noodles (see page 471)*
*55g/2oz butter, melted*
*salt and freshly ground black pepper*
*200ml/7fl oz crème fraîche*

To garnish
*1 bunch of fresh chives, chopped*

1. Make sure all the bones are removed from the salmon.
2. Mix the salt, sugar and pepper together. Lay half the dill in the bottom of a non-metallic dish large enough to hold the salmon fillets. Sprinkle half the salt and sugar mixture evenly over the dill.
3. Place the salmon fillets, flesh side down, on top of the cure. Cover with the remaining dill, salt and sugar. Cover tightly and refrigerate for 24 hours.
4. Remove the salmon from the cure, scrape off the dill and cure, and pat the fish dry with kitchen paper. Remove the skin and slice the fish on the diagonal into pieces 5mm/1/4in thick.
5. Preheat the grill and place a sheet of well-buttered kitchen foil on the top of the grill pan. Place the salmon slices on the foil and grill very quickly on one side so that the salmon is barely cooked.
6. Meanwhile, boil the pasta in plenty of boiling salted water for about 5–6 minutes until *al dente*. Drain well, toss with melted butter and season with salt and pepper.
7. Place a pile of noodles on 6 warmed dinner plates and arrange 3 slices of grilled salmon on top. Spoon on the crème fraîche and sprinkle with the chives. Serve immediately.

 *CHARDONNAY*

# SALMON AND PLAICE RAVIOLI WITH BASIL SAUCE

The egg whites and cream can be added in the food processor but they must be very cold and not over-beaten. If too warm the mixture will split (curdle) and there is no way to rescue it. The described method is foolproof.

SERVES 4

*1 egg quantity pasta dough (see page 470)*

For the filling
*55g/2oz salmon fillet, skinned*
*55g/2oz plaice fillet, skinned*
*5mm/1/4in piece of fresh root ginger, peeled and*
   *chopped*

Salad of Roast Tomatoes and Spring Onions.

Above: Dry-fried Prawns with Coriander. Right: Sea Bass with Black Bean Sauce.

Left: Skate with Spinach and Bacon. Above: Steamed Trout Fillets with Tomato and Ginger Sauce.

Above: Chicken with Prunes. Right: Mustard Grilled Chicken.

Left: Warm Chicken Salad. Above: Stuffed Boned Duck.

Above: Venison with Lemon and Redcurrant Sauce and Rösti Potatoes. Right: Partridge with Lentils.

Left: Cold Game Pie with Orange and Endive Salad. Above: Steak and Kidney Pudding.

Above: Gaeng Ped Nua (Spicy Red Beef). Right: Bacon Noisettes with Sweet Onion Purée.

Above: Lamb Steak à la Catalane with Lentils.

a squeeze of lemon juice
salt and freshly ground white pepper
1 egg white
120ml/4fl oz double cream, chilled
½ teaspoon ground mace

For the sauce
170ml/6fl oz extra virgin olive oil
1 large clove of garlic, peeled and very thinly sliced
2 tomatoes, peeled, deseeded and finely diced
1 squeeze of lemon juice
10 fresh basil leaves, torn

1. Make the pasta and leave to relax, covered in clingfilm.
2. Put the salmon, plaice, ginger and lemon juice into a food processor and pound well or chop finely, then push through a sieve. (This is quite a task.)
3. Put the fish into a bowl. Season with salt and pepper and set in a roasting pan of ice to keep the mixture chilled. Beat well, gradually adding the egg white, then the cream, making sure that the mixture does not become too runny. It should hold its shape. Season to taste with mace, and more salt and pepper if necessary. Refrigerate until ready to use.
4. Roll out the pasta very thinly into a square. Brush lightly with water. Place teaspoonfuls of filling at intervals of 3cm/1½in in even rows over half the pasta. Fold the other half of the pasta over the mounds of fish mousseline. Press together, firming all round each mound of filling. Cut between the rows, making sure that the edges are sealed. Set aside.
5. Put a large saucepan of salted water on to boil.
6. Make the sauce: heat the oil in a saucepan, add the garlic and leave to cook very slowly for about 3–4 minutes.
7. Add the tomatoes, lemon juice, salt and pepper. Warm through for 2 minutes, then add the basil.
8. Cook the ravioli in the simmering water for 3–4 minutes. Drain well.
9. Serve the ravioli with the basil and olive oil sauce drizzled over the top.

 *DRY WHITE*

# TARTARE OF SALMON AND TUNA

This recipe is taken from *New American Classic Cookery* by Jeremiah Towers.

SERVES 4
1 cucumber
salt and freshly ground white pepper
120ml/4fl oz fresh lemon juice
2 tablespoons sesame oil
225g/8oz salmon fillet, skinned
225g/8oz tuna fillet, skinned, all dark meat
    removed
2 tablespoons olive oil
4 tomatoes, peeled, deseeded and finely chopped

To garnish
rocket and chopped fresh chives

1. Peel the cucumber and cut into very thin slices. Whisk salt and pepper into half the lemon juice; then whisk in the sesame oil. Toss the cucumber slices in the sauce and leave to stand for 1 hour.
2. Finely chop the salmon and tuna separately. Into each chopped fish stir half the remaining lemon juice, a tablespoon of olive oil and salt and pepper to taste.
3. To serve: arrange the cucumber on 4 dinner plates with the slices overlapping. Spoon the 2 fish tartares in separate mounds in the centre of each plate.
4. Toss the chopped tomato with the marinated cucumber and divide between the plates. Garnish with rocket and chives.

 *CALIFORNIAN SAUVIGNON*

# GRILLED SARDINES

SERVES 4
16 small or 8 large fresh sardines
oil
freshly ground black pepper
lemon juice

To garnish
chopped fresh parsley

1. Clean the sardines: slit them along the belly and remove the entrails. Rinse the fish under cold running water and with a little salt gently rub away any black matter in the cavity. Cut off the gills.
2. Preheat the grill. Score the fish with 3–4 shallow diagonal cuts on each side, brush with oil, season with pepper and sprinkle with lemon juice.
3. Grill for about 2 minutes on each side, brushing with the hot oil and the juices that run from the fish.
4. Lay the sardines on a warmed serving platter. Pour over the juices from the grill pan, sprinkle with parsley and serve immediately.

 *CRISP DRY WHITE*

# DEEP-FRIED WHITEBAIT

SERVES 4
450g/1lb whitebait
oil for deep-frying
seasoned plain flour

To serve
lemon wedges
cayenne pepper

1. Sort through the whitebait, discarding any broken fish.
2. Heat the oil in a deep-fryer until a crumb will sizzle vigorously in it.
3. Put the whitebait into a sieve and spoon over the seasoned flour. Shake and toss carefully until every fish is coated. Do this in batches if necessary.

4. Place a small handful of whitebait (too many will stick together) into the hot oil and fry for no more than 2 minutes. Remove and repeat until all the fish are fried. They should be crisp and pale brown.
5. Drain on absorbent kitchen paper. Serve immediately with lemon wedges and offer cayenne pepper.

NOTE: If for any reason the whitebait cannot be served immediately, they should be spread out in a thin layer on a baking sheet and kept, uncovered, in a just-warm oven until wanted. They will become soggy if piled up or covered.

 *WHITE LOIRE*

# SEA BASS WITH BLACK BEAN SAUCE

A 1.85kg/4lb sea bass sounds like a huge amount for 6 people, but its very deliciousness necessitates such generosity! Black beans can be bought from Chinese supermarkets in tins or vacuum packs. If you like, the sauce can be thickened at the end with 2 teaspoons cornflour.

SERVES 6
1 tablespoon sunflower oil
1 × 1.8kg/4lb sea bass, cleaned and scaled
salt and freshly ground black pepper
4 slices of lemon

To serve
spring onion bows (see page 685)
black bean sauce (see page 259)

1. Preheat the oven to 190°C/375°F/gas mark 5.
2. Brush a large piece of kitchen foil with the oil. Place the fish on it, season with salt and pepper, cover with the lemon slices, wrap up loosely, but secure the edges firmly, and place on a baking sheet
3. Bake in the preheated oven for 40 minutes.
4. Remove from the foil wrapping to a warmed serving dish, garnish with the spring onion bows, dribble over a little of the sauce and hand the rest separately.

 *WHITE BURGUNDY*

# SEA BASS WITH WILD RICE

SERVES 4

*1 × 1.25kg/3lb sea bass, cleaned and scaled*
*lemon juice*
*freshly ground black pepper*
*55g/2oz brown rice, soaked overnight*
*55g/2oz wild rice*
*30g/1oz pinenuts, browned*
*30g/1oz sultanas*
*1 tablespoon chopped fresh dill*
*oil for greasing*
*1 onion, sliced*
*1 bay leaf*
*2 tablespoons dry white wine*

To garnish
*bunch of watercress, trimmed*

**1.** Preheat the oven to 180°C/350°F/gas mark 4.
**2.** Season the inside of the sea bass with a little lemon juice and pepper. Wash both the rices very well and cook them for 30 minutes in plenty of boiling water. Drain and rinse them under cold running water until they are completely cold. Drain them well. Add the pinenuts, sultanas and dill. Season to taste with salt and pepper.
**3.** Put the sea bass on a sheet of well-oiled kitchen foil and stuff the cavity with the rice mixture. Scatter the onion over the fish, add the bay leaf and sprinkle on the wine. Draw the foil up to make a parcel.
**4.** Place the parcel on a large baking sheet and bake in the preheated oven for 40–50 minutes. Serve hot or cold, garnished with watercress.

 *WHITE BURGUNDY*

# SKATE WITH BROWN BUTTER AND CAPERS

SERVES 4

*900g/2lb skate wing*
*570ml/1 pint court bouillon (see page 245)*
*75g/3oz unsalted butter*
*1 tablespoon lemon juice*
*1 tablespoon capers, rinsed and roughly chopped*

**1.** Wash the skate and divide into 4 portions.
**2.** Place the skate in the cold court bouillon in a shallow pan. Cover with a lid and bring slowly to the boil. Poach very gently for 15–20 minutes.
**3.** Remove the fish and drain on absorbent kitchen paper. Gently scrape away any skin. Place the skate on a warmed serving dish and keep warm in a low oven while you make the sauce.
**4.** Pour off the court bouillon, reheat the pan and melt the butter. When the butter is foaming and a rich golden brown, remove the pan from the heat, add the lemon juice and capers and pour over the skate.

 *VERY DRY WHITE*

# SKATE WITH SPINACH AND BACON

SERVES 2

*55g/2oz button mushrooms*
*15g/1/2oz fresh flat-leaf parsley, chopped*
*15g/1/2oz butter*
*juice of 1/2 lemon*
*salt and freshly ground black pepper*
*1 skate wing, filleted into 2*
*4 rashers of rindless streaky bacon*
*1 small piece of pig's caul, about 30cm/12in square*
*oil*
*2 cloves of garlic*
*2 tablespoons balsamic vinegar*
*150ml/1/4 pint white stock, made with chicken bones (see page 243)*

For the spinach
*450g/1lb fresh spinach, cooked and chopped*
*30g/1oz butter*
*1 clove of garlic, crushed*

**1.** Preheat the oven to 200°C/400°F/gas mark 6.
**2.** Sauté the mushrooms and half the parsley in the butter. Add the lemon juice and season to taste with salt and pepper.
**3.** Divide the mushroom mixture between the 2 fillets and roll each up into a ball. Wrap in the bacon and then in the caul. Secure, if necessary, with a cocktail stick.
**4.** Heat a little oil in a flameproof casserole and add the skate balls and the garlic. Sauté until the bacon is golden.

291

**5.** Cover and cook in the preheated oven for 15–20 minutes. Remove the cocktail sticks, if used.
**6.** Put the casserole back on the heat. Add the vinegar and reduce by half. Then add the chicken stock and reduce by half again. Add the remaining parsley.
**7.** Sauté the spinach in the butter and garlic.
**8.** Put the spinach on 2 plates, arrange the skate on top and pour over the reduced vinegar and stock.

 *CRISP DRY WHITE*

# SOLE AU GRATIN

This recipe was given to us by Mrs Levis of the Sign of the Angel in Lacock. The dish should be prepared 24 hours in advance.

SERVES 4
*3 soles, filleted and skinned*
*5 tablespoons sunflower oil*
*1 lemon, quartered*
*1 large sprig of fresh tarragon*
*15g/¹/₂oz butter, melted*
*grated cheese*
*dried white breadcrumbs*

To garnish
*lemon wedges*
*sprigs of fresh parsley*

**1.** Arrange the sole fillets, skinned side downwards, in a shallow dish. Pour over the oil. Lightly squeeze the lemon quarters over the soles, and leave them in the dish. Place the tarragon over the fish and leave to marinate for 24 hours.
**2.** Preheat the grill to a high setting.
**3.** Brush a large baking tray with a good lip with the melted butter. Arrange the sole fillets on top. Dust evenly with the cheese and crumbs and grill until golden-brown.
**4.** Arrange on warmed dinner plates and garnish with the lemon wedges and parsley.

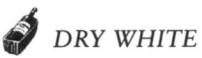 *DRY WHITE*

# SOLE BONNE FEMME

SERVES 4
*70g/2¹/₂oz butter*
*1 shallot, finely chopped*
*170g/6oz mushrooms, thinly sliced*
*290ml/¹/₂ pint hot fish stock (see page 245), made from the trimmings*
*100ml/3¹/₂fl oz dry white wine*
*¹/₂ teaspoon lemon juice*
*3 medium soles, skinned and filleted*
*salt and freshly ground white pepper*
*15g/¹/₂oz plain flour*
*150ml/¹/₄ pint double cream*

**1.** Preheat the oven to 180°C/350°F/gas mark 4.
**2.** Melt 15g/¹/₂oz of the butter in a frying pan, add the shallots and mushrooms and cook over a low heat for 10 minutes, or until the shallots are soft. Add the stock and wine and reduce, by boiling rapidly, to half its original quantity. Add the lemon juice.
**3.** Put the shallots and mushrooms into the bottom of an ovenproof dish. Arrange the sole fillets, folding the ends underneath, on top. Season with salt and pepper. Cover with a lid and bake in the preheated oven for 10–15 minutes.
**4.** Lift the fillets on to a plate and keep warm. Strain the cooking liquor into a saucepan and reserve the mushrooms as a garnish.
**5.** Reduce the fish liquor to 125ml/4fl oz by boiling rapidly.
**6.** Melt 30g/1oz of the remaining butter, add the flour and cook for 30 seconds. Remove from the heat and add the fish fumet (reduced fish stock). Stir well, return to the heat and bring slowly to the boil, stirring continuously until very thick.
**7.** Cut the remaining butter into small cubes. Gradually beat the double cream into the fish sauce – if it looks as though it might curdle, beat it vigorously. Remove the sauce from the heat and gradually beat in the cubes of butter to make it shiny. The sauce should now be of coating consistency, but if it is too thick a little milk can be added. Season to taste with salt, pepper and lemon juice.
**8.** Reheat the mushrooms. Arrange the fish fillets on a warmed serving dish. Coat the fish with the cream sauce, spoon the mushrooms down the centre and serve.

 *CHABLIS*

# SOLE WITH MUSTARD AND BACON

SERVES 4
*12 lemon or Dover sole fillets*
*Dijon mustard*
*4 thin rashers of rindless smoked back bacon*
*290ml/½ pint fish stock (see page 245)*
*1 large onion, chopped*
*8 tomatoes, chopped*
*10 fresh sage leaves, roughly chopped*
*salt and freshly ground black pepper*
*3 tablespoons Greek yoghurt*
*fish glaze to season (see page 245)*

**1.** Spread the skinned side of each sole fillet with a very little mustard. Fold into neat parcels, skinned side inside.
**2.** Cover each sole parcel with a bacon rasher and set aside.
**3.** Meanwhile, make the sauce: put the stock, onion, tomatoes, sage, salt and pepper into a saucepan and simmer for 30 minutes. Remove from the heat and allow to cool.
**4.** Liquidize the sauce ingredients very well in a blender until smooth; then pass through a sieve. Return to the rinsed-out pan and boil rapidly, stirring frequently, to a purée. Remove from the heat. Add the yoghurt and taste. It may be necessary to add a little extra fish glaze.
**5.** Grill the fillets of sole, bacon side up, for 4 minutes. Arrange on a warmed serving dish and hand the sauce separately.

 *FULL DRY WHITE*

# FILLETS OF SOLE MEUNIÈRE

SERVES 4
*3 lemon soles, skinned and filleted*
*seasoned plain flour*
*55g/2oz butter, clarified (see page 686)*
*1 tablespoon chopped fresh mixed herbs,*
*    including parsley*
*lemon juice*

To serve
*lemon wedges*

**1.** Wash the sole fillets, dry thoroughly, and roll in the seasoned flour.
**2.** Melt half the butter in a heavy frying pan and when foaming add the fillets skinned side uppermost. Cook over a medium heat until lightly browned, turn over and brown on the other side.
**3.** Slide the fish on to a plate, with the butter from the pan, and keep warm.
**4.** Wipe the pan very well, removing any bits of fish. Melt the remaining butter in the pan, heat until a delicate brown, cool slightly and add the herbs and lemon juice. Pour over the fish and serve immediately with the lemon wedges.

 *DRY WHITE*

# SOLE COLBERT

In this recipe, the backbone of the fish is loosened while it is raw and removed after cooking.

SERVES 4
*4 × 340g/12oz Dover soles*
*seasoned plain flour*
*beaten egg*
*dried white breadcrumbs*
*oil or deep-frying*
*110g/4oz maître d'hôtel butter (see page 263)*

To serve
*lemon wedges*

**1.** Skin and trim the soles, leaving the heads on. With a small sharp knife make a cut on the side of the fish that had the black skin, down the centre through the flesh to the backbone. Working from the centre of the fish, lift the fillets, loosening them with a knife, and snip the bone just below the head and above the tail.
**2.** Dip the fish in seasoned flour, shaking away any excess. Brush with beaten egg and press on the breadcrumbs. Be sure to egg-and-crumb the underside of the raised fillets.
**3.** Heat the oil in a deep fryer until a crumb will sizzle in it. Fry the whole fish until a good golden-brown, holding it down with a fish slice to

prevent it curling up. Drain well on absorbent kitchen paper.

**4.** Allow to settle for 1–2 minutes. Then carefully pull out the backbone, cutting round the breadcrumb coating to prevent too much of it being pulled off.

**5.** Fill the cavity with slivers of maître d'hôtel butter. Serve immediately with lemon wedges.

NOTE: For a light lunch dish or first course 'slip' soles are suitable. They weigh 170–225g/6–8oz.

 *WHITE BURGUNDY*

# GRILLED DOVER SOLE

*1 Dover sole per person*
*melted butter*
*salt and freshly ground black pepper*
*lemon juice*

**1.** Make a cut in the belly (near the head) of each fish and remove the entrails. Wash the fish thoroughly in cold water.

**2.** Now skin the fish: place the fish on a piece of greaseproof paper and pour a little pile of salt beside it. Snip off the fins with scissors. Make a cut across the black skin just above the tail with a sharp knife, being careful to cut only the skin and not the flesh. Dip your thumb and index finger in the salt and then gently work them under the black skin from the tail upwards until you have raised enough of the skin to be able to take a firm grasp of it. The salt prevents the skin slipping out of your grasp. Using a tea towel to help get a firm grip, pull the skin off the fish in one sharp tug. Repeat on the other (pale) side. This will prove rather more difficult, and is not strictly necessary.

**3.** Preheat the grill. Brush both the grill pan and one side of the fish with melted butter. Season with salt, pepper and lemon juice and place under the hot grill for about 4 minutes. Turn over and brush the second side with butter. Grill again.

NOTES: This method of skinning a flat fish does not work very well for lemon soles.

Alternatively, the fish can be grilled by dipping them in melted butter and then seasoned flour, which makes them crisper.

 *DRY WHITE*

# CHAUDFROID OF SOLE

This is one of the great classics of French cuisine.

SERVES 4
*4 × 560g/1¼lb soles, filleted and skinned (see page 267)*

For the stock and aspic jelly
*1 onion*
*1 carrot*
*1 stick of celery*
*heads, bones and skins of the soles*
*1 bay leaf*
*6 white peppercorns*
*100ml/3½fl oz dry white wine*
*55g/2oz powdered gelatine*
*2 egg whites and 2 egg shells, crushed*

For the farce
*170g/6oz uncooked salmon, minced*
*1 egg white*
*2 tablespoons double cream*
*salt and freshly ground black pepper*

For the chaudfroid sauce
*290ml/½ pint milk*
*6 peppercorns*
*1 blade of mace*
*1 slice of onion*
*20g/¾oz butter*
*20g/¾ flour*
*7g/¼oz powdered gelatine*
*290ml/⅓ pint aspic jelly (see above)*
*1 tablespoon double cream*
*salt and freshly ground white pepper*

To garnish
*pepper-thin truffle or mushroom slices*

**1.** Make the stock: cut the onion, carrot and celery into dice and put into a saucepan with the fish heads, bones and skins. Add the bay leaf, peppercorns and wine. Add 865ml/1½ pints cold water and bring to the boil, then skim and allow to simmer for 30 minutes. Strain the stock and leave to cool.

**2.** Preheat the oven to 170°C/325°F/gas mark 3.

**3.** Make the farce: put the salmon into a bowl. Whisk the egg white until frothy and beat slowly into the salmon with the cream. Season to taste with salt and pepper.

**4.** Wash and dry the sole fillets. Divide the farce

equally between them, spreading it on the skinned side. Roll or fold up each fillet into a neat parcel.

**5.** Put the rolled fillets into a buttered ovenproof dish and add a cupful of the stock. Cover with buttered kitchen foil or greaseproof paper. Bake in the pre-heated oven for 12 minutes, or until the fish is cooked (it should be opaque and firm). Strain off and reserve the liquid; leave the fish to cool, uncovered.

**6.** Make the chaudfroid sauce: heat the milk with the peppercorns, mace and onion. Strain and mix with the reserved cooking liquid.

**7.** Melt the butter in a saucepan and add the flour. Cook, stirring, for 1 minute. Remove from the heat and add the milky liquid. Bring back to the boil, stirring continuously, and allow to simmer for 2 minutes. Strain through a tammy sieve or piece of muslin. Leave to cool, stirring occasionally to prevent a skin from forming.

**8.** Make the aspic: put the stock into a large saucepan, sprinkle on the gelatine and set the pan over a low heat.

**9.** Put the crushed egg shells into a bowl, add the egg whites and whisk until frothy. Pour into the warming stock and keep whisking steadily (preferably with a balloon whisk) until a crust begins to form. Allow the mixture to come just to the boil. Stop whisking immediately and remove the pan from the heat. Allow the mixture to subside. Take care not to break the crust formed by the egg white. Cool for 2 minutes.

**10.** Bring the aspic up to the boil again and allow to subside again. Repeat this once more (the egg white will trap the sediment in the stock and clear the aspic). Allow to cool for 10 minutes.

**11.** Fix a double layer of fine scalded muslin over a clean basin, lift the egg white crust to the sieve and then check to see how clear the stock is. If not quite clear carefully strain the aspic through it. Strain the aspic again. Do not try to hurry the process by squeezing the cloth, or the aspic will be murky.

**12.** Soak the gelatine for the sauce in about 4 tablespoons of the cleared cool aspic in a small saucepan for 5 minutes, then melt over a low heat. Beat the liquid gelatine into the sauce with the cream. Season to taste with salt and pepper.

**13.** Lay the sole parcels on a wire rack with a tray underneath. As the sauce thickens, spoon some over each parcel, covering the top and sides. Refrigerate the coated fillets until the sauce is set. Wash the tray and place it back under the wire rack.

**14.** Garnish the fish parcels with truffle or mushroom slices. When the aspic is cold and on the point of setting, carefully coat each fillet with it. Refrigerate to set. Repeat the coating if necessary: the aspic layer should be thin, but very shiny.

**15.** Pour the remaining aspic into a shallow tray and allow to set in the refrigerator, then cut it into tiny squares with a sharp knife.

**16.** Arrange the fillets on a serving dish. Garnish with the chopped aspic and keep cool until ready to serve.

NOTE: If the aspic is less than crystal-clear do not use it to garnish. Chopping it only seems to emphasize its murkiness.

 *DRY ROSÉ*

# LEMON SOLE WITH CUCUMBER

SERVES 4

*1 large cucumber, peeled, halved lengthways, deseeded and thickly sliced*
*3 × 675g/1½lb lemon soles, filleted and skinned (see pages 267, 268)*
*seasoned plain flour*
*55g/2oz unsalted butter*
*salt and freshly ground white pepper*
*lemon juice*

**1.** Blanch the cucumber in a saucepan of boiling salted water for 30 seconds. Refresh, drain and dry well.

**2.** Dip the sole fillets in seasoned flour. Lay them on a plate but do not allow them to touch each other or they will become soggy.

**3.** Heat half the butter in a frying pan. When foaming, put in a batch of fillets. Turn them over when golden-brown (about 1 minute on each side). Dish on to a shallow platter and keep warm. Fry the remaining fillets in the same way.

**4.** Melt the remaining butter in the pan. Add the cucumber and fry quite briskly for 1 minute. Remove from the heat, add salt, pepper and lemon juice. Return to the heat, bring to the boil and tip over the fish. Serve immediately.

 *DRY WHITE*

# LEMON SOLE WITH BURNT HOLLANDAISE

SERVES 4

*12 lemon sole fillets, skinned (see page 268)*
*fish stock (see page 245), cooled*
*150ml/¼ pint hollandaise sauce (see page 251)*
*3 tablespoons double cream*

**1.** Preheat the oven to 180°C/350°F/gas mark 4.
**2.** Roll the sole fillets up, skinned side inside. Lay them in an ovenproof dish or roasting pan and pour over the stock. Cover and poach in the preheated oven for 10–15 minutes. Alternatively, poach carefully on the hob.
**3.** While the fish cooks, preheat the grill and make the hollandaise sauce, which must be very thick.
**4.** Drain the fish well and arrange on a heatproof serving dish. Mix the sauce with the cream and coat each fillet with a spoonful. Brown quickly under the grill and serve immediately.

 *WHITE BURGUNDY*

# GRILLED BRILL FILLETS WITH ANCHOVY BUTTER

SERVES 4

*55g/2oz unsalted butter, softened*
*4 anchovy fillets*
*1 teaspoon lemon juice*
*salt and freshly ground black pepper*
*8 × 85g/3oz brill fillets, skinned (see page 268)*

To serve
*rocket and radicchio leaves*
*1 quantity French dressing (see page 254), made*
*    with walnut oil*
*1 bunch of fresh chives, chopped*

**1.** Preheat the grill to its highest setting. Put the butter into a food processor with the anchovy fillets and lemon juice. Whizz to a smooth paste and season with pepper.
**2.** Fold each brill fillet into 3 with the skinned side inside. Season with salt and pepper and grill the fillets for 4–5 minutes until cooked through (they

should be opaque and firm). Brush each fillet generously with the anchovy butter to give a good shine.
**3.** To serve: toss the salad in the French dressing and divide between 4 dinner plates. Arrange 2 brill fillets on each plate and sprinkle with the chopped chives. Serve immediately.

 *CHILEAN SAUVIGNON BLANC*

# TROUT WITH ALMONDS

SERVES 4

*4 medium rainbow trout*
*seasoned plain flour*
*85g/3oz clarified butter (see page 686)*
*55g/2oz flaked almonds*
*lemon juice*
*salt and freshly ground black pepper*

To garnish
*lemon wedges*
*chopped fresh parsley*

**1.** Preheat the oven to 170°C/325°F/gas mark 3.
**2.** Clean the trout very well (if not properly cleaned they will taste very bitter). Dip them in seasoned flour and shake off any excess.
**3.** Fry briefly on both sides in all but 15g/½oz of the butter. Transfer to an ovenproof dish, pouring over the butter from the pan. Bake in the preheated oven for 15 minutes, or until firm to the touch.
**4.** Fry the almonds in the remaining butter.
**5.** Arrange the trout on a warmed serving dish, pour over the almonds and butter, then sprinkle with lemon juice, salt and pepper. Garnish with lemon wedges and sprinkle with parsley.

NOTE: The trout may be cooked entirely in the frying pan, but they must be fried slowly, for about 7 minutes a side.

 *DRY WHITE*

# TROUT EN PAPILLOTE

SERVES 2
*55g/2oz butter*
*1 tablespoon very finely shredded white of leek*
*1 tablespoon very finely shredded carrot*
*55g/2oz button mushrooms, thinly sliced*
*1 teaspoon chopped fresh tarragon or fennel leaves*
*salt and freshly ground black pepper*
*4 × 110g/4oz unskinned trout fillets, pinboned*
  *(see page 268)*
*lemon juice*
*2 tablespoons dry white wine*
*oil for brushing*

**1.** Preheat the oven to 220°C/425°F/gas mark 7.
**2.** Fold a large sheet of greaseproof paper in half and cut out 2 semi-circles, with a radius of 20cm/8in. Open out to form circles.
**3.** Melt half the butter and add the leek and carrot. Cook slowly without browning for 5 minutes, then add the mushrooms. Cook for 2 more minutes, then add the tarragon or fennel, and season with salt and pepper. Allow to cool.
**4.** Brush the inside of the paper circles with a little oil, leaving the edges clear. Sandwich the trout fillets, skinned side outside, with the vegetables. Place a sandwich on one side of each paper circle. Squeeze a few drops of lemon on each and sprinkle on the wine. Dot with the remaining butter and add salt and pepper.
**5.** Fold the free half of the papillote paper over to make a parcel rather like an apple turnover. Fold the edges of the 2 layers of paper over twice together, twisting and pressing hard to seal.
**6.** Brush a baking sheet lightly with oil and put it into the oven for 5 minutes to heat. Then put the papillotes on the baking sheet, taking care that they do not touch each other. Bake in the preheated oven for 12 minutes.
**7.** Serve immediately on warmed dinner plates. Each diner unwraps his own puffed-up parcel.

NOTES: Halibut, haddock, salmon, indeed almost any fish, can be cooked in this way. Whole trout weighing 340g/12oz will take 15 minutes to cook. Breast of chicken, boned and skinned, is also good *en papillote*, and takes 20 minutes in a piece, 15 minutes if in slices.

For a richer dish serve with beurre blanc (see page 253).

Papillotes are generally made from circular papers, as in the above recipe, but are better made from heart-shaped pieces if whole small fish or long fillets of fish are to be wrapped.

 WHITE BURGUNDY

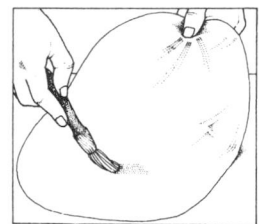

*Brush the paper with a little oil*

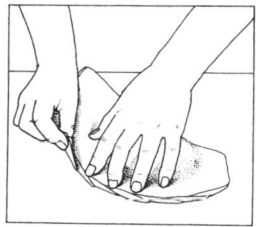

*Fold the edges of the paper together; twist and press to make a really good seal*

# STEAMED TROUT FILLETS IN LETTUCE

This recipe is taken from *Easy to Entertain* by Patricia Lousada.

SERVES 4
*2 shallots, very finely chopped*
*1 tablespoon oil*
*170g/6oz mushrooms, finely chopped*
*a squeeze of lemon juice*
*salt and freshly ground black pepper*
*8 large lettuce leaves or cabbage leaves*
*4 large trout, pink-fleshed if possible, filleted,*
  *skinned and pinboned (see pages 267, 268)*

**1.** Sweat the shallots in the oil, stirring constantly. Add the mushrooms, lemon juice, salt and pepper. Sauté until the mushrooms give off their juices, then boil hard until all the juice has evaporated.

**2.** Blanch the lettuce in a large quantity of boiling salted water for 15 seconds, until just limp. Refresh in a bowl of cold water, then spread out on tea towels or absorbent kitchen paper to dry.

**3.** Trim the fillets and remove any bones with tweezers. By running your finger against the grain of the flesh, you can feel where they are. Pat the fillets dry and season with salt and pepper. Place a spoonful of the mushroom mixture on each fillet and roll up. Wrap in a lettuce leaf and place seam down in a steamer. Continue with the other fillets. Steam until tender (about 10 minutes).

 *DRY WHITE*

# STEAMED TROUT FILLETS WITH TOMATO AND GINGER SAUCE

SERVES 4
*8 × 110g/4oz trout fillets, skinned and pinboned (see page 268)*
*1 tablespoon oil*
*8 fresh basil leaves, chopped*
*lemon juice*
*salt and freshly ground white pepper*

*For the tomato and ginger sauce*
*6 fresh ripe tomatoes, roughly chopped*
*1 teaspoon tomato purée*
*1 tablespoon ginger syrup from a jar of preserved stem ginger*
*1 slice of fresh root ginger, peeled*
*15g/¹/₂oz butter*
*salt and freshly ground black pepper*
*a squeeze of lemon juice*
*a pinch of caster sugar*

*For the watercress and coriander garnish*
*15g/¹/₂oz butter*
*1 bunch of watercress, leaves and young shoots only*
*1 small bunch of coriander, leaves only*
*1 tablespoon double cream*
*salt and freshly ground black pepper*

**1.** Put the trout fillets on a sheet of lightly oiled kitchen foil. Brush the fish with oil and sprinkle

with the basil, lemon juice, salt and pepper. Cover with foil and refrigerate until ready to cook.

**2.** Liquidize the tomatoes and tomato purée in a blender and then pass through a sieve. Add the ginger syrup, fresh ginger and butter and simmer for 15 minutes. Add salt, pepper and the sugar.

**3.** Prepare the watercress and coriander garnish: melt the butter. Add the watercress and coriander and cook for 2 minutes. Drain well in a colander. Return the leaves to the saucepan, add the cream, salt and pepper and set aside until ready to serve.

**4.** Cook the fish: lay the parcels of fish on a wire rack and steam over a pan of boiling water on top of the stove for 3–4 minutes.

**5.** Place a spoonful of the watercress mixture on each warmed dinner plate. Arrange 2 trout fillets on top and surround with the sauce. Serve immediately.

 *WHITE ALSACE*

# TROUT IN FILO PASTRY WITH LIME BEURRE BLANC

SERVES 4
*4 × 225g/8oz trout, filleted, skinned and pinboned (see pags 267, 268)*
*85g/3oz butter*
*1 large carrot, cut into julienne strips*
*1 leek, cut into julienne strips*
*4 sheets of filo pastry (see page 466)*
*4 tablespoons dry white wine*
*salt and freshly ground black pepper*
*lime beurre blanc (see page 254)*

**1.** Preheat the oven to 200°C/400°F/gas mark 6.

**2.** Cut the trout into 2.5cm/1in wide strips and divide them into 4 equal portions.

**3.** Melt a little of the butter in a frying pan, add the carrot and leek and cook until soft but not coloured.

**4.** Melt the remaining butter. Cut each filo sheet in half and brush with butter. Sandwich the halves together.

**5.** Divide the vegetables between the 4 filos and then place the fish on top of the vegetables. Sprinkle 1 tablespoon of the wine over each, brush with melted butter and season with salt and pepper.

6. Draw the edges of the pastry to form pouches.
7. Place each pouch on a floured baking sheet, dab with melted butter and bake in the oven for 8–10 minutes, or until the pastry is crisp and golden brown.
8. Serve immediately with the lime beurre blanc.

 *VERY DRY WHITE*

# BONED STUFFED TROUT

SERVES 2
*2 × 225g/8oz trout, cleaned (see page 267)*
*55g/2oz butter*
*1 tablespoon very finely shredded white of leek*
*1 tablespoon very finely shredded carrot*
*55g/2oz button mushrooms, very thinly sliced*
*1 teaspoon chopped fresh thyme*
*lemon juice*
*2 tablespoons dry white wine*
*salt and freshly ground black pepper*
*55g/2oz feta cheese, diced*

To garnish
*lemon wedges*
*1 small bunch of watercress*

1. Preheat the oven to 200°C/400°F/gas mark 6.
2. Melt the butter in a saucepan and gently cook the leek and carrot for 2 minutes. Add the mushrooms and cook for 1 further minute. Add the thyme, lemon juice and wine and cook until the liquid has evaporated. Season to taste with salt and pepper. Allow to cool. Add the feta cheese.
3. Stuff the trout with this mixture and lay in a lightly greased roasting pan. Cover and bake in the preheated oven for 15 minutes.
4. Remove to a warmed serving dish and garnish with lemon wedges and watercress.

 *DRY WHITE*

## JAPANESE FISH COOKING

SUSHI

The word sushi, literally translated, means 'happy children', which goes some way to describing the special love the Japanese have for this dish, which is served at special occasions; it is not an everyday food or one that is generally cooked in the home.

The base of sushi is sweet vinegar-flavoured rice served in various forms (for sushi recipes see page 300).

*Sushi nori maki* (literally, 'seawood roll') is cooked rice rolled in nori seaweed, often with a selection of fish fillings.

*Sushi nigiri* (literally, 'grip') is a piece of fish lying over or 'gripping' the rice.

*Plain sushi* is the vinegar-flavoured rice served on its own in a bowl with fish or meat forked through it. This is the traditional way of serving it.

SASHIMI

This consists of sheets or slices of raw fish, which is sold ready-prepared. Most Japanese supermarkets in the UK sell frozen fish especially for sashimi. As the fish is frozen while still very fresh, it tastes superb and is well worth trying. Fish traditionally served as sashimi include squid, young tuna, scallops, prawns, sea bream and yellow tail.

The fish used for sashimi in Japan is always very fresh, prepared and handled carefully by fishermen and fishmongers alike. Sashimi is kept separately from other fish at the market, to prevent cross-contamination.

Hygiene legislation in the UK now states that fish that is prepared for raw dishes, such as sushi, ceviche, gravad lax, etc. must be frozen for at least 24 hours prior to consumption, to ensure that any harmful bacteria present are kept to a minimum.

Sashimi is eaten dipped in soy sauce and traditionally served with wasabi and shredded daikon and garnished with shiso leaves.

TEMPURA

Literally translated, tempura means 'fritter'. Fish, meat or vegetables are dipped in a batter, then deep-fried (see page 198).

TEPIN-YAKI

Literally translated, tepin-yaki means 'iron-grill'. In a Japanese restaurant this method of cooking is performed in front of the diner by a highly trained tepin-yaki chef. He will demonstrate chopping, tossing, cooking and presentation techniques to the customers seated around the hot grill.

TERI-YAKI

Literally translated, teri-yaki means 'shine-grill'. The food, whether it is fish, chicken or other meat, is marinated first in soy, sugar and mirin, then grilled on a hot plate.

SUSHI SELECTION

# SWEET VINEGAR RICE

This is the recipe for the rice used in sushi. As with any cooked rice dish, keep refrigerated and eat within 24 hours of cooking.

MAKES ENOUGH FOR 15 PIECES OF SUSHI
*225g/8oz Japanese sushi short-grain rice*
*450ml/³⁄4 pint water*
*1 piece of kombu seaweed*
*75ml/2¹⁄2fl oz rice wine vinegar*
*1 tablespoon caster sugar*
*2 teaspoons salt*

1. Put the rice into a sieve and rinse under running cold water for 1 minute, to remove excess starch.
2. Put into a saucepan, cover with the water, add the kombu and allow to soak for 45 minutes.
3. After the soaking time, cover the saucepan with a well-fitting lid and bring to the boil. Reduce the heat and continue to cook the rice for 10–12 minutes or until cooked through.
4. Meanwhile, put the vinegar into a small saucepan, add the sugar and salt and heat slowly until dissolved. Remove from the heat and allow to cool.
5. When the rice is cooked, turn it on to a flat plate and remove and discard the kombu.
6. Pour the sweetened vinegar over the rice, toss with a fork and allow to cool. Use as required.

# TRADITIONAL NORI SUSHI ROLLS

Smoked or raw fish can be included in this simple roll as desired.

SERVES 4
*2 eggs*
*1 tablespoon light soy sauce*
*freshly ground black pepper*
*1 tablespoon oil*
*¹⁄2 cucumber, peeled*
*8 sheets of nori seaweed*
*1 × ¹⁄2 quantity sweet vinegar rice (see opposite)*

For dipping
*3 tablespoons dark soy sauce*
*1 red chilli, deseeded and chopped*
*wasabi paste or powder*

1. Beat the eggs and soy sauce together and season with pepper. Heat the oil in a frying pan, add the egg mixture and cook over a low heat until the egg is cooked and resembles an omelette. Remove from the pan and allow to cool.
2. Cut the cucumber into long pencil lengths. Cut the omelette into strips.
3. Lay a sushi mat or thick napkin on a work surface. Using kitchen scissors, trim the nori to fit the mat. Pass the nori sheets through a gas flame to toast them. Lay them on the mat and spoon a layer of rice over two-thirds of each sheet up to the edges.
4. Arrange a couple of cucumber and omelette strips on the rice, then roll up firmly as for a Swiss roll, using the sushi mat or napkin to help you. Press the roll well to compress it and allow it to stand for 15 minutes while you make up the rest.
5. Cut each roll crosswise into 5–6 even slices and arrange on a black or dark unpatterned plate.
6. Mix the soy and chilli together and hand separately in a little dish. Hand the wasabi separately too.

# SWEET SUSHI RICE SALAD

SERVES 6

*1 quantity sweet vinegar rice (see page 300)*
*110g/4oz smoked salmon, thinly sliced and shredded*
*½ cucumber, peeled, deseeded and diced*
*2 spring onions, thinly sliced*
*110g/4oz fine asparagus spears, blanched*
*1 tablespoon capers, rinsed*
*juice of 1 lemon*
*salt and freshly ground black pepper*

**1.** Put the rice into a large bowl, add the smoked salmon, cucumber, spring onions, asparagus and capers. Toss together.

**2.** Add the lemon juice, salt and pepper. Toss together and pile into a serving dish. Chill for 15 minutes, then serve.

# DRESSED CRAB

SERVES 3

*1 × 900g/2lb live crab*

To season
*lemon juice*
*salt and freshly ground black pepper*
*mustard*
*fresh white breadcrumbs*
*hardboiled egg yolks, sieved*
*chopped fresh parsley*

To serve
*mayonnaise (see page 250)*
*tartare sauce (see page 251)*
*brown bread and butter*

**1.** Place the crab in a pan of well-salted water (about 170g/6oz salt to 2.5 litres/4 pints water), cover and bring to the boil. Simmer, allowing 15 minutes to each 450g/1lb crab. Remove from the pan and allow to cool.

**2.** Lay the crab on its back. Twist off the legs and claws. Cracking round the natural line (visible near the edge), remove the pale belly shell and discard it. Remove and throw away the small sac at the top of the crab body and the spongy lungs which line the edge (they look rather like grey fish gills).

**3.** Have 2 bowls ready, one for white meat, one for brown. Lift out the body of the crab, cut into 2–4 pieces and carefully pick out all the meat that you can. This is fiddly and could take up to 15 minutes. If you have a lobster pick it can be very useful. Wash and dry the shell.

**4.** Crack the large claws, remove the meat and put it into the white-meat bowl.

**5.** With a lobster pick or toothpick poke out the remaining meat from the legs, and add it to the white meat in the bowl.

**6.** Dress the crab: cream the brown meat, season with lemon juice, salt, pepper and mustard. Add enough breadcrumbs to bind the mixture. Arrange this down the centre of the shell and pile the white meat up at each side. Garnish with neat lines of egg yolk and parsley.

**7.** Place on a serving plate with the claws. Serve with mayonnaise or tartare sauce and brown bread and butter.

 LOIRE WHITE

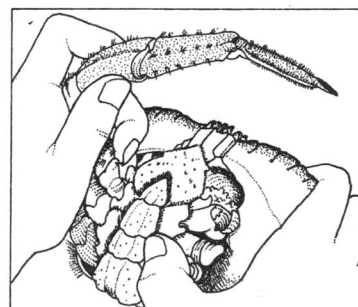 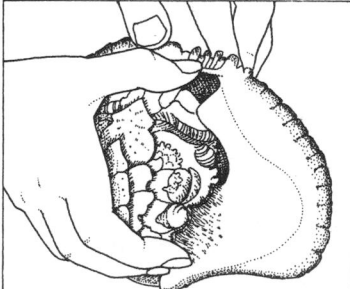 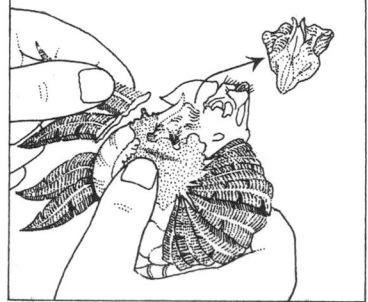

*Twist off the legs and claws; remove and throw away the pale belly shell; discard the spongy lungs and small stomach sac*

# LANGOUSTINES IN FILO WITH HERB BUTTER

SERVES 4
*12 langoustines*
*85g/3oz unsalted butter*
*6 cloves of garlic, 4 bruised and 2 crushed*
*1 tablespoon finely chopped fresh parsley*
*4 slices of white bread*
*4 sheets of filo pastry (see page 466)*
*salt and freshly ground black pepper*
*1 egg, beaten, to glaze*

To serve
*1 lemon, cut into wedges*

**1.** Bring a saucepan of water to the boil. Put the langoustines into the water and bring back to simmering point. Remove the langoustines and allow them to cool.
**2.** Remove the head, shells and legs from the langoustines. Remove the digestive tract (the black vein running down the back).
**3.** Gently melt the butter in a pan and add the 4 bruised cloves of garlic. Allow them to infuse for as long as possible – at least 30 minutes. Remove the garlic cloves and add the crushed garlic and the parsley.
**4.** Preheat the oven to 170°C/325°F/gas mark 3.
**5.** Cut 4 × 5cm/2in rounds from the bread and dry out in the oven until crisp.
**6.** Cut a sheet of filo in half and trim each half into 17.5cm/7in squares.
**7.** Brush each square with the herb butter and place one on top of the other at an angle.
**8.** Put a piece of the crisp bread in the middle. Dip 2 langoustines into the herb butter. Place them on the bread and season with salt and pepper.
**9.** Gather the corners of the pastry together to form a pouch.. Brush with beaten egg. Repeat for the other 3 parcels. Refrigerate until required.
**10.** Turn up the oven temperature to 220°C/425°F/gas mark 7. Place the parcels on a baking sheet and bake in the oven for 5 minutes or until they are a rich brown.
**11.** Remove from the oven and serve immediately with lemon wedges.

 *WHITE LOIRE*

# BOILED LOBSTER

SERVES 4
*2 × 900g/2lb live lobsters*

For the court bouillon
*1 litre/2 pints water*
*225g/8oz carrots, sliced*
*1 medium onion, sliced*
*1 bay leaf*
*1 sprig of fresh thyme*
*30g/1oz salt*
*150ml/¼ pint white wine vinegar*
*1 bunch of fresh parsley*
*10 black peppercorns*

To serve hot
*hollandaise sauce (see page 251), or melted butter*

To serve cold
*mayonnaise (see page 250)*

**1.** Combine all the court bouillon ingredients in a saucepan and simmer for 30 minutes.
**2.** Weigh the lobsters, then put them into the court bouillon.
**3.** Bring to the boil, cover and simmer for 8 minutes per 450g/1lb. Lift the lobsters out. Allow to cool before splitting if to be served cold.
**4.** Split the lobsters in half, remove the stomach sac near the head and the intestine, a thin grey or black line running the length of the body.
**5.** Serve with hollandaise sauce or melted butter if to be eaten hot, with mayonnaise if cold.

NOTE: A fresh live lobster turns bright red when cooked and the tail tightens considerably.

*CHABLIS*

# LOBSTER AND CHICKEN SALAD

SERVES 4
2 × 340g/12oz cold cooked lobsters
225g/8oz cooked chicken meat
a few drops of anchovy essence
juice of ½ lemon
a few drops of Tabasco sauce
290ml/½ pint mayonnaise (see page 250)
1 tablespoon double cream
2 hardboiled eggs
1 tablespoon chopped fresh parsley
1 hearty lettuce
French dressing (page 254)

1. Place each lobster with the head to your left
and the tail spread out flat to your right. Hold
firmly by the head and with a very sharp knife
push the point of the blade into the cross on the
top of the head. Carefully cut all the way down
the shell to the end of the tail. Turn the lobster
around and split the head in 2. Remove the small
bag or stomach sac in the head. Remove the
intestine, a thin grey or black line running the
length of the body.
2. Take out the remaining lobster meat and chop
roughly. Place in a bowl. Crack the claws and
remove the meat.
3. Cut the chicken flesh into dice about the same
size as the lobster meat. Add the anchovy essence,
lemon juice and Tabasco to the mayonnaise and
mix half of it with the lobster meat and chicken.
Pile this mixture into the lobster shells.
4. Add the cream to the remaining mayonnaise
and coat it neatly over each shell. Place on a
serving dish.
5. Halve the hardboiled eggs and sieve the yolks.
Mix the yolks with the parsley and sprinkle over
the lobsters.
6. Remove the outer leaves of the lettuce. Wash and
dry the inner leaves and shred coarsely. Shred the
egg whites and toss with the lettuce and French
dressing. Surround the lobsters with the salad.

 *WHITE BURGUNDY*

# GRILLED LOBSTER WITH RED BUTTER SAUCE

SERVES 4
4 small live lobsters
unsalted butter, melted
cayenne pepper

For the butter sauce
1 shallot, finely chopped
150ml/¼ pint dry white wine
1 teaspoon fish glaze (see page 245)
110g/4oz unsalted butter, chilled and diced
the coral from the lobster
3 tablespoons double cream
tomato purée (optional)
salt and freshly ground white pepper

To garnish
watercress, trimmed

1. Begin to prepare the butter sauce: put the
shallot into a small saucepan with the wine. Cook
slowly until the liquid is reduced to half its
original quantity. Strain into a clean saucepan.
Add the fish glaze and set aside.
2. Next kill the lobsters. Push a sharp strong knife
through the nerve centre of each lobster. This is a
well-defined cross on the back of its head. When
the middle of the cross is pierced the lobster will
die instantly, although it will still move alarmingly.
3. Lay the lobsters out flat and split in half
lengthways. Remove the stomach sac from near
the head and remove the threadlike intestine
running the length of the body. Do not mistake the
roe (or coral), which may or may not be present,
for the intestine, which is tiny. The roe, when
cooked, will be bright red and has an excellent
flavour. Reserve it for the sauce. Do not throw
away the soft grey green flesh near the head either
– it is the liver (or tomalley) and quite delicious.
4. Preheat the grill.
5. Brush the lobsters with butter and season with
cayenne pepper. Place in the grill pan, cut side
uppermost first, and grill for 5–10 minutes on
each side, depending on size, until the lobster is a
good bright red.
6. Meanwhile continue with the butter sauce. Mix
1 teaspoon of the butter with the lobster coral.
Set aside.

7. When the lobsters are cooked, crack the claws, without removing them from the body if possible, with a claw cracker or by covering with a cloth and hitting gently with a rolling pin. Keep the lobsters warm while finishing the sauce.

8. Warm up the reduced wine and fish glaze. Using a wire whisk and plenty of vigorous continuous whisking, add the butter piece by piece. The process should take about 2 minutes and the sauce should thicken considerably. Do not allow it to get too hot.

9. Whisk in the coral and cream, and any pan juices from the grill pan. Add a little tomato purée to brighten up the colour it necessary. Season to taste with salt and pepper.

10. Arrange the lobsters on a large oval dish. Garnish with watercress and hand the sauce separately.

 *CHABLIS*

# LOBSTER FRICASSÉE WITH TARRAGON CREAM SAUCE

SERVES 2
*2 × 450g/1lb live lobsters*
*45g/1½oz unsalted butter*
*1 shallot, finely chopped*
*290ml/½ pint crème fraîche*
*2 sprigs of fresh tarragon*
*salt and freshly ground black pepper*

1. Cut the lobsters in half lengthways. Remove the stomach sac and the threadlike intestine running the length of the body. Crack the claws.
2. Melt the butter in a sauté pan and add the shallot. Cook gently until softened and slightly brown.
3. Add the lobster halves, shell side down, and pour the crème fraîche over them. Add the tarragon stems, stripped of their leaves (reserve these), and simmer over a low heat until the cream comes to the boil. Cover the pan and turn the heat down to very low. Cook for 10 minutes.
4. Remove the lobsters from the cream. Carefully

pull the tail meat out of the shells in one piece. Remove the claw meat. Place all the meat in a medium saucepan and set aside.

5. Crack or cut up all the lobster shells and add to the cream in the sauté pan. Bring to the boil over a medium heat. Remove from the heat and pass the sauce through a very fine sieve into the saucepan containing the lobster meat. Season with salt, pepper and the reserved tarragon leaves.

6. Heat the fricassée through very gently and serve.

7. If making this in advance, allow the fricassée to cool, and refrigerate. About 10 minutes before serving, heat through very gently in a saucepan.

 *CRISP DRY WHITE*

# DRY-FRIED PRAWNS WITH CORIANDER

This has been adapted from a recipe by Yan-Kit So.

SERVES 4
*450g/1lb raw, medium shell-on prawns, weighed*
    *without heads*
*5 cloves of garlic*
*2.5cm/1in piece of fresh root ginger*
*3–4 tablespoons oil*
*1 tablespoon dry sherry*
*3 spring onions, chopped*
*1 tablespoon chopped fresh coriander*

For the marinade
*½ teaspoon salt*
*1 teaspoon sugar*
*1–2 tablespoons light soy sauce*
*2 teaspoons Worcestershire sauce*
*2 teaspoons oil*
*freshly ground black pepper*

1. Using a small sharp knife, slit along the backs of the prawns and remove the black vein. Cut off the legs. Wash and pat dry.
2. Mix together all the marinade ingredients and add the prawns. Leave to stand for at least 30 minutes.
3. Bruise the garlic with a rolling pin, remove the skin and leave the cloves flattened but whole. Peel the ginger and bruise it with a rolling pin.

**4.** Heat a wok or heavy sauté pan until it is very hot. Add the oil and swirl it about. Fry the garlic and ginger for about 1 minute, remove and discard.

**5.** Add the prawns. Spread them out in a single layer and fry for about 1 minute. Reduce the heat if they begin to burn. Turn over to fry the other side for about 1 minute. Turn up the heat if necessary. Splash in the sherry. The prawns are cooked when they have turned red and curled up. Sprinkle with the spring onion and coriander. Stir once or twice and serve immediately.

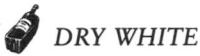 *DRY WHITE*

# PRAWN PILAF

SERVES 4
*790g/1³/4lb cooked shell-on prawns*
*570ml/1 pint water*
*100ml/3¹/2fl oz dry white wine*
*salt and freshly ground black pepper*
*1 slice of lemon*
*3–4 parsley stalks*
*110g/4oz butter*
*1 medium onion, finely chopped*
*225g/8oz long-grain rice, washed*
*2 hardboiled eggs, chopped*

To garnish
*1 tablespoon chopped fresh parsley*

**1.** Peel all but 3 of the prawns. Reserve the prawns and put the shells into a saucepan with the water, wine, salt, pepper, lemon slice and parsley stalks. Bring to the boil, then simmer for 15 minutes. Strain and reserve the liquor.
**2.** Melt 85g/3oz of the butter in a saucepan and cook the onion gently until soft. Add the rice and fry slowly until it looks opaque. Add the reserved liquor. Bring to the boil, stirring with a fork. Cover and simmer gently for 25 minutes, until the rice is tender and the water absorbed.
**3.** Meanwhile, melt the remaining butter, add the peeled prawns and eggs and heat through. Season with salt, pepper and lemon juice. Fork the shelled prawns and eggs into the pilaf rice. Pile into a warmed serving dish and sprinkle with

plenty of parsley. Put the unshelled prawns on top and serve.

NOTES: Ideally, prawn pilaf should be made with raw shell-on prawns, but they are often difficult to get hold of. If you can get them, simply cook the prawns for 4 minutes in the water and wine. Remove from the liquid and then follow the recipe as before.

If the pilaf is to be kept warm, do not garnish with the parsley and whole prawns until serving. The parsley dries out and the prawns turn chalky-white.

 *DRY WHITE*

# PRAWNS IN COCONUT SAUCE

SERVES 4
*450g/1lb raw shell-on prawns*
*2 teaspoons coriander seeds*
*¹/2 teaspoon black peppercorns*
*a few fenugreek seeds*
*2 tablespoons oil*
*a few mustard seeds*
*2 cloves of garlic, cut into slivers*
*3 shallots, chopped*
*1 teaspoon peeled and grated fresh ginger root*
*150ml/¹/4 pint water*
*1 teaspoon paprika pepper*
*a pinch of cayenne pepper*
*a pinch of ground turmeric*
*salt*
*2 teaspoons lemon juice*
*110g/4oz creamed coconut*

To garnish
*fresh coriander leaves*

**1.** Peel the prawns and remove the black veins. Rinse them out quickly under cold running water and pat them dry with kitchen paper. Cover and refrigerate.
**2.** Heat a small cast-iron frying pan over a medium heat. When hot, put in the coriander seeds, peppercorns and fenugreek seeds. Stir for about 1 minute or until lightly roasted. Remove from the heat and grind in a clean grinder. Set aside.

**3.** Heat the oil in a large frying pan. When hot, put in the mustard seeds. As soon as they begin to pop (this takes just a few seconds), stir once and add the garlic and shallot. Stir and fry until the shallot is lightly browned. Put in the ginger and stir once. Now add the water, the paprika, cayenne, turmeric, salt, the ground spice mixture and the lemon juice. Bring to the boil, then simmer for 5 minutes.

**4.** Fold in the prawns and stir until they just turn opaque. Stir in the creamed coconut. As soon as the liquid begins to bubble, turn off the heat and serve garnished with coriander leaves.

 *FULL DRY WHITE*

# FRIED SCALLOPS WITH GARLIC

SERVES 4
*16 scallops*
*55g/2oz garlic butter (see page 263)*
*salt and freshly ground black pepper*
*juice of ½ lemon*
*a little chopped fresh parsley*

**1.** Remove the hard muscle from the scallops (opposite the coral or roe, see page 128).
**2.** Melt the garlic butter in a frying pan. Add the scallops and pepper. Seal over a high heat for 30 seconds.
**3.** Add the lemon juice and parsley and sprinkle with salt. Serve immediately.

 *LIGHT DRY WHITE*

# COQUILLES ST JACQUES

SERVES 4
*150ml/¼ pint dry white wine*
*1 bay leaf*
*¼ onion*
*8 large or 12 small scallops*
*450g/1lb mashed potatoes (see page 212)*
*30g/1oz butter*
*30g/1oz plain flour*
*1 tablespoon double cream*

*lemon juice*
*salt and freshly ground black pepper*
*dried white breadcrumbs*
*a little extra butter to finish*

To serve
*4 scallop shells*

**1.** Put the wine with 150ml/¼ pint water, the bay leaf and onion into a saucepan. Bring to the boil. Turn down the heat, add the scallops and poach very gently for 5 minutes.
**2.** Lift the scallops from the liquid. Pull away the hard muscle (opposite the coral or roe, see page 128) and cut each scallop into 2 or 3 pieces.
**3.** Divide the scallops between the 4 scallop shells. Pipe or spoon the mashed potato around the edge of the shells.
**4.** Preheat the grill.
**5.** Melt the butter in saucepan, add the flour and cook for 30 seconds. Strain over the liquid in which the scallops were cooked and stir until the sauce is thick and smooth. Add the cream and season with lemon juice, salt and pepper.
**6.** Spoon over the scallops. Sprinkle with the crumbs, dot with butter and brown under the grill.

 *MUSCADET*

# FRIED SCALLOPS WITH BACON

SERVES 4
*12 scallops*
*4 rashers of rindless back bacon*
*1 tablespoon chopped fresh parsley*
*lemon juice*
*salt and freshly ground black pepper*

**1.** Clean the scallops, pull away the hard muscle (opposite the coral or roe) and discard (see page 128). Cut in half horizontally.
**2.** Cut the bacon into slivers and fry until beginning to brown. Reduce the heat and add the scallops. Fry quickly for 30 seconds. Add the parsley and lemon juice, season with salt and pepper and serve immediately.

 *CHABLIS*

# DIDIER OUDILL'S BRAISED SCALLOPS IN THEIR SHELLS

This recipe has been taken from Michel Guérard's *Cuisine Gourmande*.

SERVES 4
*12 scallops in their shells*
*75g/2¾oz butter*
*125g/4½oz flour quantity flaky pastry (see page 463)*
*salt and freshly ground black pepper*
*½ beaten egg to glaze*

To garnish
*55g/2oz butter*
*110g/4oz leeks, cut into julienne strips*
*110g/4oz carrots, cut into julienne strips*
*110g/4oz button mushrooms, cut into julienne strips*
*salt and freshly ground black pepper*
*1 teaspoon chopped fresh tarragon*
*1 tablespoon chopped shallot*

**1.** Open the scallops with a strong knife and detach the scallop from the lower shell. Scoop out the scallops with a spoon, catching all their juice in a strainer lined with a fine cloth and placed over a bowl. Pull away and discard the membrane or frill and the black stomach parts. Wash the scallops thoroughly in cold running water, and dry them on a cloth. Separate the corals and cut the white parts in 2 across the middle to obtain 24 rounds.
**2.** Scrub 8 of the shells (tops and bottoms) under running water and set aside.
**3.** Heat the butter in a saucepan and cook the leeks and carrots for 5 minutes. Then add the mushrooms and cook for a further 3 minutes. Add salt, pepper and the tarragon. Cover and simmer for 2 minutes.
**4.** Roll out the pastry and cut it into 8 strips 25 × 2.5cm/10 × 1in. Preheat the oven to 250°C/480°F/gas mark 9.
**5.** Divide half the vegetable garnish among the 8 shells and sprinkle with the shallot.
**6.** Put the coral and 3 rounds of the white part of the scallop on each shell and season with salt and pepper.
**7.** Cover the scallops with the remaining vegetables, sprinkle them with the strained scallop juice and divide the butter between them.

**8.** Put 8 empty shells on top of the filled shells and edge each with a strip of the pastry, brushed with beaten egg, to seal completely. Bake in the preheated oven for 10–12 minutes, according to the size of the scallops, and serve in the shells.

NOTE: A low-fat version of this recipe can be prepared without the butter. Steam the vegetables for the garnish instead of frying them.

 *CHABLIS*

# SCALLOPS WITH PEA AND MINT PURÉE AND DEEP-FRIED LEEK AND GINGER

*1 leek, cut into julienne strips*
*1 × 5cm/2in piece of fresh root ginger, peeled and*
    *cut into julienne strips*
*seasoned flour*
*oil for deep-frying*
*salt*
*olive oil*
*20 large scallops, prepared (see page 128)*
*juice of 1 lemon*

For the pea purée
*285g/10oz frozen peas*
*salt and freshly ground black pepper*
*2 large sprigs of fresh mint*
*4 tablespoons crème fraîche*
*1 teaspoon chopped fresh mint*

**1.** Make the pea purée: simmer the peas in salted water with the sprigs of mint until just tender. Drain in a food processor or blender and discard the mint. Process the peas until smooth. Add the crème fraîche. Season to taste with salt and pepper.
**2.** Toss the leek and ginger in seasoned flour.
**3.** Heat the oil in a deep-fryer until a crumb will sizzle and brown in jut 30 seconds. Deep-fry the leek and ginger until just golden. Drain well on absorbent kitchen paper, sprinkle with salt and keep warm.
**4.** Heat some olive oil in a frying pan and fry the scallops on both sides until brown on the outside

but translucent inside. Add a little extra oil to the pan with the lemon juice.

**5.** Stir the chopped mint into the pea purée. Divide the purée between 4 dinner plates. Arrange the scallops on top of or around the purée and garnish with the deep-fried leeks and ginger.

## FRIED SCAMPI

SERVES 4
*675g/1½lb scampi*
*salt and freshly ground black pepper*
*lemon juice*
*oil for deep-frying*
*seasoned plain flour*
*beaten egg*
*dried white breadcrumbs*

To garnish
*deep-fried parsley (see page 686)*

**1.** If using frozen scampi sprinkle with pepper and lemon juice and defrost slowly.

**2.** Heat the oil in a deep-fryer until a crumb dropped into it will sizzle and brown.

**3.** Dip the scampi in seasoned flour. Dip into beaten egg, then turn carefully in the breadcrumbs, to coat thoroughly. Deep-fry until golden-brown. Drain on absorbent kitchen paper. Sprinkle with salt.

**4.** Garnish with fried parsley and serve immediately.

 *VERY DRY WHITE*

## STUFFED SQUID PROVENÇAL

SERVES 4
*12 small squid*
*2 tablespoons olive oil*
*1 onion, finely chopped*
*4 spring onions, finely chopped*
*2 clove of garlic, crushed*
*6 tomatoes, peeled, deseeded and roughly chopped*
*2 tablespoons chopped fresh mixed herbs*

*3 tablespoons finely chopped fresh parsley*
*2 tablespoons fresh white breadcrumbs*
*2 egg yolks*
*salt and freshly ground black pepper*
*2 tablespoons brandy*
*150ml/¼ pint dry white wine*
*425ml/¾ pint tomato sauce II (see page 258)*
*3 anchovies, soaked in milk, drained and chopped*
*1 tablespoon capers, rinsed and chopped*
*12 black olives, pitted*

**1.** Preheat the oven to 150°C/300°F/gas mark 2.

**2.** Prepare the squid (see page 177), keeping the tentacles for the stuffing.

**3.** Start the stuffing. Heat half the oil in a saucepan and sweat the onions, spring onions and garlic, adding the roughly chopped tentacles to the pan for the last minute, to cook them lightly.

**4.** Mix together the tomatoes, mixed herbs, 2 tablespoons of the parsley, the breadcrumbs and the cooled onion mixture. Bind the stuffing with the egg yolks, beat well and season with salt and pepper.

**5.** Fit a piping bag with a medium plain nozzle and fill with the stuffing. Pipe into the whole squid, being careful not to overfill, or the squid will burst during cooking. Seal the ends of each squid with a cocktail stick.

**6.** Heat the remaining oil in a frying pan and brown the squid evenly all over. Then flame with the brandy. When the flames subside, remove the squid from the frying pan, and place in a casserole dish.

**7.** Add the wine to the frying pan and boil to reduce by half. Add the tomato sauce, the anchovies, capers and olives, and bring to the boil. Pour over the squid.

**8.** Cover the casserole dish and cook in the preheated oven for 25 minutes or until the squid are tender.

**9.** Using a slotted spoon, remove the squid from the casserole dish to a serving dish and keep warm while finishing the sauce.

**10.** If the sauce is too thin, reduce by boiling rapidly in a saucepan. Check the seasoning, and spoon over the squid. Garnish with the olives and the remaining parsley.

 *RHÔNE/PROVENCE ROSÉ*

# STIR-FRIED SQUID

SERVES 4
900g/2lb fresh or frozen squid
1 tablespoon sunflower oil
1 clove of garlic, cut into slivers
1cm/1/2in piece of fresh ginger root, peeled and
    finely chopped
2 sticks of lemon grass, finely chopped
4 spring onions, sliced
1–2 teaspoons sugar
1 tablespoon Shaoxing wine, vermouth or dry sherry

1. Clean the squid (see page 177). Drain well.
2. Heat the oil in a wok, add the garlic, ginger
and lemon grass and cook slowly for 1 minute.
Remove the flavourings. Add the squid and stir-
fry over a very high heat for 1 minute. Reduce the
heat, add the spring onions and cook over a low
heat for 30 seconds. Add the garlic, ginger and
lemon grass with the sugar and wine and cook for
a further 30 seconds.

 *WHITE ALSACE*

# FRITTO MISTO

SERVES 4
450g/1lb mixed raw prawns, crayfish tails, crab
    meat, sole, whiting and whitebait (prepared
    weight)
lemon juice
salt and freshly ground black pepper
oil for deep-frying

For the batter
5g/1/4oz fresh yeast
150ml/1/4 pint tepid water
110g/4oz plain flour
a pinch of salt
1 tablespoon olive oil
1 egg white

To garnish
deep-fried parsley (see page 686)

1. Make the batter: mix the yeast with the water. Sift
the flour and salt into a bowl. Make a well in the
centre and pour in the frothing yeast liquid and oil.

2. Beat the mixture with a wooden spoon,
gradually drawing in the flour. Leave in a warm
place to rise for 30 minutes.
3. Sprinkle the fish with lemon juice and pepper
and leave for 30 minutes or so.
4. Beat the egg white until stiff and fold it into the
batter.
5. Drain the fish and dry on absorbent kitchen paper.
Dip into the batter, coating each piece completely.
6. Heat the oil until a crumb will sizzle slowly.
Deep-fry the fish pieces, a few at a time, until the
batter is golden-brown. Drain on absorbent kitchen
paper, sprinkle with salt and pile on to a warmed
serving dish. Garnish with deep-fried parsley.

 *SOAVE*

# SEAFOOD GUMBO

Traditional Creole gumbo was made with okra
(ladies' fingers) which was introduced to the USA
by slaves transported from Africa. The slimy seed
interior of okra is used to thicken this spicy soup.
In the absence of okra, the Americans use filé
powder, the ground-down leaves of the sassafrass
plant, which also acts as a thickening agent.

SERVES 8
450g/1lb raw scallops, prepared (see page 128)
450g/1lb huss fillet, skinned (see page 268)
450g/1lb okra
900g/2lb raw prawns, peeled and deveined

For the sauce
110g/4oz butter
2 large onions, chopped
45g/1 1/2oz plain flour
1/2 teaspoon cayenne powder
2 teaspoons freshly grated nutmeg
2 cloves of garlic, crushed
1 red pepper, deseeded and chopped
1 green pepper, deseeded and chopped
1 teaspoon Tabasco sauce
1 bay leaf
1 × 400g/14oz can of tomatoes
1 teaspoon chopped fresh oregano
1 teaspoon chopped fresh thyme
100ml/3 1/2fl oz dry white wine
salt and freshly ground black pepper
1/2 teaspoon filé powder (optional)

1. Cut the scallops in half horizontally. Cut the huss fillet into 2.5cm/1in cubes.

2. Trim the tops of the okra carefully and set aside.

3. Make the sauce: melt the butter in a large saucepan and add the onion and flour. Cook slowly until the roux is a good russet-brown.

4. Remove the pan from the heat, add the cayenne pepper and nutmeg and cook for 30 seconds.

5. Add the garlic, peppers, Tabasco, bay leaf, tomatoes, herbs and wine. Season to taste with salt and pepper.

6. Bring to the boil and add the prepared okra. Cover and simmer gently for 40 minutes.

7. Add the prepared fish and cook for 5 further minutes or until the fish is cooked.

8. Check the seasoning, add the filé powder, if using, and serve.

 *DRY ROSÉ*

# SEAFOOD FEUILLETÉES WITH SPINACH

*340g/12oz flour quantity puff pastry (see page 464)*
*1 egg, beaten, to glaze*

For the filling
*450g/1lb fresh very young spinach*
*30g/1oz butter*
*salt and freshly ground black pepper*
*290ml/½ pint fish stock (see page 245)*
*340g/12oz peeled cooked prawns*
*3 small sole fillets*
*85g/3oz raw scampi*
*110g/4oz scallops, prepared (see page 128)*
*freshly grated nutmeg*

For the sauce
*2 shallots, finely chopped*
*225g/8oz chilled unsalted butter*
*1 teaspoon fish glaze (see page 245) (optional)*
*100ml/3½fl oz dry white wine*
*1 tablespoon double cream*
*juice of ¼ lemon*
*salt and freshly ground white pepper*

1. Preheat the oven to 220°C/425°F/gas mark 7.

2. Roll the pastry into a large rectangle and cut it into 4 diamonds, each side measuring 10cm/4in.

3. Place the diamonds on a damp baking sheet and brush with egg glaze. Using a sharp knife,

trace a line about 1cm/½in from the edge of each diamond, without cutting all the way through the pastry. A small diamond is thus traced, which will form the 'hat' for the pastry case. Make a design inside this diamond with the knife. Flour the blade of a knife and use this to knock up the sides of the pastry. Chill in the refrigerator for 15 minutes.

4. Bake the pastry cases in the preheated oven for 20 minutes, or until puffed up and brown. Using a knife, outline and remove the 'hats' and scoop out any uncooked dough inside. Return to the oven for 2 minutes to dry out.

5. Transfer the cases and hats to a wire rack and leave to cool. Reduce the oven temperature to 130°C/250°F gas mark 1.

6. Wash the spinach very well and remove the stalks. Fry quickly in half the butter until just beginning to wilt.

7. Put the fish stock into a large shallow pan. Bring up to scalding point (just below boiling), add the sole fillets and poach for 1 minute, then add the scampi and poach for 1 further minute until just cooked. Remove the fish from the pan with the slotted spoon. Strain the stock and reduce to a glaze. Reserve. Fry the scallops in the remaining butter until just cooked. Set aside.

8. Make the sauce: sweat the shallots very slowly in 15g/½oz of the butter in a saucepan. Add the fish glaze and white wine. Strain. Add the cream and reduce again. Cut the remaining cold butter into small pieces and gradually whisk it into the pan over a low heat. Remove the pan from the heat from time to time so that the butter thickens the sauce without melting. Work fairly quickly, however, as otherwise you may find that the sauce is only just warm (it does not reheat well). Add the lemon juice. Taste, add extra fish glaze if necessary and season with salt and pepper.

9. While the sauce is being made the feuilletées can be assembled and reheated. Reheat the spinach in the butter and season with salt, pepper and nutmeg. Pile some spinach inside each pastry case. Cut the sole fillets into 3–4 diagonal pieces. Arrange with the other seafood on the spinach.

10. Just before serving, spoon a generous tablespoon of sauce over each feuilletée. Set a hat on top. Hand the remaining sauce separately in a warmed sauce-boat.

 *CHABLIS*

# GRILLED SEAFOOD KEBABS

SERVES 4

*225g/8oz turbot fillet*
*12 small scallops, prepared (see page 128)*
*1 red pepper, deseeded and cut into large pieces*
*2 rashers of rindless streaky bacon*

**1.** Preheat the grill to its highest setting.
**2.** Cut the turbot into pieces similar in size to the whole scallops.
**3.** Thread the turbot, scallops and pepper on to 4 large skewers. Place on the grill pan.
**4.** Cut the bacon in half lengthways and lay a piece on each kebab. Grill for 2 minutes. Turn over, keeping the bacon on top, and grill for a further 4 minutes. Remove and discard the bacon after 2 minutes.
**5.** Serve on a bed of saffron rice or freshly cooked pasta.

NOTE: The bacon is discarded in order to make this a low-fat dish, but it can be eaten if preferred.

 *WHITE LOIRE*

# POT AU FEU DE LA MER

SERVES 6

*170g/6oz monkfish, cubed*
*170g/6oz sole fillets, skinned and sliced*
*675ml/1½ pints fish stock (see page 245)*
*4 large scallops, muscle removed (see page 128), halved*
*110g/4oz whole scampi*
*6 tablespoons dry white wine*
*8 spring onions, trimmed and cut into julienne strips*
*1 medium carrot, peeled and cut into julienne strips*
*1 large stick of celery, cut into julienne strips*
*4 large cap mushrooms, quartered*
*150ml/¼ pint double cream*
*salt and freshly ground black pepper*

**1.** Poach the monkfish and sole in the hot fish stock for 2 minutes. Remove and keep warm in a very low oven. Add the scallops and scampi to the stock and poach for 1 minute. Remove and keep warm.

**2.** Add the wine to the stock and reduce, by boiling rapidly, to 290ml/½ pint.
**3.** Meanwhile, blanch the spring onions, carrots and celery in boiling salted water for 1 minute, then drain well. Blanch the mushrooms until just cooked.
**4.** Add the cream to the reduced stock and boil to reduce to a creamy consistency. Season to taste with salt and pepper. Add the fish.
**5.** Arrange the fish in its sauce on 4 dinner plates and garnish with a scattering of warm julienne vegetables and the mushrooms.

 *WHITE BURGUNDY*

# PAELLA

There are hundreds of recipes for paella. We have chosen a good selection of shellfish, but if you are unable to find all the ingredients don't worry. A true paella is made with Valencian rice, but it is difficult to find in the UK, so we have used long-grain rice instead.

SERVES 6

*1 × 450g/1lb cooked lobster meat, removed from shell*
*16 langoustines*
*450g/1lb live mussels*
*225g/8oz shell-on prawns*
*1 × 450g/1lb single portion poussin*
*55g/2oz butter, clarified (see page 686)*
*1 large Spanish onion, finely chopped*
*2 cloves of garlic, crushed*
*225g/8oz long-grain rice*
*1 litre/1¾ pints strong, well-flavoured shellfish stock (see page 245)*
*a pinch of saffron strands*
*5 tablespoons dry sherry*
*6 plum tomatoes, peeled, deseeded and chopped*
*salt and freshly ground black pepper*
*110g/4oz whitebait (optional)*
*seasoned plain flour*
*1 tablespoon olive oil*

**1.** Prepare the shellfish and chicken: cut the lobster meat into thick slices and dice the claw meat. Set aside. Devein the langoustines. Scrub and pick over the mussels, remove the beards and

311

make sure that the shells are shut. Peel and devein the prawns. Cut the poussin into quarters.

**2.** Heat the butter in a *paellera* or large frying pan. Brown the poussin quarters well, then set aside on a plate.

**3.** Add the onion and cook over a low heat until soft. Add the garlic and rice and cook for 2–3 minutes, or until the rice is opaque.

**4.** Add the stock to the pan, with the poussin. Cover the pan and cook very slowly for 15–20 minutes, or until the rice is nearly cooked. (If the rice begins to stick, but needs longer cooking, add a little more water.)

**5.** Add the saffron and sherry to the pan with the langoustines and mussels. Cook for 3–4 further minutes until the mussel shells have opened and the langoustines and poussin are cooked.

**6.** Stir the lobster meat and tomatoes into the rice and heat for 2 further minutes, or until the lobster is very hot.

**7.** Meanwhile, dip the whitebait, if used, in the seasoned flour and fry in the olive oil until crisp. Set aside.

**8.** Season the paella very well with salt and pepper. Arrange the whitebait on the top, if using. Serve very hot.

 *WHITE RIOJA*

# BRAISED OCTOPUS WITH GLAZED ONIONS AND AÏOLI

SERVES 4
*900g/2lb octopus, cleaned*
*1 tablespoon oil*
*30g/1oz butter*
*1 onion, thinly sliced*
*1 carrot, thinly sliced*
*2 cloves of garlic, crushed*
*2 tablespoons brandy*
*100ml/3½fl oz red wine*
*150ml/5fl oz fish stock (see page 245)*
*salt and freshly ground black pepper*
*900g/2lb button onions*
*55g/2oz butter*
*1 tablespoon sugar*

To serve
*1 quantity aïoli (see page 250)*

**1.** Blanch the octopus in boiling water for 2 minutes, then drain. Peel the dark skin off the main body of the octopus and scrape the skin off the tentacles with a knife. Beat thoroughly with a rolling pin. Cut the tentacles and body into 5cm/2in pieces. Set aside.

**2.** Preheat the oven to 325°C/170°F/gas mark 3.

**3.** Heat the oil and butter in a large flame-proof casserole. When the butter is foaming, brown the octopus pieces a few at a time. Lift on to a plate.

**4.** Add the onion and carrot to the casserole, reduce the heat and cook slowly until soft. Add the garlic and cook for 2 further minutes. Put the octopus on top of the vegetables. Reserve the ink, if any.

**5.** Heat the brandy in a ladle or small saucepan, ignite and pour, flaming, over the octopus and vegetables. When the flames have died down, pour over the wine and stock and season lightly with salt and pepper. Bring to the boil and cover with a lid. Cook in the oven for 2 hours or until the octopus is completely tender.

**6.** Meanwhile, blanch the onions in boiling water for 3 minutes, then drain and peel. Taking care when removing the skin not to cut too much of the top off, or the onion will disintegrate during cooking.

**7.** Heat the butter and sugar in a second large flameproof casserole, add the onions, cover and set over a low heat. Shake the pan from time to time, but avoid removing the lid too often. When the onions are well browned all over, put into the oven and cook for 30 minutes or until tender.

**8.** When the octopus is cooked, lift out of the casserole and stir into the glazed onions. Keep warm. Strain the remaining contents of the octopus casserole into a saucepan, bring to the boil and reduce by boiling rapidly if necessary until syrupy. Add the reserved ink. Season to taste with salt and pepper.

**9.** Pour the reduced cooking liquid on to the octopus and onions.

**10.** To serve: divide the octopus, onions and sauce between 4 individual plates. Put a spoonful of aïoli on top of each and serve immediately.

 *CHILEAN CHARDONNAY*

# POULTRY
# AND GAME

# POULTRY AND GAME

TO PREPARE AND DRAW A GAME BIRD FOR THE OVEN

Some birds are easier to pluck than others, ducks being notoriously
tedious. All birds are easier to pluck if still warm when tackled. Work
away from draughts, as the feathers fly about, and pluck straight into a
dustbin. Tug the feathers, working from the tail to the head, pulling
against the way the feathers grow. If the bird is very young or if there is
a lot of fat, pull downwards towards the tail to avoid tearing the flesh.

Once plucked, the bird should be singed. This can
be done with a burning taper, or directly over a
gas flame, but care should be taken to singe only
the down and small feathers, and not to blacken
the flesh. The bird should then be rubbed with a
clean tea-towel to remove any remaining stubble.
It is now ready for drawing.

Surprisingly, birds keep better, when hanging,
with their insides intact. Once eviscerated they
must be cooked within a day or two. So when
you are ready to cook the bird, take it down, and
proceed as follows.

1. Pluck it.
2. Cut round the feet, at the drumstick joint, but
do not cut right through the tendons. Pull the legs
off the bird, drawing the tendons out with them.
If the bird is small this is easy enough – just bend
the foot back until it snaps, and pull, perhaps
over the edge of a table. Turkeys are more
difficult: snap the feet at the drumstick joint by
bending them over the end of the table, then hang
the bird up by the feet from a stout hook, and
pull on the bird. The feet plus tendons will be left
on the hook, the turkey in your arms. All too
often birds are sold with the tendons in the legs,
making the drumsticks tough when cooked.
3. Now for the head and neck. Lay the bird breast
side down on a board. Make a slit through the
neck skin from the body to the head. Cut off the
head and throw it away. Pull back the split neck
skin, leaving it attached to the body of the bird (it
will come in useful to close the gap if you are

stuffing the bird). Cut the neck off as close to the
body as you can.
4. Put a finger into the neck hole, to the side of
the stump of neck left on the bird, and move the
finger right round, loosening the innards from the
neck. If you do not do this you will find them
difficult to pull out from the other end.
5. With a sharp knife slit the bird open from the
vent to the parson's (or pope's) nose, making a
hole large enough to just get your hand in. Put
your hand in, working it so the back of your
hand is up against the arch of the breastbone, and
carefully loosen the entrails from the sides of the
body cavity, all the way round. Pull them out,
taking care not to break the gall bladder, the
contents of which would embitter any flesh they
touched. Covering the gutting hand with a cloth
helps extract the intestines intact. The first time
you do this it is unlikely that you will get
everything out in one motion, so check that the
lungs and kidneys come too. Have another go if
necessary. Once the bird is empty, wipe any traces
of blood off with a clean damp cloth.

The neck and feet go into the stockpot with
the heart and the cleaned gizzard. To clean the
gizzard, carefully cut the outside wall along the
natural seam so that you can peel it away from
the inner bag of grit. Throw the grit bag away,
with the intestines and the gall bladder. Do not
put the liver in the stockpot: it may make the
stock bitter. It may be fried and served with the
dish, or fried, chopped and added to the sauce, or

kept frozen until enough poultry liver has been collected to make pâté. But if the liver is to be used, carefully cut away the discoloured portion of it where it lay against the gall bladder (it will be bitter) and trim off any membranes.

The bird is trussed to keep it in a compact, neat shape, usually after stuffing. Trussing large birds is unnecessary as the bird is to be carved up anyway, and trussing serves to prevent the inside thigh being cooked by the time the breast is ready. Small birds, especially game birds where underdone thighs are desirable, are trussed, but their feet are left on. Their feet may simply be tied together for neatness sake, and the pinions skewered under the bird. Or they may be trussed in any number of ways, one of which is described below.

**1.** Arrange the bird so that the neck flap is folded over the neck hole, and the pinions turned under and tucked in tight. They will, if folded correctly, hold the neck flap in place, but if the bird is well stuffed the neck flap may have to be skewered or sewn in place.
**2.** Press the legs down and into the bird to force the breast into a plumped-up position. Thread a long trussing needle with thin string and push it through the wing joint, right through the body and out of the other wing joint.
**3.** Then push it through the body again, this time through the thighs. You should now be back on the side you started.
**4.** Tie the two ends together in a bow to make later removal quick.
**5.** Then thread a shorter piece of string through the thin end of the two drumsticks and tie them together, winding the string round the parson's nose at the same time to close the vent.
Sometimes a small slit is cut in the skin just below the end of the breastbone, and the parson's nose is pushed through it.

Small birds such as quail are invariably cooked whole, perhaps stuffed, and perhaps boned (see pages 316–17). But medium-sized ones, like chickens and guinea fowl, are often cut into 2, 4, 6 or 8 pieces. Use a knife to cut through the flesh and poultry shears or scissors to cut the bones.

## TO SPLIT A BIRD IN HALF
Simply use a sharp knife to cut right through flesh and bone, just on one side of the breastbone, open out the bird and cut through the other side, immediately next to the backbone. Then cut the backbone away from the half to which it remains attached. The knobbly end of the drumsticks and the fleshless tips to the pinions can be cut off before or after cooking. In birds brought whole to the table they are left on.

## TO JOINT A BIRD INTO 4
First pull out any trussing strings, then pull the leg away from the body. With a sharp knife cut through the skin joining the leg to the body, pull the leg away further and cut through more skin to free the leg. Bend the leg outwards and back, forcing the bone to come out of its socket close to the body. Turn the bird over, feel along the backbone to find the oyster (a soft pocket of flesh at the side of the backbone, near the middle). With the tip of the knife, cut this away from the carcase at the side nearest the backbone and farthest from the leg. Then turn the bird over again, and cut through the flesh, the knife going between the end of the thigh bone and the carcase, to take off the leg, bringing the oyster with it. Using poultry shears or a heavy knife, split the carcase along the breastbone. Cut through the ribs on each side to take off the fleshy portion of the breast, and with it the wing. Trim the joints neatly to remove scraps of untidy skin.

For six joints, proceed as above but split the legs into thigh portions and drumsticks. The exact join of the bones can easily be seen if the leg is laid on the board, skin side down. Cut through the fat line. With a cleaver, or the heel end of a knife, chop the feet off the drumsticks.

## TO JOINT INTO 8
**1.** Turn the chicken over so the backbone is uppermost. Cut through to the bone along the line of the spine.
**2.** Where the thigh joins the backbone there is a fleshy 'oyster' on each side. Cut round them to loosen them from the carcase so that they come away when the legs are severed.
**3.** Turn the bird over and pull a leg away from the body. Cut through the skin only, as far round the leg as possible, close to the body.
**4.** Pull the leg away from the body and twist it down so that the thigh bone pops out of its socket on the carcase and is exposed.
**5.** Cut the leg off, taking care to go between thigh bone and carcase and to bring the 'oyster' away with the leg. (Turn over briefly to check.) Repeat the process for the other leg.

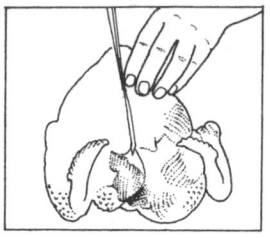 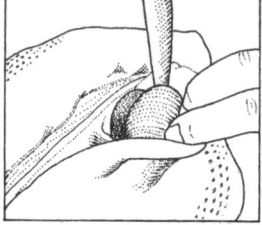 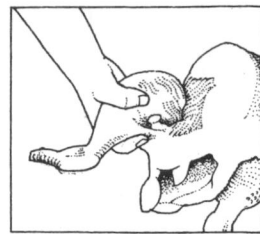

*Jointing a chicken: Stages 1 and 2 (numbers refer to text)*   *Stages 3 and 4*

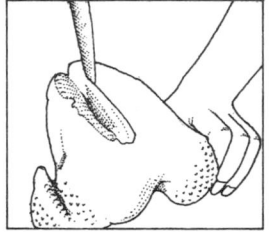 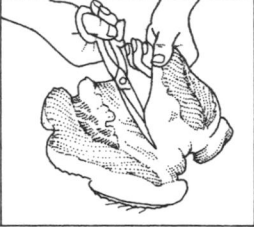 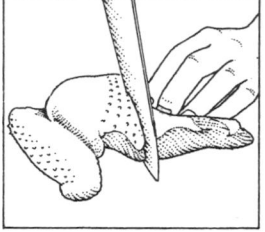 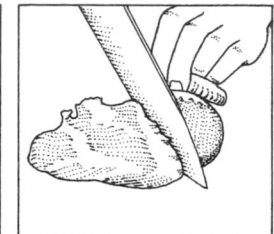

*Stages 6, 7 and 8*   *Stages 9 and 11*

**6.** Carefully cut down each side of the breast bone to free the flesh a little.

**7.** Use scissors to cut through the small bone close to the breast. Cut away the breastbone.

**8.** Open up the bird. Cut each wing and breast off the carcase with scissors. Start at the tail end and cut to and through the wing bone near the neck.

**9.** Cut the wing joint in two, leaving about one third of the breast attached to the wing.

**10.** Cut off the pinions from each wing. They can go into the stockpot with the carcase.

**11.** Separate the drumsticks and thighs, lay the legs skin side down on the board, and cut through where the thigh and lower leg bones meet, on the obvious fat line.

**12.** With a cleaver, or the heel end of a heavy knife, chop the feet off the drumsticks.

## BARDING

Poultry liable to dry out during cooking is often barded: lay fatty bacon or rindless pork back fat strips over the body of the bird, and secure or tie in place. The barding is removed during cooking to allow the breast to brown.

## BONING

**1.** Put the bird breast side down on a board. Cut through to the backbone.

**2.** Feel for the fleshy 'oyster' at the top of each thigh and cut round it. Cut and scrape the flesh

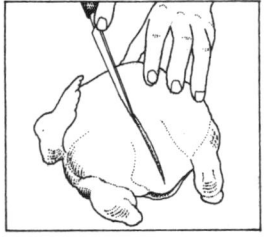 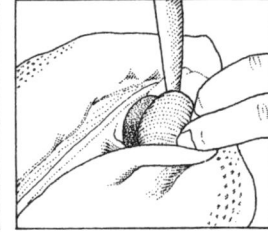

*Boning a chicken: Stages 1 and 2 (numbers refer to text)*

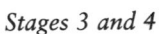

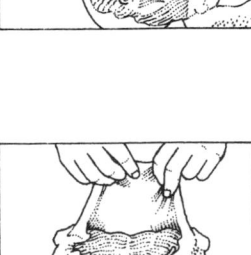 

*Stages 3 and 4*

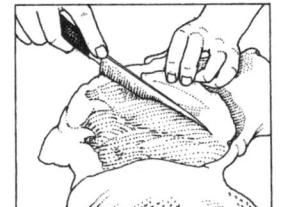

*Stages 10 and 12*

from the carcase with a sharp knife held as close as possible to the bone.

**3.** Continue along both sides of the backbone until the ribcage is exposed. At the joint of the thigh and pelvis, cut between the bones at the socket so that the legs stay attached to the flesh and skin, and not to the body carcase.

**4.** Keep working right round the bird, then use scissors to cut away most of the ribcage, leaving only the cartilaginous breastbone in the centre.

**5.** Using a heavy knife, cut through the foot joints to remove the knuckle end of the drumsticks.

**6.** Working from the inside thigh end scrape one leg bone clean, pushing the flesh down towards the drumstick until you can free the thigh bone. Repeat on the other leg.

**7.** Working from the drumstick ends, scrape the lower leg bones clean in the same way and remove them. Remove as many tendons as possible from the legs as you work.

**8.** Now for the wings. Cut off the pinions with a heavy knife.

**9.** Scrape the wing bones clean as you did the leg bones.

**10.** Carefully free the breastbone with the knife, working from the middle of the bird towards the tail.

**11.** Take great care not to puncture the skin, which has no flesh under it at this point so is easily torn.

**12.** You should now have a beautifully boned bird. Keep the neck flap of skin intact to fold over once the chicken is stuffed.

## ROASTING TABLES

If using a fan (convection) oven, reduce the cooking times by 15 per cent or lower the oven temperature by 20°C/40°F.

| Meat | | Temperature | | | Cooking time | |
|---|---|---|---|---|---|---|
| | | °C | °F | Gas | per kg | per lb |
| **Beef** | Brown | 220 | 425 | 7 | 20 mins+ | |
| | Rare roast | 160 | 325 | 3 | 35 mins | 15 mins |
| | Medium roast | | | | 45 mins | 20 mins |
| **Pork** | Roast | 200 | 400 | 6 | 65 mins | 25 mins |
| **Veal** | Brown | 220 | 425 | 7 | 20 mins+ | |
| | Roast | 180 | 350 | 4 | 55 mins | 25 mins |
| **Lamb** | Brown | 220 | 425 | 7 | 20 mins | |
| | Roast | 190 | 375 | 5 | 55 mins | 20 mins |
| **Chicken** | | 200 | 400 | 6 | 35–45 mins | 15–20 mins |
| | NOTE: Few chickens, however small, will be cooked in much under an hour. | | | | | |
| **Turkey** | Small (under 6kg/13lb) | 200 | 400 | 6 | 25 mins | 12 mins |
| | Large | 180 | 350 | 4 | 35 mins | 15 mins |
| | NOTE: For more detailed timings see chart on page 318. (Few turkeys, however small, will be cooked in under 2 hours.) | | | | | |
| **Duck, goose** | Small (under 2.3kg/5lb) | 190 | 375 | 5 | 45 mins | 20 mins |
| | Large | 180 | 350 | 4 | 55 mins | 25 mins |
| **Pigeon** | | 200 | 400 | 6 | 25–35 minutes | |
| **Grouse** | | 190 | 375 | 5 | 25–35 minutes | |
| **Guinea fowl** | | 190 | 375 | 5 | 70 minutes | |
| **Partridge** | | 190 | 375 | 5 | 20–25 minutes | |
| **Pheasant** | | 190 | 375 | 5 | 45–60 minutes | |
| **Wild duck** | | 200 | 400 | 6 | 40 minutes | |
| **Woodcock** | | 190 | 375 | 5 | 20–30 minutes | |
| **Quail** | | 180 | 350 | 4 | 20 minutes | |
| **Snipe** | | 190 | 375 | 5 | 15–20 minutes | |

## THAWING AND COOKING TIMES FOR TURKEYS

Although the thawing time in this table can be relied on, the cooking times are dependent on an accurate oven. For safety's sake, plan the timing so that, if all goes right, the bird will be ready 1 hour before dinner. This will give you leeway if necessary. To test if the turkey is cooked, press a skewer into the thickest part of the thigh. The juices should run clear. When the bird is cooked, open the oven door to cool the oven, then put the turkey on a serving dish and return it to the oven to keep warm.

Thawing in a warm room (over 18°C/65°F) or under warm water is not recommended, as warmth will encourage the growth of micro-organisms, which might result in food poisoning.

| Weight of bird when ready for the oven regardless of whether it is boned, stuffed or empty | Thawing time at room temperature 18°C/65°F | Thawing time in refrigerator 5°C/40°F | Cooking time at 200°C/400°F gas mark 6 | Cooking time at 180°C/350°F gas mark 4 |
|---|---|---|---|---|
| | hours | hours | hours | hours |
| 4–5kg/8–10lb | 20 | 65 | 2½–3 hrs | – |
| 5–6kg/10–13lb | 24 | 70 | 3–3¾ hrs | – |
| 6–7kg/13–16lb | 30 | 75 | 30 minutes then | 3¼–4 |
| 8–9kg/16–20lb | 40 | 80 | 30 minutes then | 4–4½ |
| 9–11kg/20–24lb | 48 | 96 | 1 hour then | 4–4½ |

# CHICKEN ELIZABETH

The Cordon Bleu School devised this dish for the Coronation celebration in 1953.

SERVES 4
*1 × 1.35kg/3lb chicken, cleaned but not trussed*
*white stock, made with chicken bones (see page 243), or water with 1 bay leaf, 6 peppercorns, salt, 2 parsley stalks, 1 lemon slice and 2 teaspoons fresh thyme leaves*
*225ml/8fl oz Elizabeth sauce (see page 250)*

To serve
*rice salad (see page 235)*
*1 bunch of watercress*

**1.** Place the chicken, in a saucepan of simmering stock, or water with the flavourings.
**2.** Cover the pan and cook gently for 1¼–1½ hours or until the chicken is tender and the drumsticks feel loose and wobbly. Remove the chicken from the stock and set aside to cool.
**3.** Remove the flesh from the chicken bones, and when quite cold mix with the sauce, reserving a little of it.

**4.** Pile the chicken into the middle of a serving-dish and coat with the reserved sauce. Surround with the rice salad and garnish with watercress.

NOTE: It is easier to strip chicken flesh from the bones while the bird is still lukewarm. But on no account should the sauce be added to the flesh until the chicken is completely cold.

 *WHITE LOIRE*

# POACHED CHICKEN WITH PARSLEY SAUCE

SERVES 4
*1 × 1.35kg/3lb chicken, cleaned but not trussed*

For the court bouillon
*1 onion, sliced*
*2 carrots*
*2 parsley stalks*
*salt*
*6 black peppercorns*
*2 sticks of celery*
*2 bay leaves*

For the parsley sauce
*30g/1oz butter*
*30g/1oz plain flour*
*150ml/¼ pint milk*
*2 tablespoons single cream (optional)*
*2 tablespoons chopped fresh parsley*
*salt and freshly ground black pepper*

1. Put the chicken into a large saucepan with the onion, carrots, parsley stalks, salt, peppercorns, celery and bay leaves. Half-submerge the bird with water and cover with a well-fitting lid.
2. Bring to the boil, then reduce the heat and simmer gently for 1½ hours or until the chicken is cooked, when the legs feel loose and wobbly.
3. Remove the chicken from the pan and strain the stock.
4. Carefully skim the stock of all the fat. When you have spooned off as much grease as possible, lay successive sheets of absorbent kitchen paper on the surface of the liquid to remove the remaining fat.
5. Now start the parsley sauce: melt the butter in a saucepan, add the flour and cook for 1 minute. Remove from the heat.
6. Gradually add the milk and 150ml/¼ pint of the chicken stock. Return to the heat and bring to the boil, stirring continuously.
7. Simmer for 2 minutes, then add the cream, if using, and set aside.
8. Skin the chicken and remove the bones, leaving the flesh in large pieces.
9. Reheat the sauce and add the parsley. Season if necessary with salt and pepper. Add more stock if the sauce is too thick. Add the chicken to the sauce, turn gently to coat, and tip into a serving dish.

NOTE: Do not add the parsley to the sauce in advance as it will lose its colour.

 *WHITE ALSACE*

# CHICKEN À LA KING

SERVES 6
*2 bay leaves*
*1 small onion, sliced*
*1 small carrot, sliced*
*a few parsley stalks*

*salt*
*6 black peppercorns*
*1 × 1.35kg/3lb chicken, not trussed*
*45g/1½oz butter*
*1 onion, thinly sliced*
*1 small red pepper, cored, deseeded and sliced*
*1 canned pimiento, sliced*
*110g/4oz mushrooms, sliced*
*45g/1½oz plain flour*
*1 tablespoon dry sherry*
*150ml/¼ pint milk*
*3 tablespoons single cream*
*freshly ground black pepper*

To serve
*boiled rice*

1. Put a large saucepan of water on to simmer with the onion, carrot, bay leaves, parsley stalks, salt and peppercorns. Add the chicken, breast side up. Cover and simmer until tender (about 1 hour). To test if the chicken is cooked, push a skewer into the thickest part of the thigh. It should glide in easily and the drumstick should be loose and wobbly.
2. Remove the chicken from the stock and allow both to become completely cold.
3. Skim the fat off the stock. Reduce the stock by rapid boiling to 425ml/¾ pint.
4. Skin the chicken and remove the bones. Cut the flesh into large pieces.
5. Melt the butter in a saucepan, add the onion and cook over a low heat for 2 minutes. Add the red pepper and cook for 1 further minute. Add the pimiento, mushrooms and flour and cook, stirring for 1 minute.
6. Remove the pan from the heat and add the reduced stock. Mix well and return the pan to the heat. Bring slowly to the boil, stirring continuously. Add the sherry. Simmer for 1–2 minutes.
7. Add the milk and cream and reheat without boiling. Season to taste with salt and pepper.
8. Add the chicken and allow to warm through without boiling. Check the seasoning.
9. Serve with boiled rice.

 *AUSTRALIAN/CALIFORNIAN CHARDONNAY*

# CURRIED CHICKEN AND HAM PIE

SERVES 4

*55g/2oz butter*
*1 onion, chopped*
*1 teaspoon curry powder (see page 688)*
*½ teaspoon ground turmeric*
*45g/1½oz plain flour*
*290ml/½ pint stock, reserved after cooking the chicken*
*150ml/¼ pint creamy milk*
*5ml/1 teaspoon chopped fresh parsley*
*1 teaspoon chopped fresh mint*
*a pinch of crushed cardamom seeds*
*a pinch of dry English mustard*
*salt and freshly ground black pepper*
*a squeeze of lemon juice*
*2 hardboiled eggs, chopped*
*110g/4oz ham, cut into 1cm/½in dice*
*1 × 1.35kg/3lb chicken, poached, boned and cut into large chunks*
*225g/8oz flour quantity wholemeal pastry (see page 463)*
*1 egg, beaten with a pinch of salt and a teaspoon water, to glaze*

**1.** Preheat the oven to 200°C/400°F/gas mark 6.
**2.** Melt the butter in a saucepan and add the onion. Cook gently until soft but not coloured.
**3.** Stir in the curry powder and turmeric and cook for 1 minute.
**4.** Add the flour and cook over a low heat for 1 minute. Remove the pan from the heat. Add the stock and stir well. Return to the heat and bring slowly to the boil, stirring continuously until the sauce is thick and shiny.
**5.** Add the milk and stir again until the sauce returns to the boil.
**6.** Add the parsley, mint, cardamom seeds, mustard, salt and pepper. Simmer for 2–3 minutes.
**7.** Taste, adding more salt if necessary, and add the lemon juice. Allow to cool.
**8.** Stir in the hardboiled eggs, the ham and the chicken. Pour the mixture into a pie dish.
**9.** Roll the pastry on a floured board to a rectangle about 5mm/¼in thick.
**10.** Cut a band of pastry slightly wider than the edge of the pie dish. Brush the rim of the dish with water and press on the band of pastry. Brush with a little beaten egg or water and lay the pastry lid over the pie. Cut away any surplus pastry from the sides with a knife.
**11.** Press the pie edges together and mark a pattern with the point of a small knife, or pinch with the fingers into a raised border. Shape the pastry trimmings into leaves for decoration. Make a small hole in the pastry to allow the steam to escape.
**12.** Brush the pastry with beaten egg and decorate with the pastry leaves. Brush again with egg.
**13.** Bake in the preheated oven for 30–35 minutes until golden-brown.

NOTE: If the pie is not to be baked as soon as it has been assembled it is essential that the curry sauce and the chicken are both completely cold before they are combined. Keep the pie refrigerated or frozen until ready to bake. If frozen, thaw in the refrigerator before baking.

 *DRY WHITE/ROSÉ*

# CHICKEN AND SWEETBREAD FILLING FOR VOL-AU-VENTS OR FEUILLETÉES

SERVES 4

*a pair of calves' sweetbreads or 225g/8oz lamb's sweetbreads*
*45g/1½oz butter*
*1 small onion, very finely chopped*
*55g/2oz button mushrooms, sliced*
*30g/1oz plain flour*
*150ml/¼ pint creamy milk*
*1 tablespoon dry sherry*
*150ml/¼ pint white stock, made with chicken bones (see page 243)*
*1 tablespoon chopped fresh parsley*
*a squeeze of lemon juice*
*225g/8oz cooked chicken, cut into chunks*
*salt and freshly ground black pepper*
*1 large vol-au-vent case (see page 465) or 4 feuilletée cases*

1. Soak the sweetbreads in cold water for 4 hours. Change the water every time it becomes pink (probably 4 times). There should be no blood at all when the sweetbreads are ready for cooking.
2. Place them in a saucepan of cold water and bring to the boil. Reduce the heat and poach for 2 minutes.
3. Drain the sweetbreads and rinse under cold running water. Dry well. Pick them over, removing all the skin and membrane, and chop coarsely.
4. Melt the butter in a saucepan, add the onion and cook over a low heat until soft but not coloured (this may take 10 minutes).
5. Add the sweetbreads. Stir in the mushrooms and leave over a low heat for 1 minute. Remove the sweetbreads and mushrooms with a slotted spoon.
6. Stir the flour into the pan and cook for 1 minute. Remove from the heat and stir in the milk, sherry and stock. Bring slowly to the boil, stirring continuously. Simmer for 1 minute.
7. Add the parsley, lemon juice, chicken pieces, sweetbreads, mushrooms, salt and pepper.
8. Tip the mixture carefully into the vol-au-vent case and reheat in the oven for 5 minutes.

 *SPICY DRY WHITE*

# GOUGÈRE

A gougère is a cheese choux pastry case which may be filled with a variety of mixtures such as haddock (see page 276), chicken or game (see below).

SERVES 4
*105g/3¾oz plain flour*
*a pinch of salt*
*freshly ground black pepper*
*cayenne pepper*
*85g/3oz butter*
*220ml/7fl oz water*
*3 eggs, lightly beaten*
*55g/2oz strong Cheddar cheese, cut into*
    *5mm/¼in cubes*
*425ml/¾ pint filling (see following recipe)*
*2 teaspoons browned breadcrumbs*
*1 tablespoon grated cheese*

1. Preheat the oven to 200°C/400°F/gas mark 6.
2. Sift the flour with the salt, pepper and cayenne.
3. In a large saucepan slowly heat the butter in the water and when completely melted bring to a rolling boil. When the mixture is bubbling all over, tip in the flour, remove from the heat and beat well with a wooden spoon until the mixture will leave the sides of the pan. Allow to cool for about 10 minutes.
4. Beat in the eggs gradually until the mixture is smooth and shiny and of a dropping consistency – you may not need the last few spoonfuls of egg. Stir in the diced cheese.
5. Spoon the mixture round the edge of a flattish greased ovenproof dish. Bake in the preheated oven for 25 minutes. Pile the filling into the centre and sprinkle with the breadcrumbs and grated cheese. Return to the oven and bake for about 15 minutes, until the choux is well risen and golden and the filling is hot.

# CHICKEN OR GAME FILLING FOR GOUGÈRE

SERVES 4
*30g/1oz butter*
*1 medium onion, thinly sliced*
*110g/4oz large mushrooms, sliced*
*20g/¾ plain flour*
*290ml/½ pint white stock, made with chicken*
    *bones (see page 243)*
*salt and freshly ground black pepper*
*2 teaspoons chopped fresh parsley*
*340g/12oz cooked game or chicken, shredded*

1. Melt the butter in a saucepan and soften the onion over a low heat. Add the mushrooms. Cook for 1 minute.
2. Stir in the flour. Cook for 1 minute.
3. Remove the pan from the heat and stir in the stock. Return to the heat. Bring to the boil, stirring continuously. Season to taste with salt and pepper. Simmer for 1 minute.
4. Add the parsley and game or chicken and use as required.

 *RED BURGUNDY*

# CHICKEN CROQUETTES

SERVES 4

*55g/2oz butter*
*1 small onion, chopped*
*30g/1oz mushrooms, chopped*
*55g/2oz plain flour*
*290ml/½ pint milk, or milk and white stock,*
  *made with chicken bones (see page 243) mixed*
*salt and freshly ground black pepper*
*1 teaspoon chopped fresh parsley*
*oil for deep-frying*
*1 egg yolk*
*lemon juice*
*285/10oz cooked chicken, finely diced or minced*
*seasoned plain flour*
*1 egg, beaten*
*dried white breadcrumbs*

**1.** Melt the butter in a saucepan and add the
onion. Cook until soft but not coloured, then add
the mushrooms and cook for 1 further minute.
**2.** Add the flour and cook, stirring, for 1 minute.
Remove the pan from the heat and stir in the
milk. Return to the heat and bring slowly to the
boil, stirring continuously. Simmer for 2–3
minutes, season to taste with salt and pepper and
add the parsley. Remove from the heat and allow
to get completely cold. The sauce should be very
thick.
**3.** Meanwhile, heat the oil in a deep-fryer until a
crumb will sizzle in it.
**4.** When the sauce is cold, beat in the egg yolk,
add a squeeze of lemon juice and stir in the
chicken flesh.
**5.** With floured hands, shape the mixture into
cylinders about 3.5cm/1½in long.
**6.** Coat with beaten egg and dip into
breadcrumbs.
**7.** Deep-fry the croquettes until golden-brown.
Drain well on absorbent kitchen paper and serve
immediately.

 *LIGHT RED*

# CHICKEN KIEV

SERVES 4

*110g/4oz butter, softened*
*1 clove of garlic, crushed*
*1 tablespoon chopped fresh parsley*
*a squeeze of lemon juice*
*salt and freshly ground black pepper*
*4 chicken supremes*
*seasoned plain flour*
*beaten egg*
*dried white breadcrumbs*
*oil for deep-frying*

**1.** Mix the butter with the garlic, parsley, lemon
juice, salt and pepper. Divide into 4 equal pieces,
shape into rectangles and chill well in the refrigerator.
**2.** Remove the skin and bone from the chicken
breasts. You should have 4 equal pieces of
chicken. Using a sharp knife, split the breasts
almost in half horizontally and open them out so
that you have a chicken escalope. Put them
between sheets of wet greaseproof paper and,
using a rolling pin, carefully beat the chicken
pieces to flatten the meat out thinly.
**3.** Place a piece of the chilled parsley butter in the
centre of each chicken piece. Roll up so that the
butter is completely wrapped. Dust lightly with
seasoned flour. Dip into beaten egg, then roll
carefully in breadcrumbs. Chill in the refrigerator
for 30 minutes.
**4.** Brush with more beaten egg and roll again in
breadcrumbs. Leave to chill for a further 30
minutes.
**5.** Heat the oil in a deep-fryer until a crumb will
sizzle vigorously in it. Fry the chicken pieces in
the oil for 12 minutes. Drain well on absorbent
kitchen paper and serve.

NOTES: Crushed garlic is frequently added to the
butter inside the chicken. Though frowned on by
classic chefs, this is quite delicious. Other flavourings, such as chopped tarragon, smooth liver pâté,
mashed anchovies, or a duxelles of mushrooms,
can be good too. But the butter is the essential
ingredient, providing flavour, moisture and drama
all at once.
  If desired, the small wing bone at the shoulder
end of the breast can be left in place. When the

chicken escalope is rolled up, the bone protrudes from the parcel, giving the breast the appearance of a drumstick.

 *BEAUJOLAIS*

# CHICKEN AND YOGHURT CREAM CURRY

SERVES 4
*2 medium onions, chopped*
*2 tablespoons oil*
*1 × 1.35kg/3lb chicken*
*seasoned plain flour mixed with a pinch each of turmeric, cayenne, dry English mustard and crushed coriander seeds*
*1 clove of garlic, crushed*
*1 teaspoon ground cumin*
*2 teaspoons ground turmeric*
*290ml/1/2 pint white stock, made with chicken bones (see page 243)*
*1 bay leaf*
*2 teaspoons tomato purée*
*juice of 1 lemon*
*2 tablespoons chopped fresh mint*
*1 tablespoon double cream*
*8g/1/4oz blanched almonds, browned*
*2 teaspoons Greek yoghurt*

To serve
*boiled rice*

**1.** Sweat the onions in the oil until soft.
**2.** Joint the chicken into 8 pieces and dip in the seasoned flour. Heat the oil in a sauté pan and brown the chicken all over. With a slotted spoon remove the pieces and place them in a roasting dish or casserole. Add the onions.
**3.** Preheat the oven to 180°C/350°F/gas mark 4.
**4.** Put the garlic, cumin and turmeric into the saucepan and cook for 2 minutes. Add the stock, bay leaf, tomato purée, lemon juice and mint. Season to taste with salt and pepper. Bring slowly to the boil, stirring continuously.
**5.** Pour over the chicken joints. Cover and cook in the oven for 45–50 minutes, or until the chicken is tender. Turn off the oven.

**6.** Lift the chicken pieces out of the sauce on to a warmed serving dish. Cover and keep warm in the turned-off oven. Heat the curry sauce, adding the cream and almonds. Mix the yoghurt with a little of the hot sauce and return to the pan. Pour over the chicken and serve with boiled rice.

 *SPICY DRY WHITE*

# CHICKEN WITH WHOLE SPICES

SERVES 4
*1 × 1.35kg/3lb chicken, jointed into 8 pieces and skinned*
*70g/21/2oz clarified butter (see page 686)*
*2 teaspoons ground turmeric*
*1/4 teaspoon ground ginger*
*4 cardamom pods*
*1cm/1/2in cinnamon stick, split*
*3 cloves, ground*
*a good pinch of ground mace*
*a good pinch of cayenne pepper*
*1/4 teaspoon freshly ground black pepper*
*1/2 bay leaf, crumbled*
*1 teaspoon ground mustard seeds*
*2 cloves of garlic, crushed*
*5 onions, sliced*

**1.** Lightly fry the chicken in half the butter with the turmeric and ginger.
**2.** Shell the cardamoms and crush the seeds with the cinnamon, cloves, mace, cayenne, pepper, bay leaf and mustard seeds in a pestle and mortar.
**3.** Add the garlic, onions, crushed spices and remaining butter to the chicken in the pan. Place over a fierce heat and when it sizzles reduce the temperature, cover and cook slowly for 45 minutes.

 *LIGHT RED*

# TANDOORI CHICKEN

SERVES 4

1 × 1.35kg/3lb chicken, joined into 8 pieces and
  skinned
4 cloves of garlic, crushed
290ml/½ pint plain low-fat yoghurt
1 heaped teaspoon of each of the following:
ground coriander
ground cumin
ground fenugreek
sweet paprika pepper
ground ginger
¼ teaspoon chilli powder
¼ teaspoon dry English mustard

To serve
plain yoghurt
lemon wedges

**1.** Cut a few slashes in the flesh of each chicken
piece.
**2.** Mix the garlic, yoghurt and spices together in a
large bowl. Add the chicken pieces to the yoghurt
and spice mixture, mix well, cover and refrigerate
overnight or for as long as possible.
**3.** Preheat the oven to 200°C/400°F/gas mark 6.
Put the chicken pieces on to a wire rack on a
roasting pan and bake in a preheated oven for 1
hour. The chicken should get very brown but not
burnt – it may be necessary to cover it with
kitchen foil halfway through cooking in order to
prevent it from burning.
**4.** Serve with yoghurt and lemon wedges.

NOTE: This can also be made using strips of
chicken breast. They should be marinated in the
yoghurt and spices for 1 hour and then grilled for
10 minutes.

 *LAGER OR RED RHÔNE*

# VINEGAR CHICKEN

SERVES 4

30g/1oz clarified butter (see page 686)
1 × 1.35kg/3lb chicken, jointed into 8 pieces
5 large cloves of garlic, unpeeled
5 tablespoons wine vinegar

290ml/½ dry white wine
2 tablespoons brandy
2 teaspoons Dijon mustard
1 heaped teaspoon tomato purée
290ml/½ pint very fresh double cream
2 tomatoes, peeled and deseeded

**1.** Heat the butter in a large sauté pan and brown
the chicken pieces all over, skin side first. Add the
garlic and cover the pan. Cook over a low heat
for 20 minutes, or until the chicken is tender.
Remove the chicken and keep warm. Pour off all
the fat from the pan.
**2.** Add the vinegar to the pan, stirring well and
scraping any sediment from the bottom. Boil rapidly
until the liquid is reduced to about 2 tablespoons.
**3.** Add the wine, brandy, mustard and tomato
purée, mix well and boil to a thick sauce (about 5
minutes at a fast boil).
**4.** In a small, heavy saucepan boil the cream until
reduced by half, stirring frequently to prevent
burning. Remove from the heat and fit a small
wire sieve over the saucepan. Push the vinegar
sauce through this, pressing the garlic cloves well
to extract their pulp.
**5.** Stir the sauce and season to taste with salt and
pepper. Cut the tomato into thin strips and stir
into the sauce. Arrange the chicken on a hot
serving dish, and spoon over the sauce.

NOTES: The deliciousness of this dish – and it is
delicious – depends on the vigorous reduction of
the vinegar and wine. If the acids are not properly
boiled down the sauce will be too sharp.

Five cloves of garlic seems a lot, but the
resulting smooth sauce does not taste particularly
strongly of garlic.

 *LIGHT RED*

# CHICKEN WITH TOMATO AND CORIANDER

SERVES 4

*1 × 1.35kg/3lb chicken, jointed into 8 pieces*
*seasoned plain flour*
*2 tablespoons oil*
*2 onions, finely chopped*
*1 clove of garlic, crushed*
*1 × 400g/14oz can of tomatoes*
*1 bay leaf*
*2 teaspoons tomato purée*
*salt and freshly ground black pepper*
*2 tablespoons roughly chopped fresh coriander*

**1.** Dip the chicken pieces in the seasoned flour.
**2.** Heat the oil in a large sauté pan and brown the chicken all over. With a slotted spoon, take up the pieces and place them in a roasting dish or casserole.
**3.** Preheat the oven to 180°C/350°F/gas mark 4.
**4.** Add the onions to the sauté pan and cook over a low heat for 10 minutes, or until beginning to soften. Add the garlic and cook for 1 further minute. Add the tomatoes, bay leaf and tomato purée. Season to taste with salt and pepper. Bring slowly to the boil, stirring continuously.
**5.** Pour the mixture over the chicken pieces. Cover and cook in the preheated oven for 45–50 minutes, or until the chicken is tender. Turn off the oven.
**6.** Lift the chicken pieces out of the sauce. Trim them and arrange on a warmed serving dish. Keep warm in the turned-off oven.
**7.** Skim any fat off the sauce, then boil rapidly to a syrupy consistency. Stir the sauce well to amalgamate the tomatoes and to prevent the sauce from catching. Add three-quarters of the coriander. Check the seasoning and pour the sauce over the chicken. Garnish with the remaining coriander.

 *LIGHT RED*

# COQ AU VIN

SERVES 4

*110g/4oz rindless lean bacon, diced*
*55g/2oz clarified butter (see page 686)*
*8 button onions, peeled*
*12 button mushrooms*
*1.35kg/3lb chicken, jointed into 8 pieces*
*290ml/½ pint red wine*
*white stock, made with chicken bones (see page 243)*
*1 small clove of garlic, crushed*
*1 bouquet garni (1 bay leaf, 1 sprig each of thyme and parsley and 1 stick of celery, tied together with string)*
*salt and pepper*
*20g/¾oz plain flour*

To serve
*buttered rice*
*12 small triangular croûtons (see page 686)*
*1 tablespoon chopped fresh parsley*

**1.** Drop the bacon into a saucepan of boiling water for 30 seconds. Drain and dry well.
**2.** Put half the butter into a large, heavy saucepan and slowly brown the bacon. Remove and reserve the bacon.
**3.** Add the onions, shaking the pan to brown them evenly all over.
**4.** Add the mushrooms (do not bother to peel them unless the skins are very tough). Fry fast for a further 2 minutes, then lift out all the fried food. Do not wash the pan.
**5.** Add the remaining butter to the juices in the pan and brown the chicken. Tip off all the fat.
**6.** Return the vegetables and bacon pieces to the pan and add the wine and enough stock to nearly cover the chicken pieces.
**7.** Add the garlic, bouquet garni and pepper.
**8.** With a wooden spoon move the chicken pieces about and stir the sauce until it comes to the boil. Stir well to loosen any sediment. Cover with a well-fitting lid and simmer slowly until the onions and chicken are tender (about 45 minutes).
**9.** Remove the bouquet garni. Lift out all the solid ingredients and put them on to a warmed serving dish. Keep warm while you make the sauce.
**10.** Skim all the fat from the cooking liquid, putting 1 tablespoonful fat into a cup. Measure

the liquid and make it up to 290ml/½ pint with more chicken stock or water. (If there is more than 290ml/½ pint boil rapidly to reduce it.)

**11.** Mix the flour with the fat in the cup, stir well and add a little of the hot cooking liquid to this paste. Return the mixture to the pan and bring gradually to the boil, stirring continuously. Simmer for 2 minutes until the sauce is smooth and shiny. Taste and season.

**12.** Trim the chicken pieces, arrange in a warmed deep serving platter and spoon the sauce over the chicken. Serve with buttered rice and garnish with the croûtons and parsley.

NOTE: If there is time, marinate the chicken joints in the wine and bouquet garni for a few hours or overnight – this will improve the taste and colour. Dry the joints well before frying, or browning them will be difficult.

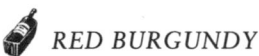 *RED BURGUNDY*

# CHICKEN SAUTÉ NORMANDE

SERVES 4
*45g/1oz clarified butter (see page 686)*
*1 × 1.35kg/3lb chicken, jointed into 8 pieces*
*1 shallot, chopped*
*1 tablespoon Calvados*
*2 teaspoons plain flour*
*225ml/8fl oz dry cider*
*150ml/¼ pint white stock, made with chicken*
  *bones (see page 243)*
*salt and freshly ground black pepper*
*1 bouquet garni (1 bay leaf, parsley stalks and 4*
  *sprigs of fresh thyme, tied together with string)*
*2 tablespoons double cream*

To garnish
*2 dessert apples, peeled, cored and cut into*
  *wedges*
*15g/½oz butter*
*a pinch of caster sugar*
*chopped fresh parsley*

**1.** Heat the butter in a large sauté pan and brown the chicken pieces all over.

**2.** Add the shallot and sauté for 2–3 minutes.

**3.** Add the Calvados, light it with a match and shake the pan until the flames subside. Remove the chicken pieces.

**4.** Stir in the flour and cook for 1 minute. Remove from the heat. Add the cider. Blend well and add the stock. Return to the heat and bring slowly to the boil, stirring continuously. Season with salt and pepper and add the bouquet garni. Simmer for 2 minutes.

**5.** Replace the chicken, cover and simmer gently for 45 minutes until tender.

**6.** Meanwhile, prepare the garnish: fry the apple wedges in the butter with the sugar until golden-brown on each side. Keep warm.

**7.** When the chicken is cooked, lift it out and trim the pieces neatly. Arrange on an ovenproof platter and keep warm.

**8.** Strain the sauce into a clean saucepan and reduce by boiling rapidly to the required consistency. Add the cream and season to taste with salt and pepper.

**9.** Garnish with the apple and sprinkle with the parsley.

 *LIGHT FRUITY RED*

# CHICKEN WITH THYME

This chicken dish is delicious but great care must be taken not to allow the sauce to curdle – make sure that there is virtually no fat in the 75ml/ 5 tablespoons liquor before you add the butter.

SERVES 4
*200g/7oz unsalted butter*
*1 × 1.35kg/3lb chicken, jointed into 8 pieces*
*2 sprigs of fresh thyme*
*½ lemon*
*a pinch of caster sugar*
*salt and freshly ground black pepper*
*4 tablespoons dry white wine*
*150ml/¼ pint water*
*2 tablespoons chopped fresh thyme*

To garnish
*1 bunch of watercress*

1. Heat 30g/1oz of the butter in a large sauté pan. Cut the remaining butter into small pieces and chill in the refrigerator.

2. Brown the chicken joints, skin side down. Add the sprigs of thyme, lemon, sugar, salt, pepper, wine and water. Cover and simmer for 25–30 minutes or until the chicken is tender.

3. Remove the chicken from the pan and keep warm while you make the sauce. Discard the lemon and thyme. Skim off all the fat.

4. Add 75ml/5 tablespoons water to the pan and mix well, scraping up any sediment. Reduce, by boiling rapidly, to about 75ml/5 tablespoons of liquor, and, when simmering, gradually add the well-chilled butter piece by piece, using a wire whisk. The process should take about 2 minutes and the sauce should become thick and creamy. Add the chopped fresh thyme. Season with salt and pepper and garnish with watercress.

 *DRY WHITE/ROSÉ*

# CHICKEN PAPRIKA

SERVES 4
*1 × 1.35kg/3lb chicken*
*1 tablespoon oil*
*15g/½oz butter*
*1 onion, thinly sliced*
*2 tablespoons paprika pepper*
*1 × 200g/7oz can of tomatoes*
*100ml/3½fl oz dry white wine*
*570ml/1 pint white stock, made with chicken*
 *bones (see page 243)*
*1 bay leaf*
*2 slices of lemon*
*1 parsley stalk*
*salt and freshly ground black pepper*
*150ml/¼ pint white sauce (see page 247)*

To garnish
*1 tablespoon soured cream*
*chopped fresh parsley*

1. Wash the chicken and wipe dry. Preheat the oven to 200°C/400°F/gas mark 6.

2. Heat the oil in a frying pan and when hot add the butter. When the butter is foaming, add the chicken and brown it well all over. Take it out and put into a casserole.

3. Fry the onion in the oil and butter and when just beginning to brown, reduce the heat and add the paprika. Cook for 2–3 minutes. Stir in the tomatoes, wine and stock. Add the bay leaf, lemon slices and parsley stalk. Season well with salt and pepper. When boiling, pour over the chicken.

4. Cover and bake in the preheated oven for about 1 hour or until the chicken is cooked.

5. When the chicken is tender, take it out of the casserole and remove the bay leaf, parsley stalk and lemon slices. Carefully skim off the fat with a spoon, or soak up and lift off the fat by laying absorbent kitchen paper on the surface of the sauce. Liquidize the sauce in a blender, then push it through a sieve.

6. Beat the paprika sauce into the prepared white sauce until completely incorporated and smooth,

7. Joint the chicken neatly into 8 pieces and arrange on a warmed serving dish. Heat the sauce and spoon it over the chicken. Trickle over the soured cream and sprinkle with parsley.

 *LIGHT RED*

# TARRAGON CHICKEN

SERVES 4
*1 × 1.35kg/3lb chicken with giblets*
*55g/2oz clarified butter (see page 686)*
*1 slice of lemon*
*4 sprigs of fresh tarragon*
*salt and freshly ground black pepper*
*150ml/¼ pint white stock, made with chicken*
 *bones (see page 243)*
*20g/¾oz plain flour*
*150ml/¼ pint double cream*
*salt and freshly ground black pepper*
*a squeeze of lemon juice*

1. Preheat the oven to 200°C/400°F/gas mark 6. Wipe the chicken inside and out. Place a small nut of the butter, the lemon slice and half the tarragon leaves inside the cavity. Season inside and out with salt and pepper.

2. Melt the remaining butter in a flameproof

casserole the size of the chicken and brown the bird on all sides. Place the giblets (except the liver) in the casserole and pour over the stock. Cover with a lid and cook in the preheated oven. Cook for 1¼ hours or until the juices run clear, rather than pink, when the thigh is pierced with a skewer.

**3.** Remove the chicken, draining the juices back into the casserole. Joint the chicken neatly and put the pieces into a covered dish. Keep warm.

**4.** Skim all the fat from the stock. Mix 15ml/ 1 tablespoon of this fat with the flour in a cup. When thoroughly blended pour more of the stock into the cup and mix well. Return this to the casserole and stir over direct heat until boiling. Simmer for 5 minutes.

**5.** Strain into a clean saucepan and add the remaining tarragon, chopped. Simmer for 1–2 minutes, then stir in the cream. Taste and season with salt, pepper and lemon juice.

**6.** Spoon over the chicken pieces and serve.

 *WHITE BURGUNDY*

# POUSSINS WITH PERNOD

SERVES 4
*4 single-portion poussins*
*seasoned plain flour*
*30g/1oz clarified butter (see page 686)*
*2 shallots, finely chopped*
*5 tablespoons Pernod*

To garnish
*lemon wedges*
*chopped fresh parsley*

**1.** Bone the poussins completely without removing the legs or wings (see pages 316–17).

**2.** Open the poussins out; put them between 2 pieces of wet greaseproof paper and flatten them with a wooden mallet or rolling pin.

**3.** Dip them in the seasoned flour and shake off any excess.

**4.** Melt the butter in a large sauté pan. When foaming, brown the poussins on each side. Reduce the heat and continue to sauté the poussins until cooked. Add the shallots and cook

for a further 1–2 minutes.

**5.** Increase the heat and pour the Pernod into the pan. When hot, set alight with a match and turn off the heat. When the flames subside, scrape the pan with a spoon to loosen any sediment stuck to the bottom.

**6.** Take out the poussins; arrange on a warmed serving dish. Boil up the pan juices and pour, sizzling, over the poussins. Garnish with lemon wedges and parsley and serve immediately.

NOTE: Two-portion poussins are called 'double' poussins, whereas one-portion birds are 'single' birds.

 *SPICY DRY WHITE*

# CHICKEN JAMBONNEAUX STUFFED WITH WILD MUSHROOMS

SERVES 4
*4 chicken drumsticks with the thighs attached*
*salt and finely ground black pepper*
*6 tablespoons dry sherry or Madeira*
*30g/1oz butter, clarified (see page 686)*
*290ml/½ pint white stock, made with chicken*
    *bones (see page 243)*

For the stuffing
*1 onion, very finely chopped*
*15g/½oz butter*
*1 rasher of rindless streaky bacon*
*55g/2oz fresh wild mushrooms, finely chopped*
*85g/3oz shiitake mushrooms, finely chopped*
*30g/1oz fresh white breadcrumbs*
*1 tablespoon finely chopped fresh parsley*
*1 teaspoon chopped fresh thyme*
*1 teaspoon dry sherry or Madeira*
*salt and freshly ground black pepper*

To serve
*Madeira sauce (see page 250)*

To garnish
*small sprigs of watercress*

**1.** Make the stuffing: sweat the onion in the butter in a frying pan until soft but not brown. Add the bacon and stir over medium heat until the bacon is cooked.

**2.** Add all the mushrooms and continue to cook until all the excess liquid released from the mushrooms has evaporated. Turn the mixture into a bowl to cool.

**3.** Cut the knobbly joint off the bottom of each drumstick. Using the point of a sharp knife, remove the bones from the leg by cutting around the flesh next to the bone, starting from the thigh end and working to the end of the drumstick. Season the chicken with salt and pepper.

**4.** Stir the breadcrumbs, herbs and the sherry or Madeira into the mushroom mixture and season to taste with salt and pepper.

**5.** Stuff the chicken legs with the mushroom mixture. Fold the chicken over to encase the stuffing and secure by tying with string.

**6.** Preheat the oven to 200°C/400°F/gas mark 6.

**7.** Heat the clarified butter in a sauté pan over a medium heat and brown the chicken well on all sides.

**8.** Place the chicken in an ovenproof dish and pour over the sherry or Madeira and the stock. Cover and bake for 30 minutes, or until the juices run clear from the chicken when it is pierced with a skewer.

**9.** Place the chicken on a warmed serving plate. Spoon over a little of the Madeira sauce and garnish with the watercress. Hand the remaining sauce separately.

 *BEAJOLAIS OR LOIRE RED*

# BONED STUFFED CHICKEN

The filling for Leith's Good Food's Boned Duck (see page 344) is also delicious in a boned chicken.

SERVES 6
*1 × 1.35kg/3lb chicken*
*55g/2oz butter, melted*

For the stuffing
*15g/¹/2oz butter*
*1 small onion, finely chopped*
*225g/8oz good-quality sausagemeat*
*2 tablespoons fresh white breadcrumbs*
*1 small dessert apple, chopped*
*1 teaspoon chopped fresh sage*
*2 tablespoons chopped fresh parsley*
*1 egg*
*salt and freshly ground black pepper*

To garnish
*1 bunch of watercress*

**1.** Bone the chicken without removing the legs or wings (see pages 316–17).

**2.** Make the stuffing: melt the butter in a saucepan, add the onion and cook until soft but not coloured. Mix together the sausagemeat, onion, breadcrumbs, apple, sage, parsley and egg and season well with salt and pepper. Beat very well.

**3.** Use this stuffing to fill the boned chicken. Draw up the sides and wrap the chicken in a piece of muslin saturated with the melted butter. Tie the chicken at either end so that it resembles a Christmas cracker.

**4.** Preheat the oven to 200°C/400°F/gas mark 6.

**5.** Place the chicken on a wire rack over a roasting pan and bake in the oven for 1½ hours.

**6.** Unwrap the chicken and serve hot or cold, garnished with the watercress.

 *DRY WHITE/ROSÉ*

# BONED CHICKEN STUFFED WITH RICOTTA AND SUN-DRIED TOMATOES

SERVES 6
1 × 1.8kg/4lb chicken
55g/2oz butter, melted

For the stuffing:
170g/6oz ricotta cheese
1 egg
85g/3oz fresh white breadcrumbs
55g/2oz sun-dried tomatoes, cut into slivers
30g/1oz black olives, pitted
1 tablespoon roughly chopped fresh basil
salt and freshly ground black pepper

To garnish
fresh basil leaves

1. Bone the chicken completely, including the legs and wings (see pages 316–17).
2. Preheat the oven to 200°C/400°F/gas mark 6.
3. Make the stuffing: beat the ricotta cheese, add the egg and beat again. Add the breadcrumbs, sun-dried tomatoes, olives and basil. Season to taste with salt and pepper.
4. Use the stuffing to fill the boned chicken. Draw up the sides and wrap the chicken up in a piece of muslin or a clean 'J'-cloth saturated with the melted butter. Tie the chicken at either end so that it looks rather like a Christmas cracker.
5. Place the chicken on a wire rack over a roasting pan and bake in the preheated oven for 1½ hours.
6. Unwrap the chicken and serve hot or cold garnished with fresh basil leaves.

 *LIGHT RED/ROSÉ*

# BONED STUFFED POUSSIN

SERVES 1
1 single-portion poussin
45g/1½oz butter
½ tablespoon chopped onion
110g/4oz chicken breast, boned and skinned
30g/1oz dried apricots, chopped
2 tablespoons mixed chopped fresh tarragon and parsley
15g/½oz unsalted pistachio nuts, skinned
salt and freshly ground black pepper
85g/3oz mixed finely diced onion, carrot, turnip and celery (mirepoix)
220ml/8fl oz white stock, made with chicken bones (see page 243)
1 bay leaf
1 small bunch of watercress

1. Bone the poussin without removing the legs or wings (see pages 316–17).
2. Make the stuffing: melt 15g/½oz of the butter in a small pan, add the onion and cook over a low heat until soft but not coloured. Remove from the heat and allow to cool.
3. Chop the chicken breast very finely or whizz briefly in a food processor. Add the cooled onion, apricots, tarragon, parsley and pistachio nuts. Mix and season very well with salt and pepper.
4. Lay the poussin, skin side down, flat on a work top. Place the stuffing in the middle and sew the poussin up using a trussing needle and or very fine string.
5. Melt half the remaining butter in a flameproof casserole. When it is foaming, add the poussin and brown lightly all over, then remove from the casserole.
6. Add the remaining butter to the casserole with the mirepoix of diced vegetables. Fry until the vegetables are lightly browned.
7. Set the poussin on top of the vegetables. Add the stock, bay leaf, salt and pepper. Bring to the boil, cover and simmer gently for 40–50 minutes.
8. When the poussin is cooked (when pierced with a skewer the juices that run out should be clear, not pink), place it on a plate and remove the thread or string. Keep warm.

**9.** Press the vegetables through a sieve to extract most of their juices, and discard the vegetables. Boil to reduce to a syrupy consistency. Season to taste with salt and pepper.

**10.** Garnish the poussin with watercress and serve the sauce separately.

 *BEAUJOLAIS OR LOIRE RED*

# BONED STUFFED POUSSINS WITH SHIITAKE MUSHROOMS AND WILD RICE

SERVES 4

*4 single-portion poussins*
*85g/3oz shiitake mushrooms, sliced*
*30g/1oz butter*
*4 spring onions, chopped*
*85g/3oz rice, cooked*
*30g/1oz wild rice, cooked*
*30g/1oz pistachio nuts, roughly chopped*
*1 egg, beaten*
*salt and freshly ground black pepper*
*a little oil*
*15g/½oz butter*
*1 small onion, finely chopped*
*1 small carrot, finely chopped*
*1 stick of celery, finely chopped*
*290ml/½ pint white stock, made with chicken*
  *bones (see page 243)*
*1 bay leaf*

To garnish
*1 bunch of watercress*

**1.** Bone the poussins without removing the legs or wings (see pages 316–17).

**2.** Make the stuffing: cook the mushrooms slowly in the butter, with the spring onions, for 3 minutes. Add to the rices with the pistachio nuts. Bind with the beaten egg and season to taste with salt and pepper.

**3.** Lay the poussins, skin side down, flat on a board. Divide the stuffing between them and sew them up, using cotton or very fine string. Try to shape them to their original form.

**4.** Heat the oil in a flameproof casserole, add the butter and when foaming add the poussins, 2 at a time, and brown lightly all over. Remove to a plate.

**5.** Add the onion, carrot and celery to the pan and fry until lightly browned. Set the poussins on top of the vegetables. Add the stock, bay leaf, salt and pepper. Bring to the boil, then cover and simmer for 40–50 minutes.

**6.** When the poussins are cooked, remove to a warmed serving plate. Remove the cotton or string.

**7.** Meanwhile, make the sauce: skim the fat from the surface of the cooking juices. Strain the sauce into a clean saucepan. Boil rapidly to a syrupy consistency. (Check that the sauce is not too strong – if necessary it can be thickened with a little beurre manié and need not be reduced). Season with salt and pepper.

**8.** Arrange the poussins on a warmed serving dish. Garnish with the watercress.

**9.** Heat the sauce, pour into a warmed sauceboat and serve separately.

 *LIGHT RED*

# FRENCH ROAST CHICKEN

SERVES 4

*1 × 1.35kg/3lb roasting chicken with giblets*
*butter*
*freshly ground black pepper and salt*
*1 slice of onion*
*1 bay leaf*
*a few parsley stalks*

For the gravy
*1 scant tablespoon plain flour*
*290ml/½ pint white stock, made with chicken*
  *bones (see page 243) or vegetable water*

**1.** Preheat the oven to 200°C/400°F/gas mark 6.

**2.** Smear a little butter all over the chicken. Season inside and out with pepper only (no salt). Put the bird breast side down in a roasting pan.

**3.** Put all the chicken giblets (except the liver) and the neck into the pan with the chicken. Add the onion, bay leaf and parsley stalks. Pour in a cup of water. Roast in the preheated oven for 30 minutes.

**4.** Take out of the oven, season all over with salt, turn the chicken right side up and baste it with the fat and juices from the pan. Return to the oven.

**5.** Check how the chicken is doing periodically. It will take 60–80 minutes. It is cooked when the leg bones wobble loosely and independently from the body. Baste occasionally as it cooks, and cover with kitchen foil or greaseproof paper if it is browning too much. Remove the cooked chicken to a warmed serving dish and keep warm while making the gravy.

**6.** Place the roasting pan with its juices over a low heat. Skim off most of the fat.

**7.** Whisk in enough flour to absorb the remaining fat.

**8.** Add the stock or vegetable water and stir until the sauce boils. Simmer for 2–3 minutes. Check the seasoning. Strain into a warmed gravy-boat and serve with the chicken.

 *LIGHT RED*

# ENGLISH ROAST CHICKEN

SERVES 4
*1 × 1.35kg/3lb roasting chicken*
*15g/¹⁄₂oz butter*
*freshly ground black pepper*

For the stuffing
*30g/1oz butter*
*1 onion, finely chopped*
*55g/2oz fresh white breadcrumbs*
*1 small cooking apple, grated*
*2 teaspoons chopped mixed fresh herbs*
*grated zest of ¹⁄₂ lemon*
*¹⁄₂ egg, beaten*
*salt and freshly ground black pepper*

To garnish
*4 chipolata sausages*
*4 rashers of rindless streaky bacon*

For the gravy
*1 scant tablespoon plain flour*
*290ml/¹⁄₂ pint white stock, made from the chicken neck and giblets (see page 243)*

To serve
*bread sauce (see page 260)*

**1.** Preheat the oven to 200°C/400°F/gas mark 6.

**2.** Start to make the stuffing: melt the butter in a saucepan and fry the onion until soft but not coloured.

**3.** Put the breadcrumbs, apple, herbs and lemon zest together in a mixing bowl.

**4.** Add the softened onion and enough beaten egg to bind the mixture together. Do not make it too wet. Season to taste with salt and pepper, then cool.

**5.** Stuff the chicken from the neck end, making sure the breast is well plumped. Draw the neck skin flap down to cover the stuffing. Secure with a skewer if necessary.

**6.** Smear a little butter all over the chicken and season with salt and pepper. Roast in the preheated oven for about 1¹⁄₂ hours, or until the juices run clear when the thigh is pierced with a skewer.

**7.** Meanwhile, make each chipolata sausage into 2 cocktail-sized ones by twisting gently in the middle. Cut each bacon rasher into short lengths and roll them up.

**8.** After the chicken has been roasting for 1 hour, put the sausages and bacon rolls into the roasting pan, wedging the bacon rolls so that they cannot come undone.

**9.** Baste occasionally and check that the sausages and bacon are not sticking to the side of the pan and getting burnt.

**10.** When the chicken is cooked, lift it out on to a warmed serving dish. Trim off the wing tips and tops of the drumsticks, surround with the bacon rolls and sausages and keep warm while you make the gravy.

**11.** Slowly pour off all but 15ml/1 tablespoon of the fat from the roasting pan, taking care to keep any juices. Add the flour and stir over heat for 1 minute. Add the stock and stir until the sauce boils. Simmer for 3 minutes. Check the seasoning. Strain into a warmed gravy-boat.

**12.** Serve the chicken with bread sauce and the gravy.

NOTES: English chicken is usually stuffed from the neck end or breast but the stuffing may be put into the body cavity if preferred.

The chicken looks neater if it is trussed after stuffing, but it is more difficult to get the thighs cooked without the breast drying out if this is done.

 *LIGHT RED*

# CHICKEN BAKED IN A BRICK

If you have no chicken brick an earthenware casserole with a well-fitting lid will do, but the brick, which is chicken-shaped, is particularly good as it fits the chicken closely, with little space for the evaporation of juices. It is a modern version of the ancient method of covering a gutted bird, feathers and all, in wet clay, then baking it. When the hardened clay was broken off, the feathers came away with it, leaving the chicken cooked, succulent and tender. Modern bricks, not made of wet clay, are designed for plucked birds!

SERVES 4
1 × 1.35kg/3lb chicken
a handful of fresh herbs
lemon
melted butter or olive oil
salt and freshly ground black pepper

1. Clean the chicken. Place the herbs and lemon inside the body cavity.
2. Brush the chicken with the butter or oil and season with salt and pepper. Place in a chicken brick.
3. Cover with the lid. Place in a cold oven. Heat the oven to 230°C/450°F/gas mark 8 and bake for 2 hours. Serve the juices with the chicken.

NOTES: If the chicken is to be served cold, remove the lid when cooked and leave to cool.

The chicken can also be put into a preheated oven. It will then take about 1½ hours.

The manufacturers of chicken bricks generally advise the user not to wash the brick in detergent. Simply rinse in very hot water and put back in the warm oven to dry out.

 *DRY WHITE/ROSÉ*

# CHICKEN WITH PRUNES

SERVES 4
1 × 1.35kg/3lb chicken with giblets
30g/1oz butter
a few slices of onion
1 slice of lemon
salt and freshly ground black pepper
1 bay leaf
a few slices of carrot

For the sauce
15g/½oz butter
12 shallots, blanched and peeled
12 cooked prunes, stoned
1 tablespoon sugar
1 tablespoon wine vinegar

To garnish
1 bunch of watercress

1. Preheat the oven to 200°C/400°F/gas mark 6.
2. Wipe the chicken inside and out. Place half the butter, half the onion and the lemon in the breast cavity. Place breast side down in a roasting dish with 5ml/¼in water. Spread the remaining butter over the chicken and season with salt and pepper. Add the giblets (except the liver), the bay leaf, the remaining onion and the carrot to the water.
3. Roast in the preheated oven for 1–1¼ hours, basting 3 or 4 times and turning the bird over half-way through. The chicken is cooked when the juices run clear from the thigh when pierced with a skewer.
4. Meanwhile, prepare the sauce: melt the butter and when foaming add the shallots. Season with salt and pepper. Cover and cook slowly, shaking the pan occasionally to prevent them from burning but allowing them to brown all over. Add the prunes to the pan and reduce the heat to a minimum.
5. Slowly melt the sugar in a heavy saucepan, tilting and turning it as necessary to get an even pale caramel colour. Add the vinegar – be sure to stand back as it will hiss and splutter. Add 30ml/2 tablespoons of the chicken stock from the bottom of the roasting pan. Simmer until the caramel is dissolved. Check the seasoning.
6. Joint the chicken and arrange on a warmed serving dish. Spoon over the prunes and shallots and glaze with the caramel sauce. Garnish with watercress.

 *CLARET*

# LEMON POUSSINS

SERVES 4

*2 small lemons*
*2 double poussins*
*55g/2oz clarified butter (see page 686)*
*2 teaspoons sugar*
*paprika pepper*
*salt and freshly ground black pepper*
*sprigs of watercress*

**1.** Prick the lemons all over with a fork and put one inside the cavity of each poussin. Tie the drumsticks together with string.
**2.** Melt the butter in a large saucepan.
**3.** Add the whole poussins and cover the pan.
**4.** Cook over a low heat for 30 minutes, turning the poussins to brown lightly on all sides. They should now be partially cooked, and the butter in the pan should be brown but not burnt.
**5.** Take out the birds and split them in two.
**6.** Preheat the grill. Lay the portions of poussin cut side up in the grill pan. Brush them with some butter from the saucepan. Sprinkle with half the sugar and plenty of paprika and pepper. Grill slowly for about 5 minutes or until a really good brown.
**7.** Turn the poussins over and brush again with butter and sprinkle with sugar, paprika and pepper. Grill for a further 5 minutes until cooked through and very dark – almost, but not quite, charred. Sprinkle with salt.
**8.** Arrange on a warmed dish, pour over the juices from the grill pan and garnish with sprigs of watercress.

 *WHITE ALSACE*

# MUSTARD GRILLED CHICKEN

Although this is called grilled chicken it is partially baked to ensure that the chicken is cooked without becoming burnt.

SERVES 4

*30g/1oz butter, softened*
*2 tablespoons Dijon mustard*
*1 teaspoon sugar*
*1 teaspoon paprika pepper*
*1 × 1.35kg/3lb chicken*
*juice of 1 lemon*
*salt and freshly ground black pepper*

To garnish
*a few sprigs of watercress*

**1.** Mix together the butter, mustard, sugar and paprika.
**2.** Preheat the oven to 200°C/400°F/gas mark 6.
**3.** Joint the chicken into 8 pieces. Cut off the wing tips and the knuckles. Remove any small feathers.
**4.** Spread the underside of each chicken piece with half the mustard mixture. Sprinkle with half the lemon juice. Season with salt and pepper. Bake in the preheated oven for 10 minutes.
**5.** Turn the chicken over and spread again with the mustard mixture. Sprinkle with the remaining paprika, lemon juice and sugar. Season with pepper. Bake for a further 10 minutes.
**6.** Preheat the grill.
**7.** Arrange the joints under the grill in such a way that the larger joints are closest to the strongest heat and the breast joints are near the edge of the grill.
**8.** Grill until dark and crisp but be very careful not to let the joints burn.
**9.** Arrange the joints neatly on a warmed flat serving dish. Pour over the juices from the pan and garnish with sprigs of watercress.

 *LIGHT RED*

# SPATCHCOCK GRILLED CHICKEN

SERVES 4
*4 single-portion poussins*
*salt and freshly ground black pepper*
*a pinch of cayenne pepper*
*lemon juice*
*55g/2oz butter*
*15g/½oz Parmesan cheese, grated*

To garnish
*sprigs of watercress*
*French dressing (see page 254)*

To serve
*sauce Robert (see page 250)*

**1.** Split the poussins down one side of the backbone with a pair of poultry shears or kitchen scissors. Cut down the other side of the backbone to remove it. Open out the chickens and flatten well on a board by pressing with the heel of your hand. Skewer the birds in position, i.e. flat and open.
**2.** Season well with salt, pepper and cayenne and sprinkle with lemon juice. If possible, leave for 1 hour.
**3.** Preheat the grill. Brush the cut side of the poussins with melted butter. Grill for about 12 minutes or until a good golden-brown, brushing frequently with the pan juices. Turn over, brush again and grill for a further 7 minutes or until the poussin is cooked.
**4.** Brush once more with the hot butter and sprinkle with the Parmesan cheese. Grill until golden-brown and crisp. Arrange on a warmed serving dish and garnish with sprigs of watercress dipped in French dressing. Serve with sauce Robert.

 *LIGHT RED*

# CHICKEN CHAUDFROID

This is a cold chicken coated with a white sauce, glazed with aspic jelly, and garnished with slices of truffle or mushroom. The chicken should be cooked the day before serving because the stock in which it is cooked becomes the aspic jelly. The recipe calls for a whole chicken but poached chicken supremes can be used in its place. When making clear jellies, all the equipment should be scalded to ensure it is absolutely clean and fat-free.

SERVES 4
*1 × 1.35kg/3lb chicken, not trussed*
*1 onion, sliced*
*½ carrot*
*2 bay leaves*
*1 sprig of fresh parsley*
*6 black peppercorns*
*2.5ml/½ teaspoon salt*

For the aspic jelly
*860ml/1½ pints white stock, made with chicken*
   *bones (see page 243)*
*55g/2oz powdered gelatine*
*5 tablespoons dry white wine*
*5 tablespoons dry sherry*
*1 tablespoon tarragon vinegar*
*3 egg whites*
*3 egg shells, crushed*

For the chaudfroid sauce
*1 bay leaf*
*4 black peppercorns*
*1 slice of onion*
*1 blade of mace*
*1 sprig of fresh parsley*
*425ml/¾ pint milk*
*30g/1oz butter*
*30g/1oz plain flour*
*salt*
*150ml/¼ pint aspic jelly (see above)*
*15g/½ powdered gelatine*
*5 tablespoons double cream*

To garnish
*1 bunch of chervil*
*1 punnet of mustard and cress*

1. Place the chicken in a saucepan, just cover with cold water, and add the vegetables, herbs, peppercorns and salt. Bring to the boil, cover and simmer gently until the chicken is tender (about 1¼ hours). When it is cooked, a skewer will glide easily into the thigh, and the drumstick should feel loose.

2. Remove the bird from the pan, allow it to cool, cover loosely with clingfilm, and refrigerate overnight. Strain the stock, taste and season very well with salt and pepper and leave to cool. If possible, refrigerate it (this will set the fat and make it easier to remove the next day).

3. The next day make the aspic jelly: remove all the fat from the chicken stock. Put the stock (which should be about 860ml/1½ pints) and gelatine into a clean pan. Add the wine, sherry and vinegar. Place over a low heat to dissolve the gelatine. Allow to cool.

4. Put the egg whites and the crushed shells into the stock. Place over the heat and whisk steadily with a balloon whisk until a crust begins to form, then allow the mixture to come just to the boil. Stop whisking immediately, and remove the pan from the heat. Allow the mixture to subside. Take care not to break the crust formed by the egg whites. Leave to cool for 2 minutes.

5. Bring the aspic just to the boil again, and again allow to subside. Repeat this once more (the egg white will trap the sediment in the stock and clear the aspic). Leave to cool for 2 minutes.

6. Fix a double layer of fine muslin or white kitchen paper over a clean bowl and carefully strain the aspic through the egg-white crust. When all the liquid is through, check and if it is not quite clear, strain the aspic again. Do not try to hurry the process by squeezing the cloth, or murky aspic will result. Allow to cool.

7. Make the chaudfroid sauce: place the bay leaf, peppercorns, onion slice, mace and parsley sprig in a saucepan with the milk. Set over a low heat and bring slowly to the boil. Remove from the heat and leave to cool for 20 minutes.

8. Melt the butter in a saucepan, add the flour and cook for 1 minute. Remove from the heat and slowly, stirring all the time, strain the milk into the pan. Return the pan to the heat and bring slowly to the boil, stirring continually until you have a slightly thickened, shiny sauce. Season well with salt and simmer gently for 2–3 minutes.

9. Put 3 tablespoons liquid aspic into a small saucepan and sprinkle the gelatine over the aspic. Allow to soak for 5 minutes, then heat gently until liquid and clear. Strain this into the white sauce with the cream. Taste and add more salt if necessary. The sauce must be very smooth and shiny: it can be strained through a tammy strainer or blended in a liquidizer to give it a good sheen. Stir the sauce as it cools and begins to set. When it is the consistency of thick cream it is ready to use for coating.

10. Prepare the chicken: skin and joint it very neatly into 4 or 8 pieces, removing the wing tips and drumstick knuckles. Place the pieces on a wire rack with a clean tray underneath.

11. Coat each chicken joint very carefully with the cold, nearly set chaudfroid sauce. Allow to set and if necessary give it a second coating, scraping extra sauce (which will need reheating slightly to return it to coating consistency) from the tray underneath the wire rack.

12. When nearly set, arrange the chervil leaves in a formal simple pattern on each chicken piece. Allow to set. Wash the tray and replace under the chicken.

13. Coat with some of the cool but still liquid aspic. Allow to set. Give a second and perhaps third coating, allowing each coating to set before attempting the next.

14. Pour the remaining aspic on to a shallow tray. Allow to set, then cut it into neat dice. Use it to cover a large flat serving dish and make a slight dome in the centre. Arrange the chicken chaudfroid around this and surround with small clumps of mustard and cress.

NOTES: Chaudfroid is classically decorated with sliced truffles. These are delicious if fresh but disappointing as well as expensive if bought in tins.

If the aspic is less than crystal-clear it is wise not to chop it, which seems to emphasize its murkiness.

 *WHITE BURGUNDY*

# CHICKEN BREASTS WITH GRILLED RED PEPPER MOUSSELINE AND BLACK OLIVE TAPENADE

SERVES 4

*4 chicken breasts*
*1 red pepper*
*½ tablespoon chopped fresh basil*
*1 teaspoon finely chopped fresh parsley*
*1 egg white*
*75ml/2½fl oz double cream*
*1 teaspoon ground mace*
*salt and freshly ground white pepper*
*1 tablespoon tapenade (see page 255)*
*570ml/1 pint white stock, made with chicken bones (see page 243).*

To serve
*tomato sauce I (see page 258)*

1. Remove the small loose fillets from the chicken breasts, chop roughly and place in a food processor.
2. Grill or roast the red pepper until the skin blisters. Allow to cool, then remove the skin, membrane and seeds. Cut the flesh into medium dice. Add to the food processor with the basil and parsley.
3. Briefly whizz the mixture, then add the egg white and cream while the machine is still running. The mixture should be smooth, but be careful not to over-process.
4. Season well with the mace, salt and pepper. Chill in the refrigerator until ready to use.
5. Cut a small pocket in the side of each chicken breast and spread a little tapenade inside it. Put a spoonful of the red pepper mousseline mixture into the pocket and pull the edges together to seal.
6. Place the stuffed chicken breasts in a large shallow pan or a roasting pan. Heat the chicken stock to boiling point and pour over the chicken. Poach over a gentle heat so that the stock barely simmers for about 15 minutes or until the chicken breasts are firm to the touch. Remove from the stock and allow to cool.
7. Serve the chicken breasts sliced with the warm tomato salsa.

NOTE: The chicken keeps its shape better if wrapped in clingfilm and then poached.

 *LIGHT RED*

# CHICKEN BREASTS WITH PARMA HAM AND SPINACH

SERVES 4

*4 chicken breasts, boned, skinned and any fat removed*
*4 thin slices of best-quality Parma ham*
*4 large spinach leaves, blanched and refreshed*
*570ml/1 pint white stock, made with chicken bones (see page 243)*

For the dressing
*4 tablespoons good-quality olive oil*
*4 tablespoons salad oil*
*2 tablespoons tarragon vinegar*
*1 tablespoon chopped fresh parsley*
*1 tablespoon chopped fresh dill*
*1 teaspoon coarse-grain mustard*
*salt and freshly ground black pepper*

To garnish
*cherry tomatoes, halved*
*pinenuts, toasted*
*chopped fresh basil*

1. Wrap each chicken breast in 1 slice of Parma ham and then in 1 large spinach leaf.
2. Place the chicken breasts in a saucepan side by side, not on top of each other, and pour over the hot stock.
3. Cover the saucepan with a lid and bring back to the boil, then turn down the heat and poach gently for 18–20 minutes, or until the breasts feel just firm to the touch.
4. Meanwhile, make the dressing: combine all the ingredients together in a liquidizer or food processor and process to a green purée.
5. Flood 4 plates with some of the dressing, then lift the chicken breasts out of the saucepan and drain. Slice each chicken breast on the diagonal and arrange overlapping in a semi-circle on the dressing. Garnish with cherry tomatoes, pinenuts and basil.

NOTE: This can be served hot or cold.

 *WHITE BURGUNDY*

# CHICKEN WITH MUSHROOMS AND CORIANDER

SERVES 4
*4 chicken breasts, skinned and boned*
*15g/¹/₂oz cornflour*
*1 large onion, thinly sliced*
*1–2 tablespoons sunflower oil*
*2 teaspoons coriander seeds, very well crushed*
*225g/8oz flat mushrooms, sliced*
*150ml/¹/₄ pint white stock, made with chicken bones (see page 243)*
*salt and freshly ground black pepper*
*2 tablespoons medium sherry*

To garnish
*fresh coriander leaves*

**1.** Trim any fat from the chicken breasts and cut the flesh into large cubes. Toss in the cornflour and set aside.
**2.** Fry the onion in 1 tablespoon of the oil and when beginning to soften add the coriander seeds, increase the heat and allow the onion to brown and the seeds to toast (1–2 minutes).
**3.** Add the chicken and fry for 3 minutes. Remove the chicken from the pan and set aside. Add the remaining oil and the mushrooms and cook until beginning to soften. Return the chicken to the pan. Add the stock and season with salt and pepper. Stir well and simmer for 4–5 minutes.
**4.** Add the sherry and boil for 30 seconds. Pile on to a warmed serving dish and garnish with coriander.

 *LIGHT RED*

# CHICKEN BREASTS WITH LEEK AND WATERCRESS SAUCE

SERVES 4
*4 chicken breasts, boned and skinned*
*30g/1oz truffle, thinly sliced (optional)*
*15g/¹/₂oz butter*
*85g/3oz white of leeks, finely chopped*
*1 small shallot, finely chopped*
*1 small bunch of watercress, carefully picked over*
*2 tablespoons port*
*290ml/¹/₂ pint white stock, made with chicken bones (see page 243)*
*2 egg yolks*
*75ml/2¹/₂fl oz double cream*

**1.** Using a sharp knife, make a horizontal incision in the thickest part of each chicken breast and insert slices of truffle, if using.
**2.** Melt the butter, add the leek and shallot and cook slowly until soft but not brown. Add all but 2 sprigs of the watercress, the port and stock and simmer for 10 minutes.
**3.** Add the chicken breasts and poach, covered, for 12 minutes. Turn the chicken over halfway through cooking. Remove from the pan, returning any watercress or leeks stuck to the breasts to the saucepan. Keep warm while you make the sauce.
**4.** Chop the remaining watercress very finely.
**5.** Reduce the poaching liquid, by boiling rapidly, to concentrate its flavour, and liquidize in a blender until very smooth. Pour into a clean saucepan. Bring to just below boiling point.
**6.** Mix the egg yolks with the cream, add a little of the hot sauce to the yolks, stir and return to the saucepan. Stir over medium heat until thickened. It is essential that the sauce does not get near boiling point or it will curdle. Stir in the remaining watercress to improve the colour.
**7.** Arrange the chicken breasts, split in 2 if liked, on warmed dinner plates. Spoon over the sauce.

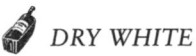 *DRY WHITE*

# CHICKEN BREASTS WITH GINGER

SERVES 4
*4 chicken breasts, boned and skinned*
*1 large onion, very finely chopped*
*2 cloves of garlic, crushed*
*5cm/2in piece of fresh root ginger, peeled and*
*    very finely chopped*
*5 cardamom pods, cracked*
*1 teaspoon ground turmeric*
*2 tablespoons light soy sauce*
*2 tablespoons dry sherry (optional)*

**1.** Place the chicken breasts in a bowl with the onion, garlic, ginger, cardamom pods, turmeric, soy sauce and sherry. Cover the bowl and leave for about 2 hours so that the chicken can absorb the flavour. Turn the chicken once or twice.
**2.** Preheat the oven to 200°C/400°F/gas mark 6.
**3.** Line a flat baking dish with kitchen foil and arrange the breasts on it. Pour over the marinade and seal the chicken tightly in the foil so that none of the juice can escape.
**4.** Bake in the preheated oven for 30 minutes.

 *AUSTRALIAN/CALIFORNIAN CHARDONNAY*

# CHICKEN BREASTS WITH RED PEPPER SAUCE

SERVES 4
*4 chicken breasts, skinned and boned*
*3 tablespoons finely shredded white of leek*
*2 tablespoons finely shredded carrot*
*salt and freshly ground black pepper*

To serve
*red pepper sauce (see page 258)*

To garnish
*watercress leaves*

**1.** Remove any fat from the chicken breasts.
**2.** Mix the leek and carrot together, season with salt and pepper and use as a stuffing.

**3.** Put the stuffing between the main part of the chicken breasts and the loose fillet. Wrap each breast in a piece of clingfilm.
**4.** Poach the chicken breasts in water for 15 minutes. Remove from the saucepan, unwrap and leave to get completely cold.
**5.** Flood the base of 4 dinner plates with the red pepper sauce.
**6.** Put a chicken breast on each plate and garnish with watercress leaves.

 *DRY WHITE/ROSÉ*

# CHICKEN CURRY WITH ALMONDS

This is a fairly mild curry. Extra spices can be added if liked.

SERVES 8
*8 chicken breasts, skinned and boned*
*4 tablespoons sunflower oil*
*85g/3oz blanched almonds*
*2 teaspoons ground cardamom*
*1 teaspoon ground cloves*
*1 teaspoon ground chilli*
*4 teaspoons ground cumin*
*4 teaspoons ground coriander*
*2 teaspoons ground turmeric*
*2 onions, finely chopped*
*2 cloves of garlic, crushed*
*2.5cm/1in piece of fresh root ginger, peeled and*
*    finely chopped*
*1 × 400g/14oz can of tomatoes, chopped*
*salt and freshly ground black pepper*
*150ml/¼ pint water*
*2 tablespoons Greek yoghurt*

To garnish
*a few fresh coriander leaves*

**1.** Preheat the oven to 190°C/375°F/gas mark 5.
**2.** Remove any fat or gristle from the chicken breasts. Set aside.
**3.** Put 1 tablespoon of the oil into a saucepan and fry the almonds until golden-brown but not burnt. Set aside. Add the remaining oil and in it slowly cook the spices for 1 minute.

**4.** In a blender, liquidize the almonds and cooked spices with enough water to make a smooth paste.

**5.** Rinse out the saucepan, add 2 more tablespoons oil and in it fry the onions, garlic and ginger until the onions are golden-brown.

**6.** Reduce the heat and add the tomatoes, spice and almond paste, salt, pepper and water. Stir well and simmer for 2–3 minutes.

**7.** Tip the sauce into an ovenproof dish. Add the chicken breasts and spoon over some of the sauce. Cover with kitchen foil and bake for 40 minutes, or until the chicken is cooked.

**8.** Transfer the chicken to a warmed serving dish. Swirl the yoghurt into the sauce. Pour over the chicken breasts and garnish with coriander.

 *RED RHÔNE*

# CHICKEN WITH CORIANDER AND SAFFRON SAUCE

This recipe has been adapted from a recipe by Shirley Gill in *Taste* magazine.

SERVES 4
*1 sachet powdered saffron*
*30g/1oz butter*
*2 onions, chopped*
*2 cloves of garlic, crushed*
*150ml/¼ pint Greek yoghurt*
*1 × 400g/14oz can of chopped tomatoes*
*5–6 tablespoons chopped fresh coriander*
*salt and freshly ground black pepper*
*4 chicken breasts, skinned and boned*

To garnish
*a few fresh coriander leaves*

**1.** Heat the saffron in a small dry saucepan for 3 seconds. Pour on 3 tablespoons of hot water and stir to dissolve.

**2.** Melt the butter in a sauté pan and fry the onions and garlic for 5–8 minutes, until lightly golden. Stir in the saffron liquid. Add the yoghurt, 1 tablespoon at a time, stir and fry until

it is well incorporated into the sauce. Add the tomatoes, coriander, salt and pepper.

**3.** Put the chicken breasts into the pan and bring slowly to the boil. Cover and simmer over a low heat for 30 minutes, or until the chicken is tender.

**4.** Remove the lid, lift out the chicken breasts and keep warm.

**5.** Reduce the sauce by boiling rapidly, stirring occasionally to prevent it catching, until thickened. Pour over the chicken breasts, garnish with coriander and serve immediately.

 *SPICY DRY WHITE*

# LEMON CHICKEN WITH MINT AND YOGHURT SAUCE

SERVES 4
*4 chicken breasts, skinned and boned*

For the marinade
*grated zest and juice of 1 lemon*
*1 tablespoon chopped fresh parsley*
*1 tablespoon fresh thyme leaves or ¼ teaspoon dried thyme*
*1.25ml/¼ teaspoon ground coriander*
*1 tablespoon sunflower oil*

For the sauce
*150ml/¼ pint yoghurt*
*1 tablespoon chopped fresh mint*
*salt and freshly ground black pepper*
*1 clove of garlic, crushed*

To garnish
*1 small bunch of watercress*

**1.** Mix together the marinade ingredients and leave the chicken breasts in it overnight or as long as possible.

**2.** Preheat the oven to 200°C/400°F/gas mark 6.

**3.** Place the chicken and the marinade in a roasting pan and cook in the preheated oven for 30 minutes.

**4.** Meanwhile, mix all the sauce ingredients together.

**5.** When the chicken is cooked, arrange on a warmed serving dish, garnish with watercress and serve the sauce separately.

 *FULL DRY WHITE*

# CHICKEN WITH BLACK BEAN SAUCE

SERVES 4

*4 large chicken breasts, skinned and boned*
*2 teaspoons cornflour*
*3 tablespoons fermented black beans*
*2 tablespoons sunflower oil*
*2 spring onions, chopped*
*1 clove of garlic, sliced*
*2.5cm/1in piece of fresh root ginger, peeled and finely chopped*
*2 tablespoons soy sauce*
*2 tablespoons dry sherry*
*1 teaspoon sugar*
*290ml/½ pint water*
*2 teaspoons sesame oil*

To garnish
*2 spring onions, chopped*

**1.** Trim any fat off the chicken breasts and cut into bite-sized pieces. Mix with the cornflour and set aside.
**2.** Wash the beans several times as they are very salty.
**3.** Heat 1 tablespoon of the sunflower oil in a small saucepan, add the spring onions, garlic and ginger and cook over a low heat for 1 minute.
**4.** Add the soy sauce, sherry, sugar, black beans and water. Bring to the boil, then simmer slowly for 10 minutes.
**5.** Heat the remaining sunflower oil in a wok and quickly stir-fry the chicken. Add the black bean sauce and cook over a very low heat for a further 5 minutes.
**6.** Add the sesame oil and pile on to a warmed serving dish. Garnish with the spring onions.

 *WHITE ALSACE*

# CHICKEN FRIED RICE I

SERVES 4

*4 chicken breasts, skinned and boned*
*170g/6oz basmati rice, soaked in cold water for 30 minutes*
*oil*
*1 onion, chopped*
*1 clove of garlic, crushed*
*2.5cm/1in piece of fresh root ginger, peeled and finely chopped*
*1 green chilli, finely chopped*
*½ teaspoon ground turmeric*
*1 teaspoon chopped fresh lemon grass or 2 teaspoons dried lemon grass*
*290ml/½ pint white stock made with chicken bones (see page 243)*
*salt and freshly ground black pepper*

**1.** Remove any fat from the chicken and cut the flesh into bite-sized pieces.
**2.** Drain and rinse the rice.
**3.** Fry the chicken lightly in a little oil in a large sauté pan. Remove from the pan. Add the onion and cook for 10 minutes. Add the garlic, ginger, chilli and rice and fry until the rice becomes slightly opaque. Add the turmeric and cook for 1 minute.
**4.** Return the chicken to the sauté pan. Add the lemon grass and enough stock to just cover the rice. Season with salt and pepper.
**5.** Bring to the boil, then simmer slowly, adding more stock if necessary, until the rice is cooked (about 30 minutes).

 *DRY WHITE*

# CHICKEN FRIED RICE II

SERVES 4

*450g/1lb boneless chicken, cubed*
*170g/6oz basmati rice, soaked in cold water for*
*30 minutes*
*2 tablespoons oil*
*1 small onion, finely chopped*
*1 clove of garlic, crushed*
*1cm/½in piece of fresh root ginger, peeled and*
*chopped*
*1 green chilli, deseeded and chopped*
*290ml/½ pint white stock, made with chicken*
*bones (see page 243)*
*2 tablespoons soy sauce*
*salt and freshly ground black pepper*
*1 tablespoon pinenuts, browned*
*1 tablespoon sesame seeds, toasted*

To garnish
*few leaves fresh coriander*

1. Remove any fat or gristle from the chicken.
2. Drain and rinse the rice.
3. Heat the oil in a large flameproof dish and
lightly fry the chicken until golden-brown.
Remove from the pan. Add the onion and cook
over a low heat for 10 minutes, or until nearly
soft. Add the garlic, ginger and chilli and cook for
1 minute.
4. Add the rice and stir until slightly opaque. Add
the stock and bring to the boil. Add the soy
sauce, salt and pepper. Simmer for 5 minutes.
5. Return the chicken to the dish and cook for a
further 25 minutes, or until the stock is absorbed,
the rice cooked and the chicken is tender.
6. Stir in the pinenuts and sesame seeds. Pile into a
warmed serving dish and garnish with coriander.

 *DRY WHITE*

# ORIENTAL CHICKEN WITH SESAME SEEDS

SERVES 4–6

*1 × 1.35kg/3lb chicken*
*oil*

For the marinade
*1 small clove of garlic, crushed*
*1cm/½in piece of fresh root ginger, peeled and*
*grated*
*3 tablespoons soy sauce*
*1 tablespoon sesame oil*
*½ tablespoon clear honey*
*½ tablespoon wine vinegar or sherry*
*a large pinch of ground turmeric*
*1 teaspoon tomato purée*

For the vegetables
*55g/2oz mangetout, blanched*
*55g/2oz baby sweetcorn, blanched*
*55g/2oz button mushrooms, blanched*
*1 red pepper, cored, deseeded and cut into strips*
*on the diagonal*
*55g/2oz French beans, blanched*
*1 tablespoon sesame seeds, toasted*

1. Skin the chicken and cut the flesh into strips
the size of your little finger.
2. Mix together the ingredients for the marinade
and add the chicken. Leave for 1 hour.
3. Heat the oil in a wok, add the chicken and stir-
fry, with its marinade, until tender (4–5 minutes).
4. Add all the vegetables and when thoroughly
heated piled into a warm serving dish and scatter
over the warm toasted sesame seeds.

 *FULL DRY WHITE*

# STIR-FRIED CHICKEN WITH CASHEWS

*450g/1lb boneless chicken meat, skinned or 4
  chicken breasts, skinned*
*2.5cm/1in piece of fresh root ginger, peeled and
  sliced*
*2 small cloves of garlic, peeled and sliced*
*2 teaspoons cornflour*
*1 tablespoon soy sauce*
*1 tablespoon dry sherry*
*150ml/¼ pint white stock, made with chicken
  bones (see page 243)*
*1 tablespoon sunflower or grapeseed oil*

*To garnish*
*55g/2oz unsalted cashew nuts*
*2 spring onions, sliced on the diagonal*

**1.** Trim the chicken of all fat and cut into even-sized pieces.
**2.** Put into a bowl with the ginger and garlic, cover and leave to stand.
**3.** Mix the cornflour with the soy sauce, sherry and stock. Set aside.
**4.** Heat the oil in a wok. Add the cashew nuts and stir-fry until lightly browned. Remove with a slotted spoon.
**5.** Add the chicken to the wok with the ginger and garlic and stir-fry until the chicken is cooked and tender (4–5 minutes).
**6.** Add the liquid ingredients and stir until well blended and thickened. Add a little water if it seems too thick. Check the seasoning. Pile into a warmed serving dish and sprinkle with the cashew nuts and spring onions.

 *FULL DRY WHITE*

# WARM CHICKEN SALAD

This salad can be adapted according to what salad ingredients you have in the refrigerator. It can easily be made into a complete meal with the addition of hot new potatoes. The essential ingredients (other than the chicken) are the rocket, chives, walnut oil and balsamic vinegar. It is also very good made with breast of pheasant instead of chicken.

SERVES 4
*4 chicken breasts, skinned*
*seasoned plain flour*
*salad leaves, such as frisée, lamb's lettuce, gem
  lettuce, rocket*
*110g/4oz baby sweetcorn*
*110g/4oz broccoli*
*salt and freshly ground black pepper*
*sunflower oil*
*110g/4oz shiitake or chestnut mushrooms*
*1 bunch of fresh chives, chopped*
*4 tablespoons walnut oil*
*1 tablespoon balsamic vinegar*

**1.** Remove any fat from the chicken breasts, cut the flesh into bite-sized pieces and coat them lightly with seasoned flour. Put them on to a plate, making sure that the pieces are not touching.
**2.** Put the salad leaves into a large salad bowl.
**3.** Cook the sweetcorn and broccoli in a small amount of boiling salted water. Drain.
**4.** Fry the chicken breasts in hot sunflower oil for about 5 minutes, until browned on both sides. Reduce the heat and continue to fry until the chicken is cooked. Meanwhile, fry the mushrooms in a second pan.
**5.** Lift the chicken pieces on to absorbent kitchen paper.
**6.** Transfer all the ingredients to the salad bowl, mix together, season well with salt and pepper and serve immediately.

 *SAUVIGNON*

# LEITH'S GOOD FOOD'S BONED DUCK

SERVES 4

*1 duck, boned (see pages 316–17)*
*1 large chicken breast, boned and skinned*
*½ small onion, chopped*
*110g/4oz dried apricots, sliced*
*chopped fresh tarragon and parsley*
*30g/1oz unsalted pistachio nuts, skinned*
*salt and freshly ground black pepper*

**1.** Preheat the oven to 200°C/400°F/gas mark 6.
**2.** Carefully remove any excess fat from the duck, especially from the vent end.
**3.** Put the chicken breast and onion together in a food processor and whizz briefly. Add the apricots, tarragon, parsley and pistachio nuts. Mix well and season with salt and pepper.
**4.** Stuff the duck and wrap it in a piece of lightly oiled muslin or a clean 'J'-cloth. Tie it at either end so it looks like a Christmas cracker.
**5.** Place the duck on a wire rack in a roasting pan. Prick lightly all over and rub with salt. Roast in the preheated oven for 1¼ hours. Serve cold with the tarragon sabayon on page 160 or hot with Cumberland sauce (see page 260).

 *SOFT LIGHT RED*

# LEITH'S ROAST DUCKLING

SERVES 3

*1 large oven-ready duckling*
*salt and freshly ground black pepper*
*30g/1oz granulated sugar*
*1 tablespoon wine vinegar*
*150ml/¼ pint duck or strong white stock (see page 243)*
*grated zest and juice of 1 orange*
*2 teaspoons brandy*
*15g/½oz butter*
*1 stick of celery, finely chopped*
*1 small onion, finely chopped*
*45g/1½oz flaked almonds, toasted*

To garnish
*1 whole orange, segmented*
*1 bunch of watercress*

**1.** Preheat the oven to 200°C/400°F/gas mark 6.
**2.** Place the duck on a wire rack in a roasting pan, prick all over with a fork and sprinkle lightly with salt. Roast in the oven for 1 hour. It needs no fat, but it is a good idea to lay it legs up for the first 30 minutes and turn it right side up for the next 30 minutes.
**3.** Remove the duck from the oven, drain well, and joint it. Put the pieces into a clean roasting pan, skin side up. Reserve the roasting juices.
**4.** Put the sugar and vinegar into a heavy saucepan. Dissolve the sugar over a low heat, then boil until the sugar caramelizes: it will go dark brown and bubbly, with large slow bubbles. Pour on the stock; it will hiss and splutter, so take care. Stir until the caramel lumps disappear. Add the orange zest and juice, the roasting juices from the duck (but no fat) and the brandy. Pour around the duck.
**5.** Return to the oven and continue cooking until the joints are cooked through (a further 20 minutes or so). Do not baste. Remove the duck joints to an ovenproof plate and keep warm. (If the skin is not truly crisp the duck can be returned to the oven for 10 minutes like this without the sauce.)
**6.** Skim the sauce to remove any fat, and strain into a saucepan. Add the celery and onion, and boil until the celery is just beginning to soften but is still a little crunchy (about 5 minutes). Check the sauce for seasoning. You should have a thin, fairly clear liquid with plenty of chopped celery and onion in it.
**7.** Serve the sauce separately, or poured round, not over, the duck. Surround the duck with the orange segments, scatter over the almonds and garnish with watercress.

 *CLARET*

# ROAST DUCK WITH APPLE SAUCE

SERVES 3
*1.8kg/4lb oven-ready duck*
*salt and freshly ground black pepper*
*½ onion*
*½ orange*
*1 teaspoon plain flour*
*290ml/½ pint duck or strong white stock, made*
*with chicken bones (see page 243)*

To serve
*apple sauce (see page 259)*

**1.** Preheat the oven to 200°C/400°F/gas mark 6.
Wipe the duck clean inside and out. Season the
cavity well with salt and pepper. Place the onion
and orange inside the duck. Prick the skin all over
and sprinkle with salt.
**2.** Put the duck upside down on a rack in a
roasting pan and roast in the preheated oven for
30 minutes. Then pour off the fat. Turn the duck
over and continue roasting until cooked (about 1
hour). Test by piercing the thigh with a skewer –
if the juices run out pink the duck needs further
cooking.
**3.** Tip the juices from the cavity into a bowl and
reserve them. Joint the duck into 6 pieces and
arrange on a serving dish; or leave the duck whole
for carving at the table. In any event keep it
warm, without covering, as this would spoil the
crisp skin.
**4.** Make the gravy: pour off all but 1 tablespoon
of the fat in the roasting pan. Stir over a low heat,
scraping the bottom of the pan to loosen all the
sediment. Whisk in the flour and add the juices
from inside the duck, and the stock, and whisk
until smooth. Simmer, stirring, for 2 minutes.
Season to taste with salt and pepper.
**5.** Strain the gravy into a warmed gravy-boat. Fill
a second gravy-boat with hot or cold apple sauce.
and serve with the duck.

 *RED LOIRE*

# DUCK BREASTS WITH GREEN PEPPERCORN SAUCE

SERVES 4
*4 large duck breasts, skinned*
*45g/1½oz unsalted butter*

For the sauce
*150ml/¼ pint dry white wine*
*3 tablespoons brandy*
*8 tablespoons white stock, made with chicken*
*bones (see page 243)*
*290ml/½ pint double cream*
*2 tablespoons wine vinegar*
*1 teaspoon sugar*
*1 tablespoon port*
*20g/¾oz canned green peppercorns, well rinsed*
*20g/¾oz canned red pimiento, cut into tiny dice*
*salt and freshly ground black pepper*

To garnish
*30g/1oz unsalted butter*
*2 firm dessert apples, peeled, cored and cut into*
*eighths*
*a little caster sugar*

**1.** Make the sauce: put the wine and brandy into
a heavy saucepan and boil gently for about 5
minutes or until reduced by two-thirds.
**2.** Add the stock and boil for 5 minutes. Add the
cream and boil for about a further 5 minutes,
stirring occasionally so that it does not catch on
the bottom of the pan, until the sauce has reduced
by about a third and is of pouring consistency
(i.e. about as thick as single cream).
**3.** Put the vinegar and sugar into a small
saucepan. Boil for 30 seconds or until the mixture
smells caramelized and is reduced to about 1
tablespoon. Add the reduced cream sauce. Stir
well. It may be necessary to replace the pan over
the heat to re-melt the caramel. Add the port,
peppercorns and pimiento. Season with salt and
pepper. Set aside.
**4.** Cook the duck breasts and the apple garnish:
melt the 45g/1½oz unsalted butter in a large,
heavy frying pan. When it stops foaming, add the
duck breasts and fry fairly fast on both sides.

Reduce the heat and fry slowly for 8–10 minutes, until browned but pink in the centre.

**5.** Melt the butter for the garnish in a second frying pan and fry the apples very slowly with a little sugar until golden-brown.

**6.** Serve the duck breasts garnished with the apples and hand the sauce separately.

NOTE: An alternative way to cook the duck breasts is to sprinkle the unskinned breasts with a little salt, roast in a hot oven for 15–20 minutes and then place them under a grill for a good crisp skin.

 *RED LOIRE*

# PEKING DUCK

The pancakes can be bought from oriental grocers, or follow the instructions below for making them.

SERVES 6
*1 × 2.3kg/5lb duck*
*3 tablespoons brandy*
*5 tablespoons clear honey*
*3 tablespoons light soy sauce*
*1 bunch of spring onions*
*10cm/4in piece of cucumber*

For the Chinese pancakes
*250g/9oz plain flour, plus extra for dusting*
*200ml/7fl oz boiling water*
*3 tablespoons sesame oil*

For the sauce
*1 tablespoon sesame oil*
*2.5cm/1in piece of fresh root ginger, peeled and*
*    sliced*
*2 tablespoons soya paste*
*200g/7oz plum jam*
*1 teaspoon chilli powder*
*30g/1oz caster sugar*

**1.** Place the duck in a colander in a saucepan. Pour over a kettleful of boiling water to loosen the skin. Pat dry, inside and out, with absorbent kitchen paper.

**2.** Brush the brandy over the duck – the alcohol has a drying effect on the skin and will help to make it really crispy. Tie a piece of string around the wings and hang the duck up in a cool airy place. Put a bowl or tray underneath to catch any drips.

**3.** Leave the duck for 4 hours, or until the skin is very dry. Mix together the honey and soy sauce and brush over the duck. Leave to dry for 1 hour, then brush again and leave to dry for 1 hour, then brush again and leave to dry for a further 3 hours.

**4.** Meanwhile, make the pancakes: sift the flour into a mixing bowl and gradually add the water to make a soft dough. Place on a lightly floured surface and knead well until smooth. Place in a bowl, cover with a clean damp tea-towel and leave to rest for 30 minutes.

**5.** Knead the dough again for 5 minutes, and dust with a little flour if it is sticky. Roll out to a roll about 2.5cm/1in in diameter. Cut the roll into 16 × 2.5cm/1in segments, then roll each segment into a smooth ball.

**6.** Work with 2 dough balls at a time. Dip one side of one ball in the sesame oil. Place the oiled side on top of the other ball, then flatten the balls together slightly with the palm of your hand. Lightly flour your work surface, then roll out to a circle of about 15cm/6in diameter. Repeat with the remaining balls of dough.

**7.** Heat a heavy frying pan over a low heat. Place a double pancake in the pan and cook for about 1 minute, or until dry on one side. Turn over and cook for 1 minute on the other side. Pull the pancakes apart and stack on a plate. Cooking the pancakes together will keep them moist, making them easier to roll around the filling.

**8.** Make the sauce: heat the oil in a small pan and fry the ginger for 2 minutes to lightly flavour the oil. Remove the ginger with a slotted spoon. Add the soy paste, plum jam, chilli powder and sugar and heat gently until smooth. Pour into a serving bowl and set aside.

**9.** Preheat the oven to 190°C/375°F/gas mark 5. Place the duck on a rack in a roasting pan and roast in the oven for 1½ hours. It is essential that the duck be placed on a rack, otherwise the fat in the pan will stop the skin browning underneath. Do not open the door during the cooking time.

**10.** Meanwhile, cut the spring onions into 5cm/2in pieces, and shred lengthways into thin strips. Cut the cucumber in half and then into batons. Arrange on a warmed serving dish.

**11.** Transfer the duck to a board. Remove the skin and cut into squares. Carve the meat into slices and place both on a serving dish. To serve: dip the meat and crispy skin in the plum sauce and brush over a pancake. Put the meat, skin, spring onion, and cucumber in the middle and roll up to eat.

NOTE: Instead of making the plum sauce, you can use hoisin sauce. Flavour the oil with the ginger, then add 125ml/4fl oz hoisin sauce and heat gently.

 *SPICY DRY WHITE*

# COLD DUCK BREAST SALAD

SERVES 6
*4 duck breasts, skinned*
*a little oil*
*salt and freshly ground black pepper*
*225g/8oz mangetout, cooked and refreshed*
*110g/4oz broccoli florets, cooked and refreshed*
*55g/2oz pinenuts, toasted*
*4 spring onions, sliced*

For the French dressing
*1 tablespoon lemon juice*
*4 tablespoons grapeseed oil*
*salt and freshly ground black pepper*
*1 tablespoon double cream*

**1.** Preheat the oven to 200°C/400°F/gas mark 6.
**2.** Fry the duck breasts, skin side up, in a little oil in a roasting pan. Season with salt and pepper, then roast in the oven for 15 minutes. Remove from the oven and allow to cool.
3. Once cool, refrigerate the duck breasts. There should be meat juices in the pan. Remove any fat and then reduce the juices to 2 tablespoons and allow to cool.
**4.** Make the French dressing by mixing all the ingredients together, and add the cool, reduced duck juices. Check the seasoning.
**5.** Slice the duck breasts on the diagonal, then toss the French dressing with the mangetout and broccoli. Arrange on a plate and scatter the pinenuts and spring onions over the top.

 *FULL DRY WHITE*

# ROAST GOOSE MARY-CLAIRE

A 4.5kg/10lb goose may sound huge for 6 people but most of a goose seems to be carcase! Therefore this goose has a lot of delicious, Middle Eastern-style stuffing. It is a similar stuffing to that made by Leith's Good Food for its famous roast stuffed duck. Be careful not to overcook the goose or it will become dry and tough.

SERVES 6
*1 × 4.5kg/10lb oven-ready goose*
*salt and freshly ground black pepper*
*½ lemon*

For the stuffing
*30g/1oz butter*
*1 onion, finely chopped*
*285g/10oz chicken breast, minced (or cut in 4 if using a food processor)*
*1 tablespoon chopped fresh sage*
*340g/12oz dessert apples, peeled and chopped*
*10 dried apricots, soaked for 2 hours, drained and chopped*
*55g/2oz unsalted pistachio nuts, lightly chopped*
*55g/2oz shredded beef suet*
*85g/3oz fresh white breadcrumbs*
*1 egg*

To finish
*1 tablespoon clear honey*

For the gravy
*570ml/1 pint potato water or goose stock*
*2 tablespoons Calvados*

To garnish
*1 bunch of watercress*

**1.** Wipe the goose all over. Season the inside with salt and pepper and rub with the cut lemon.
**2.** Preheat the oven to 190°C/375°F/gas mark 5.
**3.** Make the stuffing: melt the butter in a saucepan, add the onion and cook for about 10 minutes until soft but not coloured. Mix together the chicken, onion, sage, apple, apricots, pistachio nuts and suet. Add enough of the breadcrumbs to make a firm but not solid stuffing. Season to taste with salt and pepper. Add the egg and beat really

well. You can make the stuffing in a food
processor, but leave out the pistachios and stir
them in at the end.

**4.** Fill the goose cavity with the stuffing. Weigh
the stuffed goose, to establish the cooking time.
Allow 15 minutes per 450g/1lb plus an extra 15
minutes.

**5.** Prick the goose all over with a fork and
sprinkle with salt. Place on a wire rack over a
roasting pan. Roast in the preheated oven, basting
occasionally, but do not worry if you forget as a
goose is very fatty. Every so often you will have to
remove fat from the roasting pan with a baster.
Do not throw the fat away as it is wonderful for
cooking. If the goose gets too dark, cover it with
kitchen foil.

**6.** Ten minutes before the bird is cooked, brush
the honey evenly over the skin. This will help to
make it crisp. When the goose is cooked, place on
a serving plate and return to the turned-off oven.

**7.** Make the gravy: carefully spoon off all the fat
in the roasting pan, leaving the cooking juices
behind. Scrape off and discard any burnt pieces
stuck to the bottom of the pan. Add the potato
water or stock and, if you can, a little of the
stuffing. Bring to the boil, whisk well and simmer
for about 15 minutes. Increase the heat and boil
until syrupy, add the Calvados, season to taste
with salt and pepper and boil for 30 seconds.
Taste and strain into a warmed gravy-boat.

**8.** Garnish the goose with watercress.

 *RED BURGUNDY*

# CONFIT D'OIE
# (PRESERVED GOOSE)

This recipe, still common in France, is for goose
flesh preserved in fat. The pieces of goose are
lifted from the jar and wiped clean of fat before
being served either cold or reheated, or used in
composite dishes. The confit takes 3 days to
complete. Use a very fat goose, but if you cannot
get one, use 2 average or 3 small ducks instead.

*1 × 4.5kg/10lb goose*
*900g/2lb salt*

*7g/¼oz saltpetre*
*4 cloves, crushed*
*2 bay leaves, pounded*
*a pinch of dried thyme*
*1.8kg/4lb goose fat*
*450g/1lb lard*

**1.** Cut the goose into quarters.

**2.** Mix together the salt, saltpetre, cloves, bay
leaves and thyme and rub some of this over the
whole surface of the goose.

**3.** Put the goose into a large (about 1.8kg/4lb)
glazed earthenware pot and add the remaining
spiced salt. Cover and leave for 24 hours.

**4.** Slowly melt the goose fat in a large saucepan.
Remove the goose pieces from the salt, wipe clean
and put into the fat. Place over a low heat and
cook very gently for 3 hours. To test if the goose
is cooked, prick it with a skewer. The juices that
run out should be clear, and the flesh should feel
tender.

**5.** Drain the pieces of goose and remove the
bones. Strain a thick layer of fat in which the
goose was cooked into a large glazed earthenware
jar.

**6.** When this fat has completely solidified arrange
the pieces of goose on top, making sure they do
not touch the wall of the jar.

**7.** Cover the pieces of goose with just-liquid cool
goose fat. Put into a cool place.

**8.** Leave for 2 days. Strain some more liquid
goose fat into the jar to seal any holes which may
have occurred.

**9.** When this is set, melt the lard and pour a layer
about 1cm/½in thick over the surface. When this
is set, put a circle of greaseproof paper on top,
pressing it down to exclude any air. Cover the top
of the jar with a double thickness of paper and tie
with string. You can keep the confit d'oie in this
way for at least a month.

 *FULL RED*

# COLD BONED GOOSE WITH ASPIC

SERVES 10
*1 medium oven-ready goose*
*1 carrot, chopped*
*1 onion, chopped*
*2 leeks, chopped*
*1 stick of celery, chopped*
*6 black peppercorns*
*1 bouquet garni (1 bay leaf, 1 parsley stalk, 1*
  *blade of mace and 1 sprig of fresh thyme, tied*
  *together with string)*

For the aspic
*150ml/¼ pint dry cider*
*55g/2oz powdered gelatine*
*2 egg shells, crushed*
*2 egg whites*

For the stuffing
*30g/1oz butter*
*1 onion, finely chopped*
*225g/8oz dessert apples, peeled, cored and*
  *chopped*
*225g/8oz cooking apples, peeled, cored and*
  *chopped*
*85g/3oz fresh white breadcrumbs*
*4 dates, stoned and finely chopped*
*170g/6oz sausagemeat*
*2 tablespoons chopped fresh mint*
*salt and freshly ground black pepper*
*1 egg, beaten*

To garnish
*1 small orange*
*1 bunch of watercress*

**1.** Bone the goose completely, including the legs and wings (see pages 316–17).
**2.** Make the stock for the aspic: place the goose bones and giblets (except the liver) in a large pan with the carrot, onion, leeks, celery, peppercorns and bouquet garni. Bring to the boil, cover and simmer for 1 hour.
**3.** Make the stuffing: melt the butter in a saucepan, add the onion and cook over a low heat until soft but not coloured. Add the apples and cook for 1 further minute. Allow to cool.

**4.** Stir the apple and onion mixture into the breadcrumbs with the dates and sausagemeat. Add the mint and season well with salt and pepper. Add enough beaten egg just to bind the mixture together.
**5.** Lay the goose, skin side down, on a board. Remove any excess fat. Pile on the stuffing and roll up the goose into a neat roll, making sure that all the untidy ends are tucked in. Sew up neatly, using a needle and fine string. Wrap the goose in a piece of muslin or a clean tea towel and tie it securely.
**6.** Strain the stock and check the seasoning. Put the goose into a heavy saucepan or fish kettle and pour on the stock. Bring to the boil, cover tightly and simmer slowly for 2 hours. Turn the goose over once during cooking. Drain, reserving the stock for the aspic.
**7.** As soon as the goose is cool enough to handle, tighten the wrappings, and put on a plate. Leave to become completely cold, then refrigerate.
**8.** Pour the stock into a bowl and leave to cool overnight. If the stock can be transferred to the refrigerator once it is cold so much the better – it will set the fat and make removing it easier. Next day lift or skim off any fat from the goose stock. It must be absolutely fat-free.
**9.** Put 860ml/1½ pints of the goose stock (make up with water if necessary) into a very large saucepan with the cider and gelatine. Place over a low heat.
**10.** Place the crushed egg shells in a bowl, add the egg whites and whisk until frothy. Pour into the warming stock and keep whisking steadily with a balloon whisk until the mixture boils and rises. Stop whisking immediately, and draw the pan off the heat. Allow the mixture to subside. Take care not to break the crust formed by the egg white.
**11.** Bring the stock to the boil again, and again allow to subside. Repeat this once more (the egg white will trap the sediment in the stock and clear the aspic). Remove from the heat and allow to cool for 10 minutes.
**12.** Fix a double layer of fine muslin over a clean basin and carefully strain the aspic through it, taking care to hold the egg-white crust back. When all the liquid is through (or almost all of it) allow the egg white to slip into the muslin. Then strain the aspic again – this time through both egg-white crust and cloth. Do not try to hurry the

process by squeezing the cloth or the jelly will be murky. Allow to cool until on the point of setting.

**13.** Unwrap the goose and wipe away all the grease. Place it on a wire rack with a tray underneath.

**14.** Coat it with the nearly set aspic. Place in the refrigerator until set.

**15.** Cut the unpeeled orange crossways into very thin, even slices. You should end up with 7 or 8. Dip the orange slices in a little cool aspic and arrange them in a neat overlapping row down the centre of the goose. Leave to set. Coat the goose with more aspic. Once this layer has set, add further layers until really shiny. Place on a serving dish.

**16.** Set the remaining aspic in a shallow tray. Cut into neat squares and use to surround the goose. Garnish with watercress.

NOTE: If the aspic is less than crystal-clear, it is wise not to chop it as this seems to emphasize its murkiness.

 *RED BURGUNDY*

# ROAST TURKEY

A large square of fine muslin (butter-muslin) is needed for this recipe.

SERVES 12
*1 × 5.35kg/12lb oven-ready turkey*

For the oatmeal stuffing
*1 large onion, finely chopped*
*20g/³/₄oz butter*
*340g/12oz medium oatmeal*
*1 teaspoon rubbed dried sage, or 4 fresh sage*
  *leaves, chopped*
*170g/6oz shredded beef suet*
*salt and freshly ground black pepper*

For the sausagemeat and chestnut stuffing
*450g/1lb sausagemeat*
*450g/1lb unsweetened chestnut purée*
*110g/4oz fresh white breadcrumbs*
*1 large egg, beaten*
*salt and freshly ground black pepper*

To prepare the turkey for the oven
*170g/6oz butter*
*giblets*
*¹/₂ onion*
*2 bay leaves*
*a few parsley stalks*
*290ml/¹/₂ pint water*

To garnish
*1 chipolata sausage per person*
*1 rindless streaky bacon rasher per person*

For the gravy
*2 teaspoons plain flour*
*turkey stock (see page 244) or vegetable water*

**1.** Weigh the turkey. Calculate the cooking time with the help of the chart on page 318.

**2.** Make the oatmeal stuffing: cook the onion in the butter until beginning to soften. Mix with the oatmeal, sage and shredded suet. Add enough water just to bind the mixture together, and taste and season as required. Stuff into the cavity of the turkey.

**3.** Make the sausagemeat and chestnut stuffing: mix together the sausagemeat, chestnut purée, breadcrumbs and beaten egg. Taste and season as required. Stuff this into the neck end of the turkey, making sure that the breast is well plumped. Draw the skin flap down to cover the stuffing. Secure with a skewer.

**4.** Preheat the oven to 180°C/350°F/gas mark 4.

**5.** Melt the butter and in it soak a very large piece of butter-muslin (about 4 times the size of the turkey) until all the butter has been completely absorbed.

**6.** Season the turkey well with salt and pepper. Place it in a large roasting pan with the giblets (except the liver) and neck. Add the onion, bay leaves and parsley stalks and pour in the water. Completely cover the bird with the doubled butter-muslin and roast in the preheated oven for the calculated time (a 5.3kg/12lb turkey should take 3–3½ hours).

**7.** Meanwhile, prepare the garnishes: make each chipolata sausage into 2 cocktail-sized ones by twisting gently in the middle. Stretch each bacon rasher slightly with the back of a knife, cut into 2 lengthways and roll up. Put the sausages and bacon rolls into a second roasting pan, with the bacon rolls wedged in so that they cannot unravel. Thirty minutes before the turkey is ready, put the sausages and bacon in the oven.

**8.** When the turkey is cooked, the juices that run out of the thigh when pierced with a skewer should be clear. Remove the muslin and lift the bird on to a serving dish. Surround with the bacon and sausages and keep warm while making the gravy.

**9.** Lift the pan with its juices on to the top of the cooker and skim off the fat. Whisk in the flour and add enough stock or vegetable water to make up to about 425ml/¾ pint. Stir until boiling, then simmer for a few minutes. Check the seasoning. Strain into a warmed gravyboat.

 *RED BURGUNDY*

# CHRISTMAS TURKEY STUFFED WITH HAM

SERVES 20
*2.3kg/5lb piece of boiled bacon or ham, skinned*
*6.7kg/15lb turkey, boned (see pages 316–17)*

For the stuffing
*30g/1oz butter*
*1 large onion, finely chopped*
*900g/2lb pork belly, minced*
*450g/1lb unsweetened canned chestnut purée or*
  *mashed cooked fresh chestnuts*
*225g/8oz fresh white breadcrumbs*
*2 eggs, lightly beaten*
*1 teaspoon dried sage*
*2 tablespoons chopped fresh parsley*
*salt and freshly ground black pepper*

For roasting
*55g/2oz butter*
*1 onion, sliced*
*3 bay leaves*
*2 parsley stalks*
*425ml/¾ pint water*

For the gravy
*2 tablespoons plain flour*
*about 290ml/½ pint turkey stock (see page 244)*
*1 bunch of watercress*

**1.** Preheat the oven to 200°C/400°F/gas mark 6.
**2.** Make the stuffing: melt the butter in a saucepan, add the onion and cook until soft but not coloured.
**3.** When cold, mix with all the other stuffing ingredients.
**4.** Open the turkey out flat on a board, skin side down. Spread the stuffing on the turkey and put the ham or bacon on top.
**5.** Draw up the sides and sew together with a needle and fine string. Turn the bird right side up and try to push it into an even, rounded shape.
**6.** Smear the butter all over the turkey and put it into a roasting pan. Add the giblets (except the liver) and the neck. Add the onion, bay leaves and parsley stalks. Pour in the water. If the turkey looks too flat, wedge the sides with loaf tins to hold it in shape.
**7.** Roast in the preheated oven for 1 hour, then lower the temperature to 180°C/350°F/ gas mark 4 and roast for a further 3 hours. Baste occasionally as the turkey cooks and cover with kitchen foil or greaseproof paper if it is browning too much.
**8.** When the turkey is cooked, a skewer will glide through the thigh easily. Lift it out on to a serving dish and keep warm while you make the gravy.
**9.** Lift the pan with its juices on to the top of the cooker. Pour off as much fat as possible.
**10.** Using a wooden spoon or wire whisk, stir in enough flour to absorb the remaining fat. Add 290ml/½ pint stock and stir until the sauce boils. Strain into a warmed gravy-boat.
**11.** Garnish the turkey with the watercress and serve the gravy separately.

NOTES: This turkey is delicious served cold with a herby mayonnaise.

The turkey may be stuffed the day before cooking. If this is done, care should be taken that both the turkey and stuffing are well chilled before the bird is stuffed. Refrigerate until ready to cook.

If the turkey is roasted covered in 2 layers of muslin completely saturated in melted butter there is no need for basting during cooking, and when the cloths are removed the bird will be brown and crisp.

 *RED BURGUNDY*

# JUGGED HARE

SERVES 6

*1 hare, skinned and jointed, with its blood*
*2 tablespoons oil*
*225g/8oz mirepoix of carrot, onion and celery*
*1 bouquet garni (1 bay leaf, 2 parsley stalks, 1*
*    sprig of fresh thyme, tied together with string)*
*570ml/1 pint brown stock (see page 243)*
*salt and freshly ground black pepper*
*1 tablespoon redcurrant jelly*
*3 tablespoons port*

**1.** Wash and wipe dry the pieces of hare, removing any membranes. Heat the oil in a large saucepan and fry the joints until well browned, adding more dripping if the pan becomes dry. Lift out the joints and brown the mirepoix.
**2.** Return the hare to the pan. Add the bouquet garni, stock, salt and pepper. Cover and simmer for 2 hours, or until the hare is very tender.
**3.** Arrange the joints in a casserole.
**4.** Strain the stock into a saucepan. Add the redcurrant jelly and port and simmer for 5 minutes. Remove the pan from the heat.
**5.** Mix the blood with a cupful of the hot stock. Pour back into the pan without allowing the sauce to boil. The blood will thicken the sauce slightly.
**6.** Taste the sauce, adding salt and pepper if necessary. Pour over the hare joints in the casserole and serve.

NOTE: The sauce depends on the hare's blood to thicken it. If very little blood (less than 150ml/1/4 pint) comes with the hare, the basic stock must be thickened with a little beurre manié – flour and butter kneaded together in equal quantities – and whisked in small blobs into the boiling stock. This must be done before the addition of the blood, which would curdle if boiled.

 *CLARET*

# VENISON CASSEROLE

SERVES 4
*675g/1½lb venison*

For the marinade
*5 tablespoons sunflower oil*
*1 onion, sliced*
*1 carrot, sliced*
*1 stick of celery, sliced*
*1 clove of garlic, crushed*
*6 juniper berries*
*1 slice of lemon*
*1 bay leaf*
*290ml/½ pint red wine*
*2 tablespoons red wine vinegar*
*6 black peppercorns*

For the casserole
*1 tablespoon sunflower oil*
*30g/1oz butter*
*110g/4oz onions, peeled*
*1 clove of garlic, crushed*
*110g/4oz button mushrooms*
*2 teaspoons plain flour*
*150ml/1/4 pint brown stock (see page 243)*
*1 tablespoon cranberry jelly*
*salt and freshly ground black pepper*
*55g/2oz fresh cranberries*
*15g/1/2oz sugar*
*110g/4oz cooked whole chestnuts*

To garnish
*chopped fresh parsley*

**1.** Cut the venison into 5cm/2in cubes, trimming away any tough membrane or sinew.
**2.** Mix the ingredients for the marinade together in a bowl and add the venison. Mix well, cover and leave in a cool place or in the refrigerator overnight.
**3.** Preheat the oven to 170°C/325°F/gas mark 3.
**4.** Lift out the venison cubes and pat dry with absorbent kitchen paper. Strain the marinade, reserving the liquid for cooking.
**5.** Heat half the oil in a heavy saucepan and brown the venison cubes a few at a time. Place them in a casserole. If the bottom of the pan becomes brown or too dry, pour in a little of the strained marinade, swish it about, scraping off the sediment stuck to the bottom, and pour over the venison cubes. Then heat a little more oil and continue browning the meat.

**6.** When all the venison has been browned, repeat the déglaçage (boiling up with a little marinade and scraping the bottom of the pan).

**7.** Now melt the butter in a saucepan and fry the onions and garlic until the onions are pale brown all over. Add the mushrooms and continue cooking for 2 minutes.

**8.** Stir in the flour and cook for 1 minute. Remove from the heat, add the remaining marinade and the brown stock, return to the heat and stir until boiling, again scraping the bottom of the pan. When boiling, pour over the venison.

**9.** Add the cranberry jelly. Season with salt and pepper.

**10.** Cover the casserole and cook in the heated oven for about 2 hours or until the venison is very tender.

**11.** Meanwhile, cook the cranberries briefly with the sugar in 2–3 tablespoons water until just soft but not crushed. Strain off the liquor. Lift the venison, mushrooms and onions with a slotted spoon into a serving dish.

**12.** Boil the sauce fast until reduced to a shiny, almost syrupy consistency. Add the chestnuts and cranberries and simmer gently for 5 minutes.

**13.** Pour the sauce over the venison and serve garnished with chopped parsley.

 *FULL RED*

# BRAISED VENISON

SERVES 6–8
*2.7kg/6lb haunch of venison*
*30g/1oz butter*
*1 tablespoon oil*
*2 onions, sliced*
*225g/8oz carrots, sliced*
*4 sticks of celery, sliced*
*salt and freshly ground black pepper*
*1 bay leaf*
*chopped fresh thyme*
*chopped fresh sage*
*150ml/¼ pint red wine*
*about 290ml/½ pint brown stock (see page 243)*
*30g/1oz butter*
*30g/1oz plain flour*
*1 tablespoon cranberry jelly*

**1.** Preheat the oven to 150°C/300°F/gas mark 2.

**2.** Prepare the venison by trimming away any tough membranes and sinews.

**3.** Heat the butter and oil in a large flameproof casserole and brown the venison well on all sides. Remove from the casserole.

**4.** Add the onions, carrots and celery, and fry for 5 minutes until lightly browned.

**5.** Season with salt and pepper, add the bay leaf and sprinkling of thyme and sage. Lay the venison on top of the half-cooked vegetables. Add the wine and enough stock to come about a quarter of the way up the meat.

**6.** Bring to simmering point, then cover tightly and cook in the preheated oven for 1½ hours, or until tender.

**7.** When cooked lift out the meat, carve neatly and place on a warmed serving dish. Keep warm, covered with a lid or kitchen foil.

**8.** Strain the liquid from the vegetables into a saucepan.

**9.** Mix the butter and flour together to make a beurre manié. Add this to the liquid bit by bit, stirring, and bring to the boil. Stir in the cranberry jelly and correct the seasoning.

**10.** Just before serving spoon a thin layer of sauce over the venison to make it look shiny and appetizing; serve the remaining sauce in a sauceboat.

 *FULL RED*

# PEPPERED VENISON STEAK

SERVES 4
*4 × 140g/5oz venison collops (steaks) cut from the fillet*
*2 tablespoons black peppercorns*
*1 tablespoon oil (preferably olive)*
*30g/1oz unsalted butter*
*2 tablespoons brandy*
*150ml/¼ pint double cream*
*salt*

**1.** Wipe the steaks and trim off any gristle.

**2.** Crush the peppercorns coarsely in a mortar or under a rolling pin and press them into the surface of the meat on both sides.

**3.** Cover the steaks and leave them for 2 hours at room temperature for the flavour to penetrate the meat.

**4.** Heat the oil in a heavy pan, add the butter and when it is foaming fry the steaks as fast as possible until done to your liking (about 2 minutes per side for blue, 3 minutes for rare, 3½ minutes for medium and 4 minutes for well done).

**5.** Pour in the brandy and set it alight. Add the cream and a pinch of salt. Mix the contents of the pan thoroughly, scraping up any sediment stuck to the bottom.

**6.** Place the steaks on a warmed serving platter.

**7.** Boil up the sauce again, then simmer to a syrupy consistency and pour over the meat. Serve immediately.

NOTE: If the venison is very fresh and you want a gamier taste, marinate it for 2 days in equal quantities of red wine and oil, flavoured with a sliced onion, 6 juniper berries and a bay leaf. Dry well before frying.

 *VERY FULL RED*

# VENISON STEAKS WITH LEMON AND REDCURRANT SAUCE

SERVES 4
*For the sauce*
*1 lemon*
*110g/4oz redcurrant jelly*
*1 cinnamon stick*
*2 tablespoons port*
*45g/1½ oz butter, chilled and cut into small pieces*

*For the steaks*
*4 × 1cm/½in venison steaks cut from the leg or loin*
*salt and freshly ground black pepper*
*1 tablespoon juniper berries, crushed*
*55g/2oz butter*
*2 tablespoons olive oil*
*4 tablespoons port*

*To garnish*
*1 small bunch of watercress*

**1.** First prepare the sauce: pare the zest from the lemon and cut into fine needleshreds. Cut the lemon in half and squeeze the juice. Reserve.

**2.** Heat the redcurrant jelly gently with the cinnamon stick, port and needleshreds. Simmer for 10 minutes, then add the strained lemon juice and beat in the butter.

3. Trim the venison steaks of any tough membranes and season them with salt, pepper and juniper berries.

**4.** Heat the butter and oil in a heavy frying pan and cook the steaks over a high heat to brown on both sides. Reduce the heat and cook for a total of about 8 minutes, depending on size.

**5.** Remove the steaks to a warmed serving dish. Pour the fat out of the frying pan and deglaze with the port. Pour over the steaks.

 *FULL RED*

# ROAST PHEASANT

A piece of apple can be placed in the pheasant cavity, to help keep the flesh moist and improve the flavour.

SERVES 4
*2 medium oven-ready pheasants*
*salt and freshly ground black pepper*
*2 strips of pork fat*
*butter*

*For the gravy*
*1 teaspoon plain flour*
*1 tablespoon ruby port*
*1 teaspoon redcurrant jelly*

**1.** Wipe the pheasants and remove any remaining feathers.

**2.** Preheat the oven to 200°C/400°F/gas mark 6.

3. Season the birds inside.

**4.** Tie the pork fat over the breasts (this is called barding and is to prevent drying out during cooking).

**5.** Spread a little butter over the rest of the birds and season with salt and pepper.

**6.** Place in a roasting pan, pour 5mm/¼in water into the pan and cook in the preheated oven for about 40–50 minutes, basting frequently.

**7.** When cooked, lift the pheasants out of the pan and keep warm while you make the gravy.

**8.** Sprinkle the flour into the roasting juices and add the port and redcurrant jelly.

**9.** Place the roasting pan over heat and stir and scrape the bottom until the liquid boils.

**10.** Add a little more water or stock if it is too thick. Boil for 2 minutes, then season well and strain into a warmed gravyboat.

**11.** Serve the pheasants on a warmed serving platter. Serve the gravy separately.

 *CLARET*

# GALANTINE OF PHEASANT

SERVES 6
*1 large oven-ready pheasant*
*225g/8oz raw chicken meat, minced*
*170g/6oz sausagemeat*
*2 shallots, chopped*
*2 tablespoons Madeira*
*1 tablespoon chopped fresh parsley*
*salt and freshly ground black pepper*
*2 slices of cooked tongue, cut into strips*
*1 field mushroom, sliced*

For the stock
*1 carrot, sliced*
*1 onion, sliced*
*1 stick of celery, chopped*
*6 black peppercorns*
*1 bay leaf*
*1 parsley stalk*
*salt*
*a pinch of dried thyme*

To garnish
*1 bunch of watercress*

**1.** Bone the pheasant completely, including the legs and wings (see pages 316–17). Cut off any excess fat from the vent end.

**2.** Place the bones in a saucepan of water with the stock ingredients, bring to the boil, cover and simmer gently for about 1 hour.

**3.** Meanwhile, prepare the farce (stuffing): mix together the chicken meat, sausagemeat, shallot, Madeira and parsley. Season with salt and pepper.

**4.** Open the pheasant out on a board, skin side down. Push the meat around gently so that it is evenly distributed on top of the skin. Spread with half the farce and lay on the tongue strips and the mushroom slices. Season and cover with the remaining farce. Fold over the sides of the bird and stitch them together with a needle and fine string. Wrap the bird in a piece of muslin and tie the ends together.

**5.** Strain the stock. Place the pheasant in a heavy saucepan and pour over the stock. Bring to the boil, cover tightly with a lid and simmer slowly for 1½ hours, turning the pheasant over once during cooking.

**6.** Lift out the bird and, when cool, tighten the muslin cloth round it and refrigerate overnight.

**7.** Unwrap the cold pheasant, wipe off any grease and slice. Arrange the slices on a flat serving plate and garnish with watercress.

 *RED BURGUNDY*

# PHEASANT BREASTS WITH PANCETTA AND ROSEMARY

*4 pheasant breasts, skinned and boned*
*salt and freshly ground black pepper*
*4 sprigs of fresh rosemary, chopped*
*110g/4oz pancetta, thinly sliced*

To garnish
*1 small bunch of watercress*

To serve
*Cumberland sauce (see page 260)*

**1.** Preheat the oven to 200°C/400°F/gas mark 6.

**2.** Wipe the pheasant breasts and season lightly with salt and pepper.

**3.** Sprinkle the rosemary on each breast and cover them with the pancetta, folding the overlap underneath.

4. Wrap the pheasant in a large piece of kitchen foil and bake in the preheated oven for 5 minutes. Uncover the parcel and bake for a further 10 minutes or until the pheasant is cooked and the pancetta lightly browned.

5. Remove to a warmed serving dish. Garnish with the watercress and hand the Cumberland sauce separately.

# WHISKIED PHEASANT

This recipe is one that Nicola Cox has demonstrated at Leith's School; it was, rightly, very popular.

SERVES 2
*55g/2oz butter*
*1 plump oven-ready pheasant*
*1 onion, finely chopped*
*55ml/2fl oz whisky*
*salt and freshly ground black pepper*
*200–300ml/⅓–½ pint double cream*
*1 tablespoon Dijon mustard*
*1 lemon*

To garnish
*1 bunch of watercress*

1. Preheat the oven to 190°C/375°F/gas mark 5.
2. Melt the butter in a flameproof casserole and gently fry the onion until golden; add the pheasant and brown on all sides.
3. Pour over the whisky and set alight, shaking the pan until the flames subside. Season with salt and pepper, then cover the casserole closely and cook in the oven for 40–50 minutes, until the pheasant is tender.
4. Remove and joint the pheasant; keep warm.
5. Place the pan over a high heat and boil the juices to reduce to 2–3 tablespoons, stirring all the time; then gradually add the cream, boiling down until you have a coating sauce.
6. Remove the pan from the heat, add the mustard and season to taste with salt and pepper. Add the lemon juice, pour over the pheasant and serve garnished with the watercress.

 *FULL RED*

# MUSTARD RABBIT

Preparation for this dish begins a day in advance.

SERVES 4
*1 rabbit, skinned and cleaned*
*French mustard*
*1 teaspoon chopped fresh tarragon*
*45g/1½oz butter or bacon dripping*
*85g/3oz bacon or salt pork, diced*
*1 onion, finely chopped*
*1 clove of garlic, crushed*
*1 teaspoon plain flour*
*570ml/1 pint white stock (see page 243)*

To garnish
*chopped fresh parsley*

1. If the rabbit's head has not been removed, cut it off with a sharp heavy knife. Then joint the rabbit into 6 neat pieces.
2. Soak the rabbit in cold salted water for 3 hours. Drain and dry well. (This is to whiten the rabbit.)
3. Spread 2 tablespoons mustard mixed with the tarragon over the rabbit pieces and leave in a cool place overnight.
4. The next day preheat the oven to 170°C/325°F/gas mark 3.
5. Heat the butter or dripping in a frying pan and brown the rabbit pieces all over. Remove them with a slotted spoon and place in a casserole.
6. Add the bacon, onion and garlic to the pan and cook over a low heat until the onions are soft and just browned. Stir in the flour and cook for 1 minute.
7. Remove the pan from the heat and stir in the stock. Return to the heat and bring the sauce slowly to the boil, stirring continuously.
8. Pour this sauce over the rabbit. Cook in the oven for about 1½ hours, or until the rabbit is tender.
9. Lift the rabbit on to a warmed serving dish. Add 1 teaspoon mustard to the sauce and check the seasoning. Boil for 1 minute. If the sauce is now rather thin, reduce it by boiling rapidly until shiny and rich in appearance. Pour the sauce carefully over the rabbit pieces.
10. Sprinkle with the parsley.

 *FULL RED*

# RABBIT RAVIOLI

SERVES 4

For the filling
*450g/1lb rabbit*
*1 tablespoon oil*
*3 onions, finely chopped*
*1 teaspoon soft dark brown sugar*
*1 tablespoon balsamic vinegar*
*290ml/½ pint white stock (see page 243)*
*3 tablespoons finely chopped fresh thyme*
*juice of ½ lemon*
*a pinch of cayenne*
*salt and freshly ground black pepper*

For the pasta
*200g/7oz strong white '00' flour*
*a pinch of salt*
*2 eggs, beaten*
*2 teaspoons oil*

For the sauce
*150ml/¼ pint dry white wine*
*150ml/¼ pint white stock (see page 243)*
*2 tablespoons dry sherry*
*200ml/7fl oz double cream*
*1 tablespoon grainy mustard*
*salt and freshly ground white pepper*

**1.** Skin, bone and mince the rabbit finely and set aside.
**2.** Heat the oil in a heavy frying pan and sweat the onions until soft and translucent.
**3.** Add the sugar, increase the heat and stir until the onions are a dark golden brown. Add the vinegar and remove from the pan.
**4.** Add more oil to the pan if it seems dry and brown the minced rabbit meat thoroughly.
**5.** Return the onions to the pan with the stock, thyme, lemon juice, cayenne and salt and pepper. Simmer for about 45 minutes, or until all the liquid has evaporated. Taste and add extra salt and pepper if necessary. Leave to cool.
**6.** Meanwhile, make the pasta: sift the flour and salt on to a wooden board. Make a well in the centre and drop in the eggs and oil.
**7.** Using the fingers of one hand, mix together the eggs and oil and gradually draw in the flour. The mixture should be a very stiff dough.
**8.** Knead until smooth and elastic (about 15 minutes). Wrap in clingfilm and leave to relax in a cool place for 1 hour.

**9.** Roll the pasta out as thinly as possible and stamp out circles using a 7.5cm/3in round cutter. Put a heaped teaspoon of the rabbit mixture in the centre of half the circles, wet the edges and cover with the remaining pasta circles. Press the edges together firmly to seal well and eliminate any air bubbles. Leave to dry on a wire rack for 30 minutes.
**10.** To make the sauce: put the wine into a saucepan and boil rapidly to reduce by one third, then add the stock and sherry and boil again to reduce by half.
**11.** Add the cream and reduce again by about half or until the sauce is of coating consistency. Add the mustard and season to taste with salt and pepper.
**12.** Cook the pasta in a large saucepan of boiling salted water until tender (about 4–6 minutes).
**13.** To serve: drain the pasta well, arrange on 4 warmed individual serving plates and pour over the sauce.

 *CHIANTI OR DOLCETTO*

# PIGEON KEBABS

SERVES 4

*4 pigeon breasts*
*freshly ground black pepper*
*16 short rashers of rindless streaky bacon*
*16 mushrooms*
*oil*
*chopped fresh savory or thyme*

**1.** Preheat the grill.
**2.** Skin each pigeon breast and cut into 3 pieces. Season with pepper. Stretch the bacon on a board with the back of a knife. Wrap each breast piece loosely in a strip of bacon.
**3.** Skewer the wrapped breasts alternately with the mushrooms on 4 short skewers.
**4.** Brush well with oil, sprinkle with savory or thyme and season with pepper.
**5.** Grill the kebabs for about 6 minutes, turning the skewers every 2 minutes, until the breasts are slightly pink inside and the bacon evenly brown. Serve immediately as the meat toughens if kept for any length of time.

 *MEDIUM RED*

# WARM PIGEON BREAST AND CRACKED WHEAT SALAD

SERVES 4

*8 pigeon breasts, skinned*
*110g/4oz cracked wheat (bulghur)*
*2 tablespoons sesame oil*
*½ red chilli, deseeded and finely chopped*
*2.5cm/1in piece of fresh root ginger, peeled and grated*
*110g/4oz shiitake mushrooms, sliced*
*110g/4oz Parma ham, sliced*
*140g/5oz plum jam*
*5 spring onions, sliced on the diagonal*
*55g/2oz sun-dried tomatoes in oil, drained and sliced*
*salt and freshly ground black pepper*
*lemon juice*
*30g/1oz pinenuts, toasted*
*½ cucumber, deseeded and finely chopped*
*2 tablespoons oil*

*For the marinade*
*2 tablespoons Chinese five-spice powder*
*1 tablespoon light soy sauce*

*To garnish*
*2 tablespoons snipped chives*

1. Mix together the marinade ingredients and coat the pigeon breasts on both sides. Put into a shallow dish, cover and leave to marinate for at least 30 minutes or overnight in the refrigerator.
2. Put the cracked wheat into a bowl and cover with cold water. Leave to stand for 15 minutes. Drain thoroughly, squeeze out any remaining water and spread out to dry on absorbent kitchen paper.
3. Heat the sesame oil in a wok or large frying pan, add the chilli, ginger, mushrooms and Parma ham and stir-fry over a high heat for 2–3 minutes. Add the jam, spring onions and sun-dried tomatoes and bring to the boil. Add the cracked wheat and season to taste with salt, pepper and lemon juice. Heat thoroughly and stir in the pinenuts and cucumber. Keep warm.
4. Heat the oil in a frying pan, add the pigeon breasts in batches and fry for 3 minutes. Turn and

cook for 2 further minutes until browned but pink inside.
5. To serve: place 2 pigeon breasts on each of 4 individual plates and spoon a portion of the cracked wheat salad beside each serving. Sprinkle with the chives.

 *SPICY DRY WHITE*

# PIGEON WITH GARLIC

This recipe has been adapted from *Nouvelle Cuisine* by the Troisgros brothers. The quantity of garlic called for is not a mistake!

SERVES 4

*4 pigeons*
*100g/3½oz butter*
*salt and freshly ground black pepper*
*24 cloves of garlic, unpeeled*
*7g/¼oz foie gras (optional), or 30g/1oz chicken liver pâté (see page 149)*
*1½ tablespoons brandy*
*5 tablespoons white stock, made with chicken bones (see page 243)*

1. Clean the pigeons and reserve the livers.
2. Put 7g/¼oz butter into each pigeon and truss them, just cutting the nerve at the joint of the legs so that they do not curl up. Season with salt and pepper.
3. Separate the cloves of garlic but do not peel them. Push the foie gras or chicken liver pâté through a sieve.
4. Preheat the oven to 220°C/425°F/gas mark 7. Heat the remaining butter in a flameproof casserole, put in the pigeons and brown them lightly on all sides. Surround with the cloves of garlic and cook in the oven for 20 minutes, basting frequently.
5. Put the pigeons on a plate in a warm place with 8 cloves of garlic and their cooking butter. In the casserole, sauté the pigeon livers with the remaining cloves of garlic, deglaze with the brandy and press the livers and garlic through a sieve on to the foie gras.
6. Put the stock, or failing that, water, into the casserole, bring to the boil and thicken with the

garlic and liver purée. Untruss the pigeons, lift off the breasts, and skin them. Simmer the breasts in the sauce for 2–3 minutes and check the seasoning.

**7.** Serve the breasts on a warmed serving dish, lightly coated with the sauce and surrounded by the whole cloves of garlic.

 *RED BURGUNDY*

# JACK HORNER'S PIE

SERVES 6
*8–10 (depending on size) pigeon breasts, boned*
*    and skinned*
*oil or dripping*
*1 onion, finely chopped*
*1 large carrot, sliced*
*2 teaspoons plain flour*
*290ml/½ pint brown stock (see page 243), or*
*    water*
*150ml/¼ pint red wine*
*salt and freshly ground black pepper*
*1 tablespoon orange juice*
*2 teaspoons redcurrant jelly*
*170g/6oz prunes, soaked overnight*
*225g/8oz flour quantity puff pastry (see page 464)*
*beaten egg to glaze*

**1.** Remove any membranes from the pigeon breasts and cut each into 3–4 pieces.
**2.** Heat a little oil or dripping in a heavy frying pan and brown the pieces of pigeon breast, a few at a time, until brown all over. Remove them to a plate as they are done.
**3.** Fry the onion and carrot in the pan until slightly softened and pale brown.
**4.** Stir in the flour and cook for 1 minute. Remove from the heat and add the stock and wine. Return to the heat, bring to the boil and simmer, stirring to scrape any sediment from the bottom of the pan, for 2 minutes. Season with salt and pepper.
**5.** Return the pigeon breasts to the frying pan (or if it is too small, tip the lot into a saucepan). Add the orange juice and jelly and simmer slowly for 1 hour. Be very careful not to let the liquid evaporate and the pan burn. If it boils, add extra water.
**6.** Add the prunes and simmer for a further 30 minutes. Taste and add extra seasoning if required. Tip into a pie dish and leave to get cold.
**7.** Preheat the oven to 200°C/400°F/gas mark 6.

**8.** Roll out the pastry to the thickness of a £1 coin. Cut a long strip just wider than the rim of the pie dish, brush the lip of the dish with water and press down the strip.
**9.** Brush the strip with water and lay over the sheet of pastry. Press it down firmly. Cut away any excess pastry.
**10.** Cut a 1cm/½in hole in the centre of the pie top and cover with a leaf-shaped piece of pastry (the hole is to allow the escape of steam).
**11.** Decorate the top of the pie with more pastry leaves. Brush all over with egg. Leave in the refrigerator to relax for 10 minutes.
**12.** Bake in the preheated oven for 30 minutes, or until the pastry is well risen and golden-brown.

 *VERY FULL RED*

# ROAST WOODCOCK

SERVES 4
*4 woodcock*
*4 rashers of rindless streaky bacon*
*salt and freshly ground black pepper*
*4 rounds of white bread 13cm/5in in diameter,*
*    toasted on one side (see croûtes, page 364)*
*1 teaspoon plain flour*
*150ml/¼ white stock, made with chicken bones*
*    (see page 243)*
*a squeeze of lemon juice*

To garnish
*1 bunch of watercress*

**1.** Pluck the woodcock. Remove the heads and draw the gizzards through the neck openings, but do not draw the entrails. Truss neatly.
**2.** Preheat the oven to 180°C/350°F/gas mark 4.
**3.** Cover each bird with a rasher of bacon and season well with salt and pepper. Place in a roasting pan and roast for about 25 minutes, removing the bacon after 15 minutes to allow the breasts to brown thoroughly.
**4.** Spread the entrails on the untoasted side of the bread rounds and place a bird on top of each. Keep warm while you prepare the gravy.
**5.** Tip off all but a scant tablespoon of the fat from the roasting pan.
**6.** Add the flour to the pan and cook over heat for 1 minute until a russet brown.

**7.** Pour in the stock and bring to the boil, stirring continuously with a spoon, scraping the bottom of the pan to loosen the sediment as it comes to the boil.

**8.** Season with salt, pepper and lemon juice. Simmer for 2 minutes. Strain the gravy into a warmed gravy-boat.

**9.** Place the woodcock on a warmed serving dish and garnish with sprigs of watercress.

 *RED RHÔNE*

# ROAST PARTRIDGE WITH PORT AND GRAPES

This is a low-fat recipe; if required, a little cream can be added to the sauce to enrich it.

SERVES 4
*4 small partridges*
*1 dessert apple*
*1 onion, chopped*
*1 tablespoon port*
*55g/2oz seedless grapes*

**1.** Preheat the oven to 375°F/190°C/gas mark 5.
**2.** Clean the partridges. Cut the apple into quarters and put a quarter inside each partridge.
**3.** Put the onion into a roasting pan. Pour on 425ml/¾ pint water.
**4.** Put the partridges on a wire rack in the roasting pan. Roast in the preheated oven, basting occasionally with water, for 40 minutes.
**5.** Remove from the oven. Transfer the partridges to a warmed serving platter and keep warm. Tip the apple and any meat juices from the partridges into the roasting pan. Bring to the boil and stir vigorously to pulverize the apple. Simmer for 2–3 minutes.
**6.** Push through a sieve, pressing well to extract all the flavour, into a clean saucepan. It should be the required consistency; however, if it is too thin, boil rapidly to reduce to a syrupy consistency.
**7.** Add the port and boil for 30 seconds; add the grapes and allow them to warm through.
**8.** Serve the partridges with the heated sauce separately in a warmed sauceboat.

 *RED BURGUNDY*

# PARTRIDGE WITH PEARS

SERVES 4
*110g/4oz pancetta or smoked streaky bacon, in one piece*
*3 tablespoons olive oil*
*12 shallots, peeled and blanched*
*2 plump partridges, halved and claws removed*
*plain flour, seasoned with salt, freshly ground black pepper and ground mace*
*2 tablespoons brandy*
*150ml/¼ pint dry white wine*
*150ml/¼ pint white stock (see page 243)*
*1 small clove of garlic, crushed*
*thinly pared zest of ½ lemon*
*1 tablespoon finely chopped fresh rosemary*

To garnish
*2 medium pears (ideally Comice)*
*15g/½oz unsalted butter*

To serve
*wild rice*

**1.** Cut the pancetta or bacon into 1cm/½in chunks and blanch in a pan of boiling water for 30 seconds. Drain and pat dry with absorbent kitchen paper.
**2.** Heat half the oil in a heavy flameproof casserole and fry the bacon until brown. Remove from the pan with a slotted spoon and reserve.
**3.** Next add the shallots, shaking the casserole to brown them evenly. When brown remove from the casserole with a slotted spoon and reserve with the bacon.
**4.** Coat the partridges lightly with the seasoned flour and place in the casserole, skin side down, adding more oil if the dish is too dry. Remove when brown and tip off all the oil.
**5.** Add the brandy, set alight with a match and shake the casserole until the flames subside.
**6.** Add the wine, stock, garlic, lemon zest, rosemary and partridges. Season with salt and pepper and bring to the boil, then cover and simmer very slowly for 35–40 minutes. Add the shallots and bacon 10 minutes before the end of the cooking time.
**7.** Meanwhile, prepare the garnish: peel, quarter and core the pears and cut each quarter into 3 slices lengthways. Melt the butter in a frying pan

and when foaming add the pear slices and fry over a medium heat until golden-brown on both sides.
8. When the partridges are ready, lift them out of the casserole, trim them neatly and keep them warm on a serving dish, surrounded by the bacon, shallots and pear slices.
9. Strain the sauce into a clean saucepan and boil rapidly to reduce to a syrupy consistency. Pour over the partridges and serve.

 *RED BURGUNDY*

# PARTRIDGE WITH LENTILS

*2 partridges, drawn, trussed and larded*
*salt*
*30g/1oz lard*
*30g/1oz rindless unsmoked bacon, chopped*
*30g/1oz onion, chopped*
*110g/4oz Puy lentils, soaked in cold water for 1*
  *hour and drained*
*grated zest of ½ lemon*
*1 bay leaf*
*110g/4oz Gyula sausage or similar dried, smoked*
  *pork sausage*
*290ml/½pint white stock, made with chicken*
  *bones (see page 243)*
*75ml/3fl oz soured cream*

1. Preheat the oven to 170°C/325°F/gas mark 3.
2. Sprinkle the partridges with salt. Melt the lard in a large frying pan and fry the partridges until they are golden-brown all over. Remove from the pan.
3. Fry the bacon and onion in the same pan until golden-brown.
4. Put the lentils into a large casserole with the lemon zest and bay leaf. Add the partridges, sausage, bacon and onion. Pour over enough stock to just cover the ingredients. Cover with a lid and cook in the preheated oven until the partridges are tender (about 45 minutes). If the partridges are ready before the lentils, remove them and the sausages from the pan.
5. When the lentils are tender, pour over the soured cream and bring the liquid to the boil.
6. Carve the partridges and cut the sausages into thin slices. Place the lentils in a deep serving dish, put the partridge pieces on top and garnish with the sliced sausage.

# GUINEA-FOWL BRAISED WITH CARAMEL AND ORANGES

SERVES 4
*2 guinea-fowl*
*2 teaspoons sunflower oil*
*55g/2oz shallots, finely chopped*
*30g/1oz granulated sugar*
*1 tablespoon wine vinegar*
*175ml/6fl oz white stock (see page 243)*
*juice of 2 oranges, strained*
*salt and freshly ground black pepper*

To garnish
*1 orange, segmented*
*1 small bunch of watercress*

1. Preheat the oven to 190°C/375°F/gas mark 5.
2. Remove any feathers from the guinea-fowl and wipe clean inside with a damp cloth.
3. Heat the oil in a flameproof casserole. Add the guinea-fowl and brown them all over. Remove them from the casserole.
4. Reduce the heat, add the shallots to the casserole and cook for 2 minutes. Add the sugar and vinegar, dissolving the sugar over a low heat, then boil the liquid until the sugar caramelizes. Pour on the stock – it will hiss and splutter, so take care – and stir over a low heat until the caramel lumps disappear. Add the orange juice. Season well with salt and pepper. Return the guinea-fowl to the casserole and bring the cooking liquor to the boil.
5. Cover the casserole and pot-roast it for 1 hour.
6. Remove the guinea-fowl and joint them as you would a chicken (see pages 316–17). Arrange the pieces on a warmed serving plate. Skim as much fat as possible from the cooking liquor. Strain it into a clean saucepan, skim it again and boil rapidly for 3 minutes.
7. Garnish the guinea-fowl with orange segments and watercress, and serve the sauce separately in a warmed sauceboat.

 *RED BURGUNDY*

# QUAIL WITH CHESTNUTS AND CALVADOS

8 small quail
freshly ground black pepper
2 dessert apples, peeled, cored and diced
1 onion, sliced
1 bay leaf
3 tablespoons Calvados
1 × 140g/5oz can of unsweetened chestnuts
white stock, made with chicken bones (see page 243)

1. Preheat the oven to 200°C/400°F/gas mark 6.
2. Season the quail with pepper and stuff with the apple.
3. Place the quail in a roasting pan with the onion, bay leaf, Calvados and 4 of the chestnuts. Add enough chicken stock to come a quarter of the way up the quail. Cover with kitchen foil and roast in the preheated oven for 25 minutes. Remove the foil and roast for a further 10 minutes.
4. Transfer the quail to a warmed serving dish and keep warm in the turned-off oven.
5. Strain the cooking liquid into a saucepan, pressing the vegetables to extract their flavour. Skim off any fat from the liquid, then reduce by boiling until syrupy. You should have about 290ml/1/2 pint.
6. Add the remaining chestnuts and warm through in the sauce.
7. Spoon the liquid over the quail, garnish with chestnuts and hand any extra sauce separately.

 *LIGHT RED*

# COLD GAME PIE (I)

This pie takes 2 days to complete.

SERVES 6–8
1 grouse
1 partridge
1 pigeon
2 hare joints
110g/4oz venison
1 large carrots

2 large onions
2 sticks celery
110g/4oz butter
4 tablespoons oil
290ml/1/2 pint red wine
1 litre/1 3/4 pints white stock, made with chicken bones (see page 243)
4 bay leaves
a little fresh thyme
parsley stalks
salt and freshly ground black pepper
30g/1oz powdered gelatine
450g/1lb quantity pâte à pâté (see page 467)
beaten egg

1. Split the birds in half. Cut the venison into small cubes. Chop the carrot, onion and celery roughly.
2. Heat about 1 tablespoon each of butter and oil in a heavy frying pan, and when the butter is foaming, add a good handful of the chopped vegetables. Keep the heat at a medium temperature – enough to fry and brown the vegetables without burning the butter. Keep turning the vegetables to get an even colour all over. When they are all done, lift them out with a slotted spoon and transfer to a large, deep saucepan.
3. Add more oil and butter to the frying pan and brown the venison, the hare and finally the birds. If the bottom of the pan becomes sticky and brown, deglaze it with half a glass of the wine or stock: pour in the liquid and boil up, stirring with a metal spoon or fish slice and scraping the bottom of the pan to loosen the sediment. Tip this liquid in with the browned ingredients and continue frying the meats.
4. When all the ingredients are browned and transferred to the deep saucepan, deglaze the pan again, pouring the juices in with the meats. Add the remaining wine, the stock, and, if necessary, a little water (the ingredients must be just covered). Add the herbs, salt and pepper. Cover with a lid and simmer for 1 1/2 hours or until everything is tender.
5. Strain off the liquid and leave until completely cold. Skim thoroughly, then transfer to a saucepan and boil to reduce to about 570ml/1 pint. Add the gelatine to the liquid and leave to soak.
6. When the meat is cool enough to handle, remove all the bones from the birds and hare and

cut the flesh into small pieces (about the size of
the cubes of venison). Discard the cooked
vegetables, the bay leaves and parsley stalks. Let
the meat cool completely.

**7.** Preheat the oven to 190°C/375°F/gas mark 5.
Lightly grease a 1.8kg/4lb pie mould or a loose-
bottomed cake tin.

**8.** Roll two-thirds of the pastry into a round big
enough to cover the base and sides of the mould
or tin. Dust the pastry with a little flour. Now
fold it in half, away from you. Place one hand on
the fold of the semi-circle and with the other
gently push and pull the sides so that you form a
'bag' roughly the shape and size of the pie mould
or cake tin. Open out the bag and fit it into the
greased mould or tin.

**9.** Fill the pie with the meat. Roll out the
remaining pastry into a round big enough to
cover the top of the pie. Dampen the bottom
edge, then press this 'lid' on to the pastry case,
pinching the edges together.

**10.** Decorate with pastry trimmings, shaped into
leaves, and make a neat pea-sized hole in the
middle of the top. Brush with beaten egg.

**11.** Bake in the preheated oven for 50 minutes.
While the pie is in the oven, heat up the stock to
melt the soaked gelatine. Allow to cool.

**12.** Remove the pie carefully from the mould or
tin and stand it on a flat baking sheet. Brush the
pie all over with beaten egg and return to the
oven for a further 20 minutes. Remove and allow
to cool.

**13.** Using a small funnel, pour the cooled, but not
quite set, stock into the pie through the hole in
the pastry lid. Allow the liquid to seep down into
the pie, then pour in some more: this can be a
slow process, but the pie should take about
570ml/1 pint of liquid, and it is important that
you add it to prevent the filling becoming
crumbly and dry.

NOTE: If buying such small quantities of hare
and venison proves difficult, use 225g/8oz lean
chuck steak instead.

 *CLARET*

# COLD GAME PIE (II)

Preparation for this dish must start 2–3 days in
advance.

SERVES 6
For the forcemeat
*110g/4oz poultry livers*
*1 pheasant, boned (see pages 316-17) and skinned*
*450g/1lb pork belly, derinded*
*3 shallots, finely chopped*
*2 fresh sage leaves, finely chopped*
*1 teaspoon chopped fresh thyme*
*1 clove of garlic, crushed*
*2 teaspoons salt*
*1 teaspoon coarsely ground black pepper*
*1 tablespoon brandy*
*3 tablespoons dry white wine*

For the jelly
*1 stick of celery*
*1 carrot, sliced*
*1 slice of onion*
*1 bay leaf*
*1 sprig of fresh parsley*
*1 sprig of fresh marjoram*
*bones, giblets (except the liver) and skin of the
    pheasant*
*15g/½oz powdered gelatine*

For the pastry crust
*450g/1lb flour quantity pâte à pâte (see page 467)*
*a piece of pig's caul about 30cm/12in square*
*beaten egg to glaze*

**1.** Trim any discoloured parts and sinew from the
livers.

**2.** Reserve 1 pheasant breast, the pheasant liver
and 1 other poultry liver. Mince the rest of the
pheasant meat with the remaining livers and the
pork belly. Add the shallot, sage, thyme, garlic,
salt, pepper, brandy and wine. Mix well and put
into a deep bowl.

**3.** Lay the breast meat and livers on top, and
cover. Refrigerate for 24 hours.

**4.** Make up the pâte à pâte.

**5.** Use two-thirds of it to line a 20cm/8in raised
pie mould or loose-bottomed cake tin.

**6.** Line the pastry shell with the pig's caul,
allowing the sides to hang down over the edge.

**7.** Put half the minced mixture into the mould. Cut the pheasant breast into strips and lay them on top of the forcemeat.

**8.** Lay the livers on top of the pheasant strips. Cover with the remaining forcemeat, pressing down well to eliminate any air pockets.

**9.** Draw the caul up over the forcemeat to envelop it.

**10.** Preheat the oven to 190°C/375°F/gas mark 5.

**11.** Use the remaining pastry to cover and elaborately decorate the top of the pie. Press the edges of the top firmly to the base pastry. Make a hole in the middle of the pastry top to allow steam to escape.

**12.** Brush with beaten egg.

**13.** Bake the pie in the preheated oven for 15 minutes, then turn the oven temperature down to 150°C/300°F/gas mark 2, and bake for a further 1¾ hours. Remove the pie from the oven and allow to cool overnight.

**14.** Make the stock by simmering the jelly ingredients (except the gelatine) in 1 litre/2 pints water for 2 hours. Strain through muslin or a double 'J'-cloth and chill overnight.

**15.** Remove all traces of fat from the stock. Pour it into a saucepan and sprinkle on the gelatine. Leave to soak for 5 minutes, then bring slowly to the boil. Boil until there is 290ml/½ pint of liquid left.

**16.** Leave until cold but not set – it should be syrupy. Carefully pour, little by little, into the pie, through the hole in the pastry. A small funnel will make this operation easier. Continue until the liquid level is visible, and will no longer gradually sink. If by some mischance the pastry case has a hole in it allowing the liquid to leak out, plug the hole with softened butter.

**17.** Chill the pie until the liquid is set: about 2 hours.

NOTE: If pouring the liquid into the pie proves difficult, carefully make, with the top of a knife, another hole in the cooked pastry towards the edge, and pour the liquid through this.

 *CLARET*

# CROÛTES FOR ROAST GAME BIRDS

When roasting small game birds, such as snipe or woodcock, the 'trail', or entrails, is left inside and only the gizzard removed. After roasting, the liver and juices are spread on the uncooked side of a slice of bread which has been fried or toasted on one side only. The roasted bird is served on this croûte.

Larger birds like pheasant and grouse are drawn before roasting, but the liver may be returned to the body cavity to cook with the bird. This, plus any other scrapings from the inside of the bird, is spread on the uncooked side of the croûte, which is then cut in half on the diagonal and served as a garnish to the whole roast bird.

# FRIED CRUMBS FOR ROAST GAME BIRDS

*55g/2oz butter*
*4 tablespoons dried white breadcrumbs*

Melt the butter and fry the crumbs very slowly until they have absorbed most of it, and are golden and crisp. Serve in a warmed bowl, handed with the sauce or sauces.

NOTE: Fresh white breadcrumbs can be used, but rather more butter will be needed as they are very absorbent, and great care should be taken to fry slowly so that the crumbs become crisp before they turn brown.

# MEAT
# AND OFFAL

# MEAT AND OFFAL

The younger the animal, and the less exercise it has taken, the more tender its meat will be, but its flavour will be less pronounced. For example a week-old calf will be tender as margarine, and about as flavourless. An ox that has pulled a cart all its long life will be quite the reverse – good on flavour, but tough as old boots. A relatively young, and therefore tender, animal will have white or pale fat, rather than yellow; the meat will be less dark, and the bones more pliable than in an older, tougher animal. So rump steak with a bright red hue and white fat may well be more tender than the dark flesh and yellow fat of older meat, but it will probably lose in flavour what it gains in texture.

Because tenderness is rated highly today, the most expensive cuts of meat are those from the parts of the animal's body that have had little or no exercise. For example, the leg, neck and shoulder cuts of beef are tougher (and therefore cheaper) than those taken from the rump or loin.

But apart from the age of the animal, there are other factors that affect tenderness. Meat must not be cooked while the muscle fibres are taut due to rigor mortis, which can last, depending on the temperature at which the carcase is stored, for a day or two. The state of the animal prior to slaughter can also affect the tenderness of the meat; for example, if it is relaxed and peaceful the meat is likely to be more tender. Injections of certain enzymes (proteins that produce changes in the meat without themselves being changed) given to the animal before slaughter will produce the same result artificially.

But the most crucial factor affecting tenderness is the length of time that meat is stored before cooking. If hung in temperatures of 2°C/35°F it will, due to enzyme activity, become increasingly tender. Temperatures should not be higher than this, because although the enzyme activity would be greater, the risk of spoilage due to bacterial action would become high. For beef, 7 days is the minimum hanging time, while 3 weeks or a

month are more desirable. However, with the commercial demands for quick turnover, the weight-loss during storage and the expense of storing, good hanging is rare these days. Some enzyme activity continues if the meat is frozen, and the formation, and subsequent melting, of ice-crystals (which, in expanding, bruise the fibres of the meat) mean that freezing meat can be said to tenderize it. However, the inevitable loss of juices from the meat (and subsequent risk of dryness after cooking) is a disadvantage that outweighs the minimal tenderizing effect.

Hanging is most important in beef, as the animals are comparatively old, perhaps 2 or 3 years, when killed. It is less important for carcases of young animals, such as calves and lambs, as their meat is relatively tender anyway.

Because, inevitably, some bacterial action (as well as enzyme action) must take place during hanging, the flavour of well-hung meat is stronger, or gamier, than that of under-hung meat. The colour will also deepen and become duller with hanging. But the prime reason for hanging meat is to tenderize it, rather than to increase or change its flavour. This is not so with game, including venison, which is hung as much to produce a game flavour as to tenderize the meat.

The last, and probably most important, factor

that affects the ultimate tenderness of meat is the method of cooking. Half-cooked or rare meat will be tender simply because its fibres have not been changed by heat, and will still retain the softness of raw meat. But as the heat penetrates the whole piece of meat the fibres set rigidly and the juices cease to run. Once the whole piece of meat is heated thoroughly, all the softness of raw meat is lost and it is at its toughest. This explains the natural reluctance of chefs to serve well-done steaks – it is almost impossible to produce a tender well-done grilled steak.

But, paradoxically, further cooking (though not fast grilling or frying) will tenderize that tough steak. This is seen in stewing, when long, slow cooking gradually softens the flesh. A joint from an older animal, which has done much muscular work during its lifetime and is coarse-grained and fibrous, can be made particularly tender by prolonged gentle cooking. This is because much of the connective tissue present in such a joint, if subjected to a steady temperature of, say, 100°C/200°F, will convert to gelatine, producing a soft, almost sticky tenderness.

Joints with finer graining and little connective tissue, such as rump or sirloin, will never become gelatinous, and are consequently seldom cooked other than by roasting or grilling, when their inherent tenderness (from a life of inaction) is relied on. But they will never be as tender as the slow-cooked shin or oxtail, which can be cut with a spoon.

It does not matter that few people have any idea which part of the animal their meat comes from. But it is useful to know, if not how to do the butcher's job, at least which cuts are likely to be tender, expensive, good for stewing, or not worth having, and what to look for in a piece of meat.

## ROASTING MEAT

**1.** Weigh the joint and establish the length of cooking time (see below).
**2.** Preheat the oven (electric ovens take longer to heat up than gas ovens).
**3.** Prepare the joint for roasting; see the relevant recipe.
**4.** Heat some dripping in a roasting pan and if the meat is lean, brown the joint over direct heat so that it is well coloured. Pork and lamb rarely need this but many cuts of beef do.
**5.** Place the joint in the pan, on a grid if you have

one available, as this aids the circulation of hot air; roast for the time calculated.

ROASTING TIMES
Obviously a long thin piece of meat weighing 2.3kg/5lb will take less time to cook than a fat round piece of the same weight, so that the times below are meant only as a guide. The essential point is that meat must reach an internal temperature of 60°C/140°F to be rare, 70°C/150°F to be medium pink, and 80°C/170°F to be well done. A meat thermometer stuck into the thickest part of the meat, and left there during cooking, eliminates guesswork.

BEEF: Beef is generally roasted in the hottest of ovens for 20 minutes to brown the meat (or it may be fried all over in fat before being transferred to the oven). Whatever the method, calculate the cooking time after the browning has been done, and allow 10–15 minutes per 450g/1lb for rare meat, 20 minutes for medium and 25 for well done, roasting the meat in an oven preheated to 190°C/375°F/gas mark 5.
LAMB: Put the lamb into the hottest of ovens for 20 minutes, then allow 20 minutes to 450g/1lb at 190°C/375°F/gas mark 5. This will produce very slightly pink lamb. If lamb without a trace of pinkness is wanted, allow an extra 20 minutes after the calculated time is up.
PORK: Pork must be well cooked. Allow 40 minutes to 450g/1lb at 170°C/325°F/gas mark 3. If crackling is required, roast at 200°C/400°F/gas mark 6 for 25 minutes to 450g/1lb, plus 25 minutes over.
VEAL: Brown in hot fat over direct heat. Or roast for 20 minutes at maximum temperature. Then allow 20 minutes per 450g/1lb at 180°C/350°F/gas mark 4.

## CUTS OF MEAT
BEEF
**For roasting:** sirloin, fore rib, fillet
**For pot-roasting:** topside, silverside, brisket, thick flank
**For stewing, braising and boiling, and for salting and boiling:** chuck, shin, brisket, flank, neck, topside, silverside
**For grilling and frying:** fillet, rump and sirloin. But the names for steaks can be confusing:

*Beef cuts*

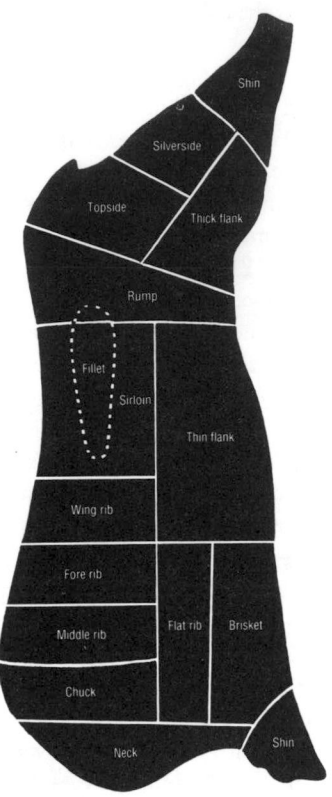

**For pies:** chuck, brisket, thick flank, shin (foreleg), shin or leg (hind leg).

VEAL

The cuts of veal, and their names, more closely resemble those of a lamb or sheep than those of grown-up beef.

As veal is more tender than beef, most of the animal is suitable for quick cooking (roasting, frying). But as there is little fat on a calf, care must be taken to moisten the meat frequently during cooking to prevent dryness. Because of the absence of fat, veal is seldom grilled.

Much Dutch veal is milk-fed and expensive. It has a pale pink colour and the best cuts are exceptionally tender. But the taste is mild to the point of insipidity, and it needs good seasoning, usually plenty of lemon, pepper or a good sauce. English veal is cheaper, has more flavour, and generally has a slightly more reddish hue. This is because the animals are killed older then their Dutch fellows, and are generally, though not always, grass-fed. But veal should never look bloody or really red.

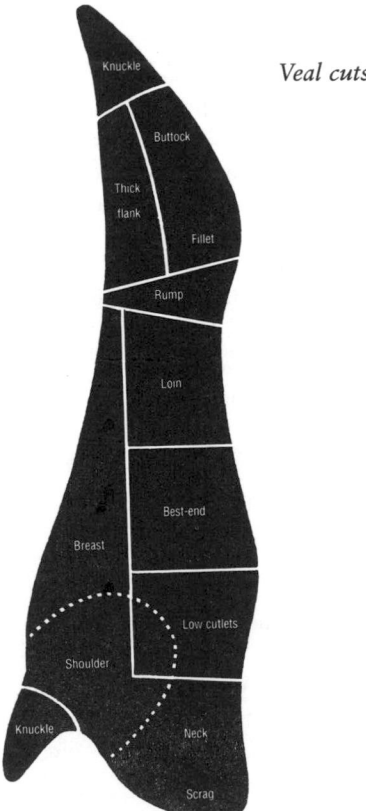

*Veal cuts*

**Rump steaks** (rumsteak or bifsteak in French): These are thick (about 2cm/¾in) slices cut across the grain of the rump, and then, if for individual servings, cut into smaller neat pieces.

**Fillet steak:** This comes in various guises. Cut across into neat thick (2.5cm/1in) slices, it becomes tournedos. A neat piece for 2–3 people, weighing perhaps 225g/8oz cut from the thick end (but with all the coarser meat trimmed from it), can be grilled, spitted or roasted as a châteaubriand. Medallions are thin neat slices cut across the fillet.

**Sirloin steaks:** The name sirloin covers steak from the upper side of the true sirloin, wing rib and fore rib. The French entrecôte means only the true tender sirloin, which is cut in individual steaks or as T-bone steaks (on the rib, with the sirloin on one side of the T and the fillet or undercut on the other). French côte de boeuf or our rib of beef are thick steaks on the rib bone, from the slightly less tender wing rib or fore rib. Porterhouse is a double-sized T bone, or double-sized wing rib.

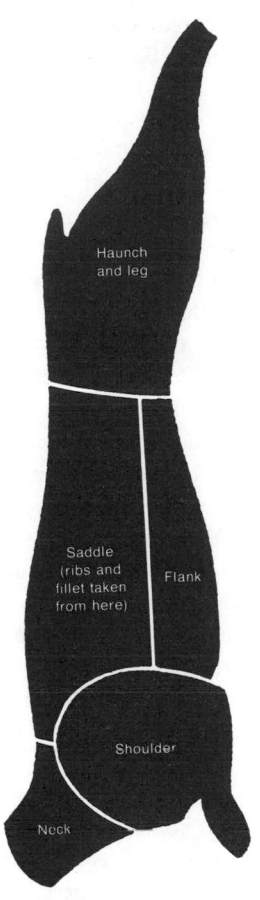

*Venison cuts*

**For roasting:** haunch, saddle, either whole or in fillets
**For grilling and frying:** steaks from the fillet or chops made from the saddle
**For stewing:** shoulder, neck, flank
**For braising in one piece:** shoulder
**For mincing:** flank, neck

PORK

Pork used to be eaten mainly in winter, or as bacon, because of the difficulty of keeping it fresh. But with modern methods of refrigeration, pork is eaten all the year round.

The flesh should be pale pink, not red or bloody. Pork killed for the fresh meat market is generally very young and tender, carrying little fat. Suckling pigs, killed while still being milk-fed, may be roasted or barbecued whole, and are traditionally served with the head on, and with an apple or an orange between the jaws.

Crackling is the roasted skin of pork. The skin must be scored deeply with a sharp knife before roasting. Salt is rubbed on the skin, making it crisp and bubbly when cooked.

**For roasting:** leg, loin, best end, breast
**For braising and stewing:** leg, shoulder, middle neck, scrag, breast
**For frying (and possibly grilling if frequently basted):** cushion (fillet), loin chops, best end cutlets, rump, round (buttock)
**For stock:** knuckle, foot or scrag end of neck.
NOTE: The more tender cuts from the forequarter, from a top-quality milk-fed calf, may also be boned out and sliced for escalopes.

VENISON

Venison is the meat of deer. Good deer meat should be dark red with a fine grain and firm white fat.
When preparing venison remove as much of the membrane as possible. Venison is very low in fat so it is often recommended that the meat be marinated before cooking. If roasting, the meat can be barded with bacon to help retain moisture.

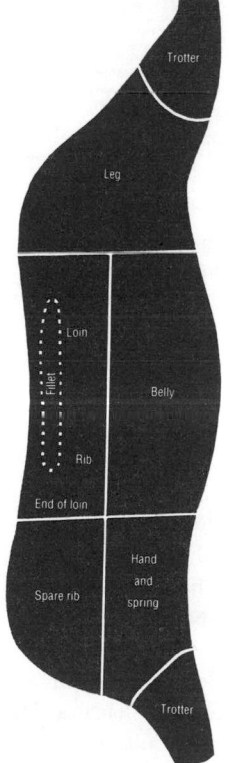

*Pork cuts*

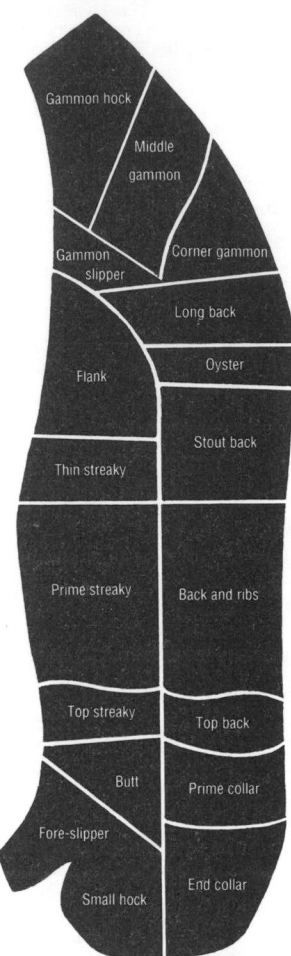

*Bacon cuts*

has been brined or cured in dry salt separately from the rest of the pig. Gammon is cured while still attached to the body. Hams are salted and possibly smoked according to varying local traditions. Parma ham and Bayonne ham, for example, are salted and smoked but not cooked further before eating. English hams are generally cooked before eating hot or cold. The most famous are the well-hung Braddenham ham and the sweet milk York ham. American Virginia hams are said to owe their sweet flavour to the fact that the hogs are fed on peanuts and peaches, and the hams are cured in salt and sugar and smoked over apple and hickory wood for a month. Westphalian ham from Germany is eaten raw in thin slices like Parma ham. Paris ham is similar to English York ham.

Since good refrigeration is now widely available, pork need no longer be salted as a preservative measure. Today pork is turned into bacon mainly for the flavour. Smoked bacon keeps slightly longer than green (unsmoked) but, again, modern smoking is done more for the flavour than for preservation.

Commercially produced bacon is generally mild. Bacon cured at home, without chemical preservatives, vacuum packs, etc., is likely to have more flavour and saltiness, but needs soaking before cooking.

Smoked and green bacon flesh look similarly reddish-pink. It should not be dry, hard, dark or patchy in colour. Smoked rind is yellowish-brown; green bacon rind is white.

English bacons vary according to manufacturer and price, some being saltier than others, so care should be taken if boiling without prior soaking. It is wise to soak large pieces to be cooked whole, such as gammons or forehocks. Smaller cuts, steaks and rashers, rarely need soaking.

Danish pigs are all cured in the same manner, giving a good quality, mild-tasting, not very salty bacon.

**For roasting:** any part of the pig (bar the head, trotters and knuckle) are suitable
**For grilling and frying:** spare rib chops, loin chops, chump chops from the saddle, best end cutlets, belly bones or American spare ribs (usually with a marinade), fillet, tenderloin, trotters
**For boiling:** leg, belly, hand and spring, trotters
**For pies:** any meat is suitable
For sausages: any fatty piece, especially belly.

BACON
Bacon pigs are killed when heavier than pigs destined for the fresh pork market, so the comparable cuts of bacon should contain more fat than those of fresh pork.

Almost the whole of the pig is salted in brine for up to a week then matured. Green bacon is sold at this stage. Smoked bacon is hung in cool smoke for up to a month. Gammon is bacon from a hind leg, and ham is bacon from a hind leg that

**For boiling and stewing:** all cuts are suitable, but the lean pieces (forehock, gammon, collar) are sometimes casseroled or stewed whole, tied with string.
**Streaky and flank** are used diced for soups, or to add flavours to stews
**For frying or grilling:** all cuts are suitable but rashers are usually cut from the back, streaky or

collar. Steaks are cut from the gammon or prime back

**For baking (usually boiled first):** large lean pieces are generally used (whole gammon or ham, whole gammon hock, large piece of back, whole boned and rolled forehock or either of the collars).

LAMB AND MUTTON

Animals weighing more than 36kg/80lb are graded as mutton. Real mutton is seldom available in butchers' shops since all the animals are killed young enough to be called lamb. But there is a difference between the small sweet joints of the new season's spring lamb, and the larger lambs killed later in the year.

Really baby lambs, killed while still milk-fed, are extremely expensive, with very pale, tender flesh. A leg from such a lamb would feed only 2 or perhaps 3 people at most.

British lamb is very fine in flavour, but good imported New Zealand lamb is usually cheaper. As a general rule, New Zealand lamb joints come from smaller animals than the full-grown English lambs, but it should be remembered that 3 grades of New Zealand lamb are imported into Britain, ranging from excellent to very tough. All New Zealand lamb comes into the country frozen, so it stands to reason that some lambs have been more recently killed than others. The best time to buy New Zealand lamb is from Christmas through to the summer months.

Lamb should be brownish-pink rather than grey in colour, but not bloody. Because the animal is killed young, almost all the cuts are tender enough for grilling, frying or roasting, but the fattier, cheaper cuts are used for casseroles and stews too.

**For roasting:** saddle or loin, best end of neck (rack of lamb), shoulder, leg, breast
**For braising:** chump chops, loin, leg
**For grilling and frying:** best end cutlets, loin chops, chump chops, steaks from fillet end of leg
**For boiling and stewing:** knuckle, scrag and middle neck, breast, leg.

## BUTCHERY AND MEAT PREPARATION

Most cuts of meat are available ready prepared from the shop or market. But it is useful to know how to bone and tie certain French and English cuts that a busy butcher may be unwilling to tackle.

BONING

Boning is easier than most people imagine. A short sharp knife is essential. Tunnel-boning – where the bone, say from a leg, is extracted from the hole from which it protrudes, without opening out the meat – is more difficult than open-boning where the flesh is split along the bone, the bone worked out and the meat rolled up and tied or sewn. But, whether tunnel-boning or open-boning, it is essential to work slowly and carefully, keeping the knife as close to the bones as possible, and scraping the meat off the bone rather than cutting it. Any meat extracted inadvertently with the bone can be scraped off and put back into the joint.

With most bones it is possible, when tunnel-boning, to work from both ends – for example, a leg of lamb can be worked on where the knuckle bone sticks out of the thin end, and the leg bone out of the fillet end. But in most cases it is simpler to cut neatly through the flesh, along the length of the bone, from the side nearest to the bone, and

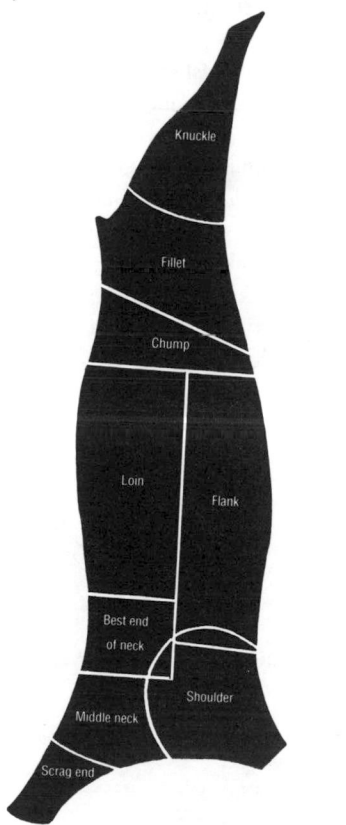

*Lamb cuts*

Knuckle
Fillet
Chump
Loin
Flank
Best end of neck
Shoulder
Middle neck
Scrag end

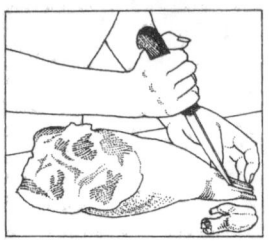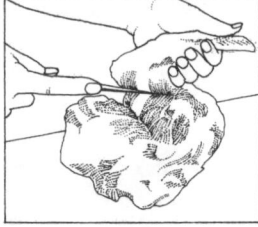

*To make a butterfly joint, work from the knuckle end*

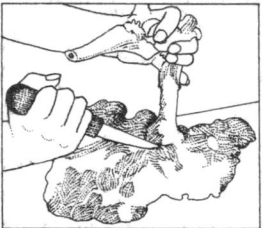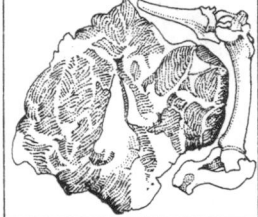

*Gradually ease out the three bones*

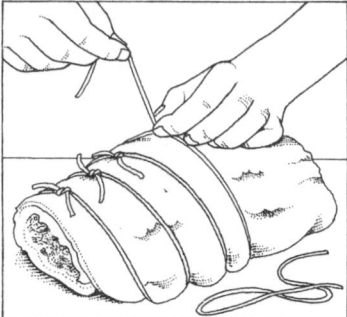

*Tie with short pieces of string or cotton*

*After stuffing, fold the butterfly flaps under the joint*

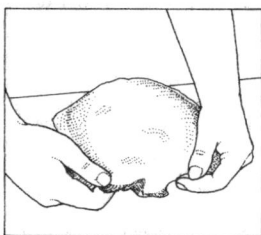

work the bone out all along its length. After all, some sewing or tying is necessary at the ends of the joints even if tunnel-boned, and it is simpler to sew up the length of the joint.

Trainee butchers are taught to use the knife in such a way that should it slip it will not hurt them. This means never pulling the knife directly towards the body. In addition, the knife is held firmly like a dagger when working, with the point

of the knife down. But the safest precaution that cooks can take is to see that their knives are sharp. Blunt knives need more pressure to wield, and are therefore more inclined to slip.

BUTTERFLY JOINTS
To make a butterfly joint, open-bone a leg of lamb. Hold a sharp, sturdy butcher's knife like a dagger and cut, from the knuckle end, down the non-fleshy side of the leg and gradually work out the three bones.

LAMB 'EN BALLON'
This is stuffed boned shoulder of lamb that is tied up to look like a balloon (see page 408 for a recipe). To reassemble the shoulder, spread the stuffing on one half of the boned lamb and fold the other half close up over to cover it. If the shoulder has been tunnel-boned, push the stuffing into it. Turn the shoulder over, skinned side up. Tie the end of a 3m/9ft piece of string firmly round the shoulder, making a knot in the middle at the top. Take the string around again, but this time at right angles to the first line, again tying at the first knot. Continue this process until the 'balloon' is trussed about 8 times. Tuck in any loose flaps of meat or skin.

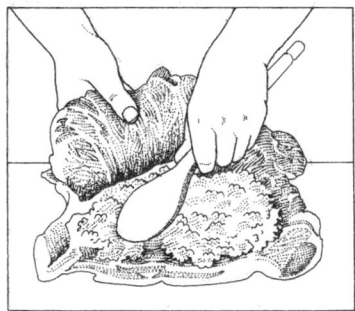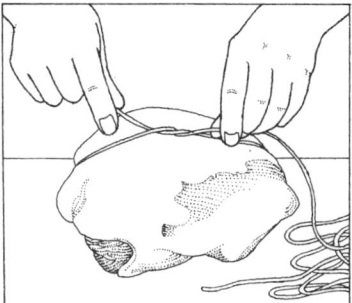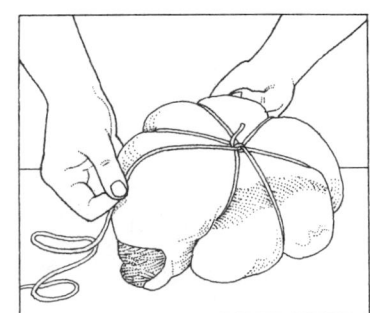

*To assemble lamb en ballon, stuff a boned shoulder and tie*

## ROLLING AND TYING

Once a joint, such as loin, is boned, remove most of the fat and lay it, meat side up, on the board. Season it or spread sparingly with stuffing. Roll it up from the thick end and use short pieces of thin cotton (not nylon) string to tie round the meat at 2.5cm/1in intervals. These can easily be cut off when serving, or the carver can slice between them when cutting the meat into thick slices.

## SEWING UP WHOLE JOINTS AFTER STUFFING

Use a larding needle or large darning or upholstery needle. Some of these are curved slightly which makes the job easier. Use thin old-fashioned white string, not nylon which will melt under heat. If the string is not very thin it can be 'untwined' quite easily and used as required. Leave a good length of string at the beginning and end, but do not tie elaborate knots, which are difficult to undo when dishing the meat. Simple, large, fairly loose stitches are best – the whole length of string can be pulled out in one movement when dishing.

## LARDING

Some very lean or potentially tough meat is larded before roasting. This promotes tenderness and adds flavour. The technique is most commonly used for slow-roasted dishes like boeuf à la mode or roast veal. A special larding needle is used.

To lard a joint, cut the larding fat (usually rindless back pork fat) into thin strips and put one of them into the tunnel of the needle, clamping down the hinge to hold it in place. The fat should extend a little way out of the needle. Thread through the meat, twisting the needle gently to prevent the fat pulling off. Then release the clamp, and trim the 2 ends of fat close to the meat. Repeat this all over the lean meat at 2.5cm/1in intervals.

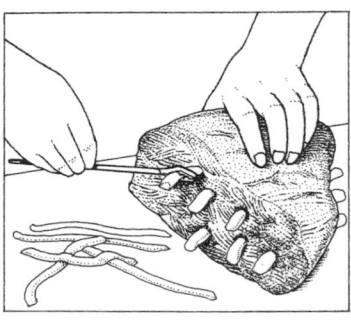

*To lard: thread with strips of pork fat*

## PREPARING BEEF

### STEAKS FOR GRILLING OR FRYING

Cut across the grain of the meat, if possible into thickish slices. Trim neatly, and cut rump slices into 2–3 individual steaks.

### MINUTE STEAKS

Cut large thin steaks. Put them between 2 sheets of paper or clingfilm and bat gently with a cook's mallet or rolling pin to flatten the meat.

### TOURNEDOS STEAKS

Cut 2.5cm/1in slices across the trimmed fillet.

### FOR STEWING

Remove the gristle, but not all the fat (it will add moisture and flavour). Cut into 2.5cm/1in cubes, or larger. Too-small pieces shred up, becoming dry and tough during cooking.

### FOR STROGANOFF

Cut into small strips about the thickness of a pencil across the grain of the meat.

### FOR ROASTING

If the meat has no fat on it, tie a piece of pork fat, or fatty bacon, round it. Tie up as described on page 372.

## PREPARING LAMB

### SADDLE

This consists of both loins of lamb, left attached at the backbone, in the same way as a baron of beef.

First remove the skin: with a small knife lift a corner of the skin, hold this firmly with a tea towel to get a good grip and tug sharply to peel off. Trim off any very large pieces of fat from the edges of the saddle, but leave the back fat. Tuck the flaps under the saddle. Cut out the kidneys but keep them (they can be brushed with butter and attached to the end of the saddle with wooden skewers 30 minutes before the end of the roasting time). Using a sharp knife, score the back fat all over in a fine criss-cross pattern.

The pelvic or aitch bone, protruding slightly from one end of the saddle, can be removed, or left in place and covered with a ham frill when the saddle is served.

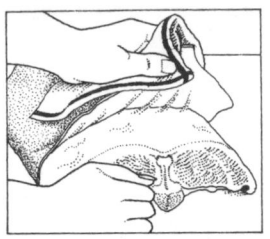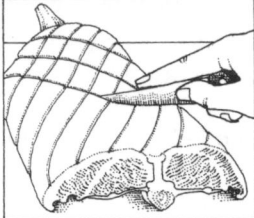

*Preparing a saddle of lamb*

### FRENCH-TRIMMED BEST END CUTLETS

Skin the best end: lift a corner of the skin from the neck end with a small knife, hold it firmly, using a cloth to get a good grip, and peel it off. Chine if the butcher has not already done so. This means sawing carefully through the chine bone (or spine) just where it meets the rib bones. Take care not to saw right through into the eye of the meat. Now remove the chine bone completely. Chop off the cutlet bones so that the length of the remaining bones is not more than twice the length of the eye of the meat. Remove the half-moon shaped piece of flexible cartilage found buried between the layers of fat and meat at the thinner end of the best end. This is the tip of the shoulder blade. It is simple to work out with a knife and your fingers. Remove the line of gristle to be found under the meat at the thick end.

If thin small cutlets are required, cut between each bone as evenly as possible, splitting the rack into 6–7 small cutlets. If fatter cutlets are required, carefully ease out every other rib bone. Then cut between the remaining bones into thick cutlets. Now trim the fat from the thick end of each cutlet, and scrape the rib bones free of any flesh or skin.

### NOISETTES

These are boneless cutlets, tied into a neat round shape with string. They are made from the loin or best end. Skin the meat: lift a corner of the skin with a small knife, holding it firmly with a cloth to get a good grip, and pull it off.

Chine the meat (see above). Now remove first the chine bone and then all the rib bones, easing them out with a short sharp knife. Remove the half-moon-shaped piece of flexible cartilage found buried between the layers of fat and meat at the thinner end of the best end. This is the top of the shoulder blade. Remove the line of gristle to be found under the meat at the thick end.

Trim off any excess fat from the meat and roll it up tightly, starting at the meaty thick side and working towards the thin flap. Tie the roll neatly with separate pieces of string placed at 3cm/1½in intervals. Trim the ragged ends of the roll to neaten them. Now slice the roll into pieces, cutting accurately between each string. The average English best end will give 4 good noisettes. The string from the noisette is removed after cooking.

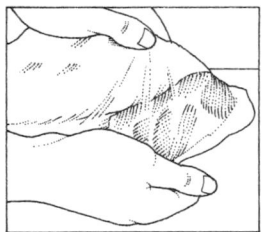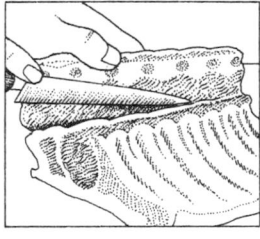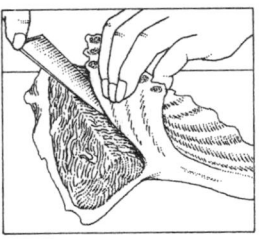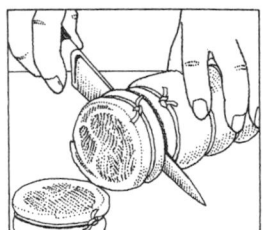

*For cutlets: skin and chine*

*For noisettes: ease out the bones, then roll, tie and cut*

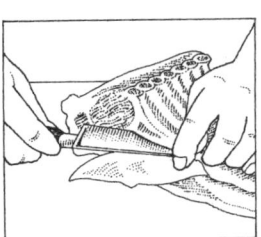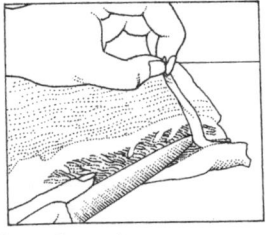

*Remove the shoulder blade and gristle*

### COLLOPS

These are small slices of meat taken from the best end neck of lamb. They are a very extravagant lamb steak (see page 402 for a recipe). Lay the best end neck down and prepare the meat partly as for noisettes (see above), i.e. remove the chine bone, gristle and shoulder blade. With a sharp knife (and making small cuts close to the rib bones), ease the bones, in one piece, away from the meat. Gradually separate the whole 'eye' of the meat (the fat-free cylinder) from the bones. Using a sharp flexible knife, remove all fat and membranes from the meat. Finally, slice into meat rounds or 'collops'.

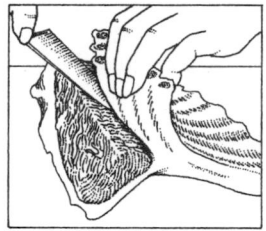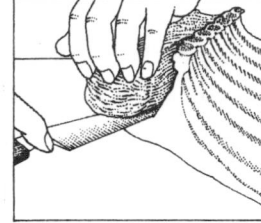

*For collops:* ease out the bones and separate the eye

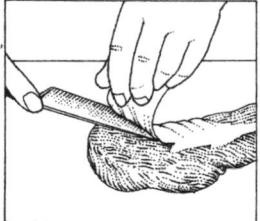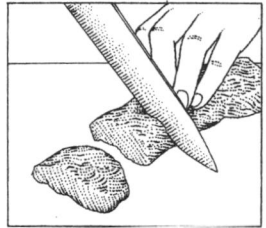

*Remove fat and membrane, and slice*

## CROWN ROAST

Two racks (best ends) are needed. The rack is prepared similarly to one destined for cutlets (see page 374) but the rib bones are left slightly longer, and the rack is not split into cutlets.

However it is skinned and chined, the shoulder cartilage and the line of gristle are removed. The excess fat is cut off (stages 1 and 2 below) and the top inch of the bones are scraped clean (stage 3 below). Remove an even layer of fat from the prepared rack (stage 4 below). Bend each best end into a semi-circle, with the fatty side of the ribs inside. To facilitate this it may be necessary to cut through the sinew between each cutlet, from the thick end for about 2.5cm/1in. But take care not to cut into the fleshy eye of the meat. Sew the ends of the racks together to make a circle, with the meaty part forming the base of the crown. Tie a piece of string round the 'waist' of the crown (stage 5 above). A crown roast is traditionally stuffed, but this can result in undercooked inside fat.

## GUARD OF HONOUR (RACK OF LAMB)

Prepare 2 best end racks exactly as for the crown roast, above. Score the fat in a criss-cross pattern.

*Stage 1*

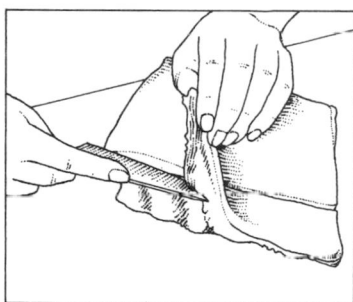

*Stage 2*

*Stage 3*

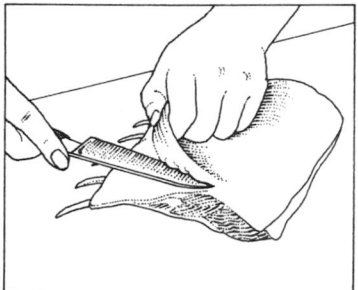

*Stage 4*

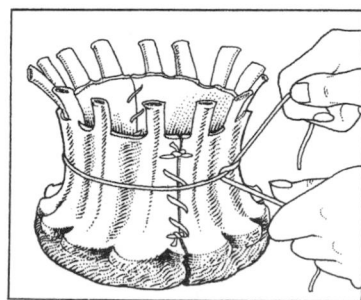

*Stage 5*

*To make a crown roast: see the numbered stages in the text above*

Hold the 2 best ends, one in each hand, facing each other with the meaty part of the racks on the board, and the fatty sides on the outside. Jiggle them so that the rib bones interlock and cross at the top. Sew or tie the bases together at intervals. Stuff the arch if required.

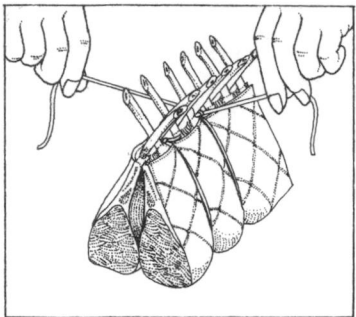

*To assemble a guard of honour: tie the prepared racks together*

*FOR ROASTING TIMES, SEE PAGE 367*

## PREPARING PORK AND BACON
### CHOPS
Chops are trimmed of rind, and the fat snipped or cut across (from the outside towards the meat). This is because as the fat shrinks during cooking, it tends to curl the chops out of shape.

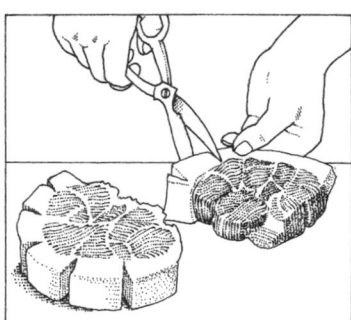

*To prepare chops: snip the fat at even intervals*

### GAMMON STEAKS OR BACON CHOPS
Snip the surrounding fat as described above. Bacon chops (really thick rashers from the prime back) are sometimes cooked with the rind left on, but snipping is essential to prevent curling.

### AMERICAN OR CHINESE SPARE RIBS
These are made from pork belly (not English spare rib). They can be cut before or after cooking. Simply cut between each belly bone, splitting the meat into long bones.

### TO SCORE CRACKLING
It is vital that crackling should be scored evenly and thoroughly, each cut, which should penetrate the skin and a little of the fat below it, being even and complete. Unscored crackling is tough and difficult to carve. Make the cuts not more than 1cm/½in apart all over the skin. Score the crackling after boning but before rolling and tying the joint.

## CARVING MEAT
The most important factor in good carving is a really sharp knife, a fork with a safety guard, and a board or flat plate unencumbered by vegetables and garnishes. Common sense usually dictates how joints are to be tackled. Meat off the bone is simple: just cut in slices of whatever thickness you prefer, across the grain of the meat. Pork, beef and veal are traditionally carved in thinner slices than lamb.

### LEGS
The legs of pork, lamb, bacon (gammon or ham), veal and venison are carved similarly. Put the leg meaty side up on the board or plate and grasp the knuckle bone with one hand, or pierce the joint firmly with a carving fork. Cut a small shallow 'V' or scoop out the middle of the top of the meat. Carve slices of meat from both sides of the 'V'. Then turn the leg over and take horizontal slices from the other side.

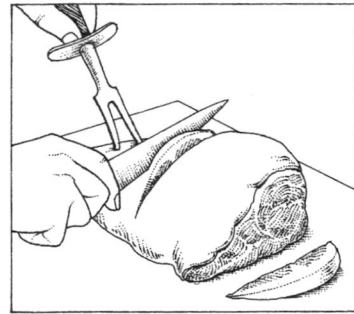

*To carve a leg of lamb: carve slices of meat from both sides of the 'V'*

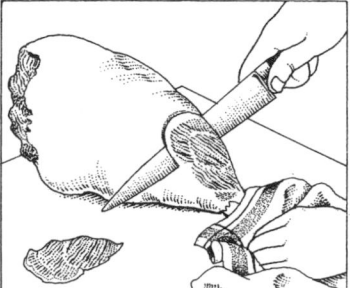

*Alternatively, carve diagonally from the knuckle end*

Legs can also be cut in diagonal slices from the knuckle end. This is more common with hams, but both methods are used for all legs.

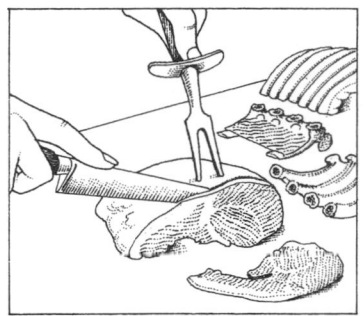

*To carve a loin of pork: remove bones and crackling before slicing*

### LOINS

Loins and best end of pork, veal and lamb are often roasted on the bone to prevent shrinkage, but to carve them it is easier to remove the meat off the rib cage and slice to the desired thickness. To carve a loin of pork, the crackling can be removed in one piece. The meat is then sliced and the crackling can be cut, with scissors, in the same number of pieces as there are slices of meat. If boned, the meat is cut similarly, but in thinner slices, about 5mm/¼in thick. Beef strip loin (boned sirloin) is cut in the same way, thinly in Britain, thickly in America.

Sirloin of beef on the bone is tackled from the top and bottom, the slices cut as thinly as possible on the top, the undercut or fillet slices being carved more thickly. Each diner should be given a slice or two from both top and bottom.

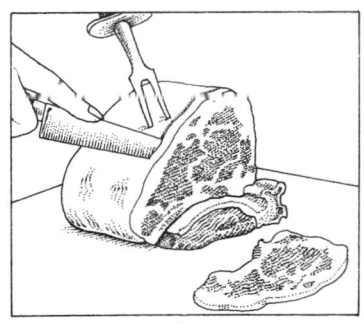

*To carve a sirloin on the bone: slice from the top and undercut*

### SADDLE OF LAMB

The chump end of the saddle is cut in thin angles across the grain of the meat, at right angles to the backbone. But the main part of the saddle, lying each side of the backbone, is cut in thin strips or narrow slices down the length of the saddle. This can be done on the bone, but it is easier if you lift the whole side of the saddle off in one piece and cut into long slices.

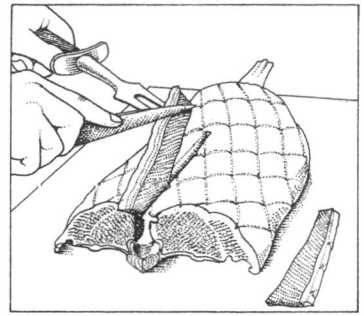

*To carve a saddle: cut in thin strips, down the length of the saddle*

### CROWN ROAST AND GUARD OF HONOUR

Remove the string and split into cutlets.

### SHOULDER OF LAMB

A shoulder is simple to carve as long as you know where the bones are. Place it fatty side up and cut like a cake on the side opposite to the bone.

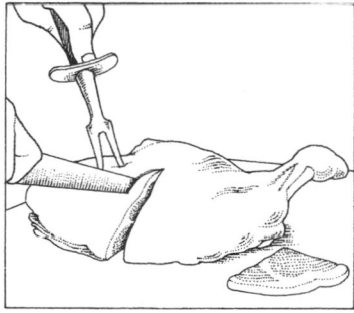

*To carve a shoulder of lamb: cut like a cake*

### SMALL FORERIB OF BEEF

A single forerib of beef is cooked on the bone and then cut off the bone in one piece. Instead of slicing into thin horizontal slices it can be cut into shorter fatter vertical slices.

### LARGE FORERIB OF BEEF

Place the roast on its side and make a 5cm/2in cut along the length of the rib. Stand the meat up, rib side down. Carve several slices and lift off and place on a warm serving dish. Turn the rib back on its side and make a second 5cm/2in cut along the length of the rib. Carve.

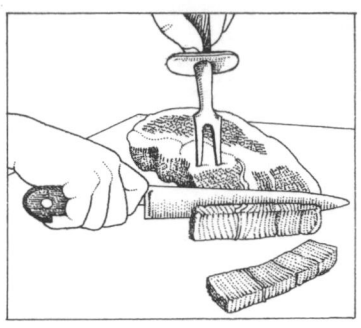

*To carve a small forerib of beef: remove from the bone and slice horizontally*

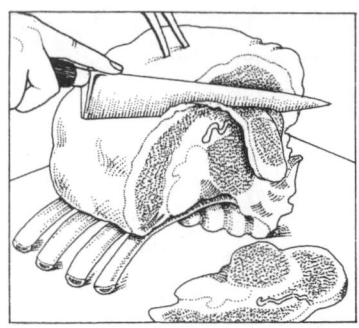

*To carve a large forerib of beef*

*FULL DETAILS OF THE DIFFERENT KINDS OF OFFAL ARE GIVEN ON PAGES 52–4*

# STEAK AND KIDNEY PUDDING

SERVES 4
*675g/1½lb chuck steak*
*225g/8oz ox kidney*
*plain flour*
*suet pastry made with 340g/12oz self-raising flour*
*    (see page 462)*
*butter for greasing*
*salt and freshly ground black pepper*
*2 teaspoons very finely chopped onion*
*2 teaspoons chopped fresh parsley*

**1.** Cut the beef into cubes about 2.5cm/1in square.
**2.** Cut the kidneys into cubes, discarding any sinews.
**3.** Place both beef and kidney in a large sieve. Pour over the flour and shake until the meat is lightly coated.
**4.** On a floured surface, roll out two-thirds of the suet pastry into a round about 1cm/1½in thick. Flour the surface lightly to stop it sticking together when folded. Fold the pastry over to form a half-moon shape. Place the pastry with the straight side away from you and roll it lightly so that the straight side becomes curved and the whole rounded again. Now separate the layers, and you should have a bag, roughly the shape of a 1kg/2¼lb pudding basin. Use it to line the lightly greased basin, easing the pastry where necessary to fit, and trimming off the top so that 1cm/½in sticks up over the edge.

**5.** Fill the lined basin with the meat, sprinkling plenty of salt, pepper, onion and parsley in between the layers.
**6.** Add water to come three-quarters of the way up the meat.
**7.** Roll the remaining third of suet pastry 5mm/¼in thick, and large enough to just cover the pudding filling. Put in place, wet the edges and press them together securely.
**8.** Cover the pudding with a double piece of greaseproof paper, pleated down the centre to allow room for the pastry to expand, and a similarly pleated piece of kitchen foil. Tie down with string.
**9.** Place in a saucepan of boiling water with a tightly closed lid, or in a steamer, for 5–6 hours, taking care to top up with boiling water occasionally so as not to boil dry.
**10.** Remove the paper and foil and serve the pudding from the bowl.

NOTES: Traditionally, steak and kidney puddings served from the bowl are presented wrapped in a white linen napkin.

As the filling of the pudding may, with long cooking, dry out somewhat, it is worth having a gravy boat of hot beef stock handy to moisten the meat when serving.

A delicious addition to steak and kidney pudding is to add a small can of smoked oysters to the meat filling.

 *CLARET*

# STEAK AND KIDNEY PIE

SERVES 4

*675g/1½lb chuck steak*
*225g/8oz ox kidney*
*oil or dripping*
*1 onion, finely chopped*
*30g/1oz plain flour*
*425ml/¾ pint brown stock (see page 243)*
*salt and freshly ground black pepper*
*1 tablespoon chopped fresh parsley*
*225g/8oz flour quantity rough puff pastry (see
    page 463)*
*beaten egg*

**1.** Trim away the excess fat from the steak and cut
the beef into cubes about 2.5cm/1in square. Cut
the kidneys into cubes, discarding any sinew.
**2.** Heat the oil or dripping in a frying pan and fry
a few beef cubes at a time until browned all over,
putting them into a flameproof casserole as they
are done. Fry the onion in the same fat until soft
and brown.
**3.** Stir in the flour and cook for 1 minute.
Gradually add the stock, stirring continuously
and scraping any sediment from the bottom of the
pan. Bring to the boil, then simmer for 1 minute.
Pour over the meat in the casserole, season with
salt and pepper and simmer slowly until the meat
is tender (about 2 hours). Add the parsley.
**4.** If the sauce is too greasy, skim off the fat; if it
is too thin, remove the meat to a pie dish and boil
the sauce rapidly until syrupy. Pour the sauce over
the meat and leave until completely cold.
**5.** Preheat the oven to 200°C/400°F/gas mark 6.
**6.** Roll out the pastry to the thickness of a £1
coin. Cut a long strip just wider than the rim of
the pie dish, brush the lip of the dish with water
and press down the strip.
**7.** Brush the strip with water and lay over the
sheet of pastry. Press it down firmly. Cut away
any excess pastry.
**8.** Cut a 1cm/½in hole in the centre of the pie-top
and cover with a leaf-shaped piece of pastry (the
hole is to allow the escape of steam).
**9.** Decorate the top with more pastry leaves.
Brush all over with egg. Leave in the refrigerator
to relax for 10 minutes.
**10.** Bake in the preheated oven for 30 minutes, or
until the pastry is well risen and golden-brown.

 CLARET

# PANCAKE PIE

SERVES 4

*8 French pancakes (see page 471)*
*450g/1lb minced beef*
*1 large onion, chopped*
*1 stick of celery, chopped*
*3 rashers of rindless streaky bacon, diced, blanched*
*1 clove of garlic, crushed*
*2 teaspoons plain flour*
*570ml/1 pint brown stock (see page 243)*
*1 tablespoon Madeira*
*1 teaspoon tomato purée*
*a pinch of chopped fresh thyme*
*1 tablespoon chopped fresh parsley*
*salt and freshly ground black pepper*
*150ml/¼ pint soured cream*
*150ml/¼ pint plain yoghurt*

**1.** Make the pancake batter first and allow it to
stand while preparing the meat sauce.
**2.** Fry half the mince in a hot frying pan.
**3.** Lift out with a slotted spoon and place in a
saucepan.
**4.** Fry the remaining mince, and transfer this to
the saucepan too.
**5.** When all the mince has been fried, fry the
onion, celery, bacon and garlic until just turning
brown. Tip off a little of the fat.
**6.** Add the flour and cook gently, stirring for 1 minute.
**7.** Stir in the stock and Madeira and bring to the boil,
stirring continuously. Pour this into the saucepan.
**8.** Add the tomato purée, thyme, half the parsley,
salt and pepper. Simmer gently for about 45
minutes, or until thick and syrupy.
**9.** While the sauce simmers fry the pancakes. Keep
them warm in the folds of a tea-towel in a low
oven while finishing off the sauce.
**10.** When the meat sauce is cooked, reduce by
rapid boiling if it is too runny. Season well.
**11.** Place one pancake on the serving dish, spoon over
some meat sauce and cover with a second pancake.
**12.** Continue to layer the meat sauce and
pancakes, finishing with a layer of meat sauce.
**13.** Mix the soured cream and yoghurt together.
Season with salt and pepper.
**14.** Sprinkle the remaining parsley over the
pancakes and serve immediately, with the soured
cream and yoghurt sauce handed separately.

 MEDIUM RED

# SHEPHERD'S PIE (I)

SERVES 4–5
*675g/1½lb minced beef*
*1 onion, finely chopped*
*1 carrot, finely chopped*
*1 stick of celery, finely chopped*
*oil for frying*
*2 teaspoons plain flour*
*570ml/1 pint brown stock (see page 243)*
*1 bay leaf*
*1 teaspoon Worcestershire sauce (optional)*
*1 teaspoon tomato purée*
*salt and freshly ground black pepper*

For the topping
*900g/2lb mashed potato (see page 212)*
*butter*

**1.** Fry half the mince in a large frying pan. Brown well all over. Remove with a slotted spoon and place in a saucepan. Brown the remaining mince and place in the saucepan.
**2.** Fry the onion, carrot and celery in the frying pan until just beginning to brown. Tip off a little of the fat and place in a saucepan.
**3.** Add the flour and cook for 30 seconds.
**4.** Add the stock and bring slowly to the boil, stirring continuously.
**5.** Now add the bay leaf, Worcestershire sauce, tomato purée, salt and pepper. Mix with the browned mince.
**6.** Set the saucepan over a medium heat to simmer. Cover and leave to cook for 45 minutes. Check it every so often and add extra water if it becomes too dry.
**7.** Preheat the oven to 200°C/400°F/gas mark 6.
**8.** Remove the bay leaf from the mince and tip the meat into a pie dish, reserving some of the liquid if the mixture is very runny.
**9.** When slightly cooled, spread the potato over the top.
**10.** Fork it up to leave the surface rough, or draw the fork over the surface to mark with a pattern.
**11.** Place in the preheated oven for 20–30 minutes, or until the potato is brown and crusty.

 *MEDIUM RED*

# SHEPHERD'S PIE (II)

This is a low-fat dish – the mince is a component part, rather than a principal ingredient.

SERVES 4
*2 teaspoons grapeseed oil*
*110g/4oz lean minced beef*
*1 onion, finely chopped*
*2 large carrots, finely chopped*
*2 sticks of celery, finely chopped*
*2 teaspoons tomato purée*
*½ teaspoon ground allspice*
*2 teaspoons plain flour*
*290ml/½ pint brown stock (see page 243)*
*1 bay leaf*
*110g/4oz cooked chickpeas*
*salt and freshly ground black pepper*

For the topping
*675g/1½lb potatoes, peeled and cut into chunks*
*150ml/¼ pint skimmed milk*
*30g/1oz low-fat spread*
*freshly grated nutmeg*
*salt and freshly ground black pepper*

**1.** Heat the oil in a large non-stick sauté pan. Add the mince and brown well all over. Reduce the heat and add the onion, carrot and celery. When the vegetables have softened, add the tomato purée, allspice and flour. Cook for 1 minute.
**2.** Remove from the heat, add the stock and stir well. Return to the heat and bring gradually to the boil, stirring continuously. Add the bay leaf, season with salt and pepper and simmer for 30 minutes.
**3.** Meanwhile, prepare the mashed potatoes. Cook the potatoes in boiling water until soft. Drain them and return to the empty saucepan. Mash over a medium heat allowing them to dry out as you do so but taking care that the mashed potato does not stick to the bottom of the pan and burn. Push the mound of potato to one side of the pan and pour the milk into the exposed side of the pan. Put this side over direct heat and get the milk boiling. Add the low-fat spread and allow it to melt. Now beat the milk and low-fat spread into the potato. Season with nutmeg, salt and pepper.
**4.** Preheat the oven to 200°C/400°F/gas mark 6.
**5.** Add the chickpeas to the pan of meat and vegetables and simmer for 2–3 minutes. Remove

the bay leaf. With a large slotted spoon, transfer the meat and vegetables to a pie dish. Boil the gravy until reduced to a syrupy consistency. Pour it over the meat and vegetables and mix well. Leave to cool for 5 minutes.

**6.** Pile the potato on top of the pie filling and fork it up roughly. Reheat in the oven for 20 minutes.

 *MEDIUM RED*

# SPAGHETTI BOLOGNESE

SERVES 4
*340g/12oz spaghetti*

*For the sauce*
*55g/2oz chicken livers*
*85g/3oz unsmoked bacon*
*oil*
*170g/6oz lean minced beef*
*15g/½oz butter*
*110g/4oz mixed onion and celery, finely diced*
*1 clove of garlic, crushed*
*110g/4oz mushrooms, sliced*
*100ml/3½fl oz white wine or Madeira*
*290ml/½ pint brown stock (see page 243)*
*1 × 225g/8oz can of tomatoes*
*1 teaspoon tomato purée*
*salt and freshly ground black pepper*
*1 teaspoon chopped fresh marjoram*
*Parmesan cheese, freshly grated*

**1.** Trim off and discard the discoloured parts from the chicken livers.
**2.** Dice the bacon and fry slowly in its own fat, in a large frying pan, until lightly browned. Increase the temperature and fry the chicken livers. Remove from the pan and set aside. Add a little oil if necessary, and fry the mince. Fry until well browned all over.
**3.** With a slotted spoon, lift the bacon, mince and livers into a saucepan. Melt the butter in the frying pan and add the onion and celery. Cook over a low heat, stirring occasionally, until soft and lightly coloured. Add the garlic and mushrooms and cook for 30 seconds. Tip into the pan of meat.
**4.** Pour the wine into the frying pan and bring to

the boil, scraping the bottom of the pan with a wooden spoon to loosen all the sediment. Stir in the stock, tomatoes and tomato purée. Pour on to the meat in the saucepan. Cover and simmer for 45 minutes, or until the meat is tender. If greasy, skim off as much of the fat as possible.
**5.** While the sauce is cooking, push the spaghetti into a large saucepan of boiling salted water and stir until the water reboils. Boil uncovered for 10–12 minutes, or until just tender. Tip into a colander, then rinse under hot running water. Drain well. Return to the rinsed-out pan and heat gently with 1 tablespoon oil, turning carefully with a wooden spoon.
**6.** Place the spaghetti in a warmed serving dish and pour over the Bolognese sauce. Serve with Parmesan cheese sprinkled on top of the sauce or heated separately.

 *VALPOLICELLA*

# BOILED SILVERSIDE

SERVES 6
*1.35kg/3lb piece of salt silverside*
*6 pieces of marrow bone*
*1 bouquet garni (1 bay leaf, 2 parsley stalks, 6*
  *peppercorns, 1 small onion, tied in muslin)*
*6 medium onions*
*4 large carrots, quartered*
*2 turnips, quartered*
*12 dumplings (see page 382)*

*To garnish*
*chopped fresh parsley*

**1.** Soak the beef in cold unsalted water for about 3 hours.
**2.** Put the bones and beef into a large saucepan of fresh unsalted water and bring slowly to the boil, skimming as the scum rises to the surface.
**3.** When simmering, add the bouquet garni and half-cover the pan. Simmer for about 3 hours. Remove the bouquet garni and skim off any fat.
**4.** Now add the vegetables and simmer for 1 hour, or until the meat and vegetables are tender.
**5.** Meanwhile, cook the dumplings: if there is room in the saucepan, float them in the liquid 20

minutes before the end of the cooking time. If not, take some of the stock (topping up with boiling water if necessary) and simmer them in a separate saucepan. Do not cover.

**6.** Place the beef on a large warmed serving dish. Surround it with the vegetables, dumplings and marrow bones. Cover and keep warm.

**7.** Taste the stock. If weak-flavoured, reduce by rapid boiling. Skim if necessary.

**8.** Ladle a cupful or so of hot liquid over the meat and vegetables, sprinkle with parsley and serve immediately. Serve more liquid separately in a warmed sauceboat.

NOTE: Dumplings are always a little soggy cooked on the stove. For a drier, fluffier version, they should be baked in the oven.

 *CLARET OR RIOJA*

# POT AU FEU ORDINAIRE

This recipe has been adapted from Time Life's *The Good Cook: Beef and Veal.*

SERVES 4–6
1kg/2¼lb beef bones, sawn into 5–7.5cm/2–3in pieces
1kg/2¼lb silverside or topside of beef, tied in a compact shape
2.25 litres/4 pints water
15g/½oz salt
200g/7oz carrots
110g/4oz turnips
200g/7oz leeks
3 onions, 1 stuck with cloves
30g/1oz parsnip
30g/1oz celery

**1.** Put the bones into the bottom of a large saucepan with the meat on top. Add the water and the salt. Place over a very low heat, so that you can skim the liquid when it boils. It should take about 30 minutes to come to the boil – it must be skimmed constantly to make a very clear broth.

**2.** When the liquid boils, splash on 3 tablespoons cold water. Skim again and, once the liquid starts to boil again, add another 3 tablespoons cold

water. This produces a third lot of scum, this time almost white. Skim. When the liquid starts to boil once more, add a further 3 tablespoons cold water. The little scum that rises this time should be perfectly white and clean. Skim it. Then add the vegetables and skim off any scum that rises. With a damp cloth, carefully wipe the inside edges of the saucepan so that no traces of scum remain.

**3.** Simmer, very slowly, for 3 hours. Keep checking and should any scum rise to the surface, remove it with a slotted spoon. It can also be cooked in a low oven or ideally in the slow oven of an Aga.

**4.** Traditionally the broth is served as a first course, either with noodles or with the vegetables cooked with the beef.

**5.** The beef is served sliced and garnished with freshly cooked vegetables. It can be accompanied by a selection of the following: pickled gherkins, coarse salt, horseradish sauce, capers, mustard and French dressing.

 *RED RHÔNE*

# DUMPLINGS

SERVES 4
225g/8oz self-raising flour
a pinch of salt
110g/4oz beef suet
about 5 tablespoons cold water
570ml/1 pint brown stock (see page 243)

**1.** Preheat the oven to 180°C/350°F/gas mark 4.

**2.** Sift the flour and salt into a bowl. Mix in the suet.

**3.** Make a dip or well in the flour. Add a little water to the well and, using a palette knife, mix in the surrounding flour. Draw the mixture together with your hands and knead gently to a soft dough.

**4.** With floured hands, shape the mixture into dumplings about the size of a ping-pong ball.

**5.** Float the dumplings in the simmering stock in a saucepan and cook uncovered for 20–25 minutes.

**6.** Remove with a slotted spoon. The dumplings should be light and not too doughy.

# FAMILY BEEF STEW

SERVES 4
*675g/1½lb stewing beef*
*dripping or oil*
*2 large mild onions, sliced*
*3 medium carrots, cubed*
*1 medium turnip, cubed*
*570ml/1 pint brown stock (see page 243)*
*salt and freshly ground black pepper*
*1 bay leaf*
*2 parsley stalks*
*a pinch of chopped fresh thyme*
*30g/1oz pearl barley*

**1.** Preheat the oven to 150°C/300°F/gas mark 2.
**2.** Remove any gristle and excess fat from the meat and cut it into 3cm/1½in cubes.
**3.** Melt a little of the dripping or oil in a sauté pan. Brown the beef cubes on all sides, a few at a time, and transfer to a casserole. If the bottom of the pan becomes too brown and sticky, pour in a little stock and swish it about, scraping the sediment from the bottom of the pan. Pour this into the casserole, and then heat a little more dripping or oil and continue browning the meat until all is transferred to the casserole.
**4.** Fry the onion, carrot and turnip in the pan until golden-brown and place them in the casserole.
**5.** Pour the stock into the pan and bring to the boil, scraping any remaining sediment from the bottom. Stir in the seasoning, bay leaf, parsley, thyme and barley and pour on to the meat. Bring to the boil, then simmer for 2 minutes.
**6.** Cover the casserole and cook in the preheated oven for 2–2½ hours. Skim off any excess fat.

NOTE: This stew is even better if kept for a day before eating – the barley swells up even more and the flavour improves.

 *FULL RED*

# BEEF OLIVES

SERVES 4
*4 thin slices of lean beef buttock*
*seasoned plain flour*
*1 tablespoon beef dripping*
*425ml/¾ pint brown stock (see page 243)*
*225g/8oz mirepoix of carrot, onion and celery*

For the stuffing
*8 tablespoons fresh white breadcrumbs*
*2 tablespoons chopped beef suet*
*2 tablespoons chopped fresh parsley*
*grated zest of 1 lemon*
*beaten egg to bind*
*salt and freshly ground black pepper*

**1.** Preheat the oven to 150°C/300°F/gas mark 2.
**2.** Put the slices of beef between damp grease-proof paper and flatten lightly with a rolling pin or mallet.
**3.** Mix together all the ingredients for the stuffing and season to taste with salt and pepper.
**4.** Divide the mixture between the slices of beef and roll up, folding in the ends to make neat parcels. Tie the beef olives with fine string and roll them in seasoned flour.
**5.** Heat half the dripping in a frying pan and brown the beef olives on all sides. Remove them and lightly brown the mirepoix in the remaining dripping.
**6.** Place the beef olives on top of the mirepoix in a shallow casserole or small roasting pan. Pour over the stock, bring to the boil and cover. Cook in the preheated oven for 1½ hours.
**7.** Dish the beef olives on a warmed serving plate. Remove the string. Skim any fat off the liquid and then strain, pressing as much of the softened vegetables as possible through the sieve. Pour over the beef.

NOTE: If the sauce is too thin, either thicken it by reduction or by adding beurre manié (see page 241). If the sauce is too thick, thin it down with a little extra stock.

 *MEDIUM RED*

# BOEUF BOURGUIGNONNE

SERVES 4
*675g/1½lb chuck steak*
*1 tablespoon beef dripping or oil*
*12 small button onions or shallots*
*30g/1oz butter*
*1 clove of garlic, crushed*
*2 teaspoons plain flour*
*290ml/½ pint red wine*
*290ml/½ pint brown stock (see page 243)*
*1 bouquet garni (bay leaf, sprig of fresh thyme, a*
 *few parsley stalks and 1 stick of celery, tied up*
 *with string)*
*salt and freshly ground black pepper*
*55g/2oz piece of fatty bacon, diced*
*110g/4oz button mushrooms*

To garnish
*chopped fresh parsley*

1. Preheat the oven to 150°C/300°F/gas mark 2.
2. Cut the beef into 3cm/1½in cubes, discarding any fat and gristle.
3. Heat half the dripping or oil in a flameproof casserole and brown the beef cubes very well, a few at a time. They must be brown on all sides. Put them into a bowl as they are done. If the bottom of the pan becomes very dark or too dry, pour in a little water, swish it about, scraping off the sediment stuck to the bottom, and pour over the meat. Heat up a little more dripping or oil and continue to brown the meat. When it is all brown repeat the déglaçage (adding water and scraping the pan).
4. Peel the shallots by immersing them in boiling water for 30 seconds and then removing the skins. Dry them and fry in half the butter until well browned.
5. Add the garlic and stir in the flour. Cook, stirring, for 1 minute.
6. Add the wine and stock. Stir until boiling, again scraping the bottom of the pan.
7. Put the meat and sauce together in the casserole and add the bouquet garni. Season with salt and pepper. Cover and cook in the preheated oven for 2–3 hours, or until the meat is very tender.
8. Meanwhile, prepare the bacon and mushrooms: cut the bacon into 1cm/½in cubes and blanch in

boiling water for 1 minute. Refresh and drain well. Wipe the mushrooms but do not peel or remove the stalks. Cut into quarters if large. Melt the remaining butter in a frying pan and, when foaming, add the bacon and mushrooms and cook fairly fast until delicately browned. Lift them out and add the bacon to the stew when it has been cooking for 2 hours. Continue for a further 30 minutes. Add the mushrooms and cook until the meat is tender (about 30 minutes).
9. When the beef is tender, use a slotted spoon to lift the meat, bacon and vegetables into a clean casserole. Remove the bouquet garni, check the seasoning and boil the sauce fast to reduce to a syrupy consistency. If the sauce is too salty do not reduce it but thicken with a little beurre manié (see page 243).
10. Pour the sauce over the beef and serve sprinkled with the parsley.

NOTES: This stew can be cooked on top of the cooker, over a low heat, for 1–2 hours, but slow oven-cooking produces a better result, with the meat as soft as butter but not shredded or falling apart and with no danger of 'catching' on the bottom.

   It can of course be made entirely with wine using no stock at all – delicious but more expensive.

 *RED BURGUNDY*

# CARBONNADE DE BOEUF

SERVES 4
*675g/1½lb chuck steak*
*1 tablespoon beef dripping or oil*
*3 onions, thinly sliced*
*1 clove of garlic, crushed*
*2 teaspoons soft brown sugar*
*2 teaspoons plain flour*
*290ml/½ pint brown ale*
*290ml/½ pint brown stock (see page 243)*
*1 teaspoon wine vinegar*
*1 bay leaf*
*a pinch of chopped fresh thyme*
*a pinch of freshly grated nutmeg*
*salt and freshly ground black pepper*
*4 slices of French bread spread thickly with*

*French mustard*

**1.** Preheat the oven to 150°C/300°F/gas mark 2.

**2.** Cut the beef into small steaks, cutting across the grain of the meat. Heat half the dripping or oil in a large frying pan and fry the steaks, a few at a time, until browned all over, putting them into a flameproof casserole as they are done. If the bottom of the pan becomes very dark or too dry, pour in a little water, swish it about, scraping off the sediment stuck to the bottom, and pour over the meat. Heat up a little more dripping or oil and continue to brown the meat. When it is all brown, repeat the déglaçage (adding water and scraping the pan).

**3.** Fry the onions slowly and, when beginning to brown, add the garlic and sugar. Cook for a further minute or until nicely brown.

**4.** Stir in the flour and cook, stirring, over the heat for 1 minute. Remove from the heat and pour in the brown ale and the stock.

**5.** Return to the heat and bring slowly to the boil, then simmer for 2 minutes, stirring continuously. Pour into the casserole and add the vinegar, bay leaf, thyme, nutmeg, salt and pepper.

**6.** Cover and bring to simmering point over direct heat, then cook in the preheated oven for 1½–2 hours.

**7.** Increase the oven temperature to 190°C/375°F/gas mark 5. Put the slices of bread, mustard-side up, on top of the stew (they are there to absorb the fat) and return the casserole, without the lid, to the oven until the bread is brown and crisp (about 15 minutes).

 *BEER OR FULL RED*

# BEEF CURRY

SERVES 4

*1 tablespoon oil*
*675g/1½lb chuck steak, cut into 5cm/2in cubes*
*2 onions, sliced*
*2.5cm/1in piece of fresh root ginger, peeled and finely chopped*
*2 cloves of garlic, crushed*
*1 teaspoon ground cardamom*
*½ teaspoon ground cloves*

*½ teaspoon ground chilli*
*1 teaspoon freshly ground black pepper*
*2 teaspoons ground cumin*
*1 tablespoon ground coriander*
*½ teaspoon ground turmeric*
*1 teaspoon plain flour*
*1 × 400g/14oz can of tomatoes*
*salt and freshly ground black pepper*

**1.** Heat the oil and fry the beef cubes, a few at a time, until well browned all over, removing them to a plate as they are done.

**2.** Fry the onion in the same oil (adding a little more if necessary), add the ginger and garlic and cook for 2 minutes.

**3.** Add all the ground spices and cook slowly for 1 further minute, taking care not to let them burn. Add the flour and cook for 30 seconds.

**4.** Add the tomatoes and bring slowly to the boil, stirring all the time.

**5.** Put back the meat, cover with a lid and simmer very slowly until the meat is tender – about 2 hours. Add a little water if it begins to dry out. It can also be cooked in a very low oven for about 3 hours.

 *VERY FULL RED*

# GAENG PED NUA (SPICY RED BEEF)

Ingredients for this recipe are available in specialist Thai shops.

SERVES 6–8

*2 tablespoons Thai red curry paste*
*3 tablespoons oil*
*1.35kg/3lb braising steak, cut into strips*
*1 stalk of lemon grass, cut into strips*
*a few makrut (citrus) leaves*
*340g/12oz creamed coconut*
*2 tablespoons nam pla (Thai fish bouillon)*
*½ teaspoon sugar*
*2 red peppers, cored, deseeded and cut into strips*
*1 bunch of fresh basil*

**1.** Fry the curry paste in the oil in a large wok or pan for 1 minute. Add the strips of beef and stir-

385

fry, then, ensuring that the curry paste coats the meat, cover with water and add the lemon grass and broken-up makrut leaves.

**2.** Simmer until the beef is tender (about 1½ hours).

**3.** Mix the creamed coconut with 570ml/1 pint water and add it to the pan. Reduce until the sauce is thick.

**4.** Add the fish bouillon, sugar and red peppers and simmer until the peppers are just cooked.

**5.** Finally add the basil leaves.

**6.** Serve with steamed or boiled rice.

NOTE: If the sauce curdles (which it often does) it can be brought back with vigorous whisking.

 *FULL SPICY RED*

# SAUTÉ OF BEEF WITH GREEN PEPPERCORNS

SERVES 4
*675g/1½lb skirt of beef*
*1 tablespoon oil*
*1 tablespoon brandy*
*450ml/¾ pint demi-glace sauce (see page 249)*
*salt and freshly ground black pepper*
*4 tablespoons double cream (optional)*
*2 teaspoons canned green peppercorns, well*
*  rinsed and drained*

**1.** Cut the beef into 6cm/2½in cubes, discarding any fat.

**2.** Heat the oil in a heavy frying pan and brown the beef pieces very well on all sides, a few at a time. Transfer them to a bowl as they are done.

**3.** Tip off any excess fat from the pan, put back the meat, add the brandy and set alight with a match. When the flames subside, pour in the demi-glace sauce, cover and simmer very gently until the meat is tender. This will take about 45 minutes, or longer, depending on the quality of the meat.

**4.** Add the cream, if using, and the peppercorns, and adjust the seasoning to taste.

 *CÔTES DU RHÔNE OR AUSTRALIAN SHIRAZ*

# BEEF CURRY WITH ALMONDS

This is an adaptation of a recipe by Josceline Dimbleby. As with many recipes using a large variety of dried spices, if you have not got them all do not worry, just use a little extra of the ones you do have. The cumin and coriander, however, are essential.

SERVES 4
*675g/1½lb chuck steak*
*2–4 tablespoons sunflower oil*
*1 teaspoon ground cardamom*
*½ teaspoon ground cloves*
*2 teaspoons freshly ground black pepper*
*2 teaspoons ground cumin*
*1 tablespoon ground coriander*
*½ teaspoon ground turmeric*
*85g/3oz blanched almonds*
*2.5cm/1in piece of fresh root ginger, peeled and*
*  very finely chopped*
*2 cloves of garlic, crushed*
*2 onions, sliced*
*1 × 400g/14oz can of tomatoes*
*salt*
*2 tablespoons Greek yoghurt*

To garnish
*fresh coriander leaves*

**1.** Trim the beef of as much fat and gristle as possible and cut into 3.5cm/1½in cubes.

**2.** Preheat the oven to 170°C/325°F/gas mark 3.

**3.** Put 1 tablespoon of the oil into a frying pan and heat gently. Add the almonds and fry until golden-brown. Set aside. Add a little more oil to the pan, add the dry spices and cook slowly for 1 minute.

**4.** Put the spices and almonds into a blender and whizz to a smooth purée with 150ml/¼ pint water.

**5.** Wipe the frying pan clean. It is important to prevent the final curry having bits of burnt dried spices in it. Add 1 tablespoon oil, heat well and brown the beef cubes well on all sides, a few at a time. Transfer to a casserole. If the bottom of the pan becomes too brown and sticky pour in a little water and swish it about, scraping the sediment from the bottom of the pan. Pour this into the casserole and then add a little more oil to the frying pan and continue to brown the meat until all is transferred to the casserole.

**6.** Add the ginger, garlic and onions to the pan and fry slowly until the onions are a deep golden-brown. Add the spice and almond mixture and the tomatoes. Stir well and bring to the boil, then simmer for 1 minute. Season to taste with salt and pour over the meat. Place over direct heat and bring back up to the boil. Cover and cook in the preheated oven for 2–3 hours, or until the meat is very tender.
**7.** Check the curry 2 or 3 times during the cooking process and if it is becoming too dry add a little water.
**8.** Just before serving, stir the yoghurt into the curry and reheat without boiling. Turn into a warmed serving dish and garnish with the coriander leaves.

 *FULL SPICY RED*

# FRIED STEAK

SERVES 4

*4 sirloin steaks, cut 2cm/³⁄₄in thick or 4 fillet*
*steaks, cut 2.5cm/1in thick*
*freshly ground black pepper and salt*
*oil or dripping*
*maître d'hôtel butter (see page 263)*

**1.** Season the steaks with pepper. Leave to warm to room temperature if they have been chilled. Sprinkle lightly with salt just before cooking.
**2.** Brush a frying pan with a little oil or dripping and place over good heat until it is beginning to smoke.
**3.** Brown the steaks quickly on both sides. For a blue or rare steak, keep the heat fierce for the whole cooking time. For better-done steaks, lower the temperature to medium after the initial good browning. Length of cooking time varies according to the type of steak, the degree of heat, the weight of the frying pan, etc. With experience it is possible to tell from the feel of the steak how well cooked it is – it feels very soft when blue; very firm when medium. But if you want to be certain, there is nothing for it but to cut a tiny slit in the fattest part of the meat, and take a look. Don't do this until you are fairly sure that the steak is ready – too many cuts will mean loss of juices. Cooking times, assuming a good hot pan, would be very approximately as below:

**4.** Serve each steak topped with a slice of maître d'hôtel butter.

**SIRLOIN**

| | |
|---|---|
| Blue steak: | 1 minute per side |
| Rare steak: | 1½ minutes per side |
| Medium rare: | 2 minutes per side |
| Medium steak: | 2¼ minutes per side |

**FILLET**

| | |
|---|---|
| Blue steak: | 1½ minutes per side |
| Rare steak: | 2¼ minutes per side |
| Medium rare: | 3¼ minutes per side |
| Medium steak: | 4½ minutes per side |

 *MEDIUM RED*

# GREEN PEPPERCORN STEAKS

SERVES 4

*2 teaspoons canned or frozen green peppercorns*
*oil*
*4 × 2.5cm/1in thick fillet steaks*
*2 tablespoons brandy*
*2 tablespoons double cream*
*salt*

**1.** Rinse the peppercorns if they are canned.
**2.** Brush a frying pan with oil. Heat until hot. Fry the steaks as fast as you dare on both sides, until done to your liking (see chart in previous recipe).
**3.** Pour in the brandy and set alight.
**4.** When the flames subside, remove the steaks to a warmed serving dish.
**5.** Add the peppercorns, cream and a pinch or two of salt to the pan. Mix well, scraping up any sediment. Boil up and pour over the steaks.

 *FULL RED*

# GRILLED STEAK

SERVES 4

*4 fillet steaks, cut 2cm/³/4in thick, or 4 sirloin
    steaks, cut 2.5cm/1in thick*
*salt and freshly ground black pepper*
*butter, melted*
*maître d'hôtel butter (see page 263)*

**1.** Season the steaks with pepper. Leave to warm
to room temperature if they have been chilled.
Sprinkle lightly with salt just before cooking.
**2.** Preheat the grill to its highest setting. Do not
start cooking until it is at maximum temperature.
**3.** Brush the grill rack and steak with a little
melted butter.
**4.** Grill the steak quickly on both sides. For a blue
or rare steak, keep the heat fierce for the whole
cooking time. For better-done steaks, lower the
temperature to medium after the initial good
browning. Length of cooking time varies
according to the thickness of the meat, the type of
steak, the efficiency of the grill, etc. With
experience it is possible to tell from the feel of the
steak how well cooked it is – it feels very soft
when blue, very firm when medium. But if you
want to be certain, there is nothing for it but to
cut a tiny slit in the fattest part of the meat and
take a look. Don't do this until you are fairly sure
that the steak is ready – too many cuts will mean
loss of juices. Cooking times, assuming a good
hot grill, will be approximately as below:

### SIRLOIN

| Blue: | 1¼ minutes per side |
|---|---|
| Rare : | 1¾ minutes per side |
| Medium rare: | 2¼ minutes per side |
| Medium : | 2¾ minutes per side |

### FILLET

| Blue: | 2¼ minutes per side |
|---|---|
| Rare: | 3¼ minutes per side |
| Medium rare: | 4¼ minutes per side |
| Medium: | 5 minutes per side |

**5.** Serve each steak topped with a slice of maître
d'hôtel butter.

 *FULL RED*

# HAMBURGER

SERVES 4

*675g/1½lb minced lean beef steak*
*1 small onion, grated (optional)*
*2 tablespoons chopped fresh parsley or mixed
    herbs*
*1 teaspoon Worcestershire sauce (optional)*
*salt and freshly ground black pepper*

**1.** Preheat the grill.
**2.** Mix all the ingredients together with a fork.
Check the seasoning.
**3.** With wet hands, shape the meat into flattish
rounds, making sure that they are equal in size.
Make a slight dip in the centre. They will shrink
and thicken when they cook.
**4.** Grill steadily, turning once. Allow 3 minutes
each side for rare burgers, 5 for well done.
**5.** Serve on a warmed dish, or between heated soft
buns sliced in half.

NOTE: See pages 662–4 for relishes.

 *MEDIUM RED*

# GREEN DRAGON WALNUT MEATBALLS

This recipe has been taken from *Marvellous Meals
with Mince* by Josceline Dimbleby.

SERVES 4
For the meatballs
*1 large green pepper*
*450g/1lb minced beef or pork*
*2 cloves of garlic, finely chopped*
*85g/3oz walnuts, finely chopped*
*1 tablespoon tomato purée*
*2 tablespoons soy sauce*
*1 teaspoon ground ginger*
*3–4 pinches of cayenne pepper*
*1 tablespoon caster sugar*
*salt*
*1 tablespoon sunflower oil for frying*

For the sauce
1½ tablespoons soy sauce
4½ tablespoons water
1 tablespoon wine vinegar
½ tablespoon caster sugar
4–5 spring onions, finely chopped

**1.** Cut the pepper in half and take out the seeds and stem. Bring a small saucepan of salted water to the boil, put in the pepper, cover the pan and boil for 6–8 minutes, until soft. Drain and chop finely.
**2.** Put the mince into a bowl and add the chopped pepper, garlic, walnuts, tomato purée and soy sauce. Then add the ginger, cayenne pepper, sugar and a good sprinkling of salt.
**3.** Mix everything together very well with a wooden spoon. If you have a food processor the mixture can be whizzed together briefly: this prevents the meatballs from breaking up when they are cooked. Then, with wet hands, form the mixture into balls the size of ping-pong balls.
**4.** Heat the oil in a large frying pan and fry the meatballs over a low to medium heat, turning to brown all over, for about 15 minutes. Transfer with a slotted spoon to a serving dish and keep warm in a low oven.
**5.** Pour most of the fat out of the pan but leave the residue of meat juices. Add the soy sauce, the water and the vinegar. Stir in the sugar and dissolve over a low heat. Then allow the mixture to bubble fiercely for a minute or two until you have a dark and syrupy sauce. Remove from the heat and stir in the chopped spring onions. Spoon the sauce over the meatballs and serve immediately.

 *RED RHÔNE*

# MEATBALLS

This version is lower in fat than most meatballs.

SERVES 4
85g/3oz burghul (cracked wheat)
225g/8oz lean minced beef
1 tablespoon roughly chopped fresh coriander
4 spring onions, roughly chopped
1 clove of garlic
2 teaspoons soy sauce
salt and freshly ground black pepper
1 tablespoon sunflower oil for frying

To serve
tomato sauce II (see page 258)

To garnish
a few coriander leaves

**1.** Soak the burghul in cold water for 20 minutes. Drain and squeeze dry.
**2.** Put all the ingredients into a food processor and process to a soft dough.
**3.** Wet your hands and shape the meat mixture into balls the size of a walnut. Fry them in the oil in a frying pan over a low heat for about 5 minutes.
**4.** Arrange the meatballs on a warmed serving dish. Heat the tomato sauce, pour it over the meatballs and garnish with the coriander leaves.

# KIBBEH

This recipe for stuffed cracked wheat shells has been adapted from one by Claudia Roden in her book *Middle Eastern Food*.

For the shells
225g/8oz burghul (cracked wheat)
450g/1lb minced beef
1 onion, roughly chopped
salt and freshly ground black pepper

For the filling
1 onion, finely chopped
2 tablespoons sunflower oil
55g/2oz pinenuts
285g/10oz minced beef
1 teaspoon ground cinnamon
½ teaspoon ground allspice
1 tablespoon chopped fresh parsley
1 tablespoon chopped fresh mint
salt and freshly ground black pepper
sunflower oil for deep-frying

To serve
plain yoghurt
sesame oil

To garnish
sprigs of watercress

**1.** First make the shells: soak the cracked wheat in cold water for 20 minutes.
**2.** Process the mince, onion, salt and pepper

together in a food processor. Drain the cracked wheat and process, in batches, with the beef mixture, until very soft. Knead well by hand.

**3.** Make the filling: fry the onion in the oil until soft but not brown, add the pinenuts and fry until golden-brown. Add the mince and fry until lightly browned all over. Add the cinnamon, allspice, parsley, mint, salt and pepper.

**4.** With wet hands, take a small egg-sized portion of the shell mixture and roll into a ball. Make a hole in the centre and shape into a thin walled pot with a pointed bottom by turning and pressing it in your palm.

**5.** Put some stuffing inside the hole and pinch the top of the pot together to seal it. Shape the top to a point. Repeat with the rest of the mixture, wetting your hands frequently.

**6.** Heat the oil in a deep-fryer until a crumb sizzles and fry 4–5 kibbeh at a time until golden-brown. Drain well on absorbent kitchen paper.

**7.** Flavour the yoghurt with sesame oil.

**8.** Arrange the kibbeh on a warmed serving plate, garnish with watercress and hand the yoghurt sauce separately.

 FULL RED

# TOURNEDOS CHASSEUR

SERVES 4

*4 slices of white bread, crusts removed*
*oil for frying*
*55g/2oz butter*
*4 × 170g/6oz fillet steaks*
*1 shallot, finely chopped*
*110g/4oz field mushrooms, sliced*
*1 tablespoon dry white wine*
*290ml/½ pint demi-glace sauce (see page 249), or*
  *good beef gravy, slightly thickened*
*1 teaspoon chopped fresh chervil*

**1.** Trim each slice of bread into a round or octagonal croûte. Heat some oil in a frying pan and fry the bread on both sides until crisp and brown. Keep warm on a serving platter.

**2.** Heat 1 teaspoon of the oil in a heavy frying pan and cook the steaks on both sides until done to your liking (4–5 minutes a side for well done, 1–2

minutes a side for rare). Lift them out when ready and place on top of the croûtes. Keep warm.

**3.** Melt the butter in the same pan in which you fried the steaks. Add the shallot and cook over a medium heat until just turning colour. Add the remaining butter and fry the mushrooms in this, scraping the bottom of the pan to loosen any of the sediment left from the fried steaks, to add flavour to the sauce.

**4.** After about 2 minutes, pour in first the wine, then the demi-glace sauce. Allow to bubble rapidly to reduce and thicken to a coating consistency. Add the chervil and spoon carefully over the steaks.

 CLARET

# FILET DE BOEUF À LA STROGANOFF

SERVES 4

*450g/1lb fillet of beef*
*55g/2oz butter*
*1 medium onion, thinly sliced*
*225g/8oz mushrooms, thinly sliced*
*100ml/3½fl oz dry white wine*
*150ml/¼ pint brown stock (see page 243)*
*1 tablespoon oil*
*2 tablespoons brandy*
*salt and freshly ground black pepper*
*2 tablespoons double cream*
*2 tablespoons soured cream*

**1.** Cut the beef into 5cm/2in strips, the thickness of a finger.

**2.** Melt half the butter in a frying pan and cook the onion over a low heat until soft and transparent. Add the mushrooms and toss over the heat for 1 minute. Add the wine and stock. Boil rapidly to reduce to about 2 tablespoons. Stir well, then pour into a bowl, scraping the pan.

**3.** Now heat the oil and the remaining butter in the pan. Get it as hot as you dare. Drop in the beef strips. Fry over fast heat to brown and seal the edges without over-cooking the middle. Remove the strips to a plate as they are browned. Then reduce the heat.

**4.** Pour the brandy into the hot pan. Set it alight.

As soon as the flames subside, pour in the mushroom and stock mixture. Return the beef strips to the pan and stir in the double cream. Season the sauce to taste with salt and pepper. If the sauce is too thin, remove the beef strips and boil rapidly to reduce to a syrupy consistency.
**5.** Reheat, then tip into a warmed serving dish and fork the soured cream in roughly. If the soured cream is very thick it can be diluted slightly with a little water.

NOTE: The essence of a perfect beef Stroganoff is the speed at which the beef strips are cooked. If using tougher meat, there is nothing for it but to stew the beef gently (after adding the mushrooms and stock) until tender. This alternative can be very good.

 *RED BURGUNDY*

# MIXED GRILL

Grilling times depend on the thickness of the ingredients and the temperature of the grill. The suggestions below should be regarded as guidelines only.

SERVES 1
*110g/4oz rump or sirloin steak*
*oil*
*freshly ground black pepper*
*55g/2oz calves' liver*
*1 chipolata sausage*
*1 lamb's kidney*
*1 rasher of back bacon*
*1 whole tomato*
*2 large flat mushrooms*
*salt and freshly ground black pepper*

To garnish
*1 bunch of watercress*

When preparing a mixed grill, begin by grilling the meat that will take the longest time to cook and then gradually add the other ingredients so that everything is ready at the same time.

STEAK: Flatten the steak slightly, brush it with oil and season with pepper. Do not use salt as this drains out the juices and makes the meat tough and dry. It should be salted just before cooking.
LIVER: Remove the membrane that surrounds the liver, cut into thin pieces, brush with oil and season with pepper.
CHIPOLATA SAUSAGES: Prick with a fork to allow the fat to escape during cooking. Do not add any extra fat.
KIDNEY: Skin and halve the kidney, snipping out the core. Brush with oil and season with pepper.
BACON: Cut off the rind. Put the bacon on a board and, using the back of a knife, stretch it. This helps to prevent shrinking and curling during grilling.
TOMATO: Cut in half, brush with a little oil and season with salt and pepper.
MUSHROOMS: Wipe and peel the mushrooms, cut the stalk to 1cm/½in, brush with oil and season with salt and pepper.

**1.** Preheat the grill to its highest setting.
**2.** When very hot, place the chipolata sausage under it.
**3.** After 1 minute, add the liver and the kidney.
**4.** After 1 further minute, add the steak and bacon. Grill for 1 minute.
**5.** Turn over the sausage and steak and grill for 1 further minute.
**6.** Add the tomatoes and mushrooms and grill for a further 2 minutes or so, turning over the tomatoes and turning the sausage if necessary.
**7.** As the items are ready, put them onto a warmed serving platter, draining the fat from the sausage and bacon carefully. Just before serving, garnish with sprigs of watercress.

NOTE: Mixed grill is traditionally served with potato chips or straw potatoes.

 *CLARET*

# STEAK WELLINGTON

SERVES 4

*4 × 170g/6oz fillet steaks or tournedos*
*salt and freshly ground black pepper*
*Worcestershire sauce*
*30g/1oz beef dripping or 1 tablespoon oil*
*55g/2oz flat mushrooms, chopped*
*85g/3oz chicken liver pâté (see page 149)*
*225g/8oz flour quantity rough puff pastry (see*
  *page 463)*
*beaten egg*

To serve
*290ml/½ pint wild mushroom sauce (see page*
  *256)*

To garnish
*watercress*

**1.** Preheat the oven to 230°C/450°F/gas mark 8.
Trim any fat or membranes from the steaks.
Season with pepper and a few drops of
Worcestershire sauce.
**2.** Heat the dripping or oil in a frying pan and
brown the steaks quickly on both sides. The
outside should be brown, the middle absolutely
raw. Reserve the frying pan unwashed. Leave the
meat to cool on a wire rack (this is to allow the
fat to drip off the steaks rather than cooling and
congealing on them).
**3.** Cook the mushrooms in the frying pan. Tip
into a bowl.
**4.** Beat the pâté into the mushrooms. Check the
seasoning. Spread one side of each steak with the
mixture. Roll out the pastry until it is about the
thickness of a £1 coin. Cut into 4 × 18cm/7in
squares.
**5.** Place each steak, pâté side down, on a piece of
pastry. Brush the edges with water and draw them
together over the steak, making a neat and well-
sealed parcel. Place them on a damp baking sheet,
pâté side up, and brush with beaten egg. Make a
small slit in the top of each parcel so that the
steam can escape. Decorate with leaves made
from the pastry trimmings. Brush these with egg
too. Place in the refrigerator for 10 minutes to
allow the pastry to relax.
**6.** Now brush the steak parcels with a little more

beaten egg. Bake in the preheated oven for 15
minutes, or until the pastry is golden-brown and
the meat pink.
**7.** Meanwhile, reheat the sauce.
**8.** Arrange the steaks on a warmed serving plate.
Garnish with watercress and serve the sauce
separately.

 *RED BURGUNDY*

# FILLET OF BEEF EN CROÛTE

SERVES 8–10

*1.8kg/4lb piece of fillet from the thick end*
*freshly ground black pepper*
*Worcestershire sauce (optional)*
*30g/1oz beef dripping or 1 tablespoon oil*
*340g/12oz flour quantity puff pastry (see page*
  *464)*
*110g/4oz flat mushrooms, very finely chopped*
*30g/1oz butter*
*110g/4oz chicken liver pâté (see page 149)*
*beaten egg*

**1.** Preheat the oven to 230°C/450°F/gas mark 8.
**2.** Skin and trim the fillet and season well with
pepper and Worcestershire sauce, if using. Heat
the dripping or oil in a roasting pan and when
hot add the meat and brown on all sides. Roast in
the preheated oven for 20 minutes.
**3.** Remove the fillet from the roasting pan and
allow to cool.
**4.** Take one-third of the pastry and roll it on a
floured board until it is a little more than the
length and breadth of the fillet. Place it on a
damp baking sheet, prick all over with a fork and
bake in the oven for about 20 minutes, until
golden-brown. Do not turn the oven off. Place the
pastry on a wire rack and leave to cool.
**5.** Fry the mushrooms quickly in the butter in a
frying pan. Mix with the pâté and spread the
mixture over the cooked pastry base. Place the cold
fillet on top of this and, with a sharp knife, cut
away any pastry that is not covered by the fillet.
**6.** Roll the remaining pastry on a floured board
into a 'blanket' large enough to cover the fillet

easily. Lift up the 'blanket' and lay it gently over the fillet. With a sharp knife, cut off the corners of the 'blanket' and reserve these trimmings.

**7.** Lift one length of the 'blanket' and brush the underside with beaten egg. With a palette knife, lift the base and tuck the 'blanket' neatly underneath it. Repeat with the other 3 sides. Shape the pastry trimmings into leaves. Brush the pastry-covered fillet with beaten egg. Decorate with the pastry leaves and brush again with beaten egg.

**8.** Bake the fillet in the preheated oven for 20 minutes, or until the pastry is very dark brown and shiny. This recipe assumes that rare beef is desired, but longer cooking in the first instance, without the pastry, will ensure a more well-done fillet. For medium beef, cook for a further 10 minutes and for well-done beef, a further 15 minutes.

**9.** Serve hot or cold. If served hot, the fillet should be carved at the table or the juices will be lost and the meat may have a grey, unappetizing look.

NOTE: The dish may be prepared in advance up to the final baking. It should be left ready for the oven on the baking sheet, loosely covered with clingfilm or kitchen foil to prevent the egg glaze from drying. If prepared in advance, it is important that the mushrooms and pâté should be completely cold before mixing together, and that the meat should be cold before covering with the pastry.

 *RED BURGUNDY*

# BEEF EN GÊLÉE

This recipe has been adapted from a Cordon Bleu recipe.

SERVES 4
*450g/1lb centre piece of beef fillet*
*salt and freshly ground black pepper*
*1 tablespoon oil*
*55g/2oz butter, softened*
*170g/6oz good-quality duck liver pâté*
*¼ teaspoon Dijon mustard*
*2 teaspoons dry sherry*

*4 slices of very good-quality cooked ham*
*850ml/1½ pints aspic (see page 244)*

To garnish
*2 tomatoes, peeled and deseeded*
*4 sprigs of fresh chervil*

**1.** Preheat the oven to 200°C/400°F/gas mark 6.
**2.** Tie the beef fillet into a neat shape. Season with salt and pepper. Heat the oil in a roasting tin. Add the fillet and brown lightly all over, then roast in the preheated oven for 30 minutes.
**3.** Remove from the oven and leave to get completely cold.
**4.** Beat the butter into the duck pâté, a little at a time. Add the mustard and sherry and season to taste with salt and pepper. Set aside.
**5.** Cut the cold beef fillet into 4 even-sized steaks about 1cm/½in thick. Spread a layer of pâté on top of each steak. Lay a slice of ham on top of the layer of pâté and press down lightly. Trim the edges neatly.
**6.** Put the steaks into a dish and carefully spoon in enough liquid, but cold, aspic just to cover them. Leave to set in the refrigerator.
**7.** Meanwhile, prepare the garnish: cut the tomato flesh into small diamond shapes and pick over the chervil.
**8.** Arrange the garnish on top of the steaks and coat again, very carefully, with a little cold aspic. Leave to set in the refrigerator.
**9.** Pour any remaining aspic into a shallow tray and chill until firm, then dice.
**10.** To serve: cut round the steaks with a round or oval cutter. Place on individual plates and garnish with the diced aspic.

 *RED BURGUNDY*

# FILLET OF BEEF WITH THREE PURÉES

SERVES 4

*4 × 170g/6oz fillet steaks*
*freshly ground black pepper*
*1 tablespoon oil*

For the mushroom filling
*30g/1oz butter*
*225g/8oz mushrooms, thinly sliced*
*salt and freshly ground black pepper*
*a pinch of chopped fresh thyme*
*lemon juice*

For the onion purée
*30g/1oz butter*
*1 large Spanish onion, finely chopped*
*1 tablespoon double cream*
*salt and freshly ground white pepper*

For the spinach purée
*30g/1oz butter*
*450g/1lb fresh spinach, destalked and shredded*
*1 small clove of garlic, crushed*
*a pinch of freshly grated nutmeg*
*55g/2oz Gruyère cheese, grated*
*55g/2oz anchovy fillets, soaked in milk*
*8 sheets of filo pastry*
*45g/1½oz butter, melted*
*1 egg beaten, to glaze*

1. Make the onion purée: melt the butter in a saucepan, add the onion and sweat until softened but not brown (at least 20 minutes). Add the cream and season with salt and white pepper. Remove from the heat and leave to cool.
2. Season the steaks with pepper. Heat the oil in a frying pan and brown the steaks quickly on both sides and quickly round the edge. Remove and leave to cool on a wire rack.
3. Make the mushroom filling: melt the butter in a saucepan. Add the mushrooms and season with salt and pepper and thyme. Cook until soft, then add a little lemon juice. Allow to cool.
4. Make the spinach purée: melt the butter in another saucepan, add the spinach and garlic and toss until limp. Season with salt, pepper and nutmeg. Remove from the heat and leave to cool.

Preheat the oven to 220°C/425°F/gas mark 7.
5. Cut 2 sheets of filo pastry in half. Brush each piece with melted butter and pile the pastry layers on top of each other.
6. Take a quarter of the mushroom filling and place it in the centre of the pastry. Place a steak on top and wrap the pastry round it to form a parcel. Turn it over and place it seam side down on a baking tray. Repeat with the other 3 steaks.
7. Brush parcels with beaten egg and bake them in the preheated oven for 10 minutes.
8. Meanwhile, heat the onion purée in a saucepan. Toss the spinach in a pan. When the spinach is hot add the Gruyère and anchovy fillets.
9. To serve: place the pastry parcels on warmed dinner plates with a spoonful of each purée beside each one.

 RED BURGUNDY

# ENGLISH ROAST BEEF

SERVES 10
*2.3kg/5lb sirloin or rib roast of beef*
*a little dry English mustard*
*salt and freshly ground black pepper*

To serve
*horseradish cream (see page 246)*

1. Weigh the beef to calculate the cooking time (see stage 5 below).
2. Preheat the oven to 220°C/425°F/gas mark 7.
3. Place the beef in a roasting pan and sprinkle with salt, a little mustard and plenty of pepper.
4. Roast in the preheated oven for 20 minutes.
5. Turn the oven temperature down to 160°C/325°F/gas mark 3 and roast for 20 minutes per 450g/1lb for medium meat or 10–15 minutes for very rare. Serve with horseradish cream in a separate dish.

NOTES: If allowed to rest for 20 minutes before serving, the meat will be easier to carve, but, naturally, not so hot.

If thickened gravy is required in addition to 'God's gravy' – the juices that will run from the meat before and during carving – pour off most of the dripping, taking care not to lose any brown juices. Add enough flour (usually about 1 tablespoon) to the remaining fat and juices and stir over the heat until the flour has browned and any sediment from the bottom of the pan is loosened. Add up to 570ml/1 pint of stock and stir or whisk until boiling. Season to taste with salt and pepper. Simmer for 2–3 minutes.

 *CLARET*

# YORKSHIRE PUDDING

SERVES 4
*110g/4oz plain flour*
*a good pinch of salt*
*2 eggs*
*290ml/½ pint milk or milk (200ml/7fl oz) and*
*    water (90ml/3fl oz) mixed*
*4 tablespoons good beef dripping or 2*
*    tablespoons oil*

**1.** Sift the flour and salt into a bowl. Make a well in the centre and break the eggs into it.
**2.** Beat the eggs with a wooden spoon, gradually drawing in more flour to the centre.
**3.** Beat in the milk little by little until the batter is smooth. Leave for 30 minutes before use.
**4.** Preheat the oven to 200°C/400°F/gas mark 6.
**5.** Heat the dripping or oil until very hot in a roasting pan, flameproof dish or Yorkshire pudding tin.
**6.** Pour in the batter. Bake in the preheated oven for 40 minutes, or until the pudding is risen and golden. Yorkshire puddings baked in individual patty moulds take about 15 minutes.

NOTES: If the pudding is to be served with roast beef, you can place it between an open rack holding the beef, and the dripping pan below. In this way any dripping juices from the beef will fall on to the pudding and improve its flavour. However, this makes for a slightly flat pudding.
    Alternatively, roast the beef directly in the pan (i.e. not on a wire rack) and 30 minutes before the beef is ready, increase the oven temperature to 200°C/400°F/gas mark 6 and pour the batter around the beef.
    If the pudding is not quite cooked when the beef is ready, keep the beef warm and increase the oven

temperature to 220°C/425°F/gas mark 7. Cook until the pudding is well risen and golden-brown.
    If making the pudding as a sweet course, use flavourless oil instead of dripping and serve with honey, treacle or maple syrup.

# SPICED BEEF

This recipe takes 8 days to complete.

SERVES 8
*1 clove of garlic*
*1.35kg/3lb boneless sirloin of beef*
*55g/2oz soft light brown sugar*
*30g/1oz ground allspice*
*2–3 bay leaves, chopped*
*85g/3oz salt*
*about 450g/1lb plain flour*

**1.** Peel the garlic and cut it into thin slivers. Stick these into the beef. Rub the surface of the joint with the sugar.
**2.** Leave in a cool place for 12 hours. Mix together the allspice, bay leaves and salt.
**3.** Take a little of the salt mixture and rub it well into the meat.
**4.** Keep for a week, turning and rubbing with more salt and spice each day.
**5.** Preheat the oven to 190°C/375°F/gas mark 5.
**6.** Mix the flour with water to make enough of a fairly thick, doughy paste to completely envelop the beef.
**7.** Wrap the joint in the paste.
**8.** Put it, paste and all, into a roasting pan and pour in a small cup of water. Bake in the preheated oven for 1¼ hours.
**9.** Remove from the oven and allow to cool. Snip off the crust and discard it before serving the beef.

NOTE: This is especially good eaten cold with Cumberland sauce (see page 260) or a sweet pickle.

 *CALIFORNIAN/AUSTRALIAN*
*CABERNET SAUVIGNON*

# STEAK TARTARE

The beef in this recipe is served raw, so it is essential that it is top quality and very fresh.

SERVES 4
*450g/1lb fillet or rump steak*
*salt and freshly ground black pepper*
*about 4 tablespoons salad oil*
*3 egg yolks*
*Worcestershire sauce (optional)*
*about 3 tablespoons finely chopped onion*
*about 1 tablespoon finely chopped green pepper*
*about 1 tablespoon chopped fresh parsley*

To garnish
*crisp lettuce*

**1.** Chop or mince the steak finely and mix with all the other ingredients.
**2.** Shape into 4 rounds and arrange on a serving dish. Garnish with the lettuce.

NOTES: To cater for varying tastes, in restaurants this dish is mixed to the customer's requirements at the table. The meat is presented in a hamburger shape on the plate, with the egg yolk in a half shell sitting on the top of it, and surrounded by the prepared chopped vegetables. The waiter then proceeds to beat the flavourings, oil and yolk into the meat with a fork.

Steak tartare is sometimes garnished with anchovy fillets or even caviar.

Steak tartare is surprisingly good with hot potatoes of some kind, rather than a salad. Chips or matchstick potatoes are best.

 *CLARET*

# BOEUF PHILIPPE

SERVES 6
*560g/1¼lb fillet of beef (ends will do)*
*Worcestershire sauce*
*freshly ground black pepper*
*1 tablespoon beef dripping or oil*
*½ cauliflower*
*170g/6oz French beans*

*3 tomatoes*
*½ teaspoon horseradish sauce*
*1 clove of garlic, crushed*
*3 tablespoons French dressing (see page 254)*
*8 black olives, pitted*

To garnish
*1 bunch of watercress*

**1.** Preheat the oven to 200°C/400°F;/gas mark 6.
**2.** Season the meat with Worcestershire sauce and pepper. Heat the dripping or oil in a roasting pan over direct heat and add the beef. Brown evenly on all sides. If the beef is in one thick piece, roast it in the preheated oven for 15 minutes, less if it is thin or in smaller pieces. It should be pink inside. Remove from the oven and allow to cool.
**3.** Wash the cauliflower and cut into florets. Plunge these into a saucepan of boiling water and cook for 4–5 minutes. Drain. Rinse under cold water to prevent further cooking. Drain again.
**4.** Wash and top and tail the beans. Cook in boiling salted water for 5 minutes, then rinse under cold running water and drain.
**5.** Plunge the tomatoes into boiling water for 5 seconds, then peel and cut into quarters.
**6.** Add the horseradish sauce and garlic to the French dressing. The salad is now ready for assembly but this should not be done until just before serving. The beef will lose its colour if dressed too soon, and the salad will look tired if left to stand for any length of time.
**7.** Cut the beef into thin slices and then into thin strips, cutting across the grain of the meat. Place in a bowl with the other ingredients, reserving 1 tomato and 4 olives for decoration.
**8.** Using your hands, mix in three-quarters of the French dressing and pile into a serving dish. Place the reserved tomatoes and olives on top of the dish and brush with a little French dressing. Garnish with the watercress dipped into the remaining dressing.

 *CLARET*

# SESAME BEEF SALAD

SERVES 6

*450g/1lb sirloin steak, about 5cm/2in thick*
*oil for frying*
*225g/8oz button mushrooms, sliced*
*225g/8oz mangetout, topped, tailed and blanched*

*For the marinade*
*2 onions, thinly sliced*
*5 tablespoons dry sherry*
*5 tablespoons light soy sauce*
*3 tablespoons sesame oil*
*plenty of freshly ground black pepper*

*For the dressing*
*6 tablespoons grapeseed oil*
*3 tablespoons white wine vinegar*
*1 tablespoon Dijon mustard*
*1 teaspoon clear honey*

**1.** Remove any fat or gristle from the steak.
**2.** Mix together the marinade ingredients, add the steak and leave to marinate overnight. Turn the steak occasionally if not completely submerged in the marinade.
**3.** Place the dressing ingredients in a bowl and whisk until well emulsified.
**4.** Remove the beef from the marinade. Strain the marinade (reserving the onions and marinade). Heat a little oil in a frying pan and brown the steak well on both sides. Turn the heat down to medium and cook for a further 4 minutes on each side (this timing assumes that you like rare steak; it can obviously be cooked for longer). Remove the steak, place on a wire rack and leave to get completely cold.
**5.** Add the onions from the marinade to the frying pan and cook over a high heat for about 4 minutes. Lift out and place in the dressing.
**6.** Add the mushrooms and the marinade to the frying pan and cook until the marinade has reduced to about 1 tablespoon. Add to the dressing and allow to get completely cold.
**7.** When all the ingredients are cold, cut the steak into very thin strips and add to the dressing with the mangetout. Toss together and pile on to a serving dish.

*FULL RED*

# FONDUE BOURGUIGNONNE

The fondue pot is placed in the middle of the table. Guests spear cubes of meat with a long fondue fork and cook them in the sizzling oil. Then they dip them into one of the sauces (guests should be provided with their own small dishes of these as well as salt, pepper and mustard) before eating them. Each guest should also be provided with an ordinary eating fork (the long one gets too hot to put in the mouth) and plenty of paper napkins for mopping up drips.

*oil for frying*
*curried mayonnaise (see page 250)*
*soured cream*
*tomato and mint salsa (see page 257)*
*170g/6oz rump or fillet steak per person*

**1.** Make the sauces or dips and put into small saucers or bowls for each person.
**2.** Using a sharp knife, cut the meat into small cubes, removing any fat, shortly before the meal. If the meat is left ready cut in pieces for too long the juices may run out. This makes the meat dry when cooked; but if it is wet when lowered into the hot fat it will splutter dangerously.
**3.** Get the fondue oil ready: do not overfill the pot – it should be just over half full. Test that the oil is hot enough by dropping in a cube of bread. It should sizzle gently.

 *RED BURGUNDY*

# DRIED-FRIED SHREDDED BEEF

This recipe has been adapted from a recipe by one of our most admired outside lecturers, Yan-Kit So.

SERVES 4–6
*450g/1lb lean beef, such as rump steak, or top round*
*3–4oz/85–110g carrots, cut into julienne strips*
*3–4 sticks of celery, cut into julienne strips*
*½ teaspoon salt*
*2½ cups of oil for deep-frying*
*1 teaspoon cornflour*
*2–3 dried red chillis, halved and deseeded*
*½ teaspoon ground roasted Sichuan peppercorns*
*1 teaspoon sesame oil*

For the marinade
*2 tablespoons light soy sauce*
*2 teaspoons sugar*
*1 tablespoon Shaoxing wine or dry sherry*
*1 teaspoon sesame oil*
*½ teaspoon ground roasted Sichuan peppercorns*

For the thickening
*1–1½ teaspoons cornflour*
*scant 1 teaspoon sugar*
*4 tablespoons water*

**1.** Shred the beef across the grain into thread-like strips 7.5cm/3in long. Put into a bowl.
**2.** Add all the ingredients for the marinade and combine well. Allow to stand at room temperature for 45–60 minutes so that the marinade permeates every sliver of beef.
**3.** Put the carrots and celery into a bowl and add a pinch of salt to draw out the water. Leave for 20–30 minutes, then drain. Pat dry, if necessary.
**4.** Mix the ingredients for the thickening in a small bowl and set aside.
**5.** Heat the oil in a wok until very hot. Remove the beef from the marinade and coat evenly with the cornflour. Tip the beef gently into the oil and deep-fry for 2–3 minutes, or until crisp. Turn off the heat, remove the beef with a large hand strainer and drain on absorbent kitchen paper. Pour the oil into a container for future use. Wash and dry the wok.
**6.** Reheat the wok over a medium heat until hot.

Add 2 tablespoons oil and swirl it around. Tip in the chillis and fry until dark in colour. Remove and discard. Add the carrots and celery. Stir for a few minutes until dry before adding the beef. Continue to stir over a low heat for a further 1–2 minutes, or until everything is quite dry and crisp. Add the thickening gradually and stir until the beef is coated.
**7.** Sprinkle with the ground Sichuan peppercorns and sesame oil before serving.

 *MEDIUM RED*

# FILLET OF BEEF CARPACCIO

SERVES 6
*675g/1½lb fillet steak, cut across the grain into very thin slices*

For the sauce
*3 tablespoons plain yoghurt*
*3 tablespoons double cream*
*3 tablespoons mayonnaise (see page 250)*
*1 tablespoon made English mustard*
*salt and freshly ground black pepper*
*½ teaspoon horseradish cream*
*lemon juice*

To garnish
*rocket leaves*
*shavings of Parmesan cheese*

**1.** Flatten the slices of beef between 2 sheets of clingfilm or damp greaseproof paper, using a mallet or rolling pin. Carefully remove all the sinews.
**2.** When the slices are as thin as possible, spread them over plates without letting them overlap.
**3.** Mix together the first 4 sauce ingredients.
**4.** Flavour to taste with the remaining ingredients.
**5.** Garnish with the rocket and Parmesan. Serve the sauce separately.

 *MEDIUM RED*

# MOUSSAKA

SERVES 4
*olive oil*
*675g/1½lb lean lamb, minced*
*1 large onion, finely chopped*
*½ clove of garlic, crushed*
*3 tomatoes*
*150ml/¼ pint dry white wine*
*150ml/¼ pint water*
*salt and freshly ground black pepper*
*a handful of fresh parsley, finely chopped*
*a pinch of freshly grated nutmeg*
*1 medium aubergine*
*1 large potato, peeled*
*15g/½oz dried breadcrumbs*
*15g/½oz butter*
*15g/½oz plain flour*
*1 bay leaf*
*290ml/½ pint milk*
*1 egg yolk*
*1 tablespoon double cream*
*55g/2oz dry Cheddar cheese, grated*

**1.** Heat a little oil in a large saucepan and brown the meat in it. Tip off any excess fat. Put the meat into a bowl.
**2.** Add the onions and garlic to the pan. Cook, stirring, for 5 minutes. Return the meat to the pan.
**3.** Dip the tomatoes in boiling water for 10 seconds, peel, chop and add to the meat.
**4.** Add the wine, water, salt, pepper, parsley and nutmeg and cook over a low heat, stirring often, for 30 minutes, or until most of the liquid has evaporated.
**5.** Preheat the oven to 170°C/325°F/gas mark 3. Cut the aubergine into thin slices, salt lightly and leave for about 30 minutes for some of the juice to drain out. Rinse and dry well on a cloth. Cook the potato in boiling salted water until just tender. Cool and slice.
**6.** Heat a little more oil in a frying pan and fry each slice of aubergine on both sides until well browned but not burnt.
**7.** Put the aubergine slices into the bottom of a large casserole. Sprinkle on the breadcrumbs.
**8.** Now tip in half the meat mixture. Put half the sliced potato in next, seasoning with salt and pepper, then the remaining meat, and then the remaining potato.

**9.** Melt the butter in a saucepan. Stir in the flour, add the bay leaf and then the milk, and stir constantly while bringing slowly to the boil. Season with salt and pepper and leave simmering while you mix the egg yolks and cream in a bowl.
**10.** Pour the sauce on to the yolks and cream, stirring all the time. Add half the cheese.
**11.** Pour the sauce over the casserole. Sprinkle the cheese on top.
**12.** Cook in the preheated oven for 1 hour, then test with a skewer; the whole mass should be soft. The top should be browned too, but if not, finish browning under the grill.

NOTE: Many chefs insist that the custard top and the inclusion of potato do not make this dish a true moussaka. But moussaka in its native Greece usually contains both, and the Greeks have as many variations on moussaka as we have on apple pie.

 *FULL SPICY RED*

# BABOTIE

SERVES 4
*1 slice of white bread*
*150ml/¼ pint milk*
*1 onion, chopped*
*1 small dessert apple, chopped*
*30g/1oz butter*
*1 tablespoon curry powder (see page 688)*
*450g/1lb cooked lamb, minced*
*1 tablespoon chutney*
*a few raisins*
*1 tablespoon vinegar or lemon juice*
*salt and freshly ground black pepper*

For the topping
*2 eggs*
*290ml/½ pint Greek yoghurt*
*salt and freshly ground black pepper*
*1 tablespoon flaked almonds*

**1.** Soak the bread in the milk.
**2.** Grease an ovenproof dish and preheat the oven to 180°C/350°F/gas mark 4.
**3.** Cook the onion and apple in the butter in a

saucepan over a low heat until soft but not coloured. Add the curry powder and cook for 1 further minute.

**4.** Mix the onion and apple with the lamb, chutney, almonds, raisins and vinegar or lemon juice. Fork the bread into the meat. Season with salt and pepper and pile into the dish.

**5.** Mix the eggs with the yoghurt. Season with salt and pepper.

**6.** Pour this over the meat mixture, place the almonds on top and bake in the preheated oven for about 30–35 minutes, until the custard has set and browned.

 *LIGHT RED*

# COTTAGE PIE

SERVES 4
*1 tablespoon oil*
*1 onion, chopped*
*340g/12oz cooked beef or lamb, minced*
*2 tomatoes, peeled and chopped*
*2 teaspoons Worcestershire sauce*
*1 tablespoon tomato chutney*
*1 teaspoon tarragon vinegar*
*1 tablespoon chopped fresh thyme*
*1 tablespoon plain flour*
*425ml/³/4 pint brown stock (see page 243)*
*gravy browning (optional)*
*450g/1lb mashed potatoes (see page 212)*
*butter*

**1.** Preheat the oven to 200°C/400°F/gas mark 6.

**2.** Heat the oil in a frying pan and cook the onion over a low heat until lightly browned.

**3.** Add the meat, tomatoes, Worcestershire sauce, chutney, vinegar and thyme. Sprinkle with the flour and stir into the meat. Cook over a low heat for 2 minutes.

**4.** Add the stock and bring to the boil, stirring continuously. Simmer for 20 minutes, adding more stock if necessary. Season with salt and pepper and add some gravy browning if required.

**5.** Tip into a pie dish and allow to cool slightly.

**6.** Spread the mashed potato on the top. Fork it up to leave the surface rough or draw the fork over the surface to mark with a pattern. Dot the top with butter.

**7.** Place the pie on a baking sheet and cook in the preheated oven for 20–30 minutes, or until the potato is golden-brown and crisp.

 *MEDIUM RED*

# MUNG BEANS WITH LAMB AND ROSEMARY

This is a bean dish with meat – in other words, the lamb is not the principal ingredient, merely one of the flavours and textures integral to the finished recipe.

*225g/8oz lean lamb, preferably leg (trimmed weight)*
*1 teaspoon sunflower oil*
*1 large onion, sliced*
*2 cloves of garlic, crushed*
*1 litre/1³/4 pints brown stock (see page 243) or water if not available*
*1 tablespoon tomato purée*
*1 tablespoon chopped fresh rosemary*
*salt and freshly ground black pepper*
*225g/8oz mung beans, soaked for 4 hours*
*5 cloves, tied together in a small piece of muslin*

**1.** Preheat the oven to 150°C/300°F/gas mark 2.

**2.** Cut the meat into 2.5cm/1in cubes. Fry in the oil, in a non-stick frying pan until well browned all over. Transfer to a casserole. Fry the onion and garlic in the pan for 2 minutes. Add the stock, tomato purée, rosemary and pepper. Bring to the boil, then pour over the meat.

**3.** Drain the beans, rinse and add to the casserole. Bring to the boil and add the little bag of cloves. Cover and bake in the preheated oven for 1½ hours.

**4.** Season to taste with salt. Pile into a clean serving dish and sprinkle with the parsley.

NOTE: Do not add salt to the beans until after they are cooked.

 *FULL RED*

# LANCASHIRE HOTPOT

SERVES 4
*900g/2lb middle neck of mutton or lamb*
*3 lambs' kidneys (optional)*
*900g/2lb potatoes*
*salt and freshly ground black pepper*
*2 large onions, thinly sliced*
*2 carrots, sliced*
*1 teaspoon chopped fresh thyme or a pinch of*
    *dried thyme*
*1 bay leaf*
*570ml/1 pint brown stock (see page 243)*
*55g/2oz butter*

**1.** Preheat the oven to 180°C/350°F/gas mark 4.
**2.** Cut the meat into chops, trimming away most
of the fat.
**3.** Skin, split, core and quarter the kidneys.
**4.** Wash and peel the potatoes, discard any eyes
and cut into slices about 5mm/¼in thick.
**5.** Butter a casserole dish and line it with a layer
of potatoes. Season well with salt, pepper and
thyme.
**6.** Layer the chops, sliced onions, carrots and
kidneys on top of the potatoes, seasoning well
with salt, pepper and thyme and adding the bay
leaf when the casserole is half full. Finish with a
neat layer of potatoes overlapping each other.
**7.** Pour in enough stock to come to the bottom of
the top layer of potatoes.
**8.** Brush the top with plenty of melted butter and
season well with salt and pepper.
**9.** Cover the casserole and bake in the preheated
oven for about 2 hours.
**10.** Remove the lid and continue to cook for a
further 30–40 minutes, until the potatoes are
brown and crisp and the meat is completely
tender.

 *CLARET*

# NAVARIN OF LAMB

SERVES 4–6
*900g/2lb middle neck of lamb*
*salt and freshly ground black pepper*
*2 tablespoons dripping*
*1 tablespoon plain flour*
*1 litre/1¾ pints brown stock (see page 243)*
*1 clove of garlic, crushed*
*1 tablespoon tomato purée*
*1 bouquet garni (parsley, bay leaf and a stick of*
    *celery, tied together with string)*
*12 button onions, peeled*
*a pinch of caster sugar*
*1 turnip, cut into sticks*
*3 carrots, cut into sticks*
*3 potatoes, peeled and cut into chunks*

**1.** Cut the lamb into pieces and season with salt
and pepper.
**2.** Heat 1 tablespoon of the dripping or oil in a
heavy saucepan and brown the meat on all sides.
Pour off the fat into a frying pan. Sprinkle the
meat with the flour. Cook for 1 minute, then stir
in the stock, garlic and tomato purée. Add the
bouquet garni. Stir until boiling, then simmer for
1 hour. Skim off any surface fat.
**3.** Heat a little more fat and soften and brown
first the onions with the sugar, then the turnips,
carrots and potatoes, adding more dripping as
needed.
**4.** Add the browned vegetables to the meat stew,
cover tightly and continue cooking over a low
heat, or in a moderate oven, for a further 30–40
minutes or until the meat is tender. Taste for
seasoning.
**5.** Remove the bouquet garni. Allow the navarin
to stand for 5 minutes, then skim off the surface
fat and spoon the stew into a warmed serving
dish.

NOTE: Fresh peas or beans are sometimes added
to the navarin after the final skimming. The stew
must then be cooked until they are just tender.

 *CLARET*

# NOISETTES OF LAMB WITH BACON AND SWEET ONION PURÉE

SERVES 4
2 × 6–7 bone best end necks of lamb, chined
10 rashers of streaky rindless bacon
unsalted butter

For the purée
30g/1oz butter
2 large onions, very finely chopped

To garnish
1 small bunch of watercress

1. First prepare the noisettes (see page 374). Surround the rolls with the bacon and tie each best end into 4–5 noisettes. Slice. Press under a heavy weight until required, ideally for 1 hour.
2. Make the purée: melt the butter in a frying pan, add the onions and cook slowly until absolutely soft (this may well take 45 minutes). Increase the heat and cook until the onions are browned but not burnt. Liquidize in a blender, then push through a sieve.
3. Fry the noisettes in the butter for 5 minutes per side, remove the string and arrange on a warmed serving plate. Garnish with watercress and serve the warm onion purée separately.

 *MEDIUM RED*

# COLLOPS OF LAMB IN FILO PASTRY

This recipe has been adapted from a recipe by Giselle Marden.

1 × 8-cutlet rack (best end) of lamb
30g/1oz butter, melted
55g/2oz green beans, cooked
8 cherry tomatoes

For the sauce
1 carrot, chopped

1 onion, chopped
2 teaspoons plain flour
1 teaspoon tomato purée
570ml/1 pint water
1 bay leaf
1 spring of fresh rosemary
1 clove of garlic, crushed

For the stuffing
110g/4oz mushrooms, chopped
1 onion, chopped
1 clove of garlic, crushed
1 sprig of fresh rosemary
225g/8oz tomatoes, peeled, deseeded and cut into slivers
salt and freshly ground black pepper
45g/1½oz feta cheese

## PREPARE THE MEAT

1. Trim the fat from the lamb and render down 2 tablespoons of dripping. Discard the remaining dripping.
2. Remove the eye or fillet from the lamb and trim off any remaining fat.
3. Heat the 2 tablespoons of dripping in a frying pan and quickly brown the lamb fillet on all sides. Cut into 4 collops 3.5cm/1½in thick. Return to the pan and quickly brown the cut sides. Remove and place on a wire rack to cool.

## PREPARE THE SAUCE

4. Chop up the bone and trimmings from the rack of lamb and brown them over a medium heat in a little dripping. Remove from the pan.
5. Add the carrot and onion and cook until well browned. Add the flour and cook, stirring, until lightly coloured, then add the tomato purée and cook for 1 further minute.
6. Return the browned bones to the pan and add the water, herbs and garlic. Bring to the boil, then leave to simmer for at least 1 hour.

## PREPARE THE STUFFING

7. In another pan heat 2 tablespoons of the dripping and cook the onions until golden. Add the mushrooms and stir until cooked and just moist.
8. Remove from the heat and add the garlic, rosemary, tomatoes, salt and pepper. When cold crumble in the cheese.

## TO ASSEMBLE

**9.** Preheat the oven to 200°C/400°F/gas mark 6. Melt the butter.

**10.** Cut the filo pastry into 12 × 30 × 20cm/12 × 8in squares. Place one square on a baking sheet and brush with butter, place a second square on top at a slight angle and place a third square on again at a slight angle. Brush with butter. (The filo pastry should look like the petals of a flower.)

**11.** Place a spoonful of the stuffing in the middle, then a collop, then another spoonful of stuffing. Gather the pastry round the meat in a pouch shape and spread the edges of the pastry like a collar. Use the remaining ingredients to make 3 more parcels.

**12.** Cook in the oven for 20 minutes or until golden.

## TO SERVE

**13.** Strain the sauce. If too thin, reduce by boiling and season as necessary.

**14.** Place a spoonful of the sauce on each of 4 dinner plates and place a parcel off-centre on each plate. Garnish each with a few green beans and 2 cherry tomatoes.

 *MEDIUM RED*

# COLLOPS OF LAMB WITH ONION AND MINT SAUCE

This dish can also be made with lamb noisettes or cutlets: simply grill until tender.

SERVES 4
*2 × 6-7 bone racks of lamb*
*thick onion and mint sauce (see page 257)*

For the sauce
*bones from the racks of lamb*
*1 carrot, chopped*
*1 onion, chopped*
*2 teaspoons plain flour*
*1 teaspoon tomato purée*
*570ml/1 pint water*
*1 bay leaf*
*1 sprig of fresh mint*
*1 clove of garlic, crushed*

**1.** Preheat the oven to 240°C/475°F/gas mark 8.

**2.** Prepare the meat: trim the fat from the rack of lamb and place in a roasting pan in the preheated oven to render down. Reserve this dripping to brown the collops and the bones.

**3.** Remove the 'eye' or fillet from the best ends in one piece and trim off all the fat and gristle.

**4.** Prepare the sauce: cut up the remains of the rack of lamb and brown over a medium heat in a little of the dripping. Remove from the pan.

**5.** Add the carrots and onions and cook until well browned. Add the flour and cook, stirring until lightly coloured, then add the tomato purée and cook for 1 further minute.

**6.** Return the bones to the pan and add the water, herbs and garlic. Bring to the boil and leave to simmer for at least 1 hour.

**7.** Strain the sauce, pressing the vegetables lightly; skim off any fat. Reduce, by boiling rapidly, if necessary, and season to taste with salt and pepper.

**8.** Brown the meat quickly in a little dripping and then place in the oven, still at 240°C/475°F/gas mark 8, for 10 minutes. Turn the oven off and leave for 5 minutes to allow the juices to set.

**9.** Warm 4 dinner plates. Heat the sauce and the onion and mint purée. Place a spoonful of the purée on each plate. Slice the fillet and arrange, in overlapping slices, on top of the purée. Spoon over some of the sauce and serve the remainder separately in a warmed sauceboat.

 *CLARET*

# LAMB DAUBE

SERVES 4
*900g/2lb lamb (preferably from the shoulder)*
*1 tablespoon oil*
*110g/4oz streaky bacon, diced*
*1 onion, chopped*
*150ml/¼ pint brown stock (see page 243)*
*55g/2oz plain flour*
*1 bouquet garni (1 bay leaf, a sprig each of fresh thyme, rosemary and parsley, and a small strip of orange zest, tied together with string)*

For the marinade
*290ml/½ pint red wine*
*1 medium onion, cut into thick slices*

1 *clove of garlic, bruised*
4 *whole allspice berries*

**1.** Trim the lamb and cut into large pieces.
**2.** Prepare the marinade by mixing all the ingredients together. Lay the pieces of meat in it and leave overnight.
**3.** Preheat the oven to 170°C/325°F/gas mark 3.
**4.** Drain the meat from the marinade. Reserve the marinade.
**5.** Heat the oil in a heavy frying pan and brown the bacon and the onion. Lift out with a slotted spoon and place in a casserole.
**6.** Brown the meat in the same pan, a few pieces at a time. Lay them on top of the bacon and onion.
**7.** Strain the marinade into the empty pan. Add the stock. Bring to the boil, scraping the bottom of the pan to loosen any sediment. Pour over the meat.
**8.** Immerse the bouquet garni in the liquid in the casserole.
**9.** Make a stiff dough by adding water to the flour. Put the lid on the casserole and press a band of dough around the join of the lid and the dish to seal completely.
**10.** Cook in the preheated oven for 1½ hours. Remove the bouquet garni.
**11.** Lift the meat out and put it on a warmed serving dish. Keep warm.
**12.** Boil the sauce to reduce to a syrupy consistency and pour over the meat.

 *RED BURGUNDY*

# LAMB CURRY

SERVES 4
30g/1oz *clarified butter (see page 686) or ghee*
1 *small onion, finely chopped*
675g/1½lb *boneless lamb, preferably shoulder,*
    *cut into 4cm/1½in cubes*
2 *teaspoons ground turmeric*
½ *teaspoon ground ginger*
1 *clove of garlic, crushed*
1½ *teaspoon ground coriander*
¼ *teaspoon salt*
¼ *teaspoon cayenne pepper*
425ml/¾ *pint brown stock (see page 243) or*
    *vegetable stock (see page 246)*
1 *tablespoon chopped fresh parsley*
½ *tablespoon chopped fresh mint*

**1.** Melt the butter in a large saucepan and brown the onion in it. Remove to a plate.
**2.** Put the meat into the pan and brown all over. Add the turmeric, ginger, garlic and coriander. Return the onions to the pan and stir and cook over a low heat for 1 minute.
**3.** Season with salt and cayenne and add enough stock to come 1cm/½in below the top of the meat. This level should be kept constant. Bring to the boil, then cover and simmer gently for about 1½ hours, until the meat is tender, adding more stock as necessary.
**4.** When the lamb is tender, remove it from the pan and keep warm. Reduce the liquid by rapid boiling. Add the parsley and mint and pour over the meat.

NOTES: More (or fewer) spices may be added according to taste.

    Ghee is clarified fat sold in tins in Indian stores.

 *LAGER OR FULL SPICY RED*

## ACCOMPANIMENT FOR CURRIES
BANANA AND COCONUT: Chop 2 bananas and squeeze the juice of 1 lemon over them. Mix in 2 tablespoons freshly grated coconut.

TOMATO AND ONION: Chop 1 large onion and 3 peeled tomatoes finely. Mix together with salt and pepper, 1 tablespoon olive oil and a squeeze of lemon juice.

CHUTNEY AND CUCUMBER: Mix 1 cupful chopped cucumber into the same quantity of sweet chutney (such as mango or apple).

GREEN PEPPER, APPLE AND RAISIN: Chop equal quantities of apple and green pepper finely, or mince them. Add 1 tablespoon raisins or sultanas and salt, pepper, lemon juice, cayenne and sugar to taste.

POPPADOMS: These are large flat wafers, available in most supermarkets. They are heated in the oven or under the grill, or fried in hot fat until crisp. They can be bought spiced or plain.

# LAMB WITH DILL SAUCE

SERVES 4

*900g/2lb boneless lamb, cut into large chunks*
*1 onion, sliced*
*1 carrot, cut into sticks*
*1 tablespoon dill seeds, crushed, or 3–4 sprigs*
  *fresh dill*
*1 bay leaf*
*12 black peppercorns*
*½ teaspoon salt*
*720ml/1¼ pints white stock, made with chicken*
  *bones (see page 243)*
*30g/1oz butter*
*1 tablespoon plain flour*
*1 egg yolk*
*3 tablespoons double cream*
*2 teaspoons lemon juice*
*freshly ground black pepper*

**1.** Put the meat, onion, carrot, dill seeds or stalks,
but not the fresh leaves, bay leaf, peppercorns and
salt into a saucepan.
**2.** Cover with the stock and bring slowly to the
boil. Turn down the heat and cook as slowly as
possible for 2–2½ hours, or until the meat is
tender.
**3.** Lift out the meat, discarding the bay leaf and
dill stalks, and place in a casserole or serving dish.
Cover to prevent drying out, and keep warm.
**4.** Strain the stock and skim off all the fat.
Measure the remaining liquid and make up to
425ml/¾ pint with water if necessary. Return to
the saucepan.
**5.** Mix the butter and flour together to a smooth
paste. Whisk this gradually into the hot stock,
and whisk steadily until the sauce is smooth.
Bring to the boil, then simmer for 2 minutes.
**6.** Mix the egg yolk and cream in a bowl. Mix a
little of the hot sauce into the cream mixture, then
stir this back into the sauce. Be careful not to boil
the sauce now or the yolk will scramble. Flavour
the sauce with the lemon juice and season to taste
with salt and pepper. Chop the dill leaves if you
have them, and stir in. Pour over the meat and
serve immediately.

 *MEDIUM RED*

# LAMB CUTLETS GRILLED WITH HERBS

SERVES 4

*12 French-trimmed lamb cutlets (see page 374)*
*30g/1oz butter, melted*
*1 tablespoon oil*
*a selection of chopped fresh herbs, such as thyme,*
  *basil, mint, parsley, marjoram, rosemary*
*salt and freshly ground black pepper*

**1.** Preheat the grill to its highest setting.
**2.** Brush the cutlets with melted butter and oil,
sprinkle over half the herbs and season with salt
and pepper.
**3.** Place the cutlets under the grill, about 8cm/3in
away from the heat, and cook for 3–4 minutes.
**4.** Turn them over, baste with the fat from the
bottom of the pan and sprinkle over the
remaining herbs.
**5.** Grill for 3–4 minutes (3 minutes each side
should give a succulent pink cutlet, 4 minutes a
well-done cutlet).
**6.** Arrange the cutlets on a warmed serving dish
and pour over the pan juices. Serve immediately.

 *CLARET*

# INDONESIAN MIXED MEAT KEBABS

SERVES 4

*225g/8oz lean lamb, cut into 1cm/½in cubes*
*225g/8oz lean pork, cut into 1cm/½in cubes*
*2 medium onions, blanched and quartered*
*1 green pepper, blanched, cored, deseeded and cut*
  *into 8*
*1 red pepper, blanched, cored, deseeded and cut*
  *into 8*
*110g/4oz button mushrooms*

For the marinade
*140g/5oz low-fat plain yoghurt*
*1 teaspoon ground ginger*
*1 clove of garlic, crushed*
*a pinch of ground cumin*
*a pinch of ground coriander*
*grated zest and juice of ½ lemon*
*salt and freshly ground black pepper*

To garnish
*1 small bunch of watercress*

1. Mix the marinade ingredients in a bowl. Add the lamb and pork, then coat well. Cover and leave for several hours in a cool place, turning occasionally.
2. Preheat the grill to its highest setting.
3. Thread the ingredients on to 4 skewers and baste with any extra marinade.
4. Place under the grill and cook for 5 minutes on each side. Garnish with sprigs of watercress.

 *FULL SPICY RED*

# LAMB CUTLETS SOUBISE

SERVES 4
*12 French-trimmed cutlets (see page 374)*
*seasoned plain flour*
*beaten egg*
*dried breadcrumbs*
*55ml/2fl oz oil*
*15g/½oz butter*

To garnish
*sprigs of watercress*

To serve
*290ml/½ pint soubise sauce (see page 248)*

1. Dip each cutlet into the seasoned flour, shake off the excess and brush with beaten egg. Press on the breadcrumbs.
2. Heat the oil in a frying pan. When hot, add the butter. Fry the cutlets for 3–4 minutes on each side, until golden-brown on the outside but not hard to the touch. Drain briefly on absorbent kitchen paper to remove any grease. Garnish with watercress and serve the soubise sauce separately.

 *LIGHT/MEDIUM RED*

# LAMB STEAK À LA CATALANE WITH LENTILS

SERVES 4
*4 lamb steaks 1cm/½in thick, cut across the upper leg, bones removed*

For the marinade
*150ml/¼ pint olive oil*
*6 cloves of garlic, crushed*
*2 tablespoons chopped fresh thyme*
*1 large onion, sliced*
*24 black peppercorns, slightly crushed*
*salt*

For the lentils
*225g/8oz (raw weight) green/brown lentils, cooked*
*4 onions, finely chopped*
*4 cloves of garlic, crushed*
*olive oil*
*2 tablespoons tomato purée*
*4 tablespoons chopped mixed fresh herbs*
*salt and freshly ground black pepper*
*sesame oil*

To garnish
*watercress*

1. Lay the lamb steaks in a shallow dish. Pour over the oil and add all the other marinade ingredients. Leave the steaks to marinate for at least 8 hours, preferably 24 hours, turning them over 2 or 3 times.
2. Sweat the onion and garlic in a little oil until completely soft and transparent.
3. Add the lentils, tomato purée and herbs, season well with salt and pepper and sprinkle over sesame oil to taste. Keep warm.
4. Meanwhile, get a heavy frying pan or griddle really hot, or preheat the grill for at least 10 minutes.
5. Remove most of the oil from the steaks and put them in the hot pan or under the grill. Fry or grill, turning once, until both sides are a good brown. Like beef steaks, they can be eaten in any state from blue to well done, but if overcooked they become very tough. They are best pink in the middle. Garnish with a bouquet of watercress.

 *MEDIUM RED*

# ROAST STUFFED SHOULDER OF LAMB

SERVES 6
*1.8kg/4lb boned whole shoulder of lamb*
*15g/½oz butter*
*1 large onion, finely chopped*
*55g/2oz mushrooms, sliced*
*1 clove of garlic, crushed*
*1 tablespoon chopped mixed fresh herbs, such as*
*    mint, thyme, parsley, rosemary*
*a squeeze of orange juice*
*salt and freshly ground black pepper*
*½ cup cooked rice*
*2 tablespoons sultanas*
*1 small bunch of watercress*

For the gravy
*2 teaspoons plain flour*
*1 teaspoon tomato purée*
*290ml/½ pint brown stock (see page 243)*
*100ml/3½fl oz red wine*

1. Weigh the lamb and calculate its cooking time:
20 minutes to 450g/1lb plus 20 minutes.
2. Preheat the oven to 190°C/375°F/gas mark 5.
3. Melt the butter in a frying pan and add the
onion. Fry over a low heat until soft.
4. Add the mushrooms, garlic, herbs and orange
juice. Cook over a low heat until the mushrooms
are soft. Season with salt and pepper.
5. Remove from the heat and mix with the cooked
rice. Stir in the sultanas.
6. Push this stuffing into the shoulder of lamb, sewing
up the edges with thin string. Place in a roasting pan.
7. Roast in the preheated oven for the calculated
cooking time.
8. Lift the meat from the roasting pan and keep
warm on a serving platter in the turned-off oven.
9. Make the gravy: pour off most of the fat from
the roasting pan, then stir in first the flour and
then the tomato purée. Cook for 30 seconds.
10. Add the stock and wine, and stir over the heat
until the sauce boils, scraping the brown bits from
the bottom of the pan as you go. Simmer for 2–3
minutes. Season to taste with salt and pepper.
Strain into a warmed gravy-boat.
11. Garnish the lamb with bouquets of watercress
and serve with the gravy.

 *MEDIUM RED*

# SHOULDER OF LAMB STUFFED WITH FETA

This dish is served with a tomato and mint salsa.

SERVES 6
*1.8kg/4lb boned whole shoulder of lamb*
*85ml/3fl oz red wine*
*20g/¾ plain flour*

For the stuffing
*225g/8oz feta cheese, cut into 1cm/½in cubes*
*2 teaspoons green peppercorns*
*1 shallot, chopped*
*85g/3oz fresh white breadcrumbs*
*2 tablespoons thinly sliced sun-dried tomatoes, or*
*    2 tomatoes, peeled, deseeded and finely*
*    chopped*
*1 tablespoon fresh thyme leaves*
*1 egg, beaten*
*salt and freshly ground black pepper*

To garnish
*sprigs of watercress*

To serve
*tomato and mint salsa (see page 257)*

1. Preheat the oven to 200°C/400°F/gas mark 6.
2. Trim the lamb of any excess fat, leaving a thin
layer on the outside.
3. Mix together the stuffing ingredients, beat
lightly and season carefully with salt and pepper
(the feta can be very salty).
4. Season the inside of the lamb and stuff it
carefully. Using thin string, sew the lamb up, but
not too tightly.
5. Weigh the lamb and for pink lamb allow 20
minutes per 450g/1lb plus 20 minutes. For better-
done lamb cook for a further 30 minutes.
6. Put the lamb into a roasting pan and roast in the
preheated oven for the calculated cooking time.
7. Thirty minutes before the lamb is ready, pour
the wine over the joint.
8. When the lamb is cooked, remove it from the oven
and place in a warm place to rest for 10 minutes.
9. Pour off all but 1 tablespoon of fat from the
roasting pan, place the pan over direct heat and
stir in the flour. Cook, stirring, for 1 minute. Add

some water and also any cooking juices. Bring to the boil, then simmer for 5 minutes.

**10.** Just before serving remove the string from the lamb. Garnish with small sprigs of watercress. Serve with the gravy and hand the tomato and mint salsa separately.

 *FULL RED*

# SHOULDER OF LAMB 'EN BALLON'

This dish is served with a sweet port gravy.

SERVES 6–8
*1 boned shoulder of lamb*
*salt and freshly ground black pepper*
*sprigs of fresh rosemary*
*290ml/½ pint brown stock made with lamb*
    *bones (see page 243) or water*
*150ml/5fl oz port*

For the seasoning in the centre of the lamb
*2 tablespoons chopped fresh parsley*
*85g/3oz smoked ham, chopped*
*salt and freshly ground black pepper*

For the glaze
*2 tablespoons redcurrant jelly*

To garnish
*watercress*

**1.** Preheat the oven to 190°C/375°F/gas mark 5.
**2.** Mix the seasoning ingredients together and push into the lamb, or, if the lamb has been opened out, spread it on one half and fold the other half over to cover it.
**3.** Using a long piece of string, tie the shoulder so that the indentations made by the string resemble the grooves in a melon or the lines between the segments of a beachball (see page 372).
**4.** Weigh the lamb and calculate the cooking time at 20 minutes per 450g/1lb plus 20 minutes.
**5.** Sprinkle with salt and pepper. Scatter a few rosemary leaves on top. Pour the stock into the pan.

**6.** Roast in the preheated oven for its calculated cooking time. Half an hour before the end of cooking, smear the lamb with redcurrant jelly and return to the oven.
**7.** Remove the string carefully and lift the lamb on to a warmed serving dish. Leave to rest for 15 minutes before serving. It will retain heat even if not placed in a warming cupboard.
**8.** Meanwhile, make the gravy: skim the fat from the juices in the pan. Add the port and bring to the boil. Boil vigorously until the sauce is syrupy and reduced to about 200ml/7fl oz. Check the seasoning. Strain into a warmed gravy-boat. Garnish the lamb with watercress and serve with the gravy.

 *CLARET*

# CROWN ROAST OF LAMB

SERVES 4–6
*1 crown roast or 2 × 7-bone matching racks (best*
    *ends) of lamb, chined*
*55g/2oz butter*
*1 large sprig of fresh rosemary*
*1 bunch of watercress*

To garnish
*paper cutlet frills*

To serve hot
*1 teaspoon plain flour*
*290ml/½ pint brown stock, made with lamb*
    *bones (see page 243)*
*salt and freshly ground black pepper*

To serve cold
*redcurrant jelly*

**1.** If the butcher has not trimmed and tied the meat into a crown, follow the instructions on page 377.
**2.** Preheat the oven to 200°C/400°F/gas mark 6. Melt the butter in a roasting pan. Add the crumbled rosemary and put in the crown of lamb. Wrap up the ends of the bones with wet brown paper, then with kitchen foil to prevent them from burning. It is easier to cover a few bones at a time

than to cover the whole crown. Brush over the melted butter.

**3.** Weigh the lamb and allow 20 minutes per 450g/1lb plus 20 minutes. Roast in the preheated oven for the calculated cooking time. Lift out the crown.

**4.** To serve hot: skim or pour off virtually all of the fat from the roasting pan, taking care not to pour away any of the meat juices. Stir in the flour, scraping any sediment off the bottom of the pan. Add the stock and stir until boiling. Simmer for 2 minutes. Season to taste with salt and pepper.

**5.** Place a cutlet frill on each cutlet bone. Garnish with sprigs of watercress in the centre. Hand the gravy separately in a warmed gravy-boat.

**6.** To serve cold: slice the meat between the bones to separate the cutlets. Trim off the excess fat from each cutlet, but take care to keep the cutlets in the right order, so you can reassemble the crown. Decorate each bone with a cutlet frill. Garnish with sprigs of watercress in the centre. Serve with redcurrant jelly.

 *CLARET*

# RACK OF LAMB WITH MUSTARD AND BREADCRUMBS

SERVES 2
*2 teaspoons Dijon mustard*
*1 tablespoon fresh white breadcrumbs*
*1 tablespoon chopped mixed fresh herbs, such as mint, chives, parsley, thyme*
*¼ teaspoon salt*
*½ teaspoon freshly ground black pepper*
*1 rack (best end) of lamb, chined, trimmed and skinned*
*2 teaspoons unsalted butter*

**1.** Preheat the oven to 220°C/425°F/gas mark 7.
**2.** Trim off as much fat as possible from the meat.
**3.** Mix together the mustard, breadcrumbs, herbs, salt, pepper and butter. Press a thin layer of this mixture over the rounded, skinned side of the best end. Chill in the refrigerator for 30 minutes.
**4.** Place, crumbed side up, in a roasting pan and

roast in the preheated oven for 25 minutes for a 7-cutlet best end, less for a smaller one. This will give pink, slightly underdone lamb. Serve with the butter and juices from the pan poured over the top.

 *FULL RED*

# ROAST SADDLE OF LAMB

A saddle of lamb is a cut consisting of both loins, left in a single piece. It can weigh anything from 2–4.5kg/4½–10lb. New Zealand lamb cuts are generally smaller than British.

*1 saddle of lamb*
*dripping*
*1 clove of garlic, peeled and cut into slivers (optional)*
*salt and freshly ground black pepper*
*sprigs of fresh rosemary*

For the gravy
*425ml/¾ pint brown stock, made with lamb bones (see page 243)*
*2 teaspoons plain flour*

To serve
*redcurrant jelly or soubise sauce (see page 248)*

**1.** Preheat the oven to 200°C/400°F/gas mark 6.
**2.** Trim off any excess fat from underneath the saddle and remove the kidneys. Trim away all but 2.5cm/1in of the 2 flaps.
**3.** Skin the saddle: the best way to do this is to lift the skin at one corner with a sharp knife and hold it tightly in a tea-towel to prevent it slipping out of your grip. Give a sharp tug and pull off all the skin in one piece. This sounds more difficult than it is. Score the fat in a criss-cross pattern with a sharp knife.
**4.** Heat 2 tablespoons dripping in a roasting pan. When it is hot, add the saddle of lamb, tucking the flaps underneath and basting well.
**5.** If liked, stick a few slivers of garlic into the saddle near the bone. Season with salt, pepper and a scattering of rosemary. Weigh the joint and calculate the cooking time at 15 minutes per 450g/1lb plus 15 minutes for pink lamb.

**6.** Roast in the preheated oven for the calculated time. If the saddle is extremely large, it should be covered with damp greaseproof paper halfway through roasting to prevent it from becoming too brown.

**7.** Lift the meat on to a warmed serving platter. Pour away all but 1 tablespoon fat from the pan, taking care not to lose any of the juices or sediment. Stir the flour into the pan to absorb the remaining fat. Cook, stirring, over the heat for 1 minute. Add the stock and stir until boiling, taking care to scrape up any sediment stuck to the bottom of the pan. Simmer for 2 minutes and season to taste with salt and pepper.

**8.** To carve the saddle: cut thin strips parallel to the backbone, down the length of the meat. The thicker, chump end may be cut across in slices if preferred but the main part is usually carved lengthways (see page 377).

 *CLARET*

# ROAST LEG OF LAMB

SERVES 4
*1 small leg of lamb*
*salt and freshly ground black pepper*
*3 large sprigs of fresh rosemary*
*200ml/7fl oz red wine*

For the gravy
*2 teaspoons plain flour*
*290ml/½ pint brown stock, made with lamb*
    *bones (see page 243)*
*1 teaspoon redcurrant jelly*
*salt and freshly ground black pepper*

**1.** Preheat the oven to 200°C/400°F/gas mark 6.
**2.** Weigh the joint and calculate the cooking time at 20 minutes per 450g/1lb plus 20 minutes.
**3.** Wipe the lamb. Season with salt and pepper and place in a roasting pan, with the sprigs of rosemary on top.
**4.** Roast in the preheated oven for the calculated cooking time. Thirty minutes before the end of cooking, pour the wine over the lamb.
**5.** When the lamb is cooked, the juices that run out of the meat when pierced with a skewer will

be faintly pink. Remove the joint from the oven and place it on a warmed serving dish, discarding the sprigs of rosemary. Keep warm while making the gravy.

**6.** Carefully pour off all but 1 tablespoon fat from the roasting pan, leaving any meat juices in the pan.

**7.** Add the flour to the remaining liquid in the pan and, using a wire whisk or wooden spoon, stir it over a low heat until a delicate brown. Remove from the heat and stir in the stock and redcurrant jelly. Return to the heat, stirring all the time, and simmer for 2 minutes.

**8.** Check the seasoning and strain into a warmed gravy-boat.

NOTE: For well-done lamb allow 25 minutes per 450g/1lb and 20 minutes extra. When cooked the juices that run out of the meat, when pierced with a skewer, should be clear.

 *CÔTES DU RHÔNE*

# GIGOT OF LAMB WITH STUFFED ARTICHOKE HEARTS

SERVES 4–5
*1 small leg of lamb*
*salt and freshly ground black pepper*
*1 clove of garlic, peeled and cut into slivers*
    *(optional)*
*a large pinch of fresh rosemary leaves*
*2 teaspoons dripping*
*8 globe artichokes or 8 canned artichoke bottoms*
*225g/8oz celeriac*
*110g/4oz mashed potato*
*30g/1oz butter*
*2 teaspoons plain flour*
*150ml/¼ pint brown stock, made with lamb*
    *bones (see page 243)*
*1 teaspoon redcurrant jelly*

To garnish
*1 small bunch of watercress*

**1.** Preheat the oven to 200°C/400°F/gas mark 6.

**2.** Wipe the lamb. Season with salt and pepper. If liked, spike thin slivers of garlic into the meat near the bone. Sprinkle with rosemary. Weigh the lamb and calculate the cooking time at 20 minutes per 450g/1lb plus 20 minutes.

**3.** Heat the dripping in a roasting pan, add the lamb, baste well and roast in the preheated oven for the calculated time. When pierced with a skewer, the juices that run out of the meat should be fairly pink.

**4.** Prepare the fresh artichokes, if using: wash them and cook in a saucepan of boiling salted water for about 45 minutes or until the leaves will pull away easily. Peel away all the leaves, keeping them to serve with a vinaigrette dressing as a first course. Using a teaspoon, scrape out the prickly choke of each artichoke, and trim the base with a sharp knife so that it will stand steady.

**5.** While the artichokes are cooking, peel the celeriac and boil in salted water until quite tender. Drain well. Push the flesh through a sieve. Beat in the mashed potato, half the butter, and salt and pepper to taste.

**6.** Pile this mixture into the artichoke bottoms. Brush with the remaining butter and place on a greased baking sheet.

**7.** When the lamb is cooked, remove from the oven. Turn the oven temperature down to 150°C/300°F/gas mark 2 and put the artichokes into the oven to heat up as the oven cools.

**8.** Place the lamb on a warmed serving dish, removing the garlic if used.

**9.** Carefully pour off all but 1 tablespoon fat from the roasting pan, leaving any meat juices in the pan.

**10.** Add the flour to the remaining liquid in the pan and, using a wire whisk or wooden spoon, stir it over a low heat until a delicate brown. Remove from the heat and stir in the stock and redcurrant jelly. Return to the heat, stirring all the time, and simmer for 2 minutes.

**11.** Check the seasoning and strain into a warmed gravy-boat. Surround the lamb with the artichokes and garnish with bouquets of watercress.

 *RED RHÔNE*

# BUTTERFLY LEG OF LAMB

SERVES 6–8

*1 large leg of lamb, butterfly boned (see page 372)*
*1 tablespoon soy sauce*
*½ onion, sliced*
*4 sprigs of fresh thyme*
*2 bay leaves*
*3 cloves of garlic, peeled and sliced*
*2 tablespoons good-quality olive oil*
*salt and freshly ground black pepper*

For the gravy
*290ml/½ pint brown stock, made with lamb bones (see page 243)*
*50ml/2fl oz red wine*

To garnish
*1 small bunch of watercress*

**1.** Weigh the boned leg of lamb and calculate the cooking time at 8 minutes per 450g/1lb plus 20 minutes.

**2.** Open the leg of lamb and place it skin side down on a large plate. Sprinkle over the soy sauce, onion, thyme, bay leaves, garlic, oil and pepper. Fold the 2 'butterfly' ends inwards to encase the flavourings, cover and leave to marinate overnight.

**3.** Preheat the oven to 230°C/450°F/gas mark 8.

**4.** Open out the boned leg and lay it, flesh side down, in a roasting pan. Sprinkle the fatty side fairly liberally with salt and roast in the oven for 20 minutes, then reduce the oven temperature to 200°C/400°F/gas mark 6 and roast for a further 8 minutes per 450g/1lb. In other words, a 1.8kg/4lb leg (boned weight) will cook for about 50 minutes.

**5.** Turn off the oven. Transfer the meat to a serving plate and leave it in the turned-off oven while making the gravy.

**6.** With a large metal spoon, skim off as much fat as possible from the cooking juices. Add the water and wine and place over direct heat. Bring to the boil and stir well to loosen any sediment stuck to the bottom of the pan. Simmer for 4–5 minutes. Check the seasoning and add extra salt, pepper or soy sauce as necessary, then strain into a warmed gravy boat.

**7.** Garnish the lamb with watercress and serve the gravy separately.

 *MEDIUM RED*

# LAMB CUTLETS REFORM

SERVES 4
*beaten egg*
*salt and freshly ground black pepper*
*12 lamb cutlets, French trimmed (all fat removed*
*    and bones shortened to about 5cm/2in)*
*2 teaspoons very finely chopped cooked ham*
*dried white breadcrumbs*
*1 tablespoon oil*
*15g/½oz butter*

For the sauce
*150ml/¼ pint demi-glace sauce (see page 249)*
*white of 1 hardboiled egg*
*1 gherkin*
*30g/1oz mushrooms*
*½ slice cooked tongue*
*150ml/¼ pint sauce espagnole (see page 249)*

To garnish
*paper cutlet frills*
*sprigs of watercress*

1. Preheat the oven to 230°C/450°F/gas mark 8.
2. Season the beaten egg with salt and pepper.
Brush the cutlets with this.
3. Mix the ham with the breadcrumbs and press this
mixture onto the cutlets, coating both sides well.
4. Heat the oil in a heavy roasting pan and add the
butter. Fry the cutlets briskly in the fat to brown
them on both sides, then cook in the preheated
oven for 5 minutes, until they are tender but still
pink. Drain well on absorbent kitchen paper.
5. Meanwhile, prepare the sauce: put the demi-glace
into a saucepan. Cut the egg white, gherkin, mushrooms and tongue into very thin strips. Add them
to the sauce and heat for 3–4 minutes. Add poiv-
rade sauce to taste. Pour into a warmed gravy-boat.
6. Place a cutlet frill on each cutlet bone. Arrange
the cutlets in an overlapping circle on a warmed
serving dish. Garnish with watercress. Serve the
sauce separately.

NOTE: The cutlets can be simply fried or grilled
if preferred. They are finished in the oven to clear
the cooker top so that there is room to make the
sauce and prepare any vegetables.

 *CLARET*

# FORCEMEAT BALLS

Forcemeat balls are traditionally made to
accompany jugged hare (see page 352).

SERVES 20–24
*450g/1lb good-quality pork sausagemeat*
*1 medium onion, very finely chopped*
*1 tablespoon finely chopped fresh parsley*
*1 tablespoon finely chopped fresh sage or 1*
*    teaspoon dried sage*
*grated zest of ¼ lemon*
*30g/1oz fresh white breadcrumbs*
*salt and freshly ground black pepper*

1. Preheat the oven to 200°C/400°F/gas mark 6.
2. Mix together the sausagemeat, onion, parsley,
sage, lemon zest and breadcrumbs. Season with
salt and pepper.
3. Using wet hands, shape into balls the size of a
ping-pong ball.
4. Place in a roasting pan and cook in the
preheated oven for 30 minutes.

# SIMPLE SAUSAGES

This sausagemeat mixture can be used to fill
sausage skins or simply made into skinless
sausages as described below.

SERVES 4
*450g/1lb minced fatty pork (e.g. from the belly)*
*1 medium onion, very finely chopped (optional)*
*4 slices of white bread, crusts removed, crumbed*
*1 egg*
*3 fresh sage leaves, chopped or 1 teaspoon dried*
*    sage*
*salt and freshly ground black pepper*
*fat for frying*

1. Mix together the pork and onion, if using.
2. Stir the breadcrumbs into the mixture with the
egg and sage.
3. Add plenty of salt and pepper and mix
thoroughly. Taste and season further if necessary.
4. Wet your hands and form the mixture into
sausage shapes.
5. Fry the sausages in hot fat, turning them
frequently. They should cook slowly, and will take
about 12 minutes if 2.5cm/1in diameter.

# PORK CHOPS WITH ROSEMARY

SERVES 4

*1 small onion, finely chopped*
*1 teaspoon finely chopped fresh parsley*
*1 teaspoon finely chopped fresh rosemary*
*1 egg*
*salt and freshly ground black pepper*
*4 × 170g/6oz pork chops, neatly trimmed*
*dried white breadcrumbs*
*oil*

1. Mix the onion, parsley, rosemary and egg together in a bowl. Season well with salt and pepper. Coat each pork chop with the egg mixture and then dip in breadcrumbs, covering them well.
2. Heat the oil in a frying pan. Add the chops and fry for 12–15 minutes, until golden brown on both sides and tender all the way through.

 *MEDIUM RED*

# SPARE RIBS

SERVES 4

*1.25kg/2½lb skinned pork belly pieces (American spare ribs)*

For the marinade
*2 tablespoons clear honey*
*2 tablespoons soy sauce*
*½ clove of garlic, crushed*
*juice of 1 lemon*
*salt and freshly ground black pepper*

1. Mix together the ingredients for the marinade and soak the spare ribs in it for at least 1 hour. The longer they marinate the better.
2. Preheat the oven to 180°C/350°F/gas mark 4.
3. Put the ribs, with the marinade, into a roasting pan and bake, covered, for a further 45 minutes. Remove the cover and cook, basting occasionally, for 45 minutes, or until glazed and sticky.

 *MEDIUM RED*

# GLAZED HAM OR GAMMON JOINT

SERVES 4–6

*1 ham or gammon joint*
*1 onion*
*1 carrot*
*1 bay leaf*
*fresh parsley stalks*
*black peppercorns*
*2 tablespoons demerara sugar*
*1 teaspoon dry English mustard*
*a handful of cloves*

1. Soak the joint overnight in cold water to remove excess salt.
2. Place it in a large saucepan of cold water and add the onion, carrot, bay leaf, parsley stalks and peppercorns. Bring slowly to the boil, cover and simmer for 25 minutes per 450g/1lb. For large joints, (i.e. 3.5kg/8lb upwards) allow 20 minutes per 450g/1lb.
3. Leave the joint to cool slightly in the stock. Then lift out and carefully pull off the skin without removing any of the fat. Reserve the cooking liquor as ham stock.
4. Mix the sugar and mustard together and press all over the joint to form an even coating.
5. Using a sharp knife, cut a lattice pattern across the joint through the sugar and fat. Press on again any sugar that falls off. Stick a clove into each diamond segment, or into the cuts where the lines cross.
6. Preheat the oven to 220°C/424°F/gas mark 7. Bake the joint for about 20 minutes, or until brown and slightly caramelized.

NOTES: If you haven't time to soak salty ham or gammon overnight, cook it for 30 minutes in plain water and then transfer to a pan of simmering water with the vegetables and herbs.

The joint can be decorated with a ham frill: to make one, cut a piece of greaseproof paper to about 12 × 30cm/5 × 12in. Fold it loosely in half lengthways, without pressing down the fold. Make 5cm/2in cuts, 1cm/1/2in apart, parallel to the end of the paper, cutting through both thicknesses from the folded side towards the open sides. Make the cuts all along the strip. Now open out the paper and refold it lengthways in the opposite direction. Wrap the frill round the ham bone and secure with a paper clip.

 *RED BURGUNDY*

# ROAST PORK

SERVES 4
*1.35kg/3lb loin of pork, with skin intact*
*oil*
*salt*

For the gravy
*2 teaspoons plain flour*
*290ml/½ pint brown stock (see page 243)*

To serve
*1 small bunch of watercress*
*apple sauce (see page 259)*

**1.** Preheat the oven to 220°C/425°F/gas mark 7.
**2.** Score the rind (crackling skin) with a sharp knife in cuts about 5mm/¼in apart, cutting through the skin but not right through the fat.
**3.** Brush the skin with oil and sprinkle with salt to help give a crisp crackling.
**4.** Place the pork in a roasting pan and roast in the top of the preheated oven for 1 hour 40 minutes (25 minutes per 450g/1lb plus 25 minutes). After 30 minutes turn down the oven temperature to 190°C/375°F/gas mark 5.
**5.** Once the pork is cooked, turn off the oven, put the pork on a serving dish and replace it in the oven, leaving the door ajar if it is still very hot.
**6.** Tip all but 2 teaspoons of the fat from the roasting pan, reserving as much of the meat juices as possible.
**7.** Add the flour and stir over the heat until well browned.
**8.** Remove from the heat, add the stock and mix well with a wire whisk or wooden spoon. Return to the heat and bring slowly to the boil, whisking all the time. Simmer for a few minutes until the gravy is shiny. Season to taste with salt and pepper. Strain into a warmed gravy-boat.
**9.** Garnish the pork with watercress and serve with the gravy and apple sauce.

NOTE: Remove the crackling before carving, then cut it into thin strips with kitchen scissors.

 *RED BURGUNDY*

# ROAST SUCKLING PIG

A traditional 'feast' food, suckling pig is always roasted whole, ideally on a spit, but if one is not available, in an oven. During Elizabethan times it was often served boned and stuffed as a chaudfroid.

Piglets up to 6 months old can be used after which time they are called porkers.

A roast suckling pig should be cooked to the point where it is just cooked inside, with a crisp and brown skin, and is served with a good gravy.

This recipe has been adapted from a recipe by Pierre Koffman.

SERVES 12–15
*1 × 6kg/15lb suckling pig with liver, heart and*
  *lungs*
*200g/7oz duck fat, melted*

For the stuffing
*2 onions, finely chopped*
*55g/2oz butter*
*6 cloves of garlic, crushed*
*600g/1¼lb boneless pork*
*400g/14oz pork fat*
*150ml/¼ pint dry white wine*
*4 egg yolks*
*200g/7oz fresh white breadcrumbs*
*2 tablespoons chopped fresh parsley*
*salt and freshly ground black pepper*

For the gravy
*2 tablespoons plain flour*
*water*

**1.** Prepare the stuffing: cook the onions in the butter until soft but not coloured, add the garlic and cook for a further minute.
**2.** Mince the pig's liver, heart and lungs, together with the pork meat and the fat.
**3.** Mix with all the remaining stuffing ingredients and season with salt and pepper.
**4.** Stuff the pig with this mixture and sew up with large, loose stitches, using a trussing needle and thread.
**5.** Roast the pig: either put it on a spit in front of the fire, with a pan below to catch the juices, and roast for 4–5 hours, turning constantly and

basting with duck fat to prevent the skin from cracking. Or roast in an oven preheated to 180°C/350°F/gas mark 4 for 3 hours, basting frequently with duck fat.

**6.** Test that the pig is cooked: a skewer inserted into the thickest part (leg or shoulder) will come out hot and the juices will run clear.

**7.** Transfer the pig to a warmed serving dish and make a gravy with the roasting juices left in the pan. Pour all the juices from the pan into a glass bowl. Deglaze the pan with water.

**8.** Put 2–3 tablespoons of the fat from the roasting pan into a large saucepan, stir in the flour and brown gently over a medium heat. Use a baster to extract the roasting juices from the bowl, leaving the fat behind. Stir the juices into the flour, add some water, bring to the boil and simmer until the gravy has a syrupy consistency.

NOTES: If you roast the pig on a wire rack the skin will crisp up all over.

Basting with duck fat (or oil) is essential for a crispy skin and to prevent cracking.

For a traditional look, put an orange in the pig's mouth during cooking (an apple will disintegrate).

The pig can be eaten hot or cold: either way the meat should be tender and succulent.

 *RED BURGUNDY*

# LOIN OF PORK WITH PRUNES

SERVES 4
*1.35kg/3lb loin of pork without skin or much fat*
*oil for frying*
*15g/¹⁄₂oz butter*
*1 onion, finely chopped*
*290ml/¹⁄₂ pint brown stock (see page 243)*
*100ml/3¹⁄₂fl oz red wine*
*110g/4oz no-need-to-soak prunes*
*1 bay leaf*
*1 tablespoon redcurrant jelly*
*2 sprigs of fresh thyme*
*150ml/¹⁄₄ pint single cream*

To garnish
*1 small bunch of watercress*

**1.** Preheat the oven to 150°C/300°F/gas mark 2.

**2.** Heat the oil in a flameproof casserole. Add the butter and, when foaming, add the pork. Fry until lightly browned all over. Add the onion and fry until golden.

**3.** Add the stock, wine, one-third of the prunes, the redcurrant jelly, bay leaf and thyme. Bring to the boil, then cover and cook in the oven for 1¹⁄₂ hours.

**4.** Remove the pork from the casserole and slice neatly. Arrange in overlapping slices on a serving dish and keep warm in the turned-out oven while you make the sauce.

**5.** Strain the cooking liquor, removing any excess fat. Boil until reduced to a syrupy consistency. Add the cream and remaining prunes.

**6.** Spoon the sauce over the pork and garnish with watercress.

 *MEDIUM RED*

# PORK MEDALLIONS VALLÉE D'AUGE

SERVES 4
*675g/1¹⁄₂lb pork fillets*
*salt and freshly ground black pepper*
*2 tablespoons oil*
*1 medium onion, very finely chopped*
*1 stick of celery, chopped*
*2 teaspoons Calvados*
*30g/1oz cooked ham, diced*
*150ml/¹⁄₄ pint dry cider*
*2 dessert apples*
*lemon juice*
*caster sugar*
*15g/¹⁄₂oz butter*
*1 egg yolk*
*150ml/¹⁄₄ pint double cream*

To garnish
*a bouquet of watercress*

**1.** Preheat the oven to 180°C/350°F/gas mark 4.

**2.** Prepare the pork fillets by trimming off any fat and membrane with a sharp, flexible knife. Season with salt and pepper.

3. Heat 1 tablespoon of the oil in a large frying pan and brown the fillets carefully on all sides. Place them in a casserole dish.

4. Lower the heat under the frying pan, add the onion and celery and fry gently until soft but not coloured. Add the Calvados and set alight with a match. When the flames subside, add the ham and cider, and allow to simmer for 2 minutes.

5. Pour the contents of the pan over the pork fillet, cover and cook in the preheated oven for about 20 minutes or until the fillets are completely tender.

6. Meanwhile, peel, quarter and core the apples and cut them into wedges. Brush each wedge with lemon juice and sprinkle with sugar. Melt the butter in the frying pan and fry the apple wedges until barely soft and brown on both sides. Keep them warm.

7. Remove the pork fillets from the oven and keep them warm while preparing the sauce.

8. Strain the liquor from the casserole (reserve the ham and vegetables) into a saucepan and bring to simmering point. Mix the egg yolk with the cream in a bowl and add a little of the hot stock to the mixture. Return this to the saucepan and set over a gentle heat until the sauce becomes creamy and thickens slightly, but take great care not to curdle it by boiling.

9. Arrange the reserved ham and vegetables neatly on a warmed serving dish. Slice the pork fillets into medallions and arrange on top of the ham and vegetables. Coat with the creamy sauce and garnish with the apple wedges and a bouquet of watercress.

 *MEDIUM RED*

# PORK FILLETS IN CIDER

SERVES 4
*1 tablespoon oil*
*15g/¹/₂oz butter*
*1 medium onion, finely chopped*
*675g/1¹/₂lb pork tenderloin (fillet), trimmed*
*290ml¹/₂ pint cider*
*salt and freshly ground black pepper*
*1 bay leaf*
*1 tablespoon single cream*

To garnish
*2 dessert apples*
*butter*
*caster sugar*
*chopped fresh parsley*

1. Preheat the oven to 180°C/350°F/gas mark 4.

2. Heat the oil in a frying pan. Add the butter and when hot add the pork and brown quickly all over. Remove to a plate. Reduce the heat, add the onion and cook slowly until soft. Return the pork to the pan. Add the cider and bay leaf. Bring to the boil, then tip into a flameproof casserole. Season with salt and pepper, cover and cook in the preheated oven for 10–15 minutes.

3. Peel, and core the apples and cut into wedges. Fry in butter, sprinkled with sugar, until lightly coloured.

4. Take out the pork and keep warm. Strain the cooking liquor, remove the bay leaf from the sieve, and place the onions in a serving dish. Keep warm.

5. Boil the cooking liquor rapidly until reduced to a syrupy consistency. Add the cream. Taste and adjust the seasoning if necessary.

6. Slice the pork thickly, arrange on top of the onions, pour over the sauce and sprinkle with parsley and garnish with the fried apple.

 *CIDER OR LIGHT RED*

# PORK FILLETS WITH RED AND GREEN PEPPERS

SERVES 4
*675g/1¹/₂lb pork tenderloin (fillet)*
*2 tablespoons sunflower oil*
*1 clove of garlic, crushed*
*1 large onion, sliced*
*1 red pepper, cored, deseeded and sliced*
*1 green pepper, cored, deseeded and sliced*
*1 teaspoon ground cumin*
*1 teaspoon ground coriander*
*1 teaspoon ground cinnamon*
*1 teaspoon ground turmeric*
*¹/₂ teaspoon ground mild chilli powder*
*2 tablespoons Greek yoghurt*
*1 tablespoon roughly chopped fresh mint*

Above: Butterfly Leg of Lamb

Above: Veal Cutlets and Grilled Vegetables with Aïoli. Right: Oxtail Stew.

Left: Cassoulet. Above: Pizza.

Above: Greek Parsley Pasta. Right: Salmon and Plaice Ravioli with Basil Sauce.

Left: Caroline's Ricotta Pie. Above: Grilled Polenta and Prosciutto Salad.

Above: Cassis Cream Pie. Right: Three-Chocolate Bavarois.

Left: Striped Chocolate and Grand Marnier Bavarois. Above: Black Coffee Jelly with Greek Yoghurt.

Above: Ballymaloe's Jelly of Fresh Raspberries. Right: Charlotte's Higgledy Piggledy Tart.

Above: Poached Pear and Polenta Tart.

**1.** Trim off any fat and membrane from the pork with a sharp, flexible knife. Cut the meat into 5mm/¼in slices.

**2.** Heat the oil in a large sauté pan and brown the meat, a few pieces at a time, until evenly coloured all over. Remove to a plate.

**3.** Add the garlic, onion and peppers to the pan and allow to soften without browning for a few minutes. Add the dry spices and cook for a further 2 minutes. Stir regularly and add a little extra oil if they are in danger of getting too dry or burnt.

**4.** Remove the pan from the heat. Return the pork and add just enough water to cover the meat and vegetables. Return to the heat and bring gradually to the boil, stirring constantly.

**5.** Simmer for about 10 minutes or until the pork is tender. Remove from the pan and reduce the sauce, by boiling rapidly, to half. Return the pork to the pan, add the yoghurt, and heat through without boiling. Remove from the heat, add the mint and serve immediately.

 *RED RHÔNE*

# MEDALLIONS OF PORK WITH PRUNES

This recipe has been adapted from *Cuisine à la Carte* by Anton Mosimann.

SERVES 4
*8 pork medallions cut 2.5cm/1in thick, well trimmed*
*8 small prunes, stones removed*
*seasoned plain flour*
*1 tablespoon olive oil*
*20g/¾oz butter*
*100ml/3½fl oz dry white wine*
*150ml/¼ pint brown stock (see page 243)*
*40g/1¼oz butter, diced*

To garnish
*50g/2oz turned carrots, boiled and refreshed*
*50g/2oz turned turnips, boiled and refreshed*
*8 small prunes, blanched, stones removed*
*20g/¾oz butter*
*a little chopped fresh parsley*

**1.** Flatten the pork medallions lightly between 2 sheets of wet greaseproof paper.

**2.** Place the prunes in cold water in a saucepan, cover and bring to the boil.

**3.** Remove from the heat and set aside for 30 minutes in the water.

**4.** Pour off the water, cut the prunes in half and dry on a cloth.

**5.** Push the prunes through the pork medallions. Dust with seasoned flour.

**6.** Heat the oil and butter in a large frying pan.

**7.** Put in the pork medallions and sauté over a low heat on both sides until juicy, basting constantly.

**8.** Remove the medallions from the pan and keep warm. Pour off all the fat from the pan.

**9.** Add the wine and stock and reduce, by boiling rapidly, to about 150ml/¼ pint. Strain through a sieve, reheat and gradually add the butter, piece by piece, whisking all the time until smooth and glossy. Season to taste and pour over the medallions.

**10.** Sauté the carrots, turnips and prunes for the garnish in the butter and scatter around the pork.

**11.** Garnish with parsley and serve immediately.

 *MEDIUM RED*

# JAMBALAYA

SERVES 4–6
*450g/1lb pork tenderloin (fillet)*
*2–3 tablespoons oil*
*1 onion, finely chopped*
*2 sticks of celery, finely chopped*
*55g/2oz garlic sausage, diced*
*110g/4oz rice*
*2 teaspoons ground ginger*
*½ teaspoon ground turmeric*
*½ teaspoon paprika pepper*
*290ml/½ pint white stock, made with chicken bones (see page 243)*
*lemon juice*
*salt and freshly ground black pepper*
*110g/4oz peeled cooked prawns*

**1.** Trim the pork and cut into 1cm/½in cubes. Heat half the oil in a heavy saucepan and quickly fry the pork until well browned. Lift the pieces out and put them aside. Add the onion and celery to the pan, reduce the heat and fry over a low heat until soft and evenly coloured. Lift them out on to a plate.

**2.** Now fry the garlic sausage, adding more oil if necessary and turning them until evenly browned. Lift them out and add to the pork. Heat the remaining oil, stir in the rice and fry, stirring constantly, until opaque. Add the ginger, turmeric and paprika and fry for 30 seconds.

**3.** Add the stock and put all the fried food back into the pan. Bring to the boil and season with a dash of lemon juice, salt and pepper. Reduce the heat, cover and simmer until all the stock has been absorbed and the rice is cooked (about 20 minutes). Add the prawns and warm them in the rice for a minute or two before serving.

 *RED RHÔNE*

# SWEET AND SOUR PORK

SERVES 4
*675g/1½lb lean boneless pork*
*½ teaspoon salt*
*1 tablespoon cornflour*
*oil for deep-frying*
*1 green pepper, cored, deseeded and sliced*

For the sweet and sour sauce
*1 teaspoon cornflour*
*4 tablespoons water*
*2 tablespoons sugar*
*2 tablespoons wine vinegar*
*2 tablespoons tomato purée*
*2 tablespoons orange juice*
*2 tablespoons soy sauce*
*2 tablespoons finely chopped pineapple*
*½ teaspoon oil*

**1.** Start with the sauce: blend the cornflour with the water and mix it with the sugar, vinegar, tomato purée, orange juice and soy sauce.
**2.** Fry the chopped pineapple in the oil for 1 minute. Add this to the sauce.
**3.** Cut the pork into 2cm/¾in cubes. Sprinkle with salt and toss in the cornflour.
**4.** Heat the oil in a deep-fryer until a crumb

sizzles vigorously in it. Deep-fry the pork for 4 minutes. Drain on absorbent kitchen paper.
**5.** Heat 1 tablespoon oil in a wide pan. Fry the green pepper quickly for 30 seconds. Reduce the heat, add the sauce to the pan and cook for 1 minute. If the sauce seems too thick, add a little water before serving.

 *BEER OR RED BURGUNDY*

# JAMBON PERSILLÉ

SERVES 6
*1 × 900g/2lb piece of mild gammon or unsmoked lean bacon*
*1 slice of onion*
*1 bay leaf*
*½ carrot*
*2 parsley stalks*
*6 black peppercorns*
*1 litre/2 pints white stock, made with veal bones (see page 243) plus 15g/½oz powdered gelatine if the stock is not jellied*
*150ml/¼ pint dry white wine*
*1 tablespoon tarragon vinegar*
*2 egg shells*
*2 egg whites*
*3 tablespoons finely chopped fresh parsley*

**1.** Soak the gammon in cold water overnight.
**2.** Simmer it in fresh water to cover with the onion, bay leaf, carrot, parsley stalks and peppercorns for about 1½ hours, or until tender. Remove from the heat and leave to cool in the liquid.
**3.** Put the stock into a large clean saucepan. If it is not set to a solid jelly, sprinkle in the gelatine. Add the wine and vinegar. Set over a low heat to dissolve the gelatine or to melt the jelly, then allow to cool.
**4.** Put the crushed shells and egg whites into the stock. Place over the heat and whisk steadily with a balloon whisk until the mixture begins to boil. Stop whisking immediately and remove the pan from the heat. Allow the mixture to subside. Take care not to break the crust formed by the egg white.
**5.** Bring the aspic just up to the boil again, and again allow to subside. Repeat this once more; the

egg-white will trap the sediment in the stock and clear the aspic. Allow to cool for 2 minutes.

**6.** Fix a double layer of fine muslin or absorbent kitchen paper over a clean bowl and carefully strain the aspic through it, taking care to hold the egg-white crust back. When all the liquid is through, or almost all of it, allow the egg white to slip into the muslin or paper. Then strain the aspic again – this time through both egg-white crust and cloth. Do not try to hurry the process by squeezing the cloth, or murky aspic will result. Allow to cool.

**7.** Cut the gammon into thick slices and then into neat strips. Arrange a neat layer in the bottom of a mould or soufflé dish which has been rinsed out with cold water or very lightly oiled.

**8.** Pour in enough almost-cold jelly to hold the gammon in place when the jelly sets. Leave in the refrigerator to set.

**9.** Mix the parsley into half the just-liquid jelly and pour 1cm/½in into the mould. Allow to set. Arrange a second layer of ham on top and set it in place with clear jelly.

**10.** Continue the layers in this way, finishing with clear jelly. Chill well.

**11.** To turn out: dip the mould into hot water to loosen the jelly. Invert a plate over the mould and turn the plate and mould over together. Give a slight shake to dislodge the jelly and remove the mould.

NOTES: A good but less elegant jambon persillé is made with uncleared veal jelly, chopped parsley and cubes of cooked ham simply combined in a dish and allowed to set.

When clearing it is advisable to scald the saucepan, sieve and whisk before use.

 *RED BURGUNDY*

# JUNIPER PORK CHOPS

SERVES 4
*4 pork chops at least 2cm/¾in thick*
*4 juniper berries*
*salt and freshly ground black pepper*
*7g/¼oz butter*

*2 tablespoons dry white wine*
*2 tablespoons water*
*4 tablespoons double cream*

To garnish
*1 small bunch of watercress*

**1.** Crush the juniper berries with a rolling pin or in a mortar.

**2.** Cut off the excess fat from the chops, leaving only 5mm/¼in all the way round. Reserve this fat. Sprinkle with salt and pepper.

**3.** Heat the fat cut from the chops in a frying pan and cook until the liquid fat has run out and the pieces are crisp. Remove the pieces with a slotted spoon and discard.

**4.** Put the chops into the hot pan. Fry for 5–7 minutes on each side until browned. Remove the chops and keep warm in a low oven.

**5.** Pour off the fat from the pan and add the butter. Toss the juniper berries in the melted butter for 1 minute. Add the wine and water, bring to the boil and reduce, by boiling rapidly, to half the original quantity. Add the cream and reduce, by boiling rapidly, to a thin but syrupy sauce. Season to taste with salt and pepper and pour over the chops.

**6.** Garnish with watercress.

 *LIGHT RED*

# GRILLED PORK CHOPS WITH CARAMELIZED APPLES

SERVES 4
*4 × 170g/6oz pork chops*
*a little oil*
*freshly ground black pepper*
*3–4 fresh sage leaves, chopped, or a pinch of dried sage*

To garnish
*2 dessert apples*
*butter for frying*
*1 teaspoon sugar*
*a few sprigs of watercress*

1. Preheat the grill to its highest setting.

2. Trim the rind from the chops and snip short cuts through the fat towards the meat, about 1cm/½in apart, to prevent curling up during grilling. Brush lightly with oil.

3. Season with pepper and sage.

4. Grill the chops for 5–7 minutes on each side, or until tender right through. Keep warm on a serving platter.

5. Peel and core the apples and cut them into quarters.

6. Melt a small knob of butter in a frying pan and when it is foaming add the apples. Sprinkle with a little sugar and fry lightly on both sides until golden-brown but not mushy. The sugar will caramelize, giving a brown, toffee-like coating to the apples.

7. Garnish the chops with the caramelized apples and the watercress.

 *MEDIUM RED*

# STIR-FRIED PORK

Although this recipe uses pork fillet it is still reasonably low in saturated fat.

SERVES 4
*450g/1lb pork tenderloin (fillet), trimmed*
*1 tablespoon dry sherry*
*1 tablespoon soy sauce*
*1cm/½in piece of fresh root ginger, peeled and*
 *grated*
*1 bunch of spring onions, cut into rings*
*110g/4oz baby sweetcorn, blanched*
*110g/4oz mangetout, topped and tailed*
*freshly ground black pepper*

For the sauce
*1 tablespoon dry sherry*
*1 tablespoon soy sauce*

1. Cut the pork into strips the size of your little finger and marinate for at least 1 hour in the sherry, soy sauce and ginger.

2. In a non-stick frying pan or wok, stir-fry the pork with a little of the marinade for 4 minutes.

3. Add the remaining marinade and the spring

onions, baby corn and mangetout. Cook for a further 4 minutes. Add the sauce and reheat.

4. Season with pepper and serve.

NOTE: If not using a non-tick frying pan or wok, the pork will have to be fried in a little oil.

 *LIGHT RED*

# PORK MEDALLIONS WITH GINGER SAUCE

SERVES 6–8
For the marinade
*225ml/8fl oz teriyaki sauce*
*110g/4oz clear honey*
*110ml/4fl oz medium-dry sherry*
*2 teaspoons peeled and finely chopped fresh*
 *ginger root*
*2 tablespoons sesame oil*
*3 pork fillets, cut into 2.5cm/1in medallions*
*oil for frying*

1. Whisk together the marinade ingredients and pour over the pork medallions. Cover and allow to marinate for 2 hours, turning the meat occasionally.

2. Drain off the marinade. Strain into a saucepan, bring to the boil and allow to reduce a little until the sauce has thickened slightly.

3. Heat a little oil in a frying pan. Fry the medallions a few at a time until cooked through. Serve with the sauce.

NOTE: This goes very well with stir-fried batons of parsnip and carrot.

 *LIGHT RED*

# BRAISED PIG'S TROTTERS

This recipe comes from Marco Pierre White's
*White Heat* He calls it Braised Pig's Trotters
'Pierre Koffman'.

SERVES 6
*6 pig's trotters, from back legs only*
*1 tablespoon oil*
*2 carrots, cubed*
*1 stick of celery, cubed*
*1 onion, diced*
*290ml/½ pint dry white wine*
*425ml/¾ pint white stock, made with veal bones*
    *(see page 243)*
*1 sprig of fresh thyme*
*½ bay leaf*
*salt and freshly ground black pepper*

For the stuffing
*40g/1½oz dried morels*
*675g/1½lb veal sweetbreads, soaked in water*
    *overnight*
*½ onion, diced*
*1 × 290ml/½ pint quantity chicken mousse (see*
    *page 422)*
*olive oil for frying*

For the sauce
*2 chicken legs*
*2 tablespoons sunflower oil*
*110g/4oz mushrooms, sliced*
*110g/4oz shallots, chopped*
*½ head of garlic, sliced across to halve each clove*
*1 sprig of fresh thyme*
*½ fresh bay leaf*
*1½ tablespoons sherry vinegar*
*1½ tablespoons cognac*
*425ml/¾ pint Madeira*
*570ml/1 pint white stock, made with veal bones*
    *(see page 243)*
*200ml/⅓ pint white stock, made with chicken*
    *bones (see page 243)*
*150ml/¼ pint water*
*4 dried morels*
*lemon juice to taste*
*a few drops of cream*
*a knob of butter*
*olive oil for frying*

To garnish
*72 wild mushrooms, chopped*
*30g/1oz butter*
*72 roast button onions (optional)*
*900g/2lb mashed potato (see page 212)*

1. Soak the pig's trotters in cold water for 24
hours. Drain and pat dry. Singe off any remaining
hairs, particularly between the toes. Scrape off the
singed stubble and any stray hairs with a knife.
2. Slit the underside of each trotter lengthways,
starting at the ankle end. Using a sharp knife, cut
the main tendon and then start to work off the
skin by cutting around it close to the bone.
(Remember that the trotter skin is effectively
going to form a sausage skin, so be careful not to
tear it.)
3. Pull the skin right down and cut through the
knuckle joint at the first set of toes. Continue to
pull the skin off as far as the last toe joint. Snap
and twist off the bones and discard them.
4. Preheat the oven to 220°C/425°F/gas mark 7.
5. Heat the oil in flameproof casserole dish and
fry the carrot, celery and onion over a medium
heat for about 2 minutes. Add the trotter skins,
outside down, and the wine and boil until the
wine has reduced by about half.
6. Add the stock, thyme and bay leaf. Bring to the
boil, then cover and cook in the preheated oven
for about 3 hours. During cooking, shake the
casserole from time to time to prevent the skins
from sticking to the pan. Remove the skins from
the cooking liquor (they should be a wonderful
oak-brown colour) and leave to cool.

TO MAKE THE STUFFING:
7. Soak the morels in cold water for 10 minutes.
Drain and rinse. Repeat this process once more.
8. Put the sweetbreads into a saucepan of clean
cold water, bring to the boil and poach for 2
minutes. Drain and refresh under running cold
water. Remove the membrane and sinew from the
sweetbreads, saving the trimmings for the sauce.
Cut the sweetbreads into cubes and fry these in
very hot oil in a large frying pan over a high heat
until they are golden-brown with a crunchy
texture.
9. Add the soaked morels and the onion and cook
for 1 minute only. (Remember that this mixture is
to be cooked again in the trotters.) Season well

with salt and white pepper, drain the mixture through a colander and leave to cool.

**10.** When the mixture is cool, stir in just enough chicken mousse to bind it together. Taste and adjust the seasoning again, if necessary.

### TO MAKE THE SAUCE:

**11.** Fry the chicken legs and sweetbread trimmings in the oil in a large frying pan over a medium heat until they are golden brown but not cooked through.

**12.** Add the mushrooms, shallots, garlic, thyme and bay leaf and stir well. Deglaze the contents of the pan with the vinegar, cooking to drive off the acidity. Deglaze in the same way with the cognac.

**13.** Add the Madeira and reduce the mixture until it has a caramelized appearance. Add the stocks and water to cover the bones and vegetables. Add the dried morels and simmer the mixture for 20 minutes. Pass the sauce through a sieve or muslin cloth several times, reserving the morels for garnish if you wish. Keep warm.

**14.** Just before serving, reduce the strained stock just a little to a coating consistency. Taste and adjust the seasoning. Add a few drops of lemon juice and one or two drops of cream, then add the butter and a little pepper. Taste the sauce while adding all these to get exactly the required flavour.

### TO STUFF THE TROTTERS:

**15.** Cut 6 large squares of kitchen foil, each big enough to wrap and seal a trotter.

**16.** Butter one side of each piece of foil, then place on a trotter outside skin side down. Pick out and discard the little pieces of fat inside the skin.

**17.** Divide the stuffing mixture between the 6 trotters. There should be enough to give each of the trotters enough bulk to hold its original shape.

**18.** Roll the foil tightly around each trotter, making a sausage shape, and twist at either end to seal securely. Chill the trotter parcels in the refrigerator for about 15 minutes to allow to set.

**19.** Poach the trotters in a large saucepan of boiling water for about 12 minutes.

### TO MAKE THE GARNISH:

**20.** Cook the wild mushrooms in half the butter in a large frying pan over a high heat until they produce their liquid.

**21.** Drain the mushrooms and cook them again in the remaining butter for 1–2 minutes. Keep warm.

### TO SERVE:

**22.** Remove the trotter parcels from the poaching water and unwrap them.

**23.** Carefully place the trotters, uncut skin side up, on 6 warmed individual serving plates.

**24.** Place 12 onions, if using, on each plate and scatter the mushrooms over the trotter.

**25.** Spoon a serving of mashed potato alongside each trotter and dot it with slices of the morels reserved from the sauce.

**26.** Coat the trotters with the sauce and spoon more sauce around the plate.

# MARCO'S CHICKEN MOUSSE

*225g/8oz chicken breast, skin and sinews*
*    removed, chopped*
*a pinch of ground mace*
*1 tablespoon chopped fresh tarragon*
*1 egg*
*2 teaspoons salt*
*200ml/7fl oz double cream*

**1.** Process the chicken flesh in a blender for 1 minute with the mace and tarragon.

**2.** Add the egg and salt and work the mixture for another minute in the blender.

**3.** Chill the resulting mixture for 10–15 minutes in the refrigerator before adding the cream (this will prevent the mixture from separating later).

**4.** Force the mixture through a sieve to ensure a velvety texture. Taste and adjust the seasoning. Store any excess mousse, wrapped in clingfilm, in the refrigerator.

NOTE: If you prefer a crisp skin, glaze the trotters with honey and grill briefly before serving.

 *STRONG WHITE, SUCH AS SAUVIGNON, OR LOIRE RED*

# PORK PIE

SERVES 8–10

*675g/1½lb pork tenderloin (fillet)*
*2 tablespoons oil*
*450g/1lb flour quantity pâte à pâte (see page 467)*
*45g/1½oz butter*
*45g/1½ plain flour*
*225ml/8fl oz white stock, made with veal bones*
    *(see page 243)*
*55ml/2fl oz dry white wine*
*2 eggs*
*55ml/2fl oz double cream*
*salt and freshly ground black pepper*
*1 tablespoon chopped fresh parsley*
*2 tablespoons chopped fresh thyme*
*beaten egg to glaze*

**1.** Preheat the oven to 200°C/400°F/gas mark 6.
**2.** Trim the pork, discarding any fat, sinew or gristle. Brown in the oil, place in a roasting pan and roast uncovered in the preheated oven for 30 minutes. Remove from the oven and allow to cool.
**3.** Place one-third of the pastry in the refrigerator. Divide the remaining pastry in half. Roll out one piece into a long strip to fit the sides of a 20cm/8in spring-clip tin. Press it neatly round the sides. Roll out the second piece to fit the base of the tin. Press the base and sides together carefully. Prick the base all over with a fork and place it in the refrigerator to chill.
**4.** Meanwhile, make the filling: mince the pork finely.
**5.** Melt the butter in a heavy saucepan, stir in the flour and stir over the heat for 1 minute. Remove the pan from the heat, add the stock and wine and mix well. Return to the heat and stir or whisk until it comes to the boil. Simmer for 5 minutes, stirring occasionally. (If the sauce is too thick add some water, but it should be a thick panade.)
**6.** Remove the pan from the heat, separate the eggs and beat the yolks into the sauce with the cream. Season carefully with salt, pepper, parsley and thyme. Add the minced pork.
**7.** Whisk the egg whites until stiff, then fold into the mixture. Check the seasoning.
**8.** Place the filling in the pastry case, making it slightly domed in the centre.

**9.** Roll out the remaining pastry for the lid. Dampen the bottom edge with water and press the lid on to the pastry case. Trim and crimp the edges. Make a neat hole in the middle of the lid. Decorate with pastry trimmings made into leaves.
**10.** Brush with egg glaze and place on a baking sheet. Bake in the preheated oven for 40 minutes. Serve cold.

 *LIGHT RED/ROSÉ*

# FLAT HAM PIE

SERVES 10

*450g/1lb flour quantity pâte à pâte (see page 467)*
*110g/4oz Gruyère or Cheddar cheese, grated*
*55g/2oz Parmesan cheese, freshly grated*
*85g/3oz butter, melted*
*110g/4oz fresh white breadcrumbs*
*450g/1lb cooked ham*
*2 tablespoons chopped fresh dill or chives*
*1 large clove of garlic, crushed*
*150ml/¼ pint soured cream*
*freshly ground black pepper*
*juice of 1 lemon*
*beaten egg*

**1.** Roll the pastry out into rectangles, one the size of a Swiss roll tin, the other slightly larger. Chill in the refrigerator for 20 minutes.
**2.** Preheat the oven to 200°C/400°F/gas mark 6.
**3.** Lightly grease and flour the back of a Swiss roll tin or a rectangular baking sheet. Put the small rectangle of pastry on it and prick all over with a fork. Bake in the preheated oven for 15 minutes, then leave to cool on a wire rack.
**4.** Mix together the cheeses, the melted butter and the breadcrumbs. Scatter half this mixture all over the baked pastry, leaving a good 1cm/½in clear all round the edge.
**5.** Chop the ham into small pieces and scatter it on top of the cheese mixture. Then scatter over the dill or chives.
**6.** Mix the garlic with the soured cream and spread all over the ham. Season well with pepper but no salt.
**7.** Sprinkle evenly with the lemon juice and top with the remaining cheese mixture. Wet the edge of the bottom piece of pastry with lightly beaten

egg and put the top sheet of pastry in place, pressing the edges to seal it well.

**8.** Use any pastry trimmings to decorate the pie and brush all over with beaten egg.

**9.** Bake in the preheated oven until the pastry is crisp and pale brown. Serve hot or cold.

 *LIGHT RED/ROSÉ*

# VEAL ESCALOPES WITH ROSEMARY

SERVES 4

*4 × 140g/5oz veal escalopes*
*salt and freshly ground black pepper*
*30g/1oz butter*
*1 teaspoon chopped fresh rosemary or*
    *½ teaspoon dried rosemary*
*2 tablespoons dry white wine*
*1 tablespoon single cream*

**1.** If the escalopes are not very thin, place them between 2 sheets of wet greaseproof paper or clingfilm and beat gently with a mallet or rolling pin. Season with salt and pepper.

**2.** Melt the butter with the rosemary in a frying pan over a medium heat. When the butter is foaming, fry the escalopes (one or two at a time if they won't fit in the pan together) for 1–2 minutes on each side until a very delicate brown. Remove the veal with a slotted spoon or fish slice and keep warm in a very low oven.

**3.** Pour the wine into the pan and heat, scraping the surface of the pan with a wooden spoon to incorporate any sediment. Boil up well and add the cream. Check the seasoning. Pour over the veal and serve immediately.

 *LIGHT RED*

# VEAL ESCALOPES WITH RAGOÛT FIN

SERVES 4

*110g/4oz calves' sweetbreads*
*20g/³⁄4oz butter*
*1 small onion, finely chopped*
*30g/1oz bacon, diced*
*55g/2oz button mushrooms, sliced*
*1 tablespoon chopped fresh parsley*
*7g/¹⁄4oz plain flour*
*150ml/¹⁄4 pint well-flavoured white stock, made*
    *with veal bones (see page 243)*
*4 × 140g/5oz veal escalopes*
*extra butter for frying*
*a squeeze of lemon juice*

To garnish
*sprigs of watercress*
*lemon wedges*

**1.** Soak the sweetbreads in cold water for 4 hours, changing the water every time it becomes pink; probably 4 times. There should be no blood at all when the sweetbreads are ready for cooking.

**2.** Place them in a saucepan of cold water and bring to boiling point, but do not allow to boil. Simmer for 2 minutes. Rinse under cold running water and dry well.

**3.** Pick over the sweetbreads, removing all the skin and membrane. Chop them coarsely.

**4.** Melt the butter and add the onion. Cook slowly until soft but not coloured. Add the bacon and sweetbreads and cook for 3 minutes. Stir in the mushrooms and parsley and leave over a low heat for 1 minute.

**5.** Mix in the flour and cook for 1 minute. Remove from the heat and stir in the stock. Return to the heat and bring slowly to the boil, stirring continuously. Season with salt and pepper. Simmer for 1 minute, then set aside to cool and solidify.

**6.** Place the veal escalopes between 2 pieces of wet greaseproof paper or clingfilm and, with a rolling pin or mallet, beat them lightly until quite thin.

**7.** Divide the sweetbread mixture between the escalopes and fold them in half.

**8.** Melt some butter in a large frying pan and when foaming, add the escalopes. Brown lightly on both sides. Reduce the heat and cook slowly for 4–5 minutes. Lift out the escalopes on to a warmed serving plate.

**9.** Increase the heat under the frying pan and brown the butter, remove from the heat and add a squeeze of lemon juice. Pour over the escalopes and serve garnished with watercress and lemon wedges.

 *MEDIUM RED*

# VEAL MARSALA

SERVES 4
*4 × 140g/5oz veal escalopes*
*30g/1oz butter*
*salt and freshly ground black pepper*
*2 tablespoons Marsala*
*4 tablespoons double cream*
*lemon juice*

**1.** Put the veal escalopes between 2 sheets of wet greaseproof paper and beat lightly with a mallet or rolling pin until thin. Season with salt and pepper.
**2.** Melt the butter in a frying pan and, when it is foaming, fry the escalopes briskly to brown them lightly on both sides (1–2 minutes per side). Remove them to a warmed plate and keep warm.
**3.** Tip off any fat in the pan. Add 4 tablespoons water and the Marsala, swill it about and bring to the boil. Add the cream and season well with salt, pepper and a squeeze of lemon juice.
**4.** Return the veal to the pan to heat through gently.

 *LIGHT RED/VALPOLICELLA*

# VEAL MEDALLIONS WITH WILD MUSHROOMS

SERVES 4
*4 × 140g/5oz veal medallions*
*110g/4oz mixed wild mushrooms, sliced*
*425ml/³/4 pint brown stock (see page 243)*
*100ml/3½fl oz dry white wine*
*170g/6oz unsalted butter, chilled and diced*

**1.** Melt 15g/½oz of the butter in a frying pan and, when it is foaming, fry the veal medallions to brown them lightly on both sides (2–3 minutes per side). Remove them to a warmed plate.
**2.** Add the mushrooms to the pan and fry for 1 minute.
**3.** Add the stock and wine and boil, scraping the bottom of the pan to incorporate any sediment, for 3 minutes. Remove the mushrooms with a slotted spoon and arrange on the veal medallions. Continue to boil the stock until reduced to 5 tablespoons.
**4.** Allow the stock to cool slightly. Using a wire whisk and plenty of vigorous continuous whisking, add the butter. The process should take about 2 minutes and the sauce should thicken. Taste, season and pour over the veal.

NOTE: Veal cutlets may be used instead of medallions.

 *LIGHT RED*

# HUNGARIAN VEAL MEDALLIONS WITH AUBERGINE

SERVES 4
*1 large aubergine*
*salt and freshly ground black pepper*
*30g/1oz seasoned plain flour*
*4 × 140g/5oz veal medallions*
*225g/8oz larding pork or 110g/4oz thin rindless*
*    streaky bacon*
*oil for frying*
*30g/1oz clarified butter (see page 686)*
*1 shallot, finely chopped*
*1 teaspoon paprika pepper*
*3 tablespoons dry white wine*
*150ml/¼ pint single cream*
*290ml/½ pint mornay sauce (see page 247)*
*1 tablespoon grated cheese*
*1 tablespoon dried white breadcrumbs*

**1.** Preheat the oven to 130°C/250°F/gas mark 1.
**2.** Cut the aubergine into 1cm/½in thick slices.
Sprinkle with salt and leave in a colander for 20
minutes to extract the bitter juices (degorge).
Rinse well, pat dry and dip in seasoned flour.
**3.** Wrap the medallions carefully in the pork fat,
cut into thin strips, or in the streaky bacon. Tie
with string.
**4.** Heat the oil in a frying pan and fry the
aubergine until golden-brown and tender. Remove
from the pan, drain on absorbent kitchen paper
and keep warm in the oven.
**5.** Dust the veal medallions with seasoned flour.
Heat the butter in the pan and fry the veal for
3–4 minutes on each side, or until just cooked.
Remove and keep warm in the oven.
**6.** Add the shallot to the pan and cook slowly for 2
minutes, then add the paprika and continue
cooking for a further 2 minutes. Pour on the wine
and boil to reduce by half. Cool slightly, pour in
the cream and season with salt and pepper. Reheat,
boil to reduce if a little thin, then set aside.
**7.** Preheat the grill to its highest setting. Reheat
the mornay sauce.
**8.** Lay the aubergine slices in an ovenproof dish.
Remove the strings from the veal steaks and lay
them on top of the aubergines. Coat with the

mornay sauce. Sprinkle with cheese and crumbs
and brown under the grill. Reheat the paprika
sauce and trickle it around the dish.

 *MEDIUM RED*

# GRILLED MEDALLIONS OF VEAL WITH GOAT'S CHEESE AND AUBERGINE PURÉE

SERVES 4
*4 × 110g/4oz veal medallions*
*4 slices of goat's cheese*
*4 tablespoons fresh white breadcrumbs*

For the purée
*2 medium aubergines*
*1 clove of garlic*
*about 150ml/¼ pint olive oil*
*225g/8oz olives, pitted and finely chopped*
*freshly ground black pepper*

To garnish
*frisée lettuce, tossed in a hazelnut oil French*
*    dressing*

**1.** Preheat the oven to 200°C/400°F/gas mark 6.
**2.** Brush the aubergines lightly with oil and put
into a roasting pan. Cook in the preheated oven
for 30 minutes, then add the unpeeled garlic and
cook for a further 30 minutes, until they are soft.
**3.** Remove the aubergines and garlic from the
oven and allow to cool.
**4.** Peel the aubergines, put the flesh into a clean
cloth and squeeze lightly to extract the bitter
juices. Peel the garlic and chop the aubergines and
garlic together. Add half the oil and the olives.
Season with pepper and leave for at least 30
minutes for the flavour to develop.
**5.** Preheat the grill to its highest setting. Baste the
veal medallions with some of the remaining oil
and grill for 2 minutes on each side.
**6.** Put the goat's cheese slices on the veal
medallions, brush lightly with oil and sprinkle
with the breadcrumbs. Grill until lightly coloured.

**7.** Place the medallions of veal on 4 warmed dinner plates. Place a generous spoonful of the warm aubergine and olive purée on each plate.
**8.** Garnish with the frisée tossed in hazelnut dressing.

 *MEDIUM RED/CHIANTI*

# VEAL MEDALLIONS AND GRILLED VEGETABLES WITH AÏOLI

SERVES 8
*8 × 140g/5oz veal medallions*
*olive oil*
*salt and freshly ground black pepper*

For the aïoli
*6 cloves of garlic, peeled and crushed*
*3 egg yolks*
*3 tablespoons fresh white breadcrumbs*
*½ teaspoon salt*
*4 tablespoons white wine vinegar*
*290ml/½ pint olive oil*
*1 tablespoon boiling water*

For the vegetables
*2 aubergines, cut in slices lengthways*
*olive oil*
*3 large red peppers, halved and deseeded*
*6 medium courgettes, cut into thin diagonal slices*
*4 onions, sliced*
*6 tomatoes, peeled, quartered and deseeded*
*balsamic vinegar*
*finely chopped fresh mint*
*finely chopped fresh basil*

**1.** Make the aïoli: put the garlic, egg yolks, breadcrumbs, salt and vinegar into a food processor. Process to a paste, then with the motor running, slowly add the oil to make a thick sauce. Add the boiling water.
**2.** Salt the aubergines and leave in a colander for 20 minutes to extract the bitter juices (degorge). Rinse and pat dry with absorbent kitchen paper. Paint each side of the aubergine slices lightly with oil and grill until dark brown but not burnt.

**3.** Preheat the grill to its highest setting.
**4.** Grill the peppers skin side up until they are charred and blistered. Remove the skin and cut the flesh into strips.
**5.** Lightly oil the courgettes and grill until just cooked.
**6.** Sauté the onions in a little oil until light brown.
**7.** Layer the vegetables, including the tomatoes in a bowl, sprinkling each layer with balsamic vinegar, mint and basil. Set aside to marinate at room temperature for 1 hour.
**8.** Brush both sides of the veal with oil and sprinkle with salt and pepper. Grill under a preheated grill for 3–4 minutes each side, depending on the thickness of the meat.
**9.** To serve: place the cooked veal and some of the marinated vegetables on warmed dinner plates. Serve a spoonful of aïoli beside the vegetables.

 *LIGHT FRUITY RED*

# OSSO BUCCO

Osso bucco looks, and is, a substantial peasant dish, made brighter by a last-minute scattering of chopped parsley and grated lemon zest (gremolata). It is quite often served without sieving the sauce.

SERVES 4
*4 large meaty pieces of knuckle of veal, cut crossways*
  *with the bone and marrow in the centre*
*3 tablespoons good-quality olive oil*
*1 large or 2 small onions, finely chopped*
*1 large carrot, finely chopped*
*2 cloves of garlic, crushed*
*2 teaspoons plain flour*
*2 teaspoons tomato purée*
*340g/12oz ripe tomatoes, peeled and chopped*
*150ml/¼ pint dry white wine*
*290ml/½ pint white stock, made with veal bones*
  *(see page 243)*
*salt and freshly ground black pepper*
*1 bouquet garni (a sprig each of fresh parsley and*
  *thyme, 1 stick of celery and 1 bay leaf, tied*
  *together with string)*

To garnish
*1 tablespoon chopped fresh parsley*
*grated zest od 1 lemon*

**1.** Put 1 tablespoon of the oil into a saucepan, add the onion, carrot and garlic and cover with a well-fitting lid. Cook over a low heat without browning.

**2.** Brown the meat on all sides, one or two pieces at a time, in the remaining oil in a large saucepan. Remove to a plate as they are browned.

**3.** When all are done, sprinkle the flour into the pan and stir well. Add the tomato purée, cooked vegetables, tomatoes, wine, stock, salt and pepper and bring to the boil.

**4.** Replace the veal, immerse the bouquet garni in the liquid and cover the pan. Simmer for 11/2 hours, or until the veal is very tender but not quite falling off the bone.

**5.** Take the veal out and place on a warmed serving platter with a fairly deep lip. Cover with kitchen foil and keep warm while you boil the sauce rapidly until thick. Stir frequently and watch that it does not catch and burn at the bottom.

**6.** Remove the bouquet garni. Push the sauce through a sieve, then pour over the meat. Sprinkle with the parsley and grated lemon zest.

 *ITALIAN MEDIUM RED/CHIANTI*

# BLANQUETTE DE VEAU

SERVES 4
*900g/2lb pie-veal*
*1 slice of lemon*
*1 bouquet garni (4 parsley stalks, 2 bay leaves,*
   *1 blade of mace tied together with string)*
*salt and freshly ground white pepper*
*2 carrots, peeled and cut into sticks*
*2 onions, peeled and sliced*
*1 teaspoon cornflour*
*1 egg yolk, or 2 for a very rich sauce*
*150ml/¹/4 pint double cream*

To garnish
*8 fried bread triangles made from 2 slices of white*
   *bread, crusts removed*
*chopped fresh parsley*

**1.** Trim the fat from the veal but do not worry about the gristle. Put the veal into a saucepan of cold water with the lemon slice. Bring slowly to the boil, skimming carefully. Add the bouquet garni and a little salt. Remove the lemon slice. Simmer gently for 30 minutes.

**2.** Add the carrots and onions and continue to simmer until the meat is really tender and the vegetables cooked (probably a further 30–40 minutes).

**3.** Strain the liquid into a jug. Skim off any fat. There should be 290ml/1/2 pint. If there is less, add a little water. If there is more, return the liquid to the pan and reduce, by rapidly boiling. Pick over the meat, removing any fat or gristle, and put the meat and vegetables into an ovenproof serving dish. Remove the bouquet garni.

**4.** Mix the cornflour in a cup with a few spoons of cold water and add some of the hot liquid from the veal. Stir the mixture into the remaining liquid in the pan and continue to stir while bringing to the boil. You should now have a sauce that is very slightly thickened: about the consistency of single cream. If it is still too thin, do not add more cornflour, but boil rapidly until reduced to the correct consistency. Season to taste with salt and pepper.

**5.** Mix the egg yolks and cream together in a bowl. Add some of the sauce, mix well, and return to the pan. Do not boil or the eggs will scramble. Reheat gently, stirring until the egg yolks have thickened the sauce to the consistency of double cream, then pour over the meat and vegetables.

**6.** Serve garnished with triangles of fried bread with their corners dipped in chopped parsley.

 *FULL DRY WHITE*

# VEAL FLORENTINE

SERVES 4
*1 clove of garlic, crushed*
*55g/2oz butter*
*6 tomatoes, peeled and sliced*
*900g/2lb spinach, cooked and chopped*
*salt and freshly ground black pepper*
*a pinch of freshly grated nutmeg*
*4 × 140g/5oz veal escalopes*
*570ml/1 pint mornay sauce (see page 247)*
*1 tablespoon grated cheese*
*1 tablespoon dried breadcrumbs*

**1.** Preheat the oven to 180°C/350°F/gas mark 4.
**2.** Fry the garlic lightly in a quarter of the butter. Then add the tomatoes and cook for 30 seconds. Place them in a dish big enough to hold the veal in one layer.
**3.** Toss the spinach in a little butter in the pan. Season with salt, pepper and nutmeg. Spread the spinach on top of the tomatoes.
**4.** Put the veal between 2 pieces of wet greaseproof paper and flatten by batting evenly with a rolling pin. Cut across the grain into strips.
**5.** Heat the remaining butter in a large frying pan. Fry the veal strips in this until lightly browned all over. Put them on top of the spinach and season well with salt and pepper.
**6.** Heat the mornay sauce and pour evenly over the veal and spinach. Sprinkle with the grated cheese and breadcrumbs.
**7.** Bake in the preheated oven for 15 minutes or until bubbly and hot, then grill to brown the top, if necessary.

NOTE: Chicken Florentine can be made in the same way using strips of poached chicken in place of fried veal. They both make excellent party dishes.

 *DRY WHITE/SOAVE*

# HUNGARIAN VEAL GOULASH

SERVES 4
*900g/2lb pie veal*
*450g/1lb onions, sliced*
*20g/³/4oz butter*
*1 tablespoon paprika pepper*
*290ml/½ pint white stock, made with veal bones (see page 243)*
*a squeeze of lemon juice*
*100ml/3½fl oz dry white wine*
*2 teaspoons tomato purée*
*salt and freshly ground black pepper*
*1 teaspoon plain flour*
*150ml/¼ pint soured cream*

To garnish
*fresh chopped parsley*

**1.** Cut the veal into 5cm/2in cubes. Trim off as much fat as possible but do not worry about any skin and gristle.
**2.** In a large saucepan, cook the onions in the butter until soft. Add the paprika and cook for 1 further minute.
**3.** Add the veal, stock, lemon juice, wine, tomato purée, salt and pepper, bring to the boil and simmer for 45–60 minutes, until the meat is tender.
**4.** Strain the stock into a jug. Skim off any fat. There should be about 290ml/½ pint. If there is less, add some water. If there is more, reduce by boiling rapidly. Pick off any skin or gristle from the veal and place the meat in an ovenproof dish. Return the stock to the pan, mix the flour with a little of the soured cream and add some of the hot stock to it. Mix thoroughly and return the paste to the stock in the pan. Bring slowly to the boil, stirring continuously; cook for 2 minutes.
**5.** Check the seasoning and pour the sauce over the veal. Streak in the remaining soured cream and sprinkle with parsley.

 *MEDIUM RED*

# VEAL AND HAM RAISED PIE

The pastry case should be made at least 1 hour in advance of the filling. The finished pie must be left overnight for the aspic to set.

SERVES 4
*675g/1½lb boned shoulder of veal*
*110g/4oz ham*
*salt and freshly ground black pepper*
*1 onion, chopped*
*2 tablespoons chopped fresh parsley*
*450g/1lb flour quantity hot watercrust pastry (see page 468)*
*1 egg, beaten*
*290ml/½ pint aspic, flavoured with tarragon (see page 244)*

**1.** Make the pastry and mould the pastry case (see pages 467, 468).

**2.** Preheat the oven to 190°C/375°F/gas mark 5.

**3.** Cut the veal and ham into cubes. Trim away most of the fat and all the skin and gristle. Season with salt, pepper, the onion and parsley.

**4.** Fill the pie with the seasoned meat, making sure that you press it firmly into the corners, then cover with the remaining pastry. Press the edges together. Make a neat hole in the middle of the lid. Secure a lightly buttered double piece of greaseproof paper around the pie with a paper clip.

**5.** Bake in the preheated oven for 15 minutes. Reduce the oven temperature to 170°C/325°F/gas mark 3. Bake for 1 further hour. Thirty minutes before the pie is due to come out of the oven, remove the paper 'collar' and brush the pastry evenly all over with beaten egg. Remove the pie from the oven and allow to get quite cold.

**6.** Warm the aspic enough to make it just liquid but not hot. Using a funnel, fill up the pie with jelly. Allow the liquid to set slightly and then add more liquid until you are sure that the pie is completely full. This will take some time. Leave in the refrigerator for the jelly to reset.

NOTE: A richer and, frankly, better result is achieved with a pâte à pâté crust, though the classic English pie is made as above. The recipe for pâte à pâté is found on page 467, and the pork pie recipe on page 423 gives instructions for shaping and baking.

 *LIGHT RED/ROSÉ*

# VEAL FRICANDEAU

This dish has been adapted from a recipe in the Time Life *Veal and Beef* book.

SERVES 8
*200g/7oz long strips of pork fat*
*salt and freshly ground black pepper*
*1.35kg/3lb piece of rump or loin of veal, cut lengthways along the grain*
*45g/1½oz unsalted butter*
*2 onions, thinly sliced*
*2 carrots, thinly sliced*
*570ml/1 pint white stock, made with veal bones (see page 243)*
*200ml/7fl oz dry white wine*

To serve
*1.35kg/3lb leaf spinach, destalked and well washed*
*15g/½oz butter*
*salt and freshly ground black pepper*
*freshly grated nutmeg*

**1.** Season the pork fat with salt and pepper.

**2.** Take a strip of pork fat and press into the tunnel of a larding needle. Push the needle right through the meat. Gently turn the needle so that the fat does not come loose. When the fat is through the length of the meat, pull the needle away, leaving the fat embedded in the meat. Repeat this 10–12 times, making sure that there is an equal distance between each strip. Leave the little ends of the pork fat sticking out of the veal flesh.

**3.** Preheat the oven to 180°C/350°F/gas mark 4.

**4.** Melt the butter in a flameproof casserole. Add the onions and carrots and cook until just beginning to soften. Add the veal and brown it lightly all over. Season with salt and pepper.

**5.** Add 5 tablespoons each of the stock and wine. Bring to the boil, then reduce the heat and simmer until the liquid has just evaporated. Add the remaining stock and wine. Bring to the boil, then cover with a piece of buttered greaseproof paper and a lid and cook in the preheated oven for 1 hour.

**6.** Using a ladle, remove half the braising liquid and place in a saucepan. Reduce by boiling rapidly until syrupy. Use this to baste over the fricandeau as it cooks. The surface of the meat should become brown and sticky.

**7.** Increase the oven temperature to 190°C/375°F/gas mark 5 and remove the covering paper and lid. Baste the veal frequently with the braising juices. Cook for 1 further hour.

**8.** Remove the veal from the casserole pot. Leave to stand, covered, in the turned off oven while you make the sauce and prepare the spinach.

**9.** Strain all the meat juices into a saucepan. Bring to the boil, then add a dash of cold water. (This will help to bring the scum to the surface.) Skim off all the scum. Repeat this process if necessary.

**10.** Meanwhile cook the spinach. Melt the butter in a large sauté pan. Add the well washed spinach and turn in the pan until wilted. Season with salt, pepper and nutmeg.

**11.** Arrange the spinach on a large warmed serving dish. Place the veal on top of the spinach and hand the sauce separately.

# ROAST LOIN OF VEAL

SERVES 6
1kg/2¼lb piece of boned loin of veal
30g/1oz butter, softened
2 teaspoons Dijon mustard
chopped fresh mixed herbs
salt and freshly ground black pepper
1 tablespoon dripping
1 teaspoon plain flour

**1.** Preheat the oven to 180°C/350°F/gas mark 4.
Weigh the veal and calculate the cooking time at
20 minutes per 450g/1lb.
**2.** Using a very sharp knife, cut away the rind and
most of the fat from the loin, leaving about
1cm/½in of fat on the joint.
**3.** Using a sharp knife, make criss-cross incisions
into the outer layer of fat.
**4.** Spread the butter and half the mustard over the
lean side of the joint. Spread mustard only on the
fat side, making sure that it goes well into the
incisions. Sprinkle with herbs, salt and pepper,
and tie up neatly with string.
**5.** Put the dripping into a roasting pan and melt
over a low heat. When it begins to spit, put the
joint into it, baste, then place in the preheated
oven. Roast for the calculated cooking time.
**6.** Remove the joint to a warmed serving dish.
Skim the excess fat from the pan. With a whisk or
wooden spoon, scrape the bottom of the pan and
beat in the flour. Stir until boiling, then simmer
for 2 minutes.
**7.** Check the seasoning and pour into a warmed
sauceboat. Serve with the joint.

 *MEDIUM RED*

# COLD VEAL WITH GREEN PEPPERCORNS

SERVES 10
2kg/4½lb piece of boned shoulder of veal
30g/1oz unsalted butter
100ml/3½fl oz dry white wine

For the stuffing
1 onion, finely chopped
30g/1oz butter
140g/5oz button mushrooms, sliced
1 small green pepper, cored, deseeded and
    chopped
1 clove of garlic, crushed
70g/2½oz fresh white breadcrumbs
salt and freshly ground black pepper
450g/1lb minced pork belly
1 teaspoon green canned peppercorns, well-rinsed
1 tablespoon chopped fresh mixed herbs
1 egg, lightly beaten

To garnish
1 bunch of watercress

**1.** First prepare the stuffing: cook the onion in the
butter in a saucepan until soft. Add the
mushrooms, green pepper and garlic and cook for
a further 2 minutes. Mix with the breadcrumbs,
salt, pepper, minced pork, peppercorns, herbs and
beaten egg. Beat well.
**2.** Lay the veal out flat, season with salt and
pepper and spread with the stuffing. Roll and tie
up to a cylindrical shape. Calculate the cooking
time at 20 minutes per 450g/1lb plus 20 minutes.
**3.** Preheat the oven to 180°C/350°F/gas mark 4.
**4.** Lightly brown the meat in the butter in a large
flameproof casserole. When browned all over, add
the wine. Cover with kitchen foil and cook in the
preheated oven for the calculated cooking time.
**5.** Remove the veal from the casserole and if it is
to be served cold, allow to cool before removing
the string. If it is to be served hot, remove the
string, and serve in thin overlapping slices.
Garnish with watercress.

 *SPICY DRY WHITE*

# BRAINS WITH BROWN BUTTER

SERVES 4
*4 calves' brains*
*860ml/1½ pints court bouillon (see page 245)*
*salt and freshly ground black pepper*
*55g/2oz butter*
*about 3 gherkins*
*about 10 capers*
*chopped fresh parsley*
*3 tablespoons lemon juice*

**1.** Wash the brains well and soak in cold water for 2–3 hours. Drain them.
**2.** Bring the court bouillon to the boil in a large saucepan, add the brains and poach for 15 minutes. Remove and drain thoroughly.
**3.** Cut the brains into slices, removing any membranes. Lay on a heated serving dish and season with salt and pepper.
**4.** Chop the gherkins, capers and parsley.
**5.** Heat the butter in a pan until just turning brown. Immediately add the gherkins, capers and parsley. Boil up, remove from the heat, add the lemon juice, pour over the brains and serve immediately.

 *CLARET*

# KIDNEYS TURBIGO

SERVES 4
*9 lambs' kidneys*
*butter for frying*
*225g/8oz small pork sausages*
*12 baby onions or shallots, peeled*
*225g/8oz button mushrooms*
*2 tablespoons dry sherry*
*425ml/¾ pint brown stock (see page 243)*
*1 bouquet garni (1 stick of celery, 1 bay leaf, 1*
*    sprig each of parsley and thyme, tied together*
*    with string)*
*salt and freshly ground black pepper*
*30g/1oz butter*
*30g/1oz plain flour*
*150ml/¼ pint soured cream*

**1.** Skin the kidneys, halve them and remove the cores with kitchen scissors.
**2.** Heat the butter in a frying pan. Brown the kidneys quickly, a few at a time, on both sides. They should cook fast enough to go brown rather than grey. Remove them into a sieve set over a bowl as you go.
**3.** Now fry the sausages, then the onions, and finally the mushrooms in the same way. Put them on to a plate, not with the kidneys.
**4.** Put everything back into the pan, except for the kidney juice in the bowl (the blood can be very bitter). Pour over the sherry and stock and immerse the bouquet garni in the liquid. Add salt and pepper and cover with the lid.
**5.** Cook over a very low heat for about 1 hour, or until the kidneys and onions are tender. Make sure that the kidneys are submerged during cooking.
**6.** Lift the meat and vegetables on to a warmed serving dish and discard the bouquet garni. Reduce the liquid by boiling rapidly to half the original quantity.
**7.** Work the butter and flour together to a paste (beurre manié). Drop about half of it into the sauce and whisk or stir briskly while bringing slowly to the boil. If the sauce is still on the thin side, add the remaining butter and flour mixture in the same way, whisking out the lumps. Boil for 1 minute.
**8.** Mix half the soured cream with some of the hot liquid. Add to the pan, stir, but do not boil, and pour over the dish. Serve the remaining soured cream separately.

NOTE: Classic turbigo does not have the soured cream but the addition is delicious.

 *FULL RED*

# LAMBS' KIDNEYS WITH MUSHROOMS IN MUSTARD SAUCE

SERVES 2
*6 lambs' kidneys*
*30g/1oz clarified butter (see page 686)*
*110g/4oz large flat mushrooms, chopped*
*4 tablespoons double cream*
*2 teaspoons Dijon mustard*
*salt and freshly ground black pepper*

To garnish
*chopped fresh parsley*

**1.** Skin, halve and core the kidneys with kitchen scissors. Cut into chunks.
**2.** Melt the butter in a frying pan and brown the kidneys quickly all over. Remove to a sieve set over a bowl and discard the juices. Return the kidneys to the pan, add the mushrooms and cook for 1 minute.
**3.** Reduce the heat and stir in the cream, mustard, salt and pepper. Garnish with parsley and serve immediately.

 *RHÔNE*

# VEAL KIDNEYS ROBERT

SERVES 2–3
*150ml/¼ pint dry white wine*
*450g/1lb veal kidneys*
*45g/1½oz unsalted butter*
*1 teaspoon Dijon mustard*
*2 teaspoons chopped fresh parsley*
*a squeeze of lemon juice*
*salt and freshly ground black pepper*
*2 tablespoons double cream*

**1.** Put the wine into a saucepan and boil until reduced by half.
**2.** Remove the membranes and cores from the kidneys, and slice them quite thinly.
**3.** Fry a handful of kidney slices at a time in hot butter in a frying pan, shaking the pan until the

kidneys are brown but still pale inside. Remove to a sieve set over a bowl and discard the juices.
**4.** Add the mustard, reduced wine, parsley, lemon juice, salt and pepper to the pan. Bring to the boil, stirring continuously. Stir in the cream. Check the seasoning. Simmer until syrupy. Stir in the kidneys.
**5.** Turn into a warmed serving dish and sprinkle with parsley.

 *FULL RED*

# VEAL KIDNEY FEUILLETÉES

If ceps, chanterelles or morels are not available, use oyster or small button mushrooms instead.

SERVES 4
*340g/12oz flour quantity puff pastry (see page 464)*
*1 beaten egg to glaze*

For the filling
*150ml/¼ pint dry white wine*
*340g/12oz veal kidneys*
*55g/2oz ceps, sliced*
*55g/2oz small chanterelles*
*55g/2oz small morels*
*2 teaspoons Dijon mustard*
*1 tablespoon chopped fresh parsley*
*salt and freshly ground black pepper*
*6 tablespoons double cream*

**1.** Preheat the oven to 220°C/425°F/gas mark 7.
**2.** Roll the pastry into a large rectangle. Cut it into 4 diamonds, each side measuring 10cm/4in. Place the diamonds on a damp baking tray and brush with beaten egg. Using a sharp knife, trace a line about 1cm/½in from the edge of each diamond, without cutting all the way through the pastry. A small diamond is thus traced, which will form the hat for the pastry case. Make a design inside this diamond with the knife. Flour the blades of the knife and use this to `knock up' the sides of pastry. Chill for 15 minutes.
**3.** Bake in the preheated oven for 20 minutes or

until puffed up and brown. With a knife, outline and remove the 'hats' and scoop out any uncooked dough inside. Transfer the cases and hats to a wire rack to cool. Reduce the oven temperature to 180°C/350°F/gas mark 4.

**4.** Meanwhile, prepare the filling: put the wine into a saucepan and boil until reduced by half.

**5.** Remove the membranes and cores from the kidneys and slice them quite thinly.

**6.** In a frying pan, fry the ceps, chanterelles and morels in a little of the butter over a very low heat for about 3 minutes. Set aside.

**7.** Fry the kidneys, a small handful at a time, in the remaining butter over a low heat. Remove to a sieve set over a bowl. Bitter juices will run out of the kidneys and these should be discarded.

**8.** Return the pastry cases to the oven for 4 minutes to reheat.

**9.** Put the wine, mustard, parsley, salt, pepper and cream into the frying pan. Bring to the boil and reduce, by boiling rapidly, for 1 minute or until syrupy. Add the kidneys and mushrooms to the sauce.

**10.** Divide the filling between the 4 pastry cases. Put on the hats and serve immediately.

 *RED BURGUNDY*

# CALVES' LIVER LYONNAISE

SERVES 4
*450g/1lb calves' liver, skinned and sliced*
*55g/2oz unsalted butter*
*1 large onion, thinly sliced*
*seasoned plain flour*
*salt and freshly ground black pepper*
*290ml/1/2 pint brown stock (see page 243)*
*1 tablespoon orange juice*
*1 tablespoon finely chopped mixed fresh herbs,*
*   such as rosemary, sage, thyme*

To garnish
*chopped fresh parsley*

**1.** Remove any large tubes from the slices of liver.

**2.** Heat half the butter in a frying pan and slowly cook the onion until first soft and transparent and then golden-brown. Set aside.

**3.** Dip the slices of liver into the seasoned flour, shaking off any excess.

**4.** Heat the remaining butter until foaming. Fry the liver pieces in it, a few at a time, for about 2 minutes each side. The liver should be nicely browned on the outside but pale pink in the middle. Drain well. Arrange in overlapping slices with the onions in an ovenproof dish. Keep warm.

**5.** Sprinkle enough of the seasoned flour (about 1 teaspoon) into the frying pan to absorb the remaining fat. Cook for 1 minute, stirring and scraping any sediment from the bottom of the pan. Gradually stir in the stock and the orange juice. Allow to boil. Season with pepper and salt and add the herbs. Simmer for 1 minute. Pour over the liver, garnish with parsley and serve immediately.

 *RED BURGUNDY*

# LIVER AND BACON

SERVES 4
*450g/1lb calves' or lambs' liver, skinned and sliced*
*seasoned plain flour*
*55g/2oz butter*
*1 onion, thinly sliced*
*6 rashers of rindless bacon*
*290ml/1/2 pint brown stock (see page 243)*
*2 tablespoons sherry*

To garnish
*1 small bunch of watercress*

**1.** Heat half the butter in a frying pan and fry the onion slowly until soft and brown. Tip the onion into a saucer.

**2.** Preheat the grill. Grill the bacon under it until crisp and brown but not brittle. Turn off the grill and leave the bacon under it to keep warm.

**3.** Remove any large tubes from the liver. Dip the slices in seasoned flour and keep well separated on a plate.

**4.** Heat the remaining butter in the frying pan and fry the liver slices, a few at a time, adding more butter if necessary. Note that liver is easily spoiled by overcooking. Arrange the slices on a warmed shallow platter and keep warm.

**5.** Put the onion, and any of its fat, back into the pan and add a sprinkling of the seasoned flour – just enough to absorb the fat. Cook for 1 minute. Pour in the stock and stir well as it comes to the boil. Add the sherry.

**6.** Boil the sauce rapidly to reduce in quantity and thicken it. This will also give a richer appearance and concentrate the flavour. Check the seasoning.

**7.** Pour the sauce over the liver, top with the bacon and garnish with watercress. Serve immediately as liver toughens on standing.

 *FULL RED*

# OXTAIL STEW

SERVES 4

*2 oxtails, cut into 2.5cm/1in lengths, total weight*
*about 1.35kg/3lb*
*seasoned plain flour*
*30g/1oz beef dripping*
*340g/12oz carrots, thickly sliced*
*225g/8oz onions, sliced*
*150ml/¼ pint red wine*
*570ml/1 pint water*
*1 teaspoon chopped fresh thyme*
*salt and freshly ground black pepper*
*½ teaspoon sugar*
*1 teaspoon tomato purée*
*juice of ½ lemon*

To garnish
*2 tablespoons chopped fresh parsley*

**1.** Wash and dry the oxtails. Trim off any excess fat and toss in seasoned flour.

**2.** Melt the dripping in a heavy saucepan, add the oxtail, a few pieces at a time, and brown on all sides evenly and well. Remove to a plate as they are done.

**3.** Brown the carrots and onions in the same pan.

**4.** Replace the oxtail. Pour over the wine and water or stock and add the thyme, salt, pepper and sugar. Bring to the boil, then simmer for 2 hours.

**5.** Preheat the oven to 150°C/300°F/gas mark 2.

**6.** Take out the pieces of meat and vegetables and place in a casserole.

**7.** With a small ladle or spoon, skim off the fat

which will rise to the top of the remaining liquid. Add the tomato purée and lemon juice and bring quickly to the boil.

**8.** Pour this over the oxtail, cover with a lid, and cook in the preheated oven for about 3 hours, or until the meat is almost falling off the bone. Sprinkle with the parsley.

NOTES: If the sauce is too thin, remove the meat and vegetables to a warmed serving dish and boil the sauce rapidly until reduced to the desired consistency.

When buying oxtail choose short fat tails with a good proportion of meat on them. Long stringy thin tails are poor value – pale in flavour and short on meat.

Oxtail is very good served with dumplings (see page 382).

 *FULL RED*

# PRESSED TONGUE

SERVES 4

*1 ox tongue, fresh or salted*
*salt*
*6 black peppercorns*
*1 bouquet garni (1 stick of celery, 1 bay leaf, 1*
*sprig each of fresh parsley and thyme, tied*
*together with string)*
*2 onions*
*2 carrots*
*1 stick of celery*
*425ml/¾ pint aspic made from brown stock and*
*gelatine (see page 244)*

**1.** If the tongue is salted, soak it in fresh water for 4 hours. If the tongue is fresh, soak it in brine (salty water) for 1–2 hours.

**2.** Place it in a saucepan and pour in enough water to cover completely.

**3.** Add salt if the tongue is fresh. Add the peppercorns, bouquet garni, onions, carrots and celery.

**4.** Bring gently to the boil, skimming off any scum. Cover tightly and simmer for 3–4 hours, or until tender when pierced with a skewer. Remove from the heat and leave to cool for 1 hour in the liquid.

**5.** Take out the tongue. Remove the bones from the root and peel off the skin.

**6.** Curl the tongue tightly and fit it into a deep round cake tin or tongue press. Cool.

**7.** Pour a little cool jellied stock or aspic into the tin.

**8.** Place a plate which just fits inside the tin on top of the tongue. Stand a heavy weight (about 4kg/8lb) on the plate and leave overnight in the refrigerator.

**9.** To carve: slice thinly across the top of the round.

NOTE: The stock in which the tongue is cooked is suitable for use in making the jellied stock if it is not too salty.

 *RED BURGUNDY*

# HAGGIS

Even in Scotland haggis is seldom made at home today, mainly because a sheep's pluck, consisting of the liver, heart and lights (lungs), makes too much haggis for a modern-sized family, and cleaning the stomach of the sheep (which forms the skin of the haggis) is a tedious and messy business, requiring much washing and careful scraping. This is a simplified haggis, cooked in a pudding basin instead of a sheep's stomach.

SERVES 4
*2 onions*
*2 sheep's hearts*
*450g/1lb lambs' liver*
*55g/2oz oatmeal*
*85g/3oz chopped beef suet*
*1 teaspoons chopped fresh sage*
*a pinch of ground allspice*
*salt and freshly ground black pepper*
*butter for greasing*

**1.** Peel the onions and put them, with the cleaned hearts and liver, into a saucepan of water. Boil for 40 minutes, then lift them out of the liquid.

**2.** Mince the hearts, liver and onions and mix with the oatmeal, suet, sage, allspice and plenty of salt and pepper. Add enough of the cooking liquid to give a soft dropping consistency.

**3.** Grease a pudding basin, fill with the mixture, cover with greaseproof paper and kitchen foil and tie down with string.

**4.** Steam for 2 hours. Serve hot.

NOTE: Very good haggis can be bought in reliable shops. Do not prick haggis before boiling or baking – it may burst. A haggis should be boiled for 30 minutes per 450g/1lb, but for a minimum of 1 hour It can also be baked, wrapped in kitchen foil, at 180°C/350°F/gas mark 4 for 3 minutes per 450g/1lb, but for a minimum of 1 hour. Place the wrapped haggis in a casserole, add a little water and cover tightly.

 *WHISKY OR CLARET*

# SUPPER
# DISHES

# FROGS' LEGS WITH ROSEMARY AND GINGER

SERVES 4
45g/1½oz butter, softened
a large pinch of ground ginger
a small piece of fresh root ginger, peeled and
    finely chopped
1 sprig of fresh rosemary, roughly chopped
½ clove of garlic, crushed
salt and freshly ground black pepper
8 frogs' legs
a little butter for frying
150ml/¼ pint dry white wine

1. Mix together the butter, ground and fresh ginger, rosemary, garlic, salt and pepper and beat well. Spread this mixture over the frogs' legs.
2. Fry the frogs' legs briefly on both sides in a little butter in a frying pan to just colour.
3. Pour over the wine and simmer for 7 minutes. If the wine evaporates too much, add a little water.
4. Remove the frogs' legs and keep them warm. Bring the sauce to a rolling boil and reduce, whisking all the time until slightly thickened.
5. Pour the sauce over the frogs' legs and serve immediately.

 *SPICY DRY WHITE*

# WILD MUSHROOMS IN A CAGE

This recipe has been adapted from one of Paul Gayler's recipes in *Take Six Cooks*

SERVES 4
For the vegetable sauce
100g/3½oz unsalted butter
¼ onion, peeled and diced
½ leek, cleaned and diced
½ stick of celery, diced
30g/1oz carrots, peeled and diced
30g/1oz cabbage, shredded
¼ teaspoon crushed garlic
¼ teaspoon crushed black peppercorns
1 teaspoon sea salt
150ml/¼ pint dry white wine
290ml/½ pint water
2 tablespoons double cream

4 slices of wholemeal bread
45g/1½oz unsalted butter
2 shallots, finely chopped
100g/3½oz selection of wild mushrooms, such as
    morels, trompettes, oyster, chanterelles, etc.,
    washed and roughly chopped if large
70ml/2½fl oz Madeira
70ml/2½fl oz dry white wine
150ml/¼ pint double cream
salt and freshly ground black pepper
100g/3½oz flour quantity puff pastry (see page 464)
beaten egg to glaze

To garnish
*fresh chervil leaves*

1. Preheat the oven to 200°C/400°F/gas mark 6.
2. First prepare the vegetable sauce: melt 30g/1oz of the butter in a medium saucepan and add the diced vegetables and garlic. Sweat gently, covered, for about 5 minutes, or until soft. Add the peppercorns, salt and wine. Bring to the boil, then simmer, uncovered, until reduced by half.
3. Add the water and bring to the boil, skimming frequently. Simmer gently for 20–25 minutes. Pass through a fine sieve. Skim off any fat that rises to the top and reserve the stock.
4. Cut out 4 × 9cm/3½in diameter circles of wholemeal bread. Brush with 30g/1oz melted butter and place in a patty tin. Press another patty tin, of the same size, on top and place in the preheated oven for 10 minutes. Remove the top tin and continue to dry out the croustades in the oven.
5. Melt 15g/½oz of the butter in a sauté pan, add the shallots and cook over a low heat for 2 minutes. Then add the wild mushrooms and cook for 1 further minute. Add the Madeira and white wine and cook until reduced by half, then add the cream and continue reducing until the mushrooms are coated with the cream. Check the seasoning and allow to cool.
6. Fill the croustades with the mushroom mixture.
7. Roll out the pastry very thinly and cut out

4 circles 6.5cm/2½in in diameter. Make 1cm/1/2in parallel gashes into the pastry at regular intervals from the centre to the rim.

**8.** Brush the pastry with beaten egg and put on top of the mushrooms, pulling downwards to stick on to the croustade. Rest the pastry in the refrigerator for 30 minutes.

**9.** Brush the 'cages' with egg wash and bake in the preheated oven for 5–8 minutes.

**10.** Boil the stock until reduced by half, add the double cream and reduce again until thickened. Whisk in the remaining butter, adding a little at a time to form an emulsion. Check the seasoning.

**11.** To serve: pour a little sauce on to a serving plate, remove the 'cages' from the oven and place on the centre of the plate. Garnish with the chervil. Serve immediately.

 *CRISP DRY WHITE*

# EXOTIC VEGETABLE COUSCOUS

*225g/8oz couscous*
*425ml/³/4 pint tomato juice*
*425ml/³/4 pint water*
*1 clove of garlic, crushed*
*1 teaspoon ground cumin*
*a few sprigs of fresh coriander*
*salt and freshly ground black pepper*

For the vegetables
*10 baby carrots, scraped, with a little green left on*
*10 baby turnips, scraped, with a little green left on*
*10 fresh okra pods, trimmed*
*10 ears fresh baby sweetcorn*
*6 tiny purple finger aubergines (if available)*
*10 pearl onions, peeled*
*225g/8oz thin asparagus, trimmed*

For the sauce
*1 teaspoon ground cumin*
*1 teaspoon ground coriander*
*½ teaspoon chilli powder*
*2 tablespoons tomato purée*
*fresh coriander leaves*

**1.** Put the tomato juice, water, garlic, cumin, coriander, salt and pepper into a large saucepan.

Bring to the boil, then simmer for 15 minutes. Strain and return to the saucepan.

**2.** Cover the couscous with boiling salted water and leave to absorb the liquid for 10 minutes. Drain off excess liquid and leave the couscous to dry on absorbent kitchen paper.

**3.** Fork the couscous to remove any lumps. Add all the vegetables, except the asparagus, to the tomato sauce and simmer for 5 minutes. Add the asparagus and simmer for a further 5 minutes.

**4.** Pile the couscous on to a warmed serving dish and keep warm. Do not worry if it feels a little tacky; it always does.

**5.** Drain the vegetables, reserving the liquor, and arrange them on top of the couscous. Drizzle over 2 tablespoons of the tomato sauce. Garnish with the coriander leaves.

**6.** Mix the remaining tomato sauce with the sauce ingredients and serve it separately. It is very hot.

 *DRY WHITE*

# HOT SWEET POTATO STEW

SERVES 4
*120ml/4fl oz oil*
*1 tablespoon yellow mustard seeds*
*1 teaspoon ground mace*
*2 green chillies, chopped*
*5 cloves of garlic, crushed*
*30g/1oz fresh root ginger, peeled and sliced*
*2 onions, peeled and sliced*
*225g/8oz sweet potatoes, sliced*
*225g/8oz parsnips, sliced*
*450g/1lb tomatoes, or 1 × 400g/14oz can, chopped*
*1 tablespoon garam masala*
*lemon juice to taste*
*salt and freshly ground black pepper*

**1.** Heat the oil in a large pan, add the mustard seeds and mace and cook until the seeds pop.

**2.** Reduce the heat, add the chilli, garlic, ginger and onion, and fry gently.

**3.** Add the sweet potato, parsnip and tomatoes. Cover and simmer very gently until the vegetables soften. Add the garam masala. Season to taste with lemon juice, salt and pepper.

 *MEDIUM DRY WHITE*

## LENTIL 'CASSOULET'

SERVES 4
olive oil
340g/12oz lamb fillet (shoulder), sliced
1 large onion, thinly sliced
1 clove of garlic, crushed
450g/1lb brown lentils
1 × 400g/14oz can of tomatoes
water to moisten
100ml/3½fl oz red wine
5 cloves, tied in a muslin bag or a clean 'J'-cloth
salt and freshly ground black pepper
1 tablespoon herbes de Provence
1 large spicy sausage, sliced

1. Heat the oil in a large, flameproof casserole and lightly brown the lamb on both sides. Remove to a plate. Reduce the heat and add the onion and garlic; cook until beginning to soften.
2. Add the lentils, lamb, tomatoes and enough water to cover. Bring gradually to the boil and add the wine, cloves, salt and pepper and herbs.
3. Cover and simmer very slowly until the lentils are soft but not mushy (about 1 hour). Check every so often to make sure that the mixture is not getting too dry. If so, add extra water.
4. Add the sausage about 10 minutes before the lentils are cooked. Serve with a green salad.

🖌 FULL RED

## CHORIZOS

This recipe is from Jane Grigson's *Charcuterie and French Pork Cookery*. The sausages are lightly smoked in a food smoker before they are cooked. The smoking, which does not cook the sausages but simply adds flavour, may be omitted.

MAKES 20
For the filling
450g/1lb lean pork (neck or shoulder)
225g/8oz pork fat
1 small red pepper
1 small chilli
70ml/2½fl oz red wine
1 tablespoon salt

¼ teaspoon granulated sugar
a good pinch of saltpetre, if available
¼ teaspoon ground mixed spice
¼ teaspoon cayenne pepper
1 large clove of garlic, crushed
sausage skins (2.5cm/1in diameter), washed
    (available from good butchers)

1. Mince the pork and fat, using the coarse blade of the mincer.
2. Cut the pepper and chilli in half, remove the seeds and stalks, put through the mincer and add to the pork.
3. Add the remaining ingredients and mix well.
4. Fill the sausage skins with the mixture, but do not pack too tightly or the sausages will burst. Twist every 12.5–15cm/5–6in.
5. Smoke for 20 minutes.
6. Cook as required.

 MEDIUM RED

## VENISON SAUSAGES

MAKES ABOUT 80
1.8kg/4lb boned venison (haunch or shoulder)
900g/2lb rump steak
675g/1½lb pork fat
225g/8oz canned anchovy fillets
4 teaspoons juniper berries, crushed
1 clove of garlic, crushed
1 tablespoon ground ginger
1½ tablespoons salt
1 tablespoon dried sage
1 teaspoon ground mace
1 teaspoon mignonette or cracked black pepper
425ml/¾ pint red wine
150ml/¼ pint Jamaica rum
340g/12oz Cox's apples, unpeeled and grated
oil for frying
sausage skins (2.5cm/1in diameter), washed
    (available from good butchers)

1. Mince together the meats, fat and anchovy fillets. Mince again. Mix in all the remaining ingredients and beat well.
2. Fry a small amount of the mixture in a little oil to test for seasoning before filling the skins.

**3.** Fill the sausage skins with the mixture; do not pack too tightly or they will burst. Twist every 10–12.5cm/4–5 in.

**4.** Cook as required.

 *FULL RED*

# BOUDIN BLANC

This recipe has been adapted from *The Observer French Cookery School*.

MAKES ABOUT 10
*1 onion, chopped*
*15g/¹⁄₂oz butter*
*150ml/¹⁄₄ pint double cream*
*100g/3¹⁄₂oz fresh white breadcrumbs*
*2 metres/6 yards pork intestine*
*225g/8oz lean veal*
*225g/8oz pork fat*
*225g/8oz boned chicken breast, or a further*
  *225g/8oz lean veal*
*3 eggs*
*1 teaspoon ground allspice*
*salt and freshly ground white pepper*
*oil for frying*

For cooking
*1.5 litres/2¹⁄₂ pints water*
*750ml/1¹⁄₄ pints milk*

**1.** Sweat the onion in the butter until soft, then cool.

**2.** Scald the cream by bringing it to just below boiling point, pour it over the breadcrumbs and leave to cool.

**3.** Soak the pork intestine in cold water.

**4.** Work the veal, fat pork and chicken, if used, twice through the fine blade of a mincer, adding the onion before the second mincing. Alternatively, work the meat and onion a little at a time in a food processor. Put the mixture into a bowl and stir in the soaked breadcrumbs, eggs, allspice and plenty of salt and pepper. Sauté a small ball of the mixture in a little oil and check the seasoning – the mixture should be quite spicy. Beat with a wooden spoon or your hand until very smooth.

**5.** Fill the sausages: drain the pork intestine – it should be pliable. Tie one end, insert the sausage-stuffer or funnel in the other and spoon in the filling, shaking it down the skins. Do not fill them too tightly or they will burst during cooking. Tie into 15cm/6in sausages.

**6.** Bring the water and milk to the boil in a large pan. Lower the sausages into the pan. Cover and poach very gently for 18–20 minutes. Allow the sausages to cool in the liquid until tepid, then drain them and leave to cool completely. They can be cooked up to 24 hours ahead and kept covered in the refrigerator. They are very good fried and served with slices of fried apple.

 *LIGHT RED*

# CASSOULET

SERVES 12
*900g/2lb dried haricot beans*
*225g/8oz salt pork or unsmoked bacon*
*1 onion, studded with 8 cloves*
*1 bouquet garni (see page 19)*
*2 cloves of garlic, crushed*
*450g/1lb pork bladebone*
*225g/8oz Toulouse sausage or Cumberland*
  *sausage*
*1 tablespoon tomato purée*
*675g/1¹⁄₂lb boned breast of lamb*
*8 large tomatoes, peeled and quartered*
*2 tablespoons chopped fresh thyme*
*2 tablespoons chopped fresh parsley*
*salt and freshly ground black pepper*
*4 tablespoons fresh white breadcrumbs*

**1.** Wash the beans well in cold water and leave to soak overnight. Blanch in clean water for 5 minutes, then drain.

**2.** Rinse well and place in a pan of fresh cold water, making sure the beans are covered. Add the rind of the salt pork or bacon, the onion and cloves, bouquet garni and garlic.

**3.** Bring to the boil, then skim and simmer for 1¾ hours, or until the beans are tender.

**4.** Meanwhile, preheat the oven to 190°C/375°F/gas mark 5. Roast the lamb, pork and sausages in the oven for 30 minutes or until the meat is cooked and the sausages brown.

**5.** Remove the meat from the oven, tip off and reserve the fat, slice the sausages into 2.5cm/1in pieces and cut the meat into 2.5cm/1in chunks.

**6.** When the beans are cooked strain them, reserving 570ml/1 pint of the cooking liquor. Discard the rind, onion and bouquet garni. Add the tomato purée.

**7.** Turn the oven temperature down to 170°C/325°F/gas mark 3.

**8.** Place a layer of beans in a deep ovenproof dish. Cover with a layer of meat, sausage, tomatoes and herbs. Season generously with salt and pepper. Continue to layer up, finishing with a layer of beans. Pour over the cooking liquor and reserved fat, and sprinkle the breadcrumbs on the top.

**9.** Cook uncovered in the preheated oven for 1½ hours. If the breadcrumbs become dry and crusty, stir them into the cassoulet and add more liquid if necessary. Sprinkle more breadcrumbs on top. At the end of the cooking time the meat and beans should be very tender and creamy and the top crisp and brown.

 *FULL RICH RED*

# BLACK PUDDING WITH APPLE SAUCE

SERVES 4
*2 black puddings*
*oil*
*apple sauce (see page 259)*

**1.** Slice the black puddings into 1cm/½in slices and fry slowly in a little oil for a couple of minutes per side.

**2.** Arrange on a warmed serving plate and serve the apple sauce separately.

 *LIGHT RED*

# ROMAN-STYLE GRILLED MOZZARELLA CHEESE

*2 loaves of ciabatta (Italian bread)*
*2 × 110g/4oz mozzarella cheeses*
*3 tablespoons olive oil, infused with garlic*
*salt and freshly ground black pepper*
*10 anchovy fillets in oil, drained and soaked in milk*
*85g/3oz unsalted butter*

**1.** Cut the bread and the mozzarella cheese into 2cm/¾in thick slices.

**2.** Preheat the grill to its highest setting.

**3.** Skewer the bread alternately with the cheese on 2 long skewers.

**4.** Pack the bread and cheese really close together.

**5.** Place the skewers on an oiled baking sheet.

**6.** Brush the slices of bread liberally with the oil and season with salt and pepper.

**7.** Lower the grill temperature slightly and grill the skewers for 6–8 minutes, turning occasionally, making sure that the bread doesn't burn.

**8.** Meanwhile, drain the anchovies from the milk. Heat the butter and, when melted, remove the pan from the heat. Add the anchovies and mash with a fork until they are well emulsified. Season to taste with pepper.

**9.** Remove the skewers from the grill, place on a large flat serving dish, and pour some of the sauce over both skewers.

 *DRY WHITE*

# PIZZA

This recipe has been taken from *A Taste of Venice* by Jeanette Nance Nordio.

MAKES 2 × 25CM/10IN PIZZAS
*10g/⅓oz fresh yeast*
*150ml/¼ pint warm water*
*200g/7oz plain flour*
*½ teaspoon salt*
*2–3 tablespoons olive oil*
*1 quantity salsa pizzaiola (see page 256)*
*225g/8oz mozzarella cheese, diced or grated*
*3 tablespoons freshly grated Parmesan cheese*

**1.** Cream the yeast with the sugar and 2 tablespoons of the lukewarm water.

**2.** Sift the flour with the salt and make a well in the centre. Pour in the yeast mixture, the remaining water and the oil. Mix together to make a soft but not wet dough. Add more water or flour if necessary.

**3.** Turn out on to a floured surface and knead well for about 5 minutes until the dough is smooth. Place in a clean bowl and cover with greased clingfilm. Leave in a warm place until the dough has doubled in bulk.

**4.** Preheat the oven to 230°C/450°F/gas mark 8. Divide the dough in 2. Roll each piece into a 25cm/10in circle. Place on greased and floured baking trays.

**5.** Crimp or flute the edges of the dough slightly to help keep in the filling. Spread with the pizzaiola sauce. Sprinkle with the cheese and pour over a little oil. (The pizza can be left for up to 1 hour before baking.)

**6.** Bake near the bottom of the preheated oven for 5 minutes, then turn down the temperature to 200°C/400°F/gas mark 6 and bake for a further 15 minutes.

 *LIGHT/MEDIUM RED*

# CHICAGO PIZZA PIE

It is essential that the canned tomatoes are very well drained.

MAKES 2 × 20CM/8IN PIZZAS
*1 teaspoon fresh yeast*
*290ml/¹/2 pint warm water*
*450g/1lb plain flour*
*¹/2 teaspoon salt*
*2 tablespoons olive oil*
*225g/8oz mozzarella cheese, thinly sliced*
*4 tablespoons tomato purée*
*a good pinch of dried oregano or marjoram*
*1 tablespoon chopped fresh basil*
*1 × 900g/2lb can of Italian tomatoes, very well*
    *drained*
*100g/4oz Italian sausage or salami, chopped*
*salt and freshly ground black pepper*

**1.** Dissolve the yeast in the water. Sift the flour with the salt and mix to a soft dough with the yeast liquid. Mix in the oil with a knife, then knead for 10 minutes until elastic and smooth.

**2.** Grease 2 deep sandwich tins or flan tins with a little more oil and divide the dough between the tins. Put in a warm place, such as an airing cupboard, for about 1 hour to rise, then push the dough flat on the bottom of the tins and press to come up the sides. Preheat the oven to 250°C/500°F/gas mark 9.

**3.** Cover the dough with half the mozzarella cheese and put the tins back in the warm place to rise again. When puffy, after about 30 minutes, push the dough down again with the back of a large spoon and once again press the edges up the sides of the tins.

**4.** Mix together the tomato purée, marjoram and basil and spread all over the dough. Cut each canned tomato in half and discard the juice. Arrange over the pizzas. Add the remaining cheese and the salami. Sprinkle with a little more marjoram, season well with salt and pepper and bake in the preheated oven for 20 minutes.

 *MEDIUM RED*

# PIZZA CALZONE

SERVES 2
*225g/8oz flour quantity pizza dough (see pages*
    *442–3)*
*2 slices of cooked ham, cut into strips*
*170g/6oz mozzarella cheese, cut into slices*
*6 tomatoes, peeled and sliced*
*salt and freshly ground black pepper*
*1 tablespoon chopped fresh basil*
*extra virgin olive oil*

**1.** Preheat the oven to 240°C/475°F/gas mark 8.

**2.** Divide the dough into 4 equal pieces and place on 4 floured baking sheets. Using the heel of your hand, push and punch the dough into 4 ovals about 20cm/8in in diameter.

**3.** Arrange the ham, mozzarella cheese and tomato slices over half of each pizza base, leaving the edge clear. Season with salt and pepper and sprinkle over the basil and a little oil.

4. Fold over the uncovered half of the pizza and press the edges firmly together.

5. Bake in the preheated oven for 15 minutes.

 *LIGHT/MEDIUM RED*

# CORNISH PASTIES

SERVES 4

*225g/8oz flour quantity shortcrust pastry (see page 461)*
*110g/4oz chuck steak, very finely diced*
*1 large onion, finely chopped*
*1 large potato, finely chopped*
*2 tablespoons water*
*salt and freshly ground black pepper*
*beaten egg to glaze*

1. Chill the pastry in the refrigerator.

2. Prepare the filling by mixing together the meat, onion and potato. Add the water, salt and pepper and mix thoroughly.

3. Preheat the oven to 200°C/400°F/gas mark 6.

4. Divide the chilled pastry into 4 equal pieces and roll each piece out to the thickness of a £1 coin. Cut out a 20cm/8in diameter circle, using a plate as a template.

5. Spoon the meat and vegetable mixture into the centre of each circle. Brush around the edge with water. Carefully bring the sides up and over the filling so that the pasties look like closed purses. Using floured fingers, crimp the edges. Place on a baking sheet. Brush with beaten egg and chill in the refrigerator for 5–10 minutes.

6. Brush again with beaten egg. Baking near the top of the preheated oven for 10–15 minutes. Turn the oven temperature down to 180°C/350°F/gas mark 4 and bake for a further 45–50 minutes. Check occasionally, and if the pasties show signs of overbrowning, move to a lower shelf.

 *MEDIUM RED*

# TOAD IN THE HOLE

SERVES 4

*450g/1lb pork sausages*
*4 tablespoons beef dripping*

For the batter
*110g/4oz plain flour*
*a good pinch of salt*
*2 eggs*
*150ml/¼ pint water mixed with 150ml/¼ pint milk*

1. Make the batter: sift the flour with the salt into a large wide bowl. Make a well or hollow in the centre of the flour and break the eggs into it.

2. With the whisk or wooden spoon, mix the eggs to a paste and very gradually draw in the surrounding flour, adding just enough milk and water to the eggs to keep the central mixture a fairly thin paste. When all the flour is incorporated, stir in the rest of the liquid. The batter can be made more speedily by putting all the ingredients in a blender or food processor for a few seconds, but take care not to over-whisk or the mixture will be bubbly. Leave to rest at room temperature for 30 minutes before use. This allows the starch cells to swell, giving a lighter, less doughy final product.

3. Preheat the oven to 220°C/425°F/gas mark 7.

4. Heat 1 tablespoon of the dripping in a frying pan and fry the sausages until evenly browned all over, but do not cook them through.

5. Heat the remaining dripping in an ovenproof shallow metal dish or roasting pan until smoking hot, either in the oven or over direct heat. Add the sausages and pour in the batter.

6. Bake in the preheated oven for 40 minutes or until the toad in the hole is risen and brown. Serve with hot gravy.

 *FULL RED*

# CRESPELLE ALLA FIORENTINA

SERVES 4–6
*30g/1oz butter*
*1 medium onion, finely chopped*
*55g/2oz prosciutto (Parma ham), chopped*
*290ml/½ pint béchamel sauce (see page 247)*
*225g/8oz ricotta cheese*
*450g/1lb spinach, cooked and chopped*
*55g/2oz Parmesan cheese, freshly grated*
*55g/2oz pinenuts, toasted*
*salt and freshly ground black pepper*
*freshly grated nutmeg*
*double quantity (425ml/¾ pint) tomato sauce II
  (see page 258)*
*16 French pancakes (see page 471)*

1. Melt the butter in a sauté pan, add the onion and cook slowly until soft but not coloured. Add the prosciutto and cook over a medium heat for 1 minute. Tip into a bowl and leave to cool.
2. Add 5 tablespoons of the béchamel sauce, the spinach, ricotta cheese, Parmesan cheese and pinenuts to the onion and prosciutto. Mix well and season to taste with salt, pepper and nutmeg.
3. Preheat the oven to 200°C/400°F/gas mark 6.
4. Tip a little of the tomato sauce into a large ovenproof gratin dish.
5. Divide the spinach filling between the pancakes and roll them up. Arrange them in a single layer on top of the tomato sauce.
6. Cover with the remaining tomato sauce and bake in the preheated oven for 30 minutes, or until the pancakes are thoroughly hot.
7. Reheat the béchamel sauce and, just before serving, dribble it over the crespelle.

 MEDIUM RED

# BOCCONCINI DI PARMA

SERVES 4–6
*900g/2lb ricotta cheese*
*4 egg yolks*
*1 whole egg*
*170g/6oz Parmesan cheese, freshly grated*
*55g/2oz butter, softened*
*freshly grated nutmeg*
*salt and freshly ground black pepper*
*16 French pancakes (see page 471), made with a
  pinch of freshly grated nutmeg added to the
  batter*

1. Drain the ricotta and put into a bowl. Using a wooden spoon, start to break it up, adding the egg yolks, whole egg, Parmesan cheese and butter. Mix well and season to taste with nutmeg, salt and pepper. Refrigerate for 30 minutes.
2. Place a pancake on a board and spread 3 heaped tablespoons of the filling along one side. Roll up. Place the rolled pancake, seam side down, on a baking sheet. Repeat until all the pancakes are filled. Refrigerate for 30 minutes.
3. Preheat the oven to 190°C/375°F/gas mark 5.
4. Grease a 33 × 22cm/13½ × 8in baking dish with butter. Using a very sharp knife, cut each pancake into thirds. Arrange them standing up in the baking dish, side by side. Bake in the preheated oven for 20 minutes and serve hot.

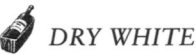 DRY WHITE

# BAKED STUFFED AUBERGINES

SERVES 4
*2 medium aubergines*
*285g/10oz lean minced beef*
*1 onion, finely chopped*
*½ green pepper, cored, deseeded and chopped*
*55g/2oz mushrooms, chopped*
*1 clove of garlic, crushed*
*1 teaspoon plain flour*
*290ml/½ pint brown stock (see page 243)*
*1 bay leaf*
*2 teaspoons tomato purée*
*1 teaspoon chopped fresh parsley*
*salt and freshly ground black pepper*
*lemon juice*
*15g/½oz butter, melted*
*grated Gruyère or strong Cheddar cheese*
*dried breadcrumbs*
*290ml/½ pint tomato sauce II (see page 258)*

1. Cut the aubergines in half lengthways and scoop out the centre, leaving the shell with about 5mm/¼in of flesh attached. Sprinkle lightly with salt and leave upside down to drain.

2. Chop the aubergine flesh and sprinkle lightly with salt. Leave to drain in a sieve for 20 minutes.

3. Fry the mince in a saucepan until evenly brown.

4. Rinse and dry the aubergine flesh. Add to the mince with the onion, green pepper, mushroom and garlic and cook for a further 3–4 minutes.

5. Stir in the flour. Cook for 1 minute, then add the stock, bay leaf, tomato purée, parsley, pepper and lemon juice. Bring to the boil, stirring continuously, then cover and simmer for 20–25 minutes. Remove the bay leaf.

6. Preheat the oven to 200°C/400°F/gas mark 6.

7. Wash and dry the aubergine shells, brush with the melted butter and fill with the mince mixture. Sprinkle over the grated cheese and crumbs.

8. Bake in the preheated oven for 30 minutes, or until the aubergine shells are tender and the cheese well browned and crusty. Serve with the tomato sauce.

 *MEDIUM RED*

# BUBBLE AND SQUEAK

SERVES 4
*450g/1lb mashed potatoes (see page 212)*
*450g/1lb cooked vegetables, such as cabbage,*
  *onion. leek or Brussels sprouts*
*salt and freshly ground black pepper*
*55g/2oz good dripping or butter*

1. Mix the potato with the other vegetables. Season to taste with salt and pepper.

2. Melt the dripping or butter in a heavy frying pan.

3. Put in the vegetable mixture, pressing it down flat on the hot dripping. Cook slowly to heat through and allow a crust to form on the bottom of the mixture.

4. Now flip the cake over on to a plate and return it to the pan to brown the second side.

5. Slide on to a warmed serving dish and serve immediately.

NOTE: Bubble and squeak is really a leftover fry-up and it does not matter if the cake is neat and even or crumbly and broken. But if you prefer it to be round and neat so that you can cut it into slices, a beaten egg added to the mixture will ensure that the ingredients hold together.

 *LIGHT RED*

# STUFFED PEPPERS

SERVES 4
*4 green or red peppers*
*30g/1oz butter*
*1 medium onion, finely diced*
*1 clove of garlic, crushed*
*100g/4oz mushrooms, thinly sliced*
*30g/1oz split blanched almonds*
*140g/5oz long-grain rice*
*290ml/½ pint white stock (see page 243)*
*1 teaspoon chopped fresh rosemary*
*30g/1oz raisins*
*1 tablespoon chopped fresh parsley*
*salt and freshly ground black pepper*
*290ml/½ pint tomato sauce II (see page 258)*

1. Cut off the tops of the peppers and remove the core and seeds.

2. Drop the peppers into boiling water for 5 minutes. Plunge immediately into cold water to cool.

3. Preheat the oven to 190°C/375°F/gas mark 5.

4. Melt the butter in a flameproof casserole and cook the onion until transparent. Add the garlic, mushrooms and almonds. Sauté (fry briskly, while tossing the contents of the pan in the butter) for a further 2 minutes. Stir in the rice and fry for 1 further minute.

5. Pour on the stock and bring to the boil. Add the rosemary, raisins, parsley, salt and pepper. Cover and bake in the preheated oven for 20 minutes.

6. When the rice mixture is cooked, fill the peppers with it and place them in a deep ovenproof dish. Pour on the tomato sauce. Cover with damp greaseproof paper and a lid and cook in the oven for 30 minutes.

 *LIGHT RED*

# RISOTTO WITH THREE CHEESES

SERVES 4–6
*110g/4oz Gorgonzola cheese, rind removed*
*110g/4oz mozzarella cheese*
*150ml/¼ pint warm milk*
*85g/3oz butter*
*1 tablespoon olive oil*
*450g/1lb arborio rice*
*860ml/1½ pints white stock (see page 243)*
*salt and freshly ground black pepper*
*30 unsalted pistachio nuts, shelled, blanched and*
*    skinned, or toasted pinenuts*
*110g/4oz Parmesan cheese, freshly grated*

**1.** Cut the Gorgonzola and mozzarella cheeses into small cubes. Place in a bowl, pour over the milk and leave to stand for 20 minutes.
**2.** Heat the butter and oil in a flameproof casserole over a medium heat. When the butter is melted, add the rice and cook over a very low heat for 4 minutes.
**3.** Meanwhile, heat the stock and gradually add it to the rice, stirring continuously but gently until all the stock has been absorbed (about 30 minutes).
**4.** Add the milk with the cheeses to the pan and stir continuously until well amalgamated (about 5 minutes).
**5.** Check for seasoning and add the nuts and Parmesan cheese. Serve immediately.

NOTE: Risotto has to be made at the last minute as it does not keep warm well.

 *LIGHT RED*

# RISOTTO ALLA MILANESE

SERVES 4
*85g/3oz unsalted butter*
*1 large onion, finely chopped*
*400g/14oz risotto (arborio) rice*
*150ml/¼ pint dry white wine*
*1.75 litres/3 pints white stock (see page 243)*
*about 15 saffron strands*

*salt and freshly ground black pepper*
*30g/1oz unsalted butter*
*55g/2oz Parmesan cheese, freshly grated*

**1.** Melt the butter in a large saucepan and gently cook the onion until soft and lightly coloured. Add the rice and wine and bring to the boil, cook until the wine is absorbed (about 3 minutes), then reduce the heat and stir gently and continuously.
**2.** Meanwhile, reheat the stock in a second pan and add the saffron. Allow the stock to simmer gently.
**3.** Start adding the hot chicken stock to the rice a little at a time, stirring gently. Allow the stock to become absorbed after each addition. Keep stirring constantly. Season with salt and pepper, and keep adding the stock until the rice is cooked but still *al dente* (about 30 minutes).
**4.** Remove the pan from the heat, add the butter and the Parmesan cheese and mix well with a wooden spoon until the butter is melted and the cheese absorbed. Serve immediately, with additional grated Parmesan cheese handed separately if desired.

 *LIGHT RED*

# MACARONI CHEESE

SERVES 4
*110g/4oz macaroni*
*20g/¾oz butter*
*20g/¾oz plain flour*
*cayenne pepper*
*a pinch of dry English mustard*
*425ml/¾ pint milk*
*salt and freshly ground black pepper*
*170g/6oz strong Cheddar cheese, grated*
*½ tablespoon fresh white breadcrumbs*

**1.** Cook the macaroni, uncovered, in plenty of rapidly boiling salted water. The water must boil steadily to keep the macaroni moving freely and prevent it from sticking to the saucepan; the lid is left off to prevent boiling over. Cook the macaroni until it is just tender. Drain well and rinse under boiling water.
**2.** Melt the butter in a second saucepan and add

the flour, cayenne pepper and mustard. Cook, stirring, for 1 minute. Remove from the heat. Pour in the milk and mix well. Return to the heat and stir until boiling. Simmer, stirring all the time, for 2 minutes.

**3.** Stir the macaroni into the sauce and reheat if necessary. Season the sauce to taste with salt and pepper. Stir in all but 1 tablespoon of the cheese and turn the mixture into an ovenproof dish.

**4.** Preheat the grill to its highest setting.

**5.** Mix the reserved cheese with the breadcrumbs and sprinkle evenly over the sauce; make sure that all the sauce is covered or it will form brown blisters under the grill.

**6.** Grill fairly quickly until the top is browned and crisp.

 *LIGHT FRUITY RED*

# SPAGHETTI CARBONARA

SERVES 4
*450g/1lb spaghetti*
*salt*
*1 tablespoon oil*
*100g/3¹/₂oz streaky bacon, cut into small strips*
*4 egg yolks*
*6 tablespoons single cream*
*55g/2oz Parmesan cheese, freshly grated*
*freshly ground black pepper.*

**1.** Cook the spaghetti in plenty of rapidly boiling salted water.

**2.** Heat the oil in a fairly large frying pan, add the bacon and fry lightly over a medium heat until the fat has melted. Remove the pan from the heat and set aside, keeping it warm.

**3.** Meanwhile, whisk the egg yolks in a bowl, then whisk in the cream and half the Parmesan cheese, and season generously with pepper.

**4.** When the spaghetti is still firm to the bite (*al dente*), drain it; transfer it to the pan with the bacon, place over a medium heat and pour the egg mixture over it. Stir quickly and serve immediately, with the remaining Parmesan cheese handed separately.

 *LIGHT RED*

# SPAGHETTI CON VONGOLE

This recipe has been taken from *A Taste of Venice* by Jeanette Nance Nordio.

SERVES 4
*900g/2lb baby clams in their shells*
*6 tablespoons olive oil*
*2 cloves of garlic, peeled and bruised*
*4 large tomatoes, peeled and chopped*
*salt and freshly ground black pepper*
*1 tablespoon chopped fresh parsley*
*450g/1lb spaghetti*

**1.** Wash and scrub the clams thoroughly.

**2.** Heat 1 tablespoon oil in a large saucepan, add the clams, cover and shake until they have opened. Discard any that have remained closed. Remove the clams and strain the juices. Reserve both.

**3.** Heat 4 tablespoons of the remaining oil in the pan, add the garlic and cook until golden-brown; remove and discard. Add the tomatoes, clam juice, salt and pepper and cook for about 30 minutes. Add the clams and cook over a low heat for 1–2 minutes. Add the parsley.

**4.** Meanwhile, cook the spaghetti in plenty of rapidly boiling salted water until *al dente*. Drain and mix with the tomato and clam sauce. Serve immediately and provide finger bowls.

 *DRY WHITE*

# SPAGHETTI EN PAPILLOTE

This is an unusual way to serve spaghetti, which keeps it moist and succulent.

SERVES 4
*150ml/¹/₄ pint good-quality olive oil*
*1 large clove of garlic, peeled*
*1 × 400g/14oz can of tomatoes, drained*
*salt and freshly ground black pepper*
*¹/₄ teaspoon chill powder*
*225g/8oz spaghetti*
*450g/1lb fresh tomatoes, peeled, deseeded and*
    *slivered*
*2 tablespoons finely chopped fresh parsley*
*28 large black Greek olives, pitted*

1. Heat all but 2 tablespoons of the oil in a heavy saucepan. Add the garlic and leave to infuse over a gentle heat for 2 minutes. Remove and add the drained tomatoes, taking care as the oil will spit. Simmer for 20 minutes, stirring occasionally. Season with salt, pepper and the chilli powder.

2. Process or liquidize in a blender until smooth, then return to the rinsed-out pan. Simmer for a further 10 minutes until reduced to a thick, shiny sauce.

3. Preheat the oven to 190°C/375°F/gas mark 5.

4. Cook the spaghetti in plenty of rapidly boiling salted water until *al dente*.

5. Meanwhile, arrange 4 × 30cm/12in circles of double greaseproof paper on a board.

6. Drain the spaghetti, mix it with the fresh tomatoes, the remaining oil, half the parsley, the olives and the tomato sauce. Mix well and check the seasoning.

7. Divide the spaghetti mixture between the 4 circles of greaseproof paper. Close each parcel up, trap a little air in the parcel and secure the edges firmly by twisting and turning them together.

8. Place in a shallow, damp roasting pan and bake in the preheated oven for 15 minutes.

9. Remove from the oven and place on warmed dinner plates. Open the parcels with scissors and sprinkle the remaining parsley over each serving.

 *MEDIUM RED*

# PASTA WITH RICH TOMATO SAUCE

SERVES 4
*2 large Spanish onions, sliced*
*1 tablespoon olive oil*
*2 × 400g/14oz cans of tomatoes, chopped*
*salt and freshly ground black pepper*
*285g/10oz pasta butterflies or spirals*
*1 tablespoon chopped fresh basil*
*3 eggs, beaten lightly*
*freshly grated Parmesan cheese*

1. Cook the onions very slowly in the oil in a saucepan for 15–20 minutes, until soft but not coloured.

2. Add the tomatoes, salt and pepper, stir well and bring the mixture to the boil. Reduce the heat and simmer for 10 minutes.

3. Meanwhile, cook the pasta in rapidly boiling salted water until *al dente*. When the pasta is cooked, drain it well and refresh with boiling water.

4. Remove the tomato sauce from the heat, check the seasoning, add the basil and then gradually pour in the lightly beaten eggs until the sauce becomes rich and creamy.

5. Mix a little of the sauce with the pasta, pile it into a warmed serving dish and pour the remaining sauce over it.

6. Serve sprinkled with a little Parmesan cheese.

 *MEDIUM RED*

# GREEK PARSLEY PASTA

SERVES 4
*340g/12oz flour quantity egg pasta (see page 470)*
*1 bunch of flat-leaf parsley, washed and dried*
*pesto sauce (see page 255)*

1. Roll the pasta out to a very thin rectangle on a lightly floured board. Cut in half. Keep well covered to prevent it from drying out.

2. Take one sheet of pasta and arrange individual parsley leaves at 3cm/1½in intervals, in even rows, all over it. Cover loosely with the other sheet of pasta and press down firmly. Roll again until the parsley can be seen between the layers of pasta.

3. Using a pastry cutter, cut between the rows, making sure that all the edges are sealed.

4. Simmer in boiling salted water for 2–3 minutes or until just tender. Drain well and toss in warm pesto sauce.

 *MEDIUM RED*

# PASTA ROULADE WITH TOMATO SAUCE

SERVES 4
*30g/1oz butter*
*1kg/2¼lb spinach, cooked and chopped*
*225g/8oz ricotta cheese*
*85g/3oz pinenuts, toasted*
*freshly grated nutmeg*
*salt and freshly ground black pepper*
*1 tablespoon roughly chopped fresh basil*
*340g/12oz flour quantity egg pasta (see page 470)*
*tomato sauce I (see page 258)*
*freshly grated Parmesan cheese*

1. Melt the butter in a saucepan, add the spinach and cook for 1 minute, stirring continuously to prevent sticking. Add the ricotta, pinenuts, nutmeg, salt, pepper and basil. Remove from the heat and leave to cool.
2. Roll out the pasta into a large thin circle. Spread the spinach filling evenly over the surface, then roll up like a Swiss roll. Wrap the roll in a clean 'J'-cloth or piece of muslin and tie the ends with string, like a Christmas cracker.
3. Cook in a large saucepan or fish kettle of salted simmering water for about 20 minutes.
4. Preheat the oven to 200°C/400°F/gas mark 6.
5. Slice the roulade thickly and arrange in an ovenproof dish. Pour over the tomato sauce, sprinkle with Parmesan cheese and reheat in the oven for 20 minutes.

 *MEDIUM RED*

# TAGLIATELLE WITH OYSTER MUSHROOMS AND SAGE

SERVES 3–4
*225g/8oz tagliatelle*
*oil*
*salt and freshly ground black pepper*
*55g/2oz butter*
*450g/1lb oyster mushrooms, sliced*
*1 tablespoon chopped fresh sage*

1. Cook the tagliatelle in plenty of rapidly boiling salted water until tender. Drain well and keep warm.
2. Melt the butter in a large saucepan and cook the oyster mushrooms for 1–2 minutes until soft. Add the tagliatelle and sage, season to taste with salt and pepper and serve immediately.

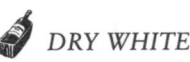 *DRY WHITE*

# TRICOLOUR PASTA SALAD

SERVES 4–6
*225g/8oz pasta twists*
*1 red pepper, cored, deseeded and quartered*
*450g/1lb broccoli*
*6 tablespoons French dressing (see page 254)*
*2 tablespoons chopped fresh parsley*

1. Cook the pasta in plenty of rapidly boiling salted water until just tender. Rinse under cold running water until completely cold, then drain well.
2. Grill the pepper until the skin is well charred, scrape off the skin and cut the flesh into 5mm/¼in wide strips.
3. Cut the broccoli into small florets and cook in boiling water for 1 minute. Rinse under cold running water and drain well.
4. Toss the pasta, peppers and broccoli in the French dressing and parsley. Serve chilled.

 *LIGHT DRY WHITE*

# RAVIOLI WITH SPINACH AND RICOTTA FILLING

SERVES 4
*340g/12oz flour quantity egg pasta (see page 470)*

For the filling
*450g/1lb spinach, cooked and chopped*
*110g/4oz ricotta cheese*
*1 egg*
*salt and freshly ground black pepper*
*freshly grated nutmeg*
*freshly grated Parmesan cheese*

To serve
*pesto sauce (see page 255)*

**1.** Mix the spinach with the ricotta cheese, add the egg and beat well. Season to taste with salt, pepper, nutmeg and Parmesan cheese.

**2.** Roll the pasta to a very thin rectangle. Cut in half. Keep well covered to prevent drying out.

**3.** Take one sheet of pasta and place half-teaspoons of filling, in even rows, all over it. Brush round the piles of filling with a little water. Cover loosely with the other sheet of pasta and press firmly round each mound of filling. Check carefully that there are no pockets of air.

**4.** Cut between the rows, making sure that all the edges are sealed. Allow to dry on a wire rack for 30 minutes.

**5.** Cook in a saucepan of simmering salted water for 4–5 minutes until tender. Drain well and serve with the pesto sauce.

 *BARDOLINO OR VALPOLICELLA*

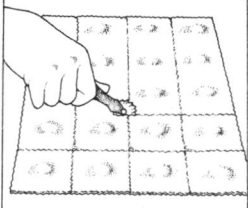

*Cut between the rows of pasta, checking carefully that there are no pockets of air*

# PASTA-FILLED BREAD

SERVES 6

*Italian bread made with 900g/2lb flour (see page 614)*

*oil*

*pesto sauce (see page 255)*

*2 avocados, peeled and sliced*

**1.** Cut the top quarter off the Italian bread and keep it to use as a lid. Hollow out the centre of the loaf. This will be used as a container for the pasta.

**2.** Cook the pasta in rapidly boiling salted water until just tender. Drain well. Toss in the pesto sauce and add the avocado slices. (Do not worry if they break up.) Tip the filling into the hollowed-out loaf.

**3.** Place the lid on top and serve immediately.

 *LIGHT DRY WHITE*

# LASAGNE VERDI BOLOGNESE

SERVES 4

*half quantity green pasta (see page 470)*
*freshly grated Parmesan cheese*

For the meat sauce
*1 tablespoon dripping or oil*
*340g/12oz lean minced beef*
*1 onion, finely diced*
*1 stick of celery, finely diced*
*4 cloves of garlic, chopped*
*30g/1oz plain flour*
*290ml/½ pint brown stock (see page 243)*
*100ml/3½fl oz dry white wine*
*salt and freshly ground black pepper*
*1 tablespoon chopped fresh parsley*
*1 teaspoon chopped fresh marjoram*
*a pinch of ground cinnamon*
*1 tablespoon tomato purée*

For the cream sauce
*45g/1½oz butter*
*1 bay leaf*
*45g/1½oz plain flour*
*570ml/1 pint creamy milk*
*salt and freshly ground black pepper*
*freshly grated nutmeg*

**1.** Cut the pasta into 5 × 3cm/6 × 1in strips. Allow to dry for 1 hour.

**2.** Heat the dripping or oil in a saucepan and brown the mince well. Add the vegetables and garlic and fry, stirring continuously, for 2 minutes.

**3.** Stir in the flour. Cook for 30 seconds. Pour in the stock and wine and add the salt, pepper, parsley, marjoram, cinnamon and tomato purée. Bring to the boil, stirring. Simmer slowly for 45 minutes, then boil rapidly, stirring, until the sauce is very thick and syrupy.

**4.** Make the cream sauce: melt the butter in a saucepan, add the bay leaf and flour and cook, stirring, for 1 minute. Remove from the heat.

**5.** Add the milk and return to the heat. Beat slowly to the boil, stirring continuously, until you have a thick, creamy sauce. Simmer for 2 minutes. Season to taste with salt and pepper and remove the bay leaf.

**6.** Preheat the oven to 190°C/375°F/gas mark 5. Butter an ovenproof dish and cover the bottom with a layer of pasta, then spoon on a thin layer of meat sauce. Cover with a layer of cream sauce. Arrange a layer of pasta on top of this. Continue the layers in this manner, finishing with cream sauce. Sprinkle with grated Parmesan cheese.

**7.** Bake in the preheated oven for 20–25 minutes until bubbling and just brown on top.

NOTE: If using bought pasta, cook according to manufacturer's instructions.

 *MEDIUM RED*

# RAVIOLI

Ravioli can be made with leftover cooked beef, veal, lamb or pork.

SERVES 4
*340g/12oz flour quantity egg pasta (see page 470)*

For the meat filling
*170g/6oz cooked meat, minced*
*15g/¹/₂oz butter*
*2 teaspoons fresh white breadcrumbs*
*2 teaspoons chopped fresh parsley*
*2 teaspoons brown stock (see page 243)*
*1 teaspoon tomato purée*
*salt and freshly ground black pepper*
*a pinch of freshly grated nutmeg*
*a pinch of ground cinnamon*
*1 small egg, beaten*
*freshly grated Parmesan cheese*
*melted butter or oil or tomato sauce II (see page 258)*

**1.** Fry the meat in the butter in a saucepan for 5 minutes. Stir in the breadcrumbs, parsley, stock, tomato purée, salt, pepper, nutmeg and cinnamon. Check the seasoning.

**2.** Add enough egg to bind the mixture together. Allow to cool.

**3.** Roll out the pasta to a very thin rectangle. Cut in half. Keep well covered to prevent drying out.

**4.** Take one sheet of pasta and place half-teaspoons of filling at 3cm/1½in intervals, in even rows, all over it. Cover loosely with the other sheet of pasta and press together firmly all round

each mound of filling. Cut between the rows, making sure that all the edges are sealed. Allow to dry on a wire rack for 30 minutes.

**5.** Simmer the ravioli in near-boiling salted water for 12–15 minutes, or until just tender. Drain well. Serve with butter, oil or tomato sauce, and hand grated Parmesan cheese separately.

 *LIGHT RED*

# CANNELLONI

SERVES 4
*225g/8oz quantity egg pasta (see page 470)*
*290ml/¹/₂ pint tomato sauce II (see page 258)*
*45g/1¹/₂oz strong Cheddar or Gruyère cheese, or*
  *30g/1oz Parmesan cheese, grated*

For the filling
*2 teaspoons oil or dripping*
*340g/12oz lean minced beef*
*1 onion, chopped*
*1 stick of celery, chopped*
*1 clove of garlic, crushed*
*2 teaspoons tomato purée*
*2 teaspoons plain flour*
*180ml/6fl oz brown stock (see page 243)*
*1 bay leaf*
*1 tablespoon chopped fresh parsley*
*1 tablespoon port or Madeira*
*salt and freshly ground black pepper*

**1.** Cut the pasta into 10 × 6cm/4 × 2½in strips. Allow to dry for 1 hour.

**2.** Heat the oil in a saucepan and add the mince. Brown well all over. Add the onion, celery, garlic and tomato purée and cook for 2 minutes.

**3.** Add the flour and cook for 30 seconds. Remove the pan from the heat, add the stock, bay leaf and parsley, stir well and return to the heat. Bring slowly to the boil, stirring continuously.

**4.** Season with salt and pepper, cover and simmer for 10 minutes. Then add the port or Madeira and continue to simmer for 10 minutes. Check the sauce every so often and if it is getting too dry add a little extra stock. Remove the bay leaf.

**5.** Preheat the oven to 200°C/400°F/gas mark 6. Preheat the grill to its highest setting.

**6.** Cook the pasta in rapidly boiling salted water

until just tender (about 5 minutes if home-made, 12 minutes if bought). Drain well and pat dry with a tea-towel or cloth.

**7.** Divide the meat mixture between the pasta strips and roll them up to form the cannelloni. Place them in a greased ovenproof dish.

**8.** Pour over the tomato sauce and sprinkle with grated cheese. Bake in the preheated oven for 15 minutes, then place under the grill until nicely browned.

NOTES: For a blander version, trickle over a little white sauce or double cream before grilling the finished dish.

Commercially made cannelloni are usually tube-shaped, and the filling is inserted with a teaspoon.

 *LIGHT RED / VALPOLICELLA*

# LEMON AND GARLIC GNOCCHI WITH WARM BORLOTTI BEANS

SERVES 4
*1 quantity well-seasoned gnocchi (see page 197)*
*3 cloves of garlic, unpeeled*
*oil*
*110g/4oz fine fresh white breadcrumbs*
*finely grated zest of 1 lemon*
*3 tablespoons chopped fresh parsley*
*freshly ground black pepper*
*1 egg, beaten*
*oil for frying*
*2 × 400g/14oz cans of borlotti beans, drained*
*150ml/¼ pint extra virgin olive oil*
*2 cloves of garlic, peeled*
*1 small red chilli, deseeded*
*2 tablespoons chopped fresh basil*
*juice of 1 lemon*
*salt and freshly ground black pepper*

**1.** Preheat the oven to 200°C/400°F/gas mark 6.
**2.** Make the gnocchi and leave to chill in a shallow square tin which has been rinsed with water.
**3.** Paint the cloves of garlic with a little oil and fry for about 10 minutes, then peel and crush.
**4.** Mix together the crushed garlic, breadcrumbs, lemon zest and parsley, and season with black pepper.

**5.** Divide the chilled gnocchi into 8 even pieces. Dip into beaten egg, then coat evenly in the breadcrumb mixture.

**6.** Heat enough oil in a frying pan to come halfway up the gnocchi and then fry until golden-brown on both sides. Drain well and keep warm in the oven.

**7.** Meanwhile, heat the extra virgin olive oil, remove from the heat, add the garlic and chilli and leave to infuse for 30 minutes. Strain.

**8.** Heat the infused oil and when hot, quickly fry the basil. When it turns bright green reduce the heat, add the borlotti beans and heat through. Add the lemon juice, salt and pepper to taste.

**9.** Divide the warmed beans between 4 warmed dinner plates, and put 2 gnocchi on each plate.

 *SPICY DRY WHITE*

# POTATO TART

This doesn't sound very exciting but is in fact a truly delicious tart.

SERVES 6–8
*225g/8oz plain flour*
*a pinch of salt*
*110g/4oz butter*
*1 egg yolk*
*very cold water*
*150ml/¼ pint crème fraîche*
*freshly grated nutmeg*

For the tomato filling
*3 tablespoons olive oil*
*1 onion, finely chopped*
*8 medium tomatoes, peeled, deseeded and chopped*
*1 tablespoon tomato purée*
*1 sprig of fresh thyme*
*a pinch of caster sugar*
*salt and freshly ground black pepper*

For the potato filling
*6 waxy potatoes, peeled and cut into even chunks*
*2 tablespoons olive oil*

For the onion filling
*85g/3oz unsalted butter*
*5 medium onions, thinly sliced*

To serve
*150ml/¼ pint crème fraîche*
*freshly grated nutmeg*

**1.** Preheat the oven to 200°C/400°F/gas mark 6.
**2.** Sift the four with the salt into a large bowl.
Rub in the butter until the mixture resembles
breadcrumbs.
**3.** Mix the egg yolk with 3 tablespoons water and
add to the mixture. Mix to a firm dough, first
with a knife and then with one hand, adding
more water if necessary.
**4.** Roll the pastry out and use to line a 25cm/10in
flan ring. Chill in the refrigerator for 20 minutes,
then bake blind in the preheated oven (see page
459) for 15 minutes.
**5.** Make the tomato filling: heat the oil in a
saucepan over a low heat and cook the onion
gently for about 10 minutes. Add the tomatoes,
tomato purée, thyme, sugar, salt and pepper.
Increase the heat and cook until all the liquid
evaporates (about 35 minutes).
**6.** Brush the potatoes with oil and sprinkle with
salt. Roast in the preheated oven for about 1
hour, until tender. Cut into 5mm/¼in slices. Turn
the oven temperature up to 230°C/450°F/gas
mark 8.
**7.** Make the onion filling: melt the butter in a
frying pan, add the onions and cook over a low
heat for about 30 minutes until soft and creamy.
**8.** Spread the onions on the pastry base and cover
with the tomato filling, then arrange the sliced
potatoes around the top. Cover with the crème
fraîche and sprinkle with nutmeg. Bake in the
preheated oven for 15 minutes, or until brown.
Serve at room temperature.

 *LIGHT RED*

# CHEDDAR AND HAZELNUT CROQUETTES

SERVES 6
*110g/4oz fresh wholemeal breadcrumbs*
*85g/3oz chopped mixed nuts, such as hazelnuts,*
*    almonds, walnuts, toasted*
*1 tablespoon chopped mixed fresh herbs, such as*
*    parsley, mint, thyme*
*1 large onion, finely chopped*
*1 teaspoon tomato purée*
*110g/4oz Cheddar cheese, grated*
*1 egg, lightly beaten*
*salt and freshly ground black pepper*
*seasoned plain flour*
*oil for frying*

To sauce
*tomato sauce II (see page 258)*

**1.** Mix together all the ingredients except the
flour. Season well with salt and pepper.
**2.** With wet hands, shape the mixture into balls the
size of ping-pong balls and roll in seasoned flour.
**3.** Heat oil in a deep-fryer until a crumb sizzles in
it. Deep-fry the cheese and nut balls until brown.
**4.** Serve with tomato sauce.

 *LIGHT RED*

# CAROLINE'S RICOTTA PIE

This recipe was devised by Caroline Yates,
co-author of *Leith's Contemporary Cooking*.

SERVES 8
*840g/1¾lb ricotta cheese*
*4 egg yolks*
*1 whole egg*
*170g/6oz Parmesan cheese, freshly grated*
*55g/2oz unsalted butter, softened*
*salt and freshly ground black pepper*
*freshly grated nutmeg*
*pesto sauce (see page 255)*

**1.** Preheat the oven to 190°C/375°F/gas mark 5.
**2.** Mix together the ricotta, egg yolks, egg,
Parmesan cheese and butter. Beat well and season
to taste with salt, pepper and nutmeg.

**3.** Turn into a buttered 1 litre/2 pint ovenproof dish.

**4.** Bake in the preheated oven for 30 minutes. Remove from the oven and cool slightly. Turn out on to a plate. Drizzle with pesto sauce and serve while still warm.

 *MEDIUM RED*

# GRILLED POLENTA WITH PROSCIUTTO SALAD

SERVES 6–8

*2 litres/3¹/₂ pints white stock, made with chicken
   bones (see page 243)*
*400g/14oz precooked cornmeal*
*285g/10oz Parmesan cheese, freshly grated*
*salt and freshly ground black pepper*
*85ml/3fl oz olive oil infused with a sliced clove of
   garlic*
*1 medium aubergine*
*225g/8oz wild mushrooms, sliced*
*110g/4oz sun-dried tomatoes in oil, sliced*
*170g/6oz prosciutto, thinly sliced*
*1 red pepper, grilled, deseeded, peeled and sliced*
*1 yellow pepper, grilled, deseeded, peeled and sliced*
*1 large red chilli, thinly sliced*
*85g/3oz black olives, pitted*
*1 × 400g/14oz can of artichoke hearts, drained
   and cut in half*
*a few basil leaves*

**1.** Heat the stock in a large saucepan until simmering. Slowly pour in the cornmeal, stirring all the time until thick. Reduce the heat as much as possible, cover the pan and cook, stirring frequently, for 5–7 minutes or until thick. Add 250g/9oz of the Parmesan cheese and season with pepper. Cover and set aside to cool slightly.

**2.** Pour the polenta on to a damp baking sheet and smooth the surface with a wet spatula. The polenta should be about 1cm/¹/₂in thick. Preheat the grill to its highest setting.

**3.** When the polenta is cool, cut into diamond shapes, place on a lightly greased baking sheet, brush with the flavoured oil and grill under the grill. When brown and crisp, turn the shapes over, brush with more oil and grill on the other side. Dust with the remaining Parmesan cheese.

**4.** Cut the aubergines into long strips 1cm/¹/₂in wide and salt them lightly. Leave for 30 minutes to extract the bitter juices (degorge), then rinse and dry the aubergine, brush with oil and grill until soft.

**5.** Toss the mushrooms with the sun-dried tomatoes and their oil in a frying pan over a high heat for 3 minutes. Remove with a slotted spoon, add the prosciutto and increase the heat. Fry, stirring, until crisp and brown.

**6.** Mix together the peppers, chilli, aubergines, mushrooms, tomatoes, prosciutto, olives and artichoke hearts. Mix 2 tablespoons olive oil with the vinegar, season with salt and pepper and sprinkle over the salad.

**7.** Arrange the polenta around the edge of a large serving plate, put the salad in the centre and garnish with basil leaves.

 *ITALIAN MEDIUM RED*

# AUBERGINE CHARLOTTE

This is a useful supper dish of a layered-up aubergine and tomato, good served with a crisp green salad and Basmati rice. It can also be made individually in small dariole moulds.

SERVES 4

*4 large aubergines*
*salt and freshly ground black pepper*
*1 onion, finely chopped*
*olive oil*
*1 clove of garlic, crushed*
*15 tomatoes, peeled, deseeded and chopped*
*290ml/¹/₂ pint plain yoghurt*
*stock*

**1.** Slice and salt the aubergines and leave to degorge in a colander for 30 minutes. Meanwhile, cook the onion in a little oil in a saucepan for 3 minutes. Add the garlic, tomatoes, salt and pepper and cook for a further 25 minutes.

**2.** Rinse and dry the aubergines. Fry in oil in a frying pan until soft and highly browned. Drain on absorbent kitchen paper.

**3.** Preheat the oven to 180°C/350°F/gas mark 4.

**4.** Arrange a layer of aubergine slices along the bottom and up the sides of a loaf or charlotte tin.

**5.** Layer up two-thirds of the tomatoes, the

yoghurt and remaining aubergines, finishing with
a layer of aubergines.

**6.** Cover with kitchen foil and bake in the
preheated oven for 40 minutes.

**7.** Remove from the oven and leave to cool for 5
minutes. Tip off any excess liquid. Turn out and
serve hot with the remaining tomatoes, thinned to
the consistency of a sauce with a little stock.

# RED ONION POLENTA TATIN

SERVES 6–8

*170g/6oz flour quantity polenta pastry (see page 468)*

For the topping
*55g/2oz butter*
*900g/2lb red onions, thinly sliced*
*2 tablespoons white wine*
*2 cloves of garlic, crushed*
*1 tablespoon soft light brown sugar*
*2 large red peppers*
*1 tablespoon capers, rinsed and drained*
*3 anchovies, slivered*
*¼ tablespoon chopped fresh rosemary*

**1.** Preheat the oven to 190°C/375°F/gas mark 5.

**2.** To make the topping: melt 30g/1oz of the
butter in a heavy, ovenproof frying pan. Add the
onions and cook, covered, for 15 minutes, until
they begin to soften. Add the wine, garlic and half
the sugar and cook for 20 minutes. Turn up the
heat and reduce, by boiling rapidly, until the
liquid coats the onions.

**3.** Preheat the grill to its highest setting. Cut the
peppers into quarters, then remove the stalks,
membrane and seeds. Grill the peppers, skin side
uppermost, until the skin is black and blistered.
Scrape off the skin with a small knife.

**4.** Melt the remaining butter in the pan, stir in the
remaining sugar and remove from the heat.
Arrange the red pepper pieces in the pan in a
daisy pattern. Place the capers and anchovies
between the peppers and cover with the cooked
onions, taking care not to dislodge the peppers.

**5.** Place the pan over a high heat until the butter
and sugar start to caramelize, which may take

5 minutes. Remove the pan from the heat and
place it on a baking sheet.

**6.** Lay the polenta pastry on top of the onions and
press down lightly. Bake for 25 minutes. Allow to
cool slightly, then invert the pan over a serving
plate and serve warm.

 *LIGHT RED*

# PROSCIUTTO AND AUBERGINE GOUGÈRE

SERVES 4

*butter for greasing*
*55g/2oz Parmesan or Gruyère cheese, grated*
*½ teaspoon dried mustard*
*2-egg quantity choux pastry (see page 465)*
*1 small aubergine, cut into small dice*
*1 tablespoon olive oil*
*85g/3oz prosciutto, cut into shreds*
*1 teaspoon chopped fresh basil*
*4 tablespoons double cream*
*salt and freshly ground black pepper*
*1 tablespoon freshly grated Parmesan cheese*

**1.** Lightly butter 4 ramekins.

**2.** Preheat the oven to 200°C/400°F/gas mark 6.

**3.** Beat the 55g/2oz cheese and the mustard into
the choux pastry. Fit a piping bag with a 1cm/½in
plain nozzle and fill with the cheese mixture. Pipe
round the bottom and sides of the ramekins,
leaving a small well in the centre.

**4.** Fry the aubergine lightly in the oil until soft.

**5.** Mix together the prosciutto, basil, aubergine
and cream. Season to taste with salt and pepper.

**6.** Spoon the filling into the centre of the
ramekins. Sprinkle with the Parmesan cheese.
Bake in the preheated oven for 15–20 minutes
until well risen and brown. Serve very hot.

 *MEDIUM RED*

# PASTRY, PASTA AND BATTERS

# PASTRY, PASTA AND BATTERS

Pastry comes in many forms. All of them are made from a mixture of flour and liquid, and usually contain fat. Variations in quantities and the ingredients themselves give each type its distinctive texture and taste. The three commonest types of pastry are short, flaky and choux, all of which have variations. The degree of shortness (or crisp crumbliness) depends on the amount and type of fat (the shortening factor) incorporated into the flour, and the way in which the uncooked pastry, or paste, is handled.

## THE INGREDIENTS

FATS Butter gives a crisp, rich shortcrust pastry with excellent flavour. Solid margarine gives a similar result that is slightly less rich and flavourful. Lard gives very short but rather tasteless pastry. It gives excellent results when used in combination with butter. Solid cooking fat and vegetable shortening give a crust similar to that produced by lard. Suet is used only in suet crust, which is a soft and rather heavy pastry. A raising agent is usually added to the flour to combat the pastry's doughiness, and to make it more cake-like in texture.

FLOUR in shortcrust pastry is usually plain, all-purpose flour. Weak or cake flour is also suitable for pastry-making. Wholemeal flour produces a delicious nutty-flavoured crust, but is more absorbent than white flour and will need more liquid, which makes it harder and heavier. For this reason, a mixture of wholemeal and white flour, usually half and half, is generally used to make 'wholemeal' pastry. Self-raising flour is occasionally used in pastry-making. It produces a soft, thicker, more cakey crust. It is also sometimes used to lighten cheese dough and other heavy pastes like suet crust. Whatever the flour, it should be sifted, even if it has no lumps in it, to incorporate air and give the pastry lightness.

The less liquid used in pastry-making the better. Some very rich doughs, such as almond pastry, which contains a high proportion of butter and eggs, can be kneaded without any water or milk at all. Others need a little liquid to bind them. Water gives the pastry crispness and firmness. Too much makes pastry easy to handle but gives a hard crust that shrinks in the oven. The addition of egg or egg white instead of water will give a firm but not hard crust. Egg yolk on its own produces a rich, soft and crumbly crust.

## MAKING PASTRY

RUBBING IN Shortcrust pastry is made by rubbing fat into sifted flour and other dry ingredients with the fingertips, then adding other ingredients such as egg yolks and any liquid. Everything should be kept as cool as possible. If the fat melts, the finished pastry may be tough. Cut the fat, which should be firm and cold but not hard, into tiny pieces using a small knife and floured fingers. The flour prevents the fat from sticking to the fingers and beginning to melt, and the smaller the pieces of fat, the better the chances of even distribution. Mix the pieces of fat into the flour, then rub in, handling the fat as quickly and lightly as possible so it does not stick to the fingertips. Pick up a few pieces of floury fat and plenty of flour with the fingertips and thumbs of both hands. Hold your hands about 25cm/10in above the bowl, thumbs up and little fingers down, and gently and quickly rub the little pieces of fat into the flour, squashing the fat lightly as you go. Do not try to mash each piece of fat; a breadcrumb texture, not doughy lumps, is what is required. Drop the floury flakes of fat from a height; this cools the fat and aerates it, making the finished pastry lighter. Shake the bowl regularly so that the big unrubbed pieces of fat come to the surface. Stop when the mixture resembles very coarse – not fine – breadcrumbs.

ADDING LIQUID Rich shortcrust pastry, with a higher proportion of fat, needs little, if any, water added. Although over-moist pastry is easy to handle and roll out, the baked crust will be tough and may well shrink in the oven as the water evaporates in the heat. The drier and more difficult to handle the pastry is, the crisper the shortcrust will be. Add only as much water as is needed to get the pastry to hold together, and sprinkle it, 1 teaspoonful at a time, over as large a surface as possible.

Mixing should be kept to a minimum. Mix the pastry with a fork or knife so you handle it as little as possible. As soon as it holds together in lumps, stop mixing. Lightly flour your hands and quickly and gently gather into a ball, rolling it around the bowl to pick up crumbs.

RELAXING It is important to chill pastry for at least 30 minutes before rolling it out, or at least before baking. This allows cells to swell and absorb the liquid evenly. 'Relaxed' pastry will not shrink drastically or unevenly as just-made pastry will. Most pastries benefit from chilling, especially in hot weather, or if they are used to line tart tins, when shrinkage can spell disaster. Relaxing is less important, though still a good idea, for pastes used to cover pies. To prevent the surface of the pastry from drying out and cracking in the dry atmosphere of the refrigerator, cover it lightly with clingfilm or a damp cloth. Ideally pastry is relaxed before and after rolling.

ROLLING OUT Lightly dust the work surface with flour. do not use much as this can alter the proportion of flour to the other ingredients. Once rolled, allow the pastry to relax in a cool place before baking, especially if it was not relaxed before rolling out.

BAKING BLIND Line the raw pastry case with a piece of kitchen foil or a double sheet of greaseproof paper and fill it with dried lentils, beans, rice or even pebbles or coins. This is to prevent the pastry bubbling up during cooking. When the pastry is half cooked (about 15 minutes) the 'blind beans' can be removed and the empty pastry case further dried out in the oven. The beans can be re-used indefinitely.

## TYPES OF PASTRY
SHORTCRUST: See recipe on page 461.
RICH SHORTCRUST: See recipe on page 461.

SUET CRUST PASTRY. This is made like shortcrust pastry except that the fat (suet) is generally chopped or shredded before use. Because self-raising flour (or plain flour and baking powder) is used in order to produce a less heavy dough pastry, it is important to cook the pastry soon after making it, while the raising agent is at its most active. During cooking the raising agent causes the dough to puff up and rise slightly and as it hardens, air will be trapped. This makes the suet crust lighter and more bread-like (see page 462).

PÂTE SUCRÉE, ALMOND PASTRY AND PÂTE À PÂTE
These and other very rich pastries are extreme forms of rich shortcrust, with all the liquid replaced by fat or eggs. Traditionally they are made by working together the egg yolks and fat, and sometimes sugar, with the fingertips until soft and creamy (see page 466). The flour is then gradually incorporated until a soft, very rich paste is achieved. To mix the paste, use only the fingertips of one hand. Using both hands, or the whole hand, leads to sticky pastry. The warmth of the fingertips is important for softening the fat, but once that is done, mixing and kneading should be as light and quick as possible. The pastry can be brought together very quickly by using a palette knife. Because of the high proportion of fat, no water is added.

Modern food processors enable the most unskilled cook to make these pastries in seconds. Simply put all the ingredients (the fat in smallish pieces) into the machine and process until the paste forms a ball. This may take a minute or so. The mixture first becomes crumbly, then as it warms up the butter softens and largish lumps appear. When these are gathered into one or two cohesive lumps the paste is made. Do not over-process as the paste will become sticky and taste greasy. The speed of the processor makes for very good pastry which becomes crisp as it cools. When biscuit-coloured and cooked it will feel soft in the centre. When completely cool, slide off the baking sheet using a palette knife.

HOT WATERCRUST This is made by heating water and fat together and mixing them into the flour. Because of the high proportion of water, this pastry is inclined to be hard. Its strength and firmness allow it to encase heavy mixtures, such as an English pork pie, without collapsing. Also, as the fat used is generally lard, the pastry can lack flavour, so add plenty of salt. Many old recipes recommend throwing the pastry away uneaten once it has done its duty as container. Our recipe for veal and ham pie (see page 423) is a better-tasting modification of hot watercrust, containing butter and egg.

Do not allow the water to boil before the fat has melted. If the water reduces by boiling, the proportion of water to flour will not be correct. Quickly mix the water and melted fat into the flour in a warmed bowl, then keep it covered with a hot damp cloth. This prevents the fat from becoming set and the pastry from flaking and drying out.

CHOUX PASTRY Like Yorkshire pudding batter, this pastry contains water and eggs and depends on the rising of the steam within it to produce a puffy, hollow pastry case. It is easy to make if the recipe is followed closely. The following points are particularly important:

1. Measure ingredients exactly. Proportions are important with choux.
2. Do not allow the water to boil until the butter has melted, but when it has, bring it immediately to a full rolling boil. Boiling the water too soon will cause too much evaporation.
3. Having the sifted flour ready in a bowl so that the minute the rolling ball is achieved, you can tip in the flour, all in one go.
4. Beat fast and vigorously to get rid of lumps before they cook hard.
5. Do not over-beat. Stop once the mixture is leaving the sides of the pan.
6. Cool slightly before adding egg, otherwise it will scramble.

7. Do not beat in more egg than is necessary to achieve a dropping consistency. If the mixture is too stiff, the pastry will be stodgy. If it is too thin, it will rise unevenly into shapeless lumps.
8. Bake until it is a good, even brown, otherwise the inside of the pastry will be uncooked.
9. If the pastry is to be served cold, split the buns/rings, or poke a hole in each of them with a skewer, to allow the steam inside to escape. If steam remains trapped inside, the pastry will be soggy and a little heavy. Opened-up pastry or small buns with holes in them can be returned to the oven, hole uppermost, to dry out further.
10. Serve the pastry on the day it is made (or store frozen), as it stales rapidly and does not keep well in a tin. See page 528 for chocolate profiteroles recipe.

FLAKY PASTRY AND PUFF PASTRY These are begun in rather the same way as the first stage for preparing shortcrust pastry, though the consistency is initially softer and less short, as they contain a high proportion of water. Then more fat, either in a solid block or in small pieces, is incorporated into the paste, which is rolled, folded and re-rolled several times. This process creates layers of pastry which, in the heat of the oven, will rise into light thin leaves. For instance, puff pastry, which is folded in three and rolled out six times, will have 729 layers.

As the whole aim is to create the layers without allowing the incorporated fat to melt, start with everything cool, including the bowl, the ingredients, and the worktop if possible. Short, quick strokes (rather than long steady ones) allow the bubbles of air so carefully incorporated into the pastry to move about while the fat is gradually and evenly distributed in the paste. Work lightly and do not stretch the paste, or the layers you have built up will tear and allow the air and fat to escape. Chill the pastry between rollings or at any point if there is a danger of the fat breaking through the pastry, or if the pastry becomes sticky and warm. It sounds like a complicated business, but it is a lot easier done than said: follow the instructions on page 464 (puff pastry), page 463 (rough puff pastry) and page 463 (flaky pastry).

Pastry rises evenly to a crisp crust in a steamy atmosphere. For this reason flaky and puff pastries (which are expected to rise in the oven) are sometimes baked with a roasting pan full of water at the bottom of the oven, or on a damp baking sheet. The oven temperature is set high to cause rapid expansion of the trapped layers of air and quick cooking of the dough before the fat has time to melt and run out.

STRUDEL PASTRY This differs from most other pastries in that it actually benefits from heavy handling. It is beaten and stretched, thumped and kneaded. This treatment allows the gluten to expand and promotes elasticity in the dough. The paste is rolled and stretched on a cloth (the bigger the better) until it is so thin that you should be able to read fine print through it. Keep the paste covered and moist when not in use. When the pastry is pulled out, brush it with butter or oil to prevent it cracking and drying, or keep it covered with a damp cloth. Strudel pastry can be bought in ready-rolled leaves from specialist food shops, especially Greek-owned ones. Called phyllo or filo pastry, it is used to make the Middle Eastern baklava. Detailed instructions for strudel pastry appear on page 466.

# SHORTCRUST PASTRY (PÂTE BRISÉE)

*170g/6oz plain flour*
*a pinch of salt*
*30g/1oz lard*
*55g/2oz butter*
*very cold water to mix*

1. Sift the flour with the salt into a large bowl.
2. Rub in the fats until the mixture resembles coarse breadcrumbs.
3. Add 2 tablespoons water to the mixture. Mix to a firm dough, first with a knife, and finally with one hand. It may be necessary to add more water, but the pastry should not be too damp. (Though crumbly pastry is more difficult to handle, it produces a shorter, lighter result.)
4. Chill, wrapped, in the refrigerator for 30 minutes before using. Or allow to relax after rolling out but before baking.

# RICH SHORTCRUST PASTRY

*170g/6oz plain flour*
*a pinch of salt*
*100g/3½oz butter*
*1 egg yolk*
*very cold water to mix*

1. Sift the flour with the salt into a large bowl.
2. Rub in the butter until the mixture resembles breadcrumbs.

3. Mix the egg yolk with 2 tablespoons water and add to the mixture.
4. Mix to a firm dough, first with a knife, and finally with one hand. It may be necessary to add more water, but the pastry should not be too damp. (Though crumbly pastry is more difficult to handle, it produces a shorter, lighter result.)
5. Chill, wrapped, in the refrigerator for 30 minutes before using. Or allow to relax after rolling out but before baking.

NOTE: To make sweet rich shortcrust pastry, mix in 1 tablespoon caster sugar once the fat has been rubbed into the flour.

# SWEET PASTRY

*170g/6oz plain flour*
*a large pinch of salt*
*½ teaspoon baking powder*
*100g/3½oz unsalted butter*
*55g/2oz caster sugar*
*1 egg yolk*
*55ml/2fl oz double cream*

1. Sift the flour with the salt and baking powder into a large bowl.
2. Rub in the butter until the mixture resembles coarse breadcrumbs. Stir in the sugar.
3. Mix the egg yolk with the cream and add to the mixture.
4. Mix to a firm dough, first with a knife and finally with one hand. Chill, wrapped, in the refrigerator for 30 minutes before using, or allow to relax after rolling out but before baking.

## PÂTE SABLÉE

*285g/10oz plain flour*
*a pinch of salt*
*225g/8oz butter, softened*
*2 egg yolks*
*110g/4oz icing sugar, sifted*
*2 drops of vanilla essence*

1. Sift the flour with the salt on to a board. Make a large well in the centre and put the butter in it. Place the egg yolks and sugar on the butter with the vanilla essence.
2. Using the fingertips of one hand, 'peck' the butter, yolks and sugar together. When mixed to a soft paste, draw in the flour and knead lightly until the pastry is just smooth.
3. Wrap and chill before rolling or pressing out to the required shape. Then chill again.


## MARTHA STEWART'S WALNUT PASTRY

*225g/8oz plain flour*
*a pinch of salt*
*100g/4oz butter*
*140g/5oz ground walnuts*
*45g/1½oz sugar*
*1 egg, beaten*

1. Sift the flour with the salt into a large bowl. Rub in the butter until the mixture resembles coarse breadcrumbs. Add the walnuts.
2. Stir in the sugar and add enough beaten egg (probably half an egg) to just bind the mixture together. Knead lightly. Chill, wrapped, in the refrigerator before use.

NOTES: If you have a food processor, simply beat all the ingredients together until lightly combined. Chill before use.

This pastry is virtually impossible to roll out: simply press into place.


## SUET PASTRY

As suet pastry is most often used for steamed puddings, instructions for lining a pudding basin are included here. Use the pastry as soon as it is made.

*butter for greasing*
*340g/12oz self-raising flour*
*salt*
*170g/6oz shredded beef suet*
*very cold water to mix*

1. Grease a 1.1 litre/2 pint pudding basin.
2. Sift the flour with a good pinch of salt into a large bowl. Stir in the suet and add enough water to mix, first with a knife, and then with one hand, to a soft dough.
3. On a floured surface, roll out two-thirds of the pastry into a round about 1cm/½in thick. Sprinkle the pastry evenly with flour.
4. Fold the round in half and place the open curved sides towards you.
5. Shape the pastry by rolling the straight edge away from you and gently pushing the middle and pulling the sides to form a bag that, when spread out, will fit the pudding basin.
6. With a dry pastry brush, remove all excess flour and place the bag in the well-greased basin.
7. Fill the pastry bag with the desired mixture.
8. Roll out the remaining piece of pastry and use it as a lid, damping the edges and pressing them firmly together.
9. Cover the basin with buttered greaseproof paper, pleated in the centre, and a layer of pleated kitchen foil. (Pleating the paper and foil allows the pastry to expand slightly without bursting the wrappings.) Tie down firmly to prevent water or steam getting in during cooking.

NOTE: Occasionally suet pastry is used for other purposes than steamed puddings, in which case it should be mixed as above and then handled like any other pastry, except that it does not need to relax before cooking.

## WHOLEMEAL PASTRY

*110g/4oz wholemeal flour*
*110g/4oz plain flour*
*a pinch of salt*
*140g/5oz butter*
*very cold water to mix*

**1.** Sift the flours with the salt into a large bowl and add the bran from the sieve. Rub in the butter until the mixture looks like coarse breadcrumbs.
**2.** Add 2 tablespoons water and mix to a firm dough, first with a knife and then with one hand. It may be necessary to add more water, but the pastry should not be too damp. (Although crumbly pastry is more difficult to handle, it produces a shorter, lighter result.)
**3.** Chill, wrapped, in the refrigerator for at least 30 minutes before using, or allow the rolled-out pastry to relax before baking.

NOTES: To make sweet wholemeal pastry, mix in 2 tablespoons sugar once the fat has been rubbed into the flour.
   All wholemeal flour may be used if preferred.

## HERB WHOLEMEAL PASTRY

*110g/4oz plain flour*
*110g/4oz wholemeal flour*
*a pinch of salt*
*110g/4oz butter, chopped*
*1 tablespoon chopped fresh thyme*
*very cold water to mix*

**1.** Sift the flours with the salt into a large bowl and add the bran from the sieve.
**2.** Rub in the butter until the mixture resembles coarse breadcrumbs. Add the thyme.
**3.** Add enough water to the mixture to mix first with a knife and then with one hand to a firm dough. Chill, wrapped, in the refrigerator for 10 minutes and use as required.

## ROUGH PUFF PASTRY

*225g/8oz plain flour*
*a pinch of salt*
*140g/5oz butter*
*120–150ml/4–5fl oz very cold water to mix*

**1.** Sift the flour with the salt into a chilled bowl. Cut the butter into knobs about the size of a sugar lump and add to the flour. Do not rub in but add enough water to just bind the paste together. Mix first with a knife, then with one hand. Knead very lightly.
**2.** Chill, wrapped, in the refrigerator for 10 minutes.
**3.** On a floured board, roll the pastry into a strip about 30 × 10cm/12 × 4in long. This must be done carefully: with a heavy rolling pin, press firmly on the pastry and give short, sharp rolls until the pastry has reached the required size. Take care not to over-stretch and break the surface of the pastry.
**4.** Fold the strip into 3 and turn so that the folded edge is to your left, like a closed book.
**5.** Again roll out into a strip 1cm/½in thick. Fold in 3 again and chill, wrapped, in the refrigerator for 15 minutes.
**6.** Roll and fold the pastry as before, then chill again for 15 minutes.
**7.** Roll and fold again, by which time the pastry should be ready for use, with no signs of streakiness. If it is still streaky, roll and fold once more.
**8.** Roll into the required shape.
**9.** Chill again in the refrigerator before baking.

## FLAKY PASTRY

*225g/8oz plain flour*
*a pinch of salt*
*85g/3oz butter*
*120–150ml/4–5fl oz cold water*
*85g/3oz lard*

**1.** Sift the flour with a pinch of salt into a large bowl. Rub in half the butter. Add enough water to mix with a knife to a doughy consistency. Turn on to a floured board and knead until just smooth. Chill for 10 minutes.

463

**2.** Roll into a rectangle about 30 × 10cm/12 × 4in. Cut half the lard into tiny pieces and dot them evenly all over the top two-thirds of the pastry, leaving a 1cm/½in margin.

**3.** Fold the pastry in 3, folding first the unlarded third up, then the larded top third down and pressing the edges to seal them. Give a 90-degree anti-clockwise turn so that the folded closed edge is to your left. Chill for 10 minutes.

**4.** Repeat the rolling and folding process (without adding any fat) once more so that the folded, closed edge is on your left.

**5.** Roll out again, dot with the remaining butter as before, and fold and seal as before.

**6.** Roll out again, dot with the remaining lard, fold, seal and roll once more.

**7.** Fold, wrap the pastry and chill in the refrigerator for 10–15 minutes.

**8.** Roll and fold once again (without adding any fat) and then use as required. If the pastry is still streaky, roll and fold once again.

NOTES: As a general rule, flaky pastry is rolled out thinly, and baked at about 220°C/425°F/gas mark 7.

If the pastry becomes too warm or sticky and difficult to handle, wrap it and chill in the refrigerator for 15 minutes before proceeding.

# PUFF PASTRY

*225g/8oz plain flour*
*a pinch of salt*
*30g/1oz lard*
*120–150ml/4–5fl oz iced water*
*140–200g/5–7oz butter*

**1.** If you have never made puff pastry before, use the smaller amount of butter: this will give a normal pastry. If you have some experience, more butter will produce a lighter, very rich pastry.

**2.** Sift the flour with the salt into a large bowl. Rub in the lard. Add enough water to mix with a knife to a doughy consistency. Turn on to a floured board and knead quickly until just smooth. Chill, wrapped, in the refrigerator for 30 minutes.

**3.** Lightly flour the board and roll the dough into a rectangle about 30 × 10cm/12 × 4in.

**4.** Tap the butter lightly with a floured rolling pin to shape it into a flattened block about 9 × 8cm/3½ × 3in. Put the butter on the rectangle of pastry and fold both ends over to enclose it. Fold the third closest to you over first and then bring the top third down. Press the sides together to prevent the butter escaping. Give it a 90-degree anti-clockwise turn so that the folded, closed edge is on your left.

**5.** Now tap the pastry parcel with the rolling pin to flatten the butter a little; then roll out, quickly and lightly, until the pastry is 3 times as long as it is wide. Fold it very evenly in 3, first folding the third closest to you over, then bringing the top third down. Give it a 90-degree anti-clockwise turn so that the folded, closed edge is on your left. Again press the edges firmly with the rolling pin. Then roll out again to form a rectangle as before.

**6.** Now the pastry has had 2 rolls and folds, or 'turns' as they are called. It should be put to rest in a cool place for 30 minutes or so. The rolling and folding must be repeated twice more, the pastry again rested, and then again given 2 more turns. This makes a total of 6 turns. If the butter is still very streaky, roll and fold it once more.

# BOUCHÉE CASES

MAKES ABOUT 20
*225g/8oz flour quantity puff pastry (see above)*
*beaten egg to glaze*

**1.** Preheat the oven to 220°C/425°F/gas mark 7.

**2.** Roll out the pastry 5mm/¼in thick. With a 4cm/1½in round pastry cutter, stamp it out in rounds. With a slightly smaller cutter, cut a circle in the centre of each round, but be careful not to stamp the pastry more than halfway through.

**3.** Brush the tops with beaten egg, taking care not to get egg on the sides, which would prevent the pastry layers from separating and rising.

**4.** Bake on a damp baking sheet in the preheated oven for about 12 minutes, until brown and crisp.

**5.** Take off the pastry 'lids' and scrape out any raw pastry left inside. Return the bouchée cases to the oven for 4 minutes to dry out. Cool on a wire rack.

NOTE: Bouchée cases, if they are to be eaten hot, should either be filled while they are still very hot with a cooked hot filling, or (if they are cooked and cold) with a cooked cold filling. Hot fillings will tend to make the pastry soggy during the reheating process. If both filling and pastry go into the oven cold, the pastry will have time to become crisp again before the filling is hot.

# VOL-AU-VENTS

MAKES 1 OR 2
*225g/8oz flour quantity puff pastry (see page 464)*
*a pinch of salt*
*beaten egg to glaze*

**1.** Preheat the oven to 220°C/425°F/gas mark 7.
**2.** Roll out the pastry to 1cm/½in thickness and cut into a round about the size of a dessert plate. Place on a damp baking sheet. Using a cutter half the size of the pastry round, cut into the centre of the pastry, but take care not to cut right through to the baking sheet.
**3.** Flour the blade of a knife and use this to knock up the sides of the pastry: try to slightly separate the leaves of the pastry horizontally; this enables the edge to flake readily when baking: it counteracts the squashing effect of the cutter used to cut out the round, which may have pressed the edges together, making it more difficult for the pastry to rise in even layers.
**4.** Mix the salt into the beaten egg. Brush the pastry carefully with this egg wash, avoiding the knocked-up sides (if they are covered with egg, the pastry will not rise).
**5.** With the back of the knife blade, make a star pattern on the borders of the vol-au-vent case and mark a lattice pattern on the inner circle. (The back rather than the sharp edge of the blade is used as this will not cut into the pastry; the idea is to make a pattern without cutting through the surface of the pastry.)
**6.** Bake in the preheated oven for 30 minutes, then carefully lift off the top of the inner circle. Keep this for the lid of the case when filled. Pull out and discard any partially cooked pastry from the centre of the case.
**7.** Return the case to the oven for 2 minutes to

dry out. The vol-au-vent is now ready for filling. Ideally the heated pastry case is filled with hot filling, and then served.

NOTE: Flaky or rough puff pastry is also suitable. But the method of cutting is different: cut the pastry into 2 rounds the size of a side plate. Stamp a circle right out of the centre of one of them. Brush the uncut round with egg and place the ring of pastry on top. Bake the middle small round of pastry too, and use it for the vol-au-vent lid.

# CHOUX PASTRY

*85g/3oz butter*
*200ml/7fl oz water*
*105g/3¾oz plain flour, well sifted*
*a pinch of salt*
*3 eggs*

**1.** Put the butter and water into a heavy saucepan. Bring slowly to the boil so that by the time the water boils the butter is completely melted.
**2.** Immediately the mixture is boiling really fast, tip in all the flour with the salt and remove the pan from the heat.
**3.** Working as fast as you can, beat the mixture hard with the wooden spoon: it will soon become thick and smooth and leave the sides of the pan.
**4.** Stand the bottom of the saucepan in a bowl or sink of cold water to speed up the cooling process.
**5.** When the mixture is cool, beat in the eggs, a little at a time, until it is soft, shiny and smooth. If the eggs are large, it may not be necessary to add all of them. The mixture should be of a dropping consistency – not too runny. ('Dropping consistency' means that the mixture will fall off a spoon rather reluctantly and all in a blob; if it runs off, it is too wet, and if it will not fall even when the spoon is jerked slightly, it is too thick).
**6.** Use as required.

# FILO OR STRUDEL PASTRY

*285g/10oz plain flour*
*a pinch of salt*
*1 egg*
*150ml/¼ pint water*
*1 teaspoon oil*

**1.** Sift the flour with the salt into a large bowl.
**2.** Beat the egg and add the water and oil. First with a knife and then with one hand, mix the water and egg into the flour, adding more water if necessary to make a soft dough.
**3.** The dough has now to be beaten: lift the whole mixture up in one hand and then, with a flick of the wrist, slap it on to a lightly floured board. Continue doing this until the dough no longer sticks to your fingers, and the whole mixture is smooth and very elastic. Put it into a clean floured bowl. Cover and leave in a warm place for 15 minutes.
**4.** The pastry is now ready for rolling and pulling. To do this, flour a tea-towel or large cloth on a work top and roll out the pastry as thinly as possible. Now put your hand (well floured) under the pastry and, keeping your hand fairly flat, gently stretch and pull the pastry, gradually and carefully working your way round until the paste is paper-thin. (You should be able to see through it easily.) Trim off the thick edges.

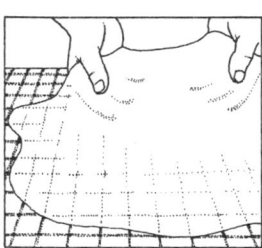 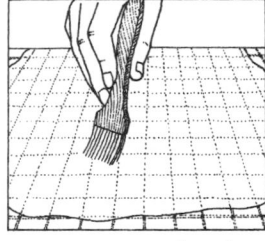

*Stretch and pull until almost transparent; brush with butter*

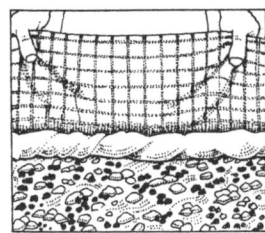

*After filling, roll up (using the tea-towel)*

**5.** Use immediately, as strudel pastry dries out and cracks very quickly. Brushing with melted butter or oil helps to prevent this. Or the pastry sheets may be kept covered with a damp cloth.

NOTE: If the paste is not for immediate use wrap it well and keep refrigerated (for up to 3 days) or frozen. Flour the pastry surfaces before folding up. This will prevent sticking.

# PÂTE SUCRÉE

*170g/6oz plain flour*
*a pinch of salt*
*85g/3oz butter, softened*
*3 egg yolks*
*85g/3oz sugar*
*2 drops of vanilla essence*

**1.** Sift the flour with the salt on to a board. Make a large well in the centre and put the butter in it. Place the egg yolks and sugar on the butter with the vanilla essence.
**2.** Using the fingertips of one hand, mix the butter, yolks and sugar together. When mixed to a soft paste, draw in the flour and knead just until the pastry is smooth.
**3.** If the pastry is very soft, wrap and chill, before rolling or pressing out to the required shape. In any event the pastry must be allowed to relax for 30 minutes either before or after rolling out, but before baking.

# ALMOND PASTRY (1) (PÂTE FROLLÉE)

Care must be taken when making this because if it is over-kneaded the oil will run from the almonds, resulting in an oily paste.

*110g/4oz plain flour*
*a pinch of salt*
*45g/1½oz ground almonds*
*85g/3oz butter, softened*
*45g/1½oz caster sugar*
*1 egg yolk or beaten egg*
*2 drops of vanilla essence*

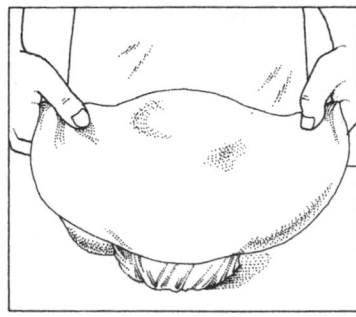 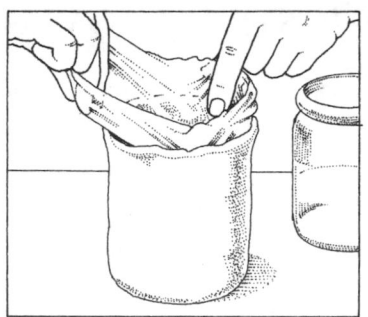 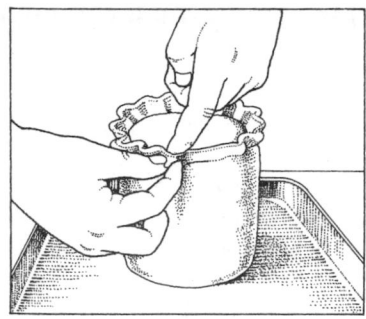

*To shape a raised pie, drape pastry over prepared jar; when cool, remove jar and carefully draw out the paper. Crimp the edges together and bake. See Hot Watercrust Pastry recipe, page 468.*

**1.** Sift the flour with the salt on to a board or work top. Scatter over the ground almonds. Make a large well in the centre and put in the butter, sugar, yolk or beaten egg and vanilla essence.
**2.** Using one hand only, mix with your fingertips. When creamy, gradually draw in the flour and almonds.
**3.** Knead gently to a paste. Chill, wrapped, in the refrigerator for 30 minutes before baking.

## ALMOND PASTRY (2)

*340g/12oz plain flour*
*a pinch of salt*
*225g/8oz butter*
*85g/3oz ground almonds*
*100g/3½oz caster sugar*
*2 egg yolks*
*2 tablespoons very cold water*

**1.** Sift the flour with the salt into a large bowl.
**2.** Rub in the butter until the mixture resembles coarse breadcrumbs. Stir in the ground almonds and the sugar.
**3.** Mix the egg yolks with the water and add enough to the pastry mixture to make a firm dough. Mix first with a knife and finally with one hand. The pastry should not be damp.
**4.** Chill, wrapped, in the refrigerator for 20 minutes before using, or allow to relax in the refrigerator after rolling out, but before baking.

## WALNUT PASTRY

*225g/8oz plain flour*
*a pinch of salt*
*110g/4oz butter, chopped*
*140g/5oz ground walnuts*
*45g/1½oz sugar*
*beaten egg*

**1.** Sift the flour and salt into a large bowl. Rub in the butter with the fingertips until the mixture resembles coarse breadcrumbs.
**2.** Stir in the walnuts and sugar and add enough beaten egg (probably half an egg) just to bind the mixture together. Knead lightly.
**3.** Chill, wrapped, in the refrigerator for 30 minutes before using.

NOTE: If you have a food processor, simply mix all the ingredients together until lightly combined. Chill before use.

## PÂTE À PÂTE

*225g/8oz plain flour*
*½ teaspoon salt*
*165g/5½ oz butter, softened*
*2 small egg yolks*
*3–4 tablespoons water*

1. Sift the flour with the salt on a work top. Make a large well in the centre and put the butter and yolks in it. Work the yolks and butter together with the fingers on one hand and draw in the surrounding flour, adding the water to give a soft, malleable, but not sticky paste.
2. Chill, wrapped in the refrigerator for 30 minutes. Use as required.

# HOT WATERCRUST PASTRY

This pastry is used for raised pies, such as pork pie and game pie.

*225g/8oz plain flour*
*½ teaspoon salt*
*1 egg, beaten*
*100ml/3½fl oz water*
*40g/1¼oz butter*
*40g/1¼oz lard*

**1.** Wrap a piece of paper around the outside of a wide jar or small straight-sided saucepan. The paper can be held in position by tucking it into the opening of the jar or saucepan. Leave it upside down while you make the pastry.
**2.** Sift the flour with the salt into a large bowl. Make a dip in the middle, break the egg into it and toss a liberal covering of flour over the egg.
**3.** Put the water, butter and lard into a saucepan and bring slowly to the boil.
**4.** Once the liquid is boiling, pour it on to the flour, mixing with a knife as you do so. Knead until all the egg streaks have gone and the pastry is smooth.
**5.** Chill, wrapped, in the refrigerator for 10 minutes.
**6.** Reserve about a third of the paste for the pie lid, keeping it covered or wrapped in a warm place. Roll out the remaining paste to a circle and drape it over the jar or saucepan. Working fast, shape the pastry to cover the jar or saucepan to a depth of about 7cm/½in (see page 467). Leave to chill uncovered in the refrigerator.
**7.** As the pastry cools it will harden. When hard, turn the jar or saucepan over and remove it carefully, leaving the paper inside the pastry case. Carefully draw the paper away from the pastry and when it is all loosened take it out. Stand the pastry case on a baking sheet and fill as required. Use the reserved third of the pastry to make the lid, wetting the rim of the pie case to make it stick down firmly. Bake as required.

# PROVENÇAL PASTRY

*340g/12oz plain flour*
*190ml/⅓ pint virgin olive oil*
*salt*
*190ml/⅓ pint lukewarm water*

**1.** Sift the flour into a bowl, add the oil, salt and water and mix as quickly and lightly as possible to a smooth dough.
**2.** Form into a ball, and chill, wrapped, in the refrigerator for 30 minutes. Use as required.

NOTE: A delicious alternative to virgin oil is a herb and chilli flavoured olive oil (available in specialist shops).

# POLENTA PASTRY

*170g/6oz plain flour*
*a pinch of salt*
*85g/3oz polenta (coarse cornmeal)*
*140g/5oz butter*
*30g/1oz Parmesan or Gruyère cheese, grated*
*1 egg, beaten*

**1.** Sift the flour, salt and polenta into a large bowl. Rub in the butter until the mixture resembles breadcrumbs.
**2.** Add the cheese and the egg and bind to a dough.
**3.** Roll into a circle 1cm/½in thick to fit the top of a 25cm/10in frying pan. Chill in the refrigerator.

# THYME PASTRY

*225g/8oz plain flour*
*salt and freshly ground black pepper*
*110g/4oz butter, chopped*
*2 tablespoons fresh thyme leaves, unchopped*
*2 tablespoons dry white wine*
*very cold water to mix (optional)*

**1.** Sift the flour, salt and pepper into a large bowl. Rub in the butter with the fingertips until the mixture resembles breadcrumbs. Add the thyme leaves.
**2.** Add the wine and mix to a firm, but not damp, dough, first with a knife and then with one hand.

Add water only if required. A crumbly pastry may be more difficult to handle but will produce a lighter result.

**3.** Use as required.

NOTES: Any herb can be used in this recipe. Rosemary should be chopped finely.

The pastry can also be made in a food processor (see page 459).

# LEMON PASTRY

*170g/6oz plain flour*
*a pinch of salt*
*1 teaspoon grated lemon zest*
*30g/1oz lard*

*55g/2oz butter*
*very cold water to mix*

**1.** Sift the flour with the salt into a large bowl. Add the lemon zest.

**2.** Rub in the fats until the mixture resembles breadcrumbs.

**3.** Add 2 tablespoons water to the mixture. Mix to a firm dough – first with a knife, and finally with one hand. It may be necessary to add more water, but the pastry should not be too damp. (Although crumbly pastry is more difficult to handle, it produces a shorter, less tough result.)

**4.** Wrap in clingfilm and chill in the refrigerator for 30 minutes before using, or allow to relax in the refrigerator after rolling out but before baking.

# REASONS FOR FAILURE IN PASTRY-MAKING

**Shortcrust, rich shortcrust, etc.**

| | |
|---|---|
| Shrinkage | Over-handled, stretched too much during rolling, not chilled sufficiently, not cooked on top shelf. |
| Tough texture | Too much water, over-handled, heavy-handed rolling. |
| Greasy appearance | Over-worked, hot hands, cooked at too low a temperature. |
| Grey appearance | Not baked blind for long enough, or not covered well in the refrigerator. |

**Rough puff, flaky, puff pastry**

| | |
|---|---|
| Tough pastry | Too much water, over-handling, fat not cold enough. |
| Fat escaping | Fat has not been incorporated correctly, pastry not chilled enough, fat not cold enough. |
| Poor rising | Incorrectly rolled and folded, final pastry rolled too thin. |
| Uneven rise | Uneven pressure when rolling. |

**Choux pastry**

| | |
|---|---|
| Flat, cracked appearance | Panada beaten too much when the flour was added. |

**Suet pastry**

| | |
|---|---|
| Grey, oily, unrisen | Water has not been boiling throughout cooking. |
| Tough, heavy texture | Over-handling, too much liquid. |

**Yeasted pastry**

| | |
|---|---|
| Tough pastry | Over-handling, too much liquid. |
| Greasy appearance | Butter has been melting while the pastry is made. |
| Poor rising | Too much sugar or salt, stale yeast, liquid too hot when added to the mixture. |

NOTE: For all pasta recipes use strong '00' pasta flour if available.

# EGG PASTA

*450g/1lb strong '00' flour*
*4 large eggs*
*1 tablespoon oil*

**1.** Sift the flour on to a wooden board. Make a well in the centre and put in the eggs and oil.
**2.** Using the fingers of one hand, mix together the eggs and oil and gradually draw in the flour, to make a very stiff dough.
**3.** Knead until smooth and elastic (about 15 minutes). Wrap in clingfilm and leave to relax in a cool place for 1 hour.
**4.** Roll out one small piece of dough at a time until paper-thin. Cut into the required shape.
**5.** Allow to dry (unless making ravioli), hanging over a chair back if long noodles, or lying on a wire rack or dry tea towel if small ones, for at least 30 minutes before cooking. Ravioli is dried after stuffing.

NOTE: If more or less pasta is required the recipe can be altered on a pro-rata basis, for example a 340g/12oz quantity of flour calls for a pinch of salt, 3 eggs and 1 scant tablespoon of oil.

# GREEN PASTA

*225g/8oz spinach, cooked*
*340g/12oz strong '00' flour*
*a pinch of salt*
*2 eggs*
*1 tablespoon double cream*

**1.** Chop or liquidize the spinach and push through a sieve to get a fairly dry paste.
**2.** Sift the flour with the salt on to a board. Make a well in the centre and put in the eggs, spinach and cream. Using the fingers of one hand, mix together the eggs, spinach and cream, gradually drawing in the flour, to make a stiff dough.
**3.** Knead until smooth and elastic (about 15 minutes). Wrap in clingfilm and leave to relax in a cool place for 30 minutes.
**4.** Roll out one small piece of dough at a time until paper-thin. Cut into the required shape. Allow to dry (unless making ravioli), hanging over a chair back if long noodles, or lying on a wire rack or clean tea-towel if small ones, for at least 30 minutes before cooking. Ravioli is dried after stuffing.

## COMMONEST NOODLE SHAPES

**Spaghetti:** originally made by pulling the dough into thin strands, now usually made by machine.
**Macaroni:** made commercially into short tube-like pieces.
**Tagliatelle (fettucine):** thin ribbons of pasta, usually served with a sauce.
**Ravioli:** flat sheets used to form small stuffed envelopes, which are then boiled and served with or without sauce.
**Tortellini:** small stuffed pasta shaped like curled half moons.
**Cannelloni:** rectangles about the size of a side plate. They are rolled and generally stuffed (like a pancake) after boiling, then reheated.

## SHAPING TORTELLINI

**1.** Cut the rolled-out pasta dough into 7.5cm/3in rounds. Put a teaspoon of stuffing into the middle of each round. Moisten the edges with water.
**2.** Fold over to form stuffed semicircles. Press the edges together.
**3.** Take each half-circle in both hands and curve it gently round the middle of the index finger. The ends should almost, but not quite, touch.
**4.** Roll the sealed curved edge of the tortellini over to make a groove around the edge.
**5.** Slip the tortellini off the finger and press the ends of the curled half-moon firmly together so that the tortellini cannot unroll.

## FLAVOURED PASTA

Follow the recipe for egg pasta (see page 470) and add the flavourings with the eggs.

**Tomato Pasta** Add about 2 teaspoons tomato purée.
**Herb Pasta** Add plenty of chopped very fresh herbs to taste, such as parsley, thyme, tarragon.
**Beetroot Pasta** Add 1 small cooked, puréed beetroot.
**Saffron Pasta** Add 1 packet of infused saffron strands.
**Chocolate Pasta** Add 55g/2oz melted plain chocolate.

# SAFFRON NOODLES

*225g/8oz strong '00' flour*
*2 eggs*
*3 egg yolks*
*1 tablespoon olive oil*
*½ teaspoon saffron filaments, dry-fried*
*salt and freshly ground white pepper*

**1.** Put all the ingredients into a food processor and process until the mixture forms a dough. (If a food processor is not available, sift the flour into a bowl, add the salt and pepper, make a well in the centre add the eggs, oil and saffron liquid. Gradually mix the flour into the liquid, using your hand. Eventually draw it together into a ball of dough and knead until elastic.
**2.** Roll the pasta as thinly as possible. Dust with flour and roll up like a Swiss roll. Cut as thinly as possible. Unravel the pasta, dust with the flour and place on a tray to dry slightly. (This is much easier if you have a pasta machine).

# HALF-HOUR PASTA

With a food processor and a pasta machine you can be eating pasta half an hour after you thought about it. Use the same ingredients as for the traditional egg pasta recipe on page 470. While the dough is resting make your favourite quick pasta sauce and sit down to enjoy the best fast food there is.

*450g/1lb strong '00' flour*
*a pinch of salt*
*4 eggs*
*1 tablespoon oil*

**1.** Put the flour, salt and the flavouring of your choice (see box) into a food processor and blend well. Beat the eggs and oil together, and with the motor running, gradually add them to the flour until the mixture resembles breadcrumbs. Remove from the processor. Bring a small amount of the mixture together with your fingertips. It should come together easily, but not be too wet. If it does feel wet, add a little extra flour.
**2.** Knead the dough briefly to bring it together, wrap it in clingfilm and leave it to relax for 10 minutes. Pass it through the widest setting of the pasta machine three or four times, then roll it through the different settings of the machine until you can get it through the narrowest gauge. Cut the pasta into the required shape and drop it straight into a large saucepan of boiling salted water.
**3.** Cook until *al dente*, then drain and serve with the sauce of your choice.

# FRENCH PANCAKES (CRÊPES)

MAKES ABOUT 12
*110g/4oz plain flour*
*a pinch of salt*
*1 egg*
*1 egg yolk*
*290ml/½ pint milk, or milk and water mixed*
*1 tablespoon oil*
*oil for cooking*

**1.** Sift the flour with the salt into a bowl and make a well in the centre, exposing the bottom of the bowl.
**2.** Put the egg and egg yolk with a little of the milk into this well.
**3.** Using a wooden spoon or whisk, mix the egg and milk and then gradually draw in the flour from the sides as you mix.

**4.** When the mixture reaches the consistency of thick cream, beat well and stir in the oil.

**5.** Add the remaining milk; the consistency should now be that of thin cream. (Batter can also be made by placing all the ingredients together in a blender for a few seconds, but take care not to over-whizz or the mixture will be bubbly.)

**6.** Cover the bowl and refrigerate for about 30 minutes. This is done so that the starch cells will swell, giving a lighter result.

**7.** Prepare a pancake pan or frying pan by heating well and wiping with oil. Pancakes are not fried in fat – the purpose of the oil is simply to prevent sticking.

**8.** When the pan is ready, pour in about 1 tablespoon batter and swirl about the pan until evenly spread across the bottom.

**9.** Place over heat and, after 1 minute, using a palette knife and your fingers, turn the pancake over and cook again until brown. (Pancakes should be extremely thin, so if the first one is too thick, add a little extra milk to the batter. The first pancake is unlikely to be perfect, and is often discarded.)

**10.** Make up all the pancakes, turning them out on to a tea-towel or plate.

NOTES: Pancakes can be kept warm in a folded tea-towel on a plate over a saucepan of simmering water, in the oven, or in a warmer. If allowed to cool, they may be reheated by being returned to the frying pan or by warming in the oven.

Pancakes freeze well, but should be separated by pieces of greaseproof paper. They may also be refrigerated for a day or two.

# FRITTER BATTER

*125g/4½oz plain flour*
*a pinch of salt*
*2 eggs*
*290ml/½ pint milk*
*1 tablespoon oil*

**1.** Sift the flour with the salt into a bowl.

**2.** Make a well in the centre, exposing the bottom of the bowl.

**3.** Put 1 whole egg and 1 yolk into the well and mix with a wooden spoon or whisk until smooth, gradually incorporating the surrounding flour and

the milk; the consistency should be thick and creamy.

**4.** Add the oil. Allow to rest for 30 minutes.

**5.** When ready to use the batter, whisk the egg white until stiff but not dry. Fold it into the batter with a large metal spoon. Use the batter to coat the food and fry immediately.

# WAFFLES

MAKES 8–10
*2 eggs*
*170g/6oz plain flour*
*a pinch of salt*
*1 tablespoon baking powder*
*30g/1oz caster sugar*
*290ml/½ pint milk*
*55g/2oz butter, melted*
*vanilla essence*
*extra melted butter*

To serve
*butter*
*honey, maple syrup or jam*

**1.** Separate the eggs.

**2.** Sift the flour, salt, baking powder and sugar together into a large bowl. Make a well in the centre and put in the egg yolks.

**3.** Stir the yolks, gradually drawing in the flour from the edges and adding the milk and melted butter until you have a thin batter. Add the vanilla essence.

**4.** Grease a waffle iron and heat it.

**5.** Whisk the egg whites until stiff but not dry and fold into the batter with a large metal spoon.

**6.** Add a little melted butter to the hot waffle iron, pour in about 4 tablespoons of the mixture, close and cook for 1 minute on each side.

**7.** Serve hot with butter and honey, maple syrup or jam.

NOTE: The first waffle always sticks to the iron and should be discarded.

# SCOTCH PANCAKES OR DROP SCONES

MAKES 40
*225g/8oz self-raising flour*
*½ teaspoon salt*
*290ml/½ pint milk*
*½ egg, beaten*

To serve
*butter*
*jam*

1. Sift the flour with the salt into a large bowl.
2. Make a well in the centre of the mixture and pour in half the milk.
3. Add the egg and beat well with the milk.
4. Stir the liquid and gradually draw in the flour from the sides of the bowl.
5. Stir in more milk until the batter is the consistency of thick cream and will just run from a spoon. Cover and leave to stand for 10 minutes.
6. Meanwhile, lightly grease a heavy frying pan or griddle iron and heat it. When really hot, drop 2 or 3 spoonfuls of batter on to the surface, keeping them well separated.
7. Cook for 2–3 minutes. When the undersides of the pancakes are brown, bubbles rise to the surface. Lift the pancakes with a fish slice, turn over and brown the other side.

# SWEET
# SAUCES

---

# CRÈME CHANTILLY

*150ml/¼ pint double cream*
*1 teaspoon icing sugar*
*2 drops vanilla essence*

**1.** Put all the ingredients into a chilled bowl and whisk with a balloon whisk, steadily but not too fast, for about 2 minutes or until the cream has thickened and doubled in volume.
**2.** Whisk faster for 30–40 seconds until the mixture is very fluffy and will form soft peaks.

NOTE: Chilling the ingredients and the bowl gives a lighter, whiter result.

# CRÈME PÂTISSIÈRE

*290ml/½ pint milk*
*2 egg yolks*
*55g/2oz caster sugar*
*20g/¾oz plain flour*
*20g/¾oz cornflour*
*vanilla essence*

**1.** Scald the milk by bringing it to just below boiling point in a saucepan.
**2.** Cream the egg yolks with the sugar and a little of the milk and when pale, mix in the flours. Pour on the milk and mix well.
**3.** Return the mixture to the pan and bring slowly to the boil, stirring continuously. (It will go alarmingly lumpy, but don't worry, keep stirring vigorously and it will become smooth.) Allow to cool slightly, then add the vanilla essence.

# CRÈME ANGLAISE (ENGLISH EGG CUSTARD)

*290ml/½ pint milk*
*1 vanilla pod or a few drops of vanilla essence*
*2 egg yolks*
*1 tablespoon caster sugar*

**1.** Heat the milk and vanilla pod, if using, and bring slowly to the boil.

**2.** Beat the yolks in a bowl with the sugar. Remove the vanilla pod, and pour the milk on to the egg yolks, stirring steadily. Mix well and return to the pan.
**3.** Stir over a low heat until the mixture thickens sufficiently to coat the back of a spoon (about 5 minutes). Do not boil. Strain into a chilled bowl.
**4.** Add the vanilla essence, if using.

# EASY CRÈME ANGLAISE

*1 egg yolk*
*30g/1oz caster sugar*
*30g/1oz plain flour*
*225ml/8fl oz milk*
*2 drops of vanilla essence*

**1.** Whisk the egg yolk with the sugar. Add the flour and beat well.
**2.** Heat the milk and bring slowly to the boil. Pour on to the egg-yolk mixture. Mix well and return to the pan.
**3.** Bring to the boil, stirring continuously. Allow to thicken. Pour into a cold bowl and add the vanilla essence.

# ORANGE CRÈME ANGLAISE

*570ml/1 pint milk*
*finely grated zest of 1 orange*
*1 vanilla pod*
*85g/3oz caster sugar*
*6 egg yolks*
*2 tablespoons Grand Marnier*
*1 drop of orange essence*

**1.** Heat the milk with the orange zest and vanilla pod and bring slowly to the boil.
**2.** Beat the sugar with the egg yolks until pale. Pour the milk on to the egg yolks, stirring steadily. Remove the vanilla pod.
**3.** Return the milk to the pan and cook over a low heat, stirring well until the custard will coat the back of a spoon (about 5 minutes).
**4.** Strain into a cold bowl and add the Grand Marnier and orange essence. Allow to cool before using.

# MOCHA CUSTARD

*290ml/½ pint milk*
*8 coffee beans*
*55g/2oz plain chocolate*
*2 egg yolks*
*15g/½oz caster sugar*

**1.** Put the milk into a small saucepan with the coffee beans. Place over a low heat and bring to the boil. Turn off the heat and leave to infuse for 10 minutes.
**2.** Break the chocolate into small, even-sized pieces and put them into a heatproof bowl set over, not in, a saucepan of simmering water. Allow to melt completely.
**3.** Whisk the egg yolks with the sugar until pale and creamy.
**4.** Strain the milk into the melted chocolate and add to the egg-yolk mixture.
**5.** Pour this mixture into a rinsed-out saucepan and place over a medium heat, stirring until the mixture thickens so that it will coat the back of a spoon (3–4 minutes), but do not boil. Strain into a bowl.

# SUGAR SYRUP

*285g/10oz granulated sugar*
*570ml/1 pint water*
*thinly pared zest of 1 lemon*

**1.** Put the sugar, water and lemon zest into a saucepan and heat slowly until the sugar has completely dissolved.
**2.** Bring to the boil and cook to the required consistency (see below). Allow to cool.
**3.** Strain. Keep covered in a cool place until needed.

NOTE: Sugar syrup will keep unrefrigerated for about 5 days, and for several weeks if kept chilled.

# CARAMEL SAUCE

*225g/8oz granulated sugar*
*290ml/½ pint water*

**1.** Place the sugar in a heavy saucepan with half the water.
**2.** Dissolve the sugar slowly without stirring it or allowing the water to boil.
**3.** Once all the sugar has dissolved, turn up the heat and boil until it is a good caramel colour.
**4.** Immediately tip in the remaining water (it will fizz dangerously, so stand back).
**5.** Stir until any lumps have dissolved, then remove from the heat and allow to cool.

# STAGES IN SUGAR SYRUP CONCENTRATION

| TYPE OF SUGAR SYRUP | BOILING POINT | USES |
| --- | --- | --- |
| Vaseline | 107°C/220–221°F | Syrup and sorbets |
| Short thread | 108°C/225–226°F | Syrup and mousse-based ice creams |
| Long thread | 110°C/230°–235°F | Syrup |
| Soft ball | 115°C/235°–240°F | Fondant, fudge |
| Firm ball | 120°C/248°–250°F | Italian meringue |
| Hard ball | 124°C/255°–265°F | Marshmallows |
| Soft crack | 138°C/270°–290°F | Soft toffee |
| Hard crack | 155°C/300°–310°F | Hard toffee and some nougat |
|  | 160°C/318°F | Nougat |
| Spun sugar | 152°C/305°–308°F | Spun sugar |

# TOFFEE SAUCE

*2 tablespoons brandy*
*110g/4oz butter*
*55g/2oz demerara sugar*
*2 tablespoons double cream*

1. Place all the ingredients in a saucepan and heat until melted. Bring to the boil and allow to thicken slightly.

# APRICOT SAUCE

*170g/6oz dried apricots, soaked overnight*
*570ml/1 pint water*

1. Drain the dried apricots and put them into a saucepan with the water. Bring to the boil, then simmer until tender.
2. Liquidize in a blender, then push through a sieve. If the sauce is too thin, reduce it by rapid boiling to the required consistency. If it is too thick, add a little water.

NOTE: This sauce can be served hot or cold.

# APRICOT SAUCE WITH KERNELS

*85g/3oz granulated sugar*
*290ml/½ pint water*
*225g/8oz apricots, halved*
*juice of ½ lemon*

1. Dissolve the sugar in the water in a heavy saucepan over a low heat. Do not allow to boil until the sugar has completely dissolved (this will prevent the syrup from crystallizing).
2. Add the apricots to the pan with the stones and lemon juice.
3. Bring to the boil and cook until the apricots are soft (about 15 minutes).
4. Remove and reserve the stones.
5. Boil the apricots rapidly for a further 5–10 minutes, or until the pulp is reduced to a syrupy consistency. Push the apricot sauce through a nylon or stainless steel sieve. Taste and add extra sugar if necessary.
6. Crack the stones and remove the kernels. Chop the kernels roughly and add to the sauce. Serve hot or cold.

# RASPBERRY JAM SAUCE

*85g/3oz caster sugar*
*150ml/¼ pint water*
*3 tablespoons raspberry jam*

1. Put the sugar and water into a saucepan and heat slowly until the sugar has dissolved. Then boil rapidly until the syrup feels tacky between finger and thumb.
2. Add the jam, stir until smooth, then sieve to remove the pips.

# HOT CHOCOLATE SAUCE

*170g/6oz plain chocolate, chopped*
*4 tablespoons water*
*1 tablespoon golden syrup*
*1 teaspoon instant coffee powder, dissolved in 1 tablespoon boiling water*
*15g/½oz butter*

1. Put the chocolate into a heatproof bowl set over, not in, a saucepan of simmering water. When melted, add all the remaining ingredients and stir until smooth and shiny.

# APPLE PURÉE

*450g/1lb cooking apples*
*110g/4oz caster sugar*
*4 tablespoons water*

1. Peel and core the apples. Cut them into chunks. Put them with the sugar and water in a heavy saucepan and simmer gently until they are a soft pulp. Beat out any lumps with a wooden spoon.
2. If the purée is too sloppy, boil it rapidly to reduce and thicken it, but leave the lid half on as it splashes dangerously.

# APPLE MARMELADE

*3 cooking apples*
*a little butter*
*a strip of thinly pared lemon zest*
*about 85g/3oz soft light brown sugar*

**1.** Wash the unpeeled apples, quarter and core them. Rub the bottom and sides of a heavy saucepan with butter.
**2.** Slice the apples thickly into the pan and add the lemon zest. Cover and cook over a low heat, stirring occasionally, until completely soft.
**3.** Push through a sieve. Rinse out the pan and return the purée to it. Add at least 55g/2oz sugar to 570ml/1 pint purée. Cook rapidly until the mixture is of dropping consistency (about 4 minutes). Allow to cool. Add more sugar if necessary.

# BRANDY BUTTER

Cream equal quantities of unsalted butter and caster sugar together until very light. Add finely grated orange zest and brandy to flavour fairly strongly.

# MELBA SAUCE

*225g/8oz fresh or frozen (not canned) raspberries*
*icing sugar*

**1.** Defrost the raspberries if frozen. Push them through a nylon or stainless sieve to remove all the seeds.
**2.** Sift in icing sugar to taste. If too thick, add a few spoonfuls of water.

# RASPBERRY COULIS

*340g/12oz raspberries*
*juice of ½ lemon*
*70ml/2½fl oz sugar syrup (see page 477)*

**1.** Whizz all the ingredients together in a food processor or blender, and push through a conical strainer.

NOTE: If it is too thin, the coulis can be thickened by boiling rapidly in a heavy saucepan. Stir well to prevent it catching.

# SWEET GOOSEBERRY SAUCE

*225g/8oz ripe gooseberries*
*150ml/¼ pint water*
*110g/4oz caster sugar*
*a pinch of ground ginger*

**1.** Put all the ingredients into a heavy saucepan. Bring gradually to the boil, then simmer until the gooseberries pop open and change to a yellowish colour.
**2.** Push through a nylon sieve and reheat.

# MANGO AND PASSIONFRUIT SAUCE

*2 ripe passionfruits*
*1 large ripe mango*
*3 tablespoons fresh orange juice*

**1.** Process (but do not liquidize) the passionfruit pulp, mango flesh and orange juice together for 2 minutes. Sieve.

# PUDDINGS

# ORANGE FOOL

SERVES 4
*2 small oranges*
*290ml/¹/₂ pint double cream*
*2 tablespoons icing sugar, sifted*

**1.** Using a potato peeler, pare about half the zest off 1 orange. The strips should have no white pith on the underside. Using a very sharp fruit knife, cut into tiny thin strips about 2.5cm/1in long.
**2.** Place these needleshreds in a saucepan of boiling water for 5 minutes. Rinse in cold water until completely cool. Drain.
**3.** Grate the remaining orange zest and squeeze the juice.
**4.** Whip the cream. When stiff, stir in the orange juice, grated zest and icing sugar.
**5.** Spoon into small glasses or little china pots or coffee cups. Scatter over the needleshreds of orange zest to decorate.

 *SWEET WHITE*

# LEMON SYLLABUB

SERVES 4
*290ml/¹/₂ pint double cream*
*finely grated zest of ¹/₂ lemon*
*juice of 2 lemons*
*2 tablespoons sweet white wine*
*icing sugar to taste, sifted*
*thinly pared zest of ¹/₂ lemon*

**1.** Place the cream in a bowl with the grated lemon zest. Whip, adding the lemon juice, wine and icing sugar at intervals. Spoon into individual glasses.
**2.** Cut the lemon zest into very thin needleshreds. Drop them into boiling water and cook for 2 minutes. Drain and dry them. Scatter on top of the syllabub.

 *SWEET WHITE*

# GINGER SYLLABUB

SERVES 4
*4–5 tablespoons Advocaat liqueur*
*2 tablespoons ginger marmalade*
*290ml/¹/₂ pint double cream*
*1–2 pieces of preserved stem ginger*

**1.** Mix together the Advocaat and ginger marmalade.
**2.** Whip the cream lightly and stir in the ginger marmalade mixture.
**3.** Spoon into small glasses, little china pots or coffee cups.
**4.** Put 2–3 thin slivers of preserved ginger on top of each syllabub. Chill in the refrigerator before serving.

NOTES: For a smoother texture the ginger marmalade and the Advocaat can be liquidized or sieved together.

In the absence of ginger marmalade use orange marmalade well flavoured with finely chopped preserved ginger and its syrup.

 *RICH SWEET WHITE*

# APRICOT MOUSSE

SERVES 4
*170g/6oz good-quality dried apricots, soaked overnight*
*1 tablespoon caster sugar*
*290ml/¹/₂ pint water*
*7g/¹/₄oz powdered gelatine*
*150ml/¹/₄ pint double cream, lightly whipped*
*2 egg whites*

To decorate
*whipped cream*
*apricot pieces*

**1.** Drain the apricots and put them into a heavy saucepan with the sugar and water. Simmer slowly until they are tender.
**2.** Liquidize the cooked apricots in a food processor or blender with enough of the liquor to make a smooth, soft purée. Taste and add more sugar if necessary.

**3.** Put 3 tablespoons water into a small saucepan, sprinkle on the gelatine and leave for 5 minutes to become spongy.

**4.** Dissolve the gelatine over a low heat without boiling until liquid and clear, then stir it into the apricot purée. Leave the mixture in the refrigerator to set slightly, then fold in the cream.

**5.** Whisk the egg whites until stiff but not dry and, using a large metal spoon, fold into the apricot mixture.

**6.** Pour into a soufflé dish and leave to set in the refrigerator for 2–3 hours.

**7.** When set, decorate with rosettes of cream and apricot pieces.

 *SWEET WHITE*

# ORANGE MOUSSE

This is a very low-fat, sugar-free mousse. Some people may find it a little tart.

SERVES 4–6
*150ml/¼ pint water*
*15g/½oz powdered gelatine*
*200ml/7fl oz carton frozen concentrated orange juice, defrosted and warmed*
*290ml/½ pint low-fat plain yoghurt*
*2 egg whites*

**1.** Put 3 tablespoons of the water into a small saucepan. Sprinkle on the gelatine and leave for 5 minutes to become spongy. Dissolve the gelatine over a low heat without boiling until liquid and clear, then add to the orange juice with the remaining water. Stir the mixture into the yoghurt.

**2.** Refrigerate until just beginning to set.

**3.** Whisk the egg whites until they are stiff but not dry. Fold them into the setting orange mixture and pour into a glass bowl. Leave it to set in the refrigerator for a few hours.

NOTE: To make orange ice cream, make the mousse as above and freeze until solid. Remove from the freezer 20 minutes before serving.

 *SWEET WHITE*

# CHOCOLATE MOUSSE

SERVES 4
*110g/4oz plain chocolate*
*4 eggs*

**1.** Chop the chocolate into even-sized pieces. Put into a heatproof bowl set over, not in, a saucepan of simmering water. Allow it to melt.

**2.** Separate the eggs.

**3.** Whisk the egg whites until quite stiff. Stir the melted chocolate into the egg yolks. Mix well.. Fold the whites into the chocolate mixture.

**4.** Turn immediately into a soufflé dish or individual pots or glasses.

**5.** Chill until set, preferably overnight, but for at least 4 hours.

 *FORTIFIED SWEET WHITE*

# RICH CHOCOLATE MOUSSE

SERVES 4
*70g/2½oz granulated sugar*
*110ml/4fl oz water*
*3 egg yolks*
*170g/6oz plain chocolate, chopped*
*340ml/12fl oz double cream, lightly whipped*

**1.** Put the sugar and water into a small heavy saucepan and heat gently until the sugar has completely dissolved, then bring to the boil.

**2.** Boil to the short thread stage (when a little syrup is placed between a wet finger and thumb and the fingers are opened it should form a thread about 2.5cm/1in long).

**3.** Allow to cool slightly.

**4.** Pour the sugar syrup over the egg yolks, whisking all the time. Carry on whisking until the mixture is thick and mousse-like.

**5.** Carefully melt the chocolate in a heatproof bowl set over, not in, a saucepan of simmering water. Fold the chocolate into the egg mixture.

**6.** Immediately and carefully fold in the lightly whipped cream. Use as required.

NOTE: Use couverture chocolate (see page 62) if available.

 *LIQUEUR MUSCAT*

# WHITE CHOCOLATE MOUSSE

SERVES 4
*30ml/1fl oz milk*
*110g/4oz white chocolate, chopped*
*2 drops of vanilla essence*
*2 egg yolks*
*15g/½oz caster sugar*
*7g/¼oz powdered gelatine*
*100ml/3½fl oz double cream, lightly whipped*
*3 egg whites*

**1.** Heat the milk in a small saucepan. Add the chocolate and stir over a low heat until melted. Add the vanilla essence.
**2.** Beat the egg yolks with the sugar until pale and creamy.
**3.** Put 3 tablespoons water into a small saucepan, sprinkle on the gelatine and leave for 5 minutes to become spongy.
**4.** While the chocolate is still warm add it to the yolk and sugar mixture.
**5.** Dissolve the gelatine over a low heat without boiling and when liquid and clear, stir it into the chocolate mixture.
**6.** Leave the chocolate mixture in the refrigerator to thicken and begin to set, then fold in the cream.
**7.** Whisk the egg whites until stiff but not dry and fold into the chocolate mousse mixture.
**8.** Turn into individual serving dishes and chill in the refrigerator until set.

 *SWEET SPARKLING*

# CHOCOLATE AND CHESTNUT MOUSSE CAKE

SERVES 4–6
*140g/5oz plain chocolate*
*45g/1½oz unsalted butter*
*225g/8oz canned unsweetened chestnut purée*
*4 eggs*
*55g/2oz caster sugar*
*1 egg white*
*icing sugar, sifted*

To serve
*double cream, lightly whipped*

**1.** Line the base and sides of a 20cm/8in diameter, 5cm/2in deep, cake tin with greaseproof paper. Lightly oil the paper and dust it out with flour.
**2.** Melt the chocolate and butter in a small heavy saucepan over a low heat. Tip into a bowl and beat well until smooth.
**3.** Preheat the oven to 180°C/350°F/gas mark 4.
**4.** Sieve the chestnut purée into the chocolate and butter mixture.
**5.** Separate the eggs. Whisk the egg yolks with the sugar until thick, pale and mousse-like. Add this to the chocolate and chestnut mixture and mix well.
**6.** Whisk the egg whites until stiff but not dry. Fold into the chocolate mixture. Pour into the prepared cake tin.
**7.** Bake in the preheated oven for 50 minutes. Remove from the oven and leave in the tin to set and cool for 5 minutes. Turn out and dust lightly with the icing sugar. Serve the cream separately.

 *LIQUEUR MUSCAT*

# CHOCOLATE MOUSSE AND GINGER SYLLABUB IN CHOCOLATE CASES

SERVES 6
*chocolate mousse (see page 483)*
*ginger syllabub (see page 482)*

For the chocolate case
*225g/8oz best-quality plain chocolate*

To decorate
*chocolate shapes (see page 649)*

**1.** First make the chocolate cases: break up the chocolate and place it in a heatproof bowl. Set it over, not in, a saucepan of simmering water. Stir until the chocolate is smooth and melted. Do not overheat or the chocolate will lose its gloss.
**2.** Brush the melted chocolate thinly over the insides of 8 small paper cases. (It is easier if you

make double paper cases by slipping one case inside another.) Repeat the process until you have a reasonably thick but even layer. Leave to harden, then carefully peel away the paper.

**3.** Make up the chocolate mousse and ginger syllabub according to the recipes but do not dish them up.

**4.** Divide the chocolate mixture between the 8 chocolate cases. Spread flat and leave to set slightly. Spoon over the ginger syllabub. Decorate each case with a chocolate shape.

 *FORTIFIED SWEET WHITE*

# CARAMEL MOUSSE

SERVES 4
*10g/¹⁄₃oz powdered gelatine*
*a squeeze of lemon juice*
*170g/6oz granulated sugar*
*3 eggs*
*45g/1¹⁄₂oz caster sugar*
*150ml/¹⁄₄ pint double cream*

*To decorate*
*55g/2oz granulated sugar*
*double cream, whipped*

**1.** Sprinkle the gelatine over the lemon juice with 4 tablespoons water in a small saucepan. Leave for 5 minutes to become spongy.

**2.** Melt the granulated sugar in a heavy saucepan with 3 tablespoons water and boil until it turns to a brown caramel. Pour in 5 tablespoons water very carefully – it will hiss alarmingly. Cook over a low heat until the caramel is dissolved. Leave to cool slightly.

**3.** Whisk the eggs with the caster sugar in a heatproof bowl set over, not in, a saucepan of simmering water until mousse-like and thick. Remove from the heat and whisk until beginning to cool.

**4.** Dissolve the soaked gelatine over a low heat without boiling until liquid. Fold into the mousse mixture with the caramel sauce. Stir gently over a bowl of ice until beginning to thicken and set.

**5.** Lightly whip the cream and fold into the mixture.

**6.** Pour into a serving dish and refrigerate until set.

**7.** Meanwhile, make the caramel chips for the decoration: lightly oil a flat dish or baking sheet. Put the sugar into a small heavy saucepan and heat gently, without any water, until it first melts, then turns to caramel. When it is evenly brown, pour immediately on to the oiled dish or baking sheet. Allow to cool until hard as glass, then immediately break into small chips with the end of a rolling pin. Keep dry and cool until needed.

**8.** Decorate the mousse with rosettes of whipped cream and caramel chips.

 *FORTIFIED SWEET WHITE*

# CHARLOTTE RUSSE

SERVES 4–6
*150ml/¹⁄₄ pint clear lemon jelly (see page 502)*
*15 sponge fingers (see page 631)*

*For the custard*
*1 vanilla pod or ¹⁄₂ teaspoon vanilla essence*
*425ml/³⁄₄ pint milk*
*45g/1¹⁄₂oz caster sugar*
*5 egg yolks*
*3 tablespoons sweet sherry*
*15g/¹⁄₂oz powdered gelatine*
*4 tablespoons water*
*235ml/8fl oz double cream, lightly whipped*

*To decorate*
*4 glacé cherries, cut in half*
*a few pieces of angelica*

**1.** Make the lemon jelly. When it is cool but not set, wet a charlotte mould and pour in a thin layer (about 5mm/¹⁄₄in) of jelly. Decorate the base with cherries and angelica and leave to set in the refrigerator. Pour in the remaining jelly and refrigerate again until nearly set. Arrange the sponge fingers, sugared side outside, standing up around the sides of the mould with their ends in the jelly.

**2.** Make the custard: put the vanilla and milk in a saucepan and heat gently.

**3.** In a heatproof bowl, mix the sugar and egg yolks well together. When the milk is almost

485

boiling, remove the vanilla pod, if using, and pour on to the yolks, stirring vigorously. Set the bowl over, not in, a saucepan of simmering water and stir until thick enough to coat the back of the spoon. Strain and allow to cool. Add the sherry.

**4.** Sprinkle the gelatine over the water in a small saucepan and leave for 5 minutes to become spongy. Dissolve over a low heat, without boiling, until liquid and clear, then stir into the cooling custard. When the custard is almost set, fold in the partially whipped cream and turn the mixture into the mould, spreading it flat. Leave in the refrigerator to set.

**5.** Trim off any biscuits sticking up above the level of the filling. Run a knife between the biscuits and the mould to make sure they are not stuck. Dip the bottom of the mould briefly into hot water to dislodge the jelly. Invert a plate over the mould, turn both over together and carefully lift off the mould.

 *SWEET WHITE*

# CHOCOLATE TERRINE WITH ORANGE AND COINTREAU SAUCE

This is a very pretty terrine of 3 coloured chocolate mousses. It can be served individually plated or as a whole.

SERVES 4
*white chocolate mousse (see page 484)*

For the milk chocolate mousse
*170g/6oz milk chocolate, broken up*
*30g/1oz unsalted butter*
*15g/½oz powdered gelatine*
*3 eggs, separated*
*30g/1oz caster sugar*
*150ml/¼ pint double cream, lightly whipped*

For the dark chocolate mousse
*170g/6oz dark chocolate, broken up*
*30g/1oz unsalted butter*
*15g/½oz powdered gelatine*

*3 eggs, separated*
*30g/1oz caster sugar*
*3 tablespoons double cream, lightly whipped*

For the orange sauce
*290ml/½ pint fresh orange juice*
*1 teaspoon arrowroot*
*juice of ¼ lemon*
*2 tablespoons Cointreau*

To decorate
*chocolate leaves (see page 649)*

**1.** Make the white chocolate mousse and pour into a lightly oiled 1.75 litre/3 pint terrine or loaf tin. Leave in the refrigerator to set for 20 minutes.

**2.** Next prepare the milk chocolate mousse: melt the chocolate and butter together in a heavy saucepan over a low heat.

**3.** Put 3 tablespoons water into a small saucepan and sprinkle on the gelatine. Leave for 5 minutes to become spongy.

**4.** Whisk the egg yolks with the sugar until very thick.

**5.** Dissolve the gelatine over a low heat without boiling until liquid and clear.

**6.** Add the melted chocolate and the gelatine to the egg yolk and sugar mixture. Stir gently until the mixture is on the point of setting. Fold in the cream.

**7.** Whisk the egg whites until stiff but not dry and fold into the mousse mixture. Pile on top of the white chocolate mousse in the terrine. Leave in the refrigerator to set for 20 minutes.

**8.** Next prepare the dark chocolate mousse: melt the chocolate with the 3 tablespoons water and the butter in a heavy saucepan over a low heat.

**9.** Pour 3 tablespoons water into a small saucepan and sprinkle on the gelatine. Leave for 5 minutes to become spongy.

**10.** Whisk the egg yolks with the sugar until very thick.

**11.** Dissolve the gelatine over a low heat without boiling until liquid and clear.

**12.** Add the melted chocolate and the gelatine to the egg yolk and sugar mixture. Stir gently until the mixture is on the point of setting. Fold in the lightly whipped cream.

**13.** Whisk the egg whites until stiff but not dry and fold into the chocolate mousse. Pile on top of the milk chocolate mousse in the terrine and leave in the refrigerator to set for 20–30 minutes.

**14.** Finally prepare the orange sauce: put the orange juice into a saucepan and bring to the boil. Mix the arrowroot with a little cold water. Add some of the hot orange juice and pour into the remaining orange juice. Return to the boil, stirring continuously, and simmer for 1 minute. Leave to cool, then add the lemon juice and Cointreau.

**15.** To serve: flood the base of a pudding plate with the orange sauce and cover with one slice of the chocolate terrine. Decorate with chocolate leaves.

 *FORTIFIED MUSCAT*

# CHOCOLATE MARTINIQUE

SERVES 4

*30g/1oz sultanas or raisins*
*2 tablespoons dark rum*
*290ml/½ pint double cream*
*110g/4oz plain chocolate, chopped*
*1 large egg*
*1 tablespoon milk*
*1 extra teaspoon rum*

**1.** Soak the sultanas in the rum overnight.
**2.** Put the cream into a saucepan with 30g/1oz of the chocolate. Bring gradually to the boil, stirring occasionally.
**3.** Meanwhile, beat the egg lightly in a bowl with a wooden spoon. When the cream comes to the boil pour it gradually on to the egg, mixing well.
**4.** Return the mixture to the pan and cook over a low heat, stirring constantly with a wooden spoon until the mixture is thick enough to coat the back of the spoon. Remove from the heat and strain into a bowl or jug. Do not let the custard boil or it will curdle and become grainy.
**5.** Distribute the sultanas with any remaining rum in the bottom of 4 ramekins. Pour the slightly cooled chocolate custard on top. Cool, then refrigerate for 1–1½ hours until set.
**6.** When the custard has set, melt the remaining chocolate with the milk and the teaspoon of rum in a heatproof bowl set over, not in, a saucepan of gently simmering water. Stir until the chocolate is melted, smooth and glossy. Pour enough on the top of each ramekin to cover with a thin coating and leave in a cool place to harden.

 *SWEET WHITE*

# PRUNE MOUSSE

SERVES 4

*110g/4oz prunes, stoned*
*30ml/1fl oz Armagnac or brandy*
*7g/¼oz powdered gelatine*
*110g/4oz granulated sugar*
*150ml/¼ pint water*
*2 egg whites*
*150ml/¼ pint double cream, lightly whipped*

**1.** Soak the prunes in the Armagnac for a day, then purée them in a food processor or liquidizer.
**2.** Sprinkle the gelatine over 3 tablespoons water in a small saucepan.
**3.** Put the sugar and water into a small saucepan and heat gently until the sugar has completely dissolved, then bring to the boil. Allow it to boil to the short thread stage (when a little syrup is placed between a wet finger and thumb and the fingers are opened it should form a thread about 2.5cm/1in long). Leave to cool for 30 seconds.
**4.** Whisk the egg whites until stiff and pour on the cooked sugar syrup, whisking all the time until they have formed a thick, shiny meringue.
**5.** Dissolve the gelatine over a low heat without boiling until liquid and clear, then add it to the prune purée.
**6.** Gradually whisk the purée into the meringue mixture. Fold in the cream. Pour into a serving dish and leave in the refrigerator to set.

 *SWEET WHITE*

# LE GASCON

This is a very complicated recipe but the end result justifies all the effort.

SERVES 8–10
*3 egg quantity sponge fingers (see page 631)*
*3 egg quantity chocolate génoise (see page 595)*
*2 tablespoons Armagnac or brandy*
*150ml/¼ pint sugar syrup (see page 477)*
*3 egg quantity rich chocolate mousse (see page 483)*
*2 egg white quantity prune mousse (see page 487)*
*110g/4oz chocolate quantity glaçage koba (see below)*

**1.** Trim one end of the sponge fingers and use to line the sides of a 20cm/8in spring-clip tin, making sure all the fingers are the same height.
**2.** Cut the chocolate génoise in half horizontally and place one half cut side up in the bottom.
**3.** Add the Armagnac to the sugar syrup.
**4.** Brush both cakes with the sugar syrup.
**5.** Pour the chocolate mousse into the centre until it comes halfway up the sponge fingers. Allow it to set.
**6.** Place the other half of the génoise cut-side up on top of the set chocolate mousse and brush with the sugar syrup.
**7.** Pour the prune mousse on top, leaving a space of 5mm/1/4in at the top. Allow to set.
**8.** Pour the glaçage koba over the top and level with a palette knife if necessary. Leave to set.

 *FORTIFIED SWEET RED*

# GLAÇAGE KOBA (CHOCOLATE ICING)

*70ml/2½fl oz milk*
*225g/8oz plain chocolate, chopped*
*30ml/1fl oz double cream*
*55g/2oz butter*
*15g/½oz powdered glucose*
*4 tablespoons sugar syrup (see page 477)*

**1.** Bring the milk to the boil in a saucepan and add the chocolate, cream, butter and glucose. Stir over a low heat until well mixed and all the chocolate has melted.
**2.** Add the sugar syrup.
**3.** Allow the icing to cool to a coating consistency. If it gets too thick, place over a pan of simmering water and stir until the correct consistency is obtained.

NOTE: Use couverture chocolate if available.

# CASSIS CREAM PIE

SERVES 6

For the base
*2 eggs, separated*
*55g/2oz caster sugar*
*30g/1oz plain flour, sifted*
*1 tablespoon blackcurrant jelly or sieved jam*

For the mousse and glaze
*340g/12oz blackcurrants*
*5 tablespoons crème de cassis liqueur*
*3 eggs, separated*
*110g/4oz caster sugar*
*15g/½oz powdered gelatine*
*150ml/¼ pint double cream*
*2 tablespoons blackcurrant jelly or sieved jam*

**1.** Preheat the oven to 220°C/425°F/gas mark 7.
**2.** Grease and flour a 20in/8in diameter loose-bottomed cake tin.
**3.** Make the base: whisk the egg yolks and half the sugar in a heatproof bowl set over, not in, a saucepan of simmering water with an electric or balloon whisk until pale, mousse-like and very thick. Remove from the heat.
**4.** Whisk the egg whites until stiff and fold in the remaining sugar.
**5.** Fold the yolk and white mixtures together, then fold in the flour.
**6.** Turn into the cake tin and bake in the preheated oven for 15 minutes until evenly brown and slightly shrunk from the tin sides.
**7.** Remove the cake from the tin and cool, upside down, on a wire rack.

**8.** When cold, spread evenly with the blackcurrant jelly or jam.

**9.** Wash the cake tin and oil its sides.

**10.** Make the blackcurrant purée by simmering the fruit with 2 tablespoons water. Keep stirring and boiling until the juice has evaporated without the fruit catching and burning on the bottom of the pan.

**11.** Push the fruit through a nylon sieve to extract the seeds, scraping the paste-like purée from the back of the sieve with a clean spoon. Take one-third of the purée and reserve it for the top. Mix the remainder with 2 tablespoons of the crème de cassis.

**12.** Make the mousse: whisk the egg yolks, 2 tablespoons of the crème de cassis and 75g/3oz of the sugar in a heatproof bowl set over, not in, a saucepan of simmering water. It will be more liquid than the first mixture and the whisking will take longer; it should thicken sufficiently to leave a ribbon-like trail when the whisk is lifted. Remove from the heat and leave to cool, whisking occasionally.

**13.** Put 3 tablespoons water into a small saucepan and sprinkle over the gelatine. Leave for 5 minutes to become spongy.

**14.** Stir the blackcurrant purée into the egg-yolk mixture.

**15.** Dissolve the gelatine over a low heat without boiling until liquid and clear, then stir into the blackcurrant mixture.

**16.** Whip the cream until it will just hold its shape, and fold into the mousse.

**17.** Whisk the egg whites until stiff and fold in the remaining sugar.

**18.** Fold the blackcurrant mousse and the meringue mixtures together lightly and without overmixing – a few air pockets are preferable to a mixture with all the air stirred out of it.

**19.** Fit the cooled and jam-spread cake back into the cake tin, and pour the mousse into it. Level the top and freeze until very solid.

**20.** To remove the mousse from the tin: loosen the sides by wrapping the cake tin in a cloth dipped in very hot water. Push the nearly or completely frozen mousse out of the tin on the base. Using a fish slice, ease the pie on to a serving plate. Allow to thaw in the refrigerator. (The only reason the pie is frozen is to make getting it out of the tin easier. But if a deep flan ring on a baking sheet is used instead of the tin, or a spring-form cake pan – with sides that unclip – then freezing is not necessary.)

**21.** Make the glazed top: gently heat together the reserved blackcurrant purée, the blackcurrant jelly or sieved jam and the remaining crème de cassis. Stir until melted, then boil hard for a few seconds to get a shiny clear syrup.

**22.** Cool the glaze until just liquid, pour over the set mousse, and ease to the edges with a palette knife. Prick any air bubbles with the knife.

 *SWEET WHITE*

# COLD LEMON SOUFFLÉ

SERVES 4
*grated zest and juice of 2 large lemons*
*7g/¼oz powdered gelatine*
*3 eggs*
*140g/5oz caster sugar*
*150ml/¼ pint double cream, lightly whipped*
*icing sugar (optional)*

To decorate
*150ml/¼ pint double cream, whipped*
*wafer-thin lemon slices*
*nibbed almonds, toasted*

**1.** Put the lemon juice into a small saucepan, sprinkle over the gelatine and leave for 5 minutes to become spongy.

**2.** Separate the eggs. Place the yolks and sugar in a mixing bowl and whisk together with an electric motor (or with a balloon whisk or rotary beater with the bowl set over a saucepan of simmering water). Whisk until very thick. If whisking by hand over hot water, remove from heat and whisk for a few minutes longer, until the mixture is lukewarm. Add the lemon zest.

**3.** Dissolve the gelatine over a low heat without boiling until liquid and clear, then add to the mousse mixture. Stir gently until the mixture is on the point of setting, then fold in the cream. Taste and if too tart, sift in a little icing sugar; if too bland, add a little more lemon juice.

**4.** Whisk the egg whites until stiff but not dry and fold them into the soufflé with a large metal spoon.

**5.** Pour the mixture into a soufflé dish and leave to set in the refrigerator for 2–3 hours. Decorate with rosettes of cream, lemon slices and almonds.

NOTE: This dish can be given a more soufflé-like appearance by tying a double band of oiled paper round the top of the dish so that it projects about 2.5cm/1in above the rim, before pouring in the mixture. (The dish must be of a size that would not quite contain the mixture without the added depth given by the paper band.) Pour in the soufflé mixture to come about 2.5cm/1in up the paper, above the rim of the dish. When the soufflé is set, carefully remove the paper and press the almonds round the exposed sides.

 *SWEET WHITE*

# COLD RASPBERRY SOUFFLÉ

SERVES 4
*3 eggs*
*110g/4oz caster sugar*
*3 tablespoons water*
*15g/½oz powdered gelatine*
*340g/12oz raspberries*
*150ml/¼ pint double cream*
*icing sugar (optional)*

To decorate
*chopped or nibbed almonds, toasted*
*150ml/¼ pint double cream, whipped*
*whole raspberries*

**1.** To prepare the soufflé dish (which should be 15cm/6in in diameter), tie a double piece of greaseproof paper around the outside and secure the ends with a paper clip or pin. The paper should stick up about 2.5cm/1in above the rim. Brush the inside of the projecting paper with oil.
**2.** Separate the eggs. Whisk the yolks with the sugar either over a low heat (with the bowl set over a saucepan of simmering water), or in an electric mixer, until light and fluffy, and thick enough for the whisk to leave a 'ribbon trail' when lifted.

**3.** Remove from the heat and whisk again until the mixture is almost cold.
**4.** Put the water into a small pan and sprinkle over the gelatine. Leave for 5 minutes until spongy.
**5.** Liquidize the raspberries in a blender and sieve the purée into the egg-yolk mixture.
**6.** Dissolve the gelatine over a low heat without boiling until liquid and clear, then stir into the raspberry mixture. Stir gently until on the point of setting. Fold in the whipped cream. Taste and sift in a little icing sugar if too tart.
**7.** Whisk the egg whites until stiff but not dry and fold them into the soufflé mixture with a large metal spoon. Pile into the prepared dish and flatten the top neatly. The soufflé mixture should come at least 2cm/¾in above the rim of the dish. Refrigerate for at least 4 hours until set.
**8.** Remove the oiled paper carefully. Spread the exposed sides thinly with cream. Press almonds gently on to the cream. Pipe rosettes of whipped cream round the top and garnish each with a whole raspberry.

 *SWEET WHITE*

# COLD PASSIONFRUIT SOUFFLÉ

SERVES 4
*8 passionfruits*
*grated zest and juice of 1 lemon*
*1 tablespoon water*
*7g/¼oz powdered gelatine*
*3 eggs*
*110g/4oz caster sugar*
*150ml/¼ pint double cream*
*icing sugar (optional)*

To decorate
*1 passionfruit*

**1.** Cut the passionfruits in half. Scoop out and sieve all the flesh.
**2.** Put the lemon juice and water into a small saucepan and sprinkle over the gelatine. Leave for 5 minutes to become spongy.
**3.** Separate the eggs. Place the yolks, lemon zest

and sugar into a mixing bowl and whisk together with an electric mixer (or with a balloon whisk or rotary beater with the bowl set over a saucepan of simmering water). Whisk until very thick. If whisking by hand over hot water, remove from the heat and whisk for a few minutes longer, until the mixture is lukewarm. Gradually add the passionfruit pulp.

**4.** Dissolve the gelatine over a low heat without boiling until liquid and clear, then add to the mousse mixture. Stir gently until the mixture is on the point of setting, then fold in the cream. Taste and if too tart sift in a little icing sugar; if too bland add a little more lemon juice.

**5.** Whisk the egg whites until stiff but not dry and fold them into the soufflé with a large metal spoon.

**6.** Pour the mixture into a soufflé dish and leave to set in the refrigerator for 2–3 hours. When set decorate with the seeds of 1 passionfruit.

 *SWEET WHITE*

# SEVILLE ORANGE SOUFFLÉ

This is a recipe of Sophie Grigson's, published in the London *Evening Standard*.

SERVES 4
*butter and caster sugar for the soufflé dish*
*110g/4oz caster sugar*
*30g/1oz plain flour*
*150–200ml/5–7fl oz milk*
*1 vanilla pod, split*
*15g/½oz butter*
*finely grated zest and juice of 2 Seville oranges*
*4 egg yolks*
*5 egg whites*
*icing sugar, to dust*

**1.** Butter a soufflé dish and dust with caster sugar.
**2.** Preheat the oven to 200°C/400°F/gas mark 6. Preheat a baking sheet.
**3.** Mix half the sugar with the flour in a saucepan. Pour in a little of the milk, warm gently over a low heat, then gradually stir in the remaining

milk, making sure there are no lumps. Add the vanilla pod, bring to the boil and simmer, stirring all the time, for 1 minute (add more milk if necessary). Remove from the heat and discard the vanilla pod.

**4.** Beat in the butter and stir in the orange zest and juice and finally the egg yolks. Transfer to a large mixing bowl.

**5.** Whisk the egg whites until stiff, then gradually whisk in the remaining sugar, continuing to whisk until the mixture is stiff and shiny. Fold gently but thoroughly into the orange mixture. Pour into the prepared soufflé dish – do not fill more than two-thirds full. Run the handle of a wooden spoon around the top edge of the soufflé mixture. This gives a 'top hat' appearance to the cooked soufflé. Bake the soufflé on the preheated baking sheet for 20–25 minutes.

**6.** Test by giving the dish a slight shake or push. If the soufflé wobbles alarmingly, it needs further cooking; if it wobbles only slightly, it is ready. Dust with icing sugar and serve immediately.

 *RICH SWEET WHITE*

# HOT CHOCOLATE SOUFFLÉ

To make a successful chocolate soufflé you must have everything organized before you start to cook and work as quickly as possible. It is quite difficult to do.

SERVES 4
*butter, melted*
*55g/2oz caster sugar plus 1 teaspoon*
*110g/4oz plain chocolate*
*4 egg yolks*
*5 egg whites*
*icing sugar*

**1.** Preheat the oven to 200°C/400°F/gas mark 6. Preheat a baking sheet. Prepare the soufflé dish by brushing the inside with melted butter and dusting it with 1 teaspoon caster sugar.
**2.** Chop the chocolate with a large knife and put it into a heatproof bowl set over, not in, a

saucepan of gently simmering water, stirring until the chocolate has completely melted.

**3.** Beat the remaining sugar and the egg yolks together for 1 minute with a wooden spoon until thick and fluffy. Add the egg-yolk mixture to the chocolate, mixing well – it will thicken slightly.

**4.** Whisk the whites until they will stand in soft peaks when the whisk is withdrawn from the bowl. Whisk in 1 teaspoon caster sugar, until stiff and shiny. Gently but thoroughly fold into the chocolate mixture.

**5.** Turn into the soufflé dish but do not fill more than two-thirds of the dish. Run the end of a wooden spoon handle around the edge of the soufflé mixture. This gives a 'top hat' appearance to the cooked soufflé.

**6.** Bake in the preheated oven on the hot baking sheet for 20–25 minutes. Test by giving the dish a slight shake or push. If the soufflé wobbles alarmingly, it needs further cooking; if it wobbles slightly, it is ready. Dust lightly with icing sugar and serve immediately.

 *FORTIFIED SWEET WINE*

# SWEET SOUFFLÉ OMELETTE

SERVES 2
*2 eggs*
*1 tablespoon apricot jam*
*1 tablespoon lemon juice*
*30g/1oz caster sugar*
*15g/½oz butter*
*icing sugar to finish*

**1.** Separate the eggs.
**2.** Preheat the oven to 180°C/350°F/gas mark 4.
**3.** Warm the jam with the lemon juice.
**4.** Beat the yolks with the sugar until light and fluffy.
**5.** Whisk the egg whites until stiff but not too dry. (The mixture should form a medium peak when the whisk is lifted from it, not too floppy, not too rigid.)
**6.** Heat a 15cm/6in frying pan and melt the butter in it.

**7.** Fold the egg whites into the yolks and when the butter is foaming, but not coloured, pour in the egg mixture.
**8.** Lower the heat and cook for 1 minute until the underside has just set.
**9.** Place in the preheated oven for 5 minutes, or until the omelette top is just set – do not overcook.
**10.** Get 2 long skewers red-hot in a gas flame. Leave them there while baking the omelette.
**11.** Spread the warmed jam over half the omelette and fold in 2 with a spatula – you may need to cut the omelette a little in the middle.
**12.** Slip on to a warmed flat serving dish. Sprinkle the surface with icing sugar.
**13.** Brand a criss-cross pattern in the sugar with the red-hot skewers. Serve immediately.

NOTES: It is not strictly necessary to finish the cooking in the oven, but it avoids the risk of burning the bottom of the omelette before the top is set.

The branding with the hot skewer is not essential either, but the omelette should be sprinkled with icing sugar before serving.

 *SWEET WHITE*

# HOT APRICOT SOUFFLÉ

SERVES 4
*20g/¾oz butter, plus extra for greasing*
*30g/1oz caster sugar, plus extra for dusting*
*110g/4oz good-quality dried apricots, soaked*
*    overnight in 200ml/7fl oz water*
*20g/¾oz plain flour*
*200ml/7fl oz orange juice*
*grated zest of 1 orange*
*5 egg whites*

**1.** Butter a 15cm/6in (1 litre/2 pint) soufflé dish and dust it with caster sugar. Preheat the oven to 200°C/400°F/gas mark 6.
**2.** Poach the apricots in the water until very tender and then liquidize in a food processor or blender with the cooking liquor.
**3.** Melt the butter in a small saucepan, add the flour and cook for 1 minute. Remove from the heat and add the orange juice and zest. Return the

pan to the heat and bring to the boil, stirring continually. Simmer for 2 minutes. Remove from the heat and add the apricot purée.

**4.** Whisk the egg whites until just stiff, add the sugar and whisk again until stiff.

**5.** Add 1 tablespoon of egg white to loosen the soufflé base and then gently fold in the remaining egg whites. Pour into the prepared soufflé dish.

**6.** Run the end of a wooden spoon handle around the edge of the soufflé mixture. This gives a 'top hat' appearance to the cooked soufflé.

**7.** Bake in the preheated oven for 12–15 minutes. Test by giving the dish a slight shake or push. If the soufflé wobbles alarmingly, it needs further cooking; if it wobbles slightly, it is ready. Serve immediately.

 *SWEET SPARKLING*

# JUNKET

SERVES 4
*570ml/1 pint fresh milk*
*2 teaspoons sugar*
*1 teaspoon rennet*

**1.** Heat the milk with the sugar to blood temperature (lukewarm).

**2.** Stir well and pour into a serving bowl.

**3.** Stir in the rennet and leave to set at room temperature. Once set, the dish may be refrigerated.

NOTE: To vary the flavour of plain junket, spoon over a little whipped cream and sprinkle with crumbed ratafia biscuits; sprinkle the surface with freshly grated nutmeg; or flavour with coffee essence, grated orange zest or grated chocolate.

# BAKED CUSTARD

SERVES 4
*3 eggs*
*1 egg yolk*
*3 drops of vanilla essence*
*55g/2oz caster sugar*
*425ml/³/4 pint very creamy milk, or milk plus*
*    single cream, scalded*
*1 bay leaf*
*freshly grated nutmeg*

**1.** Preheat the oven to 170°C/325°F/gas mark 3.

**2.** Lightly beat the eggs, egg yolk, vanilla essence and sugar together with a wooden spoon; don't make them frothy.

**3.** Pour the milk and the cream, if using, on to the eggs, stirring all the time with a wooden spoon, not a whisk, to avoid creating bubbles.

**4.** Strain the mixture into an ovenproof dish. Straining removes any egg 'threads' which would spoil the smooth texture of the finished custard. Add the bay leaf and sprinkle with nutmeg.

**5.** Stand the custard dish in a roasting pan half-filled with hot water (a bain-marie) and bake in the preheated oven for 40 minutes. The custard is set when there is a definite skin on the top and the centre is no longer liquid (although it will wobble).

**6.** Serve hot, warm or chilled.

# RICE PUDDING

SERVES 4
*a nut of butter*
*1 tablespoon caster sugar*
*55g/2oz round (pudding) rice*
*570ml/1 pint milk*
*vanilla essence*
*freshly grated nutmeg*

**1.** Preheat the oven to 150°C/300°F/gas mark 2.

**2.** Rub the butter round a pie dish. Put the sugar, rice, milk and vanilla essence into the dish. Sprinkle with nutmeg.

**3.** Stir, and bake in the oven for 3–4 hours, by which time it should be soft and creamy with an evenly coloured brown skin.

# BREAD AND BUTTER PUDDING

SERVES 4
2 slices of white bread
30g/1oz butter
2 tablespoons currants and sultanas, mixed
2 teaspoons chopped mixed peel
2 eggs
1 egg yolk
1 rounded tablespoon sugar
290ml/½ pint creamy milk
vanilla essence
ground cinnamon
demerara sugar

1. Spread the bread with the butter. Cut into quarters. Arrange in a shallow ovenproof dish, buttered side up, and sprinkle with currants, sultanas and peel.
2. Make the custard: mix the eggs and egg yolk with the sugar and stir in the milk and vanilla essence.
3. Strain the custard carefully over the bread and leave to soak for 30 minutes. Sprinkle with cinnamon and demerara sugar.
4. Preheat the oven to 180°C/350°F/gas mark 4.
5. Place the pudding in a roasting pan half-filled with hot water (a bain-marie) and cook in the middle of the oven for about 45 minutes, or until the custard is set and the top is brown and crusty.

NOTE: The pudding may be baked quite successfully without the bain-marie, but if used it will ensure a smooth, not bubbly custard.

 *SWEET WHITE*

# BREAD AND BUTTER PUDDING WITH BRIOCHE

SERVES 4–6
1 brioche (see page 620), weighing 225g/8oz
55g/2oz butter
85g/3oz dried apricots, chopped
30g/1oz raisins
2 teaspoons chopped mixed peel

6 eggs
3 egg yolks
55g/2oz sugar
860ml/1½ pints creamy milk
2 teaspoons vanilla essence
1 teaspoon ground cinnamon
5 tablespoons apricot jam

1. Slice the brioche into 1cm/½in slices, leaving the crusts on. Spread the slices with butter and cut them in half diagonally.
2. Grease a large shallow oval dish (1.75 litres/3 pints capacity) and scatter over some of the apricots, all of the raisins and the mixed peel. Arrange the brioche slices buttered side up, slightly overlapping, in the dish and scatter over the remaining apricots.
3. Mix together the eggs, egg yolks, sugar, milk, vanilla essence and cinnamon, using a wooden spoon. Strain the mixture over the brioche and leave to stand in a cool place for 30 minutes.
4. Preheat the oven to 170°C/325°F/gas mark 3.
5. Heat up a bain-marie (a roasting pan half-filled with hot water) and put the dish in it. Bake in the centre of the preheated oven for about 1 hour, or until the custard is set.
6. Meanwhile, heat the apricot jam in a saucepan with 1 tablespoon water. Push through a sieve and keep warm.
7. When the pudding is cooked, remove it from the bain-marie and using a pastry brush, brush the surface with the apricot glaze. Serve warm.

# CRÈME CARAMEL

SERVES 4–5
110g/4oz granulated sugar
4 tablespoons water
4 eggs
2 tablespoons caster sugar
570ml/1 pint milk
vanilla essence

1. Preheat the oven to 150°C/300°F/gas mark 2. Warm a soufflé or other ovenproof dish in it.
2. Place the granulated sugar in a heavy saucepan with the water and allow it to melt slowly. When melted, boil rapidly until it has turned to a good

brown toffee. Pour into the hot soufflé dish and coat all over by carefully tipping the dish. Leave until cold.

**3.** Beat the eggs and caster sugar together with a wooden spoon.

**4.** Scald the milk by bringing it to just below boiling point and stir it into the egg mixture. Add the vanilla essence. Strain into the prepared dish.

**5.** Stand the dish in a roasting pan half-filled with hot water (a bain-marie) and cook in the preheated oven for 1 hour, or until the custard has set.

**6.** Allow to cool until tepid or stone-cold, then turn out on to a dish with a good lip.

NOTE: The caramel can be made in the microwave. Put the sugar and water into a shallow dish. Cover with clingfilm and pierce. Microwave on HIGH for 2 minutes. Stir, then microwave for a further 6 minutes. Swirl it carefully around the dish.

 *FORTIFIED SWEET WHITE*

# QUEEN'S PUDDING

SERVES 4
*290ml/½ pint milk*
*15g/½oz butter*
*140g/5oz caster sugar*
*55g/2oz fresh white breadcrumbs*
*grated zest of 1 lemon*
*2 eggs*
*2 tablespoons raspberry jam, warmed*

**1.** Heat the milk and add the butter and 30g/1oz of the sugar. Stir until the sugar dissolves, then add the breadcrumbs and lemon zest. Allow to cool.

**2.** Preheat the oven to 180°C/350°F/gas mark 4.

**3.** Separate the eggs. Mix the egg yolks into the breadcrumb mixture. Pour into a pie dish and leave to stand for 30 minutes.

**4.** Place the pudding in a roasting pan half-filled with hot water (a bain-marie) and bake in the preheated oven for 45 minutes, or until the custard mixture is set. Remove from the oven and allow to cool slightly.

**5.** Turn down the oven temperature to 150°C/300°F/gas mark 2.

**6.** Carefully spread the jam over the top of the custard. (This is easier if you melt the jam first.)

**7.** Whisk the egg whites until stiff. Whisk in 2 teaspoons of the remaining sugar. Whisk again until very stiff and shiny and fold in all but half a teaspoon of the remaining sugar.

**8.** Pile the meringue on top of the custard and dust the top lightly with the reserved sugar.

**9.** Bake in the oven until the meringue is set and straw-coloured (about 10 minutes).

NOTES: This is particularly good served hot with cold whipped cream.

　　See 'Whisking egg whites', page 554.

 *SWEET WHITE*

# SEMOLINA

SERVES 4
*570ml/1 pint milk*
*a few drops of oil*
*85g/3oz semolina*
*2 eggs*
*85g/3oz caster sugar*
*juice of 1 lemon*
*a few drops of vanilla essence*
*4–5 tablespoons double cream*

**1.** Heat the milk with the oil in a heavy saucepan and when boiling, gradually stir in the semolina.

**2.** Reduce the heat and simmer for 10 minutes, or until the semolina is cooked, stirring from time to time. Remove from the heat and allow to cool slightly.

**3.** Separate the eggs. Whisk the yolks with the sugar until light and fluffy, then stir in the semolina mixture.

**4.** Beat in the lemon juice, vanilla essence and cream.

**5.** Whisk the egg whites until stiff and fold into the semolina mixture with a large metal spoon.

# PETITS POTS DE CRÈME

SERVES 6
*290ml/½ pint milk*
*just over 290ml/½ pint single cream*
*30g/1oz caster sugar*
*1 vanilla pod or 2 drops of vanilla essence*
*4 egg yolks*
*1 large egg*

For the flavourings
*1 teaspoon coffee essence*
*45g/1½oz plain chocolate, melted*

**1.** Preheat the oven to 150°C/300°F/gas mark 2.
**2.** Place the milk and cream with the sugar and vanilla pod, if using, in a saucepan and scald by bringing to just below boiling point. Remove the vanilla pod. (If using vanilla essence, add it once the milk is scalded.)
**3.** Beat the egg yolks with the whole egg and pour on the scalded milk. Strain and divide into 3 equal parts.
**4.** Flavour one-third of the custard with coffee essence, one-third with melted chocolate and leave one-third plain. Pour each flavoured custard separately into 2 ramekins. Stand the 6 ramekins in a roasting pan half-filled with hot water (a bain-marie).
**5.** Bake in the preheated oven, covered with a sheet of greaseproof paper or kitchen foil, for 35–40 minutes. Remove the covering, being careful not to let any condensed water drop on to the crèmes. Lift out of the water and allow to cool.

NOTE: Chocolate-flavoured custards may take longer to cook (about 45 minutes).

# CRÈME BRÛLÉE

Crème brûlée is best started a day in advance.

SERVES 4
*290ml/½ pint double cream*
*1 vanilla pod or 1 teaspoon vanilla essence*
*4 egg yolks*
*1 tablespoon caster sugar*

For the topping
*caster sugar*

**1.** Put the cream with the vanilla pod, if using, into a saucepan and heat to scalding point (just below boiling point), making sure it does not boil. Remove the vanilla pod.
**2.** Preheat the oven to 170°C/325°F/gas mark 3.
**3.** Beat the egg yolks with the sugar and when light and fluffy, stir in the warm cream. Place the mixture in the top of a double saucepan, or in a heatproof bowl set over, not in, a saucepan of simmering water, over a low heat. Stir continuously with a wooden spoon until the custard is thick enough to coat the back of the spoon. If using vanilla essence, add it now.
**4.** Pour the custard into an ovenproof serving dish, place in a roasting pan half-filled with hot water (a bain-marie) and bake in the preheated oven for 12 minutes to create a good skin on top. Refrigerate overnight. On no account break the top skin.
**5.** Next day preheat the grill to its highest setting.
**6.** Sprinkle the top of the custard with a 5mm/¼in even layer of caster sugar. To do this, stand the dish on a tray or large sheet of greaseproof paper and sift the sugar over the dish and the tray or paper. In this way you will get an even layer of sugar. Collect the sugar falling wide for re-use.
**7.** Put the custard under the very hot grill, as close as you can get it to the heat. The sugar will melt and caramelize before the custard underneath it boils. Watch carefully, turning the custard if the sugar is browning unevenly.
**8.** Allow to cool completely before serving. The top should be hard and crackly.
**9.** To serve: crack the top with the serving spoon and give each diner some custard (which should be creamy and just set) and a piece of caramel. Crème brûlée is also good made in individual ramekins. In this case, bake the custard for only 5 minutes.

NOTE: If making crème brûlée for more than 4 or 5 people, either make in individual ramekin dishes or in more than one large dish.

 *FORTIFIED SWEET WHITE*

# ALMOND BAVAROIS WITH APRICOT SAUCE

SERVES 8
*110g/4oz ground almonds*
*1 vanilla pod*
*290ml/½ pint milk*
*2 eggs, separated*
*55g/2oz caster sugar*
*3 tablespoons water*
*15g/½oz powdered gelatine*
*grated zest of 1 orange*
*3 drops of almond essence*
*150ml/¼ pint double cream, lightly whipped*

To serve
*apricot sauce (see page 478)*

1. Preheat the oven to 180°C/350°F/gas mark 4.
2. Place the almonds on a baking sheet and place in the preheated oven for 20 minutes or until lightly roasted. Remove from the oven and allow to cool.
3. Put the vanilla pod into a saucepan with the milk and bring to scalding point (just below boiling point), making sure it does not boil.
4. Whisk the egg yolks and sugar together in a heatproof bowl set over, not in, a saucepan of simmering water and keep whisking until very thick.
5. Remove the vanilla pod from the milk and stir the milk into the egg yolk and sugar mixture. Return to the pan and reheat, stirring continuously with a wooden spoon until the custard is thick enough to coat the back of the spoon. It will curdle if allowed to boil. Strain.
6. Put the water into a small saucepan and sprinkle over the gelatine. Leave for 5 minutes until spongy.
7. Dissolve the gelatine over a low heat without boiling until liquid and clear, then pour into the custard mixture. Stir occasionally until on the point of setting.
8. Stir in the ground almonds, the orange zest and the almond essence.
9. Fold in the cream.
10. Whisk the egg whites until stiff but not dry and fold into the bavarois mixture. Tip into 8 very lightly oiled ramekins. Cover and leave to set.
11. To serve: flood the base of a pudding plate with the apricot sauce and turn an almond bavarois out on top of the sauce.

 *SWEET WHITE*

# ORANGE BAVAROIS WITH MERINGUES

SERVES 4
For the meringues
*1 egg white*
*55g/2oz caster sugar*

For the bavarois
*3 tablespoons water*
*2 teaspoons powdered gelatine*
*5 lumps of sugar*
*1 orange*
*425ml/¾ pint milk*
*3 egg yolks*
*1½ tablespoons caster sugar*
*150ml/¼ pint double cream*

To decorate
*grated chocolate*

1. Preheat the oven to 130°C/260°F/gas mark ½.
2. Make the meringues: whisk the egg white until stiff, add 2 teaspoons of the sugar and continue whisking until stiff again; then fold in the remaining sugar. Put this mixture into a piping bag fitted with a 5mm/¼in plain nozzle and pipe into tiny button meringues on a baking sheet lined with non-stick baking parchment. Dry in the oven for about 40 minutes. Immediately peel off the paper and leave to cool.
3. Make the bavarois: put the water into a small saucepan and sprinkle over the gelatine. Leave for 5 minutes to become spongy.
4. Rub the sugar lumps over the orange until the sugar is well coloured by the oils in the rind. Put the lumps into the milk in a saucepan and dissolve over a low heat.
5. Cream the egg yolks with the caster sugar until thick and light, then pour the milk on to the mixture. Return to the pan and stir constantly

over a low heat with a wooden spoon, without boiling. When the custard is thick enough to coat the back of the spoon, strain into a bowl and allow to cool.

**6.** Dissolve the gelatine over a low heat without boiling until liquid and clear, then add to the custard.

**7.** Stand the custard in a roasting pan or bowl full of ice and stir gently until the mixture thickens.

**8.** Whip the cream lightly, then fold 2 tablespoons of it into the custard. Pour immediately into a lightly oiled plain mould. Refrigerate until set (about 3 hours).

**9.** Whip the remaining cream a little more stiffly. When the custard is set, turn out on to a plate and mask with the whipped cream. Cover with the meringues and sprinkle with grated chocolate.

NOTES: Rubbing the sugar lumps over the orange rind extracts the orange flavour, but is a little tedious. An alternative method is to pare the rind thinly from the orange and infuse it in the hot milk, then strain it.

See 'Whisking egg whites', page 554.

 *SWEET WHITE*

# COFFEE CREAM BAVAROIS

SERVES 4
*2 tablespoons water*
*7g/¹/₄oz powdered gelatine*
*225ml/3fl oz milk*
*20g/³/₄oz plain chocolate, broken up*
*3 egg yolks*
*85g/8oz caster sugar*
*1 tablespoon instant coffee powder*
*150ml/¹/₄ pint double cream*

To decorate
*grated chocolate*
*double cream, whipped*

**1.** Place the water in a small saucepan and sprinkle over the gelatine. Leave for 5 minutes to become spongy.

**2.** Place the milk and chocolate in a heavy saucepan and heat gently until the chocolate has completely melted.

**3.** Mix the egg yolks and sugar together. Stir in the warm milk and chocolate mixture. Return to the saucepan.

**4.** Dissolve the coffee in 2 tablespoons boiling water and add to the mixture. Stir continuously with a wooden spoon for 3–5 minutes until the custard will coat the back of the spoon. Be careful not to overheat or the mixture will curdle. Strain into a bowl and leave to cool to room temperature.

**5.** Dissolve the gelatine over a low heat without boiling until liquid and clear, then stir into the cooling custard. Stir occasionally until on the point of setting. Whip the cream lightly and fold it into the coffee mixture.

**6.** Turn into a large dish or individual pots and leave in the refrigerator to set. Decorate with grated chocolate and whipped cream.

NOTE: An attractive way to present this bavarois is to serve individual moulds on a plate flooded with crème anglaise (see page 476) and decorated with tiny chocolate shapes (see page 649).

 *FORTIFIED SWEET WHITE*

# THREE CHOCOLATE BAVAROIS

*6 tablespoons water*
*15g/¹/₂oz powdered gelatine*
*375ml/13fl oz milk*
*8 egg yolks, beaten*
*45g/1¹/₂oz caster sugar*
*140g/5oz white chocolate, grated*
*140g/5oz milk chocolate, grated*
*140g/5oz plain chocolate, grated*
*720ml/1¹/₄ pints double cream, lightly whipped*

To decorate
*290ml/¹/₂ pint crème anglaise, flavoured with*
*    grated orange zest and/or 1 tablespoon Grand*
*    Marnier (see page 476)*

**1.** Line a 900g/2lb loaf tin with a piece of greaseproof paper cut to fit the bottom of the tin. Lightly oil the tin.

**2.** Place the water in a small saucepan and sprinkle over the gelatine. Leave for 5 minutes to become spongy.

**3.** Bring the milk to the boil in a saucepan. Beat the eggs and sugar together with a wooden spoon and pour over the milk. Return the mixture to the saucepan and heat gently, stirring constantly with a wooden spoon until the custard will coat the back of the spoon.

**4.** Place each variety of chocolate in a separate bowl and divide the custard equally between them, pouring through a sieve to remove any egg threads. Stir well to melt the chocolate.

**5.** Dissolve the gelatine over a low heat without boiling until liquid and clear, then add half to the white chocolate custard. Stir gently and when the mixture is on the point of setting, fold in one-third of the cream. Pour into the base of the loaf tin. Refrigerate until set.

**6.** Once the white chocolate bavarois has set, reheat the remaining gelatine without boiling, and add half of it to the milk chocolate custard. When it is on the point of setting, fold in another third of the cream. Pour over the set white chocolate bavarois, very carefully. Refrigerate until set.

**7.** Once the milk chocolate bavarois has set, reheat the remaining gelatine without boiling and add it to the plain chocolate custard. When it is on the point of setting, fold in the remaining cream. Pour very carefully over the set milk chocolate bavarois and refrigerate until set.

**8.** To serve: turn the bavarois out carefully, using a knife to loosen it, or dip the tin very quickly in boiling water. Remove the greaseproof paper from the top. Slice the bavarois with a hot knife and serve with the flavoured crème anglaise.

 *FORTIFIED SWEET WHITE*

# STRIPED CHOCOLATE AND GRAND MARNIER BAVAROIS

This recipe had been adapted from *The Roux Brothers on Pâtisserie*.

SERVES 8
*3 egg quantity sponge fingers mixture (see page 631)*
*3 egg quantity sponge fingers mixture (see page 631) made with 30g/1oz sifted cocoa powder instead of arrowroot*
*55ml/2fl oz sugar syrup (see page 477)*
*30ml/1fl oz Grand Marnier*
*30g/1oz plain chocolate, grated*

For the Grand Marnier bavarois
*150ml/¼ pint milk*
*2 egg yolks*
*45g/1½oz caster sugar*
*2 tablespoons water*
*1 teaspoon powdered gelatine*
*30ml/1fl oz Grand Marnier*
*150ml/¼ pint double cream, lightly whipped*

For the chocolate bavarois
*2 tablespoons water*
*1 teaspoon powdered gelatine*
*55g/2oz plain chocolate*
*150ml/¼ pint milk*
*55g/2oz caster sugar*
*2 egg yolks*
*15g/½oz plain flour*
*150ml/¼ pint double cream, lightly whipped*

**1.** Preheat the oven to 200°C/400°F/gas mark 6.
**2.** Using 2 separate piping bags fitted with 5mm/¼in plain nozzles, pipe out the plain and chocolate sponge mixtures alternately in diagonal lines on a baking sheet lined with non-stick baking paper.
**3.** Bake in the preheated oven for 10–15 minutes.
**4.** Invert the sponge on to a clean tea-towel. Carefully peel off the lining paper and turn the sponge on to a wire rack. Leave to cool.
**5.** When the sponge is cold, trim the edges with a serrated knife. Cut 2 bands the depth of a

20cm/8in spring clip tin (i.e. 7.5cm/3in). From the remaining sponge, cut out a circle slightly smaller than the diameter of the tin.

**6.** Line the sides of the tin with the bands of sponge, and place the circle of sponge in the bottom of the tin.

**7.** Mix the sugar syrup with the Grand Marnier and brush the sponge with the mixture.

### THE GRAND MARNIER BAVAROIS:

**8.** Bring the milk slowly to the boil in a saucepan.

**9.** Beat in the yolks with the sugar in a bowl. Pour the milk on to the egg yolks, stirring steadily. Return to the pan.

**10.** Stir over a low heat, stirring continuously with a wooden spoon, until the mixture thickens enough to cover the back of the spoon.

**11.** Place the water in a small saucepan and sprinkle over the gelatine. Leave for 5 minutes to become spongy. Dissolve the gelatine over a low heat without boiling until liquid and clear, then add to the custard with the Grand Marnier.

**12.** Fold in the cream.

### THE CHOCOLATE BAVAROIS:

**13.** Place the water in a small saucepan and sprinkle over the gelatine. Leave for 5 minutes until spongy.

**14.** Cut the chocolate into small, even-sized pieces. Heat the milk with half the sugar and the chocolate.

**15.** Cream the egg yolks and remaining sugar and stir in the flour.

**16.** Pour the milk on to the egg-yolk mixture, stirring well. Return the custard to the pan and bring to the boil, stirring all the time. Simmer for 2 minutes. Allow to cool.

**17.** Dissolve the gelatine over a low heat without boiling until liquid and clear, then add to the chocolate mixture.

**18.** Fold in the cream.

### TO ASSEMBLE:

**19.** Pour the chocolate bavarois into the prepared sponge case. Ladle over the Grand Marnier bavarois to make an irregular marbled effect. (If necessary stir both mixtures together quickly.)

**20.** Allow to set for 4 hours in the refrigerator.

**21.** To serve: unclip the tin and remove the sides. Trim off any excess sponge with kitchen scissors.

Scatter grated chocolate around the edges of the pudding.

NOTE: If possible use couverture for the plain chocolate.

 *FORTIFIED SWEET WHITE*

# COEURS À LA CRÈME

These are best started 4 days in advance

SERVES 4
*340g/12oz cottage cheese, drained*
*55g/2oz icing sugar*
*290ml/½ pint double cream*
*2 egg whites*
*290ml/½ pint single cream*

**1.** On the first day: push the cheese through a sieve. Stir the icing sugar and double cream into it and mix thoroughly.

**2.** Whisk the egg whites until stiff. Fold into the cheese mixture.

**3.** Line a small sieve with a clean piece of muslin and place over a bowl. Turn the cheese mixture into the muslin and leave to drain in a cool place for 3–4 days.

**4.** To serve: turn the cheese out on to an attractive serving dish. Pour over the single cream and serve with fresh summer fruits.

NOTES: Classically, coeurs à la crème are made in small heart-shaped moulds (hence the name). If you do not have these moulds, individual sweet cheeses can be made by securing muslin with rubber bands over small ramekin dishes filled with the cheese mixture, and then inverting the ramekins on to a wire rack to drain.

For a less rich cream, substitute soured cream or yoghurt for the single cream.

# ICED SABAYON

SERVES 4
*4 egg yolks*
*4 tablespoons caster sugar*
*150ml/¼ pint sweet white wine*
*2 tablespoons Marsala*
*150ml/¼ pint double cream, whipped*

**1.** Put the egg yolks, sugar and wine into a heatproof bowl. Set over, not in, a saucepan of simmering water. Whisk for 15–20 minutes until thick and creamy. Remove from the heat and continue to whisk until cool. Add the Marsala and fold in the cream.
**2.** Serve well chilled.

NOTE: Sabayon can only be left to stand for about an hour before separating.

 *FORTIFIED SWEET WHITE*

# ZABAGLIONE

SERVES 4
*4 egg yolks*
*85g/3oz caster sugar*
*8 tablespoons Marsala*

**1.** Put the egg yolks and sugar into a heatproof bowl. Whisk well and set the bowl over, not in, a saucepan of simmering water. Continue whisking until frothy and pale.
**2.** Gradually whisk in the Marsala until the mixture is very thick. Take care that the bowl does not touch the simmering water as if it does, the eggs will scramble.
**3.** Pour into individual glasses and serve immediately.

 *FORTIFIED SWEET WHITE*

# JELLIES

These are fruit juices or syrups set with gelatine. Some are clarified in a similar manner to aspic and clear soups.

You will need:
**1.** Jelly bag, usually made of flannel, or a large double muslin cloth.
**2.** Balloon whisk.
**3.** Large saucepan.

POINTS TO REMEMBER
**1.** All equipment must be spotlessly clean and grease-free. Scalding in boiling water will ensure this.
**2.** Weigh all ingredients carefully.
**3.** Follow the whisking and clearing methods very carefully. Short cuts will only lead to murky jelly.
**4.** When turning out jellies, it is a good idea to wet the serving plate. If the unmoulded jelly is not dead centre, you can then slide it gently to the correct position. If the plate is dry, the jelly will cling to it and be difficult to budge.
**5.** Recipes often say to wet a jelly mould – if using a china mould, it may be necessary to grease it with a flavourless oil to ensure that it turns out.

# ORANGE JELLY AND CARAMEL CHIPS

SERVES 4
For the orange jelly
*3 tablespoons water*
*20g/¾oz powdered gelatine*
*570ml/1 pint orange juice*
*290ml/½ pint double cream, lightly whipped*

For the caramel
*55g/2oz granulated sugar*

**1.** Start with the jelly: put the water into a small saucepan. Sprinkle over the gelatine and leave for 5 minutes to become spongy. Dissolve over a very low heat without boiling or stirring until liquid and clear.
**2.** Mix the gelatine with 150ml/¼ pint of the orange juice, warmed. Add the remaining orange juice and pour into a wet plain jelly mould or pudding basin.
**3.** Chill in the refrigerator for 2–4 hours, or until set.
**4.** Meanwhile, start the caramel: put the sugar into a heavy pan and set over a low heat.
**5.** Lightly oil a baking sheet.

**6.** When the sugar has dissolved, boil rapidly to a golden caramel. Immediately pour on to the baking sheet. Leave to harden and cool completely.

**7.** Break up the caramel into chips.

**8.** Loosen the jelly round the edges with a finger. Invert a damp serving plate over the jelly mould, turn the mould and plate over together, give a sharp shake and remove the mould. If the jelly won't budge, dip the outside of the mould briefly into hot water to loosen it.

**9.** Spread over the cream to mask the jelly completely.

**10.** Just before serving, scatter the caramel over the jelly (do not do this in advance as the caramel softens quickly).

# CLEAR LEMON JELLY

See notes on jelly-making, page 501.

SERVES 6
*860ml/1½ pints water*
*225g/8oz granulated sugar*
*thinly pared zest of 4 unwaxed lemons*
*290ml/½ pint lemon juice*
*2 small cinnamon sticks*
*4 tablespoons dry sherry (optional)*
*55g/2oz powdered gelatine*
*whites and crushed shells of 3 eggs*
*green colouring (optional)*

**1.** Make the jelly: put all the ingredients except the gelatine, egg whites, egg shells and green colouring into a very clean saucepan. Sprinkle over the gelatine and place over a medium heat. Stir without boiling until the gelatine and sugar have dissolved. Taste, adding more sugar if necessary, and cool. Remove the cinnamon stick.

**2.** Put the egg whites and crushed shells into the jelly mixture. Place over a medium heat and whisk steadily with a balloon whisk until the mixture begins to boil. Stop whisking immediately and remove the pan from the heat. Allow the mixture to subside. Take care not to break the crust formed by the egg whites.

**3.** Bring just up to the boil again, and allow to subside. Repeat this once more (the egg white will

trap the sediment in the liquid and clear the jelly). Remove from the heat and allow to cool for 2 minutes.

**4.** Fix a double layer of fine muslin over a clean bowl and carefully strain the jelly through it, taking care to hold the egg-white crust back. Keep back as much of the lemon zest as you can as it tends to clog up the sieve. Do not try to hurry the process by squeezing the cloth, or murky jelly will result. If the jelly begins to set before it is completely strained, warm it up again to melt it just enough to filter through the muslin.

**5.** Colour it delicately with the green colouring, if using.

**6.** Pour into a wet jelly mould. Refrigerate until set (at least 4 hours, but preferably overnight).

**7.** Turn out the jelly: loosen the top edge all around with a finger. Dip the mould briefly into hot water. Place a damp serving plate over the mould and invert the 2 together. Give a good sharp shake and remove the mould.

# BLACK JELLY WITH PORT

SERVES 4
*450g/1lb blackcurrants*
*225g/8oz granulated sugar*
*190ml/⅓ pint ruby port*
*3 tablespoons water*
*20g/¾oz powdered gelatine*
*whipped cream or crème anglaise (see page 476)*

**1.** Put the blackcurrants and sugar into a saucepan and cook over a low heat until the fruit is soft. Push through a nylon sieve.

**2.** Add the port to the blackcurrant purée and enough water to bring the liquid up to 570ml/1 pint.

**3.** Put the water into a small saucepan and sprinkle over the gelatine. Leave for 5 minutes to become spongy. Dissolve over a low heat without boiling until liquid and clear. Pour into the blackcurrant mixture and mix well. Pour into a wet jelly mould or dish. Refrigerate for 2–3 hours until set.

**4.** To turn out, briefly dip the mould into hot water – just enough to loosen it without melting the jelly. Put a damp serving plate over the mould and invert it so that the jelly falls on to the plate. Serve with whipped cream or crème anglaise.

# BLACK COFFEE JELLY WITH GREEK YOGHURT

This is a sugar-free jelly and will be a shock to people with a sweet tooth!

SERVES 4
*570ml/1 pint black coffee*
*concentrated apple juice*
*30g/1oz powdered gelatine*
*Greek yoghurt*

1. Make up the black coffee using freshly ground coffee beans and, while still warm, sweeten to taste with the apple juice. Leave to cool.
2. Put 3 tablespoons of the cool coffee into a small saucepan, sprinkle on the gelatine and leave for 5 minutes until spongy.
3. Dissolve the gelatine over a low heat without boiling until liquid. Pour into the coffee and spoon into suitable small wet moulds. Refrigerate until set (about 1 hour).
4. Turn the moulds out on to individual plates and place a good dollop of Greek yoghurt on each plate.

# CLARET JELLY

SERVES 4
*570ml/1 pint claret or other red wine*
*570ml/1 pint water*
*thinly pared zest of 2 lemons*
*170g/6oz granulated sugar*
*2 small cinnamon sticks*
*2 bay leaves*
*2 tablespoons redcurrant jelly*
*45g/1½oz powdered gelatine*
*whites and crushed shells of 2 eggs*
*a drop of cochineal or carmine colouring*
*   (optional)*

1. First make the jelly: put all the ingredients except the gelatine, egg whites, shells and red colouring into a very clean saucepan, sprinkle over the gelatine and place over a medium heat. Stir until the gelatine and sugar have dissolved. Taste, adding more sugar if necessary, and cool. Remove the bay leaves, cinnamon sticks and lemon zest.
2. Put the egg whites and crushed shells into the jelly mixture. Place over a medium heat and whisk steadily with a balloon whisk until the mixture begins to boil. Stop whisking immediately and remove the pan from the heat. Allow the mixture to subside. Take care not to break the crust formed by the egg whites.
3. Bring just to the boil again, and again allow to subside. Repeat this once more (the egg whites will trap the sediment in the liquid and clear the jelly). Allow to cool for 2 minutes.
4. Fix a double layer of fine muslin over a clean bowl and carefully strain the jelly through it, taking care to hold the egg-white crust back. Do not try to hurry the process by squeezing the cloth, or murky jelly will result.
5. Add a drop of red colouring if necessary. Pour into a wet jelly mould and refrigerate for 2–3 hours, or until set.
6. Invert a damp serving plate over the mould and turn the 2 over together. Give a sharp shake and remove the mould.

# GRAPE CHARTREUSE

SERVES 6
*clear lemon jelly (see page 502)*
*110g/4oz white grapes*

1. Prepare the lemon jelly.
2. Rinse a ring mould out with water. Pour a layer of lemon jelly into the bottom of the mould, about 1cm/1½in deep. Refrigerate until set.
3. If using seedless grapes, wash them. If not, cut the grapes in half and take out the seeds. (If the skins are tough or spotted, the grapes should be peeled: dip them in boiling water for a few seconds to make this easier.)
4. Arrange the grapes in the ring mould. Pour in enough cool but not quite set jelly to come halfway up the grapes and leave in the refrigerator to set. Pour in the remaining cool jelly so that the fruit is just covered, and refrigerate until set. Continue to layer the grapes in this way until the mould is full.
5. To turn out the jelly, dip the mould briefly in hot water. Invert a wet serving plate over the jelly mould and turn the 2 over together. Give a sharp shake and remove the mould.

 *LIGHT SWEET WHITE*

# BALLYMALOE'S JELLY OF FRESH RASPBERRIES WITH A MINT CREAM

Sally Procter of Leith's spent a happy few days at Ballymaloe cookery school run by Dorina Allen in Ireland and came back with several excellent recipes. This is a particularly delicious pudding for the summer.

SERVES 6
560g/1¼lb fresh raspberries
225g/8oz caster sugar
290ml/½ pint water
4 sprigs of fresh mint
2 teaspoons Framboise liqueur
1 tablespoon lemon juice
3 tablespoons water
1 tablespoon powdered gelatine

For the mint cream
15 fresh mint leaves
1 tablespoon lemon juice
200ml/7fl oz double cream

To decorate
fresh mint leaves

1. Pick over the raspberries and reserve about 110g/4oz of the best ones for decoration.
2. Put the sugar, water and mint sprigs into a small, heavy saucepan. Bring slowly to the boil. Simmer for a few minutes, then remove from the heat and allow to cool. Add the Framboise and lemon juice.
3. Put the 3 tablespoons water into a small saucepan and sprinkle over the gelatine. Leave for 5 minutes to become spongy.
4. Oil 6 ramekins very lightly.
5. Strain the flavoured syrup into a bowl. Dissolve the gelatine over a low heat without boiling until liquid and clear, then add it to the strained syrup. Add the raspberries.
6. Pour three-quarters of the jelly into the ramekins, making sure that all the raspberries are used up. Refrigerate until beginning to set, then spoon over the remaining jelly. (This is to ensure that the jellies have flat bottoms when turned out.)
7. Meanwhile, make the mint cream: crush the mint leaves in a pestle and mortar with the lemon juice. Add the cream and stir. The lemon juice will thicken the cream. If the cream becomes too thick, add a little water.
8. Divide the mint cream between 6 pudding plates and spread it over the surface of each. Turn out a raspberry jelly on top of the cream in the centre of the plate. Decorate with the reserved raspberries and extra mint leaves.

 *LIGHT SWEET WHITE*

# APPLE CHARLOTTE

SERVES 4
1kg/2¼lb apples
85g/3oz sugar
2 tablespoons apricot jam
15g/½oz butter
8 slices of stale, medium-sliced bread, crusts removed
110g/4oz butter, melted

For the apricot glaze
3 tablespoons apricot jam
4 tablespoons water

To serve
cream or custard

1. Core and slice the apples and put them into a heavy saucepan. Add the sugar and cook, without water, until very soft. Boil away any extra liquid and push through a sieve. Whisk in the apricot jam.
2. Butter a charlotte mould or deep cake tin.
3. Using a pastry cutter, stamp one piece of bread into a circle to fit the bottom of the mould or tin and cut it into 6 equal triangles. Cut the remaining bread into strips.
4. Preheat the oven to 200°C/400°F/gas mark 6.
5. Dip the pieces of bread into the melted butter. Arrange the triangles to fit the bottom of the mould or tin and arrange strips in overlapping slices around the sides.
6. Spoon in the apple purée and fold the buttery bread back over it.
7. Bake in the preheated oven for 40 minutes. Remove from the oven and allow to cool for 10 minutes.

**8.** Meanwhile, make the apricot glaze: put the jam and water into a small, heavy saucepan and heat, stirring occasionally, until warm and completely melted.

**9.** Turn out the pudding: invert a plate over the mould and turn the mould and plate over together. Give a sharp shake and remove the mould.

**10.** Brush the charlotte with the apricot glaze and serve with cream or custard.

NOTE: This looks a little clumsy but tastes delicious.

 *SWEET WHITE*

# INDIVIDUAL APPLE CHARLOTTES

SERVES 4
*55g/2oz granulated sugar*
*5 dessert apples, such as Discovery or Cox's, peeled, cored and sliced*
*2 tablespoons Calvados*
*juice of 1 orange*
*a pinch of ground cinnamon*
*70g/2½oz butter*
*8 slices of white bread, crusts removed*

For the sauce
*55g/2oz granulated sugar*
*grated zest of 1 orange*
*1 tablespoon Calvados*

**1.** Put the sugar into a heavy saucepan with 2 tablespoons water and place over a low heat. Allow the sugar to dissolve slowly and become lightly caramelized.
**2.** Add the apples to the caramel, stir and then add the Calvados, orange juice, cinnamon and 15g/½oz of the butter. Simmer together for 2 minutes.
**3.** Preheat the oven to 225°C/425°F/gas mark 7.
**4.** Melt the remaining butter. Flatten the bread slightly with a rolling pin. Cut out 8 rounds and dip them in the melted butter on both sides. Reserve 4 of the rounds and use the remaining

4 to line the base of 4 dariole moulds. Use the remaining bread to line the sides.
**5.** Drain the apple filling (but reserve the strained liquor) and pile the apple slices into the lined moulds. Cover with the remaining rounds of bread.
**6.** Put the moulds on to a baking sheet and bake in the preheated oven for 15–20 minutes.
**7.** Meanwhile, prepare the sauce: reduce the strained apple liquor, by boiling rapidly, to half the original quantity. Set aside.
**8.** Put the sugar with 2 tablespoons of water into a heavy saucepan and place over a low heat. Allow the sugar to dissolve and then caramelize. When lightly browned add the reduced apple liquor, the orange zest and Calvados. Simmer for 1 minute.
**9.** To serve: turn the apple charlottes out on to individual plates and serve with the caramel sauce.

# CHOCOLATE ROULADE

SERVES 6
*225g/8oz plain chocolate, roughly chopped*
*85ml/3fl oz water*
*1 teaspoon strong instant coffee powder*
*5 eggs*
*140g/5oz caster sugar*
*200ml/⅓ pint double cream*
*icing sugar*

For the tin
*oil, flour, caster sugar*

**1.** Take a large roasting pan and cut a double layer of non-stick baking parchment slightly bigger than it. Lay the parchment in the pan; don't worry if the edges stick up untidily round the sides. Brush the paper lightly with oil and sprinkle with flour and then caster sugar. Preheat the oven to 200°C/400°F/gas mark 6.
**2.** Put the chocolate, water and coffee into a heavy saucepan and melt over a low heat.
**3.** Separate the eggs and beat the yolks and the caster sugar until pale and mousse-like. Add the melted chocolate.
**4.** Whisk the whites until stiff but not dry. With a

large metal spoon, stir a small amount thoroughly into the chocolate mixture, to loosen it. Fold the remaining whites in gently. Spread the mixture evenly on the baking parchment.

**5.** Bake in the preheated oven for about 12 minutes until the top is slightly browned and firm to touch.

**6.** Slide the cake and parchment out of the roasting pan on to a wire rack. Cover immediately with a damp tea-towel (to prevent the cake from cracking) and leave to cool.

**7.** Whip the cream and spread it evenly over the cake. Roll up like a Swiss roll, removing the parchment as you go. Put the roll on to a serving dish and, just before serving, sift a little icing sugar over the top.

NOTES: The cake is very moist and inclined to break apart. But it doesn't matter. Just stick it together with the cream when rolling up. The last-minute sifted icing sugar will do wonders for the appearance.

If this cake is used as a Yule log the tendency to crack is a positive advantage: do not cover with a tea-towel when leaving to cool. Before filling, flip the whole flat cake over on to a tea-towel. Carefully peel off the lining paper, then fill with cream and roll up. The firm skin will crack very like the bark of a tree. Sprigs of holly or marzipan toadstools help to give a festive look. A dusting of icing sugar will look like snow.

 *FORTIFIED SWEET WHITE*

# HAZELNUT ROULADE

SERVES 4–6
*oil for greasing*
*3 eggs*
*55g/2oz caster sugar*
*1 tablespoon plain flour*
*¼ teaspoons baking powder*
*55g/2oz ground hazelnuts, toasted*
*icing sugar*
*150ml/¼ pint double cream, whipped*

**1.** Preheat the oven to 180°C/350°F/gas mark 4.

**2.** Prepare a paper case as for a Swiss roll (see page 592). It should be the size of a piece of A4 paper. Brush lightly with oil.

**3.** Separate the eggs and beat the yolks and caster sugar together until pale and mousse-like.

**4.** Sift the flour with the baking powder and fold it into the egg-yolk mixture along with the nuts.

**5.** Whisk the egg whites until stiff but not dry and fold into the mixture.

**6.** Spread the mixture into the prepared paper case.

**7.** Bake in the preheated oven for about 20 minutes until the top is slightly browned and firm to touch.

**8.** Remove the roulade from the oven and allow to cool, covered with a sheet of absorbent kitchen paper.

**9.** Sprinkle icing sugar on to a piece of greaseproof paper and turn the roulade on to it. Remove the lining paper.

**10.** Spread the whipped cream evenly over the roulade and roll it up like a Swiss roll.

NOTE: Serve the hazelnut roulade with a raspberry coulis, or add fresh fruit to the cream before rolling up the roulade.

 *RICH SWEET WHITE*

# SPICED GINGER ROLL

SERVES 4
For the roll
*caster sugar*
*110g/4oz plain flour*
*1 teaspoon ground mixed spice*
*1 teaspoon ground ginger*
*70g/2½oz butter*
*2 tablespoons black treacle*
*2 tablespoons golden syrup*
*1 egg*
*150ml/¼ pint water*
*1 teaspoon bicarbonate of soda*

For the filling
*450g/1lb cooking apples*
*30g/1oz butter*
*1 teaspoon ground cinnamon*
*55g/2oz caster sugar*

To serve
*double cream, whipped*

1. First make the filling: peel and core the apples. Slice them roughly.

2. Melt the butter in a saucepan and add the cinnamon, sugar and apples. Cover and cook over a very low heat, stirring occasionally, until the apples become pulpy. Beat until smooth, adding more sugar if the apples are still tart.

3. Preheat the oven to 180°C/350°F/gas mark 4. Prepare a Swiss roll tin by greasing the inside, then covering the base with greaseproof paper, and greasing again. Dust with caster sugar.

4. Sift together the flour, mixed spice and ginger. Melt the butter in a saucepan with the treacle and syrup. Whisk the egg with the water and soda. Remove the syrup mixture from the heat and pour in the egg and water. Mix well.

5. Now pour this into the flour and whisk together for 30 seconds. Pour into the prepared tin and bake in the preheated oven for 12–15 minutes, or until firm to the touch.

6. Turn out on to a sheet of greaseproof paper dusted with caster sugar. Remove the lining paper. Spread the cake with the apple purée and roll up like a Swiss roll. Serve with whipped cream.

NOTE: The pudding is not pretty, being squashy and dark brown, but the taste is wonderful. A last-minute dusting with icing sugar will help the appearance.

 *RICH SWEET WHITE*

# BAKED CHEESECAKE

SERVES 6
For the crust
*12 digestive biscuits (200g/7oz), crushed*
*85g/3oz butter, melted*

For the filling
*225g/8oz best-quality cream cheese*
*5 tablespoons double cream*
*1 egg*
*1 egg yolk*
*1 teaspoon vanilla essence*
*about 1 tablespoon sugar*

For the topping
*70ml/2½fl oz soured cream*
*ground cinnamon*

1. Preheat the oven to 150°C/300°F/gas mark 2.

2. Mix together the crust ingredients and line the base of a shallow 20cm/8in pie dish or flan ring with the mixture.

3. Bake in the preheated oven for 10 minutes, or until hard to the touch.

4. Beat the cream cheese and then add the remaining filling ingredients. Beat well until smooth and pour into the crust.

5. Return to the middle of the oven and bake until the filling has set (about 30 minutes).

6. Remove from the oven and allow to cool.

7. Spread with the soured cream and dust with the cinnamon.

 *LIGHT SWEET WHITE*

# TREACLE SPONGE

SERVES 4–6
*a knob of butter for greasing*
*2 tablespoons golden syrup*
*2 teaspoons fine fresh white breadcrumbs*
*110g/4oz butter*
*110g/4oz caster sugar*
*grated zest of 1 lemon*
*2 eggs, beaten*
*110g/4oz self-raising flour*
*a pinch of salt*
*1 teaspoon ground ginger*

To serve
*custard or cream*

1. Grease a pudding basin with the knob of butter.

2. Mix together the syrup and breadcrumbs in the basin.

3. In a mixing bowl, cream the butter until very soft, then add the sugar. Beat until light and fluffy. Add the lemon zest.

4. Gradually add the eggs, beating very well after each addition.

5. Sift and fold in the flour with the salt and ginger.

6. Turn into the pudding basin, cover and steam for 1½ hours.

7. Turn out and serve with custard or cream.

 *RICH SWEET WHITE*

# SIMPSON'S TREACLE ROLL

SERVES 4
*225g/8oz self-raising flour*
*a pinch of salt*
*110g/4oz shredded beef suet*
*225g/8oz golden syrup*

To serve
*whipped cream or custard*

**1.** Sift the flour with the salt into a bowl. Stir in the suet and add enough water to mix first with a knife, and then with one hand, to a soft dough.
**2.** Roll it on a floured surface to a large rectangle.
**3.** Spread the surface with the golden syrup.
**4.** Roll up and fold the sides underneath.
**5.** Wrap first in greaseproof paper, then in a cloth.
**6.** Place in the top half of a steamer and steam for 1½ hours. Serve with whipped cream or custard.

 *RICH SWEET WHITE*

# SUSSEX POND PUDDING

This recipe has been taken from Jane Grigson's *English Food*.

SERVES 6
*225g/8oz self-raising flour*
*110g/4oz shredded beef suet*
*150ml/¼ pint milk and water, half and half*
*110g/4oz slightly salted butter*
*110g/4oz demerara sugar*
*2 large lemon or 2 limes, very well washed*

**1.** Mix the flour and suet together in a bowl. Make into a dough with milk and water. The dough should be soft, but not too soft to roll out into a large circle. Cut a quarter out of this circle, to be used later as the lid of the pudding.
**2.** Butter a 1.4 litre/2½ pint pudding basin lavishly. Drop the three-quarter circle of pastry into it and press the cut sides together to make a perfect join. Put half the remaining butter, cut up, into the pastry, with half the sugar.

**3.** Prick the lemon or limes all over with a larding needle, so that the juices will be able to escape, then put the fruit on to the butter and sugar. Add the remaining butter, again cut into pieces, and sugar.
**4.** Roll out the pastry set aside to make the lid. Lay it on top of the filling, and press the edges together so that the pudding is sealed completely. Cover the basin with pleated kitchen foil. Tie it in place with string, and make a string handle over the top so that the pudding can be lifted easily (see page 511).
**5.** Put a large saucepan of water on to boil, and lower the pudding into it; the water must be boiling, and it should come halfway or a little further up the basin. Cover and leave to steam for 3–4 hours. If the water gets too low, replenish with boiling water.
**6.** To serve: put a deep dish over the basin after removing the foil lid, and quickly turn the whole thing upside down: it is a good idea to ease the pudding from the sides of the basin with a knife first. Serve immediately. The buttery juices will flow out of the pudding to form a 'pond'.

 *RICH SWEET WHITE*

# CHRISTMAS PUDDING

MAKES 2.3KG/5LB
*170g/6oz raisins*
*110g/4oz currants*
*200g/7oz sultanas*
*85g/3oz chopped mixed peel*
*225g/8oz mixed dried apricots and figs, chopped*
*290ml/½ pint brown ale*
*2 tablespoons rum*
*grated zest and juice of 1 orange*
*grated zest and juice of 1 lemon*
*110g/4oz prunes, stoned and soaked overnight in cold tea, then drained and chopped*
*1 dessert apple*
*225g/8oz butter*
*340/12oz soft dark brown sugar*
*2 tablespoons treacle*
*3 eggs*
*110g/4oz self-raising flour, sifted*
*1 teaspoon ground mixed spice*

½ teaspoon ground cinnamon
a pinch of freshly grated nutmeg
a pinch of ground ginger
a pinch of salt
225g/8oz fresh white breadcrumbs
55g/2oz chopped hazelnuts, toasted

**1.** Soak all the dried fruit except the prunes overnight in the beer, rum, orange juice and lemon juice. Mix with the prunes.
**2.** Grate the unpeeled apple.
**3.** Cream the butter with the sugar. Beat until light and fluffy. Add the orange zest, lemon zest and treacle.
**4.** Whisk the eggs together and gradually add them to the mixture, beating well after each addition.
**5.** Fold in the flour, spices, salt and breadcrumbs and stir in the nuts, dried fruit and soaking liquor.
**6.** Divide the mixture between greased pudding basins and cover with 2 layers of pleated greaseproof paper and one piece of pleated kitchen foil (see page 511). Tie with string and steam for 10–12 hours.

 *LIQUEUR MUSCAT*

# LIGHT CHRISTMAS PUDDING

This pudding is made with no added fat or sugar and therefore is less rich and more moist and tangy than traditional Christmas pudding (see page 508). The fruit should be soaked for 1–7 days in advance.

MAKES 2 PUDDINGS
110g/4oz dried apple, chopped
110g/4oz dried apricots, chopped
110g/4oz dried figs, chopped
110g/4oz dried pitted prunes, chopped
225g/8oz raisins
225g/8oz sultanas
110g/4oz currants
55g/2oz candied orange peel
290ml/½ pint cold tea
4 tablespoons brandy or rum

4 tablespoons medium sherry
1 large banana, mashed
225g/8oz carrots, grated
30g/1oz hazelnuts, chopped
30g/1oz ground almonds
3 eggs
1 tablespoon clear honey
1 teaspoon ground cinnamon
1 teaspoon ground mixed spice
1 teaspoon ground ginger
a pinch of freshly grated nutmeg
85g/3oz plain flour
170g/6oz fresh wholemeal breadcrumbs

**1.** Put all the dried fruit and candied peel into a bowl, and pour in the tea, brandy and sherry. Mix well and leave to soak in a cool place for at least 1 day or up to 7 days.
**2.** When the fruit has soaked, add the banana, carrot, hazelnuts and ground almonds to the mixture.
**3.** Beat the eggs with the honey and stir into the fruit mixture.
**4.** Sift the spices with the flour and add with the breadcrumbs to the pudding mixture. Stir well.
**5.** Place in 2 × 1.1 litre/2 pint greased pudding basins and cover with 2 layers of pleated greaseproof paper and 1 of pleated kitchen foil. Tie with string and steam for 6 hours in the usual way.
NOTE: Christmas puddings can be kept for up to 1 year – after this period they begin to dry out. They can be frozen very successfully. Ideally a pudding should be made about 3–4 months before Christmas. To store a pudding re-cover it and keep in a cool dark place. To reheat steam for about 2 hours.

 FORTIFIED DESSERT WINE

# EVE'S PUDDING

SERVES 4
*butter for greasing*
*675g/1½lb cooking apples*
*150ml/¼ pint water*
*160g/5½oz caster sugar*
*grated zest of 1 lemon*
*30g/1oz butter*
*1 small egg, beaten*
*55g/2oz self-raising flour*
*a pinch of salt*
*1 tablespoon milk*

1. Preheat the oven to 200°C/400°F/gas mark 6. Butter a pie dish.
2. Peel, core and slice the apples and place them in a heavy saucepan with the water, 110g/4oz of the sugar and half the lemon zest. Stew gently until just soft, then tip into the pie dish.
3. Cream the butter until soft and beat in the remaining sugar. When light and fluffy, gradually add the beaten egg and mix until completely incorporated.
4. Sift the flour with the salt and fold it into the butter and egg mixture.
5. Add the remaining lemon zest and enough milk to bring the mixture to a soft dropping consistency. Spread over the apple.
6. Bake in the preheated oven for about 25 minutes, or until the sponge mixture is firm to the touch and has slightly shrunk at the edges.

 *SWEET WHITE*

# BLACK CHERRY CLAFOUTIS

This recipe has been adapted from a recipe by Raymond Blanc in *Cooking for Friends*. It should be prepared an hour in advance and served warm.

SERVES 4
*4 tablespoons Kirsch*
*450g/1lb canned black cherries, drained*
*100ml/3½fl oz milk*

*150ml/¼ pint whipping cream*
*½ vanilla pod*
*4 eggs*
*140g/5oz caster sugar*
*20g/¾oz plain flour*
*a pinch of salt*
*butter and caster sugar for greasing and*
   *sprinkling*

1. Preheat the oven to 200°C/400°F/gas mark 6.
2. Sprinkle the Kirsch over the cherries. Leave to macerate.
3. Put the milk, cream and vanilla pod into a small saucepan. Bring to the boil, then turn off the heat and leave to infuse.
4. Place the eggs and sugar in a mixing bowl. Whisk until creamy. Add the flour and salt and whisk until smooth. Strain in the infused milk and cream, and beat until well mixed.
5. Generously butter an ovenproof dish about 25 × 23 × 5cm/10 × 9 × 2in and sprinkle with caster sugar.
6. Add the cherries and pour over the batter.
7. Bake in the preheated oven for 25 minutes. Remove and allow to cool before serving sprinkled with a little extra caster sugar.

 *GEWÜRZTRAMINER*

# STEAMED VALENCIA PUDDING

SERVES 4
*15g/½oz butter for greasing*
*a handful of large seedless raisins*
*110g/4oz butter*
*grated zest of 1 lemon*
*110g/4oz caster sugar*
*2 eggs*
*110g/4oz self-raising flour*
*a pinch of salt*

To serve
*crème anglaise (see page 476)*

1. Grease a pudding basin. Line the sides of the basin with split raisins (split side against the basin), arranging them in a pattern if you like.

**2.** Cream the butter and when very soft add the lemon zest and the sugar. Beat until light, pale and fluffy.

**3.** Gradually add the eggs, beating well after each addition.

**4.** Fold in the flour, sifted with the salt, and turn into the pudding basin.

**5.** Cover with a pleated piece of double greaseproof paper or kitchen foil and tie down.

**6.** Steam for 2 hours. Turn out and serve with the custard handed separately.

 *RICH SWEET WINE*

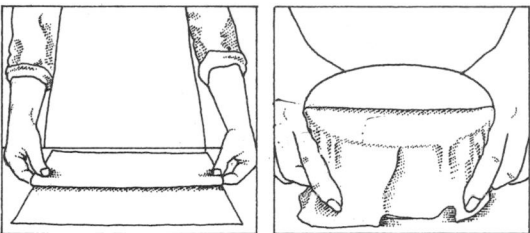

*Cover with pleated double greaseproof paper*

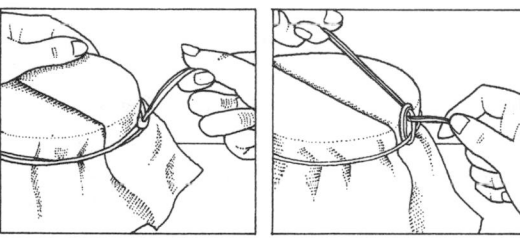

*Tie down and make a string handle for easy removal*

# INDIVIDUAL STEAMED CITRUS FRUIT PUDDINGS WITH CARAMEL SAUCE

SERVES 6

*340g/12oz flour quantity suet pastry (see page 462)*

For the filling
*55g/2oz butter*
*1 pink grapefruit, peeled and segmented*
*2 blood oranges, peeled and thinly sliced*
*6 kumquats, thinly sliced*
*4 oranges, peeled and segmented*
*55g/2oz caster sugar*

For the caramel sauce
*225g/8oz granulated sugar*
*290ml/½ pint water*
*1 cinnamon stick*
*6 cloves, lightly crushed*
*1cm/½in piece of fresh root ginger, peeled*
*3 bay leaves*
*55g/2oz butter*

**1.** Make the filling: cut the butter into small cubes and mix with the prepared fruit and sugar.

**2.** On a floured surface, roll two-thirds of the suet pastry to a 5mm/¼in thickness. Cut out 6 circles, each 12cm/5in in diameter. Grease 6 dariole moulds or heatproof teacups and line each with a pastry circle.

**3.** Pile the filling into the moulds. Roll out the remaining pastry and cut out 6 circles for the lids. Dampen the edges. Place the lids on the moulds and press the pastry firmly together.

**4.** Cover each mould with a circle of buttered greaseproof paper, pleated along the centre, and a layer of foil, also pleated. The covering should overlap the sides of the moulds so that it can be tied firmly to prevent water getting in during cooking. Tie with string.

**5.** Bring a large pan of water up to the boil, and lower the puddings into it. Cover the pan and keep the water boiling constantly for 2–2½ hours. If the water level falls below halfway up the moulds, replenish with more boiling water.

**6.** Meanwhile, make the sauce: put the sugar and

half the water into a heavy-bottomed saucepan. Dissolve the sugar slowly without stirring or allowing the water to boil. Then turn up the heat and boil the syrup until it is a good caramel colour. Turn off the heat immediately and tip in the remaining water (it will fizz dangerously, so stand back). Add the cinnamon, cloves, ginger and bay leaves. Leave to infuse in the caramel sauce while the puddings cook.

**7.** To serve: strain the caramel sauce into a clean saucepan. Bring to a simmer and whisk in the butter. Unmould the puddings on to individual plates and spoon over the sauce.

# STICKY TOFFEE PUDDING

SERVES 4–6
*225g/8oz dates, chopped*
*290ml/½ pint tea*
*110g/4oz butter*
*170g/6oz caster sugar*
*3 eggs*
*225g/8oz self-raising flour, sifted*
*1 teaspoon bicarbonate of soda*
*1 teaspoon vanilla essence*
*1 teaspoon strong coffee*

To serve
*toffee sauce (see page 478)*

**1.** Preheat the oven to 180°C/350°F/gas mark 4.
**2.** Soak the dates in the hot tea for 15 minutes.
**3.** Oil a moule-à-manqué cake tin and line the base with a circle of oiled greaseproof paper.
**4.** Cream together the butter and sugar until pale.
**5.** Beat in the eggs, one at a time, and then fold in the sifted flour.
**6.** Add the soda, vanilla essence and coffee to the date/tea water and then fold into the cake mixture.
**7.** Turn into the prepared moule-à-manqué tin and bake in the middle of the oven for 1–1½ hours, or until a skewer inserted into the centre of the cake comes out clean.
**8.** Pour the warm toffee sauce over the hot pudding and serve immediately.

 *RICH SWEET WHITE*

# PINEAPPLE AND APRICOT GÂTEAU

SERVES 6
*225g/8oz fresh apricots*
*5 thin slices of fresh pineapple*
*150ml/¼ pint sugar syrup (see page 477)*
*3 eggs*
*105g/3¾oz caster sugar*
*85g/3oz plain flour*
*a pinch of salt*
*½ teaspoon ground cinnamon*
*finely grated zest of ½ lemon*
*290ml/½ pint double cream*
*30g/1oz chopped nuts*
*3 drops of vanilla essence*
*1 tablespoon icing sugar, sifted*
*warm apricot glaze (see page 638)*

**1.** Cut the apricots in half and poach them with the pineapple in the syrup until tender (about 20 minutes). Take care that the apricots do not overcook. Remove from the heat and leave to cool.
**2.** Preheat the oven to 180°C/350°F/gas mark 4. Grease 2 × 20cm/8in sandwich tins and dust them with flour.
**3.** Whisk the eggs with the caster sugar with an electric beater (or with a hand whisk with the bowl set over a saucepan of simmering water) until thick and mousse-like. If the beating has been over heat, continue to beat while the mixture cools.
**4.** Fold in the flour with the salt, cinnamon and lemon zest. Pile the mixture into the sandwich tins and smooth with a spatula. Bake in the preheated oven for 20 minutes. Remove from the oven and allow to cool in the tins for 2–3 minutes, then turn out on to a wire rack and leave to cool completely.
**5.** Whisk the cream until stiff. Stir in the nuts, vanilla and icing sugar. Sandwich the cakes together with the cream. Decorate the top with the poached fruits and brush with warm apricot glaze.

 *SWEET WHITE*

# APPLE AND ORANGE CRUMBLE

SERVES 4
*3 oranges*
*900g/2lb cooking apples*
*3 tablespoons demerara sugar*
*a pinch of ground cinnamon*

For the crumble
*170g/6oz plain flour*
*a pinch of salt*
*110g/4oz butter*
*55g/2oz granulated sugar*

**1.** Peel the oranges as you would an apple, with a sharp knife, removing all the pith. Cut out the orange segments, leaving behind the membranes.
**2.** Peel and core the apples. Cut into chunks. Mix with the orange segments and their juice. Add the sugar and cinnamon. Tip into an ovenproof dish.
**3.** Preheat the oven to 200°C/400°F/gas mark 6. Preheat a baking sheet.
**4.** Sift the flour with the salt into a bowl. Rub in the butter and when the mixture resembles coarse breadcrumbs mix in the sugar. Sprinkle the mixture over the apples and oranges.
**5.** Bake on the baking sheet for 45 minutes or until hot and slightly browned on top.
NOTE: If using wholemeal flour for the crumble topping, use 140g/5oz melted butter. Instead of rubbing it into the flour, mix briskly with a knife.

 *SWEET WHITE*

# PLUM PIE

This recipe leaves the stones in the plums – if preferred, the plums can be cut in half and stoned. If the plums are large or not very ripe they should be cooked in a little sugar syrup before they are baked.

SERVES 6
*225g/8oz plain flour*
*a pinch of salt*
*55g/2oz lard*

*85g/3oz butter*
*2–3 tablespoons cold water*
*caster sugar for dredging*

For the filling
*675g/1½lb small plums*
*½ teaspoon ground cinnamon*
*3 tablespoons demerara sugar*

**1.** Preheat the oven to 220°C/425°F/gas mark 7.
**2.** Sift the flour with the salt into a bowl. Rub in the fats until the mixture resembles coarse breadcrumbs.
**3.** Stir in enough water to bind together. Push into a ball, wrap and chill in the refrigerator while you prepare the filling.
**4.** Wash the plums and place them in a pie dish with the cinnamon and sugar.
**5.** Roll out the pastry on a floured board. Cut a band of pastry wider than the rim of the pie dish. Wet the rim and press the band on all the way round. Brush with water and lay over the rolled-out pastry. Trim the edges, press them down firmly and mark with a fork or press into a frilly edge with fingers and thumb.
**6.** Shape the pastry trimmings into leaves. Brush the top of the pie with water and decorate with the leaves. Brush the leaves with water and dredge the whole pie with sugar.
**7.** Cut 1 or 2 small slits in the pastry top to allow the steam to escape. Bake on the top shelf of the preheated oven for 25–35 minutes.

 *RICH SWEET WHITE*

# TREACLE TART

SERVES 4
*110g/4oz plain flour*
*a pinch of salt*
*55g/2oz butter*
*2 teaspoons caster sugar*
*1 egg yolk*
*very cold water*

For the filling
*8 tablespoons golden syrup*
*grated zest of 1/2 lemon and 2 teaspoons lemon*
*    juice*
*a pinch of ground ginger (optional)*
*4 tablespoons fresh white breadcrumbs*

**1.** Preheat the oven to 190°C/375°F/gas mark 5.
**2.** Sift the flour with the salt into a bowl. Rub in the butter until the mixture resembles breadcrumbs. Add the sugar.
**3.** Mix the egg yolk with 2 tablespoons water, and add to the mixture.
**4.** Mix to a firm dough, first with a knife, and finally with one hand. It may be necessary to add a little water but the pastry should not be too wet. (Though crumbly pastry is more difficult to handle, it produces a shorter, lighter result.)
**5.** Roll out the pastry and use to line a pie plate or flan ring. Prick the bottom all over with a fork – do not prick all the way through the pastry.
**6.** Heat the golden syrup with the lemon zest and juice to make it a little runny. Add the ginger, if using.
**7.** Pour half the syrup into the pastry case.
**8.** Sprinkle with breadcrumbs until they are soaked. Pour in the remaining syrup and sprinkle in the remaining breadcrumbs.
**9.** Bake in the preheated oven for about 30 minutes, or until the filling is almost set and the edge of the pastry is brown. The filling should be a little on the soft side if the tart is to be eaten cold because it hardens as it cool. Ideally, serve warm.

 *SWEET SPARKLING*

# LEMON MERINGUE PIE

SERVES 4
*170g/6oz plain flour*
*a pinch of salt*
*85g/3oz butter*
*1 teaspoon caster sugar*
*1 egg yolk*
*very cold water*

For the filling
*30g/1oz cornflour*
*290ml/1/2 pint milk*
*30g/1oz caster sugar*
*grated zest and juice of 1 lemon*
*2 egg yolks*

For the meringue
*2 egg whites*
*110g/4oz caster sugar*
*a little extra caster sugar*

**1.** First make the pastry: sift the flour with the salt into a bowl. Rub in the butter until the mixture resembles breadcrumbs. Add the sugar.
**2.** Mix the egg yolk with 2 tablespoons water and add to the mixture.
**3.** Mix to a firm dough, first with a knife, and finally with one hand. It may be necessary to add a little water, but the pastry should not be too wet. (Though crumbly pastry is more difficult to handle, it produces a shorter, lighter result.)
**4.** Roll out the pastry and use to line a 20cm/8in flan ring. Leave it in the refrigerator for about 30 minutes to relax (this prevents shrinkage during baking).
**5.** Preheat the oven to 190°C/375°F/gas mark 5. Bake the pastry case blind (see page 459). Remove the lining paper and beans.
**6.** Turn the oven temperature down to 170°C/325°F/gas mark 3.
**7.** Meanwhile, make the filling: mix the cornflour (which should be very accurately weighed) with 2–3 tablespoons of the milk.
**8.** Heat the remaining milk. Pour on to the cornflour paste, stir well and return the mixture to the pan. Boil for 2 minutes, stirring continuously. Stir in the sugar.
**9.** Remove from the heat and allow to cool slightly, then beat in the lemon zest and juice. Add the egg yolks.

**10.** Pour this mixture immediately into the pastry case. Remove the flan ring and return to the oven for 5 minutes to set the filling. Make the meringue: whisk the egg whites until stiff. Add 1 tablespoon of the sugar and whisk again until very stiff and firm.

**11.** Fold in the remaining sugar. Pile the meringue on to the pie. It is essential to cover the filling completely or the pie will weep. Dust with a little extra sugar.

**12.** Place in the oven for 5 minutes or until the meringue is a pale biscuit colour.

NOTES: Lemon curd (see page 660) makes a good alternative to the lemon custard filling.

When making a meringue mixture with a powerful electric mixer, add half the sugar when the whites are stiff. Whisk again until very shiny, then add the remaining sugar and whisk until just incorporated. If using a hand-held electric blender, add the sugar a tablespoon at a time once the whites are stiff.

# CUSTARD TART

SERVES 6
*140g/6oz flour quantity rich shortcrust pastry (see page 461)*

For the filling
*4 eggs*
*55g/2oz caster sugar*
*290ml/½ pint milk*
*290ml/½ pint single cream*
*a few drops of vanilla essence*
*freshly grated nutmeg*

**1.** Preheat the oven to 190°C/375°F/gas mark 5. Roll out the pastry and use to line a 20cm/8in flan ring or dish. Bake blind (see page 459).

**2.** Turn the oven temperature down to 170°C/325°F/gas mark 3.

**3.** Lightly beat the eggs with the sugar. Pour on the milk and cream and add the vanilla essence. Strain into the prepared flan case and sprinkle a little grated nutmeg over the top. Place on a baking tray.

**4.** Bake in the preheated oven for 1 hour, or until the custard has set.

# BUTTERSCOTCH PIE

SERVES 4
*110g/4oz flour quantity rich shortcrust pastry (see page 461)*
*30g/1oz butter*
*55g/2oz demerara sugar*
*290ml/½ pint milk*
*1 tablespoon cornflour*
*a pinch of ground ginger*
*2 tablespoons double cream, lightly whipped*

To decorate
*chopped walnuts*

**1.** Preheat the oven to 190°C/375°F/gas mark 5.

**2.** Roll out the pastry and use to line a 15cm/6in flan ring. Bake blind (see page 459). Cool on a wire rack.

**3.** Slowly melt the butter. Add the sugar and cook until dark brown and oily; this may well take 10 minutes.

**4.** Carefully pour on three-quarters of the milk (the milk will splutter alarmingly and the butter and sugar will become toffee-like). Simmer slowly until the sugar has dissolved.

**5.** In a cup, blend the cornflour with the remaining milk. Pour a little hot milk into the cup and mix well. Pour this back into the butterscotch milk and stir while it boils and thickens. Remove from the heat and stir in the ginger. Allow to cool.

**6.** Stir in the cream. Pour the mixture into the pastry case and sprinkle over the chopped nuts.

 *FORTIFIED SWEET WHITE*

# MINCEMEAT FLAN

SERVES 8

*225g/8oz flour quantity rich shortcrust pastry (see page 461) or pâte sucrée (see page 466)*
*caster sugar for sprinkling*

For the filling
*1 small cooking apple*
*55g/2oz butter*
*85g/3oz sultanas*
*85g/3oz raisins*
*85g/3oz currants*
*45g/1½oz chopped mixed peel*
*45g/1½oz almonds, chopped*
*grated zest of 1 large lemon*
*1/2 teaspoon ground mixed spice*
*1 tablespoon brandy*
*85g/3oz soft light brown sugar*
*1 banana, chopped*

**1.** Preheat the oven to 190°C/375°F/gas mark 5.
**2.** Roll out the pastry and use to line a 25cm/10in flan ring, keeping the pastry trimmings for the lattice decoration. Bake blind (see page 459). Remove the lining paper and beans.
**3.** Prepare the mincemeat: grate the unpeeled apple. Melt the butter and add it, with all the remaining filling ingredients, to the apple. Mix well.
**4.** Fill the flan with the mincemeat. Cut the pastry trimmings into thin strips and lattice the top of the flan with them, sticking the ends down with a little water. Brush the lattice with water and sprinkle with caster sugar. Return to the oven for 10–12 minutes, removing the flan ring after 5 minutes to allow the sides of the pastry to bake to a pale brown.

 *FORTIFIED SWEET WHITE*

# RHUBARB AND STRAWBERRY LATTICE FLAN

SERVES 4–5

*170g/6oz flour quantity rich shortcrust pastry (see page 461)*
*675g/1½lb rhubarb*
*30g/1oz caster sugar*
*caster sugar for sprinkling*
*225g/8oz strawberries, hulled and halved*

For the glaze
*1 teaspoon arrowroot*
*1 tablespoon redcurrant jelly*

**1.** Roll out the pastry and use to line a 20cm/8in flan ring, reserving the trimmings. Leave it in the refrigerator for 20 minutes to relax. (This prevents shrinkage during baking.)
**2.** Preheat the oven to 190°C/375°F/gas mark 5.
**3.** Prepare the rhubarb: cut it into 3cm/1½in lengths and stew very gently in 1 tablespoon water with the sugar until tender. Drain the fruit very well and reserve the juice.
**4.** Bake the pastry case blind (see page 459).
**5.** Arrange the rhubarb and strawberries neatly in the flan case.
**6.** Mix the arrowroot with enough of the fruit juice to make it smooth. Put the arrowroot mixture and the juice into a saucepan and bring to the boil, stirring all the time. Add the redcurrant jelly and boil for 30 seconds. Remove from the heat and leave until warm, then pour evenly all over the fruit in the flan case.
**7.** Roll out the pastry trimmings into long strips 5mm/¼in wide. Twist the strips like barley sugar and arrange them in a lattice pattern over the flan, sticking the ends down with a little water. Brush each strip with water and sprinkle with caster sugar.
**8.** Return the flan to the oven until the pastry is a pale golden brown. Leave to cool on a wire rack.

 *SWEET WHITE*

# PECAN PIE

SERVES 8–10
For the pastry
*225g/8oz plain flour*
*a pinch of salt*
*55g/2oz lard*
*85g/3oz butter*
*2 teaspoons caster sugar*
*2–3 tablespoons cold water*

For the filling
*450g/1lb pecan nuts*
*4 eggs*
*225g/8oz soft light brown sugar*
*170g/6oz golden syrup*
*½ teaspoon salt*
*55g/2oz unsalted butter, melted*
*vanilla essence*
*2 tablespoons plain flour, sifted*

**1.** Preheat the oven to 200°C/400°F/gas mark 6. Preheat a baking sheet.
**2.** Sift the flour with the salt into a bowl. Rub in the fats until the mixture resembles breadcrumbs.
**3.** Add the sugar and stir in enough water to bind the pastry together.
**4.** Roll out the pastry and use to line a 28cm/11in flan case. Leave it in the refrigerator for about 30 minutes to relax. (This prevents shrinkage during baking.)
**5.** Bake the pastry case blind (see page 459).
**6.** Meanwhile, make the filling: chop half the pecan nuts. The remaining nuts will be used for the topping, so chop any that are broken, keeping back the best-looking ones. Whisk the eggs in a large bowl until frothy. Add the sugar, golden syrup, salt, melted butter and vanilla essence and beat well until thoroughly mixed. Stir in the flour, making sure there are no lumps of flour in the mixture.
**7.** Scatter the chopped pecan nuts over the baked pastry case and pour over the filling. Arrange the remaining halved pecan nuts on top.
**8.** Bake on the hot baking sheet in the preheated oven for 10 minutes, then turn the oven temperature down to 170°C/325°F/gas mark 3 and bake for a further 30–40 minutes, or until the centre is just set. Serve warm or cold.

NOTE: The filling will separate slightly when it is cooked but this is normal and quite delicious.

 *FORTIFIED SWEET WHITE*

# INDIVIDUAL APPLE TARTS

MAKES 8
*170g/6oz flour quantity sweet pastry (see page 461)*
*4 dessert apples*
*caster sugar*
*Calvados*
*warm apricot glaze (see page 638)*

**1.** Preheat the oven to 220°C/425°F/gas mark 7.
**2.** Roll out the pastry and divide into 8 equal pieces.
**3.** On a floured work surface, roll out each piece of pastry as thinly as possible. Cut each into a 12.5cm/5in circle, place on a baking sheet and refrigerate for 20 minutes.
**4.** Peel the apples, if liked. Cut in half and carefully remove the cores, using the point of a knife.
**5.** Slice the apples thinly and arrange the slices of half an apple on each circle of chilled pastry. Take care to pack the apples tightly to allow for shrinkage during cooking.
**6.** Sprinkle each tart evenly with 2 teaspoons caster sugar.
**7.** Bake on the top shelf of the preheated oven for 15 minutes, or until golden-brown. If the tarts are not quite brown, place them under a hot grill for 1–2 minutes.
**8.** Sprinkle with a little Calvados and brush with warm apricot glaze.

*SWEET WHITE*

# REDCURRANT AND BLACKCURRANT FLAN

SERVES 6

*170g/6oz flour quantity sweet pastry (see page 461)*

For the sponge lining
*2 eggs*
*55g/2oz caster sugar*
*55g/2oz plain flour, sifted*

For the filling
*170g/6oz redcurrants, fresh or frozen*
*170g/6oz blackcurrants, fresh or frozen*
*85g/3oz caster sugar*

For the glaze
*3 tablespoons redcurrant jelly*

To serve
*double cream, whipped*

1. Strip the redcurrants and blackcurrants off the stalks by holding each sprig of berries by the stalk and using a fork to dislodge the berries. (If they are frozen, thaw and drain them.)
2. Put the black- and redcurrants in separate bowls and add half the sugar to each bowl, shaking to distribute the sugar without crushing the fruit. Leave for 4 hours. (Alternatively, simmer the fruits very gently with the sugar and a few spoons of water for 3–4 minutes to soften and cook them.)
3. Roll out the pastry and use to line a deep 18cm/7in flan ring. Refrigerate for 20 minutes.
4. Preheat the oven to 200°C/400°F/gas mark 6.
5. Bake the pastry case blind (see page 459).
6. Meanwhile, make the sponge lining: put the eggs and sugar into a heatproof bowl and set it over, not in, a saucepan of simmering water. Whisk steadily until the mixture is thick and mousse-like and the whisk will leave a ribbon-like trail when lifted. Remove from the heat and fold in the flour. Remove the lining paper and beans from the half-cooked flan case and pour in the mixture.
7. Bake in the oven for a further 10 minutes, then remove the flan ring and turn down the oven temperature to 190°C/375°F/gas mark 5. Continue baking until the pastry case is crisp and

pale biscuit-coloured, then remove from the oven and allow to cool.
8. Strain the fruit well, tipping both juices into a small saucepan, and arrange the black- and redcurrants in alternate quarters of the flan.
9. Add the redcurrant jelly to the juice and boil rapidly until syrupy and smooth. Cool until near setting, then spoon over the tart to give it a good clear glaze.
10. Serve with whipped cream.

 *SWEET WHITE*

# RHUBARB TART

SERVES 4–6

For the filling
*675g/1½lb trimmed rhubarb*
*1 tablespoon caster sugar*

For the pastry
*225g/8oz plain flour*
*a pinch of salt*
*55g/2oz butter*
*55g/2oz lard*
*1 teaspoon caster sugar*

For the flan mixture
*2 eggs*
*125g/4½oz caster sugar*
*150ml/¼ pint crème fraîche or single cream*

1. Cut the rhubarb into 2.5cm/1in lengths and sprinkle with the sugar.
2. Preheat the oven to 190°C/375°F/gas mark 5.
3. Sift the flour with the salt into a medium bowl. Rub in the fats until the mixture resembles breadcrumbs. Stir in the sugar. Add enough cold water to bind the pastry together.
4. Roll out the pastry and use to line a 25cm/10in flan ring. Refrigerate for 30 minutes.
5. Place the rhubarb and sugar in a shallow saucepan and cook over a low heat until the rhubarb softens slightly but still holds it shape. Remove from the heat and allow to cool.
6. Bake the pastry case blind (see page 000). Turn the oven temperature down to 150°C/300°F/gas mark 2.

**7.** Mix the flan mixture ingredients together with a wooden spoon.

**8.** Arrange the rhubarb, without its juice, carefully in the baked flan case. Pour over the flan mixture and bake in the oven for 20–30 minutes. This tart is best served cold but not chilled.

 *SWEET WHITE*

# CHARLOTTE'S HIGGLEDY PIGGLEDY TART

SERVES 8–10
*225g/8oz flour quantity Martha Stewart's walnut*
*    pastry (see page 462)*
*150ml/¼ pint double cream, lightly whipped*
*290ml/½ pint crème pâtissière (see page 476)*
*soft seasonal fruit, such as apricots, oranges,*
*    plums, kiwis, bananas and strawberries*
*warm apricot glaze (see page 638)*

**1.** Line a 25cm/10in flan ring with the pastry, pressing it in. Refrigerate for 30 minutes.
**2.** Preheat the oven to 375°C/190°F/gas mark 5.
**3.** Bake the flan case blind (see page 459). Leave to cool.
**4.** Fold the cream into the almost cold crème pâtissière and pile into the flan case. Spread out evenly.
**5.** Prepare the fruit as for a fruit salad and arrange in a higgledy piggledy fashion in the flan case.
**6.** Brush or spoon the warm apricot glaze over the top.

 *SWEET WHITE*

# APPLE FLAN MÉNAGÈRE

SERVES 4
*110g/4oz flour quantity sweet pastry (see page 461)*

For the filling and topping
*675g/1½lb medium dessert apples*
*caster sugar*
*3 tablespoons warm apricot glaze*

**1.** Preheat the oven to 190°C/375°F/gas mark 5.
**2.** Roll out the pastry and use to line a 15cm/6in flan ring. Refrigerate for 10 minutes. Bake blind (see page 459).
**3.** Peel, quarter and core the apples. Using a stainless steel knife, thinly slice them into the flan ring (the apples will shrink considerably during cooking, so make sure that the flan is well filled). When the flan is nearly full, arrange the apple slices very neatly in overlapping circles.
**4.** Dust the apples well with caster sugar and bake in the preheated oven for about 20 minutes.
**5.** Remove the flan ring and return to the oven for a further 7–8 minutes.
**6.** When the flan is cooked, brush with warm apricot glaze and slide on to a wire rack to cool.

 *SWEET WHITE*

# DANISH STRAWBERRY SHORTCAKE

SERVES 4
*85g/3oz plain flour*
*a pinch of salt*
*55g/2oz butter*
*30g/1oz caster sugar*
*30g/1oz ground hazelnuts, browned*
*450g/1lb strawberries*

For the redcurrant glaze
*4 tablespoons redcurrant jelly*
*1 tablespoon lemon juice*

**1.** Preheat the oven to 190°C/375°F/gas mark 5.
**2.** Sift the flour with the salt into a bowl. Rub in the butter until the mixture resembles breadcrumbs. Stir in the sugar and ground hazelnuts. Knead together to form a stiff dough.
**3.** On a lightly greased baking sheet, roll or press the pastry into a flat 20cm/8in cake-sized round. Refrigerate to relax for 10–15 minutes.
**4.** Bake in the preheated oven for 8–10 minutes until pale brown all over. Loosen and leave to cool and harden on the tray.
**5.** Make the glaze: melt the redcurrant jelly with the lemon juice, but do not allow it to boil. Keep warm.
**6.** Place the baked shortcake on a serving dish, arrange the strawberries neatly over the top and brush thickly with the redcurrant glaze.

 *SWEET WHITE*

# TARTE TATIN

This tart is classically made with dessert apples. We prefer the tartness of cooking apples but have found that early in the season these tend to become soft and pulpy.

SERVES 6
For the pastry
*170g/6oz plain flour*
*55g/2oz ground rice*
*140g/5oz butter*
*55g/2oz caster sugar*
*1 egg, beaten*

For the topping
*110g/4oz butter*
*110g/4oz granulated sugar*
*1.4kg/3lb cooking apples*
*grated zest of 1 lemon*

**1.** Preheat the oven to 190°C/375°F/gas mark 5.
**2.** Make the pastry: sift the flour and ground rice into a large bowl. Rub in the butter until the mixture resembles breadcrumbs. Stir in the sugar. Add the egg and bind the dough together. Refrigerate while you prepare the topping.
**3.** Melt the butter in a 25cm/10in frying pan with a metal handle. Add the sugar and remove from the heat. Peel, core and thickly slice the apples. Arrange the apple slices over the melted butter and sugar in the base of the frying pan. Sprinkle on the lemon zest.
**4.** Place the frying pan over a medium heat until the butter and sugar start to caramelize. It may take 15–20 minutes and you will be able to smell the change – it is essential that the apples get dark. Remove from the heat.
**5.** Roll the pastry into a circle 5mm/¼in thick, to fit the top of the pan. Lay it on top of the apples and press down lightly. Bake in the preheated oven for 25–30 minutes.
**6.** Remove from the oven and allow to cool slightly, then turn out on to a plate and serve warm.

NOTE: If you do not have a frying pan with a metal handle, cook the apples in an ordinary frying pan. Let the butter and sugar mixture become well caramelized and tip into an ovenproof dish. Cover with the pastry and then bake in the oven on a hot baking sheet.

 *SWEET WHITE*

# UPSIDE-DOWN APRICOT TART

This recipe has been adapted from one in *The Josceline Dimbleby Collection* published by Sainsbury's.

SERVES 6
For the pastry
*170g/6oz plain flour, plus extra for rolling*
*85g/3oz caster sugar*
*a pinch of salt*
*85g/3oz butter*
*1 egg, whisked*

For the filling
*340g/12oz dried apricots*
*55g/2oz butter*
*85g/3oz caster sugar*

**1.** Soak the apricots in a bowl of water for 2 hours.
**2.** Make the pastry: sift the flour, sugar and salt into a bowl. Gently melt the butter in a saucepan and stir into the flour mixture with a wooden spoon. Then thoroughly mix in the egg until the dough is smooth. Press the mixture together in a ball, cover with clingfilm and refrigerate for at least 1 hour.
**3.** Make the filling: drain the apricots and pat dry with absorbent kitchen paper. Grease the base and sides of a 25cm/10in flan dish or tin (not one with a loose base) with the butter. Sprinkle all over with the sugar and arrange the apricots neatly in circles on top of the sugar, rounded side down.
**4.** Now take the pastry from the refrigerator and roll out on a floured surface to a circle slightly larger than the flan dish. (If the pastry breaks, just press it together again and don't worry if it looks messy as it won't show.) Press the edges of the pastry firmly down within the flan dish. Pierce 2–3 holes in the pastry.
**5.** Preheat the oven to 200°C/400°F/gas mark 6. Bake the tart in the centre of the oven for 25 minutes. Then turn the oven temperature down to 170°C/325°F/gas mark 3 and bake the tart for a further 30–35 minutes. Remove from the oven and allow to cool slightly. Then turn out the tart upside down on to a serving plate and serve while warm.

 *SWEET WHITE*

# MARTHA STEWART'S FUDGE TART

This tart is served with crème anglaise and orange sauce.

*a deep 20cm/8in shortcrust pastry (see page 461) tart case, baked and cooled*

SERVES 6
For the filling
*140g/5oz plain chocolate, finely chopped*
*170g/6oz unsalted butter, cut into small pieces*
*340g/12oz granulated sugar*
*95g/3½oz plain flour*
*6 eggs, lightly beaten*

For the crème anglaise
*570ml/1 pint milk*
*1 vanilla pod*
*170g/6oz granulated sugar*
*6 egg yolks*
*2 teaspoons cornflour*
*2 tablespoons brandy*

For the orange sauce
*170ml/6fl oz freshly squeezed orange juice*
*2 tablespoons Grand Marnier*
*225g/8oz granulated sugar*
*1 tablespoon grated orange zest*

1. Preheat the oven to 180°C/350°F/gas mark 4.
2. Make the filling: melt the chocolate and butter together in a heatproof bowl set over, not in, a saucepan of simmering water. When melted, remove from the heat and stir well to mix. Set aside to cool.
3. Mix together the sugar, flour and eggs in a bowl and whisk until well blended. Stir in the chocolate and butter mixture. Pour the filling into the tart case and bake in the preheated oven for about 50 minutes, until the filling is just set. Remove to a wire rack and leave to cool completely.
4. Make the crème anglaise: put the milk and vanilla pod into a saucepan. Bring to the boil. Turn off the heat under the pan and leave the milk to infuse for 6 minutes. Remove the vanilla pod. Using an electric mixer, beat the sugar and

egg yolks together until thick and fluffy. Add the cornflour. Mixing on low speed, gradually add the infused milk. When thoroughly incorporated, transfer the mixture to a heavy saucepan. Cook over a low heat, stirring constantly, until the sauce thickens to a light, creamy consistency. (Do not let the mixture boil, or the egg yolks will curdle.) Remove the mixture from the heat and whisk in the brandy. Strain the mixture through a fine sieve and cool. Refrigerate until ready to use.
5. Make the orange sauce: mix together the orange juice, Grand Marnier and sugar in a heavy saucepan and cook over a low heat, stirring constantly, until thick and syrupy and reduced by half. Remove from the heat, stir in the grated orange zest and leave to cool.
6. To serve: place a slice of the tart on a plate and spoon some crème anglaise around it. Drizzle a small amount of orange sauce into the crème anglaise in swirls.

 *FORTIFIED SWEET WHITE*

# TARTE AL' COLOCHE

This recipe has been taken from *The Roux Brothers on Pâtisserie*. The tart takes its name from the bubbling caramel, which puffs up and *coloche*s (bubbles). It makes a divine winter pudding, creamy and delicate, with the apples all coated in caramel. Christian Germain, the chef patron of the Château de Montreuil in France, makes the best tarte al' coloche in the world!

SERVES 8
*310g/12oz flour quantity shortcrust pastry (see page 461)*
*a pinch of flour*
*15g/½oz butter for greasing*
*12 medium dessert apples, preferably Cox's*
*½ cinnamon stick or a pinch of ground cinnamon*
*4 turns of the pepper mill*
*100g/3½oz butter*
*140g/5oz caster sugar*
*500ml/18fl oz double cream*
*2 eggs*
*icing sugar, sifted (optional)*

1. Preheat the oven to 220°C/425°F/gas mark 7.

2. Make the pastry base: on a lightly floured surface, roll out the pastry to a thickness of about 3mm/⅛in.

3. Grease a flan ring and place it on a baking sheet. Line the ring with the pastry, cutting off any excess with a sharp knife. Lightly crimp up the edges of the pastry to form a frill above the edge of the ring. Refrigerate in the refrigerator for 20 minutes before baking.

4. Peel, quarter and core the apples. Place 4 quartered apples in a saucepan with 2 tablespoons water and the cinnamon. Cover the pan and cook over a low heat until soft. Remove the cinnamon stick and add the pepper. Beat vigorously until the apples have the consistency of a compôte. Set aside at room temperature.

5. Bake the pastry case blind (see page 459). Remove the lining paper and beans and leave the base in a warm place. Turn the oven temperature down to 200°C/400°F/gas mark 6.

6. Melt the butter in a large, heavy saucepan, then immediately add the sugar. Cook over a low heat until it becomes a very pale caramel. Add the remaining apple quarters and roll them in the caramel for 4 minutes. They should be cooked but still firm. Set aside in a cool place.

7. Assemble the tart: spread the apple compôte over the base of the pastry case, then arrange the caramelized apple quarters on top. Pour the remaining caramel into a bowl and stir in the cream and eggs. Beat together lightly, then pour the mixture over the apples. Bake the tart in the preheated oven for 25 minutes.

8. Serve the tart warm, sprinkled lightly with icing sugar if wished.

 *RICH SWEET WHITE*

# WALNUT, PEAR AND APPLE TART

SERVES 10

For the pastry
*225g/8oz plain flour*
*a pinch of salt*
*1 teaspoon ground cinnamon*
*140g/5oz butter*
*110g/4oz caster sugar*
*55g/2oz walnuts, finely chopped*
*1 egg, beaten*

For the filling
*3 cooking apples*
*3 William or Comice pears*
*30g/1oz butter*
*200g/7oz caster sugar*
*2 teaspoons ground cinnamon*
*juice of 1 lemon*
*110g/4oz sultanas*
*3 eggs*
*150ml/¼ pint double cream*
*170g/6oz walnuts, chopped*

1. Make the pastry: sift the flour with the salt and cinnamon into a bowl. Rub in the butter until the mixture resembles breadcrumbs. Mix in the sugar, then the walnuts.

2. Add the egg to the mixture and mix to a firm dough. Refrigerate for 30 minutes.

3. Roll out the pastry and use to line a deep loose-bottomed 30cm/12in flan ring. Refrigerate for a further 30 minutes.

4. Preheat the oven to 200°C/400°F/gas mark 6.

5. Bake the pastry case blind (see page 459). Reduce the oven to 170°C/325°F/gas mark 3.

6. Meanwhile, make the filling: peel and core the apples and pears and cut into chunks.

7. Melt the butter in a large, heavy saucepan and, when foaming, add the apples and pears. Scatter on 85g/3oz of the sugar, the cinnamon, lemon juice and sultanas.

8. Toss the fruit over a medium heat for about 5 minutes, then strain, reserving the juice.

9. Reduce the juice, by boiling rapidly, until syrupy.

10. Mix together the eggs, the remaining sugar, double cream and strained juice. Add to the flan

ring with the fruit and scatter the chopped walnuts over the top.

**11.** Bake the flan in the oven for 50 minutes, or until the centre is firm. (Cover with wet greaseproof paper if the tart begins to look too dark.)

**12.** Serve warm or cold.

 *SWEET WHITE*

# POACHED PEAR AND POLENTA TART WITH SOFT CREAM

SERVES 8
*425ml/³/4 pint red wine*
*55g/2oz sugar*
*6 whole cloves*
*3 strips of thinly pared lemon zest*
*¹/2 teaspoon ground cinnamon*
*8 pears*

For the pastry
*140g/5oz butter at room temperature*
*140g/5oz sugar*
*3 egg yolks*
*200g/7oz plain flour*
*85g/3oz polenta, plus 1 tablespoon*
*¹/2 teaspoon salt*

For the soft cream
*150ml/¹/4 pint double cream*
*pear poaching liquid (see recipe)*
*brandy to taste*
*a few drops of vanilla essence*

**1.** Bring the wine, sugar, cloves, lemon zest and cinnamon to the boil in a medium saucepan and simmer until reduced by about one-fifth.

**2.** Peel the pears and cut them in half. Remove the cores carefully with an apple corer. Cut the pears into 1cm/¹/2in slices. Put the pear slices into the wine mixture and cook carefully over a low heat for about 40 minutes, or until the pears are tender. Lift them out with a slotted spoon and allow them to cool to room temperature.

**3.** Strain the wine to remove the lemon zest and cloves. Put the syrup back on the heat, bring to the boil and reduce by half. Some of this will be used to flavour the cream. Preheat the oven to 200°C/400°F/gas mark 6.

**4.** Make the pastry: cream the butter and sugar together until well blended. Add the egg yolks one at a time, beating well after each addition. Sift the flour, 85g/3oz polenta and salt together and mix into the creamed mixture. Beat until the dough comes together, then knead lightly on a floured surface, adding more flour if necessary, until the pastry is no longer sticky. Refrigerate for 20 minutes.

**5.** Cut the dough in half. Press one half of the dough on to the base and sides of a 22cm/9in flan ring. Sprinkle the base with the tablespoon of polenta. Spoon the drained pears into the pastry case.

**6.** Roll out the remaining dough 1cm/¹/2in thick. Using a fluted biscuit cutter, cut out as many circles as possible from the dough. Place them on top of the pears, starting on the outside. Overlap the shapes and continue to cover the top.

**7.** Bake the tart in the preheated oven for about 30 minutes, covering with greaseproof paper after 20 minutes if the tart shows signs of becoming too dark.

**8.** Make the soft cream: whip the double cream until soft peaks are formed. Flavour with some of the poaching liquid, the brandy and the vanilla essence to taste. Serve with the warm tart.

 *SWEET WHITE*

# NORMANDY APPLE FLAN

This recipe has been taken from *The Observer French Cookery School* by Anne Willan of La Varenne.

SERVES 6
For the rich shortcrust pastry
*225g/8oz plain flour*
*110g/4oz butter*
*1 egg yolk*
*³/4 level teaspoon salt*
*2–3 tablespoons cold water*

For the frangipane
*200g/7oz butter*
*200g/7oz caster sugar*
*2 eggs, beaten*
*2 egg yolks*
*4 teaspoons Calvados or Kirsch*
*200g/7oz blanched almonds, ground*
*4 tablespoons plain flour*

*3–4 ripe dessert apples*

To finish
*150ml/¼ pint warm apricot glaze (see page 638)*

1. Make the pastry as described on page 461 and wrap and chill for at least 30 minutes.
2. Preheat the oven to 200°C/400°F/gas mark 6. Preheat a baking sheet.
3. Roll out the pastry and use to line a 30cm/12in tart tin. Prick the base lightly all over with a fork, flute the edges and refrigerate again until firm.
4. Make the frangipane: cream the butter in a bowl, gradually beat in the sugar and continue beating until the mixture is light and soft. Gradually add the eggs and egg yolks, beating well after each addition. Add the Calvados and Kirsch, then stir in the ground almonds and the flour. Pour the frangipane into the chilled pastry case, spreading it evenly.
5. Peel the apples, halve them and scoop out the cores. Cut the apples crosswise into very thin slices and arrange them on the frangipane like the spokes of a wheel, keeping the slices of each half apple together. Press them down gently until they touch the pastry dough base.
6. Bake the flan on the hot baking sheet near the top of the preheated oven for 10–15 minutes until the pastry dough is beginning to brown. Turn down the oven temperature to 180°C/350°F/gas mark 4 and bake for a further 30–35 minutes, or until the apples are tender and the frangipane is set.
7. Transfer to a wire rack to cool. A short time before serving, brush the tart with the apricot glaze and serve at room temperature.

NOTES: Normandy apple tart is best eaten the day it is baked, but it can also be frozen. Just before serving, reheat to warm in a low oven.

   If using red apples, they need not be peeled.

 *SWEET WHITE*

# RAISIN AND YOGHURT TARTLETS

MAKES 18
*170g/6oz flour quantity, sweet wholemeal pastry*
   *(see page 463)*
*1 large egg*
*55g/2oz caster sugar*
*1 tablespoon plain flour*
*a pinch of freshly grated nutmeg*
*a pinch of ground cinnamon*
*grated zest of ½ lemon*
*2 teaspoons lemon juice*
*150ml/¼ pint plain yoghurt*
*55g/2oz raisins*

1. Preheat the oven to 200°C/400°F/gas mark 6.
2. Roll out the pastry thinly and use to line 18 tartlet tins. Refrigerate for 15 minutes.
3. Bake blind for 10 minutes (see page 459). Remove the lining paper and beans. If the pastry is not quite cooked, return to the oven for 5 minutes. Leave to cool on a wire rack.
4. Turn the oven temperature down to 180°C/350°F/gas mark 4.
5. Put the egg and the sugar into a heatproof bowl set over, not in, a saucepan of simmering water. Whisk until the mixture thickens sufficiently to leave a 'ribbon' trail when the whisk is lifted.
6. Fold in the flour, spices, lemon zest and juice, yoghurt and raisins.
7. Fill the tartlet cases with the mixture and bake in the oven for 20–25 minutes, or until the filling is just firm. Leave to cool on a wire rack.

*LIGHT SWEET WHITE*

# APPLE FLORENTINE

SERVES 4
*900g/2lb cooking apples*
*55g/2oz butter*
*50g/2oz demerara or barbados sugar*
*1 teaspoon ground cinnamon*
*grated zest of 1 lemon*
*225g/8oz flour quantity, rough puff pastry (see*
  *page 463)*
*caster sugar for sprinkling*
*icing sugar, sifted, for dusting*

For the spiced cider
*150ml/¼ pint cider*
*a pinch of ground ginger*
*a pinch of freshly grated nutmeg*
*1 cinnamon stick*
*pared zest of ½ lemon*
*55g/2oz sugar*

To serve
*ice cream or whipped cream*

**1.** Preheat the oven to 200°C/400°F/gas mark 6.
**2.** Peel, core and quarter the apples.
**3.** Melt the butter in a frying pan and, when foaming, add the apples. Fry until delicately browned.
**4.** Tip into a pie dish and mix in the sugar, cinnamon and lemon zest. Allow to cool.
**5.** Roll out the pastry on a floured board.
**6.** Cut a strip of pastry very slightly wider than the edge of the pie dish. Brush the rim with water and press the strip down all round it.
**7.** Lift the pastry with the aid of the rolling pin and lay it on the pie. Press down the edge and trim the sides.
**8.** Mark round the edge with the prongs of a fork or the tip of a knife, or crimp the edges with finger and thumb. Brush with cold water and dust with caster sugar.
**9.** Bake the pie in the preheated oven for 25–30 minutes until golden brown.
**10.** Prepare the spiced cider: heat all the ingredients together in a pan over a low heat for 10 minutes without boiling. Strain.
**11.** Remove the pie from the oven and, with a sharp knife, lift off the crust in one piece. Pour in the spiced cider.

**12.** Replace the crust on the pie and dust with icing sugar. Serve hot with ice cream or whipped cream.

NOTE: 'Florentine' is an obsolete word for pie.

 SWEET WHITE

# MILLEFEUILLES

SERVES 4–6
*225g/8oz flour quantity rough puff pastry (see*
  *page 463) or puff pastry (see page 464)*
*225g/8oz strawberries, hulled and sliced*
*290ml/½ pint double cream, whipped*
*225g/8oz icing sugar, sifted*

**1.** Preheat the oven to 220°C/425°F/gas mark 7.
**2.** On a floured board, roll the pastry into a thin rectangle about 30 × 20cm/12 × 8in. Place on a baking sheet. Prick all over with a fork.
**3.** Leave to relax, covered, for 20 minutes. Bake in the preheated oven until brown. Remove from the oven and allow to cool.
**4.** Cut the pastry into 3 neat strips, each 10 × 20cm/4 × 8in. (Keep the trimmings for decoration.) Choose the piece of pastry with the smoothest base, and reserve. Spread the other 2 strips with cream, top with strawberries and sandwich together. Cover with the third, reserved, piece of pastry, smooth side uppermost. Press down gently but firmly.
**5.** Mix the icing sugar with boiling water until it is thick, smooth and creamy. Be careful not to add too much water. Coat the top of the pastry with the icing and, while still warm, sprinkle crushed cooked pastry trimmings along the edges of the icing. Allow to cool before serving.

NOTES: To 'feather' the icing, put 1 tablespoon warmed, sieved liquid jam in a piping bag fitted with a 'writing' nozzle. Pipe parallel lines of jam down the length of the newly iced millefeuilles, about 2cm/¾in apart. Before the icing or jam is set, drag the back of a knife across the lines of jam. This will pull the lines into points where the knife crosses them. Repeat this every 5cm/2in in the same direction, then drag the back of the knife in the opposite direction between the drag-lines already made.

Millefeuilles are also delicious covered with fresh strawberries and glazed with warm melted redcurrant jelly instead of icing the top.

 *SWEET SPARKLING WHITE*

# JALOUSIE

SERVES 4
*225g/8oz flour quantity rough puff pastry (see page 463)*
*225g/8oz fresh apple marmelade (see page 479)*
*milk*
*caster sugar*

**1.** Preheat the oven to 230°C/450°F/gas mark 8.
**2.** Roll the pastry into 2 thin rectangles, one about 2.5cm/1in bigger all round than the other. The smaller one should measure around 13 × 20cm/5 × 8 in, and the larger 18 × 25cm/7 × 10 in. Leave to relax for 20 minutes.
**3.** Prick the smaller rectangle all over with a fork and bake in the preheated oven until crisp and brown. Remove from the oven and turn over onto a baking sheet. Allow to cool. Spread the apple marmelade all over the cooked piece of pastry.
**4.** Lay the larger pastry rectangle on a board, dust it lightly with flour and fold it, gently so that nothing sticks, in half lengthways. Using a sharp knife, cut through the folded side of the pastry, at right angles to the edge, in parallel lines, as though you were cutting between the teeth of a comb. Leave an uncut margin about 2.5cm/1in wide, all round the other edges, so that when you open up the pastry you will have a solid border.
**5.** Now lay the cut pastry on top of the pastry covered with apple marmelade and tuck the edges underneath. Brush the top layer carefully all over with milk (this is a bit messy as the apple keeps coming up between the pastry crust). Sprinkle well with sugar.
**6.** Bake in the preheated oven for about 20 minutes, until well browned. Serve cold or warm.

NOTE: Jalousie is French for shutters, which the pie resembles.

 *RICH SWEET WHITE*

# INDIVIDUAL APPLE TARTS WITH CALVADOS CRÈME ANGLAISE

SERVES 4
*225g/8oz flour quantity puff pastry (see page 464)*
*4 dessert apples*
*caster sugar*
*beaten egg, to glaze*
*warm apricot glaze (see page 638)*

To serve
*1 tablespoon Calvados*
*290ml/½ pint crème anglaise (see page 476), chilled*

**1.** Preheat the oven to 200°C/400°F/gas mark 6.
**2.** Roll out the pastry 2mm/⅛in thick and cut into 4 circles 12.5cm/5in in diameter. Place on a damp baking sheet. Using a sharp knife, trace an inner circle about 1cm/½in from the edge of each pastry circle. Do not cut all the way through the pastry.
**3.** Peel, core and thinly slice the apples and arrange in concentric circles within the border of each pastry tart. Using a sharp knife, mark a pattern on the pastry border.
**4.** Sprinkle lightly with caster sugar. Brush the rim of each pastry circle with beaten egg, taking care not to let it drop down the sides of the pastry.
**5.** Flour the blade of a knife and use this to knock up the sides of the pastry. Refrigerate for 15 minutes.
**6.** Bake in the preheated oven for 20 minutes. Remove from the oven and leave to cool slightly, then brush liberally with warm apricot glaze.
**7.** Add the Calvados to the well-chilled crème anglaise. Serve the tarts warm with the cold custard.

 *SWEET WHITE*

# FEUILLETÉE DE POIRES TIÈDE

SERVES 4

*2 William pears*
*290ml/½ pint sugar syrup (see page 477)*
*340g/12oz flour quantity puff pastry (see page 464)*
*290ml/½ pint double cream, lightly whipped*
*290ml/½ pint crème anglaise (see page 476)*
*55ml/2fl oz Poire William liqueur*
*icing sugar, sifted, for dusting*

**1.** Peel the pears, cut in quarters and remove the cores. Poach carefully in the sugar syrup until soft.
**2.** Preheat the oven to 220°C/425°F/gas mark 7.
**3.** On a lightly floured board, roll the pastry into 4 neat rectangles, each 10 × 6cm/4 × 2½in. Refrigerate for 20 minutes.
**4.** Bake in the preheated oven for 15 minutes until brown. Split in half horizontally, remove any uncooked dough and return to the turned-off oven to dry out. Remove from the oven.
**5.** Fold the cream into the crème anglaise. Flavour with the liqueur.
**6.** Sandwich the pastry slices together with the cream mixture and slices of warm poached pear. Dust the pastry lightly with icing sugar.

 *SWEET WHITE*

# SUMMER FRUIT FEUILLETÉES

SERVES 4

*225g/8oz flour quantity puff pastry (see page 464)*
*1 egg, beaten, to glaze*
*8 tablespoons Greek yoghurt, sweetened with 2 teaspoons sugar*
*a selection of summer fruits, such as 110g/4oz raspberries, 110g/4oz strawberries, hulled, 110g/4oz blueberries*
*icing sugar, sifted, for dusting*

*For the coulis*
*250g/9oz blackcurrants*
*110g/4oz redcurrants*
*110g/4oz caster sugar*
*45ml/3 tablespoons crème de cassis*

**1.** Roll the pastry to a 1cm/½in thickness. Cut out 4 star shapes, each 8.5cm/3½in across. Chill in the refrigerator for 30 minutes.
**2.** Preheat the oven to 200°C/400°F/gas mark 6.
**3.** Place the pastry stars on a damp baking sheet. Brush with beaten egg and bake in the preheated oven for 15–20 minutes until risen and golden-brown. Leave to cool on a wire rack.
**4.** Prepare the coulis: destalk the blackcurrants and redcurrants and place in a saucepan with the sugar. Cook over a low heat for 15 minutes or until the fruit is pulpy.
**5.** Press the pulp and juice through a sieve. Taste for sweetness and add more sugar if necessary. Stir in the crème de cassis.
**6.** Using a sharp knife, split each pastry star in half horizontally. Spoon 2 tablespoons of yoghurt on to each of the 4 bases.
**7.** Arrange the summer fruits of your choice on top. Spoon 2 teaspoons of coulis on to the fruit and cover with the pastry lids. Dust the top of the lids with icing sugar.
**8.** Spoon the layer of coulis on to 4 individual plates and place a feuilletée on each plate.

 *SPARKLING ROSÉ*

# GÂTEAU PITHIVIERS

SERVES 6

*225g/8oz flour quantity puff pastry (see page 464)*
*1 egg, beaten with ½ teaspoon salt*
*icing sugar*

*For the almond filling*
*125g/4½oz butter, softened*
*125g/4½oz sugar*
*1 egg*
*1 egg yolk*
*125g/4½oz whole blanched almonds, skinned and ground*
*15g/½oz plain flour*
*2 tablespoons rum*

1. Refrigerate the puff pastry.

2. Make the almond filling: cream the butter in a bowl, add the sugar and beat thoroughly. Beat in the egg and the egg yolk; then stir in the ground almonds, flour and rum.

3. Roll out half the puff pastry to a circle about 27cm/11in in diameter. Using a pan lid as a guide, cut out a 25cm/10in circle from this with a sharp knife, angling the knife slightly. Roll out the remaining pastry slightly thicker than for the first round and cut out another 25cm/10in circle. Set the thinner circle on a baking sheet, mound the filling in the centre, leaving a 2.5cm/1in border, and brush the border with beaten egg. Set the second circle on top and press the edges together firmly.

4. Scallop the edge of the gâteau by pulling it in at intervals with the back of a knife. Brush the gâteau with beaten egg, and, working from the centre, score the top in curves like the petals of a flower. Do not cut through to the filling. Refrigerate the gâteau for 15–20 minutes. Preheat the oven to 220°C/425°F/gas mark 7.

5. Bake the gâteau in the oven for 30–35 minutes, or until firm, puffed and brown.

6. Preheat the grill to its highest setting.

7. Dust the gâteau with icing sugar. Place under the grill until lightly glazed.

 *SWEET SPARKLING WHITE*

# TARTE FRANÇAISE

SERVES 4
*225g/8oz flour quantity puff pastry (see page 464)*
*beaten egg*
*3 tablespoons warm apricot glaze (see page 638)*
*a squeeze of lemon juice*
*fruit as for fruit salad, such as 2 oranges, a small*
*    bunch of black grapes, a small bunch of white*
*    grapes, a small punnet of strawberries, 1*
*    banana*

1. Roll out the pastry into a rectangle the size of an A4 sheet of paper.

2. Cut out a 'picture frame' 2.5cm/1in wide. Dust liberally with flour and fold into 4. Carefully set aside.

3. Roll out the remaining pastry until it is a little larger than A4 size.

4. Preheat the oven to 220°C/425°F/gas mark 7.

5. Transfer the pastry to a baking sheet and prick it well all over with water. Using a pastry brush, dampen the edges with a fork. Place the 'picture frame', still folded, on to the pastry and unfold. Trim the edges neatly. Brush off any excess flour. Knock up the pastry and brush the frame with beaten egg (take care not to dribble the glaze down the sides or the pastry will stick together). Refrigerate for 20 minutes.

6. Bake in the preheated oven for 15 minutes or until crisp and brown.

7. Remove from the oven and leave to cool on a wire rack.

8. Use a little of the apricot glaze to brush the surface of the pastry.

9. Cut up the fruit as you would for a fruit salad and lay the pieces in rows on the pastry as neatly and closely together as possible. Be careful about colour (do not put 2 rows of white fruit next to each other, or tangerine segments next to orange segments, for example). When complete, paint carefully with the warm apricot glaze.

 *SWEET WHITE*

# CHOCOLATE PROFITEROLES

MAKES 30
For the profiteroles
*1 quantity choux pastry (see page 465)*

For the filling and topping
*570ml/1 pint double cream, whipped and*
*    sweetened with 1 tablespoon sifted icing sugar*
*110g/4oz plain chocolate, chopped*
*15g/½oz butter*
*2 tablespoons water*

1. Preheat the oven to 200°C/400°F/gas mark 6.

2. Put teaspoons of the choux mixture on a baking sheet, about 8cm/3in apart.

**3.** Bake in the preheated oven for 20–30 minutes. The profiteroles will puff up and become fairly brown. If they are taken out when only slightly brown, they will be soggy when cool.

**4.** Using a skewer, make a hole the size of a pea in the base of each profiterole and return to the oven for 5 minutes to allow the insides to dry out. Leave to cool completely on a wire rack.

**5.** When cold, put the sweetened cream into a piping bag fitted with a small plain nozzle. Pipe the cream into the profiteroles through the holes made by the skewer, until well filled.

**6.** Put the chocolate, butter and water in a heatproof bowl set over, not in, a saucepan of simmering water and leave until melted.

**7.** Dip the tops of the profiteroles in the melted chocolate, then allow to cool.

NOTE: If no piping bag is available for filling the profiteroles, they can be split, allowed to dry out, and filled with cream or crème pâtissière when cold, and the icing can be spooned over the top. However, made this way they are messier to eat in the fingers.

 *FORTIFIED SWEET WHITE*

# COFFEE ÉCLAIRS

MAKES 20–25
*1 quantity choux pastry (see page 465)*

For the filling and topping
*425ml/³⁄4 pint double cream, lightly whipped and
    sweetened with 1 tablespoon sifted icing sugar,
    or crème pâtissière (see page 476)*
*225g/8oz icing sugar*
*2 tablespoons very strong hot black coffee*

**1.** Preheat the oven to 200°C/400°F/gas mark 6.
**2.** Using a piping bag fitted with a 1cm/½in plain nozzle, pipe 5cm/2in lengths of choux pastry on to the baking sheets (keep them well separated as choux pastry puffs up during baking). Bake in the preheated oven for 25–30 minutes until crisp and pale brown.
**3.** Using a skewer, make a hole the size of a pea in each éclair and return to the oven for 5 minutes to allow the insides to dry out. Leave to cool completely on a wire rack.

**4.** Put the sweetened cream or the crème pâtissière into a piping bag fitted with a medium plain nozzle. Pipe the cream into the éclairs through the holes made by the skewer, until well filled.
**5.** Mix the icing sugar and very hot coffee together and beat with a wooden spoon until smooth. The mixture should be just runny.
**6.** Dip each éclair upside down into the icing so that the top becomes neatly coated.
**7.** Set aside to dry. Alternatively, the icing can be carefully spooned along the top ridge of each éclair.

NOTE: The éclairs may be split lengthways when cooked, allowed to dry out, and filled with cream or crème pâtissière when cold. The tops are then replaced and the icing spooned over but they are then messier to eat in the fingers.

 *FORTIFIED SWEET WHITE*

# BEIGNETS SOUFFLÉS

When dropping the choux into the hot oil, grease the teaspoon to prevent sticking.

MAKES ABOUT 30
*oil for deep-frying*
*1 quantity choux pastry (see page 465)*
*290ml/½ pint crème pâtissière (see page 476)
    (optional)*
*caster sugar and ground cinnamon for dusting*

**1.** Heat the oil in the deep-fryer until a crumb will sizzle gently in it. Drop teaspoonfuls of the choux pastry into the hot oil, one at a time, so that they do not stick together. Tap them lightly with a spoon to puff them up. Deep-fry for about 5 minutes or until brown and crisp. Drain well on absorbent kitchen paper.
**2.** The beignets can be split open and filled with warm crème pâtissière, if wished. Toss lightly in sugar and cinnamon.

NOTE: Apricot sauce (see page 478) is delicious served hot with these.

 *SWEET SPARKLING WHITE*

# GÂTEAU ST HONORÉ

SERVES 6

*110g/4oz flour quantity pâte sucrée (see page 466)*
*1 quantity choux pastry (see page 465)*
*double quantity crème pâtissière (see page 476)*
*170g/6oz granulated sugar*

1. Preheat the oven to 190°C/375°F/gas mark 5. Line an 18cm/7in flan ring with the pâte sucrée. Bake blind until biscuit coloured (see page 459).
2. Make the profiteroles: increase the oven temperature to 200°C/400°F/gas mark 6.
3. Put teaspoonfuls of the choux pastry on to 2 baking sheets and bake for 25 minutes until firm and pale brown.
4. Using a skewer, make a hole the size of a pea in the base of each choux bun and return to the oven for 5 minutes to allow the insides to dry out. Leave on a wire rack to cool completely.
5. Put the crème pâtissière into a piping bag fitted with a plain nozzle and pipe into 17 even-sized profiteroles through the holes made by the skewer. Spread the remaining crème pâtissière in the bottom of the pastry case. Pile the profiteroles into a pyramid on top of the filling.
6. Heat the sugar in a heavy saucepan over a low heat until it caramelizes to a pale liquid toffee. Remove from the heat and allow the bubbles to subside.
7. Pour the caramel over the profiteroles.

NOTE: Vast pyramids of profiteroles filled as here, or with whipped cream, form the traditional French wedding cake or croque-en-bouche. Sometimes icing sugar is sifted over the whole creation.

 *SWEET SPARKLING WHITE*

# APRICOT RING

SERVES 6

*225g/8oz fresh apricots*
*150ml/¼ pint sugar syrup (see page 477)*
*1 quantity choux pastry (see page 465)*
*2 tablespoons apricot jam*
*140g/5oz icing sugar, sifted*
*290ml/½ pint double cream, whipped*
*30g/1oz almonds, toasted*

1. Preheat the oven to 200°C/400°F/gas mark 6.
2. Wash and halve the apricots and remove the stones. Poach in the sugar syrup until just tender (about 15 minutes). Drain well and leave to cool.
3. Put the choux pastry into a piping bag fitted with a large plain nozzle and pipe into a circle about 15cm/6in in diameter on a baking tray. Bake in the preheated oven for about 30 minutes until brown and crisp.
4. Split horizontally with a bread knife. Scoop out any uncooked pastry and discard. Leave the choux ring on a wire rack to cool completely.
5. Heat the jam and spread it on the base of the choux ring.
6. Mix 30g/1oz of the icing sugar with the cream and fold in the apricots.
7. Spoon the mixture on to the base and press the lid on firmly.
8. Mix the remaining icing sugar with a little boiling water until just runny. Coat the top of the choux ring with the icing and, while still wet, sprinkle with browned almonds.

 *SWEET WHITE*

# APPLE STRUDEL

SERVES 6

*285g/10oz flour quantity strudel pastry (see page
466), rolled to a rectangle at least 40 ×
60cm/16 × 24in*

For the filling
*900g/2lb cooking apples
a handful of currants, sultanas and raisins
30g/1oz soft light brown sugar
½ teaspoon ground cinnamon
a pinch of ground cloves
3 tablespoons browned breadcrumbs
grated zest and juice of ½ lemon
85g/3oz butter, melted
icing sugar, sifted, for dusting*

**1.** Preheat the oven to 200°C/400°F/gas mark 6.
Grease a baking sheet.
**2.** Prepare the filling: peel, core and cut the apples
into chunks making sure they do not have any
very sharp corners which would pierce the delicate
pastry, and mix together with the dried fruit,
sugar, spices, breadcrumbs, lemon zest and juice.
**3.** Flour a large tea-towel. Lay the pastry on this.
**4.** Brush with melted butter. Place the filling at
one end of the pastry. Using the tea-towel to help,
roll up as for a Swiss roll, trying to maintain a
fairly close roll. Lift the cloth and gently tip the
strudel on to the baking sheet. Brush with melted
butter. Trim the edges neatly.
**5.** Bake in the preheated oven for about 40
minutes until golden-brown. Dust with icing
sugar while still warm.

NOTE: In delicatessens, strudels are generally
sold in one-portion sizes. To make these you will
need leaves of pastry about 22cm/9in square. As
they are easier to handle, they can be lifted
without the aid of the cloth – jut flour the table
top to prevent sticking. Bake for 20 minutes.

 *SWEET WHITE*

# BAKLAVA

Claudia Roden's *A New Book of Middle Eastern
Food* is fascinating to read and an excellent book
from which to cook. At Leith's she is one of our
very special guest lecturers. The students love to
see her make both this baklava and the konafa.

SERVES 6

*170g/6oz unsalted butter, melted
450g/1lb filo pastry (24 sheets)
340g/12oz pistachios, walnuts or almonds,
   ground or finely chopped*

For the syrup
*450g/1lb granulated sugar
290ml/½ pint water
2 tablespoons lemon juice
2 tablespoons orange-blossom water*

**1.** Make the syrup: put the sugar, water and lemon
juice into a saucepan, dissolve over a low heat and
then simmer until thick enough to coat the back of
a wooden spoon. Add the orange blossom water
and simmer for a further 2 minutes. Remove from
the heat and leave to cool, then refrigerate.
**2.** Preheat the oven to 160°C/325°F/gas mark 3.
**3.** Brush melted butter on the base and sides of a
deep baking tray. Put half the filo sheets into the
tray, brushing each sheet with melted butter and
overlapping or folding the sides over where
necessary.
**4.** Spread the nuts evenly over the pastry, spoon
over 4 tablespoons of the sugar syrup and then
cover with the remaining sheets of filo, brushing
each one as you layer it up. Brush the top layer
with butter. Cut diagonally into lozenge shapes
with a sharp, serrated knife.
**5.** Bake in the preheated oven for 45 minutes,
then turn the oven temperature up to
220°C/425°F/gas mark 7 and bake for a further
15 minutes or until well risen or until well risen
and golden brown.
**6.** Remove from the oven and pour the chilled
syrup over the hot baklava. Leave to cool.
**7.** When cold, cut into lozenge shapes as before
and place on a serving dish.

 *RICH SWEET WHITE / SPARKLING*

# KONAFA

SERVES 8
*450g/1lb konafa pastry (available in delicatessens)*
*225g/8oz unsalted butter, melted*

For the syrup
*450g/1lb granulated sugar*
*290ml/½ pint water*
*2 tablespoons lemon juice*
*2 tablespoons orange-blossom water*

For the filling
*6 tablespoons ground rice*
*4 tablespoons caster sugar*
*1 litre/1¾ pints milk*
*150ml/¼ pint double cream*

**1.** Make the syrup: put the sugar, water and lemon juice into a saucepan, dissolve over a low heat and then simmer until thick enough to coat the back of a wooden spoon. Add the orange-blossom water and simmer for a further 2 minutes. Remove from the heat and leave to cool, then refrigerate.
**2.** Mix the ground rice and sugar to a smooth paste with 150ml/¼ pint of the milk. Bring the remaining milk to the boil and gradually add the ground rice paste, stirring vigorously. Simmer, stirring to prevent the mixture catching on the bottom of the pan, until very thick. Remove from the heat and allow to cool, then add the cream and mix well.
**3.** Preheat the oven to 170°C/325°F/gas mark 3.
**4.** Put the konafa pastry into a large bowl. Pull out and separate the strands as much as possible with your fingers so that they do not stick together too much. Pour in the melted butter and work it in very well. Put half the pastry into a large, deep ovenproof dish. Spread the filling evenly over and cover with the remaining pastry. Flatten it with the palm of your hand.
**5.** Bake in the preheated oven for 1 hour. Then turn the oven temperature up to 220°C/425°F/gas mark 7 and bake for a further 10–15 minutes or until golden-brown.
**6.** Remove from the oven and pour the cold syrup over the hot konafa.

NOTE: Konafa can be made with a variety of fillings, such as curd cheese, nuts and cinnamon or sliced bananas. They can also be made as individually rolled pastries instead of one large pastry.

 *RICH SWEET WHITE / SPARKLING*

# ALMOND PASTRY FRUIT FLAN

SERVES 6
*110g/4oz flour quantity almond pastry (2) (see page 467)*
*a selection of fruit, such as oranges, pears, grapes, cherries, strawberries, bananas, apples, plums, depending on the season*
*4 tablespoons apricot glaze (see page 638)*

**1.** Preheat the oven to 190°C/375°F/gas mark 5.
**2.** On a baking sheet roll or press the pastry into a 22cm/9in circle. Decorate the edges with a fork or the point of a sharp knife (pressed broad side into the pastry) or by pinching between fingers and thumb. Prick lightly all over with a fork. Refrigerate to relax for 15 minutes.
**3.** Bake in the preheated oven for about 15 minutes until a pale biscuit colour. Loosen with a palette knife and allow to cool slightly and harden on the baking sheet. Slip on to a wire rack and leave to cool completely.
**4.** Prepare the fruits as you would for a fruit salad, leaving any that discolour (such as apples or pears) until you assemble the flan.
**5.** Brush the pastry with some of the apricot glaze (this helps to stick the fruit in place and prevents the pastry from becoming too soggy).
**6.** Arrange the fruit in neat overlapping circles, taking care to get contrasting colours next to each other. Brush with apricot glaze as you go, especially on apples, pears or bananas. When all the fruit is in place, brush with the remaining glaze.

NOTE: This flan should not be assembled too far in advance as the pastry will become soggy in about 2 hours.

 *SWEET WHITE*

# APRICOT TART BOURDALOUE

SERVES 4–6

*170g/6oz flour quantity pâte sucrée (see page 466)*
*140g/5oz caster sugar*
*290ml/½ pint water*
*450g/1lb fresh apricots*

For the bourdaloue cream
*290ml/½ pint milk*
*2 egg yolks*
*55g/2oz caster sugar*
*15g/½oz plain flour*
*20g/¾oz cornflour*
*2 tablespoons ground almonds*
*2 tablespoons double cream*
*1 tablespoon Kirsch (optional)*
*2 egg whites*

**1.** Refrigerate the pâte sucrée for at least 30 minutes.
**2.** Now prepare the apricots: place the sugar and water in a heavy saucepan and set over a low heat until dissolved. Wash and halve the apricots and place them in the pan once the sugar has dissolved. Poach in the gently simmering sugar syrup until soft – be careful not to overcook them. Drain very well and set the apricots and syrup aside.
**3.** Preheat the oven to 190°C/375°F/gas mark 5. Line a 20cm/8in flan ring with the pâte sucrée and bake blind (see page 459) until a pale biscuit colour (about 15 minutes). Remove the lining paper, beans and flan ring and bake for a further 5 minutes until the sides are evenly coloured. Slide on to a wire rack and leave to cool.
**4.** To prepare the bourdaloue cream: scald the milk by bringing it to just below boiling point. Cream the egg yolks with half the sugar and when pale mix in the flours. Pour on the milk and mix well. Return the mixture to the pan and bring slowly to the boil, stirring continuously. (It will go alarmingly lumpy at first, but don't worry, keep stirring and it will get smooth.) Pour into a bowl. Allow to cool slightly. Mix in the ground almonds, cream and the Kirsch, if using.
**5.** Whisk the egg whites until stiff, then add the remaining sugar and whisk again until stiff and shiny. Stir in to the cool bourdaloue mixture.

**6.** Assemble the flan: fill the flan case with the bourdaloue cream and spread it flat with a spatula or palette knife. Arrange the well-drained apricots over the cream so that the tart is completely covered. Boil up the sugar syrup in which the apricots were cooked until thick enough to form a thread when tested between finger and thumb. Cool. Brush over the apricots.

 *RICH SWEET WHITE*

# CANDIED LEMON TART

SERVES 6

*170g/6oz flour quantity pâte sucrée (see page 466)*
*4 eggs*
*1 egg yolk*
*200g/7oz caster sugar*
*150ml/¼ pint double cream*
*grated zest and juice of 2 lemons*
*icing sugar, sifted, for dusting*

To glaze
*1 lemon*
*150ml/¼ pint sugar syrup (see page 477)*

**1.** Preheat the oven to 190°C/375°F/gas mark 5.
**2.** Line a 20cm/8in flan ring with the pâte sucrée. Refrigerate for 30 minutes, then bake blind for 15 minutes (see page 459). Remove the lining paper and beans and leave to cool on a wire rack. Turn the oven temperature down to 150°C/300°F/gas mark 2.
**3.** Make the filling: mix the eggs and egg yolk with the sugar and whisk lightly until smooth. Add the cream and whisk again. Add the lemon zest and juice. The mixture may thicken alarmingly but do not worry.
**4.** Put the pastry case back on to a baking sheet and spoon in the lemon filling. Bake in the oven for 50 minutes until almost set.
**5.** Meanwhile, prepare the glazed lemon rind. Using a potato peeler, pare the rind from the lemon very thinly, making sure that there is no pith on the back of the strips. Cut into very fine shreds.
**6.** Simmer the shreds in the sugar syrup until

tender, glassy and candied. Remove with a slotted spoon and leave to cool on greaseproof paper.
7. When the tart is cooked, remove the flan ring and leave to cool. Then dust thickly and evenly with sifted icing sugar and arrange the candied shreds on top.

 *SWEET WHITE*

# STRAWBERRY TARTLETS

MAKES 20
*170g/6oz flour quantity pâte sucrée (see page 466)*

For the filling
*225g/8oz petit Suisse cheese*
*55g/2oz caster sugar*
*450g/1lb strawberries, hulled*
*4 tablespoons redcurrant jelly, melted*

1. Preheat the oven to 190°C/375°F/gas mark 5.
2. Roll out the pastry thinly and use to line 20 tartlet tins. Bake blind (see page 459) until a pale biscuit colour (about 15 minutes). Remove the lining papers and beans. If the pastry is not quite cooked, return to the oven for 5 minutes. Carefully remove the pastry cases and leave to cool on a wire rack.
3. Cream the cheese with the sugar and place a teaspoonful of the mixture at the bottom of each case. Arrange the strawberries, cut in half if necessary, on top of the cheese and brush lightly with warm melted redcurrant jelly.

NOTE: If Petit Suisse cheese is not available, use Mascarpone or soft curd cheese.

 *SWEET WHITE*

# SABLÉ AUX FRAISES

This recipe has been adapted from *The Roux Brothers on Pâtisserie.*

SERVES 6
*280g/10oz flour quantity pâte sablée (see page 462)*
*675g/1½lb strawberries, hulled and sliced*
*425ml/¾ pint raspberry coulis (see page 479)*
*55g/2oz icing sugar, sifted, for dusting*

1. Preheat the oven to 190°C/375°F/gas mark 5.
2. Divide the chilled dough into 2 pieces to make for easier rolling.
3. Roll out the doughs very thinly and cut into a total of 18 × 10cm/4in circles. Refrigerate to relax for 10 minutes. Bake in the preheated oven for 8 minutes or until pale golden. Transfer to a wire rack and leave to cool.
4. Cut the strawberries in half and mix them with two-thirds of the raspberry coulis. Leave to macerate.
5. Place a pastry base on each of 6 pudding plates. Arrange a few macerated strawberries on top. Cover with a second pastry base and more strawberries. Cover with a third piece of pastry and dust generously with icing sugar.
6. Serve the remaining raspberry coulis separately or poured around the sablés.

NOTE: Do not assemble this pudding in advance as the pastry will become soggy.

# PEACH PASTRY CAKE

SERVES 6
*70g/2½oz hazelnuts*
*55g/2oz caster sugar*
*85g/3oz butter*
*110g/4oz plain flour*
*a pinch of salt*
*3 fresh peaches*
*200ml/7fl oz cream, whipped*
*icing sugar, sifted, for dusting*

1. Preheat the oven to 230°C/450°F/gas mark 8. Toast the nuts in the hot oven. When brown, rub

in a dry cloth to remove the skins. Cool. Grind the nuts with 1 tablespoon of the sugar taking care not to overgrind them or they will be oily.

**2.** Beat the butter until soft, add the remaining sugar and beat until light and fluffy.

**3.** Sift the flour with the salt and stir into the mixture with the nuts.

**4.** Turn the oven temperature down to 190°C/375°F/gas mark 5.

**5.** Divide the nut mixture into 3 and press out until thin flat 15cm/6in rounds. Refrigerate for 30 minutes.

**6.** Place on baking sheets and bake in the preheated oven for 10–12 minutes. Loosen from the baking sheet with a palette knife. Cut 1 biscuit round into sixths before it cools. Allow to cool on a wire rack. The pastry will become crisp as it cools.

**7.** Skin and slice the peaches. Mix the peach slices with the cream. Using half this mixture as a filling, sandwich the 2 whole biscuit rounds together. Spread the remaining filling on the top.

**8.** Set the cut portions of biscuit into the cream mixture, placing each at a slight angle. Dust with icing sugar before serving.

# BRIOCHE TART WITH GRAPES AND MASCARPONE

SERVES 4–6
*450g/1lb flour quantity brioche dough (see page 620)*
*170g/6oz raisins (optional)*
*340g/12oz Mascarpone*
*450g/1lb seedless grapes*
*110g/4oz soft dark brown sugar*

**1.** Preheat the oven to 190°C/375°F/gas mark 5.

**2.** Knock back the risen brioche dough and roll out to a circle about 28cm/11in in diameter. Place on a baking sheet.

**3.** If using raisins, sprinkle them over the surface of the dough and press in lightly.

**4.** Spread the Mascarpone over the surface, leaving a 2.5cm/1in border all the way around the edge.

**5.** Scatter the grapes on top and press firmly into the Mascarpone. Sprinkle over the sugar.

**6.** Bake the tart in the centre of the preheated oven for 30–40 minutes until golden brown. Reduce oven temperature if the tart shows signs of becoming too dark.

**7.** Serve the tart warm.

NOTE: Other soft fruits can be used in place of the grapes, for example pitted cherries or plums.

# RUM BABA

SERVES 4
For the sugar syrup
*170g/6oz loaf sugar*
*225ml/8fl oz water*
*2 tablespoons rum*

For the yeast mixture
*110g/4oz plain flour*
*15g/½oz fresh yeast*
*15g/½oz caster sugar*
*6 tablespoons warm milk*
*2 egg yolks*
*grated zest of ½ lemon*
*55g/2oz clarified butter (see page 686)*

To decorate
*fresh fruits, such as grapes and raspberries*
*150ml/¼ pint double or whipping cream, lightly whipped*

**1.** First make the sugar syrup: dissolve the sugar in the water in a heavy saucepan and boil rapidly for 3 minutes. The syrup should be boiled to the short thread stage (see page 477): (when a little syrup is put between a wet finger and thumb and the fingers are opened, the syrup should form a short thread). Add the rum.

**2.** Now make the yeast mixture: sift the flour into a warmed bowl.

**3.** Mix the yeast with ½ teaspoon of the sugar, 1 teaspoon of the flour and enough milk to make a batter-like consistency.

**4.** Whisk the egg yolks, remaining sugar and lemon zest until fluffy.

**5.** Make a well in the centre of the flour and add the yeast and egg-yolk mixtures. With your fingers, mix together and gradually draw in the flour from the sides, adding more milk as you take in more flour. When all the flour has been incorporated, beat with your hand until very soft and smooth.

**6.** Gradually add the clarified butter, kneading and slapping the dough until it looks like a very thick batter and no longer sticks to the palm of your hand.

**7.** Cover and leave to rise in a warm place, such as the airing cupboard, for about 45 minutes, until doubled in size.

**8.** Preheat the oven to 190°C/375°F/gas mark 5. Grease a 1 litre/1¾ pint savarin (ring) mould with plenty of butter.

**9.** When the dough has risen, beat it down again and place in the mould, which it should half-fill.

**10.** Cover and leave to prove (rise again) for 10–15 minutes in a warm place.

**11.** Bake in the preheated oven for 30–35 minutes.

**12.** Turn out on to a wire rack and, while still hot, prick all over with a cocktail stick and brush with plenty of rum syrup until the baba is really soaked and shiny. Place on a serving dish.

**13.** Serve plain or surround with fresh fruit and pile the whipped cream in the centre.

NOTE: If using dried yeast, use half the amount called for. Mix it with 3 tablespoons of the liquid, warmed to blood temperature, and 1 teaspoon sugar. Leave until frothy (about 15 minutes), then proceed. If the yeast does not go frothy, it is dead and unusable. If using easy-blend yeast, use half the quantity called for and add it to the dry ingredients.

# SAVARIN AUX FRUITS

In the absence of a savarin mould, use an ordinary cake tin. The fruit should then be piled on top of the cake.

SERVES 4
For the savarin
*110g/4oz plain flour*
*7g/¼oz fresh yeast*
*15g/½oz caster sugar*
*2 egg yolks*
*grated zest of ½ lemon*
*6 tablespoons warm milk*
*55g/2oz butter, softened*

For the sugar syrup
*170g/6oz loaf sugar*
*225ml/8fl oz water*
*2 drops of vanilla essence*

For the fruit mixture
*675–900g/1½–2lb total of bananas, cherries, plums, grapes, oranges, apricots, apples and pineapple*

To serve
*290ml/½ pint crème Chantilly (see page 476)*

**1.** Sift the flour into a warmed bowl. Mix the yeast with ½ teaspoon of the sugar, add 1 teaspoon of the flour and enough milk (about 4 tablespoons) to give a batter-like consistency.

**2.** Whisk the egg yolks, remaining sugar and lemon zest until fluffy.

**3.** Make a well in the centre of the flour and add the yeast and egg-yolk mixtures. Mix them together with the fingers of one hand, and then gradually draw in the flour from the sides, adding milk as you take in more flour. When all the flour has been incorporated, beat with your hand until very soft and smooth.

**4.** Gradually add the butter, kneading and slapping the dough until it looks like a thick batter and no longer sticks to the palm of your hand.

**5.** Cover and leave to rise in a warm place for about 45 minutes until doubled in size.

**6.** Make the sugar syrup: dissolve the sugar in the water in a heavy saucepan and boil rapidly for 2 minutes, or until syrupy. When cool, add the vanilla essence.

**7.** Prepare the fruit as for a fruit salad and moisten with 1–2 tablespoons of the syrup.

**8.** Preheat the oven to 190°C/375°F/gas mark 5. Butter a savarin or large ring mould thickly. When the dough has risen, beat it down again and place in the mould, which it should half-fill. Cover and leave to prove (rise again) for 10–15 minutes in a warm place.

**9.** Bake in the preheated oven for 30–35 minutes until golden-brown. Turn out on to a wire rack and, while still hot, prick all over with a cocktail stick and brush with plenty of warm sugar syrup.

**10.** Allow to cool. Place on a serving dish and brush again with the syrup until the cake is completely soaked. Fill the centre with the fruit. Serve with crème Chantilly.

NOTE: If using dried or easy-blend yeast see note to previous recipe.

# ORANGE AND GRAND MARNIER PANCAKES

SERVES 4
*grated zest of 1 large orange*
*290ml/½ pint crème pâtissière (see page 476)*
*2 tablespoons Grand Marnier*
*8 French pancakes (see page 471)*
*icing sugar, sifted, for dusting*

**1.** Preheat the grill to its highest setting.
**2.** Mix the orange zest with the crème pâtissère and the Grand Marnier.
**3.** Divide the mixture between the pancakes.
**4.** Fold each pancake in half and dust heavily with icing sugar.
**5.** Place under the hot grill until the icing sugar begins to caramelize.

# CRÊPES SUZETTE

SERVES 4–6
*12 French pancakes (see page 471)*

For the orange butter
*85g/3oz unsalted butter*
*30g/1oz caster sugar*
*grated zest of 1 orange*
*2 tablespoons orange juice*
*2 tablespoons orange Curaçao or Grand Marnier*

To flame
*caster sugar*
*2 tablespoons orange Curaçao or Grand Marnier*
*1 tablespoon brandy*

**1.** Put the butter, sugar, orange zest, juice and Curaçao or Grand Marnier into a large frying pan and simmer gently for 2 minutes.
**2.** Put a pancake into the frying pan and, using a spoon and fork, fold it in half and then in half again. Add a second pancake and repeat the process until the pan has been filled. If the pan begins to look a little dry, add a little water.
**3.** Sprinkle the pancakes with caster sugar and pour over the orange Curaçao or Grand Marnier and brandy. Light a match, stand back, and light the alcohol. Spoon it over the pancakes until the flames have subsided. Serve immediately.

# BAKED APPLES

*1 smallish cooking apple per person*
*soft light brown sugar*
*sultanas*

**1.** Preheat the oven to 180°C/350°F/gas mark 4.
**2.** Wash the apples and remove the cores with an apple corer. With a sharp knife cut a ring just through the apple skin about two-thirds of the way up each apple.
**3.** Put the apples into an ovenproof dish and stuff the centres with a mixture of sugar and sultanas.
**4.** Sprinkle 2 teaspoons sugar over each apple. Then pour 5mm/½in of water into the dish over the apples.
**5.** Bake in the preheated oven for about 45 minutes, or until the apples are soft right through when tested with a skewer.

 *SWEET WHITE*

# POACHED APPLES

SERVES 4
*170g/6oz granulated sugar*
*570ml/1 pint water*
*450g/1lb dessert apples*
*1 cinnamon stick*
*a squeeze of lemon juice*

To serve
*cream (optional)*

**1.** Dissolve the sugar in the water in a heavy saucepan. When completely dissolved, boil rapidly until you have a thin syrup (3–4 minutes).
**2.** Peel, core and quarter the apples. Place them in the sugar syrup with the cinnamon.
**3.** Bring slowly to the boil, then reduce the heat and poach gently for 20 minutes, or until the apples are tender.
**4.** Remove the apples with a slotted spoon and arrange in a shallow dish.
**5.** Reduce the syrup a little by further boiling, then add the lemon juice. Pour over the fruit just before serving.
**6.** Serve hot with cream, or chilled with or without cream.

 *LIGHT SWEET WHITE*

# APPLES AND BLACKBERRIES IN CASSIS SYRUP

SERVES 4
*4 Granny Smith apples, with stalks if possible*

For the poaching liquid
*225g/8oz blackberries*
*juice and 2 strips of zest from ½ lemon*
*½ cinnamon stick*
*2 strips of orange zest*
*110g/4oz sugar*
*150ml/¼ pint crème de cassis*
*150ml/¼ pint dry white wine*

To serve
*2 tablespoons of the poaching juices (see above)*
*plain yoghurt*
*225g/8oz blackberries*

1. Put the poaching ingredients into a large shallow pan and simmer over a low heat until the sugar has dissolved.
2. Peel the apples, cut in half leaving the stalk on one half, and remove the cores with a melon baller or small spoon.
3. Add to the poaching liquid, cut side up, and cover with a lid.
4. Poach the apples over a low heat for about 15 minutes, or until just tender. Baste frequently, using a wooden spoon to avoid damaging the fruit. Remove the pan from the heat. Leave the fruit to cool in the liquid. The longer the apples are left in the poaching liquid the more coloured they will become.
5. Remove the apples with two wooden spoons and place, cut side down, on a plate. Strain the cooking liquid through a plastic or nylon sieve, return to a clean saucepan and simmer over a medium heat until reduced to a thick syrup. Leave to cool.
6. To serve: put 2 apple halves on each of 4 pudding plates and spoon the syrup over and around. Add a spoonful of yoghurt if wished or serve it separately.
7. Decorate with blackberries.

NOTE: This recipe also works well with pears; cook them for 20 minutes.

# ALAIN SENDERENS' SOUPE AUX FRUITS EXOTIQUES

This recipe was taken from Robert Carrier in the *Sunday Express*.

SERVES 4
*1 small papaya*
*16 lychees*
*20 strawberries*
*2 kiwi fruits*
*8 passionfruits*

For the syrup
*6 tablespoons sugar*
*1 sprig of fresh mint*
*1 clove*
*¼ teaspoon Chinese 5-spice (from good food stores and Chinese specialist shops)*
*thinly pared zest of 1 lime*
*thinly pared zest of ¼ lemon*
*1 vanilla pod, split lengthways*
*½ teaspoon peeled and finely chopped fresh root ginger*
*2 coriander seeds*
*425ml/¾ pint water*

To decorate
*1 tablespoon finely chopped fresh mint*

1. Make the syrup: put the sugar, mint sprig, clove, Chinese 5-spice, lime and lemon zest, vanilla pod, ginger, coriander seeds and water into a heavy saucepan and bring slowly to the boil, stirring to dissolve the sugar. Reduce, by boiling rapidly, for 1 minute. Remove the pan from the heat and leave to infuse until cool.
2. Meanwhile, peel the papaya and cut the flesh into even-sized pieces. Skin the lychees and remove the stones. Wash and hull the strawberries. Peel the kiwi fruits and slice thinly.
3. When the syrup is cool, strain through a fine sieve into a bowl. Add the prepared fruits. Cut the passionfruits in half and spoon out the seeds and juice into the bowl of syrup. Chill for 2–3 hours.
4. To serve: divide the prepared fruits into 4 shallow bowls; spoon over the syrup and sprinkle with mint.

 *LIGHT SWEET WHITE*

# GRATIN DE FRUITS

SERVES 6
*4 ripe peaches*
*4 ripe plums*
*4 ripe apricots*
*2 eggs*
*2 egg yolks*
*85g/3oz caster sugar*
*a dash of Kirsch (optional)*
*55g/2oz flaked almonds*

**1.** Skin, stone and slice the peaches. Halve and stone the plums and apricots. Arrange on 6 small gratin dishes.
**2.** Preheat the grill to its highest setting.
**3.** Put the eggs, egg yolks and sugar into a heatproof bowl set over, not in, a saucepan of simmering water. Whisk for 10–15 minutes until thick and creamy. It is important that the eggs should thicken, not scramble. Add the Kirsch, if using.
**4.** Spoon the sauce over the fruits. Sprinkle with the almonds and grill until evenly browned. Serve immediately.

 *SWEET WHITE*

# FRESH FRUIT IN BISCUIT CUPS

SERVES 8
*1 quantity iced sabayon (see page 501)*
*8 biscuit cups (see page 571)*
*6 kiwi fruits, peeled and sliced*
*170g/6oz seedless grapes*

**1.** Divide the iced sabayon between the 8 biscuit cups.
**2.** Decorate with the kiwi fruit and grapes. Serve immediately.

# GREEN FRUIT SALAD

SERVES 4
*3 kiwi fruits*
*225g/8oz greengages*
*225g/8oz white grapes*
*1 small ripe melon with green flesh*
*1 green dessert apple*
*apple juice or ginger cordial*

**1.** Peel and slice the kiwi fruits. Stone and quarter the greengages and halve and seed the grapes.
**2.** Using a melon baller, scrape the melon flesh into balls, or simply cut into even-sized cubes. Core the unpeeled apple and cut it into chunks.
**3.** Mix the fruits together, moisten with the apple juice or ginger cordial and chill well before serving.

 *LIGHT SWEET WHITE*

# RED FRUIT SALAD

SERVES 4
*675g/1½lb assorted red fruit, such as raspberries, strawberries, redcurrants, watermelon, plums*
*fresh orange juice (optional)*

**1.** Wash the fruit.
**2.** Check the raspberries, discarding any bad ones.
**3.** Hull and halve the strawberries.
**4.** Wash, top and tail the redcurrants with the prongs of a fork.
**5.** Cut the melon flesh into cubes, discarding most of the seeds, but reserving the juice.
**6.** Halve and stone the plums.
**7.** Put the fruit into a glass dish and moisten with orange juice, if required. Chill well.

NOTE: Red fruit salad is also very good if sprinkled with a little triple-distilled rosewater in place of the orange juice. A teaspoonful will be plenty.

 *LIGHT SWEET WHITE*

# BLACKCURRANT KISSEL

SERVES 4
*450g/1lb blackcurrants*
*grated zest and juice of 1 orange*
*1 cinnamon stick*
*caster sugar to taste (about 170g/6oz)*
*2 teaspoons arrowroot*

**1.** Wash the blackcurrants and remove the stalks.
**2.** Barely cover with water and add the orange zest and juice, the cinnamon and sugar. Stew gently for about 20 minutes. Remove the cinnamon stick, then push through a sieve. Return to the saucepan and bring back to the boil.
**3.** Mix the arrowroot to a smooth paste with a little cold water.
**4.** Add a cupful of the boiling purée to the arrowroot paste and mix thoroughly. Add the arrowroot mixture to the fruit, stirring, and allow to thicken. Simmer for 1 minute. Pour into a serving bowl. Sprinkle evenly with caster sugar to prevent a skin from forming.

 *LIGHT SWEET WHITE*

# PINEAPPLE IN THE SHELL

*1 large pineapple*

**1.** Cut the top and bottom off the pineapple so that you are left with a cylinder of fruit. Do not throw away the leafy top. With a sharp knife, cut round inside the skin, working first from one end and then from the other, so that you can push the fruit out in one piece. Try not to pierce or tear the skin.
**2.** Slice the pineapple thinly. Stand the pineapple skin in a shallow bowl, put the fruit back in it and replace the top. Kirsch can be sprinkled in too if liked.

# FRESH PAPAYA WITH LIMES

Simply serve halved papayas, with the seeds removed, with a wedge of fresh lime. Allow one half of a papaya per head.

# TURNED MANGOES WITH LIMES

This idea for serving mangoes, from Arabella Boxer's *Sunday Times Cookery Course*, solves the problem of how to eat mangoes.

*½ mango and 2 lime wedges per person*

**1.** Cut a thick slice off the mango as close to the flat stone as possible.
**2.** Repeat on the other side. (Use the remaining mango flesh for another dish.)
**3.** With a small, sharp knife, make diagonal cuts through the flesh right down to the skin, taking care not to pierce the skin.

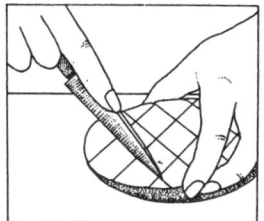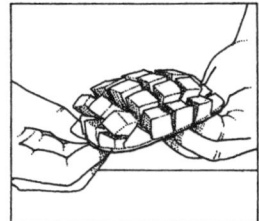

*Cut the flesh to give a lattice finish. Turn mango inside out*

**4.** Push the skin so that the mango is domed and can be eaten with a spoon. Serve with lime wedges.

# SUMMER FRUIT COMPOTE

SERVES 4–6
*110g/4oz black cherries, pitted*
*225g/8oz strawberries*
*juice of 1 orange*
*juice of 1 lemon*
*2 tablespoons caster sugar*
*2 tablespoons Kirsch*
*225g/8oz raspberries*
*110g/4oz red cherries, pitted*
*110g/4oz blueberries*
*225g/8oz blackberries*
*225g/8oz loganberries*

1. Process together half the black cherries, half the strawberries, the orange and lemon juice, the sugar and Kirsch. Taste and add more sugar if necessary.

2. Mix the remaining fruit together and pour the purée over it. Mix gently and pile into a serving bowl.

3. Keep the compote covered and refrigerated if not using immediately, but serve at room temperature.

 *LIGHT SWEET WHITE*

# WATERMELON SALAD

SERVES 6
*1 large watermelon*
*110g/4oz strawberries*
*1 tablespoon triple-distilled rosewater*

To decorate
*white gypsophilla (if available)*

1. Cut off the top of the watermelon. Remove as much of the flesh as possible. Discard the seeds and cut the flesh into neat pieces.

2. Hull and halve the strawberries.

3. Mix together the strawberries, watermelon flesh and rosewater. Pile back into the watermelon shell and replace the top. Put on a large plate and decorate with the white gypsophilla.

# ARRANGED FRUIT SALAD

SERVES 4
*2 ripe passionfruits*
*1 large ripe mango*
*3 tablespoons fresh orange juice*
*seasonal fruit, chilled, such as 4 kiwi fruits, peeled and sliced, 110g/4oz strawberries, hulled, 110g/4oz black grapes, peeled and halved*
*4 sprigs of fresh mint*

1. Process (but do not liquidize) the passionfruit pulp, mango flesh and orange juice together for 2 minutes.

2. Sieve the purée on to the base of 4 pudding plates so that each one is well flooded.

3. Arrange the prepared fruit in an attractive pattern on each plate. Decorate each with a sprig of mint.

NOTE: If you do not have a food processor, the sauce can be made in a blender if the passionfruit are sieved before 'whizzing'.

# HOT WINTER FRUIT SALAD

SERVES 4
*450g/1lb good-quality mixed dried fruits, such as prunes, apricots, figs and apples*
*1 tablespoon Calvados*
*cold tea*
*4 tablespoons fresh orange juice*
*3–4 cloves*
*1 × 5cm/2in cinnamon stick*
*¼ teaspoon ground mixed spice*
*thinly pared zest of 1 lemon*
*1 star anise*

1. Soak the mixed dried fruits in the Calvados and enough tea to just cover. Leave overnight.

2. Pour into a saucepan and add the orange juice, cloves, cinnamon, mixed spice, lemon zest and star anise. Bring to the boil, then simmer slowly until the fruits are soft (about 20 minutes).

3. Remove the cloves, cinnamon, lemon zest and star anise. Serve hot or cold.

# STRAWBERRIES WITH QUARK AND BLACK PEPPER

Quark is the German equivalent of the French fromage blanc. It is a very low-fat cheese made from skimmed milk.

Serve unhulled strawberries with a dip of Quark mixed with a little water and seasoned with freshly ground black pepper.

# ORANGES IN CARAMEL

*1 large orange per person*
*caramel sauce (see page 477)*

**1.** With a potato peeler, pare the zest of 1 or 2 oranges very thinly, making sure that there is no pith on the back of the strips. Cut into fine shreds.

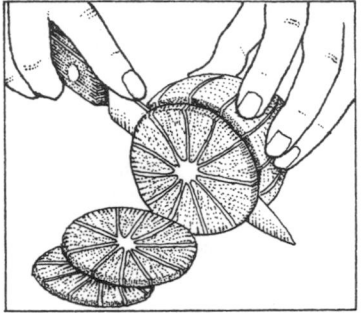

*How to prepare an orange*

**2.** Simmer the needleshreds in caramel sauce until soft and almost candied. They should be very sticky and quite dark.
**3.** Peel the remaining oranges with a knife as you would an apple, making sure that all the pith is removed.
**4.** Slice each orange crossways. Remove pips.
**5.** Place the oranges in a glass serving bowl and pour over the cold caramel sauce. Chill well.
**6.** Scatter with the needleshreds before serving.

 *FORTIFIED SWEET WHITE*

# BUTTERSCOTCH FIGS

SERVES 4
*8 ripe figs*
*140g/5oz caster sugar*
*55g/2oz unsalted butter*
*a pinch of ground cinnamon*
*4 tablespoons Grand Marnier*

To serve
*150ml/¼ pint double cream, lightly whipped*

**1.** Preheat the oven to 150°C/300°F/gas mark 2.
**2.** Prick the figs with a fork. Place them in a

casserole dish and sprinkle over 30g/1oz of the sugar. Add a little water and bake in the preheated oven for 30 minutes. Baste the figs occasionally.
**3.** Meanwhile, melt the butter in a large sauté pan, add 4 tablespoons water and the sugar and boil until lightly browned. Add the figs, sprinkle with a little cinnamon and toss gently with 2 wooden spoons so that they become lightly caramelized all over.
**4.** Heat the Grand Marnier in a small saucepan and then pour it over the figs to flame.
**5.** Serve the figs with the cream handed separately.

 *FORTIFIED SWEET WHITE*

# APRICOT CHEESECAKE

SERVES 4
For the crust
*170g/6oz digestive biscuits, crushed*
*85g/3oz butter, melted*
*a pinch of ground cinnamon*

For the filling
*3 tablespoons water*
*15g/½oz powdered gelatine*
*200g/7oz can of good-quality apricots*
*225g/8oz soft cheese*
*150ml/¼ pint double cream, whipped*
*70ml/2½fl oz soured cream*
*grated zest and juice of ½ lemon*
*sugar to taste (about 45g/1½oz)*

To decorate
*150ml/¼ pint double cream, whipped*
*nibbed almonds, toasted*

**1.** Place an oiled flan ring on a flat, lipless baking sheet. Mix together the crust ingredients and put the mixture into the flan ring, pressing down firmly. Refrigerate for 20 minutes to harden.
**2.** Put the water into a small saucepan, sprinkle over the gelatine and leave for 5 minutes until spongy.
**3.** Liquidize the apricots in a food processor or blender, reserving 3 halves for decoration. Beat the cheese until creamy, then mix with the apricot purée, creams, lemon zest, juice and sugar.

**4.** Dissolve the gelatine over a low heat, without boiling until liquid and clear. Pour this into the cheesecake mixture, stirring well. Pile the filling into the flan ring and spread it flat with a palette knife. Refrigerate for 1 hour or until set.

**5.** To serve: with a sharp knife, loosen the flan ring from the cheesecake and remove gently, being careful not to knock the edges. Using 2 palette knives, or fish slices, carefully lift or slide the cake on to a serving dish. If this proves difficult, the biscuit base can be loosened by placing the baking sheet above a low heat for 30 seconds. Decorate the edges with rosettes of whipped cream and the reserved apricot halves, each halved again. Sprinkle the almonds over the cream and serve.

NOTE: In the absence of a lipless baking sheet, use the back of a baking tray or roasting pan. The cake is easier to slide off a flat surface.

 *RICH SWEET WHITE*

# PINEAPPLE AND DATE SALAD

SERVES 4
*2 small pineapples*
*12 fresh dates*

**1.** Cut the pineapples in half lengthways, making sure that each half has an equal amount of green leaves. With a grapefruit knife, carefully remove the flesh, leaving the shells intact. Cut the flesh into cubes. Halve and stone the dates.

**2.** Mix the dates with the pineapple, keeping back 4 or 5 for the top. Pile the mixture into the shells and put the reserved date halves, shiny side up, on top.

NOTES: Preserved dates are good too, though not as good as fresh ones.

If the pineapple is very sharp, it may be sweetened with sifted icing sugar.

# BRISTOL APPLES

SERVES 4
*170g/6oz granulated sugar*
*290ml/1/2 pint water*
*4 dessert apples*
*2 oranges*
*oil*

**1.** Make the syrup: place 110g/4oz of the sugar and the water in a heavy saucepan and set over a low heat until the sugar dissolves. Once dissolved, boil rapidly for 3 minutes.

**2.** Peel, quarter and core the apples and place in the sugar syrup. Simmer very gently until just tender (about 20 minutes). Remove the apples and allow them to cool.

**3.** With a sharp knife or potato peeler, thinly pare the zest from 1 orange, taking care to leave behind the bitter pith. Cut the zest into very fine even-sized needleshreds. Put these into the syrup and boil until thick and tacky.

**4.** Peel the oranges with a sharp knife as you would an apple, making sure that all the pith is removed. Cut into neat segments, discarding any pips and membrane.

**5.** Put the remaining sugar into a heavy saucepan and let it dissolve over heat, without stirring.

**6.** Meanwhile, oil a baking sheet.

**7.** As the sugar bubbles, it will become a dark-golden colour. Pour this on to the oiled baking sheet and leave it to set into a thin layer like brown glass. When cold, break into chips, and set aside in a cool, dry place.

**8.** Arrange the apples and oranges in a glass serving bowl, pour over the sugar syrup and chill in the refrigerator. When ready to serve, scatter over the broken caramel chips and the needleshreds.

 *RICH SWEET WHITE*

# YOGHURT, HONEY AND DATES

*unsweetened plain Greek yoghurt*
*best-quality dates, fresh or dried*
*double cream*
*very cold clear honey*
*Jordan almonds, shelled but with the inner, brown*
  *skin left on, i.e. unblanched (optional)*

**1.** For each person half-fill a pudding bowl or glass with yoghurt.
**2.** Stone the dates and chop them roughly. Put a few on the top of each helping of yoghurt.
**3.** Spoon a good dollop of cream over the top, then trickle over 1 teaspoon honey.
**4.** Scatter with a few almonds, if using.

# REDCURRANT, MINT AND YOGHURT PUDDING

This is a quick and simple, light, low-fat, sugar-free summer pudding. It is better made with Greek yoghurt, but this has a higher fat content than most low-fat yoghurts. It can also be made with blackcurrants.

SERVES 4
*290ml/½ pint plain low-fat yoghurt*
*450g/1lb redcurrants, topped and destalked*
*concentrated apple juice to taste (optional)*
*1 tablespoon chopped fresh mint*
*1 egg white*

**1.** Mix together the yoghurt and the redcurrants. Sweeten to taste with a little apple juice. Add the mint.
**2.** Whisk the egg white until stiff but not dry and fold into the yoghurt and redcurrant mixture.

NOTE: The pudding should not be made more than 2 hours in advance or it will begin to weep.

# RASPBERRY AND ALMOND MALAKOFF

SERVES 6
*170g/6oz caster sugar*
*170g/6oz unsalted butter*
*290ml/½ pint double cream*
*170g/6oz ground almonds*
*3 tablespoons Kirsch*
*225g/8oz raspberries*
*1 large packet of boudoir biscuits (sponge fingers)*

**1.** Beat the sugar and butter together until very fluffy, soft and white.
**2.** Whip the cream and fold with the ground almonds, Kirsch and finally the raspberries into the butter and sugar mixture.
**3.** Put an oiled circle of greaseproof paper (oiled side up) into the bottom of a 15cm/6in straight-sided cake tin or soufflé dish.
**4.** Line the sides with the biscuits, standing them up round the edge. Spoon the mixture into the middle, pressing down gently and smoothing the top level.
**5.** Chill in the refrigerator for 4 hours.
**6.** With a bread knife, trim the tops of the biscuits to the level of the mixture. Turn the Malakoff out on to a serving plate. Remove the lining paper.

NOTE: The top can be decorated with rosettes of whipped cream and a few fresh raspberries, but the pudding also looks very pretty without further adornment.

 *SWEET WHITE*

Above: Individual Apple Tarts .

Above: Gâteau Pithivier. Right: Sablé aux Fraises.

Left: Summer Fruit Compote. Above: Arranged Fruit Salad.

Above: Raspberries and Fromage Blanc with Fresh Figs. Right: Summer Pudding.

Left: Lemon Curd Ice Cream. Above: Individual Mango Parfaits with Passionfruit Sauce.

Above: Pistachio Parfait. Right: Brandy Snap Tortes.

Left: Gâteau Nougatine. Above: Scones.

Above: Petits Fours. Right: Pickles.

Above: Canapés.

# PEACHES WITH RASPBERRY COULIS

SERVES 4
*4 large ripe peaches*
*290ml/½ pint raspberry coulis (see page 479)*
*about 30g/1oz flaked almonds, toasted*

**1.** Place the peaches in a saucepan of boiling water for 10 seconds, then remove the skins. Stone the peaches and cut into segments.
**2.** Flood the base of 4 pudding plates with the raspberry coulis. Arrange a peach attractively on each plate and scatter over the almonds.

 *LIGHT SWEET WHITE*

# SUMMER FRUIT PARCELS

SERVES 6
For the fruit purée
*¼ melon*
*4 peaches*
*2 apricots*
*150ml/¼ pint water*
*a dash of bitter almond essence*
*2 vanilla pods, split lengthways*

For the parcels
*2 bananas*
*1 orange*
*8 greengages*
*8 Victoria plums*
*24 raspberries*
*1 pear*
*3 vanilla pods, split lengthways*
*fresh mint leaves*
*55ml/2fl oz Grand Marnier*

**1.** Preheat the oven to its highest setting.
**2.** First make the fruit purée: cube the melon flesh, halve and stone the peaches and apricots and cut the flesh into cubes. Put the fruit into a small saucepan with the water, almond essence and vanilla pods. Cover and simmer for about 10 minutes or until reduced to a light purée. Remove the vanilla pods. Liquidize the purée in a food processor or blender, then sieve it. You should have about 290ml/½pint purée.

**3.** Prepare the remaining fruit: cut the bananas in half lengthways, then cut each piece in half. Peel the orange with a knife as you would an apple, making sure that all the pith is removed, then cut the orange into segments. Halve and stone the greengages and plums. Pick over the raspberries. Peel, core and quarter the pear and cut each quarter into 3 pieces.
**4.** Cut 6 × 35cm/14in squares of kitchen foil. Place 3 tablespoons purée on each square. Arrange the fruit on top. Add half a vanilla pod to each parcel, 2 or 3 mint leaves and a dash of Grand Marnier. Fold up the edges of the foil to form sealed parcels and place on a baking sheet.
**5.** Bake in the preheated oven for 7 minutes. Serve immediately on individual plates.

 *LIGHT SWEET WHITE*

# GREEK ICED FRUIT SALAD

*a selection of fruit, such as cantaloupe melon, red apples, bananas, black grapes, oranges, strawberries, cherries*
*lemon juice*
*crushed ice*

**1.** Put all the fruit, unprepared, into the refrigerator for a few hours to chill well.
**2.** Prepare the fruit for eating with the fingers: peel the oranges and divide into segments, removing any pith. Wash, quarter and core the apples and slice, using a stainless steel knife. Break the grapes into bunches of 3–4 grapes each. Peel the bananas and cut into large pieces. Cut the melon into quarters, peel and cut the flesh into fingers. Leave the strawberries whole and unhulled, washing them only if they are sandy. Wash the cherries, leaving the stalks intact.
**3.** Arrange the fruit attractively on a very well chilled dish and sprinkle with lemon juice. Sprinkle with ice just before serving.

NOTES: Apples can be peeled of course, but shiny red ones look good unpeeled.
Fruit that is liable to discolour, such as bananas, pears and apples, should be cut up shortly before serving.
To crush ice cubes, put them into a strong plastic bag or cloth and beat with a rolling pin.

# SWEET FRITTER BATTER

*125g/4oz plain flour*
*a pinch of salt*
*2 eggs*
*150ml/¼ pint milk*
*1 tablespoon oil*
*50g/1¾oz caster sugar*

**1.** Sift the flour with the salt into a bowl.
**2.** Make a well in the centre, exposing the bottom of the bowl.
**3.** Put one whole egg and one yolk into the well and mix with a wooden spoon or whisk until smooth, gradually incorporating the surrounding flour and the milk. The consistency of thick cream should be reached.
**4.** Add the oil and sugar. Allow to rest for 30 minutes.
**5.** Whisk the remaining egg white and fold into the batter with a metal spoon just before using.

NOTE: This batter can be made speedily in a blender. Simply put all the ingredients, except the egg white, into the machine and whizz briefly, then fold in the whisked egg whites just before serving.

# BANANA FRITTERS

SERVES 8
*8 bananas*
*150ml/¼ pint fritter batter (see above)*
*oil for shallow-frying*
*icing sugar to finish*

**1.** Peel the bananas and cut in half lengthways.
**2.** Dip immediately into the prepared batter.
**3.** Heat 5mm/¼in of oil in a frying pan and when hot, fry the fritters for about 2 minutes on each side until golden-brown. Drain well and dust with icing sugar.

 *RICH SWEET WHITE*

# CHINESE APPLE FRITTERS

SERVES 6
*450g/1lb granulated sugar*
*150ml/¼ pint water*
*3 dessert apples*
*lemon juice*
*85g/3oz cornflour*
*oil for deep-frying*
*2 tablespoons sesame seeds*
*1 teaspoon white wine vinegar*

**1.** Have ready a bowl of iced water.
**2.** Place the sugar and water in a heavy pan and set over a low heat to dissolve without boiling.
**3.** Peel, core and quarter the apples. Cut into chunks. Sprinkle with lemon juice and roll in the cornflour.
**4.** Heat the oil in a deep-fryer.
**5.** Meanwhile, toast the sesame seeds in a small, heavy, dry frying pan.
**6.** Deep-fry the apples in the hot oil for about 4 minutes until golden-brown. Drain well on absorbent kitchen paper.
**7.** When the sugar has dissolved, boil rapidly until the mixture caramelizes (becomes toffee-brown), then add the vinegar, taking care as the mixture will splutter and sizzle. Add the sesame seeds and stand the saucepan in a roasting pan of warm water. (This will prevent the caramel from becoming too hard.)
**8.** Turn a few apples at a time in the caramel and sesame seeds.
**9.** Dip each fritter into cold water to rapidly cool and harden the caramel, then drain and serve immediately.

 *FORTIFIED SWEET WHITE*

# MELON WITH GINGER WINE

*small melons, such as Ogen*
*ginger wine*

**1.** Halve the melons, scoop out the seeds and pour 1 tablespoon ginger wine into each.
**2.** Chill well in the refrigerator before serving.

NOTE: Buy tiny individual melons or slightly bigger ones that can be split between 2 people.

# PEARS IN RED WINE

SERVES 4
*150ml/¼ pint water*
*290ml/½ pint red wine*
*110g/4oz granulated sugar*
*1 tablespoon redcurrant jelly*
*thinly pared zest of 1 lemon*
*a pinch of ground cinnamon or 1 cinnamon stick*
*4 firm pears*
*30g/1oz flaked almonds, toasted*
*150ml/¼ pint double cream, whipped*

**1.** Place the water, wine, sugar and jelly in a heavy saucepan and heat gently until the sugar has dissolved. Add the lemon zest and cinnamon.
**2.** Peel the pears very neatly without removing the stalks. Place upright in the pan and cover with a lid. The pears should be completely covered by the wine and water mixture, so choose a tall, narrow pan. If this is not possible, wet the pears thoroughly with the mixture and turn them during cooking.
**3.** Bring the mixture to the boil, then simmer slowly for at least 20 minutes. The pears should be a deep crimson colour and very tender. The longer and slower the pears cook the better. (They can even be cooked overnight in an extremely low oven.)
**4.** Remove the pears from the pan and place in a glass serving bowl. Reduce the wine liquid by rapid boiling to a syrupy consistency, then strain it over the pears. Allow to cool, then chill in the refrigerator.
**5.** Sprinkle over the almonds just before serving and serve the whipped cream separately.

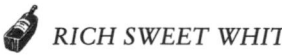 *RICH SWEET WHITE*

# PEAR SABAYON WITH PEAR SORBET

SERVES 4
*4 Conference pears*
*570ml/1 pint sugar syrup (see page 477)*
*pear sorbet (see page 578)*

For the sabayon sauce
*4 egg yolks*
*3 tablespoons caster sugar*
*55ml/2fl oz Poire William liqueur or eau de vie*
*150ml/¼ pint double cream, lightly whipped*

To decorate
*a few sprigs of mint*

**1.** Peel the pears very neatly, without removing the stalks. Place upright in a pan with the sugar syrup, which should completely cover the pears. Choose a tall, narrow pan. If this is not possible, wet the pears thoroughly in the syrup and turn them during cooking.
**2.** Cover the pan and bring to the boil, then simmer slowly for about 1 hour, until the pears are glassy and very tender. Remove from the syrup, allow to cool and then refrigerate until cold.
**3.** While the pears are poaching, prepare the sabayon sauce: put the egg yolks and sugar into a heatproof bowl set over, not in, a saucepan of simmering water. Whisk for at least 10 minutes until thick and creamy. Remove from the heat and continue to whisk until cool. Add the liqueur and cream. Chill in the refrigerator.
**4.** To serve: flood the base of 4 pudding plates with the sabayon sauce. Slice the pears in such a way that they can be rearranged on the sabayon as a whole, fanned-out pear. Place a large scoop of pear sorbet on each plate and decorate with a sprig of mint.

 *SWEET WHITE*

# RASPBERRIES AND FROMAGE BLANC WITH FRESH FIGS

This is a low-fat, sugar-free pudding.

SERVES 4
*225g/8oz fresh raspberries*
*concentrated apple juice (optional)*
*4 tablespoons low-fat fromage blanc*
*4 ripe figs, cut into quarters*

To decorate
*sprigs of fresh mint*

**1.** Liquidize the raspberries in a food processor or blender with enough water to make a smooth purée. Taste and add a little apple juice to sweeten, if required. Strain and pour on to one side of 4 pudding plates.
**2.** Mix the fromage blanc with a little water and pour on to the other half of the pudding plates.
**3.** Marble the fromage blanc and raspberry purée together with a large fork and arrange the figs on top of the sauces. Decorate with the sprigs of mint.

 *LIGHT SWEET WHITE*

# RASPBERRY PLATE

SERVES 4
*225g/8oz cooked blackcurrants*
*140g/5oz icing sugar*
*4 tablespoons crème de cassis liqueur*
*150ml/¼ pint double cream*
*fresh fruit, such as raspberries, figs, blackberries, blueberries*

To decorate
*sprigs of fresh mint*

**1.** Liquidize the cooked blackcurrants, icing sugar and cassis in a food processor or blender. Strain.
**2.** Pour this sauce on to one side of 4 pudding plates and pour the cream on the other side. Squiggle with a fork where they join to marble slightly.
**3.** Pile fresh raspberries or a mixture of sliced figs, blackberries and blueberries in the centre of each plate and top each with a sprig of mint.

# CREAMED CHEESE WITH FRESH FRUIT

This dessert is simple to prepare and particularly suitable for a buffet party.

SERVES 4–6
*225g/8oz cottage cheese*
*290ml/½ pint double cream, lightly whipped*
*55g/2oz icing sugar, sifted*
*2 drops of vanilla essence*
*3 figs, quartered*
*3 kiwi fruits, peeled and sliced*
*4 oranges, peeled and sliced*

**1.** Put the cottage cheese into a sieve and drain very well.
**2.** Push the cheese through the sieve (or process briefly in a food processor or blender) and fold in the cream. Sweeten with the icing sugar and add the vanilla essence.
**3.** Pile the mixture on to a large oval serving dish and shape into a shallow mound. Arrange the fruit attractively on top of the cheese.

 *LIGHT SWEET WHITE*

# SUMMER PUDDING

SERVES 4–6
*900g/2lb mixed redcurrants, blackcurrants, blackberries, raspberries and strawberries, or a mixture of just some of these*
*2 tablespoons water*
*170g/6oz caster sugar*
*6–9 slices of stale white bread*

To serve
*double cream, lightly whipped*

**1.** Cook the redcurrants, blackcurrants and blackberries with the water and sugar in a saucepan for 5 minutes, or until just soft but still bright in colour. Add the raspberries and strawberries. Drain off most of the juice and reserve.
**2.** Dip slices of the bread into the reserved fruit juice and use to line a pudding basin.

**3.** While the fruit is still just warm, pour it into the bread-lined basin. Cover with a round piece of bread dipped in the fruit juice. Tip the remaining juice into a saucepan and reduce, by boiling rapidly, to a syrupy consistency. Leave to cool.

**4.** Stand the pudding basin on a dish. Press a saucer or plate on top of the pudding and put a 450g/1lb weight on top. Leave in a cool place overnight. Remove the saucer and weight.

**5.** Invert a serving dish over the bowl and turn both over together. Give a sharp shake and remove the bowl. Spoon over the reserved, reduced fruit juice. Serve the cream separately.

 *SWEET WHITE*

## PASHKA

A rich, creamy cheese mixture, this is traditionally moulded in a tall wooden container, like a cut-off metronome. You can use a tall flowerpot or plastic pot instead. Whatever container you use, make sure it has a hole in the bottom for draining.

This recipe has been taken from the *Observer Guide to European Cookery* by Jane Grigson.

SERVES 8
*125ml/4fl oz double cream*
*10cm/4in piece of vanilla pod, split lengthways*
*2 large egg yolks*
*85g/3oz caster sugar*
*110g/4oz unsalted butter, creamed*
*675g/1½lb curd cheese or ricotta cheese*
*55–85g/2–3oz candied fruit and peel, chopped*
*55–85g/2–3oz blanched almonds, chopped*

To decorate
*blanched almonds*
*candied fruit and peel*
*glacé fruits or raisins*

**1.** Bring the cream, with the vanilla pod, to the boil in a small saucepan.

**2.** Beat the egg yolks with the sugar until creamy, then whisk in the hot cream.

**3.** Return the pan to the heat and cook, without boiling, until thick. Remove the vanilla pod and allow the custard to cool. Then mix it with the remaining ingredients.

**4.** Pour the mixture into your chosen mould, lined with muslin – this helps you to turn it out, and gives a good surface pattern to the cream cheese.

**5.** Chill in the refrigerator for at least 10 hours or up to 3 days. Stand the pot in a dish so that the whey can drain (some may ooze out, depending on the type of cheese that is used). Turn out and decorate. Serve with kulich (see page 600), or any brioche (see page 620) mixture you prefer, but flavoured with candied peel and cardamom.

NOTE: Chopped chocolate is a delicious addition to pashka.

 *FORTIFIED SWEET WHITE*

## TRIFLE

SERVES 6
*1 Victoria sandwich cake (see page 585), preferably stale*
*very good-quality raspberry jam*
*4 tablespoons sherry*
*2 tablespoons brandy*
*290ml/½ pint milk*
*5 egg yolks*
*2 tablespoons caster sugar*
*2 drops of vanilla essence*
*290ml/½ pint double cream*
*30g/1oz split blanched almonds, toasted*
*a few ratafia biscuits (optional)*

**1.** Cut the sponge cake into thick pieces. Sandwich the pieces together sparingly with jam. Pile them into a large glass serving dish.

**2.** Pour over the sherry and brandy and leave to soak while you prepare the custard.

**3.** Put the milk into a saucepan and scald by bringing to just below boiling point.

**4.** In a large bowl, lightly beat the yolks and sugar with a wooden spoon. Pour the scalding milk on to them, stirring.

**5.** Return the mixture to the pan and reheat carefully, stirring all the time, until the mixture is thick enough to coat the back of the spoon. Care must be taken not to boil the custard, or it will curdle. Add the vanilla essence.

**6.** Strain on to the cake and leave to get completely cold.

**7.** Whip the cream until fairly stiff and spread or pipe over the trifle.

**8.** Decorate with the almonds and the ratafia biscuits, if using.

 *SWEET SPARKLING*

# ZUCCOTTO

SERVES 8

*2 Madeira cakes (see page 586)*
*3 tablespoons brandy*
*2 tablespoons Maraschino*
*2 tablespoons Cointreau*
*170g/6oz plain chocolate*
*55g/2oz split almonds, roasted*
*55g/2oz hazelnuts, roasted and skinned*
*110g/4oz icing sugar*
*290ml/½ pint double cream, whipped*
*290ml/½ pint mocha custard (see page 477)*

**1.** Line a 1.5 litre/2½ pint round-bottomed pudding basin with damp muslin or a clean damp 'J'-cloth.

**2.** Cut the Madeira cakes into slices 9mm/¾in thick. Mix the brandy, Maraschino and Cointreau together and use to moisten each slice of cake. Line the pudding bowl as neatly as possible with these slices (as for a summer pudding, see page 548). Reserve 2 slices for the top.

**3.** Chop the chocolate into tiny, even-sized pieces. Mix half the chocolate with the nuts. Fold the sugar into the cream. Mix the chocolate and nuts with half the sweetened cream. Pile into the pudding basin and spread evenly over the sliced Madeira cake.

**4.** Melt the remaining chocolate in a small pan and mix with the remaining cream. Pile into the pudding basin and spread flat.

**5.** Cover the chocolate filling with the remaining slices of Madeira cake. Cover and refrigerate overnight.

**6.** The next day turn the zuccotto out on to a serving dish and coat with the cold mocha custard. Serve the remaining custard in a sauceboat.

 *FORTIFIED SWEET WHITE*

# NICE BISCUIT REFRIGERATOR CAKE

SERVES 4

*200ml/7fl oz double cream*
*3 tablespoons milk*
*2 tablespoons sweet sherry*
*15 Nice or 'morning coffee' biscuits*
*225g/8oz canned sweetened chestnut purée*
*110g/4oz plain chocolate*
*30g/1oz butter*
*a few walnut halves*

**1.** Whip the cream until thick.

**2.** Mix the milk and sherry together.

**3.** Soak 3 biscuits in the milk and sherry and place them side by side on a serving dish.

**4.** Spread half the cream over this.

**5.** Soak the next 3 biscuits and place them on top of the cream.

**6.** Spread this with half the chestnut purée.

**7.** Repeat these 2 layers.

**8.** Top with 3 biscuits.

**9.** Place the chocolate in a heavy saucepan with a very little water and heat gently until smooth and thick. Beat in the butter.

**10.** Pour over the biscuits and, when nearly set, decorate with the walnuts. Refrigerate.

 *LIQUEUR MUSCAT*

# ATHOLL BROSE

The Duke of Atholl's original recipe for Atholl Brose involved steeping oatmeal in boiling water and then draining off the milky liquid and mixing it with whisky and heather honey to make a warming drink. This recipe for a pudding has been adapted from the original.

SERVES 4–6

*55g/2oz medium oatmeal*
*290ml/½ pint double cream*
*2 tablespoons clear honey, or more to taste*
*85ml/3fl oz whisky*

**1.** Toast the oatmeal under the grill and allow to cool.

**2.** Whip the cream until it just holds its shape and stir in the toasted oatmeal and the honey. Add the whisky and transfer to a glass serving dish.

**3.** Cover and chill in the refrigerator for at least 1 hour before serving.

NOTE: This also freezes well. Because of the amount of alcohol it remains soft but it is very powerful and goes well with mince pies or Christmas pudding instead of brandy butter.

# CARROT HALVA

This recipe for a typical Indian pudding has been adapted from one by Madhur Jaffrey.

SERVES 6
*450g/1lb carrots, finely grated*
*6 cardamom pods*
*680ml/1¼ pints milk*
*85g/3oz clarified butter or ghee (see page 686)*
*140g/5oz caster sugar*
*55g/2oz unsalted pistachio nuts, skinned and*
*    chopped*

**1.** Put the carrots, cardamom pods and milk into a pan. Bring to the boil, then simmer for 1–1½ hours, or until most of the liquid has evaporated. Remove the cardamom pods.

**2.** Melt the butter in another saucepan. Stir the carrot mixture into the melted butter and cook for 5–7 minutes. Add the sugar and nuts. Cook for a further 5 minutes.

**3.** Pile the mixture into a serving dish and serve at room temperature.

 *FORTIFIED SWEET WHITE*

# TIRAMISÙ

SERVES 8
*6 egg yolks*
*scant 150ml/¼pint Marsala*
*5 tablespoons dry white wine*
*85g/3oz icing sugar, or more to taste*
*500g/1lb 2oz Mascarpone or cream cheese*

*10 amaretti biscuits*
*24 Savoy biscuits ('ladies' fingers')*
*5 tablespoons strong black coffee*
*unsweetened cocoa powder, for sprinkling*

**1.** Mix the egg yolks, half the Marsala, the white wine, icing sugar and Mascarpone together to make a cream, but if making this for children or teetotallers leave out the Marsala and white wine.

**2.** Dip the biscuits in the remaining Marsala mixed with the coffee (once again, leave out the Marsala if so desired), taking care not to make the biscuits so soggy that they break. Line a dish about 25cm/10in square with a layer of biscuits and a layer of the cream.

**3.** Repeat, until all the ingredients have been used, ending with a layer of cream. Sprinkle a thin layer of unsweetened cocoa powder on top and refrigerate for a few hours before serving.

 *RICH SWEET WHITE*

# CHOCOLATE CRUMBLE CAKE

SERVES 4
*85g/3oz plain chocolate*
*85g/3oz butter*
*45g/1½oz caster sugar*
*4 tablespoons golden syrup*
*340g/12oz plain biscuits, crushed*
*85g/3oz glacé cherries*
*85g/3oz flaked almonds*

**1.** Chop the chocolate and melt it slowly with the butter, sugar and syrup in a heavy saucepan, stirring all the time.

**2.** Add the crushed biscuits, cherries and almonds.

**3.** Grease a sheet of greaseproof paper and the inside of a 20cm/8in flan ring.

**4.** Press the mixture on to the paper and flatten it, using the flan ring to get a round shape.

**5.** Allow to cool until set hard.

**6.** Cut into small wedges.

 *LIQUEUR MUSCAT*

# FRENCH TOAST WITH APPLES

For the soaking liquid
30ml/1fl oz single cream
2 eggs
2 tablespoons cognac
45g/1½oz caster sugar

For the French toast
4 slices of baguette, 2.5cm/1in thick
55g/2oz unsalted butter
3 cooking apples, peeled, quartered, cored and
  each quarter cut into 3

For the vanilla crème anglaise
500ml/18fl oz milk
1 vanilla pod, split lengthways
5 egg yolks
85g/3oz caster sugar

For the butterscotch sauce
225g/8oz caster sugar
150ml/¼ pint water
225ml/8fl oz double cream
45g/1½oz unsalted butter

1. Whisk together the cream, eggs, cognac and sugar. Strain into a shallow dish. Add the baguette slices and set aside.
2. Make the crème anglaise: scald the milk with the vanilla pod by bringing it to just below boiling point.
3. Beat the egg yolks and sugar together, pour in the milk and mix well. Return to the pan and stir over a low heat with a wooden spoon, until the custard is thick enough to coat the back of the spoon. Do not allow to boil. Strain into a bowl and cover closely with a disc of greaseproof paper to prevent a skin from forming.
4. Make the butterscotch sauce: put the sugar and water into a heavy saucepan over a medium heat. Allow the sugar to dissolve completely, then bring to the boil. Cook to a golden-brown and remove from the heat. Immediately add the cream and return to the heat. Stir to dissolve any lumps of sugar. Add the butter.
5. Put the apple pieces in the butterscotch sauce and cook very gently until they are soft. Take great care as cooking apples fall apart very easily. Set them aside.
6. Drain the baguette slices. Heat the butter in a frying pan. Cook the slices on both sides until golden-brown.
7. To assemble: ladle the vanilla crème anglaise on to 4 pudding plates. Set a slice of toast on each plate and arrange the apples on top. Strain over the caramel sauce and serve.

# MERINGUES

# MERINGUES

Meringues have been made since at least 1700. Some cookery historians believe that they were invented by a Swiss pastry cook called Gasperlini, who practised his art in the small town of Meringen.

There are 3 main types of meringue: **Italian (see page 555; cuite, or cooked (see page 557); Swiss (see page 558)**. Meringues are not that easy to make, as it is possible to whisk the albumen in the egg white either too much or too little, with resulting poor volume, premature collapse, and in the case of overwhisking, some curdling.

One reason why egg whites increase in volume so dramatically when whisked is their high protein content (11 per cent). The protein forms tiny filaments which expand on whisking, incorporate air in minute bubbles, then set to form a fairly stable, puffed-up structure which can be as much as 8 times its original volume.

## WHISKING EGG WHITES

**1.** An electric mixer, hand-held electric beater or balloon whisk may be used.
**2.** Both bowl (ideally copper) and whisk (ideally balloon) must be scrupulously clean, dry and free from grease.
**3.** Do not use a plastic bowl as plastic tends to retain traces of fatty material on the surface.
**4.** When the egg yolks are separated from the whites, no specks of yolk must be allowed to remain in the whites: the fat in the yolk can reduce the whisked volume by up to two-thirds.
**5.** When the whites are half-whisked, the addition of a little caster sugar (15g/½oz per 4 whites) will assist efficient whisking and reduce the possibility of overwhisking.
**6.** When making Swiss meringues, once the whites are stiff, add half the total sugar quantity if using a powerful electric mixer, whisk again until very shiny, then add the remainder and whisk lightly until just incorporated. If using a hand-held

electric beater, once the whites are stiff add the sugar a tablespoon at a time.
**7.** Ideally egg whites are whisked by hand with a balloon whisk in a clean copper bowl (see note). A chemical reaction takes place between the egg whites and the copper which means that the egg whites are stabilized and will thus hold their shape for several minutes without separating. Egg whites whisked in a copper bowl also give you a greater volume of smooth-textured egg white foam. This foam is easy to fold into soufflé bases and makes for excellent meringues. It is difficult to overwhisk whites in a copper bowl.
**8.** Acid, usually in the form of cream of tartar, is often added to stabilize the foam. Although it has no effect on the volume of foam produced, it makes it less prone to overwhisking and resulting lumpiness, draining and collapse. Only a minute amount of acid is necessary to make a significant difference – about 1/16 teaspoon per egg white.

NOTE: A copper bowl must be cleaned before use. Rub the inside with half a lemon dipped in a generous quantity of salt. Wipe thoroughly and use immediately. The clean bowl is essential; once the copper becomes oxidized the chemical reaction between the egg whites and copper bowl is weakened. The acid in the lemon also helps to increase the volume of egg white.

## COOKING MERINGUES
Once the foam is formed it is baked to coagulate the protein, dry out the sugar to the point where it is more solid than liquid, and so leave the structure strong enough to stand up for hours. *Soft Meringues* are typically baked at 180°C/ 350°F/gas mark 4 for 15 minutes. This crisps the

surface but leaves the centre moist and chewy.
*Hard Meringues* are baked at 110°C/225°F/gas
mark ½ for an hour or two, or put into a hot
oven with the heat turned off, and allowed to dry
for several hours. Meringues can also be baked in
an airing cupboard. They come out uniformly dry
and crisp.

*Under-cooking* results in incomplete coagulation
and may cause syrup leakage, beading or collapse.
*Baking at too high a temperature* may coagulate
the proteins so rapidly that the moisture squeezed
out may not be able to evaporate before beading
up into tears of syrup on the surface. Weeping can
also be a problem in humid weather. When the
sugar in a well-dried meringue absorbs moisture
from the air and dissolves into droplets of syrup,
it makes the meringues sticky and limp.

*Paper for cooking meringues:* The best is silicone-
coated, non-stick baking parchment. Greased and
floured greaseproof paper or kitchen foil may also
be used, but the great advantage of baking
parchment is that meringues may be left to cool
completely on it and can then be easily removed
without sticking or breaking.

# FLAMING BAKED ALASKA

*1 × 18cm/7in Victoria sandwich (see page 585)*
*150ml/¼ pint sugar syrup (see page 477)*
*choice of 340g/12oz fresh fruits, such as peaches,*
*strawberries, etc.*
*1.14 litres/2 pints vanilla, chocolate or strawberry*
*ice cream*
*4 egg whites*
*a pinch of salt*
*225g/8oz caster sugar*
*3 tablespoons brandy*

**1.** Put the sponge cake on a plate and sprinkle
with a little of the sugar syrup.
**2.** Arrange the fruit on top of the cake and cover
with ice cream.
**3.** Preheat the oven to 230°C/450°F/gas mark 8.
**4.** Meanwhile, make the meringue: whisk the egg
whites with the salt to a stiff snow. Whisk in 3
tablespoons of the sugar and continue to whisk
until the mixture is stiff and shiny. Fold in the
remaining sugar with a large metal spoon.

**5.** Place the meringue in a piping bag fitted with a
star nozzle and pipe it over the cake and ice
cream.
**6.** Place the pudding in the oven for about 10
minutes until it has turned golden-brown.
**7.** Meanwhile, heat the brandy. When the
meringue is browned, light the brandy and pour it
flaming over the meringue. Serve immediately.

NOTE: See 'Whisking egg whites', page 554.

 *RICH SWEET WHITE*

# ITALIAN MERINGUE

This meringue is much more laborious to make
than Swiss meringue (see page 558), but it has the
advantage that once mixed it is extremely stable.
Provided it is covered with clingfilm or a damp
cloth to prevent drying out, the cook can leave it
for hours before using it without risk of
disintegration and, as it hardly swells at all in the
oven, it is ideal for piped meringue baskets,
vacherins, etc. It cooks rather faster than Swiss
meringue, is chalkier and more powdery, and
stays a brilliant white. Although it is not quite as
nice to eat as Swiss meringue, it is useful if
catering for large numbers, and delicious if filled
with strawberries and cream.

*225g/8oz lump sugar*
*6 tablespoons water*
*4 egg whites*

**1.** Put the sugar and water into a heavy saucepan.
**2.** Bring slowly to the boil without stirring. If any
sugar crystals get stuck to the side of the pan,
brush them down into the syrup with a clean wet
brush. Use a sugar thermometer if available.
**3.** The syrup is ready when it reaches
120°C/248°F. Alternatively, test for the firm ball
stage (see note).
**4.** While the syrup is gently boiling to the correct
stage, whisk the egg whites to stiff peaks.
**5.** If using an electric mixer, pour the bubbling hot
syrup on to the whites in a steady stream while
whisking, taking care not to pour the syrup on to
the wires of the whisk – it cools fast against the

cold metal and can harden and stick to the whisk. If whisking the whites by hand, and in the absence of anyone to pour as you whisk, pour the syrup on to the whites in stages, about one-third at a time, whisking hard after each addition and working as fast as possible. The syrup must be bubbling hot as it hits the egg white to partially cook it.

**6.** Once the syrup is all in, whisk hard until the mixture is stiff, shiny and absolutely stable. If the whisk is lifted, the meringue should not flow at all.

**7.** Keep covered with clingfilm or a damp cloth if not using immediately.

NOTES: To test the syrup, drop a teaspoonful into a cup of cold water. If the syrup has reached the right temperature, it will set into a firm ball which can be squashed between the fingers. If the syrup forms a hard ball, like a hard-boiled sweet, it has reached too high a temperature to make Italian meringue.

See 'Whisking egg whites', page 554)

# GALETTE AU CHOCOLAT CORDON BLEU

This very rich chocolate meringue pudding has come to Leith's via the Cordon Bleu Cookery School.

SERVES 6
*5 egg whites*
*285g/10oz caster sugar*
*45g/1½oz cocoa powder*

For the filling
*1 × 400g/14oz can of pitted black cherries*
*Kirsch*
*110g/4oz plain chocolate*
*70ml/2½fl oz water*
*570ml/1 pint double cream*

To decorate
*icing sugar to dust*
*150ml/¼ pint double cream*
*chocolate caraque (see page 594)*

For the cherry sauce
*the cherries not used in the cake*
*1 teaspoon arrowroot*
*the drained cherry juice*

**1.** Preheat the oven to 140°C/275°F/gas mark 1. Line 3 × 18cm/7in baking sheets with non-stick baking parchment.

**2.** Whisk the egg whites until stiff, add 1 tablespoon of the caster sugar and continue whisking for about 30 seconds. Sift the cocoa with the remaining sugar and quickly cut and fold into the whites. Spread or pipe the mixture into 3 × 18cm/7in rounds on the baking parchment. Bake in the preheated oven for 1–1¼ hours, or until dry and crisp. Remove from the oven and cool slightly, then remove the lining paper and leave to become completely cold.

**3.** Drain the cherries, reserving the juice, and leave to macerate in a little kirsch.

**4.** Break the chocolate into small pieces, put into a heavy pan with the water and stir continuously over a low heat until melted. Remove from the heat and allow to cool slightly.

**5.** Start whisking the cream and, as it thickens, add the chocolate, and then continue whisking until the cream holds its shape.

**6.** Sandwich the meringue rounds together with chocolate cream, topped with a quarter of the cherries. Dust the top with icing sugar. Decorate with rosettes of plain cream and chocolate caraque.

**7.** Make the cherry sauce: mix the arrowroot with 1 tablespoon cold water. Heat up the reserved cherry juice in a small saucepan. Add a little of the hot cherry juice to the arrowroot. Return to the pan and boil, stirring continuously, for 45 seconds until slightly thickened and shiny. Add the macerated cherries. Serve hot or cold with the galette.

NOTE: See 'Whisking egg whites', page 554)

 *FORTIFIED SWEET WINE*

# ALMOND DACQUOISE WITH APRICOT PURÉE

SERVES 6
*5 egg whites*
*a pinch of salt*
*a large pinch of cream of tartar*
*285g/10oz caster sugar*
*110g/4oz ground almonds*
*290ml/½ pint double cream*
For the purée
*225g/8oz fresh apricots, halved and stoned*
*caster sugar to taste*

**1.** Preheat the oven to 140°C/275°F/gas mark 1.
**2.** Line 2 baking sheets with non-stick baking parchment and mark a 22.5cm/9in diameter circle on each.
**3.** Whisk the egg whites with a pinch of salt and the cream of tartar until stiff, then add 2½ tablespoons of the sugar. Whisk again until very stiff and shiny.
**4.** Fold in the remaining sugar. Fold in the ground almonds.
**5.** Divide the mixture between the 2 baking sheets and spread the meringue evenly all over the marked circles.
**6.** Bake in the preheated oven for 1 hour. Remove from the oven and cool slightly, then remove the lining paper and leave to become completely cold.
**7.** While the meringues are baking, make the apricot purée. Put the apricots into a saucepan with 2 tablespoons sugar and enough water to come halfway up the apricots. Cook over a low heat, stirring occasionally, until the apricots are tender.
**8.** Process the poached apricots in a blender or food processor with enough of the liquid to make a thick purée. Taste and add extra sugar if required. Cool.
**9.** Whip the cream. Sandwich the cake together with half the cream mixed with the apricot purée. Decorate the top of the dacquoise with rosettes of cream.

NOTE: See 'Whisking egg whites', page 554.

 *SWEET WHITE*

# MERINGUE CUITE

'Cuite', or 'cooked', meringue is a professional chef's meringue used largely for frosting petits fours, for fruit pie tops and as unbaked frosting for cakes. It is only worth making if an electric whisk is handy, when it is easy. It produces an even chalkier and finer-textured meringue than Italian meringue and, if used on baked confections, comes out of the oven shiny, smooth and pale biscuit-coloured.

Like Italian meringue, meringue cuite is very stable in the oven, hardly swelling at all and unlikely to cook out of shape. For this reason it is often used for intricate work such as the meringue basket on page 558. When baked at very low temperatures, it emerges smooth and shiny white.

The proportions of egg white to sugar are the same as for most meringues, but the sugar used is confectioner's (icing) sugar, rather than caster. Sometimes a 50–50 mixture of caster and icing sugar is used and occasionally, when the meringue is for a fine cake frosting that will not be baked, the sugar content can be increased above the normal 55g/2oz per small egg white to 85g/3oz.

*4 egg whites*
*225g/8oz icing sugar, sifted*
*3 drops of vanilla essence*

**1.** Use a heatproof bowl that will fit snugly over a saucepan of simmering water without being in direct contact with the water. Whisk the egg whites until stiff, then set them over the water.
**2.** Add the icing sugar. It flies about in sugar-dust clouds, so take care. Whisk until thick and absolutely stable – there should be no movement at all when the whisk is lifted. Add the vanilla essence.
**3.** Keep covered with clingfilm or a damp cloth if not using immediately.

NOTES: If the mixture is whisked in an electric mixer, a good result can be achieved without beating over heat. But it takes a good 15 minutes to get a perfect 'cuite' consistency.
See 'Whisking egg whites', page 554.

# NOIX AU CAFÉ

SERVES 4–6

225g/8oz caster sugar
6–7 tablespoons water
4 egg whites
2 teaspoons coffee essence

**1.** Put the sugar and water into a heavy saucepan. Dissolve over a low heat and then cook quickly, without stirring, to 120°C/248°F. Use a sugar thermometer for this, or wait until the sugar syrup reaches the firm ball stage (see page 477).

**2.** Whisk the egg whites until stiff. Pour the sugar syrup steadily on to the egg whites, whisking all the time, but taking care that the syrup does not strike the whisk wires (where it would cool and solidify). Continue whisking until all the sugar has been absorbed and the meringue is completely cool. Fold in the coffee essence.

**3.** Preheat the oven to 140°C/275°F/gas mark 1. Line 2 baking sheets with non-stick baking parchment (it can be held in place with a few dots of the uncooked meringue).

**4.** Reserve a quantity of the meringue for the filling. Place the remaining mixture in a forcing bag fitted with a medium to plain nozzle. Pipe walnut-sized mounds on to the prepared baking sheets. Bake in the preheated oven for 1–1½ hours, they lift easily off the lining paper.

**5.** Allow to become completely cold, then sandwich together with the reserved coffee meringue mixture.

NOTES: The meringues feel sticky when warm but will crisp and dry in 1–2 minutes.

See 'Whisking egg whites', page 554.

# STRAWBERRY MERINGUE BASKET

This is a classic meringue cuite recipe. You will need to make this quantity of meringue in 2 batches.

SERVES 8

For the meringue cuite
8 egg whites
450g/1lb icing sugar, sifted
6 drops of vanilla essence

For the filling
425ml/¾ pint double cream, lightly whipped
450g/1lb fresh strawberries, hulled

**1.** Preheat the oven to 140°C/275°F/gas mark 1. Line 2 large baking sheets with non-stick baking parchment. Mark 3 × 18cm/7in diameter circles on each piece of paper.

**2.** Make up the first batch of meringue cuite. Put half the egg whites with half the icing sugar into a heatproof mixing bowl and set over, not in, a saucepan of simmering water. Whisk, with a large hand balloon whisk or electric hand whisk, until the meringue is thick and will hold its shape. This may well take up to 10 minutes of vigorous beating. (A very good imitation meringue cuite can also be made by whisking the egg whites and sugar together in a powerful electric mixer without needing to heat the meringue.)

**3.** Add half the vanilla essence. Remove from the pan and whisk for a further 2 minutes.

**4.** Put the meringue into a forcing bag fitted with a 1cm/½in plain nozzle. Squeeze gently to get rid of any pockets of air. Hold the bag upright in your right hand and, using your left hand to guide the nozzle, pipe a circular base on the first baking sheet, using one of the marked circles as a guide. Pipe 3 × 18cm/7in empty hoops around the edges of the 3 remaining pencilled circles.

**5.** Bake the meringue base and hoops in the preheated oven for 45–60 minutes until dry and crisp. Cool on a wire rack.

**6.** Make up the second batch of meringue cuite using the remaining ingredients. Return the baked meringue base to the baking sheet. Use a little uncooked mixture to fit the hoops on the base, one on top of the other.

**7.** Put the remaining mixture into a piping bag fitted with a rose nozzle. Cover the hoops with the meringue.

**8.** Bake in the oven at the same temperature for 45–60 minutes until set and crisp. Cool on a wire rack, then carefully remove the paper.

**9.** Fill with the cream and strawberries just before serving.

 *LIGHT SWEET WHITE*

# MERINGUES (SWISS MERINGUES)

This quantity makes 50 miniature or 12 large meringues.

*4 egg whites*
*a pinch of salt*
*225g/8oz caster sugar*
For the filling
*double cream, whipped*

1. Preheat the oven to 110°C/225°F/gas mark ½.
2. Line 2 baking sheets with non-stick baking parchment.
3. Whisk the egg whites with a pinch of salt until stiff but not dry.
4. Add 2 tablespoons of the sugar and whisk again until very stiff and shiny.
5. Fold in the remaining sugar.
6. Drop the meringue mixture on to the lined baking sheets in spoonfuls set fairly far apart. Use a teaspoon for tiny meringues; a dessertspoon for larger ones.
7. Bake in the preheated oven for about 2 hours until the meringues are dry right through and will lift easily off the paper.
8. When cold, sandwich the meringues together in pairs with whipped cream.

NOTE: See 'Whisking egg whites', page 554.

# WALNUT AND LEMON MERINGUE CAKE

SERVES 6
*4 egg whites*
*a pinch of salt*
*225g/8oz caster sugar*
*140g/5oz walnuts*
*290ml/½ pint double cream*
*4 tablespoons lemon curd (see page 660)*

1. Preheat the oven to 190°C/375°F/gas mark 5.
2. Line 2 × 20cm/8in cake tins with lightly oiled kitchen foil or simply line the base with non-stick baking parchment and oil the sides of the tin.

3. Whisk the egg whites with a pinch of salt until stiff, then add 2 tablespoons of the sugar. Whisk again until very stiff and shiny.
4. Fold in the remaining sugar.
5. Chop the walnuts roughly, reserving a handful, and stir into the mixture.
6. Divide the mixture between the 2 tins, smoothing the tops slightly.
7. Bake in the preheated oven for 40 minutes. Turn the cakes out on to a wire rack, peel off the lining paper and leave to cool completely.
8. Whip the cream and mix half of it with the lemon curd. Sandwich the cakes with this mixture.
9. Use the remaining whipped cream and nuts to decorate the top.

NOTE: See 'Whisking egg whites', page 554.

 *SWEET WHITE*

# PAVLOVA

SERVES 4–6
*4 egg whites*
*a pinch of salt*
*225g/8oz caster sugar*
*1 teaspoon cornflour*
*1 teaspoon vanilla essence*
*1 teaspoon white wine vinegar or lemon juice*
*290ml/½ pint double cream, lightly whipped*
*450g/1lb soft fruits*

1. Preheat the oven to 140°C/275°F/gas mark 1.
2. Line a baking sheet with non-stick baking parchment.
3. Whisk the egg whites with a pinch of salt until stiff. Gradually add the sugar, whisking until you can stand a spoon in the mixture.
4. Add the cornflour, vanilla and vinegar or lemon juice.
5. Pile the mixture on to the prepared baking sheet, shaping to a flat oval or circle 3cm/1½in thick. Bake in the preheated oven for about 1 hour. The meringue is cooked when the outer shell is pale biscuit-coloured and hard to the touch. Remove from the oven, carefully peel off the lining paper and leave to cool completely on a wire rack.

**6.** When quite cold, spoon on the whipped cream and sprinkle on the fruit and nuts.

NOTE: See 'Whisking egg whites', page 554.

 *SWEET WHITE*

# MERINGUE BASKETS

MAKES 6
*2 egg whites*
*a pinch of salt*
*110g/4oz caster sugar*

For the filling
*double cream, lightly whipped*
*strawberries or raspberries*

**1.** Preheat the oven to 110°C/225°F/gas mark ½. Line 2 baking sheets with non-stick baking parchment.
**2.** Whisk the egg whites with the salt to a stiff snow. Whisk in 2 tablespoons of the sugar and continue to whisk until the mixture is stiff and shiny. Fold in the remaining sugar with a large metal spoon.
**3.** Put the mixture into a piping bag fitted with a rose nozzle and pipe on to the lined baking sheets to form little baskets.
**4.** Place in the preheated oven to dry out for 2 hours. Remove from the oven, carefully peel off the lining paper and allow to cool on a wire rack.
**5.** Place a little cream in each basket and fill with strawberries or raspberries.

NOTES: Meringue baskets are also often made with meringue cuite (see page 000), which is very solid and does not rise out of shape in the oven.

See 'Whisking egg whites', page 554.

# BANANA AND GRAPE VACHERIN

SERVES 6
*4 egg whites*
*a pinch of salt*
*225g/8oz caster sugar*
*1 banana*
*lemon juice*
*85g/3oz black grapes*
*85g/3oz green grapes*
*290ml/½ pint double cream, lightly whipped*

**1.** Preheat the oven to 110°C/225°F/gas mark ½. Line 2 baking sheets with non-stick baking parchment.
**2.** Whisk the egg whites with the salt until stiff but not dry, then add 2 tablespoons of the sugar. Whisk again until very stiff and shiny. Fold in the remaining sugar with a large metal spoon.
**3.** Fill a piping bag fitted with a medium plain nozzle with the meringue. Pipe into a round the size of a dessert plate on each prepared baking sheet.
**4.** Place in the oven to dry out for 2–3 hours. The meringue is ready when light and dry and the paper will peel off the underside easily.
**5.** Cut the banana into chunks and toss in the lemon juice. Halve and deseed the grapes.
**6.** Spread three-quarters of the cream over one of the meringue bases and scatter over the banana and all but 4 each of the black and green grapes. Place the second meringue on top of this. Using the remaining cream, pipe rosettes around the top. Decorate the rosettes alternately with the grape halves.

NOTE: See 'Whisking egg whites', page 554.

 *SWEET WHITE*

# HAZELNUT MERINGUE CAKE WITH RASPBERRY SAUCE

SERVES 6
*110g/4oz hazelnuts*
*225g/8oz caster sugar*
*4 egg whites*
*a pinch of salt*
*a drop of vanilla essence*
*½ teaspoon white wine vinegar*
*225g/8oz raspberries*
*icing sugar, sifted*
*a squeeze of lemon juice*
*290ml/½ pint double cream*

**1.** Preheat the oven to 190°C/375°F/gas mark 5. Line 2 × 20cm/8in cake tins with lightly oiled kitchen foil.
**2.** Place the hazelnuts on a baking sheet and roast in the preheated oven until dark brown. Remove the skins by rubbing the nuts in a tea-towel. Leave to get completely cold. Set aside 5 nuts and grind the remainder with 1 tablespoon of the caster sugar. Do not over-grind or they will become greasy and make the meringue heavy. Add half the remaining caster sugar.
**3.** Whisk the egg whites with the salt until stiff, then gradually whisk in the remaining caster sugar a tablespoon at a time, with the vanilla and vinegar, whisking until very stiff. Fold in the nuts and sugar very gently with a large metal spoon. Pile the mixture into the prepared tins, spreading evenly with a spatula.
**4.** Bake in the oven for 40 minutes. Remove from the oven and allow to cool in the tins. Lift out the meringues in the foil, then carefully peel away the foil. Leave the meringues to cool completely on a wire rack.
**5.** Meanwhile, liquidize the raspberries in a blender with icing sugar and lemon juice to taste. Push through a nylon sieve and taste for sweetness. If very thick, add a little water.
**6.** To decorate: whip the cream and sandwich two meringues together with two-thirds of it. Dust the top with icing sugar. Pipe 5 large rosettes of cream round the edge of the top of the meringue and decorate each rosette with a reserved hazelnut. Serve the raspberry sauce separately.

NOTE: See 'Whisking egg whites', page 554.

 *RICH SWEET WHITE*

# MERINGUE MONT BLANC

SERVES 6
For the meringue
*3 egg whites*
*a pinch of salt*
*170g/6oz caster sugar*
*icing sugar, sifted*

For the filling
*1 × 440g/15oz can of sweetened chestnut purée*
*150ml/¼ pint double cream, lightly whipped*

To decorate
*chocolate caraque (see page 594) or coarsely*
*grated chocolate*

**1.** Preheat the oven to 110°C/225°F/gas mark ½. Line a baking sheet with non-stick baking parchment.
**2.** Whisk the egg whites with the salt until stiff but not dry. Add 1½ tablespoons of the caster sugar and whisk again until very stiff and shiny. Fold in the remaining sugar.
**3.** Place the meringue in a piping bag with a fitted 1cm/½in plain nozzle. Pipe the mixture into an 18cm/7in circle on the prepared baking sheet, starting from the centre and spiralling outwards. Pipe a rim 3cm/1½in deep. Dust lightly with icing sugar.
**4.** Bake in the preheated oven for at least 2 hours, until the meringue is dry and crisp. When cooked, remove from the oven, carefully peel off the lining paper and leave to cool completely on a wire rack.
**5.** Beat the chestnut purée until soft. Pile into the meringue case, cover with the cream and sprinkle the chocolate on top.

NOTE: See 'Whisking egg whites', page 554.

 *SWEET SPARKLING WHITE*

# MERINGUE CROQUEMBOUCHE

MAKES 30 MERINGUE SHELLS
For the white sugar meringue
*4 egg whites*
*225g/8oz caster sugar*

For the brown sugar meringue
*4 egg whites*
*30g/1oz caster sugar*
*200g/7oz soft light brown sugar, sifted*

To serve
*450ml/³/4 pint double cream, whipped*
*icing sugar, sifted*

**1.** Preheat the oven to 110°C/225°F/gas mark ½.
**2.** Line 4 baking sheets with non-stick baking parchment.
**3.** Make the white sugar meringue: whisk the egg whites until very stiff but not dry. Add 2 tablespoons of the sugar and whisk again until very stiff and shiny. Carefully fold in the remaining sugar.
**4.** Put the meringue mixture into a piping bag fitted with a 1cm/½in plain nozzle. Squeeze gently to get rid of any pockets of air. Pipe the meringue into 5cm/2in shells set fairly far apart on 2 baking sheets. Allow to stand.
**5.** Make the brown sugar meringue: whisk the egg whites until very stiff but not dry. Add the caster sugar and whisk again until very stiff and shiny. Carefully fold in the brown sugar.
**6.** Pipe the mixture in the same way as for the white sugar meringues.
**7.** Bake all the meringues in the oven for 1 hour, or until they will lift cleanly from the paper. Using your thumb, make an indentation in the base of each meringue (this helps to pile them up neatly). Put back on the baking sheet and continue to cook for a further 45 minutes.
**8.** Lift the meringues from the paper, transfer to a wire rack and leave to cool completely.
**9.** Sandwich the white sugar meringues then the brown sugar meringues together in pairs with the cream. Pile them into a pyramid on a serving dish and dredge with icing sugar.

NOTE: See 'Whisking egg whites', page 554.

 *SWEET WHITE*

# FLOATING ISLANDS

MAKES 12 ISLANDS
For the custard
*240ml/8fl oz milk*
*290ml/½ pint double cream*
*2 teaspoons caster sugar*
*1 vanilla pod or 3 drops of vanilla essence*
*2 teaspoons cornflour*
*4 egg yolks*

For the meringue islands
*3 egg whites*
*a pinch of salt*
*170g/6oz caster sugar*

To cook
*150ml/¼ pint milk*

To decorate
*grated chocolate*

**1.** Place the milk, cream and sugar in a saucepan with the vanilla. Bring gently to the boil, then remove from the heat and leave to infuse for 30 minutes. Remove the vanilla pod.
**2.** Mix the cornflour with a little water. Stir a little of the hot milk mixture into it, then pour it back into the milk. Place over a low heat and bring slowly to the boil, stirring continuously. Simmer for 4 minutes to cook the cornflour.
**3.** Beat the egg yolks and then pour the cream mixture on to the yolks in a thin stream, beating well all the time with a wooden spoon. The custard will probably thicken at once to a consistency that will coat the back of the wooden spoon. If it does not, return to the saucepan and stir steadily over a very low heat until it does so. Take care not to boil or it will curdle. Pour into a wide shallow serving dish, and cover with clingfilm to prevent a skin from forming.
**4.** Meanwhile, make the islands: half-fill a deep frying pan with water, add the milk and set over the heat.
**5.** Whisk the egg whites with the salt until stiff but not dry. Whisk in the sugar very gradually until you have a smooth, shiny meringue mixture.
**6.** The water mixture should now be simmering. Slip 3 or 4 tablespoons of the meringue mixture into the frying pan and cook gently for just

30 seconds on each side, by which time they will have almost doubled in size. (Do not add more than 3 or 4 islands at a time and do not overcook.) Lift out with a slotted spoon and leave on a wire rack or tea-towel to drain completely. Lay the islands carefully on the 'lake' of custard.
7. Sprinkle the islands with the chocolate.

NOTE: See 'Whisking egg whites', page 554.

 *SWEET WHITE*

# FLOATING ISLANDS WITH CARAMEL

*floating islands (see previous recipe)*
*85g/3oz caster sugar*

1. Place the sugar in a heavy saucepan and set over a low heat until it has dissolved and cooked to a golden-brown.
2. Remove from the heat and immediately trickle over the islands in the custard.

 *RICH SWEET WHITE*

# FLOATING ISLANDS WITH COFFEE CUSTARD

*floating islands (see page 562)*
*1 teaspoon instant coffee powder*
*2 teaspoons boiling water*

1. Proceed as for floating islands but dissolve the coffee in boiling water and add it to the custard sauce just before removing it from the heat.

 *RICH SWEET WHITE*

# FLOATING ISLANDS WITH ORANGE

*floating islands (page 562, omitting the vanilla)*
*thinly pared zest of 1 orange*
*1 tablespoon Grand Marnier*

1. Proceed as for floating islands, but infuse the orange zest in the cream and milk mixture in place of the vanilla pod.
2. Add the Grand Marnier to the custard before pouring into the serving dish.

 *SWEET WHITE*

# ICE CREAMS
# AND SORBETS

# ICE CREAMS AND SORBETS

Ice cream is a foam stabilized by freezing much of the liquid (even in frozen ice cream some of the liquid is left unfrozen). Ice cream contains tiny ice crystals composed of pure water, solid globules of milk fat and tiny air cells. The liquid in ice cream prevents the formation of a solid block. The ice crystals stabilize the foam by trapping air and fat in its structure and if ice creams contain a good proportion of fat they freeze to a smooth creaminess without too much trouble. If they consist of mostly sugar and water or milk they need frequent beating during the freezing process to prevent too large ice crystals from forming. In any event the more a mixture is beaten and churned during freezing the more air will be incorporated and the creamier in texture it will be. The tiny air cells are very important as they break up the solid liquid to make a lighter, softer texture. Ice cream without air would be difficult to serve, scoop or eat.

## MAKING ICE CREAM

AN ICE-CREAM MAKER The best modern method of churning ice cream is with an ice-cream maker with a built-in chiller and electric motor. These machines are expensive, scaled-down versions of the commercial machines used by caterers. Their chief advantages are that they operate independently of the freezer, and are powerful and large enough to churn even a thick mixture to smoothness. The main disadvantages are the expense and the fact that they take up valuable work space when not in use (they are too heavy for cupboard storage).

AN ELECTRIC SORBETIÈRE is useful if making small quantities of ice cream from a fairly thin mixture, such as a custard or syrup. But few are powerful enough to churn a mixture containing solid pieces (meringue or raisins, for example) or thick mixtures from, say, mashed bananas. Also, sorbetières must be put into a freezer as they have no built-in chilling equipment, and care must be taken when setting up the machine that the lead that connects the churn placed in the freezer to the plug on the wall will not be damaged by closing the freezer door, or prevent the door from closing tight.

A FOOD PROCESSOR will not chill the mixture, of course, but it is powerful enough to churn it to smoothness in a few minutes. Freeze the mixture in a shallow tray until solid, then break it up and process the frozen pieces again, using the chopping blade, to pale creaminess. Return to the tray and refreeze.

BUCKET CHURNS can be bought with electric motors or with a handle for manual operation. Most have a good large capacity and are reliable and powerful, but they require a supply of ice and of salt. Coarsely crushed ice is packed in layers, sprinkled with coarse salt, between the metal ice-cream container and the outer bucket. The ice cream in the container is churned steadily by a strong paddle for 25 minutes or so, until the ice cream is thick. It can be left, without fear of melting, in the churn for an hour or so after making.

MIXING ICE CREAMS BY HAND Finally, ice cream can be made without any special equipment. All that is needed is a shallow ice-cube tray or roasting pan, a bowl, and a strong whisk. The ice cream is half-frozen in the tray, then tipped into the bowl (which is chilled) and whisked until smooth. This is repeated until icy shards are eliminated.

SUGAR AND FLAVOURINGS Extreme cold inhibits our sense of taste, the tastebuds being too cold to operate effectively. For this reason ice creams must be sweetened or flavoured more than seems right when tasting the mixture at room temperature.

## STORAGE

Theoretically, ice cream can be stored for very long periods, but, certainly in a domestic freezer, there is some deterioration. Ice crystals may form on the surface of the ice cream after a week or so, meringue-based ices or ices containing gelatine may become rubbery, and if raw fruit (such as puréed peach) has been used, the colour will change for the worse. For total perfection, ice cream should be eaten the day it is made, but a few days' freezing is acceptable. If ices are frozen for longer periods – and obviously they often will be – poor texture can be rectified by allowing the ice cream to soften slightly, rewhisking it and refreezing it. Or the frozen mixture can be rebeaten in a processor. If fruit ices are to be stored for longer than a few days, the fruit should be cooked to preserve the colour.

## THAWING

Unless the mixture is very soft, it is wise to transfer it to the refrigerator for 30 minutes before serving to allow the ice to soften slightly. Or the ice cream may be softened sufficiently to scoop into balls, then put into a chilled serving dish and returned to the freezer until needed.

There are three basic methods of making ice cream.

CUSTARD-BASED METHOD These ice creams are made by freezing very rich, flavoured custards consisting of eggs, sugar, cream and/or milk and the required flavouring.

MOUSSE-BASED PARFAITS In a mousse-based parfait the air that will give the creaminess to the frozen mixture is beaten into the egg base over heat before cooling and freezing. This means that there is no need to churn or beat once the mixture is in the freezer, and it can be poured into a china soufflé dish with a paper collar tied round (see page 572) it so that it looks deceptively like a risen soufflé or an ice soufflé.

MERINGUE-BASED ICE CREAMS These are similar to the mousse-based parfaits, but the air is incorporated into the egg whites, as for meringue, before the flavouring fruit purée is added. The method is suitable for fruit ice creams, where the acidity of the fruit nicely cuts the sweet meringue.

THEN THERE ARE FROZEN YOGHURTS Yoghurt, because it is so low in fat, is not easy to freeze smoothly without the aid of a machine that beats or stirs constantly during freezing. It thaws and melts too fast for the processor method. The addition of large quantities of cream or sugar would make a smoother and more stable mixture, but as frozen yoghurt is often served as a healthy alternative to a fattening dessert, such additions would defeat the cook's object.

SORBETS AND GRANITA Sorbets (sherberts or water ices) are made by freezing flavoured syrups or purées. The essential thing is to get the proportions right. Too much sugar and the sorbet will be oversweet, syrupy and too soft to hold its shape. Too little and it will be icy, crystalline and hard. Chefs use a saccharimeter to measure the amount of sugar in a syrup (a 'pèse-syrop' to get the desired 37 per cent sugar), but good results can be obtained if the mixture contains about one-third sugar and two-thirds other ingredients. Bearing this figure in mind, the cook can make almost any sorbet with two-parts liquid (unsweetened) and one-part sugar, bringing the syrup slowly to the boil, cooling it, and freezing it, whisking as necessary.

There is no question but that a machine gives the best results. If no machine is available the addition of powdered gelatine (1 tablespoon for every 300ml/½ pint of liquid) or the addition of whisked egg whites does help prevent the formation of large ice crystals, and slows up melting.

If slightly less sugar is used, and the mixture is forked rather than beaten while freezing, a granita results – a granular, fast-melting sorbet.

**The recipes for ice creams assume that you do not have an ice-cream maker – if you do, however, simply follow the manufacturer's instructions. Light, sweet wines go with most ice creams, particularly Italian Muscato with fruit ices. Also, try sweet sparkling wine or champagne.**

# PLUM OR APRICOT ICE CREAM

This ice cream is made with a mousse base.

SERVES 6
*900g/2lb plums or apricots, washed and halved*
*290ml/½ pint water*
*110g/4oz granulated sugar*
*3 egg yolks*
*150ml/¼ pint double cream*

1. Stew the fruit with 2 tablespoons of the water and 55g/2oz of the sugar in a saucepan. When tender, push the fruit and the juice through a nylon or stainless steel sieve. You should have 290ml/½ pint purée. Check for sweetness.
2. Dissolve the remaining sugar in the remaining water without boiling. Then boil rapidly to the short thread stage (see page 477). (To test, take a little syrup out of the pan with a wooden spoon, dip your fingers in cold water and then dip your finger and thumb into the syrup. The syrup should feel very tacky and form short threads when finger and thumb are drawn apart.)
3. Remove from the heat and allow to cool for 30 seconds. Beat the egg yolks with a whisk. Pour on the sugar syrup, whisking all the time, until the mixture is thick, pale and mousse-like, and quite cold.
4. Add the cream to the fruit purée with the yolk mixture. Turn into a freezerproof dish.
5. Freeze for about 45 minutes or until beginning to freeze around the edges. Remove the ice cream, stir thoroughly, then return to the freezer to freeze completely.
6. If the ice cream is not perfectly smooth, tip it into a chilled bowl, beat until smooth and creamy and freeze again.

# GINGER ICE CREAM

This ice cream is made with a mousse base.

SERVES 6
*85g/3oz granulated sugar*
*150ml/¼ pint water*
*4 egg yolks*

*2 teaspoons ground ginger*
*570ml/1 pint double cream, lightly whipped*
*4 pieces of preserved stem ginger, cut into slivers*

1. Put the sugar and water into a small heavy saucepan. Dissolve over a low heat. Then boil for 3 minutes. Remove from the heat and allow to cool for 1 minute.
2. Put the egg yolks into a large bowl with the ground ginger, whisk lightly and pour on to the warm sugar syrup (do not allow the syrup to touch the whisk if doing this in a machine as it cools fast against the cold metal and can harden and stick to the whisk). Fold in the cream and pour into an ice tray.
3. Freeze until half-frozen, then whisk again and add the stem ginger. Freeze again.
4. Remove from the freezer 30 minutes before it is to be eaten and scoop into a glass bowl.

# RICH VANILLA ICE CREAM

This ice cream is made with a mousse base.

SERVES 6–8
*70g/2½oz granulated sugar*
*8 tablespoons water*
*1 vanilla pod, split lengthways*
*3 egg yolks*
*425ml/¾ pint double cream*

1. Put the sugar, water and vanilla pod into a heavy saucepan and dissolve the sugar over a low heat, stirring.
2. Beat the egg yolks well. Half whip the cream.
3. When the sugar has dissolved completely, boil rapidly to the short thread stage (see page 477): when a little syrup is placed between a wet finger and thumb and the fingers opened, it should form a sticky thread 2.5cm/1in long. Remove from the heat and allow to cool for 1 minute. Remove the vanilla pod.
4. Whisk the egg yolks and gradually pour in the sugar syrup. Whisk until the mixture is very thick and will leave a trail when the whisk is lifted.

**5.** Cool, whisking occasionally. Fold in the cream, pour into a freezer container and freeze.

**6.** When the ice cream is half-frozen, whisk again and return to the freezer.

# DAMSON ICE CREAM

This is a meringue-based ice cream.

SERVES 6–8
*450g/1lb damsons*
*340g/12oz caster sugar*
*150ml/¼ pint water*
*2 large egg whites*
*finely grated zest and juice of 1 small orange*
*290ml/½ pint double cream*

**1.** Wash the damsons and put them, still wet, into a heavy saucepan with 110g/4oz of the sugar. Stew gently, covered, over a very low heat or bake in a medium oven until soft and pulpy.

**2.** Push through a sieve, removing the stones.

**3.** Dissolve the remaining sugar in the water in a heavy pan, then bring to the boil.

**4.** Boil steadily for 5 minutes to the firm ball stage (see page 477).

**5.** Meanwhile, whisk the egg whites until stiff. Pour the boiling syrup on to the egg whites, whisking as you do so. The mixture will go rather liquid at this stage, but keep whisking until you have a thick meringue.

**6.** Stir in the orange zest and juice and the damson purée.

**7.** Whip the cream until thick but not stiff, and fold into the mixture.

**8.** Turn into an ice tray and freeze. It is not necessary to rewhisk the ice cream during freezing.

NOTE: The damson purée can be replaced by a purée of cooked plums, greengages, rhubarb, dried apricots or prunes, or a raw purée of soft fruit, such as fresh apricots or peaches.

# COFFEE ICE CREAM

This ice cream is made with a custard base.

SERVES 4–6
*4 egg yolks*
*85g/3oz caster sugar*
*a pinch of salt*
*425ml/¾ pint single cream*
*5 teaspoons instant coffee powder*

**1.** Mix the egg yolks with the sugar and salt.

**2.** Place the cream and coffee in a saucepan and heat gently until the coffee dissolves.

**3.** Add the cream to the egg-yolk mixture, stirring all the time.

**4.** Pour the mixture into the top of a double saucepan or into a heatproof bowl set over, not in, a saucepan of simmering water.

**5.** Stir continuously until thick and creamy.

**6.** Strain into a bowl and allow to cool, whisking occasionally.

**7.** Chill, then pour into an ice tray and freeze.

**8.** When the ice cream is half-frozen, whisk again and return to the freezer.

# RASPBERRY ICE CREAM

This ice cream is made with a mousse base.

SERVES 4–6
*450g/1lb raspberries*
*85g/3oz icing sugar, sifted*
*70g/2½oz granulated sugar*
*110ml/4fl oz water*
*a little vanilla essence*
*3 egg yolks*
*290ml/½ pint single or double cream*
*a squeeze of lemon juice*

**1.** Liquidize or crush the raspberries and push through a nylon or stainless steel sieve.

**2.** Sweeten with the icing sugar.

**3.** Place the sugar and water in a heavy saucepan and dissolve over a low heat.

**4.** When completely dissolved, boil to the short thread stage (see page 477): when a little syrup is put between a wet finger and thumb and the fingers opened, it should form a sticky thread about 2.5cm/1in long.

**5.** Remove from the heat and cool for 1 minute. Add the vanilla essence.

**6.** Pour the sugar syrup on to the egg yolks and whisk until the mixture is thick and mousse-like.

**7.** Cool and add the cream, raspberry purée and lemon juice.

**8.** Check for sweetness and add more icing sugar if necessary.

**9.** Chill, then pour into an ice tray and freeze.

**10.** If the ice cream is not quite smooth when half-frozen, whisk it once more and return to the freezer.

# CHOCOLATE ICE CREAM

This ice cream is made with a custard base.

SERVES 4
*340g/12oz plain chocolate, cut up into small*
   *pieces*
*570ml/1 pint milk*
*1 egg*
*1 egg yolk*
*55g/2oz caster sugar*
*570ml/1 pint double cream*
*1 teaspoon vanilla essence*

**1.** Dissolve the chocolate in the milk in a heavy saucepan over a low heat.

**2.** Whisk the egg and egg yolk with the sugar in a heatproof bowl set over, not in, a saucepan of simmering water. Whisk until light and fluffy.

**3.** When the chocolate has melted and the milk nearly boiled, pour on to the egg mixture and whisk well. Strain and allow to cool.

**4.** Whip the cream lightly and fold it into the chocolate mixture with the vanilla essence. Pour into a bowl and freeze.

**5.** When half-frozen, whisk again and return to the freezer.

NOTE: Chocolate mint crisps or mint cracknel, crumbled up and added to the mixture at the time of the final whisking, give a delicious flavour and crunchy texture.

# LEMON CURD ICE CREAM

SERVES 6
*4 egg yolks*
*grated zest and juice of 2 lemons*
*125g/4½oz caster sugar*
*110g/4oz unsalted butter, at room temperature,*
   *cut into small pieces*
*570ml/1 pint plain yoghurt*

**1.** Put the egg yolks, lemon zest and juice, sugar and butter into a small saucepan. Set over a low heat and stir with a wooden spoon until the butter has melted and the curd is thick enough to coat the back of the spoon.

**2.** Remove from the heat and allow the curd to cool, then stir in the yoghurt. Cover closely and freeze.

**3.** Transfer the ice cream to the refrigerator about an hour before serving.

NOTE: This ice cream is also delicious made with good-quality shop-bought lemon curd.

# PISTACHIO PARFAIT

SERVES 6
*170g/6oz caster sugar*
*60ml/2½fl oz water*
*3 egg whites*
*570ml/1 pint double cream*
*1 drop of green colouring (optional)*
*1 tablespoon vanilla essence*
*1 drop of almond essence*
*75g/2½oz unsalted pistachio nuts, skinned and*
   *chopped*

**1.** Put the sugar and water into a heavy saucepan. Bring slowly to the boil, without stirring, then boil the syrup to the firm ball stage (see page 477).

**2.** Meanwhile, whisk the egg whites to stiff peaks.

**3.** If the whites are in a machine, pour the bubbling hot syrup on to them in a steady stream while whisking, taking care not to pour the syrup on to the wires of the whisk – it cools fast against the cold metal and can harden and stick to the whisk. If whisking the whites by hand, and in the absence of anyone to pour while you whisk, pour the syrup on to the whites in stages, about one-third at a time, whisking hard between each addition, and working as fast as possible. The syrup must be bubbling hot as it hits the egg white, to partially cook it.

**4.** When all the syrup has been added, whisk hard until the mixture is stiff and shiny and absolutely stable. When the whisk is lifted, the meringue should not flow at all.

**5.** Lightly whip the cream and colour it a delicate green.

**6.** Fold the cream into the meringue mixture. Add the essences and chopped pistachio nuts.

**7.** Pour into an ice tray and freeze. Remove from the freezer 30 minutes before serving.

# PISTACHIO ICE CREAM IN BISCUIT CUPS

SERVES 8
For the biscuit mixture
*85g/3oz butter*
*85g/3oz caster sugar*
*3 egg whites*
*85g/3oz plain flour, sifted*

For the ice cream
*570ml/1 pint milk*
*225g/8oz caster sugar*
*1 vanilla pod*
*290ml/1/2 pint single cream*
*8 egg yolks, beaten*
*110g/4oz unsalted pistachio nuts, skinned and
    chopped*

For the sauce
*3 eggs*
*3 egg yolks*
*140g/5oz caster sugar*
*3 tablespoons Framboise liqueur*
*340g/12oz fresh raspberries, sieved*

**1.** Preheat the oven to 220°C/425°F/gas mark 7.
**2.** Make the biscuit cups: melt the butter in a saucepan, add the sugar and stir over a very low heat until dissolved. Remove from the heat and allow to cool.

**3.** Gradually beat in the unwhisked egg whites, using a balloon whisk. Fold in the flour. Spread a quarter of the mixture out in 2 very large paper-thin rounds on a greased and floured baking sheet. (Warm the sheet for easier spreading.)

**4.** Bake in the preheated oven for 4 minutes until the biscuits are just brown at the edges and pale in the centre.

**5.** While still hot and pliable, shape the discs of biscuit over greased upturned jam jars. Remove the jam jars when the paste has set. (If the cups are not quite crisp when cold, return them to the oven on the jam jars.)

**6.** Bake the remaining mixture 2 biscuits at a time, in the same way, and shape into cups.

**7.** Make the ice cream: bring the milk, vanilla pod and cream very slowly to the boil in a saucepan. Pour on to the egg yolks beaten with the sugar in a bowl, stirring well. Remove the vanilla pod.

**8.** If the mixture is still very runny return it to the pan and stir continuously with a wooden spoon over a low heat until it will coat the back of the spoon. Immediately pour into a chilled bowl and allow to cool. Add the pistachio nuts.

**9.** Pour into ice trays and freeze, taking it out and beating 2 or 3 times during the freezing process to prevent large ice crystals from forming.

**10.** When nearly ready to serve, fill each biscuit cup with ice cream, stand on a platter and put back into the coldest part of the refrigerator or into the freezer while making the sauce.

**11.** Whisk the whole eggs, yolks, sugar and liqueur together in a heatproof bowl. Then set over a saucepan of simmering water and whisk until the mixture thickens like zabaglione. Stir in the sieved raspberries and serve warm, with the biscuit cups.

# INDIVIDUAL MANGO PARFAITS WITH PASSIONFRUIT SAUCE

SERVES 8
*2 ripe mangoes*
*3 egg yolks*
*110g/4oz icing sugar, sifted*
*200ml/7fl oz double cream*
*lemon juice*

For the sauce
*4 passionfruits*
*fresh orange juice*
*sugar syrup (see page 477)*

To decorate
*8 sprigs of fresh mint*

1. Lightly oil 8 ramekins.
2. Process the mango flesh until smooth.
3. Whisk the egg yolks with the icing sugar until very thick and light.
4. Lightly whip the double cream.
5. Fold the mango purée and cream into the egg-yolk mixture.
6. Add lemon juice to taste; it may also be necessary to add extra icing sugar.
7. Pour the mixture into the prepared ramekins, cover with clingfilm and freeze for at least 4 hours.
8. Make the sauce: scoop the flesh and seeds from the passionfruit and mix with a little orange juice and sugar syrup to taste.
9. To serve: turn the parfaits out on to individual plates, spoon over a little passionfruit sauce and decorate each with a sprig of mint.

# HAZELNUT ICE

This is a meringue-based ice cream.

SERVES 8
For the hazelnut praline
*150g/5oz granulated sugar*
*3 tablespoons water*
*150g/5oz hazelnuts, roasted and skinned*

For the Italian meringue
*150g/5oz granulated sugar*
*4 tablespoons water*
*6 egg yolks*
*8 egg whites*
*290ml/1/2 pint double cream, lightly whipped*

To serve
*raspberry coulis (see page 479)*

1. Prepare a 15cm/6in soufflé dish: tie a double piece of greaseproof paper around the outside of the dish. The paper should stand about 5cm/2in above the rim. Lightly brush the inside of the 'paper collar' with oil.
2. Lightly oil a baking sheet.
3. Make the hazelnut praline: melt the sugar in a heavy saucepan with the water. When the sugar has dissolved, boil until it turns to a pale caramel. Add 130g/4½oz of the still-warm hazelnuts and cook for a further 2 minutes until a rich brown. Pour on to the oiled baking sheet.
4. Cool, until hardened, then pound or liquidize.
5. Make the Italian meringue: dissolve the sugar in the water in a heavy saucepan over a low heat, then boil until the syrup reaches the firm ball stage (see page 477). In a large bowl, whisk the egg whites until stiff, then gradually add the sugar syrup, whisking all the time. Continue to whisk until really thick and shiny.
6. Put the egg yolks into a heatproof bowl and add the hazelnut praline. Place the bowl over, not in, a saucepan of simmering water and whisk until the mixture is thick and fluffy. Remove from the heat and continue to whisk until the mixture has cooled. (If you use an electric mixer, you need not beat the mixture over heat.)
7. Fold the cream into the egg mixture and then fold in the meringue.
8. Pour into the prepared soufflé dish and freeze for at least 8 hours.
9. To serve: remove the greaseproof paper. Roughly chop the remaining hazelnuts and scatter on top of the soufflé. Serve the raspberry coulis separately.

# VANILLA AND PRUNE ICE CREAM

This is a custard-based ice cream.

SERVES 4
290ml/½ pint milk
290ml/½ pint double cream
2 vanilla pods, split lengthways
6 egg yolks
100g/3½ oz caster sugar
8 prunes, stoned, cut in half and marinated in
    brandy for 24 hours

To serve
2 ripe peaches, halved

**1.** Scald the milk and cream with the vanilla pods in a heavy saucepan by bringing to just below boiling point.
**2.** In a bowl, beat the egg yolks with the sugar until creamy, add the milk mixture gradually and whisk together.
**3.** Return it to the pan and cook over a low heat, stirring constantly with a wooden spoon, until the custard is thick enough to coat the back of the spoon. Strain through a sieve into a bowl and allow to cool.
**4.** Pour the mixture into an ice tray and freeze.
**5.** Once frozen, take the ice cream out of the freezer and allow to soften at room temperature. Either place in a food processor and whizz to remove the ice crystals or use an electric beater. Fold in the prunes and brandy.
**6.** Return the ice cream to the container and freeze again.
**7.** Serve with the peaches.

# PEACH AND BANANA ICE CREAM WITH GRAPE SAUCE

Ice creams made from yoghurt inevitably have a crystal-like texture. The more they are whisked, the smoother they become. If you have an ice-cream machine, however, they will be almost as smooth as other ice creams.

SERVES 4–6
4 ripe peaches
2 bananas
450g/1lb low-fat plain yoghurt
concentrated apple juice (optional)

For the sauce
750ml/1¼ pints black grape juice

**1.** Skin and stone the peaches. Peel and chop the bananas.
**2.** Purée the peaches, bananas and yoghurt in a food processor or blender.
**3.** Taste and sweeten with apple juice if required (it will taste less sweet once frozen).
**4.** Place in the freezer until half-frozen. Tip into a chilled bowl and whisk well. Replace in the freezer until half-frozen and whisk again. Freeze again until firm.
**5.** Meanwhile, put the grape juice into a saucepan and reduce, by boiling, to a quarter of its original quantity.
**6.** Remove the ice cream 30 minutes before serving with grape sauce.

# DRIED APRICOT ICE CREAM

SERVES 4
225g/8oz dried apricots, soaked overnight
1 strip of thinly pared lemon zest
290ml/½ pint double cream, lightly whipped
lemon juice to taste

**1.** Put the apricots, the soaking water and the lemon zest into a saucepan and bring to the boil.
**2.** Simmer the apricots until they are soft (about 20 minutes).
**3.** Remove the lemon zest and purée the apricots with the water in a food processor or blender. Allow to cool.
**4.** Fold the cream into the apricot purée. Add lemon juice to taste.
**5.** Chill, in the refrigerator, then freeze. When half-frozen, whisk well and return to the freezer.

NOTE: If you have a food processor, once the ice cream has frozen allow it to soften, cut it into pieces and process it well. If you have a *gelato chef* (electric ice-cream maker), add the unfrozen mixture to the machine and follow the manufacturer's instructions.

# BROWN BREAD ICE CREAM

SERVES 4
*110g/4oz wholemeal breadcrumbs*
*110g/4oz soft dark brown sugar*
*2 eggs*
*290ml/$\frac{1}{2}$ pint double cream*
*150ml/$\frac{1}{4}$ pint single cream*
*2 drops of vanilla essence*

1. Preheat the oven to 200°C/400°F/gas mark 6.
2. Place the breadcrumbs in the oven for 15 minutes or until dry.
3. Mix the sugar and breadcrumbs and return to the oven for a further 15 minutes or until the sugar caramelizes. Remove, allow to cool and crush lightly.
4. Separate the eggs. Beat the yolks, add the creams and fold in the caramelized crumbs. Add the vanilla essence.
5. Whisk the egg whites to soft peaks and fold into the mixture. Freeze until required.

# COFFEE AND RICOTTA ICE CREAM

*Claudia Roden inspired this very simple and completely delicious ice cream.*

SERVES 4
*255g/9oz ricotta cheese*
*1 tablespoon fine-ground coffee*
*2 tablespoons caster sugar*

1. Beat the ricotta cheese in a bowl, add the coffee and sugar and mix until smooth. Freeze for 2–3 hours.
2. Remove from the freezer 20 minutes before serving.

# MORELLO CHERRY BOMBE

*This is a cheat's bombe – simple to make and delicious to eat.*

SERVES 8
*400g/14oz can of morello cherries, pitted*
*110g/4oz meringue shells (see page 558)*
*570ml/1 pint double cream, or 675g/1$\frac{1}{2}$lb rich vanilla ice cream (see page 568)*
*1 tablespoon brandy or Kirsch (optional)*
*icing sugar to taste*
*110g/4oz raspberries*

For the sauce
*2 teaspoons arrowroot*
*1 tablespoon brandy or Kirsch*

1. Drain the cherries well, reserving the juice. Break the meringues up roughly.
2. Whip the cream until stiff, add the brandy or Kirsch if using, and sweeten to taste with icing sugar. (If using ice cream, allow it to soften but not to melt.) Mix in the cherries, raspberries and meringue. Check for sweetness.
3. Spoon the mixture into a bombe mould or freezerproof bowl and put immediately into the freezer. It will take at least 2 hours, and probably 4, to harden. It can then be turned out on to a plate and put back in the freezer until needed.
4. Make the sauce: mix the arrowroot with a little water. Heat the reserved cherry juice in a saucepan. Pour some of the hot juice on to the arrowroot, stirring to a paste then stir the paste into the saucepan. Bring to the boil, stirring. Allow to simmer for 1 minute after boiling. Add the brandy or Kirsch and serve hot with the bombe.

NOTE: This dessert can also be made with fresh or frozen strawberries, pineapple or peaches, but the fruits should be chopped rather than left whole or in large pieces.

# RUM BOMBE WITH MINCEMEAT SAUCE

SERVES 8
290ml/½ pint double cream
3 tablespoons rum
225ml/8fl oz plain yoghurt
110g/4oz meringue shells (see page 558), crushed
1 teaspoon freshly grated nutmeg

For the mincemeat sauce
1 large dessert apple
55g/2oz raisins
55g/2oz sultanas
55g/2oz hazelnuts, chopped and lightly toasted
55g/2oz soft dark brown sugar
½ teaspoon ground mixed spice
grated zest and juice of ½ lemon
grated zest and juice of 1 orange
4 tablespoons rum

1. Lightly oil 8 ramekins and line them with discs of greaseproof paper.
2. Whip the cream until it holds it shape. Whisk in the rum and fold in the yoghurt, meringues and nutmeg. Turn into the ramekin dishes and freeze until firm.
3. Make the sauce: peel, core and chop the apple and add the remaining ingredients for the sauce, with more orange juice or rum to taste.
4. To serve: run a knife around the ramekins and turn out on to individual plates. Place in the refrigerator for 10 minutes before serving.
5. Heat the sauce until very hot but not boiling and hand it separately.

# CHOCOLATE CHRISTMAS BOMBES

SERVES 6
85g/3oz plain chocolate, chopped
2 tablespoons rum
1 tablespoon water
170g/6oz unsweetened chestnut purée
30g/1oz raisins
30g/1oz sultanas

30g/1oz chopped mixed peel
55g/2oz glacé cherries
290ml/½ pint double cream
2 egg whites
45g/1½oz caster sugar

To decorate
chocolate holly leaves (see page 649)

1. Line 6 individual ramekins or large dariole moulds with clingfilm.
2. Put the chocolate, 1 tablespoon of the rum and the water into a heatproof bowl set over, not in, a saucepan of simmering water until the chocolate has just melted. Remove from the heat and stir into the chestnut purée. Set aside.
3. Sprinkle the remaining rum over the dried fruits, peel and cherries and leave to stand for 5 minutes.
4. Whip the cream lightly. Whisk the egg whites until stiff and then gradually add the sugar, a teaspoon at a time, whisking well after each addition.
5. Carefully fold the fruit into the chocolate and chestnut mixture, then add the cream and finally the whisked egg whites.
6. Divide the mixture between the ramekins, cover and freeze for at least 3 hours.
7. To serve: remove the moulds from the freezer 10 minutes before serving. Turn on to a plate, remove the clingfilm and decorate with the holly leaves.

# BRANDY SNAP TORTES

SERVES 6
110g/4oz flour quantity brandy snap mixture (see page 630)
450g/1lb damson ice cream, slightly softened (see page 569)
raspberry coulis (see page 479)
100g/4oz mixed raspberries and blueberries

To decorate
sprigs of fresh mint
icing sugar, sifted, for dusting

1. Preheat the oven to 190°C/375°F/gas mark 5. Line a baking sheet with non-stick baking parchment. Grease a palette knife.

2. Make the brandy snap mixture, adding the extra 1 teaspoon ground ginger. Bake 18 brandy snaps on the baking sheet as in the recipe on page 630 but lift them, flat, on to a wire rack and leave them to cool and harden.

3. Put a flat brandy snap on to each of 6 pudding plates. Cover with some of the damson ice cream and flatten slightly. Cover with a second flat brandy snap. Arrange some more ice cream on top of the brandy snaps and cover with a third brandy snap.

4. Pour the raspberry coulis around the tortes.

5. Arrange the raspberries and blueberries on the coulis and decorate with a small sprig of mint.

6. Dust lightly with icing sugar.

# FROZEN CHOCOLATE TORTE

SERVES 6
For the chocolate biscuit base
*170g/6oz butter*
*85g/3oz caster sugar*
*170g/6oz self-raising flour*
*45g/1½oz cocoa powder*

For the chocolate mousse
*170g/6oz plain chocolate, chopped*
*30g/1oz bitter chocolate, chopped*
*85ml/3fl oz black coffee or water*
*4 eggs, separated*
*140g/5oz caster sugar*
*290ml/½ pint double cream*

To finish
*2 teaspoons each sifted icing sugar and cocoa*
*    powder, mixed*

1. Preheat the oven to 190°C/375°F/gas mark 5.

2. Make the base: cream the butter until soft. Add the sugar and beat until light and fluffy. Sift the flour and cocoa powder together and stir into the mixture.

3. Press into the bottom of a 25cm/10in spring form tin or deep-sided cake tin lined with kitchen foil.

4. Bake in the preheated oven for 10 minutes. Do not allow to colour. Remove from the oven and leave to cool.

5. Make the mousse mixture: place the chocolates and coffee or water in a bowl set over, not in, a saucepan of simmering water. Allow to melt.

6. Whisk the egg yolks with half the sugar until light and mousse-like. Stir in the melted chocolate.

7. Whip the cream until it just holds its shape.

8. Whisk the egg whites until stiff, then gradually add the remaining sugar, a spoonful at a time, whisking well after each addition.

9. Fold the cream into the chocolate mixture, followed by the egg whites. Pour on to the cooked biscuit base, cover and freeze for at least 4 hours.

10. To serve: remove the torte from the freezer. Remove from the tin. Dust with the icing sugar and cocoa. Allow to stand for 20 minutes before serving.

# PEACH MELBA

SERVES 4
*2 large fresh peaches*
*raspberry coulis (see page 479)*
*425ml/¾ pint rich vanilla ice cream (see page 568)*

1. If the peaches are not completely ripe, split and stone them and poach gently in a little sugar syrup (see page 477) until tender. Drain well and peel. If they are ripe, simply dip in boiling water for 4–5 seconds, then peel and halve them.

2. Serve on individual plates. Place a spoonful of vanilla ice cream on each plate, cover with half a peach, round side up, and coat with raspberry coulis. Serve immediately.

NOTES: The original peach Melba, created by Escoffier for the great opera singer, consisted of plain vanilla ice cream and fresh peaches resting in the hollowed-out back of a swan fashioned in ice. Escoffier later added the refinement of a pure raspberry purée.

This recipe calls for the more sophisticated raspberry coulis rather than the Melba sauce recipe.

# MELON AND CHAMPAGNE SORBET

SERVES 4–6
*1 large Ogen melon*
*340g/12oz granulated sugar*
*10 tablespoons water*
*juice of 1 lemon*
*290ml/¹⁄₂ pint champagne*

**1.** Cut the melon into quarters. Remove the skin and seeds and purée the flesh in a food processor or blender.
**2.** Put the sugar and water into a heavy saucepan. Dissolve slowly over a low heat.
**3.** When the sugar has completely dissolved, increase the heat and boil rapidly to the short thread stage (see page 477): when a little syrup is placed between a wet finger and thumb and the fingers opened, it should form a thread 2.5cm/1in long.
**4.** Mix together the melon purée, lemon juice, champagne and warm sugar syrup. Allow to cool, then pour into a freezer container.
**5.** Freeze overnight or until icy, then whisk until smooth and return to the freezer. Serve in well-chilled goblets.

NOTE: If you have an ice-cream machine, it makes short work of this sorbet. It is a soft sorbet because of the high alcoholic content.

# TOMATO SORBET

SERVES 4–6
*110g/4oz granulated sugar*
*290ml/¹⁄₂ pint water*
*500ml/18fl oz tomato juice*
*juice of ¹⁄₂ lemon*
*fresh mint or basil leaves, roughly chopped*
*1 tablespoon Worcestershire sauce*
*Tabasco sauce*
*salt and freshly ground black pepper*
*1 egg white*

**1.** Put the sugar and water into a heavy saucepan. Dissolve slowly over a low heat. When the sugar

has completely dissolved, increase the heat and boil to the short thread stage (see page 477): when a little syrup is placed between a wet finger and thumb and the fingers opened, it should form a sticky thread 2.5cm/1in long. Remove from the heat and allow to cool for 1 minute.
**2.** Meanwhile, mix together the tomato juice, lemon juice and herbs. Season to taste with Worcestershire sauce, Tabasco, salt and pepper. Add the cooling sugar syrup. Transfer to a freezer container and cool completely, then freeze.
**3.** Once large crystals have formed and the sorbet is almost set, remove from the container and break up with a fork.
**4.** Whisk the egg white until stiff but not dry and fold into the tomato mixture. Return to the container and freeze again. Remove from the freezer 10–15 minutes before serving.

NOTE: If using a food processor, when the sorbet is partially frozen remove from the container, roughly chop and then quickly process. Add the unwhipped egg white through the lid funnel as the blade is moving. Process for about 1 minute. Return the mixture to the container and freeze again.

# APPLE SORBET

SERVES 4
*4 Cox's apples*
*160g/5¹⁄₂oz caster sugar*
*juice of 1 lemon*
*2 tablespoons Calvados*
*1 egg white*

**1.** Peel, core and quarter the apples.
**2.** Put the apples into a saucepan with the sugar and enough water to just cover them. Poach gently for 20 minutes or until glassy.
**3.** Remove the apples and reduce the cooking liquor, by boiling rapidly to the short thread stage (see page 477): when a little syrup is placed between a wet finger and thumb and the fingers opened, it should form a sticky thread 2.5cm/1in long. Purée the apples, syrup, Calvados and lemon juice together in a food processor or blender.

**4.** Allow to cool, then pour into a freezer container and freeze.

**5.** When nearly frozen, place the sorbet in a processor and whizz briefly. Gradually add the unwhisked egg white with the motor running. The mixture will fluff up tremendously. Return to the container and freeze until firm.

# PEAR SORBET

SERVES 4

*4 ripe William pears*
*160g/5½oz caster or icing sugar*
*juice of 2 lemons*
*1 egg white, lightly whisked*

**1.** Peel, core and quarter the pears.

**2.** Put the pears into a saucepan with the sugar and enough water to just cover the pears. Poach gently for 20 minutes or until glassy.

**3.** Remove the pears and reduce the cooking liquor by boiling rapidly to the short thread stage (see page 477): when a little syrup is placed between a wet finger and thumb and the fingers opened, it should form a sticky thread 2.5cm/1in long. Purée the pears, syrup and lemon juice together in a food processor or blender.

**4.** Allow to cool, then pour into a freezer container and freeze.

**5.** When nearly frozen, fold in the egg white and freeze until firm.

NOTE: If you have a food processor, allow the sorbet to freeze and then defrost until half-frozen. Whizz in the food processor and gradually add the egg white, unwhisked. It will fluff up tremendously. Return to the container and freeze until firm.

# TROIS SORBETS

SERVES 4

*pear sorbet (see above)*
*strawberry sorbet (see page 579)*
*passionfruit sorbet (see page 579)*
*fresh raspberries*
*fresh strawberries*
*fresh orange segments*

For the coulis rouge
*225g/8oz raspberries*
*1 tablespoon water*
*1 tablespoon caster sugar*

**1.** Prepare the coulis rouge: heat the raspberries, water and sugar together in a saucepan. Bring to the boil for 30 seconds to allow the sugar to dissolve. Push through a sieve and spoon on to 4 pudding plates so that the base of each dish is completely flooded. Leave to get completely cold.

**2.** Arrange the sorbets and fresh fruit on the plates as illustrated.

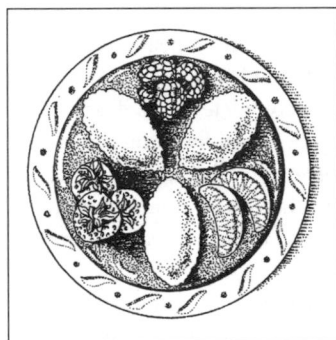

*Pear, passionfruit and strawberry sorbet with fresh fruits*

# REDCURRANT WATER ICE

SERVES 4

*450g/1lb granulated sugar*
*425ml/¾ pint water*
*425ml/¾ pint redcurrant juice*
*7g/¼oz powdered gelatine*

**1.** Dissolve the sugar in the water in a heavy saucepan over a low heat and, when completely dissolved, boil to the short thread stage (when a little syrup is put between finger and thumb and the fingers opened, it should form a sticky thread 2.5cm/1in long).

**2.** Put 2 tablespoons redcurrant juice into a small saucepan, sprinkle over the gelatine and leave for 5 minutes to become spongy.

**3.** Add the remaining juice to the sugar syrup.

**4.** Dissolve the gelatine over a low heat without boiling until liquid, then stir into the redcurrant mixture.

**5.** Allow to get quite cold. Whisk very thoroughly, preferably in a food processor or ice-cream maker.

**6.** Chill in the refrigerator, then freeze until firm.

# LEMON SORBET

SERVES 4
*thinly pared zest and juice of 3 lemons*
*140g/5oz granulated sugar*
*570ml/1 pint water*
*½ egg white*

**1.** Place the lemon zest, sugar and water in a heavy saucepan. Dissolve the sugar over a low heat and, when completely dissolved, boil rapidly to the short thread stage (when a little syrup is put between finger and thumb and the fingers opened, it should form a sticky thread 2.5cm/1in long).
**2.** Remove from the heat and allow to cool completely. When the syrup is cold, add the lemon juice and strain.
**3.** Freeze for 30 minutes, or until beginning to solidify.
**4.** Whisk the egg white until stiff and fold into the mixture.
**5.** Return to the freezer until firm.

NOTE: If you have a food processor, allow the lemon syrup to freeze and then whisk until soft. Pour in the egg white, through the funnel, whisking all the time. Freeze until firm.

# STRAWBERRY SORBET

SERVES 4
*170g/6oz caster sugar*
*570ml/1 pint water*
*juice of ½ lemon or small orange*
*340g/12oz fresh or frozen strawberries*
*1 egg white*

**1.** Place the sugar and water in a heavy saucepan. Dissolve the sugar over a low heat. When completely dissolved, boil gently for 5 minutes. Add the lemon or orange juice and cool.
**2.** Liquidize or mash the strawberries to a pulp and add the syrup. Place in a bowl in the freezer for 30 minutes or until beginning to solidify.
**3.** Whisk the egg whites until stiff and fold into the mixture.
**4.** Return to the freezer until firm.

NOTE: If you have a food processor, allow the strawberry syrup to freeze, then whisk until soft. Pour in the egg white, through the funnel, whisking all the time. Freeze until solid.

# PASSIONFRUIT SORBET

SERVES 6
*140g/5oz granulated sugar*
*425ml/¾ pint water*
*thinly pared zest and juice of 1 lemon*
*450g/1lb passionfruit pulp (from about 32 passionfruits)*
*½ egg white*

**1.** Dissolve the sugar in the water in a heavy saucepan. When completely dissolved, add the lemon zest and boil rapidly for 5 minutes, or until the syrup is tacky.
**2.** Sieve the passionfruit pulp and add to the syrup with the lemon juice. Cool.
**3.** Place in a bowl in the freezer until half-frozen.
**4.** Tip into a chilled bowl and whisk well. Refreeze until almost solid.
**5.** Whisk the egg white until very stiff.
**6.** Tip the sorbet into another chilled bowl and break up. Whisk until smooth and fold in the egg white.
**7.** Freeze again until firm.
**8.** If the ice is not absolutely creamy and smooth, give it one more freezing and whisking.

NOTE: If you have a food processor, allow the passionfruit, syrup and lemon juice to freeze. Defrost slightly, then whisk until soft. Pour the egg white in, through the funnel, whizzing all the time. Freeze until firm.

# CAKES

# CAKE-MAKING

Successful cake-making is a most satisfying activity for the cook. It is also most demanding on account of the accuracy needed in measuring the ingredients and the skill necessary in preparing certain cakes. Confidence is best built by beginning with the easier cakes, such as gingerbread or fruit cake. First attempts at making more difficult cakes such as a génoise sponge are often disappointing. Happily, practice, with good ingredients, proper utensils, careful weighing and measuring, precise oven temperatures and exact timing – in short, careful attention to detail – makes perfect.

Most cakes are made by combining fat, sugar, flour, eggs and liquid. Air or another raising agent is incorporated to make the mixture rise during baking. As it bakes, strands of gluten in the flour are stretched by the gas given off until the heat finally firms the cake. It is even rising that gives a cake a light, sponge-like texture.

## INGREDIENTS

FATS Butter makes the best-flavoured cakes. Margarine, particularly the soft or tub variety, is useful for speed but has less flavour than butter. Vegetable shortenings are flavourless but give light cakes. Lard cakes are often delicious but heavy, and for this reason lard is little used in cake-making. Oils are not much used as they do not easily hold air when they are creamed or beaten, and the resulting cakes can therefore be heavy.

SUGARS The finer creaming possible with caster sugar makes it most suitable for cake-making. Coarse granulated sugar can give a speckled appearance to a finished cake unless the sugar is ground down first in a blender or food processor. Soft brown sugars give colour and flavour to dark cakes like gingerbread, but they give sponge cakes a drab look and too much caramel flavour.

Golden syrup, honey, treacle and molasses are used in cakes made by the melting method. Such cakes are cooked relatively slowly, as these thick liquid sugars tend to caramelize and burn at higher temperatures.

EGGS Unless specified, most recipes assume a medium egg weighing 55g/2oz (UK size 3). The eggs should be used at room temperature–cold eggs tend to curdle the mixture and this results in the cake having a tough, coarse, too open texture. When using whisked egg whites in a cake, be sure not to allow even a speck of yolk into the whites. Any yolk or fat on the whisk will prevent proper whisking of the whites, reducing their air-holding ability and the lightness of the finished cake.

FLOURS Plain white flour is used in cake-making unless otherwise specified. The high proportion of 'soft' or low-gluten wheat in European plain flour makes it particularly suitable for cake-making. In North America, plain or 'all-purpose' flour is made with more 'hard' than soft wheat, so cornflour, which is also weak (low in gluten), is sometimes substituted for some of the all-purpose flour, or special soft 'cake flour' is used. Although a little gluten is needed to allow the mixture to stretch and expand as it rises, too much would given a tough, chewy cake.

Self-raising flour has a raising agent (baking powder) added to it and should be used only if specified in the recipe. All flours, even if labelled 'ready-sifted', should be sifted before use to eliminate any lumps and to incorporate air.

## RAISING AGENTS

Air is incorporated into cake mixtures by agitating the ingredients. Methods include sifting the flour, beating the butter and beating or creaming it again with the sugar to a fluffy, mousse-like consistency, and whisking the eggs. The heat of the oven causes the air trapped in the mixture to rise and leaven or lighten the cake, either by itself or in conjunction with other raising agents.

Steam raises some mixtures even when air has not been beaten into them. Flour mixtures with a high proportion of liquid in them, like Yorkshire pudding, will rise in a hot oven since, as the water vaporizes and the steam rises, the uncooked flour mixture rises with it. While in this puffed-up state, the mixture hardens in the oven heat with the steam trapped inside. The pockets of air created by steam are uneven and very open, as in choux pastry (see pages 460, 465), so steam is not used on its own for making cakes. But steam is a contributing factor in raising wet cake mixtures such as gingerbread.

Bicarbonate of soda, or baking soda, is a powder which, when mixed into cake mixtures, quickly gives off half its substance as carbon dioxide. In a cake the trapped gas causes the mixture to puff up. Heat sets the mixture once it has risen. By the time the cake cools, the gas will have escaped and will have been replaced by air. Unfortunately, the bicarbonate of soda remaining in the cake can give it a slightly unpleasant smell and taste, and a yellowish colour. For this reason, bicarbonate of soda is most often used in strong-tasting cakes such as gingerbread and those flavoured with chocolate, treacle or molasses. The carbon dioxide reaction is speeded up by acidic substances, so bicarbonate of soda is usually used in cake mixtures with ingredients such as sour milk, vinegar, buttermilk, soured cream, cream of tartar and yoghurt. This makes it especially suitable for quickly mixed items like fruit cakes, scones, soda bread and gingerbread. It also gives them a soft texture and spongy crust with a deep colour. Unfortunately the process destroys some of the vitamins present in the flour.

Baking powder in commercial forms consists of bicarbonate of soda and an acid powder that varies according to the brand, plus a starch filler, usually cornflour, arrowroot or ground rice. The starch keeps the mixture dry by absorbing any dampness in the air, which might cause the soda and the acid in the powder to react. The presence of the filler explains why more commercial baking powder than mixed 'bicarb' and cream of tartar would be needed to raise the same cake. A 'delayed action' or 'double action' baking powder is sold in the USA that needs heat as well as moisture to produce carbon dioxide. It is not widely known in Europe. The advantage of it is that it can be added to mixtures in advance of baking – it starts to work only once in the oven.

Yeast cakes caused to rise by the growth of yeast cells are really sweetened enriched breads. They are traditional in Eastern European cookery. The kulich on page 600 is a classic example.

## PREPARING A CAKE TIN

All tins should be greased before use to prevent the cake mixture from sticking or burning at the edges or bottom. Melted lard or oil are the most suitable fats. Always turn the tin upside down after greasing to allow any excess fat to drain away. Use a paint-brush to get a thin layer. Bread tins and non-stick sandwich tins need no preparation other than greasing. Tins for cakes made by the melting or creaming methods should be greased, then the base lined with greaseproof paper, cut exactly to size and the paper brushed out with more melted lard or oil. (To cut the paper accurately draw round the tin, then cut just inside the line.) For cakes made by the whisking method, a dusting of caster sugar and flour should be given after lining and greasing.

For fruit cakes, grease the tin, then line the sides and base with greaseproof paper as follows:
**1.** Cut 2 pieces of greaseproof paper to fit the base of the cake tin.
**2.** Cut another piece long enough to go right round the sides of the tin and to overlap slightly. It should be 2.5cm/1in deeper than the height of the cake tin.
**3.** Fold one long edge of this strip over 2.5cm/1in all along its length.

**4.** Cut snips at right angles to the edge and about 1cm/½in apart, all along the folded side. The snips should just reach the fold.

**5.** Grease the tin, place one paper base in the bottom and grease again.

**6.** Fit the long strip inside the tin with the folded cut edge on the bottom (the flanges will overlap slightly) and the main uncut part lining the sides of the tin. Press them well into the corners.

**7.** Grease the paper and lay the second base on top of the first.

**8.** Brush the base again with more melted lard or oil and dust the lined tin with flour.

**9.** After making the cake mixture and placing in the tin, wrap the outside of the tin in newspaper.

## METHODS USED IN CAKE-MAKING

RUBBING IN The rubbing-in method gives a fairly substantial cake (such as rock cakes) with a crumbly, moist texture. The raising agent is always bicarbonate of soda. In rock cakes the agent is in the self-raising flour. The cake is delicious served sliced and spread with butter, or eaten as a warm pudding with custard.

MELTING The melting method is used for very moist cakes like gingerbread. The fat, sugar, syrup and any other liquid ingredients are heated together to melt, then cooled slightly. The flour and other dry ingredients are sifted together and the warm sugar mixture is stirred, not beaten, into the dry mixture along with the eggs. The raising agent is always bicarbonate of soda. These cakes are perfect for the beginner – easy, reliable and delicious.

CLASSIC CREAMING Creaming fat and sugar to a mousse-like consistency, and thereby incorporating air, is the secret of lightness in cakes like Victoria sponge, although a little chemical raising agent is usually added to ensure rising. First the butter or margarine is creamed or beaten until smooth and very light in colour, but the fat is never allowed to melt. If it did the carefully incorporated air beaten into it would escape. The sugar is then beaten in by degrees, until the mixture is pale and fluffy.

The eggs are lightly beaten and added, also by degrees, to the creamed mixture. The mixture is beaten after each addition to incorporate it

thoroughly. At this point the batter can curdle, especially if the eggs are too cold, but beating in a spoonful of sifted flour taken from the recipe after each addition of eggs should prevent this. Cakes made from curdled mixtures are acceptable, but they have a less delicate, more open and coarse texture than those made from uncurdled mixture.

Plain flour, if used, should be sifted with the baking powder and salt. Self-raising flour should be sifted with salt. The flour mixture is then folded carefully into the creamed mixture with a metal spoon and with as little mixing as possible to ensure minimum air loss in the batter.

ALL-IN-ONE CREAMING The all-in-one method is an easy version of the creaming method, because all the ingredients are beaten together at the same time, but a strong electric mixer is necessary to make these cakes really successful. Soft tub margarine gives a lighter result than butter.

CREAMING FOR FRUIT CAKES Another version of the creaming method is suited to fruit cakes. Softened butter and sugar are creamed in a mixing bowl to incorporate air. The eggs and any other liquid are gradually beaten into the creamed mixture, with the flour added with the last few additions of egg to reduce the risk of curdling. After the mixture is well combined, the dry fruit is folded in well to distribute it throughout the cake. The mixture should have a soft, dropping consistency (it should fall reluctantly off a spoon given a slight shake, neither sticking obstinately nor running off) and be spread out evenly in the prepared tin, with a slight dip in the centre of the mixture to counteract the cake 'peaking'.

Because fruit cakes are generally large and dense and contain a high proportion of fruit, which burns easily, they are cooked extremely slowly. To prevent burning they can be placed on a folded newspaper in the oven and can be covered in several layers of greaseproof or brown paper, but not foil, which traps the steam and produces too doughy a result.

WHISKING In the whisking method, the only raising agent is air that has been trapped in the cake batter during mixing. As the air expands in the heat of the oven, the cake rises. Cakes like Swiss roll (page 592) and génoise commune (page 593) are made by this method.

The simplest whisked sponge contains no fat. Sugar and eggs are whisked together until they are thick and light, then flour is folded in gently to keep in as much air as possible. In a lighter but more complicated whisked sponge, the eggs are separated and the yolks are whisked with the sugar and flour. The whites are whisked in another bowl, then folded into the batter. Sometimes half the sugar is whisked with the yolks, and half with the whites to give a meringue.

The sugar and eggs (or egg yolks only) are whisked in a bowl set over a pan of barely simmering water. Make sure that the bowl does not touch the water or the heat will scramble the eggs. The gentle heat from the steam speeds up the dissolving of the sugar and slightly cooks and thickens the eggs, so encouraging the mixture to hold the maximum number of air bubbles. The mixture should change colour from yellow to almost white and increase to four times its original volume. The mixture is ready when a lifted whisk will leave a ribbon-like trail. Traditionally, a balloon whisk is used, but a hand-held electric one works excellently. If a powerful food mixer is used, the heat can be dispensed with, though the process is speeded up if the mixture is put into a warmed bowl.

When the flour is folded in, great care should be taken to fold rather than stir or beat, as the aim is to incorporate the flour without losing any of the beaten-in air, which alone will raise the cake. The correct movement is more of lifting the mixture and cutting into it, rather than stirring it.

Although they are light and springy, a drawback of these cakes is that they go stale quickly. Always plan to make fatless sponge on the day of serving, or freeze the cake once it is cool.

The génoise is a whisked sponge that has just-runny butter folded into it with the flour. Butter gives it flavour and richness and makes it keep a day or two longer than fatless sponges. The butter should be poured in a stream around the edge of the bowl and then folded in. If the butter is poured heavily on top of the whisked mixture, it forces out some of the air, and needs excessive mixing, with the danger of more air loss.

Whisked cakes are cooked when the surface will spring back when pressed with a finger. The cakes should be cooled for a few minutes in the tin and then turned out on to a cake rack. The baking paper should be carefully peeled off to allow the escape of steam.

# VICTORIA SANDWICH

*oil for greasing*
*110g/4oz butter*
*110g/4oz caster sugar*
*2 eggs*
*110g/4oz self-raising flour, sifted*
*water*
*2 tablespoons raspberry jam*
*caster sugar for dusting*

1. Preheat the oven to 190°C/375°F/gas mark 5.
2. Prepare 2 × 15cm/6in sandwich tins by lining the bottom of each with a disc of greaseproof paper and lightly brushing out each tin with oil.
3. Cream the butter and sugar together until light and fluffy.
4. Mix the eggs together in a separate bowl, and gradually beat into the creamed mixture a little at a time, adding 1 tablespoon of the flour if the mixture begins to curdle.
5. Fold in the flour, adding enough water to bring the mixture to a dropping consistency.
6. Divide the mixture between the prepared tins and smooth the tops with a spatula. Bake in the middle of the preheated oven for about 20 minutes, or until the cakes are well risen, golden and feel spongy to the fingertips.
7. Allow the cakes to cool for a few minutes in the tins, then turn out on to a wire rack to cool completely. Peel off the lining paper.
8. Sandwich the cakes together with the jam.
9. Dust the top of the cake with caster sugar.

# LEMON VICTORIA SPONGE

oil for greasing
170g/6oz butter
170g/6oz caster sugar
grated zest of 1 lemon
3 large eggs
170g/6oz self-raising flour

For the filling and topping
lemon curd (see page 660)
feather icing (see page 639)

**1.** Preheat the oven to 190°C/375°F/gas mark 5.
**2.** Prepare 2 × 20cm/8in sandwich tins (see page 583).
**3.** Cream the butter and when soft add the sugar and beat until light and fluffy. Add the lemon zest.
**4.** Beat in 1 egg at a time, each time with 1 teaspoon flour.
**5.** Beat very well. Fold in the remaining flour. Add a little water to bring the mixture to a dropping consistency.
**6.** Divide the mixture between the prepared tins and smooth the tops with a spatula. Bake in the middle of the preheated oven for 20–25 minutes, or until the cakes are well risen, golden and feel spongy to the fingertips.
**7.** Allow the cakes to cool for a few minutes in the tins, then turn out on to a wire rack to cool completely. Peel off the lining paper.
**8.** Sandwich the cakes with lemon curd.
**9.** Ice the top and 'feather' it as described in the icing recipe.

# MADEIRA CAKE

oil for greasing
170g/6oz unsalted butter
170g/6oz caster sugar
grated zest and juice of 1 lemon
a pinch of ground cinnamon
3 eggs
110g/4oz self-raising flour
55g/2oz ground almonds
milk (optional)
1 slice of candied citrus peel

**1.** Preheat the oven to 170°C/325°F/gas mark 3.
**2.** Prepare an 18cm/7in cake tin (see page 583).

**3.** Cream the butter and when soft add the sugar and beat until light and fluffy. Add the lemon zest and cinnamon.
**4.** Beat in the eggs one at a time, adding a little flour as you beat, to prevent the mixture from curdling. Add the lemon juice.
**5.** Fold in the remaining flour and the ground almonds.
**6.** Add enough milk to bring the mixture to a dropping consistency.
**7.** Spoon the mixture into the prepared tin and smooth the top with a palette knife or spatula.
**8.** Bake in the preheated oven for 45 minutes. Place the citrus peel on top of the cake, then bake for a further 30 minutes.
**9.** Cool the cake for 10 minutes in the tin before gently easing out on to a wire rack.

# MARBLED CHOCOLATE CAKE

oil for greasing
4 egg quantity Victoria sandwich cake mixture (see page 585)
1 tablespoon cocoa powder
1 tablespoon warm milk
110g/4oz plain chocolate
15g/½oz butter

**1.** Preheat the oven to 190°C/375°F/gas mark 5.
**2.** Lightly oil a 20cm/8in ring mould.
**3.** Divide the Victoria sandwich mixture equally between 2 bowls.
**4.** Mix the cocoa powder with the milk and add it to one bowl.
**5.** Place spoonfuls of the mixture, alternating the colours, in the ring mould. Use a skewer in a figure-of-eight motion to swirl the colours together.
**6.** Bake in the preheated oven for 20–25 minutes, or until the cake is well risen and feels spongy. Allow to cool for a few minutes in the tin, then turn out on to a wire rack to cool completely.
**7.** Break up the chocolate into small even pieces. Put into a heatproof bowl, add the butter and place over, not in, a saucepan of simmering water. Stir until completely melted.
**8.** Pour the chocolate over the cake, making sure that it is completely covered. Leave to cool and harden.

# LIGHT CHRISTMAS CAKE

110g/4oz glacé cherries
55g/2oz chopped mixed peel
450g/1lb raisins
285g/10oz sultanas
110g/4oz currants
225g/8oz butter
225/8oz soft dark brown sugar
5 eggs, beaten
285g/10oz plain flour
2 teaspoons ground mixed spice
grated zest of ½ lemon
2 tablespoons black treacle
200ml/7fl oz beer or sweet sherry
110g/4oz ground almonds

1. Preheat the oven to 170°C/325°F/gas mark 3.
2. Line the base and sides of a 22cm/9in round cake tin with a double thickness of greased greaseproof paper.
3. Cut up the cherries and mix with the remaining fruit.
4. Cream the butter until soft. Add the sugar and beat until light and fluffy.
5. Add the eggs slowly, beating well after each addition. If the mixture curdles, beat in 1 teaspoon of the flour.
6. Fold in the flour, mixed spice, lemon zest, black treacle and beer or sherry.
7. Stir in the ground almonds and fruit.
8. Place the mixture in the prepared tin and make a deep hollow in the middle.
9. Bake in the preheated oven for 2½ hours, or until a skewer emerges clean when inserted into the middle of the cake.
10. Allow to cool on a wire rack.

# OLD-FASHIONED BOILED CHRISTMAS CAKE

This cake is not, as its name suggests, boiled instead of baked, but the fruit is boiled in water and orange juice and allowed to stand for 3 days before completing. This gives the fruit a wonderful plumpness. Instead of being decorated with marzipan and icing, the cake is finished with a glazed fruit and nut topping and a pretty ribbon.

225g/8oz butter
225g/8oz sultanas
225g/8oz raisins
110g/4oz currants
55g/2oz chopped mixed peel
55g/2oz glacé cherries, halved
170g/6oz dried apricots, chopped
55g/2oz dried apples, chopped
110g/4oz dried dates, chopped
110g/4oz dried peaches, chopped
110g/4oz dried pears, chopped
225g/8oz soft dark brown sugar
grated zest and juice of 1 lemon
grated zest and juice of 1 orange
110ml/4fl oz water
110ml/4fl oz orange juice
110ml/4fl oz brandy
½ teaspoon freshly grated nutmeg
1 teaspoon ground cinnamon
1 teaspoon ground allspice
½ teaspoon ground ginger
¼ teaspoon ground cardamom
1 tablespoon black treacle
5 eggs, beaten
310g/11oz plain flour
1 teaspoon baking powder

For the fruit topping
340g/12oz apricot jam
340g/12oz mixed dried fruit and nuts, such as pecans, brazils, almonds, apricots, red and green cherries, prunes, peaches, pears, etc.

1. Put the butter, sultanas, raisins, currants, mixed peel, cherries, apricots, apples, dates, peaches, pears, sugar, lemon and orange zest and juice, water and orange juice into a large pan. Bring slowly up to the boil. Stir with a wooden spoon, cover with a lid, and simmer for 10 minutes.
2. Remove from the heat and allow to cool slightly. Add the brandy and spices and transfer to a large bowl. When the mixture is completely cold, cover and put in a cool place (not the refrigerator) for 3 days, stirring daily.
3. Preheat the oven to 170°C/325°F/gas mark 3. Line the base and sides of a 25cm/10in round cake tin with a double thickness of greased greaseproof paper.
4. Stir the treacle into the boiled fruit mixture and beat in the eggs. Sift together the flour and baking

powder and stir into the cake mixture, which will be slightly sloppy. Turn it into the prepared cake tin and bake in the preheated oven for about 4½ hours, or until a skewer inserted into the centre of the cake comes out clean.

**5.** Leave the cake to cool in the tin.

**6.** When completely cold, wrap up carefully in kitchen foil until ready to decorate. It will mature well for 2–3 months.

**7.** To decorate the cake: put the apricot jam into a saucepan with 1 tablespoon water. Heat until boiling and then push through a sieve. Allow to cool slightly, then brush the top of the cake with the apricot glaze. Arrange the fruit and nuts all over the top of the cake in a haphazard fashion and then, using a pastry brush, glaze carefully with the apricot glaze.

**8.** Before serving, tie a decorative ribbon round the cake.

NOTES: The glaze will remain shiny on the cake for a few days but after a week it will begin to lose its gloss so it is better not to decorate the cake too early.

If the cake top becomes very dark during baking cover it with a double layer of damp greaseproof paper.

# SIMNEL CAKE

A festive Easter cake: the 11 balls of marzipan are said to represent the apostles (without Judas). Sometimes they are made into egg shapes, the symbol of spring and rebirth.

*oil for greasing*
*225g/8oz plain flour*
*55g/2oz rice flour*
*a large pinch each of salt and baking powder*
*110g/4oz glacé cherries*
*225g/8oz butter*
*225g/8oz caster sugar*
*grated zest of 1 lemon*
*4 eggs, separated*
*225g/8oz sultanas*
*110g/4oz currants*
*30g/1oz chopped mixed peel*
*675g/1½lb marzipan (see page 643)*
*beaten egg*
*110g/4oz glacé icing (see page 639)*

**1.** Preheat the oven to 180°C/350°F/gas mark 4.

**2.** Prepare a 20cm/8in cake tin with a double lining of greased and floured greaseproof paper. Wrap the outside of the cake tin with a double thickness of brown paper to insulate the cake from direct heat.

**3.** Sift the flours with the salt and baking powder. Cut the cherries in half.

**4.** Cream the butter until soft. Add the sugar and beat until light and fluffy. Add the lemon zest.

**5.** Beat in the egg yolks. Whisk the whites until stiff.

**6.** Fold one-third of the sifted flour into the mixture. Gradually fold in the egg whites, creamed alternately with the remaining flour and the fruit and peel.

**7.** Put half the mixture into the prepared tin, spreading a little up the sides.

**8.** Take just over one-third of the marzipan paste. Roll it into a smooth round the size of the cake tin. Place in the tin. Cover with the remaining cake mixture.

**9.** Using a palette knife, make a dip in the centre of the cake to counteract any tendency to rise in the middle.

**10.** Bake in the preheated oven for 2 hours, then turn the oven temperature down to 150°C/300°F/gas mark 2. Bake for a further 30 minutes.

**11.** Roll the remaining marzipan into a circle the same size as the top of the cake. Cut a piece from the centre about 12.5cm/5in in diameter and shape into 11 small even-sized balls.

**12.** Preheat the grill to its highest setting. Lay the ring of marzipan on top of the cake and brush with beaten egg. Arrange the marzipan balls on top of the ring and brush again with beaten egg. Grill until golden-brown.

**13.** When cold, pour a little glacé icing into the centre of the cake. Tie a ribbon around the side.

# COFFEE ALMOND LAYER CAKE

*oil for greasing*
*110g/4oz butter*
*110g/4oz caster sugar*
*85g/3oz plain flour*
*a pinch of salt*
*1 teaspoon baking powder*
*2 eggs*
*2 teaspoons instant coffee powder, dissolved in 2*
*    tablespoons hot water*
*55g/2oz ground almonds*

For the filling
*170g/6oz unsalted butter*
*340g/12oz icing sugar*
*2 teaspoons instant coffee powder*

To decorate
*55g/2oz flaked almonds, toasted*

1. Preheat the oven to 190°C/375°F/gas mark 5.
2. Prepare 2 × 18cm/7in sandwich tins (see page 583).
3. Cream the butter until soft. Add the sugar and beat until light and fluffy.
4. Sift the flour with the salt and baking powder. Beat the eggs lightly.
5. Gradually add the eggs and flour alternately to the butter and sugar mixture. Stir in the coffee and the ground almonds. Divide the mixture between the prepared tins and smooth the tops with a spatula.
6. Bake in the preheated oven for 20–25 minutes, or until the cakes are firm and golden-brown. Allow to cool in the tins for 5 minutes, then turn out on to wire racks to cool completely. Peel off the lining paper.
7. Meanwhile, make the filling: beat the butter and sugar until light and fluffy and stir in the coffee.
8. Sandwich the cake layers with half the butter icing and spread the remainder around the sides and top of the cake. Decorate with flaked almonds.

# CHOCOLATE AND ORANGE CAKE

For the cake
*oil for greasing*
*85g/3oz plain chocolate*
*1 teaspoon vanilla essence*
*340g/12oz soft light brown sugar*
*290ml/½ pint milk*
*grated zest of ½ orange*
*110g/4oz butter*
*2 eggs*
*225g/8oz plain flour*
*1 teaspoon bicarbonate of soda*

For the filling
*grated zest of ½ orange*
*290ml/½ pint double cream, whipped*
*caster sugar to taste*

For the icing
*110g/4oz plain chocolate*
*4 tablespoons milk*

1. Preheat the oven to 190°C/375°F/gas mark 5.
2. Prepare 3 × 15cm/5in sandwich tins (see page 583).
3. Put the chocolate, vanilla, half the sugar and half the milk into a heavy saucepan. Cook, stirring, until quite smooth. Add the orange zest.
4. Beat the butter with the remaining sugar until very light and creamy. Beat in the eggs, then add the melted chocolate mixture and beat again. Sift in the flour and soda and beat well to get rid of all lumps. Stir in the remaining milk. The mixture should now have the consistency of pancake batter.
5. Divide the mixture between the prepared tins and bake in the middle of the preheated oven for about 30 minutes, or until the cakes have a very slightly shrunken look around the edges. Do not worry if they do not feel very firm – they should be very moist and rather sticky. Allow the cakes to cool in the tins for 3 minutes before turning out on to a wire rack to cool. Peel off the lining paper.
6. Make the filling: mix the orange zest into the whipped cream and sweeten to taste with caster sugar. Sandwich the 3 layers of cake together with the cream filling.
7. Make the icing: put the chocolate and milk into a small, heavy saucepan. Heat gently, stirring, until smooth and thick. Cool slightly, then pour or spread over the top of the cake.

# CHOCOLATE FUDGE CAKE

*oil for greasing*
*110g/4oz butter*
*110g/4oz caster sugar*
*2 eggs*
*2 tablespoons golden syrup*
*30g/1oz ground almonds*
*110g/4oz self-raising flour*
*a pinch of salt*
*30g/1oz cocoa powder*

*For the icing*
*110g/4oz granulated sugar*
*110ml/4fl oz milk*
*140g/5oz plain chocolate, chopped*
*55g/2oz butter*
*2 tablespoons double cream*
*vanilla essence*

**1.** Preheat the oven to 180°C/350°F/gas mark 4.
**2.** Prepare an 18cm/7in deep cake tin (see page 583).
**3.** Cream the butter until soft. Add the sugar and beat until light and fluffy.
**4.** Whisk the eggs together and add a little at a time to the butter and sugar mixture, beating well after each addition. If the mixture curdles, beat in 1 teaspoon flour.
**5.** Stir in the golden syrup and ground almonds.
**6.** Sift the flour with the salt and cocoa powder and fold into the mixture, which should have a reluctant dropping consistency; if it is too thick add a little water or milk.
**7.** Pile the mixture into the prepared tin and smooth the top with a palette knife. Bake in the preheated oven for 40 minutes, or until the cake is well risen and feels spongy.
**8.** Turn out and cool on a wire rack. Peel off the lining paper.
**9.** Meanwhile, make the icing: put the sugar and milk into a saucepan. Allow the sugar to dissolve over a low heat then bring to the boil.
**10.** Remove the pan from the heat and stir in the chocolate; add the butter, cream and vanilla essence. Stir until completely melted.
**11.** Put into a bowl, cover and chill for 2 hours until the icing is spreadable.
**12.** When the cake is cool, split it in half horizontally and sandwich back together again using a quarter of the icing. Spread the remaining icing on the top and sides of the cake, swirling it to give a frosted appearance.

# RICE CAKE

*oil for greasing*
*110g/4oz butter*
*225g/8oz caster sugar*
*finely grated zest of ½ lemon*
*4 eggs*
*225g/8oz ground rice*

**1.** Preheat the oven to 180°C/350°F/gas mark 4.
**2.** Line an 18cm/7in cake tin with a double layer of greased and floured greaseproof paper.
**3.** Cream the butter until soft. Add sugar and beat until light and fluffy. Add the lemon zest and mix well.
**4.** Separate the eggs. Add the yolks to the mixture one at a time, beating hard all the time.
**5.** Whisk the egg whites until fairly stiff but not dry. Take a spoonful of egg white and mix it into the creamed mixture. Stir in half the ground rice. Add half the remaining egg white. Add the remaining ground rice, then the remaining egg white.
**6.** Pour the mixture into the prepared tin. Make a slight hollow in the centre of the mixture to counteract any tendency to rise in the middle.
**7.** Bake in the preheated oven for 45 minutes, or until firm to the touch and slightly shrunken at the edges.
**8.** Allow to cool in the tin for 5 minutes, then turn out on to a wire rack to cool completely. Peel off the lining paper.

# COFFEE BUNS

MAKES 12
*110g/4oz butter*
*110g/4oz caster sugar*
*2 eggs*
*110g/4oz self-raising flour*
*2 teaspoons instant coffee powder*
*¼ teaspoon vanilla essence*
*55g/2oz chopped walnuts*
*55g/2oz plain chocolate, grated*

**1.** Preheat the oven to 180°C/350°F/gas mark 4. Grease and flour 12 bun tins or paper cases.
**2.** Cream the butter and sugar until light and fluffy.
**3.** Beat in the eggs, a little at a time.
**4.** Fold in the flour, coffee, vanilla essence and walnuts. Add a little water if necessary to make a soft dropping consistency.
**5.** Fill the tins or paper cases two-thirds full and bake in the preheated oven for 15–20 minutes. Leave to cool on a wire rack.
**6.** Melt the chocolate on a heatproof plate over a saucepan of boiling water.
**7.** Spread each bun with a little melted chocolate and leave to cool and harden.

# SQUASHY RHUBARB CAKE

For the cake
*85g/3oz butter*
*85g/3oz sugar*
*2 small eggs*
*85g/3oz self-raising flour, sifted with a pinch of salt*
*milk*

For the filling
*675g/1½lb rhubarb, cut into 2.5cm/1in pieces*
*1 tablespoon sugar*

For the crumble topping
*55g/2oz butter*
*85g/3oz plain flour*
*30g/1oz sugar*

To finish
*icing sugar*

**1.** Preheat the oven to 190°C/375°F/gas mark 5.
**2.** Prepare a deep 20cm/8in cake tin (see page 583).
**3.** First make the crumble topping: rub the butter into the flour and add the sugar. Set aside.
**4.** Now make the cake: cream the butter until soft. Add the sugar and beat until very pale, light and fluffy.
**5.** Lightly beat the eggs and add them to the sugar mixture, beating in a little at a time, and folding in a spoonful of flour if the mixture curdles.
**6.** Fold in the remaining flour and add a few dribbles of milk if the mixture is too stiff; it should be of a dropping consistency.
**7.** Turn the mixture into the tin and smooth the top with a spatula.
**8.** Cover carefully with the raw rhubarb pieces and the sugar. Sprinkle with the crumble mixture.
**9.** Bake in the preheated oven for about 45 minutes, or until the cake feels firm on top. Leave to cool in the tin.
**10.** Just before serving, remove from the tin and sift a thin layer of icing sugar over the top.

NOTE: If using canned rhubarb, you will need a 450g/1lb can.

# PAIN DE GÊNES (RICH ALMOND CAKE)

This is a difficult cake to make. If the oven door is opened too early it will sink.

*melted butter for greasing*
*110g/4oz blanched almonds*
*3 eggs*
*140g/5oz caster sugar*
*55g/2oz potato starch or plain flour*
*½ teaspoon baking powder*
*a good pinch of salt*
*85g/3oz butter, melted and cooled*
*1 tablespoon Amaretto or Kirsch*

To finish
*icing sugar*

**1.** Preheat the oven to 180°C/350°F/gas mark 4.
**2.** Brush a moule-à-manqué or 20cm/8in cake tin with melted butter, line the bottom with a circle of greaseproof paper and brush it again.

**3.** Grind the almonds finely with 1 tablespoon of the sugar.

**4.** Whisk the eggs and remaining sugar together until light and fluffy.

**5.** Sift the potato starch or flour with the baking powder and salt into a bowl. Stir in the nuts. Half fold this mixture into the egg and sugar mixture.

**6.** Carefully fold the butter into the cake mixture with the minimum of stirring. Add the Amaretto or Kirsch. Pour the mixture into the prepared tin.

**7.** Bake in the preheated oven for 35–40 minutes, or until the cake is brown on top and springs back when lightly pressed with a finger.

**8.** Allow the cake to cool in the tin for 5 minutes, then loosen the sides with a knife and turn out on to a wire rack to cool. Peel off the lining paper. When cold, sift a thin layer of icing sugar over the top.

# WHISKED SPONGE

*oil for greasing*
*3 eggs*
*85g/3oz caster sugar*
*1½ tablespoons warm water*
*85g/3oz plain flour, sifted*
*a pinch of salt.*

**1.** Preheat the oven to 180°C/350°F/gas mark 4. Prepare a 20cm/8in cake tin (see page 583).

**2.** Place the eggs and sugar in a heatproof bowl set over, not in, a saucepan of simmering water. Whisk the mixture until light, thick and fluffy. (If using an electric mixer no heat is required.)

**3.** Remove the bowl from the heat and continue whisking until slightly cooled. Add the water.

**4.** Sift the flour with the salt and, using a large metal spoon, fold into the mixture, being careful not to beat out any of the air.

**5.** Turn the mixture into the prepared tin and bake in the middle of the preheated oven for about 30 minutes. When the cake is ready, it will shrink slightly and the edges will look crinkled. When pressed gently it will feel firm but spongy and will sound 'creaky'.

**6.** Turn out on to a wire rack to cool.

# SWISS ROLL

*melted lard or oil for greasing*
*85g/3oz plain flour, sifted*
*a pinch of salt*
*3 eggs*
*85g/3oz caster sugar*
*1½ tablespoons warm water*
*2–3 drops of vanilla essence*
*caster sugar*
*3 tablespoons warmed jam*

**1.** Preheat the oven to 180°C/350°F/gas mark 4.

**2.** Prepare a Swiss roll tin by brushing a little melted lard or oil on the bottom and sides. Place in it a piece of greaseproof paper cut to fit the bottom of the tin exactly and brush again with melted fat. Dust with flour and sugar. (If no Swiss roll tin is available, a baking sheet fitted with a tray of doubled greaseproof paper can be used instead.)

**3.** Sift the flour with the salt.

**4.** Put the eggs and sugar into a heatproof bowl set over, not in, a saucepan of simmering water. Whisk the mixture until light, thick and fluffy. (If using an electric mixer, no heat is required.) Continue whisking until slightly cooled.

**5.** Using a large metal spoon, fold the water, essence and flour into the egg mixture.

**6.** Pour the mixture into the prepared tin.

**7.** Bake in the preheated oven for 12–15 minutes, or until no imprints remains when the sponge is lightly pressed with a finger, and the edges look very slightly shrunken.

**8.** Lay a piece of greaseproof paper on a work top and sprinkle it evenly with caster sugar. Using a knife, loosen the edges of the baked sponge, then turn it over on to the sugared greaseproof paper. Remove the lining paper.

**9.** While the cake is still warm, spread it with the jam.

**10.** Using the paper under the cake to help you, roll the cake up firmly from one end. Making a little cut across the width of the cake just where you begin to roll helps to get a good tight Swiss roll.

**11.** Dredge the cake with caster sugar.

NOTE: If the cake is to be filled with cream, this cannot be done while it is hot. Roll the cake up, unfilled, and keep it wrapped in greaseproof paper until cool. Unroll carefully, spread with whipped cream, and roll up again.

# NORMANDY APPLE AND NUT CAKE

For the apple filling
*3 cooking apples (about 450g/1lb)*
*a little butter for greasing*
*1 strip of thinly pared lemon zest*
*about 85g/3oz soft light brown sugar*

For the cake
*butter for greasing*
*125g/4½oz caster sugar*
*40g/1½oz ground hazelnuts, toasted*
*4 egg yolks*
*50g/1¾oz plain flour, sifted*
*50g/1¾oz arrowroot*
*3 egg whites*

To finish
*icing sugar*
*150ml/¼ pint double cream, whipped*

**1.** Wash, quarter and core the unpeeled apples. Grease the bottom and sides of a heavy saucepan with butter. Slice the apples thickly into the pan and add the lemon zest and 4 tablespoons water. Cover and cook over a low heat, stirring occasionally, until completely soft.
**2.** Push through a sieve. Rinse out the pan and return the purée to it. Add at least 55g/2oz sugar to 570ml/1 pint purée. Cook rapidly until the mixture is of a dropping consistency (about 4 minutes). Leave to cool.
**3.** Preheat the oven to 180°C/350°F/gas mark 4. Butter a 20cm/8in moule-à-manqué or sandwich tin and dust it out with flour.
**4.** Beat the sugar, hazelnuts and egg yolks together until creamy and white, then fold in the flour and arrowroot.
**5.** Whisk the egg whites until stiff but not dry and fold them into the cake mixture. Turn into the prepared tin and smooth the top with a spatula.
**6.** Bake in the preheated oven for 40 minutes, until firm to the touch. Turn on to a wire rack to cool.
**7.** Split the cake and sandwich it with the apple filling. Dredge the top with icing sugar.
**8.** Serve with whipped cream.

# GÉNOISE COMMUNE

*oil for greasing*
*4 eggs*
*125g/4½oz caster sugar*
*55g/2oz butter, melted and cooled*
*125g/4½oz plain flour*

**1.** Preheat the oven to 190°C/375°F/gas mark 5.
**2.** Prepare a 20cm/8in moule-à-manqué or deep sandwich tin (see page 583).
**3.** Break the eggs into a large heatproof bowl and add the sugar. Set the bowl over, not in, a saucepan of simmering water and whisk until the mixture has doubled in bulk, and will leave a ribbon trail on the surface when the whisk is lifted. Lift the bowl off the heat and continue to whisk until slightly cooled. (If using an electric mixer, whisking need not be done over heat.) Pour the butter over the mixture but do not stir it in.
**4.** Sift the flour over the cake mixture and fold it in with the butter, using a large metal spoon.
**5.** Pour the mixture into the prepared tin. Bake in the preheated oven – the edges should look slightly shrunken and the top should spring back when pressed lightly with a fingertip – for 30–35 minutes. Allow to cool slightly in the tin before turning out on to a wire rack to cool completely. Peel off the lining paper.

# GÉNOISE FINE

*oil for greasing*
*4 eggs*
*125g/4½oz caster sugar*
*100g/3½oz butter, melted and cooled*
*100g/3½oz plain flour*

**1.** Preheat the oven to 190°C/375°F/gas mark 5.
**2.** Prepare a 20cm/8in moule-à-manqué or deep sandwich tin.
**3.** Break the eggs into a large bowl and add the sugar. Set the bowl over, not in, a saucepan of simmering water and whisk until light, fluffy and doubled in bulk. Remove from the heat and continue whisking until slightly cooled (if using an electric mixer, whisking need not be done over

593

heat). Pour the butter over the mixture but do not stir it in.

**4.** Sift the flour over the cake mixture and fold it in with the butter with a large metal spoon.

**5.** Turn the mixture into the prepared tin and bake in the preheated oven for 30–35 minutes – the edges should look slightly shrunken and the top should spring back when pressed lightly with a fingertip. Allow the cake to cool in the tin for a few minutes, then turn on to a wire rack to cool completely. Peel off the lining paper.

NOTE: This is sometimes called a 'butter sponge'. However, this description is not culinarily correct, as a true sponge contains no fat.

# COFFEE GÉNOISE WITH CHOCOLATE CARAQUE

For the cake
*oil for greasing*
*4 eggs*
*125g/4½oz caster sugar*
*55g/2oz butter, melted and cooled*
*100g/3½oz plain flour*
*2 teaspoons instant coffee powder*

For the coffee buttercream
*110g/4oz sugar*
*150ml/¼ pint milk*
*2 egg yolks*
*110g/4oz unsalted butter*
*110g/4oz salted butter*
*coffee essence*

For the chocolate caraque
*30g/1oz plain chocolate*

To decorate
*toasted chopped almonds*
*icing sugar*

**1.** Preheat the oven to 190°C/375°F/gas mark 5.
**2.** Prepare a 20cm/8in moule-à-manqué or deep sandwich tin (see page 583).
**3.** Break the eggs into a large heatproof bowl and add the sugar. Set the bowl over, not in, a saucepan of simmering water. Whisk until the mixture has doubled in bulk. Remove from the

heat and continue whisking until slightly cooled. (If using an electric mixer, whisking need not be done over heat.) Pour in the butter over the mixture but do not fold it in.

**4.** Sift the flour and coffee powder over the cake mixture and fold in thoroughly but gently with the butter using a large metal spoon. Turn the mixture into the prepared tin.

**5.** Bake for about 35 minutes or until cooked – the edges should look slightly shrunken and the top should spring back when pressed lightly with a fingertip. Allow the cake to cool slightly in the tin, then turn out on to a wire rack to cool completely. Peel off the paper lining.

**6.** Make the buttercream: put half the sugar and the milk into a saucepan and bring to the boil. Beat the egg yolks with the remaining sugar, pour on the milk, mix well and return the mixture to the saucepan. Stir over a low heat without boiling until slightly thickened. Strain and leave to cool.

**7.** Beat the butter until creamy and gradually whisk in the custard mixture. Flavour with coffee essence.

**8.** Make the chocolate caraque: melt the chocolate on a heatproof plate over a saucepan of boiling water. Spread thinly on a marble slab or other hard cold surface. When just set, use a long knife to shave off curls of chocolate: hold the knife with one hand on the handle and one hand on the tip of the blade. Hold it horizontally and scrape the chocolate surface by pulling the knife towards you. Chill the curls to harden them.

**9.** To decorate: split the cake in half and sandwich with one-third of the buttercream. Spread the tops and sides with the remainder. Press almonds on to the sides of the cake. Cover the top with a pile of caraque chocolate and sift over a very fine dusting of icing sugar.

NOTE: If you do not want to make caraque, the cake can be very simply and attractively decorated in the following manner. Melt the chocolate meant for the caraque and stir it into the coffee buttercream. Spread the icing as smoothly as possible on top of the cake. Lightly place a lacy paper doily over it. Sift icing sugar over cake and doily. Carefully remove the doily, taking pains to prevent the icing sugar on it from falling on to the cake.

# CHOCOLATE GÉNOISE

*oil or melted lard for greasing*
*4 eggs*
*110g/4oz caster sugar*
*55g/2oz unsalted butter, melted and cooled*
*85g/3oz plain flour, sifted*
*30g/1oz cocoa powder, sifted*

1. Preheat the oven to 190°C/375°F/gas mark 5.
2. Prepare a 20cm/8in moule-à-manqué tin (see page 583).
3. Whisk the eggs and sugar together until very light and fluffy. If you have an electric mixer, this should take 5 minutes. If not, the whisking has to be done with a balloon whisk in a bowl set over, not in, a saucepan of simmering water and it can take up to 10 minutes. Be careful not to allow the base of the bowl to become too hot.
4. The mixture should then be whisked until slightly cooled. It is ready when it leaves a ribbon trail when the whisk is lifted. Do not over-whisk and stop if it begins to lose bulk. Pour the butter over the mixture but do not fold it in.
5. Fold the flour and cocoa powder into the mixture with the butter, using a large metal spoon.
6. Tip the mixture into the prepared tin and give a light tap on the work top to get rid of any large air pockets. Bake in the preheated oven for 25–35 minutes – the edges should look slightly shrunken and the top should spring back when pressed lightly with a fingertip. Allow the cake to cool in the tin for 2 minutes, then turn out on to a wire rack to cool completely. Peel off the lining paper.

# VERY RICH CHOCOLATE CAKE

This is an adaptation of a Martha Stewart recipe.

For the cake
*55g/2oz sultanas, chopped*
*55ml/2fl oz brandy*
*oil for greasing*
*3 eggs, separated*
*140g/5oz caster sugar*

*200g/7oz plain chocolate, chopped evenly*
*2 tablespoons water*
*110g/4oz unsalted butter*
*55g/2oz plain flour, sifted*
*85g/3oz ground almonds*

For the icing
*140g/5oz dark chocolate, cut into small pieces*
*150ml/¼ pint double cream*

1. Soak the sultanas in the brandy overnight.
2. Preheat the oven to 180°C/350°F/gas mark 4.
3. Prepare a 20cm/8in moule-à-manqué or cake tin (see page 583).
4. Beat the egg yolks and sugar until pale and mousse-like.
5. Put the chocolate and water into a heatproof bowl set over, not in, a saucepan of simmering water. Stir until melted, then stir in the butter piece by piece until the mixture is smooth. Stir into the egg-yolk mixture.
6. Very carefully fold the flour into the egg yolk and chocolate mixture with the ground almonds, sultanas and brandy.
7. Whisk the egg whites until stiff but not dry and fold into the chocolate mixture.
8. Turn the mixture into the prepared tin and bake in the preheated oven for 35–40 minutes (the centre should still be moist). Leave to get completely cold in the tin.
9. Remove the cake from the tin and place it on a wire rack. Peel off the lining paper.
10. Make the icing: heat together the chocolate and cream. Stir until all the chocolate has melted and the mixture is smooth. Allow to cool and thicken to a coating consistency before pouring it over the cake.
11. Leave for at least 2 hours to allow the icing to harden.

# CHOCOLATE AND ORANGE GÂTEAU

For the candied orange peel
*1 orange*
*110g/4oz granulated sugar*
*150ml/¼ pint water*
*2 tablespoons golden syrup*
*55g/2oz caster sugar*

For the chocolate sponge cake
*oil for greasing*
*55g/2oz plain flour*
*55g/2oz cornflour*
*3 tablespoons cocoa powder*
*a pinch of baking powder*
*4 eggs*
*salt*
*110g/4oz caster sugar*

For the orange syrup
*55g/2oz granulated sugar*
*85ml/3fl oz water*
*3 tablespoons fresh orange juice or Grand
   Marnier*

For the orange filling
*55g/2oz orange marmalade*
*2 tablespoons fresh orange juice or Grand
   Marnier*

For the whipped ganache filling
*340g/12oz plain chocolate*
*225ml/8fl oz double cream*

For the ganache glaze
*225g/8oz plain chocolate*
*225ml/8fl oz double cream*

## CANDIED ORANGE PEEL

1. Peel the zest off the orange and cut into strips 2mm/⅛in wide. Put the zest into a small saucepan and cover with water. Bring to the boil and simmer for 5 minutes. This softens the zest and removes the bitter flavour. Drain and rinse under cold water.
2. Bring the granulated sugar, water and golden syrup slowly to the boil in a heavy saucepan, ensuring that the sugar has dissolved before the liquid boils. Remove from the heat.

3. Stir in the zest and allow it to stand for 30 minutes. Bring it back to the boil and set aside for a further 30 minutes.
4. Remove the strips of orange zest from the syrup, one at a time, with a fork, and put them on a wire rack to dry.
5. Spread the caster sugar on a plate and roll the cooled orange zest in it. Put in a warm dry place to dry out, keeping the pieces separate. These can be made one week ahead.

## CHOCOLATE ORANGE CAKE

1. Preheat the oven to 180°C/350°F/gas mark 4.
2. Prepare a 22cm/9in cake tin (see page 583).
3. Sift the flours, cocoa and baking powder together.
4. Place the eggs, a pinch of salt and the sugar in a large heatproof bowl set over, not in, a saucepan of simmering water. Whisk until the mixture is light, thick and fluffy and holds a good trail when the whisk is lifted. (If using an electric mixer no heat is required.)
5. Carefully fold the sifted dry ingredients into the egg mixture in 2 batches.
6. Turn the mixture into the prepared tin and bake in the centre of the preheated oven for about 35 minutes, or until the cake is firm to the touch and just shrinking away from the edges of the tin. Loosen the sides of the cake and turn on to a wire rack to cool completely. Peel off the lining paper.

## ORANGE SYRUP

1. Dissolve the sugar in the water in a heavy saucepan and bring to the boil. Allow to boil for a minute, then allow to cool. Once the syrup is cool stir in the orange juice or liqueur.

## ORANGE FILLING

1. Stir the marmalade and orange juice or liqueur together in a small bowl.

## WHIPPED GANACHE FILLING

1. Chop the chocolate into small pieces. Bring the cream to boiling point in a saucepan. Remove from the heat and stir in the chocolate. Let the mixture stand for 2 minutes, then beat until smooth. Cool at room temperature. Do not refrigerate.

## GANACHE GLAZE

1. Make in exactly the same way as the whipped ganache filling. This may be made 2 hours in advance. Do not refrigerate.

## TO ASSEMBLE THE CAKE

**1.** Beat the ganache filling with an electric hand mixer for 2 minutes until it has lightened in colour and texture.

**2.** Split the sponge cake horizontally into 3 layers. Using a pastry brush, moisten the bottom layer of the cake with some of the syrup. Spread with half the orange filling and then with a quarter of the whipped ganache.

**3.** Put the second layer of sponge on top, moisten that with syrup, spread with the remaining orange filling and then a further quarter of the whipped ganache. Cover with the top layer of cake and moisten with the remaining syrup.

**4.** Spread the top and sides with whipped ganache, reserving some for decoration. Refrigerate for at least 30 minutes or until the ganache becomes firm.

**5.** Place the gâteau on a wire rack over a tray. Pour the cool ganache glaze over the top and sides. Smooth with a palette knife. Refrigerate until set.

**6.** Put the remaining whipped ganache into a piping bag with a star nozzle and pipe out 12 rosettes around the edge of the gâteau. Decorate with the candied orange peel, just before serving.

NOTE: This cake can be assembled and refrigerated overnight. It tastes better if given a day to mature. It also freezes well – without the candied orange zest.

# GÂTEAU NOUGATINE

For the cake
*oil for greasing*
*110g/4oz hazelnuts*
*4 eggs*
*1 egg white*
*110g/4oz caster sugar*
*55g/2oz butter, melted and cooled*
*100g/3½oz plain flour*

For the royal icing
*1 small egg white*
*170g/6oz icing sugar*
*a squeeze of lemon juice*

For the nougat
*45g/1½oz finely chopped almonds*
*85g/3oz caster sugar*
*½ teaspoon powdered glucose or a pinch of cream of tartar*
*1 lemon*
*a little oil*

For the crème au beurre mousseline
*85g/3oz lump or granulated sugar*
*3 tablespoons water*
*2 egg yolks*
*110–140g/4–5oz unsalted butter*

For the chocolate fondant icing
*22.5g/8oz loaf sugar*
*½ teaspoon liquid glucose or a pinch of cream of tartar*
*115ml/4fl oz water*
*30g/1oz plain chocolate*
*1 drop of vanilla essence*

**1.** Preheat the oven to 180°C/350°F/gas mark 4.
**2.** Prepare a 20cm/8in moule-à-manqué tin (see page 00).
**3.** Make the cake: brown the hazelnuts in the oven. Remove the skins. Cool and grind with 1 tablespoon of the sugar.
**4.** Separate the eggs. Beat the yolks and 1 egg white with all but 1 tablespoon of the remaining sugar, until white and creamy.
**5.** Whisk the remaining egg whites until stiff. Whisk in the reserved sugar.
**6.** Pour the butter around the edge of the egg-yolk mixture. Add the dry ingredients and the meringue and fold swiftly together.
**7.** Pile into the prepared tin and smooth the top with a spatula. Bake in the preheated oven for 40–50 minutes, or until the cake is firm to the touch and just shrinking away from the sides of the tin. Cool on a wire rack. Peel off the lining paper.
**8.** Make the royal icing: whisk the egg white until frothy. Beat the icing sugar into it with the lemon juice until very smooth, white and stiff. Cover with a damp cloth until ready for use.
**9.** Oil a baking sheet.
**10.** Make the nougat: bake the chopped almonds until pale brown. Keep warm. Put the sugar and glucose into a heavy saucepan and place over a

medium heat. When golden, add the warm
almonds and continue to cook for 1 minute.

**11.** Turn the mixture on to the oiled baking sheet.
Turn it over with an oiled palette knife, using a
half-mixing, half-kneading motion. While still
warm and pliable, roll as thinly as possible with
an oiled lemon.

**12.** Make the crème au beurre mousseline:
dissolve the sugar in the water. Boil to the short
thread stage (a little syrup stretched between a
wet finger and thumb will form a short thread).
Whisk the yolks as you pour on the sugar syrup
in a steady stream. Whisk until thick and mousse-
like. Cream the butter and, when soft, add the
mousse mixture to the butter.

**13.** Make the chocolate fondant icing: dissolve the
sugar and liquid glucose in the water in a heavy
saucepan over a low heat without boiling. Cover
and bring to the boil. Boil to the soft ball stage
(see page 477). Meanwhile, scrub a stainless steel
work top and sprinkle with water. Stop the sugar
syrup from cooking further by dipping the bottom
of the pan into a bowl of very cold water. Cool
slightly.

**14.** Chop the chocolate and melt it in a heatproof
bowl set over, not in, a saucepan of simmering
water. Pour the sugar syrup slowly on to the
moistened stainless steel top. With a wet palette
knife, fold the outsides of the mixture into the
centre. When opaque but still fairly soft, add the
melted chocolate and vanilla essence and continue
to turn with a spatula and work until the fondant
becomes fairly stiff. Put in a bowl and stand over
a saucepan of simmering water to soften.

**15.** To assemble: split the cake into 3 layers.
Crush the nougat with a rolling pin and mix half
of it with half the crème au beurre mousseline.
Sandwich the cake together with this. Pour the
melted chocolate fondant icing over the top.
Spread crème au beurre around the sides and
press on the remaining crushed nougat.

**16.** When the chocolate has set, fill a piping bag
fitted with a writing nozzle with the royal icing
and pipe the word 'nougatine' across the top.

# BLACK CHERRY CAKE

*1 × 400g/14oz can of black cherries, pitted*
*Kirsch*
*290ml/½ pint double cream*
*1 chocolate génoise cake (see page 595)*
*85g/3oz plain chocolate, grated*
*3 tablespoons water*
*110g/4oz icing sugar*
*about 55g/2oz split almonds, toasted*
*icing sugar for dusting*

**1.** Sprinkle the cherries with a little Kirsch.

**2.** Whip the cream until it just holds its shape.

**3.** Split the cake into 3 thin rounds. On the
bottom layer spread about one-third of the cream
and sprinkle with half the cherries. Place the next
layer of cake on top. Spread on another third of
cream and the rest of the cherries. Place the top
round on and flatten gently with your hands.

**4.** Place the chocolate in a small, heavy saucepan
with the water and stir over a low heat until
smooth, taking care not to boil.

**5.** Sift the icing sugar into a bowl and blend in the
chocolate, adding a little extra water if necessary. Do
this drop by drop to make a thick, pouring consistency. Pour over the top of the cake and allow to set.

**6.** Spread the remaining cream around the sides of
the cake and press the almonds against it.

**7.** Cut 3 strips of paper about 25cm/10in long and
about 2.5cm/1in wide. Place them over the cake
about 2.5cm/1in apart and sift over a heavy
dusting of icing sugar.

**8.** Remove the paper strips carefully to reveal a
striped brown and white top.

# DOBEZ TORTE

This is a cake with 5 layers. The mixture will not
deteriorate if all the layers cannot be baked at the
same time because of a lack of baking sheets or
space in the oven.

For the cake
*4 eggs*
*170g/6oz caster sugar*
*140g/5oz plain flour*
*a pinch of salt*

For the buttercream
*85g/3oz granulated sugar*
*4–5 tablespoons water*
*3 egg yolks*
*225g/8oz unsalted butter*
*coffee essence*
*55g/2oz hazelnuts, toasted, skinned and ground*

To decorate
*140g/5oz caster sugar*
*2 tablespoons toasted chopped almonds or*
*    toasted ground hazelnuts*
*6 whole toasted, skinned hazelnuts*

1. Preheat the oven to 190°C/375°F/gas mark 5. Grease and flour 5 baking sheets and mark a 20cm/8in circle on each sheet with a flan ring or saucepan lid.
2. Make the cake: whisk the eggs in a large heatproof bowl, adding the sugar gradually. Set the bowl over, not in, a saucepan of simmering water and whisk until the mixture is thick and mousse-like. Remove from the heat and whisk until slightly cooled. Sift the flour and salt and fold into the egg mixture with a metal spoon. Divide the mixture between the 5 baking sheets and spread into the circles as marked.
3. Bake in the preheated oven for 8 minutes. Trim the edges and leave to cool on a wire rack.
4. Make the buttercream: dissolve the sugar in the water and, when clear, boil rapidly to the short thread stage. (To test, put a little sugar syrup on to a wooden spoon, dip your index finger and thumb into cold water and then into the syrup in the spoon. When you pull your finger and thumb apart there should be a short thread of syrup between them.) Allow the syrup to cool slightly for about 1 minute.
5. Whisk the egg yolks in a bowl and then pour the syrup slowly on to them, whisking all the time. Keep whisking until you have a thick mousse-like mixture. Cream the butter well and beat in the egg and sugar mixture. Cool. Flavour 2 tablespoons of the buttercream with coffee essence and reserve for decoration. Mix the ground hazelnuts and the remaining coffee essence into the remaining mixture.
6. Lay one round of cake on a wire rack over an oiled tray. Melt the sugar for the caramel in a little water and, when dissolved, boil fiercely until

a good caramel colour, then pour immediately over the piece of cake, covering it completely.
7. Allow to harden slightly and mark into 6 portions with an oiled knife, cutting through the setting caramel but not through the cake. Trim the edges of excess caramel.
8. Sandwich the cake layers together with the coffee and hazelnut buttercream, placing the one with caramel on top. Spread the coffee and hazelnut buttercream thinly around the sides and press on the nuts.
9. Put the remaining plain buttercream into a piping bag fitted with a large star nozzle, and pipe a rosette on top of each portion of cake. Decorate each rosette with a whole hazelnut.

# BLACK STICKY GINGERBREAD

*butter for greasing*
*225g/8oz butter*
*225g/8oz soft dark brown sugar*
*225g/8oz black treacle*
*340g/12oz plain flour*
*2 teaspoons ground ginger*
*1 tablespoon ground cinnamon*
*2 eggs, beaten*
*290ml/½ pint milk*
*2 teaspoons bicarbonate of soda*

1. Preheat the oven to 150°C/300°F/gas mark 2.
2. Grease a 30 × 20cm/12 ×8in roasting pan with butter and line the base and sides with greaseproof paper.
3. Melt the butter, sugar and treacle in a saucepan. Cool to room temperature.
4. Sift the flour with the ginger and cinnamon, then stir in the melted mixture with the beaten eggs. Warm the milk to blood heat, pour it on to the soda, stir it in and add it to the mixture. Stir well and pour the mixture into the prepared tin.
5. Bake in the preheated oven for about 1 hour. Cover the top with greaseproof paper after 45 minutes. It is cooked when a skewer inserted into the centre comes out clean.
6. When the gingerbread is cold, cut it into fingers and serve it spread with butter. This gingerbread keeps very well: in fact, it improves.

# BANANA CAKE

110g/4oz butter
55g/2oz caster sugar
2 drops of vanilla essence
1 teaspoon ground cardamom
2 eggs, beaten
170g/6oz self-raising flour
2 ripe bananas
55g/2oz walnuts, roughly chopped
milk, if necessary

1. Preheat the oven to 180°C/350°F/gas mark 4.
2. Cream the butter in a mixing bowl, and beat in the sugar until light and fluffy. Add the vanilla essence and ground cardamom.
3. Add the beaten eggs gradually, adding a little flour every time the mixture begins to curdle. Beat very well.
4. Peel the bananas and mash well with a fork.
5. Add half the bananas to the cake mixture.
6. Stir in half the flour. Add the remaining bananas with the walnuts.
7. Stir in the remaining flour. Add a little milk if necessary – the mixture should fall reluctantly off a spoon. Pile into a non-stick loaf tin.
8. Bake in the preheated oven for 45 minutes or until the cake is risen and golden and a skewer inserted into the centre comes out clean.
9. Allow the cake to cool for a few minutes in the tin, then turn out on to a wire rack to cool completely.
10. Serve with or without butter.

# ALL-IN-ONE CHOCOLATE CAKE

85g/3oz self-raising flour
a pinch of salt
30g/1oz cocoa powder
2 eggs
110g/4oz caster sugar
110g/4oz very soft butter
2–3 drops of vanilla essence
2–3 tablespoons warm water
soured cream and chocolate icing (see page 638)

1. Preheat the oven to 180°C/350°F/gas mark 4.
2. Prepare a 10cm/7in cake tin (see page 583).
3. Sift the flour with the salt into a bowl. Add the cocoa powder.
4. Add the eggs, sugar, butter and vanilla essence.
5. Beat with an electric whisk for 2 minutes.
6. Add the warm water and beat for a further minute.
7. Turn the mixture into the prepared tin. Bake in the preheated oven for 25–30 minutes, or until firm to the touch. Turn out on to a wire rack and leave to cool.
8. Split the cake in half and sandwich it together with half the icing. Use the remaining icing to cover the top of the cake.

# KULICH

This Russian Easter cake recipe has been adapted from a recipe in the *Observer Guide to European Cookery* by Jane Grigson.

570g/1¼lb plain flour, sifted
1 packet of dried yeast
180ml/6fl oz warm milk
¼ teaspoon salt
3 egg yolks
140g/5oz caster sugar
3 cardamom pods, seeded and crushed
140g/5oz butter, softened
3 egg whites
75g/2½oz raisins
30g/1oz each candied fruit and blanched almonds, chopped

To decorate (optional):
blanched almonds, chopped, candied fruit and peel or white glacé icing

1. Mix 225g/8oz of the flour with the yeast in a mixing bowl, then stir in the milk. Put the mixture into a polythene bag and leave in a warm place until spongy and doubled in size (about 1 hour).
2. Mix in the salt, 2½ egg yolks (reserve about half a yolk for glazing the kulich later), sugar, cardamom and butter. Whisk the egg whites until stiff and fold in with 225g/8oz more flour. The

dough will be on the wet and sticky side. Add the remaining flour gradually until the dough leaves the sides of the bowl. If it is a little sticky, do not worry too much. Put in a warm place and leave to rise again (about 2–3 hours).

**3.** Knock down the dough and add the fruits and almonds. Divide between 2 buttered and floured tall round moulds, such as large brioche tins. If you have no suitable moulds, use coffee tins. The dough should come half or two-thirds of the way up the tins. Leave in a warm place to prove for about 1 hour.

**4.** Preheat the oven to 180°C/350°F/gas mark 4. Bake the kulichs for about 45 minutes. Check after 35 minutes by inserting a cocktail stick or thin skewer, which should come out clean. When the dough is cooked, the cake should have the appearance of a chef's hat.

**5.** When ready, turn out and brush with the remaining egg yolk and decorate, if you like, with chopped fruit and nuts, or icing, pouring it on so that it dribbles down the sides. At Easter time, stick a candle in the top of each cake.

# REASONS FOR FAILURE IN CAKE-MAKING

### Creamed cakes

| | |
|---|---|
| Close texture | Eggs added too quickly, making the mixture curdle |
| Flat, dense cake | Wrong flour used or no raising agent added |
| Flattish cake with large bubbles on surface | a) Long delay before cake put in oven |
| | b) Oven temperature too low |
| Base and sides of cake wet and soggy | Cake not turned on to a wire rack to cool |

### Fruit cakes

| | |
|---|---|
| Cake risen to a peak | No dip put in the cake mixture prior to baking |
| Hard, dark crust round base and sides | a) Cake tin not lined |
| | b) Oven too hot |
| | c) Cake overcooked |
| Fruit, e.g. cherries, sunk to bottom of cake | a) Not enough care taken to beat air into cake |
| | b) Cake mixture too liquid |
| | c) Too little flour |
| | d) Cherries (which can be very sticky) have not been washed, dried and dusted with flour prior to adding to the mixture |

### Whisked sponges

| | |
|---|---|
| Unrisen sponge | Not whisked enough before flour added |
| Unrisen génoise with large bubbles on the top | Butter overfolded into the mixture |
| Flat sponge with very hard crust | Egg and sugar mixture too hot when flour folded in |
| Pockets of flour in cake | Flour underfolded into cake |

## Melted method cakes, e.g. gingerbreads

| | |
|---|---|
| Slightly fizzy taste | Too much bicarbonate of soda |
| Greeny, orange colour | Too much bicarbonate of soda |
| Cake sunk in the middle | a) Open door opened during cooking |
| | b) Cake not put in oven soon enough |

## General mistakes

| | |
|---|---|
| Cake risen to high peak with the surface cracked | a) Too much raising agent |
| | b) Oven temperature too high |
| | c) Cake tin too small |
| Thick crust all around cake | Overcooked |
| Thick, crunchy crust round base and sides | Too much oil, butter or lard used to grease the tin |
| Cake sunk in middle | a) Not cooked for long enough |
| | b) Oven door opened before cake has set, causing cake to collapse |
| Hard, shiny crust | Too much sugar |
| Cake overflowed over sides of tin | Cake tin too small |
| Cake good texture but very thin and overcooked | Cake tin too big |
| Cake leaked out of the bottom of loose-bottomed tin | a) Tin not lined |
| | b) Wrong type of tin for particular cake |
| Dense, heavy texture | Cake mixed too quickly, e.g. not enough air beaten in |
| Cake stuck to tin | a) Tin not greased |
| | b) Tin not lined |
| | c) Silicone non-stick baking parchment not used when specified in recipe |

# BREADS
# AND BUNS

---

# BREAD-MAKING

With the advent of factory-made bread, bread-making became, for a while, almost a lost art amongst home cooks. It has recently been rediscovered and many people make the time to produce their own bread. Bread-making can be improved by understanding what is happening to the dough as it rises and bakes and what factors affect it. Once the process is understood, the cook can branch out from plain white bread to breads that contain nuts, herbs, fruits, vegetables, cheeses and different seeds and grains.

## YEAST

Baker's yeast, the most usual leavening agent for bread, is a single-celled organism that belongs to the fungus family. For yeast to reproduce it needs warmth, moisture and food. Given the right conditions it can reproduce very quickly, giving off carbon dioxide as it does so. This is trapped in the dough or batter and so aerates it. The optimum temperature for yeast to reproduce is 27°C/80°F. Too much heat can kill it so care must be taken to ensure that the liquid used in making bread is lukewarm. A high concentration of sugar, fat or salt can slow down its rates of reproduction. If a dough is high in these ingredients then more yeast must be used. There are three types of yeast available: fresh, dried and easy-blend dried yeast.

Fresh yeast should be beige, crumbly-soft and sweet-smelling. It is usually thought of as the most satisfactory form of baker's yeast as it is less likely to produce 'beery' bread. Fresh yeast keeps for five days or so wrapped loosely in the refrigerator, and can be frozen for short periods, though results after freezing are unpredictable. If it is difficult to obtain, use dried yeast, or buy fresh yeast in a suitable quantity, divide it into 30g/1oz pieces, wrap them individually, then overwrap and freeze. Use as soon as the yeast thaws, and do not keep frozen for more than a month.

Dried yeast is bought in granular form in airtight sachets. It will remain active for about 6 months in a cool, dry place. If substituting dried for fresh yeast when following a recipe, halve the weight of yeast called for. Dried yeast takes slightly longer to work than fresh yeast, and must first be 'sponged' in liquid, partly to reconstitute it, partly to check that it is still active. To avoid any beery taste, use rather less than the amount of dried yeast called for and allow a long rising and proving time. Using too much yeast generally means too fast a rise, resulting in bread with a coarse texture that goes stale quickly.

Easy-blend dried yeast is mixed directly with the flour, not reconstituted in liquid first. Sold in small airtight packages, it is usually included in bought bread mixtures. One 7g/¼oz package usually equals 15g/½oz conventional dried yeast or 30g/1oz fresh yeast.

## FLOUR

Flour is the main ingredient in bread and gives it its individual character. Wheat flour is the most common because it contains a large amount of gluten, a form of protein that absorbs liquid to produce elastic strands in the dough. As the yeast works, it gives off carbon dioxide, which is trapped in the expanding dough, making it rise and puff up. When the loaf is baked and set rigidly, the gas leaks out and is replaced by air.

RYE, MAIZE, MILLET and other flours contain less gluten than wheat flour. Because these flours lack the essential elasticity of wheat gluten, some wheat flour is usually added to the dough to produce a light-textured, well-risen loaf.

WHITE FLOUR is ground from wheat with the outer bran and inner germ removed, leaving 70–75 per cent of the original wheat. Removing the wheatgerm means the flour keeps longer, while removing the bran makes the flour lighter and finer. On the other hand, it will have fewer vitamins. For this reason white flours, whether bleached or unbleached, have B vitamins and other nutrients added to them in most countries. With or without such additions, bread made from white flour will have less flavour and less fibre than that made from wholegrain flour.

STRONG FLOUR is white flour made from varieties of wheat known as 'hard' wheat, which contain a particularly high proportion of gluten. Also called bread flour, the best comes from North America and is usually known as durum wheat. It is highly suitable for bread-making, giving the dough a remarkable capacity to expand and rise and produce a light, well-risen, springy loaf.

WEAK, SOFT OR HOUSEHOLD FLOUR is made from wheat grown mainly in Europe. It has less expansive gluten, produces a less elastic dough and bakes to a heavier, more crumbly bread. It makes excellent cakes and biscuits where crumbliness and non-elasticity are advantages.

PLAIN FLOUR is general, all-purpose flour suitable for sauces, cakes and breads, even though it does not have the high gluten content of strong flour. In Europe, where plain flour contains more soft wheat, it is less suitable for making breads than the plain or all-purpose flour used in North America, which contains more hard wheat.

SELF-RAISING FLOUR is usually made from soft wheat. A raising agent – usually a mixture of bicarbonate of soda and cream of tartar – is mixed with the flour. It is not used in yeast cookery, though some 'breads', such as wholemeal soda bread, are made with it.

WHOLEMEAL OR WHOLEWHEAT FLOUR is milled from the whole grain so that it contains the germ and the bran. Most of the B vitamins are in the wheatgerm, while bran provides roughage necessary for the digestive system. Bread made from wholemeal flour is undoubtedly healthier, but regardless of its natural gluten, it produces a heavier loaf. Also, the oil in the wheatgerm means that wholemeal bread will not keep as well as a white loaf. A mixture of wholemeal and white flour is a good compromise.

STONEGROUND FLOUR is usually wholemeal flour that has been milled between stone rollers rather than by modern milling methods. It is a coarser and heavier flour, even in its white version, than factory-milled flour, so more yeast or a longer rising time is needed to make it rise. It is claimed that more of the wheat's nutrients are retained as the grain is kept cooler during stone-grinding.

WHEATMEAL FLOUR, judging by its name, should refer to any wheat flour. However, the term is used by commercial bakers to describe brown bread flour that is not wholemeal. The colour may simply come from dye. Containing little or no bran or wheatgerm, it makes a lighter loaf. It is usually no more nutritious or 'healthy' than refined white flour.

## OTHER BREAD INGREDIENTS
LIQUIDS For plain everyday bread the only liquid needed is water. It gives a crisp crust and a fairly hard or chewy bread. Milk produces a softer bread and a golden crust and is said by some to increase the keeping quality of bread. Beer gives the bread an individual, malty taste.

SALT is very important in bread. It affects not only the flavour but also the rising action of the yeast, the texture of the loaf and the crust. Without salt the flavour of the loaf can be bland. If a quick rising time is required, more yeast and less salt are needed, as in a pizza dough for example. If a dough does not seem to be rising very fast it is worth tasting it. If it tastes noticeably salty, the dough will produce a tough, badly risen loaf.

SUGAR is often included in savoury recipes for bread as a starter for the yeast. Too much sugar retards the yeast, so sweet doughs usually have a high proportion of yeast. White, demerara and brown sugars are used in doughs as well as molasses, black treacle and golden syrup. Honey can be substituted for golden syrup.

FATS added to a yeast dough include butter, lard, oil and vegetable fats. Butter gives a very good flavour and a good-looking crust. It can impede the action of the yeast and so a dough that is heavily enriched with butter, such as brioche dough, may not rise as much as an ordinary dough. Oil makes bread wonderfully easy to knead even when added in small quantities, for example 2 tablespoons to 675g/1½lb flour. Olive oil is the best oil to use, but alternatives are sunflower, peanut or sesame oil.

## STAGES IN BREAD-MAKING

It is important to create the right conditions for the yeast to grow so that the dough will be elastic and accommodate the maximum carbon dioxide.

1. If the yeast is fresh, first cream it in a warm, not hot, cup with about 1 teaspoonful caster sugar until smooth, then with a spoonful of lukewarm water. Dried yeast should be mixed with a little sweetened lukewarm water and left in a warm place for about 15 minutes. Once the yeast liquid is frothy, or 'sponges', add it to the flour, and mix in any remaining ingredients specified. If it does not froth, the yeast is dead and should not be used. Some recipes, usually those enriched with fat and sugar, require the yeast mixture and all the liquid to be beaten with a small proportion of the flour to a yeasty batter, called the starter, and left in a warm place until it 'sponges'. Then the remaining flour is added and the mixing completed. This method used to be common to all breads. The process takes longer but is said by old-fashioned bakers to produce the lightest, most even-textured bread.

2. Kneading, or manipulating, the dough, is the next stage. It is necessary in order to distribute the yeast cells evenly and promote the dough's elasticity. The length of time for kneading varies according to the type of flour and the skill of the kneader, but the dough must lose its stickiness and become smooth, elastic and shiny – this usually takes about 15 minutes.

Techniques vary, but the most common is to push the lump of dough down and away with the heel of the hand, then to pull it back with the fingers, slap it on the work top and repeat the process, turning the dough slightly with each movement. Table-top electric mixers with dough hooks or robust food processors can also be used for kneading. Kneading in a machine takes less time than kneading by hand, but follow the manufacturer's instructions closely. Once kneaded, the dough is formed into a ball and put into a lightly oiled, warmed – not hot – bowl, and turned to coat it evenly with grease to prevent hardening and cracking. The bowl is covered with a piece of clingfilm or a damp cloth, put in a warm (32°C/90°F) draught-free place and left until about 1½ times its original size. The dough should spring back when pressed lightly with a floured finger. The longer the rising takes the better. Too rapidly risen or over-risen bread has a coarse texture and a beery smell.

3. Knocking back is the next process. The risen dough is knocked down, or punched with the knuckles to push out air that may have formed large, unevenly shaped holes. Punched to its original size, it is then kneaded briefly to make it pliable. Extra sugar or dried fruit are usually added at this point, before the dough is shaped and put into a loaf tin or on to a baking sheet.

4. Proving is the second rising of the dough. When this is completed, the loaf will have doubled in bulk and should look the size and shape you hope the finished bread will be. Proving can be done in a slightly warmer place, about 38°C/100°F, for a shorter time, about 20 minutes, because the previous rising and further kneading will have made the dough even more elastic and it will rise more easily. With a second rising, the bread will be lighter when baked.

5. The bread will continue to rise in the oven for a short time partly because of the rising steam in the loaf and partly because of the rising steam in the loaf and partly because the yeast keeps working until the dough reaches 60°C/140°F. Then the heat of the oven will cook the dough into a rigid shape. Called 'oven spring', this final rising is likely to push the top crust away from the body of the loaf. To avoid too much oven spring, bread is baked at a fairly high temperature to kill the yeast quickly.

6. The baked bread should be golden-brown and have shrunk slightly from the sides of the tin. To

make sure that the bread is done, it should be turned out on to a cloth and tapped on the underside. If it sounds hollow, it is done. If not, it should be returned to the oven, on its side, without the tin. Bread is cooled on a wire rack. After 2 hours, it will slice easily. Once stone-cold it may be stored in a bread tin or a plastic bag. A lukewarm loaf stored in an airtight container will become soggy, if not mouldy.

## SODA BREAD

Soda bread has bicarbonate of soda as a raising agent. However, in order to activate the soda an acid must be included in the ingredients. This is usually cream of tartar, which must be sifted with the bicarbonate of soda and the other dry ingredients to incorporate it thoroughly. When liquid is added to the dough, the alkali (bicarbonate of soda) and acid (cream of tartar) enter a chemical reaction and form carbonic acid gas. As soon as this is liberated the dough must go into the oven or the bread will not work and the flavour will be impaired. In some recipes cream of tartar is replaced by sour milk or buttermilk. These doughs are the exact opposite of yeast doughs. High-speed mixing and quick light handling are required, rather than careful mixing and vigorous kneading.

## SHAPES FOR ROLLS

These shapes are made using approximately 55g/2oz made-up bread dough each. Once the dough has had its first rising, knock it back and divide into equal-sized pieces of dough. A 450g/1lb flour quantity of bread dough will make 16 rolls. Rolls have to be made and shaped quickly or the first rolls will have overproved before the last rolls have been shaped.

PLAIN ROLLS Roll the dough into a ball on the

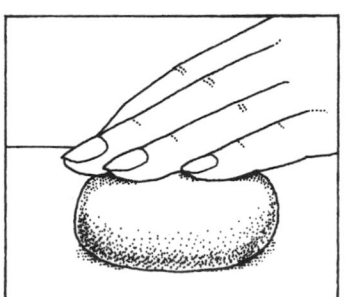

*Plain roll*

work top, pinching with the fingers to create a smooth surface on the underside. Turn the roll over, place on a baking sheet and press down slightly.

BAPS As above except that when they are placed on the baking sheet press down firmly to make them round and flattish.

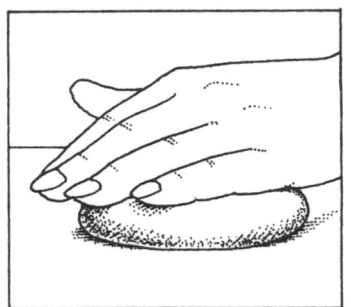

*Bap*

KNOTS Shape the dough, with your hands, into a sausage about 10cm/4in long. Carefully, without stretching, tie into a knot.

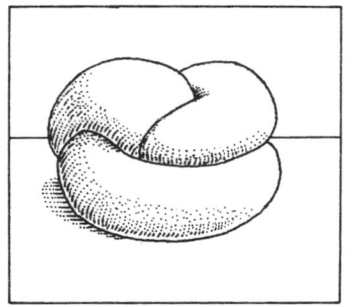

*Knot*

PLAITS Divide the dough into 3 equal pieces and shape each piece into a sausage about 10cm/4in long. Put 2 pieces parallel to each other 2.5cm/1in apart, and put the third one across them, threading it under the left-hand piece and over the right-hand piece. Starting from the middle, take the left-hand piece and place it over the right-hand piece and proceed as for a plait (see diagrams). When one end is completed turn the plait over so that the unplaited pieces are towards you and proceed as before.

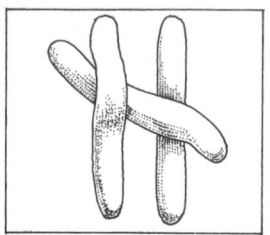

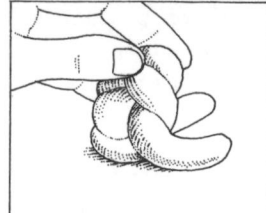

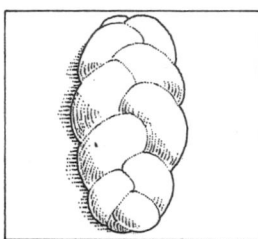

1. *Preparing to plait*
2. *Turning the plait over*
3. *The completed plait*

CROWNS Shape as for plain rolls, and cut a cross into the surface before proving.

*Crown*

COTTAGE LOAVES Divide the dough into 2 pieces, one three-quarters larger than the other. Shape both into balls as for plain rolls. Make a small indentation in the centre of the top of the larger one and place the smaller roll on it. Using a floured finger or a wooden spoon handle, press a hole through both rolls to the baking sheet below, thus fixing the top to the bottom.

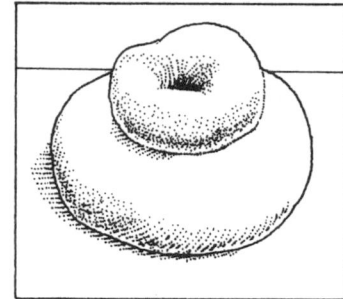

*Cottage loaf*

TWISTS OR WREATHS Divide the dough into 2 equal pieces and shape each into a sausage about 12cm/5in long. Twist each piece around the other to look like a rope, then draw round into a circle pressing the ends together.

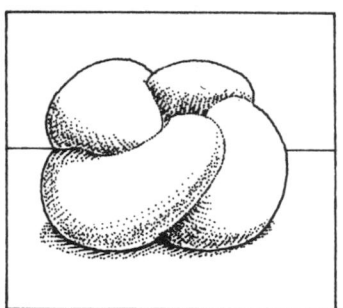

*Twist*

BLOOMERS Make as for plain rolls, except oval and not round. Make 3 diagonal slashes into the surface before proving.

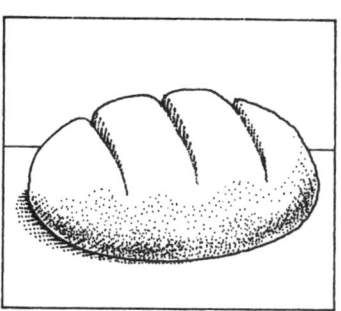

*Bloomer*

CATHERINE WHEEL Shape the dough into a sausage about 15cm/6in long. Coil the dough round from the centre, forming a Catherine wheel.

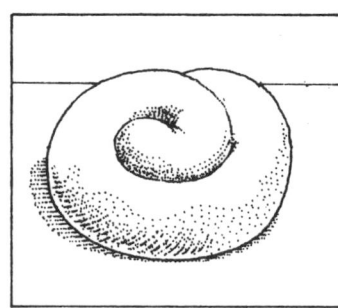

*Catherine wheel*

PAWNBROKER Divide the dough into 3 equal pieces. Form each into a neat ball and place next to each other on the baking sheet to make a triangle.

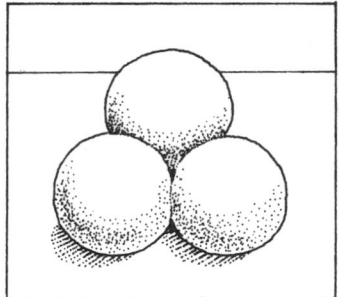

*Pawnbroker*

MALTESE CROSS Shape the dough as for plain rolls and with a pair of scissors snip into the dough in 4 places as illustrated. Prove.

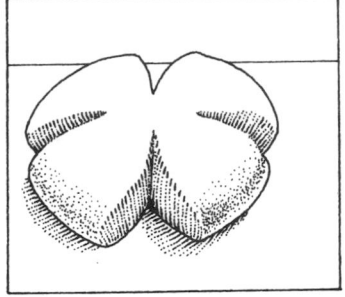

*Maltese Cross*

PROPELLER Shape the dough as for plain rolls and with a pair of scissors make 1cm/½in snips at an angle of 45 degrees all round the edge. Prove.

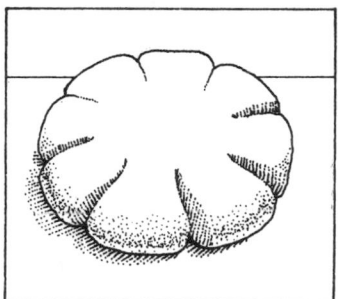

*Propeller*

HEDGEHOGS Shape the dough into an elongated plain roll. Pinch with finger and thumb at one end to form the nose and eyes. With a pair of scissors make tiny snips into the dough to form the prickles. Use peppercorns or currants for the eyes.

# WHITE BREAD

You will need a 1kg/2¼lb bread tin. If it is old and used, you may not need to grease or flour it, but if it is new and not non-stick, brush it out very lightly with flavourless oil and dust with flour.

*15g/½oz fresh yeast*
*scant 290ml/½ pint lukewarm milk*
*1 teaspoon caster sugar*
*450g/1lb strong plain flour*
*2 teaspoons salt*
*30g/1oz butter*
*1 egg, lightly beaten*
*beaten egg to glaze*

**1.** Dissolve the yeast with a little of the milk and the sugar in a teacup.
**2.** Sift the flour with the salt into a warmed large mixing bowl and rub in the butter as you would for pastry.
**3.** Pour in the yeast mixture, the remaining milk and the beaten egg and mix to a softish dough.
**4.** Add a small amount of flour if the dough is too sticky. When the dough will leave the sides of the bowl, press it into a ball and tip it out on to a floured board.
**5.** Knead until it is elastic, smooth and shiny (about 15 minutes).
**6.** Put the dough back into the bowl and cover it with a piece of lightly greased clingfilm.
**7.** Put it in a warm, draught-free place and leave it to rise until it has doubled in size (at least 1 hour). Bread that rises too quickly has a yeasty, unpleasant taste; the slower the rising the better – overnight in a cool larder is better than 30 minutes over the boiler!

**8.** Knock down and knead for a further 10 minutes or so.

**9.** Shape the dough into an oblong and put it into a 1kg/2¼lb loaf tin.

**10.** Cover again with oiled clingfilm and prove (allow to rise again) until it is the size and shape of a loaf. Brush with beaten egg.

**11.** Preheat the oven to 220°C/425°F/gas mark 7. Bake the loaf in the oven for 10 minutes, then turn the oven temperature down to 190°C/375°F/gas mark 5 and bake for a further 25 minutes, or until it is golden and firm.

**12.** Turn the loaf out on to a wire rack to cool. It should sound hollow when tapped on the underside. If it does not, or feels squashy and heavy, return it to the oven, without the tin, for a further 10 minutes.

NOTE: If using dried or easy-blend yeast, see page 604.

# PLAITED WHITE LOAF

*450g/1lb warmed strong plain flour*
*1 teaspoon salt*
*290ml/½ pint milk*
*15g/½oz butter*
*15g/½oz fresh yeast*
*1 teaspoon caster sugar*
*1 egg, beaten*
*milk and poppy seeds to glaze*

**1.** Sift the flour with the salt into a warmed large mixing bowl. Make a well in the centre.

**2.** Heat the milk, melt the butter in it and allow to cool until tepid. Cream the yeast and sugar together. Mix the milk, egg and creamed yeast together and pour into the well.

**3.** Mix and knead until smooth and elastic (10–15 minutes). The dough should be soft.

**4.** Cover the bowl with a piece of oiled clingfilm and put to rise in a warm place for about an hour. The dough should double in size.

**5.** Preheat the oven to 200°C/400°F/gas mark 6.

**6.** Divide the dough into 3 equal pieces and knead on a floured board. Form each piece into a long sausage and plait them together (see diagram, page 608). Place on a greased baking sheet.

**7.** Cover again with oiled clingfilm and prove (allow to rise again) in a warm place for 15 minutes.

**8.** Brush with milk, sprinkle with poppy seeds and bake in the preheated oven for about 25 minutes, or until the loaf is golden and sounds hollow when tapped on the underside.

NOTE: If using dried or easy-blend yeast, see page 604.

# BROWN SODA BREAD

Many soda bread recipes call for buttermilk, but we have found that ordinary milk works well too.

*900g/2lb wholemeal flour, or 675g/1½lb*
   *wholemeal flour and 225g/8oz plain white*
   *flour*
*2 teaspoons salt*
*2 teaspoons bicarbonate of soda*
*4 teaspoons cream of tartar*
*2 teaspoons sugar*
*45g/1½oz butter*
*570–860ml/1–1½ pints milk (if using all*
   *wholemeal flour, the recipe will need more*
   *liquid than if made with a mixture of 2 flours)*

**1.** Preheat the oven to 190°C/375°F/gas mark 5.

**2.** Sift the dry ingredients into a warmed large mixing bowl.

**3.** Rub in the butter and mix to a soft dough with the milk.

**4.** Shape with a minimum of kneading into a large circle about 5cm/2in thick. Dust lightly with flour. With the handle of a wooden spoon, make a cross on the top of the loaf. The dent should be 2cm/¾in deep.

**5.** Bake in the preheated oven on a greased baking sheet for 25–30 minutes. Allow to cool on a wire rack.

# WHOLEMEAL BAPS

MAKES 12 BAPS
*20g/³/4oz fresh yeast*
*290ml/¹/2 pint warm milk*
*1 teaspoon caster sugar*
*225g/8oz wholemeal flour*
*225g/8oz strong plain white flour*
*2 teaspoons salt*
*55g/2oz butter*
*1 egg, lightly beaten*
*sesame seeds*

**1.** Dissolve the yeast with a little of the milk and the sugar in a teacup.
**2.** Sift the flours with the salt into a warmed mixing bowl. Rub in the butter as you would for pastry.
**3.** Pour in the yeast mixture, the remaining milk and nearly all the beaten egg and mix to a fairly slack dough.
**4.** When the dough will leave the sides of the bowl, press it into a ball and tip it out on to a floured board. Knead it until elastic, smooth and shiny (about 15 minutes).
**5.** Put the dough back into the bowl and cover it with a piece of lightly greased clingfilm. Put it into a warm place (on a shelf above a radiator, in the airing cupboard or just in a draught-proof corner of the kitchen). Leave it there until the dough has doubled in size (at least 1 hour).
**6.** Take the dough out of the bowl, knock down and knead again for 10 minutes.
**7.** Preheat the oven to 200°C/400°F/gas mark 6.
**8.** Divide the dough into 12 equal pieces and shape them into flattish ovals, using a rolling pin if you like. Place on a floured baking sheet and prove (allow to rise again) or 15 minutes. Brush with the remaining beaten egg. Sprinkle with the sesame seeds.
**9.** Bake in the preheated oven for 20 minutes, or until firm. Leave to cool on a wire rack. Covering the baps with a tea-towel will ensure a very soft crust.

NOTE: If using dried or easy-blend yeast, see page 604.

# WHOLEMEAL BREAD

This wholemeal bread is simple to make as it has only one rising. As with all bread made from purely 100% wholemeal flour it will be heavier than bread made from a mixture of flours. The flour and water quantities are approximations as wholemeal flours vary enormously. The dough should be moist but not sticky. Use the smaller quantity called for and then add extra flour or water as necessary.

*550g–600g/1lb 4oz–1lb 6oz stoneground 100%*
*   wholemeal flour*
*2 teaspoons salt*
*3 tablespoons buttermilk*
*290–340ml/10–12fl oz warm water*
*15g/¹/2oz fresh yeast*

**1.** Warm the flour with the salt in a large mixing bowl in the bottom of a low oven for about 5 minutes. Warm 2 × 675g/1¹/2lb non-stick loaf tins.
**2.** Mix the buttermilk with the warm water. Add a little of the liquid to the yeast with a pinch of flour.
**3.** Make a well in the centre of the flour, pour in the yeast mixture and nearly all the water and buttermilk. Mix to a dough. Add extra flour or liquid as required. Knead well.
**4.** Fill the warmed tins three-quarters full of dough. Smooth the tops and cover with a piece of lightly oiled clingfilm. Leave in a warm place for 45 minutes, or until the dough has risen to the top of the tins.
**5.** Meanwhile, preheat the oven to 225°C/450°F/gas mark 8.
**6.** Bake the bread in the preheated oven for 15 minutes. Turn down the oven temperature to 190°C/375°F/gas mark 5 and bake for a further 25 minutes.
**7.** The bread should sound hollow when it is tapped on the underside. If it does not or feels squashy and heavy, then return to the oven, without the tin, for a further 5–10 minutes. Leave to cool on a wire rack.

NOTE: If using dried or easy-blend yeast, see page 604.

# BALLYMALOE BROWN BREAD

*30g/1oz yeast*
*1 teaspoon black treacle*
*350–425ml/12–15fl oz water at blood heat*
*450g/1lb wholemeal flour*
*1 teaspoon salt*
*1 tablespoon sesame seeds*

**1.** Grease a 13 × 20cm/5 × 8in loaf tin.
**2.** Mix the yeast with the treacle and 150ml/¼ pint of the water, and leave in a warm place for about 5 minutes, by which time it should look creamy and slightly frothy on top.
**3.** Sift the flour with the salt into a warmed large mixing bowl. Make a well in the centre and add the yeast mixture and enough of the remaining liquid to make a wettish dough that would be just too wet to knead.
**4.** Put the dough into the loaf tin and smooth down the surface. Sprinkle with the sesame seeds and pat down. Place the tin a warm place and cover with a dry tea-towel. Leave to rise for 15–30 minutes.
**5.** Preheat the oven to 230°C/470°F/gas mark 9.
**6.** Bake the bread in the preheated oven for 30 minutes, then remove the bread from the tin and return it to the oven to bake for a further 15–25 minutes. When cooked, the bread should sound hollow when tapped on the underside.

NOTE: If using dried or easy-blend yeast, see page 604.

# BEER BREAD

*55g/2oz butter*
*2 teaspoons soft light brown sugar*
*290ml/½ pint brown ale*
*30g/1oz fresh yeast*
*2 teaspoons salt*
*1 egg*
*225g/8oz wholemeal flour*
*225g/8oz strong plain white flour*

**1.** Grease a 1kg/2¼lb loaf tin.

**2.** Bring the sugar, beer and the remaining butter to boiling point, then allow to cool until lukewarm.
**3.** Use 1–2 spoonfuls of this liquid to cream the yeast. Add the creamed yeast, salt and lightly beaten egg to the beer mixture.
**4.** Sift the flours into a warmed large mixing bowl. Make a well in the centre and pour in the liquid. Mix, first with a knife, and then with your fingers, to a soft but not sloppy dough. Knead for 10 minutes or until smooth, a little shiny and very elastic.
**5.** Put the dough back into the bowl and cover with a piece of oiled clingfilm. Leave in a warm place until it has doubled in bulk.
**6.** Take the dough out of the bowl, knock it down and knead until smooth again. Shape the dough into a loaf shape and put into the tin. Cover again with oiled clingfilm and return in the warm place to prove (rise again) until doubled in size and the shape of the finished loaf.
**7.** Meanwhile, preheat the oven to 200°C/400°F/gas mark 6. Bake the loaf in the middle of the oven for 35 minutes, or until it is brown on top and sounds hollow when tapped on the underside. Cool on a wire rack.

NOTE: If using dried or easy-blend yeast, see page 604.

# RAISIN BREAD

*225g/8oz seedless black grapes*
*110g/4oz raisins*
*85ml/3fl oz sweet white wine*
*30g/1oz fresh yeast*
*150ml/¼ pint warm milk*
*310g/11oz strong plain white flour*
*a pinch of salt*
*130g/5oz caster sugar*

**1.** Soak the grapes and raisins in the wine.
**2.** Dissolve the yeast in some of the warm milk.
**3.** Sift the flour with the salt into a warmed mixing bowl. Add 110g/4oz of the sugar. Make a well in the centre and add the yeast mixture and enough of the remaining milk to make a soft but not sticky dough.

**4.** Knead for 5 minutes or until the dough is smooth and springy. Put to a clean bowl, cover with a clean tea-towel and leave in a warm place to rise for 1 hour or until double in size.

**5.** Knock down the dough and knead again for 2 minutes. Cut the dough in half and shape into 2 × 20cm/8in circles. Place one on a floured baking sheet and cover with three-quarters of the soaked grapes and raisins. Cover with the second piece of dough and place the remaining grapes and raisins on top. Leave covered, in a warm place, until 1½ times its original size.

**6.** Preheat the oven to 180°C/350°F/gas mark 4.

**7.** Sprinkle the bread with the remaining sugar and bake in the preheated oven for about 45 minutes, or until the loaf is risen and brown and sounds hollow when tapped on the underside.

NOTE: If using dried or easy-blend yeast, see page 604.

# HAZELNUT AND RAISIN BREAD

*225g/8oz strong plain flour*
*225g/8oz wholemeal flour*
*1 teaspoon salt*
*15g/½oz fresh yeast*
*290ml/½ pint warm milk*
*1 tablespoon olive oil*
*55g/2oz raisins*
*55g/2oz hazelnuts*
*extra flour for dusting*

**1.** Sift the flours and salt into a large mixing bowl and make a well in the centre.

**2.** Mix the yeast with 1 tablespoon of the milk. Pour into the well with the remaining milk and the oil.

**3.** Mix with a knife and then draw together with the fingers of one hand to make a soft but not sticky dough.

**4.** Knead until smooth and elastic (about 10 minutes), using more flour if necessary.

**5.** Put the dough into a large, clean bowl and cover with a piece of lightly greased clingfilm. Put in a warm place to rise until doubled in bulk (about 1 hour).

**6.** Preheat the oven to 190°C/375°F/gas mark 5.

**7.** Knock back the dough and knead the raisins and hazelnuts carefully into it. Shape into a round loaf and place on a baking sheet.

**8.** Cover the loaf with lightly greased clingfilm and leave in a warm place until it is 1½ times its original size. Dust the top with a little flour.

**9.** Bake the loaf in the preheated oven for 30 minutes, or until it sounds hollow when tapped on the underside.

**10.** Place the loaf on a wire rack and leave to cool.

NOTE: If using dried or easy-blend yeast, see page 604.

# BLUE POPPY SEED AND FRESH MINT BREAD

*675g/1½lb wholemeal flour*
*2 teaspoons salt*
*110g/4oz blue poppy seeds*
*3 tablespoons roughly chopped fresh mint*
*55g/2oz fresh yeast*
*1 teaspoon muscavado sugar*
*570ml/1 pint warm water*
*1 tablespoon oil*

**1.** Sift the flour with the salt into a warmed large mixing bowl. Stir in the poppy seeds and mint and make a well in the centre.

**2.** Cream the yeast and sugar together. Mix the oil with the lukewarm water.

**3.** Put the yeast mixture and the water and oil into the well and mix to a soft, pliable dough with a round-bladed knife, adding more water if necessary.

**4.** When the dough will leave the sides of the bowl, press it together into a ball and tip it out on to a lightly floured work surface.

**5.** Knead it until smooth and elastic (about 10 minutes).

**6.** Put the dough back into the washed and lightly oiled bowl and cover with lightly oiled clingfilm. Leave the dough to rise in a warm place until approximately doubled in size (at least 1 hour).

**7.** Turn the dough out on to a floured work top,

knock it down and knead for a further 10 minutes or so until smooth.

**8.** Shape the dough into an oval, place on a floured baking sheet, cover again with oiled clingfilm and leave to prove (rise again) for about 15 minutes. Preheat the oven to 220°C/425°F/gas mark 7.

**9.** Dust the top of the loaf with a little flour and bake in the oven for 20 minutes. Turn the oven temperature down to 190°C/375°F/gas mark 5 and bake the loaf for a further 20 minutes, or until it is brown and sounds hollow when tapped on the underside.

**10.** Leave the loaf to cool on a wire rack.

NOTE: If using dried or easy-blend yeast, see page 604.

# ITALIAN BREAD

This is a basic olive oil bread which can be easily adapted by adding a variety of herbs such as rosemary or sage or grated cheese.

*30g/1oz fresh yeast*
*225ml/8fl oz warm water*
*450g/1lb strong plain flour*
*2 teaspoons salt*
*2 tablespoons olive oil*

**1.** Dissolve the yeast in the warm water.
**2.** Sift the flour with the salt into a large bowl and make a well in the centre. Pour in the dissolved yeast and the oil. Gradually draw in the flour and when all the ingredients are well mixed, knead the dough for 8 minutes.
**3.** Put the dough into a lightly greased bowl. Cover with clingfilm and leave to rise in a warm place (about 1 hour).
**4.** Shape as required. Cover again with clingfilm and leave to prove (rise again) until 1½ times its original size.
**5.** Preheat the oven to 230°C/450°F/gas mark 8.
**6.** Place the loaf on a baking sheet and bake in the preheated oven for 10 minutes. Turn the oven temperature down to 190°C/375°F/gas mark 5 and bake for a further 45 minutes. Transfer to a wire rack and leave to get completely cold.

NOTE: If using dried or easy-blend yeast, see page 604.

# POTATO BREAD

*450g/1lb potatoes, peeled, cooked and mashed*
*30g/1oz fresh yeast*
*425ml/³/4 pint warm water*
*675g/1½lb strong plain flour*
*2 teaspoons salt*

**1.** Allow the potatoes to cool until lukewarm.
**2.** Dissolve the yeast in a little of the warm water. Mix it with the mashed potatoes.
**3.** Sift the flour with the salt into a large mixing bowl. Add the potato, yeast mixture and enough water to mix to a soft dough. Mix well. When the mixture will leave the sides of the bowl, press it into a ball and tip it out on to a floured surface.
**4.** Knead until elastic, smooth and shiny (about 15 minutes).
**5.** Put the dough back into the bowl and cover with lightly oiled clingfilm.
**6.** Put it into a warm place and leave to rise until doubled in size (at least 1 hour).
**7.** Knock down and knead for a further 10 minutes or so.
**8.** Shape into 3 loaves, cover again with oiled clingfilm and leave to prove (rise again) for 15 minutes. Dust lightly with flour.
**9.** Preheat the oven to 220°C/425°F/gas mark 7. Bake the loaves in the oven for 10 minutes. Turn the oven temperature down to 190°C/375°F/gas mark 5 and bake for a further 25minutes, or until golden-brown and firm.
**10.** Turn out on to a wire rack to cool. The bread should sound hollow when tapped on the underside.

NOTES: This recipe can be used for making attractive bread rolls. For details of making these see pages 607–9.

If using dried or easy-blend yeast, see page 604.

# SOURDOUGH BREAD

Sourdough is very popular in the USA, traditionally served with chowders and shellfish dishes. It is time-consuming to make, as the base has to be started 2–3 days in advance, but the final result is delicious.

The dough is made with the starter. Always reserve a little of the dough for the next batch: it can be frozen and used at a later date.

For the sourdough starter
*225g/8oz wholemeal flour*
*225ml/8fl oz warm water*
*225g/8oz strong plain flour*
*150ml/¼ pint warm water*

For the loaf
*225g/8oz strong plain flour*
*55ml/2 fl oz warm water or milk*
*2 teaspoons salt*

1. Sift the wholemeal flour into a bowl. Mix in the 225ml/8fl oz water to make a batter. Cover lightly with oiled clingfilm and leave to stand at room temperature for 2–3 days until slightly bubbly and smelling yeasty.

2. Stir the white flour and the 150ml/¼ pint water into the starter dough. Cover and leave to stand for a further 6 hours.

3. To make the bread dough: beat the flour into the starter dough with the water or milk and salt and tip on to a lightly floured surface. Knead well for 10 minutes until smooth, shiny and elastic. Place in a clean bowl, cover and leave to rise in a warm place until doubled in bulk. This may take some time.

4. Tip out of the bowl, knock down and remove a small quantity of the dough – about the size of a large bun. Put into an oiled plastic bag and freeze until required.

5. Knead the remaining dough well and shape into a round or oval loaf. Cover with lightly oiled clingfilm and leave to rise again. This may take some time.

6. Preheat the oven to 190°C/375°F/gas mark 5.

7. Glaze the loaf with milk or flour and bake in the oven for 35–40 minutes until risen and it sounds hollow when tapped on the base. Leave to cool on a wire rack.

# CHEESE AND CARAWAY BREAD

*675g/1½lb wholemeal flour*
*1 teaspoon salt*
*2 tablespoons caraway seeds*
*170g/6oz Cheddar cheese, finely grated*
*55g/2oz fresh yeast*

*1 teaspoon muscavado sugar*
*1 tablespoon oil*
*570ml/1 pint warm water*
*milk to glaze*

For the topping
*30g/1oz Cheddar cheese, grated*
*1 tablespoon caraway seeds*

1. Sift the flour with the salt into a warmed large mixing bowl. Stir in the caraway seeds and grated cheese and make a well in the centre.

2. Cream the yeast and sugar together until liquid and mix the oil with the lukewarm water.

3. Put the liquid ingredients into the well, and mix to a soft, pliable dough with a round-bladed knife, adding more water if necessary.

4. When the dough will leave the sides of the bowl, press it into a ball and tip it out on to a lightly floured surface.

5. Knead until it is smooth and elastic (about 10 minutes).

6. Put the dough back into the washed and lightly oiled bowl and cover with lightly oiled clingfilm. Leave the dough to rise in a warm place until about double in size (at least 1 hour).

7. Turn the dough out on to a floured work top, knock it down and knead for a further 10 minutes or so until smooth.

8. Shape the dough into a large circle, place it on a floured baking sheet, cover with the oiled clingfilm and leave to prove (rise again) for about 15 minutes. Preheat the oven to 220°C/425°F/gas mark 7.

9. Brush the loaf with milk and sprinkle on the grated cheese and caraway seeds. Bake in the preheated oven for 20 minutes, then turn the oven temperature down to 190°C/375°F/gas mark 5. Bake for a further 30 minutes, or until the loaf is brown and sounds hollow when tapped on the underside.

10. Transfer the loaf to a wire rack and leave to cool.

NOTE: If using dried or easy-blend yeast, see page 604.

# CHEESE GANNAT

This recipe is based on a cheese brioche originally from Gannat, a small town in Auvergne.

*15g/½oz fresh yeast*
*⅓ teaspoon sugar*
*225g/8oz wholemeal flour*
*1 teaspoon salt*
*55g/2oz butter*
*105ml/3½fl oz milk*
*2 eggs, beaten*
*110g/4oz cheese, preferably strong Cheddar or*
   *Gruyère, grated*
*a pinch of cayenne pepper*
*a pinch of dry English mustard*
*freshly ground black pepper*
*a little milk to glaze*

1. Cream the yeast with the sugar.
2. Sift the flour with the salt into a warmed mixing bowl and make a well in the centre.
3. Melt the butter, remove from the heat and add the milk. Mix with the eggs and the creamed yeast. Pour this liquid into the flour and mix to a soft dough.
4. Cover and leave to rise in a warm place (do not worry if it does not rise very much – it will during baking).
5. Preheat the oven to 200°C/400°F/gas mark 6.
6. Mix most of the cheese into the dough and season well with cayenne, mustard and pepper.
7. Pile into a well-greased 20cm/8in sandwich tin and flatten so that the mixture is about 2.5cm/1in deep. Put back in the warm place to prove (rise again) for 10–15 minutes.
8. Bake in the preheated oven for 25–30 minutes.
9. Brush lightly with the milk and sprinkle with the remaining cheese, and return to the oven for a further 5 minutes.

NOTES: The mixture can be divided into 6 round rolls: put 5 around the edge of a Victoria sandwich tin and one in the middle. Leave to prove and then bake. It will look like a crown loaf.

If using dried or easy-blend yeast, see page 604.

# GRISSINI

This recipe has been taken from Arabella Boxer's *Mediterranean Cookbook*.

*7g/¼oz fresh yeast*
*2 teaspoons sugar*
*3 tablespoons warm water*
*1 teaspoon sea salt*
*150ml/¼ pint boiling water*
*225g/8oz strong flour*
*1 tablespoon olive oil*
*1 egg, beaten*
*55g/2oz sesame seeds*

1. Preheat the oven to 150°C/300°F/gas mark 2.
2. Dissolve the yeast and sugar in the lukewarm water.
3. Dissolve the sea salt in the boiling water, allow to cool to blood temperature and then mix with the yeast.
4. Sift the flour into a large bowl, make a well in the centre, pour in the yeast mixture and the oil. Mix to a soft dough.
5. Tip the dough on to a floured board and knead for 3–4 minutes, until smooth and elastic. Cover with a damp cloth and leave for 5 minutes. Knead for 3 minutes and then divide into 20 equal pieces.
6. Roll each piece of dough out until it is as thick as your little finger. Place on oiled baking sheets and prove (allow to rise again) for 10–15 minutes.
7. Brush with beaten egg, sprinkle with sesame seeds and bake in the preheated oven for about 45 minutes until crisp and golden brown.

# SICHUAN-STYLE NAAN BREAD

*450g/1lb strong plain flour*
*1 tablespoon salt*
*15g/½oz fresh yeast*
*1 teaspoon sugar*
*90–150ml/3–5fl oz warm milk*
*2 tablespoons sesame oil*
*150ml/¼ pint fromage frais or plain yoghurt*
*1 egg, beaten*
*1 tablespoon Sichuan peppercorns, dry-roasted*
   *and crushed*

1. Sift the flour and salt into a bowl.

2. Cream the yeast with the sugar, then mix with the milk, oil, fromage frais or yoghurt and the egg.

3. Mix the yeast mixture into the flour to form a soft but not sticky dough. Knead for 5 minutes or until smooth.

4. Put the dough into an oiled bowl. Cover with greased clingfilm and leave to rise in a warm place until doubled in size.

5. Turn the dough on to a floured board and knead for a further 5 minutes. Knead the peppercorns into the bread.

6. Divide the dough into 8 equal pieces and roll each piece into an oval measuring about 12.5 × 20cm/5 × 8in. Place on a greased baking sheet, cover with clingfilm and leave to rise for about 15 minutes or until 1½ times the original size.

7. Preheat the grill.

8. Brush the bread with water and grill on each side for 3 minutes or until well browned. Serve warm.

NOTE: If using dried or easy-blend yeast, see page 604.

# WALNUT LOAF

This bread is particularly delicious when served with apple and walnut marmelade (see below) and Roquefort cheese.

*225g/8oz strong plain flour*
*225g/8oz malted brown flour*
*1 teaspoon salt*
*15g/½oz fresh yeast*
*290ml/½ pint warm milk*
*1 tablespoon olive oil*
*225g/8oz walnuts, roughly chopped*
*1 egg, lightly beaten*
*1 tablespoon clear honey*

To serve
*apple and walnut marmelade (see below)*
*wedges of Roquefort cheese*

1. Sift the flours and salt into a large mixing bowl and make a well in the centre.

2. Mix the yeast with 1 tablespoon of the milk. Pour into the well with the remaining milk and the oil.

3. Mix with a knife and then draw together with the fingers of one hand to make a soft but not sticky dough.

4. Knead until smooth and elastic (about 5 minutes by hand), using more flour if necessary.

5. Put the dough into a large, clean bowl and cover with a piece of lightly greased clingfilm. Put in a warm place to rise until the dough has doubled in bulk (about 1 hour).

6. Preheat the oven to 190°C/375°F/gas mark 5.

7. Knock back the dough and knead the walnuts into it. Divide the dough into 2 equal pieces and shape into ovals. Place on a baking sheet. Slash the tops with a sharp knife.

8. Cover the loaves with lightly greased clingfilm and leave in a warm place until they are 1½ times their original size.

9. Mix the beaten egg and honey together, and brush evenly over the loaves. Bake in the preheated oven for 30 minutes, or until they sound hollow when tapped on the underside.

10. Place on a wire rack and leave to cool.

11. Serve the marmelade and Roquefort cheese separately.

NOTE: If using dried or easy-blend yeast, see page 604.

# APPLE AND WALNUT MARMELADE

This recipe was first cooked for us by Lesley Waters, who served it with the walnut loaf and Roquefort cheese.

*900g/2lb dessert apples (preferably red)*
*110g/4oz unsalted butter*
*grated zest and juice of 1 lemon*
*225g/8oz soft light brown sugar*
*30ml/1fl oz brandy*
*225g/8oz walnuts, roughly chopped*

1. Quarter and core the apples.

2. In a large saucepan melt the butter with the lemon zest and juice. Stir in the sugar and add the

apples. Cover with a lid and cook very gently until just soft. Remove the lid and reduce the excess liquid over a high heat. Add the brandy and cook for 1 minute. Allow to cool.

**3.** Add the walnuts and serve with the walnut bread (see above) and a slice of Roquefort cheese.

NOTE: This should not be made too far in advance – it does not keep well for more than 2–3 days.

# DOUGHNUTS

MAKES 8
*225g/8oz plain flour*
*a pinch of salt*
*7g/¼oz fresh yeast*
*45g/1½oz sugar*
*30g/1oz butter*
*2 egg yolks*
*150ml/¼ pint warm milk*
*oil for deep-frying*
*caster sugar flavoured with ground cinnamon*

**1.** Sift the flour with the salt into a warmed bowl.
**2.** Cream the yeast with 1 teaspoon of the sugar.
**3.** Rub the butter into the flour. Make a well in the centre.
**4.** Mix together the egg yolks, yeast mixture, remaining sugar and milk. Pour this into the well in the flour.
**5.** Using the fingertips of one hand, mix the central ingredients together, gradually drawing in the surrounding flour. Mix to a smooth soft dough.
**6.** Cover the bowl with a piece of greased clingfilm and leave to rise in a warm place for 45 minutes.
**7.** Knead the dough well for at least 10 minutes. Roll out on a floured board to 1cm/½in thick. With a plain cutter, press into small rounds. Place on a greased tray and leave to prove (rise again) until doubled in size.
**8.** Heat the oil in a deep-fryer until a crumb will sizzle vigorously in it. Put the doughnuts into the fryer basket and lower into the fat. Fry until golden-brown, then drain on absorbent kitchen paper.
**9.** Toss in caster sugar and cinnamon.

# CHELSEA BUNS

MAKES 12
*15g/½oz fresh yeast*
*85g/3oz caster sugar*
*450g/1lb strong plain flour*
*1 teaspoon salt*
*85g/3oz butter*
*1 egg*
*225ml/7½fl oz warm milk*
*½ teaspoon ground mixed spice*
*55g/2oz sultanas*
*55g/2oz currants*
*sugar for sprinkle*
*apricot glaze (see page 638)*

**1.** Cream the yeast with 1 teaspoon of the sugar.
**2.** Sift the flour with the salt into a warmed dry mixing bowl. Rub in half the butter and stir in half the sugar.
**3.** Beat the egg and add to the yeast mixture with the lukewarm milk.
**4.** Make a well in the centre of the flour and pour in the liquid. Using first a knife and then your hand, gradually draw the flour in from the sides of the bowl and knead until smooth.
**5.** Cover the bowl with lightly oiled clingfilm and leave to rise in a warm place until doubled in size (about 1 hour).
**6.** Knock the dough down and knead again on a floured board. Roll into a 23cm/9in square.
**7.** Mix the remaining butter with the remaining sugar and the mixed spice and spread over the dough.
**8.** Preheat the oven to 200°C/400°F/gas mark 6.
**9.** Roll the dough up like a Swiss roll and cut into 3.5cm/½in slices.
**10.** Arrange the buns cut side up on the baking sheet and leave in a warm place to prove (rise again) for 15 minutes.
**11.** Sprinkle with sugar. Bake in the preheated oven for 20–25 minutes. Brush with apricot glaze.
**12.** Leave the buns to cool on a wire rack before separating.

NOTE: If using dried or easy-blend yeast, see page 604.

# HOT CROSS BUNS

MAKES 10
*20g/³/₄oz fresh yeast*
*55g/2oz caster sugar*
*200ml/7fl oz milk*
*2 eggs, beaten*
*450g/1lb strong plain flour*
*½ teaspoon salt*
*1 tablespoon ground mixed spice*
*85g/3oz butter*
*110g/4oz currants*
*30g/1oz finely chopped mixed peel*
*a little sweetened milk to glaze*

**1.** Cream the yeast with 1 teaspoon of the sugar.
**2.** Warm the milk to blood heat. Mix about two-thirds of the milk with the eggs and yeast.
**3.** Sift the flour with the salt and spice into a large mixing bowl. Rub in the butter. Add the remaining sugar. Make a well in the centre of the flour. Tip in the warm milk mixture and beat until smooth, adding more milk if necessary to produce a soft, sticky dough.
**4.** Turn the dough on to a floured board. Knead until the dough is very elastic (about 15 minutes).
**5.** Place in a lightly oiled bowl. Sprinkle with flour. Cover with a damp tea-towel or oiled clingfilm. Leave to rise in a warm place until doubled in size (about 1½ hours).
**6.** Preheat the oven to 200°C/400°F/gas mark 6.
**7.** Turn out on to a floured board, knock down and knead again for a few minutes. Then work in the currants and peel, making sure that they are distributed evenly.
**8.** Shape into small round buns. Mark a cross on top of each bun with a knife. Place on baking trays and leave to prove (rise again) until doubled in bulk (about 15 minutes). Brush the tops with sweetened milk.
**9.** Bake in the preheated oven for about 15 minutes. Brush again with sweetened milk, bake for a further 2 minutes, then cool on a wire rack.

NOTES: The crosses can be made by laying strips of shortcrust pastry or by piping a cross of flour and water paste on top of the buns just before baking. To make the paste, combine 110g/4oz plain flour with a pinch of baking powder and 1 tablespoon oil and mix with cold water.

If using dried or easy-blend yeast, see page 604.

# STOLLEN

*450g/1lb strong plain white flour*
*1 teaspoon caster sugar*
*15g/½oz fresh yeast*
*225ml/8fl oz warm milk*
*1 teaspoon salt*
*85g/3oz butter*
*110g/4oz currants*
*110g/4oz sultanas*
*30g/1oz chopped mixed peel*
*30g/1oz walnuts or almonds, chopped*
*2 teaspoons granted orange or lemon zest*
*1 egg*
*55g/2oz glacé cherries*
*icing sugar for dusting*

**1.** Prepare the yeast batter: mix together 110g/4oz of the flour, the sugar, yeast and warm milk. Set aside in a warm place until bubbly (about 20 minutes).
**2.** Mix the remaining flour with the salt in a mixing bowl. Rub in 55g/2oz of the butter. Add the currants, sultanas, mixed peel, nuts and citrus zest.
**3.** Beat the egg and add it to the yeast batter with the flour, fruit and nuts. Mix well to a soft but not too sticky dough.
**4.** Knead until smooth and elastic (about 10 minutes). Shape into a ball, place in a clean bowl cover with lightly oiled clingfilm and leave in a warm place until doubled in size (at least 1 hour). The dried fruits and nuts slow down the rising and proving of the dough.
**5.** Knock down, knead again for 2 minutes and shape into a 30 × 20cm/12 × 8in oval.
**6.** Melt the remaining butter and brush half of it over the dough. Spread the glacé cherries over half the dough. Fold over the other half of the dough and press down lightly. Cover with lightly oiled clingfilm and leave to prove (rise again) (until 1½ times the original size (15–30 minutes).
**7.** Preheat the oven to 190°C/375°F/gas mark 5.
**8.** Brush the remaining butter over the proved loaf and bake on a baking sheet in the preheated oven for 20–25 minutes. Leave to cool on a wire rack. Dust with icing sugar.

NOTES: An alternative version of this traditional German Christmas cake is to use 225g/8oz made-up marzipan to stuff the Stollen in place of the cherries and butter. Roll the marzipan into a sausage and place in the middle of the dough. Roll up and seal the ends by pinching them together. Bake as before.

If using dried or easy-blend yeast, see page 604.

# BRIOCHE (1)

*15g/¹/₂oz fresh yeast*
*85ml/3fl oz warm milk*
*1¹/₂ teaspoons salt*
*500g/1lb 2oz plain flour*
*6 eggs*
*350g/12oz butter, softened*
*30g/1oz sugar*

For the glaze
*1 egg yolk, lightly beaten with 1 tablespoon milk,*
  *to glaze*

1. Place the yeast and milk in a large bowl and beat with a whisk. Add the salt.
2. Add the flour and eggs and mix with a knife until a dough forms. Beat in the bowl with a wooden spoon or in a machine with a dough hook until smooth and elastic (about 20 minutes by hand and about 10 minutes in a machine).
3. Beat the butter and sugar together and, if using a machine, add to the dough at low speed, making sure everything is completely incorporated after each addition. Beat for 5 minutes. Or knead by hand for 15 minutes. The dough should be shiny, elastic and glossy. Remove to a clean bowl and cover with greased clingfilm. Leave to rise in a warm place for 2 hours or until the dough has doubled in bulk.
4. Knock back the dough by flipping it with your fingertips just a few times. Then refrigerate, covered, for several hours (but not more than 24 hours).
5. Grease a large brioche mould or 12 small brioche tins.
6. Place the dough in the brioche mould (it should not come more than halfway up the mould). If using individual brioches, divide the dough into 12 pieces. Using three-quarters of each piece, roll into small balls and place in the brioche tins.

Make a dip on top of each brioche. Roll the remaining dough into 12 tiny balls and press into the prepared holes. Push the unleaded end of a pencil or a thin spoon handle right through each small ball into the brioche base, to anchor the balls in a place when baking.
7. Cover with greased clingfilm and leave in a warm place until risen to the top of the mould or tins. Individual brioches will take 20 minutes, a large one about 1 hour.
8. Preheat the oven to 220°C/425°F/gas mark 7.
9. Glaze the brioche with the egg yolk and milk. Take care not to allow it to drip down the side of the mould or tins.
10. Bake the large brioche in the preheated oven for 40–45 minutes; the small ones for 8 minutes.
11. When the brioche is cooked it will be golden-brown, come out of the mould or tins easily, sound hollow when tapped on the underside and feel light for its size.

NOTE: If using dried or easy-blend yeast, see page 604.

# BRIOCHE (2)

This is a less rich, slightly sweeter brioche than the previous recipe

MAKES 1 LARGE OR 12 SMALL BRIOCHES
*7g/¹/₄oz fresh yeast*
*5 teaspoons caster sugar*
*2 tablespoons warm water*
*225g/8oz plain white flour*
*¹/₂ teaspoon salt*
*2 eggs, beaten*
*55g/2oz melted butter, cool*

For the glaze
*1 egg, mixed with 1 tablespoon water and 1*
  *teaspoon sugar*

1. Grease a large brioche mould of 12 small brioche tins.
2. Mix the yeast with 1 teaspoon of the sugar and the water. Leave to dissolve.
3. Sift the flour with the salt into a mixing bowl. Sprinkle over the sugar. Make a well in the centre.

Drop in the eggs, yeast mixture and melted butter and mix with the fingers of one hand to a soft but not sloppy paste. Knead on an unfloured board for 5 minutes or until smooth. Put into a clean bowl, cover with a damp cloth or lightly oiled clingfilm and leave to rise in a warm place until doubled in bulk (about 1 hour).

**4.** Turn out and knead again on an unfloured board for 2 minutes.

**5.** Place the dough in the brioche mould (it should not come more than halfway up the mould). If making individual brioches, divide the dough into 12 pieces. Using three-quarters of each piece roll them into small balls and put them in the brioche tins. Make a dip on top of each brioche. Roll the remaining paste into 12 tiny balls and press them into the prepared holes. Push a pencil, or thin spoon handle, right through each small ball into the brioche base as this will anchor the balls in place when baking.

**6.** Cover with lightly oiled clingfilm and leave in a warm place to prove (rise again) until risen to the top of the mould or tin (about 30 minutes for the large brioche, 15 minutes for individual ones).

**7.** Preheat the oven to 200°C/400°F/gas mark 6.

**8.** Brush the brioches with the egg glaze. Bake the large one in the preheated oven for 20–25 minutes, the small ones for 10 minutes.

NOTE: If using dried or easy-blend yeast, see page 604.

# CROISSANTS

This recipe has been taken from *The Roux brothers on Pâtisserie*. We have tried literally dozens of croissant recipes and this is the first one we have found that works really well. The dough for croissants should be made 10–12 hours in advance. You will need a template to make the croissants. It should be a 15 × 18cm/6 × 7in isosceles triangle.

MAKES 16–18
*45g/1½oz caster sugar*
*1 teaspoon salt*
*300ml/11fl oz cold water*
*15g/½oz fresh yeast*
*30g/1oz dried milk powder*
*500g/1lb 2oz strong plain white flour*
*285g/10oz butter*

For the glaze
*1 egg yolk, beaten with 1 tablespoon milk, to glaze*

**1.** Dissolve the sugar and salt in one-third of the cold water. In a separate bowl, beat the yeast into the remaining water, then beat in the milk powder.

**2.** Sift the flour into a bowl and, with one hand, mix in both the liquids. Mix to a smooth soft dough but do not knead.

**3.** Cover the dough with lightly oiled clingfilm and leave in a warm place to rise until doubled in size (about 30 minutes).

**4.** Knock back the dough by quickly flicking it over with your fingers to release the carbon gases – do not overwork. Cover again with lightly oiled clingfilm and refrigerate for 6–8 hours.

**5.** Shape the dough into a ball and cut a cross in the top. Roll out the dough at the 4 quarters so that it looks like 4 large 'ears' surrounding a small head.

**6.** Put the butter in the centre and fold the 'ears' over, ensuring that the butter is completely enclosed and will not ooze out.

**7.** Lightly flour the work top and then carefully roll the dough away from you into a 40 × 70cm/16 × 27in rectangle. Brush off the excess flour and fold the dough into 3. Wrap in clingfilm and refrigerate for 20 minutes.

**8.** Repeat the rolling, folding and chilling (as in step 7) at least twice more until the dough is no longer streaky.

**9.** Preheat the oven to 200°C/400°F/gas mark 6.

**10.** Roll out the dough to a 40 ×76cm/16 ×30in rectangle, flouring the surface lightly and flapping up the dough occasionally to aerate it.

**11.** With a large knife, trim the edges and cut the dough lengthways into 2 equal strips.

**12.** Lay one short edge of the triangular template along one long edge of the dough and mark out the outline with the back of a knife. Invert the triangle and mark out as before. Once all the triangles are marked out (16–18 in all), cut them with a sharp knife.

**13.** Arrange the triangles on a baking sheet, cover tightly with clingfilm and refrigerate for a few minutes. If the dough becomes too warm, it may soften and crack.

**14.** Place the triangles, one at a time, on the work

surface with the long point towards you. Stretch out the 2 shorter points and begin to roll the triangle towards you. Make sure that the central point is in the middle and underneath so that it does not rise up during cooking.

**15.** As soon as they are shaped, place the croissants on a baking sheet, turning in the corners to make a crescent shape. Since the sides of the oven are the hottest, the last row of croissants must face inwards or the points may dry out or burn.

**16.** Lightly brush the croissants with egg wash, working from the inside outwards so that the layers of dough do not stick together. Leave to rise in a warm draught-free place until they have doubled in size.

**17.** Lightly reglaze the croissants with egg wash. Bake the croissants in the preheated oven for 15 minutes. Transfer to a wire rack to cool.

NOTE: If using dried or easy-blend yeast, see page 604.

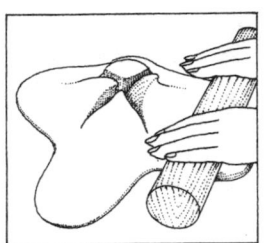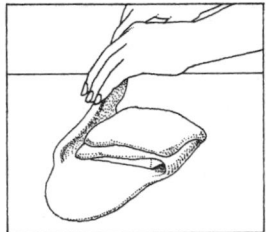

*Steps 5 and 6*

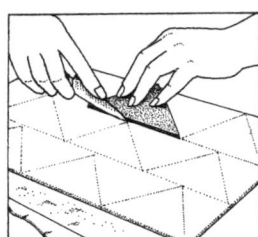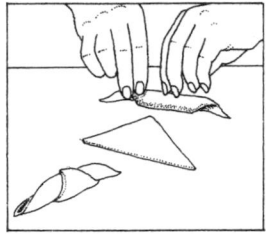

*Steps 11 and 13*

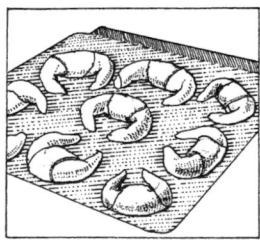

*The finished croissants*

# REASONS FOR FAILURE IN BREAD-MAKING

**1. Close texture:**

a) Stale yeast
b) Insufficient yeast
c) Too much salt or sugar
d) Insufficient kneading
e) Too much/too little liquid
f) Second rising too short
g) Dough left to rise in too warm a place
h) Oven too cool

**2. Poor rising of dough:**

a) Stale yeast
b) Too much salt or sugar
c) Mixture too dry
d) Rising time too short

**3. Uneven texture and holes:**

a) Too much liquid
b) Too much salt
c) Insufficient kneading
d) Too long/short risings
e) Dough left uncovered during rising
f) Oven too cool
g) Not knocked back enough

**4. Coarse texture:**

a) Too much/too little salt
b) Too much/too little liquid
c) Insufficient kneading
d) Too long/short rising
e) Dough left uncovered

**5. Wrinkled top crust:**

a) Second rising too long
b) Dough not covered
c) Insufficient kneading
d) Not knocked back enough

**6. Sour or yeasty flavour:**

a) Stale yeast
b) Too much yeast
c) Yeast creamed with too much sugar
d) Second rising too long – overproved

**7. Cracked crust:**

a) Second rising too short
b) Tin too small for mixture
c) Oven too cool

If the oven is too cool the bread will be pale, dry and hard, with an uneven texture. If the oven is too hot the crust will be too dark or burnt.

# SCONES,
# BISCUITS
# AND PASTRIES

# SCONES

MAKES 6
*225g/8oz self-raising flour*
*½ teaspoon salt*
*55g/2oz butter*
*30g/1oz caster sugar (optional)*
*150ml/¼ pint milk*
*1 egg, beaten, to glaze*

**1.** Preheat the oven to 220°C/425°F/gas mark 7. Flour a baking sheet.
**2.** Sift the flour with the salt into a large bowl.
**3.** Rub in the butter until the mixture resembles breadcrumbs. Stir in the sugar, if using.
**4.** Make a deep well in the flour, pour in the milk and mix to a soft, spongy dough with a knife.
**5.** On a floured surface, knead the dough very lightly until it is just smooth. Roll or press out about 2.5cm/1in thick and stamp into rounds with a small pastry cutter.
**6.** Brush the scones with beaten egg for a glossy crust, sprinkle with flour for a soft one or brush with milk for a light gloss and soft crust.
**7.** Bake the scones at the top of the preheated oven for 7 minutes, or until well risen and brown. Leave to cool on a wire rack, or serve hot from the oven.

NOTE: 30g/1oz sultanas or other dried fruit may be added to the flour. For cheese scones, substitute 30g/1oz grated strong cheese for half the butter, and omit the sugar.

# SHORTBREAD

MAKES 6-8
*110g/4oz butter*
*55g/2oz caster sugar*
*110g/4oz plain flour*
*55g/2oz rice flour*

**1.** Preheat the oven to 170°C/325°F/gas mark 3.
**2.** Beat the butter until soft, add the sugar and beat until pale and creamy.
**3.** Sift in the flours and work to a smooth paste. Chill for 15 minutes.

**4.** Place a 15cm/6in flan ring on a baking sheet and press the shortbread paste into a neat circle. Remove the flan ring and flatten the paste slightly with a rolling pin. Crimp the edges. Prick lightly.
**5.** Mark the shortbread into 6–8 wedges, sprinkle lightly with a little extra caster sugar and bake for 40 minutes, until a pale biscuit colour. Leave to cool for 2 minutes, then transfer to a wire rack to cool completely.

# FLAVOURED SHORTBREADS

Shortbread can be stamped into biscuits or made into petticoat tails and put into attractive tins. Many variations can be created by adding different ingredients to the basic recipe (see above).

### ALMOND SHORTBREAD
Replace of the flour with the equivalent weight of ground almonds.

### HAZELNUT SHORTBREAD
Add 30g/1oz roughly chopped, browned and skinned hazelnuts with the flour to the creamed butter and sugar.

### GINGER SHORTBREAD
Add 1 teaspoon ground ginger and 55g/2oz chopped crystallized stem ginger with the flour.

### ORANGE SHORTBREAD
Add the finely grated zest of 2 oranges to the creamed butter and sugar before adding the flour.

# CHOCOLATE FORK BISCUITS

MAKES ABOUT 20
*225g/8oz butter*
*110g/4oz caster sugar*
*1 teaspoon vanilla essence*
*225g/8oz self-raising flour*
*55g/2oz cocoa powder*
*extra butter for greasing*

For the filling
*7 tablespoons strong coffee*
*55g/2oz cocoa powder*
*55g/2oz butter, softened*
*icing sugar, sifted, to taste*
*vanilla extract or rum to taste*

**1.** Preheat the oven to 180°C/350°F/gas mark 4.
**2.** Cream the butter until soft, add the sugar and vanilla, and beat again until light and fluffy.
**3.** Sift the flour and cocoa powder together and carefully work into the butter mixture.
**4.** Roll teaspoons of the mixture into walnut-sized pieces and arrange well spaced on a greased baking sheet. Flatten each piece with a fork dipped in water.
**5.** Bake in the preheated oven for about 12 minutes.
**6.** Transfer the biscuits to a wire rack and leave to cool completely.
**7.** Meanwhile, make the filling: heat the coffee in a small saucepan and stir in the cocoa powder. Cook for 1 minute, then remove from the heat, when it should be the consistency of a paste. If too thick, add a little water and leave to cool.
**8.** Gradually beat in the butter and add icing sugar and vanilla or rum to taste.
**9.** Sandwich the biscuits together with the filling.

NOTE: If preferred, the biscuits may be served without the filling, simply dusted with sifted icing sugar.

# ICED BISCUITS

MAKES 20
*110g/4oz unsalted butter*
*110g/4oz caster sugar*
*1 egg, beaten*
*a few drops of vanilla essence*
*285g/10oz plain flour*
*a pinch of salt*

For the glacé icing
*225g/8oz icing sugar*
*boiling water*
*food colouring*

**1.** Preheat the oven to 190°C/375°F/gas mark 5.
**2.** Beat the butter until soft, add the sugar and

beat until light and fluffy. Gradually beat in the egg. Add the vanilla essence.
**3.** Sift the flour with the salt and mix it into the butter, sugar and egg mixture.
**4.** Roll the paste out to the thickness of a £1 coin and stamp into rounds with a small pastry cutter. Place on an ungreased baking sheet.
**5.** Bake in the preheated oven for 8–10 minutes until just beginning to brown at the edges. Leave to cool on a wire rack.
**6.** Make the glacé icing: sift the icing sugar into a bowl. Add enough boiling water to mix to a fairly stiff consistency.
**7.** Colour the icing as required.
**8.** Spoon the icing smoothly and evenly over the top of the biscuits. Leave to dry and harden.

# PEANUT BUTTER COOKIES

MAKES ABOUT 40
*140g/5oz butter*
*110g/4oz caster sugar*
*110g/4oz soft light brown sugar*
*1 large egg, beaten*
*110g/4oz crunchy peanut butter*
*½ teaspoon vanilla essence*
*200g/7oz plain flour*
*½ teaspoon salt*
*1 teaspoon baking powder*

**1.** Preheat the oven to 180°C/350°F/gas mark 4.
**2.** Cream the butter and both sugars together until smooth and soft. Beat in the egg, then the peanut butter, and add the vanilla essence.
**3.** Sift the flour with the salt and the baking powder into the mixture and stir until smooth. Do not overbeat or the dough will be oily.
**4.** Roll the mixture into small balls with the fingers and place well apart on 3 ungreased baking sheets. Flatten with the prongs of a fork.
**5.** Bake in the preheated oven for 10–15 minutes to an even, not too dark, brown.
**6.** While hot, ease off the baking sheets with a palette knife or fish slice and cool on a wire rack. Once completely cold and crisp, store in an airtight container.

# FLAPJACKS

MAKES 16
*170g/6oz butter*
*110g/4oz soft light brown sugar*
*55g/2oz golden syrup*
*225g/8oz rolled oats*

**1.** Preheat the oven to 190°C/375°F/gas mark 5.
**2.** Melt the butter.
**3.** Weigh out the sugar, then weigh the syrup by spooning it on top of the sugar (thus preventing it sticking to the scale pan) and add to the warm melted butter to heat through.
**4.** Remove the pan from the heat and stir in the oats.
**5.** Spread the mixture into a well-greased shallow tin.
**6.** Bake in the preheated oven for about 30 minutes until golden-brown.
**7.** Remove from the oven, mark immediately into bars and leave to cool in the tin.

# EASTER BISCUITS

MAKES 8
*55g/2oz butter*
*55g/2oz caster sugar*
*grated zest of ½ lemon*
*½ egg or 1 egg yolk*
*110g/4oz plain flour*
*½ teaspoon caraway seeds*
*55g/2oz currants*
*30g/1oz granulated sugar*

**1.** Preheat the oven to 180°C/350°F/gas mark 4. Line a baking sheet with greaseproof paper.
**2.** Cream together the butter, caster sugar and lemon zest. Beat in the egg.
**3.** Fold in the flour, caraway seeds and currants.
**4.** Roll out the dough 5mm/¼in thick on a floured board. Cut into large rounds and carefully lift them on to the baking sheet. Prick with a fork and sprinkle with granulated sugar.
**5.** Bake in the preheated oven for 10–15 minutes until set and pale golden.
**6.** Leave on a wire rack to crisp and cool.

NOTE: If the dough becomes soft and difficult to handle, wrap it up and chill for 15 minutes before proceeding.

# OLD-FASHIONED GINGERBREAD

These can be cut into different shaped biscuits and used as Christmas tree decorations. To do this, cut a hole in the baked biscuits while they are still hot. Leave to cool on a wire rack. When cool, thread through green and red ribbons and tie on to the Christmas tree.

MAKES ABOUT 120 SMALL BISCUITS
*340g/12oz plain flour*
*1 teaspoon baking powder*
*1 teaspoon salt*
*1 teaspoon freshly grated nutmeg*
*1 teaspoon ground cloves*
*2 teaspoons ground cinnamon*
*2 teaspoons ground ginger*
*225g/8oz butter*
*225g/8oz caster sugar*
*170g/6oz soft dark brown sugar*
*2 eggs, beaten*

**1.** Preheat the oven to 180°C/350°F/gas mark 4.
**2.** Sift the flour, baking powder, salt and spices into a large bowl.
**3.** Melt the butter in a saucepan, add the sugars, mix well and allow to cool. Add the eggs.
**4.** Make a well in the dry ingredients and gradually add the butter and sugar mixture. Place in the refrigerator until completely cold.
**5.** Cut into 4 equal pieces and roll each one out separately to the thickness of a £1 coin. Stamp into different shapes, such as stars, balls, angels, Christmas trees. Place on a greased baking sheet and bake in batches in the preheated oven for about 10 minutes.

NOTE: This mixture should be made by hand. It is very easy to overwork.

# ALMOND AND APRICOT COOKIES

MAKES 18
*85g/3oz butter*
*85g/3oz granulated sugar*
*110g/4oz ground almonds*

To decorate
*apricot jam*
*toasted flaked almonds*

1. Preheat the oven to 180°C/350°F/gas mark 4.
2. Beat the butter and when soft, add the sugar and beat until light and fluffy. Stir in the ground almonds and roll the paste into balls the size of a marble. Refrigerate for 10 minutes.
3. Place each ball in a paper case and put the cases into tartlet tins. Bake in the preheated oven for 15–20 minutes. Remove from the oven and allow to cool in the cases.
4. Remove from the cases, spread with a little apricot jam and decorate each cookie with a toasted flaked almond.

# HAZELNUT SABLÉS

MAKES ABOUT 24
*225g/8oz butter*
*110g/4oz icing sugar, sifted*
*2 egg yolks*
*340g/12oz plain flour*
*55g/2oz ground hazelnuts*

1. Preheat the oven to 180°C/350°F/gas mark 4.
2. Cream the butter and icing sugar together until light and fluffy. Beat in the egg yolks.
3. Sift the flour and mix with the ground hazelnuts. Stir into the butter mixture and bring together to form a ball of dough.
4. Roll out the dough to the thickness of a 50p coin and stamp out biscuits with a small round pastry cutter. Place on a baking sheet and refrigerate for 10 minutes.
5. Bake the biscuits in the preheated oven for 20 minutes, or until golden-brown.

# GINGERNUTS

MAKES 20–25
*30g/1oz demerara sugar*
*55g/2oz butter*
*85g/3oz golden syrup*
*110g/4oz plain flour*
*½ teaspoon bicarbonate of soda*
*1 heaped teaspoon ground ginger*

1. Preheat the oven to 180°C/350°F/gas mark 4. Grease a baking sheet.
2. Melt the sugar, butter and syrup together slowly, without boiling. Make sure the sugar has dissolved, then remove from the heat and allow to cool.
3. Sift the flour with the soda and ginger into a bowl. Make a well in the centre.
4. Pour the melted mixture into the well and knead until smooth. Roll into balls and flatten, on the prepared baking sheet, into biscuits about 3.5cm/1½in in diameter.
5. Bake in the preheated oven for 20–25 minutes, or until golden-brown. Leave on a wire rack to crisp and cool.

# BRANDY SNAP CUPS

MAKES 8
*110g/4oz caster sugar*
*110g/4oz butter*
*4 tablespoons golden syrup*
*110g/4oz plain flour*
*juice of ½ lemon*
*a large pinch of ground ginger*

To serve
*whipped cream or ice cream*

1. Preheat the oven to 190°C/375°F/gas mark 5. Grease a baking sheet, a palette knife and one end of a wide rolling pin or a narrow jam jar or bottle.
2. Melt the sugar, butter and syrup together in a saucepan. Remove from the heat.
3. Sift in the flour, stirring well. Add the lemon juice and ginger.
4. Place teaspoonfuls of the mixture on the prepared baking sheet about 15cm/6in apart.

Bake in the preheated oven for 5–7 minutes until golden-brown and still soft. Watch carefully as they burn easily. Remove from the oven.

**5.** When cool enough to handle, lever each biscuit off the baking sheet with a greased palette knife.

**6.** Working quickly, shape around the end of the rolling pin or greased jam jar to form a cup-shaped mould.

**7.** When the biscuits have been shaped, remove them and leave to cool on a wire rack.

**8.** Serve filled with whipped cream or ice cream.

NOTES: If the brandy snaps are not to be served immediately, once cool they must be put into an airtight container for storage, or they will become soggy. Similarly, brandy snaps should not be filled with moist mixtures like whipped cream or ice cream until shortly before serving, or they will quickly lose their crispness. Do not bake too many snaps at one time as once they become cold, they are too brittle to shape. They can be made pliable again if returned to the oven.

# BRANDY SNAPS

The mixture for these is exactly the same as for brandy snap cups (above) but the biscuits are shaped round a thick wooden spoon handle and not over the end of a rolling pin or jam jar. They are filled with whipped cream from a piping bag fitted with a medium nozzle.

Miniature brandy snaps (served as petits fours after dinner) are shaped over a skewer. They are not generally filled.

# FILIGREE BASKETS

These make excellent 'cups' or baskets in which to serve ice cream and sorbets.

MAKES 6
*2 egg whites*
*110g/4oz caster sugar*
*125g/4½oz plain flour*
*½ teaspoon vanilla essence*

**1.** Cut a template out of cardboard. For a basket big enough to hold a ball of sorbet, the stencil

should be about 5cm/2in across and 20cm/8in long.

**2.** Line a baking sheet with greaseproof paper and grease and flour it. Mark the shape of the template in the flour coating.

**3.** Preheat the oven to 200°C/400°F/gas mark 6.

**4.** Whisk the egg whites and sugar together in a bowl until the whisk will leave a ribbon-like trail when lifted.

**5.** Sift in the flour, add the vanilla essence and beat until smooth.

**6.** Put the mixture into a piping bag fitted with a plain 2mm/⅛in nozzle, or into a paper piping bag with the point snipped to provide the small nozzle mouth.

**7.** Pipe the mixture into the shapes on to the prepared baking sheet.

**8.** Bake in the preheated oven for 4–6 minutes or until just pale brown.

**9.** Remove from the oven and ease the biscuits off the tray. Have ready 6 smallish tea cups.

**10.** Return the biscuits to the hot oven for 30 seconds or just long enough for them to become very pliable again. While hot, curl them round and drop them into the tea cups. Leave on a wire rack to cool completely.

**11.** Once cold, store in an airtight container.

# LANGUES DE CHAT

MAKES 30–40
*100g/3½oz butter*
*100g/3½oz caster sugar*
*3 egg whites*
*100g/3½oz plain flour*

**1.** Preheat the oven to 200°C/400°F/gas mark 6. Grease a baking sheet or line it with non-stick baking parchment.

**2.** Soften the butter with a wooden spoon and add the sugar gradually. Beat until pale and fluffy.

**3.** Whisk the egg whites slightly and add gradually to the mixture, beating thoroughly after each addition.

**4.** Sift the flour and fold into the mixture with a metal spoon. Put into a piping bag fitted with a medium plain nozzle. Pipe into fingers the thickness of a pencil and about 5cm/2in long on the prepared baking sheet.

**5.** Tap the baking sheet on the table to release any over-large air bubbles. Bake in the preheated oven for 5–7 minutes or until biscuit-coloured in the middle and brown at the edges. Cool slightly, then lift off the baking sheet with a palette knife. Leave on a wire rack to cool completely.

**6.** Once cold, store in an airtight container.

# MACAROONS

Macaroons are particularly good with freshly ground blanched almonds.

MAKES 25
*110g/4oz ground almonds*
*170g/6oz caster sugar*
*1 teaspoon plain flour*
*2 egg whites*
*2 drops of vanilla essence*
*rice paper for baking*

To decorate
*split blanched almonds*

**1.** Preheat the oven to 180°C/350°F/gas mark 4.
**2.** Mix together the ground almonds, sugar and flour.
**3.** Add the egg whites and vanilla essence. Beat very well. Leave to stand for 5 minutes. Beat again for 1 minute.
**4.** Line a baking sheet with rice paper or non-stick baking parchment and with a teaspoon put on small heaps of the mixture, well apart.
**5.** Place a split almond on each macaroon and bake in the preheated oven for 20 minutes. Leave on a wire rack to cool completely.

NOTES: To use this recipe for petits fours the mixture must be put out in very tiny blobs on the rice paper. Two macaroons can then be sandwiched together with a little stiff apricot jam and served in petits fours paper cases.

Ratafia biscuits are tiny macaroons with almond essence added.

# SPONGE FINGERS

MAKES 30
*6 eggs*
*140g/5oz caster sugar*
*110g/4oz self-raising flour*
*30g/1oz arrowroot*

**1.** Preheat the oven to 200°C/400°F/gas mark 6. Line 2 large baking sheets with non-stick baking parchment. Draw parallel lines 12.5cm/5in apart on the parchment.
**2.** Separate 5 of the eggs. Beat the yolks with the whole egg and 110g/4oz of the sugar in a large bowl until nearly white.
**3.** Whisk the egg whites until stiff and gradually whisk in the remaining sugar. Fold the egg whites into the egg-yolk and sugar mixture. Carefully fold in the flour sifted with the arrowroot.
**4.** Fill a piping bag fitted with a 5mm/¼in plain nozzle with the mixture. Pipe 12.5cm/5in fingers between the parallel lines on the baking parchment. The fingers should be just touching.
**5.** Bake in the top of the preheated oven for about 10 minutes, or until the sponge has risen and is biscuit-coloured.
**6.** Remove from the oven, invert on to a clean tea-towel and immediately and carefully peel off the lining paper. Turn the sponge fingers on to a wire rack to cool.

# TUILES À L'ORANGE

MAKES 25
*2 egg whites*
*110g/4oz caster sugar*
*55g/2oz butter, melted and cooled*
*55g/2oz plain flour, sifted*
*grated zest of 1 orange*

**1.** Preheat the oven to 190°C/375°F/gas mark 5. Grease a baking sheet or line it with non-stick baking parchment.
**2.** Whisk the egg whites until stiff. Add the sugar and whisk until stiff and glossy.
**3.** Add the butter to the meringue mixture by degrees with the flour. Fold in the orange zest.
**4.** Spread out teaspoonfuls of the mixture very

thinly on the prepared baking sheet, keeping them well apart to allow for spreading during cooking. Bake in the preheated oven for 5–6 minutes until golden-brown.

**5.** Oil a rolling pin or the handle of a large wooden spoon. Loosen the tuiles from the baking sheet while still hot. While they are still warm and pliable curl them over the rolling pin or round the wooden spoon handle. When they are quite firm slip them off. Leave to cool completely on a wire rack.

**6.** When cold, store in an airtight container.

# TUILES AMANDINES

MAKES 25

*30g/1oz blanched almonds*
*2 egg whites*
*110g/4oz caster sugar*
*55g/2oz plain flour*
*½ teaspoon vanilla essence*
*55g/2oz butter, melted and cooled*

**1.** Preheat the oven to 180°C/350°F/gas mark 4. Lightly grease at least 3 baking sheets and a rolling pin or line the baking sheets with non-stick baking parchment.

**2.** Cut the almonds into fine slivers or shreds.

**3.** Place the egg whites in a bowl. Beat in the sugar with a fork. The egg white should be frothy but by no means snowy. Sift in the flour and add the vanilla essence and almonds. Mix with the fork.

**4.** Add the melted butter to the mixture. Stir well.

**5.** Place teaspoonfuls of the mixture at least 13cm/5in apart on the prepared baking sheets and flatten well.

**6.** Bake in the preheated oven for about 6 minutes until pale biscuit-coloured in the middle and a good brown at the edges. Remove from the oven and cool for a few seconds.

**7.** Lift the biscuits off carefully with a palette knife. Lay them, while still warm and pliable, over the rolling pin to form them into a slightly curved shape. Leave on a wire rack to cool completely.

**8.** When cold, store in an airtight tin.

# VENETIAN BISCUITS

MAKES 24

*110g/4oz blanched almonds*
*450g/1lb plain flour*
*a pinch of salt*
*1 teaspoon baking powder*
*140g/5oz granulated sugar*
*85g/3oz plain chocolate, chopped into small pieces*
*4 large eggs, lightly beaten*
*1 egg white to glaze*

**1.** Preheat the oven to 190°C/375°F/gas mark 5. Grease a baking sheet.

**2.** Place the almonds on the baking sheet and bake in the preheated oven until golden-brown. Remove from the oven and cool. Chop two-thirds of the almonds and grind the remainder finely.

**3.** Sift the flour with the salt and baking powder into a large bowl. Add the sugar, chocolate and chopped and ground almonds. Mix well.

**4.** Make a well in the centre and add the eggs. Gradually incorporate the dry ingredients with the eggs to make a firm dough.

**5.** Divide the dough into 4 equal pieces and roll each piece into a long thin sausage shape about 2cm/¾in in diameter and 20cm/8in long.

**6.** Place the rolls at least 5cm/2in apart on the baking sheet. Lightly whisk the egg white until just frothy and brush over the tops of the rolls.

**7.** Bake in the preheated oven for 20 minutes.

**8.** Remove the rolls from the oven and turn the temperature down to 80°C/175°F/gas mark ¼. Cut the rolls at a 45-degree angle into 1cm/½in slices and place on the baking sheet. Bake for a further hour. Leave on a wire rack to cool completely.

NOTE: Raisins or glacé fruit can be used in place of the chocolate. The biscuits are meant to be very dry and crisp and to be eaten after being dipped in a liqueur, such as Amaretto or Grappa.

# CALICIONI (ALMOND BISCUITS)

This recipe was given to us by Jeanette Nance Nordio.

MAKES ABOUT 36
*450g/1lb flour quantity pâte frollée (see page 466), made with triple-distilled rosewater instead of vanilla essence*
*450g/1lb blanched almonds, soaked overnight*
*450g/1lb caster sugar*
*1 tablespoon triple-distilled rose-water*

1. Chill the pastry in the refrigerator.
2. Drain the almonds and grind finely. Mix with the sugar and enough rose-water to bind the mixture together.
3. Preheat the oven to 180°C/350°F/gas mark 4.
4. Roll out the pastry to the thickness of a 50p coin and cut into small squares or rounds.
5. Place a little filling on top of 1 square or round and cover with another. Press the edges to seal and place on a baking sheet.
6. Bake the biscuits in the preheated oven for 10–15 minutes, being careful not to let them burn.
7. Transfer the biscuits to a wire rack and leave to cool.

# BÂTONS MARÉCHAUX

MAKES 25–30
*10 egg whites*
*225g/8oz caster sugar*
*55g/2oz plain flour*
*225g/8oz ground almonds*
*85g/3oz nibbed almonds*
*apricot jam, for filling*

1. Preheat the oven to 190°C/375°F/gas mark 5.
2. Whisk the egg whites until stiff but not dry. Gradually whisk in half the sugar and whisk again until very stiff and shiny.
3. Mix together the remaining sugar, the flour and ground almonds, and fold into the meringue.
4. Place the meringue in a piping bag fitted with a 1cm/½in plain nozzle and pipe 5cm/2in lengths on to baking sheets lined with non-stick baking parchment.
5. Sprinkle with nibbed almonds. Remove any excess almonds.
6. Allow the meringue to dry slightly, before baking in the preheated oven for 45 minutes until firm.
7. Sandwich the biscuits together in pairs with apricot jam.

NOTE: Instead of sandwiching together with jam, the back of each biscuit may be coated with chocolate couverture (see page 62) and decorated by marking with a comb scraper or the calk of a knife. (Two coats of chocolate may have to be applied to obtain a good finish.)

# FLORENTINE BISCUITS

MAKES 20
*55g/2oz butter*
*55g/2oz caster sugar*
*2 teaspoons clear honey*
*55g/2oz plain flour*
*45g/1½oz chopped mixed peel*
*45g/1½oz glacé cherries, chopped*
*45g/1½oz blanched almonds, chopped*
*85g/3oz plain chocolate, melted*

1. Preheat the oven to 180°C/350°F/gas mark 4. Line 2 baking sheets with non-stick baking parchment.
2. Melt the butter, sugar and honey together in a heavy saucepan. Remove from the heat and add the flour, peel, cherries and almonds. Mix until smooth.
3. Drop teaspoonfuls of the mixture on to baking sheets lined with non-stick baking parchment, leaving plenty of space for them to spread during baking. Spread slightly with the spoon.
4. Bake in the preheated oven for 8–10 minutes until golden. Remove from the oven and leave on the sheets for 2 minutes, then transfer to a wire rack to cool completely.
5. When cold spread the flat sides of the biscuits with melted chocolate. Leave until the chocolate is on the point of setting, then mark it with wavy lines with the prongs of a fork. Leave until the chocolate cools and hardens.

# DANISH PASTRIES

Most Danish pastries require almond filling and icing as well as the basic dough. Instructions for these are given first, followed by individual instructions for Almond Squares, Pinwheels, etc.

When rolling out Danish pastry, care should be taken to prevent the butter breaking through the paste and making the resulting pastry heavy. Use a heavy rolling pin, bring it fairly firmly down on to the paste and roll with short, quick, firm movements. Do not push it. Avoid using too much flour. If the paste is becoming warm and unmanageable, wrap it up and chill well in the refrigerator before proceeding.

The icing should not be made until the pastries are baked. Danish pastries are frequently scattered with toasted flaked almonds while the icing is still wet. Sometimes sultanas, small pieces of canned pineapple or apple purée are included in the filling.

MAKES 6
For the pastry
*15g/½oz fresh yeast*
*1 tablespoon caster sugar*
*100ml/3½fl oz warm milk*
*225g/8oz plain flour*
*a pinch of salt*
*1 egg, lightly beaten*
*110g/4oz unsalted butter, softened*
*1 egg, beaten, to glaze*

For the almond paste filling
*45g/1½oz butter*
*45g/1½oz icing sugar*
*30g/1oz ground almonds*
*2 drops of vanilla essence*

For the glacé icing
*boiling water to mix*
*110g/4oz icing sugar*

**1.** Dissolve the yeast with 1 teaspoon of the sugar and the milk.
**2.** Sift the flour with a pinch of salt into a bowl. Add the remaining sugar. Make a well in the centre and drop into it the egg and the yeast mixture.

**3.** Using a round-bladed knife, mix the liquids, gradually drawing in the surrounding flour to make a soft dough. If extra liquid is required, add a little more water.
**4.** When the dough leaves the sides of the bowl, turn it on to a floured work top and bring together gently until fairly smooth. Roll into a longish rectangle 5mm/¼in thick.
**5.** Divide the butter into hazelnut-sized pieces and dot it over the top two-thirds of the dough, leaving a 1cm/½in clear margin round the edge. Fold the pastry in 3, folding the unbuttered third up over the centre section first, and then the buttered top third down over it. You now have a thick 'parcel' of pastry. Give it a 90-degree turn so that the former top edge is on your right. Press the edges together.
**6.** Dust lightly with flour and roll again into a long rectangle. Fold in 3 as before. Chill in the refrigerator for 15 minutes.
**7.** Roll and fold the pastry once or twice again, turning it in the same direction as before, until the butter is worked in well and the paste does not look streaky. Chill in the refrigerator for at least 30 minutes, or overnight, before proceeding with one of the recipes below.
**8.** To make the almond paste, cream the butter, add the sugar and beat well until light and soft. Mix in the ground almonds and flavour with vanilla essence. Mix well but do not overbeat or the oil will run from the almonds, making the paste greasy.
**9.** When ready to use, make the glacé icing: mix enough boiling water into the sugar to give an icing that will run fairly easily – about the consistency of cream.

NOTE: If using dried or easy-blend yeast, see page 604.

# ALMOND SQUARES

**1.** Follow the instructions above.
**2.** Preheat the oven to 200°C/400°F/gas mark 6.
**3.** Roll the pastry on a floured baking sheet into a 25 × 20cm/10 × 7in rectangle. Cut into 5cm/2in squares.
**4.** Put a spoonful of the filling into the centre of

each piece of pastry. Fold each corner into the middle and press it down lightly into the almond paste to stick it in position.

**5.** Prove for 15 minutes (put into a warm, draught-free place to allow the dough to rise). Press down the middle of the squares.

**6.** Brush with beaten egg and bake in the preheated oven for 15–20 minutes.

**7.** Leave to cool completely on a wire rack, then spoon over freshly made glacé icing.

# CROSSES

**1.** Follow the instructions on page 634.

**2.** Preheat the oven to 200°C/400°F/gas mark 6.

**3.** Roll the pastry out thinly on a floured baking sheet and cut it into 13cm/5in squares.

**4.** Cut through each square and then overlap the 2 opposite corners.

**5.** Fill the central hole with almond paste filling or apple purée.

**6.** Leave to prove (rise) for 15 minutes in a warm, draught-free place.

**7.** Brush with beaten egg and bake in the preheated oven for 15–20 minutes.

**8.** Leave to cool on a wire rack, then dust with icing sugar or spoon over freshly made glacé icing.

# PINWHEELS

**1.** Follow the instructions on page 634.

**2.** Preheat the oven to 200°C/400°F/gas mark 6.

**3.** Roll the pastry out thinly on a floured baking sheet and cut it into 13cm/5in squares. From each corner, towards the centre of each square, make a cut about 3cm/1½in long. Put a blob of almond filling in the uncut centre of each square.

**4.** Fold alternate points of pastry (one from each corner) into the middle and press on to the filling to secure. This leaves one unfolded point at each corner, and the pastry should now resemble a child's pinwheel.

**5.** Leave to prove (rise) for 15 minutes in a warm, draught-free place. Press down the corners.

**6.** Brush with beaten egg and bake in the preheated oven for 15–20 minutes.

**7.** Leave to cool on a wire rack, then spoon on freshly made glacé icing.

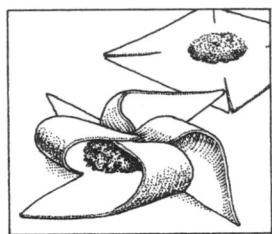

*Cut and fill pinwheels as in recipes*

# CINNAMON WHEELS

In this recipe the almond paste is replaced with a cinnamon filling.

For the cinnamon filling
*55g/2oz butter*
*55g/2oz sugar*
*2 teaspoons ground cinnamon*
*small handful of dried fruit and chopped mixed peel*

**1.** Follow the instructions on page 634, omitting the almond filling.

**2.** Make the cinnamon filling: cream the butter with the sugar. Add the cinnamon and mix well.

**3.** Preheat the oven to 200°C/400°F/gas mark 6.

**4.** Roll the pastry out to a 25 × 20cm/12 × 8in rectangle. Place on a floured baking sheet.

**5.** Spread the butter mixture over the dough, leaving a narrow margin clear all around. Scatter over the dried fruit and peel.

**6.** Roll the pastry, from one end, into a thick roll. Cut into 2.5cm/1in slices. With lightly floured hand, flatten each slice to the size of the palm of your hand. Leave to prove (rise) in a warm, draught-free place.

**7.** Brush with egg glaze and bake in the preheated oven for 15 minutes.

**8.** Allow to cool slightly on a wire rack, then spoon over freshly made glacé icing.

# CRESCENTS

**1.** Follow the instructions on page 634.
**2.** Preheat the oven to 200°C/400°F/gas mark 6.
Roll out the pastry on a floured baking sheet into
a 30 × 15cm/12 × 6in rectangle. Cut into
7.5cm/3in squares and cut each square diagonally
in half.
**3.** Place a small piece of almond paste at the base
(long side) of each triangle. Roll it up from the
base to the tip and curve into a crescent shape.
**4.** Leave to prove (rise) for 15 minutes in a warm,
draught-free place.
**5.** Bake in the preheated oven for 15–20 minutes
or until a good brown.
**6.** Leave to cool on a wire rack, then spoon over
freshly made glacé icing.

# PALMIERS

Palmiers are usually made from leftover
trimmings of puff pastry.

**1.** Preheat the oven to 200°C/400°F/gas mark 6.
**2.** Do not roll the trimmings up into a ball as you
would with shortcrust pastry – this would spoil
the carefully created layers in the paste. Lay the
strips or pieces flat on top of each other, folding
them if necessary.
**3.** Using caster sugar instead of flour, on a work
top or board, roll the pastry out into a rectangle
5mm/¼in thick. Sprinkle well with caster sugar.
Fold each end of the pastry to the centre, then
fold the pastry in half. Cut the roll across into
slices 1cm/½in wide.
**4.** Lay the slices flat on a damp baking sheet, set
well apart, and flatten well with a sugared rolling
pin or your hand. Bake in the preheated oven for
10 minutes or until pale brown, with the
underside caramelized. Turn over and bake for a
further 10 minutes.
**5.** Leave to cool on a wire rack.

NOTE: These are delicious sandwiched together
with strawberry jam and whipped cream.

# ECCLES CAKES

MAKES 6
*225g/8oz flour quantity rough puff pastry (see
 page 463)*

For the filling
*15g/½oz butter*
*55g/2oz soft light brown sugar*
*110g/4oz currants*
*30g/1oz chopped mixed peel*
*½ teaspoon ground cinnamon*
*¼ teaspoon freshly grated nutmeg*
*¼ teaspoon ground ginger*
*grated zest of ½ lemon*
*1 teaspoon lemon juice*

For the glaze
*1 egg white*
*caster sugar*

**1.** Preheat the oven to 220°C/425°F/gas mark 7.
**2.** Roll out the pastry to the thickness of a £1
coin. Cut out 12.5cm/5in rounds. Set aside to
relax.
**3.** Melt the butter in a saucepan and stir in all the
other filling ingredients. Cool.
**4.** Place a good teaspoon of filling in the centre of
each pastry round.
**5.** Dampen the edges of the pastry and press
together in the centre, forming a small ball. Turn
the balls over and roll them lightly until the fruit
begins to show through the pastry.
**6.** With a sharp knife, make 3 small parallel cuts
on the top.
**7.** Beat the egg white lightly with a fork, until
frothy. Brush the top of the Eccles cakes with this
and sprinkle with caster sugar.
**8.** Place on a baking sheet and bake in the
preheated oven for 20 minutes, or until lightly
browned.

# ICINGS,
# FILLINGS,
# SWEETS
# AND PETITS FOURS

---

# APRICOT GLAZE

*3 tablespoons apricot jam*
*2 tablespoons water*
*juice of ½ lemon*

**1.** Place all the ingredients in a heavy saucepan.
**2.** Bring slowly to the boil, stirring gently (avoid beating in bubbles) until syrupy in consistency. Strain.

NOTE: Use when still warm, as the glaze becomes too stiff to manage when cold. It will keep warm standing over a saucepan of very hot water.

# CHOCOLATE BUTTER ICING

*110g/4oz plain chocolate, chopped*
*1 tablespoon water*
*55g/2oz unsalted butter*
*110g/4oz icing sugar, sifted*
*1 egg yolk*

**1.** Melt the chocolate in a heavy saucepan with the water, stirring continuously.
**2.** Beat together the butter and icing sugar until light and fluffy.
**3.** Beat in the egg yolk followed by the melted chocolate.

# CRÈME AU BEURRE MERINGUE

This is a light, soft cake frosting.

For the meringue
*2 egg whites*
*110g/4oz icing sugar*
*85g/3oz unsalted butter*
*85g/3oz salted butter*

Suggested flavourings
*grated lemon or orange zest*
*melted plain chocolate*
*coffee essence*

**1.** Put the egg whites with the icing sugar into a heatproof bowl and set over a saucepan of simmering water. Whisk until the meringue is thick and will hold its shape. Remove from the heat and continue to whisk until slightly cooled.
**2.** Beat the butter until soft and gradually beat in the meringue mixture.
**3.** Flavour to taste as required.

# SOURED CREAM AND CHOCOLATE ICING

*140g/5oz plain chocolate*
*150ml/¼ pint soured cream*
*2 teaspoons caster sugar*

**1.** Break up the chocolate and place in a double saucepan.
**2.** Add the soured cream and sugar. Melt together over a low heat. Leave to cool and thicken.

# CRÈME AU BEURRE MOUSSELINE

This is a rich, creamy cake filling.

*110g/4oz granulated sugar*
*8 tablespoons water*
*4 egg yolks*
*grated zest of 1 lemon*
*110g/4oz unsalted butter*
*110g/4oz salted butter*

**1.** Dissolve the sugar in the water and when completely dissolved boil rapidly to the short thread stage, about 108°C/225°F on a sugar thermometer. At this point a little sugar syrup, pulled between finger and thumb, will form a thread. Remove from the heat immediately.
**2.** Whisk the yolks and lemon zest and pour on the syrup. Keep whisking until thick.
**3.** Soften the butter and whisk gradually into the mixture. Allow to cool.

NOTE: This makes quite a small quantity of icing. However, it is very rich.

# GLACÉ ICING

225g/8oz icing sugar is enough to ice an 18cm/7in sponge.

*225g/8oz icing sugar*
*boiling water to mix*

**1.** Sift the icing sugar into a bowl.
**2.** Add enough boiling water to mix to a fairly stiff coating consistency. The icing should hold a trail when dropped from a spoon but gradually find its own level. It needs surprisingly little water.

NOTE: Hot water produces a shinier icing than cold. Also, the icing, on drying, is less likely to craze, crack or become watery if made with boiling water.

# FEATHER ICING

*225g/8oz icing sugar*
*boiling water to mix*
*food colouring or melted chocolate*

**1.** Sift the icing sugar into a bowl.
**2.** Add enough boiling water to mix to a fairly stiff coating consistency. The icing should hold a trail when dropped from a spoon but gradually find its own level.
**3.** Take 2 tablespoons of the icing and colour it with food colouring or melted chocolate.
**4.** Place in a piping bag fitted with a fine writing nozzle.
**5.** Spread the remaining icing smoothly and evenly over the top of the cake, using a warm palette knife.
**6.** While it is still wet, quickly pipe lines, about 2.5cm/1in apart, across the top of the cake.

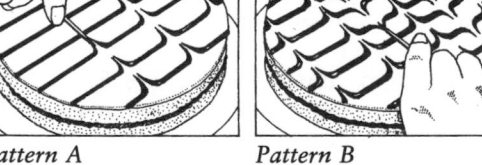

*Pattern A*          *Pattern B*

**7.** Now draw lines at right angles to the coloured lines with a pin or sharp knife, dragging the tip through the coloured lines to pull them into points. If the pin is dragged in one direction through the coloured icing lines, Pattern A will result: if the pin is dragged alternately in opposite directions through the coloured icing lines, Pattern B will result.

NOTE: Smooth melted jam can be used instead of coloured icing for the feathering.

# SUGAR PASTE

Sugar paste is a simple mock fondant icing and is easy to mould and shape; it is very useful for decorating children's party cakes.

*1 tablespoon liquid glucose*
*1 egg white*
*450g/1lb icing sugar, sifted*

**1.** Warm the liquid glucose in the bottle in a saucepan of hot water.
**2.** Beat together the glucose, egg white and icing sugar. Shape into a ball.
**3.** Knead on a surface dusted with icing sugar until pliable. This will take 5 minutes.

NOTES: Store in a polythene bag in the refrigerator for up to 3 months.
   Sugar paste can be coloured as required. Simply add food colouring and knead until thoroughly incorporated.

# FONDANT ICING

*225g/8oz loaf sugar*
*115ml/4fl oz water*
*½ teaspoon liquid glucose, or a pinch of cream of*
*   tartar plus 1 teaspoon water*

**1.** Dissolve the sugar in the water over a low heat without boiling.
**2.** Mix in the glucose or the cream of tartar and the water. Cover and bring to the boil. Boil to the soft ball stage (115°C/235–240°F on a sugar

thermometer). At this point, a spoonful of the sugar syrup dropped into a bowl of cold water will form a soft ball when rolled between the fingers. Stop the sugar syrup from cooking any further by dipping the bottom of the pan into a bowl of cold water. Let it cool slightly.

**3.** Moisten a cold hard surface and pour the sugar syrup on to it in a steady stream. With a metal spatula, fold the outsides of the mixture into the centre.

**4.** Continue to turn with a spatula and work until the fondant becomes fairly stiff. Knead into balls. Place in a bowl and cover with a damp cloth for 1–2 hours.

**5.** If the fondant is to be stored, place in a screw-top jar. When ready to use, put it into a heatproof bowl and set it over a saucepan of simmering water to melt.

NOTES: A sugar thermometer is almost essential to get the syrup exactly the right consistency: not too liquid, nor too hard.

To make coffee fondant icing, proceed as above but add 2 teaspoons coffee essence to the sugar syrup before pouring on to the work surface.

# ROYAL ICING

Icing a cake with royal icing is an advanced skill, and these notes are intended as a reminder for those who have already iced a cake or two. Royal icing is traditionally used (over a layer of marzipan) for the coating and decoration of special-occasion fruit cakes. It keeps very well.

**1.** More than with any other cooking, it is vital to clean up as you go along. It is almost impossible to produce delicate and neat work from a cluttered work surface. Get all the nozzles and piping bags lined up before you begin icing.

**2.** Never overfill the piping bag. This leads to the stick in icing oozing out of the top.

**3.** Keep all full piping bags under a damp cloth or in a polythene bag to prevent the icing in the nozzle from drying out.

**4.** Always keep the icing covered with a damp cloth when not in use to prevent it from drying out.

**5.** Always clean the nozzles immediately after use, using a pin to ensure that no icing is left in the tip.

**6.** Practise the required pattern on the work surface before tackling the cake. Don't try complicated things like roses and scrolls before you have mastered the easier decorations like trellis, shells, stars and dots.

**7.** Follow the instructions slavishly.

**8.** Never lick your fingers or equipment. Even a little wet icing can make you feel sick.

**9.** 450g/1lb sugar makes enough for a 20cm/8in cake; 900g/2lb sugar makes enough for a 25cm/10in cake.

For 1 coat of icing for a 20cm/8in cake
*1–2 egg whites*
*450g/1lb icing sugar*

Mix the egg white with 3 tablespoons of the icing sugar, and add lemon juice or glycerine if required (see below). Gradually add the remaining sugar and mix very well until the icing is soft, very white, fluffy and will hold its shape. More sugar can be added if the mixture is too sloppy. Blue colouring, if used (see below), is added last.

## FLAVOURINGS AND COLOURINGS

**1.** 1 drop of blue food colouring makes white icing a very bright white.

**2.** 1 teaspoon lemon juice to 225g/8oz sugar makes the icing a little sharper and less sickly.

**3.** ½ teaspoon glycerine to 225g/8oz sugar produces a softer icing which will not splinter when cut. Without glycerine, royal icing eventually hardens to an unbreakable cement. More glycerine can be added, but this will give a softer icing unsuitable for a tiered cake. None need be used if the cake is to be eaten within 24 hours of icing.

## CONSISTENCY

A cake is normally covered with 2–3 coats of icing and decorated with either piping or 'run-in' work. The consistency varies for each coat.

FIRST COATING: very thick – the icing should stand up in points if the beating spoon is lifted from the bowl.

SECOND COATING: a little thinner (the points should flop over at the tips, like rabbit ears).

THIRD COATING: the icing should be of thick pouring consistency.

FOR PIPING: consistency as for the first coating.

FOR RUN-IN WORK: as for the third coating.

## BUBBLES
Royal icing should be beaten as little as possible: if making it by hand or in an electric mixer, stop as soon as it is smooth and glossy. If there are any bubbles, leave the icing, covered with a damp cloth, in the refrigerator overnight.

## APPLYING THE FIRST COAT
It is easier to apply the first layer of royal icing in two (for a round cake) or three (for a square cake) stages rather than all at once. The top is iced first and allowed to dry for 24 hours before icing the sides. On a square cake two of the opposite sides are iced and allowed to dry before the second two sides are iced.

Place a small spoonful of icing on a cake board about 5cm/2in larger in diameter than the cake, and put the cake on top. It will now stick to the board. Spoon half the icing on to the top of the cake with a palette knife and spread to the edge, using a paddling action to remove any air bubbles. Then, using a clean metal ruler, a 'straight edge' or large palette knife placed in the centre of the cake, draw the icing forwards and backwards across the cake until it is completely smooth and level and can be drawn off the cake.

Carefully remove any icing that has fallen down the sides of the cake. Leave to dry for 24 hours. Put the cake and board on an icing turntable or upturned bowl and spread the icing evenly around the sides, using a special icing scraper or a palette knife held at an angle of 45 degrees to the cake. Try to turn the cake around in one movement as you ice in order to ensure a smooth finish. For a square cake, ice two of the opposite sides.

Store the cake for at least 24 hours in a clean, cool, dry place to dry before you ice the other two sides. If the storage place is damp, it will prevent the icing from during and it will slowly

slip down the sides of the cake. If it is too warm, the cake will 'sweat' and oil from the marzipan will be drawn into the icing.

## APPLYING THE SECOND COAT
This may not be necessary if the first layer is very smooth. If it is not perfect, smooth it down with fine sandpaper. Brush the surface well with a grease-free brush to remove any loose icing. Ice the cake as for the first coating, but use a slightly thinner icing.

## APPLYING THE THIRD COAT OR FLOAT
A three-tier wedding cake or a less than perfectly iced cake may need a third layer of icing. If this is necessary, proceed when the second coating is dry. Prepare the surface as previously instructed.

Before converting the icing into the desired pouring consistency, pile a little thick icing into a piping bag fitted with a no. 1 or 2 writing nozzle and cover it with a damp cloth. Add a little egg white to the remaining icing and beat until smooth and of a pouring consistency. Leave in a tightly covered container for 30 minutes. (Stretching a piece of clingfilm over the bowl will do.) This is to make the air bubbles rise to the surface. If you do not do this, air bubbles will break all over the surface of the cake, making little holes in the icing.

With the writing nozzle, pipe an unbroken line of icing around the top edge of the cake. Now pour the runny icing into a piping bag, remove the nozzle and guide it over the top of the cake, flooding the surface and carefully avoiding the piped line. With the handle of a teaspoon, work the flooding to edge of the cake. The piped line will prevent the icing running off.

## DECORATING WITH ICING
You must have a clear idea of the design before you begin. If it is a geometric pattern, draw it on a piece of tracing paper and place this on the cake. Using a large pin, prick where the lines meet. Remove the paper and you will be left with guidelines made by the pinpoints. Join these up with more pricked holes so that the design is visible. Half-fill the piping bags, fitted with the chosen nozzles, with the icing mixed to the correct consistency. Put them under a wet cloth

until needed. Get everything you will need ready on or near your work surface (such as more bags and extra nozzles, a large spoon, a palette knife, a small bowl of hot water for washing the nozzles).

## DIRECT PIPING

STAR PIPING: Fit the bag with a star nozzle. Hold the nozzle upright, immediately above and almost touching the top of the cake, and squeeze gently from the top of the bag. Stop pressing and lift the bag away. Always stop pressing before lifting the bag away.

DOT OR PEARL PIPING: Use a plain nozzle, and pipe as for stars. If the dots are too small, do not try to increase their size by squeezing out more icing; use a larger nozzle.

STRAIGHT LINES: with a plain nozzle, press the bag as for making a dot but leave the icing attached to the cake surface – do not draw away by lifting the bag. Hold the point of the nozzle about 4cm/1½in above the surface of the cake and, pressing gently as you go, guide rather than drag the icing into place. The icing can be directed more easily into place if it is allowed to hang from the tube.

TRELLIS WORK: with a plain nozzle, pipe parallel lines 5mm/¼in apart. Pipe a second layer over the top at right angles or at an angle of 45 degrees to the first. Then pipe another layer as closely as possible over the first set of lines, then another set over the second layer, and so on until you have the desired height of trellis. Six layers (three in each direction) is useful for an elaborate cake.

SHELLS: Use a star nozzle. Hold the bag at an angle of about 45 degrees. Pipe a shell, release the pressure on the bag and begin a new shell one-eighth of the way up the first shell, so that each new shell overlaps its predecessor.

SCROLLS: Use a star nozzle. Hold the bag at an angle of about 45 degrees. Pipe a scroll first from left to right and then from right to left.

RUN-IN WORK: Using a writing nozzle, pipe the outline of a design (e.g. leaf, Father Christmas, etc.) on to oiled kitchen foil or greaseproof, waxed paper or non-stick baking parchment.

'Float' runny icing in the centre, and leave to set. Lift off and stick on to the cake with wet icing.

NOTE: Variations of pressure when piping both shells and scrolls make the icing emerge in the required thickness. Shells and scrolls can be made into very attractive borders when combined with trellis work and edged with pearls.

## CAUSES OF FAILURE

BROKEN LINES
- Icing too stiff.
- Pulling rather than easing into place.
- Making the icing with a mixer set at too high a speed, causing air bubbles.

WOBBLY LINES
- Squeezing the icing out too quickly.
- Icing too liquid.

FLATTENED LINES
- Icing too liquid.
- Bag held too near the surface.

## INDIRECT PIPING

Indirect piping is done on to oiled moulds or waxed paper and, when dry, the piped shapes are stuck to the cake with a little wet icing.

TRELLISED SHAPES: Pipe as for direct piping on to waxed paper or oiled moulds (the backs of teaspoons, patty tins, cups or glasses). Leave for 24 hours, then warm over a very low heat to dislodge them. Slide off the mould and fix to the cake with a little wet icing.

FLOWERS: you need confectioner's flower nails and petal nozzles. The icing should be thick. The petals are piped individually on to the oiled surface of the flower nail, the biggest petals first and then the smaller ones. If the lower nail is covered with oiled kitchen foil, the flower can be removed carefully after piping and the nail used for the next flower. When dry, green icing leaves (piped and dried separately) can be attached to the back of the flowers with a little wet icing.

When making coloured flowers, it is helpful to tint the icing to a pale colour first. After they have dried, they can be touched up with a paint brush to give the flowers a more natural appearance. By varying the angle at which the piping bags are held, flatter petals (for daisies, violets and primroses) or thicker, more rounded petals (for roses) can be made. Sweet peas are made with 2–3 flat petals slightly overlapping each other with a smaller upright rounded petal piped on top of each flat one.

# MARZIPAN OR ALMOND PASTE (UNCOOKED)

*225g/8oz caster sugar*
*225g/8oz icing sugar*
*450/1lb ground almonds*
*2 egg yolks*
*2 eggs*
*2 teaspoons lemon juice*
*6 drops of vanilla essence*

**1.** Sift the sugars together into a bowl and mix with the ground almonds.
**2.** Mix together the egg yolks, whole eggs, lemon juice and vanilla essence. Add to the sugar mixture and beat briefly with a wooden spoon.
**3.** Lightly dust the working surface with icing sugar. Knead the paste until just smooth (overworking will draw the oil out of the almonds, giving a too greasy paste).
**4.** Wrap well and store in a cool place.

## TO COVER A ROUND CAKE WITH UNCOOKED MARZIPAN

For a 22cm/9in cake you will need:

*uncooked marzipan made with 450g/1lb ground almonds*
*apricot glaze (see page 638)*
*icing sugar for dusting*

**1.** If the cake is not level, carefully shave off some of the top and turn it upside down.
**2.** Measure around the side with a piece of string.
**3.** Lightly dust a very clean work top with icing sugar and roll out two-thirds of the marzipan to a strip the length of the piece of string and the depth of the cake. Trim it neatly.
**4.** Roll out the remaining marzipan to a circle the size of the cake top.
**5.** Brush the sides of the cake with apricot glaze

and, holding the cake firmly between both hands, turn it on to its side and roll it along the prepared strip of marzipan. Turn the cake right side up again. Use a round-bladed knife to smooth the join. Take a jam jar or straight-sided tin and roll it around the side of the cake.
**6.** Brush the top with apricot glazing and, using a rolling pin, lift the circle of marzipan on to the cake. Seal the edges with the knife and smooth the top with a rolling pin.
**7.** Leave to dry on a cake board 5cm/2in larger in diameter than the cake.

## TO COVER A SQUARE CAKE WITH UNCOOKED MARZIPAN

For a 20cm/8in square cake you will need:

*uncooked marzipan made with 450g/1lb ground almonds*
*apricot glaze (see page 638)*
*icing sugar for dusting*

**1.** If the cake is not level, shave off a little of the top. Turn it upside down.
**2.** Measure one side of the cake with a piece of string.
**3.** Lightly dust a very clean work top with icing sugar and roll out two-thirds of the marzipan into 4 strips the length of the piece of string and the depth of the cake. Trim neatly.
**4.** Roll the remaining marzipan, with any trimmings, to a square to fit the top of the cake.
**5.** Brush one side of the cake with apricot glaze. Turn the cake on to its side and, holding it firmly between both hands, place the glazed edge on one strip of marzipan. Trim the edges and repeat with the other 3 sides. Smooth the joins with a round-bladed knife. Take a jam jar or straight-sided tin and roll it around the sides of the cake, keeping the corners square.
**6.** Brush the top of the cake with apricot glaze and, using a rolling pin, lift the square of marzipan on to the cake. Seal the edges with the knife and smooth the top with a rolling pin. Leave to dry on a cake board about 5cm/2in wider, all round, than the cake.

NOTE: Square cakes are normally covered with uncooked marzipan. The cooked paste is too pliable and it is therefore difficult to get square corners.

# COOKED MARZIPAN

This recipe gives a softer, easier-to-handle paste than the more usual uncooked marzipan.

*2 eggs*
*170g/6oz caster sugar*
*170g/6oz icing sugar*
*340g/12oz ground almonds*
*4 drops of vanilla essence*
*1 teaspoon lemon juice*
*icing sugar for kneading*

**1.** Beat the eggs lightly in a heatproof bowl.
**2.** Sift the sugars together and mix with the eggs.
**3.** Place the bowl over a saucepan of boiling water and whisk until light and creamy or until the mixture just leaves a trail when the whisk is lifted. Remove from the heat and whisk until the bowl is cold.
**4.** Add the ground almonds, vanilla and lemon juice.
**5.** Lightly dust a very clean work top with icing sugar. Carefully knead the paste until just smooth. (Overworking will draw out the oil from the almonds giving a too greasy paste.) Wrap well and store in a cool place.

### TO COVER A ROUND CAKE WITH COOKED MARZIPAN
For a 20cm/8in cake you will need:

*cooked marzipan made with 340g/12oz ground*
   *almonds*
*apricot glaze (see page 638)*
*icing sugar*

**1.** If the cake is not level, shave off a little of the top. Turn it upside down. Brush lightly with apricot glaze.
**2.** Lightly dust a very clean work top with icing sugar and roll out the marzipan to a circle 20cm/8in larger in diameter than the cake.
**3.** Place the glazed cake upside down in the centre of the marzipan and, using your hands, carefully work the marzipan up the sides of the cake.
**4.** Take a jam jar or straight-sided tin and roll it around the sides of the cake to make sure that the sides are quite straight, and the edges square.

**5.** Turn it the right way up and place on a cake board 5cm/2in larger in diameter than the cake.

NOTE: Once a cake has been covered with marzipan, it should be left for a minimum of 2 days, but ideally a week, to harden before icing, otherwise the marzipan colour can leak into the icing.

# MARZIPAN DATES

MAKES ABOUT 20
*about 20 fresh or dried dates*
*225g/8oz marzipan (see previous recipe)*

**1.** Slit the dates lengthways almost in half. Take out the stones carefully, making sure that the dates stay whole.
**2.** Form the marzipan into a long sausage about 5mm/¼in in diameter. Cut it into lengths about the size of the dates.
**3.** Place a piece of marzipan in each date and half-close the opening. Place in tiny paper cases.

NOTE: The marzipan can be coloured pale green by the addition of a few drops of green colouring. Work the colour into the marzipan by kneading with one hand.

# TOMMIES

MAKES ABOUT 20
*70g/2½oz caster sugar*
*110g/4oz butter*
*85g/3oz ground hazelnuts*
*140g/5oz plain flour*
*clear honey*
*225g/8oz plain chocolate, chopped*

**1.** Preheat the oven to 180°C/350°F/gas mark 4.
**2.** Cream the sugar and butter together until white.
**3.** Stir in the hazelnuts and flour.
**4.** As soon as the mixture becomes a paste, wrap it and refrigerate for 30 minutes.
**5.** Roll out thinly and cut into 2.5cm/1in rounds with a biscuit cutter or an upturned glass.

**6.** Place on a baking sheet and bake in the preheated oven for 12 minutes. Transfer to a wire rack to cool.

**7.** Spread honey on half the biscuits, then sandwich them with the others. Return to the cooling rack.

**8.** Break up the chocolate into even pieces and place on a heatproof plate over a saucepan of simmering water until it is melted and smooth.

**9.** Spoon the chocolate over to cover the biscuits completely.

**10.** Leave until set. If there is enough melted chocolate left, place in a small piping bag fitted with a writing nozzle and pipe a design over the set chocolate. Store in an airtight container.

# CHOCOLATE CHERRIES

These chocolates should be made a week in advance to allow the full flavour of the brandy to be infused into the cherries. You will need 24 small foil cups to make these sweets.

MAKES 24
*24 black cherries, pitted*
*5 tablespoons brandy*
*225g/8oz chocolate couverture*
*170g/6oz fondant icing (see page 639)*

**1.** Put the cherries into a bowl. Heat up the brandy and pour it over the cherries. Leave to stand for as long as possible.

**2.** Break up the chocolate into even pieces and place in a heatproof bowl set over, not in, a saucepan of simmering water. When the chocolate has melted, use a teaspoon to line the little foil cups with it. Pour out any excess chocolate. Leave to dry.

**3.** Melt the fondant with 2 teaspoons of the brandy from the cherries in a heatproof bowl set over, not in, a saucepan of simmering water.

**4.** Pour in enough fondant to come a third of the way up each foil cup.

**5.** Drain the cherries very well. Add one to each cup. Fill almost to the top with more fondant. Leave to harden for 5–10 minutes.

**6.** Spoon over enough chocolate, swirling it to seal the edges, to cover the fondant icing completely. Leave to cool and harden. Serve in the foil cups.

# MARRONS GLACÉS

These chestnuts are time-consuming to prepare, but nicer than the commercially prepared ones.

*900g/2lb large, chestnuts in their skins*
*570ml/1 pint milk*
*1 vanilla pod, split*
*570ml/1 pint water*
*450g/1lb granulated sugar*
*225ml/8fl oz liquid glucose*

**1.** Put the chestnuts into a large saucepan and cover with water. Bring to the boil, then simmer gently for 5 minutes. Remove from the heat.

**2.** Remove the chestnuts one by one and peel, taking care to remove the inner membrane of the chestnut as well as the skin. It is easier to peel the chestnuts while they are still hot.

**3.** Put the peeled chestnuts into a clean saucepan, pour over the milk and add the vanilla pod. Bring to the boil, then cook the chestnuts over a low heat for 5 minutes, or until completely soft, but not breaking up. Lift the chestnuts out of the milk with a slotted spoon and leave to dry on kitchen paper. Rinse and reserve the vanilla pod.

**4.** Meanwhile, make the syrup: put the water, sugar and liquid glucose into a saucepan. Dissolve the sugar over a low heat, then bring to the boil. Simmer for 5 minutes. Add the chestnuts to the pan with the vanilla pod and bring back to the boil. Simmer for 1 further minute. Pour the chestnuts and syrup into a bowl and leave to cool overnight.

**5.** The following day, put the chestnuts back into the saucepan, bring back to the boil and simmer for 1 minute. Cool overnight. Repeat this process once more the following day.

**6.** Lift the chestnuts out of the syrup with a slotted spoon and leave to drain on a wire rack overnight.

**7.** Place each chestnut in a petit four case and store in a sealed container in a cool, dry place.

# NOUGAT

This recipe has been adapted from one by Mary B. Bockmeyer in *Candy and Candy Making*. You need rice paper to make nougat.

MAKES 850g/1¾LB
*rice paper*
*225g/8oz granulated sugar*
*140g/5oz clear honey*
*1½ tablespoons liquid glucose*
*110ml/4fl oz water*
*2 egg whites*
*1 teaspoon vanilla essence*
*285g/10oz blanched almonds, toasted, chopped*
  *and warmed*
*110g/4oz skinned pistachio nuts, chopped and*
  *warmed*

1. Line a 20cm/8in square tin with rice paper.
2. Put the sugar, honey, liquid glucose and water into a heavy saucepan and stir over a very low heat until the sugar dissolves. Then boil rapidly to the hard crack stage (160°C/318°F on a sugar thermometer).
3. Whisk the egg whites lightly, and gradually pour on the hot syrup, whisking continuously. Whisk until stiff, then add the vanilla essence and chopped nuts. The mixture must be stiff; if not, place in the top of a double boiler and stir until it dries it out a little.
4. Turn into the prepared tin. Cover with a second piece of rice paper. Place a board on top, weight lightly and leave for 1 hour.
5. Cut into diamond shapes to serve.

NOTE: We take the sugar syrup to a very high temperature. This gives the finished sweet a good texture and a very slightly caramelized flavour. For a softer nougat, take the sugar syrup to 155°C/310°F.

# FUDGE

*olive oil for greasing*
*310g/11oz sugar*
*110g/4oz glucose powder*
*290ml/½ pint double cream*
*110g/4oz butter*
*1 tablespoon icing sugar, sifted*

To flavour
*1 vanilla pod, split, or 110g/4oz chocolate*
  *couverture, melted (see page 62)*

1. Prepare 2 trays with a raised edge 2cm/¾in high all the way round by greasing lightly with olive oil.
2. Place the sugar, glucose, cream and butter in a large clean, heavy saucepan. (If a vanilla flavour is required, add the pod with other ingredients.) Bring slowly to the boil, stirring frequently.
3. When boiling, reduce the heat quickly and allow to cook to just above the 'soft ball' stage (see page 477) (remove the vanilla pod if necessary).
4. Remove from the heat and very carefully pour into a machine bowl. Place on a machine with a balloon whisk and turn on to the lowest speed (remember this mixture is very hot, so be careful to check the speed of machine before switching on).
5. Very carefully add the icing sugar and continue whisking until well mixed in. (If a chocolate flavour is required, add the melted couverture after the icing sugar while still on the machine, and mix well).
6. Now very carefully pour the mixture into the oiled trays, ensuring that they are filled to the top.
7. Allow to cool and set, preferably overnight. Cut the fudge into petit four-sized pieces and serve in paper sweet cases.

# CHOCOLATE TRUFFLES

MAKES 24
*255g/9oz chocolate couverture, roughly chopped*
*100ml/3½fl oz double cream*
*1 vanilla pod, split lengthways*
*20g/¾oz unsalted butter*
*cocoa powder, sifted, to finish*

1. Melt the chocolate in a heatproof bowl set over, not in, a saucepan of simmering water. Remove from the heat and leave to cool.
2. Put the cream into a saucepan, add the vanilla pod and bring to scalding point (just below boiling). Remove from the heat and leave to cool. Remove the vanilla pod.
3. Beat the butter until very soft. Mix it into the chocolate, add the vanilla cream and refrigerate until firm.
4. Shape into small balls and roll lightly in cocoa powder.

# GRAND MARNIER TRUFFLES

MAKES ABOUT 60
*175ml/6fl oz double cream*
*2 tablespoons liquid glucose*
*400g/14oz milk chocolate couverture, grated (see page 62)*
*2 tablespoons Grand Marnier*

To finish
*sifted icing sugar*
*grated chocolate or cocoa powder*

1. Pour the cream and glucose into a heavy saucepan. Bring to the boil without stirring. Add the boiling mixture to the couverture. Stir until smooth.
2. Add the Grand Marnier and stir until cool.
3. Pour the mixture into a stainless steel bowl and lay a piece of clingfilm on the surface to prevent a skin from forming. Cool, preferably over night, at room temperature of no more than 24–25°C/75–77°F.
4. Handling the mixture as little as possible, transfer to a piping bag fitted with a 2cm/¾in plain nozzle and pipe bulb shapes on to non-stick baking parchment. Allow to set in the refrigerator.
5. Reshape the truffles in a little icing sugar, then dip into grated chocolate or cocoa powder.

# WHISKY TRUFFLES

MAKES 24
*225g/8oz milk chocolate*
*4 tablespoons double cream*
*3 tablespoons whisky*
*30g/1oz unsalted butter*
*sifted cocoa powder, to finish*

1. Break the chocolate into even pieces and melt in a heatproof bowl set over, not in, a saucepan of simmering water.
2. In another saucepan, bring the cream to the boil, then remove from the heat and mix with the melted chocolate.
3. When well mixed, add the whisky and beat in the butter.
4. Refrigerate until firm.
5. Roll the mixture into a sausage shape, slice crossways and roll into balls the size of a walnut. Toss in the cocoa powder.

# MINT AND TEA CHOCOLATES

MAKES 24
*225g/8oz milk chocolate*
*110ml/4fl oz double cream*
*7g/¼oz Indian tea leaves*
*4 fresh mint leaves, roughly chopped*

1. Break the chocolate into even pieces and melt in a heatproof bowl set over, not in, a saucepan of simmering water.
2. In another saucepan, bring the cream to the boil, then turn off the heat and add the tea and mint. Allow to infuse for 1 minute, then strain.
3. Mix the flavoured cream with the melted chocolate and refrigerate to harden slightly.
4. Roll out the chocolate mixture between 2 sheets of greaseproof paper until 1cm/½in thick. Refrigerate until completely hardened.
5. Using a 2.5cm/1in plain round cutter, cut out the chocolates.
6. They can be served as they are or dipped in warm melted chocolate. Alternatively, the mixture can be rolled into a sausage shape, cut into lengths, rolled with the palms of the hands into balls and dipped in sifted cocoa powder.

# COFFEE AND ORANGE MINI MERINGUES

MAKES 20
For the meringues
*3 egg whites*
*170g/6oz soft light brown sugar*
*1 teaspoon instant coffee powder*

For the filling
*425ml/¾ pint double cream*
*1 tablespoon Grand Marnier*
*grated zest of 1 orange*

1. Preheat the oven to 110°C/225°F/gas mark ½.
2. Line 4 baking sheets with non-stick baking parchment.
3. Whisk the egg whites until stiff but not dry.
4. Gradually add 1½ tablespoons of the sugar and whisk again until stiff and very shiny.

**5.** Whisk in the remaining sugar gradually, with the instant coffee powder.

**6.** Put the meringue into a piping bag fitted with 1cm/½in plain nozzle. Pipe the meringue into small whirls.

**7.** Bake in the preheated oven for about 2 hours until the meringues are dry and will lift easily off the paper. Leave to cool.

**8.** Whip the cream and fold in the Grand Marnier and orange zest. Sandwich the meringues together in pairs.

NOTE: See 'Whisking egg whites', page 554.

# ORANGE TARTLETS

MAKES 24
*170g/6oz flour quantity rich shortcrust pastry (see page 461)*

For the candied orange zest
*1 medium orange*
*340g/12oz granulated sugar*
*3 tablespoons liquid glucose*
*6 tablespoons water*

For the orange curd
*1 large orange*
*1 medium lemon*
*55g/2oz unsalted butter*
*110g/4oz caster sugar*
*4 egg yolks, lightly beaten*

**1.** First make the candied orange zest: remove the zest from the orange with a potato peeler or small sharp knife and cut into 5mm/¼in strips. Put into a small saucepan with enough water to cover and boil for 5 minutes to remove the bitter taste. Drain and refresh under running cold water.

**2.** Bring 225g/8oz of the sugar, the liquid glucose and water to the boil in the saucepan. Remove from the heat and stir in the zest. Allow to stand for 30 minutes. Bring the liquid back to the boil and allow to stand for a further 30 minutes. Remove the zest with a fork and transfer to a wire rack to cool.

**3.** Put the remaining sugar on a plate and roll the orange strips in it. Once they are dry they can be

stored in an airtight container at room temperature for up to a week.

**4.** Preheat the oven to 180°C/350°F/gas mark 4.

**5.** Line small tartlet tins or petit four tins with the pastry. Prick with a fork and chill in the refrigerator to relax.

**6.** Bake the tartlet cases blind for 10 minutes (see page 459). Remove the lining paper and beans and bake until the pastry is dry and light brown. Cool.

**7.** Next make the curd: grate the zest of the orange and half the lemon on the finest gauge of the grater, taking care to grate only the zest, not the pith.

**8.** Squeeze the juice from the orange and lemon.

**9.** Put the zest, juice, butter, sugar and egg yolks into a heavy saucepan or double boiler and heat gently, stirring all the time, until the mixture is thick.

**10.** Strain into a bowl and allow to cool.

**11.** To assemble: using a piping bag fitted with a very small plain nozzle, pipe a round of curd into each shell. Cut the orange zest into small diamonds and use to decorate the tartlets.

# TINY BAKEWELL TARTS

MAKES 36
*225g/8oz flour quantity rich shortcrust pastry (see page 461)*

For the raspberry purée
*225g/8oz raspberries*
*2 tablespoons Framboise liqueur*

For the frangipane
*100g/3½oz butter*
*100g/3½oz caster sugar*
*1 egg, beaten*
*1 egg yolk*
*100g/3½ blanched almonds, ground*
*2 tablespoons plain flour*
*2 drops of almond essence*

For the feather icing
*200g/7oz icing sugar*
*boiling water*
*red food colouring*

**1.** Line 6 × 8cm/3½in tartlet tins with the rich shortcrust pastry. Chill thoroughly.

**2.** Preheat the oven to 200°C/400°F/gas mark 6.

**3.** Make the raspberry purée: put the raspberries into a small saucepan and bring to the boil. Add the Framboise and boil to reduce to a thick purée. Push through a nylon sieve and leave to cool.

**4.** Make the frangipane: cream the butter and when soft add the sugar and beat again until the mixture is light and fluffy.

**5.** Gradually add the egg and the egg yolk, beating well after each addition. Stir in the ground almonds and the flour. Set aside.

**6.** Spread a little of the raspberry purée on to the base of each pastry case. Pile in the frangipane mixture and spread evenly with a palette knife.

**7.** Place the tartlets on a baking sheet and bake in the preheated oven for 20–25 minutes, or until the filling is set and the pastry crisp.

**8.** Allow tartlets to cool completely, then remove from the tins.

**9.** Make the icing: sift the icing sugar into a bowl and add enough boiling water to mix to a soft coating consistency. The icing should hold a trail when dropped from a spoon, but gradually find its own level.

**10.** Take 2 tablespoons of the icing and colour it with the food colouring. Place in a piping bag fitted with a fine writing nozzle.

**11.** Spread the remaining icing smoothly and evenly over the top of each tartlet, using a warm palette knife.

**12.** While the icing is still wet, quickly pipe lines of coloured icing about 5mm/½in apart across the top of each tartlet.

**13.** Now draw lines at right angles to the coloured lines with a cocktail stick, dragging the tip through the coloured lines to pull them to points.

**14.** Allow the icing to set very slightly and cut each tartlet into 6 pieces. Arrange on a serving plate.

# CHOCOLATE SHAPES

*170g/6oz best-quality plain chocolate*

**1.** First make a paper piping bag. Cut a 38cm/15in square of greaseproof paper and fold diagonally in half.

**2.** Hold the paper down with a finger on the middle of the long folded edge. Then bring one corner up to the apex opposite your steadying finger, and hold it with the apex corners together.

**3.** Wrap the other side corner right round the cone to join the other 2 corners. You should now be holding all 3 corners together.

**4.** Fold the corners over together.

**5.** Cut a tear in them so that you have a lug or flange. Fold down this flange to prevent the bag from unravelling.

**6.** Meanwhile, break up the chocolate and place it in a heatproof bowl. Set it over, not in, a saucepan of simmering water. Stir until the chocolate is smooth and melted. Do not overheat or the chocolate will lose its gloss.

**7.** Fill the piping bag with some of the chocolate and snip the tip of the cone to make a small hole.

**8.** Use the chocolate-filled bag to pipe small elegant shapes on a piece of greaseproof paper. Leave to cool and harden.

**9.** Tip the remaining chocolate on to a second piece of greaseproof paper. Leave to cool and, when almost hard, cut into shapes.

**10.** Use as required.

# CHOCOLATE LEAVES

MAKES 20–30
*110g/4oz best-quality plain chocolate, melted*

Choose clean, dry, non-poisonous leaves such as bay or rose leaves. Using a pastry brush, brush the melted chocolate on to each leaf. Leave to harden, then peel the leaf to reveal a perfect chocolate replica. These are useful for decorating cakes and puddings and will keep well in an airtight container in a cool, dry place for up to a week.

# PRESERVING

# PRESERVING

The term 'preserves' covers all food that has been treated to keep for longer than it would if fresh. Frozen food, dried food, salted food and smoked food are all preserves. But in household language, the word means jams, jellies, marmalades, pickles and sometimes bottled food; in short, the sort of preserves found on a good countrywoman's larder shelf.

Jellies are clear preserves, made from strained fruit juice. They should be neither runny nor too solid. Jams are made from crushed fruit. They should almost hold their shape, but be more liquid than jelly. Conserves are jams containing a mixture of fruits, generally including citrus fruit, and sometimes raisins or nuts. Marmalade is jam made exclusively from citrus fruit. Fruit butters are made from smooth fruit purées, cooked with sugar to the consistency of thick cream. Fruit cheese are made in the same way but cooked until very thick. Butters and cheeses, because they are not set solidly and generally contain less sugar than jams, should be potted in sterilized jars. Curds generally contain butter and eggs, are best kept refrigerated, and will not keep for more than a couple of months.

## JAMS, JELLIES AND MARMALADES
These preserves depend on four main factors to make them long-lasting:

**1. The presence of pectin.** This is a substance, converted from the gum-like pectose found to some degree in all fruit, which reacts with the acids of the fruit and with the sugar to form a jelly-like set. Slightly under-ripe fruit is higher in pectin than over-ripe fruit, and some types of fruit are higher in pectin than others, notably apples, quinces, damsons, sour plums, lemons and redcurrants. Jam made from these will set easily. Jam from low-pectin fruit such as strawberries, rhubarb, mulberries and pears may need added

commercial pectin or lemon juice (or a little high-pectin fruit) to obtain a good set.

TO TEST FOR PECTIN: before you add the sugar, take 1 teaspoon of the simmered fruit juice and put it into a glass. When it is cold add 1 tablespoon methylated spirit. After a minute a jelly will have formed. If it is in 1 or 2 firm clots there is adequate pectin in the fruit. If the jelly clots are numerous and soft the jam will not set without the addition of more pectin.

**2. A high concentration of sugar.** Sugar is itself a preservative, and without sufficient sugar the pectin will not act to form the set.

**3. The presence of acid** which, like sugar, acts with the pectin to form a gel or set. Acid also prevents the growth of bacteria, and it helps to prevent the crystallization of the sugar in the jam during storage. If the fruit is low in acid, then tartaric acid, ascorbic acid or lemon juice may be added.

**4. The elimination and exclusion of micro-organisms.** The jam itself is sterilized by rapid boiling. Jam jars need not normally be sterilized since the heat of the jam should be sufficient to sterilize them. However, harmless moulds do sometimes form round the rim and on the surface of jams potted in this way, and sterilizing the jars does help to prevent this. Jam jars may be soaked in solutions bought at chemists for sterilizing babies' bottles etc. Ordinary household bleach will also be effective, but the bottles should be rinsed in boiling water afterwards. The jam funnel should be sterilized with the jars. It is not necessary to sterilize ladles or spoons except by leaving them in the bubbling jam for a minute or two. Jelly cloths or bags need not be sterilized as the juice is dripped through them before being boiled.

Once put into the clean, dry jars, the jam is sealed to prevent the infiltration of mildew spores etc. Melted paraffin wax (melted white candles will do) poured over the surface of the jam makes a good old-fashioned and most effective seal, but most cooks rely on ordinary paper jam covers and a bit of luck.

Ideally, the jam should be sealed while boiling hot, i.e. before any fresh mildew spores can enter. However, if liquid wax is used on hot jam, it may disturb the flat surface, so the slightly cooled but still clear wax is poured on once the jam is set. Two applications of wax are necessary if the first covering shrinks away from the sides of the jar, leaving a gap.

Perhaps the best method of sealing is to use metal screw-tops. They should be sterilized and checked for a tight fit. The jam should be poured up to the shoulder of the jars, leaving a good 1cm/½in. The caps are screwed on tightly as soon as the jars are filled. The cooling jar will form a partial vacuum in the neck, tightly sealing the jar. Plastic lids do not give a reliable seal.

If, in spite of all precautions, mould appears on the top of the jams, it can be scraped off and the jam beneath is perfectly good to eat. But it should be eaten quite quickly as mould spores in the air could re-infect it. Scraping off visible mould will not prevent the invisible spores from multiplying. Jam that is fizzy or fermented should be thrown away.

### YIELD

The amount of finished jam obtained from a given quantity of fruit varies according to type, jellies giving comparatively little, marmalades and whole fruit jams much more. As a general rule, the mixture will yield between 1½ times and double the weight of sugar used. It is wise to over-estimate the amount of jars needed, rather than to have to prepare more at the last minute.

### EQUIPMENT

Making jam is easy enough, but it requires a little organization. First the equipment should be assembled. You will need:

Accurate scales
Preserving pan or a large, heavy saucepan with a solid base
Sharp knives
Grater
Mincer
Long-handled wooden spoons
Slotted spoon
Metal jug with a large lip or a jam funnel
Jam jars
Jam covers, labels and rubber bands (available from chemists and stationers) or metal screw-top lids
Sugar thermometer (not essential but useful)
Perforated skimmer (not essential but useful)

### POINTS TO REMEMBER

1. Make sure all equipment is absolutely clean.
2. Use dry, unblemished, just-ripe fruit.
3. Use preserving, lump, granulated or caster sugar. Modern white sugars are highly refined and therefore suitable. They need little skimming and give a clear preserve. Using preserving sugar has a slight advantage because the crystals are larger and the boiling liquid circulates freely round them, dissolving them rapidly. Caster sugar is inclined to set in a solid mass at the bottom of the pan and takes longer to dissolve. Brown sugar gives an unattractive colour to preserves.
4. Covering lukewarm jam could lead to mildew. If the jam is covered immediately, any bacteria or mildew spores present in the atmosphere are trapped between jam and seal and will be killed by the heat. If the atmosphere is lukewarm and steamy, perfect incubating conditions are created.

### BASIC PROCEDURE

1. Wash and dry the jam jars and warm them in the oven.
2. Pick over the fruit, wash or wipe and cut up if necessary.
3. Put the fruit and water into the pan and set to simmer.
4. Warm the sugar in a cool oven for 20 minutes. When it is added to the fruit it will not lower the temperature too much, necessitating prolonged cooking which could impair the colour of the jam.
5. Bring the fruit to a good boil. Tip in the sugar and stir, without reboiling, until the sugar has dissolved.

**6.** Once the sugar has dissolved, boil rapidly, stirring gently but frequently.

**7.** When the mixture begins to look like jam – usually after about 10 minutes – test for setting. It is important not to overboil since this can make the colour too dark and the texture too solid. It will also ruin the flavour. Overboiling can sometimes even prevent a set by destroying the pectin. If you are using a thermometer, you can check the setting point: 105°C/220°F for jam and 106°C/222°F for marmalade. To test for setting, put a teaspoon of the jam on to an ice-cold saucer and return it to the ice compartment or freezer to cool rapidly. When cold, push it gently with a finger. The jam should have a slight skin, which will wrinkle if setting point is reached. If a finger is drawn through the jam, it should remain separated, not run together. Also, clear jam or jelly should fall from a spatula not in a single stream, but forming a wavy curtain and dripping reluctantly from more than one point.

**8.** As soon as a setting test proves positive, remove the jam from the heat. Skim carefully and then, if the jam contains whole fruit or large pieces of fruit, allow to cool for 15 minutes. This will prevent the fruit rising to the top of the jam jars.

**9.** Put the hot jars close together on a wooden board or tray. Fill them with hot jam with the aid of a jug or jam funnel.

**10.** Seal at once with screw-tops or put waxed paper discs, waxed side down, on the surface of the jam, and cover the tops of the jars with cellophane covers, securing them with a rubber band. Brush the cellophane tops with water to stretch them slightly. Carefully pull them tight. As they dry they will shrink tightly around the jars.

**11.** Wipe the sides of the jars with a hot, clean, damp cloth to remove any drips of jam.

**12.** Label each jar with the type of jam and the date.

**13.** Leave undisturbed overnight.

**14.** Store in a cool, airy, dark place.

MILDEW on the surface of the jam is probably caused by one of the following:

**1.** Using wet jars.

**2.** Covering the jam when lukewarm.

**3.** Imperfect sealing.

**4.** Damp or warm storage place.

**5.** Equipment that is less than spotless.

The mildew should be removed, and the jam consumed fairly quickly.

CRYSTALLIZATION of the sugar in jam is caused by:

**1.** Insufficient acid in the fruit.

**2.** Boiling the jam before the sugar has dissolved.

**3.** Adding too much sugar.

**4.** Leaving jam uncovered.

**5.** Storing in too cold an atmosphere, such as a refrigerator.

FERMENTATION of jam is caused by:

**1.** Insufficient boiling leading to non-setting.

**2.** Insufficient acid leading to non-setting.

**3.** Insufficient pectin leading to non-setting.

**4.** Insufficient sugar leading to non-setting.

**5.** A storage place that is too warm.

**6.** Jars that are less than spotless.

## PICKLES

Pickles are foods, usually vegetables or fruit, preserved in vinegar. Fruit for pickles is generally cooked in sugared vinegar, and stored in this sweetened vinegar syrup. Vegetables are usually, but not always, pickled raw, and are generally salted in dry salt, or steeped in brine, before being immersed in the vinegar. Salting draws moisture out of the food. If salting is omitted, the juices from the vegetables leak into the vinegar during storage, diluting it and impairing its keeping quality. Salt also has preservative powers, and its penetration into the food helps to prevent it going bad, but the main preservative in pickles is vinegar, which prevents the growth of bacteria.

The best salt is pure rock salt or crushed block salt. Pure sea salt is good too, but very expensive. Table salt has additives to make it conveniently free-flowing, but these may cause the pickle to go cloudy.

NOTE: Brass, old-fashioned iron or copper preserving pans or saucepans should not be used in the preparation of foods containing vinegar. The acid reacts with the metal, spoiling both colour and flavour.

BRINING

Brine is a solution of salt in water, and is suitable for the steeping of vegetables for pickling. Firm vegetables such as shallots should be pierced with a needle to allow the brine to penetrate.

*225g/8oz pure salt (not table salt)*
*2.8 litres/4 pints water*

1. Heat the salt and water slowly together until the salt has dissolved.
2. Allow to cool.
3. Prepare (peel, cut up, prick, etc.) the vegetables to be picked, put them into a bowl and pour over the cold brine. Put a plate on top to keep the food submerged.
4. After 24 hours (usually, but check individual recipes) drain well, pat dry and pack into clean jars ready for pickling.

### DRY-SALTING

This is particularly suitable for 'wet' vegetables such as marrow and cucumber.

*110g/4oz dry pure salt (not table salt) per*
*1kg/2¼lb prepared vegetables*

1. Prepare (peel, cut up, etc.) the vegetables. If they are tough (like onions or shallots) pierce them deeply with a needle.
2. Put them in a bowl, sprinkling each layer liberally with salt. Cover and keep cool for 24 hours.
3. Drain off all the liquid, rinse the vegetables in cold water and pat dry in a clean cloth.
4. Pack into clean jars ready for pickling.

### THE VINEGAR

Pickling vinegar should be strong, containing at least 5 per cent acetic acid. Most brand vinegars contain sufficient acid, but homemade vinegars or draught vinegars are not suitable. Brown malt vinegar is the best for flavour, especially if the pickle is to be highly spiced or is made with strong-tasting foods. White vinegar has less flavour, but obviously gives a clearer pickle. Wine vinegar is suitable for delicate mild-tasting foods. Commercial cider vinegar is good too. The vinegar may be spiced and flavoured according to taste by the addition of cayenne pepper, ginger or chillies, or aromatic spices such as cardamom seeds, cloves or nutmeg. Whole spices are best as they can be removed easily, and will not leave the vinegar murky. Ready-spiced pickling vinegar may also be purchased.

## CHUTNEYS

Chutneys are the easiest preserves to make. They are mixtures, always sweet and sour, somewhere between a pickle and a jam. They are generally made of fruit, or sometimes soft vegetables such as tomato or marrow, with vinegar, onion and spices.

Both sugar and salt, themselves preservatives, are present in chutneys, but they are there for flavour more than for their keeping powers. As with jams, boiling the ingredients destroys micro-organisms, but with chutneys obtaining a set is not necessary – like pickles, they depend on vinegar for their keeping qualities.

Fruit and vegetables for chutneys should be sliced or cut small enough to be lifted with a teaspoon, but not so small as to be unidentifiable in the chutney. As the ingredients are seldom used whole, you can use damaged or bruised fruit, with the imperfect bits removed.

Chutneys improve with keeping. They can generally be eaten after 2 months (before this their taste is harsh) but are at their best between 6 months and 2 years. If the chutney is to be kept for more than 6 months a more secure seal than a jam cover is advisable. See the notes for jars and lids on pages 652–3.

### BASIC PROCEDURE FOR CHUTNEY

1. Prepare the ingredients: wash fruit and vegetables, peel where necessary, cut up, etc. Wash dried fruit if bought loose. Chop or mince onions. Use a stainless steel fruit knife for fruit or vegetables liable to discolour.
2. Put all the ingredients, except the sugar and vinegar, into a saucepan (not an unlined copper, brass or old-fashioned iron one: see note on page 654). The spices should be tied in a muslin bag if they are to be removed later.
3. Add enough of the vinegar to easily cover the other ingredients.
4. Cook slowly, covered or not, until the fruit or vegetables are soft, and most of the liquid has evaporated.
5. Add the sugar and the rest of the vinegar and stir until the sugar has dissolved.
6. Boil to the consistency of thick and syrupy jam.
7. Put into clean, hot jars. Cover as for jam if to be eaten within 6 months. Use non-metal lids or stoppers if the chutney is to be kept longer.

NOTE: In recipes for chutneys that do not require prolonged cooking to soften the ingredients (e.g. apricot and orange chutney, page 663) the sugar and vinegar may be added with the other ingredients, the whole being boiled together.

## BOTTLING FRUIT

The preservation of food by bottling works on the principle of destruction by heat of all micro-organisms present in the fruit or syrup Because a partial vacuum is created in the jar, by expelling air during processing, a tight seal is formed between the lid and jar, keeping the sterilized contents uncontaminated.

The procedure described here applies to the bottling of fruit only. Because vegetables and meat contain little or no acid, and are therefore likely to harbour bacteria they need considerably longer processing at higher temperatures to become safe. This lengthy heating tends to spoil the texture and flavour of the food. In general, bottling meat and vegetables is not worth the effort, time and risks involved. But fruit and tomatoes, because they are fairly acid, do not contain bacteria; and the relatively harmless yeasts and moulds are more easily destroyed.

Fruit may be bottled in plain water or in salted water.

### JARS

Kilner jars come with a glass lid and a rubber ring. The lid is kept in place by a metal screw-band. The rubber ring must not be re-used as it will not give a good seal twice, and is perishable. Kilner jars are closed loosely before processing, and only tightened fully when they come out of the sterilizer or saucepan, while still hot. As the hot air inside cools it will contract, pulling the lid on tightly as it does so.

Parfait jars are similar to Kilner jars but the lid is held in place by a metal gimp or clip. It is clipped shut before processing. There is sufficient spring in the gimp to allow the escape of steam during heating. The lid tightens automatically as the jar cools after processing.

### PREPARING THE FRUIT

Fruit can be bottled raw or cooked. If the fruit is cooked the processing time need only be long enough for sterilization, not for tenderizing the fruit. If raw, the fruit is cooked and sterilized at the same time, and may need longer processing. Fruits that cook to a pulp easily, such as berries and cooking apples, are generally processed from raw as the minimum time at great heat is the objective. Other fruits, such as pears and peaches, which require an uncertain time to soften, are frequently precooked as it is then possible to tell if they are tender. Precooking has a further advantage. Once the fruit is cooked and softened, more of it can be packed into the jars. Also, it will not rise up in the jar when sterilized. Fruit bottled from raw frequently rises.

### POINTS TO REMEMBER

**1.** Make sure the bottling jars are not cracked and that the tops are in good condition. Jars must have new rubber rings fitted each year. Screw bands or metal clips should work properly and jars should be clean.
**2.** Make the sugar syrup before peeling the fruit.
**3.** Choose perfect, not over-ripe fruit.
**4.** If fruit needs cutting or peeling, use a stainless steel knife.
**5.** If it is likely to discolour (apples or pears), drop the pieces into cold water containing a teaspoonful of ascorbic acid (vitamin C powder or a fizzy Redoxon tablet will do) until you are ready to process them.
**6.** Pack the fruit (cooked or raw) up to the necks of the jars.

### PROCESSING THE FRUIT

The fruit can be processed (or sterilized) in the following ways:

**1.** In a sterilizer (sometimes called a pressure canner). This is a purpose-made machine like a large pressure cooker. It is reliable and easy to use, but by no means essential. Follow the manufacturer's instructions.
**2.** In a pressure cooker, which works like a sterilizer but holds fewer jars and will not hold tall ones. About 2.5cm/1in of water in the bottom is sufficient, as no evaporation will take place. The process is very quick, and the jars and fruit sterilize in the steam. Wedge the jars with cloths to stop them rattling. Allow the pressure to fall before opening the cooker. Consult the manufacturer's manual.

**3.** In a deep saucepan or bath of boiling water. Stand the jars in the container and wedge them with cloths to stop them rattling or cracking. Fill with hot water right over the tops of the jars, or at least up to their necks. Cover as best you can with a lid or foil and tea-towels to keep in the steam.

NOTES: Processing in the oven is not recommended. The temperatures cannot be reliably checked and the jars sometimes crack or explode, or boil over.

If the fruit has been cooked in an open pan with its syrup, it is possible to get a good seal by closing the jar as soon as the hot fruit and boiling syrup are in it, without further sterilization, but the method is not reliable and processing according to the instructions on page 656 is recommended.

TESTING FOR SEALING

After processing, the jars should be lifted on to a board. Kilner jars should be screwed up tight. Jars should be left undisturbed for 24 hours. They must then be tested for sealing. Remove the bands on the Kilner jars, or loosen the clips on the Parfait jars. It should be possible to lift the jars by the lids, without breaking the seal. If the lid of a jar comes off, the jar must be reprocessed with a new rubber ring or the contents must be eaten within a day or two.

STORING

Wipe the jars with a damp clean cloth, label them with the date of bottling, and store in a dark place. They will keep for at least 18 months, probably for many years.

# GOOSEBERRY AND ORANGE JAM

MAKES 675G/1½ LB
*450g/1lb gooseberries*
*grated zest and juice of 2 oranges*
*150ml/¼ pint water*
*450g/1lb warmed preserving sugar*

**1.** Top and tail the gooseberries.
**2.** Put them into a preserving pan or large saucepan with the orange zest and juice and the water. Simmer until soft and yellowish.
**3.** Add the sugar, allow it to dissolve, then boil rapidly until setting point is reached. Allow to stand for 10 minutes
**4.** Pour into warmed dry jars.
**5.** Cover and label the jars.
**6.** Leave undisturbed overnight. Store in a cool, dark, airy place.

# BLACKCURRANT AND RHUBARB JAM

MAKES 1.3KG/3LB
*450g/1lb blackcurrants*
*450g/1lb rhubarb*
*150ml/¼ pint water*
*900g/2lb warmed preserving sugar*

**1.** Wash the blackcurrants and, using the prongs of a fork, remove the stalks.
**2.** Cut the rhubarb into 5mm/¼in chunks.
**3.** Put the rhubarb, blackcurrants and water into a preserving pan or large saucepan and boil for 30 minutes.
**4.** Add the sugar to the pan and heat slowly until the sugar has dissolved. Then boil rapidly until the jam reaches setting point (about 10–15 minutes). Allow to stand for 10 minutes.
**5.** Pour into warmed dry jars.
**6.** Cover and label the jars.
**7.** Leave undisturbed overnight. Store in a cool, dark, airy place.

# PLUM OR DAMSON JAM

MAKES 675G/1½LB
*900g/2lb barley ripe plums or damsons*
*900g/2lb preserving sugar*

**1.** Halve and stone the plums Crack half the stones and remove the kernels.
**2.** Put the fruit and sugar together in a bowl and leave to stand overnight. (Do not use a metal container.)
**3.** Next day, transfer to a preserving pan or a large saucepan and heat slowly until the sugar has dissolved. Then boil rapidly until the jam reaches setting point (about 7–10 minutes). Add the kernels while the jam is still bubbling. Allow to stand for 10 minutes.
**4.** Pour into warmed dry jars.
**5.** Cover and label the jars.
**6.** Leave undisturbed overnight. Store in a cool, dark, airy place.

NOTES: If the plums are difficult to stone, or damsons or greengages are used, simply slit the flesh of each fruit before mixing with the sugar. During boiling, the stones will float to the top and can be removed with a slotted spoon.

Macerating the fruit with the sugar helps to soften the fruit before cooking and allows the cook to dispense with added water. Cooking is quicker as less liquid must be driven off.

# STRAWBERRY AND REDCURRANT JAM

MAKES 1.5KG/3½ LB
*900g/2lb strawberries*
*450g/1lb redcurrants*
*900g/2lb warmed preserving sugar*

**1.** Hull the strawberries and, using the prongs of a fork, remove the stalks of the redcurrants.
**2.** Put the redcurrants into a preserving pan or large saucepan with 1 tablespoon water. Cook to a pulp (about 5 minutes).
**3.** Add the whole strawberries and bring to the boil.
**4.** Add the sugar and, when dissolved, boil rapidly

for 10–12 minutes until the jam reaches setting point. Remove from the heat and allow to cool for 15 minutes. This will prevent the berries from rising in the jars. Allow to stand for 10 minutes.
**5.** Pour into warmed dry jars.
**6.** Cover and label the jars. Leave undisturbed overnight.
**7.** Store in a cool, dark, airy place.

# ORANGE MARMALADE

MAKES 1.5KG/3½ LB
*900g/2lb Seville oranges*
*2 lemons*
*2.8 litres/5 pints water*
*1.5kg/3lb warmed preserving sugar*

**1.** Cut the oranges and lemons in half and roughly squeeze them into a large bowl. (Do not bother to extract all the juice: squeezing is done simply to make removing the pips easier.)
**2.** Remove the pips and tie them up in a piece of muslin or a clean 'J' cloth.
**3.** Slice the skins of the oranges and lemons, finely or in chunks as required, and add them to the juice with the bag of pips and the water. Leave to soak for 24 hours.
**4.** Transfer to a preserving pan or large saucepan and simmer gently until the orange rind is soft and transparent-looking (about 2 hours).
**5.** Tip the sugar into the orange pulp. Stir well while bringing the mixture slowly to the boil.
**6.** Once the sugar has dissolved, boil rapidly until setting point is reached (106°C/222°F). This may take as long as 20 minutes, but usually less. Test after 5 minutes and then again at 3-minute intervals.
**7.** Allow to cool for 10 minutes, then pour into warmed dry jars. Cover with jam covers and leave for 24 hours.
**8.** Label and store in a cool, dark, airy place.

NOTE: Soaking overnight helps to soften the fruit. It may be dispensed with, but longer simmering will then be necessary.

# CLEAR GRAPEFRUIT MARMALADE

MAKES 675G/1½ LB
*2 grapefruit*
*4 lemons*
*2.2 litres/4 pints water*
*900g/2lb warmed preserving sugar*

1. Wash the grapefruit and lemons. Cut in half and squeeze out the juice.
2. Strain the juice into a bowl with the water.
3. Shred or chop the skins of the lemons and grapefruit. Put them into a loose muslin bag with the pips of the lemons only.
4. Put the bag into the pan of juice and water. Allow to soak overnight.
5. Transfer the juice and muslin bag to a preserving pan or large saucepan and simmer until the skins in the bag are tender (1–2 hours) and the liquid in the pan has reduced by half.
6. Remove the muslin bag, squeezing it to extract all the juice before discarding.
7. Add the warmed sugar, stir and bring to the boil.
8. Boil rapidly for 8–10 minutes and test for setting.
9. Pour the marmalade into warmed dry jars and cover. Leave undisturbed for 24 hours. Store in a cool, dark place.

NOTE: If shreds of rind are wanted in the jelly, pare the zest from the pith and shred it separately. Add to the boiling liquid.

# THREE FRUIT MARMALADE

MAKES 2.7KG/6LB
*900g/2lb oranges*
*3 lemons*
*1 grapefruit*
*2.7kg/6lb warmed preserving sugar*

1. Scrub the fruit well and put into a preserving pan or large saucepan with 3.3 litres/6 pints of water. Bring to the boil, then simmer until the fruit is tender. Test by piercing the skin with the handle of a wooden spoon. This will take about 1½

hours and the water will have reduced in quantity.
2. Leave the water in the pan and remove the fruit, allow to cool and cut in half. Scoop out the pips and tie them in a piece of muslin, leaving a long piece of string that can be tied to the pan handle.
3. Cut the fruit halves into strips or alternatively chop them, in batches, in a blender. Put back into the pan of water and add the sugar. Warm gently and stir until the sugar dissolves.
4. Bring to the boil and boil rapidly until setting point is reached.
5. Leave for 15 minutes until the peel has settled. Stir the marmalade and discard the pips.
6. Fill the warmed sterilized jars and seal. Leave for 24 hours. Label and store in a cool, dark, dry place.

# REDCURRANT JELLY

*redcurrants*
*450g/1lb warmed preserving sugar to each
   570ml/1 pint of juice extracted*

1. Place the washed redcurrants in a stone or earthenware pot, cover and place in the oven preheated to 180°C/350°F/gas mark 4. If the jar or pot used is glass rather than pottery, stand it in a bain-marie (a roasting pan half-filled with hot water) before placing in the oven. Cook until the redcurrants are tender and the juice has run from them (about 1 hour). Mash the redcurrants with a fork 3 or 4 times during cooking.
2. Alternatively, cook the redcurrants until soft in a microwave oven, or in a saucepan with a little water, stirring frequently.
3. Turn into a scalded muslin or jelly bag and allow to drain overnight.
4. Measure the juice and pour into a preserving pan or large saucepan and add 450g/1lb sugar to each 570ml/1 pint of juice.
5. Dissolve over a low heat, then boil rapidly until setting point is reached (about 5 minutes).
6. Pour into warmed dry jars.
7. Cover with jam covers and leave for 24 hours.
8. Label and store in a cool, dark, dry place.

# HEDGEROW JELLY

Pick rosehips, haws (hawthorn berries), blackberries, crab apples, sloes, wild bullaces or plums, rowanberries and elderberries in any proportions you like, making sure, however, that there is a good proportion of high-pectin fruit among them.

If the rosehips are very hard, simmer them in water until soft, then add everything else, roughly cut up if large (e.g. crab apples) but not peeled or pitted. Add enough water to cover three-quarters of the fruit. Simmer slowly, stirring occasionally, until mushy.

Drip overnight through a jelly bag or several layers of cloth, without stirring. Measure the juice and return to a clean pan, with 450g/1lb warmed preserving or granulated sugar for every 570ml/1pint of juice. Boil to 105°C/220°F for a set. Cover while hot if using screw-top jars; while cold if using paper or wax covers.

# APPLE AND SAGE JELLY

MAKES 1.8KG/4LB
*2kg/4½lb cooking apples*
*1.1 litre/2 pints water*
*150ml/¼ pint cider vinegar*
*450g/1lb warmed preserving sugar to each*
  *570ml/1 pint juice*
*55g/2oz fresh sage leaves, finely chopped*

1. Wash the apples and cut them into thick pieces without peeling or coring.
2. Put the apples and water into a saucepan, bring to the boil, cover and simmer for about 1 hour. Add the vinegar and boil for a further 5 minutes.
3. Meanwhile, scald a jelly bag twice with boiling water.
4. Hang the jelly bag from the legs of an upturned stool and place a bowl underneath it.
5. Pour the apple pulp and juice into the jelly bag and allow to drip steadily for about 1 hour or until the bag has stopped dripping. Do not squeeze the bag.
6. Measure the juice and pour into the preserving pan. Add 450g/1lb sugar to every 570ml/1 pint of juice.

7. Bring to the boil slowly, ensuring that the sugar has dissolved before the juice has boiled, and stirring constantly.
8. Boil briskly, uncovered, for about 10 minutes, skimming frequently. Test for setting point. When this has been reached, allow the jelly to cool slightly and stir in the sage.
9. Pour into the warmed jam jars and cover.

# LEMON CURD

MAKES 450G/1LB
*2 large lemons*
*85g/3oz butter*
*225g/8oz granulated sugar*
*3 eggs, lightly beaten*

1. Grate the zest of the lemons on the finest gauge on the grater, taking care to grate the zest only, not the pith.
2. Squeeze the juice from the lemons.
3. Put the lemon zest, juice, butter, sugar and eggs into a heavy saucepan or double boiler and heat gently, stirring all the time until the mixture is thick.
4. Strain into warmed jam jars and cover.

NOTES: This curd will keep in the refrigerator for about 3 weeks.

If the curd is boiled, no great harm is done, as the acid and sugar prevent the eggs from scrambling.

# ORANGE CURD

MAKES 450G/1LB
*juice of 1 lemon*
*grated zest of 2 oranges*
*juice of 1 orange*
*85g/3oz butter*
*225g/8oz granulated sugar*
*3 eggs, lightly beaten*

1. Put all the ingredients into a heavy saucepan or double boiler and heat gently, stirring all the time until the mixture is thick.
2. Strain into a bowl and allow to cool. Strain into warmed jam jars and cover.

# DAMSON CHEESE

MAKES ABOUT 900G/2LB
*1kg/2¼lb damsons*
*150ml/¼ pint water*
*450g/1lb granulated sugar to each 570ml/1 pint*
*purée*

1. Wash the damsons and remove the stalks. Put them into a saucepan with the water. Cook slowly until the fruit is very soft.
2. Sieve the fruit and discard the stones.
3. Measure the pulp and use 450g/1lb granulated sugar for every 570ml/1 pint of purée.
4. Put the pulp and sugar together in a large, heavy saucepan. Heat gently until the sugar has completely dissolved, then bring to the boil.
5. Boil steadily until you can make a clear track through the purée with a wooden spoon, showing the base of the pan. Keep stirring, otherwise the cheese will burn on the bottom of the pan.
6. Pour into warmed jars and cover with waxed discs and cellophane circles.

NOTE: Traditionally, this cheese is served as an accompaniment to lamb or game. It therefore needs to be put into a straight-sided jar or bowl so that it can be turned out and sliced. It is also delicious spread on bread.

# BOTTLED APPLES

*340g/12oz preserving sugar*
*1.1 litre/2 pints water*
*12 dessert apples*

1. Prepare the sugar syrup: dissolve the sugar in the water over a low heat. When completely dissolved, boil rapidly for 2–3 minutes.
2. Peel, core and slice the apples.
3. Pack tightly into 1kg/2¼lb jars.
4. Pour over the hot syrup.
5. Cover with the lids (not screwed tight if Kilner jars) and place in a deep saucepan. Cover with boiling water.
6. Boil steadily for 20 minutes.
7. Remove the jars and if Kilner jars seal firmly.
8. Leave for 24 hours, then test for sealing.

# SPICED PEARS

*560g/1¼lb preserving sugar*
*425ml/¾ pint white malt vinegar or white wine*
*vinegar*
*6 small whole pears, peeled*
*15g/½oz cinnamon stick*
*5 cloves*
*2 dried chillies (optional)*
*2 pieces of preserved stem ginger, diced*

1. Dissolve the sugar with the vinegar over a low heat. When completely dissolved, bring to the boil.
2. Add the prepared pears, the spices and the ginger.
3. Simmer gently until the pears are tender but not broken (about 35 minutes).
4. Remove the pears with a slotted spoon and pack into a preserving jar.
5. If the syrup is rather thin, boil it rapidly until fairly thick and tacky.
6. Pour over the pears, and add the spices and ginger.
7. Put on the lid (if using a Kilner jar do not tighten). Place in a deep saucepan and cover with boiling water.
8. Boil steadily for 10 minutes.
9. Remove the jars and (if Kilner jars) seal firmly.
10. Leave for 24 hours, then test for sealing.

# BOTTLED RASPBERRIES

*900g/2lb raspberries*
*340g/12oz granulated sugar*

1. Pick over the fruit but do not wash it.
2. Pack into 1kg/2¼lb jars, sprinkling with sugar between the layers. Shake the jars to settle the fruit. Leave overnight.
3. Top up with more fruit and sugar so that the jars are absolutely full.
4. Cover with the lids (not screwed too tightly if Kilner jars). Place in a deep saucepan and cover with boiling water.
5. Boil steadily for 10 minutes.
6. Remove the jars and (if Kilner jars) seal firmly.
7. Leave for 24 hours, then test for sealing.

# PICKLING VINEGAR

*1.1 litres/2 pints malt vinegar*
*8g/¼oz blades of mace*
*8g/¼oz cinnamon stick*
*8g/¼oz allspice berries*
*8g/¼oz black peppercorns*
*8g/¼oz mustard seeds*
*4 cloves*
*1 chilli*
*15g/½oz fresh root ginger, sliced*

**1.** Put everything into a large saucepan (not an unlined copper or brass or iron one), cover tightly and heat gently, until on the point of simmering. Remove from the heat.
**2.** Leave for 3 hours, then strain through muslin or a jelly bag. The vinegar is now ready for use.

# PICKLED SHALLOTS OR SMALL ONIONS

An example of a raw pickle, salted in brine.

*small, even-sized pickling onions or shallots*
*brine (see pages 654–5)*
*pickling vinegar (see above)*

**1.** Scald the onions or shallots to make peeling them easier. Peel them. Prick deeply all over with a needle or skewer.
**2.** Put the onions or shallots into a bowl and cover with brine. Leave for 48 hours.
**3.** Drain thoroughly and pat dry with a clean cloth.
**4.** Pack tightly, but without bruising, into clean jars.
**5.** Cover well with the cold pickling vinegar.
**6.** Seal and store for 6 months before eating.

# PICKLED BEETROOT

An example of a cooked pickle not given preliminary salting.

*small, even-sized beetroots, unpeeled*
*pure salt*
*pickling vinegar (see above)*

**1.** Cook the beetroots in boiling, heavily salted water (1 tablespoon to 1.1 litres/2 pints) until tender (1–2 hours).
**2.** Drain and allow to cool, then peel.
**3.** Pack, without bruising, into jars.
**4.** Cover well with cold pickling vinegar.
**5.** Add 1 teaspoon pure salt to each 1kg/2¼lb jar.
**6.** Seal and store.

NOTE: If a milder pickle is wanted, the vinegar may be diluted by an equal amount of water. But if this is done the beetroot must be packed in a preserving (Kilner or Parfait) jar, and must be given a sterilization treatment in a boiling water bath for 30 minutes, or in a pressure cooker or canner for 2 minutes.

# DILL CUCUMBER PICKLE

An example of a pickle dry-salted and packed in sweet spiced vinegar.

MAKES 900G/2LB
*900g/2lb cucumbers*
*pure salt*
*pickling vinegar (see above)*
*1 head of fresh dill, or 1 tablespoon dill seeds*
*2 teaspoons mustard seeds*
*2 cloves of garlic, sliced*
*170g/6oz granulated or preserving sugar*

**1.** If the cucumbers are small enough to leave whole, prick them all over with a needle. If large, cut them into chunks, without peeling. Put into a bowl, sprinkling each layer liberally with salt. Leave for 24 hours.
**2.** Put the spiced vinegar (about 1 litre/1¾ pints) into a saucepan and add the dill, mustard seed, garlic and sugar. Bring slowly to the boil, then cool.
**3.** Rinse the cucumber well and pat dry with a clean cloth.
**4.** Pack the cucumber into jars. Cover with the cooled vinegar, adding the flavourings.
**5.** Seal and store.

# GREEN TOMATO AND APPLE CHUTNEY

MAKES 2.25KG/5LB
*1.35kg/3lb green tomatoes*
*900g/2lb apples (any kind)*
*2 large onions, chopped*
*110g/4oz sultanas*
*1 teaspoon salt*
*1 teaspoon ground ginger*
*½ teaspoon freshly grated nutmeg*
*½ teaspoon freshly ground white pepper*
*a pinch of ground allspice*
*340g/12oz granulated or preserving sugar*
*860ml/1½ pints vinegar*

1. Chop the tomatoes. Peel, core and chop the apples.
2. Put all the ingredients except the sugar and a cupful of vinegar into a saucepan and simmer gently, giving an occasional stir, or 1½ hours, or until the ingredients are soft and the liquid almost evaporated.
3. Add the sugar and the remaining vinegar and stir over a low heat until the sugar has dissolved.
4. Bring to the boil and boil rapidly, stirring, until thick.
5. Pour into warmed dry jars. If the chutney is to be eaten within 6 months, cover as for jam. If it is to be kept longer, use non-metal lids or stoppers.

# APRICOT AND ORANGE CHUTNEY

MAKES 675G/1½ LB
*4 oranges*
*450g/1lb dried apricots, soaked overnight*
*1 onion, thinly sliced*
*225g/8oz sultanas*
*400g/14oz demerara sugar*
*2 teaspoons rock salt*
*570ml/1 pint cider vinegar*
*1 tablespoon mustard seeds*
*1 teaspoon ground turmeric*

1. Boil the whole oranges for 5 minutes. Pare off the zest with a sharp knife, removing all pith left on the back.
2. Shred the zest into thin needleshreds.
3. Peel the oranges and discard all the pith. Chop up the flesh.
4. Place the orange zest and flesh together with all the remaining ingredients, except for 150ml/¼ pint of the vinegar, into a large saucepan and simmer until the fruit is soft and pulpy and the mixture very thick. Add the remaining vinegar. Boil briefly.
5. Pour immediately into warmed dry jars and cover with jam covers if to be eaten within a few months, or more securely with non-metal lids or stoppers if to be kept longer.

# SPICED FRUIT PICKLE

MAKES 1.3KG/3LB
*900g/2lb mixed fresh fruit, such as plums,*
    *apricots, peaches, rhubarb*
*455g/1lb granulated sugar*
*425ml/¾ pint cider vinegar*
*grated zest and juice of 1 orange*
*1 teaspoon ground ginger*
*4 teaspoons mustard seeds*
*6 cloves*
*1 cinnamon stick*

1. Prepare the fruit by removing the stones and cutting the flesh into 1cm/½in pieces. Do not peel.
2. Dissolve the sugar in the vinegar and add the orange zest and juice, ginger, mustard seeds, cloves and cinnamon stick.
3. Add the fruit and bring to the boil. Simmer carefully for 15 minutes.
4. Strain the fruit and reduce the liquid by boiling until syrupy. Mix it with the fruit.
5. Pour the pickle into sterilized jam jars and seal with jam seals.

NOTE: This can be used straight away but is better if left to mature for at least a month. Store in a cool, dry, dark place.

# HOT PICCALILLI

MAKES 2.7KG/6LB

*450g/1lb salt*
*4.6 litres/8 pints boiling water*
*675g/1½lb cauliflower, broken into small florets*
*450g/1lb cucumber, unpeeled and diced*
*65g/1½lb pickling onions, peeled*
*450g/1lb green beans, topped and tailed and cut*
*    into 2.5cm/1in lengths*
*450g/1lb vegetable marrow, unpeeled and diced*
*45g/1½oz dry English mustard*
*15g/½oz ground turmeric*
*45g/1½oz ground ginger*
*1½ tablespoons plain flour*
*170g/6oz caster sugar*
*1.1 litres/2 pints distilled vinegar*

**1.** Mix together the salt and boiling water. Leave to cool.
**2.** Prepare the vegetables and cover with the brine (salt and water). Leave for 24 hours.
**3.** Drain and rinse the vegetables.
**4.** Mix the mustard, turmeric, ginger, flour and sugar together and mix to a smooth liquid with 570ml/1 pint vinegar.
**5.** Pour the remaining vinegar into a large saucepan. Add the prepared vegetables, and simmer until tender but still crisp. Stir in the spiced flour mixture. Cook, stirring continuously, until the pickles come to the boil and the sauce thickens. Simmer for 3 minutes.
**6.** Pack into jars and cover when cold.

# BREAKFASTS

# POACHED EGGS ON TOAST

SERVES 4
*4 very fresh cold eggs*
*4 slices of fresh toast, buttered*
*salt and freshly ground black pepper*

**1.** Fill a large saucepan with water and bring to simmering point.
**2.** Crack an egg into a cup and tip into the pan, holding the cup as near to the water as possible.
**3.** Raise the temperature so that the water bubbles gently.
**4.** With a slotted spoon, draw the egg white close to the yolk.
**5.** Poach each egg for 2–3 minutes.
**6.** Lift out with the slotted spoon, drain on absorbent kitchen paper and trim the egg whites if they are very ragged at the edges.
**7.** Place each egg on a piece of toast and sprinkle with salt and pepper. Serve immediately.

# JUGGED KIPPERS

This is a simple, labour-saving method of cooking kippers.

SERVES 4
*4 kippers*
*butter*
*freshly ground black pepper*

1. Place the kippers, tails up, in a tall stoneware jug. Pour over enough boiling water to cover the kippers and leave to stand for 5–10 minutes.
2. Serve immediately on a warmed dish with a knob of butter and plenty of pepper.

# KEDGEREE

SERVES 4
*55g/2oz butter*
*140g/5oz (raw weight) long-grain rice, boiled*
*340g/12oz smoked haddock or fresh salmon fillet, cooked, skinned and boned.*
*3 hardboiled eggs, roughly chopped*
*salt and freshly ground black pepper*
*cayenne pepper*

**1.** Melt the butter in a large shallow saucepan and add all the remaining ingredients.
**2.** Stir gently until very hot.

NOTE: If making large quantities, heat in the oven instead of on the top of the stove. Kedgeree will not spoil in a low oven (130°C/250°F/gas mark 1). Stir occasionally.

# MUESLI

Named after Bircher Muesli, a Swiss doctor and health fanatic, this should contain nothing but natural ingredients, and no refined cereals. It usually includes flaked oats and crushed or flaked wheat (including the bran and wheatgerm).

To make a family supply of Muesli mix together:

*450g/1lb instant porridge oats*
*55g/2oz dried apricots, chopped*
*55g/2oz sultanas*
*110g/4oz dried apple flakes*
*55g/2oz hazelnuts, chopped*
*55g/2oz bran*
*30g/1oz flaked almonds*
*110g/4oz 'honey crunch' or 'granola' or other toasted cereal (optional, but improves the texture)*
*30g/1oz unrefined brown sugar*

# PORRIDGE

SERVES 4
*1.1 litres/2 pints water*
*1 teaspoon salt*
*110g/4oz medium oatmeal*

**1.** Bring the water to the boil in a saucepan and add the salt.
**2.** Sprinkle in the oatmeal, keeping the water on the boil and stirring all the time.
**3.** Simmer for 30 minutes, stirring occasionally. If necessary add a little more water.

NOTE: Porridge keeps for an hour or so in a cool oven if covered with a lid, but should not be made too far in advance. Traditionally it is served with salt in Scotland, but in the south milk and sugar are added.

# CANAPÉS,
# SAVOURIES
# AND SNACKS

---

## SMOKED SALMON CATHERINE WHEELS

MAKES ABOUT 80
*1 very large square-edged wholemeal loaf*
*soft butter for spreading*
*450g/1lb thinly sliced smoked salmon*
*freshly ground black pepper*
*lemon juice*

**1.** Put the loaf of bread on a board and carefully cut off the top crust all along the length of the loaf.
**2.** Butter the top of the bread, being careful not to crumble it.
**3.** Now cut as thin a horizontal slice as you can.
**4.** Again butter the loaf and cut off the next slice and so on through the loaf. You should end up with about 10 or 12 long slices.
**5.** Cut off the crusts and lay smoked salmon on all the slices. Sprinkle with black pepper and lemon juice.
**6.** Now, starting at one short end, roll them up carefully.
**7.** Cut each roll into about 8 thin rounds.

NOTES: Unravelling can be prevented if the rolls are wrapped in clingfilm and refrigerated for a few hours before slicing.

For larger rolls or 'Catherine wheels', 2 slices of bread may be used: roll up one, then roll the next round the first roll.

## SMOKED SALMON TRIANGLES

MAKES 40 SMALL TRIANGLES
*5 slices of wholemeal bread*
*soft butter for spreading*
*freshly ground black pepper*
*110g/4oz smoked salmon*
*lemon juice*

**1.** Butter the bread, sprinkle with black pepper and lay the smoked salmon slices carefully on top.
**2.** Sprinkle with lemon juice, then cut off the crusts and cut each slice into 8 triangles.

## SMOKED SALMON ON RYE WITH HORSERADISH

MAKES 50
*12–14 slices of rye bread*
*225g/8oz cream cheese*
*horseradish cream (see page 246)*
*salt and freshly ground black pepper*
*225g/8oz smoked salmon*
*sprigs of fresh dill*

**1.** Remove the crusts from the bread. Cut each slice into 4 even-sized rectangles 4 × 3cm/1½ × 1¼in.
**2.** Season the cream cheese with the horseradish, salt and pepper. Spread it on to the bread rectangles, mounding it neatly.
**3.** Cut the smoked salmon into long thin strips and coil it neatly on top of the cream cheese mixture.
**4.** Decorate each rectangle with a sprig of dill.

## SMOKED OYSTER TARTLETS

MAKES 20
*1 carrot*
*white part of 1 leek*
*salt and freshly ground black pepper*
*20 smoked oysters*
*20 boat or oblong tartlet cases, warmed*
*55g/2oz beurre blanc (see page 253)*

**1.** Cut the carrots and leeks into very fine julienne strips. Place in a steamer, season with salt and pepper and cook until tender.
**2.** Reheat the smoked oysters in their own juice. Drain well.
**3.** Place a little of the cooked vegetables in the base of each tartlet case, cover with a smoked oyster and coat with the beurre blanc. Serve immediately.

# PEKING DUCK CORONETS

MAKES 20
*1 duck leg*
*Hoisin sauce*
*10 wonton skins*
*1 egg white, lightly beaten*
*oil for deep-frying*
*½ cucumber*
*4 spring onions*

**1.** Preheat the oven to 200°C/400°F/gas mark 6.
**2.** Brush the duck leg with Hoisin sauce and bake in the oven for 40 minutes.
**3.** CuT the wonton skins in half. Shape into cones and brush with egg white.
**4.** Heat oil in a deep-fryer until a crumb will sizzle vigorously in it. Deep-fry the wonton cornets for 1 minute. Drain well on absorbent kitchen paper. When required, they can be reheated in the oven.
**5.** Cut the cucumber and spring onions into very fine julienne strips.
**6.** Shred the duck finely.
**7.** Pipe or spoon a little Hoisin sauce into the base of each warm cornet. Stuff with the duck and julienne of vegetables. Serve immediately.

# SPINACH ROULADE WITH SMOKED SALMON AND SOURED CREAM

MAKES 36 SLICES
*450g/1lh fresh spinach or 170g/6oz frozen leaf*
*    spinach*
*7g/¼oz butter*
*2 eggs, separated*
*salt and freshly ground black pepper*
*a pinch of freshly grated nutmeg*

For the filling
*150ml/¼ pint soured cream*
*110g/4oz smoked salmon, chopped*
*1 teaspoon chopped fresh dill*

**1.** Preheat the oven to 190°C/375°F/gas mark 5.
**2.** Line a 26 × 19cm/10½ × 7½in Swiss roll tin with non-stick baking parchment.

**3.** Cook the spinach and drain it thoroughly. Push through a sieve and beat in the butter.
**4.** Gradually beat the egg yolks into the spinach and season with salt, pepper and nutmeg. Whisk the egg whites until stiff but not dry, and fold them into the spinach. Pour the mixture into the prepared Swiss roll tin and spread it flat. Bake in the preheated oven for 10–12 minutes, or until dry to the touch.
**5.** Mix all the filling ingredients together.
**6.** Turn the roulade out on to a piece of greaseproof paper and remove the lining paper.
**7.** Cut the roulade in half lengthways. Spread each rectangle with the filling and, starting with the longer edge, roll up one as you would a Swiss roll. Wrap in damp greaseproof paper and return to the oven for 5 minutes. Remove and allow to cool.
**8.** Remove from the greaseproof paper and slice each roll into about 18 pieces.

# SMOKED SALMON AND DILL PARCELS

MAKES ABOUT 16
*2 large smoked trout*
*150ml/¼ pint double cream, lightly whipped*
*a squeeze of lemon juice*
*½ teaspoon horseradish cream (see page 246)*
*freshly ground black pepper*
*8 slices of smoked salmon*
*sprigs of fresh dill*

**1.** Cut off the heads and tails of the trout. Skin them and remove the bones. Mince or pound the flesh and mix with the cream, lemon juice, horseradish and pepper to taste. It should be a firm pâté.
**2.** Cut the smoked salmon into 6cm/2½in squares. Trim off the corners. Place a teaspoon of the pâté on the centre of the smoked salmon square and fold the ends together. Turn over and place a small sprig of dill on each.

# NORI SEAWEED CANAPÉS

MAKES ABOUT 16
*140g/5oz short-grain rice*
*200ml/7fl oz water*
*a pinch of salt*
*2 sheets of Nori seaweed*

For the mushroom filling
*8 dried mushrooms*
*2½ tablespoons caster sugar*
*a pinch of salt*
*2 tablespoons vodka*
*1¼ teaspoons soy sauce*

For the carrot filling
*1 carrot, finely diced*
*1 tablespoon oil*
*2 spring onions, thinly sliced*
*1 small piece of fresh root ginger, peeled and*
*    finely chopped*
*2 tablespoon dry sherry*
*1 tablespoon caster sugar*
*1½ teaspoons soy sauce*

For the vinegar dressing
*1½ tablespoons rice wine or white wine vinegar*
*1 tablespoon caster sugar*
*½ teaspoon salt*

1. Make the mushroom filling: in a saucepan, soak the mushrooms in enough water to cover them for 30 minutes. Add the remaining ingredients and simmer for 10 minutes, or until the liquid has evaporated. Remove from the heat and set aside.
2. Make the carrot filling: cook the carrot in the oil in a small saucepan over a very low heat. When just softened, add the spring onions and cook for 1 minute, then add the sherry, sugar and soy sauce and cook for a further 3 minutes or until glazed. Remove from the heat and set aside.
3. Mix together the ingredients for the vinegar dressing and set aside.
4. Rinse the rice under cold running water until the water runs clear. Put the rice into a saucepan and add 200ml/7fl oz cold water. Leave to stand for 30 minutes. Bring to the boil and cook, covered, for 5 minutes or until the water is

absorbed. Turn off the heat and, leaving the lid on, leave the rice to sit for 15 minutes to dry out slightly.
5. Tip the rice into a large bowl, pour over the vinegar dressing and stir until cold, by which time the rice should be shiny.
6. Place the seaweed on a clean tea-towel. Arrange strips of the fillings lengthways on top of the seaweed. Leave a gap of 2.5cm/1in at the end.
7. Using the tea-towel to help, carefully roll up the seaweed from the longer edge as you would a roulade. Press firmly and cut into 1cm/½in slices.

# STUFFED DATES

MAKES 60
*60 fresh dates (about 2 boxes)*
*340g/12oz cream cheese*
*110g/4oz nibbed almonds, toasted*

1. Cut the dates open lengthways. Replace each stone with 1 teaspoon of the cream cheese.
2. Slightly close the dates, leaving the cream cheese showing. Dip the cheese into the almonds.

# CELERY AND CREAM CHEESE

MAKES ABOUT 50
*10 sticks of celery*
*340g/12oz cream cheese*
*fresh chives, finely chopped*
*salt and freshly ground white pepper*

1. Wash and scrub the celery, and cut into 5cm/2in lengths. If the sticks are very wide, they should be split in two.
2. Cream the cheese and add the chives, salt and pepper.
3. Using a piping bag fitted with a fluted nozzle, pipe the cheese into the hollow of the celery sticks. It may be necessary to trim the underside of each celery stick to prevent it from rolling over when put on a plate.

# COCKTAIL SAUSAGES WITH MUSTARD DIP

MAKES 120
*60 chipolata or 120 cocktail sausages*

For the dip
*mustard mayonnaise*

**1.** Preheat the oven to 200°C/400°F/gas mark 6.
**2.** If using chipolata sausages, make them into cocktail size by twisting each sausage in two. After twisting, cut them apart.
**3.** Put the sausages into a greased roasting pan and bake in the preheated oven for 20 minutes, or until beginning to brown. The roasting pan should be shaken at intervals to prevent the sausages from sticking. They should be stirred around to prevent those on the edges getting browner than those in the middle.
**4.** Drain well and pierce each with a cocktail stick. Serve the dip separately.

# ANCHOVY PUFF PASTRY FINGERS

MAKES 40
*225g/8oz flour quantity rough puff pastry (see page 463)*
*40 anchovy fillets*
*6 tablespoons milk*
*beaten egg to glaze*

**1.** Divide the pastry in half and roll each piece thinly to a 30 × 10cm/12 × 4in rectangle. Place on 2 baking sheets and chill in the refrigerator to relax.
**2.** Meanwhile, soak the anchovies in the milk for 15 minutes to remove any oil and excess salt. Drain and trim the fillets neatly.
**3.** Preheat the oven to 200°C/400°F/gas mark 6.
**4.** Brush one piece of pastry with beaten egg, prick with a fork and place the anchovy fillets neatly on it. You should be able to lay out 2 neat rows of 20 fillets each.
**5.** Cover with the second piece of pastry and brush again with beaten egg. Press well together and prick all over with a fork.

**6.** Bake in the preheated oven for 10–12 minutes until golden-brown. Leave to cool on a wire rack.
**7.** When cold, cut the pastry into neat 5 × 1cm/ 2 × ½in fingers so that each finger has an anchovy fillet sandwiched inside it.
**8.** Warm through before serving.

# TWISTED CHEESE STRAWS

MAKES 50
*170g/6oz plain flour*
*a pinch of salt*
*100g/3½oz butter*
*45g/1½oz freshly grated Parmesan cheese or mixed Parmesan and Gruyère or Cheddar cheese*
*a pinch of freshly ground black pepper*
*a pinch of cayenne pepper*
*a pinch of dry English mustard*
*beaten egg*

**1.** Preheat the oven to 190°C/375°F/gas mark 5.
**2.** Sift the flour with the salt into a bowl. Rub the butter into the flour with your fingertips until the mixture resembles fine breadcrumbs. Add the cheese, pepper, cayenne and mustard.
**3.** Bind the mixture together with enough egg to make a stiff dough. Refrigerate for 10 minutes.
**4.** Line 2 baking sheets with greaseproof paper. Roll the dough into a rectangle and cut into 9 × 2cm/3½ × ¾in strips. Twist each strip 2–3 times like a barley sugar stick.
**5.** Bake in the preheated oven for 8–10 minutes until biscuit-brown.

# POPPY AND SESAME SEED STRAWS

MAKES 40
*110g/4oz flour quantity puff pastry (see page 464)*
*1 egg, beaten*
*2 tablespoons poppy seeds*
*½ tablespoons sesame seeds*

**1.** Preheat the oven to 200°C/400°F/gas mark 6.
**2.** Roll out the pastry quite thinly, brush with beaten egg and cut in half.

3. Sprinkle one half with poppy seeds and the other half with sesame seeds.

4. Line 2 baking sheets with greaseproof paper. Roll each piece of pastry out very thinly. Cut into long strips and twist like barley sugar strips. Place on the prepared baking sheets.

5. Bake in the preheated oven for 10–12 minutes until golden-brown.

## CHEESE SABLÉS

MAKES 24
225g/8oz plain flour
salt and freshly ground black pepper
225g/8oz butter
225g/8oz Gruyère or strong Cheddar cheese, grated
a pinch of dry English mustard
a pinch of cayenne pepper
beaten egg

1. Preheat the oven to 190°C/375°F/gas mark 5. Line 2 baking sheets with greaseproof paper.
2. Sift the flour with a pinch of salt into a bowl. Rub in the butter until the mixture resembles breadcrumbs.
3. Add the cheese, salt, pepper, mustard, cayenne and enough egg just to bind. Work into a paste but do not over-handle or the pastry will become greasy and tough.
4. Roll out on a floured board to a 5mm/¼in thickness. Cut into rounds or triangles and brush with the remaining beaten egg.
5. Bake in the preheated oven for about 10 minutes until golden-brown. Leave to cool on a wire rack.

## PARMESAN AND CHIVE CRISPS

Use these to garnish soups and salads.

butter for greasing
110g/4oz fresh Parmesan cheese, finely grated
1 tablespoon very finely chopped chives

1. Preheat the oven to 200°C/400°F/gas mark 6. Grease a baking sheet lightly with melted butter. Heat it in the oven until really hot.

2. Sprinkle the cheese into 4 × 7.5cm/3in rounds on the baking sheet. Flatten them slightly.
4. Bake in the preheated oven for 2½ minutes, sprinkle with the chives and bake for 30 seconds.
5. Remove from the oven and allow to crisp and harden for 2 minutes. Remove to a wire rack and leave to cool.

## STILTON GRAPES

110g/4oz Stilton cheese
110g/4oz cream cheese
110g/4oz seedless grapes
110g/4oz walnuts, finely chopped

1. Beat the cheeses together. Press a little of the mixture around each grape and roll in the nuts.

## WARMED MEDITERRANEAN PRAWNS WITH DIPPING SAUCE

20 large Mediterranean prawns
sesame oil

For the marinade
3 tablespoons soy sauce
1 tablespoon sesame oil
2 tablespoons dry sherry
1cm/½in piece of fresh root ginger, peeled and
    finely chopped
1 clove of garlic, cut into slivers

For the dipping sauce
1 tablespoon sesame oil
2 tablespoons soy sauce
1 tablespoon clear honey
3–4 tablespoons ginger syrup (from a jar of
    preserved ginger)
1 tablespoon red wine vinegar
4 spring onions, chopped

**1.** Peel the prawns and remove the black vein down the back of each prawn.
**2.** Mix together the marinade ingredients and add the prawns. Leave for 3–4 hours.
**3.** Make the dipping sauce: mix together all the ingredients except the spring onions.
**4.** Fry the prawns fairly briskly in the sesame oil. They are cooked when they turn pink and begin to butterfly out.
**5.** Tip the prawns on to a serving platter. Put the dipping sauce in a bowl, add the spring onions and serve immediately.

NOTE: Serve cocktail sticks with the prawns.

# DILL PANCAKES WITH SMOKED TROUT MOUSSE

MAKES 16
*1 tablespoon chopped fresh dill*
*150ml/¼ pint French pancake batter (see page 471)*

For the smoked trout mousse
*1 smoked trout*
*70ml/2½fl oz double cream, lightly whipped*
*a squeeze of lemon juice*
*½ teaspoon horseradish cream (see page 246)*
*freshly ground black pepper*

To garnish
*sprigs of fresh dill*

**1.** Mix the chopped dill into the pancake batter.
**2.** Make the pancakes as described on page 472, then stamp out into rounds, using a small fluted cutter.
**3.** Make the mousse: remove the skin and bones from the trout. Mince or pound the flesh and mix with the cream, lemon juice, horseradish and pepper to taste.
**4.** Place a teaspoon of the mousse on each pancake and pinch the edges together to form a cone.
**5.** Garnish each pancake with a sprig of dill.

# GRAVAD LAX ON RYE

MAKES 24
*1 packet of rye bread*
*mustard and dill mayonnaise*
*lollo rosso lettuce*
*55g/2oz gravad lax (see page 172)*

**1.** Stamp out rounds of rye bread, using a small round cutter.
**2.** Spread a little mustard mayonnaise on each round.
**3.** Place a little lollo rosso on top, spread with a little more mustard mayonnaise and arrange a piece of gravad lax on top.

# TINY STUFFED NEW POTATOES

MAKES 20
*20 even-sized tiny new potatoes*
*French dressing (see page 254)*
*75ml/2½fl oz soured cream*
*black lumpfish roe*
*¼ red pepper, cut into tiny dice*
*1 small bunch of fresh chives, snipped*

**1.** Peel or scrub the potatoes and cook in gently simmering salted water until tender (about 20 minutes). Drain and, while still warm, toss in the French dressing and leave until cool.
**2.** Lift the potatoes out of the dressing and pat dry with absorbent kitchen paper. Cut a thin slice from the bottom of each potato so that it can stand upright.
**3.** With a melon baller, carefully scoop a hollow out of the top of each potato. Pipe or spoon a little soured cream into each hollow.
**4.** Top one-third of the potatoes with the lumpfish roe, one-third with red pepper and the remaining potatoes with the chives.

# TOASTIE CASES

MAKES 20
*5 thin slices of bread*
*butter, melted*

**1.** Preheat the oven to 180°C/350°F/gas mark 4. Stamp out rounds of bread, using a small fluted cutter.
**2.** Dip into the melted butter and mould into tiny patty tins. Press an empty patty tin on top and bake in the preheated oven until golden-brown and crisp.

# TOASTIES WITH SALMON ROE

MAKES 20
*20 toastie cases (see above)*
*70ml/2½fl oz soured cream*
*small jar of salmon roe*

**1.** Fill the toasties with soured cream and top with a little salmon roe.

NOTE: These must be filled at the last minute as they go soggy very quickly.

# TOASTIES WITH TUNA PÂTÉ

MAKES 20
*110g/4oz cream cheese*
*110g/4oz tuna fish*
*lemon juice*
*freshly ground black pepper*
*20 toastie cases (see above)*

To garnish
*sprigs of fresh chervil or dill*

**1.** Beat the cream cheese and tuna fish together until very smooth. Season to taste with lemon juice and black pepper.
**2.** Pipe into the toastie cases and garnish each with a sprig of chervil or dill.

NOTE: These must be filled at the last minute as they go soggy very quickly.

# MASCARPONE TARTLETS WITH SALMON ROE

*225g/8oz Mascarpone cream cheese*
*30 tartlet cases (see below)*
*1 small jar of salmon roe*

To garnish
*sprigs of fresh dill*

**1.** Beat the Mascarpone cheese lightly and place in a piping bag fitted with a fluted nozzle.
**2.** Pipe the cheese into the tartlet cases and top with a little salmon roe.
**3.** Garnish each tartlet with a small sprig of dill.

# TARTLET CASES

MAKES ABOUT 60
*225g/8oz quantity rich shortcrust pastry (see page 461)*

**1.** Preheat the oven to 190°C/375°F/gas mark 5.
**2.** Roll out the pastry 2mm/⅛in thick. Stamp out circles, using a small fluted cutter.
**3.** Press the circles into tiny patty tins or barquette (boat-shapes) moulds. Chill in the refrigerator for 20 minutes.
**4.** Bake the tartlet cases blind for about 10 minutes (see page 459), removing the lining paper and beans after 5 minutes.
**5.** Cool on a wire rack and use as required.

# DROP SCONES WITH CAVIAR

MAKES 20
*150ml/¼ pint drop scone batter (see page 473)*
*70ml/2½fl oz soured cream*
*1 small jar of black lumpfish roe*

**1.** Make up small drop scones 3cm/1¼in in diameter. Spread each drop cone with a little soured cream and top with lumpfish roe.

## STUFFED MANGETOUT

MAKES 20
*20 mangetout*
*110g/4oz cream cheese*
*a little milk*
*1 tablespoon mixed finely chopped fresh chives
    and parsley*
*salt and freshly ground black pepper*

**1.** Blanch and refresh the mangetout, then top and
tail and split them open. Soften the cream cheese
with a little milk, add the herbs and season to
taste with salt and pepper.
**2.** Put the cheese mixture into a piping bag fitted
with a small plain nozzle and pipe into the
mangetout. Close the mangetout over the filling.

## SALAMI WEDGES

MAKES 24
*170g/6oz cream cheese*
*4 spring onions, chopped*
*4 gherkins, chopped*
*1 tablespoon finely chopped fresh parsley*
*salt and freshly ground black pepper*
*15 slices of pepper salami*

**1.** Mix the cream cheese with the spring onions,
gherkins and parsley and season to taste with salt
and pepper.
**2.** Spread a little of the mixture evenly over a slice
of salami. Place another slice of salami on top,
then spread with some more cream cheese
mixture.
**3.** Continue to layer up the cream cheese and
salami until you have used 5 slices of salami.
Repeat with the remainder.
**4.** Wrap in clingfilm and chill in the refrigerator.
**5.** Cut each stack of salami into 8 wedges.

## TABOULEH IN CUCUMBER WITH GREEK YOGHURT

*1 large cucumber*
*70ml/2½fl oz Greek yoghurt*
*½ quantity tabouleh (see page 129)*

**1.** Cut the cucumber into 1cm/½in slices. Stamp
with a fluted cutter and, using a teaspoon or melon
baller, make a hollow in the centre of each round.
**2.** Spoon or pipe a little Greek yoghurt into each
cucumber cup and top with a mound of tabouleh.

## TARTLETS WITH QUAIL'S EGGS AND SMOKED SALMON

MAKES 20
*70ml/2½fl oz mayonnaise (see page 250)*
*20 tartlet cases (see page 674)*
*10 quail's eggs, hardboiled (see page 58)*
*55g/2oz smoked salmon, cut into julienne strips*

To garnish
*sprigs of fresh chervil or dill*

**1.** Spoon or pipe a little mayonnaise into each
pastry case.
**2.** Halve the quail's eggs and place a half, cut side
up, on top of the mayonnaise.
**3.** Place a little smoked salmon on the quail's egg
and garnish with a sprig of chervil or dill.

## TARTLETS WITH SMOKED SALMON AND CAVIAR

MAKES 20
*70ml/2½fl oz Greek yoghurt*
*20 tartlet cases (see page 674)*
*85g/3oz smoked salmon, cut into julienne strips*
*½ small jar of black lumpfish roe*

**1.** Spoon or pipe a little Greek yoghurt into each
tartlet case.
**2.** Fill the tartlet case with the smoked salmon and
top with a little black lumpfish roe.

# CHERRY TOMATO, AVOCADO AND MOZZARELLA KEBABS

MAKES 20
20 *cherry tomatoes*
1 *avocado, cut into cubes*
1 *mozzarella cheese, cut into cubes*
8 *fresh basil leaves, shredded*
3 *tablespoons French dressing (see page 254)*

**1.** Using 20 bamboo sticks, thread a cherry tomato, a cube of avocado and a cube of mozzarella on to each stick.
**2.** Mix the basil with the French dressing and spoon a little over the avocado and mozzarella.

# CHERRY TOMATOES WITH CREAM CHEESE AND MINT

MAKES 20
20 *cherry tomatoes*
110g/4oz *cream cheese*
1½ *teaspoons chopped fresh mint*
*a squeeze of lemon juice*
*salt and freshly ground black pepper*

**1.** Slice a quarter of each tomato off at the rounded end. Scoop out the flesh and reserve.
**2.** Mix a little of the tomato flesh with the cream cheese, mint, lemon, salt and pepper. Cut a very thin slice from the bottom of each tomato so that it can stand upright. Fill the tomatoes with the cream cheese mixture and stick the tops back at a jaunty angle.

# MINI HAMBURGERS

MAKES 40
For the buns
30g/1oz *fresh yeast*
1 *tablespoon sugar*
150ml/¼ *pint warm milk*
225g/8oz *plain flour*
1 *teaspoon salt*
55g/2oz *butter, melted*
*beaten egg*
*sesame seeds*

For the hamburgers
450g/1lb *lean minced beef*
1 *tablespoon finely chopped fresh parsley*
1 *teaspoon Worcestershire sauce*
*salt and freshly ground black pepper*
*oil for frying*

To garnish
*lollo rosso lettuce*
*tomato chutney*

**1.** Make the buns: cream the yeast with the sugar. Stir in the milk. Sift the flour with the salt into a large bowl and make a well in the centre. Pour the yeast mixture and melted butter into the well. Using one hand, gradually mix to a soft dough. Knead well (about 15 minutes) and leave to rise in a warm place until doubled in size, about 1 hour.
**2.** Shape the dough into 40 small buns. Leave to prove (rise again) for about 10 minutes.
**3.** Preheat the oven to 200°C/400°F/gas mark 6.
**4.** Brush the buns with beaten egg and sprinkle with sesame seeds. Place on a greased baking sheet and bake in the preheated oven until firm and golden.
**5.** Make the hamburgers: mix all the ingredients together and beat lightly. With wet hands, shape the meat into flattish rounds. Fry the hamburgers in hot oil in a frying pan until brown on both sides. Keep warm.
**6.** Assemble the hamburgers: split the buns in half. Arrange a little lollo rosso lettuce and tomato chutney on each base, place a hamburger on top and finish off with the top of the bun.

NOTE: If using dried or easy-blend yeast, see page 604.

# MINI YORKSHIRE PUDDINGS WITH RARE ROAST BEEF

MAKES 30
*beef dripping or oil*
*290ml/½ pint Yorkshire pudding batter (see page 395)*
*170g/6oz fillet or sirloin steak*
*horseradish cream (see page 246)*

To garnish
*1 bunch watercress*

1. Preheat the oven to 220°C/425°F/gas mark 7.
2. Heat the dripping or oil in small patty tins.
3. Pour in the batter and bake in the preheated oven for 10–15 minutes, or until risen and golden.
4. Meanwhile, grill or fry the steak and cut into thin slices.
5. Spoon or pipe a little horseradish cream into each Yorkshire pudding. Arrange a slice of beef on top and garnish with a tiny sprig of watercress.

# MINI BAKED POTATOES WITH CHEESE AND BACON

MAKES 20
*20 small new potatoes*
*55g/2oz streaky bacon, grilled and diced*
*55g/2oz Cheddar cheese, grated*
*a little melted butter*
*salt and freshly ground black pepper*

1. Preheat the oven to 200°C/400°F/gas mark 6.
2. Scrub the potatoes and bake in the oven for about 45 minutes, or until cooked.
3. Cut a slice from the top of each potato. Scoop out the centre and mix with the remaining ingredients.
4. Pile the filling back into the potatoes.
5. Heat through in the oven for about 8 minutes.

# MUSHROOMS STUFFED WITH SPINACH, BACON AND GARLIC

MAKES 20
*20 even-sized mushrooms*
*55g/2oz butter*
*225g/8oz fresh spinach, washed, destalked, cooked and finely chopped*
*55g/2oz streaky bacon, grilled and cut into tiny dice*
*2 cloves of garlic, crushed*
*salt and freshly ground black pepper*
*plain flour*
*1 egg, beaten*
*dried white breadcrumbs*
*oil for deep-frying*

1. Wipe the mushrooms and remove the stalks.
2. Melt the butter, add the spinach, bacon, garlic, salt and pepper.
3. Pile the stuffing into the mushrooms.
4. Dip the mushrooms first into the flour, then into the beaten egg and finally into the breadcrumbs, to coat thoroughly.
5. Heat the oil in a deep-fryer and fry the mushrooms until golden-brown.
6. Drain on absorbent kitchen paper, sprinkle with salt and serve immediately.

# SPINACH AND RICOTTA STRUDELS

MAKES 20
*225g/8oz frozen chopped spinach*
*110g/4oz butter*
*110g/4oz ricotta cheese*
*salt and freshly ground black pepper*
*a good pinch of freshly grated nutmeg*
*4 sheets of filo pastry*
*1 egg, beaten, to glaze*

1. Preheat the oven to 200°C/400°F/gas mark 6.
2. Defrost the spinach. Melt 30g/1oz of the butter and add the spinach, ricotta, salt, pepper and nutmeg.

**3.** Melt the remaining butter and brush it over the sheets of filo pastry.

**4.** Cut each sheet of pastry into strips 5cm/2in wide.

**5.** Place a spoonful of filling at one end of each strip. Form a triangle by folding the right-hand corner to the opposite side, and fold over and then across from the left-hand corner to the right edge. Continue folding until the strip of pastry is used up.

**6.** Brush the strudels with beaten egg. Place on a greased baking sheet and bake in the preheated oven for about 10 minutes, or until golden-brown.

# MINI CORNISH PASTIES

MAKES 20
For the cheese pastry
110g/4oz plain flour
55g/2oz butter
15g/½oz Parmesan cheese, freshly grated
a pinch of cayenne pepper
a pinch of dry English mustard
½ egg, beaten
cold water

For the filling
225g/8oz lean minced beef
1 small onion, finely chopped
1 small potato, diced
1 small carrot, diced
1 teaspoon plain flour
stock to moisten
salt and freshly ground black pepper
a few drops of Worcestershire sauce
1 egg, beaten, to glaze

**1.** Make the pastry: sift the flour into a mixing bowl and rub in the butter. Add the Parmesan, cayenne and mustard. Bind to a firm dough with the beaten egg and a little water. Chill in the refrigerator.

**2.** Make the filling: brown the mince and vegetables in a non-stick saucepan. Add the flour and cook over a low heat for 1 minute. Add the stock, salt, pepper and Worcestershire sauce and cook until the vegetables are just soft. Remove from the heat and allow to cool.

**3.** Preheat the oven to 200°C/400°F/gas mark 6.

**4.** Roll out the pastry thinly, and stamp out 5cm/2in rounds with a pastry cutter.

**5.** Place a teaspoon of filling in the centre of each. Brush the edges of the pastry with beaten egg and fold over into tiny Cornish pasties. Seal the edges well. Brush the pastry with beaten egg and place the pasties on a greased baking sheet. Bake in the preheated oven for 10–15 minutes until golden brown.

# TANDOORI CHICKEN WITH CUCUMBER AND YOGHURT DIP

MAKES 12
225g/8oz boneless chicken meat
150ml/¼ pint plain yoghurt
a pinch of chilli powder
a pinch each of ground cumin and coriander
1 teaspoon garam masala
1 teaspoon tomato purée
grated zest and juice of ½ lemon
1 clove of garlic, crushed
1 teaspoon peeled and chopped fresh root ginger
salt and freshly ground black pepper

For the cucumber and yoghurt dip
¼ cucumber
150ml/¼ pint plain yoghurt
1 tablespoon double cream
1 tablespoon finely chopped fresh mint
salt and freshly ground black pepper

**1.** Cut the chicken into bite-sized chunks.

**2.** Place all the remaining tandoori ingredients together in a food processor or blender and process until smooth.

**3.** Lay the pieces of chicken in a shallow dish, pour over the marinade, cover and refrigerate overnight.

**4.** The following day, just before serving, lift the chicken out of the marinade and place in a roasting pan. Preheat the grill or oven to its highest setting. Cook the chicken for about 10 minutes, or until reddish-brown and tender.

**5.** Make the cucumber and yoghurt dip: chop the cucumber finely and pat dry with absorbent

kitchen paper. Mix all the ingredients together and season with salt and pepper. Place in a bowl.
**6.** Spear the chicken pieces with cocktail sticks and serve on a round dish surrounding the cucumber and yoghurt dip.

# CHICKEN SATÉ WITH PEANUT SAMBAL

MAKES 60 COCKTAIL PIECES
*5 chicken breasts, skinned*

For the marinade
*1 medium onion, finely chopped*
*1 clove of garlic, crushed*
*1 teaspoon ground coriander*
*1 teaspoon ground ginger*
*3 tablespoons dark soy sauce*
*juice of 1 small lemon*
*2 teaspoons soft dark brown sugar*
*freshly ground black pepper*

For the peanut sambal
*1 small onion, finely chopped*
*1 tablespoon oil*
*½ teaspoon chilli powder*
*110g/4oz crunchy peanut butter*
*2 tablespoons dark soy sauce*
*2 tablespoons lemon juice*
*200ml/7fl oz cold water*
*soft dark brown sugar and salt to taste*

**1.** Make the sambal: cook the onion in the oil in a saucepan over a very low heat. Add the chilli powder and cook for 10 seconds.
**2.** Remove from the heat and add the peanut butter, soy sauce, lemon juice and water.
**3.** Return to the heat and stir until the sauce is thick and smooth. Season to taste with sugar and salt.
**4.** Cut each chicken breast into 12 cubes.
**5.** Mix together the ingredients for the marinade and add the chicken pieces. Leave to infuse for at least 1 hour.
**6.** Preheat the grill to its highest setting.
**7.** Skewer the chicken pieces on long wet bamboo sticks and grill for about 3 minutes each side.
**8.** Serve the peanut sambal as a dip.

NOTE: The bamboo sticks are wetted to prevent them from burning.

# CHICKEN LIVERS WRAPPED IN BACON

MAKES ABOUT 60
*450g/1lb chicken livers*
*60 small slices of streaky bacon*

**1.** Preheat the oven to 220°C/425°F/gas mark 7.
**2.** Trim the livers, discarding the discoloured parts.
**3.** Cut the livers into small pieces. Roll each piece in a slice of bacon and lay the rolls side by side in a roasting pan, fairly tightly packed to prevent unravelling.
**4.** Bake in the preheated oven for about 15 minutes or until they are just beginning to brown on top. Drain well.
**5.** Spear each roll with a cocktail stick. They are now ready to serve, but if they are to be reheated, remove them from the roasting pan and keep in a cool place until needed.

NOTE: If the cocktail sticks are stuck in before reheating, make sure that they are wooden, not plastic.

# WELSH RAREBIT

SERVES 2
*55g/2oz Gruyère cheese, grated*
*55g/2oz Cheddar cheese, grated*
*2 teaspoons French mustard*
*salt and freshly ground black pepper*
*cayenne pepper*
*½ egg, beaten*
*1 tablespoon beer*
*2 slices of bread*
*butter for spreading*

**1.** Preheat the grill.
**2.** Combine the cheeses and mix all but 1 tablespoon with the mustard, salt, pepper, cayenne, egg and beer.
**3.** Toast the bread and spread with butter.

**4.** Spoon the cheese mixture on to the toast and spread it neatly, making sure that all the edges are covered.

**5.** Sprinkle over the remaining cheese and grill until nicely browned.

 *LIGHT RED*

# ROQUEFORT TOASTS

MAKES 16

*2 rashers of rindless streaky bacon*
*110g/4oz Roquefort cheese*
*1 tablespoon tomato chutney*
*1 teaspoon Worcestershire sauce*
*1 teaspoon grated onion*
*4 slices of bread, each cut into 4 squares*

**1.** Preheat the oven to 200°C/400°F/gas mark 6.
**2.** Dice the bacon. Fry in a heavy frying pan until crisp but not brittle. Drain well on absorbent kitchen paper and break up into small pieces. Keep warm.
**3.** Mix the Roquefort, chutney, Worcestershire sauce and onion to a smooth paste.
**4.** Divide the mixture between the squares of bread and spread it evenly, being sure to cover all the edges. Place on a greased baking sheet.
**5.** Bake in the preheated oven for 5 minutes until crisp and brown.
**6.** Sprinkle with the fried bacon and serve immediately.

# CROQUE MONSIEUR

SERVES 4

*85g/3oz butter for spreading*
*8 thin slices of white bread*
*4 slices of cooked ham*
*4 slices of Edam or Gruyère cheese*
*freshly ground black pepper*

**1.** Butter the bread
**2.** Make 4 sandwiches, each with a slice of ham and a slice of cheese inside, seasoned with pepper but not salt. Press well together.

**3.** Toast under the grill until golden-brown on both sides. Cut in half and serve immediately.

NOTE: The sandwiches may also be made in a sandwich machine or fried in 5mm/¼in hot fat or oil, turning over as necessary and draining well on absorbent kitchen paper before serving.

# SAUSAGE ROLLS

MAKES 12

*15g/½oz butter*
*30g/1oz very finely chopped onion*
*400g/14oz sausagemeat*
*30g/1oz very finely chopped fresh parsley*
*salt and freshly ground black pepper*
*225g/8oz flour quantity shortcrust pastry (see page 461)*
*1 egg, beaten, to glaze*

**1.** Melt the butter, add the onion and sweat for 20 minutes.
**2.** Preheat the oven to 200°C/400°F/gas mark 6.
**3.** Mix together the sausagemeat, parsley, onion, salt and pepper.
**4.** Roll out the pastry to a large rectangle about 2mm/⅛in thick and cut in half lengthways.
**5.** With wet hands, roll the sausagemeat mixture into 2 long sausages the same length as the pastry and place one down the centre of each piece.
**6.** Damp one edge of each strip and bring the pastry over the sausagemeat, pressing the edges together and making sure that the join is underneath the roll. Chill for 10 minutes.
**7.** Brush with beaten egg. Cut into 5cm/2in lengths. Using a pair of kitchen scissors, snip a small 'V' in the top of each sausage roll. (This is to allow steam to escape during cooking. A couple of small diagonal slashes made with a sharp knife will do as well.)
**8.** Place on a baking sheet and bake in the preheated oven for 25–30 minutes until the pastry is golden-brown.

# CHEESE AIGRETTES

MAKES ABOUT 30
*105g/3³/₄oz plain flour*
*salt and freshly ground black pepper*
*½ teaspoon dry English mustard*
*cayenne pepper*
*85g/3oz butter*
*225ml/8fl oz water*
*3 eggs, lightly beaten*
*55g/2oz strong Cheddar cheese, finely diced*
*oil or fat for deep-frying*
*freshly grated Parmesan cheese*

**1.** Sift the flour with the salt, pepper, mustard and cayenne.
**2.** Slowly heat the butter and water together in a large saucepan. As soon as the butter is completely melted, bring to a full rolling boil and tip in the flour. Remove from the heat at once and beat with a wooden spoon until the mixture leaves the side of the pan. Allow to cool for 10 minutes.
**3.** Gradually beat in the eggs until the mixture is smooth and shiny and of a dropping consistency (you may not need all the egg). Add the Cheddar cheese.
**4.** Heat oil or fat in a deep-fryer until a crumb will sizzle vigorously in it.
**5.** Shape the mixture into even-sized balls, using 2 teaspoons, and deep-fry a few at a time, leaving plenty of room for them to rise, for about 7 minutes, or until they are puffed and golden.
**6.** Lift out and drain on absorbent kitchen paper. Dust with Parmesan cheese and serve immediately.

 *LIGHT RED*

# ANGELS ON HORSEBACK

SERVES 3
*12 oysters*
*6 rashers of rindless streaky bacon*
*6 small slices of bread*
*butter for spreading*

To garnish
*1 bunch of watercress*

**1.** Preheat the oven to 200°C/400°F/gas mark 6. Preheat the grill.
**2.** Prepare the oysters: wrap a tea-towel round your left hand. Place an oyster on your left palm with the flat side upwards. Slip a short, wide-bladed kitchen or oyster knife under the hinge and push it into the oyster. Press the middle fingers of your left hand on to the shell and, with your right hand, jerk up the knife and prise the 2 shells apart. Free the oyster from its base.
**3.** On a board, stretch the bacon with the back of a knife (this helps to prevent shrinking, during cooking). Wrap half a rasher around each oyster. Place the rolls on a baking sheet, tightly packed side by side to prevent them unravelling. Bake in the preheated oven for about 8 minutes.
**4.** Meanwhile, cut the bread into rounds and toast them under the grill. Butter the toast and set 2 'angels' on each round. Arrange on a serving dish and garnish with watercress.

# DEVILS ON HORSEBACK

SERVES 3
*12 prunes*
*mango chutney*
*6 rashers of rindless streaky bacon*
*6 small slices of bread*
*butter for spreading*

To garnish
*1 bunch of watercress*

**1.** Pour boiling water over the prunes and leave to soak for 30 minutes. Preheat the oven to 200°C/400°F/gas mark 6. Preheat the grill.
**2.** Remove the stones from the prunes and stuff each cavity with half a teaspoon of mango chutney.
**3.** On a board, stretch the bacon with the back of a knife (this helps to prevent shrinking during cooking). Wrap half a rasher around each prune.
**4.** Place on a baking sheet, packed tightly side by side to prevent them unravelling. Bake in the preheated oven for about 8 minutes.
**5.** Meanwhile, cut the bread into rounds and toast them under the grill. Butter the toast and set 2 'devils' on each round. Arrange on a serving dish and garnish with watercress.

 *SPICY DRY WHITE*

# PAIN BAGNA

Cut a French stick in half horizontally, remove a little of the soft bread, rub each side with a cut clove of garlic and sprinkle liberally with extra virgin olive oil. Scatter over the base any of the following ingredients.

*sliced avocado pear*
*sliced peeled tomatoes*
*sliced mushrooms*
*pitted black olives*
*chopped anchovy fillets*
*sliced artichoke hearts*

Season with salt and freshly ground black pepper. Sandwich together.

 *VALPOLICELLA*

# SCOTCH WOODCOCK

SERVES 4
*8 anchovy fillets*
*30g/1oz butter*
*freshly ground black pepper*
*4 slices of bread, crusts removed*
*4 egg yolks*
*290ml/½ pint single cream*
*1 tablespoon chopped fresh parsley*
*a pinch of cayenne pepper*

1. Preheat the grill.
2. Pound the anchovy fillets into the butter and add pepper to taste.
3. Toast the bread under the grill and spread thinly with the anchovy paste. Put on a warmed serving plate and keep warm.
4. Put the egg yolks, cream, parsley and cayenne together in a saucepan. Stir or whisk over a medium heat until thick and creamy.
5. Pour over the toasts and serve immediately.

 *SPICY DRY WHITE*

# CAMEMBERT FRITTERS

SERVES 3
*1 Camembert cheese, chilled*
*1 egg, beaten*
*dried white breadcrumbs*
*oil for deep-frying*

To garnish
*deep-fried parsley (see page 686)*

1. Cut the chilled Camembert into small wedges and roll each first in beaten egg, then in breadcrumbs. Chill again or 30 minutes.
2. Heat oil in a deep-fryer until smoking hot. Test for heat by dropping in a crumb: if it starts to sizzle immediately, the oil is ready.
3. Deep-fry the Camembert wedges until very pale brown. Drain well on absorbent kitchen paper.
4. Garnish the fritters with the parsley and serve immediately.

NOTE: These are delicious served with gooseberry sauce (see page 278).

 *LIGHT RED*

# MUSHROOM STRUDEL

SERVES 4
*225g/8oz rashers of rindless streaky bacon*
*30g/1oz butter*
*2 small onions, finely chopped*
*450g/1lb button mushrooms, sliced*
*salt and freshly ground black pepper*
*1 tablespoon chopped fresh parsley*
*225g/8oz flour quantity strudel pastry, rolled and*
   *pulled out (see page 466)*
*melted butter for brushing*
*beaten egg, to glaze*

1. Preheat the oven to 200°C/400°F/gas mark 6.
2. Dice the bacon and fry in its own fat in a frying pan until cooked and slightly browned. Remove to a plate. Add the butter to the pan.
3. Reduce the heat, add the onions and cook until soft but not coloured. Add the mushrooms and cook briskly for 30 seconds.

**4.** Season with salt and pepper and add the parsley. Boil rapidly until the liquid has evaporated. Remove from the heat and allow to cool. Add the bacon.

**5.** Cut the strudel sheets into 13cm/5in squares. Brush each square with melted butter.

**6.** With a slotted spoon, place some mushroom mixture in the centre of each square.

**7.** Using both hands, draw the edges of the pastry together so that the strudel looks like a pouch. Pinch the neck of the pouch with your fingers to secure it tightly. Alternatively, roll each strudel up into a sausage shape. Brush the pastry with beaten egg. Place on a greased baking sheet and bake in the preheated oven for 25 minutes, or until the pastry is golden-brown.

NOTE: When working with strudel pastry it is vital to prevent the thin sheets from drying out and cracking. Keep the pastry covered with clingfilm or a damp cloth, and when the sheets are exposed to the air, work fast. Brush the strudels with butter as quickly as you can.

 *SPICY DRY WHITE*

# MOZZARELLA IN CARROZZA

SERVES 4

*8 thin slices of sandwich bread, crusts removed*
*4 large slices of mozzarella cheese*
*2 eggs, beaten with a little salt*
*oil for frying*

**1.** Make 4 rounds of cheese sandwiches. Cut each round into 4.

**2.** Leave the sandwiches to soak in the beaten egg for 30 minutes. Turn them over once so that both sides are saturated with the egg.

**3.** Press the edges of the sandwiches firmly together and fry in hot oil in a frying pan until golden-brown. Drain well on absorbent kitchen paper.

 *LIGHT RED*

# CHICKPEA BREAD

When we tested this recipe at Leith's School, it was greeted with very mixed reactions. People either loved or loathed it.

*110g/4oz chickpea flour (besan flour)*
*½ teaspoon salt*
*425ml/¾ pint water*
*30ml/1fl oz good-quality olive oil*

**1.** Preheat the oven to 220°C/425°F/gas mark 7.

**2.** Sift the flour with the salt into a bowl.

**3.** Make a well in the centre and gradually add the water, mixing as you do so to make a smooth batter.

**4.** Stir in the olive oil.

**5.** Pour into a 20 × 15cm/8 × 6in greased baking tin.

**6.** Bake in the preheated oven for 25–30 minutes, or until the bread has set.

**7.** Serve warm or cold with plenty of freshly ground black pepper.

NOTE: Chickpea or besan flour is available from many Indian and Asian shops.

# BAKED BREAD WITH GARLIC AND OIL

*1 large French stick*
*5 cloves of garlic, peeled*
*coarse salt*
*extra virgin olive oil*

**1.** Preheat the oven to 200°C/400°F/gas mark 6.

**2.** Cut the bread into diagonal slices 2cm/¾in thick. Place on a baking sheet and bake in the preheated oven for about 15 minutes, or until golden-brown.

**3.** Cut the garlic in half and, when the bread is golden-brown, rub each side with the cut surface of the garlic.

**4.** Arrange the bread on a warmed serving dish and sprinkle with the salt. Then drizzle over the oil. Serve immediately.

NOTE: The baked bread may be served with the oil poured over it and the salt and garlic handed separately.

# BRUSCHETTA

To make bruschetta simply cut thick slices of French bread on the diagonal. Fry them in olive oil that has been infused with garlic until crisp on both sides. Drain well on absorbent paper. The toast should be crisp on the outside but still soft in the middle. Top with a large variety of toppings such as:

*Parma ham, rocket and Parmesan cheese*
*Grilled haloumi cheese and beef tomatoes*
*Grilled red and yellow peppers with olive oil and*
*  basil*
*Grilled marinated aubergines with sun-dried*
*  tomatoes*

# BARQUETTES OF PUFF PASTRY WITH A JULIENNE OF VEGETABLES

Use as a garnish for fish, poultry and veal dishes.

MAKES 14–16
*170g/6oz flour quantity puff pastry (see page 464)*
*2 carrots, peeled and cut into fine julienne strips*
*white part only of 2 leeks, washed and cut into*
*  fine julienne strips*
*salt and freshly ground black pepper*
*1 teaspoon chopped fresh thyme leaves*
*110g/4oz chicken beurre blanc (see page 253)*

**1.** Preheat the oven 220°C/425°F/gas mark 7.
**2.** Roll the pastry out thinly and use it to line 14–16 small pastry boats. Prick well with a fork and bake blind for 5 minutes (see page 459).
**3.** Steam the carrots and leeks together with the salt, pepper and fresh thyme leaves.
**4.** Arrange the vegetables in the warm pastry boats and spoon over the beurre blanc.

# FILO PASTRY BASKETS FILLED WITH TOMATOES AND DILL

These pretty baskets can be used to garnish chicken, lamb and fish dishes

MAKES 20
*1½ sheets of filo pastry*
*45g/1½oz unsalted butter, melted*
*2 ripe tomatoes*
*2 large sprigs of fresh dill, roughly chopped*
*salt and freshly ground black pepper*

**1.** Preheat the oven to 200°C/400°F/gas mark 6.
**2.** Brush each sheet of filo pastry with melted butter to prevent it from drying out and cracking.
**3.** Using a small pastry cutter, press out rounds of filo pastry and use to line 20 × 2.5cm/in tartlet tins, placing 3 layers of pastry in each tin.
**4.** Bake in the preheated oven for 5–7 minutes, or until golden-brown.
**5.** Meanwhile, prepare the tomato filling: plunge the tomatoes into boiling water and leave for 10 seconds. Transfer to a bowl of cold water to prevent any further cooking. When cool, peel them. Cut them into quarters and remove the seeds. Chop the tomato flesh neatly into tiny dice.
**6.** Heat 1 tablespoon of the remaining butter in a frying pan and quickly fry the tomatoes for about 30 seconds, taking care that they do not cook to a purée. Add the chopped dill and season to taste with salt and pepper.
**7.** Place a spoonful of the tomato mixture in each pastry basket and serve immediately to prevent them going soggy.

# MINI SWEET POTATO RÖSTIS

This recipe calls for roasted black peppercorns: roasting spices intensifies the flavour. Simply dry-fry them in a pan for about 5 minutes.

MAKES 25
*675g/1½lb sweet potatoes, peeled and cut into*
*  large chunks*

6 shallots, very finely chopped
45g/1½oz butter
1 × 70g/3oz packet very thinly sliced pancetta
1 teaspoon black peppercorns, roasted and
 crushed
salt, if necessary
oil

1. Preheat the oven to 200°C/400°F/gas mark 6.
2. Cook the sweet potato in boiling, salted water until just tender. Refresh under cold running water and drain thoroughly. Grate coarsely.
3. Sweat the shallots in the butter until very soft. This may take up to 20 minutes.
4. Fry the pancetta in its own fat until crisp and pale golden-brown.
5. Fork the shallots and pancetta into the sweet potato, being careful not to mash the mixture together. Taste and season well with the roasted black pepper. The mixture is unlikely to need salt.
6. Pile the mixture into well-oiled barquette moulds and place on a baking sheet.
7. Bake in the preheated oven for 15 minutes, or until very hot and golden-brown.
8. Remove from the tins and serve warm.

NOTE: If barquette moulds are not available use patty tins, but barquette moulds make for a better shape.

# SMOKED MUSSELS ON SEAWEED CANAPÉS

The pastry in this recipe is baked in mussel shells. You will need about 20 small shells, which can be re-used.

MAKES 20–25
225g/8oz rich shortcrust pastry (see page 461)
1 egg yolk, beaten
black food colouring
1 small can of smoked mussels
10–12 large spring green leaves
oil for deep-frying

1. Preheat the oven to 190°C/375°F/gas mark 5.
2. Roll out the pastry very thinly and use to line the mussel shells. Bake blind for 5 minutes (see page 459). Mix the egg yolk and colouring until really black. Use to paint the inside of the pastry shells, then put them back into the oven to cook the glaze. Make as many shells as there are mussels in the can. Cool on a rack.
3. Heat oil in a deep-fryer until a crust of bread sizzles in it.
4. Roll up the spring green leaves and cut into very fine threads. Deep-fry for a few seconds until crisp but still green. Drain on absorbent paper.
5. Put a little of the 'seaweed' into the pastry shells and place a warmed mussel on top.

NOTE: These canapés are just as nice cold.

 DRY ROSE – SPICY

# SPRING ONION BOWS

Choose large cylindrical spring onions that do not have especially bulbous roots. Cut off a large part of the green tops and the roots. With a small, sharp knife, cut vertical lines halfway through the onions at both ends (see illustration). Leave in icy water for 2 hours, by which time they will have opened out.

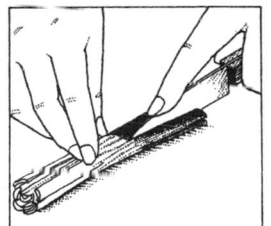 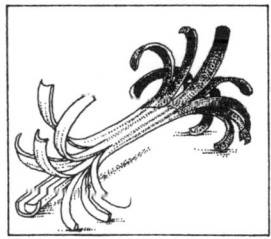

Slice from the ends towards the centre. Leave in iced water

# DEEP-FRIED PARSLEY

Pick sprigs of fresh but dry parsley and place in a frying basket. Heat oil in the deep-fryer until a crumb will sizzle in it, then lower in the basket. It will hiss furiously. When the noise stops, the parsley is cooked. It should be bright green and brittle, with a very good concentrated flavour.

NOTE: To avoid splashing any hot oil, tie the parsley on to the end of a piece of string and lower into the oil from a height.

# MARINATED GOAT'S CHEESE

SERVES 6–12
*6 crottin goat's cheeses*
*2 cloves of garlic, cut in half*
*4 sprigs of fresh rosemary*
*4 sprigs of fresh thyme*
*4 sprigs of fresh oregano*
*2 fresh basil leaves*
*10 black peppercorns*
*10 coriander seeds*
*380ml/13fl oz good-quality olive oil*

1. Cut the goat's cheeses in half horizontally.
2. Arrange the cheese, garlic, herbs, peppercorns and coriander seeds in a preserving jar in alternate layers. Pour in enough oil to cover the cheeses.
3. Seal the jar and store in a cool place for at least a week but no longer than a month. (If you leave it longer, the oil will turn rancid and the cheese will become too soft.)
4. Serve the marinated cheese sprinkled with the oil from the jar, with piping hot slices of toasted French bread.

# CLARIFIED BUTTER

METHOD 1: Put the batter into a saucepan with a cupful of water and heat until melted and frothy. Allow to cool and set solid, then lift the butter, now clarified, off the top of the liquid.

METHOD 2: Heat the butter until foaming without allowing it to burn. Pour it through fine muslin or a double layer of clean 'J' cloth.

METHOD 3: Melt the butter in a heavy saucepan and skim off the froth with a slotted spoon.

NOTE: Clarified butter will act as a seal on pâtés or potted meats, and is useful for frying as it will withstand great heat before burning.

# CROÛTONS

*2 slices of bread, crusts removed, from an*
*    unsliced slightly stale white loaf*
*oil for frying*
*salt*

1. Cut the bread into 5mm/¼in cubes.
2. Heat the oil in a frying pan until a crumb will sizzle vigorously in it. Fry the bread cubes for about 1 minute, or until golden-brown.
3. Drain on absorbent kitchen paper and then sprinkle with salt.

# WALNUT BREAD

*1½ slices of wholemeal bread per person*
*soft butter for spreading*
*chopped walnuts*

1. Place a whole loaf in the freezer for 30 minutes.
2. Using a sharp knife, cut off one crust and spread the exposed bread with butter.
3. Cut a thin slice and repeat until you have enough slices.
4. Put each slice, buttered side down, in a flat dish containing the walnuts, and press down slightly so that the walnuts stick to the butter.
5. Cut each slice in half diagonally.

# MELBA TOAST

*6 slices of white bread*

1. Preheat the grill to its highest setting. Preheat the oven to 150°C/300°F/gas mark 2.
2. Grill the bread on both sides until well browned.
3. While still hot, quickly cut off the crusts and split the bread in half horizontally.
4. Put the toast in the preheated oven and leave until dry and brittle.

NOTE: Melba toast can be kept for a day or two in an airtight tin but it will lose its flavour if kept longer, and is undoubtedly best served straight from the oven.

# FRENCH TOAST

MAKES 16 FINGERS
*4 slices of white bread, crusts removed*
*2 eggs*
*150ml/¼ pint milk*
*a good pinch of freshly grated nutmeg*
*55g/2oz butter*
*oil*

1. Cut each slice of bread into 4 fingers.
2. Beat the eggs, milk and nutmeg together in a pie dish or soup plate.
3. Dip the bread fingers into this mixture, coating them well
4. Melt half the butter with a tablespoon of oil in a heavy frying pan. When the butter is foaming, fry the bread in it until golden-brown on both sides. Drain on absorbent kitchen paper. Add the remaining butter and more oil as needed, until all the bread fingers are cooked.

NOTE: French toast is sometimes served with crisp bacon, or with marmalade, maple syrup or a mixture of sugar and cinnamon, or with strawberries sprinkled with icing sugar.

# PRALINE

*a few drops of oil*
*55g/2oz unblanched almonds*
*55g/2oz caster sugar*

1. Oil a baking sheet.
2. Put the almonds and sugar into a heavy saucepan, and set over a low heat. Stir with a metal spoon as the sugar begins to melt and brown. When thoroughly caramelized (browned), tip on to the oiled sheet.
3. Allow to cool completely, then pound to a coarse powder in a mortar or blender.
4. Store in an airtight jar.

NOTE: Whole praline almonds, as sold in the streets of Paris, are made in the same way, but are not crushed to a powder. They are sometimes used for cake decoration.

# MEMBRILLO

This is delicious eaten with cheese, or with cream cheese as a pudding or just as sweets.

*1.8kg/4lb quinces*
*290ml/½ pint water*
*granulated sugar*
*icing sugar, sifted, to finish*

1. Chop the quinces and stew in the water until soft.
2. Sieve and weigh the pulp.
3. Mix the pulp with an equal quantity of sugar. Put into a saucepan, bring to the boil and stir until the paste leaves the side of the pan. It will spit and splutter furiously so cover your hand with a cloth and stir the paste continuously.
4. Pile into flat trays lined with greaseproof paper and leave in an airing cupboard or other warm place for 3–4 days.
5. When it is completely firm, cut into small pieces and roll in icing sugar. Store between greaseproof paper in airtight tins.

# CURRY POWDER

There is no beating freshly made curry powder.
Toasting and blending all the spices together
makes a very good blend that can be used in all
our recipes specifying curry powder. This mixture
is quite hot: to increase or lessen the heat, adjust
the quantity of chillies accordingly. The art of
good curry powders is in the toasting; when the
seeds are split by the heat, their full flavour comes
through. Take care not to burn the seeds or the
powder will taste bitter.

To keep the curry powder fresh it is best stored
in the freezer or a cool, dark place. Use within 3
months: any longer and the spices lose their
flavour.

This quantity makes enough powder for
several curries; halve the amount of seeds to make
a smaller quantity. The spices can be bought from
specialist grocers and some supermarkets.

*6 tablespoons coriander seeds*
*4 tablespoons cumin seeds*
*6 dried red chillies*
*1 tablespoon black peppercorns*
*1 tablespoon mustard seeds, preferably black*
*3 tablespoons ground turmeric*
*3 teaspoons ground fenugreek*

**1.** Heat a large frying pan. Add the coriander
seeds and toss and toast over a medium heat until
they begin to pop and colour. Transfer to a plate
to cool.
**2.** Add the cumin seeds and chillies and toast in
the same way until the cumin pops and the
chillies turn dark reddish-brown in colour. Add
them to the coriander and allow to cool.
**3.** Toast the peppercorns and mustard seeds
individually in the same way and allow to cool.
**4.** When all the seeds are cold, put into a
spice/coffee grinder or mortar. Pound together
until a fine powder is formed. Stir the turmeric
and fenugreek into the powder. Transfer to an
airtight container and store until required.

# DRINKS

# MULLED WINE

The important ingredient in mulled wine is, rather surprisingly, the water. Without it it can be far too rich and sickly. This recipe is just a guideline and can be altered according to individual tastes.

*4 × 75cl bottles of full-bodied red wine*
*1.7 litres/3 pints water*
*20 cloves, wrapped up in muslin or a 'J' cloth*
*3 oranges, sliced*
*3 lemons, sliced*
*225g/8oz granulated sugar, or more according to taste*
*2 cinnamon sticks*

Put all the ingredients into a large saucepan and dissolve the sugar over a low heat. Bring up to simmering point and keep warm for at least 15 minutes. Do not boil or the alcohol will evaporate.

# CHAMPAGNE COCKTAIL

*sugar lumps*
*Angostura bitters*
*brandy*
*champagne or sparkling white wine such as Saumur or an Australian, chilled*

**1.** Put a sugar lump in each glass and add a couple of drops of Angostura bitters and 1 teaspoon brandy.
**2.** Just before serving, pour on the chilled champagne to fill the glasses.

# BELLINI

The most cheerful drink of all – the classic of Harry's Bar.
Simply mix peach juice and champagne in equal quantities. If you add the champagne to the juice, the bubbles will last considerably longer.

NOTE: It is possible to buy cartons or cans of peach juice.

# APPLE PUNCH

*1 litre/1³/₄ pints apple juice*
*5cm/2in piece of fresh root ginger, peeled*
*2 dessert apples (red ones look pretty)*
*1 litre/1³/₄ pints dry ginger ale*
*ice*

**1.** Put the apple juice into a large bowl. Bruise the ginger with a rolling pin. Quarter, core and thinly slice the apples and add with the ginger to the apple juice. Leave to marinate overnight or for at least 2 hours.
**2.** Remove the ginger and add the dry ginger ale just before serving. Chill with ice cubes.

NOTE: If a clear punch is wanted, use clear apple juice. English apple juice is cloudy but is less sweet.

# CIDER PUNCH

This is deceptively alcoholic.

*150ml/¹/₄ pint brandy, chilled*
*1.1 litres/2 pints dry sparkling cider, well chilled*
*2 dessert apples, cored and sliced*
*1 orange, sliced*
*a few sprigs of fresh mint*

Pour the brandy into a jug. Add the cider, fruit and mint.

NOTE: This should be served really well chilled. If a sweeter punch is preferred, use a medium-dry cider.

# WASSAIL CUP

This warming brew is traditionally served around Christmas time as a welcome drink. It looks wonderful presented in a large china bowl with lightly baked apples floating on the top.

*1.7 litres/3 pints brown ale*
*225g/8oz soft light brown sugar*
*1 cinnamon stick*
*½ teaspoon freshly grated nutmeg*
*½ teaspoon ground ginger*
*1 lemon, thinly sliced*
*350ml/12fl oz medium-dry sherry*

**1.** Place 570ml/1 pint of the ale in a large pan. Add the sugar and cinnamon stick and bring to the boil, stirring all the time to dissolve the sugar.
**2.** Add the spices, lemon, sherry and the remaining ale. Warm through but do not boil. Allow 150ml/¼ pint per person.

# INDEX

# INDEX